D1080158

YOUR GARDENING QUESTIONS ANSWERED

YOUR GARDENING QUESTIONS ANSWERED

PUBLISHED BY THE READER'S DIGEST ASSOCIATION LIMITED
LONDON • NEW YORK • MONTREAL • SYDNEY • CAPE TOWN

CONTRIBUTORS

YOUR GARDENING QUESTIONS ANSWERED
was edited and designed by
The Reader's Digest Association Limited, London

Printed in Italy

CONSULTANT EDITORS

Professor Alan Gemmell
Former panel member of BBC radio's *Gardeners' Question Time*

Philip Swindells, MI HORT, MISTC, FLS
Curator of Harlow Car Gardens, Harrogate

CONTRIBUTORS

John Allbutt
Technical Manager, Synchemicals Ltd

Kenneth A. Beckett

Peter Blackburne-Maze, NDH, MI HORT

Ann Bonar, BSC (HORT)

Dr Stefan Buczacki, BSC, D PHIL, FI HORT, C BIOL, MI BIOL, ARPS, FLS
Panel member of BBC radio's *Gardeners' Question Time*

John Chambers, SDH
Wild-flower seed specialist

Graham Clarke
Editor, *Amateur Gardening* magazine

Jane Courtier, HND HORT
Deputy Editor, *Amateur Gardening* magazine

Philip Damp
Former General Secretary, National Dahlia Society

Daphne Dormer
The Chelsea Gardener, London

Jim Gardiner, MI HORT
Curator, The Hillier Arboretum

Colin Hart, MI HORT, DIP HORT (KEW), CERT ED (LONDON)

David Humphries, BSC (HORT), MI HORT
Head of Horticultural Services, Institute of Horticultural Research, Littlehampton (formerly the Glasshouse Crops Research Institute)

Dr Ron McParlin, NDH
Head of Horticultural Department, Northumberland College of Agriculture

Ashley Stephenson, MVO
Bailiff of the Royal Parks

Dr David Sutton, MA, PHD, FRHS
Botany Department, British Museum (Natural History)

Mary Tyson

Dr David W. Williams, LLM, PHD, Solicitor
Senior Lecturer in Law, Manchester University

Jack Wilson

ILLUSTRATORS

Richard Bonson

Brian Delf

Colin Emberson

Nicolas Hall

Richard Lewington

Colin Newman

CONTENTS

ACID SOILS

Soil testing

I've been gardening for years and getting pretty good results without knowing whether my soil is acid or alkaline. Now the experts tell me to buy a soil-testing kit. Do I really need to bother?

There are two schools of thought on this subject. Some gardeners leave well alone until something goes wrong. Others test every part of the garden with complicated gadgets that will tell them everything about the soil content.

The happy-go-lucky gardeners are running a risk. All plants have basic needs and require a decent environment and a good standard of management to enable them to succeed. On the other hand, those scientifically minded gardeners who use gadgets to determine every trace element in their soils may well be wasting their time, because for most plants, minute variations don't matter.

The aim of all gardeners is the same: to produce strong and healthy plants. A lucky few – and you may belong to this minority group – manage this with the minimum of bother and expense, but a lot of people are dissatisfied with the results of their labours, and it might well pay them to carry out an acidity test.

The test may show that your soil is neither excessively acid nor strongly alkaline, in which case the clue to disappointing yields or performance may lie in poor soil management. All growing things need nourishment in order to thrive. They take this from the soil, and in time the soil gets depleted of nutrients. You won't need gadgets, merely an observant eye, to be aware of this state of affairs: little new growth, stunted and yellowing leaves, smaller and fewer flowers, and reduced crops. Provided that soil acidity – and drainage – is not the problem, a dose of a general fertiliser such as Growmore or, in autumn, an application of manure, will generally put things right.

How to make a home for acid-loving plants

I garden on very chalky soil which is, I understand, unsuitable for lime-hating plants. As a lover of rhododendrons, azaleas and heathers, is there any way that I can create the right soil conditions for them?

Initially, you should realise that altering the existing soil condition is not a once-for-all operation, and that the ground will need regular attention to keep it sufficiently acid for the plants to continue to thrive.

More basically, the wisdom of growing acid-loving plants in a chalky or limestone district is questionable. Such plants will always fail, partly because of the prevailing soil and partly because the climate is often wrong for them as well. In general, most acid-lovers prefer wet summers and mild winters. Even where favourable conditions exist, the soil will need to be altered radically simply to allow the plants to survive.

You might think that simply digging out planting holes and filling them with acid material like peat would be the solution. It isn't, merely a waste of time. Within three or four years at the most, chalky water will have seeped in from the surrounding soil and you'll be back to square one, with plants as yellow as quinces.

If you're hell-bent on the project, the most successful way will be either raised beds or containers for the plants. The raised-bed system relies on the fact that water flows sideways and downwards, seldom upwards. Start by marking out the growing area, then put wooden planks, bricks or, best of all, peat blocks around it to form a wall at least a foot high and, for ease of cultivation, no more than 3ft wide. You can also use large stones or small boulders for the wall, but make sure they are not limestone.

Much the same goes for filling containers for acid-loving plants with lime-free ericaceous compost, but as the operation is on a smaller scale it is less laborious and expensive. Once completed, fill the enclosed area with acid soil – a difficult and expensive task for a large bed.

ALL ABOUT pH

Soil acidity and alkalinity are measured against the pH scale – the letters stand for 'potential of Hydrogen'. The full scale runs from 1 to 14, but most garden soils are within the range 4.5-8.0. The neutral point on the scale is 7. Readings below this denote acid soil; above means alkaline. The majority of plants thrive in slightly acid soil (pH 6.5) though there are exceptions. Most vegetables, for example, do best on slightly alkaline soil (pH 7.5).

To establish the soil's acidity and consequently the types of plants it will support, you can use an inexpensive soil-testing kit, readily available from garden centres and shops. Such kits are easy to use: small soil samples are shaken with a chemical such as barium sulphate which stabilises the suspended soil while an indicator dye changes colour depending on the level of acidity around it. The result is compared with a colour-coded chart to give an approximate indication of the soil acidity. From the reading, you can assess what needs doing, if anything. Lime is used to bring an acid soil to near the neutral point; it is more difficult to turn an alkaline soil into an acid one.

Electronic pH meters, fitted with a probe for pushing into the soil, give instant readings, but are more expensive. They don't necessarily give better information than the simple soil-testing kits, and the same money might be better spent on a fertility meter. This will tell you the level and concentration of major plant foods in the soil – nitrogen, phosphorus and potassium – and help you to decide on the most appropriate fertiliser treatment.

The chart on the opposite page shows the ideal ranges of pH levels for common fruit, vegetables, herbs and flowers.

Plants that like acid

The soil in our garden is quite strongly acid with a pH of about 5. Which plants will thrive in these conditions?

A great many, headed by the rhododendrons, azaleas and callunas. These come in a wide range of shapes and colours, and in sizes to suit the smallest garden. Gaultheria, pernettya, kalmia and pieris are other shrubs that are happiest in acid conditions.

Some experts include camellias, corylopsis, ericas, hamamelis, hydrangeas, magnolias and sarcococcas in the acid-loving group of shrubs; strictly speaking, though, all they ask is a lime-free soil (pH 6.5). They aren't usually bothered about how acid it is.

Most trees tolerate most soils, but ginkgo, the tulip tree (liriodendron), stuartia and oaks positively revel in acid soil. So do perennials like alliums and campanulas, dicentras and dog's-tooth violets, primulas and cowslips, many lilies and, especially, the autumn-flowering gentian, *Gentiana sino-ornata*.

You could do worse than taking a close look at adjacent gardens. It is unlikely that yours would be an isolated plot of acid soil, and as a rule the plants that flourish in your neighbours' gardens will also thrive in yours.

Short-cut acidity tests

Can I use ordinary litmus paper to test the acidity of my soil?

Not really. Litmus paper is not accurate enough to be of any value. It will respond to strongly acid or alkaline conditions, but it will still tell you only whether the soil is acid or alkaline, and you probably know this already. It won't tell you what you really need to know: *how* acid or alkaline it is.

Sweet and sour soils

Older gardeners and gardening writers often talk about sweetening the soil. What do they mean, and what difference does it make?

Sweetening a soil is another way of saying reducing its acidity. It's as simple as that. As for the difference it makes, there are several.

First, lowered acidity increases the range of plants you can grow; the nearer a soil is to neutral the greater the number of different plants that will flourish in it.

Next, as the soil becomes less acid, some of the essential plant foods – nitrogen, phosphorus, potassium, sulphur and calcium – become more readily available, and plants will therefore grow stronger and healthier.

Third, reduced acidity encourages beneficial soil microorganisms to operate more effectively and to multiply better. Under acid conditions, soil bacteria are sluggish so that a lot of unrotted organic matter can build up in the soil, and with it an increased risk of soil-borne diseases.

Soil pollution from acid rain

Does acid rain have any effect on the garden soil and, if so, what can be done about it?

Acid rain has virtually no effect on the soil and no action need therefore be taken. For the same reason, no harm will come to the plants in your garden.

So far, the problem of acid rain has not reached serious proportions in Britain. On the Continent, and especially in Scandinavia, plantations of broad-leaved evergreens and conifers are said to suffer from the effects of acid rain, though the experts still can't agree even on that.

It's not clear, for instance, why the forests should be suffering now, when clean air laws are limiting air pollution, and why they didn't suffer in the 19th century, when there were no controls.

In any case, in a garden, the worst that years of acid rain could achieve would be a slight reduction in the pH of the soil – and that could be easily remedied with a few handfuls of lime.

How lime affects the soil

Does liming of the soil have any side-effects?

Hardly side-effects, but when you add lime in order to reduce soil acidity, you also trigger off a series of other events. The first is purely chemical and connected with the availability of some of the plant nutrients existing naturally in the soil.

When the land is strongly acid (a pH at or below 5.5), nitrogen, phosphorus, potassium, sulphur and calcium are rendered less available to most plants.

These elements are not necessarily in short supply, but the acidity has the effect of locking them up in a chemical form that the plants cannot use.

A similar chemical reaction happens on strongly alkaline soils, only here it is the iron and manganese which are immobilised. On acid land, lime liberates some of the elements that were locked up.

The second important effect from liming is purely physical. Gardeners on clay have long known that a dressing of lime or chalk after autumn digging improves the soil structure, aiding drainage and making the soil easier to cultivate.

In uncultivated, heavy clay soil, the individual soil particles are minute and stick together in a solid amorphous mass with hardly any air spaces. Thus a clay soil lies cold and wet in winter and sets like concrete in the summer.

Lime encourages the tiny clay particles to cluster together into crumb-sized lumps, thereby paradoxically breaking up the solid clods. You can see how the process works yourself by stirring a teaspoon of clay soil into a glass of water.

The liquid will stay muddy after you stop stirring because the tiny particles are too light to sink to the bottom. Now add a quarter teaspoon of garden lime to the glass. Stir it in, and you can see the soil forming crumbs and rapidly sinking to the bottom, leaving the water clear.

An excess of lime

I planted a rose hedge when I first moved here. The soil is chalky, but I put plenty of peat in the planting holes, and for the first few years the hedge grew well. Now, though, the leaves on some of the plants are turning yellow. What's wrong?

Some plants, principally those belonging to the *Ericaceae* family, will not tolerate limy soil. Others, roses among them, do better on a near-neutral soil (pH 6.5), and can sometimes be adversely affected by too alkaline a soil.

That's what is almost certainly happening to your roses: chalky water has been seeping into the rootballs, gradually overcoming the natural acidity of the peat and turning the soil alkaline. As a result, they're suffering from a deficiency disorder known as lime-induced chlorosis.

The nutrients they're short of are primarily iron and manganese, both of which tend to become chemically 'locked up' in an alkaline

THE SOIL PLANTS LIKE

pH level	Flowers and shrubs	Vegetables	Fruit
4.0-5.5	Ajuga, arbutus, blue hydrangea, spruce	—	Blueberry
4.5-6.0	Azalea, heather, kalmia, lily of the valley, pieris, rhododendron	Potato	—
5.0-6.5	Aconitum, broom, centaurea, dogwood, elaeagnus, gentian, golden rod, helianthus, holly, iris, juniper, laurel, lithospermum, magnolia, pyracantha, scabiosa, sumach, trillium, violet	Chicory, fennel, parsley	Apple, blackberry, gooseberry, raspberry, strawberry
5.5-6.5	Calendula, clematis, colchicum, fuchsia, gazania, globularia, hypericum, pansy, penstemon, primrose, rose, snapdragon, speedwell, violet	Basil, carrot, courgette, pepper, shallot, sweet potato, turnip	Cranberry, melon, redcurrant, watermelon
5.5-7.5	Aster, liatris, lupin, marigold, nasturtium, nicotiana, wallflower, zinnia	Cauliflower, cucumber, garlic, parsnip, pumpkin, sweet corn, thyme, tomato	Rhubarb
6.0-7.5	Abelia, acacia, acanthus, ageratum, alyssum, anchusa, anemone, aubrieta, bergenia, bluebell, buddleia, carnation, chrysanthemum, columbine, dahlia, deutzia, foxglove, geum, godetia, hollyhock, ivy, laburnum, lilac, lobelia, peony, poppy, pyrethrum, salvia, spiraea, stock, sweet pea, sweet william, weigela	Artichoke, asparagus, beetroot, broad bean, broccoli, brussels sprouts, cabbage, calabrese, celery, chives, french bean, horseradish, kohlrabi, leek, lettuce, marjoram, marrow, onion, radish, runner bean, spinach	Apricot, blackcurrant, cherry, damson, grape, hazelnut, mulberry, pear, quince, white currant

soil. The key is sequestrene, a fertiliser specially designed to bypass the chemical locks.

Sprinkle or spray it on the soil in spring each year before growth starts so that it is available for the roots when they start working. Use at the rate recommended by the manufacturers. If plants show the typical symptoms of yellowing leaves characteristic of iron deficiency during the growing season, you can give them a quick but temporary fillip with a foliar feed based on seaweed extract. The leaves absorb it very quickly but, as the effects last for only a few weeks, you'll need to use sequestrene as well before the foliar feed wears off.

Liming the soil

As a comparative newcomer to gardening I have joined the local garden club. The more experienced gardeners tell me to dress my plot with lime. Exactly what does that mean? When should I do it and how much should I use?

In horticultural parlance, you dress a soil rather like you dress a salad: with a thin coating of another material. Unlike a salad, you don't toss the soil in the dressing, merely scatter it evenly over the surface.

Before you add any lime, find out the pH level of the soil. On this depends the amount of lime, if any, you need to use to bring the soil to the ideal pH value of about 6.5. If the soil test shows a pH reading of 6.0 or below, you will certainly have to add lime in order to grow all but acid-loving plants.

The chart below shows how much garden (hydrated) lime you need to raise the pH value of different soils to 6.5. If you use ground chalk or limestone instead of garden lime, increase the quantity by one-third. If you use agricultural or burnt lime, reduce the quantity by one-third. Burnt lime is dangerous to handle and should be avoided if possible.

Autumn and winter are the best times for applying lime. Scatter it over freshly dug ground and leave it to be washed in by rain (on light sandy soils delay digging and liming until spring).

HOW MUCH GARDEN LIME TO USE

Soil type	Present pH level	Garden lime per sq yd
Sand	6.0	¾lb
	5.0	2lb
	4.0	3¾lb
Sandy loam	6.0	1lb
	5.0	2½lb
	4.0	4½lb
Loam	6.0	1¼lb
	5.0	3lb
	4.0	4⅔lb
Clay	6.0	1½lb
	5.0	3½lb
	4.0	5lb

ADELGIDS

Waxy wool on leaves

I have a young conifer whose leaves develop dense tufts of white waxy wool in summer. What are they and how can I get rid of them?

The tufts, which most commonly appear on the undersides of leaves and stems, are produced by adelgids, small dark insects related to aphids, which they resemble. They can be seen beneath and near the waxy tufts.

Adelgids attack the leaves and stems of pines, larches, spruces and firs, weakening them by sucking their sap. They also excrete a sticky honeydew on which sooty moulds readily develop, weakening the tree still further. The danger period is April and May. Spray infested young trees and seedlings with HCH or malathion in April and again three weeks later.

SAP-SUCKERS *Young conifers can be seriously weakened by adelgids, which cluster beneath protective white tufts in early summer. Some species also produce galls on young growth.*

ALPINES

When seeds won't sprout

I have tried to grow some of the more unusual alpines from seed. I get a few to germinate, but they are very erratic. Why is that?

Your problem is not uncommon with alpines, especially those whose true home is in the higher altitudes. Their seeds are programmed by nature to lie dormant for long periods of harsh weather. For them to be sure that spring has arrived, they need the climatic jolt which occurs when warm weather follows winter frosts. You have to recreate that sequence – by inventing a bitter winter for them.

You need a deep freeze, or the freezing compartment of a refrigerator. Start in early spring by sowing the seeds in a pan of seed compost, with about one-third by volume of sharp grit added to improve drainage. Water thoroughly, then place the pan in the freezer and leave it there for three weeks. Then bring it out into the warmth and light of the greenhouse. All the seeds will leap to life believing it to be spring, whatever the calendar says.

The lime-lovers

Do alpine plants dislike chalk and limestone soils, in the way that heathers and rhododendrons do?

There are a few alpines which detest limy soil: they include the blue autumn gentian and some of the rockery irises, for example. But a great many will put up with chalk or limy conditions, and a few positively relish them. The real lime-lover is the dianthus, or pink. It comes in dwarf varieties of many different flower shapes, but most have the same grey-green foliage. Flower colours range from dazzling white to rich port wine, and no limestone or chalk gardener would be without them. Another plant which positively thrives is the pasque flower, *Pulsatilla vulgaris*. This blooms in spring with flowers resembling purple, red or white goblets covered with a silky down.

The second category is of plants which will tolerate a limy soil without necessarily favouring it. This list is much larger, including the perennial white candytuft, *Iberis sempervirens*, and its pink cousin *I. gibraltarica*, as well as many types of aubrieta, arabis, alyssum, campanula and helianthemum. For spring-flowering bulbs in limy soil, choose narcissus, scilla, puschkinia and muscari. Among the shrubby plants, the tiny spiraeas and berberis will grow reasonably well, as will most of the dwarf conifers derived from chamaecyparis and thuja.

Edelweiss in the lowlands

I would love to grow edelweiss. But isn't it supposed to be a rare plant, even in the high Alps? How can I give it the conditions it needs in a suburban garden?

The edelweiss, *Leontopodium alpinum*, celebrated in the eternally running extravaganza *The Sound of Music*, is not especially rare in its high alpine homeland. Its name means 'noble white', and its unusual felty flowers, borne among greyish leaves, make it popular among rock gardeners. Edelweiss is by no means difficult to grow, and will tolerate bitterly cold weather as it does in its harsh natural habitat.

It does dislike getting waterlogged,

though, especially during the winter months. So a well-drained pocket in the rockery is vital. In summer, be sure to water the plant during a dry spell, so that it does not dry out completely.

Otherwise, edelweiss is surprisingly easy-going. You can raise it from seed sown in spring in a tray of John Innes seed compost mixed with about a quarter as much sharp grit. Pot the young plants individually as soon as they are large enough to handle. They will flower the following year.

Replace old plants after four or five years. Though it is possible to divide and replant them, they take a long time to settle again, and it is much simpler to raise new plants from seed.

Lifting gentians

I have some lovely autumn gentians in my rock garden. I'd like to divide them to plant a few elsewhere, but I am afraid to disturb the clumps. Are they as difficult to resettle as people say?

Gentians have a reputation for being difficult, one possible cause being that different species prefer different combinations of soil and drainage. Most of the spring-flowering varieties, for example, are tolerant of lime, while all the autumn gentians loathe it. So if you are to divide your clump, make sure that the divisions also go into a good peaty soil with no lime in it.

The most popular autumn gentian is *Gentiana sino-ornata*, and if this is your plant, you can treat it just like any other rockery perennial. After flowering in the autumn, the gentian dies back and becomes dormant through winter. You can lift and divide at any time during this dormant period, but it is best to wait for the first signs of life in early spring. Then you can make sure that each division has at least one good, strong bud.

The clumps usually divide naturally. If they don't, cut them with a sharp knife. Afterwards, plant the divisions immediately, because if the roots dry out the gentians will have a struggle to get established.

High peaks in a trough

Are all alpines suitable for a trough garden?

Most alpines will grow well enough, provided the compost is right. It should be very gritty and free-draining: about one-third of sharp grit to two-thirds of John Innes potting compost No 1, or an equal-parts mix of soil, peat and sand or grit. Though the soil should be well drained, you must also water regularly. You are trying to re-create the plants' natural mountain habitat where rain falls often, though it quickly runs away.

You must avoid over-rampant plants that will swamp the trough. The smaller the plant the better; so the little high alpine species will be especially suitable. Try, for example the tiny carpeting plant *Raoulia australis*, with its miniature silvery leaves. Most of the dwarf dianthus, or miniature pinks, will do well, including *Dianthus boydii* and *D. deltoides*, although they can be rather vigorous. The best behaved in the dianthus clan are the bright red varieties 'Huntsman' and 'Brilliancy'.

The dwarf *Aquilegia alpina* with its dangling blue blossoms lends itself beautifully to a sink garden. So, too, do many cultivated varieties of the alpine primulas, *Primula pubescens* and *P. marginata*. Another good choice for a sink is saxifrage: go especially for the lemon yellow *Saxifraga aizoon* 'Lutea' or the soft pink 'Rosea'. Lastly, consider *Draba aizoides* – a bristling little dome of closely packed rosettes, bearing bright yellow flowers in April. It is all too easily lost in a big rockery – but perfect for a garden in an old trough.

A scree garden

There is a rocky bank in our garden – so rocky, in fact, that it seems to contain more stone than soil. Can anything be done with it?

You could try making a scree garden. This is a garden devoted to those alpines which thrive naturally in the rock-strewn slopes of mountains, where soil is exceptionally sparse and rain drains quickly away. Such plants can be a bit temperamental. But, once established, they put down deep probing roots which grip even on the most perilous slopes.

Erinus alpinus is the easiest scree plant to grow, seeding itself and producing neat little mounds of foliage which bear masses of starry flowers. Some are a deep lilac-blue, but there are pink varieties and white ones, too – all flowering from late spring well into

Garden in a sink

My small terrace house has only a paved back yard that badly needs brightening up. I've been toying with the idea of alpines, but would they grow in such an environment?

No problem at all. The best thing to do is to get hold of an old kitchen sink – maybe from a demolition site – throw the plug away and stand it, raised on bricks, in a sunny and fairly sheltered corner of your yard. Fill the lower third with a layer of broken crocks covered by a layer of gravel or shale. Top up with a mixture of soil, peat and grit or sand in equal parts by volume.

Go for smaller alpines to make the most of your space. A dwarf conifer and perhaps a small rock or two among them often help to improve a design.

Alpines are usually bought as growing plants in small pots from a nursery or garden centre – try to find one which stocks a good collection. They can be transplanted from the pots to your sink at any time.

When choosing, give special consideration to dwarf species of aethionema, campanula, dianthus, gypsophila, sempervivum, saxifrage and sedum.

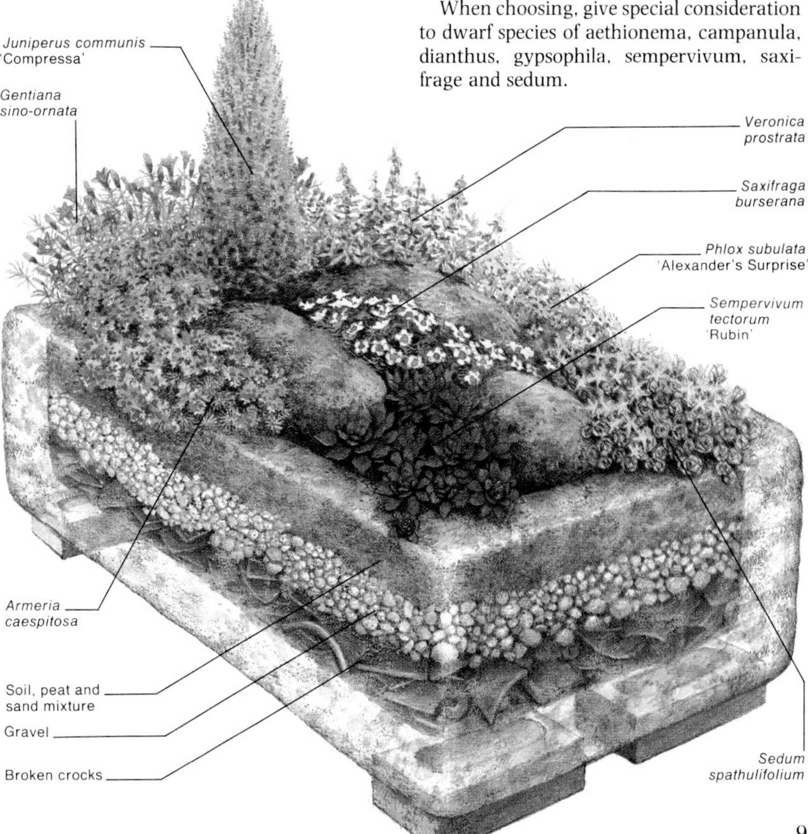

the summer. Many saxifrages are natural scree plants, as are alpine violas such as *Viola biflora*. The white-flowered *Arenaria balearica* clings to rocks and stones in a miniature green carpet, while *Gypsophila aretioides*, which is also white-flowering, grows in hard green hummocks.

The genera draba, sempervivum, rosularia, azorella and raoulia all include species suitable for a scree garden and are worth trying in your setting.

Dented cushions

My saxifrage grew in a nice tight cushion for a couple of years. But recently, the centre of the plant collapsed and now just looks straggly. What should I do?

Saxifrage is just one of a number of ground-hugging plants which spread out from the centre, seeking fresh nutrients in new ground. The healthy young growth is at the outer edge, and in time, the centre of the clump dies back. This is a natural tendency, and you can maintain a tight cushion only by the artificial means of controlled and regular feeding.

After each flowering, sprinkle some fine bone meal into the soil at the centre of the plant. Use a level tablespoonful for a plant about 9in across, proportionately less for small plants. Do not overfeed, though, or you'll get abnormal growth at the centre and ruin the cushion effect.

The stems at the centre also become straggly as they get older. The heart of the plant is the oldest part, where you get a build-up of fading leaves. To cure this, remove any fading leaves with a pair of tweezers, and each spring sprinkle some fine, soil-based compost into the centre of the plant. Eventually, a hummock of soil will build up, giving the roots more space and restoring the plant's cushioned shape.

Pot-bound plants

I have bought some alpines for the greenhouse, and plan to grow them in pots. How often should I repot them?

There are no hard and fast rules, but generally you should think of repotting every second year. The best time is early spring.

But you could also repot at any time when a plant starts to look jaded despite proper feeding and watering. It may be 'pot-bound' – that is, the roots have become so congested that the compost has dried out and lost its capacity to nourish healthy growth.

Extra watering does a pot-bound plant no good; it simply erodes the compost, which may take on a greenish, decayed look. When the compost deteriorates, the plant deteriorates too. Leaves turn yellow; flowers are disappointing; new growth is painfully slow. But if you repot every second year, your alpines should never reach this condition.

Alpine bulbs are a special case. They always benefit from being repotted every year – especially the smaller forms of narcissus, tulip and crocus.

Bulbs left to their own devices, or fed in their old compost, often emerge erratically and make a patchy display.

Dealing with weevils

I had some tiny primulas, growing in pans, which withered and died. When I emptied the pans I noticed little white grubs among the roots. What are these pests, and how can I guard against them in the future?

There can be little doubt that your plants were attacked by the larvae of a beetle called the vine weevil. The white grubs feed on the roots of a number of alpines, but primulas and cyclamen are especially vulnerable. The first sign of trouble is wilting and yellowing of the leaves, but by this stage it may already be too late to save the plant, for the roots may be damaged beyond repair. Still, it's worth a try. Knock the plant out of its pot, and put both the grubs and the compost in the dustbin. Now repot the plant in a compost incorporating an insecticide such as HCH. This treatment won't guarantee success, and insecticides can themselves damage the plants. But there is no real alternative once the roots have been attacked.

The best course is to take precautions in advance. Above all, keep your greenhouse clean and tidy. The adult beetles hide during the day in dirty pots, seed trays and plant debris. Besides tidying them up, you should occasionally dust any possible hiding places with an insecticide containing HCH.

It is much easier to eliminate the adults than to cope with the larvae once they have infested your pots. So spray the leaves regularly with an insecticide containing HCH. This will eliminate the adult weevils when they come in to feed.

ANNUALS

The right drill

I've seen some people scatter the seed of annuals over the ground and lightly rake it in, while some experts say the seed should be sown in shallow drills – like vegetables. Is there a right and wrong way?

No, but with a little time and effort spent at the sowing stage you will save time and energy later in the season.

Gardeners who sow by first raking the soil level, then taking out a shallow drill with a string line or a straight-edged board for guidance, have to spend longer getting the seed in. But they reap the benefits as the season progresses. First, the seedlings will emerge in neat straight lines. This makes the thinning out of seedlings to their required spacings a simple operation, and it makes reaching the seedlings easier, too. If the seedlings are scattered all over the ground, it may be impossible to reach the plants at the back of the bed without stepping on the ones in front. Moreover, the necessary job of weeding is made easier by drill-sowing, since it's not easy otherwise to distinguish weed seedlings from the plants you want.

One note of caution, though. Annuals in beds and borders look their best in 'drifts' – soft-edged, rounded patches of colour – rather than in squared-off blocks and regimental rows. To achieve this natural appearance without losing the advantages of sowing in drills, mark out the bed into small informal areas – overlapping circles, say – for each flower. Then draw the drills for the different areas at different angles. As the plants grow and spread, the lines of the original drills will blur and then vanish.

CIRCLE LINES *Sow bedding-plant seeds in straight lines to make weeding and thinning easier. But angle the lines in different directions within rounded areas to create, eventually, a natural look.*

Half-hardy

I understand that some annuals are tender – killed by frost – and some are hardy. But what does 'half-hardy' mean?

The meaning hangs on the nature of an annual plant. An annual is a plant that provides temporary summer colour – it grows from seed, flowers, sets seed and dies, all within one growing season.

The terms 'hardy' and 'half-hardy' relate to the plant's ability to withstand cold temperatures. Hardy plants are tough enough to stand the British winter without protection. They can be sown directly outdoors – generally in spring or, in some instances, in autumn – in the positions where they are to flower.

The half-hardies, however, are not as easy to grow. They will not germinate from seed sown in cold conditions, so the seedlings must be raised, in spring, under some form of protection – such as a greenhouse, cold frame, propagating frame or a sunny windowsill indoors. The young plants can be safely planted out in the garden only when all danger of frost is past – usually in May or June.

Doing the groundwork

I'd like a really colourful annual border. What's the best way of preparing the soil for sowing?

You are right to assume that there is more to growing annuals than simply sowing the seed. The condition of the soil is crucial. If it is too hard or dry, your seeds will have an extremely poor germination rate. A well-prepared seedbed will have a good 'tilth' – a soil raked down until its surface is like a layer of slightly damp breadcrumbs.

This crumbly surface enables the seeds to make good contact with the available soil moisture. It also enables the tiny roots to penetrate the ground easily.

Biennial mix

Is it a good idea to mix annuals and biennials in a flowerbed?

There's no botanical reason why you shouldn't, so it's up to you. The only disadvantage to mixing them up is an aesthetic one: unless you plan the border carefully, you won't get a big splash of colour from both at the same time.

Like an annual, a biennial is grown from seed, but it produces only stems and leaves in the first growing season; it flowers and dies in the next.

Most biennials are used for spring bedding, and for filling gaps in mixed borders. They are generally sown in a nursery bed out in the garden during summer, where they will grow to form small plants. In autumn they are transplanted to the positions where they will eventually flower. Since most annuals are summer flowers, sown in the spring, it is unlikely that you will have much overlapping colour.

However, there are some biennials which flower at the same time as *autumn-sown* hardy annuals. Try, for instance, any of these combinations, blooming in May-July (in the following list, *hb* stands for hardy biennial, *ha* for hardy annual):

MAY *Campanula medium*, the Canterbury bell (hb), or *Bellis perennis*, the bedding daisy (hb), with *Iberis umbellata*, the annual candytuft (ha), or *Malcolmia maritima*, the Virginian stock (ha).

JUNE *Dianthus barbatus*, the sweet william (hb), with *Eschscholzia californica*, the Californian poppy (ha); or *Matthiola incana*, in the forms known as Brompton stocks (hb), with baby blue eyes, *Nemophila menziesii* (ha).

JULY *Digitalis purpurea*, the foxglove (hb), with the nasturtium, *Tropaeolum majus* (ha); or *Papaver nudicaule*, the Iceland poppy (hb), with *Convolvulus tricolor*, the dwarf morning glory (ha).

HOW TO GET A LONG-RUNNING SUMMER SHOW

Use this list to stretch your garden's period of peak colour. By picking and combining plants with overlapping flowering periods – double bedding daisies, for instance, followed by candytuft, lobelia and clarkia – you can ensure a continuous display from March to October. In the chart, *hha* stands for half-hardy annual, *ha* for hardy annual, *p* for perennial and *b* for biennial. For details of how to grow particular annuals, see *Plants at a glance*, page 378.

		Flowering period								
Name	Type	March	April	May	June	July	August	September	October
Ageratum	hha				•	•	•	•	•
Alyssum	ha					•	•	•	
Antirrhinum (snapdragon)	ha					•	•	•	•
Begonia semperflorens (bedding begonia)	hhp				•	•	•	•	•
Bellis (double bedding daisy)	hb	•	•	•	•				
Calendula (pot marigold)	ha				•	•	•	•	•
Campanula medium (Canterbury bells)	hb			•	•				
Celosia plumosa (Prince of Wales' feathers)	hha					•	•	•	
Cheiranthus (wallflower)	hb	•	•	•					
Clarkia	ha						•	•	•
Heliotropium (heliotrope)	hha				•	•	•	•	
Iberis umbellata (candytuft)	ha			•	•	•			
Impatiens (busy lizzie)	hhp				•	•	•	•	•
Lobelia	hha				•	•	•	•	
Lunaria (honesty)	hb		•	•					
Nigella (love-in-a-mist)	ha					•	•		
Petunia	hha				•	•	•	•	•
Salvia splendens (bedding salvia)	hha					•	•	•	•
Schizanthus (butterfly flower)	hha					•	•	•	
Tagetes (marigold)	hha				•	•	•	•	•

Pots of colour

I've seen some greenhouses in gardens I've visited, which are packed with summer flowers in pots. Are these all half-hardy perennial plants or are there some annuals that are specially bred for growing in pots?

Although a number of annuals make excellent pot plants – and a few have had this useful facility attached to their common name, like the familiar pot marigold (*Calendula officinalis*) – the plants have not been bred specially for pots.

If your ambition is to have your windowsills or a greenhouse packed in summer with annual pot plants in full flower, choose your species from this list:

Love-lies-bleeding (*Amaranthus caudatus*); slipper flower (*Calceolaria multiflora*); Prince of Wales' feathers (*Celosia plumosa*); cockscomb (*Celosia cristata*); heliotrope (*Heliotropium peruvianum*); busy lizzie (Impatiens); Ten Week stock (forms of *Matthiola incana*); painted tongue (*Salpiglossis sinuata*); and youth-and-old-age (*Zinnia elegans*).

ANTS

Speeding the swarm

Are flying ants more dangerous than the crawling types? Should we spray them?

It can be off-putting to have a cloud of flying ants settle in your hair and clothes, but they do not cause any real harm. Console yourself with the thought that they may well be on the way out of your garden in any case.

Most ant colonies consist largely of wingless workers, but during warm and muggy summer weather, winged males and females are produced. When enough of the winged insects have grown, some instinct triggers the desire to swarm. For several hours before takeoff, the winged insects will be running round outside the nest. Then they will join in a mating swarm and follow the queen ant to find a new site.

So if you want to be neighbourly and prevent the ants from making a nuisance of themselves in the garden next door, those few hours are the time to act. Spray or dust around the nest and over the excited ants with HCH before they take to the air.

Guarding the aphid herds

I have noticed lots of ants running up and down the stems of my roses and the trunk of my cherry tree. How can I get rid of them?

The ants are not your real problem, as they are not directly harming the tree or the rose bushes. They are attracted by your real enemy – aphids such as blackfly or greenfly. The aphids excrete a sticky, sweet substance called honeydew on which the ants feed. The ants will even protect the aphids from predators such as ladybirds so that they have a constant source of food, and will also carry greenflies from one plant to another.

The only other trouble that ants cause the gardener is when they loosen the soil round roots as they hollow out a nest amid their shelter – and the plants wilt for lack of support. Anthills in a lawn are unsightly, too.

The most effective way to get rid of the ants directly is with an insecticide dust or spray on their nests. Much better, though, to spray the foliage of your plants to kill off the pests that started the problem in the first place (for details of how to do this, see *Aphids*, this page). The ants will then move elsewhere to look for food.

SMALL HOLDERS *Ants 'milk' their aphid herds for the sweet honeydew they excrete. In return they protect the aphids from predators.*

Beating the carnivores

Lots of tiny yellow and red ants turn up in the summer around my lawn. Will they harm my children?

No, but they might frighten them. Both types are carnivorous ants which prey on small insects. The red ones are aggressive and can give a bite which may cause irritation and even draw blood. Being nipped by a red ant might alarm a small child, but the bites are not dangerous.

Red and yellow ants are mostly found in light soils, and in areas where they can make nests in cracks and crevices in the soil as well as in walls and paths.

Boiling water poured down the crevices will easily kill off a lot of ants without using chemicals, but to get rid of an ant colony of any type completely, you have to destroy the nest itself.

If you do manage to uncover a nest by following the routes the ants take, water it thoroughly with a spray-strength solution of the relatively persistent insecticide HCH or the non-persistent pyrethrum. Usually the nest is some way from the point at which the ants emerge into the open and is difficult to get to. In this case, put down insecticide dust wherever ants are busy. The worker ants will carry the poison particles back to the nest.

It will be a while before numbers are reduced. You may have to renew the bait several times over a period of weeks. In the spring, dust the area once more to catch the ants when they come out of hibernation.

APHIDS

Blackfly blues

My garden is full of greenfly and blackfly. What's the best treatment?

Greenfly, blackfly – they are both aphids, as are other small, round-bodied insects which can be white, pink, red, yellow or even multicoloured. Between them, the various aphids are probably the commonest pests in British gardens.

The insects, which are mostly but not always wingless, feed on sap, distorting young leaves and shoots and depositing honeydew which encourages moulds. Even more serious, aphids transmit virus diseases, and while there are ways and sprays for dealing with insects and fungal moulds, there are no cures for virus diseases.

Spray with a contact insecticide such as malathion, derris, permethrin or pirimicarb as soon as you notice any of the insects on your plants. Some gardeners also swear by traditional remedies, such as spraying with soapy water, water with washing-up liquid added, or with an infusion of cigarette ends or boiled rhubarb leaves. But most scientists argue that a jet of plain water would be just as effective.

Where aphids are well protected from the effects of contact sprays by curled leaves or waxy coverings, choose a more persistent systemic insecticide such as dimethoate. These insecticides penetrate the leaves to enter the sap stream, killing any insect that attempts to feed on the plant.

The pests attack in spring and early summer outdoors, but can be a nuisance at any time under glass. At the end of summer, adult aphids lay their eggs on trees and bushes, where they hatch out in the following spring. So next year's problems can be reduced by tackling the eggs, before they hatch, with a tar-oil spray. These sprays should be used only in winter and only on bare-branched plants, because the chemicals will burn any green foliage they touch. Don't spray on very frosty days, though: the water in the spray can freeze, leaving the oil unable to penetrate the cracks in the bark where the eggs are usually laid.

COMMON PESTS *Aphids, which come in several colours, feed on almost all cultivated plants, weakening them and spreading virus diseases.*

APPLES

Outsize Bramley

We have just grubbed out a magnificent, but far too large, 'Bramley's Seedling' tree. I would like to plant another of the same variety. Is it possible to grow a small Bramley?

Yes, you can buy it on a special 'dwarfing' rootstock – meaning one that has been chosen because it will slow down the growth of any variety grafted onto it and so keep the resulting tree smaller. All modern apple trees are budded or grafted onto a prepared rootstock, usually one from its hardy relative, the crab apple. This gives the tree a better start in life, makes it fruit much earlier than it would on its own roots, and enables the nurseryman – and you – to choose how big a tree you want.

The 'Bramley's Seedling' is one of the most vigorous varieties, reaching in full growth on its own roots 25-30ft in height with a spread of up to 20ft. Taming it is difficult; the harder you prune it, the more vigorously it grows.

Look for a Bramley grafted onto either of the dwarfing rootstocks M9 or M26. These should keep your new tree to a manageable 10-15ft. Choose M9 if you have a rich soil. Go for M26 if your soil is not so good – this is the less dwarfing rootstock.

Whichever stock you use, the tree will need staking throughout its life. The root system will not be strong enough to support it without this extra help. Otherwise, treat it as a normal fruit tree.

Feeding apple trees

When should fertiliser be applied to apple trees?

Between Christmas and the end of March. The exact timing depends upon the size and age of the tree and the nature of your soil.

Your fertiliser needs to reach the roots when it is most needed – in spring when the sap begins to rise and the buds to form. Apply it in mid-winter if you are treating a tall, old tree with deep roots on heavy soil, so as to give the fertiliser the maximum time to get where it will be needed. A young tree with shallow roots in a sandy soil can be treated weeks later. Trees on dwarfing rootstock or trained to a wall or fence will have smaller root spreads whatever their age, and so can be fed later than larger specimens of the same variety.

Spread the fertiliser evenly to reach all the roots. As a rough guide, the root area will be about the same as that of the branches, so don't just pack it around the trunk. Feed trained trees up to 6ft from the trunk. Use a surface mulch of manure or compost – along with 2oz per square yard of bone meal, or 2-4oz per square yard of Growmore – on a tree which is growing at the rate you want and producing good crops. If you want to encourage more growth, use a high-nitrogen fertiliser such as dried blood; if more fruit production is the aim, use a high-potash feed such as a tomato fertiliser.

Moving stakes

I planted medium-sized 'Cox's Orange Pippin' and 'Ellison's Orange' trees two years ago. They look reasonably sturdy now; can I remove the stakes?

Leave them in. They are doing no harm, so why bother to move them. If they were properly put in, they will still be giving the tree some support. Generally, stakes can be left in the ground until the trees have outgrown them, or the stakes have rotted at the ground and are actually being supported by the tree.

Like all rules, though, this one has its exceptions. Fruit trees grown on dwarfing rootstocks such as M9, M26 and M27 will have weak root structures and will therefore need staking throughout their lives.

When staking these trees, make sure you do a really good job. Choose a stake that will be large and strong enough to support the grown tree, not just the sapling, and make sure it has been pressure-treated with preservative. Drive the stake firmly into the planting hole *before* you put the tree in. If you put it in after, you will damage the roots. Place the stake on the windward side of the tree to limit chafing of the trunk. In Britain that means generally to the south-west, the direction from which we get most of our winds.

Cut the top of the stake at a slant so water runs off it, but don't cut it so short that the top of the stake is below the first branch. The higher you set the tie holding tree to stake, the firmer the job. Check stake and tie every spring and autumn.

Mossy tree

I have an old apple tree largely covered in moss and lichen, producing only mediocre crops. Would getting rid of the moss help it?

Possibly, but it is more likely the age than the moss that is causing the trouble.

Moss and lichen themselves will do no harm to a tree; they are only hiding the bark. But they offer a cosy home for pests, and these can cause damage to a tree.

A spray of tar oil in the dormant season from December to February will clear moss and lichen. Give the tree a good drenching so that the wash soaks right into the moss. It will also seep into the nooks and crannies of the bark, killing off, as a bonus, any hibernating eggs of aphids and scale insects.

No fruit

I have had a young apple tree in my garden for about four years. There has been little blossom and no fruit. What must I do to encourage fruiting?

Try a high-potash feed, or lift it and replant it, or just wait. All modern apple trees are budded or grafted onto a rootstock specially selected to encourage early cropping. Some older varieties do take time to begin cropping. But, assuming your tree was between one and three years old when you planted out, you should have had sight of an apple by now.

The reason for the absence of fruit may be that the tree is putting all its energy into growth instead. If the tree seems to be making a lot of new shoots and foliage, there's too much nitrogen in the soil, so restore the nutrient balance with a dressing of a fruit-promoting potash fertiliser – a standard tomato fertiliser will do fine.

If growth seems to be slow, dig up the tree and replant it. This can often be enough to jolt it into action, even if you put it back in the same place.

One other cause may be an overly vigorous rootstock, which would encourage the tree to go on growing for longer before it starts fruiting. There is no reliable cure for this – you just have to wait. Root pruning does, however, sometimes help. To do this, dig a trench in winter 3-4ft from the trunk and for half the tree's circumference. Cut through all the roots you meet. Do the other half of the roots the following winter.

Falling blossom

My apple tree has had plenty of blossom in the past few years, but little fruit. What's going wrong?

Check that pests such as capsid bugs are not eating the flowers or young fruit. If pests are to blame, the flowers will go brown or the fruit shrivel and fall immediately after setting. A tar oil wash next winter will take care of them. So will regular spraying with a systemic insecticide such as dimethoate from the time the flower buds begin to open.

Otherwise it is probably frost. Balmy May days can make fools of us all. The night sky can stay as clear as the day, letting the sun's warmth escape from the soil and letting in icy air swiftly and silently behind it. The frost is gone with the first morning sunshine, so you hardly notice it, but the damage has been done. Your blossoms may look cheerful, but inside the stamens are black and dead, all chance of fruiting gone.

A net draped over branches will keep in the warm air of the day to protect your tree on clear nights. So will making sure that your tree isn't in a frost 'pocket' – an area where cool air can collect like water in a pond. If your garden is on a slope, make sure that there are gaps in any hedge on the downhill side so that chilly air can flow away. A garden at the bottom of a slope or hill is usually a frost pocket and will never be much good for fruit growing.

One other thing you can do is rough dig the soil beneath the trees. Some professional growers insist that cultivated ground releases warmth from the soil more readily than ground covered with an insulating layer of grass. Apple blossom will also fail to set in a very dry spring. Regular, and plentiful, watering will cure that.

Fruitless loner

I despair of ever getting a decent crop from my apple tree. I've only got the one tree so I can be lavish with my care, and I am. What can I do to ensure a full crop?

If you're sure that pests, frosts and age aren't the problem, the answer is straightforward: make sure there is another apple tree near yours. This is not usually a problem in most town and suburban gardens. Bees and other pollinating insects will travel many hundreds of yards in search of pollen. You would be very unlucky if there weren't another apple tree somewhere in your block.

Only in an isolated country garden are bees likely to find it difficult to pollinate a single tree, in which case you'll have to plant another apple yourself. Pick a variety that flowers at the same time (see *Pollination partners*, page 17). But if you decide to plant only one extra tree, avoid the varieties known as triploids. Triploid is the botanical name for a variety whose pollen does not pollinate other varieties of the species. Most common of these in the apple family are 'Bramley's Seedling', 'Ribston Pippin', 'Blenheim Orange' and 'Jupiter'. Where these varieties are grown, there must be at least two other apple varieties nearby to ensure adequate pollination.

Cross-pollinating trees do not have to be of the fruiting type. Ornamental crab apples, such as *Malus* 'Golden Hornet', *M.* 'Aldenhamensis' and *M.* × *hillieri*, will do.

If you have no room to plant another apple tree, graft the shoot of a pollinating variety onto a branch of your tree. It will provide all the pollen you need.

How to grow cordons

I saw some cordon apple trees in the garden of a stately home recently. Would they work in a small garden and would they give as much fruit as ordinary trees?

Yes, they are ideal for a small garden. But no, they won't give as much fruit as a standard tree because they will always be much smaller. The fruit they do give, however, can be of better quality.

A cordon is a tree restricted to a single stem. It is planted in the ground at an angle of about 45 degrees against a wall or fence. Supporting wires must be fixed first, at least three horizontal stretches of wire up to a height of 7ft. Plant the trees 3-4ft apart, training them up the wires so that the top of each tree eventually overhangs the base of the next one in the row.

No branches must be allowed to form. Cut all growths back near the stem to form short fruiting spurs. Each tree takes up so little room that a variety of apples can be grown along a single wall.

Cordons can be covered by netting, making them easier to protect from spring frosts than ordinary trees, and, because of the open nature of their growth and easy accessibility, cordons are easy to spray thoroughly against pests and diseases. They also get more sun and no rubbing or scarring from moving branches.

Good pruning is the key to good cordons. New growth shoots must be cut back ruthlessly in summer to provide fruit spurs (see *How to prune apple trees*, opposite).

SLIMLINE *Cordons need pruning up to four times a year: in July-August and again in September to cut back new growth; in winter to thin spurs; and in May to trim a mature tree's tip.*

Maggoty crop

Last year I had a lovely crop of apples – but half of them had been eaten into by maggots by the time they were ready to pick. What can I do to stop this?

Your parasite is almost certainly the caterpillar of the codling moth. It loves apples.

The adult moth emerges from its cocoon in June and flies into the trees to lay eggs on the developing fruits until early August. The tiny caterpillars hatch out and burrow, usually through the 'eye' of the fruit (the end opposite the stalk), into the apple. Once they get in there, you can't shift them and the fruit will be ruined, so you have a very short time in which to strike.

Spray with fenitrothion, permethrin or malathion in the second week of June if you live in the South of the country, in the third week if you live in the Midlands or the North, and spray again two or three weeks later. You are unlikely to kill all the caterpillars with these sprays, so plan some prevention for next year as well.

Many of the caterpillars leave the apples after they have feasted and crawl down the tree trunk and into the ground to spin cocoons for themselves. Most will stay there for the winter, dormant in their cocoons; they will emerge as adults next year to start the cycle all over again.

Wrap corrugated paper, sacking or straw around the tree in early August to intercept them. The migrating caterpillars will curl up in the first comfortable spot they come to. Take off the whole lot in November and burn it. Sticky grease bands will also do the job.

Tree from a pip

Can I raise an apple tree from a pip?

Yes, but don't expect results in a hurry – or that the tree will produce an apple like the one you took the pip from. Apple trees are cross-pollinated; they need pollen from another tree to fertilise fruit. The tree your pip grows into will be a cross between both of its parents, and may also have some characteristics from both parents of each parent tree, and from their ancestors, too. So it will be a botanical mongrel, not a named pedigree variety.

You will need to be patient as well. Trees from seed – which is what a pip is – take a long time to mature, probably several more years than those grafted at the nursery onto a vigorous rootstock. Don't expect to see a fruit for at least five years.

Start your seeds in a large pot filled with seed compost. The best time to sow is autumn; use the pips from a ripe apple and just cover them with a light sprinkling of compost. Leave the pot out in the open all winter, and the seeds should germinate in spring.

Once the seedlings are growing, keep them well watered, especially in the drier spells of summer, and pot them up separately. Plant them out in the ground when they're about 2ft high. Feed them with about 2oz per square yard of bone meal each spring and, during the summer, feed them from time to time with a balanced liquid feed such as a standard house plant fertiliser.

Give it a try – it will be fun to see what you end up with. You may even be as lucky as a retired London brewer named Richard Cox. In 1825 he planted a seed from a 'Ribston Pippin'. It grew into the 'Cox's Orange Pippin' – one of the all-time great apples and still, rightly, a favourite.

HOW TO PRUNE APPLE TREES

Pruning a new tree

A new apple tree from the nursery may be three or four years old when you buy it. At three years, an ordinary tree, though not a cordon, should have at least four strong branches extending outwards from the trunk.

After planting, cut about one-third off each branch, back to an outward-facing growth bud. This will encourage three or four sideshoots to sprout from each branch, forming the basic shape of the tree.

Don't let your tree fruit in the first year. Rub off any embryo fruits after the blossom has fallen. The stronger sideshoots and branches should fruit in the fifth and sixth years.

Pruning an established tree

There are two types of fruiting apple trees: spur-bearers and tip-bearers. They need slightly different pruning treatment.

Most apple trees are spur-bearers – meaning that they bear fruit on short woody spurs. On these trees, aim to trim three-year-old shoots back to the lowest fruiting spur. Near each such shoot, cut back a strong, one-year-old shoot by one-third to a growth bud, so it can grow into the space left behind.

A few varieties, such as 'Bramley's Seedling', 'Worcester Pearmain' and 'George Cave', bear fruit at the tips of their sideshoots as well as on fruiting spurs. These trees do not need so much pruning as spur-bearers.

Your general aim in pruning, on any ordinary apple tree, should be to keep the centre of the tree open, to encourage outward-growing branches and sideshoots, to cut out all crossing growths, and to cut back old growths which have fruited to make way for new growths. Try to create, by your cuts, about 12in of space between each branch.

Leaders – the outermost shoot of each young branch or sideshoot – should be pruned to a growth bud to encourage new fruit buds to form below it. Leaders with fruit buds at the tip should be cut only if they're overcrowded; if they are, cut them to within four or five buds of their bases.

Prune between December and February, when the tree is dormant. There are no hard and fast rules, but try to maintain a balance between growth and fruitfulness. Remember that a sideshoot of an apple tree develops fruit buds in its second year, and that these buds will produce blossom and fruit in the next and subsequent years. These are the main principles:

- Cut to a growth bud for growth.
- Cut to a fruit bud to form spurs.
- Cut back strong shoots by one-third.
- Cut back average shoots by a half.
- Cut back weak shoots by two-thirds.
- *Always* use sharp secateurs. If you saw off a branch, paint the cut surface with a pruning compound to keep out diseases.

Restoring an old tree

Cut out all dead and diseased wood. Open the centre of the tree, cutting out all crowding or crossing branches, and any heavy central branches. Aim to make the tree roughly cup-shaped. Cut back the tallest branches to a strong, healthy sideshoot. Thin out overcrowded spurs over a period of three to four years. Encourage sideshoots to develop from lower on the branches by cutting back branches by between one-third and a half. Prune each branch to an outward-facing bud.

RECOGNISING THE PARTS OF AN APPLE TREE

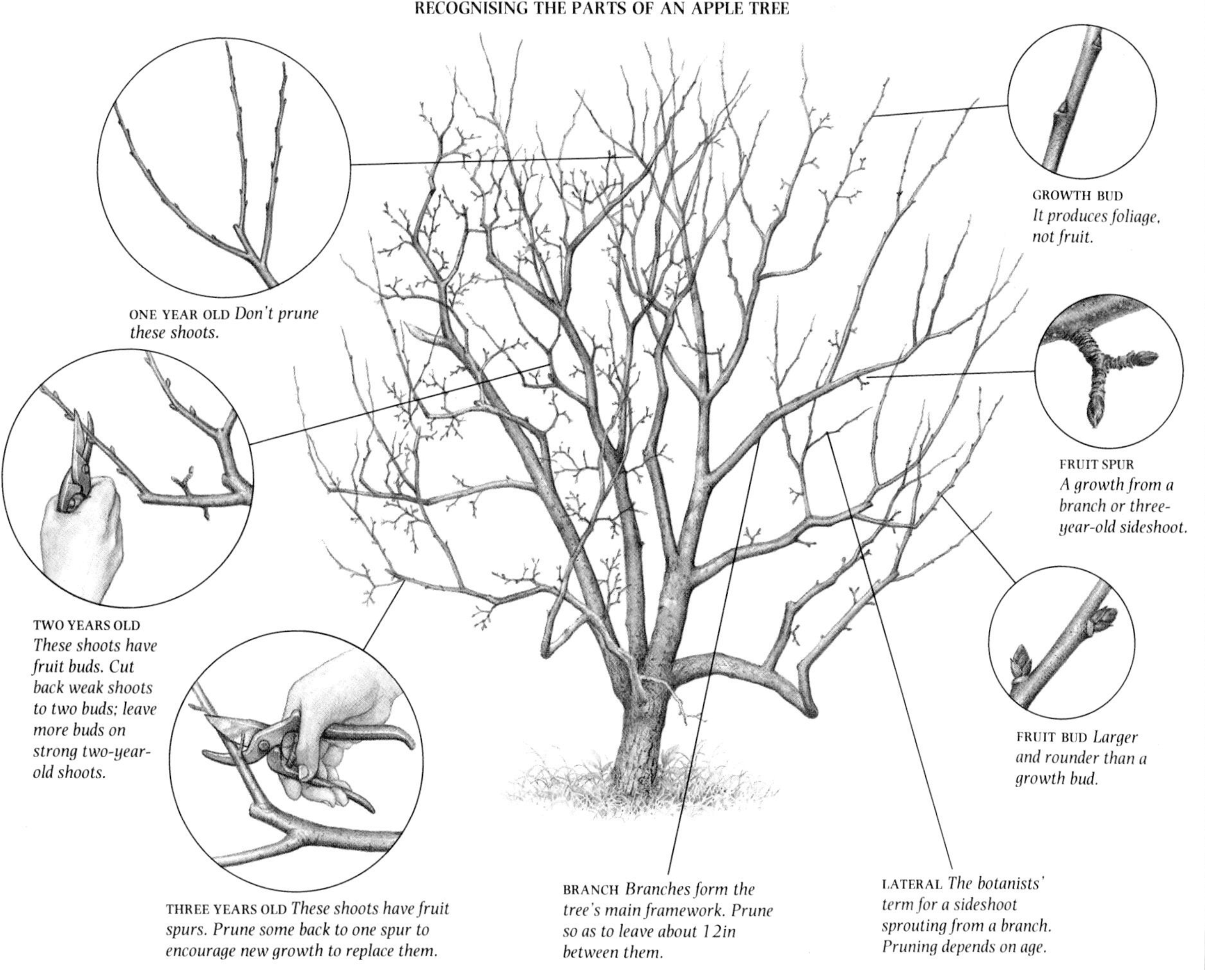
ONE YEAR OLD *Don't prune these shoots.*
TWO YEARS OLD *These shoots have fruit buds. Cut back weak shoots to two buds; leave more buds on strong two-year-old shoots.*
THREE YEARS OLD *These shoots have fruit spurs. Prune some back to one spur to encourage new growth to replace them.*
BRANCH *Branches form the tree's main framework. Prune so as to leave about 12in between them.*
LATERAL *The botanists' term for a sideshoot sprouting from a branch. Pruning depends on age.*
GROWTH BUD *It produces foliage, not fruit.*
FRUIT SPUR *A growth from a branch or three-year-old sideshoot.*
FRUIT BUD *Larger and rounder than a growth bud.*

Apple anxiety

My two apple trees set well this year, but as soon as the fruits began to swell, the skins cracked and even split. Haven't I fed the trees properly?

More likely you haven't watered them properly – or not regularly at any rate. Apple trees take up a lot of water when the fruits are setting, and what you describe is a symptom of thirst.

If your trees are growing out of grass, compensate for dry weather by giving them 4 gallons of water to the square yard each week, over the full stretch of the branches' canopy. But if you have conscientiously surrounded each trunk with a ring of bare soil, add a 1-2in thick mulch of compost, peat or well-rotted farmyard manure to the soil in spring. This will help to retain moisture.

There's no great difficulty in dealing with this disorder, but you might find it useful as well to have a checklist of other apple complaints, some of which require sterner measures. This is a list of the more common problems, and how to deal with them.

- **APPLE SAWFLY** The first sign is that fruits drop soon after forming and show holes surrounded by sawdust-like frass. When the fruit is cut open, the flesh smells strongly, and a small white grub is revealed. Combat sawflies by spraying immediately after blossom fall with fenitrothion.
- **APHIDS** Look for twisted, curled leaves and shoots covered with a sticky deposit; look under leaves for tiny green, white or black insects. Spray at the first sign of trouble with an insecticide containing dimethoate, fenitrothion or malathion.
- **CODLING MOTH** From late July onwards, watch out for tiny holes in fruit; when apples are cut through, a white or pale pink caterpillar is revealed, feeding near the core. Protect future crops by spraying in mid-June with fenitrothion or malathion. Give another spray three weeks later.
- **BITTER PIT** Signalled by brown indentations in the skin of fruit and by brown, slightly sunken spots in the flesh. Spray the tree in mid-June with 8oz of calcium nitrate in 5 gallons of water and repeat at three-weekly intervals. Never let the soil dry out.
- **RED SPIDER MITE** Mottled leaves turning yellow and rusty. Spray in mid-June with dimethoate, rotenone or malathion.
- **APPLE SCAB** Leaves, fruit and shoots become covered in brownish-black scabs. Spray with benomyl or thiophanate-methyl from when the buds first start to open until July. For how often to spray, see the manufacturer's instructions on the packet.
- **APPLE CANKER** Shows itself as oval patches of dead or dying bark on trees. The patches may extend around twigs, so killing them. Cut out and burn affected parts. Paint cut surfaces with a canker paint containing thiophanate-methyl.
- **BROWN ROT** Appears as soft brown spots surrounded by yellow-white fungal blobs on fruits. Destroy affected fruits whether they're on the tree, on the ground or in store. Spray with thiophanate-methyl or benomyl.
- **POWDERY MILDEW** White, powdery deposit visible on stems and shoots, which also become distorted. Cut out affected shoots at the first sign of trouble, and spray the rest of the tree with benomyl or thiophanate-methyl.
- **CAPSID BUG** Causes puckered leaves and misshapen fruits, which sometimes show canker-like bumps. By the time the symptoms appear, the insects have usually gone. Spray with fenitrothion.

Apple sawfly damage

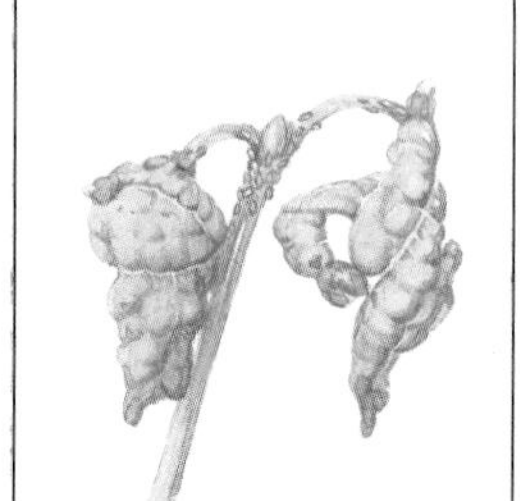
Leaf-curling aphids

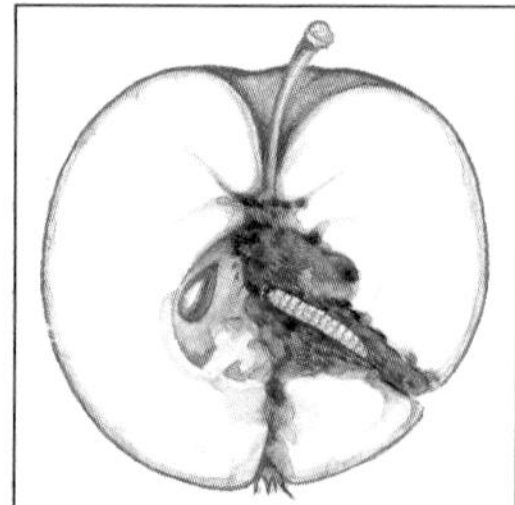
Codling moth larva

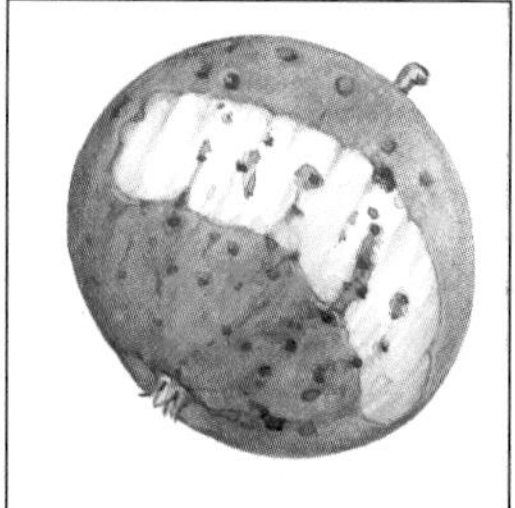
Bitter pit damage

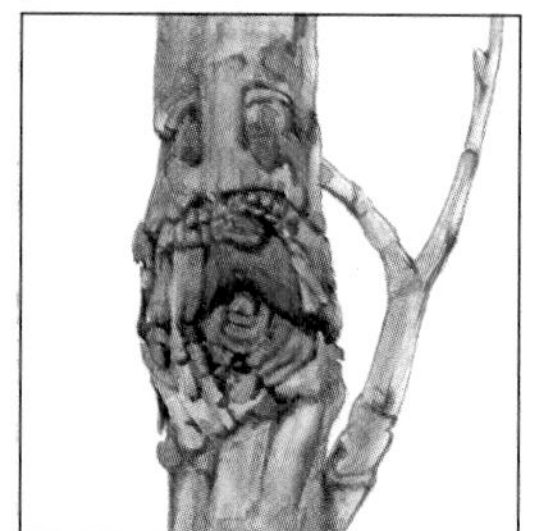
Apple canker

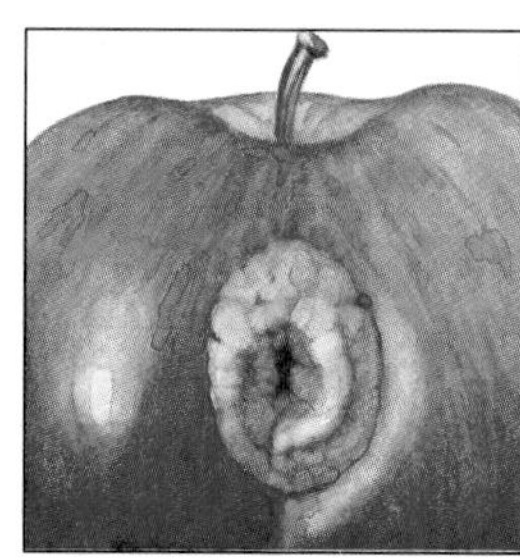
Capsid bug damage

Grease bands

I remember when almost every apple tree had a grease band around the trunk about 3ft from the ground to trap insects. Are they still in use, or have modern chemical sprays made them obsolete?

They are still available and are still used by fruit growers who don't like chemical sprays, but sprays and chemical treatments have made them a thing of the past in many orchards and gardens.

Grease bands are effective against the pests that crawl up or down a tree trunk, mainly in autumn and spring. So they do help to control two of the most troublesome apple pests: the winter moth, whose caterpillars eat leaves, buds and blossom; and the codling moth, whose caterpillars burrow into ripening fruit.

Caterpillars of the codling moth climb down the tree in summer to pupate; adult winter moths climb up the tree in winter to lay eggs. A grease band will trap many of them.

Place the bands – you can buy the fly-paper-like bands ready-made in many garden centres – around tree trunks in late August and replace them in February. Tie or glue them tightly to the surface of the trunk so that insects can't creep under them. Check every week or so that soil, garden debris or blown leaves haven't stuck to the band and made a life-saving bridge for the pests.

Insects that get stuck on the band will die off in the winter cold, and the band can be taken off when it gets crowded, burned and replaced by a new one. Grease bands are not generally as successful as sprays, however, or as quick. It'll be two or three years before bands get your pest population under control – and even then, they won't eliminate the problem altogether.

For the best chemical weapons and treatments against common apple pests, see *Apple anxiety*, this page.

Storing apples

What are the simple rules for picking and storing apples?

You must choose the right varieties to start with. All the meticulous care in the world won't keep an early 'Discovery' apple in eatable condition until Christmas. The list on the right – *Pollination partners* – shows how long you can keep, and use, some popular varieties.

As a general rule, an apple that is ready for cooking or eating before October is unlikely to store well. Varieties that mature from October onwards are the ones to store.

Pick them when they are fully grown, but before they have fully ripened. The way to tell when to pick is to lift an apple in the palm of your hand and twist it half a turn.

If it parts from the tree, it's ready to pick. If it parts readily from the tree without a twist, then it's already too ripe to be in top condition for storage. If it doesn't part with a twist, give it another three or four days and try again. Always leave the stalk on the apple.

Start picking in mid-September for the October ripeners, through to late October for those which are due to be ready from early November.

The ideal conditions for storing are a low, constant temperature with a moist atmosphere to stop the fruit shrivelling. A cellar is ideal, but few houses are built with them these days. A brick outbuilding is better than a wooden one, because it gives more insulation against sudden changes in temperature or humidity. Either is better than indoors, which is too warm and dry.

Wrap the apples up individually in newspaper and store them in boxes. If you use polythene bags, leave the tops open so that air gets to the fruit. A few can be stored in the bottom of the fridge.

POLLINATION PARTNERS

Few apple trees successfully pollinate themselves. They need pollen from another variety of apple to fertilise their fruit. Almost any apple will do – but the two varieties must flower at the same time so that bees can transfer the pollen from one to the other. This chart groups apple trees that flower together, and will therefore pollinate each other. Exceptions are the plants known as triploids, which are such poor pollinators that they need two other trees nearby – to pollinate each other and the triploid. Early-flowering varieties blossom between about May 1 and May 11 in the South, about a week later in the Midlands, and two weeks later in the North. Varieties that flower in mid-season bloom around May 7-21 in the South, and again later in the North and Midlands. Late-flowering varieties bloom from about May 11 to May 23 in the South.

Name	When to pick	When to use	Remarks
EARLY FLOWERING			
'Idared'	early Oct	Dec–Apr	Crimson-yellow dessert apple; keeps well
'George Cave'	early Aug	Aug	Green, crisp dessert
'Egremont Russet'	late Sept	Oct–Dec	Brown, nutty-flavoured dessert
'George Neal'	late Aug	Aug–Oct	Yellow-orange cooker
MID-SEASON FLOWERING			
'Discovery'	mid-Aug	Aug–Sept	Bright red dessert
'Cox's Orange Pippin'	late Sept	Nov–Jan	Red-flushed, firm dessert
'Crispin'	early Oct	Dec–Feb	Yellow dessert, resists dwarfing. Triploid
'Bramley's Seedling'	mid-Oct	Nov–Apr	Prolific green cooker. Triploid
'Grenadier'	mid-Aug	Aug–Sept	Green cooker, won't store
'James Grieve'	early Sept	Sept–Oct	Yellow orange dessert
'Fortune'	early Sept	Sept–Oct	Red-flushed dessert. Easily bruised
'Kidd's Orange Red'	early Oct	Nov–Jan	Red-grey russet dessert
'St Edmund's Russet'	mid-Sept	Sept–Oct	Golden, small dessert
'Sunset'	late Sept	Oct–Dec	Gold-speckled dessert
'Worcester Pearmain'	late Aug	Sept–Oct	Green-yellow dessert
'Spartan'	early Oct	Nov–Feb	Dark red dessert
LATE FLOWERING			
'Annie Elizabeth'	late Sept	Nov–Apr	Good-storing golden cooker
'Dumelow's Seedling'	late Sept	Nov–Apr	Small yellow cooker
'Ellison's Orange'	mid-Sept	Sept–Oct	Red-yellow dessert. Aniseed flavour; easily bruised
'Golden Delicious'	late Oct	Nov–Feb	Yellow dessert
'Lane's Prince Albert'	late Sept	Dec–Mar	Green-crimson large cooker
'Howgate Wonder'	early Oct	Nov–Feb	Big green-red cooker
'Mother'	late Sept	Oct–Dec	Yellow-red dessert
'Orleans Reinette'	mid-Oct	Nov–Jan	Red-yellow dessert

Pruning for fruit

How can I be sure when pruning that I don't cut off branches that are carrying the fruit?

Only by learning to distinguish between fruit buds and growth buds. Look at the pictures in *How to prune apple trees*, page 15, to see the difference.

Remember, too, that young growth is as important for future crops as flowers are for this year's crop. Too little pruning can lead to lots of small apples this year, too much to a few big ones next year.

Family tree

A friend of mine has what he calls a 'family' tree with several varieties of apples all growing on the one tree. Can I make my own, and do they have good fruit?

Yes, you can create your own 'family tree', and it should give good fruit.

A family tree is a single tree, grown on a rootstock, but with two or three other varieties of apple grafted onto it while still a sapling. The different apples all grow together from the same tree trunk. This gives a variety of crop in a minimum of space.

To make your own, choose combinations of apples carefully, so that the flowers will fertilise each other (see *Pollination partners*, this page). One good combination, for instance, is 'Discovery', 'Fortune' and 'Sunset', giving an early, a mid-season and a late eater. Or try 'James Grieve', 'Cox's Orange Pippin' and 'Spartan', giving an early, a late and a keeper; all of them are good eating varieties.

Don't be tempted to use 'Golden Delicious' on a family tree, however. It comes into fruit a year or two before most other varieties and may outgrow them, taking over the tree. For the same reason, avoid other vigorous varieties such as 'Bramley's Seedling' and 'Blenheim Orange'.

You can buy family trees ready-made from nurseries. Alternatively, you could try your luck at making your own. To create a family tree, take young shoots from the tree varieties of your choice and graft them to the host tree (see *Grafting*, page 160). Feed and prune as a normal tree.

Pest control

Is there a way to control pests and diseases on apple trees without spraying chemicals all over the plants?

Some control is possible with simple good plant management, but you can't eliminate pests and diseases completely this way.

A tree that was planted and staked properly, is well-fed and watered, and pruned regularly, should be strong enough to withstand most pest attacks. Snap off and burn any pest-infested or disease-infested shoots and leaves as soon as you notice them, and use grease bands (see *Grease bands*, page 16) to trap migrating caterpillars. Spray aphids with a soap and water mix or, perhaps more reliably, with an insecticide such as dimethoate or malathion.

Off-and-on fruiter

My apple tree – I think it is a 'Laxton's Superb' – crops well one year, but gives nothing the next. How can I even it out?

Thin out the newly forming fruit clusters in the good year to give a less bountiful crop. Wait until late June or early July, after the normal June drop of freshly set fruitlets.

Prune off first any apples or clusters of apples that are obviously damaged, or misshapen. Then thin clusters of fruit to a single apple. Try not to leave the 'king' fruit – the apple in the centre of the cluster – because it tends to develop a poor shape. Finally, thin out the fruits so that they are 4-6in apart.

'Laxton's Superb' is one of the few popular apple varieties with this on-off fruiting habit. If your tree is not a Laxton's, the seesaw fruiting may have been started by frost or by a vicious attack of apple sawfly (see *Apple anxiety*, page 16). Whatever the cause, the cure is the same.

Pruning for shape

How often should I prune an apple tree to keep its shape?

Regularly in winter if it is a standard or bush tree, regularly in summer if it is a cordon, espalier or dwarf pyramid.

Cordons are single-stemmed trees planted at a 45 degree angle against a wall or fence. In August, as soon as new shoots begin to harden at the base – they will probably be about 18in long by then – cut them to a fruit bud within 3in of the stem to produce fruit-bearing spurs. For details on how to recognise fruit buds, see page 15.

Espaliers are grown upright against a wall or fence with branches strung out each side at right angles, like arms held wide, and trained along wires. Cut all new sideshoots from the framework of branches back to 3in to create fruiting spurs. Spurs that have borne fruit should be cut back by at least one-third of their length in winter to encourage the growth buds which will form next year's new shoots. Cut these shoots back in turn in the following August to form new fruiting spurs.

Dwarf pyramids must also have their sideshoots cut back to form fruiting spurs. Where a greater length of shoot is required to retain the pyramidal shape, cut to the nearest suitable fruit bud.

Apple pairs

I have room to plant only two apple trees in my garden. Which would be best?

It depends in the end on how you like your apples – raw or cooked. If your family likes them both ways, go for a mid-season eater and a relatively late cooker – but make sure that both trees flower together so that they pollinate each other (see *Pollination partners*, page 17).

With only two trees, you will be looking for good, reliable croppers. Here are some combinations of compatible trees: 'Discovery' (eater) and 'Grenadier' (cooker); 'Sunset' (eater) and 'Golden Noble' (cooker); 'Rosemary Russet' (eater) and 'Lane's Prince Albert' (cooker).

A wider variety of fruit would be possible in your limited space if you decided to grow cordons or espaliers, or even a tree with several different varieties grafted onto the one trunk (see *Family tree*, page 17).

Neglected tree

How can I get an old, straggling and neglected tree back into good shape and condition?

It will need severe winter pruning, a tar oil wash, and a fertiliser feed in spring. For details see *How to prune apple trees*, page 15.

ARTICHOKES

How to store the tubers

I've been given some Jerusalem artichokes. How should I store them?

The knobbly tubers quickly lose water when they've been dug up, and even when put in a polythene bag at the bottom of a refrigerator will keep firm for only up to three weeks.

The best thing is to store them in damp peat in a cool place such as a shed. That way they will stay firm throughout the winter.

For artichokes you've grown yourself, the best storage method is to leave them in the soil until they're required – though you may find that slugs and woodlice will nibble one or two.

Tubers left in the ground after March will start growing – a good way to grow a new crop if you can't eat them all in time.

Problems of an edible screen

I've thought about using Jerusalem artichokes to screen my vegetable patch. Would this work?

Growing an ornamental sunflower-like screen that yields masses of edible tubers sounds great – but there will be problems.

The stems will not make an effective screen until June, and they could easily exceed an embarrassing 10ft by September. Some support will be necessary, and their hungry roots and the shade they cast might make it difficult to grow vegetables alongside.

The dead stems also need to be cut down close to the ground in October, otherwise the wind will loosen the roots. So, from then until June the following year, your vegetable area wouldn't be hidden from view.

The other main consideration is how many artichokes you want. Since the plant is a prolific cropper, a screen longer than, say, 12ft might well produce far more tubers than you want to eat – and the excess will spread rapidly unless you dig them all up each year.

Sisters in name only

Are globe and Jerusalem artichokes grown the same way?

They are both perennial vegetables, but that's about all they have in common. The Jerusalem artichoke is completely hardy, and spring-planted tubers can give a tenfold increase by the following autumn. The name is nothing to do with the Holy Land, but is derived from the Italian word *girasole*, meaning 'sunflower'.

The plant grows like a sunflower – to which it is closely related – and it needs hot summers to flower well, although this has little bearing on the crop.

Jerusalem artichokes are easily cultivated in ordinary soil. Plant the tubers in late February or early March (using shop-bought ones if you prefer). Set them about 5in deep and 15in apart in rows 3ft apart. Small tubers are the best for planting, providing they have at least one eye. Don't feed or manure the crop because that will encourage the growth of foliage at the expense of tubers. Lift tubers as needed between October and spring.

You need green fingers to grow good globe artichokes, especially if you try your hand at raising them from seed rather than planting rooted side growths or suckers in the spring.

The edible, fleshy scale-covered flower heads are their main attraction, and mature plants grow up to 5ft high. As a decorative bonus, the large, silvery-grey leaves look good in a roomy border.

Like the Jerusalem artichoke, the globe artichoke appreciates full sun, but it dislikes heavy clay soils. Find a well-drained spot and dig in lots of peat or garden compost before planting. It also dislikes the cold, and even in mild areas a thick winter covering of ashes, strawy manure or bracken is advisable.

ASPARAGUS

Choosing the variety

My local garden centre doesn't stock what I understand is the best variety of asparagus, 'Connover's Colossal', and they suggest I buy newer varieties which crop better. Are they right or should I try elsewhere?

Originally imported from America, 'Connover's Colossal' has been grown for a long time in this country. It's a good, reliable asparagus, but there's no denying that some of the modern ones crop more heavily, especially the all-male varieties like 'Lucullus'. These single-sex varieties tend to be more expensive, but over the years will justify the extra cost.

Nevertheless, it's a bit strange that you can't find 'Connover's Colossal' for most large garden centres and mail-order nurseries carry it. It would be well worth planting it alongside one or two other varieties just to compare performance.

Males are a better bet

I've been told that male asparagus plants grow stronger than females. Is there really much difference between the sexes?

Yes. Since they have to produce flowers and small red berries as well as edible stems, the females are worked harder, and therefore produce a lower overall yield than the males. Unfortunately, it is very difficult to distinguish between male and female plants even when they are flowering. Only when a plant produces berries can you be sure that it is a female.

If you are growing asparagus from seed, keep the plants in their seed rows for two years before moving them to their permanent bed – by then the females should have berried and can be discarded. You can, alternatively, play safe and buy crowns of the variety 'Lucullus'. It produces only male plants and, consequently, the yields are high.

WHICH VARIETIES TO GROW

A number of asparagus varieties are on the market. These are some of the best.
'Connover's Colossal' – a firm favourite with early, thick, purple-tinged stalks that freeze well. Sold as seed or crowns.
'Lorella' – very thick, succulent stems. A French variety that yields well. Sold as crowns only.
'Lucullus' – the first male-only asparagus. Higher yielding than most other varieties. Usually sold as one-year-old crowns.
'Martha Washington' – usually grown from seed. Crops in May-early June, slightly later than 'Connover's Colossal'.
'Sutton's Perfection' – available only as crowns. A sturdy variety with thick stems.

Take it with a pinch of salt

Salt is said to make asparagus grow. How does it work?

Salt's chemical formula is sodium chloride. And since all plants need sodium for healthy growth, a little salt *can* be useful. It also discourages slugs and weeds.

On the other hand, the amount of sodium required even by asparagus (which is a seaside plant) is very slight indeed. So the benefits of applying it are extremely doubtful – many successful asparagus gardeners don't bother with it.

Still, if you'd like to try it, give a light dressing of agricultural – not household – salt in spring; a level tablespoon to the square yard should be sufficient. Even better would be an application of liquid seaweed fertiliser during the growing season. Give it according to the manufacturer's instructions. Add a top-dressing of well-rotted manure in autumn to help things along.

Hold back on cutting

I planted asparagus crowns last spring. When will they be ready to cut and how long will the plants last?

Allow one year between planting and cutting the first stems or spears. The crowns were probably already two years old when you planted them.

Wait until the shoots are 4-6in long before cutting – normally this would be in April or May – and don't harvest more than two or three spears from each plant in the first season of cropping.

Use a sharp, narrow-bladed knife to cut the spears about an inch or so below the surface. Before doing so, gently scrape away the soil so you can see what you're doing; otherwise you may damage the roots and new stem growth. Don't cut later than mid-June because the plants have to regain their strength for the following year.

Strong, healthy crowns planted in a well-prepared and well-maintained bed should crop for at least 20 years and may go on for much longer.

Seed simplicity

Is it difficult to grow asparagus from seed?

No. It's fairly easy, provided the seed is sown outside in late March or April when the worst of the frost is over. Germination will occur after about five weeks. The drawback about growing asparagus from seed is that you have to wait at least three and possibly four years before cutting the first spears. 'Connover's Colossal' and 'Martha Washington' are the varieties you are most likely to find in seed form. It's hardly a wide choice, but both are good.

To hasten germination, soak the black seeds in lukewarm water for 24 hours and then sow them thinly in fine, fertile soil. If you have cloches, use them to warm up the soil for a couple of weeks before sowing. Sow the seed $\frac{1}{2}$in deep in drills 12in apart, then gradually thin the seedlings to 6in apart. You can speed the process a little by sowing in deep trays of seed compost and placing the trays in a cold frame. Transplant the seedlings into nursery rows either outdoors or in a cold frame.

Apart from weeding, and possibly watering during dry weather, the young plants won't need any other attention. Let them

ASPARAGUS GROWER'S CHECKLIST

- Choose a sunny spot for your asparagus bed – preferably one that is sheltered from strong winds which could loosen the plants. Avoid frost pockets, which may harm tender buds in the spring.
- A good asparagus bed may crop for 20 years or more – so it's worth taking the time to prepare the soil thoroughly. A deep, medium loam that drains quickly in winter and warms up quickly in spring is ideal. Dig in plenty of well-rotted manure or compost before planting. On heavy clay soils, raise the asparagus bed above the surrounding soil level to improve drainage.
- Plant one or two-year-old crowns in the spring. Set them in trenches which are about 6in deep and 12in wide. To make traditional asparagus beds, have four trenches 15-18in apart in each bed, with $2\frac{1}{2}$-3ft between the beds.
- Space the crowns 12in apart and spread their roots out in the base of the trench. Cover the crowns with 2in of soil.
- During the summer keep the rows weeded and don't let the soil become too dry. Remove berried female plants.
- In October cut the ferny growth off 1in from the ground and burn it. Mound up the soil over the plants. Apply a 2in mulch of well-rotted manure or compost over the whole area at about the same time.
- Apply a feed of liquid seaweed fertiliser at fortnightly intervals throughout the summer. Pull up any seedlings which have come from female plants.
- Cut your harvest of spears between late April and early June when the plants have been established for at least one year and the spears are 4-6in high. Avoid damaging the roots and smaller spears.

stay in their rows for one year and then set them out into a deeply dug, manured bed. Thereafter, treat them like bought crowns.

Stretching the cutting season

For a few short weeks each year, my family and I gorge ourselves on home-grown asparagus then not another spear do we get until the following year. Isn't there any way to stretch the season a bit?

Harvesting robs the plants of stems which would otherwise develop their ferny foliage and manufacture food to benefit the crowns. It's a bit of a vicious circle – being too greedy results eventually in weaker crowns, weaker plants and, thus, fewer spears.

The cutting period normally lasts for up to eight weeks – from late April to early June – and then the plants must be left to grow on. There are several things you can do to lengthen the season, although none will increase the total size of the crop.

First, grow early and late varieties. 'Connover's Colossal' and 'Larac' can be cut slightly earlier than 'Martha Washington' – although it might only extend the harvesting by about two weeks.

Second, cover some of the plants with cloches from February onwards to accelerate their growth so that you can cut them slightly earlier. 'Connover's Colossal' is suitable for this treatment.

Third, force a few plants in a heated greenhouse. Select strong, three or four-year-old crowns, cut down their yellowed tops in late October, and plant them in boxes or the greenhouse border. The crowns can be packed closely enough to be touching, and should be covered with 3in of moist soil.

With a steady temperature of 21°C (70°F) you could be cutting the first spears within four weeks, but even at 10°C (50°F) plants lifted in October will still crop several months earlier than those left out in the garden. After three or four cuts, the crowns become exhausted and should be thrown out.

AUBERGINES

Aubergine bitters

Some of my aubergines have been quite bitter. Why?

Leaving them on the plants too long until they become overripe and wrinkled – that's the reason. Try to catch them when the skin is firm and shiny.

If you don't catch them in time, the bitterness can be reduced by slicing the fruits ¼-½in thick, sprinkling salt on the slices and leaving them for 30 minutes. The salt draws out the bitter juices, and the aubergines will absorb less oil when fried.

Why eggplants like to be coddled

Do I need a greenhouse for aubergines, or could I grow them in a sunny border like my sweet peppers?

Aubergines – or eggplants, as they're often called – like more warmth and shelter than peppers. So unless your border is exceptionally well protected from the weather, or you use cloches, you do need a greenhouse.

If you do grow them in the garden, start warming the soil with cloches two or three weeks before setting out the plants. Take advantage of any spell of fine weather in late May to do this. While the soil is warming, harden the plants off gradually over two or three weeks by putting the pots outside (or by raising frame lights) for increasing periods each day. That way, the cold night air doesn't come as too much of a shock.

In a heated greenhouse, aubergines can be planted from early April, but if it's unheated, wait until early May.

The F1 hybrid variety 'Black Prince' is worth trying outside because it grows quickly and matures early.

A vegetable egg

Why is the aubergine often called the eggplant? The only ones I've seen have been large and purple.

Several older varieties had small, rounded, white fruits – hence their common name, eggplant or egg fruit.

The shiny, purple-skinned, large-fruited varieties such as 'Black Prince', 'Black Enorma' and 'Dusky' are now the most popular, but white eggplants can still be found. 'Easter Egg' is the most common: this has white fruits like large goose eggs.

How to get more fruits

When I grew aubergines last year I had only two or three fruits on each. Would pinching out the main stem have helped to get more?

It might have, if your plants were not very bushy. Aubergine plants will eventually branch out, but it's best to help them by removing the tip of the main stem when the stem is 9-12in high.

Pollinating the flowers should also help the plants to give more fruit. To do this, keep the greenhouse temperature down to 18°C (about 65°F) when the flowers are opening, then on sunny mornings lightly spray the flowers with tepid water. This will help to transfer the pollen grains onto the stigmas – the flowers' female reproductive organs. Alternatively, grow a variety such as 'Black Prince' which sets its fruit more easily than most other varieties.

Good greenhouse varieties can easily cope with two fruits per stem, but if you want really big ones, limit the total to five or six fruits per plant, pinching off the surplus as soon as they form.

Sorting out the pests

My greenhouse tomatoes and capsicums regularly get plastered in whitefly and red spider mites. Do aubergines get many pests?

Sadly, yes – in fact the same ones, with red spider mite the worst. But the pests aren't that difficult to deal with.

Spraying with dimethoate, permethrin, resmethrin or malathion every 10-14 days should do the trick, especially if you change the sprays regularly to prevent the pests acquiring resistance.

Another pest is slugs, which like the ripening fruits, so keep slug pellets handy.

AZALEAS

Halting the decline

My Japanese azaleas flower well for the first year, then fade miserably away. What am I doing wrong?

One or more of three things. To start with, your garden soil may not suit the plants as well as the acidic or ericaceous compost of the containers in which you bought them. If that's so, the azaleas won't push their roots beyond the confines of the compost. And if that happens, the nutrients in the compost will keep the plants going for the first year or two, but after that they will starve.

If you think the soil is the problem, there are two solutions. First, when removing the azalea (or indeed any plant) from its container, gently tease the roots out around the edge to encourage them to grow out into the soil. Second, enrich the soil in which the plant is being placed with both peat and a dressing of base fertiliser – Growmore is suitable. Don't use bone meal, though; it is too alkaline for such acid-loving species.

Another possible reason for the decline of your plants may be the site. Azaleas are plants of sheltered woodland. They suffer in a windswept, exposed situation and won't tolerate a waterlogged, compacted soil.

The solution to a waterlogged or compacted site is to open up the soil over the whole area by digging in bulky organic matter such as leaf mould, peat or bark. Do not merely dig a small hole in heavy soil and add organic matter to it; this will simply create a waterlogged pocket.

The third reason why your azaleas may be growing badly is the depth at which you're planting them. Azaleas and rhododendrons are surface-rooting plants and do not like being buried deeply. With a new plant, take care not to set it any deeper than the existing soil mark on its stem. An ailing plant that's already in the ground can sometimes be revived by digging it up, dressing the roots with fertiliser and replanting it more shallowly.

Raised beds

I'd love to establish a bank of azaleas, but I know that my soil is alkaline and therefore unsuitable. Is there any way round this problem?

Yes. Move house. Otherwise, you could with some effort establish a few low-growing ones. You set about it by constructing a peat bed, a small area where the addition of large quantities of peat will raise the acidity of the soil. It is best to use sedge peat in bulk for this; it is almost as good as moss peat, and usually much cheaper.

Build a raised bed 8-12in above the surrounding soil. Rocks can be used to make the walls but wood is easier, cheaper and more appealing. Half-round farm fence rails, or old railway sleepers, or logs of hardwood or of a durable softwood like larch will all do fine. If possible, buy wood which has been pressure-treated with preservative. But whether it's been treated or not, give it an additional coat of preservative to be on the safe side, taking special care to drench the surfaces of any cuts you make.

Stack the rails or logs two or three deep, according to the height required, and secure them with hardwood stakes hammered in on either side. Fill the bed with a mixture of two parts by volume of peat with one of garden soil. But if your soil is so chalky that it actually contains lumps of chalk or limestone, use ericaceous compost in the mixture instead.

Grow small azaleas in the raised bed – they have to be small to ensure that the roots do not extend into the alkaline soil beneath. Combine them with low-growing dwarf rhododendrons, summer-flowering heathers and perhaps a camellia, all of which like the same conditions.

Top-dress the bed with a 1-2in layer of peat in spring or autumn and add a sequestered fertiliser each spring. This type of fertiliser will help the plants to take up iron and other nutrients despite the alkaline soil beneath the bed. This will prevent any yellowing of the leaves.

Christmas cheer

Can the azaleas I buy as house plants at Christmas be planted out later in the garden? And how should the azaleas be treated when flowering is finished?

Sadly, they're not much good for the garden. These forced dwarf azaleas are hybrids derived mainly from two small Asian species. They do well in a cool greenhouse, but could be planted permanently outdoors only in the very mildest parts of Britain.

All the same, the Christmas plants are certainly worth keeping. Take off the dead flower heads as the blooms fade and water them with soft water – rainwater in hard-water areas. Feed them about once a fortnight with a standard house plant liquid fertiliser. Once the danger of frost has passed, bury the pots up to their rims in peat in a cool part of the garden. Keep feeding them until they are brought indoors again in early autumn.

If you have a greenhouse, put the azaleas into that for a while instead in autumn. Leave them there until the flower buds swell – and bring them into the house then.

Go for galls

My azaleas have developed small, white cheesy blobs on the shoots. What is wrong?

This is azalea gall, a common disease of both deciduous and evergreen species. The tender indoor varieties are particularly prone to it, especially when they are grown in greenhouses. If you look closely at the blobs or swellings, you will see that they are covered with a white, powdery coating. This is made

Short cuts with cuttings

What is the best way to increase my stock of azaleas?

There are two main ways, as there are with most plants – by seed and by cuttings. Raising azaleas from seed is a lengthy business and, unless you are interested in hybridising them, worthwhile only with the few true species. Reproducing by cuttings is easy and much quicker. Take cuttings in late summer when the new wood is semi-ripe; then it can be bent over but will not snap until it's been bent almost double. Cut lengths of healthy shoots about 2-3in long and trim away the lower leaves.

Use as a rooting medium a half-and-half mixture by volume of moss peat and lime-free sharp sand. Spread the mixture in a container to which a more or less airtight translucent cover can be fitted – a flowerpot with a plastic bag tied over it will do fine.

Dip the bases of the cuttings in a hormone rooting powder, and push them gently into the rooting medium. Seal the container and stand it in a well-lit spot out of direct sunlight – a cold frame outdoors would be ideal. Don't allow the cuttings to dry out. Most azaleas will root within about three months.

Layering also works well and is the easiest method of all. Simply select a low-growing shoot or branch and anchor it into the soil with a small wooden peg held down with stones. Remember where you made the layer, for it may take up to two years to root. When it has rooted, sever it cleanly from the parent and treat it like a mature plant.

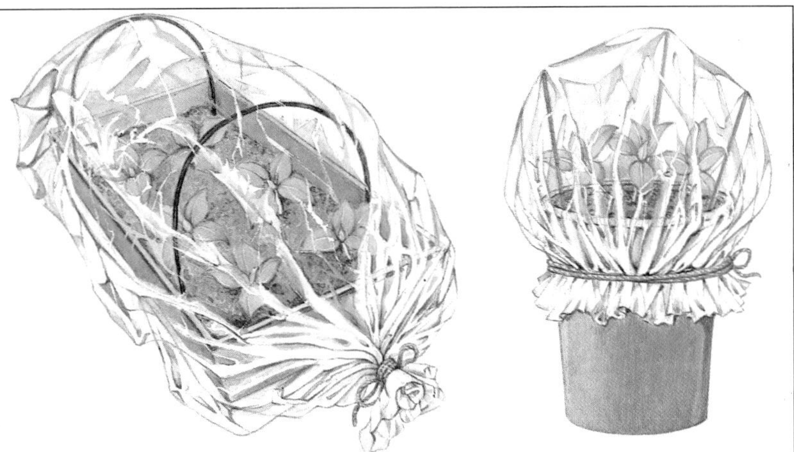

PLASTIC FOR PROPAGATING *Clear or milky plastic bags make good propagating cases for azaleas, and for any other small cuttings or seeds. One way is to upend a bag over a pot (right); another is to put the pot or tray right inside the bag and blow the bag up. Support it if necessary with canes, or wire hoops made out of old coat hangers, and seal the opening with a freezer tie.*

up of the spores of the fungus which causes the disease. There is no reliable fungicidal treatment, and affected plants soon lose their vigour.

The best antidote for azalea gall disease is to watch for any signs of an attack and then carefully cut off the infected shoots and burn them. Avoid spreading the disease by dipping your knife or secateurs into disinfectant between cuts and by taking care that you do not disturb the spores.

Bark is best

What's the best kind of mulch to use on azaleas?

Azaleas and rhododendrons have shallow roots, and can suffer badly in dry weather; a good moisture-retentive mulch is therefore vital. Peat is an obvious choice for such acid-loving plants, but only so long as it's wet. When it dries out, it forms a crust that can actually throw off water.

Shredded or pulverised bark is better, but expensive unless bought in bulk. Don't be tempted, by the way, to buy bargain lots of cheap unbranded bark. It may not have been properly composted and could still contain toxic residues.

One of the cheapest mulches is pine needles, which you can collect for nothing in woodland – provided, of course, that you have the owner's permission. Spruce or other conifer needles will do the same job, but they're more prickly and more difficult to handle.

War on weevils

Why do my azaleas have little notches extending inwards from the leaf edges?

The notches are caused by the vine weevil, a small, flightless, long-nosed beetle which attacks many types of garden plant. A menace in both its larval and adult forms, it is especially common on evergreen azaleas, rhododendrons and camellias.

It is the adult insect which is troublesome on azaleas, especially when they are grown in a sheltered spot.

The pests hide among leaf litter on the soil during the day, crawling up the plants at night to nibble the leaf edges. The females lay their eggs on or below the soil surface and the larvae burrow into the roots or tubers of almost any soft, fleshy plants they encounter. Curiously, female vine weevils very often reproduce asexually – which is perhaps just as well for the insects' survival, since males are extremely rare.

Control of such an elusive pest is difficult. It is hardly practicable to treat the entire leaf litter beneath a bank of azaleas. Fortunately, damage is not usually severe. But if it is, spray or dust the soil and litter beneath the shrubs with HCH and rake it in. This should get rid of the weevils.

Deadheading

Should dead flower heads be removed from azaleas or left to fall off of their own accord?

Take them off. By removing dead flowers – and the immature seed pods they contain – you encourage the plant to direct its energy into building up strength for the following year rather than into producing seeds, which is what it would do in the wild.

Take care, though, not to damage the young leafy shoots that originate close by the bases of the dead flowers. Old-time gardeners used to say that the dead flowers come away more easily if you bend them towards the north. Oddly enough, this does sometimes seem to be true, but it's hard to see that there could be any scientific basis for it.

Leave the dead flowers and their seed pods on the plant only if you want seed for raising new plants. Bear in mind, though, that raising azaleas from seed is worthwhile only with true species. Most azalea varieties are hybrids and won't breed true from seed. If you want seeds, leave a few pods only; more will weaken the parent plant.

Family links

What's the difference between an azalea and a rhododendron, and how important is this in the garden?

The plants we call azaleas and rhododendrons all belong to the Ericaceae family, as do heathers and the strawberry tree. Most of them prefer acid soils. At one time, azaleas were treated as a distinct genus, but they are now, botanically speaking, all considered to be forms of rhododendron.

Perhaps the most important gardening distinction between the hardy types is that most rhododendrons require greater shade than do most azaleas. This should be borne in mind when planting a mixed shrubbery.

WHICH AZALEAS TO GROW

There are scores of different azalea varieties, some of which are more fussy about their treatment than others. The varieties listed here are all fairly easy to grow and will thrive in most parts of Britain. The average fully grown height for all the species listed is 3-4 ft and the spread $2\frac{1}{2}$-$3\frac{1}{2}$ ft.

Variety	Deciduous/Evergreen	Flowers
'Addy Wery'	Evergreen	Vermilion (Apr-May)
'Coccinea Speciosa'	Deciduous	Rich orange-red (June)
'Hindodegiri'	Evergreen	Crimson (Apr-May)
'Hinomayo'	Evergreen	Clear pink (May)
'Homebush'	Deciduous	Rose-pink; semi-double (May)
'Irohayama'	Evergreen	White, with lavender edge (May)
'John Cairns'	Evergreen	Dark orange-red (May)
'Kure-no-yuki'	Evergreen	White (May)
'Mother's Day'	Evergreen	Rose-red; semi-double (May)
'Narcissiflorum'	Deciduous	Double, pale yellow with darker centre, sweetly scented (June)
'Palestrina'	Evergreen	White with faint green centre (May)
'Silver Slipper'	Deciduous	White with pink flush (May)
'Spek's Orange'	Deciduous	Orange (early May)
'Vuyk's Scarlet'	Evergreen	Vivid red (May)
'White Lady'	Evergreen	White (May)

BAMBOO

Stopping the rot

Is there any way to protect garden bamboo canes from rotting inside?

Yes. Sharpen the base of the cane to a blunt point and let it sit in a container of horticultural wood preservative. If you use a narrow container such as an old milk bottle, you can make sure that the best part of a foot of the cane is submerged. Leave it there for a day or two so that the liquid soaks right through the stem (keep it well out of the way of pets and children). Then let it dry out before use.

In addition, keep canes in a dry shed or garage in winter so that they get a chance to dry out after their season in the soil. Rot spreads much more quickly in canes that are constantly damp.

Following these tips won't stop canes rotting for ever, but it will certainly save you having to buy new ones every year.

Growing for canes

How can I tell if my bamboo canes are ready for harvesting? Is it by length, thickness, or colour, or doesn't it matter?

Canes do not increase much in girth during growth; they simply extend. Therefore you should harvest them simply when they have reached the desired length. Colour is largely irrelevant, because different species have varying stem shades, from olive-green and yellow to purple.

Harvesting is best done in autumn. With sharp secateurs, cut each cane as near to the ground as possible. Store the canes in a cool, dry place – a shed, garage or conservatory – laying them flat or hanging them from a string so that they dry straight.

The best species to grow for this purpose are vigorous large-caned plants such as *Arundinaria anceps* and *A. japonica*.

Taking cuttings

My ageing bamboo plant is going yellow. Can it be revived, should I take cuttings, or should I buy a new plant and start afresh?

Your plant has probably reached the end of its useful life. So reviving it with a sort of intensive care programme is unlikely to work for very long.

You can certainly try propagating from your plant, though with an old or sickly plant it may not be easy. The best method would be to divide the clump, or remove and plant separately any rooted suckers, during late spring.

If that doesn't work you'll have to buy a new plant. Cuttings are impossible in any circumstances. Because bamboo is a kind of grass, it can't grow from a cut stem any more than lawn clippings can.

Bamboo screens

I've seen pictures of bamboo screens. Is the plant really suitable for hedging?

Two species worth recommending for screening are *Arundinaria anceps* and *A. japonica*. The first, best for the smaller garden, has a rampant yet graceful habit. Its shiny green canes grow up to 10ft and throw out arching fronds of glossy mid-green leaves.

A. japonica reaches a height of 10-15ft. Its olive-green canes are topped by large and glossy, dark green leaves. It is an imposing, thicket-forming species, really suitable only for the larger garden.

Some types of bamboo make excellent screens – though not, strictly speaking, hedges, which are usually hardwood shrubs requiring training and clipping.

Remember that most bamboos, while hardy, dislike open gardens where they are exposed to strong winds; and although they will exist happily on many different soil types, they prefer a higher-than-average moisture content.

Blooming curiosities

I hear that some species of bamboo flower all at once – wherever they are in the world – and then die. Is this true and, if so, why have these species not become extinct?

You have hit on one of the mysteries of nature, for the flowering habits of bamboos have puzzled botanists all over the world for years.

Bamboo renews itself each year by sending up new shoots from underground stems. Each plant flowers only once in its life; then, its life cycle completed, it dies. But occasionally, at intervals of between 40 and 120 years depending on the species, the plants flower, seed and die en masse.

Sometimes the insignificant blooms appear on only a few stems of one plant, and although those particular stems die, the plant as a whole is unaffected.

Sometimes, on the other hand, the whole plant is weakened or dies. And sometimes entire forests can be killed off in this way. In one such flowering, in China's Qionglai Mountains in May 1983, much of the region's forests of arrow bamboo died. And an unknown number of giant pandas, which depend on bamboo for food, starved to death as a result.

Instances have also been known where tender bamboos grown for years in British greenhouses have suddenly flowered – and died – at roughly the same time as large numbers of plants of the same species growing wild in the tropics.

Generally, not all of the bamboos within a species flower, and so the species can survive. Moreover, many of the seeds formed in the flowers do in time germinate to grow into a new generation. A few years ago, however, a beautiful variegated bamboo (*Sasa kutilensis variegata*) did become extinct through this mass flowering and dying phenomenon. Collected seed was germinated, but the resultant plants did not possess the attractive golden leaf variegation.

If your own bamboo plant begins to produce flowers, there are two rescue options, either of which *may* save it – although neither method has won universal support from horticultural scientists.

First, you could try feeding it. Research carried out at the Pacific Bamboo Garden Nursery in California suggests that if bamboo plants are fed liberally with a high-nitrogen fertiliser, such as hoof and horn meal, at and after flowering until new growth appears, there's a good chance that they will survive. But nobody yet knows whether this method will work on all bamboo species or in all climatic zones.

Second, you could try preventing it from flowering. Some older gardeners claim that the lives of bamboos can be saved by cutting all the stems down almost to ground level at the first sign of any flowers.

BASAL ROT

Stains spreading through scales

When I dug up my overcrowded daffodils recently, intending to divide and replant them, I found that almost half the bulbs were rotten at the bottom. It hasn't been a particularly wet season, so what's wrong?

Probably they are suffering from basal rot, a fungus disease so called because it spreads from the bases of many bulbs and corms, including those of crocuses, narcissi, lilies and daffodils. The disease can attack at any time of the year.

A gardener will usually not realise his plants have basal rot until he lifts the bulbs for storage, though he will get some warning in the case of crocuses, whose growing foliage turns yellow and dies.

To confirm the diagnosis, cut a suspect bulb in half lengthways. If it has basal rot, dark strands will be visible spreading upwards from the base of the bulb, or the inner scales will be marked with chocolate-brown stains.

In the early stages of the disease, many bulbs can be saved by cutting out the affected parts and then soaking what's left for about half an hour in a spray-strength benomyl solution.

Badly affected bulbs, however, are not worth bothering with. If basal rot has been a problem before, the best way to protect bulbs and corms against it is to soak them for 15-30 minutes in a spray-strength solution of benomyl or thiophanate-methyl. Both chemicals are systemic fungicides, and both work in much the same way. A routine immersion before planting, and another before putting them into store, should keep the rot at bay.

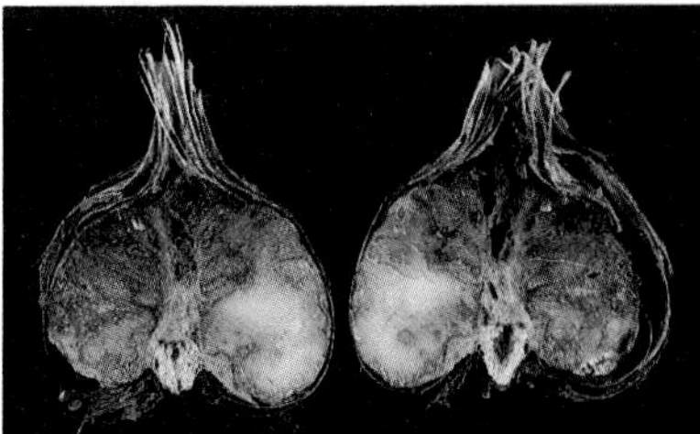

HIDDEN DANGER *Basal rot in narcissi and lilies becomes apparent only when the bulbs are dug up. Rotting roots and bases are a sure sign.*

BASIL

Out in the midday sun

I love basil in salads, and intend to grow some. Obviously, for me, the most convenient place would be outside the kitchen door. But how does basil feel about it?

Badly, unless your kitchen door is in full sun. Basil is a subtropical herb – it was brought to Britain from India in 1548 – and though you can plant it outdoors in this country once the last chance of frost is past, it requires a sunny, sheltered position. Better, maybe, to grow it in pots on a sunny windowsill. That way, you will extend its season by a month or more.

The best of basil

The local garden centre offers two kinds of basil for sale. Which has the better flavour?

There are indeed two kinds of basil plants: sweet (*Ocimum basilicum*) and bush (*O. minimum*). Sweet basil will grow to a height of 1-2ft, and has large, shiny, mid-green leaves with white flowers, or dark purple leaves with pink flowers. Bush basil is much smaller, usually about 6-12in high with small, pale green leaves and tiny white flowers. As the name implies, it is bushy in habit. Both species have an equally delicious flavour but bush basil is the better one for window boxes or pots on windowsills.

Either buy small plants, or sow in a light, rich soil, planting out seedlings 8in apart at the beginning of summer. Water lightly and pinch out the growing tips to encourage a bushy habit.

BAY

Problems with cuttings

I have tried on a number of occasions to take cuttings from a neighbour's bay tree. Each time the shoots stay dormant for months, and eventually go brown and die. I would like to succeed, as bay trees are so expensive. Any tips?

You will never succeed in rooting cuttings of bay (*Laurus nobilis*) overnight or even in weeks. There have been cases when even after 12 months roots have not formed – and this slow rooting is the main reason why the plants are so expensive. So, patience is the key.

You don't say how you were taking your cuttings. But if you follow this procedure to the letter you should have some success. During late summer or early autumn take tip cuttings from wood of the current season's growth – what the professionals call a semi-ripe or semi-hardwood cutting. Take the cuttings with a heel – that is, with a small strip of the main stem still attached.

Each cutting should be 4-6in long. Strip off the lower leaves and dip the bottom of the cutting in a rooting powder.

Set the cuttings in a half-and-half mixture of peat and sand, inserting about a quarter of their length into the compost. A shaded cold frame or propagator is the best place to keep the cuttings, but make sure they don't get frosted during the winter. Keep the cuttings moist, but not wet, and mist-spray them occasionally.

Now sit back and wait. Roots and shoots should, with a little luck, form during the spring and summer of the following year. In the autumn, set out the young plants in a sunny spot.

Standard size

I recently bought a young container-grown bay tree. How should I prune and train it to look like the bays you see outside Italian restaurants – round-headed standards about 4ft high?

If left to its own devices, a bay tree could reach 20ft or more. But a standard or mophead bay is certainly a lovely, eye-catching feature. And it need not be confined to a tub on a patio: it can be planted in a bed or border. Remember, though, that the bay, *Laurus nobilis*, originally came from Mediterranean countries. So, although it is hardy in Britain, large garden specimens can suffer in harsh winters.

Your young container-grown tree will take some years to reach the desired 4ft standard, but there's no harm in beginning training even at its present early stage.

As long as your plant has a central leading shoot you will be able to achieve the mophead. When the plant reaches 2-3ft in height, cut the lowest branches cleanly at their point of origin on the main stem. This will encourage growth in the topmost branches.

When the leading branch has reached the height you want the centre of the mophead to be, snip it off. From then on, each spring and again in summer, carefully cut back the new growths to create and later maintain the rounded head.

Drying the leaves

What's the best way to dry bay leaves for the kitchen?

On a dry day snip off some sprigs, tie them in bunches, and hang them by the stems in a warm room. Leave them for a few days. Then strip the dry leaves from the stems and store them in an airtight container so that they cannot reabsorb any moisture.

Ideally, use screw-top, non-transparent jars, or store the leaves in a cupboard. As with all herbs, the flavour deteriorates if the leaves are exposed to light.

A crushed leaf added to casseroles, chowders, prepared meats, stuffings and even milk puddings is traditional. Bay is also an essential ingredient of *bouquets garnis*. And a small leaf added to cabbage or brussels sprouts while cooking will banish the boiled greens odour from the kitchen.

BEDDING PLANTS

Bedding or annuals?

Trays and trays of bedding plants are on sale at the nurseries each spring. Are they all annuals?

No. Bedding plants are any plants set out to give bright colour in a bed for a particular season. The ones you see in spring are mostly annuals – they grow from seed, flower and die all in the same year. But there are also some biennials (plants with a two-year life cycle), and some half-hardy perennials (plants that die down each winter to return in spring).

Whatever their botanical category, however, almost all bedding plants are treated as annuals. They are usually raised from seed, brought on in a greenhouse or cold frame and planted out for summer display. Then, after a few months of glory in the garden, they are consigned to the compost heap.

The cost of colour

Bedding plants are such a price these days. What are the pros and cons of raising the plants myself?

Nursery-reared plants are much more expensive than a packet of seeds, but they do give you a wider choice. You can raise your own annuals from seed; but you'll have to weigh the fun of doing it against the cost of compost and any greenhouse heating. The savings may not be all that great. A cheaper alternative is to raise the plants on sunny windowsills, though you'll need a lot of space to grow enough for a massed display. Or you can confine your choice of bedding plants to hardy annuals, which can be sown straight into their flowering position in the garden.

You can, of course, save money by avoiding bedding plants altogether, filling your beds instead with shrubs and hardy perennials such as irises, lavender, peonies, phlox and violets. After the initial purchases, you avoid the annual outlay, but your borders will look the same each year.

Most gardeners find a happy mix: some shrubs; some borders for summer bedding plants; and some spots filled with bulbs.

Weeding problem

Which is the safest way to weed or hoe between seedlings to avoid accidental damage to them?

By hand. It's laborious, but sure. One slip of the hoe, and half a dozen baby plants can be cut off at the ground. A long-handled hoe, in any case, would be difficult to use with enough precision unless you planted your annuals in widely spaced rows like vegetables, and who wants to see flowers spaced out like brussels sprouts? For one way to simplify the job of weeding, without creating a regimented look, see *The right drill*, page 10. Make it easy for yourself as well by ensuring – with a spray or hoe – that the ground is reasonably weed-free before you plant up. Then it will be much less of a time-consuming chore to pick out by hand the ones that get away.

Alternatively, you can take the lazy but more expensive way and use chemical weed control. Brush on glyphosate gel to kill the weeds individually. Brushed by accident onto seedlings, though, it will wipe them out, too, so take care.

For particularly treasured plants, one other trick may help: use a homemade plant shield. Set a flowerpot or a bucket upside down over the plants, or lay a board on edge close beside the row (support it with stakes); then you can use a hoe freely around the pot or bucket, or up to the board.

Beating the cold

I grow all my summer bedding plants from seed and cuttings. How can I prevent them from being checked by cold weather at planting-out time?

Only by gradual hardening off, which means taking them from the greenhouse or kitchen windowsill and getting them used to a cooler atmosphere over a period of two or three weeks.

Make the process a gradual one. Start by increasing the ventilation, then later move the plants outdoors on warm days, then outside on every day. Plants in a cold frame don't need to be moved. Instead simply prop up or remove the frame top each day.

At first, bring the plants in each night. Later you can leave them out at night, but not if you think there will be a frost.

In a spring of average temperatures, it should be safe enough to put them out in the borders permanently in early May, provided that they have been hardened off. Even at that time of year, an unhardened plant can be knocked over by a cold night – which is not that rare in May.

Colour planning

I want to plan my summer borders to avoid colour clashes. Should I plot it in detail on graph paper, or is there a quick way to do it?

There is no quick way and, especially in a new garden, it is wise to draw a plan. It's also wise to keep a record of what you decide. Over the years, you will get a feeling about colour in your garden, and though you will want to change it from time to time, you

Do's and don'ts of buying plants

I have no greenhouse in which to grow summer bedding plants from seed, so I normally buy all mine. What should I look for in plants?

Primarily good, green, healthy foliage on short-jointed, stocky plants. Make sure, too, that the plants are in moist, weed-free compost.

If the leaves are yellow-green, the plants have suffered early starvation and they may take weeks to get over it. If the compost has dried out, the roots will have, too. Don't even consider buying. Go to another nursery.

These are the other rules to follow at the shops:

DON'T buy plants that are in full bloom. They will have a shorter-than-expected flowering life in the border.

DON'T buy plants just because they are cheap. If they look poor, they are poor. Forget what you will save – you will waste what you spend.

DON'T assume the plants have been hardened off. At most reputable nurseries, they certainly will have been; but if in doubt, ask.

DO, finally, make sure that each tray has a label naming variety and colour. You don't want to spoil that carefully planned border colour scheme.

HOW TO SPOT A GOOD BUY

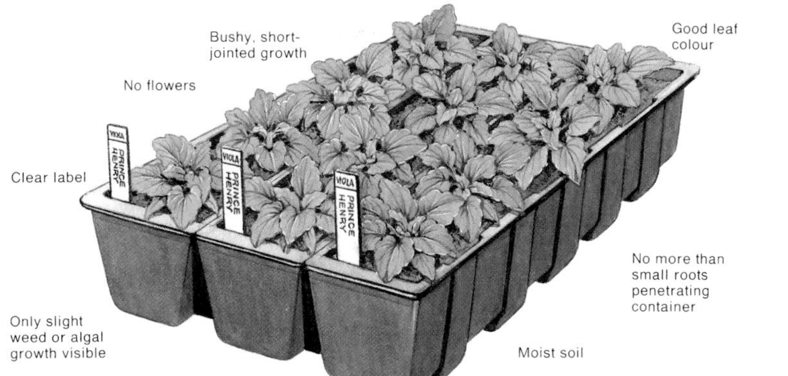

HOW TO SPOT A BAD BUY

won't want to lose the harmony. Decide whether you prefer contrast, related tones, or even monochromatic tones – different shades of the same basic colour, such as yellow, white, blue or red.

Then fill in your graph plot to scale, using coloured pencils, and write beside each section the name of the plant you will need to produce the colour, when it will flower and how many you'll need.

Planting out

I want my bedding plants to give a massed splash of colour. Should I plant them in rows, staggered, or at random?

Plant them how *you* like them best. Some gardeners say never set flowers in rows because they look like troops on parade. On the other hand, rows are easier to thin and weed, and the plants will grow together soon enough, obscuring the lines. If you set the rows for each plant at a different angle, you will also help to avoid a regimented look.

Staggering plants has the same advantages and disadvantages as rows, because the arrangement simply gives you straight lines from a different angle.

Whatever your choice about how to plant the main parts of the beds, put any edging plants in rows that parallel the edge of the display. The bed will look much neater that way.

In large areas of single-colour bedding, use 'dot' plants to break up the colour. For example, areas of red begonias (*Begonia semperflorens*) or salvia (*Salvia splendens*) can be broken up effectively by dotting among them taller plants such as *Cordyline indivisa*, *Ricinus communis* or standard fuchsias.

Winter bedding

How can I keep colour in the garden once the summer bedding plants have finished? Are there winter or spring bedding plants?

Winter, no; spring, yes. Once the summer bedding has gone over the top, lift the plants, dig over the soil and plant up straight away with bulbs and hardy perennials or biennials for spring.

Put out your favourites among the daffodils, tulips, hyacinths and crocuses. Go for biennials such as forget-me-nots, double bedding daisies, wallflowers, aubrietas, polyanthuses and primroses. They are all tough, and all make a marvellous show in spring.

Winter survivors

Which bedding plants, if any, can be lifted in autumn and stored for use next year?

Only the perennials. The annuals such as the stocks will all die off and new seeds or plants will be needed next spring. The hardy perennials such as lupins, delphiniums and hollyhocks will look after themselves where they stand. The biennials like sweet william and wallflower also need to stay put for their display next spring.

That leaves the dahlias, geraniums, tuberous begonias and the less hardy fuchsias. These are the basic rules for successful storage.

GERANIUMS (pelargoniums) Lift them in about mid-September, before the first autumn frosts. Plant them in potting compost in boxes or pots and keep them in an unheated shed or outhouse, watering only just enough to stop them drying out completely. Remove old flowers and leaves as they fade. Check the plants every couple of weeks. If they start to look brown and shrivelled, increase your watering slightly. If they're showing signs of growth, cut back the watering.

DAHLIAS Dig them up after flowering or after the first autumn frost. For storage details, see *Dahlias*, page 114. Treat cannas in much the same way as dahlias. But instead of taking cuttings from them in late winter, divide the rhizomes as they begin to shoot and pot them up singly.

BEGONIAS Showy tuberous begonias should be lifted before the first frosts and left in a dry place for the leaves and stems to die back and dry off. Store the tubers in dry peat in a cool but frost-free, airy place such as a garage or shed. Water the tubers lightly every month or so in winter to stop them shrivelling. Fetch them out and pot them up, hollow side uppermost, in March or as soon as the tubers begin shooting. Keep them in a greenhouse or on a light, frost-free windowsill until mid-May when they can be planted out again for summer flowering.

Fibrous-rooted begonias (*Begonia semperflorens*) aren't worth storing. Instead, turn them into pot plants. Trim them back in autumn, pot them singly into 4in or 5in pots and feed them with a high-potash fertiliser. They will give you good flowering plants for a cool room during the winter.

FUCHSIAS Take tender varieties in about mid-September into a greenhouse or dry shed away from any frost, and treat them like geraniums. Some hardier varieties will survive outside in moderate winters. Cut them to the ground each spring and let fresh growth form. These are, however, always later and less showy than the less hardy types which have been pampered under cover.

Hanging plants

Which plants should I choose for hanging baskets to create a cottage-garden effect?

Try these combinations, all of which should be planted up in late May or early June:

BASKET 1 Ivy-leaved geraniums 1-1½ft tall; petunias 6-12in: trailing lobelia, pale blue and white.

BASKET 2 Red, pink and white bedding begonias (*Begonia semperflorens*) 6-9in; red and orange trailing nasturtiums; blue lobelia; spider plants (*Chlorophytum comosum* 'Variegatum').

BASKET 3 Pink bedding begonias; red, white, or lilac ivy-leaved geraniums; wandering jew; and a central bedding fuchsia, up to 3ft tall.

ALL ABOUT SETTING OUT BEDDING PLANTS

Preparing the soil

Good soil will need only to be forked over lightly in spring, with a general-purpose fertiliser such as Growmore turned in as you go – about 1-2oz (a handful) for each square yard. Dig over poor or heavy clay soil in autumn, feeding in organic matter such as well-rotted compost, manure, peat or shredded bark. Smooth over and level the surface with a rake.

What to plant

As edging plants (all these are dwarf plants up to 8in tall): ageratum, pale blue and pink; lobelia, pale and dark blue; alyssum, white; tagetes, yellow, scarlet and orange; and verbena, red, blue or mauve.

As dominant groups (plants up to 2ft tall): petunia, mixed; zinnia, mixed; bedding begonia, red, pink and white; bedding dahlia, mixed; salvia, red; bedding geranium, pink, red, white, salmon or lilac; and antirrhinum, mixed.

As dot plants (tall and showy flowers or foliage to break up block planting): standard fuchsia, red, pink and white; kochia, bright green turning to copper in autumn; abutilon, brilliant white and green foliage; Indian shot plant (canna), purple leaves.

Planting out

Water the plants thoroughly before planting them out; but don't water the bed. Start planting from the back in a border and from the centre in an island bed. Lay a board across the ground to spread your weight and avoid compacting the soil.

Ease apart the roots of plants grown in boxes. Slide plants and root ball from hard-sided pots. Plants in peat pots can be planted in their pots straight into the soil.

Check the spacing between each plant on the seed packet or garden centre label. Use a trowel to make a planting hole no deeper than the soil mark on the plant stem. Set the plant in it, making sure the roots are not bent back or cramped. Firm down the soil around the base of the plant with your hands.

Aftercare

As soon as planting is finished, hoe carefully to erase any prints from your feet or planting board. Spray the plants with water. Water daily until the plants begin growing. Hand weed, and put down slug pellets to prevent damage to young plants.

Water on a general liquid fertiliser every two or three weeks. Remove faded blossoms to encourage more flowers.

BEES

Spare that spray

I am worried about killing bees with the sprays I use in my garden. How can I avoid the risk?

Far too few gardeners seem to take seriously the welfare of bees in their gardens. This is unfortunate, for not only do honeybees produce honey for someone else, but bees of all types (together, of course, with many other types of insects) play an essential role in pollination.

All insecticides are just what their name implies – killers of insects – and with few exceptions will annihilate the creatures of beneficial effect as readily as the pests. So if you use insecticides in your garden (and this applies as much to the more natural products like derris and pyrethrum as it does to the modern purely synthetic materials), there are certain precautions to observe.

The main rule is: never spray flowers of any sort while they are being visited by bees and other insects. For some plants, this could mean avoiding the flowering season altogether.

Alternatively, spray very early in the morning before bees become active or wait until late in the evening before spraying to ensure that most bees have returned to their hives or nests. This practice will limit the harm you cause the bees, but it won't eliminate the harm entirely, because the effect of most sprays lasts about a week, during which it can still affect bees visiting the flowers. Some bees will probably die, but you will not be wiping out entire populations as you might by spraying when the insects are actually on the plants.

In these circumstances, the best all-round answer is to concentrate on controlling aphids and greenflies (which are likely to be the major pests in most gardens) and to use the insecticide pirimicarb for this purpose. This chemical has the great merit of being virtually harmless to all other types of insect, including bees. Pirimicarb has a slight drawback in being fairly persistent – up to three days on outdoor plants and up to 14 days in a greenhouse – and is therefore not usually recommended for use on edible crops.

Whatever insecticide you use, never spray on windy days, even if you're spraying non-flowering plants which are never visited by bees. No matter how careful you are, if the wind is up at all, the chemical will drift onto other plants which are being visited and pollinated. Less expensive than chemicals, and held by many gardeners to be as effective, is the old-fashioned remedy of dousing the plants with soapy water. This washes off the aphids – the slippery soap makes it more difficult for them to cling on. Otherwise, it hurts nothing.

Plants to please the bees

What plants can I grow in my garden that will be attractive to bees?

Mints and thymes are among the plants which are especially attractive to bees, and they will positively hum with life in the early summer. Heathers and lavenders also make good bee plants. Others which, between them, flower for several months are *Cotoneaster horizontalis* (which flowers in June), *Mahonia aquifolium* (March-April), geranium species (May-August), *Sedum spectabile* (September-October), brooms (April-May), flowering currant (April) and michaelmas daisies (September).

Many native British flowers also bring bees in by the dozen. So even if you don't want a wholly wild garden, you can still draw in plenty of bees with a patch set aside as a conservation corner.

You could also take a leaf, or rather a flower, out of the commercial honey-maker's book. They have found that bees will fly to the brilliant yellow flowers of oilseed rape in preference to any other plant, though the flavour of the honey is thought by some to be inferior to that obtained from heather or clover. But if you merely want to attract bees, then a clump of the plants in a corner will certainly bring them buzzing.

BEETROOT

Sunshine and shade

Will beetroot grow in a shady spot?

Like most other root vegetables, it will grow in a sunless position provided it gets plenty of light. But it does prefer sunshine. Constant dark shade – beneath a tree, say – will result in weakened tops and much smaller roots.

If you have in mind a lightly shaded position protected from cold winds, use that for early sowings because they will appreciate the extra shelter.

Getting the soil right

My soil is quite limy. Is it worthwhile growing beetroot?

Not if the lime content is very high. Beetroot likes neutral or only slightly alkaline conditions. A soil pH of 7 to 7.5 is ideal. A high lime content will make the soil more alkaline than that.

Test the soil with a chemical or electronic kit. Otherwise grow a crop and see how it gets on. Slow progress and yellow leaves indicate too much lime. Digging peat in during the autumn should lower the pH. If the pH level stays high despite the peat, the soil can be dressed in winter with powdered sulphur at 2-4oz per square yard, but this is both expensive and not very effective.

Thinning the clumps

Despite sowing beetroot seed thinly I still get little clumps of plants along the rows. Should I mix sand with the seed?

No – it won't make any difference. One ordinary beetroot seed is really a cluster of two or three surrounded by a cork-like outer layer and you can't separate them before sowing.

However, when the seedlings start to spring up, they should be thinned to leave just one seedling at each position. About three weeks after that, thin the plants again so that they are 4-6in apart.

You can greatly reduce the need to thin by sowing monogerm seed, so called because it produces just one seedling from each cluster of seeds. The monogerm varieties to look out for are 'Monodet', 'Monopoly' – a good variety for early sowings because it resists 'bolting' (premature flowering) – and 'Cheltenham Mono'.

Germination agitation

Should beetroot seed take more than three weeks to germinate? I sowed it very carefully, and am now wondering if I bought a dud packet.

If the 'sow by' or 'packeted in the year ending' date hasn't expired, you can stop worrying, because beetroot seed should still germinate even when it's as much as three

HOW TO GROW THE EARLIEST BEETROOT

- In February sow the variety 'Replata' in polystyrene cellular trays – three seeds per section – and keep them in a slightly heated greenhouse with a minimum temperature of 13°C (55°F).
- Grow the plants on without thinning.
- When they're about 2in high, harden them off over two weeks and set them outside under cloches with 10in between each group.

This technique, known as multi-seeding, will produce tender beetroots in late May or early June.

years old. The seed contains naturally a chemical which inhibits germination, and often the seed won't sprout until after heavy or prolonged rain. You can, however, beat nature at her own game by soaking the seed in tepid water for an hour and sowing it immediately while it is still wet.

The first seedlings should then surface 10-14 days later.

Even if you use this trick, don't be surprised if early sowings are slow to emerge. Beetroot thrives only in warm soil; at temperatures below 10°C (50°F) progress may be very slow. In cold springs, use cloches to warm the soil before and after sowing.

How to store beetroot

What's the best way to keep beetroot?

It depends how long you want to keep them. These are the rules to follow.

- Fork up the crop when it's ripe; for maincrop sowings that means September or October.
- Twist off – rather than cut – the leaves to minimise bleeding, and store undamaged roots, stalks uppermost, in layers in boxes filled with slightly damp sand or peat. Don't let the roots touch each other, and make sure the top layer is covered.
- Left like this in a dry shed, garage or outbuilding, the roots will remain firm until small shoots and roots start forming on them in March.
- For short-term storage – up to about three weeks – put clean, sound roots in a perforated polythene bag. Tie the top, and store the bag in the bottom of a refrigerator.

Roots left in the ground will not keep as well as those which have been lifted and stored under cover. In time they will be harmed by heavy frost, although a November covering of peat, bracken or straw will provide some protection. Diseases and slugs will also take their toll.

BIRDS

Winter bud-drop

In winter, with snow on the ground, I sometimes see what look like bits of bud underneath fruit trees and bushes. What's doing this and is it cause for concern?

It will certainly worry you in the spring because what you are seeing is the scales from the tiny, immature flower buds from which the fruits will later develop. The buds are being eaten and, consequently, there's going to be a shortage of blossom.

Up to a point the weather is responsible. The damage is being caused by bullfinches, and possibly tits feeding on the buds because their natural food of weed seeds and berries is either used up or covered by snow. In a severe winter, bullfinches can cause serious damage to fruit plants, with subsequent losses of crops. The best way to protect bushes is by growing them in a fruit cage. Failing that, close-mesh nets can be draped over them from leaf fall until the spring.

Small trees can be similarly netted. This is impracticable for larger ones, but they can be given some protection with regular sprays of one of the chemical deterrents based on aluminium ammonium sulphate. The birds do not like the taste, but the chemicals will not harm them.

Sparrows and dust baths

How can I stop or better still prevent sparrows taking dust baths in carefully prepared and sown ground?

Twiggy pea sticks laid along the rows often foil sparrows, provided that the coverage is dense enough to stop the birds hopping to the ground. More effective are semicircular wire-netting tunnels erected over the rows. You can make them yourself from close-mesh chicken wire or plastic netting set on metal hoops made from galvanised wire or coat hangers.

For large areas, such as a newly sown lawn, you can make a suitable deterrent from lengths of cotton crisscrossed all over it and fastened to short sticks. Traditionally, black cotton was used for this, but as birds cannot distinguish this colour against the dark ground, they can become entangled. It's kinder to use white or coloured cotton instead.

The best way of all to prevent sparrows taking dust baths is to make sure there's no dust: simply keep the ground damp.

Sparrows and pampas grass

The moment my pampas grass produces its plumes, they're attacked by sparrows. Is there any way of preventing this?

This is a common occurrence in late summer. Netting and cotton strings are effective deterrents, but ugly unless you use material of a matching colour. You will probably have more success if you spray the plumes as soon as they emerge with chemical deterrent. Repeat the treatment after rain.

Damage to fruit crops

How can I prevent blackbirds and thrushes from eating my raspberries and strawberries before they're ready for picking?

The most effective protection against birds is undoubtedly a sturdy fruit cage. This gives complete protection.

You can also throw plastic nets over the bushes and strawberry plants during the fruiting period, but a close watch must be kept on the nets to release any birds that might get caught. Blackbirds in particular seem to have a death wish when they come across a net. Keep the net taut and raise it well above the fruit with sticks, or the birds will simply reach through it. For strawberry crops you can erect a framework of canes and stretch netting tightly over it.

Visual bird scarers seldom work for more than a day or two. After that, the birds get used to them. Humming scarers appear to be more effective.

Protection for seedlings

I have heard that birds sometimes get caught in black cotton stretched across rows of seedlings. Are there any safer ways of keeping them off?

Much safer and much more effective for rows of seedlings than cotton of any colour are wire-netting tunnels fitted over the rows. You can buy rolls of PVC-coated wire netting and cut it to suitable lengths to fit over the rows. The mesh should be no larger than 1in, and the standard width of 12in will fit over most seedling rows. It is easily bent by hand into the shape of tunnels. The netting is quite expensive but can be re-used.

If you use polythene tunnels for winter and early spring crops, you can use the wire hoops to support ordinary garden netting over the rows. Or you can make your own hoops from old metal coat hangers.

A bird-lover's garden

What can I plant to attract a greater variety of birds to my garden?

Quite apart from the plants, birds of many kinds will flock to your garden if they know they can find food and water there, especially in winter. They will roost and nest if there is sufficient cover in trees and shrubs. A pool attracts insect-chasing birds; and an open lawn area is an invitation for them to grub up undesirable leatherjackets.

Seed-eating birds such as finches and tits relish any plants with seedheads: sunflowers for instance, forget-me-nots, michaelmas daisies, teasels and both ornamental and wild species of thistles.

Berry-bearing trees and shrubs that gardeners plant for their looks also provide a rich source of food for blackbirds, all kinds of thrushes and tits, fieldfares, the occasional redwings and waxwings, and for hordes of starlings. They will feed on any berries but are especially fond of holly, rowan, berberis, cotoneaster, pyracantha, *Viburnum opulus*, hawthorn and snowberry.

BLACKCURRANTS

The need to feed

How much feeding do blackcurrant bushes need?

Enough only to encourage them to produce strong new shoots each year. In March at the beginning of the growing season, spread 2oz of Growmore evenly over each square yard of the root area. After feeding the bushes rake the fertiliser in, water the area, then spread a 3-4in thick layer of mulch over the root area to keep the moisture in and keep down weeds.

Garden compost and manure make the best mulches for this purpose.

The kindest cuts

I've never pruned my blackcurrant bushes. Is it really necessary?

Definitely. Pruning keeps the bushes young and vigorous so that they continue to produce abundant crops of good fruit each year. Since young branches – those which grew the year before – produce the best fruit, the primary aim of the pruning is to make space for these branches to develop by cutting out the older ones.

Prune the bushes after the leaves have fallen in the autumn. First cut down to the ground any outside branches that are hanging at an angle of less than 45 degrees to the ground. Even if these branches are still young, any fruit produced on them will become mud-splashed in heavy rain, and that could lead to disease. Then cut down to the ground any dead, diseased or broken branches.

Prune any branch more than four years old either down to the ground or back to a younger shoot near its base. You can tell a branch's age quite easily by starting at the tip and counting the growth sections. Each section represents a year's growth and the bark of each is a slightly different colour. The youngest section, at the tip, is the lightest and the oldest section, at the base, is the darkest. If there are more than four growth sections, the branch needs pruning.

It is not generally necessary to cut back one-year-old shoots, but if any are springing up away from the bush, cut them back to their point of origin. If a young bush is not producing enough side branches, cut new shoots back by about a quarter to encourage the bush to branch out.

Controlling the currants

I'd like to grow blackcurrants but my garden is small and I've been put off by the size to which some bushes seem to grow. Is there anything I could do to keep the size of the bushes down?

You could do one of two things – either prune the bushes harder or buy one of the newer, more compact varieties.

By cutting out branches that are more than three years old – as opposed to four – when pruning (see *The kindest cuts*, this page), you will keep the bushes much smaller. It is also possible to buy a number of new varieties which grow into smaller, more upright bushes. The 'Ben Sarek' variety, for example, which became available in autumn 1985, grows to little more than 3ft high and the bushes can be planted 4ft apart. Older, larger varieties normally need to be about 5ft apart.

Standard bushes

Picking blackcurrants and pruning the bushes is always backbreaking work. Is it possible to train the bushes into standards like roses or fuchsias, so that I can tend them standing up?

No, not really. Because the fruit is only produced on the previous year's wood, the aim when pruning is to encourage as much of that growth as possible, some of which will be new shoots from underground. This is why blackcurrants are always grown as bushes. A single stem wouldn't have enough fruiting wood to produce a good crop. Redcurrants or white currants, though, can be grown as standards about 4ft high. You can then grow another crop, lettuce for example, underneath (see *Redcurrants*, page 277).

Big bud, little menace

Last winter our blackcurrant bushes put out big, healthy buds, but in spring the buds began to wither away. What's gone wrong?

It's a case of blackcurrant gall mite, or big bud. The microscopic mite makes its home inside the bud, causing it to enlarge. Big bud is very difficult to cure, and the only effective solution is to burn the affected bushes. This is particularly important since the mites also transmit a serious plant disease known as reversion virus. It takes an expert to identify the virus positively, but virus-hit bushes produce poor crops, and there is no cure. When you replace the bushes, buy new ones certified to be virus-free.

BIG BUD *Greatly enlarged buds on blackcurrants are the symptom of an attack by microscopic mites that make their home inside.*

BORDERS

Once is enough

Is it necessary to double-dig a border before planting out?

Not really, so far as herbaceous plants are concerned. Provided that the single digging is done properly, to the full depth of the spade, then most plants will be happy. Shrubs with large root systems, however, may require deeper digging for their individual sites (see *Shrubs*, page 310).

If possible, do all your preparatory work in the autumn so that the winter weather can break down the soil before you begin planting. Incorporate all the well-rotted manure or garden compost you can get hold of – especially if you are creating a new border.

Defining the line

I would like to give the front edge of my border a curved outline. How can I achieve this?

An easy way is to lay a garden hose along the line you want. The hose is pliant, yet will not shift as a length of string would, and ensures that the curve is smooth. When you are happy with the look of the outline, cut along the inner line of the hose with a lawn edging tool.

Another way is to hammer a stake into the ground along the straight back edge of the border and tie a loose loop of rope around it. Hold the loop taut and walk round the stake, marking out a semicircle as you go with small stakes, a trickle of sand or whitewash. Adjusting the length of the loop will change the size and sharpness of the curve.

Make the curves more gentle than you initially think they ought to be. Seen from a distance, the foreshortened curves will look sharper than they actually are. For further hints, see *Garden design*, page 150.

The planting season

When is the best time to plant a herbaceous border?

During the dormant period from mid-autumn to early spring. Bare-root plants can then be moved with no check to their growth and need little if any watering.

Adapt this general rule to your type of soil, though. Plant on light, sandy soils as early as possible so that the plants have a chance to root before the spring warmth dries the ground. On heavy clay, it is better to plant in late spring, just as the shoots are emerging. Perennials planted during the autumn may well rot in the cold wet conditions of a heavy soil.

If you want to stock your flowerbed at other times of the year – in summer, say – use container-grown plants. Keep an eye on them after planting; they will need constant watering for the first month or two until they get established.

Layout problems

Can you help me with the design of my border?

There are just a couple of basic principles to follow when you plan your border. Put most of your tall plants at the back of the border, small plants in the front. Choose an odd number of plants for the best natural effect; put them in groups of five or seven, for example, rather than in sixes and eights.

The colour scheme of your border will be a very personal choice. Here are some general guidelines which may help you achieve the effect you want and avoid the patchwork-quilt look that so many borders develop.

It is best to put the strongest colours in the foreground of a border with the paler colours farther off. Colour harmonies such as soft blues, pinks and purples suggest serenity, while bright yellows, oranges and reds are more vibrant and lively.

Colour contrasts such as red and blue also work well together. A dash of white will always highlight other colours. Even a totally white border can be very striking, especially when there is plenty of green foliage (see *Colour*, page 84).

You may even decide to establish an early or late border where there is a bold show of colour for just a few weeks of the year and the rest of the season is dominated by the softer hues of foliage.

Feeding the border

What's the best fertiliser to use on an established mixed border?

A slow-release fertiliser applied each spring is the most beneficial. Quick-acting feeds may promote soft growth that is prone to disease or winter damage. Bone meal or hoof and horn are safe for all plants except those that can't tolerate any lime. Those that need extra nourishment should be treated individually with a liquid feed. Regular mulching of the border with well-rotted manure or compost will add some nutrients and, at the same time, improve the texture of the soil (see *Soil structure*, page 324).

Mixed blessing

I was advised to mulch my border with shredded bark but the leaves on many of my plants turned yellow. What went wrong?

Usually shredded bark makes an excellent mulch. It does, however, need to be properly composted before use, and it seems that yours wasn't. Instead of benefiting the soil, it was still decomposing – a process which takes up a great deal of nitrogen. In this case, the nitrogen was taken from the soil, leaving little for the plants, which announced the deficiency by turning yellow.

A lot of cheap raw bark has been offered to gardeners in recent years. It is useless unless stacked in a heap and composted in the same way as garden refuse. To help the process along a bit, stack it in layers about 6in deep and cover each layer with a generous spreading of sulphate of ammonia, which is rich in nitrogen. The bark is ready to use as a mulch only when it can be crumbled to a peat-like consistency – and that can take two or three years.

Wallflowers from seed

Can I raise wallflowers and other spring bedding plants for the border from seed?

Yes – and from seed sown in the open ground, too. To obtain the best results, sow between the end of May and mid-July. This ensures that the plants will be strong enough to withstand the winter.

Sow in shallow drills in a nursery bed. If the soil is dry, thoroughly water the open drill before sowing. Distribute the seed thinly, cover it with no more than $\frac{1}{4}$in of soil and water once again. The seedlings should appear within a few days. Young wallflowers should be dusted with a general insecticide as a deterrent to flea beetle which can cause extensive damage to young foliage.

Once the first few adult leaves appear, carefully lift and transplant the seedlings into nursery rows 4in apart with 9in between the rows. As soon as the seedlings have become established, pinch out the growing points. This helps the plants to bush out and become more substantial. Wallflowers in particular benefit from this treatment. Polyanthus and forget-me-nots grow in clumps and should be allowed to develop naturally.

You should put the young plants into their permanent positions at the end of summer, and certainly by the end of October; otherwise you will have difficulty in getting them established before winter. A generous application – 2-4oz per square yard – of bone meal a few days before planting will be of immense benefit. Don't use manure as this promotes succulent growth which is vulnerable to mildew and winter damage.

BOTTLE GARDENS

Which plants to use

I've been told that it is not advisable to include flowering plants in a bottle garden, and that I should stick to ferns and other small foliage plants. What kind of plants should I include?

It's generally agreed that three types of plant are *unsuitable* for bottle gardens:

1 Flowering plants. Once the blooms fade, they fall from the plant and start to decay – which can lead to a rotting fungal infection likely to infect the other plants in the bottle. If you do decide to include flowering plants to provide some extra colour, make sure you use a container which allows easy access to the plants inside so you can remove spent blooms.

2 Plants that grow quickly and produce a mass of foliage – such as kangaroo vine (*Cissus antarctica*) or grape ivy (*Rhoicissus rhomboidea*). If you include plants with lush foliage, in next to no time you can find yourself with a congested bottle in need of a complete replant.

3 Cacti and succulents. These desert plants are designed to tolerate dry air and lack of water – two conditions which should not exist in a bottle garden.

For a successful bottle garden choose only small, slow-growing plants, and plan the landscape before putting the plants into the bottle. You can experiment with the landscaping by placing the plants on your kitchen table and moving them around until you are completely happy with their positions. Make sure that:

- Small plants aren't hidden behind taller ones.
- The shapes and colours complement one another.
- The plants are not crowded too close together.

For a list of plants which thrive in bottle gardens, see the box opposite.

ALL ABOUT SETTING UP A BOTTLE GARDEN

Choosing the container
Early in the 19th century a London doctor named Nathaniel Ward stumbled on the fact that plants can be grown in virtually airtight containers when he found ferns and other plants happily growing in a closed bottle which he had intended to use for observing the development of a hawk moth chrysalis.

Today goldfish bowls, fish tanks, balloon brandy glasses, sweet jars and, most popular of all, carboys or other large glass bottles are all used to house bottle gardens.

Some people leave the mouth of the bottle open. Others plug it with a cork or rubber stopper. Either way, use a container with a wide neck: free access to the plants makes maintenance easier.

Making the equipment
Before you start to plant up a bottle you will need a set of special tools – which you can make yourself, quite easily, from household items attached to sticks or canes 1½-2ft long. For example, a spoon can serve as a spade: a small, sharp knife or razor blade will do for pruning: a sponge for cleaning the glass: and a cotton reel for firming the compost around the plants when you insert them. The tools which are used for manipulating aquarium plants are also well suited to the bottle garden.

Since a bottle garden is enclosed, good drainage is crucial if the plants are to thrive. You will therefore need enough clean gravel to make a layer 2in deep at the bottom of the bottle. A level sprinkling of charcoal chips on top of this will stop the compost going sour.

If you are planning to plant a garden in a narrow-necked bottle or carboy, you will need some kind of funnel (many bottle gardeners use paper or thin cardboard rolled into a cone) to keep compost away from the glass. As for compost, all you have to do is lay down a 3-4in layer of ordinary compost – peat-based or soil-based.

WHAT TO PLANT

Name	Shape and size	Leaf colour	Flowers
Begonia boweri hybrids	Creeping, height and spread 3-4in	Deep green	Pale pink
Begonia rotundifolia	Creeping, height 2in, spread 3-4in	Light green	White
Cryptanthus acaulis	Star-like, spread 5in	Bronze	White
Episcia (various types)	Creeping spread 9-12in	Green, with metallic sheen	Orange-red, white
Euonymus japonicus 'Microphyllus Variegatus'	Shrub, height and spread 12in	White-edged, dark green	Green-white
Ficus pumila	Creeping, spread 6in	Medium green	None
Fittonia verschaffeltii	Creeping, spread 6in	Bronze, red veins	Tiny, yellow
Maranta leuconeura (buy a small plant)	Spreading, height 5in, spread 6in	Medium green, spotted	None
Pellaea rotundifolia	Spreading fern, spread 3-4in	Dark green	None
Pellionia daveauana	Creeping, spread 6in	Green-edged, bronze	Tiny, dull green
Peperomia rotundifolia	Creeping, spread 3in	Light green	Green, spiked
Pilea cadierei 'Minima'	Bushy, height 4-5in, spread 6in	Bright green, silver veins	Tiny, yellow
Sansevieria trifasciata 'Hahnii'	Rosette, height and spread 6in	Dark green, yellow and silver on green	Off-white

Planting the garden
It is best to begin with the outer plants and work towards the middle. First, scoop out a hole for each plant in the layer of compost and, holding the plant between two sticks as if they were chopsticks or forceps, lower it gently into its hole.

Then fill the hole around the roots and firm in the compost round the plants, using the cotton-reel tool described above. When planting is complete, clean the inside of the glass with the dampened sponge. Then water the plants, using a long-necked watering can, and train a gentle stream of water against the inside of the glass. Very little water is needed – just enough to clean the glass and moisten the compost.

Looking after it
If your bottle garden has a cork or rubber stopper, you may find the glass misting up from time to time. Remove the stopper until the mist clears, then replace it. You may never have to water your bottle garden again, since the moisture inside the bottle will circulate indefinitely. If the plants look as if they are in need of watering, or the compost is becoming dry, it does no harm once in a while to water them sparingly. At the same time you can give them a weak liquid feed, using a plastic funnel and a narrow tube to avoid splashing the leaves and the glass.

Place the bottle garden in good light but not direct sunlight and give the bottle a quarter turn each day so that all the plants get their fair share of light. A little pruning (with the razor blade or sharp knife) may be needed every year or so. Otherwise a bottle garden will very largely look after itself.

DIGGING *An ordinary spoon tied to the end of a 2ft bamboo makes a serviceable spade and trowel.*

PLANTING *Use a couple of sticks or long kitchen tongs to lower your plants into the bottle.*

FIRMING *Push the compost back into place round the plants with a cotton reel glued onto a stick.*

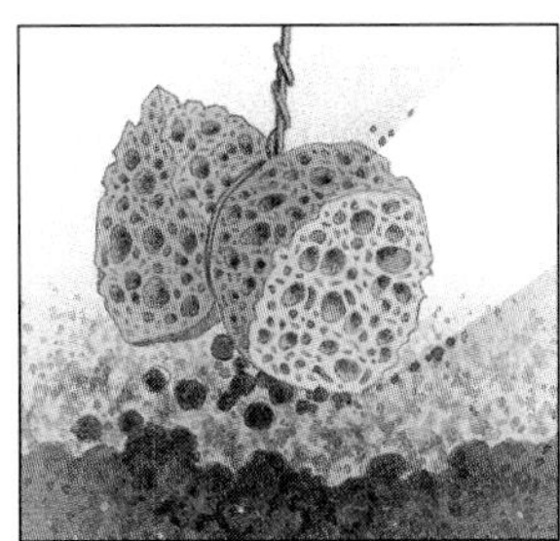
CLEANING *Mop misted or algae-stained glass with a sponge or cotton wool tied or wired to a cane.*

Misting up

My bottle garden mists up all the time. How can I keep the glass clear?

Misting is caused by the air inside the bottle heating up more quickly than the air in the room where you keep the bottle garden. Condensation can, at least partly, be prevented by keeping the bottle out of direct sunlight and away from fires or radiators.

If your bottle has a cork or rubber stopper, remove the stopper until the mist on the glass has cleared. Once the mist has cleared completely, replace the stopper and your condensation problem will, at least temporarily, have evaporated.

Carboy film

I have a bottle garden in a carboy which is gradually going green with mildew. How can I get rid of the mildew without damaging the plants or tipping the whole lot out?

Unsightly looking green mildew on the inside of the glass is caused by algae building up in the bottle, usually as a result of periods of prolonged condensation. You needn't go to the extreme of replanting the whole bottle. Instead you may be able to remove the film with one of the products designed to get rid of algae in swimming pools. Alternatively, you may find that potassium permanganate crystals dissolved in water until it is a violet colour will remove the film. Spread the cleaner on with a cotton-wool mop.

Bottle garden plants are invariably the sort which do best in shade. So, assuming the plants are healthy when planted, the build-up of algae is unlikely to block out the light so much that they will suffer serious damage.

BOX

Knot tradition

I should like to create an Elizabethan knot garden in keeping with my 16th-century house. Is it always box that is used for the edging?

No, not always. Nevertheless, box is the ideal plant for dividing up a knot garden into its sharply outlined pattern of beds, because it thrives on constant hard clipping and because it provides the neatest edging.

The knot garden was named from its patterns of low hedges resembling those made by knotting ribbons. Originally the patterns were filled in with flowers or vegetables, but after the beginning of the 16th century they became much more complicated. Meant to be viewed from the upper windows of the house, they were laid out to form coats of arms or heraldic beasts and the enclosed patches were filled with coloured stones or earths. Nowadays, most of the few knot gardens that remain seem to be stocked with herbs, with each bed containing plants whose leaf textures or colours contrast with those in the neighbouring beds.

Box itself has a distinctive fragrance, but it's not the only possible choice for a knot garden edging plant. Another traditional choice is lavender. It tolerates regular clipping and will grow into a neat low hedge up to 2½ft high. Rosemary is another scented alternative. Or, for a less formal edging, you could try sage or hyssop. All of these plants would be in keeping with the 16th-century style of your house – and all grow faster than box, too. But none gives quite the same clean lines.

Bright leaves

Are there any forms of box that have brightly coloured leaves? Most box hedges look so dark.

Common box (*Buxus sempervirens*) is the dark-leaved variety. But there are brighter-leaved, more decorative forms. Three are particularly worth looking at if you're planning to plant some box in your garden. The first is *B. s.* 'Aureovariegata'. It grows to 10ft as a shrub with a rather loose habit, and has mid-green leaves that are striped and mottled with a golden yellow. The more compact 'Elegantissima' is slower-growing with tiny cream-edged leaves of mainly greyish-green. Finally 'Gold Tip', as its name suggests, has yellow tips, usually on the leaves at the ends of the shoots.

When to clip

Can box be allowed to develop naturally or should it be clipped to keep it tidy?

Box can be allowed to develop in any way you choose, of course, but it won't be neat or much good as a hedge if you leave it to its own devices. Unclipped, it will grow to a twiggy mass 10-20ft high in time. If you want to let it grow into a tree, it's best to control this twiggy tangle by annual pruning in spring to remove dead wood.

A young plant can easily be shaped into an elegant tree by training one strong central leading shoot and removing lower side-shoots. After a few years the trunk will reach sufficient size to allow you to train the branches.

Trimming and shaping low formal hedges and topiary specimens are best done in the second half of summer.

Poison risks

Are the stories I've heard about box leaves being poisonous true?

Yes, box is toxic. But the risks are very slight. There is no case on record in Britain of any human being having died from box poisoning.

Animals have occasionally been poisoned by eating freshly cut box that has become inadvertently mixed with their food. But left to their own devices, animals never touch box hedges, so pets and wildlife are perfectly safe.

The only risks to humans are of stomach upset from eating the leaves, or of dermatitis if you have sensitive skin and you handle the plant without gloves.

BROAD BEANS

When you need to stake

I've heard that all types of broad beans should be staked and supported, to be on the safe side, but we see fields where the farmer lets them grow without any support. Who's right?

Both sides. The purpose of staking, after all, is to keep the plants upright. If the land is so sheltered from wind – or the variety being grown so small – that the plants will stay up on their own, staking is superfluous.

The dwarf varieties are least likely to need any support (unless you live on a clifftop or have a windy roof garden). But the taller varieties – those which grow to 3ft or more – should normally be staked just to make sure that they're not flattened by a storm.

Place a stout post at the end of each row, with canes at about 18in intervals. Link these with a lattice of taut string, and you should have adequate support.

It is advisable, particularly with autumn-sown varieties, to sow two separate rows, only 8in apart. The plants will then help to support and give each other some protection from the weather.

As for the fields you saw, it may be that the farmer was growing dwarf varieties, or a type known as field beans, or that the fields were well sheltered from high winds. Moreover, farmers do not necessarily treat their crops as home gardeners do. Economics and the speed required in harvesting do not allow them to stake broad beans.

Autumn versus spring

What is the theory behind the autumn sowing of broad beans? The yields don't seem any better than from those sown in spring.

The main reason for pre-winter sowing is not really the yield but the timing: to avoid attacks by black bean aphid and, incidentally, to reap an earlier harvest. For example, a November sowing will provide beans in early June; a March or April sowing will not be ready for harvesting until July or August.

Autumn sowing is worth trying, though, only if your garden is sheltered and your soil is free-draining.

Do not try if you live in a bleak, cold part of the country or if you garden on heavy clay soil. The cold and the wet will wipe out a large proportion of your crop during the winter. Far better in these circumstances to sow beans in early February, under cloches, for harvesting in late June and July.

The right varieties

I am going to try sowing a few broad beans in autumn, and a few more in spring. Can I use the same varieties, or are there types bred for different sowing periods?

Only Longpods can be sown in both seasons. Over recent years, hardier varieties have been bred for autumn sowing – they will stand severe frost without too many losses. A good tip is to sow double rows about 8in apart so that the plants give each other some protection.

Two of the best varieties for autumn sowing are 'Aquadulce', which should not be sown after January, and 'The Sutton', a dwarf Longpod variety which can be sown both in autumn and spring.

For spring-sown beans try any of these: 'Exhibition Longpod', pods of good length carrying seven to nine beans each, a good variety for showing; 'Masterpiece Green Longpod', a green-seeded variety with a good flavour, suitable for freezing; and 'Imperial Green Windsor', green-seeded and a very heavy cropper.

Language barrier

I'd like to grow broad beans but am mystified by the terms 'Longpod', 'Windsor' and 'Dwarf'. Does it make a difference which type I choose?

Longpod pods are very long – 15in or more – each carrying seven to ten kidney-shaped beans. The varieties, which include 'Aquadulce', 'Relon', 'Hylon' and 'Express' (as well as those with Longpod in the name), are the hardiest and the best for early cropping and top yields.

Windsor varieties have shorter pods – making them the broadest of the broad beans – with four to seven round beans in each pod. Generally regarded as best for flavour, they are not really hardy enough for autumn sowing, and they take a long time to mature. The two main varieties are 'Imperial Green Windsor', a heavy-cropping green-seeded form, and 'Imperial White Windsor', its white-seeded counterpart.

Dwarf varieties, by definition, make the smallest and shortest plants – no more than 18in high – and their size makes them the best choice for the small or exposed garden. They're also the best for growing under cloches. Varieties include 'The Sutton' and 'Bonny Lad'.

Inside, outside

Is there any advantage in raising broad beans in pots, rather than sowing them directly into the bed?

Not really. French and runner beans, which are tender types, are often raised under glass, singly in pots, and planted out only when all danger of ground frost is past.

Broad beans, on the other hand, are very hardy, and are quite able to exist outdoors all winter. The temperature change involved in sowing them under glass, and then planting them out, could check their growth and actually delay cropping unless they have been properly hardened off.

For details of planting and harvesting broad beans, see *Plants at a glance*, page 386.

BROCCOLI

Picking the colour

Which is the best broccoli for picking in the winter – purple or white?

The purple varieties are hardier and crop better – and so are the most widely grown. But the white varieties taste better.

Try growing some of each type. Then you will have a much longer harvest – from February right through to May.

Planting out 3in high seedlings by August will allow them to get established before winter. Planting any later can be chancy, especially in the North.

Long-distance cropper

I hear there is a broccoli that goes on cropping for years. Is it worth growing?

'Nine Star Perennial' is its name and it's raised from seed sown outside in the spring. The plants grow tall – 3-4ft. Set them out at that same spacing to ensure that they don't shade each other, and be prepared to stake them as they get older. Select a sheltered spot to minimise the battering they could otherwise get from the wind.

Twelve months after sowing, each plant should produce around a dozen small cauliflower-like heads. Cut the centre one first – that will be the largest – and let the others develop. Removing all the heads each year, before their flowers open loosely, will help the plants to go on growing.

'Nine Star Perennial' does best in a deep, rich soil. Each spring give each plant a 1-2in thick dressing of rotted manure or garden compost. Spread the dressing around the plant in a circle about 2ft across, but don't let it touch the stem.

There is another perennial spring brassica known as 'Daubenton's Kale', but you'll have to ask around for it among neighbours because seeds aren't available. Grow it from stem cuttings, which root quite easily if they're taken in July and August.

Going for green

My supermarket sells green calabrese – and it's delicious! Do you grow it the same way as purple-sprouting broccoli and is it as hardy?

Calabrese is a form of sprouting broccoli and needs similar conditions, but it isn't nearly so hardy as the purple-sprouting varieties. Depending on the variety, it matures between August and November – which makes it excellent for filling the gap between runner beans and winter greens.

Most varieties produce an abundance of small sideshoots that develop quickly after the larger, central flower head has been cut. 'Express Corona', 'Autumn Spear', and 'Topstar' are all reliable calabrese varieties. Or if you want large firm heads weighing up to 1lb, grow a variety called 'Green Comet'. It's ready for harvesting in August.

Spring is the usual sowing time. But one variety, 'Corvet', can also be sown in September for cutting the following June. It does not need winter protection except in the most severe conditions.

Of sprouts and spears

My sprouts don't grow at all well. Would winter broccoli be a better bet?

It depends on what's troubling your sprouts. If it's club root disease, that really rules out broccoli and all other brassicas for at least seven years, even if you lime the soil and use a systemic club root dip before planting.

If the reason is poor soil, broccoli should be better because it tolerates poorer soil than brussels sprouts. To improve both crops, dig in a generous quantity of manure or compost – at least 20lb or half a barrow to the square yard – a few months before planting.

Check the drainage, too. Sprouts don't like too much water. If that's the problem, broccoli won't be any happier. Double digging – that is, forking over the soil in the trench before adding the manure – may be all that's necessary. Hard work, but it will make your sprouts happier – and improve any broccoli you put beside them (see also *Heartless sprouts*, opposite).

No birds, no netting

How can I keep birds off my broccoli in winter? I don't like netting because it gets in the way when I cut the shoots.

Rectangular strips of aluminium foil suspended on string, or inverted plastic cups strung between tall canes so that they blow in the wind, may give some relief. If this fails, which is likely when birds become used to it, stretch a special 'humming line' above the plants. The line, available from garden centres, is made of thin plastic and vibrates in even a light breeze. The vibration produces a deep resonance, inaudible to humans, which scares off birds and keeps them away.

Tunnel crop

I have a polythene tunnel house. Would this be all right for raising early winter broccoli?

Yes, but it won't be much of an improvement. The only benefit will be that you should be able to harvest the spears earlier, even if you plant the crop towards the end of August instead of the more traditional late June or July.

On the other hand, winter broccoli is pretty tough, especially the purple-sprouting varieties, and doesn't really need protection. There are some drawbacks to putting the crop under cover, too. You would have to ventilate the tunnel, especially in mild weather, to harden the stems. You would also have to ventilate to control condensation because damp could rot the broccoli's leaves and buds. Cabbage whitefly will also be far more troublesome, and that means more time spent on spraying. With all that, you're probably better off growing it the old-fashioned way: outside.

Where to sow

Is it better to sow purple-sprouting broccoli and other brassicas in the garden during the spring or to raise the young plants under glass?

Many gardeners sow outside in April or May, but there is a lot to be said for using a cold frame or greenhouse to start the plants off.

The timing of outdoor sowings is governed by the weather. Waiting for a warm, dry spell to prepare the soil could hold things up for weeks, while sowing too early often results in failure.

Seedlings in the garden are also at the mercy of slugs, birds and flea beetles, and club root disease is more likely. These problems prompt gardeners to sow thickly to allow for losses, and the seedlings may as a result become drawn and spindly.

Sowing in seed trays under glass, on the other hand, or directly into a cold frame, is far less dependent upon the weather. Germination and early growth will be a good deal quicker, though you'll need to make sure, by watering and ventilation, that the seedlings do not become too dry or warm – 15°C (about 60°F) is about the maximum.

Plants raised under glass should be hardened off before they are set outside. This temperature-conditioning must be done over two or three weeks to avoid a check to growth which may not become apparent for some time. Premature flowering, often called 'bolting', is commonly the result of a setback caused by a cold spell. A plant that has been properly hardened off will be much less vulnerable to a setback of this kind.

Sowing in containers may involve more work and expense, but the plants will have better root systems than those sown in the open, so the plants should get established more quickly when they are moved outdoors, and they should produce better and earlier crops.

WHICH VARIETIES TO GROW

There are three types of broccoli grown in British gardens: purple and white (both of which are grown to be harvested in spring); and calabrese (which is harvested in the autumn). These are some of the best varieties of each type for growing at home.

'Early Purple Sprouting'

'Late White Sprouting'

Calabrese 'Corvet'

'Early Purple Sprouting' Frost-hardy, productive and prolific, even on fairly poor soils. Reaches 3ft and crops for several months starting in late February or early March.

'Late Purple Sprouting' Just as hardy and reliable as the early version, but sometimes more compact. It's ready to pick from late March.

'Early White Sprouting' Similar habit to the purple varieties but with white-tipped green shoots. Matures in March and April.

'Late White Sprouting' Crops best in April and May. The side stems stay in tight bud longer than 'Early White Sprouting'.

Calabrese varieties include:

'Corvet' High-yielding F1 hybrid variety. Grows 2ft high with a large central head followed by numerous sideshoots.

'Express Corona' Matures in August and September, as little as 45 days after transplanting. Very productive F1 hybrid.

'Green Comet' One of the fastest-growing F1 hybrids with large central heads maturing about 40 days after transplanting, but few sideshoots.

'Mercedes' Compact, fast grower, good for small plots. It is as productive as other F1 hybrid varieties, with plentiful sideshoots.

BROWN ROT

Shrivelled apples

If I believed in such things, I'd say that my recently stored apples have had a curse put on them. One by one they shrivel, turn brown and grow a nasty, yellowish mould. What's gone wrong with them?

Nothing you can counteract with a charm. This is brown rot, a common fungus which affects most types of fruit tree, particularly apples. It settles on the trees' flower stalks and young shoots, causing cracks and cankers to develop. But it doesn't normally affect the fruits until and unless they get damaged by something else – wasps, for instance, or birds or frost.

Once a fruit does get damaged, the spores can get in through the wound. Infected fruits shrivel and turn brown, and rings of pale, pimply mould form on the mummified remains. There's no way to rescue infected fruits. Simply remove them at once and burn them; otherwise they will remain as a constant source of infection. Cut out and burn any cankers and diseased shoots in winter.

The fungus can also enter harvested fruit through the stalk end, so try to leave the stalk on when picking. Check stored fruit every two weeks for signs of disease.

To prevent future attacks, protect the fruits from wasps and birds – with netting, perhaps, and by destroying any wasps' nests in the garden. If the prospect of taking on a colony of wasps bothers you, as well it might, telephone your local council's Health Department, which will normally clear the colony free of charge or for a small fee. Alternatively, contact a local pest-control firm (look in *Yellow Pages* under 'Pests and Vermin Control Services'). The firm will usually do the job sooner, but will charge you more for it.

Winter-washing with a tar-oil spray while the trees are fully dormant will curb the fungus as well as kill off any pest eggs which are spending the winter in the bark.

Remember, though, that tar-oil compounds are harmful to animals and to fish in garden ponds, and will destroy green vegetation. So spray only during still and frost-free weather, and make sure the chemical does not touch your skin. Any green plants – apart from weeds – which are near the tree being treated should be covered with sacking or newspapers.

Spraying trees with thiophanate-methyl systemic fungicide in late summer – about two or three weeks before picking the fruit – will reduce the risk of the fruit becoming infected in store.

BIRD CULPRITS *Fruits usually become mouldy after being pecked by birds or chewed by wasps. The fungus enters via the wounds.*

BRUSSELS SPROUTS

Heartless sprouts

Why can't I get my sprouts to form tight buttons? Every year they end up with a mass of leaves and no real centres.

It sounds as if you've been planting them in loose soil and overfeeding, or possibly using the wrong type of fertiliser.

The firmer the soil, the firmer the growth, although obviously it mustn't be so compacted that roots cannot penetrate freely. That doesn't mean you shouldn't dig the soil – you should dig it, and deeply because sprouts need to put their roots down. But it does mean that you should do the digging in the autumn so that the soil has plenty of time to settle before you plant in the spring. If your soil is so compacted that you have to fork it over in spring as well, that's all right provided you tread the surface when it's dry and then rake away your footprints. Use a dibber rather than a trowel when planting – it disturbs the soil less.

Sprouts thrive on farmyard manure, but it should be well rotted and dug in during the autumn. This, along with one dressing of Growmore at 2-4oz per square yard, raked into the soil at planting time, should supply enough food for the whole season.

Fertilisers which are high in nitrogen – sulphate of ammonia, for example – are fine as a one-off summer tonic for lethargic plants, but never use them for routine feeding: they encourage soft, leafy growth at the expense of firm buttons.

Persistent pests

Whitefly and aphids on sprouts are my problem. Can they be controlled?

Unfortunately, they're not going to go away, even if you spray regularly with one of the systemic insecticides such as dimethoate. The cabbage whitefly has spread widely, especially in the South, and both these sucking pests are at their worst on allotments where overlapping crops of brassicas on neighbouring plots keep them supplied with food all year round.

There is no complete answer. However, promptly digging up the stumps of all brassicas after harvest will help, especially those harvested from autumn onwards. And don't overlook swedes, because they too can remain infested during the winter.

Swap your chemicals around as well from late spring to autumn so that the pests can't build up resistance. If you use only one chemical, the few that survive will go on breeding, so that the pests can in time become almost immune. Finally, spray thoroughly the undersides of the leaves where these insects congregate.

The long and the short of it

Is it more profitable to grow short varieties of sprouts that can be planted closely together, or tall varieties which need more room?

There won't be that much difference in the overall yields, which average around 3lb per plant, or in the total number of sprouts. But the more space you give, the larger each button will be and the longer the harvest period. Also bear in mind that F1 hybrid varieties are more productive than the ordinary or open-pollinated ones.

If you want to gather sprouts over a long period, plant tall-growing varieties, such as 'Winter Harvest' and 'Bedford Fillbasket', 3ft square. Dwarf, or compact, varieties – including 'Peer Gynt' – can be set 2½ft apart each way.

Decreasing these spacings by up to 6in should still give about the same number of sprouts per plant, but they will be smaller.

Planting a medium-height F1 hybrid variety at an each-way spacing of only 20in will give you a large number of small button sprouts ideal for freezing. And normally at this spacing you would be able to harvest all the plants in one go.

Composting old leaves

Is it safe to put brussels sprout leaves on the compost heap?

It shouldn't present problems, provided they heat up and ferment with the rest of the compost to kill any pests such as aphids and caterpillars. Cut or tear up the leaves and mix them well with the other compost when you add them, so that you don't make a thick layer on top which would shed water and take longer to rot down.

The plant stems are quite woody but they, too, will slowly decompose – particularly if they're chopped into small pieces. Alternatively, when the stems are dried out, burn them on a bonfire and scatter the ash around tomatoes and soft fruit.

Never add roots from sprouts or any other brassicas to a compost heap. They won't rot down, and you could easily spread club root disease. Consign them instead to a dustbin or bonfire.

How to stop wind-rock

What's the best way to keep sprouts upright in a windy garden?

Plant them in a sunny position and mound up some soil around each stem in October. If this doesn't provide enough support, tie each stem to a stake or cane set on the windward side of each plant.

Next year, consider growing one of the shorter varieties, such as 'Peer Gynt', which are less likely to be knocked about by the wind.

Value of roofing felt

On an allotment I've seen small pieces of roofing felt laid on the ground around sprout stems. What good do they do?

They stop the cabbage root fly from laying eggs at the base of the stems. Discs of stiff cardboard, rigid plastic, or anything that forms a barrier and stays in place will do the job as well as roofing felt.

Tests at the National Vegetable Research Station have shown that foam carpet underlay works particularly well because it doesn't cramp the stem; the hole in the disc expands as the plant grows.

To make a disc, cut the material into a circle at least 5in across and make a slit from the edge to the centre so that it fits snugly around the stem. Keep the discs in position between early spring and late September.

Granular insecticides containing diazinon or bromophos are a valuable back-up against any cabbage root flies that get past your barrier, and the same chemicals will control other soil pests such as cutworms and wireworms as well. Sprinkle either insecticide around the roots and in the planting hole when transplanting.

BARRIER FOAM *Carpet underlay, cut into slit discs, prevents adult cabbage root flies from laying eggs beside the stem.*

Christmas buttons

Next Christmas I want to enjoy garden-fresh sprouts with my turkey. When do I start them off and what attention will they need?

The process starts in April when you should rake some Growmore into fine soil at the rate of 2oz per square yard, and sow the seeds thinly in shallow drills set about 6in apart.

Sowing the right varieties is also important for your timing. 'Perfect Line', 'Pegasus', 'Widgeon' and 'Wellington' should be ready on time and will crop well into the New Year.

As the seeds germinate, pull up crowded seedlings to leave the young plants 4in apart in the rows. If you wish, the excess seedlings can be planted elsewhere.

Set the plants out $2\frac{1}{2}$-3ft apart each way by the end of June – they need a long growing season. Plant them into firm soil enriched with more Growmore (at 3-4oz per square yard) and ideally manured the previous autumn. To minimise club root disease, lime the soil – use 4-6oz of hydrated or garden lime per square yard – and plant the sprouts where brassicas have not been grown for several years. Sprinkle a granular insecticide around the roots to keep soil pests at bay. Give the plants a good watering, and keep the soil moist until they are established.

During the summer, spray when needed to combat aphids, whitefly, caterpillars and other foliage pests. It may also be necessary to spray against mildew and leaf spots, though diseases should be minimal.

If tall varieties start to lean, support them with stakes or with soil drawn up around the base. Break off any leaves that go yellow to help air to circulate.

Start picking from the bottom upwards on each stem while the sprouts are still firm. Remove a few at a time from each plant once or twice a week. Strip off at once any sprouts which have opened, or 'blown'.

ALL ABOUT SPROUTS

There is no single secret of success with brussels sprouts – good harvests are the result of a combination of factors. These are the points to watch:

- Choose an open, sunny, and preferably sheltered spot.
- Dig as much well-rotted manure as you can afford into the soil several months before planting.
- To minimise the risk of club root disease, avoid planting on land which has grown brassicas within the past seven years. Sprinkle the surface with lime (4-6oz per square yard) before sowing or planting, unless you are certain the soil is not acid.
- Sow sprouts seed in April and May, beginning with early varieties – those that mature quickly.
- Space the plants $2\frac{1}{2}$-3ft square, depending on the variety and desired size of sprouts, so that each plant is equidistant from its nearest neighbours. Plant firmly.
- Spray the plants regularly to control persistent pests, including whitefly, aphids and caterpillars.
- Strip off lower leaves as they turn yellow, and harvest the lowest sprouts first when they are still firm.
- Snap off the tops of the stems when the bottom sprouts are ready for picking, to encourage faster and more uniform development of the sprouts higher up. You can cook the tops like cabbage.

BULBS

The natural look

I've got an area of rough grass which has pretty wild flowers in spring. It would be nice to plant some bulbs among them, but I don't want to spoil the natural look. How should I go about planting?

There are two points to bear in mind. First, anything too showy is likely to look out of place in a natural setting. So when you choose your bulbs, go for those which resemble the original wild species. In general, they are smaller and more delicate than the cultivated varieties.

Secondly, avoid regimenting the bulbs when you plant them. You need not follow recommended planting distances, as you would in a formal bed. Instead, just take a handful of bulbs – mixing several species together if you prefer – and scatter them gently across the area to be planted. Unless two or three fall practically on top of one another, plant them just where they fall.

Storing bulbs

Can I safely store my bulbs, for tidiness, in a polythene bag?

No – not unless you keep them in dry peat in the bag, and even then you run some risk of spoiling them. A bulb is a living organism that exudes moisture, which is liable to condense within a polythene bag. Dripping back onto the surface of the bulb, it will induce rotting. Dry peat provides a healthy medium for a bulb, and will soak up condensed moisture like a sponge. The trouble is that, sealed inside the bag, the peat itself then becomes damper, perhaps causing roots to start sprouting prematurely. By far the best storage method is to keep your bulbs loose in open wooden boxes. 'Store in a cool, dry place' is what all the books advise, and for good reasons. It should be cool to prevent too much loss of moisture – and dry to prevent the risk of rotting.

Buying bulbs

In autumn, bulbs fill my local garden centre to overflowing, each pile backed by a tempting picture of the end result. Are there any general rules I should follow when stocking up on bulbs?

There are. Rule one is that, as with life in general, you get what you pay for. There is no such thing as a good cheap bulb. Big is best, so always go for the largest examples of the varieties you want.

Rule two: make sure that the bulbs are clean and free from disfiguring blemishes.

This is especially important with bulbous irises, which should have clean white or buff-coloured fibrous tunics. Regard any dark spots with suspicion, as they are likely to be caused by ink spot disease, a contagious and lethal malady of the iris family.

Rule three: feel is important. Avoid any daffodils or narcissi with soft patches, particularly about the base. Softness there almost certainly means that the bulb has been attacked by narcissus fly or eelworm, both of which are incurable pests.

Rule four applies primarily to tulips: buy only those bulbs whose brown tunics are intact. Tulip bulbs that have been skinned and look rather like small potatoes may be all right at the time you buy them, but without their tunic for protection they are liable to catch all kinds of diseases.

Compost versus bulb fibre

Which is better for indoor bulbs: compost or bulb fibre?

It depends largely on the bulbs. Daffodils, tulips and hyacinths all do better in bulb fibre, though it is by no means essential for them.

And because this material has no nutrient value, you must add a liquid fertiliser (such as tomato feed) after flowering if you want the bulbs to bloom successfully in your garden the following year.

Compost generally yields better results for dwarf iris, crocus and other smaller bulbs. John Innes No 2 potting compost is ideal, but a peat-based compost will do fine.

Hardy summer bulbs

Can any summer bulbs be relied on to survive winter in the ground?

Yes. Most lilies, for instance, can be left undisturbed all the year round. Another hardy bulb is the large summer-flowering hyacinth, *Galtonia candicans*. This is a handsome and popular plant which bears spires of white, dangling blossoms in late summer.

Then there's *Eucomis punctata*, the so-called pineapple flower. This enjoys the dry conditions at the base of a wall, and if you plant the bulbs 6-8in deep – a couple of inches lower than gardening books traditionally recommend – they should survive the winter happily in all but the coldest parts of the country. In the North, protect them still further by putting a mound of peat or sand over the site between November and late March.

Many other plants, including anemones, ranunculus and tigridias, loosely referred to as bulbs, can be deep planted for frost protection. A depth of 4in or so should give sufficient protection in most winters, and even deeper planting will do no harm. Flowering might be delayed a little, though.

For planting under a tree

We have a big horse chestnut at the bottom of our garden. In summer, the ground underneath is very shady and the soil is dry. Realistically, can I hope to grow bulbs there?

Yes – but you will have to choose bulbs which flower very early in the year. The point is that a deciduous tree sheds its leaves in winter, and before the new green canopy starts to grow there is a period when the soil is both moist and sunlit. During this brief spell, a certain number of plants have time to produce leaves, flower and start to die back, completing their cycle before the regime of dry shadow returns.

Among the true bulbs, the most important is the snowdrop: not just the common single-flowered *Galanthus nivalis*, but its double form too, known as 'Flore-plena'. Then there are the early-flowering squills, especially the deep blue *Scilla sibirica* and the paler *S. tubergeniana*.

Crocuses would work, too. The cultivated varieties of early-flowering *Crocus chrysanthus* are particularly valuable under a tree. They are multi-flowered and come in a wide range of colours. 'Cream Beauty', 'Snow Bunting' and 'Blue Bird' are among the best, their names well describing their colours.

Strictly speaking, the winter aconites are not bulbs but tubers. Nevertheless, they are among the very earliest plants available to the gardener, coming out with the snowdrops with which they are often planted. Their lovely golden flowers are surrounded by a bright green ruff of foliage and peep out among fresh green leaves. The common variety is *Eranthis hyemalis* which can come out even before February, but the most striking is the hybrid *E.* 'Guinea Gold'.

HARDY BULBS FOR COLOUR THROUGH THE YEAR

There are few bulbs that bloom outdoors in Britain in November and December. But there are bulbs that will brighten the garden at any other time of the year. Here are some of the best for each month.

Flowering time	Name	Colour	Height
January	*Galanthus nivalis* (snowdrop) and varieties	White	4in
February	*Galanthus elwesii*	White	4-8in
	Iris danfordiae	Yellow	4in
	Iris histrioides 'Major'	Blue	3-5in
	Narcissus cyclamineus	Yellow	4-8in
	Scilla tubergeniana	Pale blue	4in
March	*Iris reticulata* and varieties	Blue and purple shades	6-8in
	Narcissus juncifolius	Yellow	4-8in
	Puschkinia scilloides	Pale blue	3-6in
	Scilla sibirica	Deep blue	4-6in
	Tulipa kaufmanniana	Pink and white	6-9in
April	*Chionodoxa luciliae*	Blue and white	6in
	Fritillaria imperialis (crown imperial)	Orange	2-3ft
	Fritillaria meleagris (snake's-head)	Purple and white	9-15in
	Narcissus triandrus albus	Creamy-white	9-12in
	Tulipa saxatilis	Lilac-magenta and yellow	12in
May	*Allium moly*	Yellow	6-12in
	Muscari armeniacum (grape hyacinth)	Blue	8-10in
	Tulipa linifolia	Scarlet	6-10in
	Tulipa marjolettii	Yellow	18in
June	*Allium ostrowskianum*	Pink, purple	8-12in
	Brodiaea laxa	Blue	1½-2ft
	Endymion hispanicus	Blue, white or pink	15-20in
July	*Allium sphaerocephalum*	Dark purple	1-2ft
	Tigridia pavonia (tiger flower)	Orange, white, pink and mauve	1½-2ft
August	*Cardiocrinum giganteum* (giant lily)	White	4-10ft
	Lilium Mid-Century Hybrids (lily)	Red, yellow, orange or white	2-3ft
September	*Amaryllis belladonna*	Pink	1½-2ft
	Colchicum autumnale (autumn crocus) and varieties	Lilac, purple or white	4-6in
	Crinum x *powellii*	Rose-pink	2-3ft
October	*Nerine bowdenii*	Pink	1½-2ft
	Sternbergia lutea	Yellow	3-5in

Bulbs which fail indoors

When I try to grow tulips or hyacinths indoors, they sometimes fail to come up in their pots. I don't get the same problem with daffodils. Why is that?

The problem is probably one of drainage. Hyacinths and tulips both come originally from warm climates where the soil tends to be dry. An ordinary potting compost can become waterlogged and stagnant, so that the bulbs' roots rot in the pot. Daffodils, by contrast, are more tolerant of wet conditions, so they are less likely to suffer in this way.

Many pots and bowls sold in the shops have inadequate drainage for the needs of tulips and hyacinths. Make sure that your containers have holes in the base, and provide plenty of broken crocks or coarse gravel at the bottom. And instead of compost, use bulb fibre – it drains more freely.

Bulbs from the indoor bowl

I grew a bowl of early tulips which made a beautiful display. Now that flowering is over, I can't bear to throw the bulbs away. Can I plant them out in the garden?

Bowls of early spring bulbs are usually grown to brighten up the dark days of January and February indoors. To get bulbs to bloom at that time, you have to 'force' them: induce them to flower earlier than their natural season. Basically, this means planting them in a bowl of compost or bulb fibre in September, and keeping them in a dark place for some weeks. They are then brought out, and the sudden light effectively tricks the bulbs into reacting as though it were spring.

The trouble is that forcing tends to exhaust bulbs. They won't be fit for flowering again in a bowl; and if you do plant them out in the garden, it may take one or two years before the plants bloom again.

If you intend to plant forced bulbs in the garden and you want them to flower next spring, then you should feed them while they are still in the bowl. If you start straight after flowering, the bulbs will build up their energy reserves and prepare healthy buds. Use a standard liquid tomato fertiliser or house plant feed at the rate recommended on the container, and keep feeding until the leaves die down. Plant the dormant bulbs in the garden in autumn in the usual way, and with luck they will flower again in spring.

Recent research at Harlow Car Gardens in Harrogate, and by the Dutch Flower Bulb Centre shows that you can further improve your chances with daffodils and tulips if you also feed *before* flowering. Start feeding, again with a standard tomato or house plant feed, as soon as you bring the bulbs out of their dark hiding place. The flowers will be better, and the bigger leaves will produce a more energy-packed bulb.

Hyacinths, though, do not benefit in the same way. Feeding after flowering helps to replenish a hyacinth's vitality; but if you feed while the young bulb is growing, the bulb tends to lose its compact form. The flower spikes become curved and elongated, with a patchy covering of blossom.

Planting depths

Does it really make much difference how deeply you plant bulbs?

Yes. The basic and traditional rule for planting bulbs is to make the hole twice the depth of the bulb, so that the bulb is covered with its own height again of soil. Plant much closer to the surface and the bulb will be vulnerable to frost damage, and to splitting in hot weather. Plant much deeper and the bulb may be too far from the sunlight to grow properly: it may come up stunted, or fail to appear at all.

The basic rule holds good in most cases. Nevertheless, there *are* occasions when you may safely plant more deeply than normal. For example, with any bulbs such as eucomis or tigridia, which are specially prone to frost damage, it is wise to go deeper – say, to four times the bulb's depth instead of twice. There is evidence, too, that deep planting of this sort also benefits some varieties of tulips and daffodils even though they don't mind frost.

Tulips, for example, have difficulty growing in a heavy clay soil. When planted at the normal depth, they cannot be relied on to flower after their first season. But for reasons not fully understood, deep planting can increase their useful life so that they come up successfully three or four years running. Not all varieties respond to this treatment, but it undoubtedly benefits *Tulipa kaufmanniana*, *T. greigii* and *T. fosteriana*. Researchers are currently exploring the merits of planting at different depths. It has been found, for example, that by planting large trumpet daffodils in a hole three times the depth of the bulb you can maintain a better flower quality from year to year. The reason seems to be that the leaves last longer so that next season's embryo flower buds grow more sturdy within the bulbs.

There are also practical advantages to deep planting: you can do jobs like hoeing with less fear of disturbing dormant bulbs. But the technique is by no means a cure-all for gardening difficulties. Hyacinths and crown imperials, for instance, definitely suffer by it.

Crown imperials

My crown imperials are a disappointment. I get plenty of leaves, but rarely a flower. What have I done wrong?

The crown imperial, *Fritillaria imperialis*, is a stately plant much loved by the early Dutch artists, who often featured it in their paintings. The red, orange or yellow flowers hang like bells from a stout stem crowned with bright green foliage. And rising to 3-4ft, it is the tallest of all the early-flowering bulbs.

To be sure of flowers, you must guard against planting too deeply. Although the bulbs are large, they dislike lying too low in the soil. A covering of a couple of inches is quite sufficient. It is also important to buy the bulbs themselves in a good firm condition. Unlike tulips and daffodils, crown imperials do not have an outer skin, or 'tunic'. They look rather like freshly peeled potatoes, and exposure to the air quickly dries them out. Always buy your bulbs from a retailer who stores them in shavings, sawdust or peat so that they do not lose moisture to the air.

Crown imperials are moisture-loving plants by nature. One of the commonest causes of reluctance to flower is dryness during the previous summer. Foliage at this time is providing sustenance for the bulb and developing the embryo flower for the following spring. So be sure to water your plant during any dry spell. And although the foliage can look untidy after flowering, always allow it to grow to the full. Never cut back the leaves just for the sake of neatness; you will damage next year's majestic display.

BUTTERFLIES

Caterpillar concern

I would like to encourage some colourful butterflies to visit my garden but am worried by their caterpillars. Is there a compromise?

Yes. Think first of the butterflies that you expect or hope to see in your garden. Most people's list will include small tortoiseshells, red admirals, peacocks, painted ladies, purple hairstreaks, the various species of blues and browns, the fritillaries, the orange tip and the skippers. These bright and familiar insects are found in most parts of the country and none of them will harm any of the plants that you are likely to cultivate in your garden. Think then of the garden plants that suffer from the attentions of caterpillars. The list will be headed by brassicas (the cabbage family) and will include peas, apples, possibly pelargoniums, tomatoes, leeks, gooseberries and perhaps a few trees, too. Yet with the exception of the brassicas, which are attacked by the caterpillar of the large white butterfly, all these plants are attacked by the caterpillars of moths, not butterflies. Few of these moth species are at all rare, and often they become a plague that must be controlled by spraying or by other methods.

There are a number of plants that will attract butterflies to your garden. Perhaps the best known is *Buddleia davidii*, which is available in several varieties, and is so effective a magnet that it is generally known as the butterfly bush. Other plants whose nectar-filled flowers regularly attract butterflies include candytuft, golden rod, hawthorn, lavender, lilac, michaelmas daisies, honeysuckle, the ice plant (*Sedum spectabile*), lady's smock, pinks, sweet violet and thyme. If you plant several of these species, you'll have fluttering visitors for as long as any one of them is in flower.

In addition, you can attract particular species to breed in your garden by planting the favourite food plants of their caterpillars in a quiet corner. For details of which caterpillars eat what, see the box below.

HOW TO MAKE A BREEDING SITE FOR BUTTERFLIES

Butterflies lay their eggs on the plants on which their caterpillars feed. So, in order to attract a particular species to breed in your garden, you need to grow one or more of its favourite food plants. This list identifies some of the more common British butterflies and the food plants of their young.

Butterfly	Food plant
Brimstone	Buckthorn
Chalk-hill blue	Trefoils and vetches
Clouded yellow	Clovers and related plants
Comma	Stinging nettles, currants, hops
Common blue	Clovers and related plants
Dingy skipper	Vetches and related plants
Gatekeeper	Brambles
Grayling	Grasses
Green-veined white	Plants of the *Cruciferae* family such as mustard and cress
Grizzled skipper	Mallows and cinquefoils

Butterfly	Food plant
High brown fritillary	Wild violets
Holly blue	Holly and ivy
Large skipper	Grasses
Large white	Brassicas, nasturtiums and related plants
Marsh fritillary	Devil's-bit scabious
Meadow brown	Grasses
Orange tip	Wild plants of the *Cruciferae* family such as mustard and cress; jack-by-the-hedge (*Alliaria petiolata*)
Painted lady	Stinging nettles
Peacock	Stinging nettles
Pearl-bordered fritillary	Wild violets

Butterfly	Food plant
Purple hairstreak	Oak
Red admiral	Stinging nettles
Ringlet	Grasses
Silver-washed fritillary	Wild violets
Small copper	Docks and sorrel
Small heath	Grasses
Small pearl-bordered fritillary	Wild violets
Small skipper	Grasses
Small tortoiseshell	Stinging nettles
Small white	Brassicas, nasturtiums and related plants
Speckled wood	Grasses
Wall brown	Grasses

CABBAGES

Where to find spring greens

I've been hunting around the shops for seeds of spring greens, but with no success. Why are they so hard to get?

For the simple reason that they are not available under that name – spring greens are merely closely planted cabbages or turnips that are harvested in the spring before they've formed hearts.

To grow cabbages for spring greens, sow varieties which mature in March-May outside between late July and early August. Transplant them about seven weeks later into rows spaced 12in apart but with only 4in between the plants in the rows. At this close spacing, the leaves will be drawn up and hearts will not develop.

In a mild winter, cabbage spring greens can be large enough to eat in late February. Before they become too crowded, pull up two out of every three plants so that the remainder, now spaced 12in square, can develop hearts in the normal way.

There is another way of growing spring greens. When you harvest cabbages in winter, leave the cut stumps in the ground. Then, in spring, harvest the new shoots that grow from the stumps. Leafy turnip tops are less productive, but many gardeners would say they are just as tasty as cabbage spring greens.

To grow these turnip spring greens, sow winter-hardy varieties such as 'Green Top' between late August and mid-September in rows 3in apart. Space the seeds about 2in apart and let all the plants grow undisturbed until they are cut in March or April when they're about 5in tall. You should be able to crop the plants two or three times for a month before they become exhausted.

Deep-bed crop

Would the deep-bed system work for cabbages?

Carried out to the letter, the system may be disappointing, but if it is modified very slightly, a deep bed is an excellent way to produce hearty cabbages where space is very limited.

A deep bed, sometimes known as a raised bed because manuring and deep digging raises its surface up to 6in higher than the surrounding soil, is simply a strip of land about 4ft wide and as long as needed. Every two or three years dig it to a depth of two spade blades and fork 4-6in of manure or garden compost into the ground (see *Digging*, page 121). Rake fertiliser over the surface before sowing or planting. Spread some compost or rotted manure over the top layer of soil each year.

Because each bed is quite narrow, it can be reached from both sides, and after it has been dug there is no need to tread upon it at all during the life of the crops. You walk only on permanent paths between the beds.

The combination of deep digging, manuring and growing compact vegetables more closely together than usual in soil which is not trodden upon can lead to yields around 50 per cent higher than crops grown in the normal way. This intensive system works for carrots, beetroot, onions, shallots, self-blanching celery, lettuce and radish. Cabbages, unfortunately, are less likely to produce firm hearts in loose soil, so it may be necessary to tread the surface just before planting. This divergence from the standard deep-bed system apart, the cabbages will enjoy all the benefits of a deep bed.

For late summer and autumn cropping, sow compact varieties such as 'Hispi', 'Minicole' and 'Quickstep' outdoors in a seedbed between March and May. When the plants are 4-6in tall, set them 12-15in apart in each direction in the deep bed.

Spring-maturing varieties suitable for a deep bed include 'Harbinger', 'April' and 'Pixie'. Sow these varieties outside between late July and early August and later transplant them to their cropping positions 12in apart each way.

Club root and small gardens

I'm worried about club root because my small garden makes crop rotation difficult. How can I keep it at bay?

You are right to be concerned because this soil-borne fungus can inflict devastating damage on cabbages and all other brassicas, including kohlrabi, turnips and swedes.

The disease strikes at the roots, distorting them into club-like swellings. It is also known, from the roots' appearance, as 'finger and toe' disease. For details on how to limit its effects, see *Club root*, page 84. But you're unlikely to get rid of it altogether because the disease can survive in the soil for up to 20 years.

How to store cabbages

To prevent bird damage, can I store cabbages indoors during the winter?

Yes, within limits. Red cabbages and the white, tight-headed Dutch cabbage varieties should keep in good condition for up to four months in a cool, dry, frost-free shed or garage. The more leafy savoy type of cabbages will store for about half this time.

In November cut firm, sound heads and pull off any loose, discoloured or damaged leaves. Store the cabbages indoors. Suspend them in open-frame hanging baskets or plastic pea and bean netting so that air can circulate freely around them. Alternatively, lay the cabbages, two or three high, on a slatted platform. Inspect the cabbages once a week, and remove any which start to rot; otherwise they will infect the rest.

Many gardeners believe, rightly, that cabbages start to lose their vitamins once they're cut. Raw cabbages have as much vitamin C, for example, as oranges – and storing them over winter can reduce the amount of vitamin C by about a quarter. But since you lose almost two-thirds of the vitamin content in cooking anyway, the loss in store is not as serious as all that. The only way to avoid any vitamin loss is to eat cabbages raw and to sow seeds of each variety over a period of several weeks. That way you'll have a longer supply of fresh heads.

Chinese puzzle

What are the secrets of success for good Chinese cabbage? My efforts have resulted in floppy leaves riddled with holes.

All varieties have a leafy habit – rather like a cos lettuce – and it may be necessary to tie a single loop of soft string or raffia around them if you want firm hearts. Do this in August when plants sown in early July start to heart up.

Plenty of water in dry weather also helps their progress; unfortunately it also encourages slugs, so you may have to use slug pellets quite liberally. Watch out, too, for caterpillars on the leaves and spray with malathion or rotenone (derris) if they become a nuisance.

CABBAGE ROOT FLY

When transplants die

My recently transplanted cabbages and cauliflowers are keeling over like dominoes. What can I do to save them?

Not much if the plants are still young. You may save some of the more established plants under attack by drenching the soil around the stems with a spray-strength mixture of diazinon. And you may be able to protect plants which have not yet been attacked by dusting the soil with bromophos. But there are no guarantees of success.

The cause of your trouble is an extremely widespread pest: the cabbage root fly. It attacks the roots of all the brassicas – a family which includes brussels sprouts, cauliflowers and broccoli as well as cabbage, and wallflowers, too. Recently transplanted plants are particularly vulnerable.

The adult flies, which are active between April and September, lay their eggs at soil level on or very near the plants' stems. The larvae – white maggots which grow to about $\frac{1}{4}$in long – burrow down into the soil when they hatch, and start feeding on the roots.

The main symptoms of an attack are blue-tinged leaves which wilt in sunny weather. Young plants usually die. Older plants grow slowly and badly: cabbages fail to develop hearts, and cauliflowers form tiny curds.

To test your diagnosis, dig up one of the plants. If the roots are blackened and tunnelled, and you can see a few white maggots, then your suspicions are confirmed. Don't put infested plants on the compost heap; burn them or put them in the dustbin.

Because treating an attack that's already under way is usually only partially successful, the best cure is to prevent the pest getting to the plants in the first place. If you've had trouble with root fly before, head off any future attack by dusting the soil with bromophos when sowing or transplanting.

In addition, since the flies sometimes seem to be resistant to insecticides, cut 5-6in discs out of cardboard or carpet underlay and fit them round the stems of the plants. The discs help to prevent the female from reaching the soil to lay her eggs.

CACTI AND SUCCULENTS

The living desert

I have a long narrow cactus with prickles on it, which hardly seems to grow above 8in tall. How can I start it growing and flowering again?

Your cactus sounds as if it is one called *Cleistocactus strausii*, which grows at least 5ft tall in the wild in Bolivia and is sometimes known as the silver torch cactus. It is covered in short white spines and hairs, with a topknot at the end of the stem. Yours has probably stopped growing because it needs water and food. Cacti are like any other plants in their need for moisture and nutrients, for even at home in a desert they receive heavy rain for a short spell in spring. Desert soil is actually quite rich in minerals, and the plant's roots absorb these in the soil water during the rainy periods.

So, in containers, any cacti should be watered during spring and summer like any pot plant, and fed with a potassium-rich fertiliser such as a tomato fertiliser. In autumn, give much less water so that the compost is only just moist. In winter, watering once a month is often enough, especially if the plants are kept in low temperatures.

Repot your cactus in fresh compost – in a larger pot, if necessary – every three years or so, and keep it in a sunny place, especially in winter.

Christmas care

My Christmas cactus produced plenty of flower buds last year, but practically all of them dropped off without opening. How can I stop it happening again?

By making sure the plant is kept at a warm and even temperature. The most common cause of this problem is a sudden drop in temperature, as occurs at night or when the plant is in a draught. Do not shut it behind the curtains. Ideally Christmas cactus should be kept at 16-21°C (about 60-70°F) from late autumn to mid-spring.

Another cause can be changing the plant's

EASY-TO-GROW CACTI

PEANUT cactus (*Chamaecereus sylvestrii*) – red flowers; a few inches tall.
Rat's-tail cactus (*Aporocactus flagelliformis*) – pink tubular flowers; trailing stems up to 3ft long.
Silver torch cactus (*Cleistocactus strausii*) – columnar cactus up to 2ft tall; cerise tubular flowers.
Echinopsis eyriesii – round, with white and pink trumpet flowers; about 3in tall.
Water-lily or orchid cactus (*Epiphyllum* hybrids) – flattened, upright stems, large trumpet-shaped flowers in pink, white, yellow, red and purple; about 12in tall.
Golden lily cactus (*Lobivia aurea*) – round, with yellow funnel flowers; 3-4in tall.
Mammillaria wildii – round; white, red-striped flowers; 3-4in tall.
Bunny ears (*Opuntia microdasys*) – oval pads 5-6in long form stems, like prickly pear; occasionally yellow flowers.
Mexican sunball (*Rebutia minuscula*) – round; red flowers; about 3in tall.
Christmas cactus (*Schlumbergera* x *buckleyi*) – flattened drooping stems 9-12in long; cerise, fuchsia-like flowers Dec-Jan.

position in relation to its light – for instance, simply turning it back to front.

A third reason is not watering enough, so that the compost becomes almost completely dry. Water the cactus as you would any house plant in flower – that is, fill the top of the pot with tepid water poured on fairly quickly, let the surplus drain through, and then leave it alone until the compost surface is dry again. In spring and summer, the plant can go outdoors in a slightly shaded place to be watered naturally.

Red seedlings

I have been trying my hand at growing cacti from seed, and have had some success with germinating them. But now the seedlings are all turning red. Is this all right?

No, it isn't. Your seedlings are turning red because they are getting too much light. Unlike adult plants, young cacti should be shaded from direct sunlight: it is too strong for them and changes the pigmentation from green to red, which halts development. Keep the seedlings from bright light for a year or so, and they will flourish.

Bugs under cover

We were given a collection of cacti for our new greenhouse last spring, and all went well until some of the plants developed fluffy white blobs, turning into patches. What can we do?

The fluffy blobs indicate the presence of insects called mealy bugs, a common pest on this type of plant. They suck the sap like greenfly, weakening the plants and slowing growth – but unlike greenfly they remain in one place. The fluffy material is a protective tent beneath which they live, breed and die.

They may have appeared because you added an infected cactus to the collection.

Get rid of the insects by dabbing the blobs with methylated spirit on a stiff paintbrush.

Limp leaves

Some of the leaves of my epiphyllums are limp and rather a poor green. Should I cut them off?

If the stems of the plant are firm at the base, leave them; otherwise cut them off at soil level.

Epiphyllums, also known as water-lily cacti or orchid cacti, are one of the epiphytic group – meaning that they perch on another plant, using it as a support only, not absorbing nutrients from it like a parasite. Usually they grow in the forks of branches, where a little vegetation collects and rots, and they have evolved a small root system to enable them to survive in such niches. They can therefore grow with little water or food, though they do need a damp atmosphere.

If they are given too much water, the roots cannot function, and eventually the stems become limp and pale green. Too little water will have the same effect. The happy medium is to keep the compost just moist and the atmosphere humid. When the buds are developing and the plant is in flower it will need more frequent watering, but even so do not drown it. Generally, let the top half inch of compost dry out between waterings. But in spring and summer, water as soon as the compost's surface dries.

How to encourage cacti to bloom

At a show I saw some lovely cacti with brightly coloured flowers. How can I get mine to flower?

Some varieties of cacti flower readily – for instance, echinopsis, epiphyllum, lobivia, mammillaria, aporocactus and rebutia. But it is still important to give them a bit of help in the form of fertiliser.

You can use a powder or a liquid, but either way it must have a high potassium content to help flower formation and colour. There are various proprietary powder fertilisers available. For the liquid, one of the tomato fertilisers, diluted as the makers direct, would be excellent; apply it about once a fortnight from early June to early September.

Powder fertiliser should be sprinkled onto the surface of the compost and watered in, at the beginning of the growing season if the plant was not repotted in fresh compost, or in early June. You can also use fertiliser spikes or tablets, once or twice during the growing season, as the makers direct.

Falling leaves

Could you tell me why the little leaves attached to the larger leaves of my plant keep falling off? The large leaves are thick, 2-3in long, with toothed edges and dark markings underneath.

The plant is probably one with the difficult name of *Bryophyllum daigremontianum*, commonly called the devil's backbone. It is a handsome plant, with purple blotches on the underside of the leaves, and grows rapidly during summer up to 3ft high.

As it grows, the tiny leaves you mention appear on the edges of the parent leaves. These mini-leaves are in fact plantlets. They fall off easily and root readily if you pot them up in the same compost as the parent plant.

This production of plantlets is a good sign and means that you are treating the plant correctly. It is usually grown for its decorative leaves, but does sometimes flower in winter with yellowish-pink tubular flowers. Another plant which carries plantlets is *Bryophyllum tubiflorum*, but its plantlets form only at the end of the leaves. Bryophyllums

EASY-TO-GROW SUCCULENTS

PARTRIDGE-BREASTED aloe (*Aloë variegata*) – black-brown stripes on triangular leaves 6in long in stiff, upright sheathed rosette; about 9in tall.
Variegated century plant (*Agave americana mediopicta*) – fleshy pointed leaves in stiff rosettes, blue-green with yellow stripes; up to 2ft wide.
Devil's backbone (*Bryophyllum daigremontianum*, also known as *Kalanchoë daigremontiana*) – fleshy, triangular, toothed leaves, blotched dark brown on underside, plantlets on leaf edges; 2-3ft tall.
Hearts entangled (*Ceropegia woodii*) – trailing stems up to 3ft long; blue-green, heart-shaped leaves with white markings on upper side; small purple tubular flowers.
Jade plant, money tree (*Crassula argentea*) – main stem trunk-like to 3ft; thick shiny green leaves about 2in wide, rounded with red edges.
Echeveria gibbiflora metallica – blue-green leaves in rosettes at end of stems, with pink-brown sheen; about 2ft tall.
Haworthia margaritifera – rosette of thick fleshy leaves, pointed and triangular in cross-section, with white warts on underside; up to 5in wide and high.
Kalanchoë blossfeldiana hybrids – fleshy, shiny, light green leaves, with red, yellow, white or orange flowers at any time; about 12in tall or 6in dwarf hybrids.
Sedum sieboldii medio-variegatum – arching stems 6-8in long with round blue-green leaves, centred pale yellow; pink-purple flowers in autumn.
Cobweb houseleek (*Sempervivum arachnoideum*) – rosette of stiff fleshy pointed leaves, forming clusters and covered in thick webbing.

need John Innes No 1 or No 2 compost, with 25 per cent volume of grit added, and a temperature no lower than 10°C (50°F). Keep the compost damp but not wet.

Cactus that needs the dark

I have had a Christmas cactus for several years, but it has not flowered since the first winter. Suggestions, please.

Lack of flower buds on a Christmas cactus is almost always because it didn't have the right amount of light in autumn and early winter. If it is kept in a lighted place after nightfall, it won't develop buds, which is why so many Christmas cacti kept in living rooms don't flower.

They need what is known as a 'short day' in autumn and early winter, and should at that time of year be kept away from artificial light in the evenings. Leave them in a dark room instead.

Occasionally the reason for lack of flower is insufficient warmth in autumn. The temperature should be above 16°C (about 60°F) from mid-autumn onwards.

On the spot

My prickly pear has round brown spots on some of its pads. Why?

Prickly pears (opuntia) can develop such spots through lack of water, often associated with too low a temperature. Cacti with similar stems – for instance, epiphyllums and Christmas cactus – are also likely to show this kind of symptom, whereas rounded or columnar varieties will shrivel when dry.

Another possible cause is fungal infection, in which case the spots will be soft and moist if pressed. To solve that problem, spray the plant lightly with a benomyl solution, and provide a less moist atmosphere.

If the spots are light brown and slightly raised, the problem is the scale insect, a sap-sucker which secretes honeydew and leaves sticky patches below the plant. If there are only a few insects they can be carefully scraped off with a fingernail, but in the case of bad infestations it is better to discard the plant altogether.

Falling stems

My cactus, which has lots of short stems with rounded ends growing in a cluster close to the soil, was being repotted when some of the stems fell off. Will it live?

Yes – and it should flourish. Your plant sounds like the peanut cactus, *Chamaecereus sylvestrii*, which has rounded stems about 3in long. The stems have rounded ends and short white spines.

All the stems grow from the same point at soil level – and they're so loosely attached that they are easily knocked off.

Your plant should not come to any harm. In fact it will probably be better for losing some stems, for they can become crowded.

Use the fallen stems to produce new plants. They will root in two or three weeks if you stick them upright into moist compost with the bases just buried. Once they've rooted, move each stem into a 2in pot, or put two or three in a 4in pot. Within a year, the young plants should start to produce large red blooms in early summer.

Treating root aphids

On repotting my collection of cacti, I discovered that some roots had a white, ash-like material on them, with patches of it in the compost. What should I do?

The villain here is the root aphid, a sap-sucking insect like greenfly but living in the soil and feeding on plant roots. It can multiply considerably without detection until the plants are nearly dying. Suspect the root aphid with any plants which, despite having the right food, water, light and warmth, are growing slowly or not at all and have a sickly grey or yellow look.

Infestation can be confirmed by turning the plant out of its pot and examining the roots and compost, when you will see the symptoms you mention. It is most likely to occur in dry soil conditions, so cacti and succulents are particularly common targets.

Treat affected plants with systemic insecticide according to the maker's instructions, or wash all the compost off the roots, wash the roots thoroughly, and then repot in fresh compost and clean containers.

Rationing water

Several of my cacti have gone rotten at the base of the stems at soil level. Can I save them?

Probably not. When cacti rot at the base, where the main body is in contact with the compost, it is usually a sign that they have been kept too moist during winter.

Such rotting rarely occurs in summer, when the growing and often flowering plants are absorbing a good deal of moisture, with any surplus evaporating.

But in winter, cacti are at a standstill. Moreover, since they are built to retain water for surviving drought, they need hardly any water at that time of year, and so a moist compost remains moist – an open invitation to any passing diseases, including rots.

Many cacti can survive low temperatures, even freezing, provided the compost is virtually dry. So the solution is to reduce winter waterings to a minimum – once a month is sufficient. If you see any signs of the stem shrivelling, the plant is getting too dry; raise the temperature a few degrees and water to keep the compost just moist. Shingle around the base of the plant on the compost surface will help to provide dry conditions and prevent rotting.

As for your present plants, you could try cutting away the rotted parts and dusting the wounds with of sulphur. But your chances of a successful rescue are not high.

ALL ABOUT CARING FOR CACTI AND SUCCULENTS

- Many cacti will flower only if kept cold in winter; allow the temperature to fall to 2-4°C (36-39°F), even to freezing, provided compost is dry – this does not apply to rat's-tail cactus, Christmas cactus, epiphyllum and prickly pears, all of which prefer to be kept at a temperature of at least 5-10°C (41-50°F).
- Drainage is very important. Put one-third part extra of grit into soil-based composts, and use drainage material such as old crocks in the base of the pot. Break up the compost surface occasionally with a table fork to prevent a caked layer from forming.
- Use gravel on the compost surface to prevent caking and to ensure that the area close to the base of the cactus or succulent is dry.
- Water cacti and succulents in the growing season like other pot plants – whenever the surface of the compost is dry. In winter, water at intervals of two to four weeks.
- Give cacti plenty of sun, but be careful with the midday sun in summer; even for cacti it can be too strong. In winter, give all the sunlight possible.
- Cacti with many prickles or spines are difficult to handle. When repotting use either kitchen tongs or wind a thick collar of paper round the base.
- Cacti grown for their long, silky or cobweb-like hairs lose their attraction when these become dirty. Clean them by spraying with a mild detergent such as diluted washing-up liquid. Leave the solution on for a few minutes, then wash it off with plain water. Do this in summer, laying the plant on its side or covering the compost with plastic.
- Feed plants during their growing season in the same way you would feed any other pot plant. Use tomato fertiliser for flowering species.
- To ensure that cuttings root, the cut surface must dry out. So leave a cutting to dry for a day or two if the cut surface is small, or for up to a week if it is large. Pot up the cuttings when the surface has formed calluses.
- Repot cacti and succulents in larger pots only when they have completely filled their pots with roots – no more than about once every three years.

CAPSID BUGS

Tattered leaves

Small brown spots appear on the leaves of my flowers and fruit trees and then turn into holes. What is the cause?

Sounds like the work of capsid bugs. They go for any number of plants – principally apples, currants and beans among crop plants – and for flowers too, especially chrysanthemums, dahlias, buddleias, forsythias and hydrangeas. The flowers become distorted and discoloured, the fruits misshapen, and the leaves develop ragged holes or become tattered and puckered. Buds and growing points may die off.

Apple capsids, bishop bugs and common green capsids, which cause similar damage, are all members of this same family of sucking insects. Adults and nymphs feed on the sap of tender growths by injecting a saliva which is toxic to plant cells; the saliva makes the sap easier to extract.

Capsids are active outdoors throughout the summer, and will be a nuisance even longer under glass. They spend the winter in leaf litter and plant debris, so the first and simplest way of keeping their numbers in check is to maintain a high standard of garden hygiene. Don't leave any plant debris lying around for them to make a home in.

Getting rid of a raiding party in summer is more difficult. Capsids are quick-moving and often they're long gone by the time you've spotted the damage. Nevertheless, you can stop further attacks by spraying affected plants with a pesticide such as dimethoate, fenitrothion, malathion or diazinon as soon as symptoms appear.

It's a good idea to hit the bugs again in winter by destroying the eggs they hide in fruit tree bark. Spray with tar oil on a still, frost-free day in winter – the spray will burn any greenery it touches.

POISONOUS SALIVA *Capsid bugs inject a substance that destroys plant tissues. The result: tattered and puckered leaves like these.*

CARNATIONS

Greenhouse varieties – for outdoor varieties, see PINKS AND BORDER CARNATIONS, page 258.

Continual cropping

I know some carnations are called 'perpetual' because they're said to flower all the year round. But surely every plant needs a rest at some time of the year – and surely even these 'perpetual' varieties are not exceptions to the rule. How long can such plants be kept?

The present-day perpetual-flowering carnations originated from a bushy strain of *Dianthus caryophyllus* and *D. sinensis*. Their descendants have been grown for many years in North America and in Europe.

True perpetuals can, in fact, grow nonstop throughout the year, without pausing for a rest. In America in the 1920s they were referred to as Tree Carnations since they were grown for three or four years and reached 6ft tall. In the 1960s, commercial growers regularly kept plants in bloom for two years without a break, and some of the vigorous red, white and pink 'Sim' varieties grew to 7ft tall.

Nevertheless, the thought behind your question is correct. Even perpetual varieties do eventually need a break. The longer they're kept in flower, the weaker they become. Modern commercial growers, raising the flowers for florists, now keep crops for 15-21 months, choosing to take the maximum numbers of blooms whilst the plants are growing most strongly. They then replant, and their pattern is perhaps a wise one to follow since you can clean up your greenhouse in winter and replant in early spring. You could in theory grow perpetuals for two or three years; but in practice they are likely to become too tall for the greenhouse by that time.

Some growers have been known to cut the plants down to half their size at this stage, but the practice is not recommended, for the plants take a long time to recover.

Growing the same plants for longer than two or three years is counter-productive, because the plants become less manageable with age. Instead, replace them with vigorous young cuttings.

Some orange and yellow perpetual carnation varieties (for example 'Joker' and 'Harvest Moon') grow less strongly in winter. Pink, white and red varieties are usually the most vigorous strains and will crop best in the duller winter months, giving you a more even harvest of blooms all year round.

Secrets of the experts

I want to grow some really spectacular carnations in my greenhouse. How important is spacing, and what are the secrets the experts keep to themselves?

The secret of growing carnations is simple: meticulous attention to detail. Preparation, spacing, correct watering and temperature control are vital. So, of course, is the greenhouse, if only to protect the plants at night.

These are the points to watch:

Preparation Wash down the greenhouse in autumn or winter with soap and a little bleach in water to improve light transmission and kill bacteria on the frames and glass.

If you plan to enter your carnations for a show, decide well ahead which classes to enter, and schedule your planting and cultivation with the show's dates in mind. The growth of carnations can be retarded by stopping (see *Building the plant*, page 46), pruning or by moving them to a cooler place.

Spacing Carnations need plenty of space. Planting 8in apart each way is well enough for normal plants in the border, but 9in gives each plant more than 25 per cent more ground space and light. This is guaranteed to produce stronger 'breaks' (sideshoots) and bigger blooms. You'll also have fewer plants to care for and so be able to give closer attention to each.

Watering Carnation growers often worry that their feeding is insufficient, when the real problem is too much – or too little – watering. You might need to water daily in a dry summer, but only once every three weeks in winter. Again, depending on the state of the weather, each plant should get from $\frac{1}{4}$ pint to 1 pint at each watering.

Temperature control The rule if you want sturdy high-quality blooms is: 'Grow cool' – and this means aiming to keep your plants in a temperature range of about 10-14°C (50-57°F). Automatic ventilation is ideal but expensive. Heat will bring the plants on fast, but they will be of poorer quality.

You may have to shade them during the day, even at the cost of reducing the energy supply from the sun. If they have been out of the greenhouse during the day, bring them in at night: temperature fluctuations encourage calyx splitting. Some cultivated varieties are more prone to this than others.

Keep up your 'intensive care' routine right up to the moment your carnations are on display. Place them in water immediately after cutting. Take special care in handling. The stems are very brittle and can easily snag at the wrong joints. If the carnations have to be transported any distance, pack them in long boxes, with the heads supported by little rolls of paper. Secure the stems with strips of paper fastened down with staples. See also *Longer-lasting flowers*, page 45.

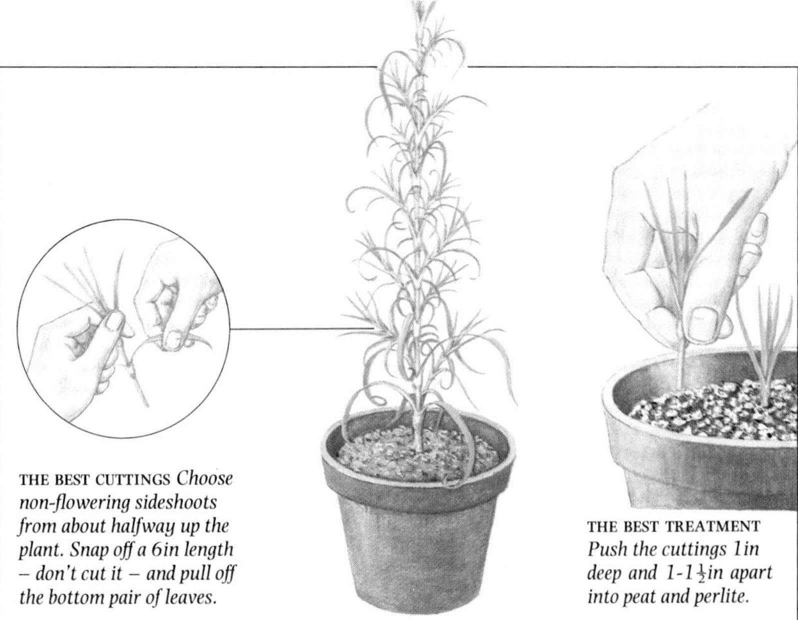

THE BEST CUTTINGS *Choose non-flowering sideshoots from about halfway up the plant. Snap off a 6in length – don't cut it – and pull off the bottom pair of leaves.*

THE BEST TREATMENT *Push the cuttings 1in deep and 1-1½in apart into peat and perlite.*

Taking cuttings

Last year I bought a collection of carnation plants and now I want to increase my stock. Can you tell me how to propagate them?

By cuttings is the best method. First, select your best plants, and take cuttings only from those. If you are not totally satisfied with their health and quality, it would be far better to buy new plants and discard the old.

When you take cuttings, do it between December and March. The spring growth will be strong and you will have flowers by midsummer. Choose the strongest sideshoots from about halfway up your plants. Shoots from the 8th, 9th and 10th 'nodes' (or joints of the stems) – counting downwards from the flower buds – are ideal, provided they have no flower buds. Snap off 6in cuttings with a sideways and downwards twist. Don't use a knife, because this can spread virus disease. Remove the lowest pair of leaves on each cutting and dip the bottom half inch in a hormone rooting powder.

You will need a propagating frame with a little bottom heat, and so many simple propagators are now on the market that it is hardly worth making your own. A bottom heat of 13°C (55°F) is needed in the rooting compost, which can be peat mixed with coarse sand, vermiculite or perlite. The ideal mix is 2 parts perlite to 1 part peat.

Water the compost before inserting the cuttings 1in deep, spacing them 1in by 1½in apart. Water them in, and put on the frame cover to prevent them drying out. On sunny days, spray the plants with water to avoid wilting, and shade them to keep the temperature down. After one week begin to ventilate the frame, and lower the bottom heat to 10°C (50°F). Aim to keep the compost temperature 1-2°C (2-3°F) above the air temperature. Control the temperature by turning up the heat or increasing the ventilation. Keep the compost moist, too, because if it dries out the cuttings will die.

Within two or three weeks the cuttings should have rooted. Pot them into 3in pots in John Innes No 1 compost. Shading should by then be needed only on very warm days. Increase the ventilation gradually and slowly reduce the bottom heat over the next two or three weeks to harden off the cuttings. It is important at this stage to develop a good root system, so don't overheat the cuttings: 10°C (50°F) is adequate.

When flowers split

When picking carnations in the greenhouse, I noticed that nearly half of the flowers had opened unevenly and split. How can I prevent this?

The petals on a carnation are enclosed by the fused green sepals that make up the bell-shaped calyx. Sometimes the calyx splits, producing a misshapen bloom.

The commonest cause is rapidly changing temperatures in spring or autumn. The flowers are most susceptible when the buds are very small (about the size of a little fingernail), and again at the point of showing colour. Aim to keep the temperature as even as possible from day to day, letting it fall gradually in the evening and rise slowly in the morning. At night close the ventilators to trap the day's heat, but open them before the sun's rays strike the greenhouse the next morning. Balance the more extreme temperature changes of spring and autumn with ventilation. Avoid changes of more than 5°C (10°F) an hour.

Other causes are varied but far less likely. Some varieties, such as 'Arthur Sim' and 'Dusty Sim', have inherently poor calyx forms – these are best avoided. Hard calyces may also develop in hot dry spells when the plant dries out more than usual. A sudden heavy watering can then cause the petals to swell and flowers to split.

Nutritional problems are occasionally the cause of splitting. Potash levels should always equal nitrogen levels in the feed; a high-nitrogen fertiliser can cause problems. In rare cases, boron deficiency can aggravate the difficulty, but you are more likely to see dead terminal buds if this is the case.

Counting the cost

I can't afford to heat my greenhouse more than is strictly necessary. How low dare I let the winter temperature fall without harming my carnations?

Carnations need very little heat. Most specialists say that 4-7°C (39-45°F) is the temperature range to aim for, but carnations will survive at temperatures a few degrees lower.

It is possible to keep greenhouse carnations through the winter without any heat at all in the extreme South, unless it is an exceptionally bad winter. Plants will survive at 1-2°C (34-36°F) for short periods, but much depends on their condition and on the humidity in the greenhouse. Condensation and damp will kill your plants, and ventilation is important even at 4°C (39°F). Air circulation is essential, and a little heating is necessary just to create this movement of air. Plants kept cool in dull weather will be less likely to suffer from thin growth, weak stems and pale flowers.

Drooping plants

My carnation plants have suddenly started wilting and dying. Have they a disease and what, if anything, can I do about it?

The most likely cause is the wilt disease *Fusarium oxysporum*. Check first, though, that you don't have a major watering or feeding problem, or that it is not a pest such as wireworm or vine weevil chewing the stems or roots (see pages 358 and 377).

There are in fact four diseases which cause carnations to wilt:

- **FUSARIUM WILT** Spread widely in the 1970s and 1980s. Infests roots at temperatures between 10°C and 25°C (50-77°F) and grows through the stems. Causes red-brown streaks in the stem a week or so before the plant wilts and begins to die.
- **VERTICILLIUM WILT** (more correctly now known as phialophora wilt). The commonest cause of carnation wilt in the 1950s and 1960s, but it has been largely eliminated by careful culturing of stock plants by suppliers.
- **PSEUDOMONAS CARYOPHYLLUS** A bacterial wilt. Very rare. Stem bases go slimy and plants die.

● ERWINIA CHRYSANTHEMI Bacterial wilt. Very rare. Causes black marks at stem base, wilting and loss of leaves.

All these diseases are quite rare. All require the same (drastic) treatment, so precise identification is not strictly necessary. There are no chemicals that can be applied to the soil or compost, or sprayed over the plants, that will move through the plant and kill the disease. There is, in fact, no cure.

Lift, bag up, and burn all dead and wilting plants. Check neighbouring plants. Any with brown streaks in their stems must be completely destroyed. These diseases rarely show up in young healthy plants, which have an inherent resistance.

If your bed of carnations has previously produced a fine crop of flowers, it is wisest to cut your losses, clear all the plants, clear all diseased soil, and start again in isolated pots, growing bags or beds. Completely clear the greenhouse if you can. Never take your own cuttings in these circumstances, as they have a high risk of being infected. Sterilise the greenhouse, washing it down and soaking the border with a solution of formaldehyde. Also sterilise your pots, canes and all other equipment.

It is best to consider a different use for your greenhouse for a year or so if possible, but if you feel you must grow carnations again immediately, grow them in pots, in growing bags or in beds isolated from the tainted ground. You can make an isolated bed by spreading heavy-grade polythene sheeting on the soil and making a new bed above it with fresh and uncontaminated compost.

Breeders are trying to produce fusarium-resistant carnation varieties. Some of these – for example, 'Saccha', a tall deep mauve-pink variety – were becoming available in the mid-1980s, but they were not fully resistant to the disease. The range of colour and the plant vigour were also limited, but there is hope for the future.

Longer-lasting flowers

What's the best way to improve the life of cut carnations?

There's no single method. It's a matter of following a number of rules, each of which will help to prolong a cut flower's life in a vase or buttonhole. Follow all these rules, and you'll at least double its life.

- Cut at the end of a fine day, when the plant is full of sugars.
- Cut the stem diagonally – don't crush it – and stand the bloom up to its neck in water for 6-12 hours before arranging it.
- Keep the flower in a cool place out of direct sunlight, and add a proprietary flower preservative to the water. Change the water after four or five days.
- Finally, keep the bloom away from ripening fruit, especially tomatoes, apples and bananas. They all give off ethylene gas, which can make carnation petals curl up within 24 hours.

Bringing a new flower to birth

The idea of breeding a new flower that nobody has ever seen before seems to me very exciting. Can I do this with carnations, and do I need any special equipment?

You *can* create your own variety, and achieve great satisfaction doing so, though your chances of making a fortune with it are slim. All you need is a steady hand, a magnifying glass and a pair of eyebrow tweezers.

The first thing is to choose the flowers you want to cross. You may have admired the shape or colour of one plant, the vigour or scent of another. This matter of choosing the right parents is the most difficult part of breeding carnations, because years of com-

PICK OF THE GREENHOUSE CARNATIONS

With so many greenhouse carnation varieties on offer, choosing which to grow is not easy. This chart helps to simplify the choice. Each of the varieties has been chosen as an outstanding example of a particular combination of colour and size. All are widely available through nurseries and garden centres. Varieties marked with an asterisk (*) are protected by Plant Breeder's Rights – the gardening equivalent of copyright. This means that you can take cuttings of your own plants for your own use or to give away to neighbours and friends – but it is illegal to sell the cuttings.

The varieties listed here are grouped into two categories: those that are suited to disbudding, and those that are not. Varieties that need disbudding should have all the flower buds on each stem removed except for the one on the end – the terminal bud. This disbudding encourages the plant to produce a few very large flowers. If the buds are not removed, you will get more, but smaller, flowers. Varieties better suited to this treatment are listed as spray varieties.

	Colour							
Name	Red	Pink	Yellow	Orange	White	Purple	Height	Scent
SPRAY VARIETIES								
Etna	●						6ft or more	●
Lilli-Anne		●					5–6ft	●
Purplette						●	5–6ft	●
Silvery Pink		●					5–6ft	●
Toni*	●		●				3–5ft	
DISBUDDED VARIETIES								
Alice	●		●				6ft or more	
Bailey's Splendour		●					3–5ft	
Calypso		●					6ft or more	
Can-can*						●	3-5ft	
Crowley Sim		●					6ft or more	
Doris Allwood		●					6ft or more	●
Fragrant Anne					●		3–5ft	●
Fragrant Rose		●					3–5ft	●
Harvest Moon			●				5–6ft	
J.M. Bibby	●						5–6ft	
Joker	●						3–5ft	
Lena		●					6ft or more	
New Arthur Sim	●				●		6ft or more	
Purple Frosted						●	5–6ft	●
Raspberry Ice					●		5–6ft	
Scania	●						6ft or more	
Tangerine Sim				●			6ft or more	●
White Sim					●		6ft or more	
William Sim	●						6ft or more	
Yellow Dusty			●				6ft or more	

mercial inbreeding have had the result that most new crosses today result in weak-growing plants. A commercial breeder trying to develop a new variety will make a great number of crosses, and keep careful records over a long period.

The amateur gardener does not usually have the time for this, so crossing can be something of a hit-or-miss affair.

Let's assume that, for better or worse, you have chosen the parent flowers. You now need to prevent either of them fertilising itself – carnations, like many other plants, have both male and female parts on the same flower. The pollen-bearing anthers, or male parts, of a carnation ripen before the stigma, the female part, is receptive – a fairly reliable built-in check on self-fertilisation.

To make this an absolute check, the flower that you've chosen to be the female parent has to be 'emasculated' – to have its anthers removed. Use eyebrow tweezers for this, practising first on flowers that you don't need for cross-breeding. To expose the anthers fully, you will probably need to take out a few central petals first.

The stigma of the emasculated flower will be receptive to pollen for two or three days if the weather is fine. You can check the plant's readiness by examining the stigmas with a magnifying glass. If the small hairs each have a shiny drop of fluid on them, they are ready.

The next step is to transfer ripe pollen from the variety you have selected as the male parent to the one you've chosen to be the female; tweezers (sterilised in a flame, but cooled) are again the best tool. Take the ripe male anther, bursting with pollen, and dab it very gently against the female stigma. Label the fertilised flower with the date and the names of the two varieties.

Repeat the process with half a dozen flowers or even more, to make success with at least a couple of plants more likely. If the pollen has fertilised the flower, the remaining outer petals of the bloom will soon collapse. Pull back the calyx with tweezers or your fingers, to stop it collecting water, and in about a month the ovary, or seed pod, will swell, ripen and begin to turn brown.

Harvest the seeds about two weeks after that. Gently break open the seed pod by hand, and shake out the dark brown seeds onto a clean sheet of paper.

Pop these seeds into an envelope, seal it and keep them in a dry place at 10-16°C (about 50-60°F) for at least three weeks. Then sow them in a seed tray in standard John Innes seed compost. Keep the seeds at 10-16°C (about 50-60°F) and keep them out of the sun.

Don't be put off by the long odds on a winner; and keep careful records – you never know.

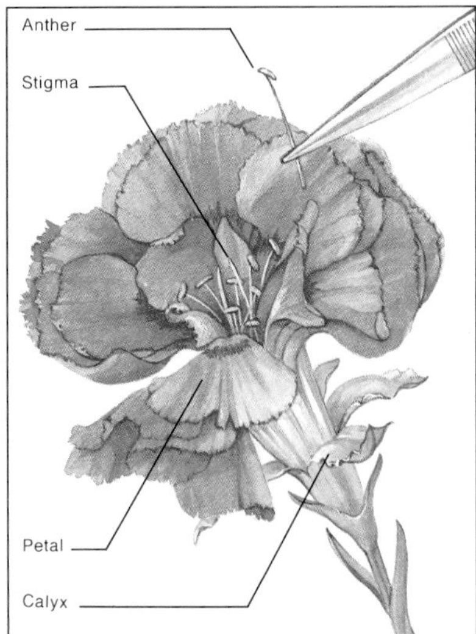

PREPARING THE 'FEMALE' *To prevent a bloom from fertilising itself, remove all its anthers – the male parts – with tweezers. Remove some petals so you can see better.*

MAKING THE CROSS *Dab a ripe anther from another flower gently onto the stigma of the prepared female. If the cross works, the seed should be ready for harvest in four to six weeks.*

Building the plant

What does it mean to 'stop' a carnation plant, and is it really necessary?

'Stopping' is the practice of removing the growing tip of a shoot. It prevents that shoot producing a flower bud, and encourages dormant buds lower on the shoot to 'break' into life and start forming sideshoots. Stopping is not necessary for the health of any carnation, but it does make a bushier plant which will produce a greater number of blooms. To stop any shoot, hold the shoot in one hand and snap out the top at the 'node', or joint, with the other.

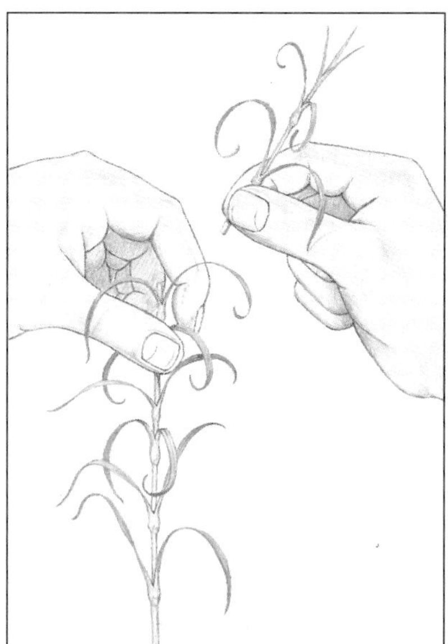

STOP AND GROW *'Stopping' a plant encourages it to bush out, and to produce more flowering stems. To do it, pinch out the top of 9in long stems so as to leave five to seven pairs of leaves.*

Young plants should be first stopped when 9in tall, leaving five to seven pairs of leaves. Up to seven strong sideshoots, or 'breaks', will grow, changing the plant from a single stem to a bushy one.

This first stopping is sometimes done while the plants are still in pots, but do not do it within two weeks before or after potting. Stopping, like potting, is something of a shock to the plant and it makes sense to let the plant get over one before jolting it again with the other.

To encourage continuity of flowering and avoid a severe check to the plant, the second stopping – of the sideshoots which you have created by the first stopping – needs to be done gradually, not all at once. Examine the plants each week, and stop only those shoots which have reached 9in and which you don't plan to leave to produce blooms. As on the main stem, stop the shoots so as to leave between five and seven pairs of leaves on each shoot.

The more shoots you stop, the bushier your plant will become and the more flowers it will eventually bear, but you will be constantly delaying flowering.

Most growers aim for a regular supply of flowers for cutting rather than stopping all the shoots at once and creating a heavy flush of simultaneous blooms. If you want autumn flowers, do the last of your stopping in July. For winter blooms, finish stopping by late August, because the buds will need longer to develop as the weather cools.

WHAT CAN GO WRONG WITH GREENHOUSE CARNATIONS		
Symptoms	**Cause**	**Action**
Ragged flowers, chewed petals	Earwigs	Spray with HCH. If the problem persists, spray again a fortnight later
Holes in buds, distorted flowers	Slugs	Apply slug pellets
Calyx splitting, distorted flowers	Fluctuating temperature	Ventilate and heat to even out fluctuations
Hollow flowers, mainly in July–Aug	Excess heat	Ventilate
Petals curling inwards. Flower fades and wilts	Ethylene gas	Keep blooms away from ripening fruit
Pale flecks on petals, distorted petals, grey flecks on leaves	Thrips	Spray with HCH. Repeat weekly if necessary
White, very small flecks on petals; bleached leaves; fine webbing on blooms and leaves	Red spider mites	Spray with permethrin, dimethoate or pirimiphos-methyl. Spray fortnightly if the problem persists. Damp down paths to discourage pests – or smoke the greenhouse fortnightly with pirimiphos-methyl
White powdery growth on calyx or lower leaves, mainly in autumn and winter	Powdery mildew	Cut back diseased areas of plant. Spray with benomyl at fortnightly intervals. Two or three sprayings will be needed
Holes in leaves; pupae in silken shelters in tips	Caterpillars of carnation tortrix moth and tomato moth	Spray fortnightly with derris or HCH
Stunted growth, yellowish plant	Root knot eelworms (microscopic worms) infesting roots	Remove and destroy all affected plants. Sterilise contaminated pots. Do not replant in the same soil
Leaf distortion; sticky deposits of honeydew on leaves and stems; black mould and visible insects on leaves and flowers	Aphids	Spray with malathion or dimethoate. Or fumigate with HCH
Lowest leaves notched and roots eaten	Vine weevil larvae	Dust soil with bromophos
Grassiness (thin shoots), no flowers	Poor genetic stock	Destroy all affected plants, and plant new varieties
Curly tips to shoots which fail to separate, and distorted growth	1 Poor light 2 Low nitrogen 3 Low phosphate	1 Clean glass 2 Check feeding 3 Check feeding
Brown (dead) tips to middle leaves – some spotting	Potash deficiency	Liquid feed with high-potash fertiliser
Thin and mauve-red tips to leaves	Phosphate deficiency	Liquid feed with high-phosphorus fertiliser
Leaf tissue collapse; rings of dead tissue; silvery-white circular scars	Frost	The plant is dead. Healthy plants will just tolerate 0°C (32°F), but no lower
Blisters on leaves which rupture, releasing rusty-brown spores. Spreads rapidly in autumn and winter	Rust disease	Keep plants dry; repair leaks in greenhouse. Spray about three times at weekly intervals with mancozeb or thiram
Holes in base of plant	Wireworms (larvae of click beetle) or larvae of vine weevil	Dust soil with bromophos
Plants go brown, wilt and die; dark streaks visible in cut stems	Bacterial wilt, fusarium wilt, or verticillium wilt (also known as phialophora wilt)	Remove and destroy all diseased plants. Do not replant in the same soil

CARROT FLIES

When sprays won't work

Carrots are among my favourite vegetables, yet I seem fated not to raise a crop without it being devastated by carrot fly. I have tried various sprays with little success – now a neighbour tells me that only a long-term effort will defeat the nuisance. Can you provide a plan of campaign?

Your neighbour is right. When the leaves of carrots, parsley, parsnips or celery turn yellow and wither without warning, it's a fair bet that the roots are being riddled by the tunnels of carrot fly maggots. Dig up a carrot or two to make sure. If the crop is infested, burn it. It's almost impossible to rescue a plant once the maggots have moved in, for the simple reason that the chemical pesticides can't reach them. What you can do, though, is start planning now to prevent or avoid attacks in future. The best way of doing it is to take advantage of the carrot fly's life cycle.

The pupae – insects in the dormant stage between maggot and adult – spend the winter in the soil. They emerge as adult flies in late May or early June, when they begin to lay eggs near carrots and other host plants. The grubs, which hatch out a week later, feed on the roots for about a month; they then begin their own metamorphoses into adult flies around early July. A second generation of maggots often appears in August or September.

By sidestepping this breeding pattern, the careful gardener can sometimes avoid the attentions of the pest. Crops sown in late May or early June will often escape the first-generation attack, because the seedlings will come through after the egg-laying season has ended.

Whenever you sow, treat the seed drills with bromophos powder or diazinon, and sow as if you were scattering gold dust; this avoids a lot of thinning later on. When young plants are thinned, it's impossible not to bruise the leaves as you pull out the rejects. The crushed foliage emits a scent which attracts egg-laying female carrot flies. Thorough watering will help to disperse the scent, but sowing very thinly to start with is a more effective way of avoiding the problem.

Protect established plants by watering along the rows with a spray-strength solution of diazinon two or three times in August and September. Do not harvest for at least two weeks after the final spray.

Lift roots as soon as they are ready, and in any event by mid-October, so that they don't remain a potential target for longer than they have to. And, finally, burn any infested carrots to reduce the number of pupae that will survive in the soil to bother you next year.

CARROTS

No roots

My carrots produce lovely ferny tops, but not much in the way of roots. What's gone wrong?

Too rich a soil will make carrots push out luxuriant foliage at the cost of roots. If, for example, you applied a generous helping of farmyard or poultry manure to the bed within the past year, then poor roots would probably result. A similar effect would arise from being too generous with such nitrogen-rich fertilisers as dried blood or sulphate of ammonia.

Grow your carrots in soil that has not been manured for at least a year. If it hasn't had any fertiliser for the past four months, rake 2oz of Growmore into each square yard about one week before sowing. Growmore contains the three major plant foods – nitrogen, potash and phosphates – in equal amounts and will provide all that is necessary for balanced growth.

Make sure that the top 12in of soil has been well dug; carrot roots can't easily penetrate a compacted layer.

Another possible cause of lush topgrowth is too much moisture. A weekly application of 2 gallons of water per square yard should be ample, even in dry weather.

If longer roots are what you want, avoid the early-season stump-rooted varieties and grow maincrop ones. Among the most reliable under average garden conditions are 'James Scarlet Intermediate', 'Chantenay Red Cored' and 'Autumn King'. These produce cylindrical carrots 6-9in long.

On stony ground

I was thinking of growing a few rows of carrots, but a neighbour tells me that the ground is too stony. Is it worth a try just the same?

You'd have to be fairly keen on home-grown carrots. Deep-rooted maincrop varieties, for instance, would almost certainly be deformed. Of course, you could copy garden exhibition enthusiasts by making deep holes with a crowbar or broom handle and filling them up with fine compost before sowing – but perhaps that's going a bit far just to produce a few carrots for the kitchen.

So try some short-rooted varieties instead; these will find the stones less of an obstacle. Round varieties, such as 'Early French Frame Rondo' and 'Kundulus', and the stump-rooted varieties such as 'Early Scarlet Horn' and 'Amsterdam Forcing Sweetheart' might well suit you. They can be sown between April and July, but you need to eat them fresh or freeze them at once. Unlike maincrop varieties that can be kept through the winter in peat or sand, they do not store well. If you can fork in some peat or fine soil before sowing it should improve matters slightly. But to clear away masses of stones would be largely a waste of time; plenty more would emerge as rain compacts the soil.

Greenhouse carrots

I'm considering sowing carrots in small peat pots next spring – in the greenhouse – and then planting them outside to get really early crops. Is it worth while?

It's a fine idea, but if you grow them entirely in the greenhouse border, you'll have a still earlier crop and save on the peat pots. Early, or forcing, varieties can be sown in a greenhouse or frame as early as February and will be ready for pulling about three weeks earlier than pot-raised carrots set outside. In other words, you could have tender young carrots on your table in mid-June.

To do this, you will need a greenhouse kept at between about 10 and 15°C (50-60°F), and you'll need to sow 'Early French Frame Rondo' – a small, round variety – at the beginning of February.

Alternatively, if you prefer to move your carrots outside later, sow the same variety at the same time – but use polystyrene cellular trays, not peat pots. Put three or four seeds in each cell. Don't thin the seedlings.

Towards the end of March, transfer the trays to a closed cold frame to harden the plants off. Then, in early April, transplant the carrots, still in their blocks of compost, to the bed. Allow 6in between blocks and cover them with cloches. This is one of the best ways to grow really early carrots, and quite cheap, too, because the polystyrene trays will last for years.

The carrot fly war

I've tried everything that's recommended on carrot fly, but still they come back. What can I do to make a permanent impression on them?

Granular insecticides, such as bromophos, diazinon and phoxim, will deter carrot fly if they are sprinkled over the soil before the pest strikes. Protect all sowings made between April and July with one of these chemicals, and repeat the application six to eight weeks later if carrot fly has been a problem in the past. But chemical controls cannot always be relied upon, so back them up with other precautions. If you have space, grow your carrots on a different site each year, and in any case, dig the soil deeply in winter to bring the dormant pests up to the surface where they will be disposed of by birds and frosts.

Delay the first sowing until June so that the plants escape the first wave of adult flies. Then sow thinly, because the odour released when crowded seedlings are pulled out attracts the egg-laying females. For the same reason, all thinning should be done on still evenings. Water the rows immediately afterwards to help to disperse the smell.

You might also try laying string soaked with creosote or paraffin down the middle of each row. Or plant garlic, onions or aromatic herbs, such as tansy or wormwood.

The carrot fly can also be thwarted with a physical barrier. Surround the area where the carrots will be grown with a 1½-2ft high wall of heavy-gauge clear polythene sheeting, firmly attached to stakes driven into the soil and pegged to the ground. No side of the wall should be longer than 12ft. The barrier helps to confine the smell of the foliage, while its height also seems to deter the winged adults from flying in.

Another kind of barrier can be made with the materials used for floating cloches (see *Cloches and frames*, page 81). Lay the material over the seeded rows, peg it down and leave it there until the carrots are ready to harvest. This will prevent the female carrot flies from laying eggs near the roots, and the extra shelter will help the crop to mature faster. For more details about this common pest, see *Carrot flies*, page 47.

CARING FOR CARROTS

For best results plant in deeply dug, light soil which has few stones. If the soil is stony or heavy, grow short-rooted varieties.

- Do not plant in soil which has been manured within the past year – it may burn the roots or make them split. Rake Growmore into the surface a few days before sowing in ½in deep drills, 6in apart.
- Water the crop once a week during dry weather, applying 2 gallons per square yard each time. Watering after a prolonged dry spell may split the roots; watering in rainy periods seems merely to encourage the foliage to grow vigorously at the expense of roots.

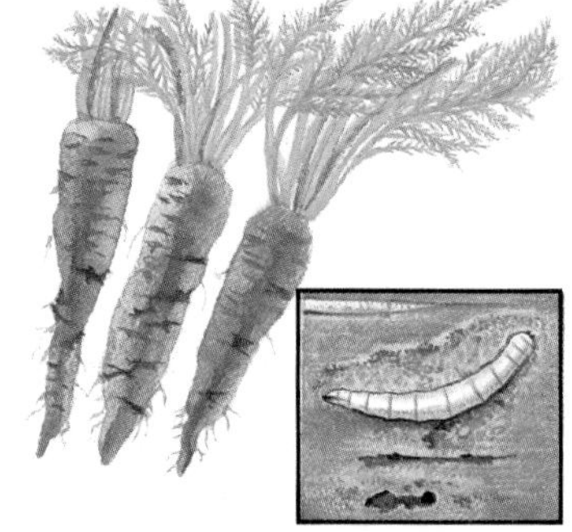

TAMING THE TUNNELLERS *Careful sowing will help to curb the damage caused by the ¼-⅓in long maggots of the carrot fly.*

CATERPILLARS

Mouths of the border

I have a plague of caterpillars in the garden that seem bent on devouring my young shrubs. Can I get rid of them quickly before they do any more damage?

With ornamental plants, you can afford to use a much tougher and more persistent insecticide than you could on vegetables. So try HCH, fenitrothion or pirimiphos-methyl. Do not, however, spray while plants – particularly fruit trees – are in full bloom, because insecticides cannot distinguish between friend and foe. Any bees in the vicinity will be killed along with the pests, and your trees will not be pollinated.

Another method of controlling caterpillars is to prevent them from being born at all.

Grease bands round fruit tree trunks will prevent female moths crawling up into the foliage to lay their eggs. The grease used for this purpose is available from garden centres. Smear it directly onto the bark, or onto 4in wide bands of paper which are then wrapped and tied around the trunk about 3ft above soil level.

Remove any loose bark before tying on the bands so that the insects cannot crawl up under them.

Shrubs and hedges are difficult to grease-band so they should be sprayed, which is probably the most effective way of dealing with large infestations of caterpillars.

Scourge of the cabbage patch

Every summer my cabbages are visited by hordes of caterpillars which reduce the leaves to skeletons. I try picking the pests off by hand, but it's a losing battle. Can you help me get on top next year?

Yes. There are several ways you can combat the pests.

Brassicas – the cabbage family – are a particularly favoured food, but most shrubs, trees and plants are popular with at least one of the more than 50 or so caterpillar species in the garden. They are the young of moths and butterflies which are themselves harmless. Most butterflies suck nectar from flowers and some never eat at all during their short existence in the winged state. But plants are at risk from caterpillars throughout the growing season outdoors, and at any time in greenhouses.

Your technique of picking the caterpillars off by hand is ideal if there are not many of them, because it cuts down the use of insecticides. Egg clusters, too, can be easily spotted – usually on the undersides of leaves – cut out and destroyed.

But as you've discovered, controlling the pests by hand alone can be a struggle if the raiders are numerous. Then, you need reinforcements.

On brassicas, and on other vegetables, the best answer is to spray with a contact insecticide such as derris or pyrethrum.

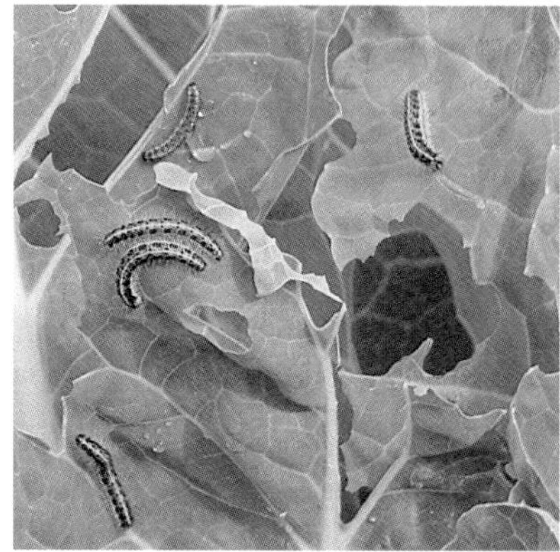

LEAF DEVOURERS *Caterpillars attack most plants and trees. These are on sprouts. Spraying and hand-picking will keep the numbers down.*

CATS

Cats on the patio

In the area where I live, most of us have small patio-type gardens where every patch of earth attracts cats. How can I keep them away?

There are two ways of keeping cats away. In spring, you can protect your seeds with twigs or netting stretched over the soil, though of course these would have to be removed when things started to grow. Or you might apply with a spray or watering can one of the chemical deterrents based on aluminium ammonium sulphate.

Cats cannot bear the smell – to humans it is noticeable but inoffensive – and after two or three doses they will stay off your garden. Stick to the instructions on the pack if you use a chemical deterrent.

The traditional antidote is to keep a dog; but dogs and gardens aren't very compatible either.

Catmint under attack

Is there any way of stopping cats rolling about on what was once a lovely clump of catmint?

Try pushing sticks into the ground amongst the catmint so that the tops stay hidden in the clump. This usually works. It stops the cats rolling about but won't prevent them from 'worrying' the plant; they find the smell absolutely irresistible.

Chemical deterrents such as those based on pepper dust and aluminium ammonium sulphate might have some effect. They're unlikely to work completely since the scent of the catmint is probably powerful enough to overcome them; but you could try.

Cat-lover's plea

Will slug pellets and weedkillers harm my cats? Are there any garden chemicals that can be used safely?

More and more people are feeling uneasy about the matter of chemicals in the garden. Paradoxically today garden chemicals are safer than they have ever been, though in their concentrated form they should always be treated with respect and stored safely.

If used according to the instructions, most garden chemicals are perfectly safe, though there could be problems in the unlikely event of a pet gorging itself on slug pellets. Slug pellets containing metaldehyde are safer than those based on methiocarb.

In addition, the mini-pellets are safer than the large ones, simply because more are needed to make up a dose that would be harmful to a cat or dog. Slug tapes and slug pastes are safer still because it's less likely that a pet would eat them.

It is best to conceal slug-killers amongst plants in little clumps and then to cover them with a tile or slate propped up on a couple of stones. The slugs and snails will still be able to reach the poisons, but birds and animals won't.

Tale of two tubs

I've got a super pair of terracotta pots on my urban patio where I love to grow colourful annuals in summer. But local cats persist in destroying my carefully sown seedbeds by using them as toilets. How can I stop them?

You can try one of the proprietary animal repellents sold in garden centres. But if they're not enough, you could try using a physical barrier.

Clip clothespegs about 3in apart all the way round the edges of the pots, or stick short canes into the soil at the same spacing.

The miniature fence should discourage the cats from jumping up. Once the flowers start to grow, and the soil becomes covered with green, the cats will leave it alone anyway, so you can safely remove the pegs before your summer display starts.

CAULIFLOWERS

Small is beautiful

My wife has heard of mini-cauliflowers that can be cooked and served whole. Is this some new variety?

No, just ordinary cauliflowers, but grown by a method developed by the Institute of Horticultural Research in Wellesbourne, near Stratford-upon-Avon. It's a technique by which up to 16 cauliflowers, with curds only 1½-3½in across, may be grown in the same amount of space that would be occupied by one plant grown in the normal way.

The mini-cauliflowers crop between late June and early November from sowings made between April and early July.

In the autumn before you sow, test the pH value of the bed and, if necessary, lime it to bring the pH up to 6.5 (see *How much garden lime to use*, page 8). This will help growth and discourage club root disease. In winter, dig the soil deeply and, just before sowing, rake Growmore into the patch at a rate of 4oz to the square yard. Firm the ground by treading it. It is important that the soil should be evenly firmed, though not compacted. It should also be moist.

Aim to grow four plants to the square foot – in other words, about 6in apart each way. Don't space the rows more than 9in apart, or uneven growth will result. Sow two seeds together in each position in the prepared soil. If both germinate, pull up the weaker seedling shortly after its first true leaves develop. The important thing, when aiming for this particular crop, is that you must always sow the seed in the cropping position; don't transplant the seedlings.

As your seedlings grow, dust them with derris or HCH to keep flea beetles away. Water only when the soil is dry, because too much moisture will lead to leafy growth and loose curds. Remove weeds by hoeing or by hand as soon as they appear, and combat aphids and caterpillars, if necessary, with derris or dimethoate. Cut the curds from late June onwards before they become loose or more than 3½in across.

The best varieties for this intensive method are the ones that mature in early summer; 'Alpha', 'Bambino', 'Perfection', 'Predominant' and 'Snowball' all give good results. Autumn-maturing varieties are not so suitable because they take longer to mature.

Autumn browning

Last autumn's cauliflowers were a bit of a disaster. None of the curds developed fully and some of them turned brown. Why?

There are three possible reasons. The most likely is the weather. Too much sun will brown the curds; so will frost. The second cause could be incorrect planting or watering. Cauliflowers need to be grown in firmly packed and moist soil.

The third reason could be boron deficiency, though this is rare. If there's not enough boron in the soil, the curds will be small and taste bitter. The leaves will also be stunted and brittle. You can confirm the diagnosis by cutting into a stem; if it is discoloured, boron deficiency is the culprit.

Boron deficiency can be treated in two main ways. The first step in either method is to check the soil pH. If your soil is very acid – in other words if it has a low pH – it's possible that it does contain boron but the plants cannot get at it because of the acidity. The solution is to add lime to bring the pH level up to about 6.5 – the level at which cauliflowers do best. For details, see page 8.

If the pH is already 6.5 or higher, the problem is more likely to be that your soil simply does not contain enough boron. In this case, rake 1oz of borax into each 20 square yards of soil before planting. You'll find it easier to sprinkle the chemical evenly if you mix it first into a bucketful of sand, then sprinkle on the mixture.

Whiter than white

Why is it that everyone else has white cauliflowers while mine are khaki? What's the knack?

Snap one or two leaves over the curds while they are small and still pure white. This will shield summer varieties from the sun, and give autumn and winter-maturing plants some protection from frost. Since broken leaves don't always stay in place, it's an even better idea to draw two or three leaves upwards around the curd and then clip the tips together with a clothespeg.

Why firm ground matters

Why do all the books say that cauliflowers must be grown in firm soil? And doesn't this contradict the other instruction that the ground must be deeply cultivated?

If cauliflowers are planted in soil that hasn't been consolidated, their curds are likely to open up. The hearts of cabbages and of brussels sprouts are affected in the same way.

Ideally, you should dig your soil deeply the winter before the plants are set out so that the ground has ample time to settle. But this isn't always possible, and you may have to prepare the soil and set out the plants very shortly afterwards.

You can get round this problem by treading the soil after it has been dug. Wait until the surface is drying out, then shuffle over the area with your feet very close together. If the ground is very soft, press down on your heels and tread the soil twice – the second time treading at right angles to the first. Rake out your footprints and level the surface. Then, just before planting, rake in 4oz of Growmore to each square yard.

When transplanting young cauliflowers – or cabbages or sprouts – into their permanent sites, don't use a dibber to make the planting holes. If you have firmed the soil as recommended, a dibber will compact the sides of the hole and hamper root growth. Use a trowel instead.

Runaway cauliflowers

My summer cauliflowers were doing fine, with heads forming early and developing well. But when the heads got to 2in across, they just stopped growing. Why?

In a word, stress. Some factor in the plants' growing conditions created so much stress that the plants became stunted. A period of drought can do this, but it's more commonly due to a cold snap in the spring that coincides with the time when the young plants are being hardened off, or becoming established in the garden. The effects would not be noticeable until early summer.

Plants that are started in a heated greenhouse in January and then transplanted to the garden are far more likely to suffer this check to growth than those sown outside during April, since the lusher growth of the early starters will be more vulnerable to the rigours of a sudden cold snap.

For this reason, it is important to harden off greenhouse-grown cauliflowers slowly – leave them in a cold frame for at least two weeks before planting them outside. Keep the frame closed for the first few days, and cover the top with polythene, sacking or old carpet if the nights are chilly. Open the frame during the warmer part of the day, then gradually increase the hours of ventilation so that the plants become acclimatised without being chilled. If the temperature takes a sudden plunge after the plants have been set out, protect them with cloches until the weather improves.

Curds for a Northern winter

I'm moving shortly to the Durham area, and when planning my future vegetable bed, I wondered if there were any winter cauliflower varieties that might be persuaded to grow that far north?

Strictly speaking no, because the so-called winter cauliflower is not really a cauliflower at all. It's a curding type of broccoli – the other type is the sprouting broccoli – and is almost identical to cauliflower except that its curd is bumpier and is a duller white. British-bred varieties are very hardy and will tolerate Northern winters. 'Asmer Snowcap March' (maturing in mid-March), 'St George' (April), 'Late Queen' (May) and 'Northern Star' (late May) are quite reliable.

Dutch varieties of winter cauliflower are also becoming popular because they are just as hardy and have larger, firmer and whiter heads than our native-bred plants, though the choice is more limited. In seed catalogues, the Dutch varieties are often listed under the heading *Walcheren Selections*. Among them, 'Walcheren Armado April' (mid-April), 'Walcheren Winter' (April) and 'Walcheren Markanta' (early May) are well worth a try.

Sow any of these varieties between March and May, or up to July in the case of 'Walcheren Winter'. Make the drills ½in deep and 6in apart. When the seedlings appear, thin them to 4in apart. Then, eight to ten weeks later, transplant to their cropping positions, allowing 2-2½ft each way between the plants.

Sooty boost

The other day, somewhat to my astonishment, I saw a neighbour spreading soot around his cauliflowers. Does it do any good?

Yes, in two ways. It discourages slugs and, by darkening the soil, helps the ground to absorb more heat from the sun. Soot also usually contains a little nitrogen, which helps to boost the plants' growth. But if you're thinking of following your neighbour's example, don't use fresh soot. It's quite caustic and will burn plant stems. Store the soot under cover for six months before using it, and it will be quite safe.

If you want to use soot in this way, put a light dusting around the plants. Repeat the dose after heavy rain.

A cauliflower for all seasons

How can I get cauliflowers all year round?

To get a crop of cauliflowers throughout the year, you'll have to grow at least three varieties. As a summer-cropping variety choose 'All the Year Round'. Summer varieties of cauliflower can be sown in a cold frame in September, in a greenhouse or on a windowsill in January, or outdoors in April. If you want to sow the seeds outside, sow them ½in deep in drills 6in apart and transplant the seedlings in May or June, setting them 1½-2ft apart each way. The variety 'All the Year Round' will crop all summer and even into early autumn.

For an autumn crop, choose 'Autumn Giant' or 'Veitch's Self Protecting'. Sow outdoors between mid-April and mid-May. Sow the seeds ½in deep in drills 9-12in apart. Thin the seedlings and transplant them to the main bed in late June. Space them about 2ft apart each way. These varieties will give a crop from late September to early December.

Cauliflowers grow according to how much daylight they receive, so the short daylight hours of winter stop any variety producing crops in the months of January and February. Winter varieties, such as 'Walcheren Winter', 'St George' and 'Late Queen', will give you crops from as early as mid-March until late May. For details about sowing see *Curds for a Northern winter*, opposite.

The variety with the longest season is 'All the Year Round' – although the name is somewhat optimistic. It signifies only that the variety can be sown over a longer period than other summer varieties. You can, for example, raise 'All the Year Round' in a heated greenhouse in January, and move the plants to fertile soil in late March or early April to crop between June and August. Or, to sample its large curds in August and September, you could sow the seeds outside in a nursery bed during March or early April, and set the young plants out into their permanent positions in June.

Wind-chill factor

Living near the East Coast as I do, my garden gets some fairly chill breezes even in summer. I'm sure these slow my cauliflowers down; what can I do to speed them up?

Better shelter is the answer. Chilling winds keep plants and soil cold, resulting in slow establishment and later cropping.

Try surrounding your cauliflower area with a screen of plastic windbreak netting, or with thick polythene sheeting sandwiched between two layers of galvanised chicken wire. Make the screen about 3ft high, attaching it to stakes driven about 18in into the ground.

Cloches would also be valuable. To get the best out of them, place them over the prepared soil to warm it two weeks before the cauliflowers are set out. Allow the plants to grow beneath for as long as there's room. A polythene floating cloche would also help your cauliflowers to get off to a good start, and because it actually rests on the plants, and would not confine growth, it could be left to cover them for a longer period than conventional glass or plastic cloches. For details about how to use these cloches, see *Floating cloches*, page 82.

Collapsing cauliflowers

During the last warm weather, some of my cauliflowers suddenly wilted, keeled over and died. Extra water made no difference. What was wrong?

Sounds very much like a visitation of the cabbage root fly, whose grubs feed on the roots and sometimes burrow into the main stem. They're unpleasant-looking creatures: white, about ¼in long, and they wriggle when disturbed. Cauliflowers, cabbages, sprouts and calabrese, and wallflowers too, are susceptible to this pest. Young plants set out in dry weather between April and July are the most liable to attack, and they can be killed off by the grubs within three weeks if the soil remains dry. Older plants may struggle on, but will be fairly useless as crops.

Raking a granular insecticide such as bromophos into the soil before planting will provide protection for about six weeks. The chemical can also be scattered around established plants to kill off the winged females – they look rather like houseflies – before they lay their eggs at the bases of the stems.

The first eggs are laid in April, and the danger continues until September, since some three generations of adults are produced each summer.

Some gardeners use discs of roofing felt, thick cardboard or plastic sheeting to deter egg-laying, by preventing the females from reaching the stem bases. Make the discs at least 5in across and cut a slit from the edge to the centre so they fit snugly around the stem at soil level.

Another good preventive measure is to dig the soil of the vegetable bed deeply during the winter. This will expose hibernating pupae to winds, frost and hungry birds. Better still, if you have room, grow cauliflowers and other greens in a different site each year; this will also help to check club root disease.

Mystery holes

Something is making tiny holes in my seedlings. What is it? How can I control it?

The striped flea beetle attacks cauliflower and other brassica seedlings when they are raised outdoors. The insects bite small, round holes in the leaves which weaken the plants and may even kill them.

Dusting the seeds with HCH often deters the beetles, and it's a good idea to spray or dust derris or HCH over the soil and young leaves as well.

If you've had trouble with these beetles in previous years, give the plants a dose of high-nitrogen fertiliser as well. That will help to speed up growth – and once the plants are beyond the seedling stage, they'll be much less vulnerable to the pests.

Keeping cauliflowers

What's the best way to store harvested plants?

Lift the plants, wash their roots and hang them upside down in a cool, dry room. They will stay firm for up to three weeks.

To keep cut cauliflowers fresh, enclose the dry curds in a ventilated polythene bag and put them in the salad compartment of a refrigerator. Preserved in this way, they will keep firm and fresh for up to a week.

CELERY

Sinister seed

I have a packet of celery seed which carries a warning that the seeds must not be used for culinary or medicinal purposes. But supposing I plant them, will it be safe to eat the crop?

Perfectly safe. Celery seed is sometimes dusted with thiram fungicide by seed firms to make sure that it is clear of leaf spot disease. The warning is given because celery seed is also used as a spice – in cabbage dishes, for example. But the fungicide will have long disappeared from seeds sold for sowing by the time you come to eat the plants. Leaf spot can also be controlled with two or three sprays of benomyl or carbendazim at ten-day intervals. Begin spraying at once if you see brown spots on the leaves in early summer.

Advice for beginners

I'm venturing into celery-growing for the first time. Which is easier – self-blanching or trenched celery?

Self-blanching. Earthing up the stems to exclude the light, an essential chore when growing trenched celery, is not necessary for self-blanching varieties, though they do require a very fertile soil – two buckets of well-rotted manure to the square yard – and copious amounts of water in dry weather. Self-blanching celery is grown in a flat bed, allowing 6-9in each way between plants, so that the foliage shades the stems and keeps them white and crisp. The stems on the outside of the bed will develop a green tinge if they're not shielded from the light. This shielding is quite easily done by placing a strip of black polythene or wooden planks so as to cast a shadow down the length of the row. One drawback of self-blanching celery is that it is badly damaged by frost, and can therefore only be cropped between August and October – whereas the traditional winter trenched celery can be enjoyed from October to February. Another is that their stems are not so tall, or as crisp or tasty as the winter-hardy varieties.

However, 'Golden Self-blanching' is a reliable variety that is ready from August onwards. 'Lathom Self-blanching' is compact with yellow stems free from stringiness. For tall, white stems grow 'Ivory Tower' – a vigorous, crisp self-blanching variety.

When to sow

Self-blanching celery is ready in early autumn – a month or so before winter celery. So shouldn't it be sown earlier?

No – sow both types at the same time. Winter (trenched) celery grows more slowly, but most varieties produce taller stalks than the self-blanching varieties.

Sow all seeds in trays of seed compost in a heated greenhouse – about 15°C (59°F) – in March or April. Cover them with the merest dusting of compost, and don't cover the trays with anything that will exclude light. The seeds don't seem to germinate as well under a heavy blanket of compost or in total darkness.

When the seedlings have developed two true leaves, prick them out into seed trays. Space the young plants about 2in apart. Harden off the plants in a cold frame for two or three weeks before setting them outside in late May or early June.

Plant self-blanching celery 6-9in apart in blocks, rather than in rows; space trenched celery 9in apart with 15in between rows. Both types must be kept well watered.

Blanching hints

Have you any tips or short cuts that might speed the business of blanching winter celery?

The traditional way of blanching celery is to pile earth up around the stalks when the plants have grown to about 12in high – usually in early August. As the celery continues to grow, continue to earth up, so that soil always reaches to the bottom of the leaves. The job will need doing about once every three weeks until about mid-September. The problem is how to keep the soil out of the plant – soil will push the stalks apart and let the light in. You can bind the stalks together with raffia before earthing up or, even better, tie a roll of corrugated paper around the stalks, and then earth up. Alternatively, wrap a black plastic bag round the stalks and unfold it as they grow.

IN THE BAG *You can keep celery stalks clean and avoid earthing them up by keeping them covered with a black plastic bag.*

CHALK

Lime-induced deficiencies

I suspect that my soil is so chalky that the plants are suffering. The leaves on some of the shrubs are going yellow. How can I find out what the problem is?

For a start you must conduct a soil test in order to find out how alkaline the soil is (see *Acid soils*, page 6). If the soil is alkaline, the reading will be pH 7 or above. It is unlikely to be higher than pH 8-8.5.

Assuming that the soil is strongly alkaline – which is almost certainly the case if your ground is chalky – the most likely cause of the yellowing of an individual plant is iron or manganese deficiency caused by the high level of chalk. Diagnosing individual mineral deficiencies is not an easy job, even for the professionals, but it is not particularly important to find out exactly which trace element the plants are lacking. If the trouble is localised and shows after prolonged rain or a long hard winter when minerals are leached out of the soil, an application of iron sequestrene fertiliser in spring, watered or raked in, will usually restore the green colour – iron sequestrene normally contains manganese as well as iron.

If, however, the problem is general, the cause is likely to be a case of starvation, and the easy answer is 2-4oz per square yard of a balanced feed such as Growmore, lightly raked in every year in spring.

Initially, as a first aid measure and irrespective of the cause, you can spray the ailing plants with a seaweed extract foliar feed. After a couple of weeks, scatter a granular feed such as Growmore on the ground. Or, where you suspect lime-induced deficiency in the soil, rake in or water on iron sequestrene. The foliar feed will quickly put the plants back on their feet, and the slower-acting feeds will keep them there.

Chalky lumps

During cultivation, I often dig up bits of raw chalk. Is this bad or can I regard it as a substitute for lime?

Chalk and lime are more or less synonymous from a gardener's point of view. Both are alkaline minerals and both make the soil alkaline. If your garden is so limy that you're digging up raw chalk, it's unlikely that your ground will ever need liming. Soil of your sort, especially if it is dug regularly, remains 'sweet' (meaning alkaline) merely by the mixing action of the digging.

Is it a good thing to bring up lumps of chalk? Not especially; it is rather like unearthing stones and bringing them to the surface on any kind of soil. Both present the same problem in that they make it harder to cultivate the ground and reduce it to a fine tilth for sowing. Lumps of chalk, and stones, should be removed.

The lime-haters

Are there any plants that won't grow on chalky soil? And if so, why?

Certainly. Such plants, called 'calcifuges' – meaning literally 'lime-fleers' – are never happy on any chalky soil and will fail if it is strongly alkaline. As to why this is so, it has to do with plant evolution. Just as many animals have adapted to specific homes and ways of life, and will thrive in no other habitat, so plants have adapted to particular combinations of climate and soil.

Top of the list of plants which require lime-free soil (pH 6.5 or less) are those belonging to the Ericaceae family, including most heaths and heathers, rhododendrons and azaleas, kalmias and gaultherias, pieris and pernettyas.

Although most maples are lime-tolerant, one species, *Acer rubrum*, is not, and the same applies to *Skimmia reevesiana*; the more common *S. japonica* is not so fussy.

Other trees and shrubs which can tolerate slightly limy soil but will do much better in neutral or acid soil include camellias, corylopsis, halesia, hamamelis, koelreuteria, liquidambar and magnolias. These plants will perform satisfactorily in chalky soil provided that it is treated annually with iron sequestrene and provided that the soil has plenty of peat worked in at planting time. Hydrangeas don't mind chalky soil, but the blue varieties will retain their colour only if the soil is treated in this way.

Iron sequestrene does not of itself make the soil less alkaline or more acid. It does, however, bypass the chemical locks which imprison some plant nutrients in alkaline soils and which lime-hating plants cannot unlock for themselves.

Chalk versus limestone

What's the difference between a chalky and a limestone soil? And what can be done to improve them?

Limestone tends to be grittier and therefore freer-draining than chalk: that's the essential difference. But there's nothing necessarily wrong with either type of soil. They merely require slightly different treatment from acid soils.

Chalky soils, which include limy ones, can be heavy or light in the same way as any other soils. They can be well or poorly drained, water and nutrient-retentive or thin and starved. The only important characteristic of chalky/limestone soils is that they are usually strongly alkaline and therefore won't support the comparatively small group of lime-hating plants. Gardening on chalky soils has certain advantages, once you have accepted that plants requiring lime-free conditions won't thrive. Soils overlying chalk are for the most part well-drained, yet moisture-retentive, thanks to the absorbent nature of the chalk. Both of these are plus factors.

On the other hand, chalky soils often have low fertility because organic matter decomposes very quickly in strongly alkaline soils and needs to be replenished annually. The art of gardening on chalk is just that: keeping up the level of bulky organic matter in the soil by regular applications of garden compost or farmyard manure. Chalky soils starved of organic matter soon turn to mud in winter and to concrete in summer.

Chalk and garden lime – the difference

Does ground chalk have the same effect on the soil as hydrated lime?

They do exactly the same job. The only difference is that one-third more of ground chalk has to be applied than hydrated (garden) lime to have the same neutralising effect. So that if the manufacturer's recommendation is for 3lb of lime to treat a given area, you would need to apply 4lb of ground chalk.

If you want to use the less common agricultural (burnt) lime, the opposite applies and you would need one-third less, in this case 2lb of agricultural lime compared to 3lb of hydrated lime. Take care when using burnt lime not to get it on your skin or clothes because it is very corrosive.

Soil starvation

I garden on thin chalky soil. Since moving here about five years ago, I have dug in peat, garden compost, bone meal and other complete fertilisers, but to little effect. The plants don't actually die but they make little headway. What else can I do?

Bluntly, exercise patience. It can take up to ten years to build up the kind of deep and fertile soil layer that most permanent plants require for continued growth.

Peat in itself does not add nutrients to the soil. It merely improves the structure of the ground by binding the fine particles together, thus helping the soil to retain water and food for longer.

Bulky organic matter, ideally well-rotted farmyard manure or garden compost, is the answer to any thin and starved soil, alkaline or acid. It is hard work to dig in, though, and in order to have any lasting benefit it should be laid at least 2in thick, either as a top-dressing or in the bottom of trenches during general cultivation. Autumn is usually considered the best time to add manure or compost on most soils, but on a thin chalky soil like yours spring is just as suitable.

Since even large quantities of organic matter go a surprisingly short way, it's worth concentrating on a small area at a time – digging in liberal amounts rather than spreading a load of manure or compost thinly over a wide area. That way at least part of your garden will begin to show encouraging results. Given time and perseverance, even the thinnest soil will eventually build up sufficient soil depth and nutrients to sustain both ornamental and food crops.

CHEMICALS

A quick way with weeds

The season is advancing and I must start planting soon. Yet my new allotment is a riot of weeds. How can I clear the ground quickly without poisoning the soil?

The fastest way to clear weeds is to spray the whole area with a contact weedkiller based on paraquat. This chemical is quickly broken down by contact with the soil, and you should be able to begin cultivating and sowing within a few days. But no single weedkiller can kill all weeds. Each works in a different way and is designed for a particular job: some kill annual weeds; others attack perennials with taproots or with creeping root systems. A paraquat-based product, for example, will permanently kill annual weeds and most grasses. But though it obliterates the surface shoots of such perennial weeds as couch grass, buttercup and bindweed, the poison is not taken down into the roots and the weeds will soon shoot up again.

Another quick killer, and one that goes right down to the roots, is glyphosate. It, too, breaks down quickly on contact with the soil, but you will have to wait a week or two before you see any particular effect on the weeds. In fact, the weeds stop growing almost as soon as the spray touches them, but only after several days will they begin to turn pale before collapsing and dying.

Glyphosate kills many annual and perennial weeds including grasses, but there are some perennials that neither it nor any other chemical weedkiller will have much effect upon – horseradish, for instance. Its very deep, thick roots will not be killed easily, and you will probably have to dig it up piece by wearisome piece.

Horsetail is another deep-rooted weed on which weedkillers make only a fleeting impression. The tops may be killed off, but they will return again and again. Worst of all, perhaps, is Japanese knotweed. This can erupt through paths, tarmac and even push paving slabs apart. It grows up to 6ft in a year – though it does die down in winter – and has an almost indestructible root system. It has been said that if you've got it, it's easier to move house than to eradicate it, though of course knotweed, like everything else, will eventually yield to sodium chlorate. The only problem with this chemical is that it creates a desert in which nothing will grow for at least a year.

You might try the non-chemical way on your allotment. Cultivate the ground thoroughly and bury the weeds deep. If they return, do it again or hoe them savagely. Or keep scything them down to ground level; after a while, they will die.

Systemic vs contact

My garden centre offers two kinds of insecticide – systemic and contact. Which would be the safer to use on my vegetable plot?

All insecticides are safe when used properly. They must be approved by the Ministry of Agriculture before they can be offered for sale, and the most significant factor in gaining this approval is that they are selective in their effects. Some chemicals are deadly to only a few species, but others are intended to kill a wide range of pests; these last types may also kill beneficial insects.

A contact insecticide will kill only the creatures it touches at the time of spraying or soon afterwards, so, to ensure that all the pests on a plant have been disposed of, spraying has to be very thorough. Contact insecticides have a short life, sometimes no more than hours, and repeat applications are often required, perhaps separated by no more than four days. A short-lived insecticide can be an advantage if you want to harvest a crop within a few days of spraying. A drawback is that it is non-selective and will wipe out bees, ladybirds and other useful insects just as readily as the pests. You can't avoid this, unfortunately, though it will help a bit if you restrict your spraying to early morning or in the evening when it is cool and ladybirds and bees are less active.

Systemic insecticides work on a completely different principle. With these, the chemical is applied to the foliage and the plant absorbs it throughout its system. It is fatal only to those insects that chew the plant or suck its sap. Those that merely visit the plant or take nectar or pollen from it are at risk only when the chemical is actually being applied.

Human consumers of sprayed vegetables are at far less risk. All the same, be sure to let the correct minimum interval pass between spraying and harvesting. This interval will be clearly indicated on the label. Also on the label is a list of plants that

GARDEN PESTICIDES AND FUNGICIDES – HOW TO CHOOSE THE RIGHT ONES

The collection of pesticides and fungicides developed by manufacturers for the gardener grows larger each year. Occasionally new chemicals are discovered and developed. More often the same chemicals are presented in new, safer or more efficient forms designed to keep abreast of rapidly evolving insect and fungal menaces. This list describes what each of the common garden chemicals does, and lists the brand names it is sold under.

The present trend is towards 'cocktails': products containing two or more chemicals and intended to exterminate several menaces at once. Thus ICI's Roseclear, for example, is made up of three chemicals: pirimicarb, a rapid killer of greenfly; triforine, a fungicide that attacks powdery mildew and black spot; and bupirimate, which also attacks black spot and powdery mildew and kills aphids as well.

Since these cocktails enable the gardener to accomplish several tasks at once, they save both time and money. But do not be tempted to make your own cocktails out of chemicals in your garden shed. Homemade mixes could nullify the effect of the ingredients or have an entirely unpredictable effect. Don't mix any chemicals unless the label specifically says you can.

Chemicals in the garden – and everywhere else, too – should be treated with respect. This means, for instance, always following the manufacturer's instructions precisely; it also means not using chemical sprays, dusts, granules and smokes indiscriminately. The continual use of a particular pesticide or fungicide can lead to the evolution of a resistant strain of the target pest or disease. There is a species of fruit tree red spider mite, for instance, that is now quite impervious to the insecticides that formerly killed it. In addition, indiscriminate scattering of a pesticide might easily kill a pest's natural predators as well, leaving the way clear for the pest to recover and multiply out of control.

This list does not include the chemical brand names of weedkillers. For details of those, see *Weeds*, page 362.

Chemical	Trade names	Description
Benomyl	ICI Benlate plus Activex	Systemic fungicide. Benomyl is not taken up readily by woody plants so has to be applied to them fairly frequently. Used as a spray against rose black spot, some turf diseases, tomato leaf mould, apple and pear scab, cane spot and spur blight of raspberries, leaf spots on ornamental plants, celery and soft fruit, grey mould and powdery mildews on ornamental plants, fruit and vegetables, but resistant strains may occur. It is harmful to earthworms.
Bitumen	pbi Arbrex pruning compound	Forms a protective seal against diseases, pests and frost over cuts in growing wood. Use after pruning.
Borax	Synchemicals Nippon Ant Killer Liquid	No harmful side effects; very persistent.
Bromophos	pbi Bromophos	Moderately persistent contact insecticide. Controls cutworms, wireworms, cabbage root fly, carrot fly and other pests found in the soil.
Bromophos in oil	Synchemicals Spring Spray	Same properties as bromophos.
Bupirimate and triforine	ICI Nimrod-T	Systemic fungicide for eradication of and protection against powdery mildew, rose black spot, scab on apples and leaf spot on blackcurrants and gooseberries; remains effective for 10-12 days. See also *triforine*.
Bupirimate, triforine and pirimicarb	ICI Roseclear	Systemic fungicide as above; also contains a systemic insecticide specific to aphids. Not harmful to other pests or beneficial insects; moderately persistent.

are particularly susceptible to damage from systemic sprays. Cherries, for example, should not be sprayed with dimethoate.

Looking after ladybirds

Aphids and greenfly are a real pest in my garden. Can I get rid of them without harming the insects that do the garden good?

Picking the right time, choosing chemicals carefully, and selecting the right kind of sprayer are the keys to saving the beneficial insects in the garden – the ladybirds, the lacewings, the beetles and the bees.

Pests such as greenfly and many diseases, like mildew, are apparent and can be dealt with at any time of day. Most beneficial insects are busy only when the sun is high. Therefore, the best time to apply a spray is early in the morning or at dusk; the air is cooler then, the bees and ladybirds settled down, and there are no warm air currents to carry the chemical about the garden.

Spray only when there is little or no wind, and direct the spray where the pest or disease can be seen. Avoid the temptation to splash it about on neighbouring plants and soil.

Choose a sprayer whose nozzle can be adjusted to applying the chemical in short bursts of fine spray. If your garden is small, then you don't need a big sprayer. Buy a small one, and mix no more than enough chemical to do the job. When you've finished, get rid of any surplus spray, by washing it down the drain. Don't spray it over plants that don't need it.

When buying an insecticide, choose one that is specific against aphids, or one that is systemic. Neither type will harm the beneficial insects.

Where pets may safely graze

Problem: my children have collected a menagerie of puppies, kittens and rabbits, and my lawn is badly in need of sorting out. Is there a lawn weedkiller that won't harm the pets?

Selective weedkillers for lawns will not harm your pets, provided you follow a few simple guidelines. Look along the shelves at the garden centre and read the labels carefully. Weedkillers that are harmful to animals are labelled so, usually on the back of the container under 'Precautions'. 'Harmful to fish', 'Harmful to livestock', or 'Keep animals out of treated areas for seven days'; these are typical of the instructions you will see on containers of products that may harm animals. For these purposes, rabbits, guinea pigs and other grass-eating pets may be classified as 'livestock'.

Once you've found a selective weedkiller that does the job you want but isn't harmful to animals, all you need to do is to keep pets and children out of the area while you spray, and until the lawn has dried – usually no more than a few hours. This kind of chemical usually works quickly on the weeds through the foliage. Few lawn weedkillers assault the roots. Those that do will bear an instruction on the label that says something like 'Do not cultivate and replant until six weeks after treatment'.

Always wash out the sprayer with water and washing-up liquid immediately after use; rinse several times, and pour the water down

Chemical	Trade names	Description
Calomel (see *mercurous chloride*)		
Captan and HCH	Murphy Combined Seed Dressing (Fisons)	Sulphur-based fungicide used against grey mould and soil-borne diseases, including damping-off. See also *HCH*.
Carbaryl	Murphy Lawn Pest Killer (Fisons); Murphy Wasp Destroyer (Fisons); pbi Autumn Toplawn	Contact insecticide for control of earthworms; moderately persistent. Poisonous to bees and fish.
Carbaryl and rotenone	Boots Garden Insect Powder	As above. See also *rotenone*.
Carbendazim	Boots Garden Fungicide	Systemic fungicide. Much the same properties and used to control the same diseases as benomyl.
Carbendazim with activator	pbi Supercarb	As above, but more efficient in control.
Chelated or fritted compounds	Murphy Sequestrene (Fisons); Chempak Trace Element Frit 253A	Compounds containing iron, manganese, magnesium and other trace elements. They overcome or prevent lime-induced chlorosis in plants growing on alkaline soil.
Chlordane	Synchemicals Chlordane 25; Synchemicals Nippon Ant Powder	Very persistent. Good for long-term control of earthworms, ants and wasps; toxic to animals, bees and fish.
Copper compound	Synchemicals Bordeaux Mixture; Murphy Liquid Copper Fungicide	Fungicide containing copper compounds and hydrated lime; toxic to livestock and fish. Can be used as a spray against azalea gall, clematis wilt, lily disease, bacterial canker, and peach leaf curl on prunus species. Also used against leaf spots on ornamental plants and against celery, potato and tomato blight, cane spot and spur blight on raspberries.
Copper sulphate and ammonium carbonate	pbi Cheshunt Compound	Fungicide that combats damping-off of seedlings, and other soil-borne diseases affecting cuttings and small plants.
Derris (see *rotenone*)		
Diazinon	Root Guard (Fisons)	Moderately persistent insecticide that controls pests living in the soil. Toxic to bees and fish.
Dichlorophen	pbi Bio Moss Killer; May & Baker Mosstox-Plus; Murphy Super Moss Killer and Lawn Fungicide (Fisons)	Contact herbicide primarily used for the control of moss, but also very effective against red thread (corticium), a disease of grass.
Dimethoate	Boots Greenfly & Blackfly Killer; Murphy Systemic Insecticide (Fisons); ICI Keriguards (with added fertiliser)	Systemic insecticide that controls aphids, capsids, scale insects, mealy bugs, leafhoppers, suckers, red spider mites, and small caterpillars. Moderately persistent; toxic to bees and fish. Keep pets and children indoors while spraying.
Dimethoate-malathion and lindane	Fisons Greenfly & Blackfly Killer	Same characteristics as above. See also *malathion* and *HCH*.
Dimethoate and permethrin	pbi Bio Longlast	Same characteristics as dimethoate. See also *permethrin*.

continued overleaf

the drain. A container used for weedkiller should never be used for anything else and should be clearly marked. The slightest trace of weedkiler can severely damage other plants if the sprayer is used on a later occasion to apply, say, an insecticide.

No wasteland if you're careful

I hear fearful accounts of weedkillers lingering in the soil and making it impossible to grow anything for ages afterwards. Is this true?

On the whole, no. With very few exceptions, weedkillers break down in the soil quite quickly once they have been absorbed through the roots of the weeds and accomplished their task. Some weedkillers such as paraquat, which act only on foliage, actually begin to break down as soon as they touch the soil. Weedkillers have little effect on soil structure. And the vital nutrients in the soil, such as nitrogen, are not affected by the long-term use of most weedkillers. Neither is plant growth hindered; in fact in the early years, the lack of weed competition produces more growth than on plants left in a weedy border.

The few total weedkillers are prominently labelled with such warnings as: 'Do not cultivate or replant for six months after treatment.' These indicate the life of the weedkiller in the soil. Such weedkillers should be used only on paths, or in areas that you do not intend to replant for some time. Be particularly cautious when using such old-fashioned weedkillers as sodium chlorate. They may persist in the soil for years. Also, they tend to 'creep' through the soil to kill plants some distance away from where they were originally applied.

Buried in the brand

Why in the garden centres do I never see the weedkillers, fertilisers and so on that the experts praise on radio and TV?

They're there all right, but they're much less prominent than the brand names. The reasons why the experts don't use these brand names is twofold. First, the radio and TV authorities are not usually very keen on casual advertising; and secondly, while brand names may come and go, those of their chemical ingredients will go on, if not for ever, at least for a very long time. Also, it's not unusual to find that two or three branded products are made up of more or less the same compounds.

So if you wish to find the chemical extolled by the experts, look at the small print on the container, ask the assistant, or look at the chart below and on pages 54-58. It shows the main brand names of most of the chemicals used in the garden.

Worried about poison

My teenage children are convinced that everyone is being poisoned by agricultural sprays, and that I too am guilty because I spray my vegetables. Surely this is nonsense?

Nobody can be absolutely sure that the chemicals we eat in any of our food, whether vegetable or other, are completely harmless.

continued from page 55

Chemical	Trade names	Description
Fenarimol	Fisons Mildew & Blackspot Killer	Moderately persistent systemic fungicide. Controls powdery mildew, rose black spot and apple scab.
Fenitrothion	Murphy Fentro (Fisons); pbi Fenitrothion	Contact insecticide that controls a wide range of insect pests, including caterpillars, aphids, capsids, sawfly larvae, thrips, gall midges, fruit fly and raspberry beetles. Moderately persistent; toxic to bees and fish. Keep pets and children indoors while spraying.
Ferrous sulphate	Fisons Lawn Sand; Fisons Mosskil Extra; ICI Mosskiller for Lawns; Boots Lawn Mosskiller & Fertiliser; pbi Velvas	Sulphate of iron to which sand is added as a carrier. Primarily used for moss control, but has some effect on fungal diseases in lawns.
HCH	Boots Ant Destroyer; ICI Fumite Loft Guard Smoke; May & Baker Greenhouse Smoke Crawling Pest Killer; Murphy Ant Killer Powder (Fisons); Murphy Gamma-BHC (Fisons)	Insecticide sometimes called lindane, and previously known as BHC. Available as spray, dust or fumigant to control ants, aphids, cabbage root flies, capsids, caterpillars, earwigs, flea beetles, fungus gnats, leafhoppers, leaf miners, leatherjackets, springtails, thrips, weevils, whiteflies, wireworm and woodlice. Moderately persistent; may taint some fruits and vegetables; toxic to bees, fish and small animals.
Latex-based pruning paint	May & Baker Seal & Heal Pruning Paint	Forms a protective seal against diseases, pests and frost on cut surfaces of wood. Use after pruning. See also *thiophanate-methyl.*
Malathion	pbi Malathion Greenfly Killer; Murphy Greenhouse Aerosol (Fisons); Murphy Liquid Malathion (Fisons); Murphy Malathion Dust (Fisons)	Compound that controls a wide range of insect pests including aphids, leafhoppers, mealy bugs, scale insects, thrips, caterpillars, fungus gnats and sawfly larvae; also fairly effective when used on red spider mite. Has an adverse effect on certain plants, so check manufacturer's label before using. Toxic to bees and fish.
Mancozeb	pbi Dithane 945	Fungicide for control of rust and black spot on roses. Also combats apple and pear scab, potato blight, tulip fire, celery leaf spot, and tomato leaf mould. Use as a regular spray to suppress red spider mite. May irritate eyes, skin or nose.
Mercurous chloride (calomel)	pbi Calomel Dust; ICI Club Root Control	Insecticide and fungicide available for use only against club root of brassicas and for the control of white rot on onion seeds and plants; a powerful purgative. See *The uses of calomel*, page 59.
Metaldehyde	Boots Slug Destroyer Pellets; Fisons Slug & Snail Killer; ICI Mini Blue Slug Pellets; Murphy Slugit Liquid (Fisons); Murphy Slugits (Fisons); Murphy Tumbleslug (Fisons); Slug Mini Pellets pbi; Slugtape (Impregnated Tapes Ltd)	Used only as a slug and snail killer, in liquid or specially formulated bait forms. Harmful to pets, to other warm-blooded animals, and to fish.
Methiocarb	pbi Slug Gard	Specially formulated bait for the control of slugs and snails; toxic to fish, pets and other warm-blooded animals.

There is, for example, some unease about the additives in processed foods and many manufacturers are beginning to omit them. So far as garden chemicals are concerned, a battery of government regulations exists to ensure that they are as safe as possible. When a new product is proposed, the manufacturer must supply a vast amount of technical information for the Ministry of Agriculture's consideration. The information must be based on the results of a series of tests designed to measure the effects of the chemical, or of the product's several chemical components, on the soil, on the fungi and bacteria of the soil, and on the cells of plants. The conclusions will determine whether the product can be sold at all, and if so, how it will be used and what interval must elapse between spraying and harvesting.

All this information must by law appear on the label of the product. So, provided you read the label carefully and apply the chemical exactly as instructed, neither you nor your children should have anything to worry about. Always use the insecticides, fungicides and so on that are specifically recommended for particular fruits and vegetables, and, where you have a choice of effective treatments, pick the one for which only a short gap is needed between spraying and harvesting.

Insect allies

Is it science fiction, or is it really true that insects are being bred to attack garden pests?

Not only are there specially bred predators available, but there are also sprays of naturally occurring diseases that are known to attack particular pests. Needless to say, such diseases are only diseases of insects. The use of biological control agents is not new: in 13th-century China, farmers put ants into orange trees to prey upon the insects that were stripping the leaves.

All the pests that attack our plants are themselves attacked by a wide variety of predators. Ladybirds and lacewings eat greenfly; frogs and hedgehogs eat slugs; thrushes and blackbirds eat slugs and snails; blue and great tits eat many pests on plants. Entomologists were commenting on the usefulness of the natural predators of cabbage caterpillars and of other pests, such as hop aphids, more than a century ago.

More recently, a number of nurseries, in Britain and elsewhere, have begun breeding insect predators for use in the controlled environment of greenhouses, and have made them available to gardeners as an alternative to chemical insecticides.

Biological controls are now widely used in the commercial production of tomatoes and cucumbers under glass. There the red spider mite is controlled by introducing another tiny mite, *Phytoseiulus persimilus*; whitefly is preyed upon by *Encarsia formosa*, a minute wasp; aphids or greenflies are kept down by spraying with a disease called *Verticillium lecani*. It is also possible to control caterpillars by spraying with the bacterium *Bacillus thuringiensis berliner*, or by introducing the ichneumon fly.

All these predators are restricted in their activity to just a small group of pests and in some cases to one pest alone. When the predators have eliminated their particular

Chemical	Trade names	Description
Permethrin	pbi Bio Flydown and Sprayday; Boots Caterpillar & Whitefly Killer; ICI Fumite Whitefly Greenhouse Insecticide Smoke; Synchemicals House Plant Leaf Shine plus Pest Killer; May & Baker Greenhouse Smoke Whitefly Killer; Murphy Permethrin Whitefly Smoke (Fisons); ICI Picket	Synthetic compound with effects similar to those of pyrethrum, but active for up to three weeks. Controls whiteflies, aphids, leafhoppers, thrips, some beetles and caterpillars.
Permethrin-carbendazim-copper oxychloride-sulphur	pbi Bio Multiveg	For the properties of each ingredient, see *permethrin, carbendazim, copper compound* and *sulphur*.
Permethrin and heptenophos	Murphy Tumblebug (Fisons)	See *permethrin*; heptenophos is a systemic insecticide for aphid control. The compound is short-lived. Toxic to bees and fish.
Permethrin-malathion	pbi Crop Saver	See *permethrin* and *malathion*.
Permethrin-tetramethrin	Synchemicals Nippon Ant & Crawling Insect Killer	Compound mostly used against ants. Available in aerosol form.
Permethrin-triforine-dinocap-sulphur	pbi Bio Multirose	Check components under individual names in this list. Dinocap is a fungicide used to fight powdery mildew. The compound may irritate skin, eyes and nose; it is toxic to fish.
Phoxim	Fisons Soil Pests Killer; Fisons Ant Killer	Insecticide with an effective life of four to six weeks; toxic to fish and bees.
Pirimicarb	ICI Rapid Greenfly Killer and Rapid Aerosol	Contact insecticide with some systemic and fumigant action; of short persistence. Specific to aphids; does not affect bees or other insects.
Pirimicarb-bupirimate-triforine	ICI Roseclear	The components and their effects are described elsewhere in this list under the names of the individual chemicals.
Pirimiphos-methyl	ICI Fumite General Purpose Greenhouse Insecticide Smoke, and ICI Antkiller, Sybol and Sybol Dust	Contact fumigant and slightly systemic insecticide. Controls aphids, caterpillars, leaf miners, beetles, whiteflies and red spider mites. The dust is effective against soil pests.
Pirimiphos-methyl and synergised pyrethrins	ICI Sybol Aerosol; Kerispray; Waspend	Similar to above. See also *pyrethrum*.
Propicanizole	Murphy Tumbleblite (Fisons)	Systemic fungicide for the control of black spot, mildew and rust on roses and other plants. Moderately persistent. Irritating to eyes and skin; toxic to fish.
Pyrethrum	pbi Anti-Ant Duster; ICI Bug Gun for Fruit and Vegetables, and Bug Gun for Roses and Flowers	Obtained from flower heads of *Chrysanthemum cinerariaefolium*. Controls aphids, whiteflies, small caterpillars, leafhoppers, thrips and beetles. Fast working, but needs to be used frequently. Non-persistent, and harmless to warm-blooded animals.

continued overleaf

prey, they do not transfer their attentions to other creatures, but die; or in some cases they begin to eat each other. You can buy ichneumon flies to keep down greenhouse pests. Or if mealy bugs are devastating your greenhouse perennials, you can fight back with a batch of *Cryptolaemus montrouzieri*, a species of black and orange tropical ladybirds. Not every garden centre sells these or other combatants in the biological war, but they are available and are increasingly widely used.

Organic chemicals

I'm into organic gardening, but I must admit that my neighbours, with their so-called 'conventional' pesticides, are getting better results with their vegetables. Are there any chemicals I could use without abandoning my principles?

This probably means that you want to use organic chemicals. But what's an organic chemical? Opinions differ. Strictly speaking, an organic chemical contains only compounds based on carbon. But in recent years, this definition has changed to include a wider range of 'natural' chemicals. Let's assume that an organic chemical is one that has been extracted either from plant materials or from the earth itself. Though such products have been refined and processed into convenient packages, they remain much the same, with few inorganic chemicals added. But whether an organic product remains 100 per cent pure during the refining process is impossible to say. To be fair, nature itself is seldom pure in its products; all naturally produced chemicals contain at least minute traces of foreign materials.

Organic growers believe that organic pesticides, almost by definition, are safer to use. This may be true of most products but some, including nicotine, are highly poisonous and are dangerous if handled incorrectly, though the same might also be said of many inorganic products. Despite the somewhat fuzzy borderline between organic and inorganic, there is wide agreement that chemicals based on the following natural products are organic – so you can spray without sacrificing your beliefs.

Pyrethrum An extract from the pyrethrum flower, mostly grown in Kenya; available both in powder and liquid form. Swift in action, and swift to break down. You will be able to harvest your crops only one day after spraying or dusting. Pyrethrum kills a wide range of plant pests, and, because its active life is measured in hours, it is very safe when used properly.

Derris Also known as rotenone, it is derived from the roots of a tropical climbing plant. Its action is more leisurely than pyrethrum's, but you may still harvest one day after spraying or dusting. It's a general-purpose insecticide that is particularly effective against the red spider mite, a serious pest of house plants, fruit, vegetables and greenhouse plants.

Nicotine An extract of the tobacco plant, nicotiana. Probably the first insecticide to be marketed as such in this country, at least as long ago as the 1880s, it is now classified as a poison, and only very diluted forms are available to the amateur. Nicotine is a highly effective contact insecticide, particularly if used in warm weather on either garden or greenhouse pests. Vegetable crops may be harvested two days after treatment.

Sulphur Widely used as a fungicide, and particularly effective against powdery mildew on most plants. It is mined as ore and

continued from page 57

Chemical	Trade names	Description
Pyrethrum and piperonyl butoxide	Synchemicals Py-Powder, and Py Garden Insecticide and Pyrethrum Garden Insect Killer	Similar to pyrethrum, but contains a booster for greater effect.
Pyrethrum and resmethrin	Synchemicals House Plant Pest Killer	See *pyrethrum* and *resmethrin*.
Resmethrin	Boots Houseplant Insecticide	Synthetic compound similar to permethrin, but of much shorter persistence. More effective than pyrethrum, however.
Rotenone	ICI Derris Dust; Synchemicals Derris Dust; pbi Liquid Derris; Murphy Derris Dust (Fisons)	Also known as derris. Obtained from the ground roots of certain species of Derris plants. Effective insecticide against aphids, small caterpillars, thrips, raspberry beetle, flea beetle and red spider mite. Short persistence. Safe for warm-blooded animals, but toxic to bees and fish.
Sulphur	Synchemicals Green and Yellow Sulphur	Fungicide used mainly to control powdery mildew and rust; also used to protect bulbs and tubers in storage. Some plants are 'sulphur-shy', so check manufacturer's instructions. Has some effect on red spider mite.
Tar oil	Murphy Mortegg (Fisons); ICI Clean-Up	Used only as a winter spray on dormant fruit trees, bushes and some woody deciduous ornamental plants to kill the eggs of aphids, suckers and winter moths, and to check scale insects and mealy bugs. Also kills lichens and mosses. May irritate skin, eyes, nose and mouth. Toxic to fish; discolours grass.
Tecnazene (TCNB)	May & Baker Greenhouse Smoke Disease Killer	Fungicide used only as a fumigant smoke in greenhouses to control grey mould on ornamental plants and on some edible crops.
Thiophanate-methyl	May & Baker Fungus Fighter; May & Baker Liquid Club Root Control; Murphy Systemic Club Root Dip (Fisons); Murphy Systemic Fungicide (Fisons); May & Baker Seal & Heal Pruning Paint	Systemic fungicide similar to benomyl, for the control of grey mould, powdery mildew, rose black spot, apple and pear scab, tomato leaf mould, club root and some grass diseases. Gives some control of apple canker. Some dessert apples may suffer adverse effects, so check manufacturer's directions before use.
Thiram/HCH-rotenone	pbi Hexyl	Sulphur-based fungicide used against grey mould, some ornamental rusts, raspberry cane spot, tulip fire, peony wilt, lettuce downy mildew, leaf spot on currants and gooseberries, pear scab and raspberry spur blight. Can be irritating to eyes, skin, nose and mouth; may taint processed fruit. See also *HCH* and *rotenone*.
Triforine-dinocap-sulphur-permethrin	pbi Bio Multirose	Triforine is a systemic fungicide used to control powdery mildew, rose black spot, apple scab and blackcurrant leaf spot. Dinocap is a fungicide used to control powdery mildew on ornamental plants, fruit and vegetables. It is toxic to fish and can irritate skin, eyes and nose. See also *sulphur* and *permethrin*.

refined usually into a powder, but produced occasionally as a liquid. It leaves an unsightly deposit, so choose green or yellow sulphur to suit the plants to be treated. Do not use it on redcurrants, white currants or such apple varieties as 'Lord Derby', 'Cox's Orange Pippin', 'Beauty of Bath' or 'Newton Wonder'. Vegetables and fruits treated with sulphur should be washed before being cooked or eaten.

Quassia A pesticide extracted from a tropical tree. Still occasionally used on its own, it's now more often used in mixtures with other pesticides such as nicotine.

Copper The base of several fungicides used against such diseases as mildew, black spot, blight, peach leaf curl and many others. Copper is also combined with other chemicals to make Bordeaux mixture and liquid copper fungicide. Bear in mind that organic chemicals are not cure-alls, however, any more than other chemicals are. Pests such as cabbage root fly and carrot fly, and diseases like onion neck rot and botrytis will not yield to them, and are difficult to control even with modern inorganic chemicals.

The uses of calomel

I've heard that there is a Common Market ban on the use of calomel in the garden, yet I see that it is still recommended as a cure for club root on brassicas. So is it safe for me to use or not?

Calomel contains mercurous chloride, a substance that a few years ago gave rise to fears of mercury poisoning. Consequently, in 1985, the nations of the European Economic Community agreed that calomel should no longer be used in horticulture – except as a cure for club root on brassicas and for onion white rot. In these two cases, though in none other, calomel is allowed to be used by both Britain's Ministry of Agriculture and the EEC. The reason behind the exemptions is straightforward. On those two diseases, no other treatment is thought to work as well.

The Brand X controversy

Some gardening books recommend adding detergents to sprays as a means of improving the chemicals' staying power. If detergents are so necessary, why haven't the manufacturers of brand-named sprays included them in their mixes?

You must have been looking at the older gardening books. In principle, adding detergents to sprays can improve their effectiveness, but may also make them useless. When a spray is applied to a plant, it arrives on the leaf surface as round droplets, whose shape needs to change into a low, flat oval that will stick to the surface and won't roll off. Most modern manufacturers now add some kind of wetting agent or detergent to make the droplets behave as they should for particular situations. So some droplets break up into lots of tiny ones, while others turn themselves into a film that covers the entire surface in a thin layer.

Pests and diseases, like leaves, come in all shapes and sizes, and manufacturers try to make their products as all-embracing as possible, adding an amount of detergent that suits as many as possible of each chemical's targets and the plants affected by them.

If you add a detergent wetting agent yourself, you upset this carefully tested balance. So, for instance, you might make a weedkiller mixture stick to the grass instead of the weeds, causing severe scorching.

Good and bad mixers

I've had an inspiration. Instead of walking round the garden three or four times, spraying with one thing and then another, why not amalgamate several sprays and do the whole job in one go?

Your inspiration sounds good, but isn't. Never mix chemicals unless the manufacturers' instructions *specifically* say that you can do so. Many products are already mixed in the container – for example there are feed-and-weed products that feed the lawn and kill weeds or moss in one swoop. You can also buy fungicide and insecticide mixtures for garden plants, vegetables and even house plants. Some insecticides, for instance, mingle contact and systemic sprays – one designed for a quick kill and the other to protect from further attack.

The labels on some sprays will say that the contents can be mixed with another product to make a combined spray that will rid you of two different pests at once. If there is no such instruction, do not experiment. You may easily create a spray that instead of killing the pest, takes all the leaves off the plant instead.

Some home-made mixtures could also be chemically incompatible, so that, when made up, one or both ingredients simply falls to the bottom of the sprayer. You would then find yourself spraying industriously but uselessly with more or less pure water – that is, until the chemical sludge at the bottom of the tank worked its way up to block filters and nozzle. Even chemicals that are compatible must be mixed in the proper manner: full instructions will be given on the label or in an accompanying leaflet. Use the mixture immediately and don't keep any for another day, not even the next. The chances are that the two chemicals will tolerate each other only for a short time.

Some gardeners worry about how much time to leave between spraying the same plant first with one chemical and then with another – in effect, if the interval were too short, might not this amount to an unsuitable mixture of chemicals on the plant? The answer is to allow time for the first chemical to dry – a day, say – before applying the next. The danger of mixing is not nearly so great as the danger of your washing off the first chemical with the second, before the first one has had time to do its job.

Hydrangea blues

Blue hydrangeas were what I ordered, but mine remain an obstinate pink. The nursery denies responsibility, saying that the fault is in my soil. Can this be so?

Your nursery sounds churlish, but is probably right. Hydrangeas grow in most soils, but the varieties that turn blue need a soil that contains a proportion of available iron and aluminium salts – in other words, an acid soil (for details on how to check your land, see *Acid soils*, page 6).

To turn blue, hydrangeas need a pH level of 5.0 or below, which is pretty acid. The reading for your soil will very likely be 6.0 or even 7.0, which is average. But do not despair. The instructions in the kit will also tell you how to increase the acidity of the soil around the hydrangeas – a matter of adding peat and some sulphur.

But even when you've increased the plot's acidity, it may still be deficient in iron and aluminium salts. This can be corrected with hydrangea colouring powder, which should be forked and watered into the soil at the rate specified in the manufacturer's instructions. Or mix the compound with water, and apply it around the base of the plant. To keep the flowers blue, you have to give regular doses, once every 7-14 days, beginning early in the spring before growth starts and continuing through the season. If you stop, then the flowers will gradually revert to pink.

The time-honoured method of obtaining blue hydrangeas is to dig old razor blades and rusty nails in among the roots – the idea being that the rusting iron will turn the flowers blue. Like most folklore, there's an element of truth in the notion, but it's slow-working and you'd probably do better with colouring compound.

Of sprays and showers

Last weekend it rained just after I sprayed my roses with a foliar feed. Will I have to do the job all over again?

Afraid so. Foliar feeds, like insecticide and fungicide sprays, vary in the speed with which they're absorbed by plants. But, as a rule of thumb, they need to remain on the leaves for at least 12 hours. If it rains much before then, you'll lose some of the benefit.

Don't be too disheartened, though, about your foliar feed. It won't all be wasted. Even if most of the feed was washed off the leaves by the rain, it will have fallen onto the soil – from where at least some of its nutrients will eventually reach the roots.

CHERRIES

Sweet cherries

I am very fond of sweet cherries and would dearly love to grow my own. Is it practical to plant a cherry tree in a small garden?

A free-growing sweet cherry is too large for a small garden, since a standard or half-standard can grow to as much as 30ft high, with a spread of about the same. Best for the small-garden owner is the rootstock called G.M.9, developed at Grand Manil, Belgium. No cherry grafted onto G.M.9 will grow taller than 6-7ft.

Another possibility is to train a sweet cherry against a wall – though a large expanse of wall is needed, because a fan-trained tree will eventually span 18-20ft.

There's also the problem of pollination. Generally sweet cherries are not self-fertile, so a second tree (of a different variety) is needed for pollination. You can now buy a variety named 'Stella', a dark red cherry with a good flavour, which is capable of producing fruit without cross-pollination – but even 'Stella' fruits more prolifically when pollinated by another variety.

On balance, if you've set your heart on growing sweet cherries, you'd better move to a house with a larger garden.

Growing a fan-trained tree

I want to train a cherry tree against a wall. How should I go about it? Will a fan-trained cherry be easier to manage than a free-standing tree?

Fan-trained cherries take up much less space than free-standing trees. Also, it is easier to drape netting over the branches so the birds can't get at the fruit. And you can cover the tree with plastic sheeting or an old bedsheet at night when there's a danger of spring frosts nipping the young flower buds.

For a fan-trained cherry, use 'Stella' or 'Morello' on the less vigorous Colt rootstock or the new dwarfing stock G.M.9.

Sweet cherries like deep, well-drained, fertile loam, preferably containing some lime, and will not thrive on poor soil. 'Morello' cherries grow quite happily on most ordinary soils, provided they are well drained.

If you buy a one-year-old tree – which nurserymen call a 'maiden' tree – plant it in the winter and cut back the main stem to 2ft after planting. Then early in the summer select two sideshoots 9-12in off the ground as the base of the fan, and rub out all others as soon as the buds appear.

Once the two sideshoots you have chosen as a base are about 18in long, tie them to canes sloped outwards at an angle of 45 degrees to the main stem, and secure the canes to strong horizontal wires fixed to the wall. Late the following winter, cut the sideshoots back to 12-18in. During the next summer, leave only four new shoots on each of the two side branches: the shoot extending from the top bud; two new shoots growing upwards from the side branches; and one pointing downwards. Tie these in as they grow.

The following February, cut back all eight shoots to an upward-pointing bud, leaving the shoots about 2½ft long, in order to produce a framework of 16 branches.

When these branches have been trained to form the main 'ribs' of the fan, new shoots are either retained and tied in – or nipped out, if they are not wanted. As a general rule, retain shoots growing parallel to the wall and nip out any growing towards the wall or away from it. The retained shoots will either be used to fill up the wall space, or kept for fruiting. To encourage fruiting, pinch out the tips of the shoots in the summer once they have produced five or six leaves; and in the autumn, once growth has stopped, shorten them to three buds.

Once a branch is as long as you want it, don't pinch out the tip. Instead, in autumn or late winter, either cut it back to a weak sideshoot or bend the tip over to encourage sideshoots and reduce its vigour.

Fan-training is a painstaking business, but it's well within the capabilities of most gardeners. All you need, besides enthusiasm, is patience and perseverance. To sum up results, occasional fruits may be produced during training, but you'll have nothing much to boast about from fan-trained cherries until three or four years have passed.

'Morello' cherries

Can I grow 'Morello' cherries successfully in my garden?

No problem. The trees are much smaller and daintier than sweet cherries (their full height when grown as bush trees is 18-20ft), so they're suitable for all but the smallest of gardens.

Fan-trained against a wall or strong fence, they reach a height and spread of even less: about 12-15ft. This is, in fact, probably the best way to grow 'Morello' – because, like all stone fruits (peaches, plums, nectarines and their relatives), they flower early in the spring. The wall or fence then gives the vulnerable blossom – from which the fruits form – some protection against frost. You'll find that they grow well even against a north-facing wall, where they are sheltered from the damaging effects of rapid thawing in the morning sun. They can also be used to pollinate sweet cherries.

'Morello' fruits can't be eaten raw – they are best used for cooking and for making jam or cherry brandy.

Keeping the birds away

Every year the birds eat the fruit on our sweet cherry tree before it is ready for picking. As a result, we end up with only a cupful of cherries. Is there any way of protecting the fruit?

Birds are a perennial problem. The chief culprits are starlings, but blackbirds are partial to cherries, too. Sweet cherry trees, unlike 'Morello', are usually so large that it's impossible to net them effectively; nor is it easy to protect the fruit by stretching cotton amongst the branches. The so-called 'scarers' aren't much use either, as the birds soon learn to ignore them.

There are a number of modern chemical deterrents, harmless to birds, which are reasonably effective. Even so, it's impossible to protect large free-standing trees completely. If you're starting from scratch, it's probably better to grow cherries fan-trained against a wall. When they've reached maturity, you can give full protection by draping wall, cherries and all, with nets.

Oozing gum

I have a ten-year-old cherry tree which periodically puts out a quick-hardening gelatine from wounds in the bark. Should I be worried about this?

This is a symptom of a disease called bacterial canker. Cherries are particularly susceptible to this disease – so are plums to a lesser extent – and it can kill a young tree.

When young shoots are attacked, they die back and the result is wilting of the shoots or blossoms. Another form the disease can take is 'shothole' damage to the leaves. The leaves develop brown spots which fall out, leaving holes which make the leaves look as if they have been blasted with a shotgun. The bacteria usually enter the tree via a wound, which oozes gum; and if the canker spreads right round to girdle a stem or branch, the parts above it die. Infection normally takes place in the autumn soon after leaf fall, and one theory is that the leaf scars may be a point of entry, though this is by no means proven.

Once the disease has struck, a tree isn't necessarily doomed. But its chances of survival are limited. Although there is no known cure, some degree of protection can be achieved by spraying your tree with a copper-based fungicide such as Bordeaux mixture during leaf fall, to protect the leaf scars, and again before the blossoms open in spring. It will also help to protect the tree if you prune it before the end of August or in April, rather than in autumn or winter – and if you paint over the larger pruning scars with a sealing compound.

CHILDREN'S GARDENS

Football crazy

My young soccer-mad sons are walking disaster areas in the garden. What can I plant that will survive their rampages?

Quite a lot, surprisingly. Look particularly for dense shrubs that will block a ball and keep out a boy, and for low-growing plants that will stand being trampled on.

Try these for tough, bushy plants: *Elaeagnus pungens, Osmanthus burkwoodii, Weigela florida, Potentilla fruticosa* or *Skimmia japonica*. Try, too, the pampas grasses, members of the genus cortaderia. Cotoneasters are pretty sturdy, as are laurels and hypericums. Hemerocallis, erigeron and kniphofia (the red-hot pokers) will also tolerate quite a bit of knocking about. So will phlox, golden rod and any mound-forming rock-garden plant such as armeria (thrift). Avoid, however, hollies, pyracanthas, berberis and any other plants with thorns or spikes – they could be dangerous. Among the bulbs, daffodils and bluebells could provide a splash of colour tucked in the shelter of the shrubs, but avoid tulips and irises – their stems are so brittle that a flying ball can snap off whole rows of them.

Mat-forming plants such as cerastium are worth considering, and herbs such as thyme will survive the occasional trampling. But perhaps the best idea is to abandon border gardening altogether until your sons get a little older. In the meantime, move your flowers and shrubs into the front garden, if you've got one, out of reach of your children. Then line the fences in the back with climbers and grass right up to their feet to make the play area as large as possible.

High-rise projects

We live in a fifth-floor flat, and there is no room on the windowsill for a window box. But my six-year-old would like to grow something for a school project. Any ideas?

Several projects, can be carried out indoors and take up little room. Here are three:

How a bean knows which way is up Take a jam jar, line it with blotting paper and pour in an inch or so of water. Put a broad bean halfway up the jar, between the glass and the blotting paper, and leave the whole thing in a dark, cool place.

Within days, roots will appear and start to grow down towards the water, while a shoot will reach upwards. Later, the jar can be turned round so the roots point upwards. Within hours, they will change direction, the pull of gravity dragging them down towards the water, while the shoot will turn upwards.

The point is that it does not matter whether a young plant is in light or darkness. Gravity will always pull the roots downwards, while the genetic structuring of the plant ensures that the shoot must always thrust upwards, against gravity – in the direction that, through millions of years of evolution, has meant light.

How light affects plants Take an old shoe box and cut a hole at one end to let in the light. Divide the inside of the box with pieces of card, one projecting halfway into the box on the left-hand side and another farther along on the right. Put a potato in the far end with an 'eye' pointing towards the light. When a shoot appears, it will grow towards the light, bending and twisting round the pieces of card to reach it. The result is a very strange-looking plant.

Another way to demonstrate the importance of light to plants is to grow two lots of seedlings such as mustard and cress in small yoghurt containers. Put one container in a dark cupboard and the other in full light. The first will produce pale, spindly plants, while the plants grown in the light will be thick, green and healthy.

How to make a miniature garden Take an old baking tray, and fill it with soil or sand. Draw a plan on a piece of paper and then, according to your design, start laying the bones of your new garden. On soil, sand or small stones make paths and terraces; a small mirror becomes a pond, and moss and small cut flowers can represent a lawn and borders. The sand can be used to make an exciting desert landscape with pebbles and sand hills strategically placed. Add dried stems or a small cactus to vary the effects.

Cuttings lesson

My small son can't understand how a whole new plant can be grown from a small cutting. He's watched me taking cuttings and I've explained. But the patience of childhood is short. Could you suggest a few dramatic examples?

Forget the big garden plants such as shrubs. By the time cuttings from most of these have taken root, a few months hence, your son will have switched his allegiance to Space Invaders. For results that are swift and satisfying, take cuttings instead from house plants at almost any time of the year except winter.

African violets (saintpaulias) are particularly rewarding. Cut a few leaves off cleanly, with a stalk on each, and insert them stalk end down in a pot containing a half-and-half mixture of peat and coarse sand. Cover the pot, maintain it at room temperature, and in 10-14 days the leaves will have grown roots; they can then be potted on.

Begonia rex has even more wondrous effects. Take a few leaves from the plant, cut a number of slits across their veins, and lay the leaves flat in a tray of compost, weighting them down with a few pebbles. Cover the tray with polythene, keep it at room tempera-

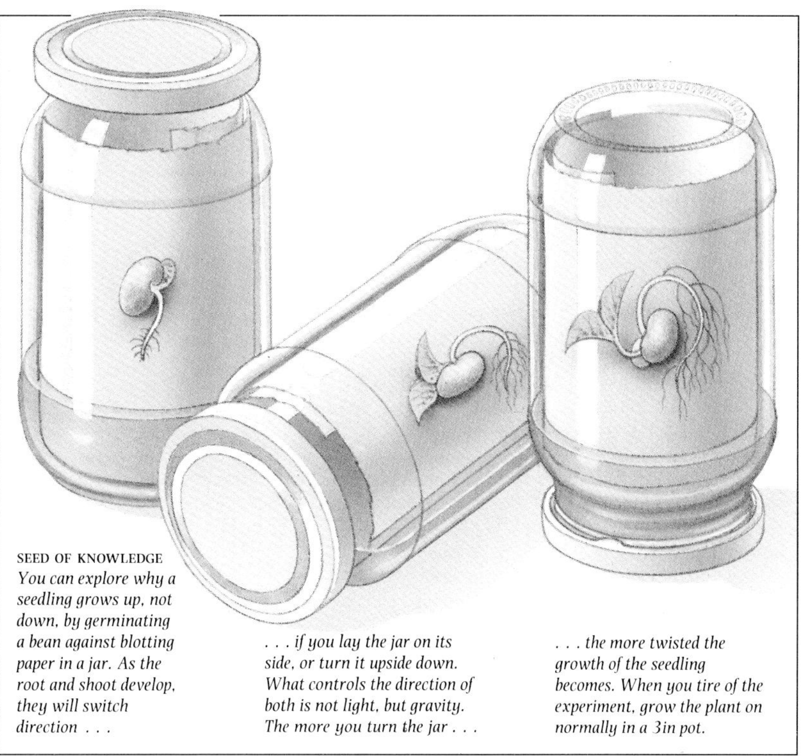

SEED OF KNOWLEDGE *You can explore why a seedling grows up, not down, by germinating a bean against blotting paper in a jar. As the root and shoot develop, they will switch direction . . .*

. . . if you lay the jar on its side, or turn it upside down. What controls the direction of both is not light, but gravity. The more you turn the jar . . .

. . . the more twisted the growth of the seedling becomes. When you tire of the experiment, grow the plant on normally in a 3in pot.

ture, and in a few weeks roots and shoots will have developed at every slit. The leaves can then be cut up to form separate plants.

Geraniums (pelargoniums), too, are most obliging. Cut off a few inches of healthy shoot, making a clean cut just below a leaf joint on the stem. Fill a pot with peat and sand, get your son to make a hole with a pencil or with his finger, then push in the cutting, firm it round and water. Growth can be speeded by making a wigwam with three sticks, covering them with polythene in which a few small holes have been punched to provide air, and putting it over the pot to make a kind of miniature greenhouse.

The fleshy 'jade' tree, *Crassula argentea*, is tough and roots readily. Two small leaves and a bit of stalk will do fine as a cutting. Succulents such as haworthia have rosettes of thick, fleshy leaves with white and green markings. They produce tiny plants at their sides which can easily be separated and potted up.

Gardening for beginners

My children are always very keen to help with the gardening, but they're still too young to manage garden tools. Are there any child-sized tools on the market?

There are, but they can be expensive. A cheaper alternative is to adapt household items – an old kitchen fork, for example, to use as a trowel, and an old spoon for a spade. An empty plastic washing-up liquid bottle with extra holes punched in the end becomes a watering can. You can show them how to fill a plastic basin with soil and turn it into a miniature garden, plant yoghurt cartons with seeds, and make a transparent-lidded plastic egg box into a miniature greenhouse. Make a few holes in the lid for air.

For hardy plants only

My small daughter would love to have some plants in her room, and I've said that she may, provided she looks after them. However, I fear that she is easily diverted, and the plants may suffer a certain amount of neglect in consequence. Can you suggest a few plants that will survive this treatment?

No plant will flourish if seriously neglected; if it is left in the dark, say, or never watered. However, there are some plants which are reasonably tough, fairly childproof, and are attractive and intriguing. Try the spider plant, chlorophytum, which has attractively striped foliage and will hang smaller versions of itself on tendrils from a shelf or windowsill. Cacti also require little attention, and produce startlingly shaped flowers in a wonderful range of exotic colours.

Try one or two of the following: *Mammillaria rhodantha*; *Notocactus tabularis*; *Opuntia azurea*; and *Aloe variegata*.

Encroaching sands

My four-year-old would love a sandpit but his father, a keen gardener, is reluctant to build one, since he suspects that sand would be scattered all over the place. Can you think of a solution to please both?

A sandpit is an ideal play-centre for a small child; it will keep him happily occupied for many hours well away from his father's important planting areas. It must of course be fairly prominently placed in order to keep it and the four-year-old under observation, but there is no need for it to be an eyesore or messy. With a little adaptation, it can even double up as a garden feature.

An ideal place for a sandpit, or box, provided the site is sunny, would be on the terrace outside the kitchen window or door. There an eye can be kept on the activities of the occupant, and the structure is out of the main run of the garden. When it's not in use, put a lid on top to keep the rain out and to protect the sand from visiting cats. A gaily coloured lidded box will make an attractive seat, while a lidded pit could double up as a platform for the barbecue. When your son has outgrown the sandpit, it can be easily turned into a small pond, a fountain or a new flowerbed.

A sandpit for older children might be established behind the vegetable plot, where it can be surrounded by trellis on which you could grow morning glory, runner beans or sweet peas.

It's quite easy to make a sandpit. Dig a shallow hole and line it with any tough plastic sheeting (with a couple of holes pierced in it for drainage); or build it above ground, holding the sand in with planks, bricks or textured concrete. Always fill it with sharp sand for good drainage. Don't use the orange-coloured sand that builders use for making concrete; it stains clothes.

Training the young

My husband and I are both keen gardeners, and would be delighted if our children followed suit. Can you suggest some plants that it would be fun and practical for them to grow, and at the same time arouse their interest in gardening in general?

Get them to plant ornamental gourds, which are easy to grow, multicoloured, and later on can be varnished and made into attractive Christmas presents. Pumpkins, too, are great fun and grow to enormous size. At Halloween, cut off the tops and put them aside for lids, hollow out the pumpkins and carve eyes, nose and a ghastly, jagged-toothed mouth in the side. Place lighted candles inside and replace the lids. Wire coathangers can be pushed through and bent to form handles for these glowing, ghostly lanterns. For more ideas, see the box on the right.

FUN GARDENING FOR CHILDREN

In gardening, indoors or out, children like fast results, novelty, colour or something edible – and, if possible, a combination of all these. Here are some ideas.

- **Chinese bean sprouts (Mung beans)** Put a 1in deep layer of beans at the bottom of a jar. Fill the jar with water, then drain it off. Seal the jar with a square cut from an old pair of tights and secure it with a rubber band. Lay the jar on its side in a bowl and raise the bottom end of the jar with a wedge to help drainage. Place the bowl in the airing cupboard. Rinse the beans twice a day for three to six days, by which time the sprouts will be 1-2in long and ready for harvesting. Use them raw in salads, or cook them as a vegetable. Japanese adzuki beans may be grown in the same way.
- **Nasturtiums** In April, plant the seeds $\frac{1}{2}$in deep and 12in apart – a poor, preferably sandy patch will suit them fine. The seeds are large, and therefore easily handled by children. The leaves and flowers – which appear from July onwards – can both be used in salads, and children love the glowing colours of the flowers.
- **Mustard and cress** Spread a layer of damp kitchen towel over the bottom of a seed tray or old ice-cream container, and scatter cress seeds evenly and thinly over it. Place the tray in the airing cupboard and make sure that the paper is kept damp. Three days later, scatter mustard seed over and around the cress, and return the tray to the cupboard. After about 14 days, when the plants are 2in high, stand the tray in the light, but not in direct sunlight, to enable the shoots to green. Harvest the plants one or two days later with a pair of scissors. Use mustard and cress in sandwiches or salads. For fun, try sowing the seeds in patterns – to spell out the child's name, say, or in the shape of a face.
- **Spring in winter** In late winter, gather bare, but just budding, twigs of forsythia and winter-flowering viburnum such as *Viburnum fragrans* and *V. bodnantense*. Bring them indoors and put them in a vase of water. In a few days they will burst into flower.
- **Giant among plants** Get the children to sow a sunflower seed apiece, and see whose plant grows tallest. In any case, children are charmed and awed by the sheer size of the flowers.
- **Fruit pips** Orange, apple, lemon and grapefruit pips sown in small pots of compost all produce pretty trees; the seeds can be sown without preparation whenever you happen to have them to hand. Avocados are best started by putting three needles into the sides of the stone and using these to balance it, pointed end down, on top of a tumbler of water, resting half in and half out of the water. It takes a long time to germinate, but usually just about the time you give up, a root appears. Take the needles out and plant the stone in potting compost.

CHIVES

Slow growth

My chives are very lethargic. What should I do to make them get a move on?

Give them a fertiliser that's high in nitrogen – the element that promotes leafy growth. Sprinkle about a teaspoon of sulphate of ammonia, or hoof and horn meal, around each plant once in late spring. Water the surrounding soil immediately afterwards.

Early each spring, too, just as the narrow grass-like leaves start growing – this could be as early as February – give each plant a dose of a standard liquid house plant fertiliser. These fertilisers contain not only nitrogen, but phosphates and potash as well, and the mixture will give the chives a quick boost, getting them off to a good start.

If you cut off most of the leaves with scissors to just above soil level at least twice a month during the summer, and remove any flower stems as soon as you see them, this will also encourage faster growth and ensure a continuous supply of fresh young leaves for the kitchen.

Winter flavour

I have a sunny windowsill in my kitchen. What's the chance of growing chives on it through the winter?

Very good – on a sunny windowsill they will produce a succession of tender green leaves which can be snipped off with scissors whenever you need them throughout the winter.

In September, plant a good-sized clump in a 3-5in pot of potting compost.

Keep the compost moist. Feed the chives every three weeks or so with a liquid house plant fertiliser. Harvest regularly, cutting off the leaves close to the base.

Time to split

When is the best time to split chives? I know that many plants are split in spring, but it can't be the case with chives because they're already growing vigorously then.

It doesn't matter. Go ahead and divide your established clumps in March or April, because chives are quite tough plants and will happily put up with a spring disturbance. If the leaves are more than 4in tall at that time, snip them off close to the soil; this will help the plants to settle in more quickly.

Dividing chives in September shouldn't present any problems either, but add peat or sharp grit to the soil if it's very full of clay and poorly drained, otherwise the roots may rot during the winter.

White chives

I thought chives had only pink flowers, until I spotted some with rather pretty white ones. Should I grow some of these for variety's sake?

If you think you'll like garlic-flavoured leaves, yes. Like the ordinary chives whose leaves taste mildly of onions, garlic chives also come up every year, but grow to 18in high – about twice as tall as the more usual kind. The plant is not so prolific as its cousin, and the leaves are broader. Starry white flowers are borne on the tall stems in August, making garlic chives an attractive plant for a sunny spot.

Sow garlic chive seeds in a cool greenhouse – at a temperature of about 12°C (54°F) – or in a pot on a bright windowsill during the spring, and transfer the seedlings to trays or 3in individual pots as soon as they are large enough to handle. Keep them in a cold frame throughout the summer. Alternatively, sow the seeds in a ½in deep drill in June, and thin the young plants to 6in apart a month or so later.

Move the chives to their permanent positions in the following autumn, and thereafter treat them like ordinary chives. Cut the leaves when required between April and September each year.

Chives for a fête

I'm thinking of adding potted chives to my usual contributions to the produce stall at the summer church fête. Do you think I could get a worthwhile number of pots out of my three 4in clumps?

It's certainly possible if you begin in March or April when the new shoots appear. Start from the outside of each clump and divide the plants by hand into single or double-stemmed segments. The centre of the plant may be too hard to split, so return it to the garden intact.

Fill a number of 3in pots with potting compost. Plant three segments in each, spacing them evenly between the rim and the centre. Stand the pots in light shade. To promote strong growth, keep the compost moist and occasionally cut down the leaves with scissors. By late summer, the chives should be large enough to take an honoured place on the stall.

CHRISTMAS TREES

Commemorative spruce

We want to buy a Christmas tree to celebrate the birth of our daughter, and then reuse it every year. What tree should we buy and how should we look after it?

Buy the traditional Christmas tree: the Norway spruce, *Picea abies*. It has a very good shape when young which, with care, it should keep throughout its life. The best time to buy is in late October or November. Many of the trees sold just before Christmas appear to have roots, but if you examine them you will see they have only a few thick ones, often torn and split. The grower did not intend that these should be replanted. Go to a nursery and explain that you want to keep the tree and must have a young specimen – 1½-2ft tall – with a good balance of branches, a well-developed root system and a strong growing point. Ideally, buy a pot-grown specimen.

At the same time buy a strong, heavy-duty pot or small tub (not a concrete tub because it will be too heavy to carry around and you'll be changing sizes in a few years anyway). For a young tree, you will need a container about 10-12in across. Don't be tempted to use a rich potting compost that will make the tree grow quickly: this will spoil its shape and create an unmanageable monster. Instead, buy a loam-based compost (such as John Innes No 3).

Before potting the tree, place a layer of broken clay pieces or a layer of shingle in the bottom of the pot. This is important for drainage, since the roots of the plant must never be allowed to become waterlogged. You may need to trim the roots – if they are too big for the pot – using a pair of secateurs, but avoid cutting into larger roots unless they have been damaged. All plants need air spaces to breathe, so when potting the tree don't ram the soil down; firm it with your hands to within ½in of the top of the pot. Next, pour on about a gallon of water. This will settle the compost and get rid of the larger air pockets.

Stand the container outside in partial shade and out of the wind. If there is no place sheltered from the wind, sink the whole container up to its rim in a shady border.

When it's time to bring the young tree indoors for Christmas, remember that, for the tree, there will be a very big difference in the temperature. If the weather is cold in the three weeks before Christmas, bring the tree into an unheated room (a shed or garage will do as long as there is some light). The week before you bring it indoors, buy one of those sprays which stop the needles drying out and falling off. Spray the whole tree thoroughly from top to bottom, reaching all parts. The reason for this is that, if the needles are lost, the tree may not recover; or it may become permanently misshapen.

Indoors, the tree should stand on a tray so that it can be watered freely without spoiling the decorations around the top of the pot. Even with the spray, it will be losing a lot of moisture in the warm room, so give it about a pint of water each day. If possible avoid standing it near a fire or beside a radiator. When it's time to take the decorations down, don't put the tree straight out into the cold (unless January is mild). Put it back into the shed or garage for a couple of weeks or until the worst of the winter is over. It is the cold east wind and hard frost that do most damage, so again, when you are replanting, a sheltered spot is best, preferably close to a building.

During the summer months the tree will lose some needles but make a lot more. It will also grow about another 3-4in in the first year. All it will need is a general liquid feed in summer. Make sure, too, that the roots never dry out or the tree will drop needles very quickly.

After the tree has been in the same container for about three years, gently ease it out and inspect the roots. If you see a tangled mass of roots, it is time to pot on into the next size up – say a 14in container. Do the repotting in the autumn or early spring. This may be the last time that you pot on your tree because by the time it has outgrown a second container it will be too big to carry around and will probably be top-heavy for the pot. So, pick a spot in the garden where the tree will be a Christmas feature, complete with lights, and plan a layout now (including a power supply) ready for planting the tree into the ground when it outgrows its 14in pot in a year or two.

When the time comes to put the tree in its final position, buy a bag of sedge peat and some bone meal. Prepare the hole carefully: it should be wider and deeper than the rootball. Soak the rootball, ease it out of the container and place it in the centre of the hole. Mix the peat with about three times its own volume of soil, add a handful of bone meal for every bucket of the mixture and fill in all around the rootball, firming it down as you go. Leave a dish-shaped depression around the tree and flood the area slowly, leaving the hosepipe running for 10-15 minutes.

The tree will need regular watering during any dry periods throughout the first and second years in its new position. If it is in an exposed spot, protect it with more Christmas tree spray and use three guy ropes to steady it in the wind. The ropes should be padded where they pass over a branch to avoid any chafing.

The tree may not grow very much for a few years to start with, but in time it will quickly outgrow your daughter and may reach 20-30ft or even more.

Shock treatment

Last year I put my Christmas tree, still in its pot, out in the garden. In the spring it went yellow except at the ends of the branches. Is it finished or can I rescue it for another year?

You have described the typical symptoms of shock suffered by a tree when it is moved after Christmas from a heated room to a frosty garden. It has recovered and is now trying to grow again, but it may not reclothe those bare branches and you may end up with a tree which is skeletal in appearance, with green shoots growing only from the ends of the branches.

But don't despair yet. Take a look at the roots by easing the tree out of its pot. If the roots look cramped, repot into the next size up using a soil-based compost. Sink the pot into soil up to its rim in a shaded spot sheltered from cold winds, and, during warm weather, water it thoroughly each week so the roots don't dry out. When watering, make sure to soak the ground all around the pot as well as the compost in the pot. If you don't, the dry surrounding soil will quickly rob the tree of moisture.

If your tree has not recovered enough to look good within two years, throw it away and start again. For details on how to care for the new tree, see *Commemorative spruce*, page 63.

Fed up with needles

We love having a real Christmas tree, but hate the mess they make dropping their needles all over the carpet. Any ideas?

The simplest is to buy one of the proprietary sprays designed to slow down the rate at which a tree loses moisture, and thus enable it to hang onto its needles for longer. That's only a partial answer, though. Even a tree which has been sprayed by the grower when it was lifted, and sprayed again by you, will still drop a fair pile of needles.

A less orthodox solution is to change trees. Instead of using the traditional Norway spruce as your Christmas tree, try the native Scots pine, *Pinus sylvestris*, or the Caucasian fir, *Abies nordmanniana*. Both species look good, and both hold their needles better than the spruce.

To improve any Christmas tree's neatness, keep it in a cool spot out of the sun until the last minute before Christmas. Spray it against needle-drop before you bring it indoors, and at the same time trim a 2in slice off the cut bottom end of the trunk. Stand the tree in a container of wet sand, and damp the sand once a week throughout Christmas. The tree will be able to soak up some moisture from the sand, and it will be able to do so more effectively through freshly cut wood.

CHRYSANTHEMUMS

Where to plant them

Where's the best place in the garden to grow chrysanthemums?

They like light, sunshine and a well-drained soil. Keep them away from overhanging trees, sheds, fences and the shade of your house. Sunshine encourages strong stems, healthy leaves and brightly coloured blooms.

Find a spot with some protection from strong winds. Wherever you put them, even in the herbaceous border, chrysanthemums will need staking. Choose your position in the autumn, so that the ground can be prepared for spring planting. Dig it deeply in the autumn (see *Digging*, page 121). Chop in some well-rotted organic matter and, on heavy land, add some coarse grit or sharp sand to open up the soil so that air will get in and it will drain well. Light, sandy soil will need leaf mould, manure or coarse peat worked in to enrich it, and hold moisture. Chop up manure or leaf mould as you add it, because thick mats of organic matter can slow drainage.

The right soil

The soil in my garden is slightly acid. Is this all right for chrysanthemums?

Yes. Like most garden plants, chrysanthemums thrive on an acid soil, although they can tolerate some lime. They grow best at a pH of between 5.8 and 6.5. Soil, on the pH scale, is neutral at 7; below that it is acid, above alkaline. For details of how to measure your soil's acidity and, if necessary, adjust it, see *Acid soils*, page 6. Chrysanthemums planted in soils with a very high or a very low pH will have leaf mottling, discoloured patches and poor growth and blooms.

Firm start

Gardening instructions always say firm down chrysanthemums when planting. Why is this?

Firming them into the soil will get the roots quickly into contact with the damp, surrounding earth. Young chrysanthemums need their roots in the shallow upper surface of the ground where a good oxygen supply will help early growth. Firming helps to prevent them being uprooted by spring winds despite the shallow anchorage. Don't use the handle of your trowel to press down the soil, though; this can damage the young roots. Use your hands and fingers, leaving a small depression around the stem. Water in the plants immediately, but then leave them for three or four days before you water again.

Time to feed

I dug in plenty of manure and compost in autumn in the border where I plan to put my early-flowering chrysanthemums. Do I have to feed them as well?

Yes, you must if you want good blooms or sprays for indoor displays, or flowers for exhibiting. Chrysanthemums are strong-growing plants with sturdy stems, lots of leaf and big, showy flower heads. So they have a large appetite for nutrients in the soil.

Digging in organic material in autumn, as you did, gives the plants a good start in the spring.

By early July, though – even if you added fertiliser over winter – the soil and the plants will need a boost. Use for this purpose a good compound fertiliser containing all three of the major plant nutrients – nitrogen, phosphorus and potassium – and traces of iron and magnesium.

Generally, it is wise to have more potassium than nitrogen (too much nitrogen can lead to lush growth at the expense of blooms). Rose or tomato fertilisers, most of which have this balance built in, are ideal.

Sprinkle the fertiliser onto the soil, following the manufacturer's instructions about dosage. Don't be tempted to give your plants a touch more than the recommended dose. The rule for feeding chrysanthemums, as all other plants, is: little and often. Apply another feed in early August, and again later in the same month.

Don't apply granular fertiliser if the ground is dry; it can scorch the root hairs. But you can use liquid fertilisers during dry weather. With these, you can feed the plants as often as once or even twice a week during June, July and August. Stop feeding when the flower buds show their first signs of colour, but keep on watering regularly.

Leggy stools

The shoots on the chrysanthemum stools I keep in my heated greenhouse over the winter often become very leggy, usually around December. What's wrong?

A combination of too much heat and poor light. The roots of garden and greenhouse varieties need only to be kept frost-free during the winter, so aim for a temperature around 4°C (40°F) increasing it to 13-16°C (55-60°F) about three weeks before you intend to propagate.

Spindly cuttings rooted from stools that have been kept too warm may develop a clustered rosette of leaves at their base instead of growing normally.

Inadequate light can also make the shoots drawn and pale. So aim to keep the stools on top of your greenhouse staging, not underneath, and make a yearly point of cleaning the glass or polythene.

Choosing composts

I have a well-heated greenhouse and want to bring on some pot chrysanthemums. Should I choose a peat compost or a soil-based mix?

Start off with a soil-based John Innes compost. It is easier to manage than peat. Use John Innes No 1 for the initial potting, thereafter No 2.

Pot chrysanthemums will need feeding with chrysanthemum or tomato fertiliser in late summer and early autumn. The clay particles in a soil-based compost will to some extent control the release of nutrients, reducing the dangers of over or under-feeding.

Despite the advantages of soil, small pot chrysanthemums, with their short growing period of only 10-12 weeks, will also do well in a peat-based compost. November-flowering, large exhibition plants will be in pots for six to eight months, however. With these plants, stick to a soil-based compost.

Good pot mix

I am ready for the final potting of my chrysanthemums. Should I use a mix of peat and loam or leaf mould and loam?

A mixture of 3 parts by volume of loam, 2 parts of coarse peat, 2 parts of coarse sand and a dressing of a proprietary chrysanthemum fertiliser should be ideal. This will give good aeration and drainage – both of which are vital for good growth during the months that your plants will be in their pots – and will encourage fine blooms in October and November. You can buy ready-made compost; but if you decide to make your own, take care with the mixing. Its quality will decide the quality of your flowers.

For the loam, use your best garden soil and mix with every two buckets of it a spadeful of crumbly garden compost. If possible, sterilise the mixture before use.

When to stake

Stake before you plant, say the experts. But do I really need an unsightly 4ft cane towering for weeks over slow-growing new plants?

No. When you first plant out in garden or pot, use 18in split canes. Tie each plant to a cane with one or two plastic or wire rings.

Place the 18in cane in the pot or soil before planting because, as the experts rightly say, this prevents damage to young roots. You will be potting up the pot-grown ones, so you can change to a larger stake as you move into the bigger containers.

In the garden you will need a 4-5ft stake by midsummer. By carefully removing the small cane, you can ease your new, larger stake into the same hole, so minimising any damage to the roots.

It is also possible to use a plastic net with a 4-5in mesh to support a whole bed of chrysanthemums. It needs to be staked at the corners and along the sides. Drop the net gently over the young plants, and raise it with them as they grow. In an exposed area, two layers of net may be needed. Use great care when you move the net, or the mesh may strip leaves from the stems.

SAFETY NET *As an alternative to staking plants individually, protect the entire bed against wind by letting the plants grow through a plastic net.*

Choosing fertiliser

I haven't a lot of money to spend on my garden. Can you recommend an inexpensive compound fertiliser for border chrysanthemums and later pot-grown blooms?

Two options. First, choose a large economy pack of a good all-purpose chrysanthemum, rose or tomato fertiliser – what you don't use on the chrysanthemums, you can put on the vegetable patch and the flower borders.

Alternatively, make up your own fertiliser by mixing together 2 parts by volume of hoof and horn, 2 parts of superphosphate and 1 part of sulphate of potash.

War on pests

Are any chrysanthemum varieties resistant to the almost endless list of pests and diseases?

No. Indeed, one or two all-year-round spray chrysanthemums suffer even more than most from aphids – possibly because their thin leaf cuticles are easier for these insects to penetrate. The wide range of pests and diseases means that chrysanthemum growers, like all other gardeners, must use good husbandry and vigilance to keep their plants healthy. To complicate the problem further, some insects have become resistant to the standard chemicals used in the past. These include the peach-potato aphid, the leaf miner, the whitefly and the red spider mite. Switch between several insecticides to clear the attacks.

Changing colour

My bright pink chrysanthemum has suddenly produced a pale salmon flower, and I am told this is called a 'sport'. How did it happen, and can I reproduce it?

Faulty cell division during the growth of the plant has thrown out a mutant shoot – what garden experts call a sport – with characteristics different from those of the plant itself. Chrysanthemums seem to do this more than any other garden plant, and it is usually the flower colour which changes.

All the showy chrysanthemums grown by gardeners for display are cross-bred plants, and they inherit their characteristics from more than one ancestor. No matter how many times you take cuttings from a chrysanthemum, or cuttings from those cuttings, it is the genes mixed in the original cross-breeding which determine how the plant grows.

Sometimes, though, the genes go awry. That is what has happened to your plant, and it is no surprise that it is a pink one. Pink chrysanthemums throw out more sports than any other colour. Usually the sports are paler or darker than the rest of the blooms. Sometimes they are white or yellow.

Reproducing the sport is not easy, because there is no way of knowing where along the branch the genetic abnormality began. The change is a small one, altering the balance of carotenoids and anthocyanins, the pigments which determine the flower's colour.

If you want to reproduce your sport, there are several approaches you can try. Try, for instance, taking cuttings from sideshoots on the affected stem; some may show the mutant characteristics.

Alternatively, you could cut out all the other branches of your plant, keeping just the mutant. If you keep it growing, the mutant colour may develop in new shoots.

Another way to get a mutant cutting is to remove all the plant's leaves, lay the plant on its side and cover it thinly with a sandy compost. This will encourage shoots from the leaf axils, and some should have the characteristics of the sport.

All this effort may do nothing more than produce a plant that has reverted to an original parent, so don't be too optimistic. There is just a tiny, tiny chance your sport could become accepted as a new variety.

Protecting blooms

I have been quite successful with my chrysanthemums and fancy exhibiting some at the local show this year. How can I protect the blooms from the weather?

Cover them with greaseproof bags as soon as the first colour shows. You can buy the ready-made bags in garden centres in various sizes to suit different sizes of blooms. Place two bags over each bud, one inside the other, and tie them tightly with plastic-coated twist ties immediately under the bud.

Before bagging, check the plant for pests and spray or dust with an appropriate insecticide if you see any symptoms. Write the date of the bagging on the bag with a waterproof marker pen, so that you know roughly in what order to pick the blooms (remember the bags are quite hard to see through).

The drawbacks with bagging are that you cannot watch the development of the bloom, and that most of the colours other than white or yellow will tend to be duller than those grown in the open air.

An alternative method is to build an open-sided shelter over the bed rather like a carport. You could use corrugated plastic sheets on a wooden framework, or a transparent awning tied on poles.

IN THE BAG *Guard blooms against the rain by putting them in double bags. Pierce holes in the outer bag to drain off moisture.*

Cutting back

After my early border chrysanthemums have finished flowering, should I cut them back at once, or wait until the frosts arrive?

Cut as soon as flowering has ended, trimming back the main stems to 8-12in. This will let air and light around the base of the plant and encourage the new growth which will give you some small blooms for late cut flowers indoors. It will also keep away damp, and that will lessen the dangers from slugs and mildew.

Wait until the sap has stopped rising to cut back farther and lift the stools. Damp is generally a bigger danger than frost, although frost will damage some varieties if you are late bringing them in.

Lift the stools between mid-October and mid-November, but be guided by the weather. Don't leave it too late in a wet autumn. As you lift, remove all remaining leaves and cut back basal growths, leaving plenty of light and air for the new shoots that will give you your spring cuttings.

What is a stool?

I heard radio gardening experts recently discussing chrysanthemum stools. What exactly is a stool?

It is the clump you dig up and keep through the winter and from which you get next year's chrysanthemums. The stool consists of the cut-down stem of the summer's growth and the rootstock.

Storing stools

What is the best way to keep a chrysanthemum stool over winter?

Store it in a dry, airy place away from frost. Lift the stools in late October or early November before the ground gets wet. Cut the stems back to about 4in after the sap has stopped rising. Slide a fork under the roots, prising them gently free of the ground.

Place the stools in boxes in a compost made up of half-and-half peat and sand. Water very lightly – just enough to settle the compost around the stools. Dust each plant with flowers of sulphur on top of the stems to prevent mildew.

Keep the boxes in a cool greenhouse, frost-protected frame, or a dry shed. Air is more important than heat. Stools will stay dormant at 2-4°C (about 36-40°F). Raise the temperature to 7-10°C (45-50°F) in January as the light improves, to encourage new shoots for spring cuttings.

Taking cuttings

When should I take cuttings from my chrysanthemum stools, and which is the best way to do it?

Take them any time from mid-January to April. The new shoots will begin to grow from the stored rootstocks and the base of the stems in January at temperatures above about 7°C (45°F). In two to four weeks they will be 1-4in long and will be ready for taking.

Choose healthy-looking sideshoots, those

which are firm and about as thick as a medium-sized knitting needle. Hold them between the finger and thumb and snap them off at the base. Dip the cut ends into hormone powder and put them into a cuttings compost in 3in deep seed trays. Aim for about 24 cuttings to a tray. Keep the compost moist, and encourage a humid atmosphere by enclosing the trays in clear or white plastic bags.

Bottom heat – via soil-warming cables, say – will encourage root formation, and you can buy propagators which contain such cables. Cuttings will root in about 10-14 days at a temperature of 10-13°C (50-55°F). Check the temperature regularly, and don't let it rise above about 16°C (60°F).

Once the cuttings have rooted – you can tell because new growth will begin to appear – ventilate them for three or four days and turn off any soil-warming heat. They're then ready for potting up individually in 3 or 3½in pots in John Innes No 1 compost and growing on in a cool greenhouse or a cold frame.

Wintering outdoors

I have some perennial chrysanthemums in the garden. Should I lift them each autumn, or can they stay for the winter where they are?

Leave them where they are only if they are hardy – and if they are early-flowering, they are unlikely to be.

All chrysanthemums are perennial; they will flower again, year after year. During the past 100 years or so, increasing demand for new varieties has been met by crossing the hardy chrysanthemums with tender ones. These half-hardy plants can't tolerate the winter unprotected. Instead they must be lifted and stored in the dry, and away from frosts. New cuttings are then taken from them in spring. Hardy chrysanthemums such as the Korean or pompon types, however, will survive outdoors all winter in most parts of Britain.

Despite the flowers' toughness, many gardeners do lift their hardy chrysanthemums each year. And there are some arguments in favour of this. Damp, disease and slugs lurk in the soil and can do much damage. Lifting the stools gives a gardener the chance to dig over the border, work in some compost, divide crowded clumps, and choose the most vigorous shoots for next year's growth.

Potting programme

I have lifted my chrysanthemum stools and want next season to bring on in pots some mid-season and late-flowering blooms. What are the rules for success?

Follow roughly the timetable outlined below. The precise timing of each stage will depend on the time you initially take your cuttings, subsequent temperatures, and the progress of your young plants. The colder the weather and the later you take your cuttings, the later each of the potting operations will be. Use a soil-based compost such as John Innes, at each stage, and you should have few problems.

First potting February in the greenhouse, using 3 or 3½in pots and a John Innes No 1 compost. Give the cuttings at least ten days to get established, then move them into a cold frame. Guard them from frosts, but watch for overheating, too, on sunny March days – open the frame if the temperature is above 16°C (about 60°F).

Potting on Mid-March in 5in pots using John Innes No 2. Delay the change of pots if the roots have not filled the first pot.

Final potting Mid-March to the end of May in 8-10in pots. Your plant will now be about 2ft tall. Use John Innes No 2, or No 3. Pot into moist compost and leave 3½in space at the top. Top-dress in mid-July with a ¾in layer of the compost you potted up with, and add the same amount in early August. These dressings will feed existing roots and encourage root spread.

Breeding a new variety

I would like to breed my own variety of chrysanthemum. Is this difficult?

Yes, but with care and patience and a lot of luck, you might be successful. Chrysanthemums are complex hybrids of the Compositae family. They will not breed unless they have been cross-pollinated. Before you can attempt this, you must be able to distinguish between the two kinds of florets that make up the flower heads.

Disc florets form the tightly packed centre of the flower. These have the male anthers, which contain pollen.

Ray florets, the female florets or petals which surround the disc florets, have only stigmas which can receive pollen, and ovaries which, if pollinated, produce the seed.

Choose the two plants you want to breed from, and make sure that they bloom at the same time. Prepare the bloom which is to carry the seed by pulling out with tweezers all the disc florets, the pollen-bearing male part of the plant. Then cut back the ray florets with fine scissors to expose the female stigmas.

On the pollen-bearing bloom, cut back the ray florets so that the male disc florets grow more vigorously and produce plenty of pollen.

Cross-pollinate on a fine, warm day, preferably in clear sunshine. Take a camel hair brush and use it to take the pollen from the male plant and place it very delicately against the stigmas on the other bloom. Repeat this task over three or four days, making sure that as many as possible of the female ray florets are pollinated. Seeds take five to ten weeks to ripen after pollination. When the seedhead falls apart, the seeds are ready to harvest. Sow the seeds in a sandy seed compost in February. Keep them at 16°C (about 60°F) and prick out the seedlings into pots after about three or four weeks, by which time they will be about 1½in high.

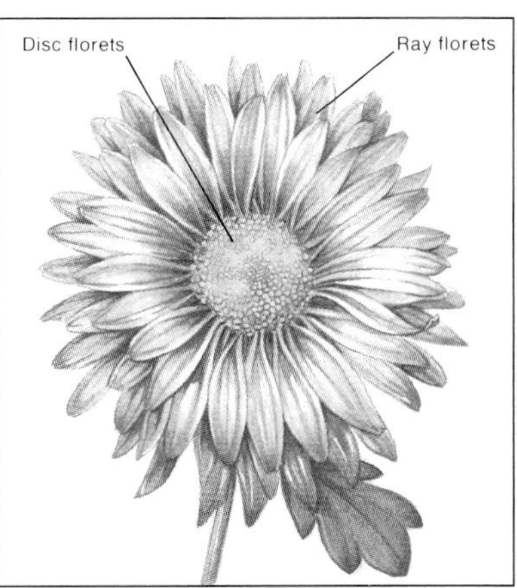

TELLING THEM APART *The male parts of a chrysanthemum are in the central disc florets. Ray florets are always female.*

Your new plants cannot be properly assessed until the second year, after you've grown on cuttings from them. Don't be too optimistic about breeding a winner – there is no telling what you will get for your efforts.

Lost flowers

My chrysanthemums were cut down by the frosts before they had finished flowering. Did I take my cuttings too late, or did I choose the wrong varieties?

Probably both. To be sure of getting the best of outdoor blooms before the first winter frost, choose early-flowering varieties and get your cuttings in at the right time.

Follow these guidelines for when to take cuttings of each chrysanthemum type. The dates given here are for growers in the South of Britain. In the Midlands and the North, aim to take cuttings a week or two later.

November Large specimen plants.

December and **January** Large exhibition varieties.

January and **early February** Incurved exhibition varieties.

Late January and **February** Decoratives, late-flowering singles and pompons.

Mid-February and **March** Early-flowering outdoor varieties.

April and **early May** Decoratives for pots.

Flowering can be advanced or slowed by 'stopping' the shoots (see *All about stopping*, page 68). Early cuttings allowed to flower on the first terminal, for instance, will bloom about two weeks earlier than those where the first terminal is stopped.

Cottage choice

We have bought an old cottage and are creating an old cottage garden around it. Which chrysanthemums should we choose?

The pompons and the Koreans will look lovely among your other cottage plants. Both are sturdy perennials, branch freely, need little staking and have a fine range of colours. The spray varieties give good cuttings for indoor display.

Choose early-flowering varieties and plant them in rich soil in full sun. Careful choice (see *Pick of the chrysanthemums*, pages 70-72) can give you blooms from August to November on 15-30in tall plants.

Growing from seed

I don't keep my greenhouse heated all winter, and I haven't the time or space to store stools. Can I grow chrysanthemums each year from seed?

Yes, you can. The Charm pot chrysanthemums make spectacular bush plants with masses of single blooms, in all colours from white to bronze and crimson, and including all the pastel shades. They will flower from late September to November.

Sow seed in late January or early February, using a sunny windowsill indoors. Pot up as growth progresses, first in 3½in pots, eventually up to 7in or even 9in pots. Stop the main stem once, when it is 6in tall. The plants will then branch naturally, producing strong stems which need little support.

Young plants should be moved to a cold frame in May, then fed weekly and watered often – up to twice a day in hot August spells. Spray to control pests and turn the plants in the frame every two or three days so that you get all-round development of shoots and buds.

Alternatively, grow the hardy annual *Chrysanthemum carinatum* (also sold as *C. tricolor*). Good varieties include 'Court Jester' and 'Rainbow Mixed'. Sow the seed from April onwards in a sunny border to have a colourful display from June.

Bigger flowers

Some chrysanthemums have large blooms, others small ones. Is it due to variety or to disbudding?

You must disbud to get bigger blooms, but disbudding will not make a small variety throw out exhibition-sized flower heads.

Left to grow naturally, a chrysanthemum will have a mass of small flowers which can make up as much as 40 per cent of the plant's weight. Removing all the unwanted flower buds and all the young shoots that start in the leaf axils – where the leaf stalks join the shoot or stem – directs the plant's reserves to the terminal bud at the end of each branch, giving blooms which are larger than usual.

To get rid of the unwanted shoots and buds – the process known as disbudding – grip the shoots and buds between your thumb and forefinger and snap them off as soon as you spot them. Disbud systematically until, by about early August, each plant is carrying a maximum of eight main shoots, each with one terminal bud. In 6-12 weeks, the terminal buds should flower.

You can reverse the effect by pinching out the terminal buds of each branch and allowing the axil shoots to develop. This will give a bushy plant with hosts of smaller blooms, ideal for garden display or for sprays of cut flowers.

When buying chrysanthemums, check with the nursery or catalogue to find which varieties are best for disbudding and which for sprays (see also *Pick of the chrysanthemums*, pages 70-72).

All about stopping

What is 'stopping' a chrysanthemum? When and how should you do it? And why?

A chrysanthemum is stopped by nipping out the top ½in of the growing stem about 10-14 days after planting out. Sideshoots then sprout, each ending in the terminal buds which produce the flowers.

The purpose of stopping is to encourage the plant to branch evenly (in the case of spray varieties) or to limit the number of flowers and so increase their size (in the case of disbudded varieties).

Aim for six to eight blooms to a plant, so pinch out the weakest-looking sideshoots if more than this number grow. Disbud each sideshoot – by pinching out unwanted buds along its length – to get a larger flower from the terminal bud. Stopping chrysanthemums does delay flowering, by two or three weeks, so do it as soon as you can on outdoor, late-flowering varieties.

Blooms for the vase

How do I grow spray chrysanthemums for flower arranging?

Follow the routine below and you can get a tremendous variety of flowers for cutting in October and November. Choose any of the American spray varieties. All need to be grown in a greenhouse. The range is extensive – from 'Green Nightingale', a greenish, spidery chrysanthemum specially bred for arrangers, to 'Rytorch', a late single which shades from gold to orange at the tips.

1 Choose short or medium-sized varieties. Tall ones grow to 6ft and they will become unmanageable in the greenhouse.
2 Take cuttings from stored stools in February.
3 Stop the young plants grown from the cuttings in April. Use sideshoots from these plants as second-generation cuttings.
4 Root these second-generation cuttings in mid to late May, no sooner.
5 Pot up the young cuttings in 3-3½in pots in June, and move them on to 8in pots in mid-July.
6 Stop all plants at the end of June.
7 Keep the plants in a minimum night-time temperature of 13°C (55°F) from mid-August to mid-September, and then at 14-16°C (about 57-60°F) night and day.
8 Give a liquid feed of chrysanthemum fertiliser once a week. Keep the compost moist, but don't let leaves stay damp overnight.
9 Watch for pests such as red spider mites.
10 Store the stools over winter in a half-and-half mixture (by volume) of peat and sand. Start the cycle again in February.

All-year chrysanthemums

Florists have chrysanthemums in bloom all year. Can I do the same?

Yes, but it is expensive, technically difficult and pretty time-consuming. You will need a well-heated greenhouse, artificial lights, and black polythene sheets for use as blinds.

Light and heat are the critical factors. A chrysanthemum needs at least 12 hours of continuous darkness each day in order to develop a flower bud. With this condition and at a temperature of about 16°C (60°F), a chrysanthemum will move from the initial development of the bud to full bloom in 9-14 weeks. So, if you heat the greenhouse to that steady level and control the light by either shutting out light with black polythene in summer or illuminating with artificial light in winter (to make the 'day' length close to, but not as much as, 12 hours), you can get chrysanthemums to bloom at any time of the year.

For lighting, use ordinary household 100 watt light bulbs suspended 4ft 6in above the plants, one bulb for every 3 square yards. Control the lighting with a 24-hour time clock, setting it so that the lights come on for a couple of hours every night between about 11pm and 1am. This will stop the plant's flowering until you decide to trigger the process by giving them a longer period in the dark.

Pots in the garden

After my pot chrysanthemums have flowered in the greenhouse, can I put them outside?

Not if you are serious about growing chrysanthemums, because it will be more by luck than judgment if they survive. Most chrysanthemums bred for the greenhouse or for indoor decoration are just not suited to a garden. Unless they flower in January or February, it will always be the wrong time when they are ready to go out. Moreover, a pot chrysanthemum is small because it has been treated with a dwarfing chemical before you buy it; planted out in the garden, it will soon revert to full size.

If your indoor pot does finish flowering in February and the spring is not too cold, you could be lucky – otherwise, you are filling up garden space with an almost certain failure. A much better bet is to buy some hardy Korean varieties that will go on flowering outdoors for years.

Outdoor checklist

I have grown outdoor chrysanthemums for years and done well with them, but this year growth is poor and there are few blooms. What can have gone wrong?

Disease, soil deterioration, inferior cuttings or, perhaps, just a little lack of care. Go through the following checklist. These are the things you should do each year for maximum success:

1 Destroy all weak, diseased or doubtful stock plants in autumn.

2 Clear weeds, rubbish and plant debris from the border or greenhouse; they will otherwise become hosts to pests and diseases.

3 Replace ageing or declining plants by taking plenty of cuttings from them, then throwing away the parent plants.

4 Consider heat-treating your stools as a last resort to kill off viruses and eelworms (see *Heat treatment*, this page).

5 Dig your border deeply each year and work into it plenty of compost.

6 Grow on only the healthiest cuttings and use only sterilised compost.

7 Give your border plants space – 12-18in depending on the variety. Don't crowd them.

8 Spray regularly against pests and diseases.

9 Check your feed programme (see *Time to feed*, page 65).

Yellow warning

The leaves on several of my chrysanthemums are turning yellow. Obviously something is wrong, but what is it?

It could be one of several things. Too much water is often to blame, a fault that is easily corrected by repotting the plants and adding sand to the compost to improve drainage. Or it might be lack of nitrogen, in which case you should feed your plants with a high-nitrogen fertiliser. You might also run a test on the pH level of your soil. Iron or manganese deficiency are frequent causes of yellowing, and the deficiency can be induced by soil that's excessively alkaline or acid. For details of how to adjust your soil to the pH range that best suits chrysanthemums – 5.8 to 6.5 – see *Acid soils*, page 6.

Another thought that occurs is that your problem may be with greenhouse chrysanthemums, the *edges* of whose leaves are turning yellow. In this case, it may well be that the plants were scorched the last time you fumigated the greenhouse to get rid of insect pests. If you fumigate again, don't use a nicotine smoke; chrysanthemums hate it. Or, if you do, take the chrysanthemums out of the greenhouse while fumigating.

Apart from yellowing, chrysanthemums are prone to all sorts of complaints, a number of which are the subjects of questions and answers in this section.

Here are some of the other problems you may encounter.

- **GREEN, CAPSID OR BISHOP BUGS** These pests cause blind shoots, twisted tips and lopsided buds. Spray the plants, and surrounding ones, with malathion, fenitrothion or pyrethrum.
- **WIREWORM OR WEEVIL LARVAE, AND LEATHERJACKETS** Look out for golden-brown, white or grey grubs in the ground, and for drooping foliage, wilting shoots and root-base damage. Dust or drench the top 2in of soil with HCH, or work diazinon into the soil before planting. Clear garden rubbish away from plants in autumn.
- **FUNGUS GNATS (SCIARRIDS)** The symptoms are poor roots on cuttings and small black flies on compost. Drench the compost with malathion or diazinon.
- **EARWIGS** Half-opened blooms and florets look chewed and bedraggled. Dust around the plants with HCH. Trap the insects in pots upturned on support canes. Stuff the pots with nesting material – crumpled newspaper, straw or dried grass.
- **LEAF SPOT** Round black spots appear under leaves. Keep plants dry and ventilated, even in cool weather. Spray with benomyl or fumigate with tecnazene smoke.
- **MILDEW** Shows as white powder on leaves. Treat in the same way as leaf spot.
- **PETAL BLIGHT** Recognisable by brown-pink spots on outer petals, which turn to sunken, wet patches of decay. Treat in the same way as leaf spot.
- **GREY MOULD** The name is the description: a grey, spreading mould. It's also known as botrytis. On older plants, it may be a secondary infection from other fungal blemishes; treat it in the same way as leaf spot. If it appears on young plants, use soil-warming cables to speed rooting, and keep the plants ventilated. Use a more free-draining compost in future.

Heat treatment

Chrysanthemum stools, I have heard, can be heat-treated. What is this? Can I do it?

Yes, you can. It is a quick way to kill off eelworms and some diseases.

Lift the stools in November and wash off all soil from the roots. Warm some water to 46°C (115°F). Plunge the stools into the water for five minutes. Take them out and plunge them into cold water. Drain off the stools, then store them in their usual winter bed – a box containing a half-and-half mixture of peat and sand. Don't use for this purpose a mixture you've used before; make a fresh batch. It is vital that you get the temperature of the water right. Much cooler and you won't kill the eelworms; much hotter and you'll kill the stool.

White rust

There have been warnings in the gardening magazines about white rust reaching Britain from the Continent. How do I recognise it and can I stop it hitting my chrysanthemums?

Look out for yellow-green spots about $\frac{1}{8}$in across on the upper surface of the leaves. These turn to pink-buff pustules, containing spores, on the undersides of the leaves. Once you have detected it, there is really nothing much you can do about it. There are proprietary brands of fungicide that can be sprayed on chrysanthemums to protect them from white rust – but if the rust is there in the plant, they will not stop it from developing.

The disease's Latin name is *Puccinia horiana*. Widespread in Europe, but not established in Britain, it would devastate the cultivated hybrids if allowed to go unchecked. It is quite different from the ordinary rust disease, *P. chrysanthemi*, which is endemic in Britain.

White rust occurs only in the florists' chrysanthemum species, *Chrysanthemum morifolium*. It does not affect the wild or cultivated annual chrysanthemums, nor *C. maximum*, the Shasta daisy.

Any infected plant must be destroyed. But before you do this, you are obliged by law to report the disease to the nearest office of the Ministry of Agriculture, Fisheries and Food. The nearest office will be listed in your phone book under 'Agriculture'.

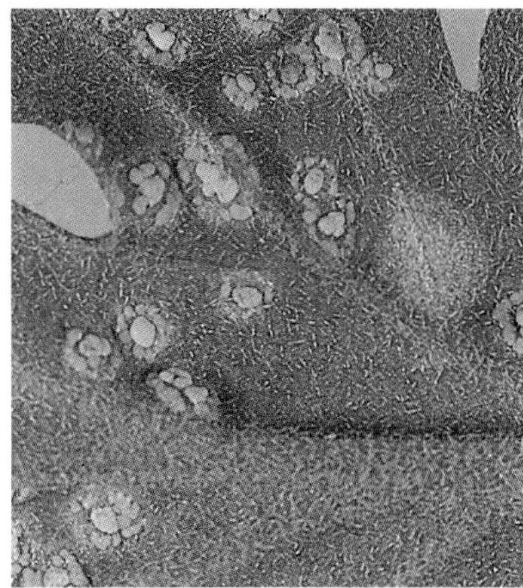

DEADLY DISEASE *Characteristic pustules of white rust dot a leaf. All infected plants must be reported and destroyed.*

PICK OF THE CHRYSANTHEMUMS

This guide will help you to choose from among the hundreds of chrysanthemum varieties those which will suit your taste in flowers. The chart on these three pages groups the varieties into greenhouse and border types. It also separates the labour-intensive chrysanthemum varieties, which need to be disbudded to give one large bloom on each stem, from the easier-to-grow varieties which can be left to throw out multi-flowered sprays.

S = single D = double
L = large exhibition blooms

Name	Type		Flower shape							Flower colour and season
	Spray	Disbudded	Incurved	Reflexed	Intermediate	Anemone	Pompon	Korean	Spider	
GREENHOUSE VARIETIES										
Allouise		•	•							Pink (Oct)
Christmas Greeting	D									Red (Nov)
Dark Westland	•								•	Red-bronze (Nov)
Elegance	D									White (Nov)
Fandango	S									Cerise (Nov)
Futura	S									Yellow (Nov)
Golden Elegance	D									Yellow (Nov)
Green Nightingale	•								•	Greeny-yellow (Nov)
Hifi	D									Pink (Nov)
James Bond		•			•					Red (Oct)
Karen Rowe		•		•						Rose-pink (Oct)
Kingpin	•						•			Yellow and gold (Nov)
Legend	•						•			Pink (Nov)
May Shoesmith		•	•							White (Nov–Dec)
Peter Rowe		•	•							Yellow (Oct)
Peter White		•	•							White (Oct)
Pink Champagne		•			•					Rich pink (Nov–Dec)
Princess Anne		•								Various (Nov–Dec)
Record	•								•	Pink (Nov)
Red Galaxy	S									Red (Nov)
Remember	•					•				Pink (Nov)
Rivalry		•								Deep golden-yellow (Nov–Dec)
Rysheen	S									White (Nov)
Rytorch	S									Gold, shading to orange (Nov)
Salmon Pinklea		•			•					Salmon (Oct)
Sampford		•		•						Orange (Oct)
Shane	•					•				Yellow (Nov)
Snow Westland	•								•	White (Nov)

Incurved

Reflexed

Intermediate

Pompon

S = single D = double
L = large exhibition blooms

Name	Type: Spray	Type: Disbudded	Flower shape: Incurved	Reflexed	Intermediate	Anemone	Pompon	Korean	Spider	Flower colour and season
Spinnaker	•					•				White (Nov)
Steve Ovett		•	semi							Light pink (Nov–Dec)
Sulphur Westland	•								•	Yellow (Nov)
Tuneful	S									Bronze (Nov)
White Sands	•					•				White (Nov)
Yellow American Beauty		•	•							Yellow (Nov–Dec)
Yellow Flying Saucer	L					•				Yellow (Nov)
Yellow Galaxy	S									Yellow (Nov)
BORDER VARIETIES										
Abundance		L		•						Yellow (Aug–Sept)
Agnes Anne	D							•		Plum-red (Sept–Oct)
Allouise		•	•							Pink (Aug–Sept)
Anastasia	•						•			Rose-pink (Aug–Sept)
Anne Marie	S									White (Aug–Sept)
Aunt Millicent	S							•		Silvery-pink and yellow (Sept–Oct)
Autumn Days		•			•					Red, gold reverse (Aug–Sept)
Beautiful Lady	•					•				Pink (Aug–Sept)
Bessie Rowe		•	•							White (Aug–Sept)
Bob	•						•			Red (Aug–Sept)
Breitnor		L			•					Rose-pink (Aug–Sept)
Bronze Margaret	D									Bronze (Aug–Sept)
Caliph	D							•		Red (Sept–Oct)
Cameo	•						•			White (Aug–Sept)
Carnbrae		•		•						Red, gold reverse (Aug–Sept)
Claret Flow		•			•					Deep pink (Aug–Sept)
Claudia	S									Orange (Aug–Sept)
Cream Bouquet	•						•			Cream (Aug–Sept)
Cricket		•			•					White (Aug–Sept)
Crimson Yvonne Arnaud		L	•							Crimson (Aug–Sept)
Denise	•						•			Yellow (Aug–Sept)
Ermine		L	•							White (Aug–Sept)

Korean

Anemone

Spider

Double Spray

continued overleaf

S = single D = double
L = large exhibition blooms

Name	Type: Spray	Type: Disbudded	Flower shape: Incurved	Reflexed	Intermediate	Anemone	Pompon	Korean	Spider	Flower colour and season
BORDER VARIETIES *continued*										
Escort		L			•					Red (Aug–Sept)
Evelyn Bush		L	•							White (Aug–Sept)
Fairie	•						•			Pink (Aug–Sept)
Fairy Rose	S							•		Rose and yellow (Sept–Oct)
Flying Saucer	•					•				White (Aug–Sept)
Golden Margaret	D									Yellow-gold (Aug–Sept)
Golden Orfe	S									Yellow (Aug–Sept)
Golden Treasure	D							•		Gold and bronze (Sept–Oct)
Grace Riley		L		•						Bronze (Aug–Sept)
Hamburg		•	•							Yellow (Aug–Sept)
Hazy Days		•	•							Bronze (Aug–Sept)
Imp	•						•			Crimson (Aug–Sept)
Karen Rowe		•		•						Pink (Aug–Sept)
Keystone		L			•					Purple (Aug–Sept)
Lucinda	•						•			Yellow (Aug–Sept)
Lyndale		L			•					Yellow (Aug–Sept)
Margaret	D									Pink (Aug–Sept)
Martin Riley		•	•							Yellow (Aug–Sept)
Olivero	•					•				Purple (Aug–Sept)
Pennine Anne	•					•				White and yellow (Aug–Sept)
Pennine Gambol	•					•				Pink and yellow (Aug–Sept)
Pennine Light	S									Yellow (Aug–Sept)
Pennine Mist	D									Pink (Aug–Sept)
Pennine Punch	•					•				Bronze and yellow (Aug–Sept)
Pennine Signal	S									Red (Aug–Sept)
Pennine Tango	S									Bronze (Aug–Sept)
Red Gambit		L		•						Red (Aug–Sept)
Red Mist		•			•					Purple, silver reverse (Aug–Sept)
Red Rose Stevens		•			•					Red (Aug–Sept)
Red Wendy	D									Red (Aug–Sept)
Salmon Margaret	D									Salmon (Aug–Sept)
Sunny Day	D							•		Yellow (Sept–Oct)
Susan Rowe		•		•						Pink (Aug–Sept)
Tommy Trout	•						•			Bronze (Aug–Sept)
Tracy Waller		L		•						Pink (Aug–Sept)
Trugold		•			•					Gold (Aug–Sept)
Vivien	•					•				Red (Aug–Sept)
Wendy	D									Bronze (Aug–Sept)
White Karen Rowe		•		•						White (Aug–Sept)
Yellowmoor		•	•							Yellow (Aug–Sept)
Yvonne Arnaud		L	•							Cerise-pink (Aug–Sept)

CLAY

Getting a start on a clay soil

I have just moved into a house where the garden is not only neglected, but on clay too. Where do I start?

Before tackling the soil problem, clear the garden completely, except for the trees and shrubs that you want to keep.

There are three keys to improving clay soil: the weather, organic matter and time. Time is the key, because nothing has ever been achieved quickly with clay. You could get some sort of immediate result by raking in peat, pulverised bark or an artificial soil conditioner, but the effect is likely to be short-lived. To make a lasting improvement you need time which, depending on the severity of the problem, could mean anything from about three to ten years.

The weather's contribution towards a reasonable soil lies in its shattering effect on the clay's structure. The two principal agents are alternate freezing and thawing. When the ground freezes, the water in it expands and breaks up the clay. In the subsequent thaw, cracks and fissures remain to collect water for the next freeze. And so on. This is a continual process in winter, and the effect reaches down as far as the limit of the frost. So dig deep in autumn, most usefully with a fork that has broad, flat tines. Leave the ground in heavy clods to give larger surfaces for the frosts to work upon. In spring, rake what remains of the clods into an even tilth for sowing and planting.

The third essential ingredient when putting together a workable soil is organic matter. Use plenty of it, and the bulkier the better – farmyard or stable manure, or garden compost. This begins the long-term build-up of the humus on which plants feed. Fork the manure or compost into the ground in autumn, to mingle and break down with the top 6in of soil, ready for planting or sowing in the spring.

Crops that thrive on clay

Is there anything I could grow that would speed the break-up of a clay soil? And are there any vegetables or fruit that actually don't mind clay?

The traditional crop to break up a clay soil has always been potatoes. They don't need a fine tilth, and the action of earthing up the rows two or three times during the early summer helps to break up the soil, as well as keeping the weeds down.

Well-cultivated heavy soils are excellent for growing runner, french and broad beans, peas, cabbages, brussels sprouts and kale (though not cauliflowers). Root crops such as carrots and parsnips do not like clay; they tend to fork or branch underground, making them useless for the kitchen. Most soft fruits do well on clay and, provided the ground does not get waterlogged, so do many fruit trees including apples, pears and plums.

Timing it right

I have a clay problem that's been going on for some years now. I dig the ground immediately after harvesting the vegetables to get it ready for another crop, but within a few weeks it's as sticky or brick-like as ever. What can I do?

Always try to do your digging in the autumn, when the ground will lie vacant for several months to come. This will give the frost time to work on it. By digging deep immediately after harvesting a crop, you have brought to the surface raw and unweathered clay which will be compacted by the rain. If you have to prepare land in spring or summer for another crop, keep the digging as shallow as possible so that the surface tilth is retained.

Summer problems

When my clay soil dries out in summer, it goes so hard that I feel I need a road drill to break it up. Is there any less drastic means?

Lots of compost or manure is the answer. Any soil which dries out and 'caps' to this extent is clearly short on organic matter. If you are already digging it in regularly, keep at it. If not, then start the next time you dig. Depending on the heaviness of the clay, it could take several years to overcome this fault – but you will win in the end.

To speed the process, it would also pay you to work peat or pulverised bark into the surface before sowing or planting. In addition, spread a 1-2in thick layer of manure or compost in spring around the bases of your roses, trees and shrubs.

Packaged help

Will proprietary soil conditioners do anything towards making the heavy clay in my garden more workable?

Some will, some won't, though they all do a certain amount of good in that they improve the surface tilth of the soil. Those based on composted seaweed are highly successful because they contain naturally occurring gluey substances called colloids which gather together the individual clay particles into crumbs or blocks so that the ground drains better. Surprisingly, colloids also help sandy soils to retain more water and nutrients. Calcified seaweed conditioners act in much the same way as ground chalk or garden lime which open up clay soils and improve their drainage. These two types of conditioner also contain trace elements beneficial to plants.

There is another group that is purely chemical. These products are more expensive, and are usually based on compounds called polymers. They work well for a short time so that sowing or planting can be carried out in the improved tilth. But they contribute nothing else to the soil.

None of the concentrated conditioners has the same permanent value as bulky organic matter, but they can be used to get you off to a good start.

Best for roses

Everyone says that roses thrive on clay. If this is true, why?

The conditions associated with clay soils suit roses. Clay is a good provider of plant foods, especially potash which encourages flowering. It is also moisture-retentive so that roses grow well without check, even during very dry summers. The heaviness of the soil, too, makes a solid anchorage for the roots and minimises wind-rock.

Using lime wisely

I know that lime is important on a clay soil, but when should I apply it and how often?

Most clay soils, but not all, are acidic. Your first step is to buy a simple test kit from a garden shop or centre. Follow the instructions to ascertain the pH level of your soil. It is likely to show a reading between 4.5 and 6.5 (see *All about pH*, page 6).

The application of lime on an acidic soil will neutralise the acidity and so encourage worms and beneficial bacteria. It also improves the soil by assisting the clay particles to collect into crumbs, which makes for quicker drainage and better rooting.

Lime contains calcium which is essential for plant growth and acts as a catalyst that releases other nutrients bound up in the acid clay. Another great advantage is that it seems to discourage pests such as wireworms, slugs and leatherjackets, and it certainly checks club root, a disease often found in acid soils. How much lime to add to your soil will depend on the results of your soil test. The more acid your soil, the more lime it'll need to bring it up to the level that most plants prefer. For details of exactly how much to add, see the chart on page 8.

Generally, test again a year after giving a first lime treatment, before applying the next lot. As your soil improves with regular manuring and liming, it's very likely that you will need to lime only once in every two or three years. The best time to add the lime is in early winter, after digging over the ground.

Caution: do not mix lime with other soil dressings, most especially not sulphate of ammonia or general chemical fertilisers. Do not use lime until a month after chemical fertilisers have been applied, and allow three months to elapse after manuring.

Stable tips

There's a livery stable up the road, and I can get horse manure cheaply, or even for nothing. Would this be useful as a bulky conditioner on a clay soil?

This is probably the best type of manure for your type of soil, because it normally contains a good deal of straw, excellent for bulk.

Since it is readily available, stack each delivery into a separate pile and cover each one with polythene until it rots down. When it is well rotted, fork it into the top 9in of soil, preferably in autumn, or use it as a spring mulch for trees and bushes.

Salad days

I should like to grow some early salad vegetables, but my garden is mostly clay. Would this make a difference?

The short answer is: don't try unless the soil has been first well warmed under cloches. In any part of the country, clay soil is so cold in early spring that crops such as lettuces, radishes and spring onions will be bound to fail in the open. Instead, concentrate on bringing on seedlings in a greenhouse. Transplant them out in April, and they will be ready for picking in June.

If your garden has been well cultivated over many years, put cloches out in early March to warm the soil for at least a fortnight before planting or sowing.

Seaweed bonus

The beach near my home is covered in seaweed after every storm. I know seaweed has been used as a fertiliser for centuries, but would it do any good to my clay soil?

You are very lucky to have such a valuable source of manure at hand, especially since it will cost no more than the transport from beach to garden.

Collect it in winter or spring, when storms dump the stuff on the beach. Mix it with alternate layers of garden compost in the compost heap, and in the following autumn, fork it into the topsoil at the rate of 2 buckets to the square yard.

CLEMATIS

Wilting away

Clematis start off well in my garden but then gradually wilt and fade away. Is there something poisonous in my soil – or is it just me?

No, it is not you, nor is it likely to be poisonous soil. The problem is called clematis wilt, and it differs from almost all other wilt diseases of plants in that there is no obvious fungal or bacterial cause. The symptoms are always the same: the plants grow well for two or three years and then simply fold up, with blackening of the shoot tips and dark scars on leaves and stem.

The cause is not fully understood and treatment is difficult to prescribe, but the following routine may help.

Because a leaf-infecting fungus may be involved, spray with a systemic fungicide such as benomyl, thiophanate-methyl or carbendazim as soon as the wilt appears. Use one of the same fungicides to drench the soil around the plants. Then cut the plants back hard, either to a live bud (if there is one) or right back to ground level. Often plants affected with wilt will regenerate from the base in the following year.

If the treatment fails and the plants do not recover, dig them up. If you plan to try another in the same spot, dig out a hole – at least a 3ft cube – and replace the soil with a fresh supply from somewhere else in the garden.

Clematis wilt does not affect any other type of plant, so it will be quite safe to use the soil on beds and borders. Unfortunately, no varieties of clematis are known to be genuinely resistant to the disease although, in some gardens, some fare better than others. The moral, therefore, if you have experienced clematis wilt is to try several different varieties and species when you replant.

PICK OF THE CLEMATIS

Name	Height	Flowers	Remarks
Clematis alpina 'Frances Rivis'	About 10ft	Mauve-blue (Apr–May)	Particularly effective on a north wall. Prune lightly after flowering.
Clematis armandii 'Apple Blossom'	15–18ft	Creamy-white with pink tinge (Apr–May)	Hardy evergreen species, best grown against a south-facing wall. Prune lightly after flowering.
Clematis campaniflora	18–20ft	Pale blue (July–Sept)	Too vigorous for a confined area. In March, cut back all of the previous year's growth to just above a pair of strong buds near the base.
Clematis 'Comtesse de Bouchaud'	15–18ft	Pink-mauve (July–Aug)	In Mar cut back all of the previous year's growth to just above a pair of strong buds near the base.
Clematis heracleifolia 'Côte d'Azur'	3ft	Light blue (Aug–Sept)	In autumn or Mar cut back all the previous year's growth to just above a pair of strong buds near the base.
Clematis x 'Jackmanii Superba'	Up to 15ft	Dark velvet purple (July–Sept)	In Mar cut back all of the previous year's growth to just above a pair of strong buds near the base.
Clematis lanuginosa 'Henryi'	15ft	White with dark brown sepals (May–June, repeating Aug–Sept)	Cut back dead or feeble shoots in Mar. Cut back others by about one-third to a pair of strong buds.
Clematis lanuginosa 'Nelly Moser'	8–10ft	Pale mauve with dark bar on sepal (May–June, repeating Aug–Sept)	Cut back dead or feeble shoots in Mar. Cut back others by about one-third to a pair of strong buds.
Clematis montana 'Elizabeth'	25ft or more	Soft pink, scented (May–June)	Not suitable for a confined space. Cut out old flowering shoots and tidy up after flowering.
Clematis montana rubens	25ft or more	Rose-pink (May–June)	Vigorous, bronze-green leaves. Cut out old flowering shoots and tidy up after flowering.
Clematis orientalis 'Bill Mackenzie'	Up to 18ft	Deep yellow (July–Sept)	Fern-like leaves. In Mar cut back all of the previous year's growth to just above a pair of strong buds near the base.

Herbaceous clematis

I have been advised to try growing herbaceous clematis, but my local garden centre doesn't seem to have heard of them. Can you explain what they are and how they should be grown?

There are several species of clematis that scramble rather than climb and never reach more than 3ft or so above the ground, although the individual stems may be longer. They are called herbaceous clematis and, although garden centres may ignore them, any specialist nursery should have some.

Those seen most frequently are *Clematis heracleifolia* and its varieties, including 'Wyevale', 'Crepuscule' and 'Côte d'Azur', which have powder-blue flowers in late summer. *C. integrifolia* is perhaps the commonest of all. The two best varieties of the species are the blue 'Hendersonii' and the pink 'Rosea'.

The herbaceous species require the same soil conditions as their climbing relatives: well-drained, fertile and preferably slightly alkaline ground with shade at the roots. Don't stake them. Either allow them to scramble over themselves and other strong plants nearby, or give them a framework of twiggy branches a couple of feet high.

Pruning the herbaceous forms amounts to simply cutting away all topgrowth in the autumn. After this treatment, protect them from frost with a 2-3in thick layer of straw, bracken or shredded bark spread over the crowns of the plants. In the North, leave the pruning until spring so that the stems provide additional protection from the cold.

Repeat-flowering clematis

What is the best all-round variety of clematis to grow in a small garden where it is important to have as long a flowering season as possible?

If clematis has a drawback as a garden plant, it is that the flowering season of most individual varieties is not very long. They display their unopened buds for weeks before anything happens and all is then over relatively quickly. Some varieties, however, do flower in early summer and then give a smaller repeat showing later; in a small garden it would be wise to select from these.

Perhaps the longest flowering season among the species is that of *Clematis durandii*, which may display its rich blue blooms intermittently from June until well into September. Among the hybrids that reliably give a repeat showing are: 'Dr Ruppel', with large, banded flowers in shades of pink; 'Elsa Spath', which can be expected to have at least some of its blue flowers open at almost any time between June and late August; 'John Warren', which has a good show of pink flowers at both the beginning and the end of summer; and the old favourite 'Nelly Moser' with its familiar large lilac-striped flowers on and off from May until autumn.

For extending the season even farther, some of the varieties of *C. viticella* like 'Mme Julia Correvon' will flower in most years from June until the beginning of October, while *C. tangutica*, which most gardening books describe as flowering from August to October, can be expected to show the first of its yellow bells at the beginning of July in milder parts of Britain.

Name	Height	Flowers	Remarks
Clematis patens 'Marie Boisselot'	10ft	Creamy-white (July–Sept)	In Mar cut back dead or feeble shoots. Cut back others by about one-third to a pair of strong buds.
Clematis patens 'The President'	10ft	Deep purple with silvery undersides (intermittently from May to Sept)	Cut back dead or feeble shoots in Mar. Cut back others by about one-third to a pair of strong buds.
Clematis patens 'Vyvyan Pennell'	10ft	Deep blue-violet doubles followed by lavender-blue singles (May–July, and again in the autumn)	In Mar cut back all of the previous year's growth to just above a pair of strong buds near the base.
Clematis rehderana	20–25ft	Pale yellow, scented (Aug–Oct)	Suitable for growing through an old tree. In Mar cut back all of the previous year's growth to just above a pair of strong buds near the base.
Clematis texensis 'Duchess of Albany'	10ft	Rich pink with darker central band (Aug–Sept)	In Mar cut back all of the previous year's growth to just above a pair of strong buds near the base.
Clematis texensis 'Gravetye Beauty'	10ft, scrambler	Ruby-red (Aug–Sept)	In Mar cut back all of the previous year's growth to just above a pair of strong buds near the base. Benefits from a mound of peat around the crown during the winter.
Clematis viticella 'Mme Julia Correvon'	Up to 10ft	Deep wine red (July–Sept)	Can appear straggly if trained upwards. Let it ramble through shrubs or tumble from a small tree. In Mar cut back all of the previous year's growth to just above a pair of strong buds near the base.
Clematis viticella 'Purpurea plena elegans'	Up to 10ft	Red-purple (July–Sept)	In Mar cut back all of the previous year's growth to just above a pair of strong buds near the base.
Clematis viticella 'Royal Velours'	Up to 10ft	Dark purple (July–Sept)	In Mar cut back all of the previous year's growth to just above a pair of growing buds near the base.

Pruning a rambler

I have a clematis growing through an old apple tree. It is beautiful in summer but looks straggly in winter. Would it do any harm to cut it back in the autumn?

The chances are that a clematis growing through an apple tree is likely to be one of the more vigorous varieties – perhaps the yellow, autumn-flowering *Clematis tangutica* or one of the spring-flowering forms of *C. montana*. To obtain the very best results from these plants in a fairly confined space, a strict pruning routine should be followed (see *Perfect pruning*, page 76). But when the plants are growing semi-wild, such respect is hardly necessary. Simply cut them back to a good bud at any convenient height.

Growing from seed

Can clematis be grown easily from seed? My plants produce enormous quantities of seed, but I never find any seedlings in my garden.

Yes, clematis can be grown from seed, but many of the plants grown in gardens are hybrid varieties and will not come true to type if raised in this way – normally they are propagated from cuttings.

There are several excellent garden plants among the species, though – such as *Clematis tangutica, C. rehderiana, C. campaniflora, C. flammula* and *C. alpina* – and some of these will produce good seed.

If you see seed as a means of producing a large number of additional plants for your garden, you will be in for quite a long wait. Collect the seed heads in the autumn and sow the seeds immediately into trays of a soil-based seed compost. Place them in a cool spot in the garden, out of direct sunlight, and forget about them until the spring.

Once the seeds have been subjected to the rigours of frost and snow during the winter, bring the trays into the warmth of the greenhouse and keep them under close observation, for germination can occur at any time thereafter.

When the seedlings emerge, prick them on into 3in pots. Thereafter, treat them in the same way as cuttings (see *Success with cuttings*, below).

Success with cuttings

I thought that striking clematis from cuttings was easy, but I rarely get more than the odd one or two to take. How can I improve my average?

Striking *some* clematis from cuttings is easy, but others can be obstinate. First, the easy ones, which comprise most of the true species like *Clematis montana, C. viticella* and *C. tangutica*. The best way is to take semi-ripe shoots around late July or the beginning of August.

Take sections of shoot, about 6-8in long, from the central part of the stem to form the cuttings. Where you trim the sections doesn't matter much. It was traditionally said that nodal cuttings should be used, but this is now known to be unnecessary. A nodal cutting is one trimmed so that the 'node' – the small swelling on the stem from which the leaves arise – is about half an inch above the base of the cutting. In order to form roots, certain hormones must be present inside the shoot, and although most plants have the highest concentration of these hormones *at* the node, it has been discovered that some types of clematis actually have the highest concentration *between* the nodes. Hence it makes sense to try inter-nodal cuttings, too – those cut at the mid-point between two pairs of leaves.

The answer is to try both sorts of cuttings, and see which works best for each of the varieties you grow. Dip the base of the cutting into hormone rooting powder and insert about an inch of it into a pot or tray containing a well-moistened mixture of 1 part by volume of peat and 2 parts of sharp sand or perlite.

Cover the pot with a plastic bag or rigid propagator lid and place it in a fairly warm place out of direct sunlight.

The cuttings should root in six to eight weeks, when they may be potted on into a proprietary potting compost – John Innes No 2 would do fine – in a 3in pot. After one year, pot them on into a 5in pot to give a strong plant ready for planting out in the following season.

The most difficult of the common garden varieties to root are the large-flowered hybrid forms such as 'Nelly Moser'. Clematis nurseries raise plants under glass to produce soft shoots that are more likely to root than the tough, woody ones that outdoor plants tend to form. This is not practical in a garden where a gardener usually wants to take a few cuttings from an existing, established plant. The best chance of success with these more tricky varieties will come from taking the cuttings in the second half of June and ensuring that they are taken from no more than 9-12in back from the shoot tip, where the tissues are likely to be less woody. Alternatively, propagate the varieties by serpentine layering in July-August (see *All about layering*, page 110).

A companion for 'Nelly Moser'

Can you suggest any other climbing plants to combine with a 'Nelly Moser' clematis on the front wall of the house?

Many plants combine well with clematis, but this particular variety is difficult for two reasons. First, because if it is to be grown in combination, a clematis really needs to be trained over a more substantial plant, such as a shrub or tree, rather than be embraced by another climber. Secondly, 'Nelly Moser' has a colour pattern that doesn't blend well with most other flowers. But its advantage as a companion for other plants is that it requires only light pruning. So you won't have the problem of disentangling offcuts from other vegetation.

Perhaps the best choice is a climbing rose of appropriate colour and robustness. Because 'Nelly Moser' begins flowering in May or early June, it will probably miss the first flush of rose bloom, although the second crop of clematis flowers in late summer should coincide with the rose, provided the rose has a fairly long flowering season.

Given the pale mauve-pink and crimson stripe of the clematis, the climbing forms of dark red roses such as 'Souvenir de Claudius Denoyal', 'Guinée', 'Josephine Bruce', 'Ena Harkness' or 'Crimson Glory' would look splendid.

Clematis also look handsome when trained through trees, especially through old, worn-out fruit trees, and over large evergreen shrubs such as cypresses.

PERFECT PRUNING

Gardeners often fall out about how to prune clematis, largely because different types need different treatment. All the types fall into one of three groups:

Group One comprises the early-flowering species, such as *Clematis alpina, C. macropetala* and *C. montana*, and their varieties. Prune them immediately after flowering to remove dead shoots and to keep the plants within their allotted space.

Group Two is the early large-flowered hybrids such as 'Nelly Moser' and 'The President', together with mid-season large-flowered forms such as 'Marie Boisselot'. These should have dead or weak shoots cut away in early March. Flowers in these varieties are produced on wood which grew the previous year, so aim to keep as many year-old shoots as you can. Cut out shoots which have flowered after the blooms fade.

Group Three includes *C. viticella* and its varieties, C. x 'Jackmanii Superba', and the late-flowering species such as *C. rehderiana, C. tangutica, C. campaniflora* and *C. texensis*. These should also be pruned in March, but harder, with the previous year's growth being taken back to a strong pair of buds just above the base. On these varieties, the flowers are produced on new shoots each year.

CLIMBERS

Climbing a north wall

What attractive evergreen and flowering climber will give year-round colour to a north wall?

Surprisingly, you can plant some of the more tender shrubs against a north wall. North would seem to spell cold, because the north wind really does give rise to some of the coldest winter days. But, in fact, most frost damage to plants arises through over-rapid thawing of frozen tissues in early spring, and this occurs when the early-morning sun strikes them. Hence more damage is likely to arise when plants face east than when they are tucked on a slowly warming north side. That's the good news. The bad news is that there aren't many evergreen climbers with attractive flowers anyway – and few plants produce as many flowers when facing north as they do in a more sunny spot. Here are some of the best options:

- *Trachelospermum jasminoides* is the star jasmine. It takes two or three years to settle down and is rather too tender for exposed or cold gardens, but it's self-clinging and clothes the wall with fairly small, elliptical and very glossy, dark green leaves. Towards the end of the summer it produces masses of white, jasmine-like flowers with a rich perfume.
- Among evergreen honeysuckles, *Lonicera japonica* is the most frequently seen and the best known. The flowers are fragrant, large, white becoming yellow later and appear, even on north-facing plants, throughout the

summer. This is a vigorous plant, and although it reaches its greatest growth in a fairly sunny spot, it needs a large wall wherever it is planted. The related *L. sempervirens* will also succeed on a north wall. Its flowers have yellow interiors with scarlet on the outside.

- *Pileostegia viburnoides* is related to the hydrangeas. It grows much more slowly than the honeysuckles and has long, narrow and rather leathery leaves and masses of creamy-white flowers late in the summer. It is self-clinging and, as it benefits from shelter, it is an especially good choice for a north wall.
- The self-clinging, evergreen climbing hydrangea, *Hydrangea serratifolia*, is much less well known than its deciduous counterpart, *H. petiolaris*, possibly because it is more tender and its flowers less spectacular. It is perhaps best considered as a very good foliage plant, with its large, dark glossy leaves; consider its creamy-white flowers as a bonus.
- *Holboellia coriacea* is yet another valuable plant. A vigorous grower, it can reach 20ft. Rather unusually for an evergreen climber, it bears its flowers, which are greenish-white, early in the season – in April-May. The dark purple, pea-like pods remain after the flowers have faded.

Because of the protection afforded by a north wall, some flowering climbers which are normally deciduous will – in gardens in the South of Britain, anyway – retain their leaves through most winters. Some roses come into this category, including one with attractive greyish-green foliage, *Rosa brunonii* 'La Mortola'.

Wisteria woe

I planted a wisteria about seven years ago on a south-facing wall. It has produced masses of leaves – but no flowers. Have I put it in the wrong position, or should I have pruned it?

Just be patient a little longer. If you have waited seven years, it is highly likely that your plant is about to burst forth from its flowering dormancy, for this is roughly the time taken for a newly established plant to settle into a flowering rhythm. The position you've chosen is also correct, for a wisteria benefits from having its head in the sun, although it will thrive perfectly well, if with fewer flowers, on a north-facing wall. Nonetheless, there are two techniques that will help it on its way.

First, other than in the most impoverished of soils, don't give your wisteria any nitrogen-rich fertiliser, for wisteria are naturally vigorous plants and tend to produce masses of foliage anyway. Nitrogen merely stimulates them to produce more leaves.

Second, establish a pruning routine to stimulate the production of the short, flowering shoots rather than long, whippy green growths. Wisterias should be pruned twice a year, in summer and in winter. In July or August, cut back all the long shoots to about six leaves from the base. In December, cut these shoots back farther to two buds.

After a few years, you'll find that the plant will produce fewer long growths and more shorter, flowering ones. Individual plants vary considerably in the rapidity and the completeness with which they achieve this condition. There are some that seem always to require considerable pruning, whereas others become virtually self-sufficient in time. Don't overlook the pruning. Just one or two years of neglect can set even an established plant back to producing masses of leafy shoots once again.

Boosting honeysuckle

I planted a honeysuckle against an east-facing fence about two years ago. It is beneath a cherry tree and doesn't get much sun. The honeysuckle is thin, and hasn't yet flowered. What can I do to boost its growth?

The honeysuckle, perhaps because it is so common, is probably the most undervalued of all garden climbers. It has a long flowering season and an incomparably evocative perfume. Although gardening books often suggest that it should always be planted in full sun, this is not strictly correct.

Consider the natural habitat of the native British honeysuckle, the wild woodbine, and you will recall that it is a plant not only of hedgerows – where obviously it is usually fairly well exposed – but also of woodlands and copses, where it will be in at least partial shade for much of the time.

The difficulty is getting the plants started in shady conditions and persuading them to grow sufficiently well to raise at least their tops into the sunlight. Your plant, having spent the first two years of its life beneath the considerable shade cast by a cherry tree, has never really had an opportunity to establish itself satisfactorily. It would have been wiser to have bought a larger plant, or to have given the existing one an additional year or two in a fairly large container before transferring it to its permanent position.

For the time being, forget about flowering and try to build up the plant's structure. In fertiliser terms, this means feeding it plenty of nitrogen and phosphorus to promote the growth of leaves and roots. An excellent way of providing this is with the organic fertiliser mixture of blood, fish and bone meal.

A top-dressing with this at the start of the growing season in March or April should be followed by weekly applications of a liquid general fertiliser. By the end of the first year this treatment should have begun to promote a more sound structure, and in the following year the same treatment should be applied with the addition of a light top-dressing with sulphate of potash in early spring. Half an ounce per square yard should be about right. In addition to the fertiliser treatment, prune out any weak and spindly growths and also any dead shoots, and cut back all others by about one-third.

Root problem

Will the roots of large climbing plants undermine or damage the foundations of my house?

By and large, the answer's no, judging by the countless walls that for centuries have played host to some very large climbers, wall shrubs or even wall trees like *Magnolia grandiflora*. The problem plants are large trees, particularly willows – not climbers. Damage is most likely to occur in peaty soils or heavy clays during drought conditions when the soil shrinks through loss of water extracted by the plants.

Among large species, magnolias, wisterias, climbing hydrangeas and the more vigorous vines are the least likely to cause problems. The numerous fruit trees such as figs, pears and cherries which are often trained against walls, are also unlikely to be damaging, even on clay or peat.

Fruits for a north wall

I have a north-facing wall on which I would like to grow something productive rather than just decorative. Any suggestions?

The traditional answer is to train a 'Morello' cherry tree against a north wall, but this has rather limited uses. Culinary varieties of gooseberry, such as 'Careless' and 'Invicta', are perfectly satisfactory if trained as cordons; red or white currants (but not black) would also do well. The best way to train these bush fruits is as U-shaped cordons with the two vertical branches 12in apart.

The main features of a north wall are that it sees little of the sun and that fruits trained to it flower and mature later than normal. This, however, is not always a drawback because late flowering can avoid frost damage, while later ripening will extend the cropping season.

Hiding unsightly pipework

Our sitting-room window looks out onto a wall disfigured by several drainpipes and a large stack pipe. What can I plant to screen the pipes without damaging them? The wall faces south, but for much of the day is shaded by the house next door.

Drainpipes and stacks, like oil storage tanks and gas cylinders, are unsightly and cry out to be covered with vegetation. But they are constructed of smooth, unyielding material to which plant life will adhere only with difficulty. Pipes usually have the merit that twining plants will wrap around them, or can at least be tied in place, whereas tanks and other larger objects need covering in some sort of trellis or plastic netting first.

In suggesting plants to use, it is assumed that the pipes are no nicer to look at in winter than summer.

Evergreens, or those having a close mat of stems after the leaves have fallen, will do the trick. Two plant genera provide the best choices for these two categories.

The best self-clinging evergreens without doubt are the ivies, and there is now an enormous range of varieties fairly widely available. The best non-evergreen species are the parthenocissus vines, although they will need regular cutting back to stop them straying from the pipes onto the walls and roof.

Three of the parthenocissus species are self-clinging: the Boston ivy, *Parthenocissus tricuspidata*; *P. henryana*; and *P. quinquefolia*, the Virginia creeper. A fourth species, *P. inserta*, climbs by means of tendrils and can be used to cover pipes if you tie wires around the pipes first.

An alternative to planting a climber to camouflage piping is to use a tall evergreen shrub. This will work best if the screening is required only from one direction, and if you don't mind waiting for a few years. If this appeals, go for a narrow conifer such as *Juniperus scopulorum* 'Skyrocket'.

Pyracanthas under attack

My pyracanthas lose masses of berries to birds. Still more drop off prematurely, and the few remaining are turned black and blotchy by some disease. What can I do about these problems?

Pyracanthas make excellent wall shrubs, with the possible drawback that they are prone to being browned by frost in severe winters. There's not much you can do about that. As for the birds, you could try spraying the plants with a proprietary chemical bird repellent as the fruits first set. It is important to apply the repellent before the birds have discovered the berries, because even the manufacturers admit that its effectiveness is dubious thereafter. Netting is a more effective alternative, but it is also unsightly and its presence defeats the object of cultivating an attractive plant.

Your second problem – premature dropping of the berries – is very common on a wide variety of shrubs. The reason that pyracantha seems especially prone to the problem is that the base of a wall, where its roots lie, is one of the driest parts of any garden and it is dryness, above all, that causes the dropping. The best answer is to ensure that the soil around the base of the plant is well mulched with a 3-4in layer of peat or compost in early spring while the ground is still moist, and that you pour on plenty of water throughout the season.

The disease that takes care of your remaining berries is pyracantha scab, which is similar to the more familiar scab disease of apples. The symptoms are rough, brownish scars on the fruit, the leaves and the twigs. Like apple scab, it is most prevalent in wet seasons. Spraying the bush with a fungicide such as benomyl every three weeks from mid-March to July will help.

Magnificent magnolias

I have seen some beautiful magnolias trained against a wall. What varieties can you recommend to grow in this way, and would they be equally suitable for north and south-facing sides of the house in my neutral loam?

The magnolia family contains some of the best flowering trees for gardens. There are more than 200 species and varieties; only about 30 are seen at all frequently in gardens, and you're likely to find less than half a dozen at most garden centres.

There are both deciduous and evergreen species, and it is one of the evergreens – *Magnolia grandiflora* – that lends itself particularly well to being grown against a wall. At a distance its pointed shoots and large, glossy and leathery leaves give it something of the appearance of a rubber tree, although on close inspection the underside of the leaves of most forms have an attractive brownish felt. The creamy-white flowers are the crowning glory, appearing in ones and twos towards the end of summer and sometimes reaching 12in across.

Grown from a seedling, *M. grandiflora* can take 25 or 30 years before flowering, but the grafted forms such as 'Exmouth' or 'Goliath' flower at an early age and are fairly readily obtainable. When it's planted against a wall you'll need to do some pruning, especially in the early stages of growth, in order to shape the plant. But once it's established, little further attention is necessary.

Bear in mind that it can reach 30ft in height and is especially likely to do so with the benefit of wall protection. Best against a south or south-west wall, it can also be grown successfully against a north-facing wall, although it's likely to produce fewer flowers there. Your neutral soil will suit it fine. Like most magnolias, it is somewhat intolerant of very limy soils. If mortar has made the soil near your wall alkaline, dig in plenty of peat at planting time to make it more acid (see *Acid soils*, page 6).

In mild parts of the country, another evergreen species, *M. delavayi*, can be breathtaking against a wall, with large white flowers and leaves well over 12in in length. Among the deciduous species, *M.* x *soulangiana* in its many varieties is probably the easiest to grow and can be wall-trained quite simply by tying its branches to horizontal wires strung between eye-bolts. Alternatively, consider what is arguably the most beautiful of all magnolias, *M. campbellii mollicomata*, with its large pink flowers.

Winter cutbacks

My gardening books tell me to remove the dead flowering shoots from my forsythia and winter jasmine each year. My plants are fairly big and there are hundreds of flowering shoots. Would it do any harm to use shears rather than secateurs?

Not at all. Removing the dead flowering shoots serves three purposes. It makes the plants appear much tidier. It removes dead tissue on which pests and diseases might become established. And, most importantly, it stimulates the development of otherwise dormant buds, leading to new leafy growth and new flowering shoots for the following season.

Secateurs make a neat job and ensure that all the dead shoots are removed and the non-flowering ones are not. But on a large plant this is impracticable and shears are essential.

If you do use shears, carry out the work immediately the flowers fade, for the longer you leave it the more likely you are to cut away large numbers of new leafy shoots on which flowers will later be borne.

Lack-lustre passion flower

After growing a passion flower from seed three years ago, I planted it against a sheltered, south-west wall in good loamy soil, but it has never flowered. Why?

The seed may be to blame. The passion flower is one of the most exotic-looking of all the plants that can be considered hardy in British gardens. It is a native of South America and the species seen most frequently is one of the hardiest of all, *Passiflora caerulea*, which normally has blue, white and purple-tinged flowers. There is also a form called 'Constance Elliott', whose flowers are pure white.

You have certainly placed your plant in the best possible position, for other than in the very mildest parts of the country it will need this kind of protection to survive in winter.

There are two possible reasons why your plant has failed to flower. Passion flowers raised from seed are not always true to type. The only way to be certain that you have a plant of true flowering stock is to buy one raised from a cutting. The other possibility is that you've treated the plant too well. Grown unrestricted in good loamy soil, even the best-quality plant may spend its energy on producing leaves instead of flowers.

With this and other vigorous climbers it is often a good idea to confine the roots in order to supply the necessary degree of 'threat' to survival, which so many plants need before they will start to flower.

This is best done at the initial planting time by setting the plant in a hole about 2ft square, with bricks or slabs around it to confine the roots. The same trick is less likely to jolt your established plant into bloom because, once planted, the passion flower does not readily tolerate being moved.

Thorn in the side

Generations of cats have been brought up to consider my garden a right of way. Can you think of anything I could grow along the fence that's tough enough to stop them?

Something climbing, spiny and impenetrable is what you want. And while we're at it, let's make it something beautiful as well. Be careful, though, that the plant doesn't become as big a problem as the cats. If you choose something too vigorous, its weight is quite likely to pull the fence down when winter gales blow.

There are no better thorny climbers than the rose family – either roses themselves or their relatives, the brambles. The thorniest of all roses is almost certainly *Rosa sericea pteracantha*, a shrub rather than a climber, but one that could be used more or less as a hedge against the fence. Its huge, translucent red thorns will stop the most determined intruders, and it produces masses of small white flowers in spring.

Then there are three similar climbers among the Species roses, that also produce small white flowers: the banana-scented *R. longicuspis*; the bluish-leaved *R. brunonii* 'La Mortola', and *R. helenae*. All are vigorous but easily kept within bounds by pruning.

Or consider the old China rose 'Mme Alfred Carrière'. It can be grown very successfully in a north-facing situation – an important consideration if you plan to clothe the entire garden boundary.

Many of the Rambler roses, too, are fairly thorny. The coppery-pink 'Albertine' would be many people's choice, although 'New Dawn' has a similarly attractive pink flower and the additional merit of blooming on and off throughout the summer rather than all in one early flush like most Ramblers. Toughest of all perhaps is 'Albéric Barbier' which produces massed clusters of white flowers in June and July. Its thorns would make an elephant quail.

Although many of the climbing versions of Hybrid tea roses have large thorns, they are much less robust than the Species and Ramblers. Their thorns, especially on young shoots, are often softer, the shoots are more brittle and they require fairly rigorous pruning if they are to go on producing an abundant crop of flowers. The need to cut away a large part of the plant each season really defeats your objective of having a year-round barrier against cats.

Among the brambles is one that is really a loose shrub rather than a climber, but it would do the job you want, provided you have a strong fence to support it. The plant is *Rubus ulmifolius* 'Bellidiflorus', and, as well as thorns, it has lovely double pink flowers.

Sudden death

I have a fremontodendron trained against the south-facing wall of my house. It has grown well for three years and flowered for the first time this summer. Suddenly, just as the flowers were fading, the whole plant gave up and died. What has gone wrong, and would it be safe to plant another in the same spot?

The chances are that nothing has gone wrong. It's just that old age has caught up with a plant that is often short-lived. Fremontodendrons, or, as they used to be called, fremontias, can be guaranteed to turn heads when they are in flower. They are tall, virtually evergreen shrubs with fairly large, lobed leaves. Their stunning flowers appear superficially like very large buttercups, although the yellow colour derives not from petals, which fremontodendrons lack, but from sepals. The flowers are produced intermittently throughout the summer but, because the plants originate in California and Mexico, wall protection is essential if they are grown outdoors (they also do well in a large conservatory). The form grown most commonly is a hybrid called 'California Glory'; it, too, is short-lived.

The plants sometimes, and quite inexplicably, die without warning. No one has determined why this should be but it seems possible that, like clematis wilt, it is at least partly the result of a disease. Some plants last for several years, others for only a few, and the only advice that can be offered is to ensure that they are grown in the warmest possible spot in light, free-draining yet nutrient-rich soil. Water them regularly when they are in bloom.

Whenever a plant has died, especially from unknown causes, it makes sense not to plant another of the same type in exactly the same spot. It is always possible that some soil factor has contributed to the plant's death. If replanting somewhere else is impossible because there is only one spot in the garden that is really suitable for a fremontodendron, dig a hole about 2ft long, wide and deep and fill it with fresh soil from another part of the garden.

No bees, no berries

My Cotoneaster horizontalis *is trained against my house wall and every year it has masses of flowers but very rarely sets any berries. Am I growing it in the wrong place, or does it not like being trained vertically?*

It's a case of wrong position – not direction. Cotoneaster is a large genus of excellent garden plants. Most are deciduous, but there are several evergreen forms, too. *Cotoneaster horizontalis* is the most familiar species; its herringbone branching pattern is uniquely attractive, and its flowers, although unspectacular, are a magnet for bees. The familiar red berries are among the most splendid sights of autumn.

Nonetheless, occasionally, a plant fails to oblige. The flowers come out but the fruits never set. Despite the fact that its name is *C. horizontalis* and this particular plant is growing vertically, the direction of growth is not the reason for the absence of berries. When flowers are not followed by fruit, the reason is usually either that the flowers are being imperfectly pollinated, or that the young fruit do set but then part company with the plant.

Imperfect pollination usually happens because the plant is in a spot which is not liked by bees and other pollinating insects, perhaps because it is cold and windy. It may be possible to put up a screen around the site, but usually the answer is to move the shrub to a less exposed place.

When fruits set but then drop off, dryness at the roots is a very common cause. This applies to all plants and shrubs but it can be a particular problem with wall shrubs, whose root area tends to be sheltered from rain by the eaves. Applying a 2-3in thick mulch of well-rotted manure, compost, shredded bark, peat or other organic matter when the soil is moist in spring will generally solve this problem. A general fertiliser such as Growmore applied around the plant at the same time will also help to get the plant back into peak condition.

Beating the east wind

What climbing plant will grow against an east-facing wall that gets strong, cold winds for much of the winter?

Only the hardiest plants will survive this tough assignment because an east-facing wall really is a stern test of any plant's durability. An east wall catches the first warmth of the winter sun, so any plant you put there risks being damaged by rapid thawing after frost; and it bears the full brunt of the cold east wind.

Not only are all tender plants out of the question, but most evergreens are as well. Because evergreen plants retain their leaves throughout the year, they are always likely to lose water through them – and the cold, drying winds of winter will be drawing water from the plants at a time when they are not in active growth and when the frozen soil makes it impossible for the roots to make good the loss. Only evergreens with tough, durable leaves, able to provide some protection against water loss, will stand any chance of survival.

Moreover, any plant that doesn't cling tightly to the wall is likely to be blown away or suffer damage from the wind.

Among evergreens the choice is limited to ivies. Even among these durable climbers, the variegated forms cannot be considered totally reliable. Any variegated plant is almost always less tolerant of poor conditions than a normal green one because it has a lower level of energy-generating chlorophyll – the green pigment in plants – and is therefore inevitably less vigorous.

Among deciduous climbers there is more choice. The self-clinging climbing hydrangea, *Hydrangea petiolaris*, is tough and attractive in leaf and produces greenish-white flowers in early summer. Its relative, *Schizophragma hydrangeoides*, has even more attractive white flowers and foliage. *Celastrus orbiculatus* is a tough, twining climber always at its best in the autumn when the leaves turn yellow and provide a foil for the red and golden seed heads (be sure to buy this plant from a reliable supplier, as not all forms are equally dependable at fruiting). *Akebia quinata* is another fairly vigorous twining climber and produces small, scented purple flowers in early spring. It is partially evergreen, but on an east wall it will almost certainly lose its leaves during winter.

Finally, consider planting one of the most valuable of climbing plants, parthenocissus, of which there are three common and one less frequently seen species. All are suitable for an east-facing wall. *Parthenocissus tricuspidata* is the Boston ivy, although it is often incorrectly called Virginia creeper. It has three-lobed, ivy-like leaves that flare into the most vivid red in autumn. The true Virginia creeper is *P. quinquefolia*, a plant with five-lobed leaves, but less assertive autumn colour. The most beautiful leaves in the genus are those of *P. henryana*, which have a rich purple-bronze colour and a silvery tint to the veins.

These three species are self-clinging, but where you want to cover an old wall a better bet is the tendril-forming *P. inserta*. Curiously, this is the least frequently seen species, but it is just as vigorous and just as easily grown as the others. The only real problem with parthenocissus species in general is that a large plant will drop a huge quantity of leaves in autumn.

PICK OF THE CLIMBERS

Name	Height	Flowers	Remarks
FAST-GROWING CLIMBERS			
Actinidia chinensis (Chinese gooseberry, kiwi fruit)	More than 30ft	Creamy-white (June–Aug)	Take out old wood and trim to shape in spring
Aristolochia durior also known as *A. macrophylla* (Dutchman's pipe)	At least 20ft	Brown, green and yellow (June)	No pruning needed
Cobaea scandens (cup and saucer vine, cathedral bell)	At least 20ft	Purple with green calyx (May–Oct)	If grown as an annual, no pruning needed. If grown as a perennial, cut back old shoots after flowering
Hedera colchica 'Dentata' (Persian ivy)	More than 30ft	Greenish (summer)	No pruning needed
Lonicera japonica 'Halliana' (Japanese honeysuckle)	More than 20ft	White to yellow (June–Oct)	After flowering, cut out old wood
Passiflora caerulea (passion flower)	30ft	Purple and white (June–Sept)	Remove dead wood in spring
Polygonum baldschuanicum (Russian vine, mile-a-minute)	More than 50ft	Pale pink or white (July–Sept)	No pruning needed
Rosa filipes 'Kiftsgate'	More than 50ft	White (June–July)	Best grown into and over an old tree. Remove dead shoots in Mar
Vitis coignetiae (vine)	Up to 50ft	Greenish (May)	Rich red autumn foliage, inedible black berries (autumn). No pruning needed
OUTSTANDINGLY ATTRACTIVE CLIMBERS			
Lapageria rosea (Chinese bellflower)	15ft	Rose-crimson (July–Oct)	Remove dead shoots in Mar
Lonicera periclymenum 'Belgica' (early Dutch honeysuckle)	About 20ft	Pale yellow with purple-red exterior (May–June)	After flowering, cut back old wood
Rosa banksiae lutea	20ft	Yellow (May–June)	Best grown against a sunny, sheltered wall. Remove older shoots about every two years
Trachelospermum jasminoides (star jasmine)	About 20ft	White (July–Aug)	Prune to retain shape
Wisteria floribunda 'Macrobotrys' (Japanese wisteria)	More than 20ft	Lilac-blue (May–June)	Shorten all new shoots to about 9in in July, and again to two buds in Dec

Climbers from seed

I would like to ring the changes when choosing climbing plants – just as I do in my beds and borders. What varieties of annual or short-lived climbers can I raise easily from seed?

Too many people think of climbers as permanent residents in the garden, yet many excellent types can be grown from seed. Perhaps the most familiar is the climbing form of nasturtium, often used to cover walls during the summer. Nasturtiums are easier than almost any other plants to raise from seed, and the only mistake you can make is to treat them too well. They thrive in poor, undernourished soil, though they relish sunshine. Climbing nasturtiums are usually sold as seed mixtures containing a range of yellow, red and orange-flowered forms.

Anyone who has tried to eradicate bindweed will wince at the prospect of deliberately planting one of its relatives, although the ornamental convolvulus is a much more amenable plant that will rapidly cover a trellis. Like the nasturtium, the convolvulus prefers poor soil and is most often sold as a mixture containing white, cream, blue and rose-pink shades.

For a sunny position, try a relative of the convolvulus, the half-hardy morning glory or ipomoea. The most reliable blue form is 'Heavenly Blue', although red and white-flowered types are available. The seed may need nicking to aid germination. For really quick cover, use *Humulus japonicus variegatus*, the ornamental hop. The more familiar golden hop, *H. lupulus* 'Aureus', cannot be raised from seed.

Sweet peas are excellent as informal climbers. Give them a start with twigs, and let them romp away. Probably the most suitable for your purpose are the ever-blooming forms like the mixture 'Galaxy'. Alternatively, consider the runner bean. After all, it was first introduced to Europe from South America in the 16th century as an ornamental climber. Choose a mixture of red and white-flowered varieties and you will have not only a most attractive climbing plant, but one that will feed you, too.

The growing season in Britain is not really long enough for most of the half-hardy climbing plants to make sufficient growth to cover much more than a small trellis. On a small scale, though, ivy-leaved pelargoniums will make an excellent display, although they are better trailers than climbers. The orange-flowered *Thunbergia alata*, or black-eyed susan, is also easily grown from seed and climbs to about 6ft.

Long-flowering jasmine

I have a 6ft high fence which faces south-east, and I want to grow something that will give colour for as long as possible in the summer. I am a little tired of roses and clematis; do you have any other ideas?

In most parts of the country the most reliable and rewarding of summer-flowering climbers is the common summer jasmine, *Jasminum officinale*, which flowers intermittently from early summer until the autumn. Its perfume is surely unsurpassed by any other easily grown garden plant. It will flourish against a south-east wall in most areas, although in colder regions it may die back in the winter.

Pineapple surprise

I have seen a fantastic yellow-flowered shrub trained against a wall. The flowers are like laburnum, but it smells of pineapples. What is this plant, and is it difficult to grow?

Is is one of the most under-appreciated shrubs, the pineapple broom, *Cytisus battandieri*. Although it can be grown as a free-standing plant, when it will reach well over 10ft, it is best trained against a warm wall. The leaves are fairly narrow, greyish and silky, rather like those of the laburnum, to which it is related. Pineapple brooms are also sometimes grafted onto laburnum.

The plant will grow in most well-drained soils, apart from those that are shallow, chalky or extremely acid. It flourishes in full sun, and is seen at its very best when trained as an espalier against a wall. At the end of June or in early July, there are few sights and scents in gardening more likely to arouse admiration and comment.

Short catkins

Why does my Garrya elliptica *have very tiny catkins? The plant is about eight years old, trained to a west-facing wall and growing well.*

The reason for your shrub's disappointing performance is simply that you are growing the female of the species. *Garrya elliptica* is an evergreen with leathery dark green foliage and, some say, a dismal appearance. But it tolerates atmospheric pollution, winter winds, and salt-laden air, too, making it extremely useful for seaside gardens.

Devotees argue that its main merit lies in the greenish catkins which are produced in February, a time of year when almost any flowers are welcome.

The male catkins can be up to 9in long, but the female's are barely half this size, although rather attractive dark brownish-purple fruits are produced on the female plant if a male is nearby to pollinate them.

Because of this fruiting habit, it makes sense to plant garryas in pairs in order to obtain the best of both worlds. The most decorative form is 'James Roof', which is male; it has very long catkins.

CLOCHES AND FRAMES

DIY frames

Cold frames are quite expensive to buy and I would like to knock one up myself. Suggestions please on size and materials.

The most important thing is to make it large enough. For hardening off plants, and perhaps growing one or two ridge cucumbers during the summer, consider a minimum size of 4ft by 3ft. Old windows make ideal tops – two or three laid side by side can make a good-sized frame. For flexibility make two frames instead of one – this will allow you to keep different plants at different temperatures.

Use bricks, railway sleepers or thick wood to make long-lasting sides for the frame. Or, make the top and sides by covering a wooden framework with thick polythene or rigid plastic sheeting. Either will keep the soil warm almost as well as glass. Line the sides with ceiling tiles or expanded polystyrene sheeting during the winter to help to keep more warmth in.

For good light penetration and to help water drain from the top, make the back wall higher than the front. A frame 6ft deep should have its back wall about 18in high and the front wall 12in high.

Ventilate the frame by sliding the tops to one side, or raise them with bricks or blocks of wood. Hinged tops are more secure in windy weather, but they can be a nuisance because you may want to remove them completely during the summer.

Outdoor melons

I'm short of space in my greenhouse, and I wonder if it's possible to grow melons outdoors or in a cold frame?

Outdoors, no. Cold frame, yes. Melons, being a tropical member of the cucumber family, definitely need the shelter and warmth of a frame or cloche.

If you don't have a greenhouse, or don't have space in it, sow the seeds in late March or early April into peat compost in 3in peat pots. Put the pots indoors on a sunny windowsill. Set them out in rich soil in the frame or cloches at the end of April in the South, and about one month later in the North. Each planting hole should be about 9-10in across, 12in deep and filled with soil which has been heavily enriched with well-rotted compost or manure. Set the young plants in the prepared soil, pots and all, with the rootball about 1in above the surface to minimise the risk of neck rot. Each plant will need at least 6sq ft of growing space, but it doesn't matter whether that is an area of 6ft by 1ft (as it might be under cloches) or 3ft by 2ft (as it might be in a frame). Keep the frame or cloches tightly closed at first while the plants get established.

Later, because a south-facing frame will become quite warm during sunny weather,

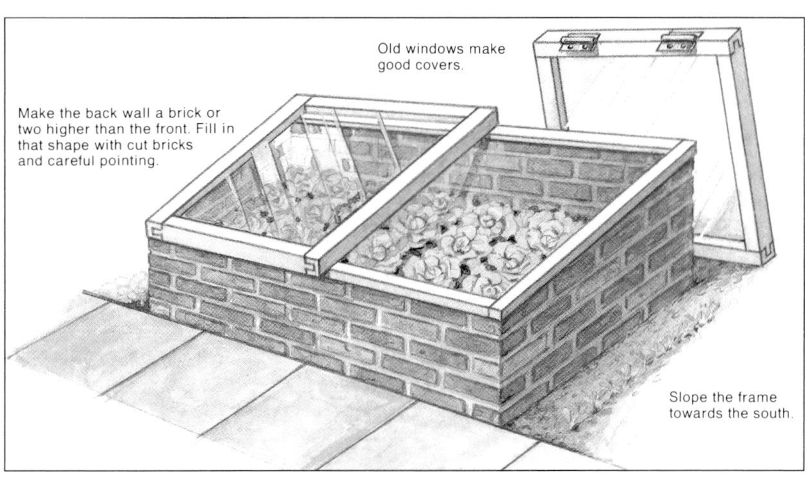
Old windows make good covers.
Make the back wall a brick or two higher than the front. Fill in that shape with cut bricks and careful pointing.
Slope the frame towards the south.

don't hesitate to open or remove the top. But do keep the rain off because too much water can lead to stem canker. Ventilate cloches as best you can – without creating draughts – and be prepared to shade them during bright sunshine to avoid leaf scorch.

When the plants are growing strongly, pinch out the main stem beyond the second leaf (not counting the seed leaves). This will encourage two 'laterals', or sideshoots, to form. Pinch the laterals out beyond the seventh leaf to encourage the development of the sub-laterals that will bear the flowers and fruit.

Melon plants usually produce more male flowers than females, but it's the females (distinguished by their short bulging stems) that become fruits.

To encourage the fruits to set, dab a male flower onto the females. Then, once the fruits have set, pinch out the sub-laterals two leaves beyond the fruit, pick off all but four fruits on each plant and pinch out any sub-laterals that have no fruit.

Set the growing fruits on upturned pots to keep them clean and discourage rots, and keep the ground moist as the fruits swell. The melons are ready to pick when a crack appears around the base of the stem.

Cantaloupe melons are the best types for growing in this way. 'Sweetheart' is the most tolerant to cold, but 'Ogen' and 'Charantais' are also worth growing.

Hardening off

I haven't got a cold frame and am thinking of using cloches to harden off my bedding plants. Does this sound like a good idea?

Yes – provided you take precautions to avoid fluctuating temperatures.

During sunny weather keep the plants cool by draping plastic shadecloth over the cloches, or by lightly applying to the cloches a liquid shading paint which can be rubbed off in the autumn. Ventilate the plants cautiously at first to avoid jolting them with chilling draughts, and don't unblock both ends of the cloches at the same time because this will create a wind-tunnel effect.

If the nights are cool, conserve the heat built up during the day by covering the cloches with polythene sheeting, rugs or matting well before dusk.

Tunnel trouble

I've seen strawberry fields covered with polythene tunnel cloches. Are they worth using in a small garden?

Unless your rows are at least 6ft long, the answer is: probably not. The trouble is that tunnel cloches shorter than this tend to be too fiddly to use. And cutting long sheets of polythene into small sections isn't economical because the ends of each row have to be pulled in, tensioned and secured to pegs in the ground. Conventional cloches are better in confined spaces because they are easier to place in position and to move when you want to get at the plants.

Unless tunnel cloches are adequately ventilated, they also tend to become rather humid, which can encourage grey mould.

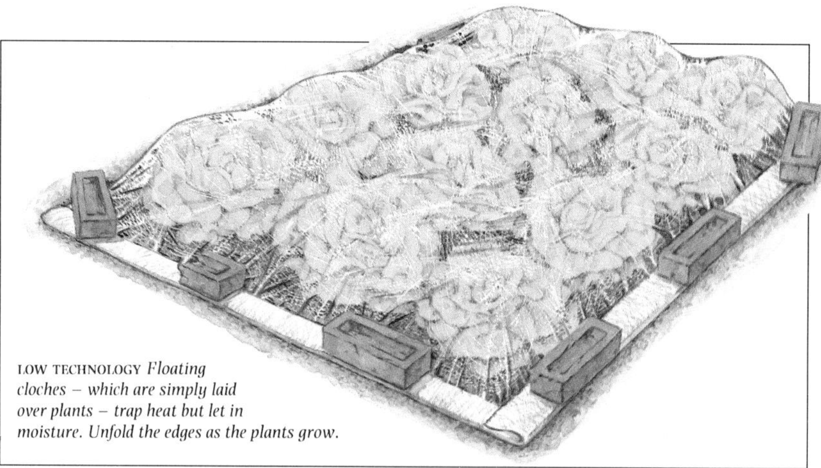

LOW TECHNOLOGY *Floating cloches – which are simply laid over plants – trap heat but let in moisture. Unfold the edges as the plants grow.*

Floating cloches

Are floating cloches really as good as the manufacturers claim?

Follow the instructions and you will get good results, but bear in mind that floating cloches are used in a different way from traditional cloches. Basically a floating cloche is just a sheet of clear polythene – slitted or perforated – or a very light, open-textured cloth that is laid over plants or soil to keep wind out and warmth in. It has no framework to hold it off the ground. The edges have to be weighted down, normally with soil or bricks, and sufficient free play allowed for the plants to grow.

As with other cloches, the main benefit is that you can sow and plant earlier than you would otherwise be able to. And because the plants and soil are kept warmer, the crop naturally matures faster. It's a cheap form of protection and with care the material can be used several times.

The main snags are anticipating how slack to leave the cloche, and then securing it in position. Ventilation takes place through the material, but the plants cannot be gradually hardened off. The material has to be either wholly on or wholly off. To avoid the plants suffering, a floating cloche should be finally taken away only when a period of warm, still weather has begun and is expected to continue. Many vegetables, such as lettuce, radish, onions, brassicas and early potatoes, are successful under floating cloches, and the same material can also be used to keep birds off newly seeded lawns.

Research work at Reading University published in 1984 showed that bush tomatoes covered with clear, perforated polythene for just two weeks developed leaves and lower branches more rapidly. This led to a higher yield as the season progressed.

Outside watering

My light soil dries out very quickly under cloches and a neighbour suggests I apply water on the outside to avoid shifting them. Will this work?

Certainly. Pour the water, gently, from a can or hosepipe over the outside of the cloches to drench the soil thoroughly.

The water will soak in beside the cloches and then spread sideways through the ground for an inch or two. Don't worry if a dry patch remains down the middle under the cloches because exploring roots will soon seek out the moisture.

Problems with paraffin

I am toying with the idea of heating my garden frame with a small paraffin heater, so that I can go on using the frame all winter. Does this sound risky for the plants?

Yes. A car sump heater, or even a hurricane lamp, might provide enough heat to raise the temperature in the frame by a few degrees, perhaps enough to protect bedding plants from spring frosts. But keeping tender plants alive during the winter this way sounds pretty doubtful.

The other snags are that you won't be able to grow plants close to the heater (because they would get scorched), and prolonged use could lead to a shortage of oxygen if the frame was well sealed.

Burning paraffin also produces a lot of moisture, which could encourage mould.

If you want to try it out despite these difficulties, experiment on a small scale first. Keep the wick trimmed, and the flame fairly low, and watch the ventilation.

Heartless lettuce

Every winter my frame lettuces rot before they develop hearts. I change the soil once a year, so what's going wrong?

Grey mould disease (botrytis) is the culprit. This fungus lives in the soil and enters through wounds, quickly destroying whole lettuces if conditions allow.

Renewing the soil helps, but before planting make a point of working a light dusting of a systemic fungicide – benomyl or thiophanate-methyl – into the surface. Plant the seedlings shallowly – so that they flop over on the soil – and never use any which are damaged or have brown marks on their stems. Water sparingly, keeping the foliage dry, and ventilate the frame whenever possible to dispel humid or stagnant air.

If the disease strikes again, remove all the affected plants and spray the remainder with the same fungicide.

Hyacinth starter

I would like to grow hyacinths to flower indoors next Christmas. Can I start them off in a cold frame?

Certainly. In fact a cold frame with a good depth of moist peat or sharp sand is the best place of all for starting off indoor hyacinths. Pot the bulbs – and you will have to buy bulbs which have been specially prepared for early flowering – in a bulb fibre between August 15 and October 7. Dutch bulb-growers have worked out that these are the best dates. Bury the pot up to its rim in the peat or sand, and then cover it with at least 3in of the same material. Leave the cover of the frame slightly open for ventilation.

After 11 weeks, uncover the pot and take it indoors. Many gardeners take the bulbs inside when the shoots are 2-3in tall, but the duration of the cold dark burial in the frame – when roots actively grow – is far more important for good flowering than how long the shoots are at the end of it.

If there's sand in the frame, lightly top-dress the bulb fibre with peat before you bury the pot. The peat can easily be shaken off when you bring the pot indoors, to leave the underlying surface nice and clean.

The value of cloches

I am thinking of buying some cloches. What difference will they make to my vegetables and could they create any problems?

With cloches, you should be able to advance your sowing and planting by at least two weeks at the beginning of the season – particularly if you set the cloches in position a couple of weeks beforehand to help to dry and warm the soil.

Early protection is especially valuable for February and March sowings of radish, lettuce, beetroot, carrots and peas. As the season progresses, use cloches to establish frost-tender crops, such as french and runner beans, sweet corn, ridge cucumbers and bush tomatoes, keeping them in place for as long as possible to hasten growth.

In September, when the weather turns cooler, you can use cloches to cover up August-sown carrots and forcing varieties of lettuce, as well as beetroot, tomatoes and other crops which are still maturing. You can also keep harvested onions under cloches until their foliage turns brittle.

Cloches actually prevent some problems – bird damage, for instance. But the warmer and often humid environment afforded by cloches can make slugs, greenfly and fungal leaf diseases more troublesome. And weed seedlings will certainly grow faster.

The most important way of avoiding problems is to keep an eye on ventilation. Leave a small gap between conventional cloches placed in rows, or raise the polythene covering of tunnel cloches during the day. Never ventilate just by removing both ends from a row of cloches, because this may create a wind tunnel. On a hot, still day take out every second or third cloche to avoid the risk of the plants burning.

Vegetables grown under cloches will be more lush than those not protected, and that will make them more vulnerable to frost. So don't remove the cloches completely as spring advances until you are sure that the weather won't turn cold again. As to which type of cloche to buy, there are advantages and disadvantages to both traditional glass types and newer plastic ones. Glass is stronger, doesn't blow away so easily and lets

How to make a hot bed

What's the best way to make a manure hot bed for a garden frame? My gardening books don't provide any information.

The traditional hot bed technique is not so widely used in these days of heaters. But it's a marvellous way to turn a cold frame into a heated greenhouse in spring. And if you've got access to the raw materials, it won't cost you a penny.

To make the bed, thoroughly mix together equal parts of fresh horse manure – the fresher, the better – and deciduous leaves, and turn the heap three or four times during the course of a fortnight. The leaves will help to moderate the heat and release it over a longer period.

Dig a hole 3ft deep and about 18in longer and wider than the frame. At the end of the two weeks, fill the hole with the fermenting mixture, firming it in layers, and position the frame on top.

Level the surface, cover it with 6-8in of fine soil and close the frame. Allow the heat to build up for a day or so before sowing or planting. Don't sow or plant directly into the soil because the young roots could get damaged by the powerful mix. Instead sow or plant as usual in pots or seed trays, then bury the containers up to their rims in the warm soil. Open the frame whenever the air temperature inside tops 21°C (70°F).

A hot bed made in February or March – when vegetable sowing and planting gets under way – will release its heat for up to eight weeks. Afterwards, you can plant ridge cucumbers, marrows or melons directly into the soil – they will enjoy the rich root run.

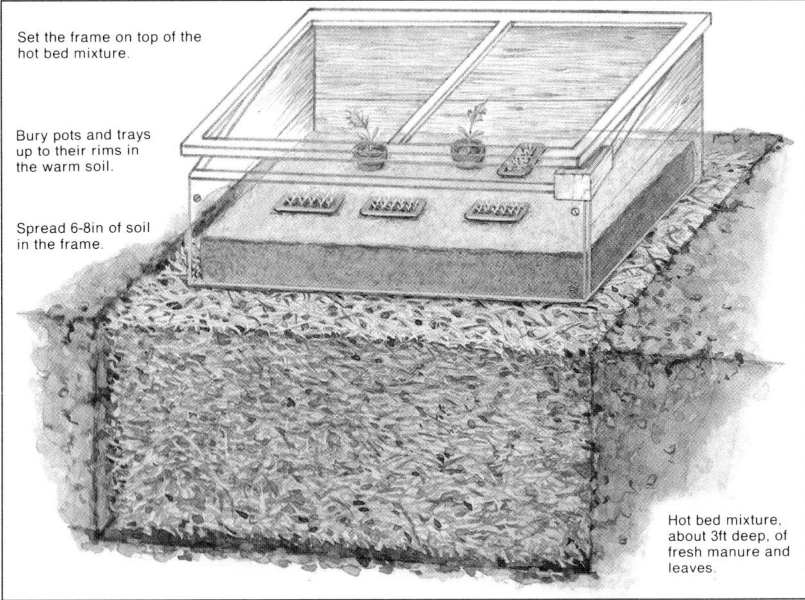
Set the frame on top of the hot bed mixture.
Bury pots and trays up to their rims in the warm soil.
Spread 6-8in of soil in the frame.
Hot bed mixture, about 3ft deep, of fresh manure and leaves.

more light through. On the other hand, good-quality plastic is cheaper, safer, easier to move, and does not break easily.

Soil 'fur'

For several years a green, furry coating has invaded the soil under my cloches. Is it harmful and how can I get rid of it?

Relax – it's only moss and it won't damage your plants. Moss likes moist, organic conditions, and using peat, compost and organic fertilisers such as blood and bone will encourage it. If, nevertheless, you want to deter its spread, lightly stir the surface with a hand fork or trowel now and again in sunny weather, especially if the soil has recently been watered. This, and better ventilation, will make the moss dry out. If your soil contains a lot of clay, work in some grit or perlite to improve the drainage. As a last resort, water the soil with a lawn mosskiller containing dichlorophen – this should kill the moss without harming the plants.

ALL ABOUT USING A COLD FRAME

There is no difference in principle between a cold frame and a small greenhouse, except for the height of plants you can grow. Nevertheless, there are some special rules to bear in mind when using a cold frame.

- Position a cold frame facing south in full sun. Protection from north or east winds will keep it warmer in the winter.
- A 3-6in layer of good, quickly draining soil makes a suitable basis for growing. Fork over the soil inside and prepare a fine, crumbly tilth each time before sowing vegetables such as carrots, lettuce and radish. Incorporate peat and fertilisers to maintain the soil in good condition.
- Keep pots and trays containing young plants near the glass to prevent them becoming leggy. Set the pots and trays on old bricks to achieve this. Clean glass will also help.
- If possible, ventilate on the side away from the wind. Avoid high temperatures and musty air – both can encourage the rapid development of fungus diseases.
- Protect tender plants by draping sacking, rugs or ground sheets over the frame at night when frosts are expected. Cover up before sunset, rather than after dark, to help to trap the day's warm air inside the frame.
- Use plastic netting, or a liquid shading paint which can be rubbed off in the autumn, to prevent sunscorch and high temperature damage in warm weather. Ventilate fully during hot weather – by taking the frame tops right off – but remember that even then you may have to shade the plants.
- Keep the frame in good condition and free from debris such as broken flowerpots and decaying wood. Otherwise woodlice, slugs and snails may congregate. If necessary, use slug pellets to protect susceptible plants.
- Root diseases or soil sickness may occur if the soil is regularly used for the same types of plants. To prevent this, shift the position of the frame each year if possible. Otherwise move the crops or replace the soil each year.

CLUB ROOT

Outlook glum

I've just moved house and found that my new garden is infected with club root. My neighbour says there's nothing much to be done about it. Is he right?

To a large extent yes. The spores of the fungus can remain in the soil for 20 years or more, germinating whenever a potential host is planted, probably due to some chemical reaction from the roots.

Wallflowers and stocks fall victim, as do radishes, brussels sprouts, cabbages, cauliflowers, swedes and turnips.

Don't give up hope entirely, though. A few painstaking measures will reduce the worst effects. Because the disease thrives on soggy, acid soils, make sure your soil is well drained, and spread about 8oz of hydrated lime on every square yard. Then, when planting susceptible seedlings, treat the planting holes with calomel (mercurous chloride). Dip the seedling's roots in a solution of calomel as well (make up the solution according to the manufacturer's instructions). Alternatively, try treating the soil with Armillatox.

If the plants later begin to look limp, try earthing up the stems. That encourages more roots to form from the newly buried sections, and helps to keep the worst of the disease at bay until after harvest time. Club root, by the way, does not affect the edibility of a crop, only its yield.

Finally, good garden hygiene will also help. Dig up all diseased plants when cropping has finished and burn them.

Don't forget that you yourself can spread the infection – so whenever you have finished working on a contaminated patch make sure you scrub boots and tools with hot, soapy water before moving to a clean area. And, of course, never take an infected transplant to a disease-free site.

ROOT AND BRANCH *Weak and yellowing leaves are the visible warning signs of club root disease. The clinching symptom, though, is underground: knobbed and swollen roots.*

COLOUR

A spring colour theme

My garden always seems to be such a muddle of colour in spring – very pretty but rather disorganised. Can I introduce a seasonal theme that would bring some order to the scene?

Your simplest approach is to select a single colour that reflects or evokes the seasonal mood, and then build a tonal blend around the colour. For example, you could make yellow your base colour and combine it with dabs of white and blue. To set the scene and bring you out of winter into spring, there is the evergreen shrub *Mahonia japonica*, whose fragrant, lemon-yellow blooms appear from January to March. From March to April, the yellow catkin-like flowers of *Corylopsis willmottiae* provide a brave show; you could also use *Forsythia suspensa* which has a rather more delicate appearance than the large-flowered forsythias.

Jew's mallow (*Kerria japonica*), with its bright, butter-yellow blooms, will continue the colour theme through April and May. Indeed, the shrub show could be brought to a climax in May with the 6ft arching cascade of creamy-yellow flowers of 'Warminster Broom' (*Cytisus* x *praecox*).

Bulbs immediately spring to mind for spring planting – and for your yellow theme, you have a huge selection. Among the earliest, try planting *Narcissus cyclamineus* 'February Gold' mixed with clumps of *Crocus aureus* 'Dutch Yellow'. To follow on immediately, you could use the trumpet daffodil *Narcissus* 'Golden Harvest' which naturalises well in grass. Among tulips, try the water-lily tulip, *Tulipa kaufmanniana*, with its creamy star-shaped flowers (March-April), or the lily-flowered varieties 'West Point' and 'Arkadia', both of which bloom in April. One of the smallest of all tulips, the March-flowering *T. tarda*, produces several white and yellow blooms from each bulb, and is perfect for the border edge or a rock garden.

Continue the yellow spring theme in border perennials, with jaunty yellow primroses (*Primula vulgaris*), flowering in March and April. Behind these you could plant *Paeonia mlokosewitschii*, with its 4in wide lemon-yellow blooms, or one of the hellebores, either *Helleborus foetidus* (bell-like blooms of pale greenish-yellow from March to May), or the Corsican hellebore, *Helleborus argutifolius*, which has yellow-tinged, lime-green flowers. For late spring, try the short but bushy *Euphorbia polychroma*.

For a dash of white, use *Anemone blanda* 'White Splendour', snowdrops (*Galanthus nivalis*), snowflakes (*Leucojum vernum*), or the robust *Narcissus triandrus* 'Thalia'. If you have space for a white-flowered shrub, you could plant *Camellia* x *williamsii*, *Viburnum* x *burkwoodii* or *Skimmia japonica*, all of which bloom in spring.

For blue, the bulbs of the brilliant glory of the snow (*Chionodoxa luciliae*) are hard to beat. A little later – April – and sporting subtle lilac-blue flowers is *Ipheion uniflorum*. You could also select a rhododendron such as 'Blue Tit', which is small enough (3ft high) to fit most gardens without becoming obtrusive. If you have enough space, it could be backed by the 4-8ft rhododendron 'Yellow Hammer', which will continue the yellow background into May.

Bridging the gap

As the year advances, my garden builds up to a crescendo of colour with the spring bulbs. In high summer, too, the effect is gorgeous as the herbaceous borders and bedding plants assert themselves. But in early summer there's a gap between the two displays when the garden seems positively dull and bedraggled, almost boring in its lack of colour. Can you suggest a few plants that might cheer it up a bit?

The 'June gap', the brief hiatus between the two great flowering periods of the year, is a phenomenon that vexes many gardeners. It seems unfair. The air is balmy, the light is brilliant, fading to long sunsets and hushed twilights. Things grow apace, but flowers are few and far between. Actually, there are quite a lot of plants gardeners could grow to fill the gap, but perhaps in the excitement of planning the spring and summer displays, the June plants simply get overlooked.

SPRING CLEAN *The lemon-fresh blooms of* Paeonia mlokosewitschii *open in April-May.*

Against the solid green of the summer foliage try some flowers which come in rich reds and purples. Start off with some early-flowering gladioli, for instance, among which is *G. byzantinus*, with flowers of a vivid

COLOUR SPREAD *A host of golden daffodils gleam beneath and beyond a canopy of blossom on a flowering cherry,* Prunus serrulata.

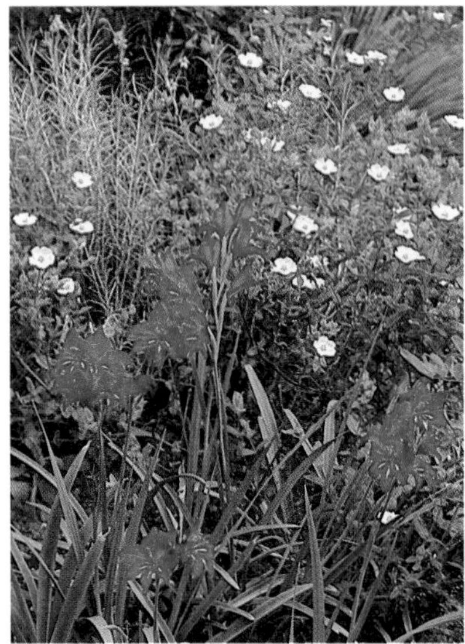

RICH RED *Miniature gladioli flame below a white-flowered* Cistus x platysepala.

GLOWING PINK *A rhododendron bursts into bloom beside* Cytisus scoparius *'Burkwoodii'.*

RED SPIKES *A forest of* Primula *'Bonfire' crackles against* Rhododendron *'Brocade'.*

MINI-MAUVE *Tiny blooms of* Oxalis articulata *twinkle between large oriental poppies.*

dark purple. Reinforce this with the brilliant cerise and maroon of peonies, and perhaps the deep purple and mauve of honesty, *Lunaria annua*. Foxgloves are almost the badge of midsummer, and might look well with the vast papery flowers of oriental poppies, *Papaver orientale*.

Among useful shrubs is the cheerful crimson broom *Cytisus scoparius* 'Burkwoodii', while on acid soils you could try the rhododendrons 'Bagshot Ruby' or the blood-red 'Grenadier'. Good companions for these would be bright clusters of the tall (2½ft) *Primula japonica* 'Miller's Crimson'.

June is also the month for early roses. This is the time of the crimson *Rosa californica* 'Plena' or 'Zéphirine Drouhin' with its cerise flowers, and of the red and velvety rugosa 'Roseraie de l'Hay'.

All in all, there's no reason for June despondency. But, should doubts still linger, here are a few more suggestions:

Aesculus indica (Indian horse chestnut, 25ft tall, white flowers).
Camassia cusickii (bulb, 2-3ft tall, mauve-blue flowers).
Campanula carpatica (perennial, 9-12in, blue flowers).
Cistus x *corbariensis* (rock rose, shrub, 3-4ft, white flowers).
Cistus x *purpureus* (shrub, 3-5ft, pinky-mauve flowers).
Cornus canadensis (dogwood, shrub, 4-6in, spread 2ft, white flowers).
Cotoneaster dammeri (shrub, 2-4in, spread 7ft, white flowers).
Dicentra formosa (perennial, 12-18in, pink flowers).
Epimedium grandiflorum (perennial, 12in, pink flowers).
Gaillardia 'Goblin' (perennial, 9-12in tall, red and yellow flowers).
Gaultheria shallon (shrub, 4-6ft, pink or white flowers).
Geranium endressii 'Wargrave Pink' (perennial, 12-18in, pink flowers).
Hypericum calycinum (St John's wort, shrub, 18in tall, yellow flowers).
Iris kaempferi (perennial, 3ft, blue colours).
Kalmia latifolia (shrub, 6-8ft, pink flowers).
Lupinus arboreus (tree lupin, perennial, 3-4ft, yellow flowers).
Olearia ilicifolia (shrub, 7-9ft, white flowers and silvery leaves).
Philadelphus 'Virginal' (mock orange, shrub, 10ft, scented white flowers).
Phlox subulata 'Bonita' (perennial, 2-4in, light blue flowers).
Potentilla fruticosa 'Mandschurica' (shrub, 1-2ft, white flowers).
Prunus laurocerasus 'Otto Luyken' (shrub, 15ft, white flowers).
Sempervivum montanum (houseleek, perennial, 2in, spread 9in, purple flowers).
Vaccinium vitis-idaea (mountain cranberry, shrub, 6in, pink flowers).
Weigela 'Abel Carrière' (shrub, 4-5ft tall, rose flowers).

The cool summer look

I'm tired of my summer garden scheme – its reds and oranges and yellows are much too 'hot' and are rather startling to the eye on a bright, sunny day. I want to cool the whole flower display down and introduce a more sophisticated look. What should I do?

For something different, try basing the colour scheme on the primary colour blue to give the garden a cool look on those hot midsummer days.

Obviously, you must build other tones into the scheme – lilacs, mauves and purples –

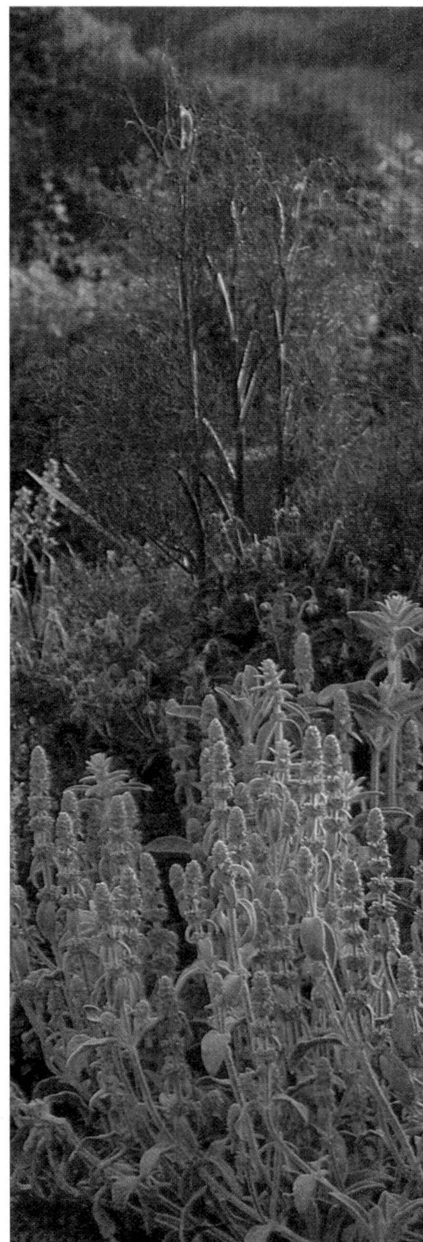

to prevent the scheme from becoming too cold. Nor should you be afraid of introducing a touch of white which will make the blue tones more telling by contrast.

Among the shrubs you could use are: *Buddleia alternifolia* (soft purple in June); the scented *Buddleia fallowiana* 'Lochinch' (soft lavender-blue from July to September); *Ceanothus* x 'Gloire de Versailles' (soft blue from July to September); Himalayan honeysuckle, *Leycesteria formosa* (purple leaf-like bracts covering white flowers in July and August); and the lilac, *Syringa microphylla* (June).

Summer is herbaceous-border time and there are numerous perennials that flower in glorious shades of blue and complementary colours. Among the most popular plants in this group are delphiniums and lupins (which flower from June to August).

You could also try: *Anchusa azurea* 'Loddon Royalist' (deep pure blue in July); *Campanula lactiflora* 'Pritchard's Variety' (lavender-blue from June to September); hound's tongue, *Cynoglossum nervosum* (vivid blue in June and July); catmint, *Nepeta* x *faassenii* (lavender-blue in June); *Salvia* x *superba* (deep purple from July to September); varieties of *Scabiosa caucasica* (blue shades from June to September); and *Veronica incana* (clear blue from June to August).

To add contrast to your blue scheme, a touch of long-lasting pink could be introduced with the purple cone flower, *Echinacea purpurea* (July to September). You could also add a splash of white to the canvas with *Lychnis coronaria* 'Alba' (June to September); the madonna lily, *Lilium candidum* (June); the turk's-cap lily, *Lilium martagon* 'Album' (July); or *Phlox maculata* 'Alba' (July to September).

SUMMER BLUES *Purple spires of* Campanula grandis *rise among the paler stars of* C. lactiflora. *Beyond are the blue spires of* Delphinium elatum, *in front a pink* Erigeron speciosus.

FLOWERLESS *You don't need flowers for colour. Here it comes from the burgundy leaves of* Berberis thunbergii *'Rose Glow' and the yellow berries of* Pyracantha rogersiana *'Flava'.*

PINK PERENNIAL Polygonum affine *makes a valuable and colourful ground-cover plant.*

BRIGHT-EYED *Michaelmas daisies bloom in a variety of colours from September to November.*

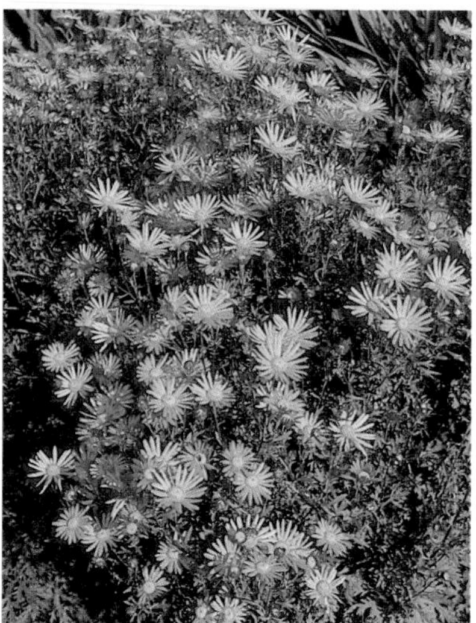

EASY TO GROW Chrysanthemum rubellum *needs no specialist care to produce its display.*

A splash of autumn flowers

The deciduous trees and shrubs in the gardens either side of mine provide a splendid autumn show. With youngsters in the family, I can't spare the space for such plants, but is there something I could grow that would liven up my garden at this time of year.

Yes, there are plenty of herbaceous perennials you could grow to reflect the colours of the dying leaves on the trees and shrubs surrounding your garden. Fiery reds, oranges and bronzes will also add a touch of warmth to the garden during those cool autumn days.

For a start, there's a huge selection from the Michaelmas daisies, both *Aster novae-angliae* and *A. novi-belgii*. They provide a wealth of colour from September through to November, from bright pink to deep carmine-red. Some of the perennial chrysanthemum species are also worth looking at – though maybe not the florists' types which need a fair amount of specialist care. For bright crimson, plant *Chrysanthemum rubellum* 'Duchess of Edinburgh', or, for a purple-red, 'Royal Command'. Both make a good link with your summer flowers (see *The cool summer look*, page 86) and bloom between August and October. Then there are the varieties of *Helenium autumnale*, most of which start flowering in late summer but continue their show into September. They include 'Baudirektor Linne' (orange and mahogany-red) and 'Bruno' (mahogany).

AUTUMN SUN *The bright yellows of* Helenium autumnale *glow on into early autumn.*

LATE STARTER Zauschneria californica *opens its flowers only in September and October.*

PINK POWDER-PUFFS Sedum spectabile *'Carmen' holds its fluffy flowers until October.*

You might also like to try the stonecrop *Sedum* x 'Autumn Joy', which in August bears flat heads of deep pink starry flowers; the colour deepens in autumn to bronze-red and lasts until the first frosts. Another late summer and early autumn perennial is *Polygonum affine* which will provide a pinkish-red carpet beneath your asters.

To sound the last notes of the autumn symphony there is *Zauschneria californica*, which bursts into colour in September and October with flaming scarlet flowers. Though essentially a rock garden plant, and not hardy enough to withstand severe winters, it is very vigorous and is probably better planted on a wall or bank where there is room for its 1½-2ft height and spread.

Berry brightness

My garden gets terribly drab in winter. I've seen many lovely evergreen shrubs, but can you tell me which ones will give me berries so that I can have a bright splash of colour in the garden from late autumn through winter until my bulbs start to flower?

You don't say how large your garden is, but if it's on the small side you'll probably have room for only a few specimen evergreens. Try, for instance, *Aucuba japonica* 'Variegata', or *Pyracantha coccinea* 'Lalandei', both of which have red berries. For ideas on deciduous shrubs with berries, see *Mostly for the birds*, page 312.

Autumn spectacular

We've just moved into the country and for the first time we have quite a sizable garden. There's an area of rough paddock at the bottom where I'd like to plant a few trees to complement the view from the house and especially to get some autumn colour. Can you suggest some that will provide a really brilliant spectacle?

Certainly. All the information you need – name, height and colour – can be found in *Trees for autumn colour*, page 348.

Winter wonderland

I do get tired of the camouflage-net look my garden has in winter – all muted greens and browns. Can you suggest a planting scheme to brighten the dreary months?

Not every gardener would agree with you. Winter is a breathing space, both for man and garden, and the season is by no means devoid of charm. The skeletal trees have great beauty, whether whipping in a gale or drooping in a mist, and on bright mornings when twigs are painted with hoar frost and ice sparkles in the gullies of flowerbeds the scene is invigorating, not dreary.

All the same, there are days when it seems that the sun will never return, and on these occasions a little colour does give some reassurance. You might, for example, lighten dark December with the white and gold flowers of the Christmas rose, *Helleborus niger*, or a bed or tub of the varieties of *Viola* x *wittrockiana*, tough winter-flowering pansies that are indifferent to weather and appear in a multitude of colours. On sandy soil you could plant winter-flowering heathers, such as varieties of *Erica carnea*.

For January colour, try aconites and snowdrops and a witch hazel, *Hamamelis mollis* 'Pallida', which has dense yellow flowers, faintly flushed with claret red. Several heathers come into flower at this time, and it's a splendid month for foliage – the blue leaves of the gum tree *Eucalyptus gunnii*, for example, or the golden glow of the cypress *Chamaecyparis pisifera* 'Gold Spangle'.

February is a month that sometimes could induce garden-lovers to emigrate, but it has its compensations: the superb honeysuckle shrub *Lonicera fragrantissima*, for instance, with its sweetly scented creamy flowers; and such harbingers of spring as *Mahonia lomariifolia* with its yellow, trailing, fragrant flower spikes. Quite a number of early narcissi force their way through the icy turf this month, as do some forsythias; and it's a great time to see the brilliant stems and decorative bark of willows and dogwoods before they put on their leaves.

All in all, British gardens have much to offer in winter, and a little planning and a few hours of browsing in the garden centre can put yours among the liveliest.

Below are some more suggestions for winter colour. When you're thinking about where to position any of these winter plants, give a thought to how they'll look from the house. Since you often can't get out into the garden in winter, try to place them so that you can enjoy them from the living room or kitchen window. The dates given apply to an average winter in the South of England. In a warm season in the West, against the shelter of a south-facing wall, some of the flowers might appear as much as a month earlier. In an exposed position in a bitter Northern winter, they might be weeks later.

DECEMBER

Acacia longifolia (tree or shrub, 12ft tall, yellow flowers, suitable only for mild districts in the South and West).

Acer griseum (tree, 10-20ft, peeling cinnamon bark).

Arundinaria nitida (grass/bamboo, 7-9ft, purple stems).

Betula utilis (tree, 50ft, cinnamon-coloured bark).

Chimonanthus praecox (winter sweet, shrub, 6-8ft, yellow flowers).

Cornus alba 'Sibirica' (dogwood, shrub, 4-6ft, red shiny stems).

Cotoneaster frigidus (shrub, 8-10ft, red berries).

Crocus imperati (bulb, 4in tall, violet flowers).

Crocus laevigatus (bulb, 4in tall, lilac flowers).

Elaeagnus pungens 'Maculata' (shrub, 6-8ft, gold splash on each leaf).

Erica carnea 'Winter Beauty' (shrub, 12in tall, pink flowers).

Erica x *darleyensis* 'Silver Beads' (shrub, 12-18in, white flowers).

Euonymus fortunei 'Coloratus' (shrub, trailing habit, purple-green leaves).

Iris unguicularis (perennial, 15in tall, blue flowers).

Lonicera auriculata (shrub, 4-6ft, white flowers).

DOUBLE YELLOW *The Chinese witch hazel,* Hamamelis mollis, *has sparkling yellow flowers in winter – and bright yellow leaves in autumn.*

WINTER MIXTURE *Variegated holly, white* Viburnum tinus *and a red-berried pyracantha.*

ERICA PAIR E. carnea *'Myretoun Ruby' and the white* E. x darleyensis *'Silberschmelze'.*

SCENT ON HIGH *The 10-12ft tall* Mahonia lomariifolia *has fragrant winter flowers.*

SPRING CUP Helleborus lividus corsicus *opens its flowers in late winter or early spring.*

Lonicera standishii (shrub, 6-8ft tall, creamy scented flowers).
Lunaria annua (biennial, 2-2½ft tall, silvery seed pods).
Nandina domestica (shrub, 3-5ft, scarlet or white berries).
Thuja occidentalis 'Rheingold' (conifer, 4-5ft, gold foliage).
Thymus 'Andersons Gold' (perennial, 2in, scented golden foliage).
Vaccinium vitis-idaea 'Koralle' (mountain cranberry, shrub, 6-9in, coral berries).
Viburnum davidii (shrub, 2-3ft tall, blue berries).

JANUARY

Camellia reticulata 'Captain Rawes' (shrub, 8ft, carmine flowers).
Camellia sasanqua (shrub, 6-8ft, white flowers).
Camellia x *williamsii* 'J.C. Williams' (shrub, 10ft, pink flowers).
Chaenomeles speciosa (shrub, 6-8ft, red flowers).
Erica carnea 'King George' (shrub, 12in, pink flowers) and *E.c.* 'Vivellii' (shrub, 8in tall, red flowers).
Hedera helix 'Buttercup' (climber, 12ft tall, yellow foliage).

Iris histrioides 'Major' (bulb, 4in, blue flowers).
Lonicera x *purpusii* (shrub, 8ft, scented cream flowers).
Senecio x 'Sunshine' (shrub, 3ft, silver foliage).
Thymus x *citriodorus* 'Silver Queen' (shrub, 9-12in, silver leaves).
FEBRUARY
Betula costata (tree, 50ft, creamy-white bark).
Camellia x *williamsii* 'Donation' (shrub, 8ft tall, pink flowers).
Chaenomeles x *superba* 'Etna' (shrub, 6-8ft, red flowers).
Crocus tomasinianus (bulb, 3-5in, lilac flowers).
Cyclamen coum (bulb, 4in, pink flowers).
Daphne mezereum 'Album' (shrub, 3-5ft tall, scented white flowers).
Daphne odora 'Aureomarginata' (shrub, 3-5ft tall, scented pink flowers).
Erica carnea 'Aurea' (shrub, 10in tall, yellow foliage and red flowers).
Galanthus elwesii (snowdrop, bulb, 4in tall, white flowers).
Garrya elliptica (shrub, 10ft, greenish catkins).
Ilex aquifolium 'Golden Queen' (shrub, 15ft, golden foliage).
Iris reticulata (bulb, 4-6in, purple and yellow flowers).
Jasminum nudiflorum (shrub, 6-8ft, yellow flowers).
Leucojum vernum (snowflake, bulb, 8in, white flowers).
Narcissus 'W.P. Milner' (bulb, 8in tall, yellow flowers).
Narcissus cyclamineus 'February Gold' (bulb, 12in, yellow flowers).
Prunus davidiana (tree, 20ft, pink flowers).
Salix aegyptiaca (willow tree, 50ft, yellow catkins, violet bark on young stems).
Salix alba 'Chermesina' (shrub, 10-12ft, orange bark).
Salix daphnoides (shrub, 12-20ft, violet stems and yellow catkins).
Skimmia japonica 'Rubella' (shrub, 3ft, red flowers).
Viburnum x *bodnantense* 'Dawn' (shrub, 8ft, scented pink flowers).

Concealing a wall

I've built a garage-cum-workshop down the side of my garden. Useful though it is, its long wall – of rather dull brick – does seem to crowd in, and on sunless days can look quite oppressive. What do you suggest that might add a little joy to the scene?

The swiftest cure for claustrophobia of this kind is *Polygonum baldschuanicum*, the Russian vine. To say that it is vigorous is an understatement. It can throw out 10ft of growth in a year, and between July and November, if you give it some wires to climb, it will smother any eyesore in a froth of pale green foliage and long greenish-white flower sprays. But it can take over, with awesome results, and if you can bear with your wall a little longer you might do better to plant some clematis instead. These, too, given a little support, will grow over, through and around anything, and come in all kinds of cheering colours – shades of blue, purple, yellow, red and white. You will find a number of clematis species and varieties suggested in *Pick of the clematis*, pages 74-75.

Excellent though these plants are, perhaps a better idea still would be to create your own entirely original colour scheme with a mingling of climbers. The choice is wide, but just to get inspiration started, how about planting the ivy *Hedera helix* 'Goldheart' along the wall. Or try the yellow-edged leaves of *Hedera colchica* 'Dentata Variegata' married with the brilliant red and yellow flowers of *Tropaeolum tuberosum*.

Making a white garden

I recently visited the gardens at Sissinghurst Castle and was entranced by the cool beauty of the White Garden. I'd like to introduce some of the effects into part of my garden. Could you tell me how to go about it?

I should imagine Vita Sackville-West had a lot more space to play with at Sissinghurst than you have in your garden. So the general scheme here is designed to be expanded or contracted according to the amount of space you have available.

To get the best effect, start by creating a special area that will become a cool oasis of calm among the other colours of your garden. You could base this on a patio with beds on all sides – it doesn't have to be rectangular. Just make it fit, as artistically as possible, the area you have available. Enclose it with a pergola.

Now to your planting scheme. To avoid making the show insipid, grow a low hedge of evergreen box behind the beds and between the pergola posts. The slow-growing *Buxus sempervirens* 'Elegantissima', with its green leaves edged with silver, is a good choice, and can be clipped to a height of about 3ft. It should take only three or four years to reach that height.

You'll need some more height in the scheme, so place a few shrubs around the arbour. There are quite a few white-flowered ones you could try.

About 5ft high is the rock rose *Cistus* 'Pat'. It's evergreen and you'll get a succession of exquisite 5in wide blooms from late May until early July.

Larger and more spectacular is bridal wreath, *Spiraea* x *arguta* (height and spread 6-8ft). In May it explodes in a fountain of white spray, with masses of flowers carried

OVER THE WALL *Purple* Clematis *'Perle d'Azur' and the white-flowered* Rosa *'Mermaid'.*

on slender, arching stems. Another evergreen of the same size, *Choisya ternata* – commonly known as the Mexican orange – gives you a bonus. Its numerous clusters of flowers are sweetly scented, and while its main show is in April and May, there's a good chance of flurries of white later, especially in a mild autumn.

If you don't mind deciduous shrubs, you could do worse than plant a tree peony such as *Paeonia suffruticosa* 'Rock's Variety'. It won't get much bigger than 5ft in height or spread and you'll be delighted by its enormous 6in wide flowers in May. If you prefer a smaller deciduous shrub (under 4ft high), consider planting the mock orange *Philadelphus* 'Bouquet Blanc'. Clusters of delicately orange-scented, double flowers flood the bush in June and July.

There's no harm in imitating Sissinghurst in your selection of border plants – among the taller ones are the waving white spires of *Eremurus himalaicus*, *Thalictrum aquilegifolium* 'Alba' and *Iris florentina*.

Towards the front of the border, plant 'White Dame' wallflowers mixed with tulips – try 'White Parrot' or the double late variety, 'Mount Tacoma' – and underplant with delicate pansies such as 'White Swan'.

All these will give you a late spring show in May, but the climax of your white garden is in June and July. For this focal summer display (and depending on the amount of space you've got), make your selection from *Campanula persicifolia* 'Planiflora Alba', the pure white Belladonna delphinium 'Moerheimii', the hardy *Geranium dalmaticum* 'Album', *Galega officinalis* 'Alba' (which grows to 3-5ft), and the white turk's-cap lily, *Lilium martagon* 'Album'.

You can let some grey-mauve creep in – say, *Campanula* x *burghaltii* – as well as a few silver foliage plants, such as *Salvia argentea* (which also has white flowers), *Artemisia absinthium* 'Lambrook Silver', *Senecio maritimus* 'Silver Dust' or 'Silver Dwarf', *Cerastium biebersteinii* (snow-in-summer), *Stachys lanata* (lamb's tongue) and *Pulmonaria saccharata* 'Argentea'.

BRIDAL WHITE *A magnificent* Spiraea x arguta *froths above clipped hedges in the White Garden at Sissinghurst Castle. The tulips in front are the variety 'White Triumphator'.*

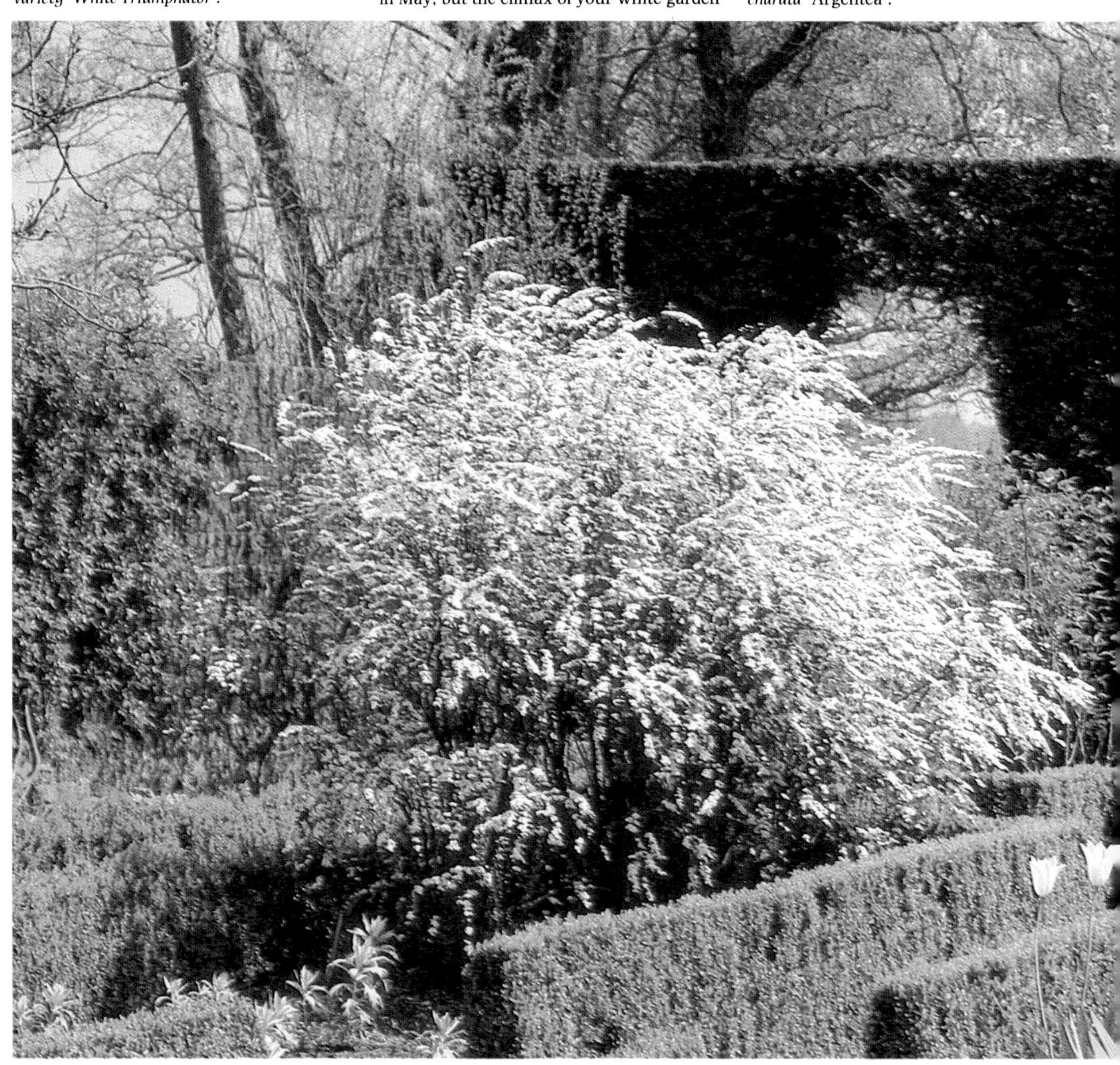

A few large ornamental containers will help break up the formal lines of the patio. You could fill these with *Dianthus deltoides* 'Albus' – it will also grow happily in cracks in the patio – and *Anaphalis triplinervis*. Though it's a tender plant, *Helichrysum microphyllum* is also well worth growing – its leaves will tumble and trail from the pots in a silvery-grey mass.

To put the lid on the scene, so to speak, you can enclose your cool white oasis with a blanket of roses around the pergola. There's the magnificent and vigorous rambler 'Bobbie James', and the climber 'Mme Alfred Carrière'. Both are deliciously scented. The first bears ivory-white blooms in June and July; the second has pink-blushed, white blooms throughout the season.

A garden to touch and smell and hear

My mother's eyesight is fairly bad now, but she still loves gardens and gardening. The other day I began to wonder if it would be possible to design a garden for my mother and for people like her, to whom colour is no longer very important, but whose other senses are just as acute as ever. For such a garden, which plants would you choose?

It's an interesting and challenging proposition, but not an easy one to answer. Obviously there should be a pattern of scented plants, but maybe there should be plants to feel as well, not only for the pleasantness of their touch, but also to help to orientate the garden's owner.

So far as scent is concerned, it might be better to begin with those that have scented foliage, since leaves generally last longer than flowers. Herbs come to mind – marjoram and mint, rosemary and sage, balm, thyme and the rest. All of them are instantly recognisable as individuals, especially if the leaves are crushed in the hand. Grown together, they make a heady bouquet that will flavour the air for yards around on summer afternoons.

Other plants with distinctively aromatic foliage include eucalyptus, geranium (the plant family known to botanists as pelargonium), lavender, burning bush (dictamnus) and the poplar known as balm of Gilead. Strongly fragrant flowers are legion, but among the best are wallflowers, daphne, carnations, heather, broom (genista species), freesias, hyacinth, jasmine, magnolia, tobacco plants, syringa, verbena and, of course, roses and violets.

Plants for touching are not so easy to come by. But how about the chilly smoothness of laurel, and the curves and strong veins of hosta leaves?

Or perhaps the delicate brush of feather grass and the waxy touch of magnolia? Moss roses do indeed have a cool, mossy feel, although they have thorns as well.

Certain poppies seem almost to rustle like expensive wrapping paper, while the gentle silkiness of the leaves of *Stachys lanata* – lamb's tongue – suggest the affection of a young animal. It might be fun, in addition, to add a novelty or two, such as paper birch, with its peeling bark, and the sheer craziness of corkscrew hazel.

As a last thought, what about *sounds*? Consider the gentle susurration of a weeping willow, for instance, or the trembling of an aspen (*Populus tremula*), both of which voice their own individual murmur in the slightest breeze.

Or consider laying out some plants which will attract birds, so as to enliven the garden with their songs. For some suggestions, see *A bird-lover's garden*, page 28, and *Mostly for the birds*, page 312.

POTTED PINK Sedum sieboldii *'Medio-variegatum' will thrive in a pot in mild areas.*

Olde worlde colour

I've moved into a wonderful little stone cottage with a well-established old-fashioned garden. The cottage is divided from the rear part of the garden by a terrace which has a dark and rather dull hedge down one side. Can you suggest something to enliven it?

Your new domain sounds idyllic, so it's all the more important to devote particular thought and care to the curing of your dull, and presumably fairly sunless, patch. There are many alternatives, but the vital thing is that the scheme must not clash with the old-fashioned air of the rest of the garden. Yet it is important, too, to turn your dismal terrace side from a liability to an asset. So here's a scheme that might fit the bill – a mixture of deep reds, purples and greens that would stand out well against both hedge and stone, and unite the two.

Get half a beer barrel – you can buy them in most garden centres – bore holes in the bottom for drainage, and fill it with a mixture of garden soil and peat or compost and add a little bone meal. This will give your scheme height. Plant three or four fuchsias in the barrel. They should be purple-petalled varieties, such as 'Cascade' or 'Mrs Popple', that will arch and tumble over the sides.

Close by you could place an ornamental stone or terracotta pot. The price of such pots is steep, but there are moulded imitations in reconstituted stone and even plastic that will serve just as well, and from even a foot or so away are indistinguishable from the real article. In your pot, plant *Heliotropium* x *hybridum* 'Royal Marine', which grows to 18in and has dark blue-green leaves and large, deep violet flower heads. Round the heliotrope's base, grow begonia varieties such as 'Carmen', which has purple-brown foliage and rose-pink flowers. Begonias need a light soil; John Innes No 2 compost would do admirably. To help your scheme fit into its old-fashioned background, paint your pot with a mixture of milk and cow manure, mixed to a semolina-like consistency. This will encourage the swift growth of mosses and lichens, and rapidly give even a brand new pot a patina of age.

THREE FOR A TREE *Purple-blue* Muscari armeniacum *and creamy* Erythronium revolutum *'White Beauty' make a cheerful spring cluster with yellow jonquils.*

CYCLAMEN CARPET C. hederifolium *will bloom under a tree from August to November.*

EARLY SHOW Anemone blanda *displays its mauve flowers from February to April.*

Colour under trees

A few venerable fruit trees – you could hardly call them an orchard – grow out of the grass at the far end of my garden, and I've been thinking of brightening the patch by turning it into a sort of ornamental wilderness. What should I grow? Bulbs, perhaps?

Bulbs, certainly. The problem with this kind of wild garden is that it will be almost impossible to maintain anything like a continuous display. It will probably be limited instead to the period just before the leaves grow on the trees, and just after they fall off. At those times, of course, bulbous plants are at their most glorious.

The situation you describe sounds extremely hopeful. It is most unlikely that you will have bothered to feed grass growing beneath ancient fruit trees, and it is against this rather starved backdrop that your spring and autumn tapestries will best reveal themselves. Too lush grass will conceal the smaller plants, and too rich soil will encourage the stronger plants to develop at the expense of the rest. Also, since bulbous plants store nutrients manufactured in their leaves after flowering is over, you want them growing in grass that doesn't have to be mowed too often. Ideally, you should mow in late July or early August, and again a few weeks before the autumn bulbs come into flower. As for what to plant, the tapestry image is not a bad one, since what you are planting is not really a wild garden, but an imitation of what, in the Middle Ages, was called a pleasaunce or an arbour.

Begin with the yellow winter aconites that come out in January or February, only a short head in advance of snowdrops. Plant clumps of these, and accompany them with drifts of mauve and lilac *Crocus tomasinianus*. Next on stage could be the anemones: *Anemone blanda*, for instance, which is 6in high and comes in various shades of pale blue, mauve, pink and white; and the native *A. nemorosa*, about the same size and white, pink-flushed or lavender-blue. Next, bring on a grand parade of daffodils, the yellow trumpets of hoop petticoats (*Narcissus bulbocodium*) and the dog's tooth violets, *Erythronium dens-canis*, whose many varieties come in pale purple, clear pink, deep pink or rich purple spotted and striped with brown. If you've got room, you might add primroses to the cast. Altogether the great spring show will last at least until your fruit trees draw a curtain of leaves across the sky.

Not quite so much is available for your autumn display, but it can be impressive enough if you establish a wide girdle of mauve, pink and white *Cyclamen hederifolium* round the base of each tree, and supplement them with colchicums – crocus-like flowers available in a wide array of colours – or with a crocus, *Crocus speciosus*. By the way, when establishing your 'natural' garden, it's a good idea to stand in the middle of the patch and scatter the bulbs and corms about you, pretty well at random. Then plant them where they fall. You'll be surprised, when the flowers appear, how effective this haphazard arrangement can be.

Plotting the plot

With a new plot to work upon, I have a clear canvas on which to compose my own individual gardening colour scheme. Yet, as I go through the catalogues to make my selection, I get more and more perplexed by plants' advertised demands – 'alkaline, clay, sun, moist', 'acid, sand, shade, dry' and so on. Is there an easier rule of thumb I could follow?

Most outdoor plants you are likely to encounter will manage perfectly well in any fertile, well-drained soil that has been reinforced with plenty of well-rotted manure or compost. What the catalogues mean is that certain plants will do better in, say, alkaline soil, or in full sun rather than in partial shade. But provided you've met their basic requirements of adequate light and reasonably good ground to grow in, they'll survive happily enough, and give you a good show year after year.

The exceptions are the acid-lovers. These really will keel over and die in an alkaline soil. There aren't very many of them – a few dozen perhaps among the plants commonly found in British gardens – and even some of these can be grown in raised peat beds, provided that they are divorced from the basic soil. Here are the most usual; to find out if your garden's soil will support them, see *Acid soils*, page 6.

Arctostaphylos (bearberry) – small trees and shrubs; may be grown in peat beds.
Calluna (ling, heather) – shrub; may be grown in peat beds.
Camellia – shrub.
Daboecia (St Dabeoc's heath) – shrub; may be grown in peat beds.
Enkianthus – shrub.
Erica (heather, heath) – shrub; may be grown in peat beds.
Eucryphia – shrub.
Fothergilla – shrub.
Gaultheria – shrub; may be grown in peat.
Gentiana (gentian) – perennial; may be grown in peat beds.
Kalmia (calico bush) – shrub.
Lapageria (Chilean wallflower) – climber.
Lithospermum – perennial.
Magnolia – shrub or tree.
Menziesia – shrub.
Nomocharis – bulb; may be grown in peat.
Nyssa – shrub.
Pernettya – shrub; may be grown in peat.
Philesia – shrub; may be grown in peat beds.
Phyllodoce – shrub; may be grown in peat.
Rhododendron – shrub; may be grown in peat beds.
Vaccinium (bilberry, blueberry, cranberry) – shrub; may be grown in peat beds.

Relieving the gloom

There's a clump of dark firs at the far end of the garden. Each year, they grow taller and more melancholy. Can you suggest something that might cheer them up a bit?

With such a dramatic backdrop of blacks, dark greens and deep shadows – no doubt shot through from time to time by shafts of sunlight – you are luckier than you realise.

There are all sorts of schemes open to you, as garish or as subtle as you like. You might, for instance, make a contrast of trees by putting in a weeping birch, *Betula pendula* 'Youngii', whose drooping branches and silver bark would be admirably set off by the dark, upright habit of the firs. Or there's the golden-leaved form of *Cupressocyparis leylandii* called 'Castlewellan' for year-round brightness. In the South and West, try combining it with a *Photinia villosa*, the ornamental Japanese tree whose leaves flare to brilliant red and gold in autumn. You wouldn't go far wrong, either, by planting a stag's horn sumach – droopy green and fernlike in summer, and a firework display of yellow, crimson and purple in autumn. Partner it, perhaps, with a Japanese maple, *Acer palmatum* 'Senkaki', whose foliage progresses from bright to pale green to yellow as summer advances, and when the leaves fall, displays its branches and twigs of brilliant coral. Any or all of these trees or shrubs would be enhanced by a swathe of naturalised spring bulbs planted in the foreground.

Here's another, and quite different, scheme. Since your firs seem to be thriving, your soil must be at least reasonably acid, so you might think of the trees as the focal point of a piece of idealised moorland and surround them with the kind of companions – or variations of them – that they might have in the wild. Begin with the extraordinary blue-white spruce, *Picea pungens* 'Glauca', and grow a few gorse bushes nearby. Once established, these will put out a mass of yellow, honey-scented flowers from March to May. And even through the rest of the year, one or the other of the bushes will show a golden flash. Spanish broom produces similar fragrant yellow flowers in July and August, but grows taller than gorse and has bright green stems. Alternatively, go for a yellow rhododendron such as *R. campylocarpum*. At the foot of the spruce, you might have a few patches of the trumpet gentian, *Gentiana acaulis*, which puts out vivid blue fanfares in May – though it needs very well-drained soil to thrive.

Finally, as a frame for the group, there could be a collection of heathers, carefully chosen to present a changing pattern of bright flowers and foliage throughout the year. To help you to make your choice, see *Pick of the heathers*, page 180.

HIGHLIGHT *A slender* Acer japonicum *'Aureum' shines against a dark Lawson cypress.*

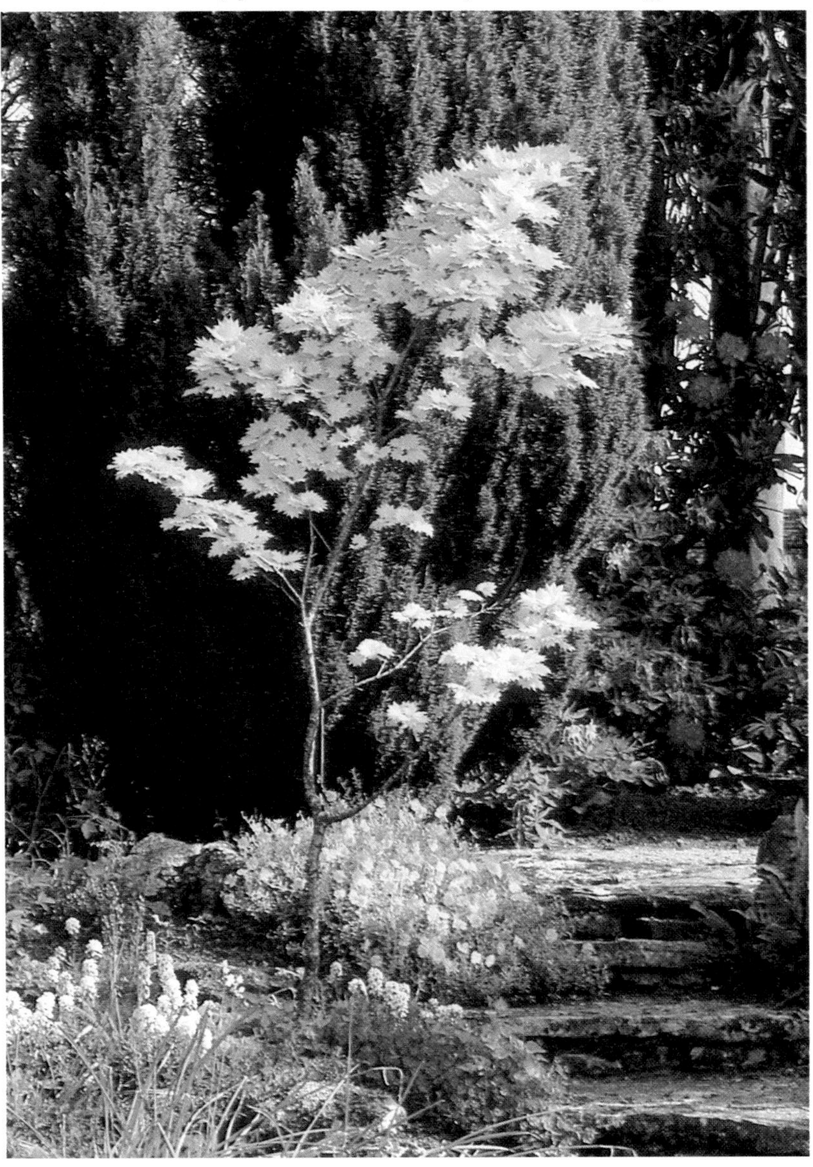

COMPOST

Composting on a small scale

Is a compost heap worth having in a small suburban garden?

Yes. A compost heap is a marvellous investment for any garden, large or small. It gives you a humus-rich soil conditioner for nothing, disposes of vast amounts of kitchen waste and gets rid of lots of garden debris too, including vegetable tops, old bedding plants and grass and hedge cuttings. If you feel that as a feature it doesn't do much to enhance the garden, let the compost build up in a lidded plastic bin instead.

Alternatively, make your compost underground. Dig a trench about two spade blades deep and dump all your waste in that. It won't be as obtrusive as an above-ground heap. As it fills, tread it down and sprinkle it with an activator. Finally, cover it with soil from a new trench. That way you can gradually turn every flower and vegetable bed in the garden into compost-rich earth.

When bins are best

Are ready-made composting bins better than the traditional heaps?

Bins are best in a small garden where there isn't much raw material being produced and it is difficult to hide the heap.

Bins make small amounts of compost much more effectively than open heaps do, mainly because the whole thing is contained. In an enclosed bin, the heat is retained and this improves the conditions for the microorganisms that do the decomposing. Rainwater is prevented from getting at the raw material as it rots down. This results in a drier, hotter compost that is ready sooner than in a heap. And, of course, the lid helps to contain any unpleasant smells.

The case against bins is that good ones can be pretty expensive, and they become full in rather a short space of time.

Speeding the process

Is there any difference between compost activators and accelerators, and are they really necessary?

They're different names for exactly the same thing. They are materials which are added to compost heaps or bins to initiate and maintain the composting process.

All contain nitrogen to feed the microorganisms responsible for decomposition, and some also have a neutralising agent to stop the heap getting too acidic. The best also incorporate microbes to start the composting process. Microbes do not like acid conditions, so to get the fastest and most thorough decomposition the heap needs to be neutral or, preferably, alkaline – which is why many experts recommend that a compost heap should be sprinkled with lime every foot or so as it is built up.

Activators are not essential for compost making. The microorganisms from the soil will go to work on the heap anyway. But an activator will speed up composting by as much as two or three months and, more importantly, will ensure that composting is even throughout the heap.

The case for a shredder

I'm thinking of buying a compost shredder. How do I justify the expense?

It's worth having a shredder only if you have enough work for it to do. Shredders are designed to chop up raw material that would otherwise have to be left out of a compost heap or bin because of its coarseness.

The material includes prunings, twigs, small branches, tough hedge clippings (especially those from conifers), brassica stalks (brussels sprouts and sprouting broccoli), and old newspapers which have been used in the bottom of a pet's cage.

If you have enough material of that sort to warrant spending £50 to £100, then it's well worth it. Much of the hard, woody vegetation that would have to be dumped or burnt without a shredder is the very stuff that is best for composting and returning to the ground. Even if you haven't enough material of your own, it might be worth sharing the cost with someone else. As to which type to buy, the best for an average garden is probably an electrically driven machine. It's effortless to use and far quicker than a hand-operated type.

Getting started

Is there any recommended way to begin a compost heap? And what sort of compost should I aim for?

There are two types of compost the gardener can make; each requires a slightly different treatment, but the results are approximately the same. The first comes from the conventional compost heap of lawn mowings, vegetable peelings, tea leaves and all kinds of garden rubbish except fallen leaves. The second type is made from these leaves, put in a separate heap and converted into a compost called leaf mould.

The reason for separating fallen leaves from the main heap is that when layered with mixed compost they form a soggy mass that defies decomposition. The flat surfaces of the leaves press together, excluding air and the microorganisms that help the pile to decompose. Then, too, the leaves are fibrous and dry, and therefore decompose more slowly than living green material, slowing down the activity of the whole heap.

The best way to compost leaves is in a small wire-netting enclosure, 4in layers of leaves being interspersed with light coverings of soil. If left alone, such a heap will break down to leaf compost in about a year.

Mixed compost requires about six to eight months. Adding a proprietary compost activator may cut the time by two or three months. As with leaves, a container is required to hold the refuse, and although elaborate compost bins are available from garden centres, you will do nearly as well with something knocked up from old planks, wire mesh or corrugated iron.

All that is needed is a three-sided container with a removable roof, though even this may be left out if the heap is covered with a plastic sheet or a layer of soil to throw off rain. Prepare two containers, and use them so that one is full of decomposing compost while the second is being filled with waste material. By the time the second is full, the compost in the first should be ready.

Each heap should be as big as practicable – the larger the heap the hotter it gets and the more efficiently it decomposes. For an unenclosed heap, aim for a minimum size of 5ft by 5ft and about 3ft high.

Choose a dry, free-draining position for the heaps. Wet, soggy material takes considerably longer to decompose than refuse stacked on a quick-draining base and it often becomes stagnant and unpleasant to handle. Stack the waste in 4-6in layers, making, if possible, alternating layers of tough, coarse material such as torn newspaper with soft green weeds or lawn mowings. If farm manure is available, spread a layer of it about every 12in. Soil may be used instead, but in any event a 3in thick layer of one or the other should be introduced at regular intervals.

Throughout the stacking process, keep the heap level by lightly treading the raised areas. This breaks up stems which cause air pockets and hamper decomposition. Regular additions of fresh waste will do a better job than occasional large deposits, for small quantities of green matter 'feed' the action of decomposition, maintaining a steady temperature in the heap which will turn it into compost quicker. You need, too, a constant heat within the pile to destroy weed seeds and diseased plant remains.

Keep an old damp sack on top of the heap; this will prevent the top layer from drying out. The lower layers will shrink as they break down into compost, so keep adding new material until the heap is full and firm. Top up with a 4in thick capping of soil and leave the heap for a minimum of six months or so before use. The final capping with soil is essential not only to retain heat and exclude rain, but also to absorb the ammonia that is given off during decomposition. Ammonia is a form of soluble nitrogen-rich fertiliser which should be retained if possible.

Stick with rhubarb

I'm told that rhubarb leaves shouldn't be put into a compost heap. Why is this, and are there any other things that should be avoided?

Don't you believe it. In the sort of quantities the normal household gets through, rhubarb leaves are no problem at all on the compost heap. The reason behind the legend is that rhubarb leaves are extremely acid and take longer to rot down than other materials because the alkali-loving microorganisms in the heap tend to avoid them.

Most things are perfectly safe to compost provided there is a good mix. Certain plant substances, such as tough evergreen leaves, pine needles, sawdust and wood shavings, newspaper and dry autumn leaves should not be piled on in large quantities. All make valuable compost in time but are best mixed with softer, greener material so that they decompose more quickly.

Dwellers in compost

My compost heap is covered in little flies, and I find red worms wriggling through it. Are these a good or bad thing?

More or less anything that you find crawling or flying around a compost heap is beneficial. They're part of nature's machinery for disposing of dead organic matter.

You should never do anything to get rid of the red worms but, if the flies become troublesome, a thorough dusting with HCH will dispose of them.

You may also notice a fungus developing on many of the woodier raw materials. This is also perfectly harmless and is just another of the organisms necessary to the breaking down of organic matter.

Off-the-shelf compost

Is it worth buying ready-made garden compost from the shops?

Yes and no. Most ready-made garden composts (as opposed to potting composts) are based on concentrated or composted manure, which is of course valuable as a soil conditioner and, to some extent, as a fertiliser. It also saves you the trouble of having to make your own compost.

Despite these advantages, shop-bought compost has one major disadvantage: cost. The main benefit of any garden compost – homemade or shop-bought – lies not in its quality, but in its quantity. It's the sheer bulk of organic matter that helps the soil to which it's added drain more freely and yet absorb water and nutrients more readily. To make an appreciable difference to any sizable patch of soil takes barrowloads of compost – which would be vastly expensive to buy.

Manure versus compost

Is farmyard manure better than garden compost?

There's nothing between them. Obviously the quality of both materials is going to vary, sometimes greatly. However, comparing a good sample of each, there is virtually no difference at all – either in their value as soil conditioners or in the amount of plant food they contain.

This may appear to be odd, for many gardeners hold to the belief that manure is the answer to all soil problems.

In fact, though, both manure and compost are made from the same raw vegetation and they have both been decomposed by microorganisms. The only real difference is that one has been transformed in a compost heap and the other inside an animal.

Re-using seed compost

When I've bought a fairly expensive bag of seed compost, it seems an awful waste to use it only once. Can I use it a second time?

As a seed compost, no. The whole point of buying a special compost for sowing seeds and rooting cuttings is that it is – or should be – sterile and, therefore, completely free from diseases that could kill the young plants.

Once a compost has been used, that guarantee no longer holds good. In addition, many of the nutrients present in the original compost will have gone.

You can, however, keep used composts of this sort for other garden purposes, such as forcing rhubarb. You don't need a compost of the same high standard for this as you do for sowing seeds or raising young cuttings.

Composting newspaper

A friend tells me that old newspaper is good for the garden. Is this true?

Yes indeed – and in two main ways. Newsprint is made of plant cell material and so is a perfect ingredient for your compost heap. Tear the pages into strips, then mix them with lawn clippings, hedge clippings and other green waste, all in equal volumes. Damp the mixture lightly with a watering can as you add it to the heap.

Thereafter, keep the compost covered so that it does not get too wet, and also to conserve the heat being generated inside as the materials decompose.

Newspaper is also good as an underground moisture reservoir for vegetables such as peas and beans. When you dig the trenches for these crops before sowing, mix thin strips of torn paper with earth and peat, then spread the mixture along the bottoms of the trenches. The paper will not rot as quickly as in a compost heap, but it still makes a very useful addition to the soil.

A deodorant for compost

My compost comes out as a horrible slimy mess that smells frightful. Is this stuff any use at all, and how can I make that lovely crumbly material that we're always being told about?

You've got the mixture all wrong. Use a greater variety of raw materials, and go easy on the grass mowings. Nearly always the cause of wet compost is too great a proportion of grass.

The answer is to buy some straw and mix it in with the mowings when building the heap. This helps to dry out the mowings, allows air to circulate, and keeps the rain off. The problem is always worst in heaps that aren't covered. Don't overdo the straw, though; too much will deplete the nitrogen in the compost.

If you've already got slimy compost, don't despair. It's still usable, but it should be spread out and dried before you use it. This will allow it to drain and make it easier to spread evenly. The wetness is only a handling problem.

Alternatively, if you're not in a hurry, simply fork over your slimy heap, cover it with a 6in thick layer of soil sloped so that rain runs off it – and leave it for at least two years. By then, you should have the crumbly compost you've been yearning for.

The waiting game

How long does it take to produce good, usable garden compost?

That all rather depends on the raw material and the time of year. There's no hard and fast rule about the minimum length of time required except that the longer a heap or bin is left, the better the resulting compost will be as a soil conditioner. On the other hand, compost made quickly can be richer in plant nutrients than compost made slowly.

Probably the shortest time possible is about six weeks. This would be for compost in a bin during the height of summer when the outside temperature is high, there is plenty of green material in the heap and it has all been firmed down and sprinkled with an activator.

Heaps without sides or in mesh bins will take longer to mature. So will those started in the autumn or winter. In these cases, or when the mix contains a lot of dry autumn leaves, it can take more than a year to form usable compost.

CORAL SPOT

Pink spots on trees

A lot of my trees and shrubs are covered in pink spots. Should I cut off the affected branches or will this just let in more disease through the cuts?

Certainly any wood affected by this disease – and there's no question that what you've got is coral spot – should be destroyed. The disease is found in many trees and woody shrubs, particularly maples, magnolias, figs and redcurrants. It's caused by a fungus which breeds on dead wood. Airborne spores infect trees through dead twigs or branches, pruning cuts or wounds, especially in early spring. Sometimes the spores can get a hold through the base when plants are growing in damp conditions such as dense grass. The first visible sign of the disease is the appearance of coral-red, spore-filled pustules on diseased branches, which begin to die back. Sometimes the whole tree dies.

Strict garden hygiene will help greatly. Never leave any dead wood lying about.

Soft fruit bushes with coral spot are best dug up and burned. More valuable trees and shrubs should be pruned to at least 4in below the affected area, and the wound painted over with a proprietary sealant that contains a fungicide.

Spray the remaining healthy parts with thiophanate-methyl at once, and spray twice more at three-weekly intervals. Encourage stronger growth in future by feeding, mulching and watering the plants.

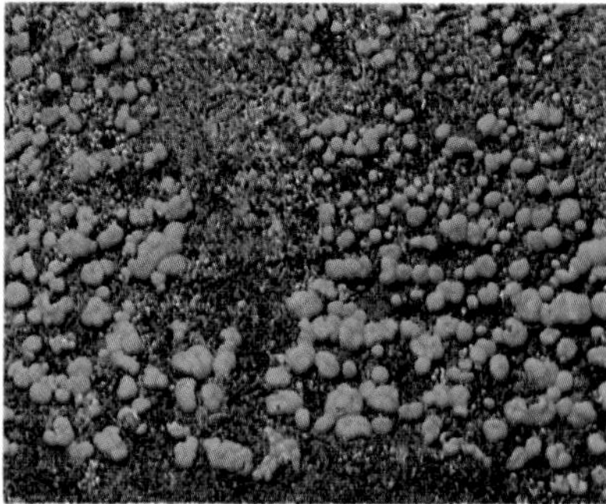

BORNE ON THE WIND *Coral spot fungus grows on dead wood, and spreads through wind-blown spores to infect and kill living woody plants. It can often be seen on old pea sticks.*

CORE ROT

How to rescue gladioli

I am particularly fond of gladioli, but am seriously considering giving them up as mine always seem prone to core rot. If I decide to try again, how long should I wait before replanting?

The fungus that causes this disease, the most serious disorder affecting gladioli, can survive in the soil for years. Do not replant for at least three years – and more than five for safety. You could try planting them in another part of the garden, but only if you can ensure that you don't carry infection from the old site to the new on your boots or tools.

The foliage on infected plants turns yellow or brown, and a rot covered with greyish mould spreads out from the leaf bases. The corms are particularly at risk during storage in moist conditions, when a spongy, dark rot develops so that the centre often drops out completely.

The fungus also affects acidantheras and causes leaf spotting in freesias. To reduce the likelihood of the disease reappearing, there are a number of things you can do. But they will only improve your chances; they won't guarantee you a disease-free garden, no matter how careful you are.

First, follow the old garden advice that every bulb or corm should be handled gently, especially when it's being lifted for winter. Before storage, soak the corms in a solution of fungicide such as benomyl or thiophanate-methyl for about 30 minutes. During the winter, keep them in cool, dry, well-ventilated conditions out of direct sunlight. Check the corms weekly for signs of the disease, and destroy any affected corms.

Growing plants showing symptoms of core rot should be dug up and burned. Even if years later you decide to replant gladioli in the old site, before you do so, soak your fresh stock for 30 minutes in a solution of benomyl or thiophanate-methyl.

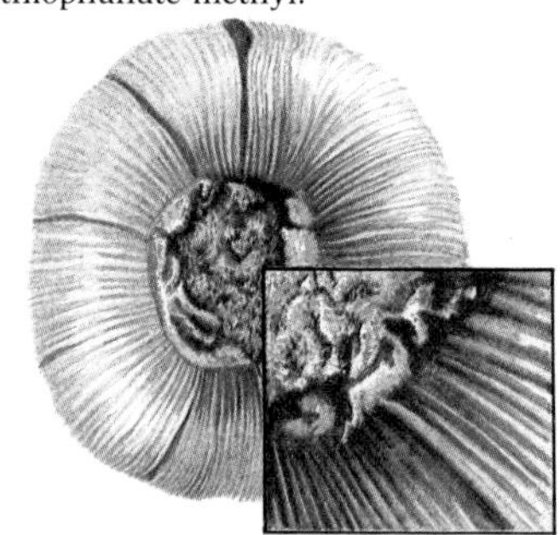

SPONGY CENTRE *First noticed in England in the 1920s, core rot is a scourge of gladioli, acidantheras and freesias.*

CORMS

Bulbs and corms: the differences

How do corms differ from bulbs – and does it matter for practical gardening purposes?

Bulbs and corms both occur on plants which have evolved reservoirs in which to store energy during dormant periods. But the plants swell in different parts of their anatomy. A bulb is a swelling of fleshy scales at the base of the leaves. The scales enclose next year's stem and flower bud; the onion is perhaps the best-known example.

A corm, on the other hand, is the swollen base of a stem. The new corm grows on the back of the old one, which starts to wither once the plant has finished flowering. Crocuses and gladioli are familiar examples. For practical gardening purposes the differences have little importance. The key thing is to understand the likes and dislikes of the individual plants and varieties.

Flowerless acidantheras

I have tried to grow acidantheras, but they seem to be a waste of effort. I am careful to protect the corms from frost – and the leaves certainly grow – but the flowers don't.

Acidantheras resemble small white gladioli and their flowers are sweetly scented. The problem with them is that, coming originally from tropical Africa, they cannot abide frost, and need a longer growing season than most parts of Britain can provide. If you plant them towards the end of May when the frost danger is past, they won't start to flower until September – just in time for the next frosts to kill the buds.

There is a way around the problem: plant the corms in pots and later 'plunge' the pots out in the garden – that is, bury the pots up to their rims in the ground.

For acidantheras you will need to use good-sized pots – say 6in – filled with John Innes compost No 3. Plant the corms in March and keep them on a sunny frost-free windowsill, or in a greenhouse. They don't need special heating, just sunlight and the absence of frost. At the end of May, or in early June, the plants should be several inches high and well ahead of any outdoor plantings. Take them out into the garden for plunging. They should flower in the second half of August, so missing the first frosts of autumn. If by any chance flowering is delayed, you can still lift the pots and bring them indoors before the first frosts, so that you can enjoy your acidantheras as house plants instead.

Dividing corms in spring

I can understand people digging up corms to protect them from winter frosts if necessary. But why do gardening books sometimes advise lifting and dividing clumps in spring?

Some corms grow in clumps which can become very congested. The young, healthy cormlets are found at the edge of the clumps, while those in the centre are often dried up or decaying. If you are lifting a clump for winter protection in autumn, you can always do your dividing at that stage. But the clumps of hardy species tend to get neglected – which is when a spring division becomes necessary.

Crocosmia provides a good example. This is a genus of yellow and orange plants which came originally from southern Africa. Despite their tropical origin they are usually very hardy so you don't need to lift them for winter. However, the groups can become overcrowded, so it is wise to lift and divide them in spring. Do it just as the young shoots are breaking through to the surface. Replant them immediately in soil enriched with plenty of rotted manure or compost.

Bargain-price perils

I often see corms being sold off in shops at the end of the season at a bargain price. They look healthy enough, except that their skin is often missing. How important is it that the skins should be intact?

It is very important. The outer skin, or 'tunic', is a corm's protection against disease and drying out. Corms that have been lying around in a warm shop unprotected are likely to have become very dry, and the loss of moisture will affect their performance. Worse still, disease easily penetrates unprotected tissue. The best advice, therefore, is to avoid end-of-season corms – and bulbs and tubers too, for that matter. They aren't bargains at all – they're liabilities.

Protecting corms from frost

Is there any way of protecting gladioli from frost while they are still in the ground? Digging them up in the autumn and replanting them in spring is such a chore.

There are certain hardy corms, such as crocuses, which need no protection. But most gladioli and other corms grown in Britain are damaged by frost. Unless you lift and store them in a cool, dry place for the winter months you are liable to lose them.

If you find lifting a chore, go for the hardiest corms. A few of the less showy gladioli will survive a British winter in the ground. The hardiest of all is the wine-red *Gladiolus byzantinus*. Otherwise, the only possible alternative is to try giving the soil a top-dressing of organic material to act as a protective winter blanket. The method is by no means guaranteed to work, but scientific research suggests that a layer of straw or dried bracken acts as a good insulator. Remove it in spring. Aim to make the layer at least 3-4in thick. There is no point in using peat or rotted manure, since both tend to become waterlogged and freeze.

Storing corms

When I store corms in winter I tend to lose a lot of them: they either go mouldy or shrivel up. What am I doing wrong?

Disease can very easily enter a corm at the top, where the leaves once sprouted. For this reason you should never lift green plants and cut off the foliage; it will leave a gaping wound. Instead, leave the plants in the ground until the first frost has blackened the foliage. This seals the tissues naturally.

Having lifted the corms, discard any which appear to be damaged already, or which have unusually wide, open necks. These will be prone to disease and may infect healthier specimens. Having made your selection of sound, narrow-necked corms, spread them out upside down in a shed out of the sun and allow them to dry. It is best to allow them to dry out naturally, since heating tends to shrivel them. When they are dry, after about 10-14 days, rub off any excess soil, taking care not to damage the fibrous skin, or 'tunic'. Do not wash the soil off, since this will encourage the development of storage moulds later.

When the corms are clean, spread them out and dust them with flowers of sulphur. This helps to keep mould at bay. For storage, place the corms in trays or nets and keep them in any cool, dry, frost-free building. Inspect them from time to time and remove any suspect corms before they infect the others. Small corms are particularly vulnerable to drying out and shrivelling, so store these in dry sand or peat in a sealed polythene bag.

Do make sure, though, that the storage site is properly cool and dry. If the sand or peat moistens, the corms may start to root prematurely, before you get them back into the ground next spring.

How deep to plant corms

Can I plant corms extra deep as is sometimes recommended for bulbs?

Some bulbs, a number of daffodils and tulips among them, definitely benefit from deep planting. But corms do not. New corms are produced each season on top of the dying originals, and they alter their position in the soil, automatically adjusting themselves over a period of years to the depth that suits them best. Planting too deep seems merely to stunt their natural development, so for corms stick to the basic rule: place each one in a hole twice its depth so that the top of the corm is covered by a layer of soil as thick as the corm is high.

CORM TROUBLES – AND HOW TO CURE THEM

Symptoms	Cause	Action
Stems, leaves or flower buds covered with small green or black insects, and often stunted or malformed	Aphids (greenflies or blackflies)	Spray with derris, malathion or a systemic insecticide such as dimethoate
Flowers and foliage of gladioli have silvery streaks and patches which ultimately turn brown	Thrips	Dust corms with HCH powder before storing; spray affected plants outdoors with malathion
Leaves of gladioli turn yellow and topple over, usually before the flowers appear. Corms show black spots or lesions and later the whole corm shrivels	Dry rot	Remove and burn infected plants; soak the remainder in benomyl or thiophanate-methyl before storing. Replant in a fresh site
Soft rot at the base of leaves, often causing plants to topple and die. Corms have round, shrunken craters with distinct shiny margins	Scab	Remove and destroy infected plants, and treat healthy stock with a fungicide as for dry rot
Foliage on anemones has patches of waxy whitish powder; sometimes leaves are also distorted	Downy mildew	Spray with mancozeb
Leaves, particularly on narcissi, show yellow or grey streaking or mottling; vigour gradually diminishes	Virus	No cure available. All infected bulbs must be destroyed

COTTAGE GARDENS

IN AN ENGLISH COUNTRY GARDEN *Traditional plants laid out almost haphazardly are the hallmarks of a cottage garden. The result is a riot of colour and charm.*

Making a start

We've just bought a small country cottage with an overgrown garden that needs completely remaking. How do we turn it into a traditional cottage garden to go with the house?

The essence of the cottage garden was that it was unplanned. The typical 'cottager' was a farm worker whose small garden had to supply vegetables and fruit, herbs for flavouring and medicines, as well as flowers for decoration. There wasn't much time for carefully tending difficult plants, so cottage garden flowers had to be tough and easy to grow. No space was wasted, either. Walls, paths, windowsills and every nook and cranny were pressed into use.

The traditional cottage garden doesn't usually have a lawn. If you want to include a lawn, surround it with wide, flower-filled borders to preserve the cottage garden effect.

Informality is one of the two keys to making your garden. The other is the choice of plants. They should be simple, free-flowering, colourful, preferably scented and easy to grow. There are many suitable plants, most of them perennials (see *Cottage garden favourites* on the opposite page for some suggestions). Mix them with a sprinkling of shrubs, climbers and bulbs. Many cottage garden plants have been 'improved' by plant breeders and are now available in brighter colours with double or frilled flowers and shorter stems that need no staking. While some of these can be incorporated into your plan, the unimproved, old-fashioned varieties will give a more authentic effect.

Forget about careful colour planning. Cottage gardens should provide a confusion and profusion of colours, and should not be planted to any strict scheme. Try dotting taller plants in among shorter ones to give occasional spires of interest. Avoid an organised graduation of heights from back to front.

Money-saving ideas

Every cottage garden I see has a profusion of plants which suggests to me that establishing one would be very expensive. How can I cut down on costs?

It *is* important to pack the plants closely for the best effect, but there are ways to keep the costs down.

Choose a number of key plants and shrubs to start with and get them established. It's worth spending a little extra on large well-grown specimens. Before planting, take some cuttings, offsets or small divisions from the plants and grow them on in a nursery bed.

Once you have the key plants set out, fill in the gaps in the first year or two with annuals, sowing direct in the positions where they are to grow. Many annuals fit in well in a cottage garden (for some recommended types, see *Annuals*, page 11).

Meanwhile increase your stock of perennials by raising plants from seed, taking more cuttings from your own stock, and begging offsets or cuttings from friends and neighbours.

Perennials raised from seed take a year or two to reach flowering size, and cuttings too will need time before they are ready for planting in the main garden. It's worth keeping a small area, perhaps part of the vegetable plot, as a nursery bed to grow on seedlings, cuttings and small divisions until they are large enough to plant in their permanent positions.

Traditional look on a new estate

I'd like a country cottage but I have to make do with a terraced house on a new estate. How can I make the garden, at least, the sort of place I dream about?

Not easily. Cottage gardens generally go best with cottages, and can sometimes look uncomfortably out of place in the wrong setting. By all means incorporate some cottage garden ideas into your new garden, but don't overdo the olde worlde theme.

The front gardens of modern terraced houses are usually open-plan, and look better if they conform to the same style. You may, however, have much more opportunity for individuality in the back garden. If you are lucky enough to have a fully walled or fenced private garden, there's no need to take neighbouring gardens into account. On most estates, however, the back gardens are more open, and you will need to make concessions to the way the gardens of the houses either side are laid out if they are not to spoil the effect of your own garden.

A new house may clash with an old-style garden, so one of the first things to do is to plant a variety of creepers and climbers against the walls (see *Climbers*, pages 76-81). These will disguise the newness of the wall and help the house to complement the garden. Give the same treatment to walls and fences.

Keep the lawn small and the borders wide. If space is short, one very wide border at the far end of the garden may be more effective than narrower borders round the edge. Spreading plants, such as London pride (*Saxifraga* x *urbium*), catmint (*Nepeta* x *faassenii*) or snow-in-summer (*Cerastium tomentosum*), will help to soften the lines of the garden, but do not use them to excess; plants that look charmingly informal in the garden of a thatched cottage can look merely untidy in the more formal setting of an estate.

Grow rambling roses and honeysuckle over walls and fences, and among perennials plant neat shrubs such as rosemary, pink or white-flowered cistus and scented, silver-leaved artemisias. Clumps of golden-headed achillea or tall-growing campanulas, summer-flowering dicentra, scented phlox and mat-forming pinks are the plants to give the right sort of effect.

Fill gaps in corners and against walls with small plants such as creeping thyme, primroses and spring-flowering bulbs.

Brightening up a winter garden

What can I do to make my cottage garden more interesting in winter after the perennials have been cut down?

The cottage garden was not originally intended to be of interest all year round. But you can extend its season and brighten its appearance with winter-flowering plants.

Evergreen shrubs form the garden's winter architecture. The golden-splashed varieties of elaeagnus and euonymus are particularly attractive and the dark-leaved *Viburnum tinus* carries its heads of pink-tinged, white flowers from November until May. The variegated forms of ivy look colourful on walls and fences throughout winter.

There are several plants that flower in the

COTTAGE GARDEN FAVOURITES

Plant	Height	Spread	Colour	Flowering
Bellflower (*Campanula persicifolia*)	4ft	12in	Blue, white	June–Aug
Canterbury bell (*Campanula medium*)	1–3ft	14in	Pink, blue, white	May–July
Columbine (*Aquilegia vulgaris*)	2ft	12in	Blue, purple, pink	May–June
Crane's-bill (*Geranium sanguineum*)	6–9in	18in	Crimson, magenta	June–Sept
Crown imperial (*Fritillaria imperialis*)	3ft	12in	Orange, yellow	Apr
Daisies (*Bellis perennis*)	4in	3in	Pink and white	Mar–Oct
Delphinium hybrids	3–5ft	9–12in	Blue, purple, pink	June–Aug
Foxgloves (*Digitalis purpurea*)	3–5ft	12in	Purple, maroon	June–July
Hollyhock (*Althaea rosea*)	5–6ft	2ft	Pink, white, red	July–Sept
London pride (*Saxifraga* x *urbium*)	12in	12in	Pink	May
Lupin hybrids	3–4ft	14in	Varied	June–July
Peony hybrids	3ft	3ft	Red, pink	June–July
Pinks (dianthus)	10in	18in	Pink, red, white	July–Sept
Shasta daisy (*Chrysanthemum maximum*)	2ft	15in	White	June–Aug
Yarrow (*Achillea filipendulina*, 'Gold Plate')	4ft	2ft	Golden-yellow	July–Aug

COTTAGE GARDEN ANNUALS AND BIENNIALS

In the early years of a newly established cottage or country garden, there will be gaps before the perennials and shrubs spread to cover the ground completely. These gaps can be filled with annuals and biennials which will flower through the summer and autumn. Sow annuals directly into the soil in spring, scattering the seeds and thinning when they are about $1\frac{1}{2}$in high.

Sow biennials in a seedbed in spring and transplant them to their flowering positions in autumn. Sow half-hardy annuals under glass in March and plant out in May.

(ha = hardy annual, hha = half-hardy annual, hb = hardy biennial)

Name	Type	Height/Spacing	Flowers
Brompton stocks (matthiola)	hb	15in/9in	Red, yellow, blue and white (June–July)
Candytuft (iberis)	ha	15in/6in	White, red, pink, purple (May–July)
Chrysanthemum (*C. carinatum*)	ha	2ft/12in	Yellow, orange-red rings (July–Oct)
Clarkia	ha	2ft/9in	Rose, purple, pink, white (Aug–Oct)
Forget-me-not	hb	12in/6in	Sky blue (May–June)
Love-in-a-mist (*Nigella damascena*)	ha	2ft/9in	Blue and rose (July–Aug)
Marigold (calendula)	ha	2ft/15in	Orange, yellow (June–Oct)
Nasturtium 'Gold Gleam'	ha	15in/15in	Yellow, orange (June–Sept)
Poppy (papaver)	ha	2ft/12in	Red (June–Aug)
Spider flower (cleome)	hha	3ft/18in	White and pink (July–Oct)
Sweet william (*Dianthus barbatus*)	hb	1–2ft/10in	White, pink and red (June)
Tobacco plant (*Nicotiana affinis* 'Sensation mixed')	hha	2–3ft/12in	White, crimson and yellow (June–Sept)

coldest months. *Iris unguicularis*, for instance, forms a large clump of untidy leaves in summer, but its strongly scented blue flowers appear between about October and March. Witch hazel, *Viburnum fragrans*, the shrubby honeysuckle *Lonicera standishii*, and *Daphne mezereum* are also valuable plants because they carry their sweetly scented flowers when there is little else of interest in the garden.

You can brighten the early days of spring by planting early-flowering narcissi and tulips, and choosing shrubs such as Japanese quince, forsythia and flowering currant.

Time-saving tips

I don't have a lot of time to spend on the garden. How can I cut maintenance to the minimum?

Cottage gardening is not the most labour-saving of gardening styles. Because of the dense planting and tangled informality of cottage gardens, weeding is more difficult.

Make sure you get off to a good start each year. Once young shoots show on the herbaceous plants in spring, hoe off or pull out weeds growing between them, then mulch all round the plants with peat, well-rotted manure or spent mushroom compost. The crowded plants make it difficult to use chemical weedkillers, but glyphosate painted on the leaves of perennial weeds such as bindweed will deal with the problem.

Stake tall plants early in the year before they begin to flop. As soon as you can identify the clumps of plants, give them twiggy branches, circles of canes or grow-through supports. If you want to avoid staking, plant short, sturdy varieties that are self-supporting. These varieties are easier to look after, but they won't give such an authentic cottage garden look.

Choosing the right sort of path

I want to get rid of some unsightly concrete slab paths in my cottage garden. What paving material would look best and what sort of ornaments, if any, are suitable?

Modern, regular paving slabs are not ideal for a cottage garden, but their appearance can be improved by clever planting. Spreading and mound-forming plants such as pinks, thyme and lavender planted close to the path will grow over the edges and help to disguise its geometric look.

Natural stone is a traditional material, either as flagstones or crazy paving, but it's expensive. Modern concrete paving slabs with a riven stone finish look like natural stone and are much cheaper.

Generally, try to match the paving material to the building material of the house. A brick path will look more in keeping with a brick house than a stone path. Brick paths can be laid in a variety of patterns, such as herringbone, basket or basket weave (see the pictures below). Basket weave is one of the most difficult patterns to lay because it involves cutting a lot of bricks into thirds.

Ideally, buy old bricks to give the path an instant patina of age, but this may be slightly more expensive because of the labour involved in cleaning the bricks.

Gravel is cheap, practical and attractive, but use edging stones to prevent the gravel from spilling into the borders. Control weeds with an application of path weedkiller every spring. In a traditional cottage garden, the paths usually went straight from the gate to the front door, but the straight lines were softened by a variety of plants spilling over the edges.

Gentle curves to paths don't look too out of place, but keep them gentle. Try laying out a hose along the line you want, and adjusting it until it looks right from all the surrounding viewpoints. Any ornaments you decide to put along the path should be simple and practical. You might try a natural wood or white-painted seat, a stone sundial or birdbath.

Large pots planted with lilies, a prized shrub or a flowering plant often stood by the door of old cottages. A porch not only provided shelter from wind and rain; it also became an ornament in its own right when covered with a climbing rose or honeysuckle.

PLANTS FOR A COTTAGE PATH

Sprawling, low-growing plants can disguise the stark edges of paths. These perennials, growing 3–12in high, can be planted when soil and weather conditions are suitable between September and March. Within a year, they will spread and tumble over the path.

Name	Spread	Flowers
Alyssum (*A. saxatile* 'Gold Dust')	12–18in	Yellow (Apr–June)
Aubrieta (*A. deltoidea*)	1½–2ft	Purple-rose (Mar–June)
Crane's-bill (*Geranium sanguineum*)	14in	Crimson (June–Sept)
Marjoram (*Origanum onites*)	2ft	Mauve-white (July–Aug)
Periwinkle (*Vinca major*)	3–4ft	Purple (Apr–June)
Pinks (*Dianthus plumarius*)	1½–2ft	Pink-white (June–Sept)
Viola (*V. biflora, V. cornuta*)	12–15in	Yellow-blue (Apr–June)
Violet (*Viola odorata*)	12in	Purple-white (Feb–Apr)

HERRINGBONE *Pinks and* Viola cornuta *line a brick herringbone pattern.*

BASKET *Leave holes in a basket pattern for plants such as alyssum and aubrieta.*

BASKET WEAVE *Periwinkle and pink crane's-bill soften the corner of a weave-pattern path.*

COURGETTES

When is a marrow not a marrow?

What actually is the difference between marrows and courgettes? They both look the same to me.

A courgette is simply a small, cylindrical marrow, gathered before it is fully grown and usually when about 4-6in long. Ordinary bush, or trailing, varieties of marrows can be used as courgettes – so long as the fruits are cut while they are still immature.

Varieties listed as courgettes are usually compact and bushy, and begin bearing usable fruits in July, unlike traditional marrows which often aren't ready until August. If courgettes are harvested regularly – a good plant can produce 15 or more fruits – they may crop until September. But if you fail to cut the fruits when they're young, they will quickly become overgrown and you will get far fewer fruits overall.

'Golden Zucchini' and 'Zucchini' (green-skinned) are popular courgette varieties with early, slender fruits. Another variety, 'Gold Rush', bears shiny golden-yellow courgettes in profusion and is sufficiently decorative to grow in the flower border.

Poor germination

I find that few of my courgette seeds sown straight into the garden come up. Is there anything I can do to give them a boost?

In a well-drained, sunny position most seeds sown between late May and mid-June should germinate within ten days. But if you're having trouble, here are two well-tried methods – one for outdoors and one for indoors.

To grow seeds outside, dig a hole about 12in across and 6-12in deep in the growing position, and almost fill it up with a mixture of soil and compost, leaving a shallow hollow at the top. Sow three seeds in the mixture, slightly apart and 1in deep. Some people believe that laying the seeds edgeways rather than flat reduces the risk of rotting. But there's no real evidence to support this view. There's no need either to use a fungicidal seed dressing. Cover the hollow with a sheet of glass to keep the compost warm and dry. Should more than one seed germinate, remove the weaker seedlings leaving only one plant in each planting hole. As the plant grows, take off the glass. But don't fill up the remainder of the hollow. Leave it so that water runs towards the roots rather than away from the plant.

If this outdoor system sounds too complicated or if you can't make it work in your garden, try growing the seeds indoors. Sow each seed ½in deep in a 3in pot of seed compost. Stand the pots on a sunny window-sill or in a greenhouse and keep them at a temperature of at least 18°C (about 65°F) until the seedlings emerge.

The case against mounds

An old allotment holder I know always grows his courgettes in piles of manure or compost heaped up on the ground. Is this better than digging the stuff into the soil?

Not really. Courgettes and other marrows revel in soil that has been well mixed with rotted manure or compost. Some gardeners dig over the planting spot, heap piles of manure or compost on top, to a height of 2ft or more, and then set a single plant in the middle of each mound. The argument for doing this is that the plant is kept above soggy ground and thus is protected from rotting. It saves digging, too.

The danger is that unless the organic matter is well mixed with soil, the mixture may be too rich, forcing quick growth and too much foliage at the expense of fruit. Also, stuck up on top of a pile, the plants will be less sheltered, which may delay maturity, and even if plenty of soil is added to the mounds, the plants still dry out more quickly than in a well-dug bed.

Courgettes under attack

Most years I get one or two courgette plants that start off well, then turn into a tangle of distorted, yellowing leaves. They don't seem to affect their neighbours, but I burn them anyway. What's the cause? Is there anything I can do about it?

This is probably the cucumber mosaic virus, a disease which is spread by greenfly. Destroy any diseased plants at once. Wash your hands and tools afterwards to avoid spreading the infection to other plants. There is no treatment for the disease, but you can stop it spreading by spraying its greenfly carriers with permethrin or malathion.

Several other problems can also afflict courgettes. Here are the common ones:

- **SLUGS AND SNAILS** Scatter slug pellets around the plants at the first sign of attack. Put polythene under the fruit and keep rubbish away to discourage future raids.
- **WITHERED FRUIT** Normally caused by poor drainage or over-watering. Treat by removing the damaged fruit and spraying with a foliar feed – a fertiliser that's absorbed through the leaves. Do not water the plants for at least a week afterwards.
- **FOOT ROT** Blackens and rots the base of the stem, and kills off the roots. Dig up and destroy affected plants. Avoid planting courgettes in the same spot next year.

Late fruiting

Last year, I planted my courgettes at the right time – early June – but they took ages to fruit. How can I stop the problem recurring this year?

Courgettes are generally planted out in the first half of June, and there can still be some cold winds then. So give the plants some shelter – in the form of a windbreak, say. This will help them to get established, will speed growth, and make it easier for the bees to visit the flowers.

Protect the plants with cloches for the first three weeks or so after planting, but if the flowers begin to open, open the cloches so that bees can enter freely during the day.

Cold and windy weather discourages bees from flying, and in these conditions it may be necessary to hand-pollinate the first flowers. When they are fully open, identify the female flowers – these have a baby marrow already formed behind their petals – and pick one of the stalked male flowers and push it into the depths of the trumpet. The operation is more effective if you carefully remove the petals from the male flower first to expose its pollen-bearing organs. Several female flowers can be pollinated by one male.

Too much manure

I gave my courgettes plenty of manure and water, but they didn't crop nearly as well as the same variety next door, whose plants were only half the size of mine. What's the reason?

You've been far too generous with the food and water. Fresh manure is rich in nitrogen, which makes leaves and stems grow quickly. That's fine for leafy crops such as lettuce and rhubarb, and even for brassicas a month or two after they are planted out – but not for courgettes or other plants which are primarily grown for their fruit.

Too much water in the early stages also results in too much leafy growth. The solution is to give your plants a tougher time: make them work a bit harder. Plants under stress will always flower and fruit more prolifically – to ensure the continuance of the species – than those which are being looked after too well.

Next year, plant your courgettes in 12in square holes filled with equal quantities of well-rotted manure and soil, and, after the initial watering-in, do not water them again (unless the soil becomes very dry and the plants are obviously suffering) until flowers appear. When the fruits begin to swell, water frequently, especially in dry spells. Give each plant 2 gallons of water once or twice a week, and add a high-potash tomato fertiliser to the watering can every 10-14 days to promote faster growth.

CRAB APPLES

Best variety

Which variety of crab apple tree gives the best fruit for jelly?

The 'John Downie'. It yields the largest and finest crab apples year after reliable year. A handsome tree that grows to some 15ft in ten years, it also has beautiful springtime blossoms of pale pink buds opening to white flowers. The conical fruits are yellow flushed with crimson and they also make good wine. The tree starts cropping in about its fifth year after planting.

A few nurseries stock 'John Downie' specimens that have been grafted onto dwarfing rootstock and are admirably suited to the small garden.

These trees are slower-growing and crop some two years earlier than the standard variety, reaching a maximum height of 10ft. The fruit makes excellent crab apple jelly. Here's how to prepare it.

Wash 6lb of fruit and quarter it without peeling or coring. Put it in a saucepan with enough water to cover it (about 4 pints), and add to the mixture the juice of a lemon. Bring it to the boil and simmer gently for about 1½ hours or until the fruit is mashed. For extra flavour, include some bruised root ginger or a few cloves in the cooking.

Strain the mixture through a jelly bag, then dissolve 1lb of sugar in each pint of extract. Boil this syrup rapidly until it reaches the setting point. You can test whether setting point has been reached by dropping a teaspoonful onto a cold saucer. Let it cool for a minute or two. If it has reached setting point, the surface will wrinkle when pushed with a finger. Skim, pot and cover.

Crabs and apples

Is it true that crab apple trees make good pollinators for other apple trees?

Some varieties do. Though all crab apple trees are self-fertile, meaning that they do not themselves need to be pollinated by another tree, ordinary apples are not. And some crab apple varieties do indeed make very effective pollinators for other types of apple trees. The reason is that the crab apples produce blossoms, and therefore pollen, over a long period which overlaps well with fruit trees.

Commercial apple growers favour *Malus* 'Aldenhamensis', *M.* 'Golden Hornet' and *M.* x *hillieri*. Besides being effective pollinators, all of these varieties are also decorative trees. Apart from 'Golden Hornet', however, they do not produce particularly useful fruit.

CROCUSES

Naturalising corms in a lawn

How do I plant corms through established grass?

If you intend growing just a few crocuses in your lawn, plant each one individually using a small trowel or dibber to cut through the turf. Cover each corm with a little less than its own depth of soil to allow for the thickness of the turf.

The tops of the corms should end up about 2in below the surface and 3in apart.

If you are planning a large expanse of crocuses, remove a thin layer of turf across the whole area, plant the corms and relay the turf. Don't set them in orderly ranks. Instead, scatter them gently over the prepared soil and plant them where they land.

Plant autumn-flowering varieties during late July or early August, and the spring-flowering kinds during September and October.

Colour splashes on a grassy palette

Which crocuses would you recommend planting to brighten a grassy bank?

Crocus tomasinianus is the first one that comes to mind. Its starry lilac flowers open in January or February, bringing colourful relief after the winter. It is one of the fastest-spreading crocuses, too. As well as the mauvish-blue species, there are several named varieties such as 'Barrs Purple', 'Whitwell Purple' and the rich port-wine 'Taplow Ruby' that will naturalise well in the bank. To add a regal touch, plant some of the large Dutch varieties such as: 'Remembrance', purple-blue; 'Pickwick', silver and lilac stripes; and 'Golden Yellow', the best of the large-flowered Dutch yellows.

If they are left undisturbed in the grass, they will gradually increase into dense clumps. It is important to allow all these spring-flowering crocuses to have some leaf growth after flowering, in order to build up new corms for the following year, before you mow them along with the grass. If possible, delay mowing until late spring when the crocus leaves have withered.

For autumn interest, plant *Crocus speciosus*. Its 4in high bright lilac-blue flowers open between August and October. It, too, multiplies quickly, and there are several colour varieties such as the pure white 'Albus', the violet-coloured 'Pollux' and the dark blue 'Oxonian'.

PICK OF THE CROCUSES

Name	Colour	Height	Flowering
SPRING-FLOWERING CROCUSES			
Crocus ancyrensis	Orange	3in	Jan–Feb
C. chrysanthus	Deep yellow to bright orange	3in	Feb
C. chrysanthus 'Blue Pearl'	Pale blue	3in	Feb
C. chrysanthus 'Cream Beauty'	Cream	3in	Feb
C. chrysanthus 'E.A. Bowles'	Yellow and bronze	3in	Feb
C. chrysanthus 'Snow Bunting'	White	3in	Feb
C. susianus	Deep orange	3in	Feb–Mar
C. tomasinianus	Lilac-mauve	3in	Jan–Feb
C. tomasinianus 'Whitwell Purple'	Purple-mauve	3in	Jan–Feb
AUTUMN-FLOWERING CROCUSES			
Crocus kotschyanus (*C. zonatus*)	Rose-lilac	3in	Aug–Sept
C. medius	Lilac and purple-mauve	3in	Oct–Nov
C. sativus	Purple	3in	Sept–Oct
C. speciosus	Bright lilac-blue	4in	Aug–Oct
C. speciosus 'Oxonian'	Dark blue	4in	Aug–Oct

Keeping out mice

How can I prevent mice from eating my crocus corms?

With difficulty, at least in the open ground. There is no perfect method of preventing the mice digging through the soil to get the corms. A method that often works, however, is to make the corms inedible by tainting them with paraffin. Sprinkle some sand with a little paraffin, and rub the corms in the sand for a few minutes before planting them as usual. The smell will discourage the mice while it lasts – usually for about a year. Corms planted in turf can be protected for longer. The method here is to cover the soil below the turf with small-mesh galvanised wire – the kind used for rabbit hutches. Lift the grass and plant the corms as you would normally. Then, before replacing the turf, lay mesh across the whole area planted with corms and extend it about a foot beyond the edges. Mice will find it difficult to burrow round the edge of the wire – and your corms should be safe for at least 15 years, until the wire disintegrates.

CROP ROTATION

How to manage

My allotment neighbour produces massive onions and carrots from the same beds every year. I religiously rotate my crops and still only get middling results. What's going wrong?

The two facts you mention are simply not related. You're assuming that crop rotation is the be-all and end-all of vegetable growing. It's just one facet.

It's perfectly possible to produce excellent crops in the same piece of ground for years on end. However, it does mean that you have to keep the soil fertility up and the pests down – and, clearly, your neighbour is doing just that. Probably the most important aspect of all is the fertility of the soil. Make sure, first, that it's well supplied with bulky organic matter – garden compost or manure – to improve the condition of the soil, and then that the crops are fed with an appropriate fertiliser (see *Fertilisers*, page 131). Rotate the crops as well and you'll soon be outshining your neighbour.

Is it worth doing?

Is crop rotation really worth bothering with in a small garden?

On balance, yes. But the decision is not nearly as clear-cut as traditional gardening advice might lead you to believe. Modern crop rotation – the practice of growing the cabbage family, root crops and other crops such as peas and beans in succession on each part of a vegetable patch in a three-year cycle – is a relatively recent custom. It gained widespread acceptance in Britain only in the late 18th century.

It had, and has, two main purposes. First, since each type of crop makes different demands on the soil, changing crops each year ensures that the soil does not become exhausted of particular nutrients, and gives it a chance to recover its balance during the two years it is used for other crops.

Second, moving crops discourages the build-up of pests and diseases which feed on one crop, and which starve without it.

The trouble is that neither of these two purposes has nearly as much force as it once had. Modern fertilisers – organic or artificial – can keep any patch of soil well stocked with all the necessary nutrients even if the same crop is grown year after year, as it often is on modern farms; and modern pesticides can successfully keep most predators at bay.

Moreover, in a small garden, crop rotation won't stop pests and diseases from following their favourite crops around the vegetable patch. Some pests can make their own way across the few yards involved; others will get a lift on garden tools or your boots. Nevertheless, crop rotation does still have some value for the home gardener with a small patch, though not the traditional value.

By carving up the vegetable patch into three plots, it makes the annual chores of manuring, liming and fertilising seem less daunting – and encourages many gardeners to do a more thorough job.

ALL ABOUT CROP ROTATION

When planning a crop rotation system, think of vegetables in three groups: brassicas (the cabbage family, which includes some root vegetables such as turnips); roots; and pulses (peas and beans) and others. There is also a permanent group which remains in its own ground undisturbed by rotation. The main crops in each group are listed in the chart, along with the order in which the crops should be grown in each part of your patch and how to prepare the soil for each group.

HOW TO GROUP VEGETABLES

Permanent crops	Brassicas	Roots	Pulses and others
Rhubarb Globe artichoke Asparagus	Brussels sprouts Cabbage Cauliflower Kale Savoy Sprouting broccoli Kohlrabi Radish Swede Turnip	Beetroot Carrot Chicory Jerusalem artichoke Parsnip Potato	Peas Beans Celery Onion Leek Lettuce Peppers Spinach Sweet corn Tomato Marrow

HOW TO PREPARE THE GROUND

For permanent crops	For brassicas	For roots	For pulses and others
Dig the soil thoroughly in autumn or spring, adding as much compost as you can afford.	Rake in 2oz of a general fertiliser. Add lime – 4–6oz per sq yd – on all but chalky soils.	Don't apply any manure before sowing root crops, except for potatoes in poor soil. Also avoid lime, but rake in a general fertiliser such as Growmore about two weeks before sowing or planting.	Dig in rotted manure or compost (about 10lb per sq yd) during the winter before planting. Or dig in peat and apply 1oz of Growmore per sq yd in the spring. Lime should not be needed once a rotation is established.

WHAT TO GROW WHERE

	Plot one	Plot two	Plot three
1st year	Brassicas	Roots	Pulses and others
2nd year	Roots	Pulses and others	Brassicas
3rd year	Pulses and others	Brassicas	Roots

For details on the fertiliser needs of individual crops, see *Fertilisers*, page 131.

CUCUMBERS

Greenhouse inspiration

A brainwave. To save space in my tiny garden, is there any reason why I shouldn't grow outdoor cucumbers as climbers – the way they're grown in greenhouses?

None at all. It does indeed save space. It also reduces the chances of rotting and helps the long-fruited varieties to grow straighter.

Use plastic pea and bean netting for support, or galvanised wires rigged horizontally about 2ft apart between posts. Ridge and all-female varieties will need a 3ft or so high support, but the more vigorous Japanese climbing types may reach twice this height. When the plants have grown five or six leaves, remove the tip of the stems to make the plants bush out. Pinch out the tip of any stems which have not flowered by the time the sixth or seventh leaf has opened, to encourage flowering sideshoots to form. The sideshoots can then be tied into the supports, or left to cling with their spring-like tendrils.

You may have to prune the plants as much as once or twice a week to keep them under control. Shorten both the leading stems and the sideshoots as necessary once the plants are bearing a reasonable number of fruits – say 12 or so per plant.

If you are going to train outdoor cucumbers to grow upwards in this way, plant them in a sheltered spot – preferably against a sunny fence – since they will be more vulnerable to wind damage than plants left to trail over the ground.

Some die, others don't

Last year I was saddened – and astonished – to see quite a few of my baby cucumbers rot or wither away while others, on the same plant, did well. How is this possible?

Embryo cucumbers sometimes rot when a plant is overloaded with fruits. The plant then sheds or aborts those it can't carry. Cutting out surplus fruits will reduce the number of withered fruits and strengthen the plant.

If you get any more rotting fruits, cut them off to stop them spreading disease.

Counting cucumbers

To settle an argument, how many ridge cucumbers would you expect from one plant?

How they're grown would make a big difference to the argument. A strong trailing variety such as 'King of the Ridge', left to grow more or less at will in a sunny frame, should produce at least 12 fruits between July and September. On the other hand, a cucumber trained upwards on netting or wires and regularly pruned to remove surplus growth and to encourage more flowering sideshoots, might yield as many as 20 fruits.

If quantity is important, grow 'Patio Pix' or 'Bush Crop'. Both are compact, non-trailing varieties, ideal for small gardens, and even for growing in 9in pots. Either of these varieties might give you 25 cucumbers, each about 6in long. 'Crystal Apple', which sprawls over the ground, is nearly as prolific. Its yellow-skinned, tennis-ball-shaped fruits will surprise any of your friends who think that all cucumbers are long and green.

A time for planting

In the East Midlands, where I live, the dividing line between the seasons is often blurred. When is the earliest I might plant outdoor cucumbers?

If the cucumbers are to be grown in a frame, or under cloches, it should normally be safe to plant them in the middle of June. In the South, by contrast, you could plant a little earlier – say, the first week of June. Unless your garden is particularly sunny and sheltered, the cucumbers will almost certainly need some protection – especially in the first month after planting.

Outdoor cucumbers may take several weeks to settle down if their roots have been disturbed in the process of transplanting. Raising the plants in peat pots or in peat blocks overcomes this problem – there is no need to take them out of their pots before planting because the roots grow through the sides of the pots when they are set out in the soil. The alternative is to sow three seeds an inch or two apart, and $\frac{3}{4}$in deep, directly into the growing position. Do this between late May and mid-June, and cover the sown area with jam jars or cloches to speed up germination. If two or more seeds germinate, remove the weakest seedlings, leaving one plant to develop in each spot.

Naming names

How did ridge cucumbers get their name? They don't look very ridged to me.

Outdoor cucumbers are so called because the traditional way of growing them is on a low ridge or on mounds of soil piled up over a trench or hole filled with rotted horse manure or compost. This method is much less common now, but one old trick which is still worth using is to bank up some of the soil from the planting hole on the north side of the plant to give the young crop extra protection from chilly north winds.

Cucumbers bred for greenhouse culture are sometimes referred to as frame varieties, though nowadays most gardeners grow them in a greenhouse, not in a cold frame. These varieties need higher temperatures than outdoor cucumbers. To add confusion to the issue, ridge varieties actually perform better when grown in frames than outdoors. It isn't the raised temperature they respond to so much as protection from the wind.

Many of the time-honoured outdoor varieties tend to be stumpier and thicker-skinned than greenhouse cucumbers. But even 'King of the Ridge', the oldest variety commonly offered by seed firms, can produce fruits around 15in long.

Another outdoor variety, 'Burpless Tasty Green', rivals any greenhouse variety because its 10-12in long fruits have very tender skins. Its American and Japanese breeders gave it its name because they say that it is less likely than some other varieties to cause indigestion, but there is no hard evidence for the claim. Other outdoor varieties recommended for their quality are the Japanese-bred 'Kyoto' and 'Tokyo Slicer'.

The gherkin myth

Gherkin plants, like spaghetti trees, are old gardening jokes, aren't they? Surely gherkins are simply baby cucumbers?

Not at all. The gherkin is a type of cucumber whose short, bumpy fruits are particularly suitable for pickling. Grow them in the same way as you would any outdoor cucumber, and cut the fruits when they are 3 or 4in long. 'Venlo Pickling' and 'Hokus' are dependable varieties.

Bitter fruit

Last year, my cucumbers looked fine, but when they were served at table, they were horribly bitter. Did they pick this up from the soil?

No. It's more likely to have been the result of pollination – the transference of pollen from male to female flowers. The condition can be avoided by growing varieties which produce only female flowers, such as 'Amslic', 'Sweet Success', or 'Pepinex', or by picking off the male flowers on greenhouse varieties before they open. Curiously, outdoor varieties need exactly opposite treatment. Except for all-female varieties, whose fruits need no pollination, all outdoor varieties *do* need to be fertilised, and so the male flowers should always be left on. Male flowers are the ones which do not have the bulge of an immature cucumber behind the bloom.

Some gardeners also believe that, regardless of pollination, fruits which grow from the main stem of the traditional, bi-sexual varieties are more likely to be bitter than those grown from sideshoots. But modern researchers insist that there is no foundation for the belief.

CULTIVATORS

How they work

What different types of powered cultivators are there, and what are their pros and cons?

There are two basic designs, but both work on the same principle. They consist of an engine driving rotating tines or blades which churn up the soil as they advance along the ground.

Type 1 has the engine set immediately above the rotor blades. They are simple to maintain and reasonably cheap to run, but they are heavier to work and harder to control than the other type. They are best for digging heavy clay soils.

Type 2, which is less common nowadays, has the engine set behind the rotor blades. This type moves more easily across the ground and is easier to control. But because the weight of the engine does not press down so directly on the blades, a machine of this type tends not to dig so deeply. It is better suited, therefore, to light, sandy soils.

Whichever type you use, you may have to make more than one pass over the ground, particularly on heavy soils, to get it properly dug. Most cultivators are powered by petrol engines, although there are a few mains electric models. Electric motors require less maintenance, usually, than petrol-driven ones and are a lot easier to start; on the other hand, the cable limits the machine's range and has to be watched to make sure you don't cultivate through it.

TROUBLE-FREE DIGGING *Most cultivators have their engines set over the blades to help to push them deeper into the ground.*

Some of the more expensive cultivators have a range of working attachments, such as grass cutters, scythes, sprayers and lawn rakes, as well as the basic cultivating rotor blades. All help to cut down the effort of gardening – at a price.

If you want to avoid the cost of buying a cultivator, consider hiring one from a tool hire shop – especially if you're going to use it only once or twice a year.

The risk of panning

I've read somewhere that cultivators can cause pans in the earth. Is there any way of getting around this?

Heavy farm machinery can cause 'pans' – layers of hard, compacted earth immediately beneath the cultivated soil – because they always till the ground to the same depth each year. Ordinary powered cultivators designed for the garden, however, are not really heavy enough to cause this kind of problem. All the same, just to be on the safe side, don't use a cultivator on heavy soil when it's wet. Otherwise, the spinning tines could smear the clay beneath, polishing it into an almost waterproof layer and leaving you with a serious drainage problem.

Digging depth

Some cultivators dig down only a few inches. Others can turn over 8-9in. Is this a real advantage?

Yes, particularly if you regularly have to tackle rough digging. These deep-reaching cultivators, which are generally the ones with the engine set directly over the rotor blades, can turn over compacted or neglected soil, leaving it ready for shallow digging by hand later. They do need some practice, though, because their extra power makes them more difficult to control.

The shallower-cutting cultivators are for digging between rows, for weeding and for preparing the crumbly surface needed for a seedbed. They won't do for heavy digging on virgin land. But once you have mastered the handling of them, you will find it possible to work close to growing plants without damaging their roots.

ALL ABOUT CARING FOR A CULTIVATOR

- Check the oil regularly. In cars, the oil is pumped around the engine. In garden machinery, it lies in the crankcase, collecting all the dirt and rubbish which finds its way into the engine. Change the oil after every 25 hours of use, or yearly, whichever is the sooner.
- The rubbish you find in the crankcase will have found its way in through the carburettor – so keep the air filter clean and efficient by washing it with clean petrol or detergent. This is especially important in dry and dusty conditions.
- Cultivators often stand idle for long periods, so starting can be a problem. Always keep a new spark-plug handy.
- Stiff bearings on the drive wheels or stabilising wheels can turn what should be a comparatively easy job into a hard slog. Clean and grease the bearings regularly.
- After each outing, clean as much of the mud and dirt off the machine as you can.
- Towards the end of each year, get the machine serviced (the queues at the local repair shop will be shorter then than at the start of the spring). Before storing, wipe the rotors and the other metal surfaces with an oily rag to keep rust at bay.

CUTTINGS

Cuttings puzzles

Is there any real need for so many different kinds of cuttings? Do they do different jobs?

They all do the same job, which is to reproduce exactly the parent plant and incidentally to keep your garden well stocked at minimal expense. The principle is straightforward enough – to take a leaf, bud, section of stem or piece of root from a living plant and grow a new plant from it. The reason for there being different kinds of cuttings is that some species will propagate more readily from, say, a stem cutting rather than a root cutting, or more readily at one time of year rather than another. But many plants will happily reproduce from more than one type of cutting.

For details of which type of cutting to take from any particular plant, look up the plant in the *Plants at a glance* section on pages 378-441. For details on how to carry out each method, see *How to multiply your shrubs* on page 314.

The various kinds of cuttings are encouraged to grow roots by different means, but all types have these requirements in common – light, warmth, moisture and a clean, free-draining soil. The soil usually provided is a seed and cuttings compost, or a half-and-half mixture by volume of peat and coarse sand. The amount of warmth needed varies according to the type of cutting and the plant species, but 13-18°C (55-65°F) is usually considered adequate. A dusting of hormone rooting powder over the base of the cutting before planting will also help it to take root.

A good many plants may be propagated by leaf, leaf-bud or root cuttings, but by far the most widely used are those taken from stems. They should never be too short, for the infant plant needs food reserves to see it through until it takes root. The longer the rooting time, the longer the cutting needs to be. The shortest cuttings – some 2-4in – are from softwood. These are taken in the spring and early summer when growth is vigorous and the cutting will root quickly.

Intermediate-length cuttings are from semi-ripe wood, usually taken in late summer when growth is not so vigorous and the cutting needs greater food reserves to maintain it until the roots form; these cuttings are generally made 6-8in long.

Most widely used of all are the hardwood cuttings, which are generally planted outdoors and may take a year to root. Their food requirements are the greatest of all, and consequently they are 9-12in long.

Everything about cuttings techniques is concerned with the race between rooting and plant starvation. Thus all kinds of stem cuttings are made just below leaf nodes. Cellular activity is strongest there and roots will form more rapidly from such a wound. By the same token, it is best to strip most of the leaves from the cutting, allowing only a few to remain at the top. This will cut the amount of moisture lost through transpiration, while the remaining leaves will add to the food reserves through photosynthesis. It's all a matter of balances.

Cutting time

Can you give some guide to the time it takes cuttings to root?

Yes. This list will give you some idea, but remember that different species take different times to 'strike' – take root – and growing conditions too will have an effect.

HOUSE PLANTS
Stem cuttings – 3-6 weeks.
Leaf-bud cuttings – 3-6 weeks.
Leaf cuttings – 6-10 weeks.

OUTDOOR PLANTS
Softwood cuttings – 4-8 weeks.
Semi-ripe cuttings – 1-6 months (depending on when the cutting is made).
Hardwood cuttings – 5-12 months.
Root cuttings – 4-8 weeks.
Leaf-bud cuttings – 4-8 weeks.

Powder power

The books tell us that, as a matter of course, we should dip the bottoms of cuttings into rooting powder before planting. Is the powder really essential to successful propagation?

Considering how very little rooting powders cost, why not give them a try? It's true that they aren't always necessary, but at the very worst they'll have no effect at all, and at best, with nine cuttings out of ten, they'll help. Rooting powders contain a growth hormone – usually naphthylacetic acid – which speeds up the production of callus tissue, the corky scar tissue that forms at the base of a cutting. Some also incorporate a fungicide as a counter to rot. In most cases, the new roots develop from the callus, rather than from the plant tissue of the cutting.

Provided that the cutting has been correctly made, and that the growth conditions are adequate, most cuttings will root without the aid of a hormone. However, this can take a considerable time with some plants, and the longer it takes the greater the chance of the cutting dying from starvation or rot before it roots. So anything that speeds the process can only be of help.

Propagating begonias

My Begonia rex *hybrid is both glorious and extremely unusual. All efforts to find it a look-alike companion have failed, and I wonder what the chances might be of propagating it. I'm afraid I'm a complete novice in these matters.*

Nothing could be easier, or more economical, than to propagate a whole host of plantlets from a *Begonia rex* hybrid. You can, in fact, obtain quite a number of plants from a single leaf. What you do is this. Fill a shallow box with seed and cuttings compost and water it well. Take a few mature, healthy leaves from your begonia, and on the underside, where the veins show, make about a dozen widely spaced cuts across and through the main veins of each leaf.

Lay the leaves cut side down on the compost, and weight them with small stones to ensure that the cuts are in contact with the soil. Plantlets will arise from the cut veins; once these are well rooted, pot them on into individual pots.

Alternatively, cut a leaf into small sections, ensuring that there is a part of at least one main vein in each. Either way, make sure that the compost is kept moist and that, while rooting is taking place, a temperature of around 18°C (65°F) is maintained. Several other plants, African violets and peperomias among them, may also be propagated by these methods.

TURNING OVER A NEW PLANT *Begonias root swiftly from leaf cuttings. Cut the veins on a leaf and put it, cut side down, onto seed and cuttings compost. Hold it in place with stones.*

THE LANGUAGE OF CUTTINGS

In cuttings phraseology, the terms softwood, semi-ripe and hardwood are what infant, teenager and adult signify in people. That is, the terms refer to the same object at different stages of its growth. As the year progresses, the same young stem would be suitable for making each of these three types of cutting in turn.

- **SOFTWOOD CUTTINGS** These are taken very early in the growing season before there is any sign of hardening in the new shoot. They are green both at the tip and the base.
- **SEMI-RIPE CUTTINGS** These are taken towards the end of the growing season (July-August), when the tip of the stem is soft and green but the base is hardening, browning and becoming woody.
- **HARDWOOD CUTTINGS** These are taken between October and March when the stem has hardened and become woody throughout its length.

Three other terms used in cuttings jargon are heel, stem and tip. These define the part of the stem used for the cutting.

- **HEEL CUTTING** A type of cutting in which the stem is torn off in a way that retains a portion of the parent branch – a heel – at its base. Heel cuttings are most often made from softwood or semi-ripe wood. They are normally 2-8in long.
- **STEM CUTTINGS** Most often used for hardwood cuttings. As hardwood cuttings, they normally include 9-12in of the stem to provide a reservoir of nutrients so that the cutting can survive through the winter until growth begins in spring. As softwood cuttings, they are normally 2-6in long, depending on the species.
- **TIP CUTTINGS** Short portions – usually 2-6in long – taken from the tips of stems. These are the parts used for most softwood and semi-ripe cuttings.

Seeds versus cuttings

Why are some plants propagated from cuttings and others from seed?

The cuttings method is generally used to propagate plants whose seeds may be infertile, difficult to germinate or simply scarce. It is also used to propagate hybrid plants, most of which fail to come true from seed.

Take apples, for example. If you sow seeds from, say, a Cox, the progeny will be enormously variable and totally unlike the parents because it will be a genetic mixture, part Cox and part the variety that the pollinating bee happened to visit last.

The way around this problem is to propagate from vegetative parts of the plant: to produce a genetic replica, or clone. Actually, it is difficult to root apple cuttings and in their case budding or grafting is used instead; but the principle is the same. The great advantage with vegetative propagation is that it produces any number of new plants all completely identical to the single parent.

Watching the pennies

I'm interested in increasing my plant stock by cuttings. But I don't have a heated greenhouse, and I find all the talk about cable-heated trays daunting from the expense point of view. Are there any cheaper methods around?

Provided you're not thinking of producing forests of plantlets, there are quite a few worthwhile and inexpensive dodges. To start with, you don't need a greenhouse to produce plants from cuttings; an indoor windowsill will do just as well. In any case, some cuttings, especially root cuttings, prefer to be outdoors. For the others, you can make a propagating frame by making hoops out of bent coathanger wire and inserting the ends in a pot or tray of compost. Cover hoops and pot with a plastic bag – either a transparent one, or a milky opaque one if the windowsill is in direct sunlight. Cuttings like plenty of light, but direct sun will scorch them. Alternatively, do you know those plastic 2 litre lemonade bottles with the black bases? The whole of the black base is easily removed by soaking the bottle's base in boiling water, leaving a round-bottomed flask. Cut off the top of the bottle at the shoulder with a craft knife, or with a razor blade in a holder, and make three or four holes in the black base. Upend the base, set a flowerpot on it, fit the bottle onto the base over the pot – and hey presto! a propagator.

Finally, you don't have to buy special seed and cuttings compost. Make your own with a half-and-half mixture (by volume) of peat and coarse sand.

Saved by the roots

My herbaceous border phloxes have suffered a number of casualties recently through the depredations of stem eelworms. I'm afraid they've had it. But what are the chances of replacing my stock with cuttings?

Not good; the chances are that the infestation will be carried on into the cuttings. But what you might consider is to make root cuttings instead. These will be free of infestation, and may be taken at any time, though preferably in February or March. Take sections, 3-4in long, from the thicker roots and lay them horizontally in a tray of cuttings compost before covering them with a thin layer of the same material. Place the tray in an unheated frame or in a sheltered position outdoors. New roots will form and young plants arise in spring. Grow them on in nursery rows and plant them out in autumn.

While on the subject, there are quite a number of woody or fleshy-rooted shrubs and perennials that can be propagated in a similar way. They include hollyhock, anchusa, verbascum, romneya, phlox and gaillardia. In these cases, take two or three cuttings 2-6in long from a ½in thick root in February or March. Cut the bottom ends of the cuttings diagonally and the top ends square, so you know which end is which. Plant them, slanted end downwards, in a pot of rooting compost and cover the tops with a ½in layer of sand. When the young plants appear in spring, grow them on in nursery rows and plant them out into their permanent sites in autumn.

Taking a leaf-bud cutting

I find propagating by cuttings a bit hit and miss – and, besides, their removal doesn't do much for the appearance of a small parent plant. Are there any fast and sure ways to multiply my stock without waiting for seeds to set?

Try leaf-bud cuttings. The technique is easier than you might think, and they will root and break into growth more quickly than traditional stem cuttings.

A leaf-bud cutting consists of a single leaf, its stalk, and a sliver of wood – including a bud – from the stem to which the leaf stalk was attached. Use a sharp knife to make a crescent-shaped cut in the stem around the stalk. Set the cuttings – several to a pot – in a half-and-half mix of peat and sharp sand, with the bud just showing, and the bud will rapidly start throwing out the roots and shoots of a new plant.

LEAF-BUD CUTTINGS *Cut round the bud which is in the angle between stalk and stem.*

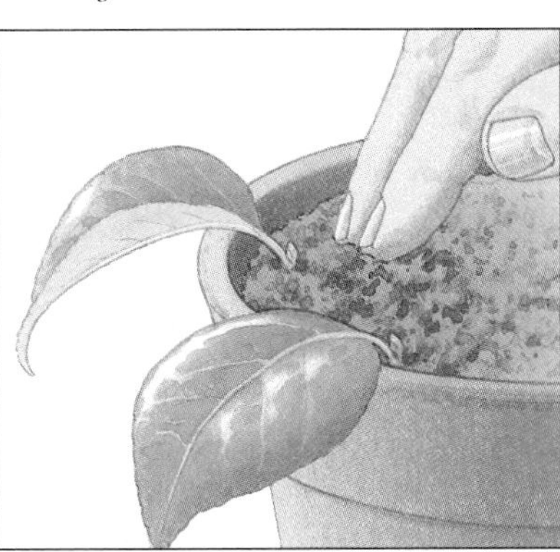

POTTING UP *Start the cuttings into life in a mixture of peat and sharp sand.*

Quite a number of plants – ivy, *Camellia japonica* and grapevines among them – respond well to this method.

Short cuts and long

How do I know what kind of cutting to take and when to take it?

The only practical answer is by learning through reading and experience. There are no rules, apart from those with many exceptions, to govern the taking of cuttings from particular groups of plants. In some cases, cuttings may not even be the best method of propagation.

As a rough guide, though, herbaceous plants – those that die down each winter – are usually best propagated by 3-4in softwood cuttings taken in spring. Most trees and shrubs propagate more reliably and easily from semi-ripe cuttings taken in summer and from hardwood cuttings taken in late autumn. For more details, have a look at this checklist, which tells you the size and type of cutting to take from some common perennial herbaceous plants and when to take them. For information on shrubs, see pages 314-15.

African violet – leaf cuttings with 2in stalk, June-Sept.
Aloe – offsets (sideshoots with a crown developed, usually underground), summer.
Aralia – rooted suckers, Oct-Mar.
Begonia – (large-leaved rhizomatous) – leaf cuttings, May-June.
Ceanothus (some) – 2in root cuttings, Feb-Mar.
Chrysanthemum – 3in softwood tip cuttings, early spring.
Crassula – leaf cuttings, spring or summer.
Currant (fruiting) – 10-14in hardwood cuttings, Oct-Nov.
Dahlias – 3in softwood tip cuttings, spring.
Delphiniums – 3-4in softwood tip cuttings, spring.
Echeveria – leaf cuttings, spring and early summer.
Eryngium – 2in root cuttings, Feb.
Fuchsias – 2-3in softwood tip cuttings, spring and summer.
Gloxinia (*Sinningia speciosa*) – leaf cuttings, June-July.
Gooseberry – 12-15in hardwood cuttings, Oct.
Hydrangea – 3-4in softwood tip cuttings, spring and summer.
Lewisia – offsets, June.
Loganberry – tip layering, July-Aug.
Pelargoniums – 3-4in softwood tip cuttings, Aug.
Peony – rooted suckers, Sept.
Phlox (perennial) – 4in root cuttings, Feb-Mar.

Pinks and carnations – 3-4in softwood tip cuttings, June-July.
Poplar – 10-12in hardwood cuttings, Oct-Mar.
Poppy (*Papaver orientale*) – 2in root cuttings, Feb-Mar.
Rhus (sumach) – rooted suckers, Oct.
Rubber plant – 2-4in semi-ripe cuttings (the tips are green, the base woody or hard), Apr-June.
Sansevieria (not variegated forms) – 3-4in long leaf sections, May-Aug.
Sedum (large-leaved varieties) – leaf cuttings, Apr-Sept.
Streptocarpus (tufted species) – 3in long leaf sections, May-July.
Tayberry – tip layering, July-Aug.
Willow – 9-15in hardwood cuttings, Oct-Mar.

How to multiply a fig

I have a fig tree growing by my south wall and would like to provide it with a few companions. Can these trees be propagated by cuttings?

Yes, but take plenty of them to allow for a high failure rate. Probably the best method is to gather hardwood cuttings in December. They should be 6-12in long, sturdy, and with only short stretches of bare stem between buds or leaves. Dip the bases in hormone powder and plant them in a half-and-half mixture of peat and sharp sand.

Thus far, straightforward enough. But the trouble is, to root reliably, fig cuttings require a bottom heat of 18-21°C (65-70°F). This can be provided by standing the container above heating pipes, or by using a heated propagator. Maybe it would be easier, though slower, to increase your fig by layering. In summer, peg a couple of young, vigorous shoots to the ground and cover them with soil. Within 12 months they will have taken root. They can then be severed from the parent tree and planted out in their permanent positions.

Compost for cuttings

Which medium should I use for my cuttings?

The material is generally sold as seed and cuttings compost. There are several brands available on the market, all of them fairly similar, so which one you choose is really a matter of economics or personal preference.

It is essential that the compost should

ALL ABOUT LAYERING

Provided that time is of no particular concern – the process can take anything from six weeks to two years – then layering is perhaps the best and surest means of plant propagation. The great advantage of the system over cuttings is that throughout the period when the new plant is developing roots, it is still part of the parent plant and is receiving nourishment from it. Not until the root system is fully grown is the offspring severed from the parent plant; consequently, the failure rate is very low indeed.

There are five layering methods, used for different types of plants and in different circumstances. Four of the methods involve taking stems to the ground and rooting them there.

In the fifth method, air layering, the soil, in effect, is taken to the stem.

SIMPLE LAYERING Used to propagate many shrubs, especially those with low-growing stems, and some perennials, such as carnations. Some shrubs – rhododendrons and magnolias, for example – reproduce naturally by layering their branches in this way.

- At some time between April and August, choose a low-growing, flexible stem, no older than last year's growth and preferably this year's.
- About 12in back from the tip, make a 1in long cut in the bottom side of the stem and insert a matchstick to hold the wound open. Dust the cut with a hormone rooting powder.
- Make a hole about 6in deep and peg the cut part of the stem into the bottom of the hole. Use a bent piece of wire or a couple of twigs for the pegs. Fill the hole with a mixture of one-third each by volume of peat, soil and coarse sand.
- Stake the tip of the layered stem to give it stability.
- About 12 months later (six weeks for carnations), gently scrape the soil away to see if new roots have developed. If they have, sever the stem from the parent plant, replant it in its new and permanent site and water it thoroughly. If, on the other hand, no roots are yet showing, replace the soil, leave the whole thing for a few more months and try again.

TIP LAYERING This follows much the same principles as simple layering, except that the tip of the stem is cut, pegged and buried rather than the middle, so that the new plant grows from the bud at the end of the stem.

Carried out in July or August, tip layering is the best way to propagate cane fruits such as blackberries and loganberries.

SERPENTINE LAYERING Like simple layering, serpentine layering should be done between April and August. It is most often used to propagate such climbers as clematis, honeysuckle, jasmine or wisteria.

- Select a long, trailing, many-jointed shoot of this or last year's growth.
- Make cuts not more than halfway through the stem at the leaf joints, cutting as many joints as the number of plants you wish to propagate.
- Dust the cut joints with rooting powder and peg and plant each of them in the same way as for simple layering – leaving a series of low hoops visible above ground, rather like the traditional image of the Loch Ness Monster.
- Stake the tip of the stem to prevent disturbance of the rooting leaf joints.
- About a year later, scrape away the soil to see if the joints have rooted. If they have, sever them from the parent stem, and from each other, and replant them in their permanent site. If they haven't rooted, put the soil back and leave them for a few more months.

RUNNER LAYERING The classic method of propagating strawberry plants, which also applies to spider plants (*Chlorophytum comosum*) and mother-of-thousands (*Saxifraga stolonifera*). All these plants send out runners which develop small plants along their lengths and at the tips.

- In June, peg the young plants, still attached to the parent, into pots of potting compost.
- In August, or at the latest in September, sever the plants from the parent and transplant them into their permanent site.

AIR LAYERING This very different method is used to propagate trees or shrubs whose stems are too stiff or too high to be easily bent to the ground.

- In March or April, select a one or two-year-old stem and strip the mid-part of its leaves.
- About 12in from the tip, make a shallow, slanting cut, dust it with hormone rooting powder, and pack it with sphagnum moss.
- Pull an 8-10in sleeve of transparent polythene over the stem and firmly tie the bottom end in about 3in below the cut.
- Pack the sleeve with a mixture of 2 parts sphagnum moss, and 1 part each of peat and coarse sand by volume. Thoroughly wet the mixture and tie in the top end of the sleeve to the stem. The joints must be airtight to prevent the mixture from drying out.
- Support the stem against the extra weight by tying it to a cane or to an adjacent branch.
- When roots are visible through the polythene, which can take a year or more, cut the stem off just below the plastic, take off the plastic and pot up the new plant in its growing mixture. Harden the new plant off before transferring it to its permanent position.

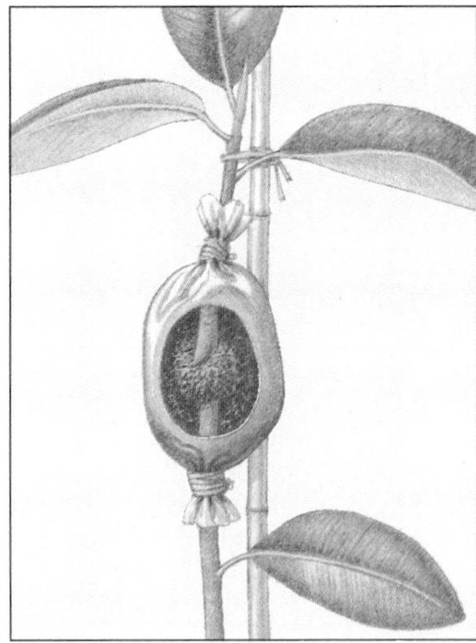

HIGH-RISE PROPAGATING *To make an air layer, cut part of the way through a stem, pack the open wound with sphagnum moss, peat and sand, and seal the area with plastic.*

drain easily: cuttings cannot root properly if they are waterlogged and, in addition, a waterlogged compost usually turns sour and acidic. Paradoxically, as well as being free-draining, the compost must also be water-retentive, rather in the manner of a sponge which holds water but expels it easily. Provided the material has these two attributes, it should be fine for rooting cuttings in. Usually a proprietary compost is made up of fibrous moss peat to which horticultural grit or sand has been added to ensure good drainage and to add weight and stability.

You can make your own compost with a half-and-half mix by volume of peat and coarse sand. Or, if you prefer, replace the sand with grit, vermiculite or perlite. Sowing and cuttings composts bought from the garden centre usually have some plant foods in them as well. This is intended to help seedlings, but it won't do cuttings any harm. There's no need to add fertilisers to a home-made cuttings compost.

Roses from cuttings

Gardening friends tell me that nothing could be easier than to propagate roses by cuttings. But I can't say that my efforts have been very successful. Is there a knack I don't know?

Despite what your friends say, very few people have great success with rose cuttings, whether from Hybrid teas, Floribundas or Species roses: none gives particularly good results. Nor does the timing of the cuttings seem to make much difference. Perhaps hardwood cuttings, taken in autumn, are the most likely to succeed, though even with these, professional gardeners would not expect to get more than a 50 per cent take.

The reason for this lack of success is not entirely clear, but it obviously has something to do with the nature and structure of rose stems – soft, pithy cores surrounded by thin wooden tubes. Some progress has been made recently by storing hardwood cuttings in heated bins through the winter before planting them out in spring. But there's still a long way to go before propagating roses from cuttings can be considered commercially viable. In the meantime, the production of hybrids by budding and Species roses from seed will remain the standard methods.

CUTWORMS

Plant stems nipped through

My morning inspections of the vegetable patch are blighted by the sight of my lettuces lopped through and toppled on the ground. I'm told this is the work of cutworms, operating under cover of darkness. How do I get rid of them?

Cutworm is a general name for several different kinds of caterpillar, all of which have similar habits. The main pest species in gardens are the larvae of the large, yellow underwing moth, the turnip moth and the heart and dart moth.

Adults emerge from the soil in June or July and almost at once the females begin to lay eggs – up to 500 a week – on living plants and dead leaves. The eggs hatch within two weeks and the resulting caterpillars feed for a month or two before spinning themselves into cocoons.

From these, a second generation of adults emerges in August or September. The autumn cutworm hatching spends the winter in the soil, feeding whenever weather permits, and metamorphoses into adult forms in the following spring.

The different species of cutworms feed between them on a wide range of vegetables and ornamental plants – lettuces, the cabbage family, carrots, celery, beetroot, potatoes, chrysanthemums, dahlias, marigolds – and even on very young trees. The only fruit plants likely to suffer are strawberries.

Damage is likely at almost any time of year, but is worst on light soils during dry summers.

Cure is difficult, but prevention relatively easy. Clear away dead plant debris, keep the weeds down, and hoe regularly through the year to expose the creatures to frost and birds. Watch the soil round the plants when you're out hoeing and you are likely to spot a few of the pests, which can be dealt with there and then. Protect seedlings with insecticidal seed dressings. Where older plants are infested, fork bromophos into the soil around the stems.

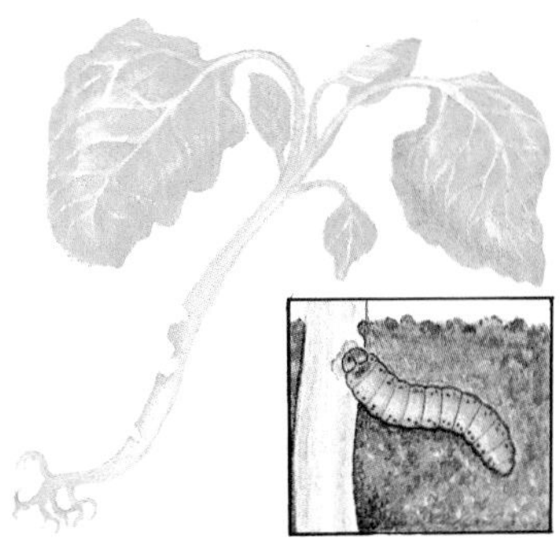

MENACE IN THE SOIL *Cutworms are fat, brown or grey caterpillars 1½-2in long. They are usually found just below the soil surface.*

DAFFODILS AND NARCISSI

Too crowded to flower

The clumps of narcissi scattered in my established borders have healthy leaves but give me very few flowers. Can you tell me what's wrong?

They have become overcrowded, that's all. You just need to lift them, separate them gently – and replant them farther apart.

The time to lift the clumps is after the narcissi have finished flowering and the leaves are turning yellow. The leaves are useful in that they remind you of the exact whereabouts of the bulbs.

Unfortunately this is not always the best season to replant because the soil can be too dry: so keep the bulbs in a cool dry place until autumn rain begins to moisten the ground in about September. Sort the bulbs out before storing them. Throw away any soft or damaged ones and rub off excess soil from those you are keeping, then spread them out on a tray. As the summer progresses, remove any leaves, roots and skins that become dry and brittle.

If you want to plant the bulbs back in the same positions in your borders, prepare the soil thoroughly first.

This is important, for when narcissi are grown in the same soil for many years, it becomes very impoverished. Dig in some well-rotted compost or manure and add a generous dressing of bone meal.

When you put the bulbs back in the border, set them in holes at least three times the depth of the bulb. A bulb 2in deep, for instance, should go into a hole at least 6in deep – deeper if you hoe the ground at all, to protect the bulb from disturbance – and should be covered with at least 4in of soil. Set the bulbs 4-8in apart if they're the large varieties, 2-3in apart if they're small. You should get a refreshed display full of flowers the spring after next.

What's in a name

What is the difference between a daffodil and a narcissus?

There isn't any. The botanical name narcissus is used for both plants.

The separation into narcissus and daffodil is an entirely artificial one that has been created by gardeners. Gardeners tend to use the name daffodil for narcissi with long trumpets. When they talk about narcissi, they are referring to flowers with short, cup-like trumpets.

Do not disturb

I remember my father digging up all his daffodils and keeping them in the shed over winter. People don't seem to bother these days. Was he right – or are they?

There is no need to lift daffodils annually: they generally grow better when left undisturbed for a number of years. The only reason for lifting is to break up clumps which have become too congested, or to make space for summer bedding plants.

Lifting daffodils annually – and mostly after flowering – was much more common in the days when people went in for ornate summer bedding displays, and wanted to move the bulbs and their declining foliage to an out-of-the-way corner of the garden.

For an alpine meadow

I tried to create the effect of an alpine meadow in a small area of my garden, but it came out all wrong. The alpines were smothered by weeds and long grass, and all you could see were a few big yellow daffodils poking up. Frankly it was a mess; I think I'd better start again. How should I go about it?

To create the effect of an alpine meadow in an English garden, you have to use some cunning. To begin with, forget the bulk of the plants listed in the catalogues as alpines. Concentrate instead on snake's-head fritillaries, squills, and the tiny hoop petticoat daffodil, *Narcissus bulbocodium*. This is the perfect daffodil for your purpose: a true wild flower of the high meadows in Europe, and quite unlike the normal garden varieties. It is a dwarf species which flowers in February and March, with very open trumpets borne on slender stems.

Your small bulbous plants will be too delicate in appearance to compete with any long or coarse grasses. These not only hide the bulbs, but also use up the nutrients in the soil so that the bulbs are eventually starved out. To get your alpine meadow going, you really need to dig up the area and remove all grass and weeds, then re-sow from scratch.

Plant the bulbs in early September. For a natural look, scatter them over the surface of the soil, planting them where they fall. Firm the soil gently after planting and then sow with one of the finer grasses with a good proportion of fescue. Remove any weeds that appear in the seedling grass, but don't use a lawn weedkiller, because it can damage emerging bulbs.

After the springtime display, let the daffodils and the other bulbs die down naturally. Then, when the leaves have faded, rough-cut the meadow with a rotary mower. Don't let the grass grow too long, or the coarser species will start to dominate, their roots competing with the bulbs for food and moisture. You need not feed the area much, but the bulbs will benefit from an early spring application of bone meal at the rate of about 1½oz per square yard. It won't do the grass any harm, either.

Poison in the stems

It occurred to me the other day that cut daffodils are always massed on their own, rather than mixed with other spring flowers. When I asked why, I was told that daffodils are poisonous to other plants. Is this true?

When daffodils are cut, their stems give off a slime which dissolves in water and is poisonous to other cut flowers. If you want to mix daffodils with other blooms, you must stand the daffodils in water on their own for 24 hours, and then wash the stems. This will drain off the toxic content and you should have no further problem – unless you cut the stems again when the flowers are being arranged.

As a further precaution, you can add activated charcoal to the water in the vase. This will absorb the slime. Use 1 tablespoon of charcoal for every 2 pints of water, stirring steadily all the time as you add it.

Alternatively, you can add household bleach to the water: about three drops to each pint. This is effective as long as the daffodils are present in no more than equal proportion to the other flowers.

When there are more daffodils, you need to add more chlorine in the form of extra bleach – and this in itself can damage more sensitive plants.

Growing daffodils indoors

I would like to grow a pot of daffodils to brighten up the house early next spring. Are any of them specially recommended for indoor growing?

Almost all daffodils can be grown indoors, so the simple recommendation is: choose whichever takes your fancy. If you want a big trumpet daffodil, you should go for the popular 'Dutch Master' or 'Golden Harvest'. For something more unusual, consider the double daffodils or one of the 'split corona' varieties (see *Unusual daffodils*, opposite).

There is another point worth considering. A pot of daffodils is especially welcome during the bleak days of early spring when there is little or no colour in the garden. To get bulbs to bloom in February, for instance, you normally have to 'force' them – a technique which involves keeping them in the cold for several weeks in autumn to trigger them into flowering sooner than normal. However, a few types of daffodil flower naturally in February and so need less attention than the others. Among these early kinds are varieties of the miniature *Narcissus cyclamineus* such as 'Peeping Tom', 'Jenny' and 'February Gold'.

Whatever you decide to grow, the basic planting methods are the same. Use a pot rather than a bowl, because a daffodil's roots go quite deep. For the best results, fill it with bulb fibre rather than garden soil or compost. Plant two layers of bulbs, one beneath the other and staggered to allow the plants of the lower layer to come up between those of the upper.

That way, you'll get a good, dense clump in which each plant supports the others. In a 5-6in pot, for instance, you could fit six bulbs in two layers of three.

When you have potted the bulbs in the autumn, bury the pot up to its rim in the garden and cover it with peat, soil or straw. This helps to produce a vigorous root system. The bulbs should remain out in the cold for at least ten weeks before being brought into the warmth of the house.

If you have used bulb fibre, remember that it is just a growing medium and contains no nutrients, so you must feed your plants at fortnightly intervals from the time the shoots turn green. Use a standard house-plant feed.

After the flowers have gone, keep on feeding right up until the time when the leaves start to wither; it will improve the quality of your bulbs. When the leaves have died down, plant the bulbs in the garden and they should give you a good display in the following spring.

For a rock garden

Which daffodils are best for a rock garden?

The plants will have to be small varieties to suit the shallow soil and miniature scale of a rock garden. Among dwarf replicas of the larger trumpet kind, many gardeners consider the loveliest to be *Narcissus lobularis*, *N. asturiensis* and *N. nanus*. They rarely exceed 6in in height.

For contrast, you can plant *N. bulbocodium*, the hoop petticoat daffodil. This is a wild species and, as its name implies, the trumpet is very open, resembling a hooped crinoline. The petals are very small by comparison with modern varieties, and the flowers are borne amid narrow, rush-like leaves. Besides plain yellow, there are lemon and cream varieties.

Equally unusual in appearance is *N. cyclamineus*. The flowers recall those of cyclamens, having elongated trumpets and petals sweeping right back against the stem. Some of its hybrids are rather too large to be suitable for a rock garden, but the original wild species is perfect.

When to divide the clumps

I like to see massed daffodils bursting with colour in spring. But how can I tell when a clump should be divided?

So long as a clump is bursting with colour, you need not disturb it. The simple rule is to divide when a mass of tightly packed foliage produces only a scattering of flowers. Timing will depend upon the variety of daffodil you are growing, but as a rough guide it will generally be no more than once every five or six years. Lift the clump when the foliage has died down, and separate the bulbs. Prepare the ground for planting, incorporating plenty of well-rotted manure or compost, and replant in the usual way. Replanting should be carried out as soon as possible after lifting and dividing. Naturalised bulbs go on a lot longer. However, if you are growing for show and want perfect individual specimens, you should aim to lift your bulbs at least every other year to allow room for development and to enable the soil to be revitalised.

Knotting leaves for tidiness

My neighbour ties a knot in the foliage of his daffodils after they have flowered. He says it's a good way of tidying up the leaves and stalks while keeping the bulb nourished in the ground. Do you agree?

This is a common practice – but not a very wise one. The bulb needs its green foliage after flowering in order to replace the energy spent on the bloom. It recharges its botanical batteries by exposing green leaves to the sunlight. If you bundle the leaves up, you reduce their surface area and so reduce their sun-trapping efficiency. You also tend to split and distort the tissues which transport nutrients and moisture down to the bulb.

Knotting the leaves is certainly better than cutting them off completely. But for the health of the bulb and of next season's flower, it is much better to let the foliage die down naturally. If you must knot for tidiness, at least wait until the leaves start to fade at the tips and become limp.

Bulbs in the lawn

My daffodils look marvellous flowering in the lawn. But when the blooms have faded, the bare green stalks and leaves are very much less attractive. Can I mow over them straight away?

Not if you hope for a good display next year. Those leaves nourish the bulbs after the flowers have gone. Mow them too soon and you are mowing off the plant's energy supply. Next season's growth will be weaker, flowers will be more frail – and in some cases they may fail to appear at all.

There are no hard and fast rules about when it is safe to mow. Some years ago, experiments with a limited number of daffodil varieties suggested that it would be safe to mow six weeks after the last flower had faded. In reality, that is the barest minimum for some bulbs – and a recipe for disaster for others. Ideally, you should allow the bulbs to die down naturally. The earliest time to consider mowing is during late June or early July when the leaves start to yellow at the tips. Some gardeners suggest as a guide that you should never mow over daffodils until Henley Regatta is past.

But your problem would be considerably diminished if you planned for foliage when you first planted the bulbs in the lawn. It's a good idea, for instance, to leave a central area of grass free of flowers so that you can start mowing at least that section when the grass needs it. Or you can group the bulbs all in one corner of the lawn. Daffodils and other bulbs can be strategically placed to catch the eye when in flower – without being too conspicuous as bare stalks at the centre of the stage.

Natural narcissi

Which narcissi can I grow in grass?

The best ones are the small varieties. *Narcissus cyclamineus* will give you a good deep yellow display early on in the year, in February and March. Its flowers have long trumpets and petals curved back on themselves – very like the cyclamens it's named after. Cultivated varieties of this narcissus such as 'February Gold', 'Peeping Tom' and 'Jenny' rarely grow more than a foot high and are perfect for naturalising in grass.

N. lobularis is another species to choose if you want early spring flowers. It is a complete miniature version of the trumpet daffodil, rarely more than 6in high.

You can follow these two, for a March and April display, with the delightful 2-5in hoop petticoat *N. bulbocodium conspicuus*. It, too, is deep yellow and has small narrow petals and a broad trumpet that looks like an old-fashioned hoop petticoat blown up in the wind. For advice on how to care for bulbs which have been planted in grass, see *For an alpine meadow*, opposite, and *Bulbs in the lawn*, on this page.

The narcissus fly

My narcissi were a great disappointment last year. They didn't flower and what few leaves emerged were very thin, stunted and twisted. I lifted the bulbs to have a look at them and found that they were all soft and rotten. What should I do?

Unfortunately there isn't a lot you can do, other than burn them and start afresh. Your bulbs were attacked by the narcissus fly, a devastating pest that also hits hyacinths.

The adult fly looks very like a small bumblebee. It is on the wing from late April to June, laying its eggs around narcissi bulbs left in the soil. The emerging grubs burrow into the bulbs and remain safe there for the winter, eating away at the succulent food reserve.

The flies are most active on warm sunny days and tend to lay their eggs around plants growing in full sun. There is no effective way to stop them. Occasionally you may buy narcissi with the grubs already inside them. You can check for this by feeling under the bulb. If the round flattened plate from which the roots appear is soft, then the bulb is almost certainly maggoty.

Commercial growers often give dormant bulbs hot-water treatment after lifting them in order to kill the grubs. They immerse them for three hours in water kept at 43-44°C (109-111°F). The exact temperature is critical. Lower than this, it won't kill the grub; higher, it'll kill the bulb.

Unusual daffodils

I've seen some rather unusual daffodils in the florists' shops this spring; frilly ones that seem to have no trumpets, and ones with the trumpets turned back. You don't see them so often in gardens. What are they, and can I grow them outdoors?

These pretty, rather pampered-looking daffodils are the so-called 'double' and 'split corona' varieties. Double daffodils are the ones which seem to have no trumpet at all, but to have several flounced rings of petals. You can certainly grow them in the garden if you like, and people sometimes naturalise them in the lawn. The trouble is that their flower heads are easily damaged by wind and rain, so they are really better grown indoors.

A split corona daffodil is one whose trumpet – known to specialists as the 'corona' – is split in several places, and often crimped back against the petals. The trumpet may also differ in colour from the petals, so that it appears blazoned against them. The effect is very attractive, and split corona varieties are valued as cut flowers. However, like the doubles, they are prone to damage by wind and rain, so are more safely grown indoors.

DOUBLE OR SPLIT *Double daffodils such as 'Mary Copeland' (top) and split-corona types like 'Parisienne' are best grown indoors.*

DAHLIAS

Keeping out frost

I have heard that frost is the worst enemy of dahlias. What is the best way to protect the plants?

Frost is so damaging to dahlias that normally it is unwise to set plants out in the open ground until late May – even early June in Northern England and in Scotland. And when frost strikes hard in late autumn or early winter, then that is the end of the dahlia season.

Can you protect your plants? No, not really, except that you can plant slightly earlier, say in mid-May, if you are prepared to cover the plants at night when frosts are forecast.

Fighting the sap-suckers

Greenflies and thrips are a nuisance in my garden – they seem to get on all the flowers I grow. Do they attack dahlias?

Yes, unfortunately. The dahlia has no exemption. Keep the creatures at bay with regular applications of an insecticide based on malathion or a systemic insecticide such as dimethoate. Apply it at ten-day intervals. These sap-sucking invaders can spread virus disease amongst dahlias, so it is particularly necessary for them to be controlled.

Alternatives to staking

I am not particularly taken with staking and tying plants. Are there any dahlias that do not demand such support?

The only dahlias that need no staking and tying are the low-growing bedders, very useful for garden decoration but of little value as cut flowers. If you do not like the chore of tying, then look around your local garden centre. There are some very efficient mesh devices that eliminate individual staking and tying, though of course at a price.

One plot, two shows

Will growing other flowers or bulbs in my dahlia plot affect my dahlias?

If you mean to have other flowers in the plot at the same time as the dahlias, you'll have trouble because of the competition for root space – especially if the plants are grown close together. But if you plan to have two shows a year, spring and summer, from the same plot, you will have to compensate the soil for its double effort by a double effort on your own part.

Before planting spring bulbs and seeds, enrich the soil with compost and a top-dressing of bone meal. Repeat the dressing after you clear the bulbs in the spring and before planting your dahlias.

In search of a scent

Are there any scented dahlias?

The dahlia has an aroma all of its own, though it is hardly a distinctive scent like that of the rose or the sweet pea.

Like that other elusive dream, the blue dahlia, the scented dahlia is constantly being sought after by dahlia hybridists the world over. There is a fortune waiting for the first breeder of either.

Hide the hoe

After planting my dahlias in late May, I kept them hoed well until the end of June, when I noticed a lot of tiny roots coming to the surface near the plants. Can you tell me what was causing this?

Your hoe was cutting into the expanding feeder roots that spread out around each dahlia plant, sometimes as far as 3ft in every direction. From these, the dahlia gets its flowering power. By the end of June, the best place for your hoe is on the back of the garden shed door.

Stick to mulching for weed control and moisture conservation, and to regular feeding to keep the plants growing strongly.

No cheer for slugs and aphids

Is there a non-chemical way of controlling slugs and aphids on my dahlias?

Although strictly speaking a chemical, pyrethrum is unlike most other insecticides in that it is natural – it is made from the dried flowers of a species of chrysanthemum. It is also perfectly safe, and can be used as a spray against aphids.

The population of slugs, and their equally destructive relatives, snails, can be reduced by setting open-topped cans of beer into the ground with about an inch of can sticking above soil level. The creatures fall into the cans and drown.

Superdahlias

Do I need a greenhouse or any special equipment to grow really large dahlias?

No. Contrary to popular belief, giant dahlias are rarely grown in a greenhouse. They are huge because they are bred to be that way. You do not need special equipment either, so long as the plants you start with are giant varieties, which are intended to carry only three or four blooms a season. Limit the plant to this number of flowers by pinching off stems on each plant until only three or four are left. These will then give you blooms as big as footballs.

In place of muck

I live in a suburban area and cannot get any farmyard manure or stable manure to help my dahlias grow. Can you suggest an alternative?

There are many substitutes available – homemade compost from vegetable peelings and grass cuttings, for example. There is also mushroom compost, litter (mostly peat and straw) from poultry farms – which needs to be composted for 12 months to reduce its potency – and enriched peat products.

Apply your manure substitute twice a year – in the autumn when you dig and in the summer as a mulch. Spread one standard-sized barrowload to each square yard, and do not bother to dig it in: earthworms and the action of sun and rain will do the job for you in two or three months.

Earwigs out

I'd love to grow dahlias, but my friends tell me that they're always infested with earwigs – an insect I can't stand. Is this so, and can I get rid of them?

Earwigs do get into the rolled petals of dahlias and, occasionally, into the hollow stems after blooms have been cut – but no more than they do into other flowers such as lupins, delphiniums and chrysanthemums.

And yes, you can get rid of them. Set empty flowerpots, filled with straw or dry grass, upside down on canes or stakes stuck into the soil near the plants. Earwigs, which feed during the night on foliage and petals, will collect in the pots to rest during the day, when they can be tipped from the pots into paraffin or neat insecticide. Another method is to spray or dust the plants with HCH.

To keep the insects out of the flower heads, smear the top 10in of each stem with petroleum jelly. If this is done before the buds open, it will prevent earwigs from reaching the blooms.

Double trouble

Why do some of my double dahlias look like singles, with large, open centres?

Your dahlias have become what gardeners call 'daisy-eyed'. Such singling is often accompanied by a stem weakness which makes the bloom unfit for anything other than the compost heap. What causes the problem is a mystery. Sometimes growers will blame the weather – and there is no doubt that long, dry spells do encourage singling. It has also been suggested that some singling is due to excessive use of fertilisers, either in the autumn or during the growing season.

Fortunately, singling is not a major problem and the percentages that make the change are low and bearable. Nevertheless, it's best not to store any affected stock for replanting in the following season. Only rarely do dahlia plants that have singled reappear as doubles next time.

Many dahlias from one

How do I go about increasing my stock of dahlias?

There are two methods – taking cuttings and dividing the tubers – and both will give you replicas of the parent flower. If you have a greenhouse, the best way to increase dahlias is by cuttings. If not, you can divide the overwintered tubers into several sections, but this, of course, will give you fewer plants.

For details of both methods of propagation, see the panel on the left.

To give you some idea of numbers, a tuber may be divided into three or four, yielding three or four plants. Or it could be allowed to shoot and produce a dozen or more offspring from cuttings.

To lift or not to lift

Do I really need to lift all my dahlias every winter, or can I safely leave them in the ground?

No question about it: it's always safer to lift and store. If you don't, your dahlias will be in peril from slugs, wireworms, such fungal diseases as the devastating *Botrytis cinerea* (grey mould) and, of course, frost.

Even in the milder parts of the country, frost can take its toll in a bad winter, as many a Devonian and Cornish dahlia grower will ruefully admit.

Amateur gardeners, though, can point just as ruefully to the losses they have experienced when, dutifully cutting back dahlias after the first hard frost of winter has blackened the foliage, they have lifted and stored the tubers. By far the most likely cause of such failures is inadequate preparation for storage.

After lifting, take the tubers to a greenhouse or garden shed and allow them to dry thoroughly. This is best achieved by standing them right side up on the staging or bench and allowing air to circulate by leaving open ventilators or windows on every occasion that our contrary climate permits.

After ten days or so, it will be possible to remove any soil trapped between the fatter tubers by shaking them vigorously. Next, cut back the old stem to an inch or so in length,

TWO WAYS TO MULTIPLY DAHLIAS

How to take cuttings

Take the old tubers out of store in February or March, and cut out any diseased parts, dusting the wounds with sulphur.

Place the tubers in shallow trays, and cover them with moist compost to just below the crowns. Keep the greenhouse at 16-18°C (about 60-65°F), with an overnight minimum temperature of 13°C (55°F). Within a couple of weeks the tubers will produce small growth 'eyes'.

Two or three weeks later, when the new shoots from the eyes are about 3in long, remove them from the tuber with a sharp knife, cutting just below a node, the point where the leaves join the stem.

Prepare a rooting mixture from equal parts by volume of peat and coarse sand, and use it to fill 3in pots or trays.

Dip the base of the cuttings lightly in a rooting powder, then push them about 1in deep into the pots. Each pot can take up to four cuttings. Water, label the pot or tray with the variety's name and mark the date.

Keep the cuttings in an unheated propagating frame in the greenhouse, shading them on bright, sunny days. After about two or three weeks, depending on the variety, they will have rooted – you'll see signs of new growth.

Now is the time for potting up your new plants. Use John Innes No 1 potting mixture or a peat-based potting compost. If you use peat pots, the young dahlias can be transferred to their final positions without disturbing the roots. In any case, keep them in the greenhouse until the end of April, then set them in a cold frame to harden off for a week or two before finally setting them out in the open garden.

If you live in a chilly part of the country, do not plant out before early June. Elsewhere you should be safe enough in late May.

1 *In February or March, take out the stored tubers and put them in trays of moist compost. Keep them in a temperature above 13°C (55°F).*

2 *After three or four weeks, new shoots will have grown from the tubers. When the shoots are about 3in long, cut them off just above the base.*

3 *Trim the cuttings back to just below a leaf joint and set them in sandy compost, four to a 3in pot. They should root in two or three weeks.*

How to divide the tubers

Start tubers for division in the same way as for cuttings, though maybe a little later – say March to early April. If you have a greenhouse or a cold frame, set the old tubers in trays of moist compost some time during March or early April. If not, simply wait a month until the weather is warmer, and set them outdoors in April-May.

When the eyes develop, aim a sharp knife down the centre of the tuber, cutting clean through the old flower stem, which will give you two portions. It will then be clear whether further cuts can be made: each one must have a growth 'eye' and a piece of old root to survive.

Sometimes, as many as five or six divisions can be achieved in this way – as many as most gardeners would require from one variety. Plant out the divisions of the tubers where you want them, and the roots will develop.

1 *In March or April, take out the tubers you want to divide and put them in compost, as for cuttings.*

2 *When 'eyes' develop, a week or two later, cut each tuber through the old stem, between the 'eyes'.*

3 *Plant out the divisions when frosts end. They should flower two or three weeks earlier than plants from cuttings.*

and then 'core' out the centre of the stem by thrusting a screwdriver down the middle until it emerges at the bottom of the rootball. This coring will get rid of any surplus moisture still remaining in the stem base; coring is now widely regarded as a better technique than the traditional practice of standing the lifted plants upside down. Finally, trim off all roots less than ½in thick, leaving a small, compact tuber that will not take too much room in store.

You can prevent any – or at least most – fungus attacks during winter by dipping the whole of the prepared root in a benomyl solution following the instructions on the bottle. Dusting the tubers with flowers of sulphur is an old-fashioned, but still reliable, alternative precaution.

Store the tubers in wooden boxes in a frost-free shed, in peat which is almost, but not quite, dry. Tomato boxes – those with corner posts which are taller than the sides – are ideal, because air can continue to circulate round the tubers even when the boxes are stacked.

The hungry dahlia

I've been told that dahlias need a lot of feeding. What's the best fertiliser to use?

Dahlias are such vigorous plants that they will bloom even without fertilisers. But there's no doubt that they'll do much better if they're well fed.

First, make sure that the soil is in good heart by spreading a barrowload of compost or manure over each square yard in autumn when you dig the bed.

Second, give the plants a fortnightly feed with a high-nitrogen fertiliser from June until the flower buds form, then switch to a high-potash feed such as a tomato fertiliser. Stop feeding in mid-October.

A clamp for winter

I do not have a greenhouse or a garden shed, or anywhere to store my dahlia tubers indoors. Is there a reliable method of outdoor storage?

Have you thought about building a dahlia clamp? This is similar to the clamps that farmers traditionally use to store root crops like potatoes. Choose a well-drained position in your garden – under a large tree can sometimes be perfect, with its network of roots to help drainage. Dig a hole about 2ft deep and large enough to accommodate all your tubers.

Dry and trim the tubers and treat them with a fungicide, as for storage indoors (see *To lift or not to lift*, page 115). Line the bottom of the hole with a 10in bed of straw and lay the tubers on it, roots downwards.

Cover with another 10in of straw, then carefully replace the excavated soil and mound it over the clamp.

When cuttings wilt

I have found that dahlia cuttings wilt rather quickly in the peat compost that I have used. Is this normal, or have I done something wrong?

Cuttings strike better in a half-and-half mixture of peat and coarse sand rather than just peat. They will tend to wilt initially, of course, but the secret of good rooting is to keep them erect until the new roots have formed. To do this, shade with newspaper on bright or sunny days; that helps to cut down the moisture loss which causes wilting.

In addition, each morning and again in the evening, aim a mist-spray over the heads

WHAT CAN GO WRONG WITH DAHLIAS

Symptoms	Cause	Action
Refusal to grow, yellowing of the foliage and distortion of the leaves	Dahlia mosaic (stunt virus)	No cure – burn any affected plants
Foliage, especially at growing tips, peppered with small holes. Leaves distorted	Thrips	Spray with malathion at ten-day intervals
Leaves are eaten, usually from the edges inwards. Shoots also eaten and slime trails are readily seen	Slugs or snails	Use anti-slug/snail bait or treat soil with a watering of similar mixture. Remove dead slugs regularly each morning
Stems – especially larger, hollow ones – cut and chewed, to the point where they may topple in the wind	Wasps	Trap wasps with half-and-half mixture of jam and water. Place the mixture in a jar, with a polythene top with a small hole in it. Smear the entrance with jam, and wasps will enter and be unable to leave, drowning in the mixture
Partial collapse of foliage	Ants	Use commercial ant-killer. If left, they are not harmful to tubers, just a nuisance
Leaves badly eaten, some with isolated holes in the centre of a leaf. Small droppings on larger leaves	Earwigs	Spray with malathion or HCH to deter the insects. Or trap them in pots placed upside down on the top of stakes or canes
Curled leaves containing caterpillars. Large pieces bitten from young foliage	Caterpillars	Pick off and destroy. Spray at ten-day intervals with malathion
Starting at the base, foliage changes colour from pale green to yellow, then withers to brown. Higher up the plant, leaf edges yellow first	Red spider mites	Remove affected foliage, even that just yellowing. Burn for safety. Then spray with malathion after first washing down the affected plant with water
Physical presence noted when lifting tubers or, later, in store	Woodlice and wireworms	Woodlice are fairly harmless, but if you want to get rid of them, treat with insect dusting powder containing malathion, HCH or pyrethrum. A single application is usually enough, but examine when in store and dust again if necessary
White mould visible on the stems and fat tuberous parts; especially common on stored tubers	Fungus	Wipe away any mould with a soft cloth impregnated with flowers-of-sulphur dust. Cut away any infected part of the root, back to clean flesh. Allow wounds a day or two to heal, and then dip the whole root in a benomyl solution before returning to store
Distortion of the growing tips, and uneven leaf formation. Distortion not quite so marked as for dahlia mosaic virus (see top of this chart)	Cucumber mosaic and spotted wilt virus	Some growers ignore this virus, believing that the plant will grow through it. It won't. Dig up and burn affected plants or put them in the dustbin
Clusters of shoots, scores on occasions, appear on the base of the tuber when lifted (leafy gall), and as small, brown nodules on the skin of the root when lifted (crown gall)	Leafy gall and crown gall	Destroy severely affected roots

of the plants so that water falls on them. This will certainly help to prevent wilting and assist speedy rooting.

Splitters and cutters

My father always splits his dahlia tubers to increase stock, and says there is no need to take cuttings. Is he right?

If you only want a few plants each spring, then splitting or tuber division is the answer. If you are looking for a lot of plants, then the only sensible answer is to take cuttings (see *Two ways to multiply dahlias*, page 115, for how to do both).

Planting time for tubers outdoors

I have no greenhouse or cold frame. When should I plant whole tubers that I have saved from the previous summer?

You can set out whole tubers, unsprouted, from early May onwards. Mark the spot where you plant with a cane or stake, and set the tubers on a bed of moist peat. Plant them at least 2½ft apart depending on variety. Position the roots of each tuber so that the base of the old stem (where the new growth comes from) is about 2-3in below the level of your garden soil.

If the weather is dry after planting, water regularly until it rains. If the weather is wet, there's no need to water.

Growth is unlikely to surface before the end of May, when, normally, all frosts are over and the emerging green shoots are perfectly safe.

If the new growth comes up too early, then mound up the soil to cover the shoots temporarily, or cover them at night with large pots or inverted jam jars.

Where to see the best of British blooms

I would like to see a selection of dahlias in the ground before I make my final choice about which sorts to grow. Where are the best places to see top-class dahlias?

Visit any of the country's major dahlia shows, held every autumn. There are local garden shows, too, of course, but the major national shows include:

August Shrewsbury; Southport.

September National Dahlia Society's Show at the Royal Horticultural Society's Hall in London; Scottish National Show at Stirling; Risca Show at Risca, Gwent.

Mid-August to end September Joint RHS/NDS dahlia trials at Wisley, Surrey; NDS trials at Bradford, Yorks.

If you want further details of these shows, with locations, send your enquiry, with a stamped self-addressed envelope for the reply, to the National Dahlia Society at 26 Burns Road, Lillington, Leamington Spa, Warwickshire CV32 7ER.

The value of compost

I can get plenty of straw and mushroom compost from a farm near my home. Can I use this to improve the quality of my dahlias?

Yes, but probably not in the way you may think. Mushroom compost (unless it has been given added nutrients commercially) has little to offer except its value as a mulch and soil conditioner, consisting as it does mainly of peat. Used as a mulch, however, to suppress weed growth, and to retain moisture, it is invaluable, assisting the feeder root system to work at maximum potential. Straw – particularly wet straw – is also useful as a mulch if dug in in autumn, but it, too, adds nothing in the way of feed.

If you mulch with straw, remember that when you dig it in, it will leach a great deal of nitrogen from your soil as it decomposes. Add a high-nitrogen fertiliser to the soil when digging in a straw mulch to counteract this. Either that, or rake off the straw and burn it when it has dried out.

Late show

My dahlias flower late into the autumn. Should I let them continue flowering into the early winter or lift the tubers earlier?

Let them flower. If you are lucky enough to live where frosts are late in coming, then November and even December blooms will be a welcome bonus. If you need the space for your spring bulbs, you'll have to lift a little earlier. The tubers, however, will come to no harm, so long as you lift them as soon as the first frost has blackened the leaves. Severe frosts can kill them.

Weakest near the wall

The dahlias in my herbaceous border, next to a 6ft garden wall, always grow tall and willowy, whatever types I grow. What am I doing wrong?

You are, unwittingly, not giving your dahlias much of a chance. Firstly, dahlias do not relish being grown in a crowded border, herbaceous or otherwise, simply because there is too much competition for root room. Rather, they prefer a bed of their own in which the energetic but delicate feeder roots can spread unhindered.

Secondly that 6ft wall is 'drawing' the plants, causing lanky sub-quality growth. You'd get the same inadequate thin stems if you planted dahlias next to a high hedge or beside tall shrubs.

Ideally, choose an open site that gets full sunshine until the late afternoon, and give dahlias their own bed. Your reward will be better, brighter blooms on sturdy stems. Dahlias come from Mexico – once the home of the sun-worshipping Aztecs – and the sun remains equally important to the plants.

Conversation piece

Does it help your dahlias to talk to them?

It won't help the dahlias, but it might help you. And certainly there's a lot of benefit, as with other plants, to be had from talking *about* them – to other growers.

When days grow short

I have grown dahlias for several years now, and noticed that their quality deteriorates dramatically from the end of September onwards. How can I improve their performance?

By the end of September, you will have had almost three months' flowering and the plants are feeling the strain somewhat. What's more, they are preparing for a natural rest period as the days shorten. You can improve quality marginally by extra disbudding (taking away several buds and shoots down each stem), but the colours will fade in the very nature of things.

Saving the seed

Can I increase my stock of dahlias by saving seed from my plants?

Yes, you can increase your stock by saving your own seed, but seed-sown dahlias are never the same as the parent, which is a natural hybrid. To obtain seed, leave some blooms to die down naturally from August onwards. Each of these blooms will form a conical seedhead that may ripen on the plant if there's reasonable weather in September and October. If the weather's bad, cut off the seedheads in late September and take them indoors to finish drying out. Store the seedheads by hanging them up in a paper bag in a cool, airy shed. During the winter, when the seed becomes ripe, the seedhead will burst and scatter seeds within the bag. Keep them there until you sow them in the following March or April.

There is one exception to the rule that dahlias grown from seed do not come true – the bedding dahlias. Seed saved from these will give you more bedding dahlias, providing the parents were not F1 hybrids.

Tips for the shows

I am thinking of putting some of my dahlias in the local flower show. Any tips?

The first lesson about showing dahlias is that beauty is not in the eye of the beholder, but in the National Dahlia Society's book of

'Ideals' (known as the *NDS List of Rules for Judging*). This book sets out requirements for the perfect dahlia, covering such matters as size, formation, depth of bloom (distance from front to back of the flower), cleanliness and freshness. Study the rules carefully before attempting to compete. Once you've absorbed these, then you should master the skill of disbudding.

This disbudding is a matter of removing the ancillary buds, so that the plant's growth energy concentrates on main buds. Each bud cluster has three buds, and, as soon as they appear, disbud by pinching out the two smaller buds with your fingers.

Finally, haunt your local flower show when dahlia showmen are exhibiting – there is no better way of learning how they do it.

HOW DAHLIAS ARE CLASSIFIED

The National Dahlia Society (NDS) divides dahlias into ten groups:

1 Single-flowered

2 Anemone-flowered

3 Collerette

4 Water-lily

5 Decorative

6 Ball

7 Pompon

8 Cactus

9 Semi-cactus

10 Miscellaneous

A number of these groups are subdivided by size, according to the diameter of the blooms.

Water-lilies, Cactus and Semi-cactus, Decorative
Giant-flowered: more than 10in across
Large-flowered: 8-10in
Medium-flowered: 6-8in
Small-flowered: 4-6in
Miniature-flowered: usually not more than 4in

Ball dahlias
Small ball: 4-6in. Miniature ball: 2-4in

Pompon
No dahlia in this group should have a flower more than 2in across.

Colours
The NDS recognises the following 13 colour sections: white; yellow; orange; bronze; flame; red; dark red; light pink; dark pink; lavender, mauve and lilac; purples, wines and violets; blends (of any colours); and bicolours and variegated.

Troubled by gall

When taking my dahlia tubers from the garden last autumn, I found clusters of shoots at the base of the stem and largish nodules on the fleshy parts. Should I be worried about this?

You should burn the tubers or put them in the dustbin. But there is no need to worry about the condition spreading to other plants. The shoot clusters are known as leafy gall and the nodules as crown gall. Both types of gall are rare.

Take them on trust

I am told that dahlias imported from abroad do not grow as well as home-produced roots. Is this the case?

No, of course not. Foreign imports of tubers, especially from important exporting countries like Holland and Belgium, are very strictly controlled. Health certificates come with every batch, and while some disease may be found on occasion, the same can happen with home-grown tubers.

Longer life for cut flowers

My dahlias wilt very quickly when cut. How can I keep them looking fresher for longer?

Cut the flowers early in the morning when they are full of sap and take them indoors immediately for arrangement. Cut the stems at an angle, so that they do not sit flat on the bottom of the vase and thus fail to take up water. Indoors, place them away from bright sunlight in a shady corner.

Plant with a thirst

In a hot, dry summer my dahlias wilt very quickly. I water regularly, but am never sure how much they need. Is there a simple rule?

Dahlias are very largely composed of water, so in a dry spell they need plenty of help. Each plant should receive at least 2 gallons every other day when in full growth – that is, during August and September.

A cage to grow in

What is the best way to support my dahlias?

All dahlias, bedding types apart, need support. Good stakes or strong 4ft canes are necessary unless you want a mid-season disaster as your promising plants are flattened by a summer gale. Place three canes around each plant at planting time. It is then an easy matter to wind string around them to form a cage that will hold even the most exuberant dahlia plant.

No true blue

I understand that the dahlia has every colour except blue. Is this true, and if so why?

Absolutely true. There is no blue in the world of dahlias – that is to say, no blue as clear as the blue of a cornflower. When the dahlia was first encountered by Europeans in Central America, it was already a hybrid. The cultivated varieties which eventually found their way into Europe, some 200 years ago, contained no chemical element from which a blue could be derived.

We do, however, have lilacs, lavenders and mauves that are very close to that elusive blue. In fact many raisers of new varieties have optimistically called their new arrivals 'blue' this or that. All, however, have had to be classified as lilacs or mauves by the National Dahlia Society.

No cure for this virus

Last year a number of my dahlias grew only a foot high when the label on the packet said they should be 3-4ft high. The blooms were twisted and the foliage had yellow markings. How could I prevent this?

Your problem was a disease popularly known as 'stunt' virus – its full name is dahlia mosaic virus. There is no cure; the plants must be burned. Otherwise the disease, which is spread by aphids, could contaminate your other dahlias.

PICK OF THE DAHLIAS

There are thousands of named dahlias to choose from, and the business of selecting what to grow can be daunting, especially for a beginner. The table below, which continues on the following page, narrows the choice by listing recommended varieties, grouped according to the purpose for which they are normally used.

There are three categories: bedding dahlias; dahlias for cut flowers; and exhibition dahlias. For details of what a variety in any particular group typically looks like, see *How dahlias are classified*, opposite.

Name	Group	Colour: White	Yellow	Orange	Bronze	Flame	Red	Dark red	Light Pink	Dark Pink	Lavender, mauve, lilac	Purple, wine, violet	Blends	Bicolour and variegated	Diameter of bloom	Height of plant
BEDDING DAHLIAS (All are under 18in high and have flowers about 3in across)																
Border Prince	Cactus										•					
Border Princess	Cactus			•												
Butter Ball	Decorative			•												
Coltness Gem	Single-flowered	MANY COLOURS														
Corona	Semi-cactus						•									
Exotic Dwarf	Miscellaneous Lilliput									•						
Fascination	Miscellaneous											•				
Gaiety	Decorative				•					•			•			
Inflammation	Miscellaneous Lilliput (single)				•		•						•			
Nellie Geerlings	Single-flowered						•									
New Fun	Decorative			•												
Park Delight	Cactus	•														
Park Princess	Cactus									•						
Piper's Pink	Semi-cactus									•						
Princess Marie-Jose	Single-flowered										•					
Redskin	Single-flowered	VARIED COLOURS														
Rocquencourt	Decorative					•										
Rothesay Herald	Decorative	•					•							•		
Yellow Cheer	Decorative		•													
Yellow Hammer	Single-flowered		•													
DAHLIAS FOR CUT FLOWERS																
Cheerio	Semi-cactus	•					•							•	4–6in	3ft
Cherida	Ball										•				Less than 4in	3½ft
Cherry Wine	Decorative							•							4–6in	3ft

continued overleaf

continued from page119

Name	Group	White	Yellow	Orange	Bronze	Flame	Red	Dark red	Light Pink	Dark Pink	Lavender, mauve, lilac	Purple, wine, violet	Blends	Bicolour and variegated	Diameter of bloom	Height of plant
Connoisseur's Choice	Ball						•								Less than 4in	3½ft
Dana Audrey	Cactus											•			Less than 4in	2½ft
Doris Day	Cactus						•								4–6in	3ft
Gerrie Hoek	Water lily								•	•			•		4–6in	4ft
Giraffe	Miscellaneous (Orchid-flowered)		•		•									•	Less than 4in	2½ft
Glorie Van Heemstede	Water lily		•												4–6in	3ft
Hamari Fiesta	Decorative		•				•							•	4–6in	3½ft
L'Ancresse	Ball	•													Less than 4in	3ft
Mariner's Light	Semi-cactus		•												4–6in	3½ft
Nettie	Ball		•												Less than 4in	3ft
Peace Pact	Water lily	•													4–6in	3½ft
Rokesley Mini	Cactus	•													Less than 4in	3ft
Twiggy	Decorative		•							•			•		4–6in	3½ft
Vicky Crutchfield	Water lily									•					4–6in	3ft
Vicky Jackson	Water lily									•					4–6in	3ft
Willos Surprise	Pompon						•								Less than 2in	3ft
Wootton Cupid	Ball									•			•		Less than 4in	3ft
EXHIBITION DAHLIAS																
Athalie	Cactus									•					4–6in	4ft
Bonaventure	Decorative			•											More than 10in	5ft
Cryfield Bryn	Semi-cactus		•												4–6in	3½ft
Daleko Jupiter	Semi-cactus										•				More than 10in	4ft
Eastwood Moonlight	Semi-cactus			•											6–8in	4ft
Hallmark	Pompon										•				Up to 2in	3ft
Hamari Gold	Decorative				•										More than 10in	2½ft
Klankstad Kerkrade	Cactus		•												4–6in	4ft
Lady Linda	Decorative		•												4–6in	4ft
Majestic Athalie	Cactus		•							•			•		4–6in	4ft
Moor Place	Pompon										•				Less than 2in	3ft
Nina Chester	Decorative	•													4–6in	3½ft
Reginald Keene	Semi-cactus		•												8–10in	4½ft
Salmon Keene	Semi-cactus								•						8–10in	4½ft
Salmon Symbol	Semi-cactus				•				•			•			6–8in	4ft
Sherwood Standard	Decorative			•											6–8in	4ft
Symbol	Semi-cactus			•											6–8in	4ft
White Moonlight	Semi-cactus	•													6–8in	3½ft
William B	Decorative								•						More than 10in	3½ft
Wootton Cupid	Ball									•					2–4in	3ft

DIGGING

Opening up derelict land

What exactly do the terms 'double digging' and 'bastard trenching' mean? I often see them mentioned in older gardening books.

The terms are both used today to mean the same operation. Double digging is a method of cultivating soil to a depth of two spade blades, or 'spits'. It is especially valuable for opening up land that hasn't been cultivated before or has lain derelict for some years.

The first step is to take out a trench along the edge of the plot to be dug. It should be one spade blade deep, 9-12in from front to back, and as long as the plot is wide. Put the soil in a wheelbarrow and take it to the far end of the plot. Alternatively, make the trench half as long as the plot is wide, and move the soil to the other side of the plot. Then you can dig your way down one half of the plot, and back up the other side – thereby saving yourself a bit of barrowing.

Either way, once you've dug the trench, dig over the bottom to the depth of a second spade blade. This is normally best done with a fork because the object is simply to open the ground up, remove any compaction and improve the drainage.

The earth doesn't have to be turned over. Nor is it usually beneficial to bring this less fertile, deeper layer of soil to the surface. If you have any compost or manure, work as much as you can spare into this lower layer with the fork.

Put the fork aside and dig with the spade a second trench beside the first, turning the earth from it over onto the first trench. By the time you've finished this second trench, the first will be full and the ground beneath it will have been thoroughly loosened to a depth of about 2ft.

Continue the forking and digging until you get to the end of the plot. Then fill the last trench with the soil you brought in the wheelbarrow.

Single digging is the same procedure except that the bottom layer, the subsoil, is left intact and isn't dug.

When to dig

When is the best time to dig the soil?

To start with, you need to know what type of soil you've got: heavy (a soil with a high proportion of clay); light (a soil with a high proportion of sand); or medium (a soil with a balance of sand and clay). To work out which category your garden falls into, see *Soil structure*, page 324. Once you know, there is one simple rule to follow: the heavier your soil, the longer you should leave it to weather after digging.

Clay is best dug early in the winter after the ground has been cleared of plants, and then allowed to weather until the spring. Frost will break down the clods during the winter so that by spring the ground can be raked into a crumbly surface suitable for seeds. It doesn't matter if you stand on the soil to dig, or if you use a plank to spread your weight. But during the winter, keep off the ground completely if you can: nothing needs to be, or should be, done to it.

If you have to dig a clay soil between about April and September in preparation for another crop, dig it as shallowly as possible to avoid bringing unweathered clay to the surface.

Light, sandy soils require the opposite treatment. Leave digging until the last minute in spring. There's no problem on sand in creating a crumbly tilth; the main difficulty is retaining water and nutrients. Leave the soil firm over the winter, and it will be holding the maximum amount of moisture, and

HOW TO DOUBLE DIG A BED

1 *The easiest way to dig over a vegetable patch or flowerbed is to take out a trench about 12in wide and one spade's blade deep, stretching across half the width of the plot. Barrow the earth from the trench across to the other half of the plot and dump it there.*

2 *Use a fork to open up the ground in the bottom of the trench. There's no need to turn this subsoil over; just loosen it thoroughly to the depth of a second spade's blade. As you go, work into the ground as much well-rotted manure or garden compost as you can spare – at least a bucketful per yard of trench.*

3 *Fill each trench with soil from the next. Don't lift each spadeful bodily; lever it free, then roll it off the blade into the empty trench. You may find this easier, especially on heavy soil, if you work with the empty trench beside you, not in front. Work your way down the first half of the plot and back up the other side. Fill the last trench with the soil you barrowed across the plot from the first.*

therefore nutrients, in the spring. If it's dug before winter, you may kill a few hibernating pests by exposing them to birds and the cold, but you will also allow nutrients to be washed out by the winter rains.

Medium-textured soils can in practice be dug at any time, but since a medium soil will have some clay, it's best to get the job over in the early winter rather than later on.

How to make light of a heavy job

I recently took over a garden of thick yellow clay. It's going to be a struggle to get it into a reasonable state, but for the moment I simply want to dig it. Do you have any tips for lightening the job?

- Avoid digging when the ground is wet or frozen, or dry and hard. It's almost impossible to do it then anyway. Do it when the soil is just moist.
- Use a fork, not a spade. It's far easier to drive in to the full depth and, because the soil clings together, there's no need for a spade. Remember, a spade is only that shape in order to lift and turn soil that would otherwise fall to pieces.
- Don't try to lift each forkful of earth bodily. Instead work with the trench you're filling beside you rather than in front of you. Simply rest the shaft of the fork on the lip of the hole you've dug. Pull the handle back to loosen the forkful and move it forwards and slightly upwards. When the forkful is free, twist the handle to turn the forkful over into the empty trench beside you. Work into the bottom of each trench all the compost and manure you have available.
- Take small bites with the fork, not large ones. The job will take longer, but your back will be grateful.
- If the work really gets too much for you, consider hiring a heavy-duty cultivator for the day. The machine will at least get part of the job done.

The value of the deep-bed system

Digging my vegetable patch is getting increasingly difficult as I get older. Is there any way of avoiding it?

There's really only one way and that is by adopting what's called the bed system or deep-bed system. The idea is to grow all your crops in beds, and to make the paths between them permanent ones. That way you never need to dig the area of the paths. And since you won't be walking on the beds, the ground won't get compacted, so you won't need to dig the beds deeply, either.

The biggest job with the bed system is setting it up. Dig the ground as deeply as possible beforehand to ensure perfect drainage in the early years. Then mark off the ground into beds 4-5ft wide with 1-2ft paths between each. Choose the final width of the bed by the length of your arms. You should be able to reach comfortably into the middle from each side.

Have short rows of vegetables running across the beds; you will get in just as many plants as if the rows ran along the bed in the traditional pattern, and it makes harvesting and cultivation much easier.

After a crop has been cleared, the bed needs only to be lightly forked over and a good helping of garden compost or manure added. The compost can either be left on top or lightly worked in. This bulky organic matter is important because, in the absence of deep digging, it's the only way the soil can be kept open.

Over the years, the bed system will improve the drainage and depth of your soil radically – and almost effortlessly. It has a useful bonus, too: crop rotation is very easy to plan and keep track of.

If you want to cut down digging in the flower garden as well, try to use perennials, trees and shrubs instead of bedding plants. Permanent plantings require little work, and the ground around them can be mulched with peat or bark, thus avoiding the need for any but shallow cultivation.

When a machine is best for digging

Using a mechanical cultivator is obviously easier than a spade or fork, but are there other advantages?

A cultivator is not simply a mechanical digger taking the place of a spade or fork. It works differently in a number of important ways.

To start with, on most soils a domestic cultivator will penetrate only 6-9in deep. To dig it effectively, you need to go to 12in at least – about the depth of a spade blade. Unless you have or hire a really large cultivator, the only way to dig those extra 3in is by hand.

A cultivator normally chops the soil up into small lumps and leaves it in a puffy condition. If this is done in the autumn, by spring the soil will be wet and compacted – the very thing that digging with a spade or fork avoids.

Digging by hand buries crop debris and weeds. Mechanical cultivating simply churns the whole top layer of soil up together so that many weed seeds will be near the surface, ready to germinate and grow.

All these are disadvantages of mechanical digging. On the plus side, a cultivator is an easy way to give permanent vegetable beds a light going-over between crops.

A cultivator is also good for chopping up plant debris ahead of digging by hand, and for preparing a seedbed in the spring where the weather has not had long enough to break the clods of earth into a layer of breadcrumb-sized particles – what expert gardeners call a fine tilth.

It can also be used for weeding and for breaking up a surface crust between the rows of a standing crop or between fruit canes and bushes.

One final tip: just as you should avoid digging in the wet, so you should keep a cultivator off wet soil. If the soil is wet enough to stick to the blades, it will clog the machine up rapidly and, even if you clear the blades, cultivating soil in that condition will turn it into pudding and ruin its structure.

Digging without backache

After a couple of hours of digging in the garden I find it hard to stand up straight for a while; I'm seized up solid. Is there any way round the problem?

There are no complete cures, but there are some things you can do to lessen the strain on your back.

- Take it easy and don't rush at the job. Remember you are using muscles that may not be used for much else.
- Avoid digging in windy weather. Strong winds and cold chill the muscles and accelerate fatigue.
- Do a little at a time. When you get the first twinge of pain, stop.
- Think about your digging technique. If you find yourself lifting each spadeful bodily, try to adopt a less arduous technique. Stand so that you're facing along the trench you're digging, with the trench you're filling beside you rather than in front. Push the blade into the ground as usual, then pull back on the handle. Using the lip of the cut as a fulcrum, lever the spadeful of earth free, then simply roll it sideways off the blade into the trench you're filling.
- Try to keep a hollow back as you dig, and bend your knees rather than your back.
- Consider buying a special spring-assisted spade that flicks the soil forward. Try one out in a shop or, better still, at home to see whether you feel comfortable using it.

To dig . . . or not to dig

Some people say that digging to prepare a flower garden is not only a waste of time but actually harmful. Is there any truth in this or is it simply wishful thinking?

It's a total myth; pay no attention to it at all. Ground needs to be prepared thoroughly, whether it is to take vegetables or flowers.

Just like vegetables, trees, shrubs and herbaceous plants do best in a ground which has been dug deeply to ensure that it drains well and that roots can penetrate without difficulty. They also prefer soil which has been enriched with compost or manure so that it holds moisture and nutrients well. It's possible that the no-digging-in-flowerbeds myth comes from a misunderstanding of the perfectly correct view that once flowers and shrubs are established and flourishing, they should, generally speaking, not be disturbed. This precludes digging the ground around them, for whatever purpose. But leaving established plants undisturbed does not mean that the ground should not be dug thoroughly *before* planting.

The worst thing that can happen to any plant is to have its root system constantly messed about, particularly the fine surface roots that do most of the searching for food and water.

If these are cut off every so often, either by digging or by deep hoeing, the plant is forced to divert energy from flowering to renewing the damaged roots.

If the ground around established plants needs weeding, use a hoe only with great caution. It's better instead to apply an appropriate weedkiller or to spread a mulch of well-rotted garden compost around the base of each plant, though not touching it. This thick weed-suppressing layer will also help the soil to keep cool and retain moisture in the summer.

How deep the layer of mulch should be depends on the plant. Generally, the larger the plant the thicker the layer – 2-3in, say, for herbaceous plants, and up to 6in for a large shrub or tree.

In short, always dig thoroughly in advance of planting, but disturb the ground as little as you can afterwards.

DOGS

Dogs versus lawn

My black Labrador bitch regularly urinates on the lawn. This results in brown and often dead patches wherever she has been. How can I get rid of them?

This is a problem that has been with us ever since dogs encountered lawns. The only real answer is to train her to go elsewhere. Unfortunately, once a patch of lawn has turned brown, nothing can be done to restore the grass, and it will very likely die.

The reason that such patches are normally caused only by bitches, not by male dogs, is simply a matter of quantity. Bitches usually empty their bladders all at once in a single spot; dogs, by contrast, tend to spray small amounts of urine in many places as a device for marking their territory. The common belief that a bitch's urine contains some special ingredient or hormone which kills grass is a myth.

The only magic material that can be applied to solve the problem in future is plain water. If a couple of buckets are emptied over the spot as soon as the bitch has been on the lawn, it will dilute the urine and make it harmless. If you are too late for this, give the dead patch a good soaking and re-sow or repair with a patch of turf from another part of the garden.

Vanishing terrier

My terrier has a passion for digging holes all over the garden – holes so big that he can disappear into them. Is there anything I can do to stop him?

Virtually nothing. At least nothing that's easy. This is more a matter of dog training than of gardening.

You might, however, like to try one of the harmless chemical deterrents based on aluminium ammonium sulphate. If the deterrent is applied sufficiently often to the areas where the dog is digging, it may succeed in putting him off.

DRAINAGE

Clay versus sand

How crucial is a well-drained soil to an attractive and productive garden? I've seen some marvellous gardens on solid clay and some terrible ones on free-draining sand.

It's not really surprising that great gardens are often created on clay, for it doesn't necessarily follow that because some clay soils are badly drained, all sandy soils are therefore much better. A clay soil can actually be better for gardening because it retains moisture and nutrients well, and the plants get a better grip with their roots.

On a free-draining sandy soil, water and nutrients are often quickly leached out, and the loose structure gives little support to plants. The important thing, with either clay or sand, is to understand the nature of the soil and work with it to create good gardening conditions.

Apart from water and bog gardens, it is absolutely essential that all cultivated soil should be well drained.

Some plants, it is true, need more water than others during the summer, but that doesn't mean that they can tolerate a badly drained soil. The vast majority of plants need air around their roots, regardless of their water requirements.

If drainage is poor, so too will be the air supply, and the plants will suffer in consequence.

The fine gardens you have seen on clay have been tended by people who know better how to manage their soil – and the plants in it – than those who have produced poor results in sandy gardens. Successful gardening, on clay or sand, begins with knowing your soil and learning how to maintain it in good condition.

Almost as important is knowing which types of plants do best in particular conditions. It is no use trying to grow plants with a preference for heavy, moist ground in a thin, sandy soil, or those that like light, free-draining soil in near-solid clay.

Plants with wet feet

Are there any plants that tolerate or actually like poorly drained ground?

Very few thrive in it – and remember that poorly drained soil is also poor all round. It is not wet enough for the true moisture-lovers, like bog plants, and it is too wet for the majority of garden plants. In addition, badly drained soil is infertile soil, with little air and reduced bacterial activity, which slows down decomposition and therefore the release of nutrients.

Another characteristic of poor drainage is that the ground is usually only wet at certain times of the year, notably the winter. This is why moisture-lovers must be excluded; they prefer soil that's evenly moist all year round. Despite all these drawbacks, some trees and shrubs will tolerate poor drainage. They include willows (especially those grown for their coloured stems in winter), alders, poplars, hornbeam, sycamore, dogwood, elder, as well as some of the bamboos, such as *Arundinaria murielae* and *A. nitida*.

Soggy clay

My garden is on heavy clay and poorly drained. How can I put it right?

First of all, accept that the clay is there to stay, though there's plenty you can do to make it easier to cultivate and more hospitable for plants.

Bulky organic matter is nearly always the best answer to poor drainage on heavy soil. The best material is well-rotted garden compost or farmyard manure, which should be dug into the ground every year, preferably in autumn. Spent mushroom compost is another possibility, but because it has chalk in it, it won't be suitable near acid-loving plants.

In order to open up the heavy clay and thereby improve drainage, the organic matter must be *bulky*: peat and bark are excellent as mulches and for improving the soil surface, but expensive.

Whatever the material you add, it's almost impossible to have too much of it. Aim to use as much as you can get hold of. Anywhere from a quarter of a barrowload to a whole barrowload per square yard will be fine. If you've got a large area to do, and not much organic material available, do a small patch thoroughly rather than spread the benefit thinly. That way, you'll have the encouragement of seeing substantial improvement each year on at least part of your garden.

Excessive drainage

My soil is sandy and drains freely. Is there a risk that the goodness might be washed out in wet seasons?

Most sandy soils quickly lose any nutrients they're given, unless steps are taken to increase their water-holding capacity. That done, plant foods are also more likely to be retained.

The most effective long-term solution is the regular addition of plenty of organic matter. Dig it into the soil, in the form of well-rotted garden compost or manure.

Correct management of a sandy soil also affects drainage. Never dig it deeper than the depth of one spade blade (9-10in). Deep digging merely opens up the soil still further, increasing its tendency to lose water and nutrients. For the same reason, it often helps to delay digging the ground until the time for spring sowing and planting. This will allow the soil to remain more compact during the winter and retain more moisture.

Finally, always firm the soil well after digging and planting. There is no need to worry about creating a hard 'pan' – an impermeable underground layer of compacted earth. On sandy soil, that will be the least of your problems.

Drains and soakaways

One particular area of my garden lies lower than the rest and is permanently wet. What can I do about it?

Ideally, consult an engineer with a view to having the whole area properly sorted out with land drains. However, this is expensive and may well be unnecessary. There is another and cheaper solution which can actually turn the situation to your advantage.

Instead of trying to improve drainage, why not change the lowest-lying area into a water garden? This could be either a bog garden or a proper pool. For a true water garden, you will probably have to install a water supply and a pump unit to supplement the natural wetness, and you will certainly need to dig out the soil to lay the foundations for the pool (see *Ponds and pools*, page 261).

A bog garden is much easier; it is simply an area devoted to the cultivation of moisture-loving plants, and apart from laying a few stepping stones you probably need do nothing more in the way of construction. For some suggestions on what plants to grow, see *Water gardens*, page 360.

If you have set your heart on drying out the area and including it in the rest of the garden, you will have to dig out a hole about 3ft square and 3-4ft deep in the lowest part of the garden – preferably in a corner. Fill it with brick rubble or stones to within 12in of the top and place a metal grid or upturned turf on top of this to stop soil from falling into the rubble. Add soil until it is level with the surrounding area.

Surplus water will drain into this soakaway and plants or grass will grow on top quite happily. Depending on the area and how wet it is, one soakaway may not be enough, but give it a year or two to see if drainage improves before constructing another. If, after that, waterlogging persists, it is probably due to a high water table; soakaways will then be of no use. The alternatives in that situation are to install a network of land drains – a very effective solution provided you have somewhere to drain the water to – or to settle for a bog garden.

HOW TO DRAIN WET GROUND

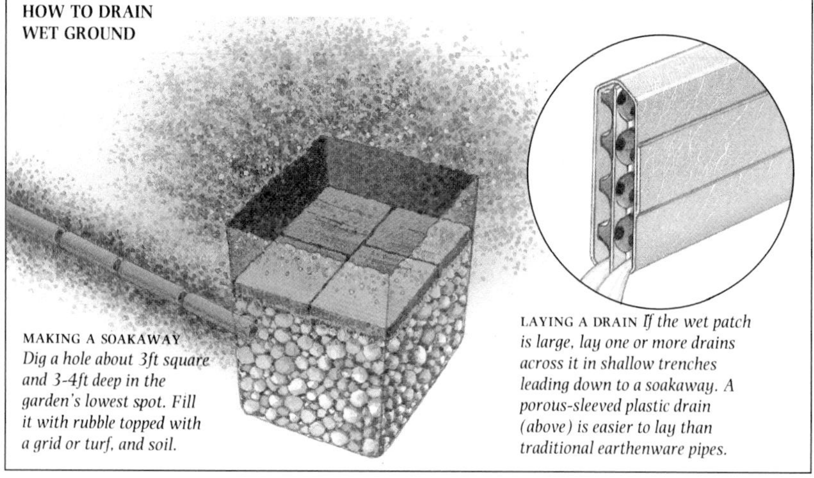

MAKING A SOAKAWAY *Dig a hole about 3ft square and 3-4ft deep in the garden's lowest spot. Fill it with rubble topped with a grid or turf, and soil.*

LAYING A DRAIN *If the wet patch is large, lay one or more drains across it in shallow trenches leading down to a soakaway. A porous-sleeved plastic drain (above) is easier to lay than traditional earthenware pipes.*

DROUGHT

Correct watering

I'm baffled by the way experts talk about watering. Terms like 'sparingly', 'moderately' and 'heavily' seem rather vague. Are there any rules of thumb?

Yes, but not many. This is partly because deciding exactly how much water each plant needs is an art, not a science – and partly because garden experts themselves often use watering terms to mean slightly different things. Having said that, there are three broad rules worth keeping in mind:

1 Terms such as 'sparingly' indicate how *often* a plant needs watering, not how *much* water you should put on at each occasion. If you know a plant needs watering 'heavily', water it just before the surface of the ground around it dries out. Water a plant with 'moderate' needs when the top ½in of the soil feels dry to your finger. A plant that needs watering 'sparingly' should be watered when the top 4in of the soil feels dry.

2 Always water thoroughly or not at all. Merely darkening the soil surface is positively harmful (see *Deep-down watering*, page 126). Each time you water, aim to make the ground wet to a depth of at least 6in. Check by digging out a spadeful of soil the first few times you do the watering, until you learn how much water it takes to soak your soil to that depth.

3 If you're using a sprinkler, a simpler system is to make sure that each patch of ground gets at least 1in of water. Check by standing jam jars in the sprayed area. Note the time you switch on, and leave the spray going until each jar has at least 1in of water in it. If you time the operation when you first do it, you will know how long to keep your sprinkler going on subsequent occasions.

Cool, clear water

The effect of drought on plants is only too apparent. But why do they need so much water?

Soil moisture is vital for plant growth, for several reasons. Minerals and other essential nutrients are dissolved in water, absorbed by the plant roots and carried around the plant to maintain growth. Simultaneously, a plant loses water through the leaves by transpiration, in direct response to the air temperature: the warmer the weather, the higher the transpiration rate.

In a healthy plant with adequate soil moisture, water constitutes at least 75 per cent of the weight. Trees can be a little below this figure, but non-woody plants can be much higher: a lettuce, for instance, is 96 per cent water. When a plant runs short of water, the various chemical functions slow down or stop altogether. The first indication is normally that the plant wilts.

The process of wilting is somewhat complicated and is influenced by the nature of the plant, its stage of development and its general health. In the first stage of wilting, the damage is reversible: the plant will revive if given enough water. However, unless moisture remains available, the plant will weaken again, the extremities drying and dying first, and finally the whole plant. This is unusual in Britain, especially with established plants, and more usually the result of wilting is a halt in growth leading to stunted plants with smaller leaves. In the case of vegetables, crops are seriously reduced.

Curiously, drought can also accelerate flowering, because many plants react to diminishing water levels by racing to reproduce themselves before death.

Sometimes, the wilting and death of young seedlings are caused not by drought but by heavy watering, which makes the soil so waterlogged that the roots are deprived of oxygen and die.

Seasonal drought

Is it possible to predict a water shortage and when does it have the most serious consequences?

Rainfall depends on too many variables for it to be predicted with any degree of confidence more than about three days ahead. Meteorological statistics assess fairly accurately the average yearly rainfall for most areas, ranging from about 80in a year in north-west Scotland to as little as 20in in East Anglia. However, conditions can vary widely within quite short distances, so that local water shortages can also be influenced by the type and depth of the soil layer, from which water is lost by evaporation and drainage, the prevailing wind and the amount of sunshine.

Predicting such shortages comes down in the end to learning the weather patterns around your own home, and watching your plants for signs of drought – particularly at the height of the growing season when the plants are growing fastest and their need for water is greatest.

You may be comforted, though, to know that in an average year most British gardens need very little extra watering.

Planning for the dry

I've just moved to a sandy part of Norfolk and suspect that I'm about to be introduced to a new and drier kind of gardening. Can you suggest some suitable plants for my new garden?

Plenty of plants revel in dry conditions, notably those of Mediterranean ancestry and plants with grey or silver foliage covered with fine hairs – a common plant defence against sun and drought. The amount of acidity in your soil will obviously influence your choice of plants; so will the plants' degree of tolerance to wind, of which there is no shortage in Norfolk. Many plants, though drought-resistant, cannot abide persistent wind, particularly wind carrying salt spray.

If your garden is near the coast, you should create a shelterbelt – a dense windbreak rather than a wall. Suitable plants for the job are described under *Hedges* on page 190.

The majority of plants that enjoy dry conditions also prefer full sun. Those that are tolerant of shade are indicated in the list at the foot of this page.

Holiday drought

How can I make sure that my garden does not dry out while I am on holiday in the summer?

Luckily, in nine years out of ten, we get sufficient rain in Britain for plants to survive quite well for a couple of weeks in summer.

However, survival is not really enough – most gardeners want their plants to go on

PLANTS FOR DRY SOIL

* = suitable for dappled shade; † = suitable for full shade

TREES AND SHRUBS			
Arbutus *	Crataegus *	Leycesteria *	Rosmarinus
Berberis *	Cytisus	Ligustrum *	Rubus *
Buddleia *	Deutzia *	Lippia	Ruscus †
Carpenteria	Escallonia	Olearia	Santolina *
Carpinus *	Euonymus *	Phlomis	Senecio
Ceanothus	Fatsia †	Potentilla	Sorbaria
Choisya	Forsythia *	*Prunus laurocerasus* *	Sorbus *
Cistus	Hebe *	*P. lusitanica*	Spartium
Coronilla	Hippophae *	Pyrus	Symphoricarpos *
Corylus	Ilex *	Rhus *	Syringa
Cotinus	Juniperus	Ribes *	Tamarix
Cotoneaster *	Lavandula	Robinia	*Vinca major* †
PERENNIALS			
Acanthus	Centranthus	Euphorbia	Malva *
Achillea	Corydalis	Gaillardia	Nepeta
Anchusa	Cynoglossum	Gypsophila	Platycodon
Artemisia	Dianthus	*Iris foetidissima* †	Rudbeckia
Campanula *	Dictamnus	Kniphofia	Stachys
Catananche	Echinops	Limonium	Stipa
Centaurea	Eryngium	Linum	
BULBS			
Allium	Chionodoxa	Gladiolus	Ornithogalum *
Alstroemeria	Crocosmia	Hyacinthus	Tulipa
Anemone 'De Caen'	Cyclamen †	Nerine	
ALPINES			
Achillea	Campanula *	Gypsophila	Sedum
Aethionema	Cerastium *	Helianthemum	Sempervivum
Alyssum	Dianthus	Linum	Teucrium
Arabis	Draba	Penstemon	Thymus
Armeria	Dryas	Potentilla	Veronica
Aubrieta	Erinus	Pulsatilla	
ANNUALS/BEDDING			
Antirrhinum	Dianthus	Kochia	Petunia
Briza	Dimorphotheca	Layia	Portulaca
Campanula *	Echium	Limnanthes	Pyrethrum
Centaurea	Eschscholzia	Limonium	Reseda *
Calendula	Felicia	Linaria	Scabiosa
Cheiranthus	Gazania	Lunaria †	*Senecio maritima*
Clarkia	Gypsophila	Mesembryanthemum	Tagetes
Convolvulus	Helianthus	Nigella	Tropaeolum
Coreopsis	Helichrysum	Papaver	
Cosmos	Iberis	Pelargonium	

thriving. For that purpose, a friendly neighbour who will look after things for you is worth more than all the gadgets and precautions ever invented. Failing a friendly neighbour, start preparing for the holiday at least a month in advance to avoid having young and/or recently set-out plants in the garden. Try to ensure that everything, including vegetables, is well established by the time the holiday begins.

Arrange for vegetables, fruit and flowers to be harvested during your absence or they will stop producing. Before you leave, water the whole garden thoroughly if the weather is at all dry; this is very often enough to keep it going for a week, and for a fortnight in a poor summer.

Inherent in all good gardening policy is plenty of bulky organic matter and firm but not compacted ground. Water retention is much better in such soil, and a good thick mulch, up to 4in deep if possible, between and around plants acts as a further lifesaver. Trees are the least susceptible to drought, followed by shrubs, herbaceous plants and, finally, annuals and vegetables. But all will benefit from a moisture-retaining mulch.

Deep-down watering

Is there any truth in the common belief that 'once you start watering, you have to carry on'?

It depends how well you do your watering. All plants do, of course, need constant soil moisture while they grow. But that does not mean that they need to be watered constantly.

The old belief is a legacy from the days before garden standpipes and hoses, when water had to be carried everywhere. The temptation then was for a gardener to make each bucketful stretch as far as possible; and if you water plants sparingly, the old adage does apply. The reason is that water does not diffuse through soil like dye in a bath. Instead it works much more like a stream flowing down a series of dry pools; each layer of soil, like each pool in the series, gets wet only when all the higher layers are saturated. You can confirm this for yourself by watering a patch of ground, then digging out a spadeful of soil. You'll see that the darker, wet area near the surface does not fade out gradually; instead there's an abrupt line between the wet layer and the dry soil beneath.

If you water sparingly during dry weather, only the top inch or two of soil becomes wet. And since plants form roots only where the soil is moist, roots will grow only in this shallow layer, where they are constantly vulnerable to the drying effects of the sun and in constant need of more watering.

The correct way to water is to give as much as is necessary for it to soak the soil to a depth of at least 6in. Roots will then be encouraged to grow downwards rather than outwards, and the whole plant system will benefit. Moreover, the deeper soil layers, insulated from the sun, will stay moist for much longer, so that you can probably get away with watering no more than once a week even during hot weather.

Coping with water restrictions

What sources can be used if water restrictions are imposed during a drought?

The obvious alternative to tapwater, if garden watering is banned during a severe drought, is rainwater collected in a butt. Water butts are available in a range of different materials, including metal, plastic and wood. Wood is the most pleasing in appearance but also the most expensive; metal butts have a tendency to rust after a while; plastic is cheap and long-lasting, but less attractive.

For greenhouse watering, store a butt inside the greenhouse and collect rainwater through tubes fixed to the drainage channels along the roof; in this way the water will be kept at much the same temperature as the plants in the greenhouse. Of course, you must acquire a water butt well in advance of a drought to give it plenty of time to collect rain, but once you have, you need never be caught short of water for your garden.

Water from wells, ponds and streams can be a lifesaver. No restrictions are normally placed on the use of such sources unless you plan to install a pump-operated watering system. In this case, obtain advice and permission from the local water authority.

Most gardens lack such handy resources and must rely on secondhand water. Bathwater is perfectly good and saved the lives of thousands of plants in the hot, dry summer of 1976. The easiest way of handling it is to siphon it out of the bathroom window into a suitably placed water butt. You can also use water saved from ordinary household chores, from defrosted freezers and the rinsing water from washing machines. It is better, though, to avoid water containing detergents, such as washing-up water, unless you are absolutely sure that the detergent is biodegradable.

Irrigation systems

What is the difference between the various watering gadgets, and which is the most suitable for the average-sized garden?

Apart from specially designed and individually installed underground irrigation systems, the basic designs are the rotary sprinkler, oscillating sprinkler and the sprinkler hose.

Rotary sprinklers throw water over a circular area, up to 25ft across. Some models can be set to spray only part of a circle. Oscillating sprinklers throw water over a square or rectangular area – which makes it easier to get water into the corner of the garden without drenching your neighbour. A sprinkler hose – an oval tube with tiny holes along one side – will water a narrow strip; with the tap turned down low, it can be used to provide trickle irrigation for a single row of plants. It's particularly valuable for precise watering of a limited area.

DRY ROT

Sunken marks

On checking my stored potatoes I noticed that some of the tubers had dark, sunken marks. Will the disease spread to my sound potatoes?

Not unless they've been damaged in some way. The pitted potatoes have dry rot, a fungal disease that must have got into the tubers through a bruise or some other damage that was inflicted on them before storing. Potatoes should be handled gently when lifting. Avoid infection by storing only sound, mature tubers; immature ones are particularly prone to the disease. There is no cure. All you can do is burn the affected tubers, or put them in the dustbin. Gladioli, acidantheras, montbretias, snowdrops, crocuses and freesias are also subject to dry rot, both on the corms and on the growing plants.

When infection occurs in growing plants, leaves brown and decay, and the plants may topple. Stored corms and tubers develop dark, sunken patches which grow and merge until the corms shrivel and die.

Destroy affected plants at the first sign of the disease. Protect the sound ones by dipping them in a solution of benomyl or thiophanate-methyl before storing or replanting. Plant the corms in a different site each year.

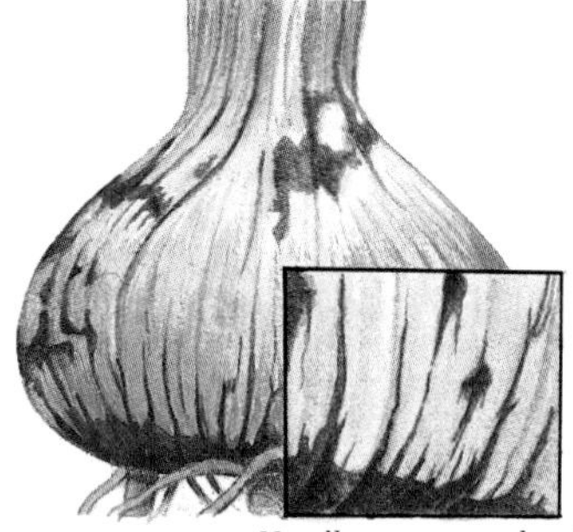

TROUBLE IN STORE *Handle corms and tubers gently when lifting them for storage in autumn. Any wound may let dry rot fungus in.*

DWARF CONIFERS

Aftercare

Do dwarf conifers need a lot of maintenance – clipping or trimming for instance?

No. It is their nature to form bushy growth, so you don't need to encourage it by pruning. Rare exceptions to this rule include the prostrate conifers which, once established, may send out an odd branch in an unwanted direction. If so, remove it as soon as it appears. In addition, a golden or variegated specimen may occasionally send out a plain green shoot – again, remove it at once.

Brightening the garden

Won't conifers tend to darken my garden – even the dwarf varieties?

It is true that a mass of plain green conifers can produce a sombre effect. But the dwarf varieties come in a range of golden and variegated tones which actually brighten a garden – especially in winter. You can plant them on their own, or mix them with the plain greens. The following are particularly valuable for their bright shades: *Chamaecyparis pisifera* 'Filifera Aurea' (bright yellow); *Thuja orientalis* 'Aurea Nana' (golden-yellow); and *T. occidentalis* 'Rheingold' (gold, turning bronze in autumn).

Bulk buying

My local garden centre is offering a collection of dwarf conifers at a reduced price. Can I risk buying them?

There may be no risk involved. Collections of plants are often offered at a lower price than they would cost if bought individually. A reputable nursery or garden centre will guarantee that they are true to their name, and the collection may well be worth buying.

Look over the trees carefully, of course, to make sure that they meet your needs for size and colour, that there are no pests on them and that the foliage is bright and healthy. And if they pass those tests, go ahead and take the plunge.

Brown sides

Why do my conifers go brown down one side in winter? Is it frost damage?

Probably not. Frost tends to damage leaves all around a plant rather than down one side only. The discoloration probably results from wind burn. This is something that particularly affects trees in exposed positions. It is most damaging to young trees, which have less resistance than well-established specimens. The searing north and east winds of a cold winter are usually the culprits. To protect your conifers, you can now buy a special plastic netting with a fine mesh. It breaks the force of the wind, but doesn't stop air reaching the tree. Simply wrap it around any vulnerable plants each winter.

As for existing brown areas, there's nothing you can do to cure them. All you can do is be patient; new growth should cover the burns in a year or two.

When is a dwarf not a dwarf?

Some years ago I bought a dwarf conifer for my rock garden. It has now grown to such a size that it shields the sun from other plants and will have to be removed. Are dwarf conifers really miniature trees – or just young ones?

The term dwarf is slightly misleading. Many so-called dwarf conifers are really slow-growing forms of normal-sized trees – which means that, in time, they grow as big as the standard forms. Others will always be smaller than the standard forms no matter how long they're grown; but since the standard forms of many conifers are forest giants, smaller versions can still grow into alarmingly big trees.

The slowest-growing put on little more than a foot in ten years and can be treated, to all intents and purposes, as true miniatures. But there are more vigorous dwarfs which grow to well over head-height in that period. So be sure to buy from a reputable nursery or garden centre which will guarantee that your dwarfs will stay small. Otherwise you may well find your dwarf turning into a sturdy forest giant.

High spot for a sink garden

I am making a sink garden and would like to include a small tree. But I don't want it to crowd out the other plants. Would a dwarf conifer be suitable?

A tree lends a wonderful sense of scale to a sink garden; with a few stones at the base you can even create the effect of a mountain outcrop. Certain dwarf conifers are ideal, particularly the column-shaped types which take up the least ground space. Among these, one of the best is *Juniperus communis* 'Compressa' – a real gem for a sink garden. Its dense grey-green foliage always looks neat and tidy, and in the confines of a sink it will grow only about an inch a year. A taller column-shaped tree is *J. c.* 'Sentinel' which reaches 3ft. If you want a rounded tree of golden foliage, use *Chamaecyparis lawsoniana* 'Minima Aurea', which will grow from a tiny cutting to about 2ft after ten years.

Some rounded dwarf conifers grow lower still, but they spread to take up more ground space in the sink. The best examples of this group are probably the dark green *C. pisifera* 'Nana' and its golden variegated form *C. p.* 'Nana Aureovariegata'. Both grow to a maximum height of 8in and spread to 12in after ten years. They are domed or 'bun-shaped' and are true miniature conifers rather than just very slow-growing ones.

HOW TO PLANT DWARF CONIFERS

- Always try to plant bare-root trees in spring, when the growing season begins. If you cannot do this, plant in early autumn while the soil is still warm. Container-grown trees can go in at any time of year, provided that the soil is not frozen.
- Choose the site carefully. Remember that even dwarf conifers grow a little each year. Remember, too, that junipers prefer a sunny position (though they will tolerate some shade).
- Prepare the site well, incorporating plenty of moisture-retaining material: well-rotted manure, compost, peat or pulverised bark. Most conifers thrive on a slightly damp soil – but they dislike permanently wet roots. If your soil is waterlogged, you will need to provide drainage (see *Drainage*, page 123).
- Make sure the planting hole is rather larger than the rootball, to allow easy root growth. If the weather is dry, fill the hole with water and leave it overnight so that the surrounding soil is fully moistened before planting the next day.
- Place the plant in the hole. Mix soil from the hole with some peat, sand and a handful of bone meal, and use the mixture to fill the hole. Firm the plant in well, and stake any larger specimen which is planted in an exposed position.
- Soak the area well after planting and mulch the surface with a 2-3in layer of compost, peat or bark chippings.
- Keep the plant well watered during its first season. Spray it from above during warm spells and give it a thorough soaking whenever the soil looks dry. Besides encouraging healthy growth, these sprayings will help to ward off the red spider mite – a hot-weather pest which is a common problem on cypresses, junipers and firs. If the mites do attack – the symptoms to watch for are yellowing foliage, dropping needles and fine webs on the leaves (the mites themselves are too small to see with the naked eye) – spray the tree three times at seven-day intervals with an insecticide such as malathion or dimethoate.
- If the site is exposed, protect the young plant against winter winds by wrapping fine-mesh plastic netting, available from garden centres, around it. Protect it in this way each winter until the conifer is firmly established – usually one or two years later.

PICK OF THE DWARF CONIFERS

A bewildering range of dwarf conifers is available. There are plants shaped like columns, domes, pyramids and sprawling sheets, while colours range from green through grey-blue to bronze, gold and variegated. The figures given here for height and spread refer to the plants' size after ten years – most will grow bigger over a longer period. No figure is given for spread where a plant's habit is to grow chiefly upwards and it covers only a very small area of ground.

Name	Height/Spread	Remarks
Abies balsamea 'Hudsonia'	1ft/1-2ft	Rounded shape, flattened at the top, with dark green leaves. A neat bush for the rock garden.
Chamaecyparis lawsoniana 'Gimbornii'	2ft	Rounded shape with a compact mass of blue-grey leaves. Ideal for a rock garden.
Chamaecyparis lawsoniana 'Minima Aurea'	2ft	Rounded shape with bright golden foliage all year round.
Chamaecyparis lawsoniana 'Minima Glauca'	2ft	Rounded shape with sea-green foliage. Ideal for a rock garden.
Chamaecyparis obtusa 'Nana Gracilis'	2-3ft/2ft	Rounded bush with dark foliage growing in shell-shaped sprays.
Chamaecyparis obtusa 'Pygmaea'	1ft/2ft	Flattened shape with bright green foliage borne on fan-shaped branchlets, slight bronzing in winter.
Chamaecyparis pisifera 'Boulevard'	3-4ft	Pyramid shape with silvery-blue foliage, popular plant, ideal for a heather bed.
Chamaecyparis pisifera 'Filifera Aurea'	2-3ft/2-3ft	Broad pyramid shape with golden foliage hanging in long threads.
Cryptomeria japonica 'Vilmoriniana'	1½ft/1½ft	Neat, rounded shape with grey-green foliage turning reddish-purple in winter.
Picea glauca albertiana 'Conica'	3-4ft/3-4ft	Cone shape with bright green foliage. Ideal for a heather garden.
Picea mariana 'Nana'	9in/1½ft	Low, rounded shape with blue foliage.
Pinus aristata	4-5ft	Pyramid shape with blue-green leaves bearing whitish markings. Commonly called the 'bristlecone pine', this plant is immensely long-lived. One specimen in eastern California, USA, is 4600 years old.
Pinus mugo 'Mops'	1-1½ft/2ft	Rounded bush with densely packed grey-green foliage.
Thuja occidentalis 'Rheingold'	3-4ft/2-3ft	Broad bushy, rounded shape with golden foliage in summer, turning to copper and gold in winter.
Thuja plicata 'Rogersii'	1-1½ft	Rounded shape with foliage of golden-bronze and green.
PROSTRATE AND SEMI-PROSTRATE PLANTS		
Juniperus communis 'Depressa Aurea'	1ft/4-5ft	Semi-prostrate juniper with bronze winter foliage turning gold in spring and early summer. Should be planted in full sun.
Juniperus x *media* 'Old Gold'	3-4ft/4-5ft	One of the brightest of the semi-prostrate junipers, with rich golden foliage.
Juniperus sabina 'Tamariscifolia'	1ft/4-5ft	Popular prostrate juniper with dark, blue-green foliage bursting from a mass of horizontal shoots.
Juniperus squamata 'Blue Carpet'	1ft/3-4ft	Low-growing and semi-prostrate with vivid silver-blue foliage. Good for ground cover. Leading shoots may require trimming.
Microbiota decussata	2-3ft/3ft	Low-growing plant with lacy, densely packed foliage. Colours are rich green in summer, bronze in winter. Ideal for ground cover.
Taxus baccata 'Repens Aurea'	2ft/3-4ft	Spreading yew with golden-yellow foliage.

Ten years is about the limit for any conifer in a sink garden. After that, buy a new young plant and move the old one out into the open garden.

For some ideas about what to plant in a sink garden around the tree you choose, see *Garden in a sink*, page 9.

Trees for a tub

I have acquired a splendid pair of 2ft diameter urns that I have mounted at each end of the patio. I have a fancy to grow dwarf conifers in them. Is the notion practical?

Perfectly. Dwarf conifers can be grown almost anywhere provided you give them soil with plenty of humus. You won't need to change the soil completely for about ten years. Just scrape away the top inch or so of compost every third year in spring and top-dress with fresh compost. The only problems with urns are possible drought, and freezing winds in winter, which have the same effect of denying moisture to the plant inside. So water your plants in drying weather, and stand the urns in places where they are sheltered from east and north-east winds.

Almost any dwarf conifers would do well, but for dramatic effect you might consider these, any of which can be grown in an urn which is at least 2ft across and 2ft deep:

Abies nordmanniana 'Aurea Nana' (2ft high) Wide-spreading golden branches.

Cedrus deodara 'Golden Horizon' (2ft) Forms a mound of weeping grey-gold.

Chamaecyparis lawsoniana 'Minima Aurea' (2ft) Golden-yellow bush.

Juniperus squamata 'Blue Carpet' (12in) Prostrate. Blue-green leaves.

Picea glauca albertiana 'Conica' (4ft) Very compact, dark green pyramid.

Taxus baccata 'Standishii' (4ft) Very slow-growing, golden columnar yew.

Thuja orientalis 'Aurea Nana' (2ft) Rounded tree with golden-yellow foliage.

Increasing stock

Is it possible to raise new dwarf conifers from existing plants – by taking cuttings, say?

Some dwarf conifers are raised by grafting, and the process is too specialised for the average home gardener. If, nevertheless, you want to try your hand at the technique, see *Grafting*, page 160. However, many other conifers can be raised from cuttings: mainly species of juniperus, chamaecyparis, thuja and cryptomeria.

Almost without exception, the dwarf conifers on the market today came into being as 'branch sports' of standard conifers. That is, they originated from some abnormal growth noticed on a branch. The growth was removed and grown as a tree in its own right. So, for example, a tall column-shaped conifer may have developed on one branch a congested growth which, when rooted on its own, produced a ball-shaped bush.

Such a bush can then be used to produce any number of replicas. But once in a while, one of the bushes may throw out an upright branch like those of the original tree. Obviously, you should remove that branch and never use it as cutting material if you want to grow a rounded bush – you should look for growth that is neat and tight. The same principle applies with all shapes. In taking cuttings of a prostrate conifer, for example, select material that is growing horizontally.

Apart from considering the shape of a shoot, you should also choose growth which is a good, healthy colour and free from any blemishes caused by wind damage. These discolorations rarely do serious damage to mature plants, but can lead to fungal infections when you are growing cuttings.

Unless you have expensive heated propagating equipment, the best times to take your cuttings are March or October. All you need then for a propagating frame is a deep box, with a sheet of glass over the top, placed in a sheltered part of the garden. Having selected a suitable shoot, take your cutting with a 'heel' – a strip of wood and bark from the main trunk at the base of the shoot. To get a good heel, you may find it easiest to tear off the shoot rather than cut it off. Afterwards, trim the heel to get rid of any trailing threads of bark, and dip the raw end of the cutting into a hormone rooting preparation.

Cuttings from green or bluish conifers seem to root much more easily than those from the golden-leaved varieties. So, to give yourself the best chance of success, take more cuttings of the golds than you would with the others – though it's always worth taking at least two cuttings for every one plant you want, since some are almost certain to fail. Insert your cuttings into a tray of peat and perlite (or peat and sharp sand) mixed in equal volumes. Place the tray in your propagating frame and keep the mixture moist but not wet. Cuttings taken in October are usually ready for potting up separately in 3in pots in March; those taken in March should be ready in midsummer.

A heather mix

I am planting a heather bed and would like to mix in some dwarf conifers. Will they need any special treatment?

No. Heather and dwarf conifers make one of the great gardening partnerships. Both are evergreen, and the conifers thrive in the same acidic, peaty soil favoured by heather. Both also share the same general dislike for chalky soil. Their shapes harmonise, too: while heathers spread out at a uniform level, most dwarf conifers grow upwards and can be planted among them for vertical accents and colour contrasts. Additionally, you can use the trees as dividers to separate heathers of different types. Some catalogues offer special collections of heathers and conifers, with suggested planting schemes.

As long as the soil is suitable, neither the trees nor the shrubs will need much attention once they're established – so they're ideal as a labour-saving feature. The main point to watch is the trees' rate of growth. Heathers do best in full sunshine, so it is wise to choose slow-growing conifers which will not quickly overshadow them.

Soils and specimens

Do dwarf conifers grow well on all soils?

Dwarf conifers are not very choosy about soils, but they do have their preferences. Many, for example, do best on a damp soil which is neutral or slightly acid. Dry, chalky soils are a problem for many conifers, but dwarf forms of the following trees will grow well on them: *Juniperus communis*, *J.* x *media*, *Pinus mugo*, *Taxus baccata* (yew), *Thuja occidentalis* and *T. plicata*.

EARWIGS

Traps can save your dahlias

I suspect that my dahlias are under attack from earwigs, for both leaves and petals have ragged holes in them. Is there any truth in the old tale that you can trap them in flowerpots?

There most certainly is. Earwigs spend the day hidden in crevices, often under loose bark, coming out after dark between May and October to feed on clematis, dahlias and chrysanthemums, as well as the leaves of beetroot, parsnips and carrots, which they can reduce to skeletons.

Any trap which satisfies their fondness for dry, upright hiding places will serve very well. Earwigs will readily crawl into flowerpots that have been raised upside down on canes next to the dahlias and stuffed with hay, straw or old newspapers.

You can trap them in rolls of corrugated cardboard, sacking, or partly opened matchboxes suspended from plants. Old, hollow broad bean stalks placed among the foliage also make effective earwig traps.

Removing dead leaves and twigs will cut down the insects' hiding places and limit their numbers. Spraying or dusting the soil and plants before flowering time with HCH, malathion or carbaryl will eliminate both young and adult earwigs. Greenhouses should be fumigated with HCH.

FORKED PROWLER *The idea that earwigs crawl into human ears may arise from the insect's fondness for small crevices. The forked tail is probably for defence.*

FERNS

How to grow ferns from spores

My daughter tells me that her botany class at school have been studying ferns and spores. Sounds complex but fascinating. Is there any way I can grow them at home?

It is a bit complex. To start with, spores are not seeds, but something more primitive, and more comparable in some ways to the pollen grains of a flowering plant. Ferns have neither flowers nor seeds. Instead, each frond bears on its underside clusters of dust-like fruiting bodies that, when ripe, rupture and cast spores upon the wind.

On coming to earth, the spores germinate, and produce minute heart-shaped growths called *prothalli*, which have both male and female organs. Cells from the male organ swim across the surface moisture of the prothallus to fertilise the female organ's egg cells. The result of the union is a tiny fern with fronds that are already recognisable under a magnifying glass.

There are several ways of increasing your own fern stocks from spores, but here's one that seems to work well for all popular varieties, indoors and out. Detach a mature frond on which the fruiting clusters are turning brown, and put it in a white paper bag or fold around it a sheet of clean white paper. In a few days, the frond will release a fine dust of spores.

Fill a small, well-scrubbed flowerpot with a compost of 3 parts peat, 1 part loamy soil and a pinch of charcoal dust, and cover the surface with a layer of finely crushed brick dust. Place a sheet of glass over the pot to keep out airborne spores. Then, with the point of a knife, pick up a tiny portion of spores from your sheet of paper, lift the glass and scatter them over the compost. Replace the glass and stand the pot in a saucer of soft water – rainwater if you live in a hard-water area. Keep the saucer topped up with water even after the compost has become thoroughly moist. Keep the pot in a shady spot in the greenhouse or on a windowsill, topping up the saucer whenever the water level in it gets low.

Not much will happen for some time – 3-12 weeks, depending on the variety of fern – but after a while the surface of the compost will become covered by a low mossy growth.

It is essential that the pot does not dry out at this stage, so make sure that the saucer is kept full. Shortly afterwards minute fronds will appear among the layer of mossy growths, and at this stage remove the glass to permit air to circulate.

Leave the ferns in the pot until they are large enough to handle, then prick them out in the same way as seedlings. Depending on the species, the seedlings may take up to two years to grow to mature plants.

Rock garden ferns

I would like to put some ferns on my rock garden. Which should I choose?

Pick from the spleenworts or aspleniums. The slender, arching fronds of *Asplenium trichomanes*, the maidenhair spleenwort, grow about 6in on slender, black stalks. *A. viride* is similar with green stalks, and *A. ruta-muraria*, which grows well in rock crevices, has stiff, wedge-shaped fronds.

The Kashmir maidenhair, *Adiantum venustum*, grows to a height of 6in with soft, green filigree foliage that turns russet at the first touch of frost but clings to the fronds like beech leaves in winter.

Tiny *Blechnum penna-marina* is evergreen with dark, leathery fronds, but it doesn't like lime. The green parsley fern, *Cryptogramma crispa*, needs an open compost of equal parts of peat and coarse grit. So does *Ceterach officinarum*, which has lance-shaped fronds with undersides of reddish scales.

For elegance, choose the dainty lady fern, *Athyrium filix-femina* 'Minutissima'. Its pale, lime-green fronds, no more than 9in high, emerge from a creeping rootstock that will soon carpet a vacant pocket of the rock garden.

Indoor rambler

I have been given a climbing fern, but I've no idea how to look after it. Can you help?

First, check which plant you have. It's almost certainly one of a genus known to botanists as lygodium. But you'll have to check which species it is, because only one, *Lygodium palmatum*, is hardy. All the others have to be grown indoors.

L. palmatum has quaint, heart-shaped leaves on thin, wiry stems. It is a woodland plant, scrambling in the wild among low shrubs, and that is how it will do best in your garden.

Plant it in a peaty soil and cover the roots with leaf mould or bracken. As it grows, let it wander among azaleas or other shrubs that do not have dense leaf cover. It will look much better naturally like this than trailed around twiggy supports.

The most common of the indoor varieties is *L. japonicum*. It has bright green, hand-shaped leaves and will ramble up to a height of 5-6ft.

Pot it in a mixture of soil-based compost and peat in equal parts, and make a slender trelliswork for it to grow through, from garden canes bound together and pushed into the pot.

Give it a liquid house plant feed two or three times in summer. The stems can become untidy and bedraggled in winter, so cut the fern down to soil level when it begins to look scruffy, and let new shoots sprout in the spring.

Dividing roots on a pot-bound fern

I split up my maidenhair fern, and it died. Now my ladder fern is pot-bound. Should I take the risk of dividing it?

Yes, you can try. The ladder fern has matted, fibrous roots, and should divide up easily. Do it in the spring, selecting the vigorous outer portions for repotting.

Your maidenhair died because, unlike the ladder fern, it has a hard, woody rootstock with just a few fibrous roots. Cut open, the woody centre is exposed and is unlikely to survive; for this reason, maidenhair ferns are best propagated from spores.

Pot up your divided ladder fern roots into 3in pots. Don't be tempted to use bigger pots, even if there is an abundance of foliage.

PICK OF THE OUTDOOR FERNS

Ferns, like other plants, vary in their needs, although they all need moist soil. This chart of hardy ferns – ones that will survive outdoors all year round – will help you to choose species that will thrive in your garden's conditions. Some ferns grow well in more than one kind of soil or position – *Athyrium filix-femina*, for instance, thrives in both acid and alkaline soils. For details on how to check whether your garden has acid or alkaline soil, see *Acid soils*, page 6.

		Soil		Position	
Name	Evergreen	Acid	Alkaline/ Neutral	Sun	Shade
Adiantum pedatum		•			•
Athyrium filix-femina and varieties		•	•		•
Blechnum penna-marina	•	•		•	•
Blechnum spicant	•	•		•	•
Blechnum tabulare	•	•			•
Cryptogramma crispa		•		•	
Cystopteris fragilis			•		•
Dryopteris carthusiana		•			•
Dryopteris filix-mas and varieties		•	•		•
Gymnocarpium dryopteris			•		•
Matteuccia struthiopteris		•	•	•	
Onoclea sensibilis		•	•	•	
Osmunda regalis		•	•	•	
Phyllitis scolopendrium and varieties	•		•	•	•
Polypodium vulgare and varieties	•		•	•	•
Polystichum acrostichoides	•	•	•		•
Polystichum aculeatum		•	•		•
Polystichum lonchitis	•	•	•	•	•
Polystichum setiferum and varieties		•	•		•
Thelypteris oreopteris		•		•	
Thelypteris phegopteris		•		•	

Over-potting is one of the main causes of house plants failing, especially ferns. Use a soil-based compost, such as John Innes No 3. Peat-based composts will be exhausted before the fern is ready for potting again.

Fading maidenhair

My mother has kept an enormous maidenhair fern in the house for years and doesn't seem to do anything to it. Mine struggles along, whatever attention I give it, and drops its leaves. What am I doing wrong?

Possibly nothing. The cause may simply be that there are gas appliances in the house or in the room where the fern stands. Maidenhairs always tend to drop their foliage if there is gas about.

Another cause could be over-potting. Keep maidenhair ferns in containers with their roots packed tightly together. They will do much better than if their roots are encouraged to spread.

Check the compost, too. Many garden centres sell ferns in peat-based composts, and this is good commercial sense. Long-term, though, maidenhairs need something more substantial. Pot up in a soil-based compost and your problems may be over. Try a monthly feed in summer as well, using a standard liquid house plant fertiliser, to keep the foliage in tip-top condition.

Hardy evergreen

Can you recommend a hardy fern that is evergreen. All mine die back to the ground in winter?

Try the hard fern, *Blechnum spicant*. It is a bold character that will thrive in a moist acid soil and will throw out central fronds up to 2ft tall. It is not just hardy, but also one of the loveliest of Britain's native ferns.

Polypodium vulgare, another native, has bright green, lance-shaped fronds 9in high. There are frilled and crested varieties available that will do well on a rock garden, but all will lose some of their foliage in a severe winter, where the blechnum won't.

Another you could try is the North American *Polystichum acrostichoides*. It will grow best in moist soil and dappled shade. Its glossy fronds, 2ft high, have small, holly-like leaves. In parts of the United States they are used for Christmas decoration.

Hanging fern

I have bought a staghorn fern which is clinging to a piece of wood. 'Keep it moist and hang it in the greenhouse,' the nurseryman told me. Wouldn't it be happier in a pot with proper compost?

No, it wouldn't. The staghorn, or platycerium, ferns grow naturally in the crooks and branches of forest trees, feeding on accumulated moss and debris and thriving in an atmosphere moistened by regular warm rain.

They are not parasites, so they are quite happy attached to a piece of log. To start a young plant off, you will need to mix up a little soil-based compost and sphagnum moss or coarse peat, and wire it up with the plant to the side of a convenient piece of wood. Once the plant is established, though, it will cling on by itself. Mist it daily with clear water from a hand sprayer and give it a monthly spray with a foliar feed in summer.

FERTILISERS

Liquid versus solid

What are the pros and cons of solid fertilisers and liquid fertilisers and does it matter if the liquids are applied as foliar feed or directly to the soil? Do different plants require different types of feeding?

In answering this question, the analogy between fertilisers and headache treatments is a useful one to draw: if you want the quickest possible results to alleviate the pain, you take a soluble aspirin or similar product which will be absorbed into your system very much more quickly than a solid tablet, which has to dissolve first. But you can expect to pay more for the added benefit.

So it is with fertilisers. A liquid is taken up quickly by plants and can thus be put to use more quickly than can a solid, but generally it costs more, too. Because of this extra expense, it makes sense to use a liquid fertiliser only when it will definitely achieve some positive benefit – in other words during high summer, the season of most active growth. This applies whatever the vegetable. Indeed, with some plants, like tomatoes, even liquid feeds barely keep pace with their needs at peak growth times.

Conversely, at the beginning or end of the growing season, a liquid feed is wasted – it will have been washed from the soil long before the plants can derive any benefit, or applied too late to make much difference. At these times, therefore, use a solid fertiliser that lasts in the soil for very much longer.

As for applying the liquid to soil or leaves, this too is largely a matter of speed. Applying a foliar feed is perhaps the fastest way of all to nourish a plant. Roots are more efficient than leaves at absorbing liquids, but the feed has to filter down through the soil to reach them, and that slows up the speed at which the fertiliser reaches the plants. Moreover, some nutrients, especially phosphorus, are actually needed by the roots not the leaves – so there is little point in applying these nutrients via the leaves. Apart from being used as a quick pick-me-up, therefore, there is no particular advantage to foliar feeds, and most gardeners manage very well by applying all of their fertilisers to the soil.

The need to feed

Do established trees and shrubs need fertilisers or can they look after themselves?

Shrubs benefit from being fed twice a year, however big they are. Feed them once when growth starts in early spring, and again after flowering or in midsummer, whichever is sooner. Use a special tree and shrub fertiliser or, failing that, a proprietary rose fertiliser which works just as well upon shrubs as upon roses.

For trees, the answer to this question depends on three factors. First, are the trees being grown in good, fairly deep soils and in situations not much different from their natural habitats? Second, are they fairly mature and deep-rooted so that they do not need to compete much for nutrients with weeds or other vegetation? And, third, are they being grown as ornamentals rather than for fruit? If the answer to all three questions is yes, then the trees are unlikely to benefit from artificial feeding, because their root systems will be extensive and tapping nutrient reserves deep in the soil.

If, however, the answer to any of the three questions is no, then the trees will almost certainly benefit from being fed twice a year in the same way as shrubs.

Organic versus artificial

I seem tp be reading all the time about the desirability of using organic fertilisers rather than artificials. But are they really worth the extra cost?

Gardeners probably argue more about this subject than about any other. Part of the argument arises out of the confusion about what exactly the terms 'organic' and 'artificial' mean. A good working definition of an organic fertiliser is one derived from a once-living organism. The names of the substances generally confirm this – dried blood, fishmeal, bone meal and hoof and horn, for instance.

This definition leaves every other fertiliser in the category of artificial, although not all are, in fact, manufactured in the way that the word implies. The straight chemical compounds such as ammonium sulphate generally come from chemical factories; but others, such as rock phosphate, are dug from holes in the ground.

Both organic and artificial fertilisers supply

NPK – WHAT THE LETTERS MEAN AND WHY THEY MATTER

All fertiliser packets sold in Britain carry somewhere on them a group of three numbers. Sometimes the three numbers are divided by colons. Sometimes the letters NPK appear by them. Whatever the form, the numbers always mean the same thing: the percentage in the fertiliser of the three main plant nutrients – nitrogen, phosphorus and potassium, in that order. A fertiliser marked 5:8:10, for instance has 5 per cent nitrogen, 8 per cent phosphorus and 10 per cent potassium – making it a high-potash type suitable for such plants as roses and tomatoes.

Initial	Name	Description
N	Nitrogen	Essential to plant growth because it helps to build protoplasm, protein and other components of plant cells. For gardeners, its greatest significance is its role in promoting leafy growth. Nitrogen is very rapidly washed from the soil and needs replacing regularly by top-dressings.
P	Phosphorus (but generally used to mean phosphate – P_2O_5 – a compound of phosphorus and oxygen)	Important in the ripening of fruits and in the germination of seeds. Phosphorus is also associated with root development and, for this reason, a slow-release form of phosphate such as bone meal is valuable in the establishment of perennial plants.
K	Potassium (but generally used to mean potash – K_2O – a compound of potassium and oxygen)	Essential for good flower and fruit development, although the details of the way that it functions are not fully understood. A liquid feed containing a high level of potash is invaluable in promoting good bloom and fruiting on a wide range of plants.

greater or lesser amounts of the three main plant nutrients – nitrogen, phosphorus and potassium – together with some of the minor or trace elements. Organic fertilisers generally contain more trace elements than do most artificials, although it is perfectly possible to buy specially blended artificial trace element fertilisers. By choosing or making blended mixtures, it is also possible to achieve roughly the same overall balance of nutrients using either organic or inorganic sources.

On the other hand, it is not always possible to obtain fertilisers of both types which act in exactly the same way. Bone meal, for instance, is an organic fertiliser containing mostly phosphorus with a small amount of nitrogen. It is a slow-release fertiliser, breaking down over a long period. Superphosphate, which is the principal artificial phosphorus-containing fertiliser, is much quicker-acting and therefore has a rather different effect in the soil.

So if you want a fast-acting fertiliser, an artificial one is usually best – although there are some fast-acting organics too, such as dried blood. If you want a fertiliser that will go on feeding for a longer period, an organic one will probably be the best bet.

But for many people the speed of release is not the only or, indeed, the most important factor in making the choice. They believe, with some justification, that the extensive use of artificial fertilisers in commercial farming has led to contamination of rivers and lakes because the chemicals are washed rapidly from the soil.

It is also said that the manufacture of the so-called 'straight' chemicals contaminates the environment and that extensive quarrying and mining of phosphates and other materials has despoiled large areas of many countries of the world. Many gardeners feel they do not want to be part of this, even on the small scale of their own gardens. Hence they use only organic fertilisers and are prepared to pay a premium for doing so.

Many gardeners will also argue passionately that vegetables grown with organic fertilisers have a better flavour than those grown with artificials. Of course, the fact that they *do* argue is evidence that there are conflicting points of view.

Ultimately the choice between organics and artificials is personal; but it is more likely to be made on moral rather than economic or scientific grounds.

High-speed feeding

What is a slow-release fertiliser, when do I need to use one – and why have I never heard of a quick-release fertiliser?

A slow-release fertiliser is simply one that breaks down in the soil physically – and, more important, chemically – over a fairly long period. This results in its nutrients being released gradually over a period of weeks or months. Bone meal, a good example of a slow-release fertiliser, is very useful in aiding the establishment of perennials like trees and shrubs, whose roots benefit from the gradual 'trickle' of phosphate as they grow.

The term quick-release fertiliser is not in general use, but there are numerous quick-release fertilisers about. All liquid fertilisers, for instance, are very quick-release in that their nutrients are almost instantly available for use by plants.

Fertilisers such as Growmore, which provide nutrients for a few weeks, but certainly not for months, are the joggers of the fertiliser world – midway between the liquid sprinters and the long-distance walkers.

A slow-release fertiliser is best applied at the start of the growing season to give long-term benefit to relatively slowly growing plants. A quicker-acting product is best used during the growing season, especially with fast-growing annual flowers and vegetables.

How to make the grass grow greener

I am confused about the various fertilisers sold for use on lawns. Do I really need a different fertiliser for each season of the year?

Because gardeners these days do not need to go to all the trouble of mixing their own fertilisers, life should be very much simpler. Standard formulas should by now have produced a small number of standard fertilisers in place of the dozens of homemade recipes that gardeners once had to choose between. But with lawn fertilisers, the trend seems to have been the other way – towards a proliferation of branded mixes, variously labelled Spring, Summer, Autumn and Winter and with or without various additives.

It all seems immensely complex, but it isn't. The simple truth is that grass grows actively in the spring and summer, and very little in the autumn and winter. When it is in active growth, the element that it needs more than any other is nitrogen. Hence the reason for using a fertiliser in the spring and early part of the summer, and hence the reason that all these fertilisers have a fairly high nitrogen content.

At the height of the summer, lawn grasses respond very rapidly indeed to nutrients – and yet this often coincides with the time that the effects of the early-season feeds are wearing off and the grass itself is looking decidedly brown. This is the time to apply a summer 'green-up' fertiliser, which has an even higher nitrogen content and which will have a very quick, although short-lived, effect in restoring some of the green colour to your turf.

The autumn and winter feeds have an entirely different purpose, and a different chemical balance: they are low in nitrogen, and fairly high in potash and phosphates. The potash has the effect of producing a harder leaf, better able to withstand the cold winter weather and the possible effects of fungal diseases.

The phosphate is vitally important in aiding root growth (especially in early spring, by which time the fertiliser will be readily available in the soil). It also promotes the development of sideshoots – thereby encouraging a thicker sward.

Remember to use the different mixes only at the appropriate season. If you are tempted to use up some of the spring and summer feed after the end of August, you stand a high risk of producing soft, lush growth which is liable to be browned and attacked by diseases when the weather turns cold. And a winter feed used in spring or summer will do nothing to turn a dull mat into a gleaming emerald.

There are two main additives used in lawn fertilisers – and both are of doubtful value. The spring feeds often contain a weedkiller. But they are generally applied rather too early for the chemical to have a great deal of effect and, as a result, you will have to apply follow-up treatments anyway of specific lawn weedkillers. Autumn feeds sometimes contain a worm killer; but many gardeners believe that the benefits of worms in a lawn actually outweigh the disadvantages. Worms aerate the soil, bring fresh soil up from below, and speed the breakdown of decaying vegetable matter into humus. Beside all this, the inconvenience of a few wormcasts seems paltry.

How to trace missing elements

I keep reading about the importance of trace elements for plants. How can I tell whether my garden is short of them and what can I do about it if it is?

Trace elements are indeed vital to plants. But your garden is unlikely to be short of them. Trace elements are those plant nutrients that, whilst essential for good growth, are required in very much smaller amounts than the major nutrients – nitrogen, phosphorus and potassium. The main ones are iron, manganese, boron, copper and molybdenum. Calcium and magnesium, which are required in rather larger quantities, are sometimes grouped with them. Most garden soils contain adequate amounts of all of these nutrients, although an alkaline soil can act as a chemical lock, preventing the plants from getting at them.

To tell if your soil has a shortage – whether the shortage is a real deficiency or simply unavailability – the plants themselves are the best guide. Use the chart below to check any plant that looks off-colour. It is possible to apply specific elements to correct specific deficiencies, but much the simplest plan is to apply one of the proprietary blends of so-called sequestered trace elements.

On very chalky soils, whose alkalinity can leave plants unable to take up the trace elements, you may need to apply one of these blends each year in early spring. The treatment supplies the elements in a form that does not become locked up in the soil, but it will not make the soil less alkaline.

On the shelf

Do fertilisers have a 'shelf life' or can I keep them from season to season provided they are stored carefully?

All chemical compounds undergo change after a period, as they react with other chemicals. Since fertilisers are essentially mixtures of chemical compounds, they too will react with the air, with any moisture present, or possibly with other fertilisers or chemicals in contact with them.

Once a fertiliser has reacted in this way, it will be unreliable for its original purpose because its chemical properties will have changed.

The only way to prevent such chemical reactions is to store fertilisers of all kinds in dry stores and out of contact with other chemicals. Nevertheless, try as you may, it is impossible to prevent stored fertilisers from coming into contact with the air and so some will inevitably deteriorate in time. Happily, some of the worst offenders in this respect, like potassium chloride, tend to be little used by gardeners today and others have so-called anti-caking agents added to them, which extend their life in store.

By following these few rules, it should be perfectly possible to store fertilisers reliably for about four years.

Never store bags or sacks of any sort in contact with bare earth. Even on the concrete floor of a garage or wooden floor of a shed, they are better raised a few inches on slats to allow air to circulate beneath.

Try to store fertilisers in a building that is well aerated and not one that is left shut for weeks on end. A regularly used garage is particularly useful.

Always ensure that bags are kept dry and carefully closed after use. If you are mixing your own compound fertilisers, try to do this as close as possible to the time when they

DEFICIENCY DISEASES – HOW TO SPOT AND CURE THEM

Lime-induced chlorosis

Symptoms Yellowing between veins; most noticeable on young leaves.
Cause Iron deficiency.
Plants affected Many plants growing on alkaline soils, particularly hydrangeas, ceanothus, raspberries and acid-loving plants such as rhododendrons and camellias.
Danger period Throughout the growing season.
Treatment Dig in acidic material such as peat. Do not add lime or chalk. Apply a sequestered iron compound.

Magnesium deficiency

Symptoms Yellowish bands between veins, becoming brown. Affected leaves may wither.
Cause Magnesium deficiency.
Plants affected All types, especially apples and tomatoes.
Danger period Throughout the growing season, or after applications of a high-potash fertiliser.
Treatment Spray with a solution of magnesium sulphate (8 rounded tablespoons to $2\frac{1}{2}$ gallons of water) plus a few drops of washing-up liquid.

Manganese deficiency

Symptoms Yellowing between veins of older leaves.
Cause Manganese deficiency.
Plants affected Many types.
Danger period Throughout the growing season.
Treatment Spray with a solution of manganese sulphate (2 tablespoons to $2\frac{1}{2}$ gallons of water) plus a few drops of washing-up liquid, or apply a proprietary blend of sequestered trace elements.

Whiptail

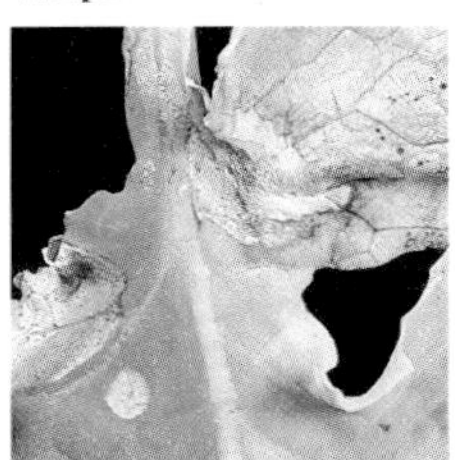

Symptoms Leaves ruffled, thin and straplike.
Cause Molybdenum deficiency.
Plants affected Broccoli and cauliflowers.
Danger period Throughout the growing season in acid soils.
Treatment Water with a solution of sodium molybdate (1 rounded tablespoon in 2 gallons of water for every 10 sq yds of soil).

Boron deficiency

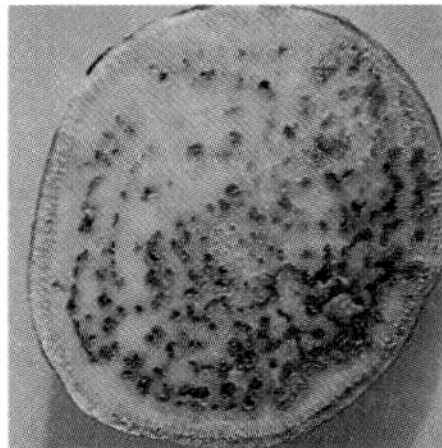

Symptoms Edible roots turn brown inside, cauliflowers develop brown curds, and celery develops brown corky mottling and cracked stalks.
Cause Boron deficiency.
Plants affected Beetroots, swedes, cauliflowers, turnips, radishes and celery.
Danger period Throughout the growing season.
Treatment Apply 1oz of borax to every 20 sq yds before planting. Mix the dose with light sand to ensure even distribution.

will be used – certainly avoid doing it in damp weather.

Always store bags of any potash fertiliser several feet from other types. Take special care to keep any sort of lime or basic slag away from ammonium sulphate, ammonium nitrate, nitro-chalk or superphosphate, with all of which they will readily react.

Don't store bags of quicklime; they should be used immediately after purchase because they are prone to bursting. Ground limestone, on the other hand, can be kept safely for long periods.

Mixing your own

Is there any real benefit in mixing your own fertilisers? There seem to be so many different ones available ready mixed that it scarcely seems worth while.

Very few gardeners, even professionals, have the time to mix their own fertilisers nowadays, and for most gardening purposes there is little real merit in turning back the clock. There are, in any case, some sound reasons for always buying your fertilisers as branded mixtures. Companies that produce fertilisers for amateur gardeners also manufacture products for the professionals, whose livelihood depends on the quality of the results they obtain. As a result, the companies exercise the most stringent quality controls to ensure that the fertilisers are true to the stated formula.

If it is good enough for the professional, it is good enough for you.

But if quality is not in question, why is it even possible still to buy so-called straight fertilisers, the basic ingredients for making compound mixtures? The answer to that is three-fold.

First, most straight fertilisers can and, indeed, should be used on their own for some purposes – sulphate of potash alone makes a fine spring feed for soft fruit, for instance. Second, it's cheaper to mix your own fertilisers from the basic ingredients, since you don't put a price on your own time and labour. And, third, there are occasions when it may be useful to double or triple the amount of one particular ingredient of a fertiliser mixture to suit the needs of one particular plant.

Despite these lingering advantages, the single-ingredient fertiliser seems to be on the way out. The ready-made branded mixes represent some 95 per cent of the market.

The benefits of bacteria

How do bacterial fertilisers differ from ordinary fertilisers and are they likely to be used more frequently in the future?

Bacterial fertilisers have given rise to a certain amount of confusion among gardeners, for they are not by any means alone in being associated with bacteria. Many fertilisers – and all manures and composts – are very largely dependent on the activities of soil-inhabiting bacteria to function at all.

It is bacteria that attack the chemicals contained in such materials and convert them into simpler forms that plants can more readily take up. In order to do their work, the bacteria must themselves grow and multiply, and for this they need nitrogen.

The purpose of adding accelerators or stable manure to a compost heap is to supply nitrogen. And since bacteria have such an appetite for nitrogen, unrotted organic matter should not be added to the soil in spring. This is precisely the time that plants have *their* greatest need for nitrogen, and adding unrotted manure could lead to a serious depletion of nitrogen in the soil.

A bacterial fertiliser differs from an ordinary one because it contains not only nutrients but also the bacteria needed to break them down. Yet very few garden soils are so short of bacteria that they cannot achieve a satisfactory breakdown of nutrients in the conventional way. Bacterial fertilisers are generally more expensive than other types and have had very limited acceptance by the commercial plant-growing fraternity – a fairly sure indication that the benefits they confer are limited.

SIX ESSENTIAL FERTILISERS

GARDEN centres offer a bewildering range of fertilisers – some balanced, some providing high rates of particular nutrients, some designed to be used during particular seasons, with and without weedkillers, pesticides and fungicides. In the perfect garden, all can have a place. But most gardeners can do perfectly well with just six.

1. Granular general fertiliser
A granular formulation of a balanced general fertiliser, such as Growmore, which contains 7 per cent each of nitrogen, phosphorus and potassium. Gardeners who prefer to use organic fertilisers should go for blood, fish and bone meal instead. Use either fertiliser ahead of planting and sowing.

2. Liquid general fertiliser
A balanced liquid fertiliser for general feeding during the growing season.

3. Liquid tomato fertiliser
A liquid tomato fertiliser containing a high proportion of potash for swift results on flowering and fruiting plants as well as on tomatoes.

4. Spring lawn feed
A lawn fertiliser for spring and summer use that contains a high proportion of nitrogen. It can also be used to encourage leafy growth on shrubs and fruit trees in spring.

5. Autumn lawn feed
A lawn fertiliser for autumn use containing a low proportion of nitrogen. The same fertiliser can also be used as a pre-seeding or pre-turfing dressing for new lawns.

6. Bone meal
Sterilised bone meal as a source of phosphorus to aid root development. Mix it into the soil when planting out herbaceous perennials, shrubs, roses, bulbs, climbers and trees.

Ashes and potash

I burn logs on an open fire. Does the ash help to add potash or other nutrients to the soil, and when would be the best time of year to spread it on the garden?

Ash, from an indoor fire or from a bonfire, does have some value as a plant food – but not nearly as much as many gardeners imagine.

Certainly wood ash does contain a variable amount of potash (between about 3 and 12 per cent), derived from the wood, but it is important to distinguish between old heartwood (logs burned on a domestic grate) and the twiggy material burned on a bonfire. Ash from twigs has a moderate potash content. Heartwood ash has very little.

On balance, bonfire ash is useful for such purposes as top-dressing soft fruit bushes in early spring. Domestic fire ash, on the other hand, even if it is derived only from logs rather than coal, is of very little value and can even be counterproductive. It can, for instance, make sticky clay soils even stickier. Domestic ash does have some uses, however: it makes an excellent slug deterrent when sprinkled around susceptible plants such as lettuces. And, if sieved, the coarser material makes excellent base material on which to stand cold frames.

Going it alone with manure

If I use plenty of manure and compost in my garden, can I manage without fertilisers?

Ultimately, the answer must depend on your soil, the types of plants that you want to grow and the amounts of manure and compost that you have available. But the question is important because manures and composts on the one hand, and fertilisers on the other, have rather different roles to play in gardening.

A fertiliser is a substance added to the soil or applied directly to plants solely for the purpose of supplying one or more nutrients that the plants require. With most fertilisers, almost the entire bulk of the product can be used by the plants in some way.

A manure or compost on the other hand is added to soil primarily as a conditioning agent, to improve soil structure – either to open up a clay soil or to help to bind a sandy one. Most manures and composts (peat and shredded bark are notable exceptions) also supply some nutrients to the soil, but they supply very much less than any fertiliser. Farmyard manure and garden compost, for instance, both contain less than 1 per cent of each of the major nutrients: nitrogen, phosphate and potash.

So if you use composts and manures as your sole source of plant nutrients, you will need a great deal of them and it could be that the structure of your soil could be affected adversely. In general, it is much better to strike a balance. Use composts and manures primarily for the value of their physical bulk, and fertilisers to feed.

Cabbages and ale

An old gardener I know swears that a pint or two of ale works wonders for his vegetable patch. Does it act as a fertiliser?

Yes, but not nearly as effectively as a normal bag of fertiliser – and what a price to pay! However, there are gardeners who like to bury a few jars or containers flush with the top of the soil among growing vegetables, then fill them with beer.

The smell attracts any slugs about and they forget to eat and make for the beer – only to drown in it. Slug pellets or slug tapes are more effective – and cheaper.

How to match the feed to the soil

Is it correct that I need different amounts of fertilisers on different soils?

Yes, but only to a limited extent. There are three main soil features that are likely to affect the ease with which plants can absorb nutrients from fertilisers.

First is drainage. A free-draining soil not only permits the easy passage of water; it also permits the easy passage of any nutrients contained in the water. Nutrient loss through drainage will also be higher in regions or seasons with an abnormally high rainfall. Since nitrogen is the most soluble nutrient, it is the one most affected by soil drainage. So perhaps twice as many doses of nitrogen will be needed on very light, free-draining, sandy soils as on heavy, poorly draining clay soils.

The second factor is the proportion of organic matter and clay in the soil. Both will act as a reservoir for nutrients, releasing them gradually to the plants over a long period. So the more clay or the more humus in your soil, the less – and the less often – you will need to feed it.

The third, and perhaps the most important factor, is the soil's acidity or alkalinity – its pH. The pH affects the availability of the three main nutrients – nitrogen, phosphorus and potassium – in different ways.

In an acid soil, phosphates and potash become more soluble and thus more prone to being washed out by rain; hence more fertiliser will be needed. On a very chalky soil (one with a pH above 7.5), phosphate in particular combines with calcium to become highly insoluble, preventing plants from taking it up. The result, again, is that more fertiliser will be needed.

Nitrogen is partly unavailable to plants from fertilisers at both high and low pH levels because these conditions limit the activity of the microorganisms that break down fertilisers into forms that plants can use. Again, therefore, additional fertiliser will be needed to counteract the deficiency.

The net result, then, is that a neutral or nearly neutral soil needs less fertilising than one at either end of the acid-alkali spectrum.

Diet guide for vegetables

I understand that different vegetable crops take different nutrients from the soil. Does this mean that I must put on different types of fertiliser in order to obtain the best results?

You understand quite correctly: different crops do have different needs, though this does not mean that you must have a shed full of specialised fertilisers. There are probably no two species of plant that have exactly the same nutrient demands, and this is one important reason why so many different types of plant can grow happily together in a natural habitat like a wood or a meadow – they are all tapping slightly different nutrient reserves in the soil.

In a garden, the plants have more space to themselves and so do not compete with each other to the same degree. As a result, small and subtle differences in nutrient demand really don't matter. As long as you provide a fertile soil, the plants will extract from it what they need.

This means that, in practice, you can very probably manage with only one type of fertiliser in the vegetable garden, and can tailor it to suit the variation in plants' needs by applying it in different doses. The type you need is a balanced fertiliser with carefully devised proportions of the major nutrients: nitrogen, phosphorus and potassium.

The most widely available artificial balanced fertiliser is Growmore, a granular mixture containing 7 per cent of each of the three major nutrients – the remaining 79 per cent is simply inert bulk.

The chart on the right shows how much Growmore to apply for each of the major vegetable crops. The doses have been calculated on the basis of the amount of nitrogen each crop needs, because this is the most important of all the nutrients. But because Growmore is a balanced fertiliser, the amounts of phosphorus and potassium will be about right, too.

To make sure that you put on the right amount of Growmore, use kitchen scales to weigh out the dose you want – 2oz, say – then empty it into a plastic drink cup and mark the level with a waterproof pen such as a freezer bag marker. You can also get good results by spreading comparable doses of a general organic fertiliser such as a dried blood, fish and bone meal mixture. But because the organic mixture may not be so uniform or precisely balanced as the manufactured one, there may be some slight danger of giving too much of one nutrient and too little of another.

HOW MUCH TO USE

Sprinkle half the recommended amount on the soil a week before planting or sowing. Sprinkle the rest around the plants, but not touching them, halfway between sowing or planting and the expected start of harvesting.

Vegetable	Growmore, ounces per square yard
Beetroot	7
Broad beans	3
Broccoli	5
Brussels sprouts	10
Cabbage	10
Carrots	
Cauliflower	8
French beans	5
Leeks	7
Lettuce	4
Onions	4
Parsnips	3
Peas	0
Potatoes	7
Radishes	1
Runner beans	2
Spinach	7
Swedes	3
Turnips	5

The value of seaweed

Some fertilisers are made from seaweed. What's special about them and are they worth their relatively high price?

Seaweed has been used as a manure and fertiliser for centuries in seaside areas; it is only fairly recently that branded products derived from seaweed have become generally available all over the country.

Like all plant materials, seaweed contains nutrients. But since seaweeds are rather unusual plants – they're actually algae – and since they grow in a rather unusual environment, it is not surprising that they contain a rather unusual blend of nutrients.

Seaweed contains all three of the major plant foods – nitrogen, phosphate and potash. It contains about 1 per cent of potash, rather more than most composts, and for this reason can be valuable on flowering and fruiting plants. One popular brand of seaweed-derived fertiliser is recommended especially for tomatoes, which have a high potash requirement.

On the other hand, seaweed has precious little phosphate, the nutrient that promotes healthy roots.

Seaweed also contains fairly high levels of trace elements such as iron and magnesium. Many gardeners feel that this confers special advantages, but, since most soils aren't short of trace elements anyway, there is little evidence for the belief. On balance, therefore, seaweed makes a useful fertiliser, but by no means an exceptional one. You'll have to decide for yourself whether its potash and its trace elements are worth paying more for.

Not surprisingly, considering its origin, fresh seaweed also has fairly high levels of sodium and chlorine, the chemical raw materials of common salt. That's fine if you want to grow the very few plants which need plenty of sodium – sugar beet, for example – but it can be a problem in gardens. The solution is to compost any fresh seaweed you buy or collect: partly to allow the salt to be washed out by rain; partly to ensure (as with any fresh organic material) that the soil is not depleted of nitrogen while it rots down; and partly to avoid the swarms of flies that always seem to congregate whenever piles of seaweed are left uncovered.

FIRE BLIGHT

Withered leaves

My apple tree shoots have wilted and died, leaving withered brown leaves which do not fall. Is the condition serious, and is there anything I can do about it?

You have described the classic symptoms of a devastating bacterial disease called fire blight. It is a notifiable disease, which means that by law you must inform the Ministry of Agriculture, Fisheries and Food as soon as you can. The Ministry's nearest office will be listed in your local phone book under 'Agriculture, Ministry of' and the officials there will tell you what has to be done.

Almost certainly they will insist on any diseased wood being cut out and burnt, or even that the tree or shrub is felled and destroyed to prevent this virulent disease from spreading.

Fire blight, so called from the scorched appearance of an affected tree, most commonly occurs on pears. But it also attacks apples, quinces, cotoneasters, hawthorns, mountain ash, pyracantha and whitebeam.

The disease is most prevalent at flowering time. Infection starts at the blossom, which blackens and withers. It passes back into the stems, which die back, while cankers develop at the bases. Finally, the disease spreads into the trunk and the tree dies.

In this country fire blight is largely restricted to the southern half of England.

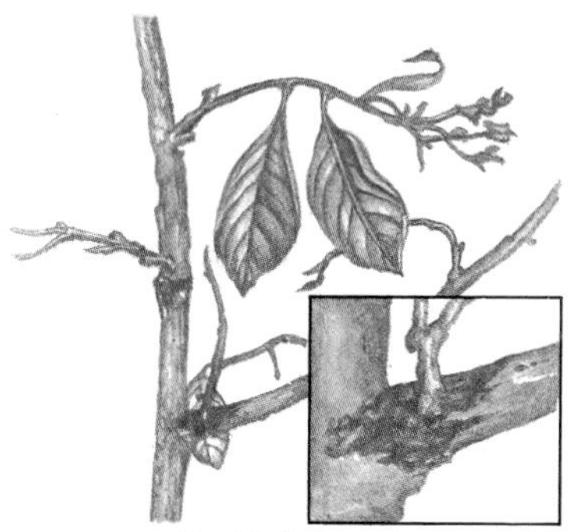

TREE KILLER *Fire blight bacteria can wreak havoc in an orchard. Any suspected infection must be reported to the Ministry of Agriculture.*

FLEA BEETLES

How to stay a jump ahead

No sooner did my wallflower and turnip seedlings get under way this year, than the leaves were riddled with holes. What did it?

Sounds like flea beetles, a great nuisance during warm weather, particularly in April and May. Their attacks on the leaves of young plants slow the rate of growth and may eventually kill off the seedlings.

One way out is to encourage speedier growth with plenty of watering and a dose of a high-nitrogen fertiliser. Once plants have passed beyond the seedling stage, they are less susceptible to attack by the insects.

The black or black and yellow flea beetles, about $\frac{1}{4}$in in length, jump when disturbed, hence their name. They feed on seedlings of the crucifer family – stocks, wallflowers, aubrieta and alyssum, as well as on turnips, swedes and cabbages – leaving small holes or pits, about $\frac{1}{8}$in across.

If you prefer more direct measures than fertiliser, try an insecticidal seed dressing before sowing. If the beetles still get through, dust or spray with derris or HCH as soon as you see the telltale holes. Plants that are already damaged will also benefit from a good watering if the weather is dry.

Brassicas that wilt and die are sometimes the victims of cabbage stem flea beetle. Check by cutting open a stem – you may find the small, cream-coloured grubs inside. The only remedy is to burn the plants, and to grow brassicas elsewhere next year.

PINHOLE PIERCER *Tiny holes mark a raid by flea beetles. Watering and a dose of fertiliser offer some protection.*

FLOWER ARRANGING

Fresh or fading

How do I know if the flowers I buy are fresh?

There are a number of pointers to watch out for when buying cut flowers. For a start, take note of where they are being displayed: a cool, shady interior is best. The lives of cut flowers kept under hot lights, or exposed to sun or wind, will already have been shortened by the time you buy them. Be wary, too, of bunches of flowers which are ready-wrapped – a way sometimes of concealing telltale brown stalks.

Some flowers, particularly roses, are often packed in Cellophane for ease of handling. Look at the outside petals through the plastic: if they are discoloured, the flowers won't last long. Double flowers of dahlias or chrysanthemums should have tightly packed centres of petals still to come out. If the centres are wide open, or have browning petals at the back of the flowers, they are already past their best.

There are giveaways with many varieties. For instance, the calyx of a carnation, below the petals, should feel solidly packed when it is squeezed gently between thumb and forefinger. If it is hollow, the flower is old. A bunch of daffodils should rustle when given a little shake; if it doesn't, the flowers are stale. Sniff the foliage of plants, too; if it has even the tiniest whiff of rotting cabbage, it is old.

Check the stems of cut flowers as well. If they are brown, they have been standing in water too long. Look at the stamens to see they are not dry; they should be fluffy with pollen. In general, flowers should have a bright, crisp look when they are fresh.

Opening time

I bought some anemones the other day and they took a long time to open. Is there some way of getting them to bloom sooner?

Yes. Anemones hate to be put into cold water. So, cut the stalks, put them into tepid water and leave them there for two hours. That will encourage the flowers to open.

The same trick will also work on most other cut flowers.

Florists' favourite

How can I grow those brightly coloured anemones sold as cut flowers?

This favourite from the florist is the *Anemone coronaria*, originally from the eastern Mediterranean. It is grown from a tuber, and a succession of them can be planted at regular intervals through the year to provide a constant supply of blossoms.

However, tubers which are planted in autumn will not normally flower in cold weather unless they're protected under a cloche. At other times, you can expect blossoms about six to eight weeks after planting. Mind you, this will work only in the year you plant. If you leave the tubers in the ground, the following year they will all flower at about the same time.

Surprisingly, the smaller tubers, ¾-1¼in long, often produce the finest flowers. The tubers look like hard, shrivelled raisins, and should be soaked for 24 hours before planting, to soften them. Plant them about ¾in deep and 2in apart in rich, well-dug soil. Surround the whole planting area with a ring of cinders to discourage slugs, which love the emerging young shoots.

Two or three weeks after the first growth shows above ground, a ruff of fresh, green foliage develops, containing the flower buds. When it does, water the soil round the plants with a weak liquid tomato fertiliser to give the developing blossoms a boost. If you intend cutting the flowers, spread straw around the bottom of each plant just before the buds open, so that rain doesn't splash mud onto the blossoms.

Of the many varieties available, a beginner should do well with 'De Caen', which has flowers 2-2¾in across in glorious shades of red, pink, blue, violet and white. Alternatively, try the variety 'St Brigid', which comes in identical colours but is semi-double – meaning that it has more petals than single anemones. Each tuber should produce up to four flowers.

When you've had some experience with anemones, try 'His Excellency' (scarlet), 'Mr Fokker' (blue), 'Sylphide' (violet) and 'The Bride' (pure white).

Dyeing art

I've seen branches of preserved beech leaves on sale which have been dyed. How is the dyeing done and can I use the same technique on the leaves and branches I collect?

One of the lesser-known uses of the antifreeze we put in our cars in winter is for dyeing plant material for preservation.

When you leave your specimens with the stems standing in the undiluted fluid, they will take on its hues – whether green, blue or pink – although the eventual, muted tones will depend on the natural colour of the plant.

Pale green beech, for instance – left in the fluid for about two weeks – will finish up a lighter, clearer colour than dark green laurel, which will turn almost black with this kind of treatment.

It is fun to experiment and see the effects you can achieve. Ferns, for instance, can be immersed in the liquid, rather than just stood in it, for about three days. And large-leaved plants, such as fatsia, often look best if the liquid is wiped over the leaves as well as soaked into the stems.

Split ends

I like to use flowers such as hyacinths in my arrangements, but the stem ends are so soft that they keep splitting as I try to push the flowers into place. How can I hold them together?

Sticky tape will prevent the stems from splitting if you do your arrangement before the moisture in the plants dislodges the tape. Wrap it around each stem just before you position it in the arrangement. The tape will stiffen the stem enough for you to be able to push it into florist's foam or a wire holder. Or use soft darning wool, wrapped around the base of the stalk and tied gently; it's kinder to the plant tissue and holds for longer. Either way, cut the stalks freshly below the binding before positioning the plants in your arrangement.

Sealing the sap

Someone told me not to use euphorbias in arrangements because the milky sap is poisonous. Is this true?

Yes, the latex-like fluid which oozes from the cut stalks of euphorbias (commonly called spurges) is an irritant: it causes inflammation and blistering on some people's skin. But the sap has no harmful effects on other plants in the same flower arrangement.

If you're one of those people whose skin is sensitive to the sap, the answer is to seal the ends of the stalks as soon as possible after picking them.

Do this by plunging the bottom 2-3in of stem into boiling water, or searing the base in a flame for 30 seconds, then standing the plants in a bucket of tepid water. If you have a hotplate, the base of the stem can also be pressed down on that for half a minute to seal it, although this leaves rather a mess. Wash your hands afterwards to get rid of any sap on your skin.

Tall order

I've been asked to provide some tall arrangements for a party in April. But the spring flowers I can get hold of are mostly daffodils with shortish stalks. How can I make them seem tall?

The way to increase the height of flowers with short stalks is to fit them with false stems, rather like those skyrockets where the firework cartridge is bound to a long stick. To do this, you'll need some thin green plant canes and containers for the flowers. Improvised holders, such as empty cigar tubes, work fine. You'll also need some sticky tape, or, better still, some dark green fabric tape which will be stronger and more permanent than paper tape and will not be affected by water.

Start wrapping the tape around the green cane, a few inches from one end, until you have built up sufficient thickness to form a ledge on which to rest the container. Now place the container alongside the cane, its base held firmly against the 'ledge', and continue taping round both cane and container until they are firmly bound together. You can if you like tape two or three containers on one cane, one above the other.

If your design is large, such as a pedestal arrangement, put the foliage in first and then position your extended 'stalks' so that they will be hidden among the leaves. Finally, fill the containers with water, ready for the short-stemmed flowers such as tulips, daffodils or freesias. Check the water level daily, and top it up if necessary.

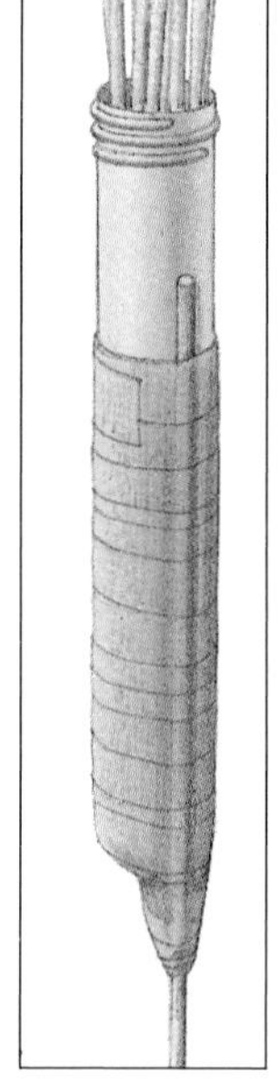

UPLIFT *Tape an empty cigar tube to a stick to hold short flowers higher.*

Deadly daffodils

Is it true that, if daffodils are put in a vase with other flowers, they will kill them off?

Yes, it is true. The slimy sap from freshly cut daffodils contains a chemical which shortens the life of other flowers, especially tulips, when they are brought into contact. But you can render daffodils harmless by cutting an inch off the stalks and putting them into water on their own for at least 24 hours. By this time the stems will be sealed and if you then rinse off the stems and move the daffodils into new water with other flowers, your arrangement will be safe. Don't trim the stems when you move the plants, or you may start the sap flowing again.

Fluffy heads

How can the fluffy heads on mimosa be kept in good shape? Mine usually shrivel within 24 hours.

Mimosa thrives in a humid atmosphere, but dries up quickly in a centrally heated room. The flowers will keep their fluffy blossom if you put them under a glass or Perspex dome. Or, put a plastic bag over the arrangement each night to create humidity.

Symbolism from the East

What is ikebana?

Ikebana is the name given today to the Japanese art of flower arrangement, a very old art form which was taken to Japan by Chinese Buddhist missionaries in the 6th century AD. The word comes from the Japanese for 'living flowers'.

Classical *ikebana* arrangements are usually based on three elements, each of which may be a single flower, leaf or branch: a low-lying element representing the Earth; a tall element representing heaven; and a central element representing man. To find out more about it, write to the Ikebana Trust, 75 Kenton Street, London WC1N 1NN.

SIMPLE LINES *A handful of catkins arch over irises in a small* ikebana *display. Large leaves hide the supporting holder.*

Use a stiffener

Many spring bulb flowers have thick, fleshy stems which are difficult to push into florist's foam. What is the best way to support this kind of stem?

The trick in supporting thick stems is to insert a wooden cocktail stick up the fleshy centre, leaving half an inch protruding. Then poke the exposed stick into the foam. For larger flowers with longer stems, such as arum lilies, a kebab stick is more practical. Neither of these stiffeners will show in the arrangement. Alternatively, make a hole for the stems in the foam with a meat skewer.

Soak to save

How can I keep cut foliage fresh?

There is a very reliable method of treating hard foliage such as laurel, bergenia, ivy, fatsia and mahonia to keep it fresh.

First, trim away any damaged leaves from the stems and also any which would otherwise be underwater in the vase. Remove dirt from the leaves by rinsing them under running water. Or fill a sink or bath with tepid water, with a few drops of washing-up liquid added, and swirl the foliage around in this. Rinse the leaves in clear water and leave them lying in a bath of water overnight. Leaves with a shiny surface (such as those of the varieties mentioned above) will look better still and keep even longer if a few drops of salad or olive oil are added to the water.

The next day, stand the foliage in an empty bucket, or give it a good shake to get rid of excess moisture, and then put it into a large polythene bag. Tie up the end of the bag and put it outdoors in a cool, shady spot such as a shed or garage, or indoors in a cool room in a box with the lid closed.

Treated this way, leaves will keep for weeks as long as they do not get heated (they seem indifferent to cold). But this method is not successful with grey foliage, which does not tolerate moisture on its leaves, or with pale green spring leaves, which tend to stain when soaked.

How to force flowers for early colour

How can I bring some colour to large indoor decorations in spring when the choice of flowers is so limited?

One way of contriving additional colour is to bring plants indoors so that they bloom sooner. If brought into the warm about a month before their normal flowering time, shoots of forsythia, flowering currant, plum and cherry blossom and lilac will usually produce blossom in two to three weeks. Lilac leaves should be stripped from the branches to allow the blossom to develop. The flowers of flowering currants brought on in this way will often be white or very pale pink instead of the customary red.

Stopping the rot

Short of changing the water in my arrangements every day, is there any way to stop the smell of rotting foliage?

It is the leaves rotting underwater which disintegrate and cause the bad smell. So the simple answer is to strip away from the stem all foliage which is likely to be submerged.

Some flowers, particularly stocks, should have all their leaves removed anyway; otherwise the leaves tend to droop and, when wet, smell like rotten cabbage. Strip off all chrysanthemum leaves, too; the fading foliage will otherwise start spoiling the look of your arrangement long before the flowers are past their best.

How to avoid spillage

Even though I am careful not to overfill my container, occasionally I find small pools of water on the furniture beneath. Why is this?

Some flower stems are covered with tiny hairs and these can effectively siphon water out of the container. But more often the puddle happens because water siphons along the surface of a partly submerged leaf stalk, over the edge of the vase and onto the stand beneath. The best answer, then, is to make sure that no part of any leaf is underwater. As an extra precaution, always put a mat under any flower arrangement.

Velvet-covered cake-boards, made to match the decor of the room, give a finishing touch and soak up any spillage, which can, of course, ruin wood. Worst of all is the mark left by a wet metal container on wood; this could require specialised treatment to remove the stain.

How to help bulrushes to keep their heads

Is there any way of stopping bulrushes and pampas grass from shedding their woolly tops after they have been indoors for a while?

If bulrushes (also known as reedmace) and pampas grass shed their tops in this way, it is because they have been picked too late. Bulrushes should be cut when their heads are green; they will turn brown if left to stand in a few inches of water.

Pampas grass is best cut just as the silky heads are emerging from their sheaths. Both these plants can be kept for years, and will remain at their most pliable if preserved with glycerine (see *Four ways to preserve your flowers*, pages 142-3).

Thirsty lilac

There's a lovely lilac in my garden, but the blooms on the shoots wilt almost as soon as I cut them. What am I doing wrong?

The problem is lack of water. You are expecting the lilac branches to carry water up into the blossom and the leaves. The trouble is that the cut branches cannot carry enough moisture for both.

When you cut lilac, prepare it by taking off almost all the leaves, then scrape the bark from the base of the stem to allow water to penetrate more easily. Plunge the lilac in hot water in a bucket for five minutes, then add tepid water and leave it to stand in this for several hours before arranging. That should ensure that enough water gets up the stem to stop the flowers wilting.

Soaking succulents

I like using rosette-shaped succulents, such as the echeverias, to make a focal point in a foliage arrangement. But their stalks soon rot, causing the heavy heads to fall. How can I keep them upright for longer?

You will find that any sort of succulent or cactus leaf rots if it is left in water for a long time. To overcome this, raise the stalks out of the water by holding them on a false stem, such as a slim stick or a piece of stiff wire. Poke the wire or stick into the cut end of the stem. Alternatively, insulate the submerged section of the stem by dipping it in melted candle wax or wrapping it with water-resistant tape.

Echeverias can be used for a few weeks in an arrangement, and then, with their stems re-cut, be replanted in a gritty compost where, with a little luck, they should take root again.

The best time to pick

What is the best time of day to pick flowers?

The best time to go looking for flowers to pick is around sunset, in the moist coolness of early evening. At this time, the plants will contain a full load of water, making it easier for you to keep them topped up with moisture after cutting. Never cut during the heat of the day. The flowers will already be sagging to some degree as the sun's heat sucks moisture from their tissues – and it will then be more difficult to restore and maintain their freshness.

Whenever you cut, it's also worth standing the cut stems in water at once so that the plant's supply of moisture continues with as little interruption as possible.

Prolonging cut flowers

Which plants last longest as cut flowers? And which are the quickest to wilt?

In general, flowers with hard stems (however thin) last best when cut. On the other hand, some soft-stemmed varieties, such as petunias, last pretty well, too. So, it is a question of experimenting. Bearing in mind always that the aim is to transfer the plant from its natural supply of food and water – lost at the moment of cutting – to an artificial supply as smoothly and as quickly as possible.

There are powdered and liquid cut-flower preservatives which help to lengthen the vase life of flowers. Some household products can be of use, too. For instance, some flowers – carnations, roses and gerberas in particular – seem to last longer than usual if put into fizzy lemonade. All cut flowers also appreciate two other additions to each pint of their water: a rounded teaspoon of sugar (which replaces some of the nutrient supply lost when the flowers are cut); and half a teaspoon of liquid bleach (to kill any bacteria and keep the water fresh).

Whatever nutrients are added, it is essential to begin with clean containers and not to allow arrangements to dry out.

Reviving cut flowers

My cut flowers always start to droop after a few days. How can I revive them?

If cut flowers drop their heads, it is usually due to airlocks in the stems, which means that fluid is not reaching the blooms. Roses, gerberas and pyrethrums are especially prone to this trouble.

There are several ways to revive them. The first is to put the cut end of the stalk into about 3in of boiling water, then add tepid water and cut an inch off the stem underwater. Leave the flowers in the water for at least an hour, by which time the heads should be standing up. Alternatively, cut an inch off the stems and lay the flowers flat in a bowl of water for two hours. Another way of reviving flowers is to cut an inch off the bottom of the stems underwater and place the flowers upright, up to their heads in water, to push moisture up through the entire length of the stems.

Where to learn more

The flower exhibits at our last harvest festival were disappointing. Where can we get some ideas on how to improve them?

Most enthusiasts learn their skills at local flower-arranging clubs, where experts are on hand to give tuition and demonstrations. For anyone thinking of making a career of flower arranging, some colleges of further education offer a three-year City and Guilds course. For further information (including the address of your nearest club secretary), write to: The National Association of Flower Arrangement Societies of Great Britain (NAFAS), 21a Denbigh Street, London SW1V 2HF.

Keep the leaves dry

I'd love to use the furry, silver leaves of lamb's tongue in my arrangements, but they always seem to turn blackish and soggy after a few hours. Is there any way to stop this happening?

Yes. All you have to do is to keep any grey or hairy leaves dry and they will stay looking good. The problem is that lamb's tongue (*Stachys lanata*) has very little stem and water often creeps along the leaves. So, using a small pair of scissors, snip part of the leaf away close to the stem, thus effectively extending the length of the supporting stem. This treatment also works well for the large artichoke and cardoon, where the stems and leaves are almost in one piece.

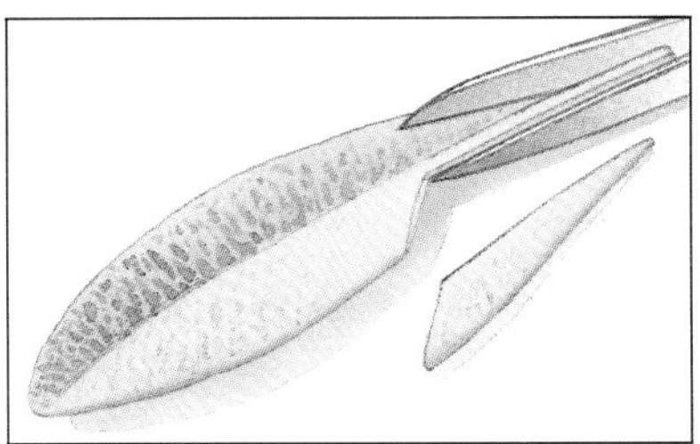

CUT AND DRY *Trim leaves such as lamb's tongue to extend the stem and keep the leaves dry. They'll last longer that way.*

Pressing pictures

I'd like to make pressed flower pictures. Which are the best flowers to use?

The best plants for pressed flower pictures are those with a flat structure and rather thin tissue. For ideas on which plants make the best raw material, see *Four ways to preserve your flowers*, page 142.

An elegant fraud

I've seen some dazzling displays with what seemed like fountains of flowers in narrow-necked vases. I've tried making these, but I can't fit many stalks in. How is it done?

The arrangements you are talking about are really a bit of a fraud, albeit an elegant one. For, of course, no one can fit many stalks into a slim-necked vase, and what skilled arrangers do is to superimpose a wider vessel on the original container and then drape flowers and foliage over it so that it's hidden.

One way of doing this is to roll up a piece of Plasticine and plug the neck of the main container, then bed a small plastic funnel

HIGH AND WIDE *Bed a funnel in Plasticine to give yourself more space in a narrow-necked vase. Hide the funnel with leaves.*

firmly down into this. Both vessels should be absolutely dry when this is done, and so should the Plasticine, otherwise the assembly will come apart when you start to use it. Leave the whole thing standing overnight in a warm place, after which you can fill the funnel with water and insert foam ready for your arrangement.

Another way of getting round the problem is to use wire netting. Cut a piece of netting 6in longer than the height of the vase. Form the netting into a tube and push it firmly into the vase. Fashion the remaining section of wire into a bowl shape. Fit a piece of florist's foam into the 'bowl', and fold the wire round it to hold it in place. Fill the vase with water so that it just reaches the foam.

In both methods, it is essential to keep topping the arrangement up with water so that the foam does not dry out.

Ivy – the arranger's friend

Is it asking too much to grow flowers to cut for arrangement when I have only a balcony and a few tubs?

No, it isn't. But if you are severely restricted for space, with room perhaps for only one plant, the ivy provides practically everything a flower arranger needs, including large base leaves (useful to cover the bottom of an arrangement), long sprays to flow down over a container, and tall climbing branches.

What is of special value to the arranger is that the ivies do not object to being cut back hard. So a few plants will ensure that there is always cuttable material on hand. Even when ivy is old, the thick, twisted stems (stripped of their bark) make intriguing shapes to combine with a few bought flowers.

Christmas cheer

How can I make a festive wreath for Christmas?

Once the province of the expert, the Christmas wreath is now well within the scope of the inventive amateur. The simplest solution is to buy from a florist a circular plastic container, ready filled with florist's foam, which (after soaking) can be filled with sprigs of box, holly and other evergreens. The fun comes in adding colour in whatever form you like – bright red carnations, berries, painted fir cones, small red apples on cocktail sticks, silk flowers, glass baubles or ribbons.

Judicious cuts

How can I cut branches from shrubs for my arrangements without spoiling the look of the plants?

Cutting from the garden – whether flowers, leaves or blossom – must be done judiciously so that it is not obvious what you have been up to. Often drooping branches, spoiling the shape of the shrub, are just the ones to use for indoor decoration. Or shrubs can be trimmed from the back. Look, too, for crossing and overcrowded branches in the centre of trees and shrubs – these must come out anyway to allow air to circulate more freely through the plant. When cutting material for arranging, always cut just above a bud or leaf joint – just as if you were pruning – so that you don't leave the dying stumps.

Invisible means of support

I find that florist's foam keeps breaking up. Is there anything I can use instead?

A simple alternative to florist's foam is the pin-holder, devised by the Japanese for their system of flower arrangement known as *ikebana*. The basic pin-holder is a lead base into which brass nails are embedded, points upwards. Flower stems are then impaled on these prongs or poked between them. Pin-holders made of plastic are of little use for anything other than soft, light plants.

Another popular means of support is thin-gauge chicken wire, with a 2in mesh. Crumpled into the container, wire mesh can sup-

FLOWERS FOR AN ARRANGER'S GARDEN

Name	Flowers
Acer pseudoplatanus 'Brilliantissimum' (sycamore)	Shrimp-pink young leaves (spring and summer)
Achillea filipendulina 'Gold Plate' (yarrow)	Deep yellow (summer)
Aconitum orientale (monkshood)	Creamy-yellow (summer)
Ajuga 'Jungle Beauty'	Gentian blue (May–June)
Alchemilla mollis (lady's mantle)	Yellow-green (June–Aug)
Allium sphaerocephalum	Wine purple (late summer)
Arabis albida 'Flore Pleno'	White (spring)
Artemisia lactiflora (white mugwort)	Creamy-white (Aug–Sept)
Arum italicum 'Pictum'	Green (spring); white-veined leaves
Ballota acetabulosa	White with purple spots (summer); woolly leaves
Bergenia cordifolia (elephant's ears)	Pink-purple (early spring); purple-tinged leaves
Buxus sempervirens (common box)	Pale green, inconspicuous (Apr)
Crocosmia 'Lucifer'	Flame red (summer)
Cytisus x *praecox* (Warminster broom)	Creamy-white (Apr–May); grey-green leaves
Digitalis purpurea (foxglove)	Purple (June–July)
Eryngium alpinum	Metallic blue (July–Sept)
Euphorbia epithymoides	Yellow bracts (spring)
Fatsia 'Variegata'	White (autumn)
Griselinia littoralis	White, inconspicuous (Apr–May)
Hedera helix 'Buttercup' (ivy)	Flowers insignificant; yellow foliage all year
Helleborus orientalis (Lenten rose)	Crimson, purple, pink or white (Jan–Apr)
Heuchera sanguinea 'Greenfinch'	Green (midsummer)
Hosta 'Honeybells'	Mauve (late summer)
Hypericum patulum 'Hidcote'	Golden (July–Oct)
Ilex aquifolium 'Perry's Silver Weeping' (holly)	White, inconspicuous (Apr–May); silver-edged leaves; red berries in winter

port stems of varying sizes at all angles. However, unless it is plastic-coated, it is not suitable for use in a glass or fine china container because it will scratch the surface.

For large arrangements, or those which may have to be moved around, use florist's foam secured on a pin-holder. To keep it stable, wrap wire mesh round it. Hold the whole assembly together with rubber bands or special adhesive tape obtainable from florists. All these means of support can be camouflaged with flowers and foliage so that they are invisible when the arrangement is complete.

Treating young ferns

I like using ferns as background material in my flower decorations. How can I stop them wilting?

Ferns stand up and last for a week or so in an arrangement when they are mature – that is, when the pinhead brown spores can be seen on the backs of the leaves. However, this only happens late in the season. Meanwhile, to keep young fern leaves fresh, dissolve a tablespoon of starch in half a bucket of water. Pour the mixture into a wide container such as a washing-up bowl and immerse the ferns in it for about an hour. Let them dry before use. This technique also helps to keep arum leaves in good condition.

Long-life branches

Is there a way to extend the life of woody branches?

Yes. The key is to recognise that woody branches do not take up moisture easily, and so you have to encourage absorption. A simple way of helping the situation is to hammer the bottom few inches of the stems to expose a greater area of wood to the water and thus allow the stems to absorb more water more quickly. A gentler but slower way of achieving the same result is to take off the lower leaves, scrape away the bark from the bottom 2in of stem and cut the wood on the slant. Put several inches of hot water in a bucket and stand each branch in this as you prepare it. Then add tepid water to fill the bucket and put it aside in a cool place until the branches are needed.

Name	Flowers
Iris foetidissima 'Variegata'	Purple, insignificant (June); orange-red seeds in autumn
Kerria japonica 'Pleniflora' (Jew's mallow)	Orange-yellow (late spring)
Lavatera trimestris 'Silver Cup' (mallow)	Pink (July–Sept)
Ligustrum ovalifolium 'Aureomarginatum' (golden privet)	Cream (July); yellow-edged leaves
Lonicera japonica 'Aureoreticulata' (Japanese honeysuckle)	White to pale yellow (June–Oct); yellow-veined leaves
Mahonia aquifolium (Oregon grape)	Yellow (Mar–Apr); blue-black berries in summer
Nicotiana alata 'Lime Green' (tobacco plant)	Yellow-green (summer–autumn)
Phlomis samia	Creamy-yellow (May–June)
Phormium tenax	Red (July–Sept); leathery leaves
Photinia x *fraseri* 'Red Robin'	White (early spring); crimson leaves
Pieris formosa 'Forrestii'	White (spring); bright red young leaves
Polygonatum multiflorum (Solomon's seal)	White (June)
Prunus triloba 'Flora pleno'	Pink (Mar–Apr)
Ribes sanguineum (flowering currant)	Red (Mar–May); blue-black berries in autumn
Salix matsudana 'Tortuosa' (willow)	Yellow male catkins (Apr)
Senecio greyi	Yellow (June–Aug); silver-grey leaves
Skimmia x 'Foremanii'	Creamy-white (Mar–Apr); red berries in winter
Spiraea x *bumalda* 'Goldflame'	Pink to rose (late summer); red-gold leaves in spring
Tellima grandiflora 'Purpurea'	Green-yellow (Apr–June); purple-bronze leaves
Verbascum chaixii 'Album'	White (July–Aug)
Veronica virginica 'Alba'	White (July–Sept)
Viburnum tinus 'Eve Price'	Pink (Nov–May)
Weigela florida 'Variegata'	Pale pink (May–June); cream-edged leaves
Yucca gloriosa	Creamy-white (Sept–Nov)
Zantedeschia aethiopica 'Crowborough'	White (Mar–June)

Wiring up cones

Pine cones are lovely to use in Christmas decorations, but I am fed up with mine always sitting at the bottom of a display. Is there another way?

The trick with pine cones is to thread them with wire so that you can make more versatile use of them in decorations and displays. Easily obtainable from flower shops, medium-grade stub wire is suitable for making false stems on cones.

Select cones which are dry or at least slightly open. Now, holding the cone upside down, insert the end of the wire between the scales about halfway along its length. Wind the wire round and round between the scales, working in the natural spiral towards the point where the scales recede into the base of the cone.

The free end of the wire is left as an artificial stem, and the cone – painted or covered with glitter, if you wish – can now be used in your arrangement in the same way as flowers with fresh foliage.

Clean as a new pin-holder

To make my arrangements more stable, I often fix a heavy pin-holder to the base of a dish and then put foam on top. But the foam clogs up the pin-holder so much that it is a nuisance to clean. Is there any way round this?

To begin with you can buy a special kind of foam pin-holder which will not clog because the pins are double length and widely spaced. However, if you want to make regular use of pin-holders, there is a very simple way to avoid getting them clogged up as you describe. All you need to do is to stretch an old piece of stocking tightly down over the pins before putting the foam on top. When you want to remove the foam, simply pull out the nylon and all the particles will come with it, leaving the pin-holder clean.

Staggered development

Sometimes I need to accelerate a flower to add colour, while at other times I need to delay maturity. Are there any simple ways of doing this?

The basic rules are that cold and dark delay the development of flowers, warmth and light accelerate it. Whichever you want to do, the first step is to cut the stems and leave them standing in deep water for an hour. Flowers that are just in bud can then be held back by sealing them in a polythene bag and putting them in the refrigerator. Flowers that are already open can be slowed down by putting them in water in a cool, dark room or – to a lesser degree – in a cool, light room.

To accelerate any flower, simply move it, in water, close to light and warmth.

FOUR WAYS TO PRESERVE YOUR FLOWERS

There are various ways to preserve plants so that you can capture the beauty of cherished specimens and always have material on hand for arrangement. Berries, for instance, shrivel as soon as they dry out. But, if picked when plump and fresh, and sprayed with clear varnish, they will keep their shape and lustre for weeks. In general, however, depending on the use to be made of preserved plants, flower arrangers rely on four principal methods of preservation. These are: air-drying; pressing; silica gel; and, for foliage and woody stems, glycerine.

AIR-DRYING

The cheapest, simplest method of flower preservation, air-drying guarantees a supply of plant material for use during the winter months. For this purpose, pick only perfect flowers and seedheads, at a point where they are fully developed (except in the case of helichrysums, whose centres should be tightly furled).

The best time to gather a flower for air-drying is when it is warm and dry – at the end of a sunny day, for instance – because the aim is to eliminate all moisture as quickly as possible. Remove all leaves immediately after picking; they rarely dry well. If you have space in a dry, airy room or shed, hang wire coat-hangers from a high washing line and tie your stems, individually, upside down to the hangers.

To avoid crushing the flower heads against each other, it helps to vary the length of the stems. If you are short of room, suspend flowers upside down in bunches to dry. Some flowers, such as delphinium and larkspur, keep their colour better if they are hung upside down in a dark airing cupboard for quick drying.

In all cases, flowers should be left to dry until they are crisp to the touch. All air-dried material is best stored in the dark. One method is to leave them on the drying hangers with a sheet of tissue paper over the hook to protect them from dirt. Packing them inside a flower box, with tissue in between, is inclined to flatten them, but it does keep out dust. Air-dried flowers can be used to make plaques or flower pictures. They make a good contrast, too, against glycerine-preserved foliage. Alternatively, spray them with paint or glitter for Christmas decorations.

Plants suitable for air-drying Acanthus; achillea; alchemilla; allium; amaranthus; anaphalis; ballota; cimicifuga; cynara; cytisus; delphinium; eryngium; foxglove; globe thistle; grasses, sedges and reeds; gypsophila; helichrysum; honesty; hosta; humulus; iris; lamb's tongue; lavender; liatris; lilies; moluccella; nicandra; physalis; poppies; sedum; sisyrinchium; and verbascum.

BUNCHED UP *If space is short, hang the blooms in bunches. Set them with the flower heads at different levels so that the petals don't get crushed.*

TIE-DRIED *Coat hangers make good drying racks for flowers. Hang them upside down until dry. Then drape tissue paper over them for storage.*

PRESSING

Pressing flattens and dries plant material so that it can be used for all kinds of decorative purposes, including pictures under glass, in paperweights or under Perspex door-plates, and as decoration for candles or greetings cards. However, this is not a method to use with thick or succulent material. Pick only thin-petalled flowers or tendrils and thin-stalked grasses or ferns. Grey leaves press well and keep their colour.

It is possible to buy special flower presses, but weighty books like telephone directories will serve the purpose just as well – and they will hold plenty of material.

Pick on fine days throughout the year, laying the material flat between the covers, with each item separated from its neighbour. Label each entry and also mark each group of materials with an exterior tag to avoid undue disturbance when you come to look through for specimens.

Keep plant material pressed under a heavy weight. The longer it can be kept under pressure, the better: three months is the minimum, and a year is not too long. When you make up pictures with pressed flowers, hang them out of the sunlight to avoid fading.

Plants suitable for pressing *Flowers*: alchemilla; aubrieta; daisy; delphinium; forget-me-not; golden rod; gypsophila; hawthorn; heather; hellebore; honeysuckle; hydrangea; lilac; love-in-a-mist; pansy; rose petals; spiraea and winter aconites. *Leaves*: acaena; bracken; cineraria; cypress; ferns; maple; parsley; rose; and rue.

INTERLEAVED *Tape stems flat to keep them in the shape you want. Separate layers of plant material with sheets of paper.*

PRESS AND HOLD *Use an old book as a press, or make one with thick wood and bolts. Label the contents with jutting tabs as you add them to the press.*

GLYCERINE

Preservation by means of glycerine – ideal for foliage and woody stems – changes the colour of plant material, but leaves it soft and pliable and likely to last for many years if it is carefully stored. Most plants treated this way take on shades of cream, beige and brown, although eucalyptus turns various shades of grey, maroon or purple, and laurel goes almost black. In general, the lighter the green of the original foliage, the more golden it is when preserved. If you want a lighter effect, leave the material in a sunny position for a few days after it has been treated.

The treatment needs to be applied when the sap is still rising – July to August in most cases – so that the mixture will be absorbed to the tips. Treat only mature foliage, and, since glycerine is expensive, select only perfect material. Put branches in a bucket of tepid water while awaiting treatment. To treat plants, mix up a solution of one part of glycerine to two parts of hot water, thoroughly stirred. Fill as many glass storage jars as you need to a depth of about 3in (coffee jars are ideal). Cut the stem ends on the slant and split woody stem ends, then scrape away the bottom 2in of bark, to speed the plant's absorption of the liquid. Stand the plants in the liquid, leaving them to absorb it for the intervals recommended on the right. To avoid spillage, stand individual jars within a larger container.

With large, flat leaves such as those of aspidistra or fatsia, mop each side with the solution first to prevent them drying out and to speed up preservation. Ferns and brackens should be laid in a tray of the solution for about three days, then placed between sheets of paper under a weight for storage. Remember that, as you take each batch of material out, you can strain the solution and store it for re-use.

Once out of the solution, preserved plant material must be kept dry, otherwise it soon turns mouldy. Do not use polythene, which traps moisture and encourages mildew. Instead, store plant material between layers of tissue paper in a closed cardboard box, kept in a dry place, or wrap it lightly in paper and hang it upside down.

When preserved material is used among fresh flowers, the stem ends become moist. They should be wiped clean and dried before being returned to storage. Or you can seal the ends against moisture by dipping them in varnish or melted candle wax.

Plants suitable for glycerine Alchemilla (1-2 weeks); allium (1-2 weeks); angelica (1-2 weeks); aspidistra (3-6 months); aucuba (3 weeks); beech (2-3 weeks); box (3-4 weeks); choisya (2-3 weeks); corn (2 weeks); dock (1-2 weeks); fatsia (2-5 weeks); garrya (3 weeks); grasses (1-2 weeks); grevillea (1-3 weeks); iris (2 weeks); mahonia (2-3 weeks); moluccella (3 weeks – hang upside down after treating); reedmace (3 weeks); solomon's seal (1-2 weeks); sweet chestnut (1-2 weeks); and teasels (2 weeks).

WOODCUT *Strip bark off stem bases so that the liquid soaks in faster.*

BUCKET TIP *Avoid the risk of accidentally knocking jars over by putting them in a bucket or washing-up bowl.*

SILICA GEL

There are several chemical drying agents, known as desiccants, which can be used to preserve plants almost indefinitely in their true colours. They all act in the same way, by leaching moisture from the plant's tissues without changing its structure or form.

By far the best desiccant is silica gel, which is obtainable as powder or fine crystals from a chemist or florist.

To start with, spread the silica gel out on a baking tray and warm it in a slow oven for about an hour to dry it. Cool it before use.

You will also need a container which can be sealed, such as a plastic food box with a lid or a small, wide, screw-top jar; and you'll need a small, soft paintbrush to brush away the silica gel from between the petals when you remove the preserved flowers after treatment.

Some delicacy of touch is needed, both in covering the plant with silica gel and in handling it afterwards. It is a good idea, therefore, to experiment with just one perfect specimen – a rose, say, which is halfway out. Put an inch of silica gel into the container and stand the flower in this. Then, using a spoon, gradually sift silica gel over the flower and through the petals until it is covered to a depth of at least ½in over the top of the bloom. Put the lid on and leave it for three days.

After three days, gently remove the flower from the container, carefully tipping the bloom into the palm of your hand. Do this over a sheet of paper on a table so that you don't lose the gel; it can be used over and over again. If the process of desiccation is complete, the petals will be dry and papery. If they're not, replace the flower in the container and check again the following day.

When treating long-stemmed flowers, it is more economical to cut the stem off and insert a wire (hooked at one end) through the front centre of the flower, gently drawing it down until the hook is concealed among the stamens. The wire can then be coiled temporarily, jack-in-the-box style, beneath the specimen, so that it takes up less room in the container.

Flowers which have been preserved with desiccants are too fragile to be exposed to the air. They must be displayed in a Perspex dome or clear-glass storage jar, where their full beauty should persist for years.

Plants suitable for silica gel Silica gel will work on any plant material. But, because the gel is expensive, the method is usually reserved for especially treasured flowers such as bridal bouquets.

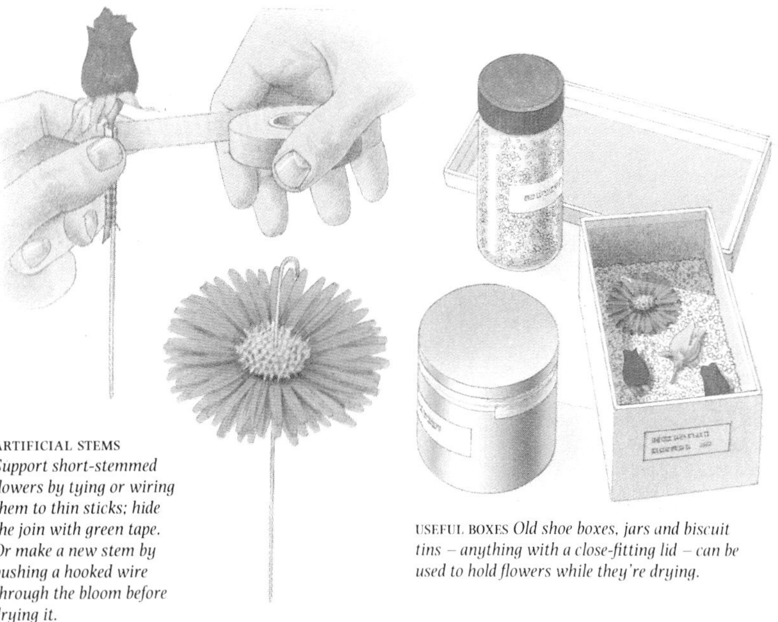

ARTIFICIAL STEMS *Support short-stemmed flowers by tying or wiring them to thin sticks; hide the join with green tape. Or make a new stem by pushing a hooked wire through the bloom before drying it.*

USEFUL BOXES *Old shoe boxes, jars and biscuit tins – anything with a close-fitting lid – can be used to hold flowers while they're drying.*

FOOT ROT

The malady that lingers on

The stems of my tomato plants are discoloured and dark rings are showing on the roots. I believe this to be caused by foot rot; will the disease linger in the soil?

Yes, it will. And it's not merely a threat to tomatoes. The several soil-borne fungi that cause foot rot may also affect bedding plants, sweet peas, peas, beans and asparagus elsewhere in the garden. So watch out for danger signals – roots that show dark patches and stem bases that discolour and rot. Yellowed, collapsing foliage follows. In such a case, the only thing to do is to dig up the plants and burn them.

But if the infection is slight – as it appears to be with your plants – then mulch the bases of the stems with moist peat, and water them with a fungicide based on copper sulphate and ammonium carbonate.

If your garden, or those of near neighbours, has been hit by foot rot, adopt a few preventive measures. Always raise bedding plants in sterilised soil or compost; and, when you plant them out, water them in with the same fungicide. If in doubt, give further weekly doses of the solution. Tomatoes may be protected from water splashes from possibly infected soil by spreading a layer of straw around the stems or by tying up the trusses. But in the case of peas and beans, which are difficult to treat for foot rot, leave at least five years before planting similar crops in the same ground again. Alternatively, try treating the soil in autumn with Armillatox.

You may be able to save greenhouse plants by packing moist peat round the stem bases and giving a fungicide spray. The peat will encourage the plants to form new roots above the diseased sections.

FRENCH BEANS

Beans means beans

Why do greengrocers seem to have so many varieties of french beans? There are flageolets, kidney beans, haricots verts *and more. What are the differences?*

There aren't any. All these categories are merely the same beans harvested at different ages. *Haricots verts* – of which you eat both the pods and their contents – are the youngest. Flageolets are harvested a little later; with those, you eat the beans fresh like peas, but not the pods. Kidney or haricot beans – often called *haricots secs* – are the oldest; again, you eat only the beans, but they're dried before cooking. All of these are french beans and, despite their name, they all come originally from South America.

Having said that, there are varieties which are particularly suited to one treatment or another. And there are some which are suitable for more than one treatment.

'Chevrier Vert', for instance, can be harvested and cooked as a flageolet bean; or the beans can be allowed to dry to a cream colour on the plant, then harvested and cooked as haricot beans.

Cook for safety

I'd like to grow some red kidney beans but I've been told that they can be poisonous if they are not well cooked. Is this true?

Yes it is. But only if the beans have been dried. The dried beans contain large amounts of the chemical lectin, a poison which can cause severe stomach upsets. They must be boiled for at least 10 minutes to destroy the poison. Soaking and washing the beans softens them, improving their texture and flavour, but does not get rid of the poison.

To prepare the dried beans, place them in a large colander or sieve and wash them under cold water, running your fingers through them as you do so. Put the beans into a large saucepan and add plenty of water – about 4 pints to one cup of beans. Either leave them to soak for 6-8 hours or bring them to the boil for 2 minutes, then remove from the heat and soak for 45-60 minutes. Discard the liquid that remains at the end of the soaking period and add fresh water for cooking. This helps to remove the oligosaccharides which cause flatulence.

Whether you opt for a long cold soak or a short hot one, the beans should be turned back into a colander afterwards and rinsed thoroughly under cold water. To cook them, put the rinsed beans into a large saucepan and cover them with fresh water. Bring the water to the boil and continue boiling rapidly for 10 minutes. After this, the beans can be simmered gently until they are tender – approximately 1-1½ hours.

Or you can cook beans in a pressure cooker in about a third of the time it would otherwise take. Boil the beans for 10 minutes as before. Then cook them at 15lb pressure for 20 minutes to half an hour.

Tinned red kidney beans do not need to be boiled before use, because the poison is destroyed in the canning process.

Firm support

How do climbing french beans compare with runners for yield and flavour? Do they need similar supports?

Climbing french beans are grown like runner beans and some people claim they have a better flavour than runners. French beans are quick growers and crop earlier than runner beans. They are very productive for the space they occupy, giving an average yield of about 18-24lb from a 10ft row.

French bean plants, which can grow to a height of 6-7ft, must be grown up strings, canes or nets supported by poles. There are many ways of arranging the supports, but the important thing is that the plants should be firmly anchored. The crop will be poor if the plants are allowed to wave about on insecure supports.

Plan for a 4ft wide bed and two rows 1½-2ft apart, with each row set 12-15in from the edge of the bed. Use crossed poles or canes at least 8ft long, firmly tied to cross-members along the tops. For economy, use a combination of canes and string. Insert the canes at 2ft intervals along the row, then fix a horizontal string 6in above soil level and tie it securely to the canes. Vertical strings can then be tied at 4in intervals along each row, running from the ridge to the horizontal string. Plant at the rate of one bean to each cane or string. Alternatively, sow two seeds by each string and thin to the stronger. If you require no more than a single, short row of beans, use bean netting supported between two strong upright posts.

A wigwam constructed of 8ft poles or canes tied together about 12in from the top is another space-saving way to support climbing french beans. The only problem with this method is that, growing in a circle, the plants on the north side are shaded by the others, so they will not do so well.

Snappy cropping

I grew french beans for the first time last year and they were tough and stringy. Surely this shouldn't have happened?

No, it shouldn't. It's just that you waited too long to pick the crop. Over-mature pods always tend to be tough and stringy. You should start picking the pods when they are about 4in long. At this size, all varieties (not just the stringless ones) will snap crisply in half when you bend them. Keep picking regularly to encourage further cropping and better quality. Remove the pods carefully so as not to damage the plants. They should be snapped off cleanly – there is no need to use a knife.

Dwarf beans produce their pods over a relatively short period – hence the importance of successional sowing. Recommended dwarf varieties include: 'Chevrier Vert', 'Comtesse de Chambord', 'Contender', 'Harvester', 'Horsehead', 'Limelight' and 'Longbow'.

Climbing types such as 'Blue Lake' and 'Marvel of Venice' continue to crop all summer.

Beans for drying

I want to grow some haricot beans. Are these raised in the same way as other dwarf beans? When do you pick them?

These small, oval, white beans belong to the kidney bean category. They are most familiar as baked beans and have a delicious, slightly sweet flavour and a mealy texture.

If you intend to dry your haricot beans, leave the pods on the plants until they turn brown or straw-coloured. At this stage, pull the whole plant from the ground and hang it up in a dry, airy shed. When the pods are at the point of cracking open, shell them out. Store the beans in a screw-top jar or some other airtight container.

Although the dried beans will keep for many years, they become harder and drier with time. So finish up each batch before starting on the next.

Water the roots, not the flowers

A lot of my dwarf bean flowers withered away before they formed pods. Didn't I water them enough?

French bean flowers develop under the shade of the foliage so they do not suffer (as do those of runner beans) during periods of strong sunshine. As long as you water regularly, so that there is no lack of moisture at the roots, the flowers will stay intact and will 'set' a crop – meaning that they can be successfully pollinated, thereby triggering the development of the beans – right through the hottest of summers.

For years, people believed that flower drop and poor setting of dwarf beans was associated with dry air around the flowers. The traditional method of overcoming the problem was to create humid conditions around the flowers by misting or spraying the plants once or twice a day during a dry spell. However, it is now thought that the practice has no beneficial effect and may actually reduce the number of pods that set.

Watering the soil at the base of the plant does however have a helpful effect on flowering and pod-setting. It seems to increase the number of beans which set within the pods and delays the onset of stringiness. In addition, a plentiful supply of moisture to the roots as the pods are swelling increases the size of the individual beans.

Water twice a week, throughout the flowering and pod-growing periods, at the rate of 1-2 gallons per square yard. Direct the water at the base of the plants, and avoid wetting foliage and flowers.

Bean bags

What are the chances of raising french beans in a growing bag on a sunny patio?

By using growing bags, crops can be grown where they have never succeeded before, including patios and balconies and in sun lounges and back yards. French beans are particularly successful in growing bags, and by making sowings at monthly intervals from late March to mid-July, beans can be picked from late June until October.

It is best to raise the plants indoors and then transplant them into the growing bags. About four weeks before planting out, sow the seeds singly 1in deep into 3in pots containing a good peat-based potting compost. After germination, grow the plants on in their pots in a cold greenhouse or frame, keeping the compost moist. Don't move the beans outside until after the risk of frost is over – in May, or even June in colder areas.

It is best not to open the growing bags until just before planting, in order to keep out weed seeds. Put 12 plants into each bag, spacing them 3-4in apart. For early crops, place the growing bags on polystyrene slabs to insulate them from cold surfaces. Immediately after planting, give each growing bag a good soaking with about 2 gallons of water. After that, water whenever the compost shows signs of drying out. Make sure the compost remains moist throughout the bag, not just in the top couple of inches. A liquid feed can be given when the first beans are picked.

Fertilise afresh

Since the french bean can make nitrogen with its roots, does it need any fertiliser before planting?

Although, like all pulse crops, the beans are capable of making nitrogen with their roots, it is still a good idea to give the plants a little extra. French beans like a rich, fertile soil which has been dug the previous autumn and given plenty of well-decayed farmyard manure or garden compost.

Prepare the seedbed about a fortnight before you intend to sow. At the same time, work a general-purpose fertiliser such as Growmore into the top few inches of soil at the rate of about 2½oz per square yard. When preparing the seedbed for an early planting, don't work the ground too deeply, since this will bring the lower soil layers, chilled and dampened by winter, to the surface.

FROGHOPPERS

Unsightly cuckoo spit

My lavender and chrysanthemums are full of cuckoo spit. It isn't very attractive, but, this apart, does it damage plants?

Cuckoo spit itself is harmless, but the frothy bubbles hide small pink insects that can injure plants, though usually not severely. Cuckoo spit gets its name simply because it begins to appear in April, when the call of the cuckoo is heard. The insects are the young of froghoppers, of which there are many species in Britain.

Only two are pests in the garden: the common froghopper, a froglike insect with prominent eyes and powerful hind legs; and its slightly larger and more vividly marked cousin, the red and black froghopper. Both grow up to ¼in in length and have similar habits. Females lay eggs in batches of about 30 in the stems of shrubs and herbaceous plants during the autumn.

Apart from lavender and chrysanthemums, roses, perennial asters, campanulas, blackberries and raspberries are also subject to infestation. The young feed on the plants' sap and the adults cause occasional damage to leaves. Nymphs of the red and black froghopper also feed on root sap.

The insects and their froth can be easily dislodged by hosing the plants with jets of water. If you want to make absolutely sure they won't come back, follow this up with a spray of malathion or HCH.

Though outdoor plants are the principal victims, the insects are sometimes a nuisance in the greenhouse, too. They are usually brought in with chrysanthemums and other plants moved indoors for the winter.

UNDERCOVER AGENTS *The young of froghoppers cover themselves with froth to hide from predators and to keep from drying out. The froth has nothing to do with cuckoos, except that it appears about the same time as the birds do.*

FUCHSIAS

Hanging baskets

This summer I want to make up some hanging baskets with fuchsias. Which varieties should I choose and how should I plant them?

Hanging baskets look particularly attractive with a bushy fuchsia or another upright plant in the middle and trailing fuchsias, perhaps mixed with some trailing lobelia, dangling over the rim. Good varieties for hanging baskets include: 'Auntie Jinks' (purple and white); 'Marinka' (rich red); and 'Golden Marinka' (like 'Marinka', but with golden variegated foliage).

The basket can be made of either wire or plastic. Whichever you use, line it with about 2in of sphagnum moss or with a peat liner to conserve moisture and prevent the compost washing out.

To make up a basket, rest it on the rim of a bucket to keep it steady. Partly fill the basket with potting compost and plant the trailing fuchsias (a good-sized basket will probably take four or five) evenly spaced around the rim. Add some more compost and work it around the rootballs, leaving a space for the central plant. Put the central plant in position, top up the basket with compost and firm lightly, leaving a slight hollow in the middle to stop water running off. As the plant in the middle grows, pinch out the shoot tips regularly to encourage it to bush out and fill the basket.

Aftercare is simple: just regular watering and liquid feeding every 10-14 days. If the basket is in a sunny position, make sure the compost does not dry out; in hot weather, it will need watering every day or two.

High standards

I'd like to plant some standard fuchsias in the middle of the flowerbeds in my garden. Can I grow my own?

Yes. All you need is a little patience and persistence, and some knowledge. The essential requirements are strong, rooted cuttings from a variety which has an upright growth. Suitable types are the *Fuchsia magellanica* varieties 'Gracilis' and 'Alba', and the hybrid 'Madame Cornelissen'. The best time to take cuttings for standards is mid to late summer. The cuttings can then be kept in a frost-free greenhouse or shed over the winter (like geraniums) and grown on again for the following year (see *How to take fuchsia cuttings*, opposite.)

When selecting cuttings, choose stem tips with whorls of three leaves. These will produce three shoots at each node and so make a denser head with more flowers. Initially, pot up the rooted cuttings in 3in pots, and insert a split cane near the main stem (taking care not to damage the roots), otherwise a kink will develop at the base. Tie the cutting to the cane as low down as possible and, as growth continues, make further ties every 2in to keep the stem straight.

As the plant develops, remove all side-shoots sprouting in the leaf axils – the joints between the leaves and the main stem – but do not remove any leaves. Inspect the root system regularly to ensure that the plant does not become pot-bound. When the roots reach the outside of the compost, transfer the plant to a pot one size larger. It is vital to keep the plant growing fast, because any check will lead to premature flowering and may stop upward growth. The final pot size

PICK OF THE FUCHSIAS

Name	Flowers	Remarks
GREENHOUSE VARIETIES		
'Auntie Jinks'	Single. Tube pink-red, sepals (the outermost flower parts) white; corolla (the central petals) purple	Excellent basket variety. Small flowers, but very profuse. Colour very bright. Flowers from top to bottom
'Celia Smedley'	Single. Tube and sepals pale pink, almost white; corolla currant-red	Strong-growing variety. Can be used for bushes, standards or pyramids. Large flowers
'Checkerboard'	Single. Tube red, sepals red changing abruptly to white; corolla deep red, white at base	Strong, upright grower. Excellent for standards and bushes. Good contrasting colours. Flowers small and profuse
'Citation'	Single. Tube and sepals rose-pink; corolla white, veined with light pink at base	Large, freely produced flowers. Corolla flares open to saucer shape. Excellent for standards or as a bush
'Lye's Unique'	Single. Tube and sepals waxy white; corolla salmon-orange	Strong upright grower. Flowers of medium size, but very profuse. A very old variety, well worth growing
'Marin Glow'	Single. Tube and sepals pure waxy white; corolla purple, aging slowly to magenta	Flowers of medium size, but profuse. Easy to grow and shape. An outstanding variety. Makes a fine standard or pyramid
'Marinka'	Single. Tube and sepals rich red; corolla darker red, almost self-coloured	Profuse bloomer, with medium-size flowers and lax growth. Popular for hanging baskets. Can be trained into any shape
'Mieke Meursing'	Single/semi-double. Red tube and sepals; pale pink corolla, with deeper pink veining	Classic shapely blooms in great profusion. An upright and bushy plant. Probably one of the most common fuchsias seen at shows
'Royal Velvet'	Double. Tube and sepals crimson-red; corolla deep purple, changing to rose-purple	Very free-flowering, with large flowers. Upright habit. Can be used for standards, bushes or baskets
'Snowcap'	Semi-double. Tube and sepals red; corolla pure white, veined with cerise	A profuse bloomer, with medium-size flowers. Growth vigorous and upright. Ideal for bushes, pyramids and standards
'Swanley Gem'	Single. Tube and sepals rich scarlet; corolla violet, veined with scarlet	Profuse medium-size flowers. The four petals of the corolla open flat, making a perfect circle. Growth upright and bushy. A good exhibition variety
'Swingtime'	Double. Tube and sepals rich red; corolla milky white, veined with pink at base	Flowers are large and extremely freely produced. Growth upright and free-branching

for a full standard is about 9in. A full standard has at least 2½ft of bare stem, but you can grow standards to any size you like.

When the required height is reached (including the stem and the desired height of head), pinch out the top of the main stem. The head should then bush out as sideshoots develop. Pinch out the growing tips of these shoots after two or three leaves have formed to encourage subsidiary sideshoots to grow. Continue the pinching-out process until the head is the size you want. Once the head is established, remove the leaves from lower down the main stem. It will take about two years to achieve a good strong stem and a balanced head.

Fuchsia fruits

Some of my fuchsias have produced red and green fruits. Can I grow new plants from the seeds inside? If so, how do I remove the seeds and when should I sow them? Are the fruits edible?

You can grow fuchsias from the seeds, but the seedlings will be very mixed in flowers, colour and habit since they will be hybrids. They probably won't look anything like the parent plant. To save the seeds, leave the fruits on the plant until they are ripe – at that stage they will be pale green, deep mauve or almost black, and soft to the touch. Pick them, cut through the segments with a sharp knife and remove the seeds. Leave the seeds to dry on a sheet of kitchen paper and, once they are dry, store them in an airtight tin in a cool, dry place.

Sow the seeds during March or April in a pot of seed compost. Place about ½in of peat at the bottom of the pot, fill it to within ½in of the top with compost and lightly firm down. Cover the surface with ⅛in of sharp sand and sprinkle the seeds thinly on the surface, gently pressing them into the sand without covering them. Soak the pot in water and allow it to drain. Place the pot in a propagator or cover it with a sheet of glass, and shade it with paper to exclude light. Leave it in a minimum temperature of 18°C (65°F). Once a day, wipe condensation from the glass or turn it over. Germination time can vary from 14 to 120 days; the average time is 30 days.

As soon as the seedlings appear, remove the paper, and when the first true leaves appear – the ones after the initial pair of seed leaves – prick the seedlings out around the rim of a 3in pot (five to a pot) or in a small seed tray, using a potting compost such as the soil-based John Innes No 1. When the plants look larger and stronger, put them singly in 3in pots in John Innes No 2 compost. Thereafter move them to larger pots as necessary. To prevent damping-off fungus from attacking the seedlings, treat the surface of the compost with a fungicide, watering it on every ten days from sowing time onwards. The seedlings may flower in the first year after planting, but the second year will show their true potential.

The fruits can be eaten. They're sweet, with a slightly aromatic flavour.

How to take fuchsia cuttings

What time of the year should I take fuchsia cuttings and how's it done?

You can grow fuchsias from softwood or semi-ripe cuttings very easily. Softwood cuttings are taken at any time throughout the summer and are usually very successful; semi-ripe cuttings are taken in August or September. A fuchsia cutting is best taken from the tip of a shoot with at least three pairs of leaves, four if possible. Remove the bottom pair of leaves and trim off the base of the cutting, with a sharp knife or razor blade, just below the joint where the leaves

Name	Flowers	Remarks
'Tennessee Waltz'	Semi-double. Tube and sepals dark rose-pink; corolla lilac-lavender, with rosy flush	Free-flowering. Medium-size flowers with upswept sepals. Excellent bush or standard
'Ting-a-ling'	Single. Tube, sepals and corolla all white	Flowers profusely. Suitable for bushes, standards and baskets
HARDY VARIETIES		
'Abbe Farges'	Semi-double. Tube and sepals (the outermost flower parts) cerise; corolla (the central petals) lilac	Best grown as a bush. Has brittle branches. Flowers small, but profuse
'Alice Hoffman'	Single. Tube and sepals rose; corolla white	Dwarf, upright and very bushy. Flowers small, but profuse
'Chillerton Beauty'	Single. Tube and sepals rose-pink; corolla mauve-violet	Growth upright and naturally bushy up to 3ft. Flowers small, but profuse
'Corallina'	Single. Tube and sepals bright scarlet; corolla deep purple	Strong growing, but lax in habit. Flowers large and freely produced
'Doctor Foster'	Single. Tube and sepals scarlet; corolla violet	Makes a colourful hedge. Flowers large and profuse
'Drame'	Semi-double. Tube and sepals scarlet; corolla violet	Vigorous and very hardy. Yellow-green foliage
'Empress of Prussia'	Single. Tube and sepals scarlet; corolla scarlet	Growth short, sturdy and upright. Flowers large and prolific
'Ethel Wilson'	Single. Tube and sepals pale pink; corolla deep pink, aging to cerise	Strong, upright grower up to 3ft. Flowers medium size and profuse
'Margaret Brown'	Single. Tube and sepals rose-pink; corolla light rose-pink	Strong and upright. Flowers small and profuse
'Mrs Popple'	Single. Tube and sepals scarlet; corolla deep violet-purple	Erect habit, upright and vigorous. Flowers large and freely produced
'Reading Show'	Double. Tube and sepals waxy rose; corolla deep blue, almost purple	Growth upright and vigorous. Flowers large and plentiful
'Riccartonii'	Single. Tube and sepals scarlet; corolla dark purple	Probably the finest hedging fuchsia. Flowers small and profuse
'Tom Thumb'	Single. Tube and sepals light carmine; corolla mauve-purple	Dwarf and upright. A prolific bloomer
'Wilson's Fairfax'	Single. Tube and sepals red; corolla violet-blue, shading to white at base	Strong, upright growth. Very bright appearance

have been removed. The best way to root the cuttings is to make up a half-and-half mixture by volume of peat and sharp sand (not builder's sand) or perlite. Fill a 3in pot with the mixture and insert five cuttings around the edge of the pot, using a pencil or plant label to make holes for the cuttings.

The cuttings should be inserted so that the bottom pair of leaves is just above the surface of the potting mixture. On completion, water the mixture well and place it in a propagating frame, or tie a plastic bag upside down over the pot. The time taken to root will depend on the temperature, but it's usually 12-20 days. The cuttings must be shaded from strong sunlight and be kept moist. Once rooting has taken place – you can tell that this has happened when the plants look firmer and the tips begin to grow – pot them up separately in 3in pots using a standard potting compost.

Winter survival

I grow fuchsias as pot plants every year but they cost so much to buy these days. Can I keep mine over the winter and so avoid buying each spring?

Yes, fuchsias can be kept alive over the winter in much the same way as geraniums. Store them in a frost-free place such as a garage or shed in their pots. The plants should be kept dry during the winter and watered only if the stems look in danger of drying out completely. Do not give them sufficient moisture to start them into growth until March or April, when you can increase the watering. If you don't have a frost-free place for them, bury the pots and plants in the garden so that the top of the pot is at least 9in below ground level. Cover them with straw topped off with soil. Make sure to mark their position as it is easy to forget where they are.

Of bugs and pests

Every year I plant out about a dozen fuchsias to give some height among the bedding plants in my garden. This summer some of the fuchsias have failed to produce flowers and their foliage has been damaged, yet the fuchsias in my greenhouse are unaffected. What should I do?

Your fuchsias have probably been attacked by capsid bugs. When capsid bugs attack a plant, clean-cut or tattered holes appear where part of the leaves have fallen out. Often the leaves develop raised surfaces and become discoloured or have reddish patches. The whole leaf has an undulating appearance and the leading buds go 'blind' – meaning that they fail to produce flowers – usually in early summer.

The bugs puncture the leaves to get at the sap and inject saliva before feeding. The saliva causes the leaves to blister and inhibits the growth of buds nearby. Sometimes whole shoots die back or buds lower down fail to develop. The eggs are laid on shrubs and trees and in plant debris, where they spend the winter.

The remedy is to spray your fuchsias with an insecticide such as dimethoate, HCH or diazinon as soon as the symptoms appear. To prevent attacks in future years, spray the plants early in July.

Capsid bugs also cause damage to chrysanthemums, buddleias, dahlias, hydrangeas and other ornamental plants, as well as fruit trees and vegetables, including apples, currants and beans. They occasionally attack plants in greenhouses, but are more common outdoors.

Despite their delicate appearance, fuchsias are fairly tough and reasonably resistant to pests and diseases. Nevertheless, apart from capsid bugs, they may also suffer from time to time from one or another of the following complaints:

- **APHIDS** The presence of these creatures is signalled by yellowing, curling and sticky leaves. Spray young plants with malathion. In the greenhouse, fumigate every two weeks with HCH smoke pellets after flowering has started.
- **CYCLAMEN MITE** The signs are thin, stunted plants that produce small leaves with rusty patches; often new shoots are distorted and flowers fail to open. Infestation is most likely to occur in a dry greenhouse. Badly infested plants should be burnt, but less serious cases may be cured by removing the plant from the pot, shaking off the soil and soaking the rootball in HCH or malathion. After repotting the plant in fresh soil, fumigate the greenhouse with HCH smoke pellets.
- **LEAFHOPPERS** Pale green jumping and flying insects give the leaves a mottled, speckled appearance. Spray at first sight of the insects with a systemic insecticide such as dimethoate, and in following years spray the plants early in July as a preventative measure.
- **MEALY BUGS** Leaves wilt, yellow and fall; small insects covered with white, cottony fluff are visible. Deal with isolated infestations by wiping the insects off the leaves with damp cotton wool. If attacks persist, spray the plants about once a week with malathion or dimethoate.
- **RED SPIDER MITES** A minute insect pest on greenhouse plants, the mite turns foliage bronzed and spotted. Leaves curl and fall prematurely and sometimes white webs can be seen among leaves and stems. Mist-spray with water daily to discourage attacks, and spray with pirimiphos-methyl.
- **THRIPS** The symptoms are silvery streaks on leaves and spotted, distorted flowers. Tiny black insects fly or jump from leaf to leaf. Spray with permethrin, and spray again if attacks persist.
- **TORTRIX MOTH CATERPILLARS** Watch out for leaves that look scorched on their upper sides and gnawed underneath. Spray the plants with fenitrothion at the first sign of damage.
- **VINE WEEVILS** Plants wilt; grey or creamy-white grubs are visible among the roots of lifted plants. Control is difficult, but as a precautionary measure maintain good garden hygiene and destroy plant debris – a favourite hiding place of adult weevils. In the greenhouse, drench pots in a solution of HCH.
- **WHITEFLY** Leaves become badly wilted and a cloud of small white flies rises up when infested plants are disturbed. Spray with permethrin and repeat the dose every three days for three weeks – seven sprays in all – to get rid of eggs, nymphs and flies. Alternatively, in the greenhouse, fumigate the greenhouse three times at seven-day intervals with permethrin smoke.

Show timing

I am thinking of exhibiting some fuchsias at our local flower show. How can I ensure that they will be at their best when the show begins?

If you are growing for a show and have the bush or standard in good shape, then the last stopping should be made six to eight weeks before the show date.

Stopping is the process of pinching out the growing tips of the shoots, a technique resulting in the development of at least two sideshoots from the stopped shoot, and often four. These in turn can be stopped when they're the size you want. This leads to more flowers and a bushier plant.

Six to eight weeks should be about right to have the plant blooming at show time. But since a lot depends on the condition of the plant and the weather, work on several plants and give each its final stopping at different times over a period of two or three weeks. That way you'll ensure that at least one is a mass of flower on the required date.

Hardy rules

I want to plant some hardy fuchsias permanently outdoors. Any tips?

Fuchsias like a half-shaded, dappled position, a slightly humid atmosphere to prevent bud-drop, and a rich soil. They dislike hot, sunny positions, too much water at the roots (the soil should never be sodden) and high temperatures. Follow this checklist and you won't go far wrong.

- Dig the ground thoroughly, in the autumn before planting, to a depth of at least one spade blade. Fill each trench with compost before you turn the soil onto it.
- Make sure the site drains well.
- Scatter a general fertiliser such as Growmore at the rate of 2oz per square yard on the surface, and lightly fork it in about two weeks before planting in early June.

• When planting, allow at least 2½ft between the plants, and set the top of the rootball just below the surface of the soil.
• In autumn, leave the stems on the plants and cover the top of the rootball with a layer of straw or bracken about 2in thick.
• In spring, trim all the top growth back to ground level and sprinkle more general fertiliser around the plants – again about 2oz per square yard.
• During the summer, spray once or twice with a systemic insecticide such as dimethoate to ward off capsid bugs and aphids, or with a relatively persistent contact insecticide like fenitrothion.

When to repot

The new fuchsias I have just bought are in 3in pots. When should I repot them?

Repot when the pots are full of roots. Lift each plant out of its pot to check. What you're looking for is a network of fine root hairs visible all round the rootball. When you see that, transfer the plant to a pot a size or two larger, using potting compost.

How to thicken a leggy bush

I have a large fuchsia which is getting rather leggy. A neighbour told me that if I cut it back to ground level in the autumn it will grow into a dense bush the following year. Is this true?

It's halfway true. Hard pruning will encourage a leggy fuchsia to bush out. But autumn is the wrong time.

Even hardy fuchsia varieties need the protection from frost that the old shoots can give them. Prune them instead in spring when the buds are just breaking, so that you can see what is living wood.

If your fuchsia is one of the hardy species, such as *Fuchsia magellanica*, trim out any overcrowding in the centre and remove all dead wood. Then cut back the stems to within 6in of the ground, cutting each to just above a new shoot. If your fuchsias are greenhouse varieties which have been planted out in the garden – ideally in a sheltered spot – cut back the stems to ground level, again in spring. With this treatment, all your fuchsias should form dense bushes, provided frost hasn't damaged the roots.

ALL ABOUT GROWING FUCHSIAS IN A GREENHOUSE

FUCHSIAS are ideal pot plants for a heated greenhouse, where they will flower in flushes of blossoms from April to November. In unheated greenhouses the flowering season is from May until early October.

With a little care, fuchsias can easily be trained into a variety of shapes by pinching out the tips of the main stems and the sideshoots that grow from them: a technique known as stopping.

Each time a shoot is stopped, the stump of the shoot branches into two or more new shoots. The more shoots you encourage the plant to form, the more bushy it will become. And, since fuchsias flower mostly from the tips of the shoots, the more shoots there are, the more blooms there will be. Greenhouse fuchsias, like their outdoor relatives, are not difficult to grow. These are the ten principal rules to follow for success with them.

1 Always use a good potting compost. John Innes composts – which are soil-based – are ideal for fuchsias. Use No 1 for freshly potted young plants, the richer No 3 for older plants.
2 When potting up, firm the compost lightly with your fingers. Shake the compost well into the root system by tapping the pot sharply on the edge of a bench or with a trowel.
3 Start training early, wrapping plastic ties firmly around the supporting cane – then slacken as the plant grows.
4 Do not let your fuchsias become pot-bound. Examine the rootball regularly – and when the roots become visible as a network on the outside of the compost, pot on.
5 Label all plants clearly after potting – it's easy to forget which is which.
6 Water regularly, early in the day. Keep the compost just moist – it's important neither to let it dry out nor become sodden.
7 In hot weather keep the doors and windows open, and draw the blinds or cover the outside of the glass with shading paint. Dampen the floor and staging at midday to increase humidity and keep the temperature down. In extremely hot weather move the plants to a shady position outside. Aim to keep the plants in a fairly even temperature of no more than 24°C (75°F).
8 To avoid bloom-spotting, don't spray plants when the blooms are open.
9 Once a week give the plants a liquid feed of a balanced fertiliser (one with roughly equal proportions of all the major plant nutrients). Most house-plant feeds are suitable for this purpose.
10 Inspect regularly for pests – whitefly is the main problem – and fumigate or spray as necessary.

FUSARIUM WILT

Lingering fungus

The lower stems of my cherished sweet peas are discoloured and entire plants are dying. What can the trouble be?

It sounds very much like fusarium wilt, a disease that can linger in the ground for years. It is caused by soil-borne fungi and is tricky to tackle in the garden. Many plants are affected – in particular carnations and pinks, sweet peas, peas and beans.

The fungus blocks the water-conducting tissues of the stem and has toxic effects, too. The leaves, and often the stem bases, become discoloured and the plants wilt.

Remove and burn diseased plants, and avoid growing any similar ones in that spot for several years. It is difficult to be precise; the only way you can tell whether the disease has departed is by trial and error. But this doesn't mean that the ground has to stay bare. Carrots, parsnips and parsley, for instance, are not prone to fusarium wilt. In the case of trees and shrubs, drench the soil around them with spray-strength benomyl or thiophanate-methyl every couple of weeks until the symptoms vanish – otherwise uproot and destroy. Give four or five drenches, and if the symptoms haven't gone by then, get rid of the plant.

It's a bit more complicated dealing with an outbreak in the greenhouse due to the difficulty of providing adequate sterilisation after an attack. As a precaution, propagate only from healthy stock and do not plant too early or into cold soil. It sometimes helps to raise the temperature in the greenhouse and to spray the plants with fungicide from above instead of round the roots.

A mild attack can be combated by packing damp peat round the stems of affected plants. This should encourage healthy roots to grow from the newly buried portions. If the wilt has established itself in the greenhouse, try spraying with benomyl first. If the symptoms do not vanish, destroy all the fungus's victims. Then disinfect the greenhouse and every pot, box, bench and tool in it. Raise the next crop in sterilised soil, fresh potting compost or growing bags.

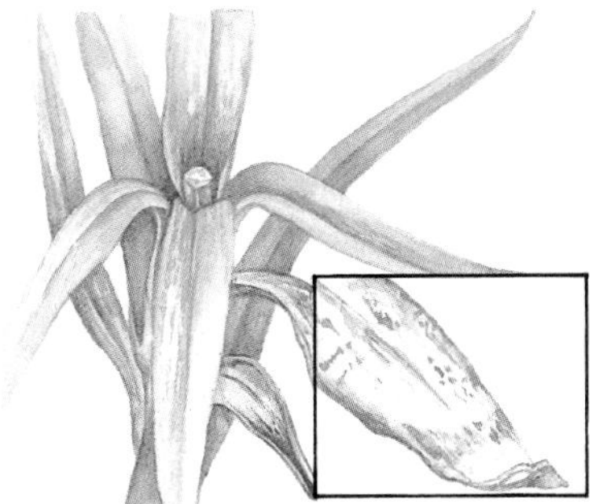

LEAVES DISCOLOUR *If not eliminated, fusarium wilt fungi will build up in the soil year after year. The first sign of an attack is often a change of colour in the leaves.*

GARDEN DESIGN

Starting from scratch

We have just moved into a new house and the garden looks like a building site. Where do we begin?

You must start with a plan. Take a large sheet of graph paper and sketch to scale the outline of the whole site, then draw the house in position. Work to a scale of about one square per foot, so you can get some detail into the plan.

Keeping to scale, draw in the features you want in your garden – paths, borders, patio, shed, greenhouse, pool, clothes line, rose beds, even a swing or a child's sandpit. Use a pencil, so you can rub out and draw again as your plan develops.

Alternatively, draw each feature to scale on separate sheets of paper, cut them out and shuffle them around your outline drawing in jigsaw fashion.

Once you are satisfied with your plan, draw up a work project.

- Get rid of weeds. Use a paraquat or glyphosate weedkiller which will clear the site but allow you to plant without risks.
- Tackle the heavy earth-moving work. Clear any old bricks or building material, or move them into position to become the core of a rockery or a bank, or the foundation for a patio or path. Dig the ground and break up the soil.
- Build the permanent features – walls, fences, pond, paths and patio (see *Ponds and pools*, page 261, and *Paths and paving*, page 246). If the garden is too big or the work too expensive to contemplate doing it all at once, consider achieving your plan in a series of stages.

This might involve completing one part of the garden at a time over a period of years. It might also involve temporary solutions to some immediate needs – a mud-free place for the children to play, for example, or somewhere close to the house to hang out washing.

- Lay the lawn areas. Sow grass – or lay turf – over a slightly larger area than your design allows for the finished lawn. This will give you some extra room to change the shape of any borders if you wish, and also allow you to cut a neater and firmer edge to the lawn.
- Plant trees. These will be the biggest and slowest-growing features of the garden. See how they look in the positions you have planned for them. In practice you may find it better to alter your plan slightly as you go along.
- Finally, fill in the borders with your choice of border plants.

One last principle worth remembering is that your plan should be a guideline, not a straitjacket. Don't let it constrict the living garden you create with it. Over the years your preferences and the garden's character will change. Allow it to develop.

Pointed garden

Our back garden is a triangular shape and the house faces one point of the triangle. What can we do to make it feel wider?

Avoid all strong lines that lead to the point of the triangle. Move any central features – trees, beds or pond – between the house and the end of the garden, so as to screen at least part of the garden's narrowest section. A pergola or trellis across the garden, short of the end, could achieve the same effect. Don't have tall trees at the point of the triangle. They'll just draw attention to the garden's constricted shape.

Soften the edges of the lawn, which should be the central feature. Don't let the edges run in straight lines to the triangle point. Instead, curve the edges away from the centre near the house to emphasise the width. The curving lines can turn towards the point farther down the garden and finish in a blunt, rounded curve.

Design a low feature where the boundaries of the garden meet. This could be a pond with a low rockery, a statue, or a sundial in a paved surround. Run a path to it down the side of the lawn, following its curve, and not straight down the middle of the garden. Set the surface of the path just below lawn level, so that you can mow over it.

VANISHING POINT *One way to disguise a narrow garden is to create a broadly curving lawn and to position, say, a jutting flowerbed between the tip and the house.*

Create some strong features at each side of the garden – a few tall conifers, say, or a herbaceous border with soaring hollyhocks and delphiniums. Get some taller features close to the house. Combine these characteristics on an outline plan (see *Starting from scratch*, this page) and juggle the elements until you're happy with the overall effect.

Snapshot mapping

All my attempts to draw a layout for the garden of our new home have failed. I can't seem to get the scale right. Isn't there some other way I can do it?

Yes – try taking photographs. Use blown-up prints of shots taken from the garden's main vantage points – a patio, perhaps, a garden seat, or through the windows of the house. The prints don't have to show the whole garden, or be of superb quality; they don't even have to be in colour. Draw on them with a wax coloured pencil the features you want in your garden.

Sketch in on the photographs the patio, the conifers, borders, vegetable patch and lawn. You will be able to see in your mind's eye at once how it will look, and you can tell from the print where in the garden to start each project.

Alternatively, try once more to make a proper map. Buy a surveyor's tape measure and start by measuring a base line. The base line could be the back corners of the house or two pegs driven in nearby.

Then build up your map as a series of triangles – with each spot identified by its distance from *two* known points.

Covering fences

My garden is surrounded by 6ft high wooden fences, and I feel shut in. How can I make them look attractive?

Line them with a variety of wall shrubs and climbers chosen for their flowers, foliage, berries, shape and habit. Intersperse evergreen and deciduous shrubs with rambling roses and clematis. Plant spring-flowering shrubs beside autumn-flowering ones. For ideas on which species to go for, see *Climbers*, page 76, and *Shrubs*, page 310.

But first check that the fence is yours. Unless there is anything in the deeds of the house to the contrary, the usual rule is that any fence is owned by the person on whose side the supports or fence posts are.

Few neighbours are likely to complain if

you add colour and interest to the garden, and some of it is bound to spill over. But they will not be happy if a prolific grower invades their garden or damages the fence. If the fence is not yours, it may be advisable to put in your own posts and wires on your side of the border to hold up your climbers and to train your shrubs along.

Watch, too, which way a fence faces. It is no good putting a climber that wants the protection of a south-facing wall on an east-facing fence, where all it will get is a little morning sun and cold winter winds. Plan your fencing plants so that they vary in height, shape and texture, and so that not all are in bloom at the same time. That way, you will have a succession of colourful focal points through the year. For suggestions on which plants to use for different times of the year, see *Colour*, page 84. Some of your choices will take several years to cover their section of the fence. Use quick-growing annual climbers such as nasturtiums to fill in the gaps meantime.

Stepped garden

We have a garden that slopes away below our house and want to create a series of terraces and steps. How should we go about it?

Don't crowd together a long run of steps; aim for terraces as wide and as shallow as possible, and soften each step with banks of flowers above and below the retaining walls.

Your scope for this will, of course, depend on how steep the garden slope is. Mark out

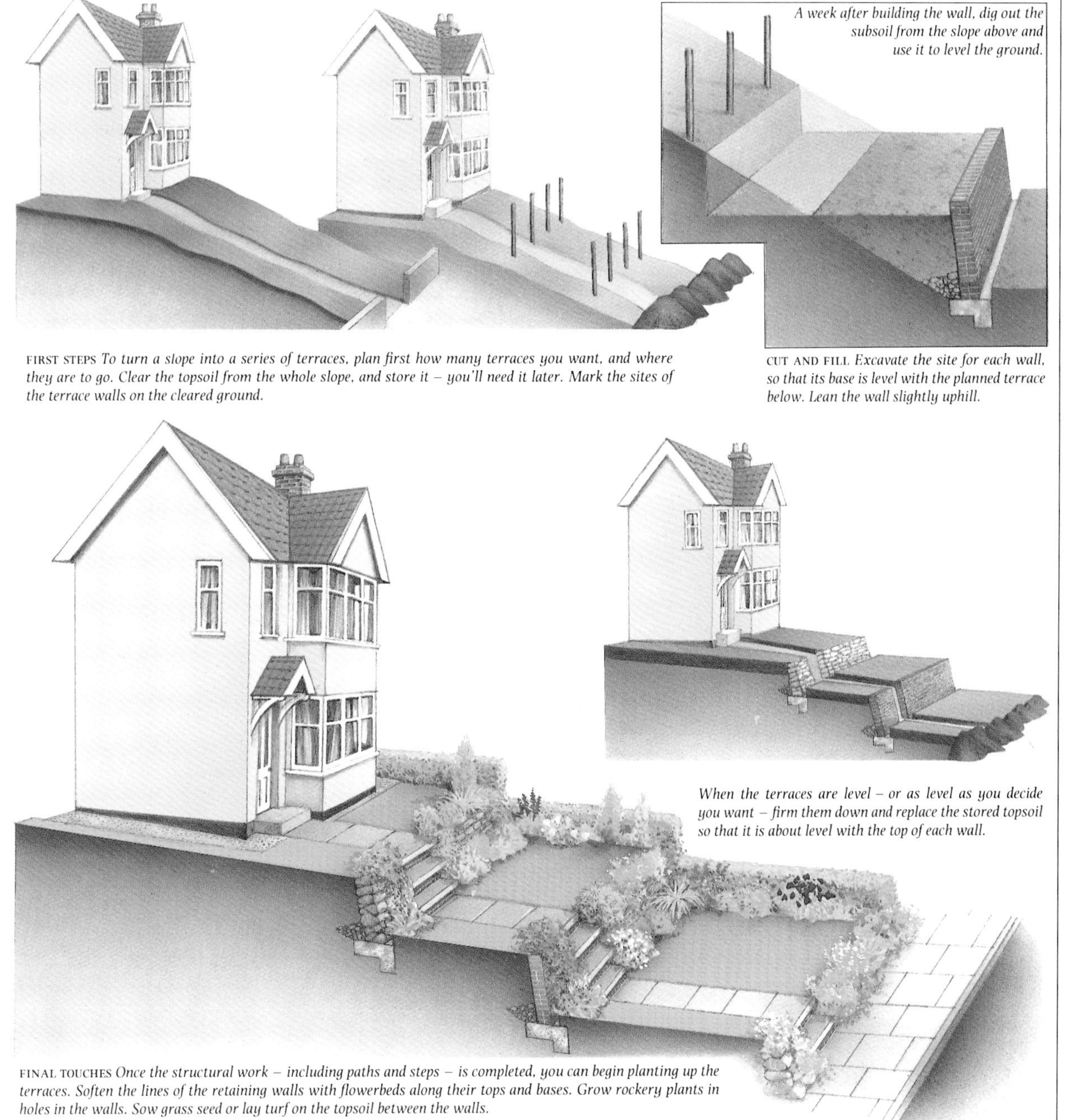

A week after building the wall, dig out the subsoil from the slope above and use it to level the ground.

FIRST STEPS *To turn a slope into a series of terraces, plan first how many terraces you want, and where they are to go. Clear the topsoil from the whole slope, and store it – you'll need it later. Mark the sites of the terrace walls on the cleared ground.*

CUT AND FILL *Excavate the site for each wall, so that its base is level with the planned terrace below. Lean the wall slightly uphill.*

When the terraces are level – or as level as you decide you want – firm them down and replace the stored topsoil so that it is about level with the top of each wall.

FINAL TOUCHES *Once the structural work – including paths and steps – is completed, you can begin planting up the terraces. Soften the lines of the retaining walls with flowerbeds along their tops and bases. Grow rockery plants in holes in the walls. Sow grass seed or lay turf on the topsoil between the walls.*

the extent of each terrace with stakes. Don't dig at random. Plan each step so that when you are digging out soil you know exactly where it has to go to form the next bank. Clear the topsoil before excavating each terrace, and replace it afterwards; otherwise the finished terraces will have varying depths of topsoil, which will cause permanently uneven growth in your plants.

Check the length of the retaining walls and the amount of material you will need before you start – you may find it quite expensive. Dig proper foundations and fill in with rubble and supporting material where necessary. Make sure to leave enough holes to drain off water from the ground above, or your foundations may be undermined.

Start by building the terrace where it is most needed, immediately against the house. Then work your way down to the lowest level. At each stage build the retaining wall first, leaning it slightly uphill to counteract the weight of the soil that it will have to support. Leave it for at least a week before piling up the soil behind it.

You can cut costs by giving each terrace a gentle slope, so reducing the number of retaining walls you need to build.

A final note of caution: don't underestimate the work involved in shifting even a small volume of earth. If in doubt, get professional advice from a builder.

Cracked wall

Frost has cracked our 5ft high front garden wall. What should we do?

First, check just how badly damaged it is. Examine the bonding between the bricks. Grip the top of the wall with both hands and see if there is any movement. If it rocks, or telltale cracks open between cement and bricks, then the wall is dangerous. Take it down to the level of the lowest crack on each part of the wall, and rebuild it from there.

If, however, the wall is still firm, you can simply mask the damage with a concrete rendering. This will protect the bricks from

How to build steps

I have a flight of 12 concrete steps down to my lawn. They are old and crumbling and need to be renewed or replaced. What's the best way to tackle the job?

They can be repaired with a layer of fresh concrete if the damage is not too bad. Ready-mixed packets specially for repair jobs are available at most do-it-yourself stores. Alternatively, if you're going to need quite a bit of concrete, buy cement and builder's sand and aggregate separately – it's less convenient because you have to mix it yourself, but cheaper.

If the steps are really bad, this is an ideal time to replace them. Using slabs, stones or bricks, you can make steps look much more attractive than you can with plain concrete. Decide, too, whether you are happy with the position of the steps and with the size of each step. Once you have decided on a new set of steps, check the total fall of the flight using two wooden posts. Get a friend to hold one post vertically from the bottom of the bottom step. Lay the other post from the top step, keeping it horizontal with a spirit level. Measure up the vertical post from the ground to the point where the posts cross.

STEP BY STEP

The smaller the gap – the 'riser' – between one step and its neighbours, the broader each step needs to be from front to back – the 'tread'. This chart shows how to pair up tread and riser sizes for maximum safety. Steps shallower than 4in or steeper than 7in are best avoided altogether.

Riser	Tread
4in	18in
4½in	17in
5in	16in
5½in	15in
6in	14in
6½in	13in
7in	12in

Decide the height you want for each of your steps. Don't make this height – what builders call the riser height – more than 7in. Divide the total height by the height of each riser to give you the number of steps you need. For a 4ft fall, say, with risers 6in high, you will need 8 steps. Then look at the chart below to see how deep each tread should be from front to back to suit the riser height you've chosen. For a 6in riser, for instance, the treads should be about 14in. Multiply the number of steps you need by the tread size to see how far your flight will stretch; in this case, with 8 steps, the flight will be 9ft 4in long.

Start building your steps at the base. Dig out a trench at least 4in deep and the full width of the steps. Fill it with a ready-mixed concrete base, or mix your own: 1 part cement, 3 parts aggregate and 2 parts sand. Mix the ingredients dry before adding enough water to make a stiff mud.

Let the base set for at least 24 hours, then build on it your first riser, using bricks, slabs or whatever material you have chosen. If each tread is to be a slab, allow at least 2in height for each one. Lay each slab in a bedding mix of approximately 1 part cement to 4 parts sand. Place the slab to overhang the riser by at least 1in. Build your second riser on the back of the first tread; and so on to the top of the flight.

Make sure each step slopes very slightly forward, so that rain will run off it. Line the sides of the finished steps with leafy plants and dwarf perennials.

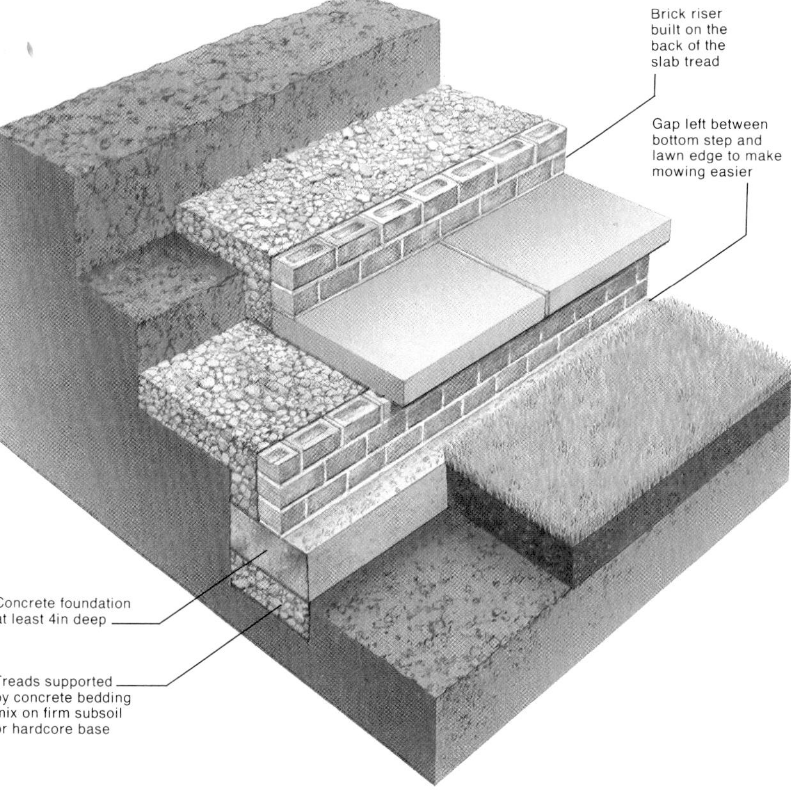

any further damage and you can pebbledash or paint it. Otherwise, grow shrubs to screen the wall; for suggestions, see *Climbers*, page 76, and *Shrubs*, page 310.

Where frost has flaked off the surface of the bricks, you can cover the wall with facing stones – a sort of stone veneer – to give the wall a whole new look and make it a feature of the garden. If you do, put a layer on top of the wall. Otherwise seepage will cause further damage and may in time dislodge the facing.

Widening vistas

How can I make my small back garden seem bigger?

The basic rule is to keep taller plants and shrubs close to the house. Large, bulky trees or shrubs standing around the edges of the garden merely restrict the horizon and exaggerate the closed-in feeling.

Keep the centre of the garden open. Plan a feature that's not too tall at the bottom of the garden: a seat, a slightly raised bed of lilies, say, or an elegant but low shrub in a paved setting. Avoid straight lines. Instead let the lawn edges bulge so that the grass is a rough hourglass shape. Run paths or lawn steppingstones in a curve along the side of the garden, not down the centre.

A second approach is to abandon the idea of a central lawn, and instead to pack the garden space with a variety of shapes and features. Wind a narrow path among some island beds, each with a different theme.

Tuck a seat or a statue as a surprise feature behind a raised bed of shrubs. Design it so that it is partly hidden from the house and can be discovered as you wind among the beds. Plan features or feature plants that can be seen only from one corner of the garden. A crowded garden such as this needs careful planning (see *Starting from scratch*, page 150). Aim to mix low-lying plants with the odd raised bed of dwarf conifers, say, and break up the beds with the occasional soaring yet slim plant, such as *Juniperus* 'Skyrocket' or *Phormium tenax*.

Consider making one bed a scree garden. Cover an irregularly shaped mound with about 2in of small pebbles or stone chippings, and grow creeping or prostrate rockery plants and dwarf conifers with a few spring and autumn-flowering bulbs.

For suggestions about which plants to grow, see *Dwarf conifers*, page 127, and *Rock gardens*, page 280.

Planning for herbs

I like to use fresh herbs when cooking. Can you advise me on laying out a herb garden?

Position is the first consideration. Plan it as near to the kitchen as you can – you don't want to have to march about in boots and a raincoat every time you need fresh herbs in winter.

Put your herb garden at the edge of the patio, or alongside a slab or concrete path, so that you have easy access to the herbs. Many are annuals, and can be planted out each spring. Some, such as rosemary, can grow into fair-sized shrubs. They may be better off in a border with plenty of room.

Other herbs, particularly mint, can be vigorously invasive. Drive some slates or plastic lawn edging into the ground vertically around them to restrict the roots. Or set the plant in a bottomless plastic bucket buried to its rim in the soil.

Many herbs – among them parsley, chives and thyme – will thrive in pots and can be brought into the kitchen or utility room in winter. Others, such as thyme, can be grown in the cracks between patio slabs – and they give off a lovely smell when walked upon. For ideas on how to grow and use particular herbs, look under the names of the individual plants, such as *Parsley*, page 244, or see *Herbs*, page 194.

Once you've worked out where to put your herb garden, and what to grow in it, you can arrange the size of each herb's patch to suit the amounts you use, and arrange the patches in any pattern that pleases you. Two ideas look particularly attractive. One is to lift a checkerboard pattern of small slabs on a patio, and grow one herb in place of each slab. The other is to get hold of an old wooden cartwheel, paint it white and lay it flat on the ground; then plant the herbs between the spokes (see, for example, the picture on page 195).

Restrain an invasive herb such as mint by concealing slates or strips of lawn edging beneath the rim and under the spokes on either side of its triangular bed.

Planning for fruit

How can I grow some fruit trees in my small garden without them taking over?

Train them up the walls and fences. Cordons, espaliers and fan-trained fruit trees can give you a fine variety of fruit in a small space. For details of varieties and how to train them, see *Apples*, page 13, and *Pears*, page 251.

Measuring a slope

I have a 50ft long sloping garden and plan to lay a few steps in it, but I am baffled as to how to find the total height of the drop from one end to the other so that I can work out how many steps I need. Is there a simple method.

Yes. Run your hosepipe from the top to the bottom of the slope and turn on the tap gently. Now, go to the bottom of the slope, taking with you a tape measure and someone to help you. Take hold of the end of the hosepipe and raise it vertically until the water is barely bubbling out. Send your helper to turn the tap off.

Lower the hosepipe end until the water level inside just reaches the nozzle. Measure the height of the hosepipe end from the ground. At the other end, measure the height of the tap nozzle from the ground. Subtract the tap height from your other measurement and what's left is the height of your drop.

Children's corner

We want to make a play area in the garden for our young children without letting it take over the garden. Any tips?

A good patch of grass is the best playing area for children. Make it fairly level, but don't aim for a bowling green. Get some sturdy rye grass in the mix, and keep the grass at least an inch long to avoid wearing bare

MEASURING A SHORT SLOPE *Use a spirit level to hold a piece of wood horizontally from the top of the slope, and another piece vertically from the bottom. Measure from the crossing point.*

MEASURING A LONG SLOPE *Fill a hosepipe, from a can or tap, until the water is level with both ends at once. Measure the height of each end above the ground and subtract the smaller figure.*

patches. Unprotected, the borders and the vegetable patch will soon be damaged by feet and footballs, so consider putting up trellisworks, or move the borders closer to the house or farther down the garden, away from the play area.

Fixtures such as swings and slides can be a problem – and they take up a lot of space, too. There are, however, easy-to-erect wood and plastic kits available from garden centres and toy shops. These can be taken down and stored away in winter, and moved easily when you want to cut the grass beneath them. An old tyre, swinging by a rope from a tall and sturdy tree, if you have one, is still a favourite with children.

A sandpit can be simply made. Make it about 3ft by 3ft and dig out to about 12in deep at the sides, sloping to about 16in in the middle. Cut planed boards to fit the sides and extend 3in above the level of the pit, and soak them in wood preservative.

Fix them into position with a square wooden peg in each corner. The wood is better planed because it cuts the risk of splinters. Line the pit and boards with heavy-duty polythene to hold in the sand, and make a few small holes in it at the bottom to allow moisture to drain away. Make a cover, using polythene-lined wood, to keep out rain and stray cats.

If you live near the seaside a good load of beach sand will be ideal. Otherwise use silver sand. It is expensive, but it doesn't stain clothes and it drains well.

Children love swingball games, but posts knocked into the ground directly can quickly loosen soil and cause holes in the lawn. Instead use the rotary washing line idea – sink a length of pipe into the lawn to hold the post. If necessary, set the pipe in concrete to hold it permanently in position.

Formal lines

I'm redesigning the beds and borders in my garden, and would like to give them a more formal shape. How can I get my curves and angles right?

You'll need a good length of rope, at least 20yds of it, and at least half a dozen sturdy pegs. See below for how to make a circle, a right angle and an oval. Using combinations of these three shapes, you can create a variety of formal shapes.

To make a circle Drive a peg into the ground in the centre of the planned bed. Take a length of rope, half the diameter of the bed. Tie one end loosely to the peg, the other end to a second peg. Hold the second peg firmly and, as if using a huge pair of compasses, walk around the central, fixed peg, scoring a furrow into the ground. If marking a furrow is difficult – on a lawn, say, or on hard ground – use the same method, but plant a series of pegs as you trace out the circumference. Dig out the circle inside the furrow or pegs. You can use the same technique to mark out quadrants or semicircles.

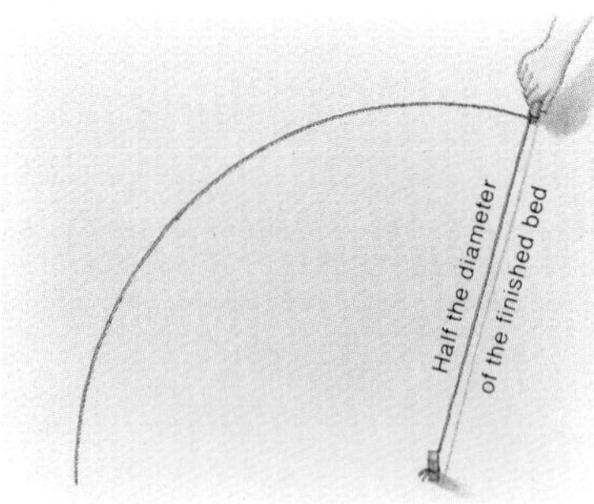

To make a right angle Knock a peg into the ground at the spot where you want the point of the corner to be. Knock a second peg into the ground along one side of the planned bed 3ft from the first. Tie a stretch of rope 9ft long to the two pegs. Put a dab of paint on the rope – or tie a piece of string around it – 4ft from the peg marking the corner.

Hold a peg against the dab of paint and pull the rope taut. It will mark an exact right angle at the corner. Knock in the peg to hold the rope steady, then use the rope as a marker for your digging.

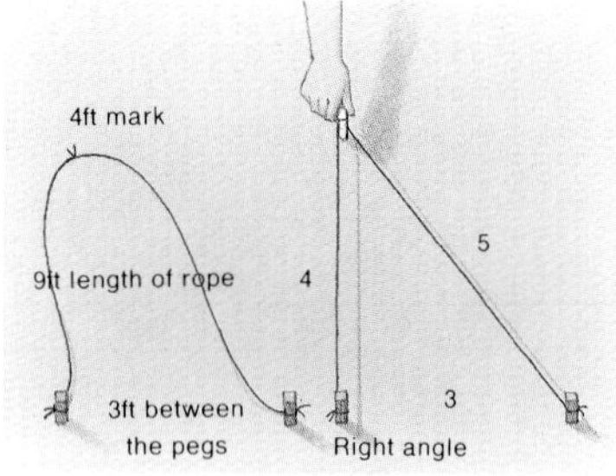

To make an oval First (1) knock in a peg each end of the long axis of the oval. Place another peg halfway between them. At right angles to the central line, across the central peg, mark the ends of the short axis with two more pegs. Mark a piece of rope to the exact length of the long axis.
2. Take the pegs from the ends of the long axis and tie one to each end of the rope at the marked point. Loop the mid-point of the rope round one of the pegs marking the short axis. With help, pull the rope taut and knock in the pegs on the line of the long axis. They will each be the same distance in from the original peg hole.
3. Remove the two unused pegs, then pull up the one at the centre of the rope. Keeping the rope taut, score a furrow in the ground with the tip of the peg, by sliding it along the length of the rope. This will give you one half of the oval. Repeat on the other side to mark the second half.

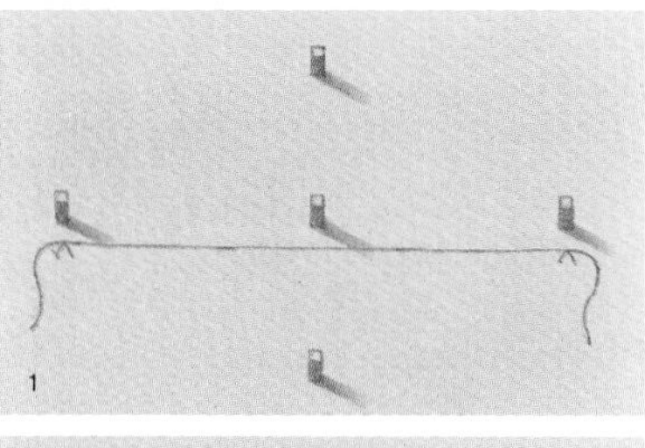

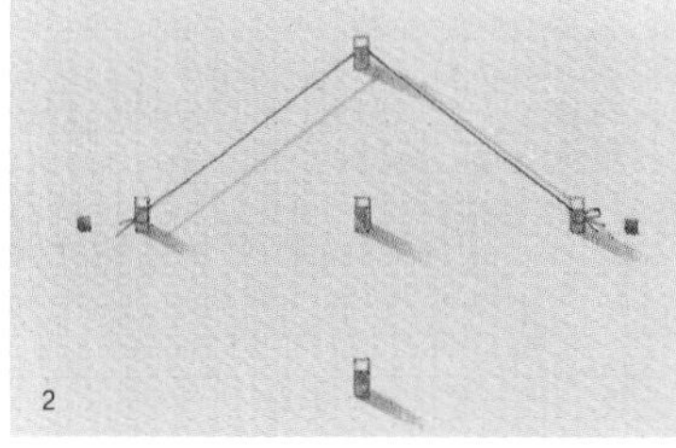

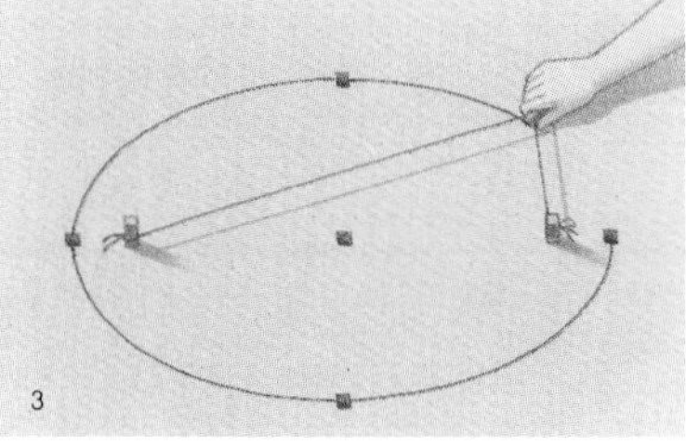

Go for curves

My garden consists of a square of grass with a narrow border around it. What is the simplest way to make it more interesting?

Curves – and be bold with them. Don't rush the job, take some time to plan where you want your new borders to be and, before you shape them, decide which plants you intend to feature in them.

To get an idea of how it will look, take a length of rope or hosepipe and lay it out across the lawn in the shapes you wish to make. Avoid tight curves and scallops, which are fussy and difficult to maintain. Go for broad sweeps. Look at your new curves from all angles. Go upstairs, if you live in a house, and look down on the garden to get the feel of the shapes you are looking for.

When you have settled on a plan, cut out the new borders and curves with a half-moon edging iron. Don't cut tight up to the rope or pipe which is your guideline for the shape. Allow about 3in for error. This will enable you to alter the shape slightly if you want to, and will make it easier for you to cut a neat, firm edge to the lawn when you are finally satisfied.

Choose your plants carefully. To get perspective and give the garden depth, you will need to put the taller trees and shrubs near to the house. Plan a feature, such as a statue, pond or archway to one side of the garden. This will draw the eye and counteract the squareness of the garden.

Stagger the heights of the plants you choose to break up the symmetry. Plant shrubs, perennials and annuals for a succession of colour and interest (see *Annuals*, page 10, and *Colour*, page 84). Spread the costs by shaping and planting up one border each month or each year.

Tackling neglect

We have just bought a house with an overgrown and neglected garden. Is there a quick way of getting it back into shape?

This is not a job you should rush. Certainly you can quickly put the garden back into some sort of shape just by cutting back the grass, weeding out the borders and trimming back overgrown shrubs, hedges and borders.

Once the garden looks halfway tidy again, find out what you have actually got in it before you start demolishing things. Give yourself time to get a feel about the garden – perhaps as much as a year. You may want to change the shape completely, or work in some new features. But you may also find some interesting plants already there that you want to keep.

Be ruthless with any plants or shrubs that are past their best or do not come up to scratch – get them out. Dig over compacted soil. Cover up the patches you have cleared with a mulch of compost, manure or peat and composted bark. This will do the soil good and improve its appearance.

Then wait, at least until winter, when you can see what, if any, spring bulbs are coming up. You may get some pleasant surprises (see *Starting from scratch*, page 150).

Concrete garden

My back garden is just a small area of concrete. What can I do to make a garden out of it?

Pots, to start with. Or, as a lower-cost alternative, growing bags. It is amazing what colour and life they can bring to a confined area. Buy some big tubs for permanent planting, some hanging baskets, and plenty of pots. Pots that you can pick up and move about to give rotation of interest, and pots you can hang on the walls for colour.

Consider also building low retaining walls along some of the fences to make raised beds which you can fill with soil or peat, and plant with honeysuckle and clematis. Rhododendrons, camellias and the versatile *Pieris formosa* 'Forrestii' can be planted in the tubs to make permanent features.

Consider, too, breaking through the concrete in one or two places so that you can plant permanent shrubs, or even a small tree, into the ground beneath.

For your pots, buy a mixture of stone and terracotta ones – they give a warm, Mediterranean look to a garden. Fill some with spring bulbs, early-flowering violas and polyanthus. Keep others for a bright summer display of geraniums and begonias, alyssum and lobelia. They will often do better in pots than in the ground.

Pot up some dwarf azaleas for spring; grow a pyramid bay tree; pot mesembryanthemum in the sunniest corner; try lilies and fuchsias, which love being in pots, and even the miniature roses, such as 'Little Flirt', 'Yellow Doll' and 'New Penny'. Hydrangeas, pansies, busy lizzies, petunias and chrysanthemums will all thrive in pots, too.

Feed your pot and growing-bag plants regularly – about every third week – and choose a general fertiliser such as a liquid house plant feed or Growmore. Water each evening to avoid leaf scorch, and never let your plants wilt in their pots.

If all goes well with the flowers, keep a couple of troughs or growing bags free to grow tomatoes, peppers and cucumbers. And you can always grow a strawberry pot. They look attractive and taste lovely – if you keep the birds away (see *Birds*, page 28).

GARLIC

How to grow cloves

Can I grow successful plants from the cloves of shop-bought garlic?

You certainly can. What you buy is the bulb of the plant after it has been hung and dried. The cloves are the softer segments you get after the bulb has been split apart.

Plant the cloves upright 6in apart in your garden in spring, burying them so that their tops are about 2in below ground level. Choose a sunny spot, preferably one with a light soil. They will sprout within a couple of weeks and need no attention apart from watering in dry spells.

In late summer the tall, thin, dark green leaves will begin to turn yellow. When they do, lift the whole plant and leave it to dry under cover; the bulb may rot if it gets wet.

When the leaves die off, remove them and store the bulbs in a cool, dry, frost-free shed for use as needed. Or leave the foliage on and use it to plait the harvest into a string of bulbs in the same way as for onions (see *Rope trick*, page 236). A few cloves can also be planted under cloches in autumn for a fresh supply early the following spring.

Natural pesticide

I have heard old gardeners claim that garlic grown between plants will fend off pests and diseases. Can this be true?

Possibly, but it is uncertain. Roses seem to benefit because aphids don't appear to like the smell of garlic plants. And aphids are not alone. Garlic has been used for years – and with some success – in homemade sprays against blackfly, greenfly, snails, cabbage flies, mosquitoes and some caterpillars.

You can make it by pulverising three large garlic cloves with 6 tablespoons of paraffin. Leave the pulp in a bowl for about 48 hours.

Grate a tablespoon of soap into a pint of hot water and stir until it melts. Mix with the garlic pulp, cool, and strain. Use 2 tablespoons of the mix in 4 pints of water for use in the sprayer. Whatever harm it does to garden pests, garlic is good for people. It contains chemicals called allyl disulphide, allicin and allicetoin, which are thought to improve digestion and help to fight dysentery, typhoid and the common cold.

Warm favourite

Garlic seems to flourish in warm countries, where it is most widely used in cooking. Can it be grown successfully in a temperate climate like Britain's?

Yes, but unless you use lots of it in the kitchen, you may not find it worthwhile, as a little goes a long way.

Garlic comes from the hot, desert regions of central Asia. It found its way centuries ago to the Mediterranean, where it thrives, and has become a characteristic ingredient of the regional cuisine.

It was once considered too tender for cooler climates, but it is, in fact, a sturdy plant and will do reasonably well even in the North of Britain.

GERANIUMS

Born for hanging

Can you suggest suitable geraniums for a hanging basket?

The most suitable geraniums for this purpose are the ivy-leaved types. Smaller than those of the zonal geraniums, the leaves are roughly ivy-shaped, and the plants have a trailing habit.

Until recently, these plants were all propagated from cuttings taken either during August or in spring. There were a number of named varieties, but 'L'Elegante', with its green and cream variegated leaves, was the most common. This is still very popular, although there are now good seed-raised alternatives which are likely to oust the more traditional plants. These newcomers, although not variegated like 'L'Elegante', have the ability to produce a good show at the end of May from a February sowing, and have done away with the problem of keeping plants alive for the winter. At the end of summer, these plants are discarded and fresh seed is sown in spring.

Supreme among the new seed-raised varieties is 'Summer Showers', with its mixed flower colours.

Well-drained soil

What's the best compost to use for greenhouse pelargoniums?

Coming from South Africa, greenhouse pelargoniums are used to warm, dry conditions and a free-draining soil. While it is possible to get young plants growing vigorously in a peat-based compost, once they have reached the 3in pot stage they should be transferred to a soil-based compost – ideally John Innes No 3. Ensure that each pot has plenty of drainage material in the bottom. To improve the free passage of water, a generous sprinkling of sharp grit – about a handful to a 5in pot, proportionately less for a 3in pot – can be mixed in with the compost. Water them freely during the growing season.

Confusion of terms

Could you explain the difference between a pelargonium and a geranium? I have been told that geraniums are hardy, but I always bring mine inside for the winter.

There are in fact two separate genera: pelargonium and geranium. The reason there is such confusion over geraniums is because the popular bedding and house plant known as the geranium is, botanically, a pelargonium. The cultivated pelargoniums – none of which is hardy – are divided into two main groups by experts: the regal pelargoniums, usually referred to as pelargoniums; and the zonal pelargoniums, which are called geraniums. The regal pelargoniums are probably derived from the species *Pelargonium cucullatum* and *P. grandiflorum*, while the so-called geraniums, with their distinctive leaf zoning, are hybrids from *P. zonale* and *P. inquinans*. The ivy-leaved geraniums used in hanging baskets are largely derived from *P. peltatum*.

The true geraniums, belonging to the genus geranium, are popularly known as crane's-bills. They include several native plants like herb-robert, *Geranium robertianum*, and the wild crane's-bill, *G. sylvaticum*. Two species widely grown in gardens are the pink *G. endressii* and purple *G. psilostemon*. True geraniums are indeed hardy, can be left in the ground over winter and are easily propagated from division or seed.

The bedding geraniums you're talking about, however – which are botanically pelargoniums – need the winter protection you give them.

Stopping the rot

When I take geranium cuttings, some always turn black at the base and rot. How can I prevent this happening?

This problem is a very common one, especially with cuttings taken from outdoor bedding geraniums. The rotting is due to a disease called black leg, which invades the basal tissue of the cutting, causing it to collapse. It is usually associated with over-watering or an unsuitable rooting medium. Often the kind of cutting material that is used has a bearing, too.

Geraniums are plants from fairly arid regions of the world. Although very adaptable, they prefer dryish conditions. Black leg is most likely to occur if the cuttings are rooted in a medium which does not drain freely. A mixture of equal parts by volume of peat and sharp sand, or peat and perlite, both of which drain well, are the best composts in which to root geraniums.

Soft green cuttings are very vulnerable as well; so, when taking cuttings, choose material which has a pinkish flush. This colour change indicates that the tissue is toughening up, either by virtue of being grown under harsher conditions, or else because it is ripening. It is much less likely to succumb to black leg.

Winter schedule

How can I keep my bedding geraniums alive through the winter?

Do you really need to hang on to your old bedding geraniums? There are so many good seed-raised kinds on the market now that, unless you have a special desire to keep one of the older cultivated varieties, there is little point in going through the laborious business of looking after the plants through the winter.

The main advantages of the older varieties (which are not found with the modern seed-raised kinds) are variegated foliage and double blossoms.

If you really feel you have to keep some geraniums alive over the winter, there are two methods of doing so.

First, if you have a greenhouse, use rooted cuttings. Take 3in tip cuttings during August, dip the bases in a hormone rooting powder, and insert them into pots of a half-and-half mixture of peat and coarse sand. By the end of September they should be well rooted. Pot them on in a compost with few nutrients (John Innes No 1 potting compost is ideal) so that no vulnerable soft growth is made before the onset of winter. Keep them in a frost-free greenhouse, or on the window-sill in a cool room, give them a light watering no more than once a fortnight, and they should survive the winter. As soon as there are signs of life in spring, repot them into a stronger compost (John Innes No 2) to encourage growth.

If you don't have a frost-free place in which to keep young plants for the winter, try to keep the old ones. Select plants with stems which have a pinkish cast, for these will be fairly hardy and are less likely to rot in store. Discard plants with soft green succulent stems; these are vulnerable to storage moulds.

Lift the plants before the first frost and stand them in boxes of peat in a cool, frost-free place such as a shed or garage. The peat should be just deep enough to cover the roots. Do not water the plants. Instead, keep them cool and allow the foliage to die back naturally. When the leaves have faded, pull them off.

The plants are then ready for storing. Wrap the roots of each one in polythene with a little peat – just damp enough to prevent the roots from drying out completely, but not enough to stimulate growth. Then tie the plants in bundles and hang them up in a frost-free shed or garage.

Alternatively, wrap the plants individually in sheets of newspaper and store them, again in a shed or garage. Inspect the plants regularly and remove any stems that show signs of disease.

In spring, the plants should be potted and watered. Use the new young shoots for cuttings; it is rarely worth trying to grow old plants for a second year.

Maintaining light and heat

I've not had much luck raising geraniums from seed. What's the secret of success?

The problem most gardeners encounter with seed-raised geraniums is ensuring sufficient heat to enable them to germinate properly and then maintaining enough heat and light to produce a bushy plant. This is especially difficult without a greenhouse.

For this reason, although most seed companies recommend that seed should be sown in January, you'd do better to delay until the end of February. The higher light levels and greater ease with which a stable high temperature can be maintained then mean that there is less risk of damaging checks to growth. On the other hand, plants from a later sowing are likely to be smaller.

Use a peat-based seed compost which will warm up quickly. Germinate the seeds in the airing cupboard, in a temperature of around 18°C (65°F), but remove them as soon as you see signs of life, because darkness rapidly elongates seedlings. Grow the freshly germinated seedlings on with a minimum night temperature in the greenhouse of 7°C (45°F) – although they'll do better if you can keep them warmer than this. About 13°C (55°F) is the ideal.

The most important factor is the correct balance of light and heat: often you'll get better plants from a lower temperature regime provided there's plenty of light. The same applies to consistency of temperature: a low but stable temperature yields far better plants than a higher but wildly fluctuating temperature.

Prick out the seedlings, as soon as the first true leaves have appeared, into 3in pots in any good potting compost. As the plants grow, give them plenty of space. A good rule of thumb is to leave a gap as big as the pot each plant is in. So by the time the plants are in 5in pots, you should be leaving a 5in gap between each pot; if the plants' leaves are touching, they're too close. Pinch out the growing tips of any plants which start to become leggy, in order to encourage them to bush out.

Chemical aid

I understand that it's possible to make ordinary bedding geraniums into dwarf plants and encourage early flowering by using a chemical. How safe is this?

The chemical – known as cyclocel – is widely used by commercial growers to produce short, stocky plants which are in flower at planting time. Applied when the foliage is about the size of a penny, it stunts growth and encourages early flowering.

Only a tiny quantity of the chemical is required, and the secret is in getting the dose right. Too much and it can cause scorching round the edges of the leaves, or even kill off the plant.

While cyclocel is a useful aid for the professional nurseryman, though, it cannot legally be sold to amateur gardeners. Moreover, recent experiments, which have involved treating a number of different seed-raised geranium varieties with cyclocel, have indicated that it does the plants little good in the long term.

GLADIOLI

Hardy species

I believe there are some hardy gladioli that can be left out as perennials. Can you tell me something about them?

There are a few perennial gladioli, but their blooms are very modest when compared with the splendid showy hybrids that have been developed. Even so, they can be quite pretty and they do have an old-fashioned charm about them.

The toughest is *Gladiolus byzantinus*, which has 15in spikes of magenta-crimson flowers in June and July. It will not look out of place in a herbaceous border; it can also be naturalised in grass, doing best among short-growing grasses such as fescues, that won't hide the flowers.

G. illyricus, another of the tough species, has fewer blooms than *G. byzantinus*, and they are more purple in colour. *G. tristis* has sulphur-yellow flowers with a reddish tinge. All three species grow to about 2ft tall and all work well in a mixed border. They like a damp, rich soil, so choose a patch which has had plenty of well-rotted manure or compost dug in, and give them plenty of sun.

The foot of a south or west-facing wall would be ideal, but they'll also produce a good show in the open garden.

The lifting controversy

To lift, or not to lift my gladioli corms? That is the question; what is the answer?

Lift. The flashy hybrid gladioli – both the large and the miniature varieties – are not tough enough to survive a British winter in the open ground. For the best storage method, see *Winter quarters*, this page. Replant the corms between mid-March and mid-April.

On light, sandy soil, plant them so that the tips are covered by about 4in of earth; on heavy clay, put a little sharp sand in the bottom of the planting hole below the corm to aid drainage, and cover the tips, again, with about 4in of soil. Some varieties may get through a winter in well-drained soil in a sheltered space in the southern part of the country. But even if they do survive, they'll probably have been weakened by the cold and their appearance the next season is likely to be sparse and patchy. Don't risk it.

Corm clusters

When I lift my gladioli in autumn, I find clusters of little corms around the flowering ones. Can I grow these into full-sized corms and will they flower? If they do, will they be different from the parent?

Yes, you can grow them into flowering corms, though it is a slow and tedious business – they will eventually produce flowers exactly the same as the parent.

Keep the little corms in a cool place for winter, then in spring plant them out in a soil-based compost in trays. They will mature enough in a year to plant out in the garden, but it may be the third year before they flower, and you will need to lift them each winter during this period.

Most gladioli can also be grown from seed. However, the corm method is more reliable in that the new plants will be identical to the parents. With seeds, you will get unpredictable variations. For an explanation of why this happens, on all plants, see *Why F1 seeds are OK*, page 308.

Winter quarters

Can you tell me the best way to lift and store gladioli corms for winter?

Wait until frost has blackened the foliage before lifting. A couple of degrees of frost will be enough to do this, so it won't get into the ground to damage the corm. Fungal disease can get into the corm if you cut down the old flower spikes and leaves while the stems are still green. The blackening caused by frost has the side-effect of sealing the tissue naturally. Chop off the frost-bitten foliage, and lay out the corms to dry, taking care not to damage the protective skin. The best method is to stretch a net a few inches above the ground and dry the corms on that for seven to ten days. Alternatively, spread the corms out on a wooden tray in a cool, airy shed or garage. Turn the corms upside down, so that any moisture can drain out of the stems. Let air circulate freely around them. Rub off any dry soil, but don't wash the corms – the damp will encourage moulds to develop later in store.

Store the dried corms in trays or nets strung from the garden shed roof. If you have only a few corms, use an old pair of tights, putting a knot above each corm to separate them. Then, if one rots, the others are less likely to than if they were touching. Dust the corms with a sulphur fungicide as an extra protection against fungal diseases which can lead to rotting. For advice on how to cope with these and other diseases of gladioli, see *Corm troubles – and how to cure them*, page 99.

Growing for showing

I want to grow top-quality gladioli for our local show. Do I need to make any special preparations?

Yes, you need a top-quality soil. That is, one that drains well and is rich in plant nutrients. So you need to start in autumn, digging in plenty of well-rotted manure and other organic material such as compost. Let winter rain and frost weather the soil, then rake it down to a fine tilth just before planting. By the time you plant, the surface should be about the consistency of breadcrumbs. This preparation is vital because extremes of drought and damp are both bad for the gladioli. The organic material acts as a buffer for the corms, evening out the fluctuating levels of rain-fed moisture in the soil.

However, all your autumn work will be wasted if you don't buy the best. Top-quality gladioli cannot be grown from second-grade corms. So go for the largest corms you can afford. On heavy loams or clays, work into the soil some sand or grit during your autumn digging. Then, at planting time, put a ½in layer of sharp sand at the bottom of each planting hole. It will improve the drainage and encourage the growth of roots.

Finally, feed the plant with a liquid fertiliser every two weeks from the time you see the first buds. You should end up with gladioli that'll be the envy of your neighbours. They may catch the judge's eye, too.

Stuck with sticks

No matter which way I try staking my gladioli, some always get spoiled. Is there a successful way to do it?

Strong canes, one for each plant, is the neatest way. All the same, however careful you are, you're almost bound to spoil a few plants. There's no foolproof method, but following these rules will minimise the risks.

- Place the canes in the soil at planting time rather than later, so that the plant roots do not get damaged.
- Set each cane upwind from the plant – on the side from which the wind usually blows. That way the plant won't chafe against the stake.
- Tie each developing flower spike to the cane with soft string or raffia.
- Don't tie the upper part of the spike; it needs to be able to move freely. If it's tied tightly all the way up, the top will be snapped off by the wind.

An alternative way of staking is to plant your gladioli in rows and dig in strong stakes at regular intervals along the rows. Stretch wire between them at intervals of about 12in, and tie your flower spikes to the wires. This method takes up more space than canes and you need wider gaps between the rows so that you can get in to hoe the ground, but it does work.

Gladioli in pots

I have been given some dwarf gladioli, but I know little about them. Can I grow them in pots?

Yes, you can, and you can also treat them as forced spring-flowering bulbs for indoor decoration. The dwarf corms you have are probably *Gladiolus* x *colvillei* hybrids, which grow to between 12in and 2ft tall. For pot cultivation, plant five or six corms in a 6in pot in October or November, using a soil-based compost such as John Innes No 2. Stand them, pot and all, in a cold frame to develop a healthy root system.

About 10-12 weeks after planting, take them into the greenhouse or the living room for forcing. Use only gentle heat. Too much warmth in moderate winter light will lead to spindly flower spikes. As the spikes develop, feed them with a standard liquid house plant fertiliser every two weeks. Stop feeding as soon as the flowers fade; otherwise luxuriant growth will tend to make the corm soft and difficult to keep.

Other dwarf gladioli are the primulinus hybrids, which grow to between 18in and 3ft, but flower later than *G.* x *colvillei*. These hybrids do best in groups in a mixed border; they need no staking and give colourful decoration.

Alternatively, primulinus hybrids can also be forced for an indoor display in spring. Pot them up in a cold frame in March – five or six corms in a 6in pot – and take them indoors as soon as the flower spikes start to develop. Start feeding at the same time with a standard house plant fertiliser every two weeks. After flowering finishes, stop feeding but don't stop watering. The idea is to keep the foliage healthy and growing for as long as possible, because the leaves are the factory that will stockpile energy for next year's blooms. Finally, when the foliage fades, dry off the corms and store them (see *Winter quarters*, page 157); then replant them out in the garden the following spring.

Best for cutting

Which are the best kinds of gladioli to grow for cut flowers?

The large-flowered, showy hybrids are best. Choose varieties such as the orange 'Saxony', soft pink 'My Love', and the pink and apricot 'Praha'. Others which will give you a good garden display, as well as good blooms for cutting, are the rich red 'Hunting Song', the pure white 'Teach In', and the bright yellow 'Flower Song'.

GLASSHOUSE AND CABBAGE WHITEFLIES

Whiteflies in the greenhouse

The trouble began with my greenhouse fuchsias – masses of small white scales on the undersides of the leaves. Now it's starting to spread onto the leaves of my tomatoes. What is it? And is it serious?

The scales are the immature stage of the glasshouse whitefly, which, as its name implies, is a pest on many greenhouse plants all the year round.

A very similar sap-sucking pest, the cabbage whitefly, afflicts cabbages and other brassicas outdoors from about May to September. The young whiteflies of both species feed on plant sap and exude sticky honeydew, which encourages sooty moulds. You will also see small clouds of adults – which look like tiny, pure white moths – flying about, especially if you shake the plants.

An infestation by either pest is serious, because it weakens plants and can check their growth if left untreated. Crops from affected plants do, however, remain edible. With either pest, spray affected plants with permethrin or pyrethrum. You'll need to spray repeatedly at weekly intervals because the sprays kill only the adult whiteflies; the aim is to kill the adults before they lay the eggs of the next generation.

With glasshouse whiteflies, it is also worth fumigating the greenhouse in autumn with permethrin smoke.

WHITE PEST *Winged adults, less than ⅛in long, lay up to 200 eggs, often in neat circles, on leaves. Eggs can grow to adults in three weeks.*

GOOSEBERRIES

Pruning gooseberries

What's the best way to prune a gooseberry?

The approach to pruning gooseberries varies with the age of the bush. The ideal you are working towards is a bush consisting of 10-12 permanent branches (furnished with fruiting spurs) growing on a short trunk, or 'leg', about 9in high.

In the early years, all pruning is done in winter, when the plants are dormant. The aim is to keep the leg free from shoots and branches and to build up the framework of the bush, and this is best done by shortening by half all the new growth on shoots which are wanted for permanent branches. The rest of the shoots on a young bush should be cut out completely.

Once a bush is three or four years old, it should start fruiting. At this stage, your pruning should aim to go on encouraging the growth of the branches, and to increase fruit production as well.

To this end, carry on cutting off half the new growth on the permanent branches in winter; but, at the same time, instead of cutting off the other shoots completely, leave them about 2in long.

At this stage, summer pruning, too, can be introduced. Carried out towards the end of June, it simply involves cutting back all sideshoots not wanted for permanent branches to a length of 4-5in. This is not essential, but is particularly helpful to dessert varieties, since it removes much of the leaf growth which would otherwise shade the berries and slow their ripening.

Newcomers to gardening can take heart from the fact that, if gooseberry bushes are not pruned at all, or if they are pruned badly, the worst that can happen is that they will carry less fruit and soon become very overgrown. They won't actually come to any harm at all.

Colour no guide

Can you tell from the colour of a gooseberry whether it's a variety that's good for eating raw or one that has to be cooked first?

No, there is no connection at all between colour and character. One of the best dessert varieties for gardens, 'Leveller', is a greenish-yellow, while the good all-rounder, 'Whinham's Industry', is red.

The most heavily cropping and most popular commercial cooker, 'Careless', is bright green; so is a more recent cooker, 'Invicta', but the dessert variety 'Langley Gage' is also bright green.

Creating a cordon

I'd love to grow gooseberries in my garden, but I haven't got room for full-sized bushes. Can they be grown any other way?

Where space is at a premium, the alternative to full bushes is the cordon system of growth – training the plant to grow as a single stem. Gooseberries (and white and red currants) lend themselves particularly to this system because the branches are more or less permanent and they bear their fruit on spurs. The system also makes fruit picking easier and a good deal less painful.

Cordons can be bought ready trained or they can be developed from one or two-year-old bushes. Single cordons are rather uneconomical because of the number of plants required. The normal practice, therefore, is to grow the plants as U-shaped cordons, with two vertical branches. Or they can be grown as double U-cordons, with four branches.

With cordons, the vertical arms are trained to wires or canes, spaced 12in apart, against a wall or fence or in the open garden. Where you place them depends on where you have room, but the site must be sunny so that the fruit ripens well and develops a good flavour.

Cordons should be pruned in late June to help the fruits develop and prevent them becoming overshadowed by too much new growth. All that is needed is for every new shoot (except the leading one at the very top of the branch) to be cut back to a length of about 4-5in. In winter cut them back to 2in. Trim the leading shoot to the height you want in winter as well.

Once you've established your cordon, it should go on cropping happily for between 10 and 12 years before needing replacement.

How old is a cutting?

Does a cutting from a ten-year-old gooseberry bush start life anew or is it ten years old from the moment it goes into the ground?

The notion that a cutting starts out as old as its parent is by no means new. In the early 19th century, no less a figure than the second president of the young Horticultural Society (now the Royal Horticultural Society) applied it to apples.

The president, Thomas Knight, firmly believed that not just each individual tree but each variety had a definite life span, after which it would go into decline. What was probably happening was that the trees were becoming infected with viruses. But, since viruses hadn't been heard of in the 19th century, the 'decline' theory seemed to make a lot of sense.

Of course, if this idea were taken to its logical conclusion, an apple tree of the variety 'Decio', for instance – which came to Britain with the Romans – would be more than 1500 years old.

Today, however, scientists know that this idea is wholly unfounded. Gooseberries, and many other plants, are propagated by cuttings taken from shoots which grew in the previous growing season. This means that the cells in the cutting are less than a year old. It's that cellular age which determines the age of the new plant, not the age of the parent bush.

So if a gooseberry variety, or any other plant, is propagated from healthy stock – and re-propagated as it ages – there is no reason why it should not survive for ever.

Trouble with lichen

The older branches of my gooseberry bushes have green stuff over them. Will this affect the crop at all?

This is simply a combination of lichen and moss – the same as you see on rocks or old trees. It won't affect your crop at all, though it will probably harbour some insects and fungi that might. But if the appearance bothers you, spray the bushes in winter with a tar-oil wash.

There are some pests and diseases, however, that can seriously damage your gooseberries. Here are the most common ones.

- **APHIDS** Can stop the growth of plants. Look for tiny green insects on the tips of shoots. Treat by applying a systemic insecticide such as dimethoate.
- **AMERICAN GOOSEBERRY MILDEW** Turns the fruit 'furry'. Young leaves and shoot tips develop a white fungus. Discard all affected fruit.

  To prevent attacks in future years, spray the plant regularly, from the time the buds start to open, with a systemic fungicide such as benomyl.
- **GOOSEBERRY SAWFLY** Leaves stripped to main veins. Caterpillars usually visible on edges of leaves. Spray with permethrin or rotenone (derris).

Choosing gooseberries

Which are the best cooking and the best eating varieties?

It is very difficult to say which are the best eaters because individual tastes vary so much. However, reliable croppers among the dessert varieties include 'Broom Girl', 'Keepsake', 'Leveller', 'Langley Gage' and 'Whitesmith'.

Similarly, it is hard to define a cooker as such, since cookers are really those varieties which are not sweet enough to be eaten raw – and, in any case, many gardeners grow dessert varieties but use them only for cooking. Good dual-purpose varieties – useful for eating raw or for cooking – include 'Jubilee' and 'Whinham's Industry'. 'Invicta', a new cooking variety which crops twice as heavily as most others, also has a good flavour.

Life expectancy

I have some gooseberry bushes which are about ten years old and still as productive as ever. How long will it be before they age and die?

Don't worry, they should be good for a long time yet. Properly looked after, gooseberry bushes should have a useful life of about 15 years. However, to attain maximum span they need regular feeding, correct pruning and protection from pests and diseases. If any of these aspects is neglected, their fruiting life will be shortened.

Bushes which show signs of deteriorating prematurely can sometimes be rejuvenated by pruning out about half the branches and training up new ones. But in any case it is wise to replant with new bushes every 10-12 years. That way, by the time the originals finally die, the new bushes will be cropping nicely.

GRAFTING

Two in one

I'm fairly new to gardening, but fascinated by all aspects of it. What about grafting, for instance? Is it really so difficult?

To most amateur gardeners, the very idea of grafting is daunting – a mystery best left to nurserymen. In fact, as in most aspects of gardening, all that's required is enthusiasm, patience and a reasonably deft hand. Marry these to an understanding of what the technique is about, and you're there.

The various types of grafting are simply means of propagating plants that don't come true from seed, or that for some reason or other are difficult to increase by cuttings, division or layering. Grafts are also used to control the vigour of plants – to form a dwarf version of an apple variety, say, or to strengthen the growth of a highly inbred rose.

The principle of grafting is to join a piece of the variety to be increased – the scion – to the rootstock of another, and make of them a single living unit. This new plant will have the fruiting and flowering ability of the scion and the strength and growing qualities of the rootstock. The character of the new plant will be entirely that of the scion. All the rootstock supplies is vigour and nutrients; it can no more change the character of the plant than a blood transfusion will change the hair colour of a human patient.

Depending on the method used, the scion may vary in size from a single bud to a shoot several inches long. The rootstock usually consists of an established root system with a main stem to which the scion is joined. Scion and stock are usually, but not always, of the same genus. Pears (*Pyrus communis*), for example, are often grafted onto quince (*Cydonia oblonga*) rootstock.

Merely pressing one bit of plant into another is unlikely to produce great results. Grafting, to be successful, must be carried out at a certain time – generally the very end of the dormant season – and in a certain way. Immediately beneath the outer skin or bark of every plant there is a layer of cells called the cambium layer. During the growing season, these cells constantly multiply, and they are responsible for the thickening of trunk, branches and roots. Upward, outward and downward growth are the department of the growing tips on branches and roots.

For a good graft, it is essential to expose as much as possible of the cambium layers of the two pieces of plant material to be joined – which is why grafting cuts are always made on the slant. When the pieces are put together and tied, and when the growth season begins, the nutrients from each piece pass to the other via the united cambium layers. By the autumn, the scion will have fused to the rootstock and the union will have become permanent. For details on how to graft, see *Common grafting methods*, opposite page.

Cheap options

Can any plant be grafted, or is it only fruit trees and roses which are propagated in this way?

An extraordinary number of plants *can be* propagated by grafting. For a time, even tomatoes were grafted onto disease-resistant rootstocks. That grafting was done in spring, with young scion and rootstock plants pressed together in neighbouring pots; when the graft had taken, after a few weeks, the scion plant was cut off just below the union, the rootstock just above.

The operative phrase, though, is 'can be'. In many cases it is quicker, cheaper and easier to propagate by seeds or cuttings instead. So, in practical terms, it's the second half of your question that's right – provided you add a number of ornamental trees and shrubs to your roses and fruit trees. Most named varieties of maples and sycamores, crab apples, flowering cherries, ornamental hawthorns, rhododendrons, some laburnums and beeches, whitebeam and rowan are all *best* propagated by grafting. So, too, are tree peonies and some of the more exotic and colourful cacti.

Time for change

Is there any way in which I can change a fruit tree to another variety? I'm fed up with my present apple and would like something different?

Provided the tree is less than about 30 years old and in good health, it can be changed by cutting it down and grafting shoots of another variety onto the stump. But it is a waste of time grafting onto a much older tree because the life expectancy of the resulting plant is correspondingly short. Similarly, it is pointless trying to do anything with a tree which is riddled with disease. In either of these cases, you'd do much better to buy a new tree – which will itself probably have been grafted – and cut down the old one when the new one starts bearing fruit.

Tools for the job

I'm thinking of trying my hand at grafting. Will I need any special tools?

If you go to a garden centre, you may find all kinds of grafting tools on offer, some of which are pretty expensive. But for the amateur, even the keen one, most of them are unnecessary. There are two basics you must have: a knife with an edge like a razor to prevent you from tearing the delicate tissue you'll be working on; and raffia, to bind your grafts together.

Of the many kinds of knives available, an ordinary craft knife is all you'll need. You might also add to your shopping list grafting wax, or wound-sealant latex paint, to make the joints airtight and keep out diseases.

However, no matter how efficient your tools, without skill and experience your chances of success are quite small. Even professional nurserymen have their failures when grafting, and beginners can reckon on a success rate of not much more than one in ten in the first year. But stick with it, and once you have mastered the skill it will stay with you for ever.

The art of pleaching

The other day, while visiting a stately garden, I was much impressed by what I was told is a 'pleached lime walk', in which the branches of an avenue of limes were knitted together to form a green, flower-hung tunnel. Could I emulate this in a small way – to make an arch, say?

Certainly, provided you intend to be fairly long-lived. Pleaching – the word comes from an old French term meaning 'to braid', or 'interweave' – is a technique in which grafting, plant training, pruning, hedging and topiary come together to allow the gardener in effect to crochet with live trees. Not only limes, but hornbeam, willow, whitethorn and fruit trees have been used as materials in this art which has swum in and out of favour down the centuries. The Elizabethan sage Francis Bacon said 'I doe not like Images cut out in Juniper or other Garden Stuffes', but his contemporaries were the most enthusiastic creators of secluded walks of pleached limes and hornbeams. Later, the Victorians wove living branches through and over iron frames to make bowers.

In basic pleaching, you plant trees about 8ft apart and allow them to grow naturally until they're firmly established, when you lop them at the same height. Then make a connecting frame of wires or bamboo canes along which new growth can be trained until the branches interweave – a process which will take at least three years. Cut off all shoots which grow out of line. You can achieve all sorts of effects in time, from a thick hedge raised on stilts to a green cave, depending on how you train the trees.

Another form of pleaching is to tie the shoots into a frame shaped, for example, like a window or a heart, and when they reach the top of the frame, graft them into a single stem. After some years, the frames can be removed, leaving the branches growing as shaped apertures through which other species can be trained.

COMMON GRAFTING METHODS

There are four common grafting techniques which are straightforward enough to be carried out with good results by the everyday gardener. The four are: budding; crown grafting; saddle grafting; and bridge grafting. Each is slightly different. Nevertheless, a few general rules apply.

- Generally, carry out grafting in March or April – that is, at the end of the dormant season. Choose your scions – the stems you want to unite with new roots – only from shoots that have grown in the previous year.

  Budding, however, is an exception; it is best done in July or August using the current season's wood for the scions.
- Make sure there is a bud close to the base of each scion so that, when it is tied in to the rootstock, the bud will be beneath the binding raffia or tape.
- The joint between scion and rootstock must be as flush as possible. Cut the scion on the slant so as to expose the maximum amount of the crucial cambium layer.
- Do not allow the cuts to dry out during grafting. Prepare the scion first, then leave it in water while you prepare the rootstock.
- Having laid the two cut edges together, bind up the union as tightly as possible with raffia. This is to ensure that the two parts of the graft are immovably held together, and that the joint is airtight and cannot dry out.
- Cover the joint completely with sealant paint, taking special care with the top of the rootstock. The tiniest gap left in the sealant at this point will result in loss of moisture and an increased risk of the graft failing.
- New shoots sprouting from the scion tell you that the graft has taken. When this occurs, slit the raffia on the side of the graft opposite the shoot so that growth will not be restricted. But leave the raffia on until it falls off naturally, so that it goes on providing some support and protection for the graft.
- Push a cane into the ground and loosely tie in both scion and rootstock to give some support to the new growth.

BUDDING

An economical way to propagate ornamental shrubs, roses and fruit trees, since no more than a single bud is used as the scion, while the rootstock can be raised from seeds or cuttings.

Remove all shoots from the rootstock in autumn, and prune it to the required height – about 12in for bush roses, for example, and 4-6ft for apples. In July or August the following year, cut the scion bud from a well-ripened shoot of the current season's growth.

Use a razor-sharp knife to cut out the bud in a shallow, curving slice, leaving $\frac{1}{2}$in of stalk above and below the bud (1). Peel back the shield of bark; remove and discard the sliver of wood.

Make a T-shaped cut in the side of the rootstock about $1\frac{1}{2}$in long and $\frac{1}{2}$in wide. Make the cut just deep enough to penetrate the bark, and gently pull the flaps back (2). Insert the scion (3), trim off the top edge of the shield flush with the bar of the T, replace the flaps and tie in with raffia (4). When growth begins, cut or loosen the raffia (5). Finally, prune the rootstock to just above the new shoot (6).

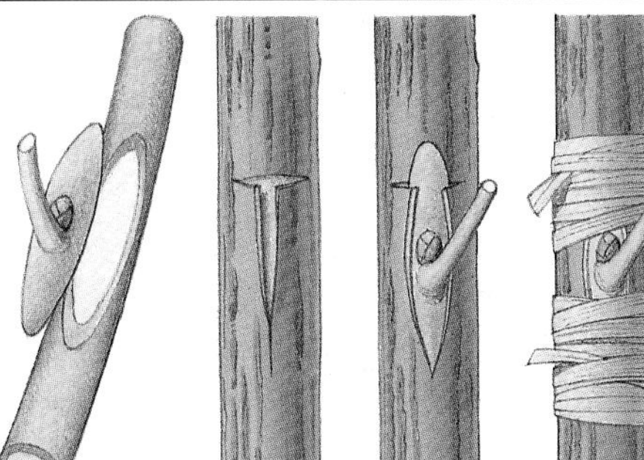

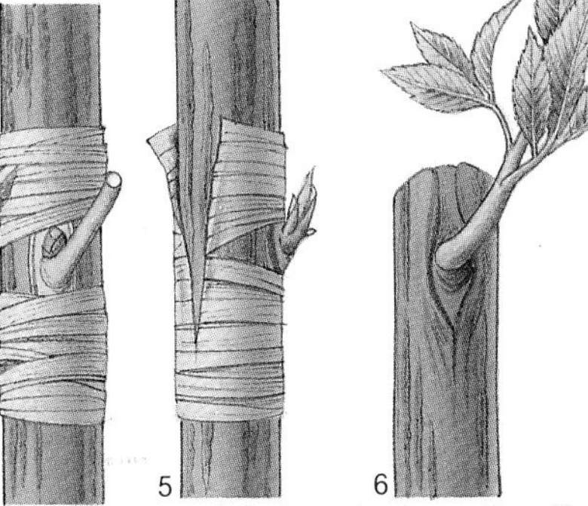

CROWN GRAFTING

A technique which is generally used to give new life to old fruit trees. It is done by inserting several scions into a cut-back branch or main stem, or even into the stump of the trunk.

Take shoots from the variety you want to propagate, and make a slanting cut about 1in long at the lower end of each; prune each upper end just above a bud (1). Make 2in vertical slits in the bark at the top of the rootstock and push in the scions, with their cut faces towards the exposed wood beneath the bark (2).

Tie the grafts in firmly with raffia and seal over and around with wax or sealant paint (3).

Signs of growth in the scions – fattening buds, or the development of leaves – are an indication that the grafts have taken. It may be several months before any signs appear.

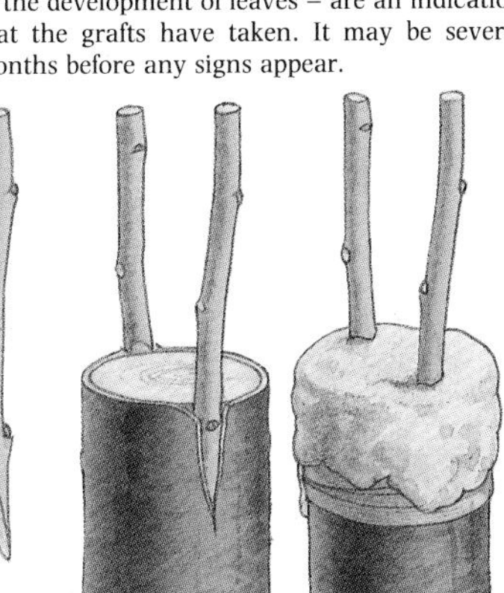

SADDLE GRAFTING

A method often used to propagate rhododendrons. Cut the rootstock into a wedge and slice a corresponding notch out of the base of the scion to fit the wedge (1).

Marry the two (2), bind them with raffia (3) and cover the joint with sealant paint.

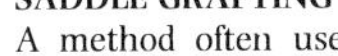

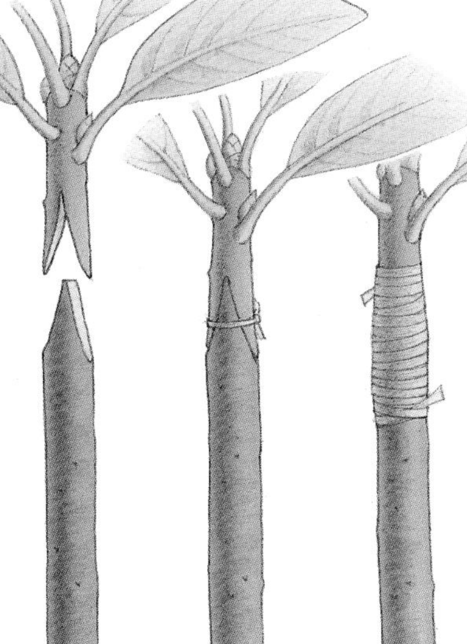

BRIDGE GRAFTING

Really a form of tree surgery by which a damaged branch or main stem can be repaired – for example, when the bark of a young fruit tree has been chewed by hares.

Take two or three scions of the same variety (or the same tree) and make 2in slanting cuts at each end (1).

Insert the scions, cut faces inward, into vertical incisions made in the undamaged bark above and below the injured part (2).

Bind the joints with raffia (3) and cover them with sealant paint.

Nutrients will pass via the scions to the upper part of the tree, keeping it alive until the task is taken over by new bark growing round the scions.

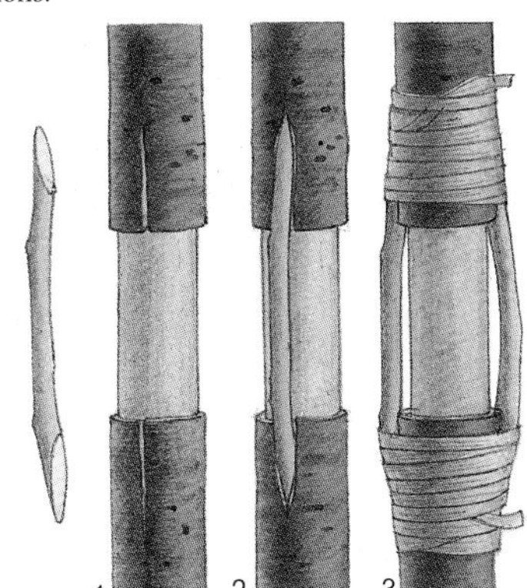

GRAPES

Growing for dessert

Can I grow proper dessert grapes outdoors?

No, high-quality dessert grapes cannot be grown outdoors in Britain, only in a greenhouse. The ones you buy from the greengrocer are normally imported from the Mediterranean area, where they can mature in the open air during summers which are warmer and longer than in Britain.

There are, however, some adequately hardy (if not top-notch) dessert varieties which can be grown outside in Britain without too much bother. 'Royal Muscardine' is one of the best of these, and can be expected to grow well from the Midlands southwards. The berries are white, quite large and with a Muscat flavour.

Possibly the hardiest of them all, the 'Strawberry' vine from America, also does very well in the South. It yields a small grape, pink and with a faint strawberry flavour, but the skin is rather tough.

'Black Hamburgh', normally regarded as the best dessert variety for growing under glass in Britain, also thrives outdoors in the South (although it needs to be grown against a south or west-facing wall).

'Buckland Sweetwater' is another greenhouse dessert grape which crops well outdoors in the South in a good summer. Elsewhere, or in a bad summer, it is less reliable. Classified as 'white', this is a good variety, with – at its best – big bunches of large grapes. It is a vigorous grower but rather susceptible to mildew.

Choice for wines

I'd like to grow some grapes to make my own wine. Which are the best varieties?

One of the most successful varieties in Britain is 'Triomphe d'Alsace'. It ripens early, crops heavily and produces an excellent red wine. Another good one is 'Brant' (or 'Brandt'). This has small, black fruits and is a prolific cropper. As an added attraction, the leaves often take on a good autumn colour. One that leads to an excellent wine is 'Müller Thurgau', a golden-brown grape which ripens in mid-October. Or, very popular with amateur wine-makers, 'Seyve Villard 5276' produces regular and heavy crops which give a delicately flavoured wine.

'Madeleine Angevine' is a good dual-purpose variety: it makes good wine or serves as a passable dessert grape. Pale green, it does well in cooler districts, ripening in early October. 'Perlette' is another dual-purpose or even triple-purpose variety, because it is good for wine, as a dessert grape and also for drying to make raisins.

Two-phase pruning

How should I prune greenhouse grapes? I'm frightened of doing the wrong thing.

The pruning of greenhouse grapes is a two-phase operation. With the vertical rod system of pruning and training – the one normally employed in a small greenhouse – the main pruning takes place in the winter; this is

HOW TO TRAIN A GRAPEVINE

There are numerous methods of training a grapevine, some of them extremely complex. The system explained here is one of the simplest and is ideally suited to vines in a small greenhouse. Two vines grown on the single-rod system described in these pictures should yield enough grapes for the average family.

To support the vines, fix wires running the length of the greenhouse. Set the wires 12in apart and 18in from the glass, attaching them to the framework with vine eyes – specially made metal spikes.

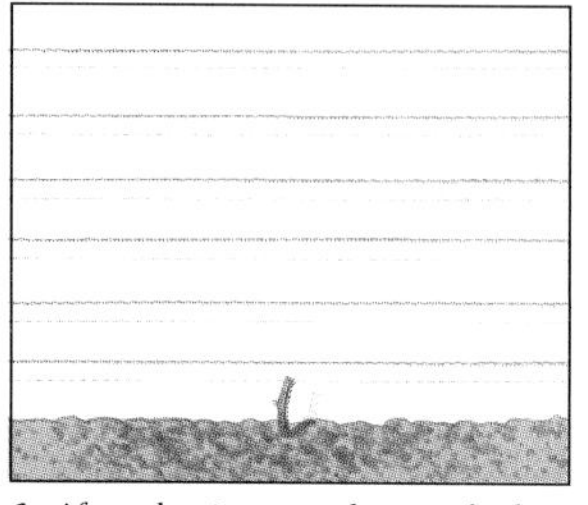

1 *After planting, cut the vine back to a bud, leaving only about 6in above ground – or in the greenhouse, if the roots are outside.*

2 *In summer, shoots will grow from the stump. But keep no more than five. Pinch out all the rest as soon as possible.*

3 *Next winter, cut the strongest shoot – known to growers as a 'rod' – back by half. Cut out the other four shoots completely.*

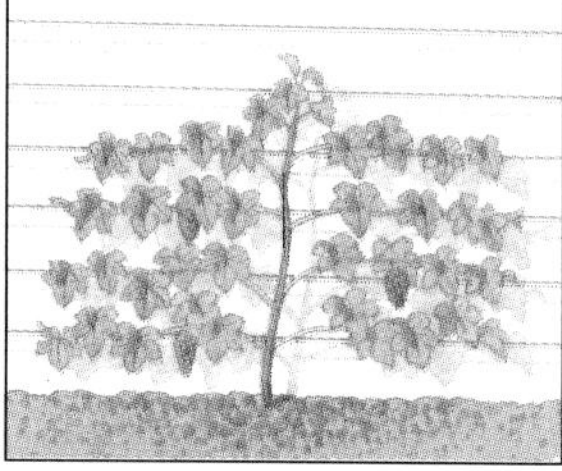

4 *As sideshoots grow in summer, tie them to wires 12in apart. Pinch out the tips when they're 2-3ft long. But leave the top shoot to grow.*

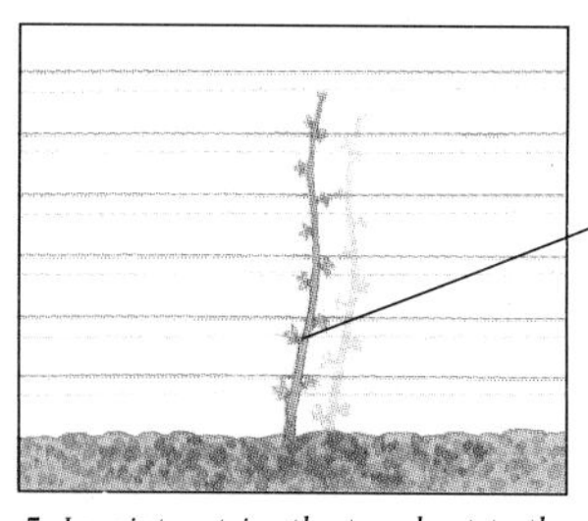

5 *In winter, trim the top shoot to the final height you want (leave it unpruned if it's still too short). Cut back each sideshoot to two buds.*

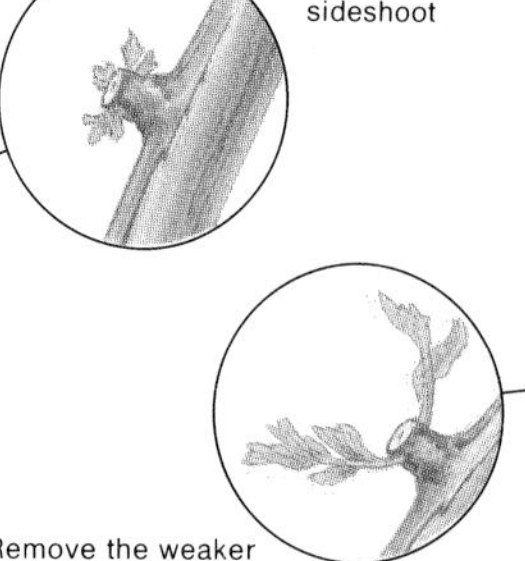
Leave two buds to grow on each sideshoot
Remove the weaker shoot when they are 3-4in long

6 *In early spring, cut off the weaker of the fruiting shoots that grow from the two buds. Cut off any other unwanted shoots. Tie in the rest.*

7 *As each flower truss forms in summer, cut off the fruiting shoot two leaves beyond the truss. In later years, repeat steps 5, 6 and 7.*

followed by trimming and tying in the new shoots in spring and summer. The important thing with the winter phase is that the stems must be completely dormant when they are pruned – around Christmas is a good time – otherwise they 'bleed', seriously weakening the plant.

After planting, cut the vine back so that only a short length (6in or so) is left above ground – or inside the greenhouse, if the roots are outside. In summer, shoots will grow from the stump but no more than five should be kept; the rest should be pinched out as soon as possible. Next winter, cut the strongest shoot back by half and remove all the others completely.

The following summer, this strongest shoot – known to growers as a 'rod' – will develop sideshoots (laterals). All of these except the top one, known as the leader, should have their tips nipped out when they are 2-3ft long.

In winter, cut the leader back to the point that is to be the permanent end of the vine rod (if the leader hasn't yet reached the final length you want, leave it unpruned). Cut back each sideshoot to two buds from its base, leaving it about 1in long. In spring cut off the weaker of the fruiting spurs that will by then have grown from these two buds.

Repeat the same routine every year from then on. In winter, cut back the canes which have fruited to two buds from the base. In spring, cut off the weaker shoots (see *How to train a grapevine*, opposite).

The other pruning operation, carried out as the vine grows, is necessary to prevent the whole thing getting out of hand and to encourage the vine to produce good grapes. When a flower truss has formed, cut off the sideshoot at a point two leaves beyond the truss. Trim off any subsidiary sideshoots – those which grow from the fruiting canes – to leave just one leaf. Cut off completely any surplus sideshoots from the main stem. Remove all tendrils as they form, and tie the young shoots to the supporting wires regularly and gently.

In the first year after planting, remove the flowers to prevent fruiting and encourage the development of the rod. In the second year, allow one truss to grow on each sideshoot. Thereafter, leave two or three trusses on each sideshoot.

Each January, too, untie the rod and let it arch over to encourage an even flow of sap. Tie it back again in February.

Promoting pollination

Do grapes need to be pollinated to produce good crops?

Yes. But some are more easily pollinated than others. Outdoor grapes, like most other fruits, need no special attention: these varieties crop perfectly well on their own pollen without any assistance. In the greenhouse, the situation is different – because, of course, there aren't nearly so many pollinating insects about. These varieties need help.

The time to intervene is when the grapes normally come into flower, during May and early June. They should be kept rather drier at the roots than usual at this time. But occasional spraying of the open flowers with clean water helps fertility. This wet-and-dry regime mimics natural conditions in that the pollen spreads best when dry, but the occasional damp period among the foliage helps the flowers to produce more pollen.

The ideal routine is to tap the branches in the morning so that the flowers release their covering cap. This makes them ready for pollination. At about midday, run your hand down a bunch of flowers so that it gets covered in pollen. Move on from bunch to bunch so that each one is pollinated. This procedure has to be repeated daily for about a week to make sure that every flower on each bunch is pollinated.

This method yields a very heavy set of fruit, which must then be thinned out, but this is better than getting only an indifferent set. You'll be able to see after a while which are going to be the best bunches. Remove any which are not up to scratch. Thin out small fruits in the centre of each bunch when the grapes start to swell.

GREENHOUSES

Best for begonias

Should I use a peat or soil-based compost for sowing bedding begonias? How much heat do they need and when should I start?

Peat compost will give the best results. Seed sown at the beginning of January should produce plants for bedding out in late May; plants from an early March sowing will be ready in July. Whenever you sow, don't be tempted to put the plants outside until all risk of frost is over.

To ease the job of sowing evenly and thinly, mix the dust-like seed with a small quantity of dry silver sand and then sprinkle it evenly over the compost's surface. It's easier that way to see where the seed is going. Don't cover the seeds with compost or black polythene because they germinate better in the light. Simply cover the containers with clear glass or polythene, topped with a single sheet of newspaper to prevent sun scorch if necessary. Use a propagator or a warm windowsill to keep the seeds in a daytime temperature of 18-24°C (65-75°F), with a minimum of about 16°C (60°F) at night. Sown in this way, the seeds will take two or three weeks to sprout.

Keep the compost moist all the time. Water it with a half-strength soluble pot plant fertiliser every ten days once the seeds sprout, and prick out the seedlings into pots or trays as soon as they're large enough to handle, which is usually when the first true pair of leaves (not the seed leaves) has expanded fully. Ease the seedlings out of the compost gently, using a small spatula or plant label and holding them by the leaves, not the stem. Set them 1½-2in apart in their new homes.

Poinsettias in bloom the second time around

Is it possible to get poinsettias to flower for a second time? I've tried once or twice, but all I get is a mass of green leaves, and no scarlet.

You can do it, provided you follow a regime of almost Prussian precision. Let's suppose your poinsettia, like most people's, has flowered over Christmas. Once the red 'bracts' – they're actually modified leaves, not true flowers – have faded, cut the plant down to 1-2in from the base.

Let the potting mixture almost – but not quite – dry out. Keep the plant in a warm and sunny part of the greenhouse until June or July, then water it freely. It will soon begin to grow again, whereupon it should be repotted in the same pot or in a pot no larger than the original. Replace the top ½in or so of compost with fresh compost when you do this.

Give the plant a monthly feed of liquid fertiliser until mid-September, the start of the most critical part of the operation. For the next eight weeks you must ensure that the plant has at least 14 hours of *total* darkness a day. You might do this by putting it inside a black polythene bag in the evening and taking it out again next morning. However you do it, the time and the complete exclusion of any light are critical. Keep the temperature at about 18-21°C (65-70°F) during this period.

Once the buds have begun to form and the bracts have coloured, you can relax and stop putting the plant in the dark. Simply bring it back indoors again for Christmas. It will, by the way, be almost certainly considerably larger than the previous year.

Gift rap

Christmas is plant time – every year I get two or three. But by spring they look awful. How best can I prolong their active lives?

All pot plants sold at Christmas have been used to a fairly high temperature, and so must be kept in a warm room or greenhouse if they are to prosper. Light, too, is vital to their wellbeing, so get into the habit of keeping them on a windowsill or at least near a window during the day (this is more important for flowering plants than for some foliage species). But remember, too, to move them back into the room at night. Shut in behind curtains they can easily become chilled, which will make the leaves turn limp, yellow, and even brown and parchment-like around the edges.

These symptoms can also be caused by over-watering, the single most common cause of house plant failure. Compost should be no more than moist to the touch, and should certainly not exude water when pressed. Overfeeding is another very common fault. Poinsettias, chrysanthemums, cyclamen and other flowering plants appreciate a liquid feed every couple of weeks while they are growing actively, but foliage plants such as ivies need much less feeding. About once a month will suit foliage plants, but during the winter they don't need feeding at all. Too much feeding results only in soft growth and poorly coloured leaves.

Another way to keep most pot plants perky – though not cacti and their relatives – is to keep the air around them moist. Put the pot in a larger bowl and fill the extra space with peat. Keep this peat continually moist, and it will create valuable humidity.

Why seedlings wilt

Every year I sow the seeds of greenhouse plants thinly in fresh compost, but the seedlings still collapse with rot. Why?

Over-wet compost and high humidity are the most likely causes. The fungus – and it's the damping-off fungus that is your problem – can infect seeds before they germinate properly, and seedlings which are infected topple over.

If your usual compost holds water like a sponge, improve the drainage by mixing in grit or a manufactured aggregate such as perlite before sowing. While the seed is germinating, ventilate the propagator or remove any glass or polythene coverings for a short spell each day to lower the humidity.

Fresh compost is not necessarily any protection because the fungus can survive in old compost sticking to trays and pots, so wash them thoroughly before use. Also, use only fresh tap water for the seeds because rainwater or water which has been stored in uncovered containers for several months may be infected.

Copper sulphate and ammonium carbonate can prevent damping-off disease, but the compound needs to be watered on before the disease strikes. Follow the manufacturer's instructions on the packet about how much of the chemical to use and at what strength. Additionally, immediately after pricking out the seedlings, spray the plants with a systemic fungicide such as benomyl to control the grey mould fungus, botrytis. This often attacks young seedlings and can be mistaken for damping-off disease.

The shading debate

Which is best for greenhouse shading: paint, blinds or plastic netting?

Liquid shading paints are cheap, popular and easy to brush or spray onto the outside of the glass. One application should last all season, but a thick coat could draw plants towards the light during dull weather, unless of course you remove it when appropriate. Removing the paints is not difficult – you wipe them off with a dry, clean cloth or wash them off – but it does involve wiping down the greenhouse, which takes time. Alternatively, some shading paints respond to the weather, becoming more opaque in bright sunlight, more translucent on rainy days.

Roller blinds, fixed inside or outside, are initially much more expensive, but they last for years and can be used as needed. If the greenhouse is heated during the winter, you can also pull them down at night to retain more heat and reduce fuel costs. Go for outside blinds if you can; inside ones tend to get tangled up with the plants.

Plastic shading mesh and woven polyethylene cloth are fairly easy to obtain and can be used either side of the glass, although they're best used outside to keep them out of the way of the plants. Outside, you may need a simple wooden framework or guide wires to keep the cloth permanently in place. But check around if cloth appeals, because some manufacturers supply fixing kits so that it can be rolled up when not required. The fixing kits are handy because the cloth is not so durable as plastic netting.

One advantage of mesh and cloth is that you have more choice in choosing the degree of shading required. But bear in mind that shading materials used internally merely cut the light level; they don't stop the sun's heat from penetrating the glass. Outside, they have the effect of keeping the greenhouse cooler as well as dimmer.

Mixed salad

Please settle the old question of whether tomatoes and cucumbers can be grown together in the greenhouse.

Yes they can, although their requirements are different. Tomatoes prefer cooler and drier air, so grow them near the door of the greenhouse. It won't be so stuffy there – especially if the door is kept open during hot weather.

Put cucumbers at the back – they'll enjoy the extra heat – and consider shielding them from the rest of the greenhouse with a polythene dividing screen to keep the air even more humid. Growing both crops together is easier than it used to be, because some modern cucumber varieties conveniently tolerate cooler air. Three good varieties for this purpose are the all-female F1 hybrid cucumbers 'Diana', 'Athene' and 'Brunex'.

Cyclamen pest

When I tipped out my cyclamen plants I found white grubs in the compost. What are they?

Vine weevil larvae. They nibble the roots of various ornamental plants in the greenhouse and garden, leading to stunted growth and sometimes wilting and collapse. Cyclamen are particularly vulnerable.

You'll be lucky to spot the beetle-like adult weevils because they hide in the compost or debris during the day. Eggs are laid in the pots from spring to early summer.

As a precautionary measure, add HCH dust to the compost before potting. And during early spring, lightly dust the same chemical around the growing plants, or soak the compost with a solution of it. For more details, see *Vine weevils*, page 358.

Where to put a thermometer

Where is the best place to position a thermometer in a greenhouse so that it gives a fairly accurate indication of the overall temperature?

Suspend it about 4ft off the ground in the centre of the greenhouse, in a spot where it will be shielded from draughts and direct sunlight.

Placing the thermometer close to the glass will not give a representative reading because the temperature there could be much higher or lower than in the main part of the greenhouse.

If you have an automatic greenhouse heating system, the same spot is also ideal for the controlling thermostat.

Creosote caution

I want to use creosote on my wooden staging to stop it rotting. How soon will it be safe to put the plants back?

That's a tricky question because it depends upon the air temperature and how quickly the creosote is absorbed by the wood. This could be about one month in the summer, and twice as long during the winter. The main thing is to wait until the fumes are barely discernible – good ventilation will speed this up – and then to replace the plants gradually in case the fumes are still too much for them.

Better still, don't bother with creosote at all – it's too risky. Modern water-based wood preservatives are just as easy to brush on, and far safer.

Soil sickness

I am worried about diseases building up and affecting my tomatoes. Is digging out all the soil and replacing it the only answer?

If you want to grow tomatoes in the greenhouse border, the answer has to be yes, because chemical sterilants such as Jeyes Fluid are not fully effective against all soil diseases, although they can lengthen the interval between replacing the soil.

In a new greenhouse, tomatoes can usually be cropped in the border soil for two or three years, and sometimes a lot longer, before diseases such as fusarium and verticillium wilt infect the roots. Pests also multiply in time, with eelworms often being the most troublesome.

The only way to go on using the border soil in the face of this inevitable and menacing build-up is to renew it every year to a depth of at least 2ft. An easier alternative is to abandon the border soil permanently as soon as you notice a build-up of pests and diseases. Use growing bags instead, buying new ones each year.

Money-wise heating

My paraffin heater uses an alarming amount of fuel during the winter. Is there a more economical way to heat an 8ft by 6ft greenhouse in the Midlands?

Natural gas could easily halve the cost, but you must take installation charges into account.

At 1986 prices, to maintain a minimum temperature of 7°C (45°F) in a fully glazed, non-insulated greenhouse from October to April would cost you about £34 with a paraffin heater. Natural gas would cost only £14, with electricity a poor third at £59.

Keeping the same greenhouse at a higher minimum temperature would, of course, cost more. If you wanted to keep the temperature at 21°C (70°F), the costs would be much higher: about £296 for paraffin, £117 for gas and £511 for electricity. Gardeners in the milder Western and Southern regions of Britain could expect slightly lower bills than these figures. Once you've chosen your fuel, there are a number of other ways you can keep costs down.

- Use thermostatically controlled heaters, and check the thermostat's accuracy with a maximum-minimum thermometer. A thermostat that is only a degree or two slow in turning the heat off can cost you pounds in unnecessary warmth.
- Set the greenhouse's minimum temperature as low as your plants will tolerate. Running a greenhouse at a minimum of 10°C (50°F) costs about twice as much as keeping it at 7°C (45°F).
- Insulate the greenhouse with polythene sheeting, or quilted bubble film.
- Draw down any blinds at night to provide an extra layer of insulation. But roll them up again during the day to let in the maximum light and warmth.
- Repair broken glass at once and seal gaps around doors and vents to block heat-draining draughts.
- Consider partitioning off a small area in the greenhouse with polythene sheeting and heating just that section.
- If the heating fails wholly or partly, protect plants until repairs are carried out by keeping them drier than usual and by covering them, especially at night, with several layers of newspaper.

When damp is good for plants

An old gardener once told me that he used to damp down his greenhouse two or three times a day. I always thought that damp air encouraged disease, so what was he trying to achieve?

Damping down the greenhouse structure, though not the plants, increases the humidity of the air and provides a healthier environment for warmth-loving plants that enjoy moist conditions – for example, cucumbers, orchids, caladiums, African violets and many popular foliage plants, including ferns.

Provided the greenhouse temperature is at least 13°C (55°F), spraying water over the floor and staging from a can or hosepipe should not encourage diseases. It's the combination of damp and cold that is really hazardous. Don't soak the plants, though, because that is inviting trouble.

Normally, damp down the greenhouse in this way in the morning as the temperature starts to rise, at midday, and again in the late afternoon or early evening. As well as improving humidity, damping down also reduces the air temperature slightly for a short while – useful for cooling down a greenhouse in very hot weather.

If you've got tomatoes in the greenhouse, be cautious about your damping down. Early in the season, the extra moist air may help the first flowers to set their fruits more quickly; but high humidity can also lead to a higher risk of leaf mould and grey mould.

Second-hand bags

Thanks to growing bags we've had super crops of tomatoes and cucumbers. But it seems a waste to use them just once. Could we grow anything else in them afterwards?

Yes, you can use them for a second crop. Lettuces and radishes will thrive, and for longer-term use consider mint, chives, small herbs, flowering bulbs and strawberries.

If bags of summer colour take your fancy, fill them with petunias, busy lizzies, pansies and other common bedding plants.

Before sowing or planting again, always remove as much as you can of the previous crop's roots, and thoroughly loosen the compost with a fork. Don't add any fertiliser to start with because the compost should still be quite rich following your summer feeding of the tomatoes and cucumbers. Wait until the plants are growing strongly and then feed them with a liquid fertiliser.

Don't expect perfect results every time from a second-hand bag, though. Depending on how enthusiastically you fed your first crop, and on what the crop was, there could be a build-up of undesirable salts in the compost, and that could undermine your success with the next crop.

When you've used the bags the second time around, you still won't have exhausted their usefulness.

You can use their compost to top-dress lawns, to mulch trees and shrubs, and to enrich the soil before planting almost anything. It also serves as a good potting compost for established plants if you mix in a generous amount of grit or perlite to improve the drainage. Otherwise, it may remain quite sodden in containers.

Tiny fruits

No matter what I do, my greenhouse cucumbers produce lots of tiny fruits that shrivel and rot. What's the solution?

The plants are under stress because the conditions aren't good enough for them to carry all their fruits. Natural abortion, if you like.

This disorder is fairly common early in the season when low air temperatures cause a check in growth. All-female varieties are especially vulnerable – they prefer more heat than varieties that bear both male and female flowers.

With warmer weather, or extra heat, the plants should grow out of the condition. If they don't, check that the roots are not waterlogged because over-wet compost can have the same effect.

Cut off the shrivelled fruits and take them out of the greenhouse to stop the fungal rot spreading.

Three into one will grow

I grew tuberous begonias for the first time last year and was delighted to see three flowers on each stem. But a friend tells me I should have let only one flower grow. What difference would it have made?

A big difference, because picking off the two single female flowers on the side of the stem when they were in bud would have helped the more attractive double male flower in the centre to grow much larger.

By leaving all three buds on the stem – a choice you were quite entitled to make, of course – you got much smaller blooms but three times as many of them.

WAX WORKS *Most greenhouse openers contain a special wax that expands in heat, pushing a piston to open the vent.*

How to choose an automatic ventilator

My neighbour's automatic ventilator opener leaked after a few months and became useless. Are these openers worth buying?

Yes they are. Even if, as happened to your neighbour, the seals prove faulty, the units can usually be repaired.

At the heart of most openers is a sensitive wax inside a cylinder. The wax expands or contracts according to the temperature and moves a piston rod attached to the vent. Louvre vents can also be automated in the same way. The openers cost nothing to run or maintain, and perform silently. They can also be adjusted to operate at set limits, usually within the range 10-29°C (50-84°F).

Models are available for virtually all aluminium and wooden greenhouses, but check that the opener you like can cope with the weight of your vents. Automatic openers are usually marked with the weight they can lift. If you can't take your vents off easily to weigh them, you can weigh them in position. Set some kitchen scales on the bottom edge of the vent frame with the opened vent resting on top. The vent you buy should be capable of lifting at least twice the weight shown on the scales.

Fertiliser dust-up

I insist that liquid fertilisers are better for tomatoes than wood ash, but my neighbour disagrees. Who's right?

You are if you're referring to fertilisers specially designed for tomatoes, because they will have more potash than nitrogen or phosphate, and that will encourage speedy ripening. Many ordinary garden fertilisers, on the other hand, are higher in nitrogen than the other two nutrients in order to encourage faster stem and leaf growth.

If you're not sure which does what, just remember this saying – 'nitrogen for shoots, phosphates for roots, and potash for flowers and first-class fruits'.

Wood ash is not very high in potash; the level varies between 3 and 12 per cent, compared with sulphate of potash at 48 per cent. So, it's useful for tomatoes, but not very. Ash is better used more generally as a tonic for flowers or shrubs. Mix it into the border soil or growing bags when planting, and sprinkle it on as a monthly top-dressing. Store it under cover and apply it at the rate of 4-8oz (2-4 good handfuls) per square yard.

Hollow side up

Which way up to plant begonias always foxes me and I invariably get it wrong. Is there an easy way to tell the difference?

Begonia tubers have one side which is rough and concave – it dips in the middle. The other side is rounded and smooth. Plant them so that the rounded side is facing downwards – shoots will grow from the hollow in the knobbly top.

Putting insiders outside

I am thinking of standing some of my pot plants outside during the summer to have more room for tomatoes in the greenhouse. Which ones could I safely leave out?

Cacti and succulents (though they do need protection from heavy rain), yuccas, busy lizzies, citrus plants (orange, lemon and grapefruit), aspidistras, geraniums, wandering jew *(Zebrina pendula)*, tradescantias, mother of thousands and the spider plant will all thrive in a sheltered spot outside from late May to September. If possible, protect them with a cold frame that can be closed up when the weather is cool and wet.

It is often assumed that foliage plants, such as tradescantias, will be harmed by strong sunshine. But this applies only if they are kept indoors close to a sunny window, where they will be scorched by the excessive heat through the glass. Outdoors, strong sunshine will do them no harm at all.

Plants that can't cope even with mild British weather outdoors and that do need to stay under cover include African violets, tuberous begonias, hibiscus, regal pelargoniums, asparagus ferns, palms, and ornamental-leaved begonias.

To cut down on watering the plants you take outdoors, bury the pots up to their rims in moist peat. Some roots may emerge through drainage holes, but those can easily be trimmed off when you bring the pots back inside at the end of summer.

Geraniums and blackleg

What is the best way to beat blackleg on greenhouse geraniums? Every year many of my cuttings rot before they have the chance to root.

Take heart; this common disease can be prevented. Select tip cuttings in July or early August from firm, healthy shoots – preferably ones not in flower. With a sharp knife or razor blade trim them just below a leaf joint so that they are about 3in long. Cut off any buds or flowers, and carefully remove the leaves and accompanying small green bracts (stipules) on the stem that would otherwise be covered by compost.

Dip the bases of the cuttings in a hormone rooting powder containing a fungicide, and push the bottom ½in firmly into a half-and-half mixture of peat and sharp sand. Any pot or pan will do to hold the cuttings. The main thing is to space the cuttings far enough apart that they don't touch each other.

Place the containers in a shaded and ventilated cold frame or greenhouse, and water the compost (with fresh tap water) only if it becomes very dry. When the leaves flag, occasionally mist them with water.

Should any cuttings rot, remove them promptly to prevent the disease from spreading to the others. New growth – indicating that the cuttings have rooted successfully – should become visible after 10-15 days.

Smoking: the risk to tomatoes

I have been told that my smoking could pass on a disease to greenhouse tomatoes. Surely this can't be true?

Afraid so. Tobacco mosaic virus can be transmitted by the fingers of smokers. It's best not to smoke in the greenhouse, and you should wash your hands thoroughly before handling your plants.

The disease distorts leaves, turning them patchy yellow and green, and the weakened plants bear fewer fruits. Those that do develop are often pitted, streaked and unevenly coloured.

Unfortunately, as with other virus diseases, there is no cure, although extra feeding may partly compensate for the weaker growth.

Leggy seedlings

My seedlings usually become far too leggy before they are ready for pricking out. How can I keep them stocky, and would it be all right to plant them deeper in the compost?

More light and sowing thinly will solve your problem. Remove any coverings as soon as the first seedlings appear, and keep the containers in good light – for example, on a shelf above the staging. Cleaning both sides of the glass, and even wiping off condensation during the day, will improve matters. Check, too, that the temperature is not too high, because this will make seedlings grow spindly if the light is poor.

Thin sowing is important because crowded seedlings inevitably become leggy as they compete for light. Many seeds, including those of lettuce and tomatoes, can be sown individually – allow about $\frac{1}{4}$in between each one if you can sow in this way. But if individual sowing is difficult, see if you can obtain the seeds in an enlarged pelleted form for easier handling. Fine seeds, such as those of begonias and petunias, can be mixed with dry silver sand to make thin sowing easier.

Seedlings will not usually suffer if they are pricked out with their lowest leaves resting on the surface of the compost – don't plant them any deeper than this – but deep planting won't be necessary if your seedlings are stocky to start with.

Colour for a cold greenhouse

Heating my greenhouse is out of the question – I can't afford it – but I want some easy plants to grow in it for colour from winter to spring. What can you suggest?

A mixture of bulbs, spring bedding, rockery plants and shrubs can create a lot of interest in a cold greenhouse. Suitable bulbs include snowdrops, scillas, crocuses, grape hyacinths and miniature iris. For later flowering choose daffodils, narcissi, garden hyacinths and tulips. Dwarf or species narcissi and tulips are particularly good for small containers.

Pot up all these bulbs in September and stand them outside for 10-12 weeks until their leaves emerge. Then bring them into the greenhouse.

Winter-flowering pansies, primulas and forget-me-nots are also worth considering because these, too, provide a bright splash of colour with little attention.

Among perennial garden plants, evergreen candytuft (iberis), forsythias, dwarf evergreen azaleas, camellias and winter-flowering heathers all flower reliably well in containers.

You can move them into the shelter of your greenhouse in October or November and watch them grow during the winter.

Tunnels versus glass

Polythene tunnels are so much cheaper than conventional greenhouses that they tempt me. Would you recommend one for a complete beginner who wants to grow pot plants and tomatoes.

No. Invest in a glass-covered greenhouse because it will be easier to ventilate and shade. In addition, your heating and maintenance costs should be lower.

Polythene structures demand more skill because unless they're adequately ventilated – and with some models this can only be done at each end – the air inside becomes stagnant and plants do not grow as well. In addition, they may become very damp, which increases the risk of fungal diseases.

However, the tunnels are good for lettuce and potted hardy shrubs and bulbs during the winter, and in late spring they can be used to harden off chrysanthemums, dahlias and summer bedding plants. In summer, sweet peppers, aubergines and courgettes are also fairly easy crops to look after in a polythene tunnel.

Cheesed off with a cheese plant

Trying to grow the Swiss cheese plant from seed has got me fed up. None of my young plants has those attractive holes in the leaves. Have I bought the wrong variety?

Not if you've grown the common Swiss cheese plant known to botanists as *Monstera deliciosa*. Its leaf serrations and perforations develop with age. There are none on young plants, but by the time the plants are two years old the holes should be quite pronounced.

In its native Mexico, the Swiss cheese plant may scramble 50ft or more up trees. The leaves are so shaped to allow the maximum amount of rain to reach the roots.

A few monstera species have smooth-edged leaves – *M. obliqua* from Brazil, for example. But most still have holes.

HOLED AGE *Swiss cheese plants develop holes in their leaves as they age. Young leaves and young plants have no holes.*

The right angle

Does it really matter which way a greenhouse faces?

Yes. The ideal alignment depends on when the greenhouse will get the greater use – winter or summer. Site it with the ridge running east-west only if you want to grow lettuces or other plants that need maximum light during the winter.

For normal summer use, it is better to have the ridge running north-south because plants will be less shaded by each other. To reduce draughts from cold north winds, have the door at the south end.

As for a conservatory or lean-to, it receives less light than a free-standing greenhouse and so, ideally, should be set up against a wall that faces south or west.

Capillary concern

I've become a great fan of capillary matting because it cuts down on watering time, but the roots penetrate the surface and some tear off when the pots are shifted. Can I prevent this, or am I worrying unnecessarily?

No, it can't be avoided – unless you move the pots daily – but the plus points of the matting outweigh the slight setback caused when the roots are disturbed.

The wet matting – which carries water to the bases of the pots – encourages roots to grow through the drainage holes of the pots, and because the plants are never short of water they should grow faster and stronger as a result.

When you move the plants, break their roots off flush with the bottom of the pot. The cuts will soon heal over and the plants will not be unduly harmed.

If any plant seems to be constantly getting tangled in the matting, though, it's worth taking it out of its pot to have a look at the rootball. You may find that, with all the extra growth, it has outgrown its pot sooner than you would normally have expected, and needs moving to a larger pot.

Persistent whiteflies

My greenhouse fuchsias and tomatoes get covered in whitefly every summer. Are modern insecticides as effective as the old ones, or have the pests become resistant? What do you recommend?

Repeated spraying with just one type of chemical can allow the pests that survive to build up resistance to it, and for this reason it is better to use two or three insecticides on different occasions during the season. Some of the older insecticides were more persistent, but they were also, in some cases, more hazardous for gardeners and so they have been replaced with chemicals that are less toxic to humans and to the pests.

The effects of these milder chemicals wear off more quickly – useful if you're harvesting vegetables or fruit shortly afterwards – but more frequent spraying will be necessary as well.

To attack tenacious whitefly, spray with products containing permethrin, resmethrin, pyrethrum or malathion. These insecticides kill by contact. Smoke fumigants can be useful in a greenhouse, too.

To gain control, spray two or three times at weekly intervals, and then as necessary to maintain control during the season. Spraying less frequently than once a week will not break the insects' life cycle, which can be as short as three weeks in hot weather.

Biological control using a parasitic wasp, *Encarsia formosa*, is worth considering, but this method rules out chemicals – including the chemicals you might want to use against other pests.

There are no reliable chemical methods of preventing an attack by whitefly, but some gardeners swear by a traditional technique involving rhubarb.

Collect rhubarb leaves as early as possible in spring, and crush them up. Put the leaves in jars, fill them with water and leave them in the greenhouse throughout spring and summer. The smell is said to repel whitefly, although there's no scientific evidence for the belief.

Grapevines – inside right

My local nursery says that grapevines grow better with their roots outside the greenhouse. My four-year-old 'Black Hamburgh' vine is planted inside – so should I move it?

No. Moving a well-established vine will severely check its growth – you could lose it.

The advantage of planting a vine with its roots outside the greenhouse is that the plant will find more water and food for itself in the open ground. On the other hand, cold outside soil can lead to the fruit stalks shrivelling, which affects yield and quality.

So, if you plan on planting a new vine, set the roots outside if you're in the warmer South or West of Britain, inside if you live in the chillier East or North. Either way, the bulk of the plant needs to be inside a greenhouse – guide the stem through a hole in the wall, if necessary – for it to produce a good crop in any but the most sheltered parts of the country.

For suggestions on which varieties to grow, see *Grapes*, page 162.

How to sow cyclamen

Tips please on sowing pot plant cyclamen. My seeds take weeks to germinate and then struggle for ages. I keep the propagator at 21°C (70°F).

Your propagator's too warm. Aim to keep the temperature between 16°C and 18°C (about 60-65°F).

The most reliable way to get cyclamen started is to soak the seed in tepid water for 24 hours. Then sow it in a peat-based compost, and cover the trays or pots with a thin layer of moist peat to prevent the seeds drying out. Set the trays in your cooler propagator, and don't expect to see any change for three or four weeks.

Prick out the seedlings into 2½in pots when they're large enough to handle and keep them at a steady temperature of 16°C (about 60°F) with protection from strong sunshine. Seeds sown by this method in August or September should be good-sized flowering plants by winter a year later.

How to use foliar feeds

What are your views on foliar feeding versus feeding via the roots? I have been foliar feeding my greenhouse plants, but I can't see much difference.

The foliar method certainly works because leaves can absorb food, but roots are still more efficient than leaves at absorbing nutrients. So regard feeding through the leaves as a supplement to the plants' diet, not as a replacement for feeding via the roots.

The main difference is in the speed of the feeds' effect. Foliar feeds get into a plant's sapstream more quickly than a feed via the roots. But the difference is not great – only a day or two.

Your plants probably show little improvement with foliar feeds because they were getting well fed anyway.

Foliar feeding is particularly useful when a low air temperature or over-wet compost rules out normal feeding. This is because nutrients can still be taken in by the leaves even when the roots are not active. To feed plants in these circumstances, make up a normal-strength solution of a liquid fertiliser and spray it on; don't water it on. The finer droplets of a spray are more readily absorbed.

For maximum effect, don't use any foliar fertilisers when the greenhouse is very hot or when all the vents are open. Otherwise the spray will dry before the leaves have had a chance to absorb its nutrients.

Small peaches

My conservatory peaches and grapes crop well but the fruits are so small, even though I feed them generously with Growmore each spring. Should I prune them harder?

It's thinning that's needed, not pruning. Wait until the peaches reach the size of hazelnuts, and then cut out some of the crowded fruits so that the remainder are spaced about 3in apart.

Repeat the thinning process as the peaches swell until, finally, each one is 9-12in from its neighbour.

Thinning grapes is more tricky and you really need a pair of long, pointed scissors to cut out crowded berries. Support each truss while you thin the grapes to ½in apart. This spacing will allow them to swell evenly and the berries are less likely to rot.

No berries on my Christmas cherry

How can I get a Christmas cherry to form berries? I grew some last summer in the greenhouse and they flowered well, but berries were few and far between.

It's not surprising – the greenhouse would have been far too dry and hot for berries to form. To improve your berry display this year, stand the plants in a cold frame during the summer. Open the frame top as often as possible to allow the flowers to be pollinated by insects. Spraying with tepid water during dry weather will also help pollination, without which the orange or red berries won't form.

One other factor that may have a bearing on your berries is the age of the plants. The Christmas cherry (*Solanum capsicastrum*) can be grown on for several years, but mature plants often start flowering in early spring – after which it becomes very difficult to get berries to form.

The answer is to grow more plants from seed. Sow the seed in February or March on a warm windowsill, transplant the seedlings into 3½in pots and then finally into 5in or 6in pots as they grow.

These young plants should flower later in the year, when cooler weather will encourage the formation of berries.

Survival in the cold

Will geraniums survive the winter in an unheated greenhouse? I overlooked some cacti last year, and much to my surprise they came through without damage.

It depends on the winter, and whereabouts in Britain you live. It's a risk worth taking in mild areas of the South and West, but gardeners elsewhere ought to keep their fingers crossed for a kind winter – or take the plants, properly known as pelargoniums, indoors. To keep geraniums alive during winter, the important thing is to keep them almost completely dry. For more advice, see *Winter schedule*, page 156.

In areas where the winters are harsh, consider keeping some of your plants growing indoors. If cut back a little in autumn, geraniums usually flower throughout the winter on a sunny windowsill. That way, even if your greenhouse gamble fails, the plants indoors will survive.

The cacti you overlooked probably survived because of your neglect. Although cacti are plants of the desert, they can survive surprisingly low temperatures so long as they're kept perfectly dry. After all, even in the Sahara, temperatures in winter can plummet to −4°C (25°F) after dark. You'll improve their chances of surviving in the greenhouse next winter by covering them with newspaper during frosty weather.

Split tongue

My mother-in-law's tongue takes up too much room in the greenhouse and I want a smaller one. When should I split it?

Spring, just as growth starts up, is the best time; but you can divide mother-in-law's tongue (*Sansevieria trifasciata*) any time up to late summer. After that, this tough succulent will take longer to recover from the disturbance and the plant may rot if the compost remains wet.

On the other hand, why not take leaf cuttings instead of splitting the plant? That way, you can get lots of small young plants from the one parent. Slice a mature leaf into 2in long pieces, and push the bottom end of each piece ½in into a gritty compost. A half-and-half mixture of peat and sand is ideal. Keep the cuttings warm – on a windowsill, say – and fairly dry. In a few weeks they will root – and new shoots will grow from the bottom edge of each piece of leaf.

A word of warning, though. Green-leaved cuttings will grow exactly the same as their parents, but cuttings from variegated plants will produce only all-green plants. The yellow areas do not contain the green, energy-producing pigment chlorophyll, and cannot root. So an all-yellow cutting will die. If you want variegated offspring from a variegated mother-in-law's tongue, split the plant instead of taking cuttings.

Mottled ivy

What's the reason for my greenhouse ivies turning mottled and brown? My busy lizzies went the same way – and they became horribly sticky too.

Red spider mites, without a doubt. These tiny pests – barely visible to the naked eye – congregate underneath the leaves and feed on the sap. The mites spread quickly, drying out the leaves, which become speckled and bronzed. Badly affected busy lizzies may wilt in hot sunshine even if their compost is quite moist.

The mites' sticky secretion, honeydew, also gives them away. Being sweet, the honeydew attracts a fungus which gradually turns it black. The fungus is known, from its appearance, as sooty mould.

Humid air slows down the spread of red spider mites, so spray the plants regularly with water – daily in hot weather. But water alone won't control the mites. For that you'll need permethrin, derris, dimethoate or malathion, all of which are effective. You will have to spray several times at intervals of 10-14 days to cure a bad outbreak.

Why paraffin keeps plants in the pink

My paraffin heater has a water tray built into the top to provide extra humidity. Do I need to use it?

No, and it's better for the plants if you don't. Paraffin gives out all the humidity your plants are likely to need as it burns. Every gallon you burn releases about a gallon of water vapour – more than enough for plants unless you're trying to create a steamy jungle environment. At more familiar tempera-

Success with pricking out

Most of my greenhouse seedlings keel over and die as soon as I move them from their sowing containers to seed trays. What are the secrets of successful transplanting?

Pricking out – transferring seedlings from their original container to another one where they have more room to develop – is a delicate operation. Seedlings suffer less root damage and become established more quickly if they are pricked out as soon as they are large enough to handle.

The ideal time to move seedlings is when they have developed their first pair of adult leaves (the two that appear immediately after the initial seed leaves). In the case of bedding plants, this could be within 14 days of germination. When the time is right, follow these rules to maximise your chances of success.

- Water the seedlings so that they and their compost are moist.
- Fill the new seed trays with compost. If it feels dry, gently water the trays using a can fitted with a fine rose and leave them to drain for at least ten minutes before inserting the seedlings.
- Use a table fork, a wooden lollipop stick or any similar plastic or metal tool to ease the seedlings out of the compost. Pulling them up may damage them.
- Carefully lift each seedling by the tip of a leaf and insert it into a hole made in the compost with a pencil or thin bamboo cane. You could also use a dibber – a short, pointed piece of wood or plastic. Never hold seedlings by their stems because the fragile tissues bruise easily.
- Position the seedlings so that their lowest leaves – their seed leaves – rest on the top of the compost.
- If the seedlings are tall or inclined to flop over, use the dibber gently to firm the compost around the stem.
- To prevent rapid wilting, don't disturb more seedlings at a time than you can prick out within two or three minutes. Keep them out of draughts and strong sunshine while you work.
- As soon as each seed tray is finished, apply water from a can fitted with a fine rose. Go over the container slowly, two or three times, so that the water levels the surface of the compost and settles it around the stems. Start and finish watering away from the containers to avoid the risk of heavy drips from the sprinkler rose knocking the seedlings over.
- Keep the pricked-out seedlings shielded from draughts and strong sunshine for a couple of days. If they flag – if, say, their leaves droop or they begin to topple to one side – mist them with water several times a day, or cover the tray with a single sheet of thin, clear polythene or newspaper during the day. This will help to increase the humidity around the plants and speed them back into active growth.

1 *Mark out planting holes 1-2in apart, depending on the seedlings' size, with a pencil or thin cane.*

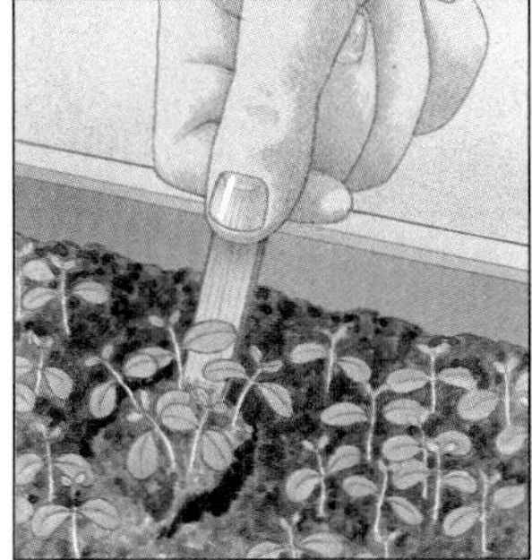

2 *Lever up the seedlings with a plant label or lollipop stick and tease them gently apart.*

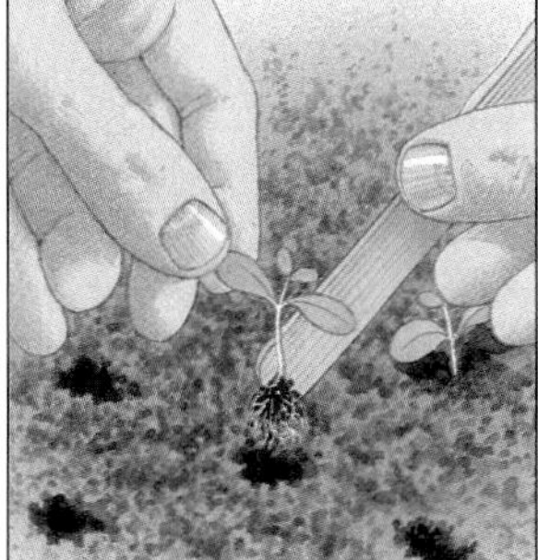

3 *Holding each seedling by a leaf – not the stem – lower it into the prepared hole and firm it in.*

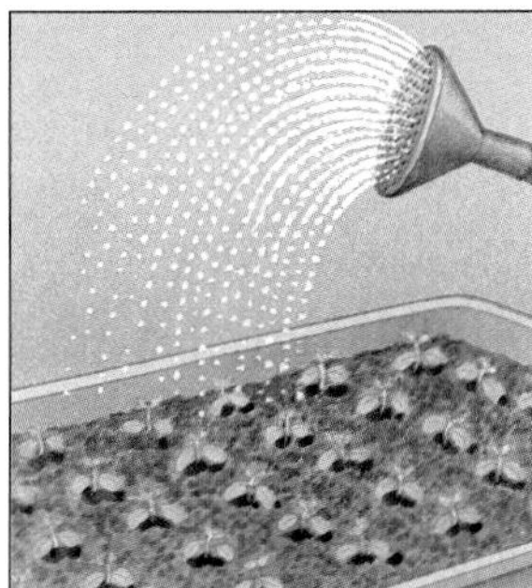

4 *Water the seedlings with a fine-rose can, and keep them in a warm sheltered spot for a day or two.*

tures, the additional humidity generated by using the water tray could expose your plants to fungus diseases in winter.

Paraffin has another great virtue, too: as it burns it gives off plenty of carbon dioxide gas, which leaves and stems need during daylight hours to manufacture food. So paraffin heating can help growing plants along even faster than heating by gas or electricity.

Tomato surprise

On holiday in Guernsey, I've seen nurseries raising their tomatoes in white plastic pots which are then half buried in growing bags. Surely this technique restricts the plants' roots?

It's what you couldn't see that matters. The bottoms of the pots are made from coarse mesh which extends partly up the sides, allowing the roots to grow through into the compost.

The tomatoes are pricked out as young seedlings into the pots – they're usually 5½in across – and are later pushed into the growing bags so that the mesh is just covered. The roots are contained within the pot until the first flower truss opens – this encourages better setting and earlier development – but are able to grow into the growing bag when they are ready. By then the compost has warmed up nicely.

As a result of this smooth undisturbed growth, the tomatoes never experience any setbacks and they crop earlier. Watering and feeding are carried out normally through the pots and over the compost.

You can buy these growing-bag pots in garden centres, but you could easily adapt large round margarine or ice cream containers for the purpose. Simply cut off the bottoms of the tubs and tie on pieces of wide-mesh plastic netting.

Low-cost flowers

To save money on buying cut flowers, I want to grow some easy plants that won't need much heat and that will provide colour all the year round. Any ideas?

Bulbs, anemones, the Peruvian lily (*Alstroemeria aurantiaca*), and gladioli don't require any heat, and all are straightforward to grow. A minimum temperature of 10°C (50°F) would also allow you to pick chrysanthemums from about October to January, perpetual-flowering carnations occasionally in the winter, and freesias during the spring and summer.

To get bulbs to flower out of season, pot up daffodils, narcissi and tulips in September, and keep the containers buried up to their rims outside in peat until their shoots are several inches high.

Then move the plants inside the greenhouse to bring their flowering time forwards by four to six weeks.

Corms of the florists' anemones – *Anemone coronaria* 'St Brigid' and *A. c.* 'De Caen' – can be planted at any time, although they flower best between February and July. Plant them in September to get winter blooms. Good varieties for greenhouse culture can also be grown from seed – 'Royal Event' and 'John Innes Mixed' are particularly suitable for this treatment. All these anemones can be grown in 5in pots.

The Peruvian lily needs a larger pot – ideally 9in or 10in – although it can also be grown in a greenhouse border. Established plants bear long-stemmed showy flowers during the summer which last for up to three weeks in water. The Ligtu hybrids are particularly good as cut flowers, but need gentle heat during the winter.

Gladioli can be grown to perfection in a greenhouse. Plant them in large pots or the greenhouse border during February for cutting in May.

Late-flowering chrysanthemums are best grown in large pots which are left outside for the summer and returned to the greenhouse in late September or early October before the frosts begin. Their cultivation needs more skill, but they will produce large bunches of flowers right through Christmas into the New Year. Raise new plants from cuttings in the spring (for details, see *Taking cuttings*, page 66).

Perpetual-flowering carnations will crop winter after winter for several years in 7in pots. They can grow several feet high, though, so they do need staking. Like chrysanthemums, they can be grown from spring-rooted cuttings.

Raise freesias from corms, rather than seeds, because corm-grown plants flower much sooner – usually between January and April if they're planted between July and November. Put six corms in a 5in pot and keep the pot outside until late September. Then bring it into the greenhouse to encourage the plants to bloom in the following spring and early summer. Freesias are renowned for their bright colours and scent, and they last well in water. Healthy corms will flourish for years.

Seeds that like the light

According to a gardening friend of mine, some seeds germinate better in the light. My gardening books and seed packets don't say anything about this. Can you help?

Certainly. It's mainly the fine seeds, which are traditionally sown on the surface of the compost, that germinate better in full light.

Sometimes the sowing instructions on the packet will recommend that the seeds be thinly covered. If so, use fine sand for the covering because it is less likely to block out all the light; don't attempt to cover the seeds completely. Watch, too, that the surface does not dry out or become too hot in strong sunlight because this could impair germination. You can avoid this risk by laying a sheet of glass or a sheet of thin, clear polythene over the containers or by misting the compost with a sprayer.

All the seeds in the following list germinate best when they're sown on the surface of compost in full light.

Best sown at a temperature of 16-18°C (about 60-65°F): Azalea, berberis, celery, papaver and primula.

Best sown at a temperature of 18-21°C (about 65-70°F): Achillea, ageratum, antirrhinum, aubrieta, cacti and succulents, calceolaria, digitalis, erica, erigeron, gloxinia, helichrysum, hollyhock, kochia, lobelia, mimulus, petunia, salvia and smithiantha.

Best sown at a temperature of 21-24°C (70-75°F): Achimenes, begonia, coleus, fuchsia, impatiens, kalanchoe, peperomia, saintpaulia and streptocarpus.

Pansy and cyclamen seeds, by contrast, need to be completely covered. But most other seeds will germinate equally well – provided they're kept moist – whether they're covered with compost or not.

Peppers in the greenhouse

Sweet peppers are quite expensive and I would like to grow my own. Would they be all right in an unheated greenhouse?

Yes, but it's unwise to plant them before early May, because of the risk of frost. You might plant them two weeks earlier inside the greenhouse under a cloche, or without a cloche if you are prepared to cover them with large flowerpots, newspaper or polythene on frosty nights.

Sow the seeds indoors in February or March and prick out the seedlings into 3in pots. Keep the plants on a sunny windowsill, or put them in the greenhouse on warm days, until May. Then plant them in the greenhouse border 15-18in apart or into 7-9in pots, or into growing bags (three plants per bag).

Sweet peppers need warmth, sunshine and fairly dry air – similar conditions to tomatoes. So if you keep the greenhouse right for the tomatoes, the peppers should thrive as well.

Cold air may prevent the flowers becoming fertilised, so don't open the vents until the temperature reaches 18°C (about 65°F). During warm weather spray the open flowers with tepid water to aid setting. Start feeding with a tomato fertiliser at ten-day intervals when the first peppers form, and keep feeding until the fruits start to turn red.

The fruits should be ready for picking in August or September, and you can expect six to ten fruits per plant. Green fruits, once mature, will turn red after about three weeks. But the change in colour makes little difference to the flavour. 'New Ace' and the F1 hybrid 'Gypsy' are both good varieties for growing in an unheated greenhouse.

Forcing rhubarb

What is the best way to force rhubarb crowns in the greenhouse? Could they be forced again the following year?

You should force them only once because the crowns become exhausted. With care, they slowly recover when returned to the garden, but many gardeners prefer to throw them away afterwards.

Forcing rhubarb starts with digging up strong, healthy and well-established clumps in the garden between late October and December, and leaving them unprotected on the ground until they have had a couple of severe frosts. The frost changes starch in the clumps into sugar, which will help them to grow quickly.

Partly fill a deep box with a half-and-half mixture of well-rotted horse manure and good soil and pack the clumps tightly inside. Lightly cover the roots with the same mixture, and then give them a good watering.

Cover the box with thick sacking or black polythene sheeting, or possibly an inverted dustbin, to exclude light. Keep the greenhouse between about 10°C and 18°C (50-65°F) and the first sticks will be ready for pulling after about four weeks. If the greenhouse is unheated, you'll normally have to wait about two months.

To extend the cropping period, keep the plants moist and feed them every 10-14 days with sulphate of ammonia (1oz in 2 gallons of water). Exposing the plants to full light when they have virtually stopped producing sometimes results in one or two additional sticks. All varieties respond to forcing, although 'Timperley Early' and 'Early Superb' are especially good.

Melons without flowers

My greenhouse water melons grew well, but didn't produce a single flower. Why not?

Over-rich soil, too much watering or poor light. Any of these will make water melons produce leaves and stems, instead of flowers and fruits. Try following these tips with your next crop.

- Grow the melons in a sunny part of the greenhouse border where they can scramble over the soil.
- Use Growmore sparingly when planting (no more than 2oz – about a handful – per square yard).
- Try to keep the temperature around 21-

GREENHOUSE TYPES – THE PROS AND CONS

Aluminium
Glass-to-ground aluminium greenhouses are the most popular types in Britain. Maintenance work is minimal because aluminium doesn't rust or rot, and the slender glazing bars allow plenty of light to reach the plants – especially at soil level.

Most aluminium greenhouses need a base, although a few models can be secured with long anchoring pegs if the ground is firm. Erecting an aluminium greenhouse is sometimes tricky, though, with hundreds of parts to identify and assemble. You'll need help from at least one other adult to move completed sections into position.

Wood
Wooden greenhouses are much more straightforward to erect because they usually come in six prefabricated sections which are bolted together. They look more attractive than aluminium greenhouses, but need more maintenance work. Softwood needs to be painted every two or three years and even decay-resistant cedar benefits from periodic applications of linseed oil or a proprietary preservative. Wooden greenhouses also need a firm base of bricks or concrete.

Glass or plastic?
Plastic-covered greenhouses, including polythene tunnels, are initially more economical than conventional structures clad with glass. But polythene sheeting – even if it has been treated with an ultraviolet light inhibitor, which slows down the rate at which sunlight attacks the plastic – rarely lasts for more than three years. It's also easily punctured or torn.

Some rigid plastic materials, including acrylic and fibreglass, have a useful life of around ten years, but they are at least as expensive as glass. Glass doesn't deteriorate with age, so it is the best choice, provided that pets, children, vandals and sonic booms from overflying jets are not likely to break it.

Choosing the shape
A greenhouse with parallel sides usually has more headroom at the eaves, which is convenient for working and for tall plants. A Dutch light greenhouse, which has sloping sides, provides greater stability in exposed positions because wind buffeting is reduced, and it lets in more of the low-angled winter sunlight.

Buyer's checklist
- Before ordering, inspect a model on display or one that's being used in a garden.
- Find out exactly what the basic price covers. Does it include the base, staging and guttering? Is there a separate charge for delivery?
- Buy a greenhouse that will be large enough for your future needs, as well as your present ones. Second-hand greenhouses don't fetch very high prices. Consider buying a model that can be extended later.
- Order extra vents if their number is inadequate. Ideally, the roof ventilation area should be not less than 20 per cent of the floor space. Fitting extra vents after the greenhouse is erected may be difficult, and will be more expensive.
- Check that the doors open widely enough to admit your wheelbarrow, and that the sill is not so high as to obstruct it, or to trip you.
- Ask about an erection service if self-assembly seems daunting. Many dealers advertise it as an optional extra to the price of the kit. The erection charge does not normally include the price of the base, which you will have to install yourself, or get a builder to erect for you.

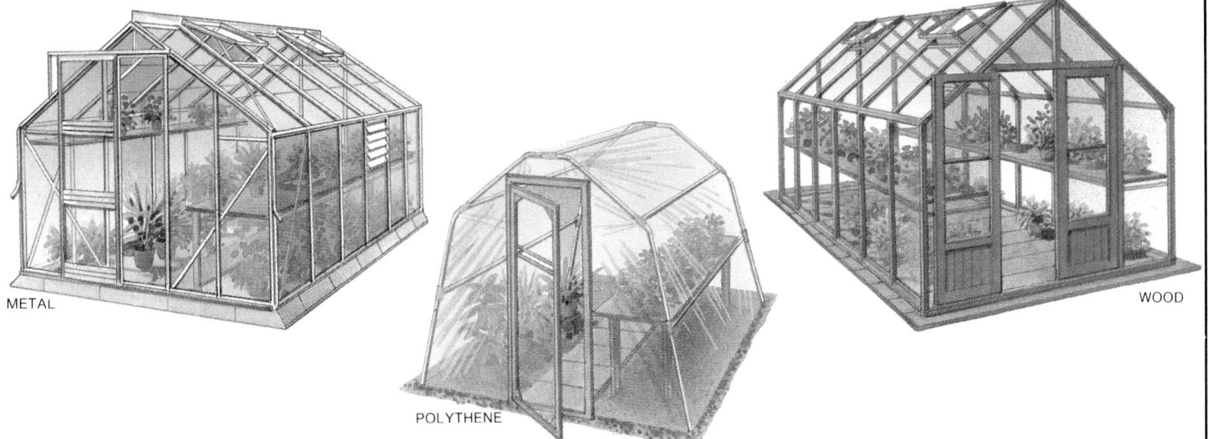

27°C (70-80°F), but don't shade the greenhouse on hot days to hold it at that level – shading will simply cut down the light, which is vital for the flowers to form. Instead, control the temperature by ventilating the greenhouse as much as possible and by hosing down the path (not the plants) during the heat of the day.

● Don't over-water – let the top ½in of soil dry out between waterings.

● Cut back the trailing stems if they interfere with greenhouse routine.

If you still don't have any luck, switch to Cantaloupe or Casaba melons – they're much more likely to succeed. 'Blenheim Orange', 'Superlative', 'Ogen', 'Sweetheart' and 'Tiger' are all good varieties. For details of how to grow these melons, see *Outdoor melons*, page 81.

Tangled cucumbers

My greenhouse cucumbers always become a tangled mess by the end of the summer. Is there a simple way to train them?

Yes there is, and it takes only a few minutes each week to keep them under control. Space the plants 2ft apart in the border (or two per growing bag) and, using soft string or raffia, loosely tie the main stem to a 6-8ft upright cane.

Cut off the spring-like tendrils as they grow, and continue to tie the stem until it reaches the top of the cane. Then pinch out its tip. The first cucumbers will form in the leaf axils on the main stem – the spots where the leaf stalks join the stem – and sideshoots will quickly grow from the same areas. Allow one sideshoot to grow from each axil and remove their tips in turn when two leaves have unfolded. Additional cucumbers will grow from the leaf axils on the sideshoots.

You could let the sideshoots grow several feet long if they were tied to horizontal wires, although of course each plant would then need much more room. You would also run a higher risk of exhausting the plant. Consider this method only if you want a lot of cucumbers from just one plant – and keep your fingers crossed that it doesn't die.

Winter vegetables

Are there any vegetables I could grow in my unheated greenhouse during the winter? They would have to be cleared by late May to make room for tomatoes.

Certainly you can grow winter crops in a greenhouse. It just takes a little planning. You could, for instance, sow greenhouse lettuces and Japanese greens (Mizuna) in seed trays at the end of August. Prick the seedlings out as soon as possible so that the young plants are ready to go into the greenhouse border towards the end of September – by then the tomatoes should be virtually finished. Before planting, dig the soil deeply and apply a light top-dressing of Growmore – about a handful per square yard. Plant the lettuces 8-12in apart, and allow 1½-2ft between the Japanese greens.

Leave enough room to put carrots in the border at the same time. Sow them in rows 6in apart, and later thin the seedlings to about 2-3in apart. For best results, choose early, quick-growing varieties such as 'Early French Frame', 'Amsterdam Forcing' and 'Early Nantes'. The first roots will be ready to pull in February.

As soon as the carrots are harvested, sow radishes in the same spot. Early, round-rooted varieties such as 'Scarlet Globe', 'Cherry Belle' and 'Robino' should be ready four or five weeks after sowing.

You could also grow parsley and chives in pots – both will grow slowly during the winter – and mint runners potted in the autumn will provide fresh pickings early in the spring.

Invisible nibbler

The leaves on some of my pot plants have been mysteriously nibbled, and the seedlings are being attacked at the base. Despite a good search I can't find the culprits. Can you help?

Look out for woodlice – they're sure to be sheltering nearby under pots, trays or the staging, and in fact anywhere else that provides a daytime refuge. Rotting wood is a favourite haunt.

Clear away all rubbish and debris to deny them their hiding places, and then dust the area with HCH. Alternatively, set out bait with cheese or mashed potato to which HCH has been added. Slug pellets that contain methiocarb are also effective; sprinkle them on the compost and around the pots.

Second-hand compost

To save money would it be all right to sow seeds in used potting compost if I mixed in some fertiliser beforehand?

There are two main disadvantages to using second-hand compost. First, adding fertilisers by guesswork is chancy and the results are unlikely to be as good as from a branded compost. Second, there is a greater risk of the compost being contaminated with fungal disease – and that could quickly spell disaster for your seedlings.

Having said all that, you *might* get away with sowing quick-germinating seeds in old compost – seeds of plants such as lettuces, cucumbers, marrows, runner beans and sweet peas. Soak runner bean seeds and sweet pea seeds overnight before sowing, in water that's lukewarm to start with; this promotes even quicker germination. If the compost has become compacted, open it up and let air into it by digging it over and working into each tray a handful of grit or perlite before sowing. Water sparingly so that the surface stays barely moist. That way you will limit the chances of damp-loving fungi getting a hold.

Flowerless amaryllis

Should an amaryllis flower every year? It's now three years since mine bloomed. What treatment does it need?

Keeping amaryllis plants alive is easy, but getting them to flower regularly can be difficult. Most bulbs sold in the autumn already contain embryo flowers, and they've been specially treated to make them grow quickly.

Once they have flowered, however, it is quite usual for the bulbs to take 15 months or more to repeat their spectacular performance. It's only after this second flowering that, with special care, they can settle down into a yearly routine.

The first step is to plump up the bulb. Do this by watering it to keep the compost evenly moist and by giving it a proprietary liquid feed every ten days while it has green, healthy leaves.

You then have two choices. First, when the foliage starts to turn yellow, stop watering and feeding and let the bulb dry out in its pot. Cut off the dried-out leaves just above the neck of the bulb.

The other method is to reduce, but not totally withhold, water and feed the bulb only about every 21 days after the first leaf goes yellow.

In both cases, sun and warmth are essential. Try to keep the greenhouse at about 18-27°C (65-80°F) during this period.

A bulb treated by either method will be ready to start growing quickly again during the winter. Gradually increase the watering again and keep the bulb in temperatures of around 21°C (70°F). Don't bother to repot the bulb at this stage unless it is obviously too big for its pot, because amaryllis plants resent disturbance. Given this treatment, your bulb should be ready to flower again after six to eight weeks.

Clean and decent

Greenhouse cleaning time has come round again, and I must say I rather dread it. All the same, I'd like to be as thorough as possible and would be grateful for a checklist I could pin to the wall.

The first tip is to keep the greenhouse neat and tidy on a regular basis so that you won't accumulate a mountain of work.

That apart, there are no short cuts. Any labour you save by skimping when you clean the greenhouse, you'll have to expend later in keeping down pests and diseases. So give the greenhouse a thorough clean some time in winter or very early spring when it is largely empty. Here's a list of what you should do.

- Clear out all the plants and all the empty seed trays, boxes and pots. Put the plants under cover – in a cold frame or indoors, if necessary.
- Scrub the staging with a disinfectant such as Jeyes Fluid. Beside checking algae and moss, the liquid will also repel woodlice.
- Clean algae-stained capillary matting, gravel and shingle with diluted household bleach. Rinse thoroughly.
- Drain rainwater butts, scrub them with disinfectant, rinse them and cover them with a tight-fitting lid to keep the water clean and free of algae.
- If falling leaves are finding their way into the butt, wedge a nylon pot-scourer into the top of the downpipe, or tie an old pair of tights over the bottom.
- Clean the greenhouse glass and glazing bars with a proprietary greenhouse glass cleaner. These cleaners shift green and slimy algae quickly and are designed to discourage its return. Use an old toothbrush or plant label to scrape out dirt from corners and between overlapping panes.
- Clean empty seed trays, boxes and pots with Jeyes Fluid or bleach, and rinse them thoroughly. If you normally store them in the greenhouse under the staging, put them on planks resting on bricks rather than on the ground. You'll be able to spot any weeds that appear underneath, and you won't be creating a sanctuary for pests such as woodlice and slugs.
- Burn greenhouse smoke cones or pellets to get rid of any remaining pests and diseases.
- When the smoke has done its work, open the greenhouse door and vents and leave them open until all traces of the smell of the chemicals you've used have disappeared completely.
- Move the plants back in.

Early strawberries

Could I make use of surplus strawberry plants from the garden and bring them on in the greenhouse? How much earlier would they fruit?

Strawberries grow well in cold and unheated greenhouses. With gentle warmth, early varieties can start fruiting in April, and even without heat you could be picking strawberries a month early.

Pot up rooted runners in 5in pots by late August and stand them outside in full sun. Move the plants to a cold greenhouse in November, or wait until late January if you heat the greenhouse – don't let the temperature rise above 18°C (about 65°F).

Once the plants are under cover, keep the compost moist and spray the crowns once a week with tepid water to encourage new growth. As the plants develop and flower buds form, start feeding them every 10-14 days with a high-potash liquid fertiliser – a tomato fertiliser would be excellent. Pollinate the flowers by gently dabbing them with a twist of cotton wool or a child's paintbrush.

Let all the berries develop if you want lots of them and you're not too bothered about their size.

For really big berries, pinch out the fruits as they start swelling until you've left only about 12 berries on each plant. Once the early harvest is over, the plants will be pretty exhausted. Don't attempt to grow them in the greenhouse the following year. Return them to the garden or throw them away.

Easy orchid

At our local horticultural show the poor-man's orchid took first prize in the pot plant section. Is this a difficult flower and will it keep from year to year?

Schizanthus, which is what botanists call the poor-man's orchid, is surprisingly easy to grow from seed. But, like other annuals, it dies after flowering. So you can't keep it from year to year. The plant, which is not a true orchid, is also known as the butterfly flower. It bears masses of brightly coloured, orchid-like blooms.

For summer and autumn flowers, sow between January and May in a temperature of 16-18°C (about 60-65°F). After the plants have been pricked out, reduce the temperature to a maximum of 16°C (60°F), otherwise the soft stems will become spindly and flop over. Use 5in pots for the final potting.

Sowing in August and September will produce flowering-size plants by the spring. Keep the temperature low during the winter – just enough to prevent frost.

Sown under glass in late winter, schizanthus also makes a good summer bedding plant for a sunny position sheltered from wind. Pinch out the tips of young plants to encourage them to bush out, and support the stems with twiggy branches, or canes and string. Compact varieties, which require less staking than tall forms, include 'Star Parade' (6-8in high) and 'Dreamland' (15in). 'Hit Parade' (12in) is particularly colourful. Most seed catalogues offer several varieties.

POOR-MAN'S ORCHID *Schizanthus does well in pots or for bedding. This is 'Giant Pansy Flowered', which grows to 18in.*

Where to cut a cutting

Why is it so important to trim cuttings just below a leaf joint? My greenhouse fuchsia and chrysanthemum cuttings root just as well when I cut them between joints.

The natural hormones that help cuttings to root are, in most plants, concentrated at their leaf joints, or 'nodes'. Because you want roots to develop at the base of the cuttings, it makes sense to cut them just below the lowest joint.

As you have discovered, fuchsia and chrysanthemum cuttings are not fussy where they are trimmed. However, it is still safer to trim all cuttings to a joint because, if the bare portion of stalk cannot root, it may decay back to the leaf joint and could, therefore, cause the cutting to fail.

With hollow-stemmed cuttings, including dahlias, lupins and delphiniums, it is particularly important to cut slightly below the solid leaf joint because of this risk of rotting.

One other rule to which chrysanthemums are an exception is the one that says you should always use a sharp knife, razor blade or secateurs to trim cuttings, because clean cuts heal faster than ragged or bruised ones. Many nurseries snap chrysanthemum cuttings off the plants and don't trim them at all, except to strip off the lower leaves which would otherwise be buried in the compost. Chrysanthemums don't seem to mind, and it does save time when dealing with large numbers of plants. Moreover, it may cut the risk of virus diseases being spread through contaminated sap sticking to the knife blade.

Mushrooms under glass

The space underneath my greenhouse staging is quite musty. Would it be a good place to grow mushrooms?

Only if you can keep the temperature within the range 10-18°C (about 50-65°F). Contrary to popular belief, the reason mushrooms are grown in cellars and the Paris sewers is not because they hate light; it's because these places maintain a constant moderate temperature. Mushrooms do not mind light, though they dislike full sun. After all, their natural habitat is the damp, shady end of a meadow, and you will have to emulate this, as far as you can, by shading the glass in summer.

The air should be kept moist, and even on cool days you'll need to give them a little draught-free ventilation to let carbon dioxide escape from the greenhouse, because it hinders growth.

Mushrooms grow best in a bed made from well-rotted horse manure. The bed should be about 12in deep and at least 3ft across with a length to suit the size of your appetite.

If you can meet all of the mushroom's exacting requirements, you can expect to harvest about 2lb per square yard. On the other hand, you may find that a DIY mushroom kit which can be kept indoors is more convenient (for more details, see *Mushrooms*, page 234).

The rainwater controversy

My husband prefers to use stored rainwater – which is often green and slimy – for our seedlings and plants, but I say tap water is better. Who's right?

You both are. Generally speaking, rainwater is fine for established plants, but it could spread damping-off disease to seedlings, especially if it has been stored for some time.

Tap water, too, is fine as a general rule. But if it is 'hard' water – which means that it contains a high level of lime – avoid using it for African violets, citrus, indoor azaleas, palms, and other pot plants that dislike lime. Use rainwater on these to help keep the leaves a healthy colour.

You can prevent stored rainwater from turning green and slimy by storing it in a lightproof and lidded container. Add enough crystals of potassium permanganate to keep the water just visibly pink. Check the colour by filling a milk bottle with water and holding it up to the light.

One other tip about tap water: to avoid chilling the roots of greenhouse plants and thereby causing a slight setback, leave tap water standing in the greenhouse overnight before using it.

Overcrowded seeds

Owing to failing eyesight, I get too many seeds crowded together in the trays. What advice can you give an elderly gardener?

Try pelleted seeds. An increasing number of flowers and vegetables are now covered with an inert material to increase their size and thus make them easier to handle. They cost more than ordinary seeds, but you should save money by sowing much more thinly. You could even 'space-sow' – sow them at measured 2-3in intervals – to avoid having to do any pricking out at all. Keep the compost slightly moister than you normally would, while pelleted seeds are germinating, in order to encourage the inert coating to dissolve. Otherwise the seeds may sprout erratically.

Another method is to cover the compost with a thin layer of silver sand or sieved perlite before sowing. That will make small seeds more visible against the lighter background. Or you could mix the seeds with dry silver sand and sow the two together.

You may also find it easier to sprinkle the seed accurately from the palm of your hand, rather than shaking it out of the packet. And dividing the quantity in half and sowing over the whole seed tray twice should help, too.

Cable hitch

I hope to make a 2ft by 3ft propagator heated with electric cables. How much and what type of cable do I need, and what should it be covered with?

For safety reasons, attempt this only if you really know what you are doing. If you've any doubts, call in an electrician, particularly if the power supply has yet to be taken to the greenhouse.

Insulated and earthed soil-warming cables are obtainable in different lengths: the longer the cable, the more power it uses and the higher the wattage. For general propagation, 8-10 watts per square foot is sufficient, so for your propagator you would need a 10ft long cable with a 50 watt rating.

Controlling the temperature manually can prove very difficult, especially during unsettled weather when the greenhouse air temperature can rise and fall quickly during the day. For this reason, consider wiring a rod thermostat into the circuit to control the temperature automatically. Alternatively, switch the propagator off during warm days, but leave it on at night if the greenhouse isn't heated.

Lay the cable on a 2in thick layer of a half-and-half mixture of fine builder's sand and peat. Cover it with another 2in layer, this time using a half-and-half mixture of peat and sharp sand, not builder's sand, if you want to root cuttings directly in the mixture. If, on the other hand, you plan to root cuttings in pots or trays placed on the mixture, then it doesn't matter which type of sand you use for the top layer.

All-in feeding

To save buying different types of fertilisers, would it be all right to top-dress all my greenhouse plants with Growmore?

Not really. Growmore is risky for plants in pots because stems and roots could easily be scorched, even if you gave the plants a good watering immediately afterwards. Play safe and feed pot plants with a liquid fertiliser instead. Once a liquid feed has been diluted according to the maker's instructions, it cannot harm roots. Ideally, use a fertiliser that meets each plant's specific requirements – a high-potash or tomato fertiliser for flowering plants, or a high-nitrogen feed for plants grown just for their foliage. You can tell which fertiliser is high in which element by looking on the packet for the letters N, P and K, followed by numbers. The letters are the chemical symbols, respectively, of the three main plant nutrients: nitrogen, phosphorus and potassium. The number signifies the percentage of each nutrient in the mix. The three numbers usually add up to much less than 100 per cent. The remainder is an inert substance such as clay or water which acts as a carrier for the active ingredients. If the numbers appear on their own without the letters beside them, as is often the case, they refer to the same elements always in the same N-P-K order. A high-nitrogen fertiliser will have an N number higher than either of the others. A high-potash, or high-potassium, fertiliser will have a K number higher than the other two.

Growmore, which is a balanced fertiliser with an NPK rating of 7:7:7, denoting an equal proportion of each nutrient, is more useful for plants which are permanently in the greenhouse border, such as grapevines, bougainvillea and jasmine. All such plants would benefit from a light sprinkling of Growmore around the root area in the spring. Apply the granules evenly (avoiding the stems) when the soil is moist, gently hoe it into the surface and then water the area.

Dying fly traps

Twice I have bought pre-packed Venus fly trap plants only to find that they fade away in my heated greenhouse. Should I complain?

Perhaps. If this happened within a month or so of purchase, take the remains back because the bulbs may have been diseased or dead. In future, look out for plants with strong, green leaves and don't accept any which are apparently lifeless, no matter what time of year you buy (for more detailed advice, see *Law*, page 205).

On the other hand, the plants' decline may have been your fault. Check what you did against this list of do's and don'ts.

- Do pot the bulbs in a mixture of 3 parts of sphagnum moss to 1 part of sharp sand.
- Do keep the plants almost soggy with rainwater during the summer.
- Do place the plants in full sun, except during very hot weather when they need light shade.
- Do maintain a minimum winter temperature of 10°C (50°F) and water them less often until the weather warms up again.
- Don't keep them in deep shade.
- Don't give them any fertiliser.
- Don't use hard tap water to water them.
- Don't overfeed them with insects or pieces of meat, or you will turn the traps black.
- Do aim to give each trap on the plant one fly or one ladybird-sized piece of raw meat every two months during the summer. It is better to underfeed than overfeed, and there's no need to feed the plant at all during the winter.

Flies on compost

Every time I water my greenhouse pot plants, tiny black flies run over the compost. Are they harmful?

The flies aren't, but their white grubs or larvae sometimes feed on the young roots of ornamental plants, cucumbers and mushrooms. Cuttings are occasionally nibbled beneath the surface.

These pests, gnats of the genus *Sciaridae*, are more generally known as mushroom flies. They lay their eggs in moist soil; peat composts are more likely to attract them than the soil-based John Innes mixtures.

Watering less often, or using a compost that drains more freely (you can achieve this by adding sand to your existing compost) should deter them. You could also dust the surface with malathion powder or HCH. If the infestation is severe, lightly water the compost with diluted malathion. Read the instructions on the packet before using either chemical, though, because some greenhouse plants can be harmed by them.

No buds on an African violet

Do African violets grow well in a greenhouse? Three years ago a friend gave me some rooted leaves, but there are still no buds.

They do if you provide the right environment. Try to keep the temperature in summer between about 16°C and 21°C (60-70°F). And if you want the plants to flower in winter, don't let the temperature fall below 13°C (55°F). Stand the plants in their pots on shingle or capillary matting, and keep the base moist because they like humidity.

Shade is essential during the summer, otherwise the soft leaves will quickly become scorched. However, insufficient light stops flower buds forming and you have to reach a happy compromise. Try reducing the shading or moving your plants to a different part of the greenhouse, ideally a spot that isn't bathed in full sunshine from midday onwards. But give the plants plenty of light in dull weather.

Leaf-stalk cuttings sometimes produce several plants on each cutting. So since crowded growth also inhibits flower buds, it's worthwhile picking off all but one of the plantlets on each cutting.

Pruning a passion flower

I have a passion flower in the greenhouse border. Should it be pruned and will it fruit?

Unless you carry out a regular pruning programme, the plant will probably take over most of your greenhouse. The passion flower is a vigorous, scrambling vine and is best grown in 12in pots or tubs to restrict root and shoot growth. If your plant in the border is already too large to move, limit the spread of its roots with corrugated-iron sheeting, or planks of wood sunk into the soil. Aim to form a bottomless box about 2ft across around the stem. The barrier will have to go down at least 2ft to be effective.

Basic pruning is quite simple. In late February cut back all the side stems growing off the older framework stems to two or three buds. This will encourage short, flowering sideshoots to grow. Prune in the same way, but more lightly, in the summer if flowers don't appear. Remove any crowded, spindly stems at the base of the plant in winter.

Plants that flower well should set fruits under glass, particularly if you lightly spray the open flowers with water daily during hot, sunny weather.

Conserving camellias

Would camellias be happy in large pots kept inside a conservatory for the winter?

Certainly. This is the best way to prevent frost and icy winds from damaging their delicate spring blooms.

Move the pots inside in October and return them to the garden in May when the risk of severe frosts is over.

The conservatory needn't be heated, but a temperature around 7-10°C (45-50°F) will make them flower a couple of weeks earlier. Keep the roots moist, preferably with rainwater because camellias dislike the calcium often contained in tap water.

Coddling an oleander

I've bought a Mediterranean oleander and Australian bottle brush to grow in my greenhouse. How warm will I need to keep them in the winter?

A temperature of 7°C (45°F) will be fine, but you could let it drop to just above freezing without harming these shrubs. The oleander tolerates slight frost, and the bottle brush is hardy enough to grow outdoors alongside a sunny wall in Southern counties and on the West and South coasts of Britain.

Provide plenty of ventilation during the summer to keep the plants sturdy. Or, if they are in pots, stand them in a sunny part of the garden until frost danger looms again in autumn.

Cuttings keel over

Even when my greenhouse cuttings are sealed in polythene bags they wilt in the sun. How can I stop this happening?

You must keep them shaded, because cuttings that wilt in hot sunshine will have difficulty in rooting. Plastic netting or a liquid shading paint on the outside of the glass will help, or you could attach the green polythene that's designed for greenhouse shading to the undersides of the glazing bars. On a small scale, one or two sheets of newspaper draped over the bags that are in the sun may do the trick.

A cheap and easy way to shade, and the one that's best for cuttings, is to enclose each container inside a milky-white polythene bag. The bags filter the sun without restricting too much light, even in dull weather.

Keep the bags from touching the cuttings. If you don't, there is a risk that leaves and stems will rot where the polythene makes contact, and chafing could also loosen the cuttings. There are several ways of keeping the bag off the new plant. You can support it on a framework of galvanised wire loops, or on three or four short pieces of cane stuck in around the edges of the container. Alternatively, if the bag is large enough to fit right round the container, you could blow it up like a balloon and seal its neck with an elastic band or a wire tie.

Clay versus plastic

Are there any greenhouse plants that prefer clay pots to plastic ones?

Yes, cacti, succulents, geraniums and many alpines grow better in clay pots because they prefer a compost that dries out within a day or two of being watered. Unglazed clay, known as terracotta, is porous and so absorbs moisture from the compost, making it dry out more quickly. This is particularly advantageous if you use a peat-based or heavy loam compost which holds a lot of water.

Immediately before using dry clay pots, it's a good idea to soak them in water for a couple of hours – or until air bubbles stop rising to the surface – otherwise the compost may dry out too quickly during the first few days after potting.

Although compost in a porous clay pot will invariably be up to 2°C (3°F) cooler than it would be in a plastic pot (due to water evaporating from the clay and cooling it), this doesn't unduly slow down the growth of the plants. In fact, cuttings inserted around the edge of a clay pot sometimes root faster than those set in the middle, and faster than cuttings put in a plastic pot. This is because the compost is less soggy near the outside of a clay pot and contains more air.

The value of rooting powders

How useful are the chemical rooting preparations for greenhouse cuttings? I've never used one because I don't usually have any difficulty in getting my cuttings to grow.

Rooting compounds contain minute quantities of synthetic hormones which can stimulate cuttings to make roots faster and in greater numbers. However, don't regard them as being the single sure-fire route to successful propagation. They won't make cuttings root if the cuttings are too weak, taken at the wrong time, or not provided with the right environment. In short, they are useful only for cuttings that are able to root without them. Given that limitation, though, they will increase the chances of more of your cuttings rooting successfully.

Many gardeners use these rooting hormones – available in powdered and liquid form – as a matter of course. Some brands contain a fungicide which helps to protect the base of the cutting from rotting. This is particularly useful for fleshy cuttings such as geraniums, cacti and African violets.

A word of caution: don't dip the end of the cuttings deeper than 1in into the powder or liquid in the belief that more powder will make them root better. If too much rooting hormone adheres, the roots may be burnt as they emerge and the results could be worse than if the chemical hadn't been used at all.

Because most of the hormone is absorbed by the cut surface of the stem, it's far safer, and also more economical, just to dip the extreme end of each cutting into the preparation. Then tap the cutting lightly against the edge of the tin to shake off any excess before inserting it into its new home.

GREY MOULD

Mouldy raspberries

How can I rid my garden of grey mould? Whenever the weather turns damp my raspberries and strawberries go mouldy, and even my flowers are affected.

Grey mould is very common on a wide variety of plants in humid weather during the growing season. Glasshouse chrysanthemums, cyclamen, dahlias, peonies and roses hit by the fungus develop spots on the blooms which later rot and become covered with a fluffy mould. Diseased buds fail to open.

Leaves and stems of many bedding plants such as godetia, clarkia, petunia and zinnia are attacked by the mould, as are all soft fruits, strawberries and raspberries being the most likely to suffer. The danger period for fruit is flowering time, although the mould does not become visible until the fruit matures. Grey mould spores spread on the wind, and the infection gets a hold by contact or through wounds and decaying tissues. Even weeds can catch it.

Wherever grey mould occurs, and whichever plants are affected, there is no cure. Remove and burn any mouldy fruit, flowers, leaves and stems as soon as signs of the disease appear.

Grey mould can be prevented by spraying with a systemic fungicide such as benomyl or thiophanate-methyl as soon as the flowers open. Repeat the treatment twice more at fortnightly intervals. Allow at least two weeks to elapse between the last application of spray and harvesting.

Longer term, the best method of prevention is good garden hygiene. Pick up any plant litter. And deadhead all flowers as a matter of routine. Mould will soon show up once a bloom begins to decay. The fungus also flourishes in the damp, still atmosphere of a greenhouse, so make sure there is good ventilation to discourage any spores from multiplying.

SPORES IN THE AIR *Damp, shady conditions and overcrowded plants provide an ideal breeding ground for the wind-blown spores of grey mould.*

GROUND COVER

Keeping a balance

If I plant ground-cover plants, will they compete with my shrubs for food in the soil?

Yes they will, but so will the weeds. And, in the case of the deep-rooted perennial weeds, the competition is so effective that the growth of shrubs can be seriously hindered. On the other hand, ground-cover plants and shrubs will grow happily together, provided the soil is well enough prepared before planting and that both the shrubs and the ground-cover plants are looked after properly.

The border must, for instance, be well manured when you dig: use rich compost or well-rotted manure generously. Add a handful of bone meal in each planting hole, too. For small ground-cover plants, work the bone meal, compost or manure into the top 3in of soil before planting. Finally, when planting is complete, cover the whole area in a generous layer of compost or chopped bark – not only to improve the appearance, but also to smother weeds and conserve valuable moisture.

Until the surface is covered in plants, add another layer of organic material each spring. On poor soil mix more bone meal or a slow-release compound fertiliser into this mulch before spreading it.

The shrubs will have deeper roots than the ground-cover plants and, although there will be some overlap, they should have feeding roots at two different levels.

When the border has been established for a few years and the cover is too dense to apply a mulch, it is time to change the method of feeding. Buy a cheap hose-end diluter and a fertiliser which feeds through the leaves (foliar feed) as well as the roots. Follow the instructions on dilution carefully, and thoroughly water the whole border once in the spring and again in June or July. Avoid feeding if any of the plants are in flower, because some spotting might occur and spoil the show of bloom.

Pruning plays an important part, too, in keeping a balance between ground cover and shrubs. The shrubs should not be allowed to grow into a dense mass above the ground-cover plants. You won't need to prune drastically (which looks ugly anyway). It is much better to trim a little each year.

The ground cover also needs attention: trim the plants according to their needs. Some you can lift and split after a few years, otherwise they will slow down in growth and may even start to die back. If they begin to look untidy and pruning doesn't help, replace them, using the opportunity to add more organic matter. With a little effort, you can have many years of lovely display with a good balance of growth.

Banking on success

Our garden is spoiled by a bank rising at the end. Too steep to mow, it is covered in rough grass and weeds. How can we make it look attractive without spending a lot of time on it?

Like so many jobs in the garden, the secret of success lies in the preparation of the area. It is essential first of all to clear the bank of all weed growth.

The best way of tackling the job without a lot of very hard work is to use a weedkiller such as glyphosate that will kill the weeds (and grass) right down to the roots.

Because the bank is steep, it is better not to dig it all over, otherwise most of the valuable topsoil will tumble down the slope and heavy rain will cause further erosion. Instead, dig individual holes for each plant (for suggestions on which plants to grow, see *Colour*, page 84, and *Shrubs*, page 310).

War on weeds

How long must I wait for my ground-cover plants to grow over the soil? Is there anything I can do meanwhile to stop the weeds taking over?

Ground-cover plants should spread to carpet the soil in two or three years, although this does depend on what you plant and on planting distances. If you have chosen some slow-growing plants such as cotoneasters (which can take three or four years to provide dense cover), consider planting some fast-growing temporary plants in between. You could, of course, simply plant more cotoneasters closer together to get a quicker carpet. But that would add to the expense and would in time lead to the plants becoming overcrowded. Some of the herbaceous perennials provide fast cover, are inexpensive and need in any case to be lifted, split and replanted every four years or so. This rhythm of growth fits in well with the development of the permanent ground cover, with the herbaceous perennials giving way eventually to the main planting. Plants such as *Geranium macrorrhizum* and *Brunnera macrophylla* are ideal for this purpose.

Another idea for keeping the area weed-free while you wait for the plants to cover over is to apply a 2in thick mulch of compost or bark once a year in spring to smother any weed seedlings. Alternatively, use a weed-killer stick which you can wipe onto individual weeds without harming your plants.

QUICK Geranium macrorrhizum *can be used to cover the ground quickly.*

QUICK Brunnera macrophylla *is also ideal as a temporary ground-cover plant.*

SLOW Cotoneaster horizontalis *plants set 2ft apart will meet in three to four years.*

Friend or foe

I keep hearing about companion plants. Is this just an old gardener's tale? If some plants are good companions, are others not?

Gardeners have long suspected that some plants grow better when planted near certain others – and the reverse also seems to be true. But there is very little scientific evidence about companion plants: what little is known is all from personal observation and experience.

The main idea behind companion planting is that each plant exerts an influence on its surroundings, on the soil in particular. Plants are complex organisms and it is thought that their influence is mainly by means of chemical exudations from root, leaf and stem. Certain plants are believed to create better conditions in the soil for a following crop, leaving behind beneficial elements which will boost subsequent growth. The most familiar example of this process is the nitrogen that legume crops such as peas and beans leave behind in their roots, which can be used by subsequent vegetable crops such as cabbages.

Then, too, many pests identify the plants they feed on by smell. Where a single crop – for example, carrots – is grown in quantity, it gives off a powerful smell, especially during thinning. But if the rows of carrots are interspersed with rows of another plant with a different smell – onions, say – the insects are less likely to attack the carrot crop.

Some plants, such as garlic, lavender, sage and chives, are said to have insect-repellent properties – with obvious benefit to other plants. The same plants are also thought to keep diseases such as mildew away from shrubs and roses. Similarly, marigolds are said to keep whitefly away from vegetables and flowers; one species of marigold, *Tagetes minuta*, is also claimed by organic gardening researchers to be a natural weedkiller, capable of destroying couch grass, bindweed and ground elder. And yellow-flowered agricultural mustard, dug into the soil as a green manure, is held by most farmers to drive off soil-borne pests.

But not all plants make good companions. Like humans, some varieties do not get on well together and are best kept apart. For instance, many gardeners avoid putting potatoes and onions or beans and onions together in the belief that each will diminish the performance of the other.

PICK OF THE GROUND-COVER PLANTS

Name	Spacing	Remarks
Acaena buchananii	10in	Good on rockeries and between paving stones
Ajuga reptans	12in	Grows well in damp spots
Alchemilla mollis	2ft	Plant in groups
Cotoneaster dammeri *C. horizontalis* *C. microphyllus*	2–3ft 2ft 2ft	Grows in most soil types. Suitable for banks, paved areas, under trees or against a wall
Euonymus fortunei	2ft	Grows well in most soils, including chalk
Geranium macrorrhizum	12in	Grows well in most soils
Hebe alpina	2ft	Mound-forming. Looks good with other hebes
H. pinguifolia 'Pagei'	18in	Mat-forming. Ideal under shrubs
Hypericum calycinum	2ft	Ideal for dry bank. Trim back each spring
Juniperus communis depressa	4ft	Ideal for banks, or for cloaking manholes
J. chinensis 'Pfitzerana'	5ft	Low-spreading shrub, ideal for banks
Lamium maculatum	12in	Very vigorous; prefers shade
Mahonia aquifolium	2ft	Best under tall shrubs and trees
Pulmonaria	12in	Useful in the front of a border
Sarcococca humilis	18in	Tolerates acid soil; flowers in winter
Vaccinium myrsinites	2ft	Requires an acid soil
Vinca major variegata *V. minor*	18in 18in	Grows well in most soils. Use under shrubs, trees and on steep banks

HARD ROT

Sunken spots on gladioli

I'm very careful when lifting gladioli to store only apparently healthy corms, yet a disease seems to be spreading among them which marks a lot of the corms with dark, sunken spots. So what am I doing wrong?

Your use of the word 'apparently' is significant. The corms are suffering from a fungus disease called hard rot, which is active in the soil in winter.

So for the corms to show symptoms in store, they must already have been infected when you lifted them – even though they looked perfectly all right.

The disease is found chiefly on gladioli, and less commonly on crocuses, freesias and acidantheras. The spores develop on diseased tissues and spread quickly in humid weather, often being carried from one plant to another by rain splashes.

On leaves and flowers, the symptoms are small brown-purple spots with tiny black bodies on them. Corms develop brownish patches which grow into sunken scars, often with tiny black spots. Severely affected corms also become shrivelled.

Spray plants with a copper compound in August and again in the following May to disrupt the life cycle of the fungus; this will prevent it from getting a hold in your garden.

Diseased plants and corms cannot be rescued. They can only be destroyed.

Next time, protect your corms in store by soaking them for 15 minutes in a solution of benomyl or thiophanate-methyl. Give the treatment before you store in autumn and again just before replanting.

HEATHERS

The right soil

I am told that heathers will grow only in acid soil. How acid should it be, and how can I tell if my soil is right?

Ideally the soil should have a pH of between 5.5 and 6, and you can measure this with a simple testing kit.

The pH scale is a measure of acidity and alkalinity and stretches from 1 to 14, though very few soils fall outside the range 4.5 to 8. At pH 7, the ground is said to be neutral. Below that it is acid: the lower the measurement, the higher the acidity. Above pH 7, soil is alkaline – this means it has a high lime content, and the higher the measurement, the greater the concentration of lime.

Very few plants like an alkaline soil. Lime makes it difficult for roots to draw up vital nutrients, such as iron and manganese.

Heathers and other plants in the *Ericaceae* family, which includes rhododendrons and azaleas, are simply not as good as other species in overcoming this problem. They make poor growth and may die.

You can get a good idea of the type of soil in your garden by looking at the plants which flourish naturally in the district where you live. If there are lots of tall rhododendrons, the soil is predominantly acid. Where beech trees do well, the soil is chalky, and that means lime.

A simple testing kit or pH meter can be bought at your local garden centre. Follow the instructions and take tests from several parts of your garden.

Growing in chalk

My soil is chalky. Are there any heathers I can grow, or would it be a waste of time to try?

No, it's not a waste of time; there are some heathers that will grow in a moderately alkaline soil. All of them are species of erica. The general rule is: winter-flowering ericas will tolerate some lime; summer-flowering types won't. Take a pH test first. If your soil measures above 7.8, then even winter-flowering species are unlikely to survive.

Erica carnea is the hardiest and probably the most popular of the lime-tolerant heathers. It gives thick ground cover up to about 12in in height, and spreads 2-3ft. There are varieties with pink, rose, carmine, purple, deep red and white flowers, and foliage that varies from deep green, blue and bronze to a bright gold. Many have new growth in spring of a different colour, giving a two-tone effect.

E. erigena (also known as *E. mediterranea*) is less hardy and less varied. It grows into rounded bushes up to 3ft tall, with white, pink or purple flowers between December and June. Severe winters may damage it.

E. x *darleyensis*, the Darley Dale heath, will flower from December to early summer. Its purple, pink or white blooms are at their best in March and April.

E. arborea, a tree heather, grows up to 15ft tall in the best conditions in the warmer South, but generally not more than 8ft. It carries white flowers in late spring.

E. terminalis is the heather that breaks all the rules. It is a tree heather growing up to 8ft in height; it is hardy; it will live quite happily in a limy soil; and it flowers in summer. In a mild year, its pink or purple blooms can glow at the tips of the apple-green foliage from as early as June until as late as December, when the dying flower heads turn a rich bronze.

Correcting the soil

I have tested my garden soil, and it is very alkaline. I really want to grow some summer heathers. Is it hopeless, or is there anything I can do?

Treat the soil with sulphur, or dig out a bed and fill it with peaty, acidic soil.

Those are about your only options, unless you confine your planting to varieties of one of the tree heathers, *Erica terminalis*, which tolerates very alkaline soil and flowers in summer and autumn, longer in mild years.

It's easy to correct an over-acid soil by adding lime. It's much more difficult to turn an alkaline soil – one containing a lot of lime – to acid. In a borderline soil it may be enough just to dig in plenty of peat and leaf mould to push it into the acid category.

A very alkaline soil can be altered with sulphur, easily obtainable from garden shops. Generally, 12oz to the square yard will lower a pH measurement by one point. But the treatment is not without hazard. Too much sulphur will harm the growth of most plants. The treatment will also need to be repeated every few years.

The surest way to correct your soil is to make a special acidic bed, by creating a raised bed above the existing soil level. A raised bed is better than a ground-level one because it will drain more freely, and there's less danger of alkaline water seeping in from the surrounding soil. Line the sides and bottom with peat blocks or heavy-duty plastic to keep out the alkaline soil. Puncture the plastic with a spike in several places for drainage, then fill up with a peaty topsoil – ask a local garden centre for advice on a good nearby supplier.

Then you can plant out as many summer-flowering heathers and other lime-hating plants as you've made room for.

Unhappy in clay

My garden soil is a fairly heavy clay and quite acid, yet my heathers don't look at all happy. What can have gone wrong?

Too much water in the soil, making it sticky, and the clay is probably too rich. Heather's natural habitat is a wide, open heath or moorland, where the soil is soft, sandy and peaty and rain drains quickly away.

A rich, fertile soil such as your clay will tend to produce lush, soft growth, which can be knocked over by a bout of hard weather. A damp, heavy clay also stays cold and shuts out the air which is vital for root growth.

These are not ideal conditions for heather. To open up the soil and improve drainage, dig in sharp sand – not builder's sand – and peat in equal quantities. Peat is like a sponge, holding water without making the soil wet and sticky. Sand will break up the soil, allowing air to reach the roots more freely.

For a really heavy soil, you may need large quantities of peat, which will make it an expensive job. If so, substitute well-rotted garden compost and leaf mould for some of the peat. Do not, however, use spent mushroom compost. Chalk is used in growing them, so the lime content will be too high for heathers.

Preparing the ground

I am planning a heather bed. How should I prepare the ground to give them the best possible start?

You want a well-mixed, free-draining, crumbly soil that won't stick together in a ball when you squeeze it in your hand. Start with rough digging to at least a spade blade's depth in autumn.

Clear out the weeds, and let winter frosts break down the soil. In spring, test the soil's level of acidity – its pH value – with a testing kit. Add peat, compost and manure to bring up the acidity if necessary, and sharp sand if the soil is a bit clayey and does not drain well.

Some superphosphate worked into the soil – about 2oz per square yard – will encourage the plants to root. Use superphosphate in preference to bone meal, because bone meal, being made from bones, is rich in calcium which most heathers dislike. Wait until some breezy, sunny spring days have dried out the soil, then rake it, firm it down by treading, then rake it again.

Most pot-reared heathers can be planted out at any time, but to give them their best chance, plant them in April as the ground warms up.

How to design the layout

I can't make up my mind about my heather bed. Would it look better in a formal or informal layout?

Heathers are free-growing wild plants and naturally informal. That is how they look on the hillsides, and, if you have room, that is how they will look best in your garden.

A formal design suggests straight lines and squares and regular groupings. Heathers fit more easily into curves and sweeps, and shapes where they can merge softly together. Don't go for fussy shapes like scalloped edges or sharp corners. In island beds, break up the low-growing spread with one or two specimen shrubs or small trees to give height.

Heathers make bold splashes of colour, so don't cram too many varieties together. Put three or four plants of each variety in a group and let them merge with each other and the surrounding varieties. If you have plenty of room, lay a meandering path of ornamental bark mulch through or around the bed to give different views of your design.

Close order

How far apart should I plant heathers to give quick ground cover?

Give them about 12-18in on each side – measuring from the centre of each plant to the centre of its neighbour – and your bed should be filled out in about three years. Where you mix species, remember they don't all grow at the same rate.

Vigorous varieties such as *Erica carnea* 'Springwood', *E.* x *darleyensis* 'Darley Dale', and *Calluna hammondii* can be spaced 2ft apart and fill up the space in the same time. Smaller, slower-growing forms such as *C.* 'Humpty Dumpty', *E. carnea* 'Eileen Porter' and *E. c.* 'Cecilia M. Beale' must be planted more densely, about 9-12in apart.

Go for bold groups of colour, not a patchwork of different types. Mark out the area you have chosen for each type. If they are pot grown, stand them all out in their pots where they are to be planted, so you can gauge the overall effect. Then switch them around if you want to.

Bare-root plants should not be allowed to dry out – get them in the ground as quickly as possible after you get them home.

Plant heathers deeply, with their lower branches resting on the soil. Bury the stems if they are bare. Firm them in gently and water them unless the soil is already really moist. Trim off dead shoots or faded flowers as soon as you have planted.

Starting from seed

Can heathers be grown from seed?

Yes, but there is no knowing what you will finish up with. Like all cross-bred cultivated plant varieties, they have mixed parentage. You cannot be sure what pollen fertilised them, so your seeds will give you new crossbreeds, and most will be disappointing. But try if you want to – in the lottery of nature you might come up with a winner.

To collect seeds, leave faded flowers on the plant for three or four weeks, then cut them and put them in paper bags. Leave them in a warm, dry place and the seed capsules should split after a few weeks to release the seeds. As soon as they do, sow the seeds in pans (shallow, wide pots) of peat and sand, mixed in equal quantities. Cover them with a thin layer of fine silver sand.

Leave the pans outside over winter, protecting them from driving rain, but not from the cold. Germination is likely to be slow and sporadic. Keep the soil just moist, and prick out the seedlings into individual pots as they become large enough to handle. Grow them on in a sheltered spot for at least two or three years before putting them out in their flowering position.

Before you get too excited about any promising-looking new seedlings – and it may be several years before they get big enough for you to assess them properly – remember that they may be throwbacks to an ancestor plant, not brand new varieties.

Registering a new variety is expensive, and you won't get nurserymen to take up a new plant unless it is outstanding.

Propagating heathers

I have a large area to plant and buying heathers to fill it will be expensive. What is the best way to propagate the plants and so save money?

By layering, but in saving money you will pay in time. Heather layers – and cuttings, too, come to that – take two or three years to form plants strong enough to put out. Add another three years for them to fill out and you could have a good deal of bare ground for a long time.

Layering is simple, and heathers in the right soil will propagate themselves naturally in this way.

Mix some sharp sand into the soil near the mother plant. In March, take two or three young shoots.

Either wound or twist the shoots, then peg them down with a bent wire or stone into the soil and sand so that only their tips are showing.

In 6 to 12 months a strong root system should have formed under each shoot. Separate the new plants from their parent and grow them on either in a nursery bed or where they have rooted, until they are ready to plant out a couple of years later.

One plant can be multiplied into numerous new ones by using a variant of this layering technique – provided you don't mind sacri-

LAYERING *Nick or twist young shoots in March, and peg them down in sandy soil. Separate them 6-12 months later.*

ficing the mother plant. Simply spread out all the branches and bury the entire centre of the plant in an equal-parts mix of soil, peat and sand, leaving just a ring of shoots showing at the edge. In 6-12 months all the shoots will have rooted separately. You can then separate all the new plants and grow them on. As for the old one you buried, dig it up and discard it.

Cuttings should be taken in late summer. Go for strong, non-flowering sideshoots about 1in long, and tear them off, keeping a heel of the older stem attached. Insert them in a seed tray or in pots containing a half-and-half mixture of peat and sand. Leave only about ½in showing.

There's no need to remove the lower leaves on the cuttings, or to dip them into a rooting compound.

Water the cuttings, cover the tray with a sheet of plastic or a plastic lid to retain moisture and keep it in a cold frame or greenhouse. They should root in 8-10 weeks. When they do, pot them up individually into 1½in pots and pot on as they grow. Keep them protected until spring.

Weeding the beds

I have bare patches among my young heather plants. How can I keep weeds down until the heathers fill out the beds?

Use a mulch of peat and pulverised bark. It will do the job, and it looks good, too. Get out all the weeds you can first, water the ground, then spread the mulch about 2in deep between the plants. Any weeds that do show through will have tenuous footholds and can be easily pulled out.

PICK OF THE HEATHERS

Matching soil to species is perhaps the most difficult part of starting a heather garden; once established, heather requires little attention. This chart of easy-to-grow varieties can help you in two ways. If you have a variety in mind, you can check whether it will grow well in your garden. If you have in mind a particular spot or colour plan you can use the chart to find the varieties that will fit in best. If you're not sure whether your soil is acid, alkaline or neutral, check it by buying a soil-testing kit (see *Acid soils*, page 6). Plants are listed under the soil in which they do best. Varieties of *Erica carnea* will *tolerate* alkaline soil, but they will do much better in neutral or even slightly acid soil.

Heather thrives best in sunny conditions. On this chart, 'Shaded' means the sort of dappled shade cast by a tree. The column headed 'Colour' describes the colour of a variety's main feature, which is marked by a spot in the 'Why it's grown' column. Where a variety is valuable both for its flowers and its foliage, both colours are given. A variety's 'Peak display' period is when it looks its best – not necessarily when it's in flower.

	Soil			Position		Why it's grown			
Name	Acid	Neutral	Alkaline	Sunny	Shaded	Flowers	Foliage	Colour	Peak display
Calluna vulgaris 'Alba Minor'	•			•		•		White	July–Aug
C. v. 'Arran Gold'	•			•		•	•	Mauve flowers; gold foliage (orange in winter)	All year
C. v. 'Beoley Gold'	•			•		•	•	White flowers; gold foliage	All year
C. v. 'Blazeaway'	•			•		•	•	Lilac flowers; green foliage (red in winter)	All year
C. v. 'C.W. Nix'	•			•		•		Deep crimson	Aug–Sept
C. v. 'Crimson Glory'	•			•		•	•	Crimson flowers; gold foliage (bronze in winter)	June–Sept
C. v. 'David Eason'	•			•		•		Red	Aug–Sept
C. v. 'Dixon's Blazes'	•			•		•	•	Mauve flowers; cream, pink-tipped foliage	Mar–May
C. v. 'Durfordii'	•			•		•		Pale pink	Oct–Nov
C. v. 'Fairy'	•			•		•	•	Pink flowers; yellow foliage (orange in winter)	All year
C. v. 'Firefly'	•			•		•	•	Red flowers; bronze-red foliage	Nov–Feb
C. v. 'Gold Haze'	•			•		•	•	White flowers; gold foliage	All year
C. v. 'Golden Carpet'	•			•			•	Gold (orange-red in winter)	Sept–Oct
C. v. 'Goldsworth Crimson'	•				•	•		Deep crimson	Sept–Oct
C. v. 'Hookstone'	•			•		•		Salmon-pink	Aug–Sept
C. v. 'Ingrid Bouter'	•			•		•	•	Red flowers; deep green foliage	Aug–Oct
C. v. 'Inshriac Bronze'	•			•		•	•	Mauve flowers; multicoloured foliage tips in spring	Mar–May
C. v. 'J.H. Hamilton'	•			•		•		Pink, double	July–Aug
C. v. 'Mrs Pat'	•			•		•	•	Lavender flowers; pink, red-tipped foliage	July–Sept
C. v. 'Multicolor'	•			•			•	Orange, yellow, bronze and red	Nov–Feb
C. v. 'My Dream'	•			•		•		White	Sept–Oct

You can also use a chemical. Glyphosate is a gluey weedkiller which can be painted onto the leaves of problem weeds such as bindweed, usually with a special applicator. It will kill any plant above and below the soil – and that includes heathers, so apply it carefully. Alloxydim-sodium will wipe out grasses – often a problem among heathers – and you can splash it about because it won't harm the heathers.

As with all weed problems, prevention is the best cure. Dig the soil well in the autumn before planting. At the same time clear out all weeds and stubborn roots. In spring, hoe off any young weeds that appear from seed. Then plant. Then mulch.

Shady patch

Beneath my conifer tree is a shady patch where nothing flourishes. Heathers would look good there, but would they grow?

Not if the soil is dry and poor and the shade permanent. Heathers are plants of the open heaths. They flower best in the sun and air. They can cope with the acidity created by falling pine needles, but not the soil-sapping roots of conifers.

Even so, heathers and conifers do look good together and, with care, you may make the combination work.

Trim out the lower branches of your conifer to give sun at the base; heathers will battle on even in dappled sunlight.

Pack the soil surface around the tree with organic matter such as peat, rotted manure and compost to hold in moisture. Put in your heathers and water them often in dry spells.

	Soil			Position		Why it's grown			
Name	Acid	Neutral	Alkaline	Sunny	Shaded	Flowers	Foliage	Colour	Peak display
C. v. 'Orange Queen'	•			•		•	•	Pink flowers; orange foliage (gold in spring)	Sept–Oct
C. v. 'Peter Sparkes'	•			•		•		Deep pink, double	Sept–Oct
C. v. 'Prostrate Orange'	•			•			•	Gold and orange	Nov–Feb
C. v. 'Sir John Charrington'	•			•		•	•	Crimson flowers; gold and orange foliage	All year
C. v. 'Sister Anne'	•				•	•		Pink	Aug–Sept
C. v. 'Spitfire'	•			•		•	•	Pink flowers; gold foliage (bronze in winter)	All year
C. v. 'Spring Cream'	•			•		•	•	White flowers; cream foliage tips in spring	Mar–May
C. v. 'Sunset'	•			•		•	•	Pink flowers; yellow, gold and orange foliage	June–Sept
C. v. 'White Gown'	•			•		•		White	Sept–Oct
C. v. 'White Lawn'	•				•	•		White	Aug–Sept
Erica carnea 'Ann Sparkes'		•				•	•	Purple flowers; orange and yellow foliage	Oct–Mar
E. c. 'Aurea'		•		•		•	•	Pink flowers; gold foliage	All year
E. c. 'January Sun'		•		•		•	•	Pink flowers; gold foliage	All year
E. c. 'King George'		•		•		•		Rose-pink	Dec–Mar
E. c. 'Myretoun Ruby'		•		•		•		Deep pink	Feb–Apr
E. c. 'Springwood White'		•		•		•		White	Jan–Mar
Erica cinerea 'Alba Minor'	•				•	•		White	June–Sept
E. c. 'C.D. Eason'	•			•		•		Deep pink	June–Sept
E. c. 'Constance'	•			•		•	•	Red flowers; yellow foliage	All year
E. c. 'Golden Hue'	•			•			•	Gold (red in winter)	All year
E. c. 'Rock Pool'	•			•			•	Gold (copper in winter)	All year
E. c. 'Startler'	•			•		•		Bright pink	July–Aug
E. c. 'Windlebrooke'	•			•		•	•	Purple flowers; gold foliage (orange in winter)	Nov–Feb
Erica terminalis			•	•		•		Rose-pink	Aug–Sept
E. t. 'Thelma Woolner'			•	•		•		Deep rose	Aug–Sept
Erica tetralix 'Alba Mollis'	•			•		•		White	June–Oct
Erica vagans 'Cream'	•			•		•		White	July–Oct
E. v. 'Mrs D.F. Maxwell'	•			•		•		Deep cerise	July–Oct
E. v. 'Valerie Proudley'	•			•		•	•	White flowers; gold foliage	All year

But don't be too disappointed if the plants sprawl and go leggy with pale little blooms and soft growth.

How to prune heathers

My heathers were fine after I first planted them. Now they have grown straggly and bare at the base. What can I do to rejuvenate them and keep them neat?

Prune them hard – but not below the lowest healthy leaves. They should send up fresh shoots from the older wood.

Prune summer-flowering varieties in early March, winter-flowering ones in late April after they have bloomed. Leggy plants can also be lifted and replanted more deeply so that the base stem is buried and only the leafy shoots show above the soil.

Heathers need regular pruning to keep them neat. The dead flower heads of summer-blooming types can look attractive if left over winter, and they'll help to keep off frost as well. Then in spring, trim to just below the old flower stems, using secateurs. Cut out dead, damaged or diseased branches and trim straggly shoots hard. Sharp shears can be used when pruning a very large area of heathers; they are quicker but less accurate than secateurs.

Summer-flowering heathers can, alternatively, be trimmed in autumn to give a bright flush of new young growth in spring. Winter-flowering heathers are often more compact, and may not need cutting more than once every two years. Trim them in spring, cutting off dead flower heads.

Tree heathers don't usually need pruning at all. Clip them only to improve their appearance or shape, and do the trimming after they have flowered.

Hardy heathers

My garden is cold and exposed. Are heathers generally hardy enough to cope, or must I choose my varieties carefully?

Most popular heathers are hardy enough for any English garden. Many flourish, after all, on cold, open, windswept moors, which are their natural habitat. One or two varieties, though, mainly of South African or Mediterranean origin, will not do well in an exposed garden.

In cold areas, do not plant the tree heathers *Erica arborea*, *E. australis*, *E. canaliculata*, and *E.* x *veitchii* 'Exeter'. *E. terminalis*, however, should not be damaged by the cold, though snow may break its branches unless you shake it off. Others that may fall to a severe winter are *E. pageana*, *E. umbellata* and *E. multiflora*, and *Daboecia azorica* and *D. cantabrica*.

Biting winds will do more damage than intense cold, drying out leaves and scorching new growth. Protect young plants with a windbreak of poles and woven netting in a chill, windy spot.

When buying young heathers, ask whether the plants have been grown outside or under cover. They may need hardening off over a period of weeks before you can safely plant them out.

Right fertiliser

Most heathers do not like lime. Which fertilisers can I safely give them?

Superphosphate, potash or fertilisers containing sequestered iron – but not too much of any of them.

When preparing a heather bed, dig into the soil about 2oz per square yard of superphosphate. On established beds, give a light dressing of sulphate of potash, no more than 1oz to the square yard, in late summer and again in early spring. A dose of sequestered iron in autumn will give iron and manganese, vital plant nutrients, in a form that heathers can absorb even in limy soils.

Heathers do not need much fertiliser. They flower best in relatively poor, easily drained soils. Soils rich in nitrogen tend to encourage soft leafy growth at the expense of blooms.

Avoid all fertilisers containing free lime or calcium, such as nitrate of lime, nitro-chalk, calcified seaweed, calcium cyanamide and basic slag. It's worth steering clear of bone meal for the same reason. But superphosphate of lime cannot harm heathers; paradoxically, it actually makes the soil slightly less limy and more acid.

Heath or heather?

Some books I have read talk of heaths and heathers, and I am confused about which is which. What is the difference?

It is in the flowers. Heathers have smaller blooms, and their colour comes from the conspicuous and papery 'calyx' – the outer leaves of the bud. Heaths have bigger flowers and their colour comes from the 'corolla' – the inner leaves, which make the petals.

So, all the species of ericas and their many varieties are actually heaths, although most people call them heathers; and the single species *Calluna vulgaris*, known as ling, is the only true heather.

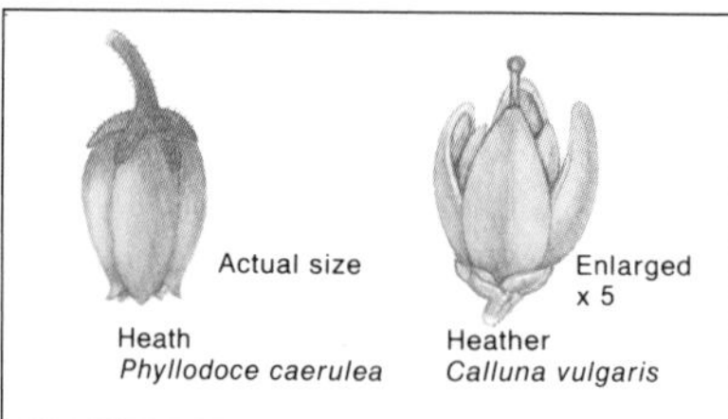

LITTLE AND LARGE *Heaths have larger flowers than heathers, and coloured petals. A heather's colour comes from its conspicuous calyx.*

Erica tetralix is commonly called the bog heather and *E. cineria* the bell heather. Botanically, both are heaths. And *Daboecia cantabrica*, called St Dabeoc's Heath, which has flowers like the heathers, is in fact neither a heath nor a heather – just another relative of the ericas and, like them, a member of the *Ericaceae* family.

It sounds confusing, but as far as garden cultivation is concerned, it does not matter. It's much more important to know the differences between the erica species – in particular which ones will tolerate lime and which won't – than it is to know the differences between erica and calluna. Treat them all, as many books and catalogues do, as heathers – and you won't go far wrong. After all, they mostly like the same soil and growing conditions.

Lucky heather

We are going to Scotland on holiday and would like to bring back some traditional lucky white heather to grow in our garden. Will it survive south of the border?

Yes, it will grow anywhere in Britain, and you needn't go to Scotland to get it. It is sold in nurseries everywhere.

Lucky white heather is a mutant of the purple-flowering heather, *Calluna vulgaris*. Its white flower heads crop up spontaneously among wide stretches of purple, and so are reputed to bring the finder luck. Bunches are sold to tourists all over the country.

The white form of *C. vulgaris* may have a reputation for not flowering south of the border because holidaymakers have snatched it from clumps in the wild, put it in a hot car boot, and driven for hours or even days with it before arriving home to plant it out. Few plants could take that.

There are several varieties of the white heather, including 'Alba aurea', with gold-tipped foliage, 'Alba Carlton', which flowers very freely, and 'Alba Pumila', a dwarf form.

If you must have yours from Scotland, don't pinch it off a hillside – under the Wildlife and Countryside Act 1981, it's illegal to dig up any native wild plant without the landowner's permission. Instead, buy a pot plant from a nursery. It will survive the journey . . . and get off to a good start in your garden.

Tree heathers

What are the tree heathers? I imagine they are not really trees, but how tall do they grow?

Some will grow into small trees in their native Mediterranean, but in Britain they remain as shrubs, reaching a maximum of about 15ft.

Tree heathers are not as hardy as other heathers and need protected positions in cold gardens in severe winters. In warmer,

Southern gardens, though, they survive most winters unscathed.

The tree heathers are:

Erica arborea – 8-15ft; conical, with pale green foliage and scented white flowers at the tips in early spring. The variety *E. a.* 'Alpina' has deeper green foliage, and is hardier than the species.

E. australis – 4-10ft; known as the Spanish heath, it has deep green foliage and, in April, purple flowers. It needs support especially when young, and it is not hardy. *E. a.* 'Mr Robert' has white blooms.

E. canaliculata – up to 15ft in the warm South-west. Pinkish flowers in late winter.

E. lusitanica – 8-15ft; known as the Portugal heath. It has pink buds and white blooms from early winter to May. The light green foliage has a red tinge in winter.

E. scoparia – 4-9ft; known as the Besom heath. Foliage is apple green and the flowers are greenish and insignificant, appearing in early summer. It is not widely grown.

E. terminalis, also known as *E. stricta*, *E. corsica* and the Corsican heath. It thrives even on alkaline soils. Flowers are deep rose or purple in summer, fading to brown in autumn. The foliage is bright green.

E. x *veitchii* 'Exeter' – up to 7ft; it is derived from a hybrid seedling found in Devon in the 19th century. It has bright green foliage and, in spring, scented white flowers.

Heather mixers

I don't want a bed filled entirely with heathers. I have seen them planted beside dwarf conifers. Are there other plants that will grow happily with heathers in the same conditions?

Yes, plenty – but don't put too many among your heathers or you will turn the display into a mixed shrub border.

The plants to go for are those that will tone or contrast with the heathers, or those that will provide colour during the heathers' off season. Any of the numerous varieties of dwarf rhododendrons or azaleas will do well beside heathers.

Here are some others for you to choose from. All need the same acid conditions that best suit most heathers.

Andromeda polifolia – evergreen, 15in high, with pink, bell-shaped flowers in May.

Gaultheria procumbens – ground-hugging evergreen, 6in, with pink flowers in July and August followed by red berries.

Kalmia angustifolia – evergreen, 2-4ft. Pink flowers in May.

Pernettya mucronata – evergreen, 2-3ft. Small white flowers in May followed by long-lasting berries of pink, red and purple on female varieties, which the majority are. A male form should be planted with female forms for good berrying. Male forms are 'Edward Balls' and 'Thymifolia'.

'Lilacina' is available in both male and female forms, and 'Bell's Seedling' is hermaphrodite, carrying both male and female elements in the same flower.

Pieris formosa 'Forrestii' – evergreen, 5ft. White flowers resembling lilies of the valley in April, and brilliant red spring foliage.

Vaccinium corymbosum – deciduous, up to 6ft. Bell-shaped pinkish flowers in May followed by edible blueberries and beautiful autumn colours.

Alternatively, if you're growing lime-tolerant heathers, you could set with them any of a much wider group of plants. All the following plants grow well in acid or alkaline soils, and look good with heathers.

Acer palmatum 'Dissectum' – a spreading, shrubby tree, growing eventually up to about 6ft, with brilliant autumn colours.

The variety 'Atropurpureum' has purple summer foliage.

Betula pendula – deciduous, 20-30ft, weeping birch tree with mottled bark. It casts only light shade.

Cytisus praecox – deciduous, 4ft high, spreading shrub with cascades of creamy blossom in May.

Cornus alba 'Sibirica' – deciduous dogwood shrub up to 4ft high. Cut to the ground each spring, it produces scarlet winter stems.

Salix caprea 'Pendula' – small deciduous weeping willow tree, growing to about 8ft. It has silky catkins in spring.

Limy tap water

Heathers like moisture, so I know that I will have to water them fairly often in my free-draining soil. My tap water is limy, though – will this hurt the plants?

Not if your soil has been prepared with plenty of acidic peat before planting. There simply won't be enough lime in the water supply to affect soil acidity. If, on the other hand, you are watering heathers in pots, there's so little soil to soak up the lime in the water that you could affect the acidity and thus the plants' health. So the rule is: rainwater for pots whenever possible; any water will do for open ground.

Free-draining, quick-drying or sandy soils like yours must have plenty of peat and well-rotted garden compost dug in when preparing a heather bed, in order to help the ground to retain moisture.

It's also worth planting out new heathers in winter or early spring when the ground is wettest, so as to give the plants plenty of time to establish themselves before the summer dry spells.

You may need to water them, too, during their first summer. But heathers are reasonably tough. Once they have set out a good root formation in well-prepared soil, they will survive all but the driest conditions.

If you must plant in summer, water the bed heavily beforehand and put the plants out in the evening. Water regularly if the following days are dry.

Pests and diseases

Are heather plants prone to any devastating pests and diseases?

No, they are not. In gardens, they are among the most pest-free and disease-free of all plants.

The heather beetle does a little damage on the moorlands, but is rare in the garden. Honey fungus will attack heather and almost any other garden plant (see *Honey fungus attack*, page 204).

Erica wilt is a fungus that occurs in some wet conditions, causing shoot tips to wilt and finally turning the whole plant crisp and brown. It is rare. The same symptoms are more often caused by parched or waterlogged soil, or by cold winds. Check these possible causes first. If it is wilt, then there is no cure. Dig up the plant and burn it, and plant fresh heathers in a new bed. The infected soil will be no good for heathers, but it won't harm other garden plants.

Rabbits sometimes eat foliage in rural areas in hard winters. Netting is the only way to stop them.

In town gardens, cats are the most common problem, crushing stems, trampling flowers and fouling plants with their urine, which can scorch the foliage. Repellent sprays and nets are the only safeguards (for more details, see *Cats*, page 49).

Hedge of heather

I believe that certain heathers can be grown as hedges. Which varieties would be the most successful?

Vigorous heathers can make a decent dwarf hedge, but you won't get such a hedge any taller than about 4ft, so it's not much good as a boundary hedge, for creating privacy, or as a windbreak. Around a bed or path though, it can look very attractive; it's also easy to keep, evergreen and with long-lasting flowers.

Plant a double row, setting each heather 1½-3ft apart depending on the variety, and allow 18in between the rows, staggering the plants. Prepare the soil just as you would for any other heather bed.

Erica arborea, a tree heather, will form a hedge up to 4ft tall, but it is not hardy enough for cold areas of Britain and is unlikely to survive many winters outside the South-west. *E. a.* 'Alpina' is a hardier relative, but smaller and often expensive to buy. It does, however, make a good, firm, upright hedge.

Erica erigena 'Superba' will make a sturdy, 2ft tall hedge with mid-green foliage and rose-pink flowers in late winter and early spring. It is scented, too. For smaller, informal hedges up to 18in, choose a variety of *E. vagans*.

Alternatively, *E.* x *darleyensis* makes a

good edging for a flower border because it tolerates lime. *E. terminalis* is another possible choice for a hedge on alkaline soil. Its purple or pink flowers add colour in summer and autumn; and it's hardy.

Calluna vulgaris 'Alportii' has brilliant red blooms in summer, making it particularly striking as a hedge.

Trim most heather hedges once a year after flowering or in early spring to keep the plants compact and the shape neat. But *Erica vagans*, commonly known as the Cornish heath, can be made into a neat, formal, non-flowering hedge if it is closely clipped several times during the growing season.

Tender visitor

I bought a very attractive Cape heath as a pot plant, but it soon died. Would it have done better outside?

It certainly would not. This pale green and feathery plant is an import from South Africa, and simply is not hardy enough to take our northern climate.

It does not much like being indoors, either. The hot, dry air of a centrally heated house will kill it off very quickly in winter. You picked a real challenge with this one.

The Cape heath is one of the true heaths, *Erica hiemalis* or *E. gracilis*. They are grown as house or greenhouse plants, and insist on lime-free conditions – which means they need to be grown in ericaceous (lime-free) compost and, ideally, they should be watered only with rainwater.

In winter they like a steady 4°C (40°F), which is a bit chilly for humans. They might survive in an unheated spare room or entrance hall, but the spot also needs to be light and airy, and you must keep the compost just moist – if it dries out completely or gets waterlogged, the plant will die.

The best place is a frost-free greenhouse with plenty of ventilation.

In summer you can move the plant outside and sink it in its pot in your heather bed. It won't be displaying its white or pink flowers – those appear in winter – but the pale green feathery foliage will add an original touch. Get it back under cover, though, before the first frosts.

Heathers for cutting

I like my garden plants to give cut flowers for the house. Which of the heathers are best for this?

Most heathers can be cut for display in the house, but you will get the best results and the most long-lasting blooms from the callunas.

Cut the flowers when they are in full bloom, and take as long a length of stem as possible. Slit the base of the stem – make the slit 1-2in long, if possible – and stand the flowers in cold water for at least two hours before arranging them.

Foliage, too, can be attractive. Cut and treat it the same way as the flowers. Older leaves often have deeper colours. Use these, too, for cutting.

Sprayed with anti-transpirant – the same spray which is widely sold and used to stop the needles of Christmas trees dropping – the branches will last well. Otherwise they tend to lose their leaves quickly in the warm, dry atmosphere of a house.

Dead heather flowers can also be cut and displayed indoors. They are papery and dry, and, although their colours may fade in bright sun, they are virtually everlasting. Cut them on a sunny day and let them dry in a warm, airy place before arranging them.

The best heathers for cutting are: *Calluna vulgaris* 'Anne Marie', a light pink flower opening to carmine; *C. v.* 'C.W. Nix', tapering deep crimson heads; *C. v.* 'Elsie Purnell', double flowers, pink to silver-pink; *C. v.* 'Golden Feather', bright gold summer foliage, orange in winter; *C. v.* 'H.E. Beale', long racemes of double pink blooms; *C. v.* 'J.H. Hamilton', large double pink flowers; *C. v.* 'Kinlochruel', long-stemmed white flowers; *C. v.* 'Peter Sparkes', pink double flowers; *C. v.* 'Schurig's Sensation', spikes of rose-pink double blooms; and *C. v.* 'Silver Rose', which has bright pink blooms.

Best of the ericas for flower arrangements are: *Erica* x *darleyensis* 'Silberschmelze', long-lasting white flowers; *E.* x *d.* 'Arthur Johnson', rose-pink; *E. carnea* 'Foxhollow', golden leaves; *E. c.* 'Springwood White', which is specially good when dried; and *E. c.* 'Myretoun Ruby', which has large pink flowers.

Window show

My window box stands empty all winter. Would flowering heathers be a good choice to fill it?

Yes, they would. Their prostrate and semi-trailing growth would be ideal. Make sure your window box has plenty of drainage holes and put a layer of pebbles or broken clay pots in the bottom to stop the compost washing out. Use a peat-based compost.

Winter-flowering heathers are lime-tolerant, so you don't have to be too careful about using ericaceous (lime-free) compost. But you must be careful how much you water the heathers. The small amount of compost you can hold in a window box will be prone to both drying out and waterlogging.

Keep the box sheltered in severe weather, too. Peg down sacking or newspaper over the box on very cold nights. Otherwise the compost and roots can freeze solid, which will damage the plants severely and could kill them.

Choose compact heathers for your window box. *Erica carnea* varieties such as 'King George' (pink), 'Ruby Glow' (red) and 'John Kampa' (rose-pink) are ideal. *E.* x *darleyensis* varieties are a little larger, but 'Ada S. Collins' (white) and 'Archie Graham' (deep pink) won't be too big. *E. erigena* 'W.T. Rackliff' makes a small and tidy mound of deep green foliage with white flowers.

Give your box a little height with a conical dwarf conifer or some spring bulbs. Try the miniature narcissi, such as *Narcissus bulbocodium*, which grows to only 6-8in high, *N. cyclamineus* (8in), *N.* 'February Gold' (10in), or *N.* 'Peeping Tom' (10-12in). In a sheltered spot with the warmth of a house wall behind a box, these bulbs could give you colour as early as late January – just when it is most welcome.

Rockery heathers

I have a small rock garden with a mixture of alpines. Would heathers fit in with them?

They will fit in very well. Apart from showing attractively against stone, the heathers will give valuable out-of-season colour. Most rock gardens are at their best in late spring and early summer, so some late summer-flowering and autumn-flowering callunas, and winter-flowering ericas, will give the rock garden a lift when it most needs it.

You needn't worry if the soil is alkaline; it is easy on a rockery to create a lime-free planting pocket by lining a peat-filled patch with rocks.

Water heathers well after planting to get them established. Rock gardens are almost always raised, so they will tend to dry out before the rest of the garden.

Alpines are small and delicate, so choose heathers that are compact. Vigorous, spreading types might swamp the alpines. On smaller rock gardens a single heather will do.

Any of this list should work well: *Calluna vulgaris* 'Californian Midge', which has pink flowers; *C. v.* 'Foxii Nana', small, bright green hummocks and purple flowers; *C. v.* 'Tib', double rose-pink flowers; *Erica carnea* 'Vivelli', slow-growing with bronze foliage and red flowers; *E. c.* 'Golden Drop', a prostrate variety with gold-copper foliage and purple flowers; and *E. vagans* 'Valerie Proudley', which has gold foliage and white flowers.

Divide – and fail

Do heathers benefit from being lifted and divided every few years, like herbaceous plants?

No, certainly not. They can't, in any case, be split into sections like the crowns of herbaceous plants. Leave them alone to become well established, just as you would do with a shrub.

Neglected heathers may become straggly and ungainly after a few years. But this is best controlled by regular pruning after flowering, not by trying to split the plants (see *Propagating heathers*, page 179).

HEDGEHOGS

When hedgehogs sleep

Where do hedgehogs go in the winter? Do they hibernate?

Yes. You are not likely to see a hedgehog between late November and mid-March, for this is when they take shelter for the winter. Occasionally during a mild spell, the creatures may come out to feed, but will return to their winter sleep as soon as the weather turns colder again.

Hedgehogs hibernate – and lie up during the day – in stacks of leaves, fallen branches or in an unenclosed compost heap.

So never set fire to any pile of garden rubbish without first turning it over to make sure that it does not harbour a hedgehog. And when you stir the heap, don't use a garden fork. Rather, work from the base with a spade or shovel, so as to give any snoozing hedgehog time to escape.

Tempting hedgehogs to your garden

Can hedgehogs be tamed? If so, how do you do it?

Hedgehogs are nocturnal creatures, rarely seen in daytime. If there are any in your neighbourhood, you can tempt them to make nightly visits by leaving out food for them. Try a saucer of bread and milk, or a tinned dog food that contains liver, though never anything that includes fish. The dog food should be left in a saucer, not in its tin which may trap the hedgehog.

Hedgehogs are not particularly shy. To watch the creature feed, just wait quietly near the saucer with a torch. You'll probably hear it approach: hedgehogs make a lot of noise, rooting and snuffling when feeding and searching for food, rather in the manner of pigs.

To encourage a hedgehog to take up residence, you will have to leave a patch of wild garden where it can find shelter. But though a hedgehog will wander openly and noisily about your garden in the evening, this does not mean that you have tamed it, or that it has any particular feelings about you. From whatever can be understood of hedgehog psychology, it would seem that they feel that their spines will confound any enemy, and therefore it does not matter what sort of racket they make.

A winter sanctuary

Can a hedgehog be kept in captivity?

Hedgehogs are creatures of the wild and it would be quite wrong to cage them. An exception to this rule might be in the case of an orphaned youngster. Hedgehogs sometimes give birth late in the year when their young do not have the time to build up enough reserves of fat to survive hibernation. The creatures need to weigh at least 1lb to see them through the winter, and those below that weight in November are almost certain to die.

So if you find an underweight hedgehog even as early as late September, it is a kindness to house and feed it. A shed is fine, with a box of clean hay or dry leaves in a corner. Feed the hedgehog on minced meat, fresh liver or tinned dog food – but nothing with fish in it. Vary the diet and bulk it out with bread or bran and provide plenty of water or milk. When the youngster's weight reaches 1-1½lb you can release it. Wait for a period of fairly warm, dry weather so that the hedgehog has time to find and make a nest of its own before going into hibernation.

Pest controllers

Is it wise to encourage hedgehogs? Do they harm plants?

The hedgehog is the gardener's friend, with an enormous appetite for pests. Beetles, caterpillars and earthworms comprise over 60 per cent of its diet, and it also accounts for large numbers of earwigs, millipedes, bees, leatherjackets (the larvae of daddy longlegs), snails and slugs. Hedgehogs vary this diet with birds' eggs, small birds, snakes, lizards and even mice and voles – dead or alive. But they never eat plants, and do no damage to them unless, through characteristic clumsiness, they tread on them.

Garden hazards

Are pesticides harmful to hedgehogs? Are there any other hazards for them in the garden?

Slug pellets are the main chemical danger to hedgehogs: they are poisonous and should be used only if you have a serious slug problem. If you do use pellets, put them under a slate or in a pipe where slugs can get to them, but hedgehogs can't. Other hazards include garden ponds and cattle grids; steep-sided pools can be death traps to any small animal, and if it fell into the concrete trough below a grid, a hedgehog would most likely starve to death. Always ensure that there are several slipways or ramps around the edge of the water or the trough so that animals have a means of escape. Alternatively, hang a piece of chicken wire over the edge, so that they can climb out if they fall in. Tennis nets present hazards too. Hedgehogs can become entangled in them, so make a point of furling them up well above the ground in the evening.

Natural climbers

I have slugs on the lower part of an apple tree. I know that hedgehogs eat slugs – but can they climb to reach them?

Surprisingly, yes. In fact, they have been known to scale drainpipes as well as trees in search of food. Some zoologists believe that hedgehog spines evolved not only to deter predators but also to protect them when they fall. It seems that when a hedgehog drops from a height, it bounces.

HEDGEHOGS – THE GARDEN'S NIGHTWALKERS

The common hedgehog (*Erinaceus europaeus*) has been known for centuries in Britain. Shakespeare writes of 'hedgepigs' and 'urchins' as well as referring to them under their more familiar name in the fairy song from *A Midsummer Night's Dream*:

'You spotted snakes with double tongue,
Thorny hedge-hogs be not seen.'

Hedgehogs are found all over Europe and everywhere in Britain apart from a few Scottish islands. Nevertheless, they do have preferences about where they live. They are rarely found, for example, in wetlands or pine forests, and shun areas of very dark and dense vegetation. They also tend to avoid bare uplands, probably because these areas lack suitable shelter and food. But they thrive in cities, where they especially favour cemeteries, railway cuttings, waste ground, parks and gardens.

The creatures' spines are really modified hairs, and the average adult hedgehog has about 5000 of them. But they are not really very sharp to the touch, and there are no spines on the chest, belly, throat or legs – those areas are covered instead with coarse grey-brown fur. Hedgehogs breed once a year, usually in early summer, when they give birth to four to eight young. Foxes and badgers are natural enemies, and when threatened, hedgehogs curl up into a motionless ball for protection. Their habit of doing this in front of vehicles helps account for the number of hedgehog casualties seen on roads and motorways.

Long established legend says that hedgehogs suck milk from cows' udders, but this is unlikely. Their teeth are very sharp, and would cause the cow to move away. However, they do lap milk from the ground as it seeps from the udders of cows when they are lying down, which may account for the stories. Unfortunately, hedgehogs also carry foot and mouth disease between cattle and other farm animals, so that farmers are less keen on them than gardeners.

For further details, contact the British Hedgehog Preservation Society, Knowbury, Ludlow, Shropshire SY8 3JT.

HEDGES

Choosing an easy hedge

I've moved into a new house and want to plant a hedge as I don't like fences. Which is the easiest one to maintain?

It depends on the type of hedge you want, and how high you want it to grow. For an average garden 5ft is ideal because it will be easy to trim and not cause too much shade. Then how fast do you want it to grow? To produce a screen quickly, the plant most often recommended is x *Cupressocyparis leylandii*, the Leyland cypress; but it grows up to 3ft a year and maintains that rate.

The tallest Leyland cypress on record is at Bicton in Devon. After 70 years, it's 120ft high and still growing.

For easy maintenance, choose a hedge which does not grow too quickly, is evergreen and requires trimming only once a year. Your choice should be between *Chamaecyparis lawsoniana* 'Green Hedger' and *Thuja plicata* 'Atrovirens', a form of Western red cedar that grows bushy and upright. Plant either variety 2ft apart and trim it in late summer, using secateurs on thuja to retain its natural bushiness.

Common yew, beech and hornbeam do not require too much work, either. Flowering hedges such as *Escallonia macrantha* and *Escallonia* 'Crimson Spire' are also worth considering – but only if you live in the South or West, or near the coast. Escallonias are not fully hardy in colder parts of Britain, such as the North and East.

HOW TO PREPARE THE SOIL FOR A HEDGE

1 In autumn or winter, mark out a 4ft wide strip along the length of your planned hedge. Dig a trench a spade's blade deep along one side of the strip and move the soil, directly or in a barrow, to beyond the other side. Remove all the weeds you come across, particularly the roots of perennial weeds.

2 Spread compost or manure in the bottom of the trench. Use as much as you can spare; once the hedge is in place, it will be difficult to weed or cultivate the ground thoroughly. Dig a second trench, turning the soil into the first.

3 Continue digging, weeding and manuring until you get to the other side of the strip. Then fill the last trench with the soil you took from the first. Leave the soil to settle for at least two weeks before planting the hedge. As a final fillip for the site ahead of planting, scatter and hoe in Growmore at the rate of about 4oz per square yard (about 5oz per yard of hedge).

Preparing the site

How should I prepare the site for a hedge which will be a permanent feature?

The best time to prepare the site is autumn or early winter. Place two marking lines 4ft apart. Dig a trench the depth of a spade blade along the inside of one line, moving the soil to the outside of the other line. Fork into the bottom of each yard of the trench a bucket of well-rotted compost or manure. Place soil from the second row into the first trench. Continue in this way until you reach the final trench beside the second marking line. Fill it with the soil removed from the first trench.

During digging remove all perennial weed roots, but simply bury annual weeds. They'll rot down and add humus to the soil. If you're not sure which weeds are annual and which perennial, remove them all and add extra manure or compost to replace their bulk. This deep digging gives good results on all soils as no subsoil is brought to the surface, which is important when shallow soil overlays chalk or clay.

After digging, hoe in a general fertiliser such as Growmore at about 4oz per square yard. Let the soil settle for at least two weeks before planting.

Privacy provider

I want a hedge that will grow quickly, provide plenty of colour and be thick enough and high enough to give some privacy. What do you advise?

Among evergreen hedges, the golden-flowered *Berberis* x *stenophylla* (6-8ft after six years) has all these qualities. *Escallonia macrantha* (6-10ft, bright pinkish-red flowers) would be another good choice near the coast, or in the South and West.

Suitable deciduous species include: *Chaenomeles speciosa* (japonica) which has crimson flowers and grows up to 6ft high after five years; and the yellow-flowered *Forsythia* x *intermedia*, 6ft after six years.

Yew for formality

What's the best plant for a formal evergreen hedge which needs little clipping?

The best formal plant is yew, but whether it will suit your garden depends on how much land you have. If you have a small garden the best plant is *Lonicera nitida*. This will need clipping at least three and possibly four times a year. It is suitable for hedges up to 5ft.

The yew (*Taxus baccata*), contrary to general opinion, is not a slow grower. It grows as much as 9in a year, although the golden variety, *T. b.* 'Elegantissima', which is more colourful, grows more slowly. Because of its slightly slower growth compared with other hedge plants, yew needs less trimming and it forms a denser hedge. It is suitable for hedges up to about 7ft and grows well on all types of prepared soil, even on shallow chalk. Clip it in late summer.

Tackling whiteflies

My beech hedge is infested with whiteflies. How do I get rid of them?

Drench the hedge with malathion and repeat the dose three times at weekly intervals.

Honeysuckle hedge

I want to plant a honeysuckle hedge. Would this be more difficult to maintain than any other type of hedge?

The best type for a hedge is *Lonicera nitida*, known as the shrubby honeysuckle. It is a small-leaved evergreen, growing to 4-6ft, which makes a good informal hedge for a small garden. The golden form *L. n.* 'Baggesen's Gold' turns green in late July or early August. Once established, it's not difficult to look after; simply clip it to shape twice a year, in May and September. Remember, though, that this species does not resemble the familiar climbing honeysuckles; its flowers are insignificant and the foliage looks more like that of a cotoneaster or privet.

Repairing a leggy hedge

My privet hedge has become bare at the base. What can I do about it?

In spring, cut back your privet with a saw and secateurs to within a few inches of the main branches. Trim the top back a few inches below the height you want. Clean around the base, removing all rubbish, weeds and dead growth. Fork the soil around the stems and give the soil a top-dressing of a 1-2in layer of new soil or well-rotted compost, then lightly fork in a general fertiliser such as Growmore at 4oz per square yard. Your hedge should then break from dormant buds at the base to fill in with new foliage.

The right level

I have a long hedge and it's difficult to keep the top level. How can I do this?

The best way is to use a garden line stretched tightly on stakes placed upright along the hedge. Always set the line so that you are cutting to the lowest dip in the hedge.

On the other hand, perhaps you're worrying unnecessarily. Many gardeners nowadays consciously choose to encourage natural curves in their hedges, as in their lawns – because it looks nice. If you do experiment with this approach, there's only one rule: go for longer, shallower curves than you think are appropriate at first. Otherwise you run the risk of creating a scalloped effect that may look fine on a pie crust, but at a garden scale just looks fussy.

Barrier to animals

I am bothered by neighbours' animals. Which hedges are reasonably animal-proof?

The best kind of hedge to give this sort of protection is one that is thorny, dense at the base and strong-growing. Plants with most of these good points include hawthorn, blackthorn, *Berberis darwinii*, *B.* x *stenophylla*, holly and roses.

There is no hedge, though, that can keep out all small animals on its own – nor even relatively large animals such as cats. Even with careful training and constant trimming, gaps appear which become pathways for small animals.

To block these pathways cut the hedge back hard and stake small-mesh wire netting along the base.

How to lay a hedge

My garden borders a field and I'd like to lay the hedge to make it neat and fill in gaps. How do I go about it and where can I get expert advice?

Hedge laying is a long and skilled process, and must be done in winter. There are several regional variations of hedge-laying techniques; this is one of the simpler methods. First take out all dead and diseased wood, leaving sound wood about 8ft high.

Starting at one end of the hedge, partly cut through saplings near their base and bend them over and down without snapping the stem. Trim off branches on the underside of the stem, then weave the stem through other branches and stems farther along the hedge. Always point the bent sapling uphill on a slope to prevent the rain collecting at and possibly rotting the growing tips. Work your way along the hedge, reducing it to an even height of about 4ft.

Push trimmed-off branches horizontally along, across and through the hedge as you work to hold the cut saplings in place. For the same reason, you may also need to hammer some branches into the ground as stakes – tying them to or hooking them over the horizontal branches.

Courses in hedge laying are organised by county branches of The British Trust for Conservation Volunteers, which can be reached at 36 St Mary's Street, Wallingford, Oxfordshire OX10 0EU; telephone Wallingford (0491) 39766.

FILLING THE GAPS *To lay a hedge, clear out dead and diseased timber, then use an axe or billhook to cut partly through the stems of saplings. Cut them just enough to enable you to bend them down to hedge height.*

KNITTING THE GROWTH *Weave the cut stems through other branches and stems along the hedge. Hold them in place with spare cut-off branches. By the time they rot, new growth will have taken over the job.*

Safety first

I have a long hedge and would like to use an electric trimmer on it; but I fear that I might cut the cable and get electrocuted. Are there alternative trimmers?

The traditional non-electric trimmer is a sharp pair of shears, but the blades must be kept sharp to make the work easy. Alternatively, use a small battery-powered hedge cutter which gives about 30 minutes' cutting time before needing a recharge. It is suitable for hedges such as privet or honeysuckle but not for beech or roses, unless the wood is green. Petrol-driven hedge cutters are twice as heavy and about three times as expensive as electric models.

If you use an electric hedge cutter, connect it to the mains through a 13amp earth leakage circuit breaker. Circuit breakers – which are on sale at most hardware shops – provide protection against shock from the hedge cutter, and from a cut or frayed cable.

Two other safety tips: always work with the cable slung over one shoulder so that the trailing lead is well out of the way behind you. And, if your cable isn't orange, change it for an orange one to make it more visible against the dark colours of the garden.

CHOOSING A HEDGE

There are so many different varieties available for hedging that making the choice can be a bewildering business. This chart is designed to help simplify your decision. The first step is to decide how high you want the hedge to be when fully grown. The chart uses three categories: low (2-4ft), medium (4-6ft), and tall (over 6ft). Hedging plants can of course be trimmed to any number of heights; the figures given are the most suitable for the named species when used for hedges.

Next, decide whether you want a flowering hedge or one whose appeal lies in its foliage alone; and, finally, decide if you want the year-round cover of an evergreen hedge or not.

TALL — FLOWERING — *EVERGREEN*

Olearia x *haastii* (daisy bush)
Height 6-7ft, spacing 18in. Clusters of white flowers in July; slightly scented. Remove dead shoots in Apr.

Pyracantha angustifolia (firethorn)
Height 6-8ft, spacing 2-3ft. White flowers in early summer followed by masses of berries. Flourishes only in the South. Trim established hedges between May and July.

Viburnum tinus (laurustinus)
Height 6-8ft, spacing 18in. The only good winter-flowering hedge. White flowers Nov–May, if grown in the South. Thin out old wood in May.

TALL — FLOWERING — *DECIDUOUS*

Cotoneaster simonsii
Height 7-8ft, spacing 18in. White flowers in June, brilliant autumn colour, vermilion berries. Trim in Feb if necessary.

Crataegus monogyna (common hawthorn)
Height 8-10ft, spacing 2ft. Quick-growing, thorny. White, scented flowers in May, red berries in autumn. Trim July–Mar.

Deutzia longifolia 'Veitchii'
Height 8ft, spacing 2-3ft. White, or pink and white flowers in June and July. Trim after flowering.

Forsythia x *intermedia* 'Spectabilis'
Height 8-10ft, spacing 2ft. Golden flowers in spring. Trim after flowering.

Prunus cerasifera (cherry plum)
Height 9-10ft, spacing 12-18in. White flowers in the spring. Strong grower, makes a hedge quickly. Trim at any time.

Prunus cerasifera 'Pissardii'
Height 10ft, spacing 2ft. Whitish-pink flowers in spring, purple leaves. Trim at any time.

Ribes sanguineum 'King Edward VII'
Height 6-8ft, spacing 18in. Blood-red flowers in spring, bright green leaves. Cut out old wood in May.

Sambucus nigra (elder)
Height 10-14ft, spacing 2-3ft. White flowers in June followed by black berries. Trim Oct–Mar.

Syringa (lilac)
Height 10-12ft, spacing 3ft. Many varieties with flowers from white through pink and red to purple in May. Unsuitable for a windswept garden. Remove flowers as they fade, and from Oct cut out crossing and weak branches.

Tamarix pentandra (tamarisk)
Height 8-10ft, spacing 2ft. Feathery foliage with pink flower spikes July–Sept. Suitable for coastal gardens. Cut back hard in spring.

TALL — NON-FLOWERING — *DECIDUOUS*

Carpinus betulus (hornbeam)
Height up to 15ft, spacing 1½-2ft. Makes a good formal hedge; hardier than beech. Clip in the autumn to encourage it to hold its leaves all winter.

Fagus sylvatica (beech)
Height up to 12ft, spacing 18in. The best formal deciduous hedging plant. Grows well in most soils. Trim late in Aug to make it retain its brown leaves all winter.

TALL — NON-FLOWERING — *EVERGREEN*

Buxus sempervirens (box)
Height up to 10ft (if left untrimmed), spacing 12-15in. Excellent formal hedge for all soils and situations. Trim Aug–Sept.

Cupressus macrocarpa 'Goldcrest'
Height 8-10ft, spacing 2ft. Fast-growing conifer with dense golden foliage, suitable for shelterbelt in coastal areas. Trim only to reduce forked trees to one leading shoot in Mar.

Euonymus japonicus
Height 10ft, spacing 18in. Strong-growing. Suitable for hedging in coastal areas. Clip to shape in Apr and trim mid-Aug to mid-Sept.

Ilex aquifolium (holly)
Height 12-15ft, spacing 2ft. Very hardy; good animal barrier and formal hedge. Berries are produced where male and female plants are grown together. Trim in Apr.

Prunus laurocerasus (laurel)
Height 6-8ft, spacing 2ft. Prune in Mar and Apr, or Aug, always with secateurs.

Taxus baccata (yew)
Height 7ft, spacing 2ft. The best of all evergreen formal hedges; hardy. Trim at any time of the year, ideally in late summer.

Thuja plicata (western red cedar)
Height 10-12ft, spacing 2-3ft. Little trimming required.

Care for conifers

I have a newly planted coniferous hedge. How should I look after it?

Stake the plants until they become established and screen them on exposed sites to prevent wind burn. For screening, use small-mesh plastic netting to cover the plants on both sides. Remove the covering after the first two years. Do not cut back the leading shoots until the plants have reached at least the height you want.

In the first two seasons ensure that the plants do not dry out at the roots by watering them thoroughly in spring, then mulching – that is, covering the soil with a 1-2in layer of peat, compost or well-rotted manure.

No fertiliser will be required in the first two seasons, but subsequently hoe in a general fertiliser, such as Growmore, at 2oz per square yard in spring.

Planting beeches

I'd like a beech hedge. Should I plant two staggered rows or only one row?

The reason why a staggered row of beech is sometimes recommended is that a single row

MEDIUM — FLOWERING

EVERGREEN	DECIDUOUS
Berberis darwinii Height 5-6ft, spacing 2ft. Orange flowers in Apr, purple berries in autumn. Trim after flowering.	*Cytisus scoparius* (broom) Height 3-7ft, spacing 18in. Flowers in cream, yellow, pink or crimson in Apr and May. Trim back only to the base of flowering shoots.
Berberis x *stenophylla* Height 6-8ft, spacing 2ft. Pendulous. Golden flowers in spring. Trim after flowering.	*Genista aetnensis* (Mount Etna broom) Height 3-7ft, spacing 18in. Yellow flowers in July–Aug. No trimming required.
Escallonia macrantha Height 6-10ft, spacing 18in. Red flowers from June. One of the best hedges for seaside gardens. Trim after flowering.	*Rosa* 'Penelope' Height 3-7ft, spacing 2ft. Pale pink flowers and colourful hips. Trim in spring.
Hebe brachysiphon (veronica) Height 5-6ft, spacing 18in. White flowers in June. Thrives in coastal gardens. Little trimming needed.	*Rosa rugosa* 'Frau Dagmar Hartopp' Height 3-7ft, spacing 2ft. Sturdy shrub with prickly, hairy branches. Delicate, carnation-pink flowers and orange-red hips. Trim to shape in early spring if needed.
Ulex europaeus (gorse) Height 6ft, spacing 2ft. Yellow flowers Mar–May. Forms an almost impenetrable hedge and fine windbreak. Cut down leggy plants in Mar.	

LOW — FLOWERING

EVERGREEN	DECIDUOUS
Berberis buxifolia (barberry) Height 2-3ft, spacing 12in. Yellow flowers in Mar followed by blue berries. Trim after flowering.	*Berberis wilsoniae* Height 3ft, spacing 18in. Yellow flowers in May. Brilliant autumn colour. Trim after flowering.
Buxus sempervirens 'Handsworthii' Height 2-4ft, spacing 12-15in. Pale green flowers with yellow anthers in Apr. Clip to shape in Aug and Sept.	*Fuchsia magellanica* 'Riccartonii' Height 4ft, spacing $1\frac{1}{2}$-2ft. Red and purple flowers. Suitable for coastal gardens. Trim in spring.
Cotoneaster microphyllus Height 3ft, spacing 18in. White flowers in May followed by red berries. Little trimming required.	*Potentilla* 'Elizabeth' Height 3-4ft, spacing 12-18in. Golden rose-like flowers June–Oct. Cut out old stems after flowering.
Lavandula (lavender) Height 2-3ft, spacing 12-18in. Aromatic. Flowers July. Trim after flowering.	*Rosmarinus officinalis* (rosemary) Height 4ft, spacing 18in. Scented foliage; blue flowers in May and June. Cut out dead growths in Mar.
Mahonia aquifolium (Oregon grape) Height 4ft, spacing 18in. Golden flowers in Feb, violet berries from July. No regular pruning needed.	*Spiraea japonica* 'Anthony Waterer' Height 4-5ft, spacing $1\frac{1}{2}$-2ft. Red flowers July–Oct. Trim hard in spring.

MEDIUM — NON-FLOWERING

EVERGREEN	DECIDUOUS
Chamaecyparis lawsoniana 'Green Hedger' Height 5-8ft, spacing 2ft. Rich green foliage. Trim in Aug.	*Carpinus betulus* (hornbeam) Height up to 15ft (if left untrimmed), spacing $1\frac{1}{2}$-2ft. Makes a good formal hedge; hardier than beech. Clip in the autumn to encourage it to hold its leaves all winter.
Ligustrum ovalifolium (privet) Height up to 15ft (if left untrimmed), spacing 12-18in. Plant with dark green leaves that will grow anywhere. Trim the hedge to shape at least twice a year in May and Sept.	*Fagus sylvatica* (beech) Height up to 12ft (if left untrimmed), spacing 18in. The best formal deciduous hedging plant. Grows well in most soils. Trim late in Aug to make it retain its brown leaves all winter.
Lonicera nitida Height 4-6ft, spacing 12-18in. Formal honeysuckle hedge. Shear to shape in May and Sept.	

LOW — NON-FLOWERING

EVERGREEN	DECIDUOUS
Buxus sempervirens 'Elegantissima' Height up to 10ft (if left untrimmed), spacing 12-15in. Grey-green leaves edged with silver. Clip to shape in Aug and Sept.	*Berberis thunbergii* 'Atropurpurea' (barberry) Height 4ft, spacing 2ft. Reddish-purple leaves turning scarlet in autumn. Little trimming needed.
Ligustrum ovalifolium (privet) Height up to 15ft (if left untrimmed), spacing 12-18in. Dark green leaves; consider alternating the plants with the golden privet, *L. o.* 'Aureo-marginatum'. Clip to shape at least twice a year in May and Sept.	

of small young plants looks insignificant. To give an immediate appearance of an established hedge, buy plants about 2½-3ft high and plant them in a single row only 18in apart.

After planting, trim the leading shoots back by about 6in to promote bushy growth right from the start.

How to grow a windbreak hedge

I've just bought a house on the coast where onshore winds make it difficult to grow my favourite shrubs. Would a hedge planted as a windbreak help?

In most gardens a hedge is an attractive screen. In seaside gardens it's a necessity. Most plants can't survive winds gusting from the sea without the shelter of a hedge. Many plants used for inland hedges would not survive either, but the plants listed in the chart below, *Plants for a seaside shelterbelt*, have adapted to their inhospitable environment and make excellent windbreaks to shelter other plants while adding their own beauty to the garden.

On the most exposed sites, hedges should be planted in two, three or four rows if space allows. Indeed, it is often necessary to sacrifice some space to provide satisfactory shelter. The most effective windbreak is provided by planting two kinds of hedges: a sturdy wind-resister such as blackthorn or euonymus, set in two rows 4ft apart on the side facing the sea; then 4ft inside that a hedge of hebes or escallonia to filter out what gets past the outer defences.

Prepare the site by digging over the soil in the same way as for other hedges (see *Preparing the site*, page 186). You'll need to stake the plants or use wire-mesh supports for the first couple of years, or until they are well established.

Dividing line

I want a hedge to divide my vegetable patch from the rest of the garden and to act as a windbreak. Any suggestions?

There are several good shrubs to choose from and, since you want a low windbreak, aim for an evergreen which can be maintained at a height of 3-4ft.

Plants fitting these requirements are: the shrubby honeysuckle (*Lonicera nitida*), which requires trimming twice a year; *Berberis* x *stenophylla* 'Irwinii', a compact evergreen with deep yellow flowers in the spring, which needs a trim only after flowering; and rosemary (*Rosmarinus officinalis*), an old favourite with grey foliage and blue flowers in May and June, which needs trimming only to shape.

For more suggestions, see *Choosing a hedge*, page 188.

Where the east wind blows

I want to plant a hedge on my eastern boundary as a windbreak. What plants are best?

To give protection, the hedge should be high enough to shield the garden both from wind and from the turbulence caused by the hedge itself. Wind striking any obstacle is diverted upwards and hits the ground some distance away on the other side.

This distance depends on the wind speed but is usually from 6 to 12 times the height of the obstacle. The turbulence at this point is worst when the obstacle is solid, such as a wall or close-boarded fence.

It's less with a hedge because only part of the wind is blocked and diverted; the rest filters through the branches. The thinner the hedge, the less the turbulence – but the less the shelter, too.

Using these figures, you can calculate that a 6ft hedge will protect a garden up to 72ft wide. Calculate what height you need for your garden and make your choice from the following list, or from the plants recommended in the chart on pages 188-189:

PLANTS FOR A SEASIDE SHELTERBELT

Name	Foliage	Flowers	Spacing	When to prune
VERY EXPOSED GARDENS				
Blackthorn (*Prunus spinosa*)	Evergreen	White (Mar)	15in	Mar or Aug
Euonymus japonicus	Evergreen	White (July)	18in	Apr
Golden elder (*Sambucus nigra* 'Aurea')	Gold turning to green, deciduous	White (June)	18in	Apr and Sept
Gorse (*Ulex europaeus*)	Spiny, evergreen	Yellow (Mar)	2ft	Mar
Olearia x *haastii*	Evergreen	White (July)	18in	Apr
Sea buckthorn (*Hippophae rhamnoides*)	Silver, deciduous	Yellow, inconspicuous (Apr)	1½–2ft	Aug
Tamarisk (*Tamarix pentandra, T. gallica*)	Feathery, deciduous	Pink (Aug)	2ft	Oct–Feb
LESS EXPOSED GARDENS				
Broom (cytisus varieties)	Evergreen	Various (July)	18in	July
Deutzia longifolia 'Veitchii'	Pale green, deciduous	White (June)	18in	July
Dogwood (*Cornus alba* 'Elegantissima')	Green to red, deciduous	White berries (July)	15–18in	Apr
Escallonia macrantha	Evergreen	Red (June)	1½–2ft	June
Hebe 'Autumn Glory'	Evergreen	Violet-blue (July)	18in	Apr
Ribes sanguineum 'Pulborough Scarlet'	Green, deciduous	Red (Mar)	12–15in	May
SHELTERED GARDENS				
Fuchsia magellanica	Green, deciduous	Purple (July)	12in	Oct–Mar
Hydrangea macrophylla	Green, deciduous	Pink or blue (July–Sept)		None needed
Lilac (*Syringa vulgaris*)	Green, deciduous	White or purple (June–Sept)	6ft	Oct–Jan
Spiraea x *arguta*	Green, deciduous	White (May)	15–24in	Immediately after flowering

Chamaecyparis lawsoniana 'Green Hedger', 5-8ft, rich green.
Ligustrum lucidum, 10-18ft, dark green.
Prunus laurocerasus, 15-20ft, mid-green.
Thuja plicata 'Atrovirens', 8ft, bright green.

All of these hedging plants need to be spaced 2ft apart.

Roses for rows

I want a rose hedge about 4-5ft high. Which variety should I choose?

There is a wide choice. Most of the more vigorous varieties – in particular those listed in the chart on the right – can be used for hedges. For a 4ft hedge you can choose between large-flowered and cluster-flowered hybrids, modern shrubs, hybrid perpetuals, hybrid musks and some species which have attractive rose hips.

If you want a hedge that will flower through the whole season, choose the large-flowered or cluster-flowered hybrids.

Whichever type you pick, space the roses 2ft apart, taking care that the bud joint is 1in above the surface. After planting, prune back to 6in above ground level.

Feed regularly in spring with a proprietary rose fertiliser and spray during the spring and summer with an all-purpose insecticide and fungicide. From the first year of growth, prune with secateurs in autumn and early spring to maintain the hedge's shape and size.

PICK OF THE HEDGING ROSES

The Royal National Rose Society lists in order of merit the following roses for a hedge. The column headed 'Type' uses a number of abbreviations. MSR = Modern shrub recurrent. HMsk = Hybrid musk. LF = Large-flowered (Hybrid tea). CF = Cluster-flowered (Floribunda).

Name	Height	Type	Flowers
'Queen Elizabeth'	5–6ft	MSR (CF)	Clear pink
'Fred Loads'	6ft	MSR (CF)	Light orange-vermilion
'Chinatown'	5ft	MSR (CF)	Bright yellow
'Scabrosa'	6ft	MSR	Mauve-red
'Roseraie de L'Hay	6ft	MSR	Purple
'Alexander'	4ft plus	LF	Vermilion
'Penelope'	5ft	MSR (HMsk)	Shell-pink fading to white
'Iceberg'	4ft plus	CF	White
'Anne Harkness'	4ft plus	CF	Saffron-yellow
'Dorothy Wheatcroft'	5ft	MSR (CF)	Bright orange-red

The fine art of topiary

I'd like to try my hand at topiary. How do I start?

Topiary, the art of training trees, bushes or shrubs in various shapes, is living sculpture. It's not necessarily the exclusive field of the professional, for it can be done by amateurs with a good eye and lots of patience. One of the best plants to train is common yew (*Taxus baccata*), but many good shapes have been achieved with privet and box. Buy a good strong plant about 3ft high between October and April and plant it firmly. As the plant becomes established, examine the shape from all angles, then decide what shape you want to create from it. The leading growths are the most important, because their strength and direction will help you to produce your desired shape.

Start encouraging branches to form a framework from the outset. You may find that the bush has three or four vigorous leaders plus two or three good branches. Out of this you might want to form, say, a peacock. One branch can be the head and neck and the other one or two the tail.

To form the neck, bend the nearest leader in the same direction as the branch you've chosen for the head and wind round it some stout wire so that the ends of the leader and the branch are brought firmly together.

To form the tail, make a wire framework the same shape as a peacock's fantail. Wire the branch you've chosen for the tail to the middle of the frame and fix one leader on each side of it. Clip the base to shape a round-topped column. To form the body, bend more wire into shape as if you were wrapping a live peacock, fitting it around the centre of the plant as you go. Push some small branches into the middle and tease smaller growths out through the wire.

To form the head and crest, shape the framework and wire to the neck, pushing some small branches inside and pulling other growth out through the wire.

Once the shape and form are set, the wire can be removed, but this is not essential because the growth will in time cover it completely.

Be careful, however, that the wire does not cut into the bark and strangle the branches, or foul the shears or trimmer.

The ends of the wire should always be free so that as the branches grow the wire expands with them. Trim the bird to shape every late summer and tidy up loose ends through the year.

Follow a similar method of wiring a framework for whatever shape you decide on.

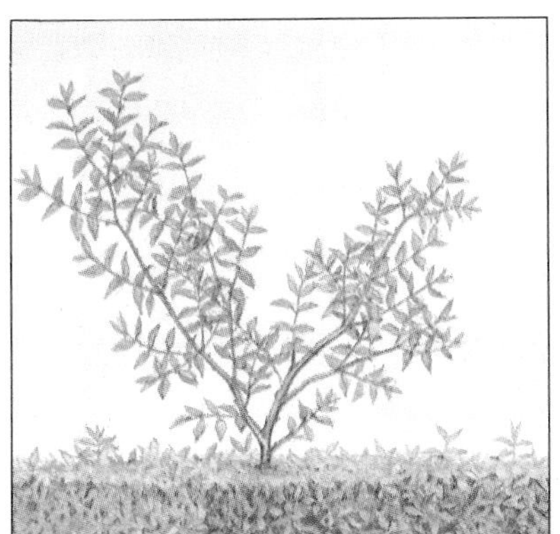

CHOOSING THE SHAPE *Let the growth of the bush guide your choice of shape. Here, the three branches could form a peacock.*

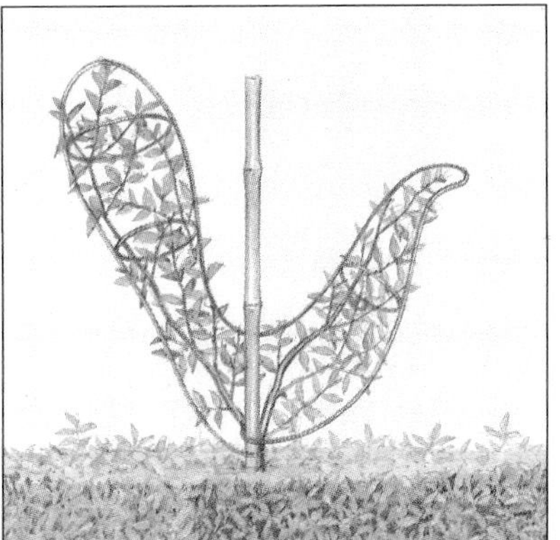

WIRING IT IN *Use fairly stiff wire to mark the main lines of the bird. Hold the framework together with thinner wire.*

LIVING SCULPTURE *Train new growth inside the wire frame, and trim off excess shoots as the bush grows, to complete the bird.*

HERBACEOUS BORDER PLANTS

What is it?

Many gardening books talk of the herbaceous border as if everyone had one. I am not sure if I have . . . how do you define it?

The word 'herbaceous' refers to plants that are herb-like in having fleshy stems, rather than the woody tissue of trees and shrubs.

The true herbaceous border is a long, narrow border backed by a wall or a clipped hedge and filled with a mix of mostly hardy perennials, rising from edging plants at the front to soaring 8ft giants at the back. It is also, largely, a thing of the past.

It belonged to the Victorian age of space, time and elegance – even in the garden. It used to be one feature of a large garden: a border edged by a long, unswerving path down which crinolined ladies could walk at their leisure to admire the rising display of colour and perfume, and which could be left to die back to bare earth in the winter, and to burst afresh from the soil each spring.

The modern gardener has virtually abandoned the pure herbaceous border, because few gardens can afford to be that profligate with their land. The traditional Victorian favourites today find their way into the more general mixed border, climbing up each summer among evergreen and deciduous shrubs, flowering bulbs and bedded-out annuals.

Some gardeners keep a small stretch of the mixed border for a purely herbaceous show, and in variety and colour it can be well worthwhile, with violets hugging the path, red and orange poppies and white daisies behind, and the whole tapestry topped by statuesque delphiniums.

Planning the border

I have a large rear garden with a long, straight stretch which would make an ideal herbaceous border. How do I go about making one?

You must plan carefully, or the effect will be lost. Draw a plan of your border – including where the sun falls at different times of the day – and plot on it where each set of perennials will go. Note on the plan the colour of each group of plants, its flowering time – and its height. The crucial rule is: small to the front; tall to the back.

The herbaceous border needs to reach backwards and upwards from the path or lawn edge where it begins. Some of the great Victorian herbaceous borders were very long and up to 10ft wide. Yours will probably be smaller and it need not follow the rigid straight lines of the past. Let it follow any curve in the lawn; this will add interest.

Choose your own plants so that the colours of those which bloom at the same time will harmonise. Don't plan for them all to burst into flower together, though. The idea is to have an everchanging, unfolding interest as the colour focus shifts throughout the summer.

Cutting back

I am told that in autumn all plants in the herbaceous border should be cut back. Can this be true, and if so, why?

Most of them should be, but there are exceptions. Cutting back is necessary to stop dead top growth falling to the ground and rotting on the soil, creating the perfect breeding ground for pests and diseases. It also gives you a chance to aerate the soil with a hoe or fork and to clean away weeds and debris.

Start once autumn frosts have brought an end to the border's growth and flowering. Choose a day when there is no frost, but the ground is damp. Use secateurs, shears or loppers to cut most plants down to about 4in from the soil.

Start at the back and, as you work forwards, fork over the top 2in of soil, taking care not to disturb the roots of the plants.

Now the exceptions. Do not cut back any plantain lilies (hostas) you have, or bergenias, or plants grown for their winter flowers, such as hellebores – the plants better known as Christmas and Lenten roses. Leave alone, too, the little border plants such as violas and primulas.

In colder parts of the country, top growth can be left on some of the more tender plants. This will protect the crowns from the worst of the winter weather, but you will need to cut the dead stems away before growth starts again in spring.

Sulky peony

My peonies were taking up too much room, so a couple of years ago I moved them. They haven't flowered since. Should I have moved them?

No, never move peonies unless there is no alternative or you want to get rid of them. They are sulky characters and, once they are established, they resent being disturbed. They settle their tubers in a comfortable position, put down their roots, and that is where they like to stay.

How long yours will take to get over the upheaval is pure guesswork. All you can do is pamper them, and wait. Hoe some bone meal, about 4oz to the square yard – equivalent to two good handfuls – into the top 4in of soil, avoiding the roots. Then give the plants a spring mulch of well-rotted manure or compost. In dry spells water them well. They may forgive you and flower again.

If, in future, you *must* move peonies, do it in early autumn in about September – not in spring – and plant them with the tops of their crowns no more than 1in deep.

Daisy mildew

My michaelmas daisies never seem to make a decent show and they're forever getting mildew. What can I do?

Before the plants flower, spray them with a systemic fungicidal solution containing benomyl, carbendazim or thiophanate-methyl. Mildew causes browning and withering of the plant and works upwards. It is encouraged by dry weather and lack of sunshine. Badly affected plants should be dug up and burnt.

Treat them in time, and your michaelmas daisies (*Aster novi-belgii*) will give you a mass of blooms of blue, pink, white and mauve, with bright yellow eyes. In a good season they will flower right through from July to November.

Perfumed border

Which plants should I choose to create a traditional perfumed country-style border?

Add some scented roses, such as 'Souvenir du Docteur Jamain' (dark red), 'Mme Hardy' (white) and 'Mme Isaac Pereire' (deep pink), some culinary herbs such as thyme or sage, and a few annuals such as tobacco plants (*Nicotiana alata*), night-scented stock (*Matthiola bicornis*) and mignonette (*Reseda odorata*), to your herbaceous border and you can get all the fragrance and mixed colour of an old-fashioned nosegay.

Choose lily of the valley (*Convallaria majalis*) for a show of white, bell-shaped, highly scented flowers in April and May. This is a low-growing perennial that likes shady spots.

Carnations and pinks will give you scent and white, pink, red, salmon and cream colours in summer. The old-fashioned pinks (varieties of *Dianthus plumarius*) are the true cottage garden pinks, and will add to the pastoral feel of your border.

The spikes of flag irises – part of every true country garden – will give you every colour except true red in June and July, and they have a subtle but fine scent.

The old-fashioned sweet violets (*Viola odorata*) won't give you the dramatic blooms you get from their relatives the pansies, but they do make an excellent and beautifully scented border plant: 4-6in high with purple, pink and white flowers about 1in across.

For a final touch, add sweet peas (*Lathyrus odoratus*) and verbena (*Verbena* x *hybrida*). Both are annuals. The sweet peas are hardy and can be sown outdoors in autumn for flowering next summer. Verbena are not so tough and need to be raised under glass from seed in spring. Both varieties will give you most colours except yellow, and both smell delightful (for more ideas on traditional borders, see *Cottage gardens*, page 100).

Blue hydrangeas

What must I do to make my pink hydrangeas flower blue, and how should I look after them in winter?

You will probably have to replant them. It is the acid in the soil that makes hydrangeas flower blue. So what you get are pink flowers on an alkaline soil, blue on acid – the opposite of what happens when a chemist tests for acid with litmus paper. If your soil is at all chalky, it is alkaline and you are probably wasting your time trying to change the colour.

Even the true blue varieties such as 'Altona' or 'Blue Prince' will edge towards pink on a chalky base, so you will end up with a dirty mauve bloom, neither one thing nor the other. On an acid soil, such as peaty ground, the more common pink varieties will shade towards purple.

To get the proper blue effect, dig up your plants in spring and fork plenty of peat into the surrounding soil. Replant and lay a thick, peat mulch on the surface of the soil beneath the branches.

The peat will counteract the alkalinity of the soil. To give the plants an even better chance of success, add a blueing agent containing aluminium sulphate every 7-14 days during the flowering period.

There is not a lot you need to do to look after hydrangeas in winter. When you first plant them, keep them out of positions where early morning sun after a sharp frost can cause a rapid thaw that will damage shoots. The shrubs need little pruning except to remove dead flower heads. Do this pruning in late February or March. That way the old, dead blooms will help to shelter the following summer's flowering buds from winter frosts. At the same time as you prune, take out any very old, weak or damaged branches by cutting them off at the base.

If a hydrangea has been badly hit by a severe winter, cut back to vigorous buds. If no buds appear, the plant is dead.

Spring colour

I have plenty of rock plants flowering in May and June, but few herbaceous plants. Can you recommend some colourful varieties for this period?

Yes. Spurge, cornflower, Shasta daisies and delphiniums will all brighten this late spring and early summer time. Here are some varieties worth considering:

Bugle (*Ajuga reptans*) produces small blue flowers, but gives most colour from its leaves. It spreads rapidly and needs to be kept under control. *A. r.* 'Burgundy Glow' has wine-red edges to its young leaves. This is a low-spreading plant, 4-6in high, ideal for a moist, shady border.

Perennial cornflower or knapweed (*Centaurea dealbata*) has thistle-like blooms in early summer and a second flush of colour in autumn. Choose *C. d.* 'John Coutts', pink with yellow centres, or *C. d.* 'Steenbergii', crimson with white. This is not the true blue cornflower (*Centaurea cyanus*) which is a hardy annual.

The Shasta daisy (*Chrysanthemum maximum*) has white, daisy-like blooms, up to 4in across, each with a bright yellow eye. You can choose forms with single, double or semi-double blooms.

Delphiniums come in white, cream, pink, mauve and purple varieties as well as the popular blue. They need careful growing. Plant them in early spring in a fertile and well-drained soil, and protect them from slugs with pellets, and from powdery mildew with a spray of benomyl or thiophanate-methyl every two or three weeks. Support them with canes, and never let the soil around the roots dry out.

Spurge (*Euphorbia polychroma*) has sulphur-yellow flowers in April and May. It grows to about 18in tall and likes full sun.

Crane's-bill will form a mound about 18in high, spreading out as far as 4ft and throwing up masses of open blue flowers from May until August. *Geranium* 'Johnson's Blue', which is hardy, is the most popular variety. Don't confuse these tough perennials with the more tender pelargoniums so commonly called bedding geraniums. The hardy crane's-bill geraniums will bloom happily for years in a well-drained soil.

Winter colour

As flowering ends and I start cutting back my perennials the border gets more and more bare. Is there anything I can do to brighten it in winter?

Yes, there is. Plant out heathers, the large-leaved bergenias, Christmas roses, snowdrops and crocuses and some early-flowering polyanthus. You won't get a lot of height, because these are all low-lying plants, but you will get colour – almost the whole range except red.

Bergenias, or elephants' ears as they are often known, will give an excellent show from January, and their bright green leathery leaves, up to 14in across, give almost year-round cover and help to stifle weeds. Try *Bergenia crassifolia*, one of the best winter flowerers, which throws up pale, pink, bell-shaped blooms on 12in stalks.

Frost and wind can spoil the Christmas and Lenten roses (hellebores), but given some protection they will carry white, cream-green, pink or purple flowers, some spotted, for weeks. They can be cut for indoors, too.

Heathers offer a vast range of height, spread and colour (see *Heathers*, page 178). Polyanthus primroses planted out in autumn can reach 12in in height and flower in purple, pink, crimson, red, yellow and cream from late winter onwards.

All these plants, along with any early crocuses you have, need guarding from birds, which are attracted by the colours and will often peck off the flower heads. Tie threads of black cotton across the beds over the flowers to keep the birds off.

Don't let the plants dry out after they have finished blooming, or you will weaken them, damaging their ability to produce a good display next year.

Spreading polyanthus

Should polyanthus be divided each year?

No. You can divide them up once, but after a second year the plants gradually lose vigour and flowering drops off. The best results are from seed sown afresh each year for flowering the following spring. In other words, treat the flowers as what they really are – biennials. Some people do divide polyanthus up year after year, but what they save in time and money they lose in display.

To divide, lift the plants after flowering, and ease the roots and leaves apart with your fingers. Plant them in a moist and shady spot where they can stay until autumn, then lift them again and plant them where they are to flower in spring.

To grow them from seed, sow in a greenhouse in January-March, or April-May if you are using a cold frame. Once the seedlings are large enough to handle, prick them out into trays. When they are 4in high, plant them in a cool, moist nursery bed. Plant them out in September or October for flowering the following spring.

Dividing plants

When should I divide my herbaceous plants – in autumn or spring?

Spring is the best time. The plants are starting to stir and the ground is getting warmer. These are the right conditions to ensure that your new plants will get off to a good start.

Don't split plants up every year, though. Wait until they have formed large clumps, or until they show any hint of a decline in vigour which can lead to poor flowering. Division will give the plant a new lease of life, keeping it young and vigorous – and, incidentally, multiplying your stock.

Some division can be done in autumn if, for example, you are replanning a border during winter. But it's a more risky business. The soil then is wet and cooling down. As a result, the divided plants may not settle and could suffer from rotting.

HERBS

Herbs that are tops in sinks

I used to have two old sinks in which I grew parsley and mint. They seemed to go on year after year with little attention. Are there any other herbs that I can grow this way?

Provided that they are given a free-draining compost, an open sunny position and are not allowed to go short of water, there are many herbs that would grow under these conditions. All the decorative and culinary thymes, for instance, will do well – the lemon-scented and pine-scented varieties as well as the golden foliage kinds. Other mints would respond to such conditions if replanted every couple of years: the apple mint and pineapple mint for instance, as well as ginger mint and the eau-de-cologne mint. Hyssop would adapt well to sink culture; so, too, would sage and pot marjoram.

Parsley is also well-suited to this situation in that, though a biennial, it will re-seed itself in the ground surrounding the original plant. The most important factor in growing herbs in a container such as a sink is to ensure that there is adequate drainage. This is rarely a problem in summer, but herbs dislike the sogginess of winter, and will die if the container becomes waterlogged. So leave the plug out of the sink and cover the plughole with a layer of loose crocks to prevent it being blocked by soil.

In summer, there is a contrary problem. Then, the small volume of soil in the sink may quickly dry out; the remedy is to water evenly every day or so in dry weather.

FIVE WAYS TO PRESERVE HERBS

1 Divide the herbs into the amounts required for a single recipe, place them in polythene bags and seal. Small recipe-sized collections can also be made; a mixture of thyme, rosemary, chives and tarragon, for example, is good with chicken. Put the bags into a plastic box, and the box into the freezer. Keep the various herbs well apart to ensure that their aromas do not pervade each other.

2 Pick the leaves, chop them if necessary, put them in water in an ice-cube tray and freeze. Use the cubes in cooking as needed.

3 Pick the sprigs early on a dry day when the plant is coming into flower. Dry them on newspaper in the airing cupboard or in the plate-warming drawer of the cooker. Exclude light with more newspaper. Dry the sprigs slowly over a period of several days, until they are brittle to the touch. Then hang them in bunches in a cool, dry place. Herbs left on the stalk stay fragrant longer.

4 For mint sauce in winter, chop the leaves, put them in a jar and cover with golden syrup. Take out spoonfuls of the mixture as required and mix with vinegar to taste. Or reverse the process: cover the mint with vinegar for storage, and mix it later with syrup or sugar.

5 For horseradish sauce in winter, grate the horseradish (an agonising, tearful business, far worse than peeling the strongest onion), put it in a jar and cover it with vinegar. Extract spoonfuls as required and mix with cream.

Pleasurable plants

Are herbs easy to grow?

It depends on what you mean by herbs. A few have special requirements, but the ones most widely used have been grown in this country for centuries, and are easy to raise in the garden provided you meet their straightforward needs.

They like to be in a sheltered sunny spot, in well-drained ground. And they will thrive in most soils except heavy clay.

Whether you decide to grow them in pots, in a separate bed, or in between your other flowers, fruit or vegetables is up to you.

For more details, see also the sections on individual herbs, such as *Basil*, *Chives*, *Mint*, *Parsley* and *Sage*. For planting details, see *Plants at a glance*, page 378.

Preparing the site

I would like to make a small herb bed. What should I do first?

Decide on the best place for herbs in your particular garden – and this doesn't automatically mean near the kitchen. Just keep the bed small, or grow your herbs round the edges of flower or vegetable beds. The point is that you will be making frequent harvestings, and should be able to do so without treading on other plants.

Before you do any planting out, prepare the soil, preferably in early autumn. Cover the ground with a 3in layer of well-rotted compost or manure and dig it in. In the following spring, fork the bed over once more a couple of weeks before planting. Don't bother about fertiliser; most herbs grow better if they are left slightly short of nutrients.

Growing from seed

Is it going to be expensive to stock a herb bed?

Not at all, since most herbs can be grown from seed. Annual species such as dill, coriander and chervil must be sown fresh each spring; and even perennial species such as chives, sage and thyme can be raised from seed. As soon as any frost danger is over, sow the seeds thinly, and cover them with a light coating of soil. Many herb seedlings hate being moved, so sow the seeds where you want the plants to grow. When the seedlings are 2-3in high you can thin them out to give the best plants growing space.

Water the seedlings in dry weather, using a fine rose on your watering can, and keep the bed weeded.

Perennial herbs may also be bought as young plants, which saves you a year or so of waiting before you begin to use them. Plant them out in summer in a sheltered site and water them each evening until they are established.

For oregano, read marjoram

Will you settle an argument, please? Are oregano and marjoram the same thing?

Yes. Oregano gets its name from the Latin name for marjoram, although there are several different kinds. The herb popularly sold by supermarkets as oregano is wild mar-

HOW TO MAKE ROSEMARY JELLY

Rosemary jelly goes marvellously with any lamb dish. This recipe makes 2-3lb of jelly.

4lb cooking apples
Water to cover
$\frac{1}{4}$ pint malt vinegar
8-10 sprigs of rosemary
About 2lb sugar

Wash and quarter the apples, and bruise six of the rosemary sprigs slightly with a rolling pin. Put apples, bruised sprigs, water and vinegar in a large saucepan or preserving pan and bring them slowly to the boil.

Simmer for an hour, stirring occasionally to break up the apples. Remove from heat and strain the mixture through a jelly bag or several layers of muslin for at least 4 hours, catching the juice in a bowl. Don't squeeze the bag or you will make the resulting jelly cloudy. Discard the bag's contents after straining.

Measure the amount of juice and add 1lb of sugar (warm it in a low oven first to make it dissolve more quickly) for every pint of juice. Boil the mixture briskly for about 10 minutes until it reaches the 'setting point' – when a dollop spooned onto a cold saucer forms a skin which wrinkles when pushed with a finger. Then remove it from the heat and let it stand for 5-10 minutes without stirring. Pour it into clean, dry jars – adding a single fresh sprig to each jar for decoration – cover and seal.

joram, *Origanum vulgare*, a rather lax and untidy plant, but one that produces highly flavoured foliage.

Then there is pot marjoram, *O. onites*, a neat and compact plant that is perfect for growing in a pot or window box, and finally the very aromatic sweet marjoram, *O. majorana*, which is the herb commonly sold as marjoram. All are used in much the same way and all are easy to grow (for details, see *Marjoram* in *Plants at a glance*, page 414).

Propagation of all the species is by seed, or by taking cuttings of young shoots.

Space invaders

Herbs are invasive and my garden is small. Is there any way I could grow a useful selection for the kitchen without them taking over the ground entirely?

It's true that herbs tend to be exuberant, which is one of the reasons why in the grander and older herb gardens, groups of plants are assembled in neat rectangles and divided from one another by brick or grass paths and by low hedges, usually of box. This prevents the plants from overwhelming one another, and at the same time gives the cook easy access to the herbs.

Such an arrangement would be impractical in a small garden, but you might adapt the idea a little.

A most attractive way of doing so is to obtain an old cartwheel, lie it on the ground and dig out a circular bed to fit it. Push it firmly into the soil and insert slates on edge down into the ground along the line of the spokes, so that each segment becomes a separate box (see the picture on the right).

Another adaptation would be to make a chequerboard out of, say, 12in by 12in paving stones, the black squares being beds for different herbs. Here, too, you should surround the beds with slates on edge.

A scented lawn

Is it worth planting herbs in grass to make a fragrant area of lawn?

The idea of re-creating an Elizabethan flowery mead is very pleasant, but rather impractical unless you have a lot of time. Considering that a true mead should contain harebells, daisies, tansy, columbines and a host of other flowers and herbs, it takes a good deal of management if it's going to look tidy after midsummer.

A better way, perhaps, to make a scented lawn would be to use chamomile. This makes a solid green sweetly scented turf, but it takes two or three years to become established and durable. During its development, you'll have to remove by hand all the weeds that appear; you can't use selective weedkillers on chamomile in the same way that you can on grass. The weeding and maintenance work will get

HARVESTING HERBS

Herb	Which part to use	When to use it fresh	When to cut it for preserving
Basil	Leaves	July–Sept	Just before flowering
Bay	Leaves	All year round	All year round
Borage	Young leaves and flowers	All summer	Whenever there are suitable young shoots
Chervil	Leaves	Summer	Summer, before flowering
Chives	Leaves	May–Sept	When leaves have reached full size
Dill	Leaves and seeds	All summer from successional sowings	Just before flowering for foliage. Gather seedheads just before they ripen
Fennel	Leaves and seeds	All summer	July–Oct
Horseradish	Roots	Nine months after planting	Nine months after planting
Hyssop	Flowers and shoots	When flowering starts	As flowers appear
Lemon balm	Leaves	June–Sept	June–Sept
Lovage	Leaves, stalks and seeds	All summer	May–Sept
Marjoram	Leaves and flowers	July–Sept	July–Sept
Mint	Leaves	June–Oct	Just before flowering
Parsley	Leaves	All summer	June–July
Rosemary	Leaves	All year round	June–Aug
Sage	Leaves	June–Oct	Just before flowering
Salad burnet	Leaves	All summer	When flower shoots appear
Savory (summer)	Leaves and flowers	July–Oct	When flowering
Savory (winter)	Leaves	Mar–May	Mar–May as young shoots emerge
Sorrel	Leaves and shoots	May–Aug	Before flowering
Tarragon	Leaves	June–Sept	June–Sept
Thyme	Leaves and flowers	June–Sept	Before and at flowering time

IN THE ROUND *A cartwheel with slates set on edge beneath the spokes makes an attractive bed.*

easier once the chamomile is established, but it will always be time-consuming. If you still think a chamomile lawn is a good idea, buy the vigorous, non-flowering variety called 'Treneague', rather than raising the ordinary variety from seed. Flowering chamomile does not yield a very satisfactory sward.

Cut and dry

Which herbs can I dry to use in winter and how do I go about it?

Thyme, marjoram, sage, rosemary, mint and bay leaves are all good candidates for preserving.

The leaves reach their aromatic peak when the flowers are just in bud but before the flowers open, so this is the best stage of growth at which to harvest. Pick them on a dry day, preferably in the early morning when the sun is not too hot and the oil content, which gives the herbs their flavour, is at its best. Gather only as much as you can dry at one time. Any delay in drying after cutting lessens the strength of the oils. Cut annual herbs to within a few inches of the ground when you harvest, but don't cut more than one-third off the stem of a perennial herb, to allow for regrowth. Moreover, do not harvest perennial herbs after September because the new growth triggered by the cutting will probably be too tender to survive the winter. For details on how to treat the plants after cutting, see *Five ways to preserve herbs*, page 194.

Seeds for cooking

Which seeds can I collect to store and use in cooking?

Those of dill, fennel, lovage and coriander are worth gathering at the end of the flowering season. Dill and fennel seeds are widely used in pickles, coriander in bread and curries, lovage in soups, bread, biscuits and cakes. As soon as the flower heads show signs of becoming brown, make daily inspections of them. Gently turn the flower heads upside down and shake them over an open bag. The seeds will fall out when they are dry.

Flavour at your fingertips

Can I grow herbs on my kitchen windowsill?

Yes, so long as you don't mind replacing them fairly regularly for they won't survive there for very long. All herbs make pretty and aromatic house plants, but unfortunately the kitchen is the site that suits them least. Herbs like neither the sudden changes in room temperature caused by cooking, nor the steamy atmosphere.

Within these limitations, the best ones to try are thyme, chives, mint, parsley, marjoram and basil.

HOLLY

Cutting a holly down to size

My two holly bushes are more than 10ft tall and growing far too big for comfort. Can I cut them down to size?

With difficulty and with care. Cut them back too harshly and they will forever appear just what they are; truncated. On the other hand, there is no entirely satisfactory way of bringing an overgrown holly back into line. Whatever you do – cut it back a foot or so a year, or chop it back almost to ground level – it's not going to look its best again for several years.

If you do decide to prune your bushes back, tackle the job in late March or early April, and wear thick clothes and sturdy but pliable gloves. Avoid the 'armoured' gloves which have metal staples stamped into them, however; they make it difficult to handle shears or saws.

The ideal way to keep a holly within bounds is to begin the shaping early, when the plant is about seven years old and 3ft high. If you want to try topiary on a holly, avoid planting any of the large-leaved varieties. They're extremely difficult to prune with secateurs, and pruning them with shears leaves the foliage looking mutilated.

Go instead for a small-leaved type such as the hedgehog holly, *Ilex aquifolium* 'Ferox'. Wear gloves when you tackle it, though. It's extremely prickly.

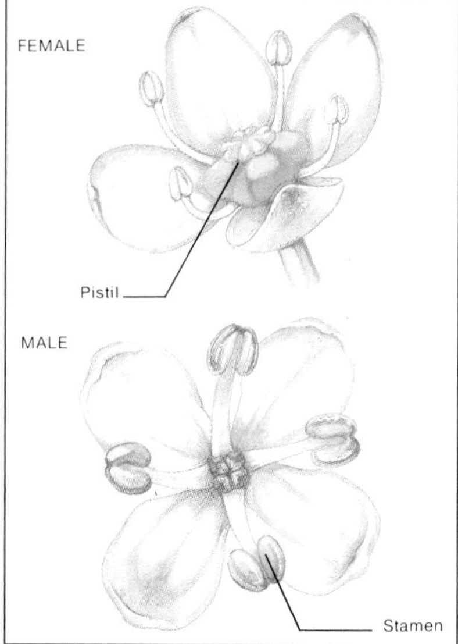

TELLING THEM APART *Male holly flowers have four large stamens; the pistil is more prominent on the berry-bearing females.*

Company for a holly

How can I persuade my 20-year-old holly tree to produce berries?

The tree must be lonely – it needs a mate. Almost all varieties of the common holly, *Ilex aquifolium*, and the larger-leaved *I.* x *altaclerensis* have male and female flowers on separate plants. Pollen from one must pass to the other before berries will develop.

To find out the sex of a tree, examine a flower to see if it has male stamens or female styles. Nurseries and garden centres often list individual named varieties as either male or female.

Many of the male varieties have extremely attractive foliage – the unexpectedly named 'Silver Queen', for instance. But only the female varieties have berries. The chart below lists some of the most attractive and popular forms.

PICK OF THE GARDEN HOLLIES

Name	Description	Sex
VARIETIES OF *ILEX* x *ALTACLERENSIS*		
'Camelliifolia'	Large, spineless camellia-like leaves	Female
'Golden King'	Bright yellow leaf edges	Female
'Mundyi'	Large spiny leaves	Male
'Silver Sentinel'	Mottled leaves with creamy edges	Female
VARIETIES OF *ILEX AQUIFOLIUM*		
'Argentea Pendula'	White-edged leaves; weeping	Female
'Ferox' (hedgehog holly)	Small leaves with spines on surface	Male
'Golden Queen'	Broad yellow edge to leaves	Male
'J.C. van Tol'	Large, almost spineless leaves	Female
'Ovata Aurea'	Thick leaves with gold edges	Male
'Pyramidalis'	Conical shape, bright green leaves	Female
'Silver Queen'	Mottled leaves with cream-white edges	Male

HYACINTHS

Standard height

Florists' hyacinths in bowls always seem to grow to the same height. Why won't mine?

There is no magic in it . . . just selection. Commercial growers bring on scores of bulbs, and when it is time to pot them up into bowls they simply choose plants of the same height.

You can try it, too, if you are potting up more than just the odd bowl of three. Plant the bulbs in deep trays in September and stand them outside, covered with peat and straw. After about ten weeks, as the shoots push through the compost, take them into the greenhouse for forcing.

Once the buds show their first hint of colour, lift the bulbs and group them in bowls. Use a sharp knife to dig out each bulb from the tray, cutting around the roots in a cube shape. This will do no harm to the plant, and will make potting up easy.

If you are planting only a few bulbs, choose the same variety. This will give you a better chance of growing plants of the same size.

Bending stems

I keep my hyacinths in full sunlight and turn them regularly, but they still bend at an angle as the flowers develop. How can I stop them?

Cut down on feed and turn off the heat. Either one could be causing the problem.

The weaker daylight of winter will not allow hyacinths to take more than a very gentle heat. Too much warmth will make the plants longer and softer, and so they bend. You want stocky, firm plants. Kept in a greenhouse which is heated just enough to keep it free of frost – but no more – they will take a week or two longer to come into flower, but they will stay upright. Feeding might also be the root of your problem, because a too-rich compost turns out hyacinths with elongated and twisted stems. Even a standard potting compost can have this effect.

Put your plants into a bulb fibre that has virtually no nutrients in it. Then let the bulb do the work. Don't feed it until after flowering is over. At that stage, extra nutrients will help the foliage, which is providing the bulb with a store of strength that will bring on more blooms next year.

Encouraging bulbs

I am told that the best way to propagate hyacinths is to slit the base of the bulb. How is this done?

Take a mature bulb in September-October and make a cross in the base with a sharp knife, cutting out two V-shaped trenches, each about $\frac{1}{4}$in across and $\frac{1}{8}$in deep. Try not to cut beyond the thick baseplate of the bulb into the softer tissue above because you risk creating openings for fungal diseases. Plant the cut bulb in a good potting compost and grow it outside just as you would normally. Do not, however, try to use it for forcing indoors. By the time the leaves die down, in about June, numerous tiny bulbils will have developed along the cuts. Lift the bulb, separate the bulbils, and plant them out separately in seed trays. They will take two to four years to reach flowering size.

Christmas bulbs

I had some hyacinths in pots over Christmas, and I want to put them out in the garden. How should I do this?

Don't plant out until after all danger of frost has passed, and in the meantime keep up the watering and feeding of the bulbs. Although the flowers will have finished, the foliage will still remain, and it's the foliage that will be generating energy for next year's flowers. Water often enough to keep the compost damp, and feed every ten days or so with a standard liquid house plant fertiliser. Keep both up until the foliage withers and dies down. Even after you plant the bulbs outside, you'll need to go on watering them if the weather is dry.

All indoor, Christmas-flowering hyacinths have been forced. They have used up a lot of energy and this needs replacing. The foliage will do the job if you treat it with care, but it will be too soft to cope with frost.

Plant the bulbs in rich soil, with plenty of good organic matter worked in. But don't expect too much from the bulbs in their first spring outdoors.

Hyacinths that have been forced often have open and unbalanced spikes instead of neat flower heads in their first year outdoors. And if the bulbs did not put up a good show in their bowls, then it is not really worth transplanting them at all.

The timing of the colours

My white hyacinths always flower later than the other varieties. Is this something to do with their colour?

No. It's an accident of gardening fashion. There's nothing special about the colour of white hyacinths – or white varieties of any other flower – which would make them flower later or earlier than any other variety.

The reason your hyacinths flower later is probably that you're growing 'L'Innocence', which is the most popular white variety. It flowers a week or two later than the common pink and blue varieties, but not later than all the pink and blue varieties. The delay is just a feature of the variety – it has nothing to do with its colour.

HYDROPONIC GARDENING

Caring for a house plant

What is the best way to look after a hydroponically grown house plant?

It should be very easy. Hydroponically grown house plants are much simpler to look after than ordinary ones.

Most hydroponically grown house plants are grown in special double containers, sometimes known as hydropots. The plant itself grows in the inner container, which is filled with aggregate – particles of any inert, sterile material. The plant's roots develop among the aggregate, which keeps the plant upright. Specially made clay granules – rather like lightweight gravel – are most widely used as aggregate, but perlite, vermiculite and clean gravel can also be used.

The base of the outer container forms a reservoir for the nutrient solution. This seeps through holes into the inner container where it is absorbed by the plant's roots.

To look after the plant, all you have to do is to make sure it has enough nutrient solution. The level of solution in the container is usually indicated by a water gauge. Keep the level between the maximum and minimum marks on the gauge, adding clean, fresh, lukewarm water when necessary. There is usually a special inlet for adding the water. Don't keep the level permanently topped up to maximum. It is better to allow it to fall almost to the minimum mark before adding more – this lets more air come into contact with the roots and so encourages them to develop healthily.

Occasionally (it can be as little as once a year) you will have to add more fertiliser. It is best to use one of the specially formulated hydroculture fertilisers which provide essential trace elements that ordinary fertilisers normally don't.

The instructions with your pot plant should recommend which brand to use; different brands are applied in different ways.

In all other respects the plant should be treated just as if it were growing in compost.

It has the same requirements of light and temperature.

Many house plants are killed either by too much watering or by too little. One of the advantages of growing them hydroponically is that it is very difficult to get the watering wrong. It is also a much cleaner way of growing plants indoors.

Growing in water

I've been given a pot plant which the label tells me is 'hydroponically grown'. What exactly does this mean?

'Hydroponically grown' means that the plant has been grown, not in soil or compost like most plants, but with its roots suspended in water with essential plant foods dissolved in it. All a plant needs to grow is light, air, water and nutrients such as nitrogen, phosphorus and potassium. Plants grown in the normal way receive water, air and nutrients from the soil – which also provides a support system to keep them upright. But soil is by no means essential. So long as some kind of support is provided, the nutrients can equally well be fed to the plants in water which also contains dissolved oxygen. This is the principle behind the hydroponic cultivation of plants, or 'hydroculture'.

One advantage of hydroculture is that you can control very precisely the amount of nutrients fed to the plants. With soil you never know exactly how much of each particular nutrient it contains, and sometimes it is deficient in certain important trace elements such as magnesium. Another advantage of hydroculture is that the risk of disease is smaller. Many plant diseases are carried by organisms in the soil – a nutrient solution can be kept sterile.

Hydroculture is most commonly used by amateurs as a way of growing house plants. But it is also used commercially to grow, for example, tomatoes and lettuces and can be used in an ordinary garden greenhouse to grow vegetables such as aubergines, cucumbers and sweet peppers as well (see *Tomatoes in a trough*, below).

Tomatoes in a trough

Growing greenhouse crops, such as tomatoes, hydroponically sounds interesting. Will it save me time and effort, or is it just a novelty?

It's unlikely to save you time or effort initially, although in the long term it can be worthwhile. If you really are interested in the idea of growing tomatoes and other greenhouse crops without soil, it is perfectly possible.

The system of hydroculture generally used in greenhouses is different from that used for house plants. You will need to buy a special hydroculture trough from a garden centre. Most troughs are long and narrow. The bottom is filled with nutrient solution which may be circulated round it by a pump, or which may seep along capillary matting. The solution is often warmed to improve the plants' growth.

To start, you can either take a cutting and raise it hydroponically as for a house plant (see *How to convert a plant to hydroculture*, this page) or you can convert a young plant grown in soil, first washing its roots carefully in water. Unlike house plants, the trough plants are not generally held in place with aggregate. In commercial systems, there are commonly two strips sloping downwards from each side of the trough to form a kind of valley. At the foot of the valley is a narrow gap which helps to hold the plants in place. The plants are further supported by strings suspended from the roof of the greenhouse. Tie a string under a leaf shoot on each plant; then as the plants grow, train them up the strings.

Greenhouse hydroculture has two main disadvantages. You need to buy and set up special equipment, which can be both expensive and time-consuming. Depending on which system you buy, you may also need an electricity supply to the greenhouse to power a pump and warm the solution.

The advantage is that once set up the system is easy to use. There are no heavy bags of compost to carry into the greenhouse, and at the end of the growing season all you have to do is drain the nutrient solution out of the trough. You don't have to dispose of barrowloads of soil. You should also be able to get very heavy crops because the solution supplies nutrients in exactly the right quantities for maximum growth and fruiting.

Hydroculture is also a way to get round the problem of infected soil. Tomatoes, for example, are prone to a number of serious diseases which are carried in the soil. Once the soil in a greenhouse is infected, the disease organisms will stay there for years to come. You will either have to remove and replace all the soil in the greenhouse, or sterilise it; or grow future tomato crops so that they are isolated from the infected soil. Hydroculture is one way of doing this, though, to be fair, it is more common to use growing bags or large pots filled with sterile compost.

Labour-saving growing

I see that a lot of big plant displays in offices and showrooms are grown in hydroponic troughs. Why are they so popular there?

Because office life is hard on plants, and hydroculture is one of the best ways of dealing with the problems it presents. Office displays, which don't belong to any member of staff, are generally neglected or mistreated. Nobody bothers to water them for weeks, then suddenly everyone decides to do it and the plants become waterlogged. The dry, centrally heated air provides poor growing conditions, and over weekends and Bank Holidays plants are simply abandoned to fend for themselves. Specialist outside companies are often contracted to supply and look after the displays – but frequent maintenance visits from the company can be expensive.

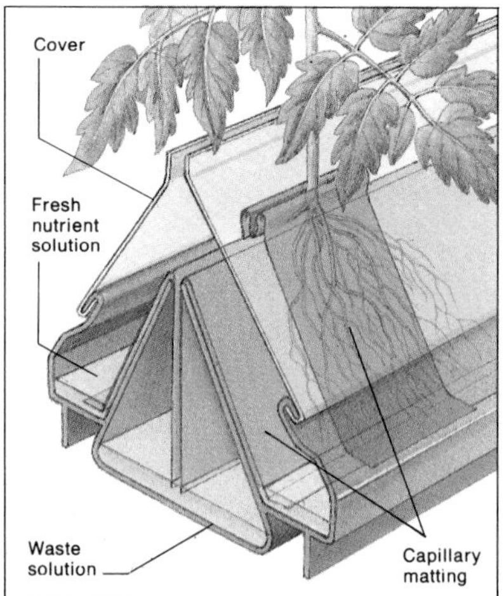

TROUGH CULTURE *One new hydroponic system introduced for amateur gardeners in 1987 makes use of capillary matting instead of a pump to circulate nutrient solution over the roots. Seeds are sown in a fold at the top of the matting, and the roots grow down the sides. The matting acts as a siphon, drawing fresh solution up the sides, then down into a central waste trough. A plastic cover keeps out the light.*

In these circumstances, hydroculture is often the most suitable way of growing plants. Plants grown hydroponically need the minimum of care and can be left for weeks on end without coming to much harm. If no company is contracted to look after the plants, the water gauge is usually clearly visible so that anyone working in the vicinity can see at a glance if the plants need watering or not.

How to convert a plant to hydroculture

I'd like to give hydroculture a go. Can I take one of my house plants that's growing in compost and try growing it hydroponically?

You could – but you'll stand a better chance of success if you start afresh with seed, or if you take a cutting from one of your plants and grow it in water from the beginning. Choose one of the plants that are best suited to hydroculture (see the list opposite).

Break off a strong, healthy shoot, preferably in spring when it will root most rapidly. If the shoot doesn't break off cleanly, trim it with a very sharp knife or razor blade just below a leaf joint. Remove the lower leaves from the stem and put the cutting in a jar of plain water. Keep the jar in a light place, but out of direct sunlight. A few lumps of charcoal in the bottom of the jar will help to keep the water fresh by absorbing impurities.

The roots that form will be different from those that develop in compost, being specially adapted to growing in water. They will be long and slender, with a large number of fine root hairs. Once the root system is well established, pot the plant up into a hydropot or similar hydroponic container (for details on how to look after it after potting, see *Caring for a house plant*, page 197). While potting up, handle the plant very carefully; water roots are especially delicate.

Transferring plants from compost is a much trickier operation. Only attempt to do it with a young, strongly growing plant. First, gently wash the plant's roots to remove all traces of compost. Take a pond planting basket (made from an open plastic mesh which allows air and water to come and go freely) and fill it with an inert aggregate, preferably soaked clay granules. Pot the plant up into the basket, then put the basket in a large bowl of lukewarm water. The water should come about one-third of the way up the sides of the pot.

Keep the plant in a warm place in bright light but out of the sun, and keep the granules damp. Use specialised hydroculture fertiliser to, feed the plant, following the manufacturer's instructions. Some ordinary liquid fertilisers can also be used successfully – but you must follow the specific instructions for their use in hydroculture.

The plant should gradually develop water roots in place of its original roots. Once the roots are well established and the plant looks healthy, pot it up into a proper hydroponic container. But be warned: while some plants transferred from compost will soon start to grow quite happily, others will look very sick for a while and still others may well die.

House and greenhouse plants that have been found to be good for cultivating hydroponically include: the fern *Adiantum fragrans*; *Aglaonema* 'Silver Queen'; *Asparagus sprengeri*; *Begonia rex*; *Caladium bicolor*; the cabbage palm *Cordyline terminalis*; umbrella grass *Cyperus alternifolius*; *Dieffenbachia picta*; *Dracaena marginata*; *Fatsia japonica*; *Ficus benjamina*; the india-rubber plant *Ficus elastica*; *Ficus lyrata*; *Fittonia argyroneura*; *Hoya carnosa*; *Monstera deliciosa*; nephrolepis; philodendron; *Pilea cadierei*; mother-in-law's tongue *Sansevieria trifasciata*; *Spathiphyllum wallisii*; the arrowhead plant *Syngonium podophyllum*; and *Yucca elephantipes*.

Tasty . . . or not?

I've heard that hydroponically grown vegetables are flavourless. Is it true?

There is no doubt that vegetables, such as tomatoes, grown outside in a vegetable plot often have a better flavour than those grown in the greenhouse. This is partly because garden soil contains large numbers of minerals and trace elements which may not be essential for plant growth but have a marked effect on flavour. Another reason is that garden vegetables aren't watered so much, relying largely on natural rainfall. Generally, the more water a vegetable receives, the more dilute its taste will be.

Hydroponically grown vegetables receive only the nutrients you give them and have as much water as they can possibly absorb. As a result, their flavour will never be quite as good as the flavour of the best garden-grown vegetables.

Flavour, however, does not depend solely on how a plant is grown. Variety is another important factor. Often varieties are bred more for qualities such as weight of crop, shape, size, colour, earliness and resistance to disease than for flavour. If, however, you choose a variety with a good flavour, you should be able to raise a reasonably tasty crop hydroponically.

For some vegetables, flavour is less important than, say, texture and juiciness, and these can actually be better on crops grown hydroponically. Lettuces, for example, will be much juicier grown with plenty of water, and will have crisp and tender leaves.

Vegetables and fruits particularly suited to hydroponic culture are: aubergines; cucumbers; lettuces; melons; strawberries; sweet peppers; tomatoes; and watercress.

INSECTS AND CRAWLING PESTS

(See also ANTS, page 12; BEES, page 27; and WASPS, page 359)

Night-time nuisance

I recently noticed a mass of woodlice sheltering under a stack of flowerpots that I keep in my greenhouse. Are these animals harmful?

Yes, they can be, especially in a greenhouse or cold frame, and in the vegetable garden as well. They tend to gather in the bottom of pots in which seedlings are growing and block the drainage holes. They also eat the soft leaves of young plants. Outdoors – under tubs on a patio, say – they're less of a nuisance because they also eat dead and decaying wood and fungi, acting as scavengers and natural composters, breaking down waste and returning goodness to the soil. That's little compensation for damaged plants in your greenhouse, though.

Strictly speaking, woodlice are crustaceans – related to lobsters – not insects. They're nocturnal creatures which come out to feed at night when the air is moist. During the day they hide among leaves and rubbish in the garden, under stones, logs, paving slabs, pots and boxes and in cracks in brickwork. Dampness is essential to them. They have no waterproof covering on their bodies and would dry out in two hours in sunshine.

To get rid of them in the greenhouse or the vegetable garden, start by removing all the likely hiding places. Clear up leaves and debris. Don't stack pots and bags on the greenhouse floor, and try to keep your vegetable garden as tidy as possible.

If the woodlice persist, buy the powder form of an insecticide designed to kill crawling insects. One based on pyrethrum or HCH will do fine. Puff the pesticide into all the places where you know woodlice are lurking. Repeat this treatment weekly or according to the instructions.

As with all pesticides, read the instructions carefully, because some chemicals aren't suitable for use near food crops and this will be pointed out on the label.

Lethal ladybirds

Are ladybirds really useful in the garden?

They most certainly are. They eat pests such as aphids, mealy bugs, thrips and mites. The adult ladybird has a pretty good appetite, but the crawling grub can eat as many as 50 aphids a day.

Ladybird beetles hibernate in winter, often in groups of a few hundred, under loose bark, among leaf litter, under stones and in cracks in a wall or fence. They emerge in spring as soon as the weather warms up. By June you will see ladybirds on your early vegetables and fruit, on your roses or on any plant that is infested with aphids. The female lays her eggs, about 200 in all, on the undersides of leaves of affected plants.

After a week the eggs hatch out as slate-blue larvae, each about $\frac{1}{8}$in long. They feed continuously and voraciously on the aphids for three weeks. Then they attach themselves firmly to the leaves and stems of the plant they are on and pupate. A week later, once the transformation is complete, the adult beetles hatch out.

To avoid harming them, if you decide to use an insecticide in the garden, choose a chemical such as dimethoate, which is systemic – in other words, is absorbed by plants. That way, it will be mostly the insects that actually attack your plants which will be affected, not the carnivorous ladybirds.

Beetles good and bad

I find more beetles than any other insect in my garden. Is this a bad thing?

Not necessarily. It comes as no surprise to learn that you see so many of these creatures, for they are in fact the biggest group of insects in Britain. Most of the beetles that you come across in your garden are harmless, and many are even helpful.

However, a number are harmful. The two most monumental destroyers are the elm bark and Colorado beetles. Dutch elm disease is caused by a fungus whose spores are carried from tree to tree by the elm bark beetle. The Colorado beetle is found only along the South coast at the moment. The yellow and black striped adult is a very serious pest to potatoes; both larvae and adults eat the leaves. If you see what you think may be a Colorado beetle, collect it and put it in a matchbox if you can, and mark the site. Report your find immediately to your local police station or, if possible, to your nearest Ministry of Agriculture office.

Other pests include the reddish-brown cockchafer which eats the leaves of shrubs, soft fruit, potatoes and herbaceous plants; its grubs eat roots, especially those of soft fruit. The long thin-bodied click beetle, or skipjack, eats nectar, pollen, leaves and flowers; its larvae, the wireworms, are a serious pest, damaging the fleshy roots of many plants. Flea beetles – there are 130 British species – feed on crop plants, especially brassica seedlings, leaving the leaves ragged and covered with tiny holes.

Weevils, a group of beetles with peculiar long 'noses', can also be destructive. The apple blossom weevil damages the flower buds, stopping fruit from developing. The vine weevil is a pest that was once confined to pot plants such as begonia and cyclamen, eating through the roots so that the plants eventually collapsed. Now this weevil is being found in borders and the grubs are attacking not only vine roots but bulbs, corms, tubers and other roots.

To reduce, and with luck eliminate, these pests you can either use a soil insecticide to kill the soil-invading larvae or a contact spray where the larvae and adults are seen on the leaves or shoots of the affected plants.

So if you do discover these beetles in your garden then, yes, it is a bad thing; but, to be fair, the pests are just a few of the nearly 4000 British beetle species. Many of them – including ladybirds, which eat aphids, ground beetles, which eat slugs, and dung beetles, which eat animal dung – actually perform a useful function.

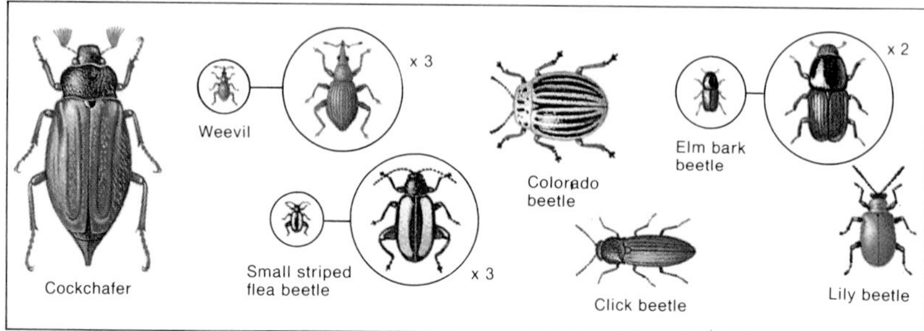

BEETLE PESTS *All these beetles are common garden pests in Britain. The species have been drawn actual size; small species are also shown enlarged for clarity.*

IRISES

Rhizome rot

When lifting my bearded irises, I found one rhizome soft and apparently rotting at one end. What can I do about this?

Cut out all the affected parts and destroy them. Plant any healthy rhizomes you have salvaged as far away as you can in the garden from the spot where the damaged rhizome was lifted.

This is rhizome rot, a troublesome and common complaint among overcrowded irises, particularly at the end of a wet season. Plant irises wherever possible in loose, free-draining soil. In heavier loams and clays, don't let them become congested.

It is best, if you can, to throw away a whole plant once rhizome rot has set in. Where it is not too severe, cut away the affected parts with a sharp knife, trimming back to firm tissue. To avoid spreading the disease with the knife, keep a jar of methylated spirit handy, and dip the knife into it after each cut. Seal any wounds with sulphur or powdered charcoal. Then plant in a new spot. Choose a well-dug soil, which is as free-draining as possible and in full sun.

Rhizome rot is only one of several afflictions that irises are heir to. These are the other common ones:

- **IRIS LEAF SPOT** Causes brown tips and brown patches on the leaves of rhizomatous irises. To treat the disease, spray affected plants at once with a copper compound fungicide.
- **IRIS SCORCH** Causes a reddish flush on the leaves of rhizomatous irises, followed by death; the youngest leaves are affected first. Lift the irises, cut off and replant unaffected offset rhizomes – then burn the rest of the plant.
- **RUST DISEASE** Causes red-brown pustules on the leaves of rhizomatous irises; the leaves later turn yellow and die. Spray slightly affected plants with a copper compound; burn severely affected plants.
- **APHIDS** Can affect bulbous and rhizomatous irises, crippling the flowers and distorting the flower stems. Treat by applying derris or malathion, or a systemic insecticide such as dimethoate.
- **VIRUS DISEASE** Stunts the growth of plants, causes petals to develop with broken patches or stripes of colour, and induces yellow streaking in leaves. There is no cure. Lift and burn all affected plants.
- **INK SPOT DISEASE** See *Failed bulbs*, page 202.

Out of the sun

I would love to grow irises, but I know they like full sun, and my garden is shady. Are there any varieties I could try?

Yes, have a go with the early-flowering, dwarf bulbous irises. These flower in February and March, so they're capable of giving you a good show before deciduous trees form a new leaf canopy over your garden, if that's the reason for the shade. Choose from *Iris reticulata*, which includes such fine varieties as the lovely blue 'Joyce', the mid-blue 'Harmony' and the plum-coloured 'J.S. Dijt'. If you have a free-draining position, try the white-flowered *I. vartani alba* or the chunky *I. histrioides* 'Major'.

If the shade in your garden is cast by buildings, then you have a much more difficult problem. Only the native stinking gladwyn (sometimes written as gladdon), *I. foetidissima*, will put up with it. It has more or less glossy, evergreen sword-shaped leaves and bluish-lilac flowers. In autumn, bold green seedpods split open to reveal rich orange-red seeds.

The variegated forms of the stinking iris will tolerate shade without enjoying it. They will give you good leaf colour, but don't expect much in the way of flowers.

Feed with care

Can you recommend a fertiliser for an iris bed? Do they need feeding every year? If so, when should I do it?

You can certainly use a slow-release fertiliser such as bone meal or hoof and horn, but it should not be necessary every year.

What is necessary is well-prepared soil before you plant. So, if you are breaking up your rhizomes and replanting every two or three years as you should be, get the goodness in the soil first. Thin sandy soil will need some peat and well-rotted compost dug into it. Heavy loams and clay will need some chopped compost, but dig in grit or sharp sand as well.

Good drainage is essential. Most of the troubles with irises stem from dampness or lack of sunshine. Two other rules worth remembering are:

- Don't apply rich compost or manure after you have planted. This will encourage the soft growth that can lead to rhizome rot (see *Rhizome rot*, opposite).
- Feed only with a little bone meal or hoof and horn, which will release topping-up nutrients slowly into the soil.

Tricky customer

I am told that Juno irises are difficult to grow. What conditions do they need?

They like a heavy soil and plenty of moisture during the flowering season from April to early summer. Once the leaves fade, towards the end of June, place a cloche over them: Juno irises like nothing better than a good summer baking.

The really interesting thing about Juno irises is the fleshy root system which grows beneath the bulb. Take care when planting not to damage this. It is from here, and not the bulb, that the vital lateral roots will sprout that sustain the plant during the growing season.

Start off with the yellow-flowered *Iris orchioides* and *I. bucharica*. They are attractive plants and the least tricky of the Junos.

Plants for the pond

I'd like to grow irises in my fish pond. Which should I choose, and will I need special compost?

Among the most attractive of the pond irises – and the best of those suited to Britain's climate – are varieties of the blue *Iris laevigata*. They are hardy and will tolerate several inches of water.

Don't confuse them with another Asiatic plant, *I. kaempferi*, the clematis-flowered iris of Japan, hybrids of which are sometimes listed under *I. laevigata*.

The Japanese one loves pond life in the summer, but is likely to die of waterlogging in a British winter. If in doubt, check that you have the right plant by running your fingers down the leaves. *I. kaempferi* has a pronounced midrib. If you can feel that, it is not for your pond.

Another good pond iris is the bluish-purple North American *I. versicolor*. Try its plum-coloured hybrid, 'Kermesina'. Our native yellow flag, *I. pseudacorus*, thrives in water, but it can swamp even the biggest ponds. Try instead the variety 'Variegata' – it has few flowers, but attractive cream and green leaves, and it grows more slowly than the species.

Aquatic plants do not need a special compost. Plant them in pots in a heavy soil – and dig the soil from a corner of your garden that has not been treated with fertiliser for a year or so. A soil rich in fertiliser will only add nutrients to the pond water and turn it green.

As you plant, drive all the air out of the soil to stop debris floating to the top of the pond. Stand the container with the plant in on a ledge in the pond about 4-6in down, so that the top of the container is just below the surface.

Cover the soil with pebbles or gravel to hold it in and to stop the fish stirring it up as they hunt water insects.

Plant the irises in the pots between April and July. But once they are in, you can move them around the pool at any time.

Hidden beauties

I tried growing dwarf bulbous irises in bowls in my greenhouse, but the leaves hid all the flowers and the plants looked untidy. What did I do wrong?

Too rich a compost, and too much heat. Your plants got too much good living too soon, so all you got was prolific leaf growth.

Use a soil-based compost such as John Innes No 1, and for each bowl mix in a generous handful of grit. Plant the bulbs, then give them between eight and ten weeks in the cool and the dark, so that they can develop a strong root system.

When you do bring them out into the light, keep them as close to the greenhouse glass as possible for maximum light, and keep the temperature down. On sunny days give full ventilation.

Bold show

Is it easy to grow Dutch irises in the garden?

Yes. Treat them as you would the bulbs of daffodils and tulips.

Plant them in autumn in open, free-draining positions. Put the bulbs 3-6in apart and cover them with 2in of soil.

In spring, as the first shoots appear, scatter a few slug pellets about. Then sit back and wait for a bold show.

Dutch irises need little attention, and they will soldier on in the herbaceous border year after year in all but the heaviest of soils – that is, soils which are almost all clay. Unless the irises are in an exposed position, they won't even need staking. Plant a few extra for cutting. Dutch irises are the ones that florists usually sell, and they are ideal for home decoration.

The most popular variety is the light blue 'Wedgwood', a fine early bloomer with distinctive yellow markings. You can force it, too, for indoor display. To force it, plant several bulbs in a pot in autumn and leave them outside in a cool place for at least ten weeks.

Then bring the pot into a light, warm room for an early show.

Other good garden varieties that will

Lifting time

When is the best time to lift and divide bearded irises?

Immediately after flowering at the end of June or in early July. Ease a fork underneath the rhizomes and prise them carefully out of the ground.

Separate the outer portions from the old, central part of the rhizome. This central section may have a few leaves on it, but its vigour will have gone, and it can be discarded. Look for the newer parts, particularly smaller ones with a healthy fan of leaves. Peel off withered leaves, trim off about half the remaining foliage and cut back any long, trailing roots.

Plant each new, young rhizome level with the soil surface, easing out the roots underneath it. As the roots grow, they will lift the rhizome to its correct position just above soil level.

Choose a sunny spot to plant out, and set the rhizome so that it points south from its leaves. Irises like maximum sunshine. Planted pointing north, the rhizome will eventually become shaded by its own leaves, and in a poor summer this could lead to dampness and rotting.

1 *Loosen the plants with a fork after flowering finishes, and separate the young rhizomes.*

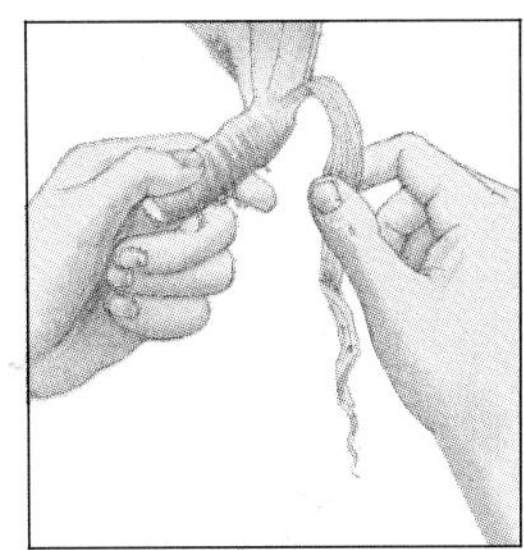

2 *Tidy up the severed portion, pulling off any old leaves and trimming the roots and foliage.*

3 *Replant with the top of the rhizome at ground level and the leaves to the north.*

enhance any border are 'White Superior', 'Golden Harvest', the dark blue 'Imperator' and the bright golden 'Yellow Queen'.

Leave them in

Do I need to lift Dutch and English irises each winter?

Only if they are planted in heavy clay, or in a very soggy area of the garden. And even then it's not in winter that they need lifting, but late summer and early autumn, after they've flowered.

Wait until the foliage has died back to a straw colour, which usually happens in July. Then dig up the bulbs, dry them off in a cool and airy shed or garage, brush off surplus soil and keep them in trays or in a net suspended from the potting-shed roof. Replant them in October.

If your soil is very heavy or soggy, dig in some compost and sand when you replant, to improve the drainage.

If the irises are in any other kind of soil than soggy or heavy ground, they don't need lifting at all. Unless you want to divide overcrowded clumps, leave them be.

Growing for the vase

Which are the best irises for cut flowers?

The Dutch iris varieties. They have long, slender stems and beautifully sculptured blossoms that last for a long time in the vase.

You can grow them in the border and take those you want for display. But you will get the best results for cutting if you grow them under glass.

Plant the bulbs in autumn in deep boxes in a good soil-based compost, and leave them to root in a cool place outdoors.

Once they are established, after 10-12 weeks, move them indoors where they will give you a steady supply of blooms between about February and May. They are pretty easy-going, and they will give you a good show even if they're stood in a porch or unheated greenhouse.

Failed bulbs

Last autumn I planted out some dwarf irises. Few came up and those that did produced only a few leaves, then died. What went wrong?

Sounds like ink spot, a troublesome disease which can devastate dwarf bulbous irises. It is no good waiting for the foliage to appear – or not to appear, in fact – to identify ink spot. By then it is too late.

Look for it when you buy. Check the bulbs. If there are any black marks on the white or yellow tunic – the outer covering of the bulb – it is infected. The signs of this fungal disease look just like ink spots, hence the name. In the soil, it will rot right through the bulbs before more than the odd leaf or two can grow.

There is no cure. If any bulbs you see in a shop have the tell-tale ink spots, don't buy. If the spots are on bulbs you already have, burn them, and dip all your healthy bulbs in benomyl as a precaution.

One other thing could have caused the failure of your bulbs. If it was not ink spot, it could have been damp. In very wet soil, iris bulb roots will rot, the first few leaves will grow, then the plant will fade without flowering. If this seems a likely cause, there is no need to burn the bulbs. Instead, try moving them to a drier spot.

Missing flowers

Two years ago I planted some dwarf bulbous irises and the next spring they flowered well. This year all I got was leaves and a handful of blooms, particularly from the yellow variety. What has gone wrong?

Nothing. Several of the dwarf irises, especially the yellow *Iris danfordiae*, split up naturally into smaller bulblets after flowering. It will take a couple of years for these to mature and flower.

If you want regular annual blooms, plant bulbs near each other in three successive years. Then you will get a natural succession of flowers.

Some alpine growers plant the dwarf iris bulbs up to twice their normal depth in the ground – that is, with the top of the bulb 4in deep instead of 2in. This does seem to keep the bulbs flowering every year and it does stop the natural break-up of the bulbs, but nobody knows why it works.

Growing from seed

How can I raise irises from seed?

Slowly. Sow home-raised seed, as soon as it ripens, in a soil-based compost and in a seed tray. Alternatively, store the seed in a refrigerator and sow it in spring. Or buy dried seed and sow in spring. Then wait. It will take several years for your plants to reach full-flowering maturity.

The soil-based compost is important. Germination is slow – sometimes taking months – so a long-lasting growing mixture is necessary; peat-based composts tend to start decomposing before the seedlings come up.

You can encourage the seeds to germinate more quickly by putting the seed tray in a freezer for a couple of weeks. This has the effect of jolting them out of their dormancy.

Bulbous irises should be pricked out into trays, with the seedlings about 2in apart, as soon as they are large enough to handle. The bearded and beardless types can be moved into individual $2\frac{1}{2}$-3in pots and then regularly repotted until they're starting to outgrow a $3\frac{1}{2}$in pot. By that time, they'll be large enough to put out in the ground.

Iris kaempferi, unlike most other irises, needs a lime-free compost.

Don't plant the seeds of any irises in the open ground. Results are likely to be poor.

Small blooms

Can you tell me how best to grow the Japanese clematis-flowered irises? I get only small blossoms from mine.

Grow them individually in pots with an acid, peaty compost, keep them moist and guard them from the weather.

The seed-raised strains of *Iris kaempferi*, the Japanese clematis-flowered iris, do have small flowers, but with their variety of colours – they come in almost every hue except yellow and bright red – they're fine plants for the bog garden or for general garden planting.

The more sophisticated, large-flowering forms, such as the Higo strain, were developed for the pot plant and cut flower trade and for greenhouse culture. They won't do well in a bog garden.

So, to get the biggest blooms, choose a colourful large-flowered variety such as 'Landscape at Dawn', and make a fuss of it in its own pot of moist and peaty compost. For the open garden, grow the smaller-flowered varieties. No amount of careful pot cultivation will do anything to improve their modest blooms.

Too much leaf

All I ever get on my winter-flowering Iris unguicularis *is leaves. What must I do to make it flower?*

Move it – the soil is probably too rich. This iris likes a hot dry place, preferably at the foot of a wall, in a free-draining and hungry soil. A rich soil merely encourages luxuriant leaf growth at the expense of flowers – an illustration of the general botanical rule that most plants flower best when there is some threat to their survival. When living is easy, plants tend to concentrate on growth instead of reproduction, on leaves instead of the blossoms that will bear the seeds for a new generation. The same principle lies behind the advice to gardeners to deadhead fading roses regularly and to keep picking sweet peas and runner beans. Neglect this job and most plants will stop producing new flowers once enough seeds have developed to ensure the continuation of the species.

In the case of your winter-flowering iris and its need to be dug out from its luxury bed, the solution presents its own problem, though. *Iris unguicularis* does not take kindly to being moved. In your case, however, it seems necessary to take the risk. The best time to take it is in the spring.

IVY

Heavy hangs the crown

Some of my old trees have a massive growth of ivy in the crowns. Will this harm them?

Not directly. Ivy's surface-clinging roots do not penetrate deeply to harm bark or wood. However, a dense growth may deny the tree some of the light and air it needs and could act like a sail in high winds, making the tree unstable. For this reason, it is worth getting rid of ivy from old or large trees close to houses. Sever the ivy stems at ground level, leave them to dry for a few months, then peel them away from the tree.

On large trees elsewhere, leave the ivy alone – a large ivy-clad tree makes a splendid shelter for wildlife. On a younger tree though, whether it's near a house or not, try to keep any ivy growth under control. Otherwise a very large ivy could deprive a young tree's relatively shallow root system of water and nutrients.

The risk with bricks

Can you settle the old argument about whether ivy damages walls?

The short answer is that it is harmless to new walls, but can be a nuisance on old ones. Modern bricks and mortar tolerate ivy. But on old walls, the roots take a very firm grip which can cause soft, old bricks to flake away. An even greater potential danger is that the roots and shoots can penetrate the old, soft mortar or get between bricks and door or window frames, sometimes working their way right through the walls and threatening their stability.

If you have a wall threatened in this way, sever the plant from its root at the base. The whole covering of ivy can then normally be pulled away like a carpet.

Wire-brush the wall vigorously to get rid of the remaining growth and scars made by the roots. Then repoint the brickwork. Watch out for green leafy shoots appearing from the stump; treat them promptly with glyphosate systemic weedkiller.

ALL ABOUT GARDEN IVY

THREE main species of ivy are grown in British gardens. The native British common ivy, *Hedera helix*, is the most popular and is available in more than 100 varieties. *H. canariensis* has larger leaves, and *H. colchica*, the Persian ivy, has the largest leaves of all. Most *H. helix* forms will thrive on walls in most parts of the country, though not all varieties of any of the species are fully hardy.

Best among the many *H. helix* forms are:
'Buttercup' – bright golden-yellow leaves if in a chalky soil and full sun.
'Erecta' – small, leathery dark green leaves on a slow-growing upright plant. It makes a fine feature in a large tub.
'Goldheart' – rich green leaves with a gold centre.
'Green Ripple' – dark green leaves with elongated and pointed lobes.
'Hibernica' – dark green foliage, and a vigorous grower for ground cover.
'Little Diamond' – fairly small leaves with silvery variegation.
'Sagittaefolia' – long, light green leaves.

The most popular form of *H. canariensis* is 'Gloire de Marengo' – shiny, deep red stems and dark green centres with silvery-grey and white borders to the leaves. In exposed gardens it needs the shelter of a patio.

Two varieties of *H. colchica* are widely grown – both of them are hardier than 'Gloire de Marengo':
'Dentata Variegata' – elongated leaves with bright green centres fading to grey and yellow or white edges.
'Sulphur Heart' (sometimes called 'Paddy's Pride') – a marked central splash of yellow on a large variegated green leaf.

JASMINE

Lasting sprays

Can I do anything to make cut sprays of jasmine last longer indoors?

Pour boiling water about 1in deep into a jug and put the stems into it immediately after cutting. Leave them there for one minute, then fill the jug with cold water and leave the jasmine to stand in it for an hour or more before arranging.

The rapid climb of the boiling water up the stem prevents air bubbles from forming in the sap; it is these bubbles which later stop the flowers drawing up the water they need to remain fresh and fragrant.

Both the white summer jasmine and yellow winter jasmine benefit from this treatment. Once treated, they will fill a room with their heavy scent for a week or even more.

Problem cutting

I have heard of several 'best' ways to prune yellow, winter-flowering jasmine. How should it really be done?

Winter-flowering jasmine, *Jasminum nudiflorum*, basically needs fairly severe pruning every year immediately after flowering. The reason you've seen conflicting advice about the plant is that it doesn't fit neatly into any of the standard pruning categories (see *All about pruning shrubs*, page 272).

For best results, cut out all old and straggly growths, and all the branches that have flowered, pruning them back to any promising shoots at the base of the plant. The young, green branches that remain will then

PICK OF THE JASMINES

Name	Type	Flower colour/season	Where to grow it
Common jasmine (*Jasminum officinale*)	Deciduous climber	White (summer)	Through large trees or up walls and pergolas.
Winter jasmine (*J. nudiflorum*)	Deciduous shrub: needs the support of a trellis or wall	Yellow (winter)	Will thrive in almost any position, but is best in the shelter of a north wall.
J. polyanthum	Half-hardy semi-evergreen climber	White, crimson in bud (spring-summer)	In a cool greenhouse or conservatory, or in a sheltered spot outdoors in the warmer Southern counties.
J. revolutum	Evergreen shrub	Yellow (summer)	Trained against a wall, sheltered from north-east winds.
Primrose jasmine (*J. mesnyi* or *J. primulinum*)	Evergreen half-hardy shrub: needs the support of a trellis or wall	Pale yellow (spring)	In a cool greenhouse, conservatory or on a south or south-west facing wall in a sheltered garden.

receive all the plant's energy. These are the branches that will brighten the dark weeks of the following winter with lively, yellow blooms.

It's important not to miss the yearly pruning. If you forget about it, in a year or two you will have old wood choking the young, leaving an untidy and straggling mass of dead shrub which will require major surgery to put right.

The right place

Plant winter jasmine on a north wall, say the experts. But wouldn't an east wall with its morning sunlight be even better?

No. Even Britain's short, weak bursts of winter sunlight would hurt the plant, not help it. On any wall, the warmth of the morning sun would bring a swift thaw after a night frost – and turn the flowers brown. Only on a north wall will the plant be able to thaw slowly and safely each day. In addition, the extra shade provided by a north wall encourages it to grow taller.

Jasmine is not the only plant that should be kept away from east walls. Other familiar flowering heralds of spring such as camellias and magnolias would also be damaged if planted in that situation.

LABURNUM

Striking curiosity

I saw a most unusual laburnum in a garden I visited recently. Among the golden flower chains were equally large heads of deep pink florets, giving a dramatic colour clash. What variety is it?

What you saw was not a true laburnum, but a remarkable graft hybrid. It is a cross between common laburnum (*Laburnum anagyroides*) and its close relative, the purple broom (*Cytisus purpureus*). It originated when the two plants were mistakenly grafted together by Jean Louis Adam at his nursery at Vitry, near Paris, in 1825; and it now bears his name *Laburnocytisus adamii*.

The broom forms the core of the tree, throwing out its pink clusters. The yellow, pea flowers of the laburnum hang on the outer branches. Both sets of flowers appear in the second half of spring. Some specimens also carry coppery-pink intermediate blooms.

The hybrid will grow to a normal height and spread for a laburnum, and needs no special care or pruning.

Sometimes, though, it reverts to a full laburnum because the laburnum's tissue is more vigorous than the broom's.

Pruning for shape

My laburnum flowers beautifully but it's too large. Can I cut it back without harming it?

Yes, if you do it correctly. The laburnum is a fast-growing tree, with a lifespan of only 15-20 years, which reaches its natural mature height in about ten years. It will then be about 15ft high with a 10ft spread.

If you don't plan a major change in the tree's dimensions, spur prune it in winter, when growth is dormant, to control the shape and size. This means cutting sideshoots back to two or three buds from the point where they join the larger branches.

If your tree needs more drastic surgery, tackle the job in July or August, after flowering and when growth is not too vigorous. This should not affect next year's blooming.

All cuts more than 1in across should be treated with a tar-like bituminised paint to seal them against disease. The heartwood in mature laburnums can rot quickly when exposed to air and moisture. Once the tree is back to the overall size you want, spur pruning it each winter will keep it within the bounds you've set.

Dangerous seeds

I know laburnum is poisonous, but just how dangerous is it?

There is no danger just in handling the plant, but simply sucking or swallowing the seeds or pods can make you quite ill. Laburnums are dangerous trees: all parts are poisonous, the seed pods particularly so.

Symptoms of poisoning show about 30 minutes after the plant has been swallowed. The symptoms can include sweating, burning in the mouth and vomiting, which can be severe for up to 24 hours. Consult a doctor at once if part of the plant is swallowed, particularly if the victim is a young child. But don't take wild risks when driving to the surgery – Britain's National Poisons Information Service reported in 1986 that there were no cases on record of anyone ever having died as a result of eating the plant.

LAVENDER

Honey fungus attack

My lavender looks very sickly, and a neighbour has indicated a clump of toadstools as a possible cause. They are browny-yellow and grow round a tree stump on the far side of the garden. How could they affect the lavender?

Very easily. What you have is almost certainly an infestation of honey fungus – also known as bootlace fungus. The toadstools are the fruiting part. What causes the damage are the black, cord-like rhizomorphs that can stretch out for perhaps 40ft to attack the roots of living trees and shrubs.

Honey fungus is generally a woodland pest, but where it occurs in gardens, lavender, privet and rhododendrons are particularly susceptible to attack. It is unlikely that your bush will survive; it should be dug up and burnt – likewise the old tree stump. Then treat the soil with Armillatox. Wood that has been infected by the fungus glows in the dark – country people used to use it to mark woodland paths. But probably this is no more consolation to an anxious gardener than the fact that the young toadstools are delicious, fried or grilled.

Flower failure

I've had my lavender bush for three years, but in all that time it's never put out a flower. What's wrong?

Maybe an embarrassment of riches. Your soil might be too high in nitrogen due to over generous fertilising in the past. You might correct this with light spring and summer dressings of sulphate of potash. Sprinkle about a handful at a time around the plant and lightly rake it in. Potash hardens tissues, and could encourage the plant to bloom.

Alternatively, give the bush a jolt by clipping it hard all over in spring, removing up to one-third of the old wood. If none of this works, dig the thing up and replace it with a new plant. But the fault may simply be that the site is too shady.

Cutting back

When should I prune lavender, and how hard?

Trim off all dead flower stems and lightly trim the plant with shears in April or in late summer. If it has a straggly appearance, cut it back by 6-9in each year until you get it to the size you want. Trim lavender hedges in March or April as well.

Lavender blue

I have several large lavender bushes and would like to make use of their flowers. Any suggestions?

The Romans used lavender water – made by crushing the plant and boiling it in water –

as a bath scent and to soothe away aches and pains.

Indeed the plant gets its name from the Latin *lavare*, meaning 'to wash'. A cold compress of lavender water is also said to relieve headaches and faintness.

Lavender oil – made by crushing the flower heads – can be used as a wound dressing; and lavender tea – made by infusing the leaves and flowers in boiling water – was traditionally taken for migraine, or simply as a refreshing drink.

You can also dry the stalks by hanging them downwards in bunches in a cool, dry place. The leaves and flowers can then be stripped off and made the filling for a scented cushion, or used as the base of a potpourri.

Hung among clothes, lavender will certainly scent them, but there seems to be no scientific evidence for the belief that it will keep moths away.

LAW

Mail-order plants

I ordered a strawberry tub and plants through a mail-order offer in a Sunday newspaper. When the tub arrived, the plants looked in a pretty sorry state. Most died soon afterwards. Can I get my money back?

Yes – if you act quickly. When you buy through the post, you are entitled to receive goods that match the description in the advertisement. If the strawberry plants were not up to scratch, you have the right in law to reject them, return them and demand your money back – provided you do so within a reasonable time of getting them. In these circumstances, a reasonable time would be a day or two. You may find that the company has enclosed with the plants a note explaining its usual procedure for dealing with complaints. If you think the procedure fair, use it. If not, write to the company giving all the details, and stating what was wrong with the plants.

The company may offer to replace the plants. It is up to you whether you accept this, but you have the right to demand cash instead, including the cost of posting the plants back. If the company does not deal with your complaint to your satisfaction, write to the newspaper and complain. It is a good idea for this reason to keep a copy of the letter you send to the company. Most newspapers expect their advertisers to deal with complaints properly, and will help a dissatisfied reader.

Seeds that cost a packet

Hardly any of the seeds from the expensive packet I bought in the spring have grown. Is it too late to complain now?

Probably, unless you have kept the seed packet, can prove where you bought the seeds, and can show that the seeds were of poor quality. But the seeds' failure to germinate may be due to all sorts of reasons to do with the soil and the weather, which are beyond the control of the seed sellers.

So, in practice, if you do go back to the shop, you may find that it will replace the packet of seeds – or you may find that it won't. Either way, you almost certainly won't get any compensation for the row of lettuce, or whatever, that should by now have grown. The moral is to make sure you buy good seeds. The marketing of most kinds of vegetable seed (but not flowers) is subject to strict control under European Economic Community rules, and all packets should bear marks indicating that the quality-control rules have been met. The marks should include a note of the year in which the seed was packeted.

Market gardening

Is there anything to stop me selling the flowers and vegetables I grow in my garden and allotment?

Not unless you're going into the big time straight away. If you're going to sell so much that you turn your garden or land into a business, you will hit problems – for a start you may need planning permission. But if you're not planning to make a full-blown business of it, you can go ahead quite legally.

One thing that worries many people is whether they ought to be telling the taxman about money they make from selling their vegetables. First, forget all about Value-Added Tax unless you really are going into business. VAT is charged on fresh food at a zero rate, anyway.

As to income tax, you are liable to pay tax on any trading profits you make. Technically, selling your lettuces to neighbours might amount to trading, but you probably won't have much, if any, profit to declare by the time you've deducted all the expenses you incur in producing those lettuces, such as fertiliser, seed, sprays, use of land and use of tools.

Weedy neighbour

The bachelor next door is often away for long periods, and entirely ignores his garden. As a result, it is a disgrace and full of weeds. The hedge has gone wild, and brambles keep growing into my land. What can I do?

You've the right to cut down the brambles and hedge on your land, but not to go next door and cut his side of the hedge down. I wonder, however, if you've been round to see him about the problem. After all, he might be happy to pay you to do it for him – or even let you take over his garden.

If asking does not work, you may have two other ways of getting help. First, on some estates there may be a legal requirement in the deeds of the houses to keep gardens in good order. Check the deeds by asking your solicitor or your building society for a copy. Second, you could ask your local council's Health and Environmental Department (the names vary) if it has any powers to intervene. In some areas, local rules allow the council to take action.

Permission for a greenhouse

I want to put a greenhouse in my garden. Do I need permission for this?

Probably not. You don't need planning permission to erect an ordinary greenhouse in the garden of a house, unless it is being built in front of the house. If you are building it onto the house though – as a conservatory, for example – you do need to comply with building regulations, which deal with such structural issues as the thickness of the glass. Your local council planning department can give you details.

It is rare, even on new estates, for you to need permission from the developer or from neighbouring home-owners to erect a greenhouse in a side or back garden.

Moving house – and garden

I am just about to buy a house on an 'open-plan' estate, with an all-grass unfenced front garden. I want to move the rose bushes from my present garden and put them in front of my new house. Can I do that?

Hold on! That's two problems in one. First, can you plant anything in your new front garden? Second, can you take the rose bushes from your present garden?

The answer to the first question depends on what limits, if any, are imposed upon you in the deeds of the new house. On many estates, restrictions – which lawyers call covenants – are placed on the person buying the house from the developer, and on all subsequent owners. The covenants are put there either because the planning authority imposed limits on the development when granting planning permission, or because the developers themselves wanted the limits in order to maintain the design or quality of the estate.

It is common for new estates to be 'open plan' and for the title deeds of all the houses to contain strict limits on what can be built or planted in the front gardens. The deeds may also contain other limits – for instance, the kinds of fences that may be erected or trees that may be grown. Once covenants are imposed on land, it is very difficult to remove them – however absurd they may seem to later generations. There are, for instance, several big housing estates near Bristol where the Duke of Beaufort still has the right to hunt the land – because he had that right when the estates were still farmland. You need to make sure, therefore, when buying a new house, that you see a copy of the deeds, and know what limits are placed on the property. Better still, keep a copy if there are conditions.

Mind you, even if there are planting restrictions in the deeds, all is not entirely lost, because very few people have the right to go to court to stop you planting your roses. In this case, only the original developers, if they still own some of the land, and any of your neighbours on the estate have that right. If the developers have sold out completely, they've lost the right to enforce the covenant. And if all or any of your neighbours are already growing plants in their own gardens, you have little to lose in going ahead.

On the other hand – and this is where the second half of the problem returns – you can't take the roses with you from your old garden unless your own purchaser agrees. Roses – or any other plants – technically form part of the land you are selling. You can remove growing plants only if you make it clear that they are not included in the sale. Tell your solicitor you intend removing the roses and ensure that the house contract covers the point. If you remove them without the buyer's agreement, he could demand a cut in the price of the house.

Fighting with shadows

My neighbour has applied for planning permission to extend the back of his house. His house and mine are the two halves of a semi-detached pair, and his is on the south side of mine, so my garden will lose a lot of light. Can I stop him?

You can try, but you may not succeed. Your neighbour needs planning permission only if he is building a big extension – one which will add more than 10 per cent to the floor area of his house. If he is, he must send full details, including plans, to the local council planning department.

You can ask the department to show you his plans and application, and if you do not like it, you can write to the council setting out your objections. These should be considered by the councillors or department when reaching their decision; but there's not much you can do about it if the council's decision goes against you. You may possibly have a right of light to a window (see *Room with no view*, page 209).

Bringing plants back from abroad

My husband and I are keen on foreign holidays. Next summer we are going to the Greek Islands again. Can we bring back some of the beautiful wild flowers that grow there for our own garden?

It's tempting to do so, but may be very unwise. You probably don't know anything about Greek property laws or conservation laws, so you might find you have dug up a rare plant, or that the land on which it grows – wild as it looks – is someone's property, and that you are guilty of theft. It may even be a nature reserve. The same considerations apply to collecting plants from any other country where you might go for a holiday.

Even if you can get away with it at the foreign end of the trip, you may still be liable to have the plants seized from you by British Customs. The United Kingdom has very strict plant health rules – and one of them says that you should not bring plants into this country with soil round their roots unless you have an import licence issued before you try to import them. Note that the rule is primarily aimed at soil; there's no objection to your bringing in seeds or seedheads. There are penalties for those who break the rule.

The reason is simple – soil harbours all sorts of diseases that can wreak havoc with our native flowers and trees. It took just a few careless importers to let the Dutch elm beetle in – and the awful results of that slip are visible in woods and hedgerows all over the country.

So, unless you know *exactly* what you are up to, and get a licence, don't try it.

Collecting in the wild

I'm becoming a specialist in growing honeysuckle, and know a place where I can get some beautiful wild specimens. They grow on a common that nobody bothers to tend, so is it okay if I take a couple?

In practice, if you take a couple of cuttings without damaging the honeysuckle, nobody is likely to complain. But before you venture out to strip the hedgerows and fields, remember that all land belongs to somebody, and taking growing things from someone else's land without the owner's permission is a form of trespass and, possibly, theft.

More seriously, before taking any cuttings from the wild, make sure you are not interfering with protected plants. Some 60 kinds of wild flower – including several orchids, sandworts and the Snowdon lily – are protected under the Wildlife and Countryside Act 1981 (for a list of these plants, see the chart on page 374). It is a serious offence intentionally to pick, uproot or destroy any protected wild plant. The maximum penalty for interfering with protected plants is a fine of £1000 for *each* plant affected.

Many people now know of these conservation laws, and how they guard the survival of particular rare species. But few realise that the 1981 Act also makes it an offence to uproot *any* wild plant of *any* species, unless it is done by the owner or occupier of the land, or with his permission or with a government licence, or as the incidental result of some other lawful action. In theory, even uprooting a dandelion from someone else's land without permission is an offence. So, don't try digging up the honeysuckle.

Bothered by birds

Some house martins have built a nest on the side of our house. They're a nuisance because their droppings keep landing on the glass roof of our lean-to greenhouse, but I am told it is illegal to move them. Is this true?

Yes – because, like most kinds of wild bird, house martins are protected by law. It is an offence to take, damage or destroy the nest of any wild bird while it is being built or is in use, or to take the eggs, or to kill, injure or take any bird. The only exceptions are the few birds treated as pests – house sparrows, wild pigeons, crows, magpies, jackdaws, jays, starlings and some gulls.

House martins are not one of the exceptions, so you'll just have to put up with them until they leave. Once they do, though – which will be in October – you can remove the plastered mud nest, and string netting under the eaves to prevent them nesting there again next spring. Alternatively, once you've removed the nest, hang strips of kitchen foil or polystyrene from the eaves. Their fluttering will frighten the birds away.

The rarer birds are even more heavily protected. In the case of what the law calls 'specially protected' birds (barn owls, hawks, bearded and crested tits and some 100 other species), it is an offence even to disturb a bird while it is nesting.

The same laws protect bats roosting in your house and garden. It is an offence to clear out a bat colony – even from your home – without official permission (which may not be obtainable).

Fuming about bonfires

I live next to an allotment area. The fellow who has the allotment nearest my garden seems to spend the whole of each weekend lighting bonfires, which nearly always blow smoke across my garden. How do I stop him?

Before anything else, make sure you tell the offender politely but firmly what you think of him – or, rather, of his bonfires. If you don't complain to him, he may at least claim he didn't know he was being a nuisance.

If he ignores your complaints, the best bet

is to get in touch with the local council. You may find that there are local bylaws or conditions covering the allotments which restrict the lighting of bonfires and which, if enforced, could stop the offender. Even if there are not, if the allotment user is behaving unreasonably, the council is still in a strong position to make the offender behave himself. If council officials don't seem sympathetic, get in touch with your local councillors and ask them for help.

If all else fails, consider taking action against the council and the allotment holder for creating a nuisance – that is, interfering with your land in a way that you should not be expected to tolerate. You'll need the help of a solicitor if you decide on this course.

An 'actionable nuisance' – that is, one you can take legal action about – exists when you find the use or enjoyment of your land is unduly interfered with by some continuous or recurring state of affairs which the law regards as unreasonable. So, one or a few bonfires have to be tolerated, even in a smokeless zone. But an excessive number – particularly if they are badly tended – will amount to an actionable nuisance.

If a nuisance exists, courts can do two things. They can award you financial compensation for the damage caused by the nuisance, or they can in more serious cases award an injunction (a sort of banning order) against the person causing the nuisance, formally ordering her or him to stop it.

Overhanging pears

My neighbour's pear tree grows almost on the border of our garden. Can I pick the fruit that grows in my garden? And what can I do about the shoots which keep growing from the tree's roots into my lawn?

A neighbour's tree growing into your land is in law a nuisance, but the tree still belongs to your neighbour. You have the legal right to end the nuisance by cutting off the branches, fruit or roots that grow in or over your land. But, strictly speaking, the parts cut or picked from the tree remain his property and should be given back.

Unless your neighbour agrees, therefore, you cannot pick the fruit for your own use. Nor, without his permission, can you eat windfalls that land in your garden.

Who mows the verge?

Am I responsible for mowing the grass verge between my front fence and the road?

This is a tricky question. In law, the owners of land adjoining a road usually also own the land under the road, the boundary being the mid-point of the road. They also own the land surface up to the road edge. But this is not always so. The only way to find out is to look at the deeds of your home to see where the boundary is. If your land extends right to the edge of the tarmac, as it usually does in the country, the verge is your problem. But if the deeds show that your land ends at the front fence, as is common in towns, then the local council is responsible for looking after the verge.

How to patent a plant

After years of trying, I have produced a new kind of tomato of an unusual colour. It has won prizes in local shows, and I have been told I ought to do something to protect my new variety and then try and sell it. Where do I start?

You can, if you are really serious, protect your interest in many kinds of new plant by claiming plant breeder's rights under the Plant Varieties and Seeds Act 1964. Effectively the rights allow you to patent your plant in much the same way as you protect any other invention. But the procedure is expensive and complicated.

Get in touch with the Plant Variety Rights Office of the Ministry of Agriculture, White House Lane, Huntingdon Road, Cambridge; it is their job to register all new plant varieties of protected species. In this context, 'protected species' covers most vegetables, including tomatoes, and some flowers.

Warning label

Why does the label on the African violet I recently bought tell me it is illegal to propagate them?

Saintpaulias (African violets) are one of the kinds of flower which are protected – as most kinds of vegetables are – under the Plant Varieties and Seeds Act 1964. Under the Act a plant breeder can be granted the exclusive right to propagate commercially a species or variety that he has bred. The idea is to allow him to reap, through sales, a reward for his breeding work.

It is not illegal for you to take cuttings of your own plants for your use, or to give away to neighbours and friends. But it is illegal for you to sell the cuttings without the permission of whoever holds the plant breeder's rights.

Anyone convicted of infringing the breeder's rights can be fined up to £400.

Mending fences – but who pays?

I want to rebuild part of the sagging fence between my house and the neighbour's. But the posts are on his land, and he says the fence is his. Any ideas?

Deciding who owns fences or hedges between properties is often tricky. To start with, look at the title deeds to your house, and get your neighbour to look at his. The deeds may show who owns which fence (on plans the ownership is marked with a 'T'), or they may show that the fence is jointly owned.

If the deeds do not specify the ownership, there is a general rule that a fence is owned by the person whose property is on the same side as the fence posts, though in some areas special rules apply. Check with your solicitor or the local council about this.

If the fence is his, he is under no general duty to repair it – though the title deeds will usually impose a duty to repair on a housing estate. So there may be nothing you can do to *make* him do the repairs. But he may be willing to come to an agreement with you if, say, you offer to share the cost of the repairs.

Of course, there is nothing to stop you building another fence alongside the existing one, provided it is entirely on your land. Unless there are special restrictions in the title deeds, you can build your fences how you like, provided their height does not exceed $6\frac{1}{2}$ft. You need planning permission to build fences higher than that.

Why I'm sour about limes

A large lime tree grows in my neighbour's front garden. In the summer it drips sticky syrup all over my car and the pavement and path to my house. Everything gets filthy, and my wife is fed up with the mess caused to the carpets in our house. The neighbour has refused to cut the tree, and the council say it is not their fault. So what can I do?

Not a great deal except move house. The key question in law is whether suffering from a lime tree like this is an actionable nuisance (see *Fuming about bonfires*, opposite). You can cut back the branches of the tree that are over your land, but that doesn't solve the whole problem. Beyond that, a court would order the neighbour to curb the nuisance only if it felt that the interference with your land or car was substantial. It is not clear that a court would take this view.

After all, there is little long-term damage caused by lime trees, and they drip only for a limited period of the year.

Peril of a neighbour's pond

My little grandson nearly drowned when he fell into the pond in a friend's garden. It is deep and unfenced and the edges grow wild. My daughter's friend often lets my grandson and other children play there, and doesn't seem particularly bothered about the accident. Shouldn't the friend make the pond safe?

These dreadful accidents happen all too frequently, and landowners often assume they need do nothing about them. But they're wrong. Landowners are legally, as well as morally, responsible for seeing that their land is reasonably safe for all those entitled or likely to use it.

If the neighbour lets young children play on her land without their parents being there, she is responsible for their safety. If she has done nothing either to fence the pond or to warn the children about it and watch them, the courts could order her to compensate anyone who suffered loss because of an accident. But that is of little use where a child might die.

The real answer, both in law and in common sense, is that parents are primarily responsible for how their small children behave. If a parent lets her toddler play unsupervised in a neighbour's garden beside an unfenced pond, it is a bit unfair to put all the blame on the neighbour if an accident happens.

Football menace

While I try to be a tolerant neighbour, I am getting fed up with the football played by the children next door. When a ball isn't landing on my head, it's smashing down my favourite plants. Would I be within my rights to confiscate it next time it lands in my garden?

No, tempting as it might be. But you could refuse to hand it to the children, and give it back instead to their parents with a few well-chosen comments. To keep the ball permanently would amount to theft.

If the ball causes damage to plants or greenhouse windows, you would also be entitled to ask the parents to pay for repairs or replacements. In law, they are responsible for damage caused by their children's carelessness, and you can recover damages through the courts – including the cheap-to-use small claims court – if the parents refuse to pay.

In an extreme case, if you are constantly bothered by flying balls – whether from the neighbour or from the local golf course or cricket ground – you could seek the help of the courts to stop it as an actionable nuisance (see *Fuming about bonfires*, page 206).

Pestered by cats

I like to encourage birds to feed and nest near my house, but they are often scared off by cats. One nearly killed a baby blackbird recently, though I scared it off with a water pistol. I think it was a stray, but others belong to nearby houses. Just what am I allowed to do to keep them out?

Not very much. Cats are merely behaving naturally when chasing birds, and cat-owners are not legally responsible for this sort of behaviour. Nor is a dog-owner liable for the ordinary behaviour of a dog.

You have authority to kill or injure a cat belonging to someone else only if this is absolutely necessary to protect your own livestock (your pet pigeons, say) or crops – but not to protect wild birds. A dog can be shot by a farmer only if it is worrying livestock and only if there is no other means of dealing with the problem – and the police must be informed within 48 hours.

In your situation, killing or injuring is out, as is using any cruel method to chase or keep them out. So the law will help you very little, though it does not stop you using deterrents like cat 'pepper' or cat-proof fencing.

The shed that has to stay

I am the tenant of my house, but will shortly be giving up the tenancy after several years. I have installed a garden shed there, and planted many new bushes at my own expense, but the landlord says I can't take them with me. Is the law really that unfair?

Is your garden shed a permanent fixture with sunk foundations? If so, the landlord is right. If the shed is free-standing, and can be removed without damage, you can take it – but you cannot in any case take the bushes.

The law is very clear. A tenant cannot remove anything which has become a fixture or fitting, where the removal would cause extensive damage, or where the addition has made a permanent improvement to the value of the property. Nor does the tenant of a private house have any right to compensation for improvements he or she makes.

How to get rid of rats

We are very bothered by rats that come into our garden from an empty building along the road and nest under our shed. What can we do?

Contact the local council's Environmental or Health Department (different councils use different names) and ask its experts to deal with the rats. The council also has powers to order the owners of the empty property to deal with the problem at source. You are, of course, also entitled to deal with rats or mice yourself by killing them, provided that you do so without causing unnecessary suffering. Buy a proprietary poison or trap and set it in places where you've seen the rats.

Buried treasure – who gets what

What happens if I really do dig up buried treasure on my land?

Treasure trove – gold or silver hidden on your land by an untraceable owner – must be declared to the police, because it belongs to the Crown. The local coroner will determine if a find is treasure trove. If it is, it will be handed over to a museum, but you will be rewarded with the full value of the find.

If what you find is lost property, where the owner could be traced, you should also notify the police. You must take reasonable steps to trace the owner, or ask the police to do so. If no owner claims the items, the police return them and you can keep them.

If you find other old items – a fossil or a relic from an ancient battle – on your land, then you can keep them. Property found in this way belongs to the landowner, even if someone else actually does the finding.

Impounding hooves

Sheep and cattle from nearby pasture often get out on the road, and from the road into my garden, causing a lot of damage. How can I stop this and get the damage made good?

While you may be wise to ensure your land has stock-proof fences, you are under no general obligation to fence it. A farmer, on the other hand, does have a duty to stop his stock getting out. So if the animals do trespass on your garden, you can claim from him the cost of repairing any damage they do.

To enforce your claim, you also have the right, under the Animals Act 1971, to impound the trespassing animals and to keep them until their owner pays you satisfactory compensation. If you impound stock, you must tell the police and the owner within 48 hours. You can charge the owner for the cost of looking after impounded animals.

The only exception to this rule applies to stock on common land, which by law cannot be fenced. In this case, it's not up to the owners of the livestock to keep the animals in. It's up to you to keep them out – you have no right to impound them or claim for any damage they cause.

Stung to anger

I've been stung several times in the past two years since my neighbour started keeping bees in his garden. My protests have been answered with the bald statement that he doesn't intend to do anything about it, and that there's nothing I can do about it. Is this really so?

More or less. Provided your neighbour is not deliberately setting out to make your life unbearable, there isn't much you can do to force him to change his ways, because the law holds that landowners have to accept the presence of bees as an inevitable consequence of cultivating land. Mind you, since many plants need bees to pollinate them, the advantage isn't all on your neighbour's side. Your garden is benefiting, too.

On the question of spraying, the law tries to draw a balance between a hive-owner's right to keep bees, and his neighbour's right to protect his crops. Each side, though, has to take account of the other's interests. A farmer, for instance, who sprays his crops with a chemical that is toxic to bees – knowing that there will be bees on the field and without warning nearby beekeepers of his plans – could be held responsible for the death of the bees caught in his spray.

On the other hand, a hive-owner who lets his bees out at a time when he knows that a neighbour plans to spray will have little chance of winning a claim for compensation if the bees die.

Worried about a wall

My mother's neighbour has just 'landscaped' his garden. This involved digging 2ft of earth away from his garden immediately beside our wall, exposing the foundations. Mother is worried the wall might subside and collapse. What can we do about it?

All landowners have a right of support from adjoining land. If the neighbour has removed earth in such a way as to cause subsidence on your mother's land, the neighbour will have to pay for any damage caused by depriving her land of support. But you can't make him pay, or make him put the earth back, just because you're worried that the wall *might* collapse. You can take legal action only when it *does* collapse.

The same principle applies where the effect of a neighbour's action is to drain water onto your land, or to cause flooding. If water flows onto your land from, for example, the neighbour's guttering or building work, or if the neighbour allows a ditch on his land to get blocked, so causing your land to flood, it can constitute what the law calls an 'actionable nuisance', and you can make him pay for the damage (see *Fuming about bonfires*, page 206).

Sprayed by accident

Our house adjoins farmland. Recently the farmer sprayed his crops on a windy day, and ended up spraying our garden. As a result, a number of plants were killed. Can we get compensation?

You can claim compensation – through the courts, if necessary – from anyone whose carelessness causes you damage. And that includes a farmer. If you can show that his spray killed the plants and that he should have foreseen that it would happen, you have a right to take legal action against him. It's better, though, to talk to him first and try to settle it by negotiation. In practice, the money you get from him to pay for new plants is likely to be much less than the legal costs involved in claiming it.

Room with no view

My neighbour has planted a Leyland cypress not more than 10ft from my house. Already, it is 7ft or so tall, and soon it will cut the light to my kitchen. Am I entitled to tell him he must keep the tree pruned?

You can tell him – but he might well have the right to refuse. Much depends upon how old your house is. If your window has had uninterrupted light for 20 years or more, the right to light may be protected in law, preventing anyone from blocking, or substantially reducing, the light by putting up a building or planting a tree or hedge.

However, you may have to wait for the offending tree to grow further before seeking legal restraint; the law can deal only with an actual nuisance, not a potential one.

If you are worried, and a polite request has no effect, get advice from a solicitor or your local Citizens Advice Bureau. Remember, though, that if your house is modern – and especially if it is on a residential estate – the deeds may well contain a clause that excludes buyers from acquiring rights of light. The deeds may also, on the other hand, specifically ban planting large trees near any of the houses.

LAWNS

Treating the lawn

There is a bewildering number of lawn fertilisers available. Is there one I can use all year round?

Yes, you can use a general fertiliser such as Growmore, which contains equal proportions of the three main plant nutrients: nitrogen, phosphorus and potassium. Sprinkle on about 2oz per square yard in early April as growth starts, the same amount in June, and the same again in late September. Keep an eye on the weather each time. If it doesn't rain within two days of sprinkling on the fertiliser, water the lawn thoroughly. This pattern of feeding will be adequate for a family garden. Don't expect it to give you the perfect lawn, though.

Grass ideally needs a different treatment at different times of the year. During the growing season, from mid-March to September, it needs a good supply of nitrogen. This will keep it growing strongly and give the rich green colour we look for in a lawn. A high-nitrogen fertiliser, such as a standard spring or summer lawn feed, will mean regular mowing as well, because the nitrogen will also make the grass grow faster.

From October to mid-March, the aim is to keep the grass in good condition but not to encourage growth. So give it a fertiliser high in potassium, such as a standard proprietary autumn lawn feed. This will toughen the grass and prevent the lush growth which is more likely to suffer disease and cold in a harsh winter. In essence, the aim is to make the grass grow up in spring and summer, down in autumn.

Summer feed can be applied in granules or liquid. Most granules need to be watered in: check the maker's instructions and scatter the granules just ahead of rain if possible. Granules release their constituents into the ground more slowly than liquid feeds, so you won't need to treat the lawn so often – every five or six weeks from early April instead of every three or four weeks, as would be the ideal with a liquid feed.

Apply an autumn feed of high-potassium fertiliser, at the rate recommended by the maker, only once – in October.

When to feed

How often should I put fertiliser on my lawn?

At least twice a year – once in April with a high-nitrogen feed, once in October with a high-potassium feed. That will be enough for the average lawn. If you want something just a cut above the average, add another high-nitrogen feed in July.

If you are looking for something a little more like a bowling green, then little and often is the best policy in summer. Some keen gardeners divide the maker's recommended monthly dose of fertiliser in half then treat their lawns with this amount fortnightly. This pattern of feeding releases nutrients more evenly into the ground, and gives a steadier growth rate.

Toadstool crop

On my lawn is a double ring of dark green grass which produces a crop of toadstools. How can I get rid of it?

With great difficulty, for it sounds as if you have the worst type of fairy-ring fungus: *Marasmius oreades*. The best thing you can do is to dig up the lawn to a depth of 12-18in and over an area extending to 12in on either side of the infected patch. Then get rid of the soil and replace it with new soil and new seed.

Alternatively, you can try to sterilise the

GROWTH TARGET Marasmius oreades *forms a bull's-eye pattern of two lush green rings separated by a brown ring of dying grass.*

soil where it lies. To do this, dig up and burn the diseased turf to a depth of at least 9in. Then drench each 10sq yds of soil with a solution of formalin, made up of 6 pints of commercial formaldehyde with 10 gallons of water. Cover the treated area for seven to ten days, then uncover it, fork over the soil and leave it for another two weeks before reseeding. Another, simpler method is to treat the soil with Armillatox.

Like other fungi, marasmius breaks up decaying organic matter beneath the lawn, releasing nitrogen as it does so and thereby stimulating the growth of grass. That's why the outer ring on the fringe of the fungus-hit patch is lush and green.

But the fungus is also waxy and actually waterproofs the soil it infects, cutting off moisture to the grass roots. This creates a characteristic strip of brown, dead or dying grass up to 6in wide inside the outer ring. Inside that strip there is a second green ring – marking the area where the fungus is dying and giving up its own nitrogen in the process.

Some systemic fungicides, such as benomyl, give a degree of control. But a proper cure means complete soil sterilisation or replacement. Be careful when you do it. A few crumbs of infected soil dropped onto the lawn will start the whole grim process all over again.

There is one other option: feed the lawn to disguise the symptoms; and harvest the toadstools as they appear, usually between July and November. The toadstools are tasty fresh and, if dried, can be used to flavour soups and stews (for a close-up picture of the toadstools, see opposite).

Killing lawn weeds

When is the best time to treat a lawn with selective weedkiller?

In May and June, when the leaves are young and growing fast and the plants have not yet flowered. Selective weedkillers contain plant growth hormones which are taken up by the leaves, not the roots. They upset the growth pattern, causing the plant to die.

Apply the chemical in a dry spell. It will need at least six hours without rain for the leaves to absorb the hormones – any showers would wash off the weedkiller before it had a chance to work. Begin your treatment in May, as soon as the weeds are growing vigorously. Some well-established weeds may need a second dose a month later in June. If you start too late, you give the stubborn weeds a chance to seed before you can get in a second treatment, storing up more trouble for next spring.

Spray it on

Which is better for lawns, a granular weedkiller or a liquid one?

The more prevalent your weeds, the better it is to use a liquid control. It gives more even coverage and is absorbed by the plants more quickly. Where one type of weed in particular is troublesome, a specialised liquid weedkiller is again the best choice because you will be able to pick the selective treatment best suited to eradicate it.

Granular weedkillers tend to contain a more general-purpose weedkiller and usually a lawn fertiliser, too. They do a good job on lawns with just average weed infestation. And, by feeding the soil, they encourage the grass to grow where the weeds have died – although large bare patches will still need reseeding or returfing.

Curved edges

My garden is long and narrow, so I tried to curve the lawn edge to break up the parade ground effect. The result, far from graceful, looks a drunken mess. How can I get good sweeping curves in the lawn?

Lay out the garden hose in the shape you want. The hose's stiffness will help to smooth the curves you make. Go and look at the curve from inside the house – including from upstairs where possible – to make sure that it also looks pleasing from a distance. When you're happy with the shape from all angles, peg the hose in position and cut alongside it with an edging tool or a flat-bladed spade. Well-cut curves will help to make your garden look shorter and wider.

Starling invasion?

In autumn, starlings crowd on my lawn. Are they doing any harm?

No, they are doing a good job for you – eating leatherjackets, the larvae of the daddy longlegs. Left in the soil, the larvae will eat the roots of the grass, making patches of it pale green or even brown.

A gathering of starlings on your lawn almost certainly means that the leatherjackets are there.

Normally, the birds will control the grubs without any help from you. If not, take a tip from the starlings and treat your lawn with a soil insecticide in autumn, when the grubs are near the surface and active. If you don't want to use a chemical, try another trick. Water the infested area thoroughly and cover it overnight with a sheet of black plastic. When you take the sheet off in the morning, you'll find that the grubs have collected on the surface under the plastic. Collect and kill them yourself, or leave them for the birds to eat. If the larvae are a serious pest, repeat the treatment at the insects' other period of peak activity – in spring.

No-grass lawn

Are there any attractive, easy-to-care-for alternatives to a grass lawn?

Among plants there are really only thyme and the traditional chamomile lawn which until the 18th century graced the gardens of many of Britain's stately homes. Chamomile does not need mowing, spreads thickly and, used as a lawn, gives off a pleasing scent when walked upon. It won't stand up to rough treatment from a family of boisterous children playing all over it, however.

If you fancy a chamomile lawn, plant the non-flowering variety, 'Treneague', about 4in apart. If you want thyme, plant seedlings of *Thymus serpyllum* about 6in apart. Chamomile does especially well on a sandy soil. It's also unusually resistant to drought. When grass has gone brown from lack of water, a chamomile lawn will still be bright green. On the other hand, it needs careful hand-

ROUGH *Lots of curves in a lawn's shape can seem spacious and interesting when you're close to them, laying them out. When they're accentuated by foreshortening, however, they may merely look fussy or even untidy.*

SMOOTH *The same garden looks shorter, broader and much more elegant with long sweeping edges to the lawn. The trick is to make the curves more gradual than instinct might suggest – use a stiff hose to plan the shape.*

weeding, both before you plant and for the first year or two afterwards, to allow the new sward to become established.

In a small garden, there is another, non-plant option you might consider: paving. An urban patch with elegant paving in place of grass, dotted with tubs and raised beds and surrounded with shrubs and climbers, can look extremely attractive. And once the borders are established, the garden requires almost no maintenance at all.

One other alternative to a grass lawn is what you might loosely call woodland. In other words, turn the garden into a network of narrow paths – which can be paved or could be left to grow with shin-high meadow grass – meandering between border plants, shrubs and trees. There won't be any open space to kick a ball around in such a garden, so it might not suit a family with children. But it can be rich in plant life, providing interest and an air of tranquillity.

Puddles on the lawn

Every time there is heavy rain, parts of my lawn lie wet for anything up to a day afterwards. Is this harming the grass?

Yes, it is, and you need to do something about it or you will get progressive deterioration of the grass.

The problem is most likely caused by compaction of the soil in the lowest-lying parts of your lawn. Drive the prongs of an ordinary digging fork deep into the wet patches at 4in intervals and wiggle them about to loosen and open up the soil. Then brush into the damp areas a top-dressing made up of half-and-half fine peat and coarse sand. This will keep open the new drainage holes you have created, and will provide air and a good channel in which new grass roots can form.

If this fails, you may have to lift a section of the lawn and lay a soakaway (for detailed advice on how to do this, see *Drains and soakaways*, page 124).

Bulbs in lawns

How do I cope with a lawn that has bulbs growing naturally in it? How soon after flowering can I cut the grass?

Leave the grass until the leaves of the bulbs have died down – which means *at least* six or seven weeks after flowering – and don't apply any selective weedkillers during that period, either.

Before the foliage dies down, it feeds the bulbs, putting back into them the strength they will need to flower next year. If you cut back the leaves or tie them in a knot, as some people do, the bulbs suffer. Do it year after year and you will end up one spring with 'blind bulbs', which have foliage but no flowers – and that defeats the whole point of having naturalised bulbs in a lawn. Daffodils look lovely flowering in a lawn, but once they are over, you are left with this rather wild patch for a good part of early summer. So, it is important to plan carefully when filling part of a lawn with spring bulbs.

Choose an area that is not in general view all the time – under a deciduous tree with low branches, say, or a spot which will be shrouded later by early-flowering shrubs or plants, so that these will draw the eye from the untidy aftermath of your early daffodils.

Another trick is to plant the bulbs in staggered rows diagonally across the viewing angle. They look from the house as if they are crowded together, but there is room to run a mower between the rows.

Every other year, give the bulbs a teacup of bone meal per square yard after they finish flowering. This will help them to compete with the grass for the nutrients they need.

Using a roller

Does it help or harm to use a heavy roller on the lawn?

Nine times out of ten it does more harm than good. The main rules about rollers are:

- Never try to level an uneven lawn with a heavy roller.
- Never flatten newly laid turf with it.
- Never use a roller when the lawn is wet.
- Never roll when the soil is rock-hard.

Most of the time all you are doing with a roller is compacting the surface soil, blocking natural drainage channels, pressing the air out of the ground and making it harder for the roots to penetrate.

The one exception to these general rules is that a heavy roller can safely be used just before the first mowing of the season. Frost often lifts the soil, leaving hard bumps and loosening the ground and surface grass. Brush off the winter wormcasts and roll to even off the surface before you take the mower to it.

If you haven't got a heavy roller, use the roller of a mower, holding down the handles if necessary so that the cutting blades are clear of the grass. If you do decide to roll, wait until the soil is merely moist – not too hard, not too sticky.

Fairy ring

Parts of my old lawn are developing bands of grass which grow faster than the rest. What can I do about this? It is spoiling the look of the garden.

Give it a good feed of a high-nitrogen fertiliser such as a standard spring lawn feed, used at the rate recommended on the packet. What you have is probably an attack of fungus. There are three likely candidates: the field mushroom, *Agaricus campestris*; the common puffball, *Lycoperdon perlatum*; or the fairy-ring champignon, *Marasmius oreades*. All

THREE LAWN INVADERS

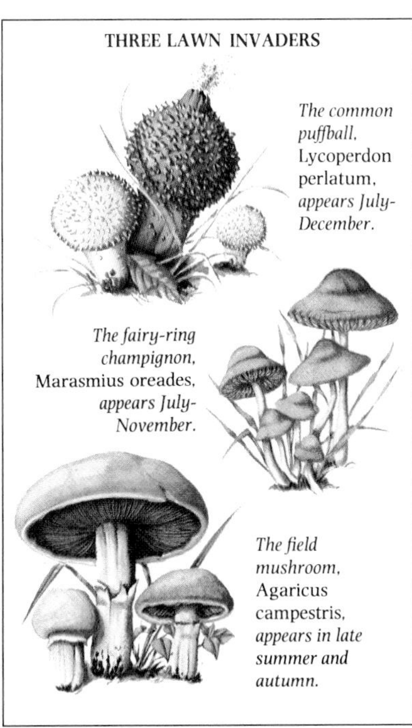

The common puffball, Lycoperdon perlatum, *appears July-December.*

The fairy-ring champignon, Marasmius oreades, *appears July-November.*

The field mushroom, Agaricus campestris, *appears in late summer and autumn.*

three fungi help to decompose dead organic matter in the ground, releasing its nitrogen and thus causing the grass nearby to grow more quickly. The effect shows up most on an underfed lawn, which is why one answer is to conceal the symptoms by feeding the rest of the lawn to the same degree.

Controlling the fungi is not easy. A copper compound fungicide or one based on benomyl applied in spring or early summer may restrict them to some extent. Otherwise the only cure is soil replacement or sterilisation (see *Toadstool crop*, page 209).

There is one bright aspect to all this, however. The fruiting bodies (the parts that grow above ground) of all three fungi are edible and tasty. So you could decide to live with your free crop.

Lawn labour

My next-door neighbour spends hours raking and brushing his lawn, and I admit it looks a little bit better than mine. But is all that work really necessary?

With lawns, like so many things, you get out of them what you put in. The more effort, the more silky will be your finished sward. But you needn't make hard work of it. Just do the right things at the right time.

In spring, rake out the 'thatch' – the bits of old and dead grass, moss and debris. Sweep up any leftover winter leaves and wormcasts, and lightly roll the surface. As growth accelerates, feed the grass from time to time and treat any weeds that develop (see *The lawn-grower's calendar*, page 216).

In autumn, give a high-potassium feed. Spike and aerate any compacted areas. And end as you started, by raking up any thatch that has built up during the summer.

None of this should swallow up hours of your time. Do it as and when it is necessary, and you will find it easy.

On the other hand, there are some perfectly good back garden patches of grass that survive summer after summer with little care other than an occasional mowing. And if their owners are happy with them, that's good enough.

Spiky stalks

Every summer I get those tough and stringy stalks sprouting out of my lawn that seem to defy the sharpest mower. Can I get rid of them or, better still, stop them coming?

No, you can't stop them growing, they are simply a natural process – the grass is flowering. You can snip them off with the shears, or you can try raking up the lawn before you mow.

The springy stalks you talk of are sometimes called bents. Top-quality lawn seed contains few of the kinds of grasses which develop these stalks, and some of the new mixes are grasses bred specially not to flower vigorously. But, even if you have laid your lawn with these, weed grasses will still invade.

Perennial rye grass and agrostis are the main culprits. Once they get a foothold, all that can be done is to kill them individually or fork them out – a long and tedious job.

A mower with a front roller tends to flatten the bents as it comes to them, and the cutters pass harmlessly over. A rotary mower or one with side wheels is generally more effective. All will work better if you rake up the grass before cutting. With regular mowing you will get fewer bents, as less grass grows long enough to flower; and any bents that do develop will be cut off before they reach an uncuttable length.

Repairing lawn edges

How can I mend a lawn edge that has broken?

If it is on a curved or shaped edge, you can simply cut out the broken section, altering the curve or shape of the edge as you do so. A squared or straight edge presents a different problem, but there is a simple way round it.

Cut round a section of the lawn about 12-18in square, including the broken edge. Slide a spade or turf float underneath it, and lift it. Turn the turf around, so that the broken section is away from the edge. Line the turf up with the grass alongside and tread it down. Fill in the patch left by the broken edge with a little sifted soil and a sprinkling of seed, and the job is done.

Repairing a dead patch in the middle of a lawn – one perhaps caused by bitches or a petrol spillage – can be done in a similar

PATCH REPAIR *To tidy a damaged lawn edge, cut out a square or rectangular patch of turf around it, and lift the turf.*

FILLING THE GAP *Turn the turf so that the damaged part is away from the edge. Fill the hole with soil and a pinch of seed.*

way. You won't find a grass seed mixture that will exactly reproduce the mixture in your lawn, so any seeded section in such an obvious place will stick out like a sore thumb.

Instead, cut out the bare patch. Go to a less conspicuous part of the lawn, and lift a piece of good turf of the same shape and size. Use this to repair your lawn centre. Fill in, level and reseed the place you took the turf from.

Where areas of grass are merely thin, scratch the surface to roughen up the soil, reseed and water in. The new grass will blend in with your existing lawn.

How high the grass?

What is the ideal height to cut a lawn?

On the finest quality lawns, aim for $\frac{1}{4}$-$\frac{3}{8}$in. On domestic lawns go for $\frac{1}{2}$-1in, and make it nearer 1in if the children run riot over it.

Never shave the lawn. For a really close cut you must have a surface almost as flat as a billiard table. If you haven't, you will end up in a mess, with hollows not cut at all and bits of sliced bare ground on all the humps. Mow regularly, too – twice a week, if possible. Lawns that are cut little and often thrive better than those left to grow several inches, then cut down. Irregular cutting merely weakens the grass and encourages invasion by weeds and moss.

In spring and autumn, and in hot dry spells during the summer, keep the blades $\frac{1}{2}$in higher than usual.

Measure the cutting height by turning the mower on its side and holding a straight-edge across the mower from the front to the rear rollers. The distance between the cutting edge of the machine and the straight-edge is the height of the cut. Always check or adjust it before you start cutting.

Holiday cut

When I am going away for a holiday, should I cut the lawn an extra bit closer, so that it will last for a fortnight?

No. You will do more harm than good, weakening the lawn, and leaving it open to invasion by moss or weeds. It is always bad policy to cut the lawn shorter than normal for whatever reason.

Just trim the lawn, as usual, the last chance you have before you go away. If you can get a neighbour to run over it for you, so much the better.

Any lawn left for a fortnight in summer will grow more than is good for it, but it may not turn out as badly as you fear. After the first flush of growth, the speed at which grass grows slows down. When you get back, treat the lawn as if you were starting out in spring again. Don't slice it down to its normal height in one go. Set the mower to about $1\frac{1}{2}$in for the first couple of cuts, then reduce it to about $\frac{3}{4}$in for another cut before going back to your usual setting.

Finally, although there is a chemical available to professional greenkeepers and groundsmen which is used to slow down the growth of grass, there is nothing you can spray on your own lawn to cut down the chore of mowing before or after a holiday. The chemical is not legally available in any form for amateur gardeners.

Cutting down cutting

I have a large lawn and I am becoming fed up with all the mowing. How can I cut down on the time spent and still do a good job?

You can't, unless you buy a mower with a wider cut, or get someone else to do the job for you. Both mean extra expense.

You could reduce the size of the lawn. One of the great gardening fallacies is that the easiest way to cut down work in a garden is to lawn it. There is less planning, less digging, less finicky work than in a flower border or vegetable garden, but there is no end of labour. After all, it will want mowing week after week for nearly half the year. A shrub border is probably the most labour-saving feature in a garden. Once it has been laid out and planted and the shrubs have filled out, it is very undemanding. A little pruning, some weed control, and a few annuals to fill the gaps are all that is needed. So try cutting down on the size of the lawn and putting in a few shrubs instead.

A larger mower sounds like an over-simplification of the problem, but it would make the job easier. You may even find a rotary mower will do the job more quickly than a cylinder at the expense of a few neat lines.

If all these sound like long-term solutions, consider letting your lawn become an orchard-type sward with much longer grass that will be cut only once every two or three weeks. Alternatively, you can save time on your current mowing if you change the pattern. Instead of mowing up and down the lawn in strips – wasting time turning round at the end of each run – consider mowing in a spiral pattern, working your way round and round the lawn from the outside edge. You won't get stripes that way, but you will avoid mowing the same piece of grass twice – and cut the time you spend.

Winter hangover

Every spring my lawn takes weeks to recover from the winter. Is there anything I can do to speed up the process?

A good autumn feed is probably what it needs. And spike it at the end of summer to open up the soil and prevent it compacting and so causing waterlogging.

A lawn goes through a good deal of stress in summer. It is continually mown, trampled upon, and probably not fed enough. The rigours of winter on top of all that can leave it in a sorry state come March.

A feed of high-potash fertiliser in October will give it the strength to survive the worst conditions. Take a garden fork and spike the lawn with the prongs before the really damp weather sets in. Then brush into the holes a half-and-half mixture of peat and sand. This will improve drainage and prevent waterlogging, which chokes roots, rots the grass, and leaves the way open for moss and weeds.

War on weeds, not pets

How long must I keep my pet and children off a lawn I've treated with weedkiller?

It all depends. Any weedkiller in its concentrated form – in the bottle – is highly toxic, and must be kept well out of reach of small children. In its diluted form – once it's been spread on the grass – it's less dangerous. But it can still be hazardous.

To be on the safe side, keep your pet – a cat or dog, say – indoors at least until the weedkiller has dried into the grass. This normally takes about two hours in good weather. But if you have a young child whose fingers are constantly on the ground and in his or her mouth, or if you have a puppy or kitten which is likely to roll on the grass and then lick its fur, keep the child or the animal off the whole area for several days or until there has been some rain to wash the chemical into the soil, or until you have watered the whole lawn thoroughly to achieve the same end.

The risk is much less acute with animals which merely play on grass than with those which eat it. If you have a grazing animal for a pet – for example, a rabbit, a tortoise or a goat – keep it off a treated lawn for at least four weeks until the chemical has been thoroughly washed in by rain and the weeds have all died.

Controlling rye grass

Some years ago I sowed a lawn with just fine grasses, no rye. Now there seems to be more rye than fine grass. How did this happen?

Fine grasses need careful looking after. Any lapse in attention and rye seeds will invade from neighbouring lawns and grasslands and eventually take over, simply because they are tougher.

The sort of fine grass you sowed needs all the help it can get in the average garden. That means monthly feeds in the summer growing season and mowing two or three times a week from May to September at a height of between $\frac{1}{4}$in and $\frac{3}{8}$in. This type of mowing will be too hard for the rye grasses, wiping them out before they get a foothold. At the same time, it will thicken and strengthen the fine grasses.

Making a lawn

I've just moved into a new house on a new estate and what – I hope – will one day be the lawn is now a mixture of builder's tip and jungle. How do I begin?

There are two ways of making a lawn – laying turf or sowing seed. Turf is for people in a hurry who don't mind paying, and seed for people who aren't and do. Either way, the initial stages are much the same. Clear the debris, old tree roots and any brambles, couch grass, ground elder and so on. Dig the site over to a spade's depth, to break up the soil and aid drainage. Old turfs should be buried grass side down.

Ideally, leave the site clear for three months, spraying or hoeing and digging out weeds as they appear, and removing stones. On heavy clay, improve fertility and drainage with a bucket of well-rotted manure or compost and two buckets of coarse sand to each square yard. Improve the water-holding ability of light, sandy soils by raking in a bucket of peat to the square yard. Meantime, the weather can work upon the site, helping to break down clods and consolidate the ground.

Plan your lawn, allowing for paths and beds. On the whole, it's best to shun neat rectangles and to add interest instead with bays and curves. For details on how to mark out beds of unusual shapes, see *Formal lines*, page 154. If you want to build paths, or put a concrete mowing strip around the edges of the lawn, construct them at this stage (see also *Paths and paving*, page 246). Now is the time to make the final preparations – breaking up remaining clods, treading the ground to firm it, and raking the soil to make a fine tilth.

By the time you finish, the ground should be flat and the surface layer should be about the consistency of breadcrumbs. About a week before sowing or turfing, rake in a general fertiliser such as Growmore at the rate of 2oz per square yard.

Turfing is best done from September to March; this gives the turfs time to settle before they begin their spring growth. When laying them, work forwards so as not to disturb the soil, and kneel on a plank while doing so.

Turfs should be laid in a staggered pattern, as when laying bricks. Fill cracks between the turfs by brushing into them a mixture of 1 part peat, 2 parts of good soil and 4 parts of sand. Roll the turfed site lightly – with the back roller of a mower, say – brush it to lift the grass and finally water it thoroughly with a sprinkler.

Sowing, on the other hand, is best carried out in April or September. Lightly rake the ground to create a fine tilth at least 1in deep, and sow the seed at a rate of about $1\frac{1}{2}$oz to the square yard – though if you're using a proprietary mixture, follow the supplier's instructions. Ensure even coverage by marking out 3ft strips with string and sowing half the seed down the strips and the other half across. Gently rake so as just to cover the seeds. Don't roll the ground – you will compact it or pick up seeds on the roller.

LAYING TURF *Kneel on a board to spread your weight, and lay the turfs in a staggered pattern, like bricks in a wall.*

Leave the lawn, merely watering it with a fine sprinkler, until the grass is about 1½in high; then roll it with a light roller or the back of a cylinder mower. About six weeks after sowing, the grass will be about 1½-2in long – and ready for its first cut. Brush the lawn lightly to get rid of debris and worm-casts, and cut with the blades set 1in high. Thereafter, gradually lower the blades until the grass is the height you want.

Wild garden

I fancy the idea of letting my lawn go wild to go with my deliberately wild garden. How should I tackle this?

You could let your existing lawn return to nature by simply not cutting it, but this could lead to problems with tough perennials like rye grass, timothy and cocksfoot taking over – and they quickly get out of hand.

A better idea may be to start from scratch by laying a new lawn with a mixture of the modern and dwarf lawn grasses, which would give a meadow-like turf and be easier to control. You could include some wild grassland flowers in the seed mixture. Most seed firms include these now in their catalogues.

Don't think, however, that a wild area can be left with little or no attention. It needs careful conservation; neglect will simply produce disorder and will look quite different from the way you imagine.

Proper paths must be cut and maintained – there is nothing worse than wet grass to walk through. And don't throw your mower away – a rotary model will be particularly useful. Wild grass will need to be cut down in July or August after it has flowered. For more details about the problems and the pleasures of back-to-nature gardening, see *Wild gardens*, page 370.

Best grass

Which is the best grass I can buy?

Traditionally, the best in Britain is Cumberland sea-washed turf. It consists of the finest fescues and is called sea-washed because it grows most widely just above the high-water mark on the south side of the Solway Firth and is often drenched by the sea.

Being the finest, it takes the most careful looking after. Amateur gardeners may find it disappointing, because without the best attention it can rapidly deteriorate.

Two other excellent grasses, but somewhat coarser than Cumberland, are New Zealand Browntop (agrostis) and Chewing's Red Fescue (festuca). Both can be bought as seed and, like Cumberland, they need a lot of looking after.

For a more easily maintained greensward, avoid these top-grade grasses. Go instead for local turf or for a proprietary seed mixture designed for a hard-wearing family lawn.

Worms – or not?

Some experts say that wormcasts damage lawns, others that worms help drainage. Should I get rid of them from my lawn?

On an ordinary, domestic lawn it is probably not worth the trouble. Wormcasts do look ugly, but they cause no damage and they can easily be brushed off.

Get rid of the worms – the best way is to use a proprietary worm-killer – only if you are after a sward with a billiard-table look or if the casts are a serious nuisance. You'll lose the benefit of the aeration and the improved drainage that the worms provide with their tunnels. But you can achieve much the same effect on your own by spending five or ten minutes every now and then spiking the grass.

Dog patches

My dog urinates on the lawn, causing discoloured patches. Is there anything I can do to prevent this?

The problem is most often caused by female dogs. Ideally, walk your dog somewhere else, but if this is not possible keep a watering can or hose handy and water the patch thoroughly straight after she urinates. If the grass is dead, replace the top inch or two of soil and re-seed, or patch with new turf.

Incidentally, the idea that there's something especially damaging about bitches' urine, that it contains some sort of harmful hormone, is a myth. The urine of both sexes is much the same: a strong concentration of urea and other chemicals. It is the quantity that does the damage, not the ingredients. Bitches are more often the cause of the problem simply because they empty their bladders in a single spot. Male dogs tend to urinate a little at a time because they use urine to mark territory – so there's rarely enough to damage the grass in any one place.

The grass-box controversy

For years I've listened to conflicting opinions about the advisability of using a grass-box when mowing the lawn. Should the mowings be collected, or left where they fall to nourish the soil? What's the straight answer?

This is an argument that will continue so long as grass is mown, but the answer seems to be that in normal conditions it's healthier for the lawn to let the cuttings lie.

During the past ten years or so, Reading University's Department of Agriculture has run a research programme on the best way to mow a lawn. The programme was based on 48 plots, each measuring 6ft by 6ft. They were mown in 16 different ways at different intervals. Richard Bisgrove, the lecturer who led the team, says: 'Allowing clippings to return to the turf recycles nutrients, invigorates the grass and makes it better able to compete with weeds and moss.' In other words, take care of the grass, and the grass itself will take care of the weeds.

One plot, for instance, was cut low and the clippings were collected – it was found, after a time, to be 60 per cent covered with moss. Another plot had exactly the same treatment except that the clippings were *not* collected; it remained almost totally free of moss.

The team's other findings were that it is better to mow frequently (at least once a week) than infrequently, and that it's better to set mower blades high (around ¾in) than low, because close mowing restricts the development of the grass roots.

It depends in the end on what you want from your lawn. There is no doubt that a grass-box will make it look tidier, and prevent the messiness of clippings being trampled into the house after rain. They can be dumped on the compost heap instead to do good work there. Remember, though, that each grass-box of clippings disposed of in this way is depriving the lawn of nutrients that will have to be replaced by fertilisers.

Then, too, there are the special problems of heavy, damp or acid soils whose bacteria population is too low to break down a heavy carpet of mowings. In this case a damp thatch of cut grass lies upon the soil, creating an ideal habitat for moss.

So what to do on the average family lawn? Try compromise, the gardener's friend, and for the first mowings of the vigorous spring grass, use a grass-box. After that, leave the box off and the clippings on, but mow frequently – twice a week if possible. Keep using the box only if you can't mow as often as this. Set the blades at about ¾in. Frequent mowing ensures that only tiny crumbs of mown grass fall on the soil – feeding the earth without smothering the lawn.

How to get rid of moss

I've tried a number of highly recommended moss-killers but they don't seem to work, and I've virtually become resigned to having a moss lawn. Is there anything I can do to get rid of this pest?

Moss-killers – many of which are based on iron sulphate – will work, but moss is a symptom of an ill-treated or badly constructed lawn, and unless you cure the underlying problem it doesn't matter how often you kill the moss; it will swiftly return.

A common feature of mossy lawns is an accumulation of 'thatch' – dead fibres – in the sward, which chokes the grass. This must be raked out. Contrary to popular belief, raking need not spread the moss since, having cleared up the rakings, you then apply moss-killer. As another reason for mossy lawns is under-feeding, it is a good idea to use a moss-killer that contains a fertiliser. Proprietary compounds, granular or liquid, are available at garden centres.

Compaction of the soil surface will also seriously affect the health of the grass and invite moss to spread. This can be counteracted by spiking the lawn, which aids drainage and allows air to penetrate to the roots. If you are on heavy clay use a hollow-tine aerator for the job, but for most lawns a garden fork is perfectly adequate. Drive the tines about 4in into the soil, allowing about 4in between each spiking. Wiggle the fork each time to enlarge the holes slightly. Follow the spiking with a top-dressing of peat and horticultural grit or sand in equal parts. Work it well into the sward at a rate of about 2lb to the square yard.

Starring stripes

My wife yearns for a lawn with elegant stripes – the kind you see on the covers of gardening catalogues. Is it so difficult to achieve?

Not really. The striping is caused by the grass being pushed in opposite directions by the roller at the back of the mower as you mow up and down the lawn. The best effects are produced by cylinder mowers – which always have rollers. After the mower, the most important factor is a good eye. A striped lawn *is* smart, but not if the lines are wiggly. Wheeled rotary mowers will also produce stripes, if more faintly.

The tearing of the green

My lawn turns brown each time I mow it and quite often stays that way for two or three days. What am I doing wrong?

Almost certainly, you are using a cylinder mower whose blades have blunted or are not tightly set. Cylinder mowers cut scissor-fashion, with the rotating blades slicing against a fixed one. If the edges of the moving blades are dulled, or if the blades don't meet properly, they will tear and mash the grass rather than cutting it. The roots survive, but the upper parts of stalks so mistreated turn brown and wither within 24 hours. Cure: get your mower blades sharpened and reset as soon as possible.

Beating the bumps

My lawn is disfigured by bumps and no amount of rolling makes any impression upon them. Should I buy a really heavy roller or is there some other solution?

Forget the roller. It only compresses and compacts the soil, making the bumps all the more intractable. Tackle the problem the other way round by removing some of the underlying soil instead. Use the corner of a spade or an edging tool to cut an X shape across the centre of the bump. Peel back the tongues of turf, remove the soil down to just below the level of the surrounding lawn, and tread the turf back into place. Hollows can be treated in a similar way. Peel back the turf, fill up with soil and put the turf back again. Always use soil from your own garden; otherwise you may get patches of grass of different colours.

Moving moles on

My lawn has recently become dotted all over with molehills. I don't want to hurt the moles. Can they be persuaded to go away?

It doesn't take an army of moles to do that kind of damage – three or four can manage it quite easily. As for showing them the exit, there are a few old folklore methods that can – surprisingly – work. You can sink a bottle, with the open neck upwards, into a run. It's said that the noise the wind makes blowing across the open top scares them off. Whatever the reason, it does seem to bother them. The problem is finding the main runway. Putting the bottle in a secondary run does no good at all, since once it has been dug, the mole will seldom use it again.

Putting crushed eucalyptus leaves in the tunnels also seems to help – moles seem to dislike strange or pungent smells. Proprietary mole smokes are worth trying, too. For more detailed advice, see *Moles*, page 232.

Choosing the grass

I was just about to sow my new lawn, when it occurred to me that there is more than one kind of turf. I want a lawn that is going to look good, yet will stand up to the pressures imposed by three energetic children, a couple of pets and the occasional summer party. What do you suggest?

There are three basic types of lawn. The grandest is the games lawn, as for bowling greens, a highly enviable sward of Cumberland, or sea marsh, turf that should be laid and maintained by a professional greenkeeper. Next comes the fine lawn, meant for show rather than tramping upon. What you require is the utility lawn, which contains a large proportion of tufted grass, such as Chewing's Fescue, which grows well on both acid and alkaline soils. A number of seed firms make up packeted mixtures to suit all kinds of gardens. Look for a mixture marked as containing plenty of rye grass.

Where the grass ends

My trees and shrubs grow straight out of the lawn, but I have been told that this is bad for them – that they should have clear soil around them. Is this true?

In a perfect world, yes. But even in an imperfect one, you should certainly have a clear space around *young* trees and shrubs. Grass competes with the plants for water and nutrients, and until the shrub or tree is well established – four or five years on, perhaps – it should grow in the middle of a turfless

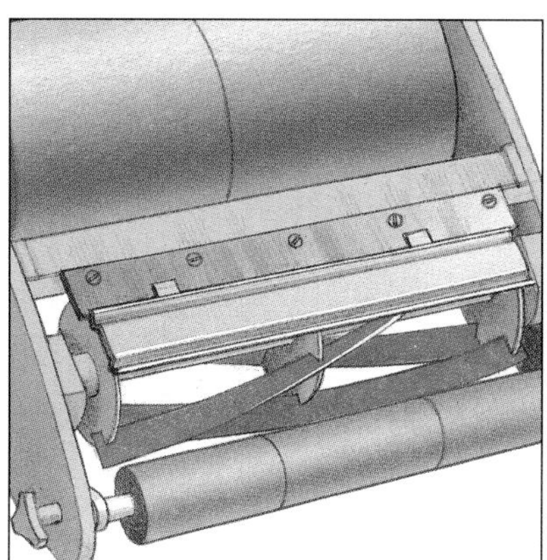

MOWER MATE *To sharpen a mower yourself, clip an abrasive strip to the fixed blade. Run the cylinder forwards for two or three minutes.*

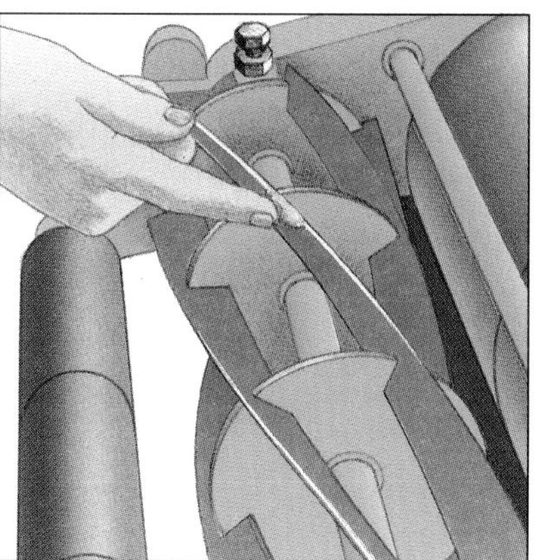

GRINDING PASTE *Alternatively, set the blades so they just rub. Spread on grinding paste and turn the cylinder backwards by hand.*

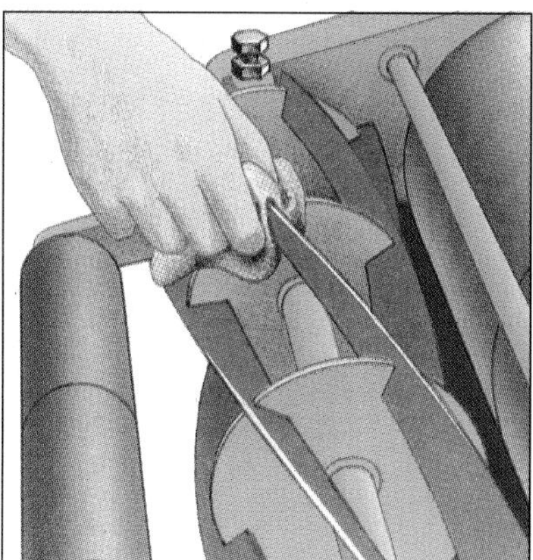

CHECKING THE EDGE *Wipe the paste off and readjust the blades so they kiss. They should cut paper as cleanly as scissors.*

circle at least 3ft across. True, this adds to the weeding chore, but it will improve the tree or shrub's health and growth rate.

For interest, plant a few spring bulbs in the circle; these make little demand on the soil. Then, once the tree or shrub is established, you can safely let the turf grow back.

Consolidating a short cut

There's a worn, bare trail across my lawn, mainly caused by my family and myself taking a short cut to the greenhouse. How can I repair the damage and prevent it happening again?

What you're talking about is the right and proper route to your greenhouse, which you and your family will continue to use, no matter how often you repair the damage or try to persuade yourselves to follow a more meandering path. So why not turn your short cut into a permanent and useful feature? Get some smallish paving slabs – say, about a foot square, though the sides need not be even – and lay them along the short cut as steppingstones. Space them to suit your average stride – you want neither to mince nor stretch along the path – and sink them into the ground by cutting round them and excavating their shape. Allow for the thickness of the slab plus a couple of inches.

Line the bottom of the hole with an inch or so of sand, the idea being that when the slabs are in place they will be just below ground level and you will be able to mow straight over the top of them. The sand lining is important; without it, the slab will in a few years sink out of sight.

Once your steppingstones are laid, scratch up the worn ground around them and sow it with grass seed that's been treated with bird repellent. Since you won't be walking on it, the new grass will quickly blend with the remainder of the lawn.

THE LAWN-GROWER'S CALENDAR

January Clear dead and dying leaves. Trim lawn in very mild spells. Shape up edges. Clean and overhaul mower.
February Sweep away wormcasts. Move stones, twigs and other debris.
March Rake off moss and old grass. Spike and open up the soil. Treat with a spring feed containing nitrogen. Re-turf worn or damaged edges.
April Begin regular mowing, cutting grass at first by one-third, then lower blades to about ¾in. Give new lawns their first cut. On established lawns, break up bare patches and re-seed.
May Apply selective weedkiller to infested lawns.
June Raise cutting blades ½in in very dry spells. Consider cutting without the grass-box, so that cuttings form a surface mulch (see *The grass-box controversy*, page 214). Apply second dose of weedkiller to eradicate stubborn weeds.
July Give a summer feed of liquid fertiliser. Water during dry spells – and don't cut too short.
August Keep edges trimmed and mow less frequently if growth slows because of very dry weather. Root out by hand any weeds which earlier treatment missed. Remember to cut just before you go on holiday.
September Watch for any mushroom-type growths, which may be encouraged by damp nights and mornings. Treat any affected areas with fungicide. Re-seed worn patches. Re-turfing can take place any time between September and December, or in spring. Use worm-killer, if necessary.
October Spike and ease open any areas which have compacted during the hot weather. Tackle moss. Apply an autumn top-dressing high in potash.
November Give the lawn a last cut. Sweep clear; check for weeds. Clean the mower, grease and store.
December If you have done all the right things during the rest of the year, take the month off and give the lawn a rest, too.

How much is a handful?

When setting out to feed my lawn, I read the fertiliser manufacturer's instructions carefully – 2oz of this, 3oz of that to the square yard. But you can't walk up and down the lawn carrying a pair of scales. Isn't there a more practical measurement? So many handfuls, perhaps?

Fine, but how big is your hand? And do you mean a closed handful or an open one? And a handful of what? A large hand closed would hold rather more than 3oz of bone meal, but only about 2oz of Growmore, and a small hand about half the amount of either. Open hands would contain almost double the weight of either Growmore or bone meal.

A similar difficulty applies to tablespoons. You can get a lot more weight of bone meal, a fairly dense powder, into a tablespoon than you can of Growmore's coarse granules. And is the tablespoon heaped or flat?

Maybe the best thing to do is to weigh out one basic dose of the fertiliser and hold it so that you get to know what it looks and feels like. You can then scatter and replenish, being fairly accurate each time. In gardening, after all, such weights are not intended to be critical to the last grain anyway.

Geese as lawn mowers

I've recently moved to the country, to an old house with quite a lot of land. Could I use geese to help keep the grass down?

Certainly, but don't expect to get an exquisite lawn out of them. If you've got a rough paddock, well fenced in, then geese will save you mowing time. But don't have them anywhere near your real garden. Geese will strip your vegetable and flowerbeds, and make a fair start on the bark of young shrubs before beginning to think of grazing – as well as covering the ground with their droppings.

All the same, given the right conditions, they're not a bad idea. You need a basic nucleus of three – two female geese and a gander – which you can buy as goslings in the spring. They'll need about a quarter of an acre of grass between them. If you've as much as an acre of grass, you could keep roughly a dozen birds of the lighter breeds of geese. You will have to supply night shelter as well. A simple three-sided pen roofed with corrugated iron and floored with clean straw would do, but unless you have a guarantee that your area is clear of foxes – and poachers – then the fourth side of the shelter should be filled with heavy wire mesh and a lockable door. Give the basic family of three a shelter 6ft by 6ft by 3ft high.

Being aquatic birds, they will also need water, though not as much as you might think. An old cistern, sunk into the ground and kept well topped up, is sufficient. They don't want to swim so much as totally immerse their heads in water several times a day. Given adequate grazing, they will require no other feeding from spring until autumn, when the grass stops growing. Michaelmas, at the end of September, is the traditional date when geese are sent to market, and you had best follow suit. Keeping geese through the winter is time-consuming, messy and expensive.

Perhaps the best reason for keeping geese as an amateur is not financial, but for fun. They're companionable, inquisitive, attractive creatures and superb watchdogs; not a thing will move on your property without them letting you know about it, loudly and clearly. The only trouble is, the neighbours may not share your enthusiasm.

War on weeds

My lawn has been taken over by plantains, dandelions and daisies to the point where there seems to be more weeds than grass. Any ideas for a cure?

The broad leaves of these plants will readily absorb selective weedkillers and the plants will quickly wilt and die. The trouble is that you are then left with patches of bare ground that will be colonised by yet more weeds. To get round this problem, encourage growth in your lawn first by applying a spring feed in March. Use a proprietary mixture for this at the manufacturer's recommended rate, or use one-third fine peat and two-thirds sand mixed with turf fertiliser and applied at the rate of about 2lb to the square yard.

Mow the lawn at least once a week with the blades set high, so that both weeds and grass make plenty of leaf.

Then, after about a month of growth, apply a proprietary lawn weedkiller. Repeat after another month if any weeds remain.

HOW TO RECOGNISE THE WEEDS ON YOUR LAWN

No single remedy is appropriate to all lawn weeds. Which treatment is best depends on which weeds you've got. Yet recognising weeds can be extremely difficult, particularly if you've just mowed the grass. This page shows 12 of the most common lawn weeds, both in their complete form and how they look from above on the lawn. Captions under each picture give the name of the weed and explain how to get rid of it.

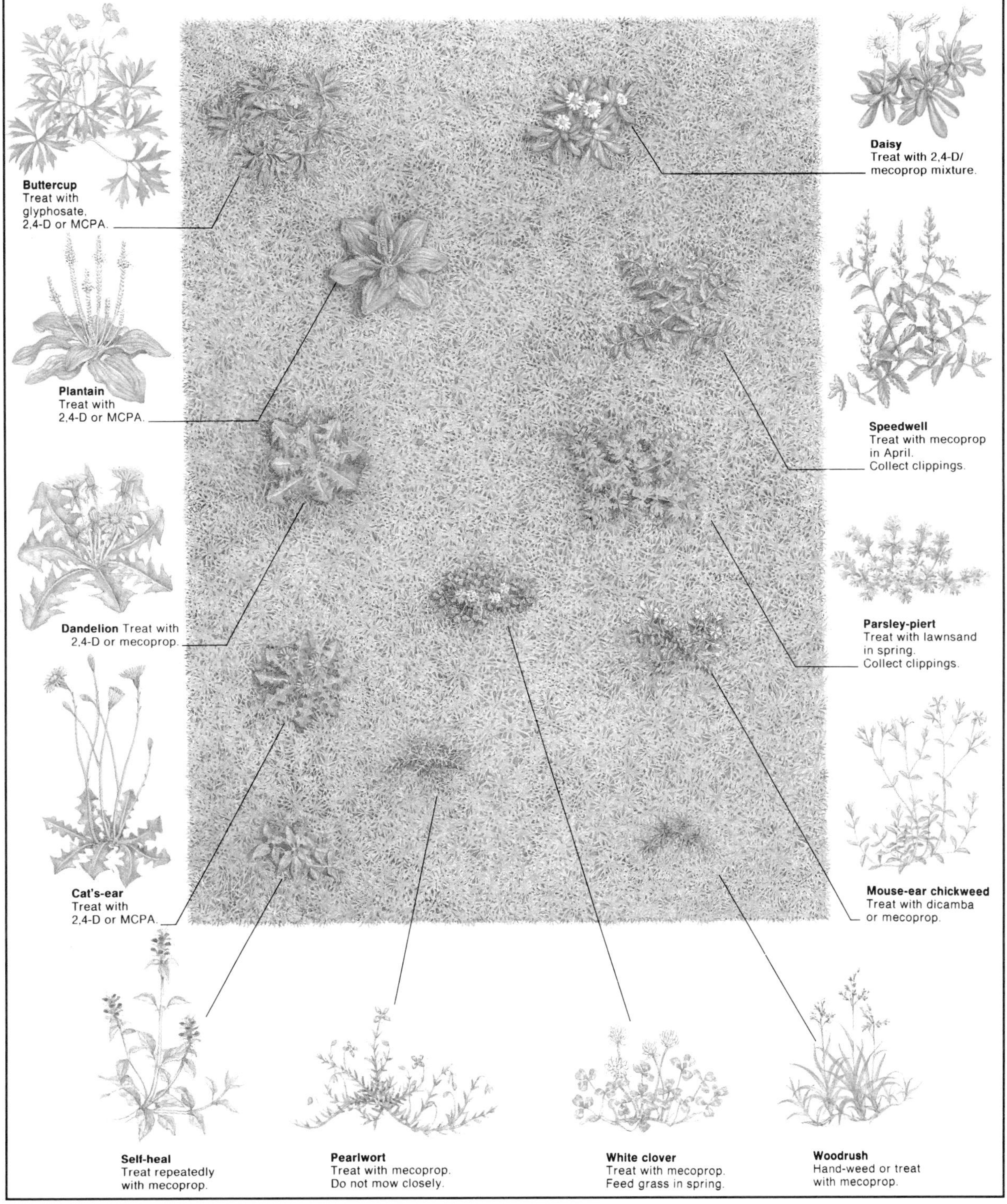

Buttercup Treat with glyphosate, 2,4-D or MCPA.

Plantain Treat with 2,4-D or MCPA.

Dandelion Treat with 2,4-D or mecoprop.

Cat's-ear Treat with 2,4-D or MCPA.

Daisy Treat with 2,4-D/ mecoprop mixture.

Speedwell Treat with mecoprop in April. Collect clippings.

Parsley-piert Treat with lawnsand in spring. Collect clippings.

Mouse-ear chickweed Treat with dicamba or mecoprop.

Self-heal Treat repeatedly with mecoprop.

Pearlwort Treat with mecoprop. Do not mow closely.

White clover Treat with mecoprop. Feed grass in spring.

Woodrush Hand-weed or treat with mecoprop.

LAWN MOWERS

Choosing a machine

What are the advantages and disadvantages of cylinders, rotaries and hovers? Which, in fact, is the least bother?

All three types of machine are really best suited to different jobs. Try not to think of them as simply different machines for doing the same job. To help you to make up your mind, here are the points for and against each type.

CYLINDER MOWERS

For Closer mowing of fine turf; more accurate setting for height of cut; cleaner cut; better finish; available in hand-powered, petrol-driven or electric forms; all can collect mowings.

Against Motorised models more expensive than other types to buy and maintain; suitable only for true lawn areas, not for rough ground; should not be used on wet grass.

ROTARY MOWERS

For Cheaper to buy and maintain than motorised cylinder mowers; can cut grass of any length; can be used in the wet; easy to clean; changeable and cheap blades ensure sharpness at all times; petrol-driven or electric versions available.

Against They don't give as fine a cut as cylinder mowers; not all are sturdy; not all can collect mowings.

HOVER MOWERS

These really have many of the same attributes as rotaries which, of course, they are.

For Light to handle; can be used in hard-to-mow places, such as on steep banks; petrol-driven or electric versions available; they ride well over obstacles; they are relatively cheap.

Against They do not cut long and wet grass as well as wheeled rotaries; few models collect mowings; light and sometimes flimsy; difficult to keep the blades sharp; they do not give as good a finish as a cylinder cutter.

VERDICT

- Cylinder mowers are best on fine lawns and where a good finish is wanted.
- A wheeled rotary is suitable for utility lawns and rough grass.
- Hovers are suitable for utility lawns and ideal for cutting in awkward and steeply sloping places.

Are better things electric?

I have decided to buy a powered mower but cannot make up my mind whether to get a petrol-driven machine or an electric one. Is one better than the other?

It's not a straightforward decision. Here are the considerations you'll have to bear in mind and weigh against each other.

Cost Electric mowers are generally cheaper than those driven by a petrol engine. An electric motor also costs less to maintain.

Ease of use Electric mowers start at a touch; petrol mowers sometimes won't start at all. Because they are lighter, electric mowers are easier to handle and manoeuvre. You do, however, have the awkwardness and potential hazard of a cable trailing around after you. This is a more important consideration in a larger garden. Battery-operated electric mowers overcome this limitation, but tend to run out of power on a large lawn.

Noise An electric mower is quieter – almost as quiet as a hand mower. It is also pollution-free and less messy than a petrol-engined machine.

Power A petrol mower is usually much stronger and more powerful than an electric one. It may do a better job if the grass has got out of hand.

Size Electric mowers generally have a narrower cut than petrol mowers. So they tend to take longer to cut a given area.

On balance, an electric mower is your best bet if your lawn is small and easily managed. A petrol-driven mower makes a better choice for larger areas and on rough ground where extra power is needed.

Striped grass

After mowing the other day, I noticed that many of the longer blades of grass on my lawn had pale stripes on them. How did this happen?

The grass is being squeezed instead of being cut between the mower bottom plate and the cylinder blades. This means there is a gap between them. The stripes are caused by each cylinder blade making a crush mark on the grass.

This happens only on cylinder mowers, all of which cut with a scissors action. Rotaries and hover mowers cannot crush the grass because they cut with a single blade like a high-speed scythe.

To solve the problem, use the adjusting nuts to move the fixed base plate closer to the cylinder. As soon as winter comes, overhaul the mower and get the cutting blades

THE RIGHT MOWER FOR YOUR LAWN

Manual cylinder mower

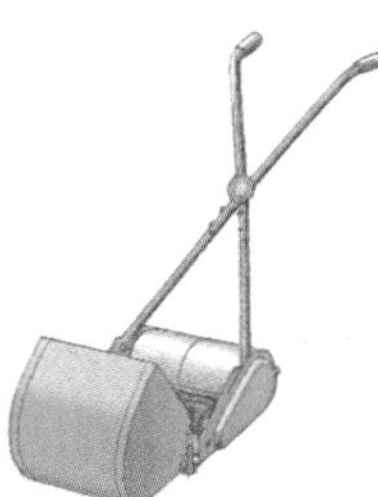

A hand mower is most practicable on a small lawn – less than about 250 square yards – whose surface is fairly flat. Use a model with a roller if you want stripes; otherwise go for a side-wheel model, which will be lighter and easier to push.

Petrol-driven cylinder mower

A petrol-driven mower is the best type for a lawn of more than 250 square yards. Use a cylinder model, like this one, for a flat lawn, and make sure it has a roller if you want a striped finish. On a very large lawn, get one with a powered roller or wheels.

Electric cylinder mower

Electric mowers are best suited for lawns of less than about 250 square yards, where the cable is not so long as to be a nuisance. Battery models do not, of course, need a cable, but their limited power makes them suitable only for a very small, flat lawn.

Petrol-driven rotary mower

A petrol-driven rotary can cope with a lawn of any size, and with rough ground that would quickly blunt the blades of a cylinder mower. It requires more maintenance than an electric mower, though, and unless it has a rear roller it won't make stripes.

Petrol-driven hover mower

A hover mower is a reliable choice on a lawn of less than about 250 square yards, or to cope with banks, rough ground or hard-to-reach spots under shrubs. Motor and blades need little maintenance. On the other hand, it doesn't make stripes.

sharpened. You may even have to fit a new base plate. For advice on how to sharpen the blades yourself, see the pictures on page 215.

Signs of a blunt rotary mower are just as clear. The ends of the grass are left ragged and tattered instead of clean-cut. They have been torn, not sliced. The answer is to fit new blades, or sharpen the existing blades with a file, whetstone or grinding wheel.

Value of rollers

Some mowers have front rollers, others rear rollers, some no rollers at all. What difference does this make?

Rollers, front or rear, give a better finish and a mower with rollers should always be used on a fine lawn. Mowers without rollers are good for cutting rough and long grass, and that is all they should be used for.

Front rollers lay out the grass ahead of the cutting blades, clear obstructions and flatten wormcasts. Rear rollers drive the cylinder blades in a hand mower and flatten out the grass behind the cutters, leaving those dark and light stripes which give a good lawn such a polished finish.

Mowers with no front roller are better at clearing bents – the stalky flower heads of grass – because they do not flatten the stalks before the cutters get to them. On the other hand, you shouldn't find many bents on a well-kept lawn.

Measuring the cut

According to the experts, I should cut my ordinary, domestic lawn to a height of ¾in. How can I set my mower to this height?

On a cylinder mower, you must turn the machine on its side and place a straight-edge between the front roller and the rear roller.

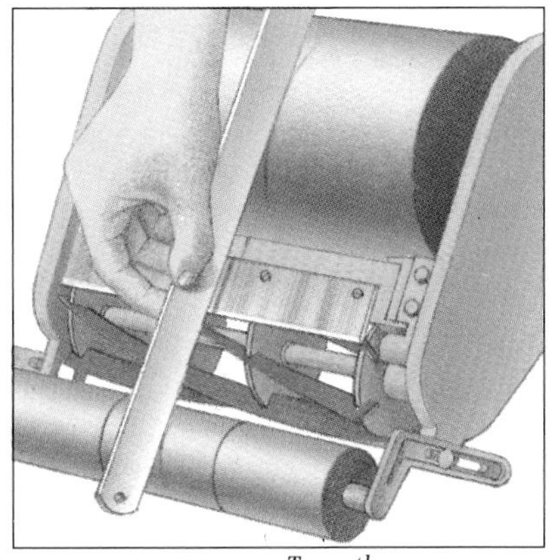

CHECKING THE HEIGHT *Turn the mower over and measure the distance from the blades to a straight-edge laid across the rollers.*

Then measure the distance between the straight-edge – which can be any straight piece of wood or metal – and the upper edge of the base plate, where the cylinder blades cross it. Adjust the height settings to make this distance ¾in. Use the same principle on any other type of mower.

Side-wheel mower Lay the straight-edge from one wheel to the roller at the rear; measure to the blades.

Four-wheeled mower Run the straight-edge from a front wheel to the diagonally opposite rear wheel.

Rotary mower Run the straight-edge from a front wheel to the diagonally opposite rear wheel. Measure from the straight-edge to the front of the cutting plate, which is usually slightly lower than the rear.

Hover mower Lay the straight-edge across the skirt and measure to the cutting blade. This will always be a slightly imprecise measurement because the height of the hover above the grass is not consistent, but it's accurate enough for mowing purposes.

When measuring the cutting height of a petrol-powered mower, empty the petrol tank first, to avoid spillage. Similarly, lift off the battery of a battery-powered model, or the acid may spill.

Check the cutting height regularly, and, with a machine which has a front roller, make sure that both sides of the front roller are locked at the same height. Otherwise you'll get a lopsided cut.

How to undo worn nuts

I've been trying to change the blades on my rotary mower, and after four hours of unavailing toil I've given up. The trouble is that the heads of the bolts on the underside of the rotary plate have been worn smooth – by flying pebbles, I suppose – and no spanner will grip. Any ideas?

It sounds as though you've let rather too much time elapse between maintenance checks, but even so there are still a few ways out of the problem. The easiest is to turn the mower over and construct a little wall of Plasticine or putty around each bolt head. Fill these wells with penetrating oil and leave it overnight to soak in. This may ease the bolts sufficiently for them to be undone.

If this doesn't work, file new flats round the edges of each bolt so you can get a grip with a smaller spanner. Another, but very laborious, method is to cut through both nuts and bolts on the underside of the rotary plate with a hacksaw. Or cut into the nuts with a cold chisel and hammer, tapping them round the thread to loosen them.

If all else fails, and you don't want to hand the job over to a mower maintenance centre, get a nut-splitter – they're available from most tool-hire shops.

LEAFCUTTER BEES

Shrubs disfigured

A lot of my bushes have had semicircular pieces sliced out of the edges of their leaves and are looking extremely tatty. What has caused this and what can I do about it?

The culprits are leafcutter bees – small, hairy insects nearly ½in long – which are close relatives of the honeybees, though they do not live in communal nests.

The females cut pieces from the leaves of roses, laburnums, privet, lilacs, rhododendrons and other shrubby plants, and use the fragments to make a series of thimble-shaped breeding cells in old brickwork, dead branches or light soils.

A single egg is laid in each cell, which is provided with a stock of pollen and honey before the top is sealed with another fragment of leaf. The larvae live off their supplies through summer and the following winter before they metamorphose into the adult form in spring.

The young bees eat their way out in June and begin their own leafcutting activities, which generally last until August.

Leafcutter bees are not usually numerous enough to cause severe damage, though their handiwork can be extremely unsightly. Sustained attacks might also eventually weaken the plants.

If you feel that your garden is not big enough for you and leafcutter bees, there are ways of getting rid of them.

One way is to follow working bees back to their nests, which you can then destroy. Alternatively, if this seems too time-consuming, spray or dust affected plants with HCH, which will kill the bees.

BUSY BEES *Slices out of leaves can spoil the look of a hedge, though serious infestations of leafcutter bees are rare.*

LEAFHOPPERS

Persistent nuisance in the greenhouse

I keep finding in my greenhouse small greenfly-like insects which thrive through the winter, apart from those that leave their corpses stuck to the undersides of leaves. How can I get rid of these pests?

What you have is an infestation of leafhoppers or frog flies, so called from their summer habit of jumping, apparently aimlessly, from leaf to leaf.

There are numerous species of leafhopper, which feed on many different plants. Tomatoes, primulas, rhododendrons, calceolarias, fuchsias and pelargoniums are all liable to infestation. The pests are active from April to October outdoors, and – as you've noticed – all year round under glass.

The adult females live on plants for two or three months, laying about 50 eggs each and inserting them into leaf veins, shoots or flower buds. After a week or two, the eggs hatch and the young hoppers suck sap from the undersides of the leaves, moulting five times as they grow.

It is not corpses that you see stuck to leaves, but the pale, shed skins from each insect. The hoppers mature to winged adults in a month or two.

To get rid of the insects, remove and destroy old leaves bearing colonies of eggs and young hoppers. Then spray the rest of the plant thoroughly with resmethrin or malathion two or three times at fortnightly intervals to protect new growth.

Systemic insecticides such as dimethoate, with their more prolonged effectiveness, can also be used.

Some types of leafhopper are found on apples, strawberries, raspberries and other fruit. In these cases it would be wiser to avoid the use of systemic chemicals – in case the fruit is eaten too soon after spraying – and go for contact insecticides instead. If you do use a systemic insecticide, study the manufacturer's instructions on the packet and follow them carefully to ensure that the minimum interval at least has elapsed between spraying and harvesting.

SKIN SHEDDERS *Empty moulted skins are the telltale evidence of infestation by sap-sucking young leafhoppers.*

LEAFY GALL

Distorted shoots

My sweet peas have developed thickened and distorted shoots near the ground, while the rest of the plant appears to be all right. What is the cause?

It sounds as though they are suffering from leafy gall, which is caused by soil-borne bacteria entering the plant through tiny wounds. The disease won't kill a plant, but it does distort the shoots and leaves.

Many types of plants are affected, chiefly sweet peas, carnations, chrysanthemums, dahlias, gladioli, geraniums, nasturtiums and strawberries. On bedding plants it sometimes results in blindness (absence of flower buds); and while petunias may grow out of this and recover, antirrhinums seldom do.

The thickened and distorted stems you describe are the result of the bacteria stimulating dormant basal buds into growth. The bacteria are active throughout the growing season, and can be spread from infected tools and by planting diseased stocks or seeds.

There is no reliable chemical method of dealing with the disease. Any infected plant should be removed and destroyed, and susceptible varieties should not be planted in contaminated soil for as long as possible.

When replanting, choose a fresh site and species that are not so prone to the disease. Disinfect hands, tools, pots and boxes with a Jeyes Fluid solution before planting.

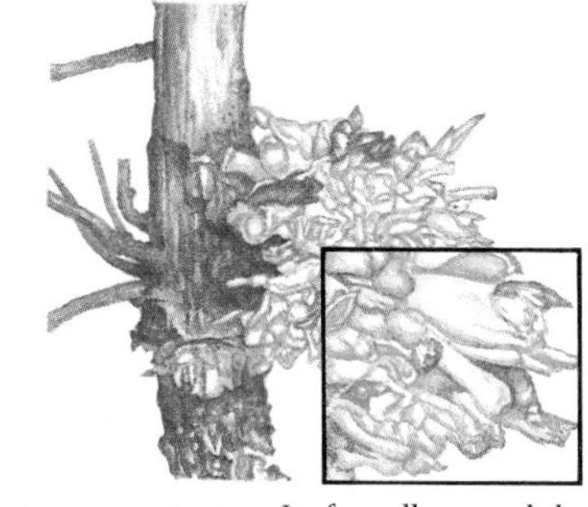

SOIL-BORNE BACTERIA *Leafy gall, caused by microscopic underground bacteria, usually has its biggest effect at or near ground level, though there may be some stunting of the plant.*

LEATHERJACKETS

Collapsing cabbages

One or two cabbages in the middle of the row began to wilt without any visible cause. I dug them up, and there, burrowed into the roots, were a number of greyish, fat, repulsive grubs. Identification and cure please.

Leatherjackets. They are the larvae of daddy longlegs – otherwise known as craneflies – and a real nuisance in the garden.

The grubs, which grow up to 2in long, do most damage to young plants in spring. But they can turn up at any time during the growing season. They're most common on land which has been cultivated only for a few years. Severely affected plants turn yellow, wilt and may die. And, as you imply, because the pests live underground feeding on roots, you can't see that a plant's in trouble until it's too late to do anything.

As well as attacking vegetables, leatherjackets are a particular pest on lawns, where they can kill off quite large areas of grass. The best treatment is to cultivate the soil thoroughly before planting, and, if you suspect infestation, to protect established plants by raking bromophos or HCH into the soil.

So far as lawns are concerned, you should water the infested area thoroughly, then cover it with a sheet of black plastic. When you remove the sheet in the morning, you will find that the grubs have come to the surface; simply leave them there for the birds.

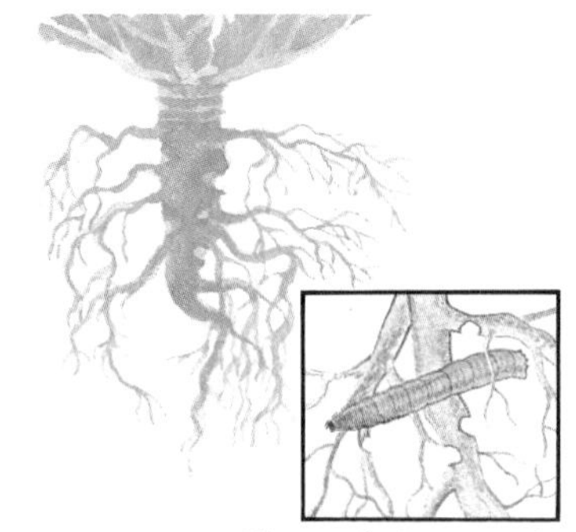

UNLOVELY LARVAE *Plump, legless, tough-skinned leatherjackets are the grubs of daddy longlegs, and a major pest in many gardens.*

LEEKS

Fiddly collars

Putting collars around leeks to make the white stems longer seems such a fiddly business. Couldn't I get the same results just by earthing up with soil?

You could get similar results, but not as good. Absence of light is what makes leek stems white, and a collar of some sort – a length of plastic drainpipe, say – can block light from a longer stretch of stem than heaped-up earth, which will constantly be washed away by rain.

You're right, though, that traditional collars are extremely fiddly. Once they're in position over the plant, you have, ideally, to trickle soil in gradually – an inch or so at a time – as the leek grows, to keep the stem in the dark. Trying to get the soil into the gap between plant and collar is tedious, but it's vital to keep soil out of the leaves, otherwise you'll wind up with gritty leeks.

A much simpler method is to use a black plastic bag in place of a rigid collar. Cut the bottom off the bag so that it's a tube, and set it concertina-fashion over the plant. Pin one end of the tube to the ground with earth or stones, and tie the other end with soft string round the stem just below the spreading leaves. Then, as the plant grows, all you have to do is slide the top end upwards – there's no need to add any soil at all.

How to store leeks

Late leeks tend to get in the way of my winter digging. Is it possible to store them, and how long will they keep?

Leeks can occupy the land for a long time and interfere with winter digging operations, for they are traditionally grown as a winter crop. The plants are famed for their ability to survive just about any weather conditions. But, unfortunately, the crop can't be lifted and stored like onions or roots.

What you can do is to lift the plants and heel them in at the corner of the plot (provided it is not too exposed, for wind can dry the plants out very quickly). This leaves most of the plot free for winter digging. When heeling in the plants, do not pack them tightly together, otherwise they will sweat and start to rot. Give each one an inch or two breathing space.

Next time, consider growing an early crop. It would be ready for harvesting from September to December, and, if you began pulling when the plants were quite small, the crop would be cleared well before Christmas. To prepare for an early crop, sow the seed in a heated greenhouse during February or March and move the seedlings outdoors in April or early May. Recommended early varieties include: 'Alma', 'Autumn Giant – Autumn Market', 'Autumn Giant – Argenta', 'Autumn Giant – Goliath', 'Autumn Giant – Walton Mammoth', 'Genevilliers – Splendid' and 'Lyon Prizetaker'.

Traditional trimmings

I'm told that it's essential to trim the tops and bottoms of leeks before transplanting them. I'll go along with most over-the-garden-wall advice, but I can't see the point of doing this.

Trimming leeks before transplanting is traditional. It's done for a number of reasons, none of which is actually of any great merit. Chopping off about half of the topgrowth is the only part of the trimming that is at all valuable. It helps to reduce moisture loss through the leaves (thus easing the strain on the roots which have to supply the water). And it makes the plants neater – that is, it prevents leaves from flopping onto the ground and picking up soil-borne diseases.

But the reasons for trimming roots are obscure indeed. Leeks, transplanted bare-rooted, suffer considerable damage when the plants are lifted, resulting in the loss of as much as half of their root systems. This delays recovery from the shock that all plants suffer when they are transplanted. In the case of leeks, it induces stress which may lead to premature flowering and running to seed, as well as reducing the plants' resistance to pests and diseases. Trimming the damaged roots merely makes things worse, though it does make it easier to drop the transplants into their holes.

The best advice is to keep root damage to an absolute minimum; this will encourage the speedy re-establishment of your plants. Best of all, really, is to sow your leek seeds in peat modules or blocks, or in peat pots. This way, when it comes to moving the plants on, their rootballs will remain intact and undamaged, enabling the leeks to survive the transfer with the minimum amount of disturbance.

If you can't be bothered with peat blocks or pots, at least give the ground a good soaking a few hours before lifting the young leeks. Then ease the plants out gently with a fork rather than pulling them; this will help to reduce root damage.

Buying in

Some garden centres sell young leek plants in trays. Would I get as good a crop from these as from plants raised in an outside seedbed?

Much the same, really. The amount of root damage that would take place when you took the plants from the tray would just about equal that incurred when extracting them from the seedbed. In some cases, the tray-grown plants could be worse – if, say, their roots had become tangled in the tray. One category of bought plants, though, would be well worth a try – those that have been raised in modules or peat pots. You could plant those straight into their permanent site without any risk of root damage to the young leeks.

Growing better leeks

What can I do to get my leeks to grow long and sturdy? I raise good seedlings, earth them up carefully after transplanting, yet really, from the time they're set out, they never seem to do very well.

Earthing up leeks will increase the length of blanched stem, and thus the usable weight, but it won't improve their quality. If you are raising good young plants, then the chances are that the trouble lies in the soil, or in the way it's been prepared. Check what you're doing against this step-by-step list.

- Prepare the main bed thoroughly some time between December and February. Choose a sunny spot, dig the ground well and incorporate a bucket of well-rotted compost or manure in each square yard. Leave the ground rough for frost to work upon it. Work plenty of peat into the seedbed as well.
- Sow maincrop leeks in March, in drills about ½in deep and in rows 6in apart. Later, thin the seedlings to 1½in apart. Alternatively, raise the seedlings in peat pots or modules in a cold frame or greenhouse.
- In May, three or four weeks before transplanting, work into the top few inches of soil in the main bed 1oz of superphosphate and ½oz of sulphate of potash per square yard.
- Transplant the seedlings to the main bed in June or early July. They are ready for the move when they are about 8in long and as thick as pencils. Trim off about half the length of the leaves to help to compensate for any root damage during transplanting.
- Make a series of holes 6in deep with a dibber. Allow 6-9in between holes and 15in between rows. Drop a seedling into each hole, setting each plant so that its leaves lie along the row, not across it. That way you'll be able to hoe more easily between the rows without damaging the leaves. Gently dribble water in to wash soil over and through the roots. Do not fill the holes with soil. The reason for this dribbling is, again, to minimise damage to the delicate roots.
- Keep the weeds down by hoeing carefully between rows and weeding by hand between the leeks. Water the plants well in dry spells. Every 10-14 days until late August, give them a liquid feed containing 1oz nitrate of soda and 1oz superphosphate to each gallon of water.

• About a month after transplanting, put a collar – a bottomless black plastic bag or a roll of corrugated paper – around each stem (see *Fiddly collars*, page 221).
• Begin harvesting maincrop leeks in November. Lift them gently from the soil with a fork; never pull them. Take them as required – the remainder will be quite happy left outside in the wintry garden until they are needed.

Shot full of holes

My leeks are very disappointing this year. On half of them, the leaves and stems are twisted and there are ragged holes in the bases of the stems. Is it some sort of disease?

Sounds much more like cutworms, a serious but by no means unbeatable pest. The cutworms, which are actually the caterpillars of various species of moth, feed on the leaves of a number of herbaceous plants and vegetables. Regular hoeing will discourage them, as will a sprinkling of bromophos around the stems. You could also scatter a bran bait mixed with HCH about the plants. Nuisance though they are, cutworms are one of the milder of the many complaints that leeks suffer from. Here are some of the others.

• **APHIDS** They cause leaves to turn yellow and become crinkled and twisted, particularly on young plants. Spray with pirimicarb or malathion.
• **BEAN SEED FLY** Seeds fail to germinate, and seedlings collapse rapidly. Control the fly by taking care not to over-manure the ground. Dress seed with bromophos.
• **LEEK MOTH** Watch out for a shot-holed appearance on young leaves as they unfold, and for damaged growing points; later, leaves rot and plants die. Deep digging and cultivating after the leek crop is over helps to reduce the numbers of this pest on future crops. So does the application of a foliar spray containing derris.
• **ONION FLY** Leaves yellow and wilt, eventually killing the plant. Prevent the creatures from getting a hold by dressing seed with bromophos and by sprinkling bromophos or diazinon along the drill before sowing. Dust the planting holes with the same chemicals.
• **ONION THRIPS** The symptoms are white or silvery blotches on leaves; later, the leaves curl and die, causing a check in the growth of young plants. Control with sprays of malathion.
• **SLUGS** The telltale signs are ragged holes in leaves and chewed or chopped-off seedlings. A scattering of slug pellets round the plants should get rid of the pests.
• **STEM AND BULB EELWORMS** These microscopic creatures will cause seedlings to turn soft and bloated, leaves to grow twisted and malformed, and plants to rot and die. There is no cure. Dig up and burn all affected plants.
• **BOTRYTIS** A fungal disease, also known as grey mould. The first symptoms are bleached markings on leaves, which rapidly die back, become soft and put out a grey fungal growth. Burn severely infected plants and prevent the infection from spreading by spraying with benomyl. Good drainage, keeping the bed tidy and cutting back on nitrogen-rich fertilisers will also help.
• **FUSARIUM FOOT ROT** Plants show decay at stem bases and have a pinkish tinge; leaves wilt successively from the outside inwards. Finally, stems and leaves collapse. There is no cure, and leeks should not be grown again on the same site for at least five years. Guard against the disease by dipping bare-root transplants in benomyl and applying a benomyl soil drench to modules and peat pots immediately after transplanting.
• **LEAF BLOTCH** The signs of this disease are white oval spots that shortly turn to greenish-brown. Spray with mancozeb.
• **PURPLE BLOTCH** Look for white, oval leaf wounds that develop purple centres. No cure; burn infected plants and never grow leeks again on the same site.
• **RUST** Orange, elongated spots on leaves warn of this disease. Growth is delayed and lower leaves wilt or die. Remove and burn infected leaves and spray the rest with benomyl or mancozeb.
• **WHITE ROT** Seedlings collapse at soil level, while the leaves of older plants turn yellow and wilt. Dig up and burn infected plants and spray the rest with thiophanate-methyl. To discourage future attacks, treat the soil with Armillatox before planting.
• **WHITE TIP** A disease whose signature is the bleaching of older leaves; leaf tips become white and papery. Remove and burn infected plants and do not grow leeks again on the same site for at least four years. Plants can sometimes be saved by spraying with mancozeb at the first signs of infection.
• **YELLOW STRIP VIRUS** An infection that robs leaves of their colour and stains them with blotchy streaks. Remove and burn affected plants; there is no treatment.

LEOPARD MOTH CATERPILLARS

Burrow in a branch

Perhaps I should have investigated earlier when I noticed that the leaves on one part of my cherry tree were beginning to droop. Now they are definitely wilting, and I see that below the affected leaves there is a long, straight burrow into the branch. Could it be caused by a woodpecker?

No. Almost certainly the culprit is a leopard moth caterpillar, a spotted creature about 2in long that spends its larval life burrowing into fruit trees, willows, birches, rhododendrons, lilacs, cotoneasters and a good many other things besides. It lives in the host tree for two or three years, chewing away at the wood. Eventually, it will kill the branch, or if there is a colony of caterpillars in the trunk, kill the tree itself. The books say you should inject HCH into the tunnel to kill the caterpillar, but that isn't easy in practice. If it isn't going to affect the look of your tree too drastically, it's better to cut off the branch and burn it. Paint the end of the stump afterwards with a sealant compound.

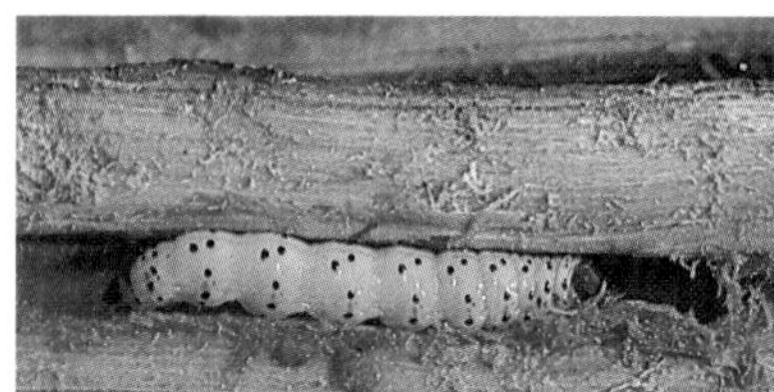

TUNNELS THAT KILL *Leopard moth caterpillars feed upon the inner wood of branches, killing the foliage beyond their tunnels.*

LETTUCES

A response to stress

How can I stop my lettuces bolting?

By looking after them more carefully. The factors that trigger the premature flowering of plants are complex. They vary from species to species and even between varieties of the same plants. Bolting – premature flowering – in outdoor lettuce usually takes place shortly after their hearts form in the long, warm days of summer. At this time, there is a space of only a few days between the hearts growing to maturity and their shooting up into flower stalks. But the process can be accelerated by stress, since the common reaction of plants that feel endangered by adverse conditions is to reproduce themselves by flowering and setting seed. A common cause of such stress in lettuce is lack of water.

You can minimise the risk considerably by giving additional water – 2-3 gallons per square yard per week while the weather stays dry. Transplanted crops, too, should be watered regularly until the plants have become established. Another method is to wait until two weeks before harvest and then apply 4 gallons of water per square yard. This will encourage the hearts to swell quickly and reduce the likelihood of bolting.

Other factors which induce stress in plants include: pest and disease attack; overcrowding; poor and infertile soils; bad drainage; chill winds; and transplanting.

A spring crop

Can you recommend some lettuces to grow during the winter for cutting in spring? When and how should I raise the plants?

The productive season for outdoor spring lettuce can be a long one, especially in milder parts of the country. To obtain a crop that will run from mid-March to early May, sow the seed directly in the ground from mid-August to early September. No need to make a fuss about soil preparation. A bed dug over and mulched for an earlier vegetable crop will do perfectly well. Nevertheless, it would do no harm to apply sulphate of potash at 2oz to the square yard two or three weeks before sowing. This strengthens the plants against the chills of winter and encourages heart formation in the spring.

Water the bed well to ensure even germination, then sow the seed thinly in ½in deep rows 12in apart. Thin the seedlings to 2-3in apart when they are about ½in high. In late February, thin the plants to their final spacing of 12in apart. Stagger the plants in neighbouring rows to give maximum growing room. Give the crop a late dressing of high-nitrogen fertiliser at the rate of 2oz per square yard in mid-January in the South or Midlands, or in mid-March in the North.

Where the harvest is late, make sure that the plants do not dry out, which can easily happen in a dry spring. In this case, water your lettuces, giving them 3-4 gallons per square yard two weeks before harvesting. You would, of course, get a crop two or three weeks earlier by growing under cloches or in a cold frame.

Recommended varieties for a spring crop include: 'Arctic King' (very hardy cabbage variety); 'Imperial Winter' (large butterhead type); 'Lobjoit's Green Cos' (cos type); 'May King' (cabbage variety, requires frame protection in most places); 'Valdor' (butterhead type); and 'Valmaine' (large, self-folding cos type).

A steady supply

I either get far too many lettuces at one time or long periods with none at all. How can I even out the supply?

Gluts usually occur when two separate sowings are ready for cutting at the same time – often due to a slow-germinating first crop being overtaken by a faster-maturing second one. Dearth, on the other hand, is frequently due to making sowings too far apart in time. To be sure of a continuous supply of lettuce, you have to make successive sowings. But if you stick to a rigid pattern, say a sowing every two weeks, this does not take into account the vagaries of the weather and its effect on germination and the emergence of seedlings. Hence gluts and shortages.

To overcome these difficulties start by preparing a good seedbed. Make sure it is evenly moist, and in dry conditions trickle water along the drill bottom before sowing. Or use the fluid sowing technique, in which the seed is mixed in a gel made from wallpaper paste and piped into the drill. This will help you to sow the tiny seeds thinly, and keep them moist while they germinate.

When sowing direct, make successive sowings just as the seedlings of the previous crop have emerged. A good scheme would be to sow in late February for a harvest in late May to early June. Follow this with March-July sowings for June-October pickings, and sow between mid-August and early September for a March-May harvest. Finally, you could make an undercover sowing in October for lettuces in early May.

Propagating plants in blocks or unit pots and then transplanting into beds can also help in adjusting crops to your needs and to the weather. It is also possible to buy packets of mixed lettuce seed. These contain several varieties which, if sown on the same date, mature at different times.

Temperature control

I tried to raise some lettuce seeds in a propagator, but not one germinated, even though it was a new packet and I used fresh compost. What could account for this?

The reason the seed failed to germinate was possibly that the temperature was too high. The optimum germination temperatures for lettuce are 10-16°C (about 50-60°F). Much higher than this, the seed enters a condition known as thermo-dormancy and remains inactive. The answer is to lower the temperature. Also, take care not to sow too deeply, because this, too, can inhibit germination. In a propagator, seedlings should start to emerge within five or six days.

The aphid and the lettuce

My neighbour tells me there's a plague of aphids in the neighbourhood and to watch out for my lettuce. Are aphids a serious pest on lettuce and how do I get rid of them?

There are several species of aphid that infest outdoor lettuce. The most troublesome are the lettuce aphid, the peach potato aphid, the potato aphid and the glasshouse and potato aphid. All of these infest leaves, which often become curled or blistered. Cast or moulted skins and honeydew excreted by the aphids further disfigure the crop and lower its quality and kitchen appeal. The honeydew excretion usually becomes covered with sooty mould, a black, or dark brown, soot-like fungus. In addition, the peach potato aphid and the glasshouse potato aphid spread a number of virus diseases, at least three of which – lettuce mosaic virus, cucumber mosaic virus and beet western yellow virus – may affect lettuce.

The lettuce aphid survives the winter as clusters of eggs on twigs of currants and gooseberries. Winged insects emerge in May and fly to summer host plants which include lettuce and a few related plants; in autumn, the creatures return to the gooseberries and currants to lay their eggs.

The green, or pink, peach potato aphid feeds on lettuce at any time of the year, checking the growth and affecting the plant's vigour. It spends the winter in the adult stage on weeds and brassica crops, migrating to its summer hosts from May onwards.

The shiny, green-yellow glasshouse potato aphid feeds on a wide range of plants, including lettuces, tomatoes, and many flower crops and weeds, both outdoors and under glass. Colonies spend the winter in greenhouses and other protected situations. They increase in spring and early summer and the winged adults disperse from June onwards.

To prevent the spread of aphids, and of virus diseases, maintain firm weed control, and clear away plant debris after harvest. Spray aphid eggs on deciduous woody plants with a tar oil wash in winter to kill the eggs and break the life cycle of the colonies. If possible, grow young lettuce plants away from older crops. Keep an eye on the plants and spray at the first sign of infestation. A routine spray is a good idea at the start of the hearting stage, with further treatment if infestations are heavy. There are quite a number of anti-aphid insecticides on the market. They include systemic sprays such as dimethoate, and non-systemic, like derris. Systemic insecticides don't need to be used as often as non-systemic ones, since the chemical enters the plant's system and lingers there, killing the insects that feed upon its juices. But you will have to allow at least a week between spraying and harvest, and, if you don't want to wait so long, use a non-systemic contact spray instead. You must apply this thoroughly, so as to reach every part of the plant. Whichever type you choose, follow the maker's advice on the label about the safe harvest interval.

The loose-leaf option

A friend tells me there are lettuces whose leaves can be pulled off as needed, leaving the remainder of the plant to grow on. Is this so?

Your friend is right: these are the so-called loose-leaf or gathering lettuces. The leaves can be picked individually as required, and this actually encourages further growth. The plants continue to grow for many weeks, and are less likely to run to seed than the more conventional kinds of lettuce. 'Salad

Bowl' and 'Red Salad Bowl' are the most common varieties of this type, but there are others, many of them highly decorative.

The plants do best in a fertile, humus-rich soil. A plot that has been well manured in the previous autumn or winter is ideal. A couple of weeks before sowing or planting, apply a general fertiliser at 2-3oz to the square yard. The crop can be sown either directly into the ground or raised under glass in boxes, modules or peat pots. If you sow direct, prepare a good seedbed with soil raked to a fine 'tilth' – about the consistency of breadcrumbs.

Sow the seeds thinly in ½in deep drills. As the seedlings grow, thin them frequently, using the thinnings in salads. The final spacing will vary according to the variety, but a good idea is to grow them in staggered rows so that each plant is about 12in from its neighbours. This will give good yields.

Sowing under glass ensures a consistent quality of seedlings and a good survival rate after transplanting. Set the plants out when they have grown four or five adult leaves.

There is no need to make successive sowings to ensure continuity of supply. Only a few plants need be raised at any one time. One sowing in April followed by another in midsummer should be ample. A space-saving method of producing a family-sized crop is to raise eight plants in a growing bag. A mixture of green and coloured varieties will look very attractive, and provide pickings over a long season.

Collapsing lettuces

My lettuces were hearting up nicely until a few weeks ago when the leaves of half a dozen or so simultaneously wilted and collapsed. The stems of these lettuces seemed soft to the touch, and later they began to grow an unpleasant white fungus that in some cases turned to black. Obviously they have a fairly serious disease; what is it, and what can I do about it?

Sclerotinia, almost certainly, and yes, it is serious. Dig up and burn all affected plants immediately. Spray the remaining plants with benomyl. This may save them from infection, but there's no guarantee. Sclerotinia is only one of quite a large number of plagues that attack lettuce. While on the subject, here are some of the others.

- **BACTERIAL WILT** This causes a soft rot on stems which discolours them and creates cavities. There is no treatment; burn affected plants. In future, prevent attacks by not planting in poorly drained soils or in wet conditions. Avoid over-watering.
- **BOTTOM ROT** Seedlings collapse; mature plants rot at stem bases. Large, blackish, water-soaked patches appear on the undersides of outer leaves and brown fungal threads become visible on the soil surface. No cure. Prevent the disease from spreading by spraying with benomyl at the first signs.

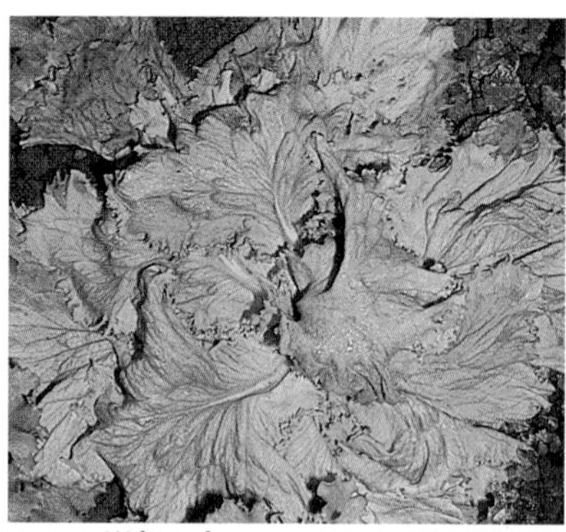

ON TOP *Wilting leaves are one of the signs of sclerotinia, a serious disease.*

UNDERNEATH *Soft stems covered with white or black fungus confirm the diagnosis.*

- **DOWNY MILDEW** The symptoms are yellowish patches on older leaves in autumn, grey or white spores on the undersides of the patches, later turning brown. There is no cure. To prevent it in future, grow mildew-resistant varieties, and spray them with mancozeb at regular intervals from the seedling stage. Make sure that all debris from infected crops is removed.
- **RING SPOT** Round spots and holes in leaves; sunken brown markings on stems. The symptoms appear most frequently in cold weather. Destroy affected plants and do not plant lettuce on the same site again for at least three years. In future, avoid badly drained sites.

For details on how to recognise and combat other pests and diseases, see: *Aphids*, page 12; *Caterpillars*, page 49; *Leatherjackets*, page 220; *Slugs and snails*, page 322; *Viruses*, page 359; and *Grey mould*, page 176.

Bonus crop

I've noticed that lettuce stumps often sprout new leaves. Could these grow into decent lettuces eventually?

Usually the cut stumps of all types of lettuce are capable of regrowth. However, not all of them necessarily make a good heart. Looseleaf types, such as 'Salad Bowl', are non-hearting to start with and when they regrow they will have outer leaves only. But cos lettuces such as 'Erthel', 'Paris White' and 'Valmaine' will almost certainly produce new hearts with the regrowth.

Make sure that, once the plants are cut, the roots are never allowed to dry out. If the weather is dry, water the plants at a rate of 2-3 gallons per square yard per week and keep the ground free of weeds that will be competing for moisture.

As the regrowth gets under way, lettuce, being a leafy vegetable, will need a high-nitrogen fertiliser such as nitro-chalk. Give it at the rate of 1 teaspoon to a gallon of water to the square yard, and repeat the feed at fortnightly intervals until the crop is ready for cutting.

Persevering with cos

Growing cos lettuces for the first time, I found their centres were very loose and leafy. Is this why they're not very popular?

It may well be that all you need do to overcome the problem is to tie in the outer leaves and the heart with string. This is practically essential with some of the older and larger-leaved varieties, such as 'Lobjoit's Green Cos'. More modern varieties, and those of compact habit, such as 'Little Gem' and 'Winter Density', don't need to be tied.

Cos's lack of popularity is more likely to be due to its being not quite so easy to grow as the tightly self-hearting butterhead or crisphead varieties. All the same, its crisp texture and flavour make it well worth persevering with. You shouldn't have much difficulty if you grow it in a well-cultivated, moist soil in which you have incorporated plenty of well-rotted compost or manure.

Early crops can be sown under glass from late January to early February. Prick them off into small pots for planting out in early spring. Sow your main crop directly into the ground at regular intervals from March to June. Winter-hardy varieties can be sown from mid-August to early September for cutting from mid-March to the end of May. Give a final spacing of 9in between plants and 12in between rows. Compact varieties, such as 'Little Gem' and 'Winter Density', require no more than 6 x 9in or 6 x 6in if grown on deep beds.

Start cutting the crop as soon as the centres begin to form. By the time the last few plants are harvested, the hearts will be fully developed. This avoids waste, since, once the hearts are fully mature, the plants won't hold and will quickly bolt, especially in dry weather. Here are some reliable cos lettuce varieties well worth trying:

'Balloon': large white heads; suitable for spring sowing.

'Barcarolle': medium to large heads, tightly enfolded leaves; attractive appearance.

'Erthel': medium size; very crisp and sweet;

resistant to mildew; very slow to run to seed.
'Little Gem': semi-cos type, very compact; solid, crisp and crunchy heart; very sweet.
'Lobjoit's Green Cos': old favourite – large imposing variety; delicious flavour; may need tying in.
'Paris White': large variety with solid white heart; crisp and sweet; slow to bolt.
'Romance': strong-growing variety; large, tightly folded head with a crisp, sweet heart.
'Valmaine': similar to 'Lobjoit's Green Cos' but more resistant to lettuce mildew; self-folding type, very robust; ideal for summer and autumn cropping.
'Vaux's Self Folding': erect, self-folding habit; very compact, always reliable.
'Wallop': erect habit, with dense heads and few outer leaves; excellent flavour and texture; stands in good condition for 10-14 days; highly resistant to root aphid, botrytis and downy mildew.
'Winter Density': semi-cos type, very hardy, crisp and sweet; holds in condition; ideal for summer or winter use.

Maintaining moisture

Is it all right to cover lettuce seeds with polythene until they germinate? My soil dries out quickly and this might save watering.

It could be all right, but it could also be a disaster. It depends on how you do it. In a hot summer, for instance, covering the soil with polythene can build up very high soil temperatures. If the temperature rises much above 21°C (70°F), the lettuce seed simply will not germinate.

Before laying the polythene, give the sowing area a thorough soaking with water at about 4-5 gallons per square yard. Then immediately stretch the film over the ground to prevent evaporation and cool the soil. Pin the polythene in place with stones. A day or so later, sow the seed – ideally between 2 and 4pm. If the weather is really hot, erect a temporary screen to give shade.

You also mention that your soil dries out quickly in the summer. This indicates that it may be sandy and low in organic matter. Improve its moisture-retentiveness by working in well-decayed farmyard manure or garden compost. These should be added each year during winter digging. But, instead of spading the stuff into the bottom spit as is generally recommended, mix it well into the soil throughout the full depth. You could also give an additional feed between the finish of one crop and the start of another by applying a surface mulch of garden compost at the rate of 1 bucket per square yard. Let the earthworms work it in and, provided you keep topping up between crops, you'll be able to sow or plant indefinitely without further labour. Make sure, though, that the compost is well rotted. The ammonia in immature compost may retard the growth of young seedlings and small transplants.

Keeping seeds fresh

I always have far too much lettuce seed left over each year. If I keep it, how long will it remain in usable condition?

Seeds start to deteriorate as soon as they are taken from the parent plant, and will eventually die. However, not all seeds deteriorate at the same rate. Some, like lettuce, lose their viability after two or three years, while others – tomato is an example – can keep for five years or more. Much depends on how the seed is stored from one season to the next. Seed kept in warm, humid conditions, for instance, will fail to germinate even after just a few weeks.

Lettuce seed should be particularly cherished, since successive sowings are often made from the same packet. After the first batch is sown, many people simply leave the packet in the greenhouse or on a shelf in the garden shed. It is not surprising in these circumstances to find a steady deterioration in the germination rate of later sowings as the season progresses.

Opened containers of lettuce seed, whether paper packets or tinfoil vacuum packs, should be stored in a cool, dry place at a temperature of around 10°C (50°F) throughout the year. The best course is to place the opened packet in an airtight jar with a small amount of silica gel (obtainable from garden centres) placed in a separate, open-topped container within the jar. The silica gel will absorb moisture from the surrounding air, and the dry air will in turn draw moisture from the seeds, thus preserving them.

A summer pest

Some of my lettuces weren't so good last summer, and later I found masses of small grey insects on the roots. What were they?

The problem was undoubtedly lettuce root aphid. It is harmful mainly to outdoor lettuce in summer, especially in dry weather. The lettuce root aphid is a migratory species which survives the winter in the egg stage on Lombardy and black poplars. In spring, the newly hatched insects live inside flask-shaped galls on the leaf stalks. During June, winged aphids fly from colonies inside the galls to lettuce and certain weed hosts where they produce several generations of wingless aphids on the roots. These wingless aphids can be recognised by the whitish-grey, waxy secretion that covers them. The creatures return to the poplars in late summer and autumn. Some root aphids may survive the winter in the soil, even in the absence of host plants, and can attack lettuce planted in the same ground the following spring.

Only crops sown between mid-April and late June are liable to attack by the lettuce root aphid. The best defences for crops sown in this period are regular watering and weeding. Once the aphids establish themselves on the roots, they are virtually invulnerable to chemicals.

Clearing away weeds and plant debris, particularly root stumps, after autumn lettuce crops discourages aphid colonies from remaining in the soil over the winter. Next year, plant your spring-sown lettuce in a new site if the autumn crop was infested.

A winter crop grown in pots

I'm thinking of growing winter lettuces in pots because my greenhouse soil isn't very good. What growing medium should I use and what size pots?

John Innes or a peat compost would be fine. However, John Innes contains loam, which will act as a buffer against problems such as over-watering. Use a John Innes No 2 potting compost for the best results. A 5in pot is adequate. Anything larger will increase the volume of compost, which increases the risk of over-watering.

It is important to choose the right variety of lettuce. For instance, it must be a short-day variety as it is only these types which have been bred specifically to grow under poor light conditions. The following varieties are ideal for growing in pots in winter: 'Ambassador', 'Claret', 'Columbus' and 'Cynthia', all butterheads; and the crispheads 'Kelly's' and 'Marmer'. You will be able to harvest them from October to mid-May.

Leaves all summer

I've heard about the NVRS method of growing leaf lettuce, but don't know what it is. Can you explain?

This method of lettuce growing, developed at the National Vegetable Research Station at Wellesbourne in Warwickshire, involves growing the plants very close together in order to boost the total weight of the crop. The NVRS is now known as the Institute of Horticultural Research, but the method it devised lives on under the old initials.

To use the method, it is absolutely essential to prepare a first-class weed-free seedbed. On most garden soils a general fertiliser (about 1-2oz per square yard) should be applied two or three weeks ahead of sowing. The seed must be sown in rows 4-6in apart, thickly enough to establish between 15 and 20 plants per square foot. Sow the seed in drills no deeper than ½in. Once above ground, the seedlings should be kept well watered in order to keep them growing quickly.

By sowing a succession of crops, it is quite easy to obtain lettuce leaves every week from the end of May until October. The first sowings can be made in early spring, and the first harvest will be ready about seven weeks later. To collect the crop, cut off all the leaves about 1in above soil level, using a pair of scissors or a sharp knife and leaving a short stump. After this, give the soil a thorough soaking. New leaves will start to grow from the cut ends about ten days later, and, after a further seven or eight weeks, a second harvest can be taken. After this second harvest the plants must be dug up and destroyed in order to prevent any build-up of pests and disease.

Later sowings can continue until late summer, and these will mature more rapidly, allowing the first cut to be made after about three weeks, and the second four weeks or so later. Not every variety is suitable for this method of growing. In some cases, the young leaves are too bitter to harvest. The most suitable varieties are the cos types, particularly 'Avoncrisp', 'Erthel', 'Lobjoit's Green Cos', 'Paris White' and 'Valmaine'.

Winter crispheads

I like 'Webb's Wonderful' for its crunchy hearts. Is there anything like it that can be grown for winter use?

Winter crops of crisp lettuce can be obtained from October to May if they're grown under the protection of a greenhouse or walk-in polythene tunnel. Use varieties such as 'Mariner' and 'Kelly's' – 'Kelly's' being very much a Webb's type. To obtain the best results, raise the crop from transplanted seedlings rather than by sowing directly into the site.

The seed can be sown in early August in trays containing a peat-based compost. After sowing, cover the seed to a depth of $\frac{1}{8}$in. Prick off the seedlings into further trays as soon as they can be handled. Alternatively, sow the seeds singly into blocks, peat pots or unit pots and leave them to germinate at around 15-20°C (about 60-70°F). The plants will be ready for planting out when they have made two or three true leaves.

Whatever method of propagation you use, keep the growing medium moist, though not wet. Otherwise the plants can be severely checked; they may also become susceptible to disease.

Prepare the greenhouse border by raking it thoroughly. But there's no need to dig it deeply. If you are following on from a previous well-fed crop, no additional fertiliser is necessary; otherwise apply a general-purpose fertiliser at 2oz per square yard.

Spacing depends on harvest time. Plant an autumn crop 7in apart with 7in between rows. Winter and spring crops, coming along when growing conditions are at their worst, require slightly wider spacing: 8 x 8in or 9 x 9in.

Water little and often for the first week to keep the soil surface moist. After the first week, do not water until the plants reach the rosette stage – that is, when they begin to form hearts. Then give the border about 2 gallons per square yard. This should see the plants through to harvest time.

Growing space

Seed firms don't seem to agree when it comes to recommended spacing for lettuces. How close can they be planted and is there an ideal distance for the cos and cabbage types?

Recommendations in catalogues for the spacing of lettuce vary a great deal because many factors must be taken into consideration, such as the type of lettuce, the variety, whether it is grown on flat or deep beds, outdoors or indoors, and at what time of year. But as a general rule you should thin most varieties down to a final spacing of 12in apart each way. Exceptions are 'Tom Thumb' and 'Little Gem' which need only 9in, and 'Salad Bowl', which requires no more than 6in.

What is equally important is the plant arrangement. The most efficient pattern is to stagger the plants in adjacent rows, to allow the maximum of growing space for each.

Keep a cool head

Lettuces wilt so quickly once they've been cut. What's the best way to keep them fresh?

Always cut a harvest-ready lettuce first thing in the morning. After that, because lettuces deteriorate quickly at high temperatures, the sooner it is moved into cool conditions the better. So, place the entire lettuce in the refrigerator and leave it for an hour or so. Then wrap it in clingfilm and return it to the refrigerator to prevent wilting. A lettuce kept like this will remain fresh for up to 14 days.

If there is no room in the refrigerator, keep cut heads cool by spraying them with water once or twice each day. In this case, do not wrap the lettuces in plastic.

Ready or not?

Several times I've cut lettuces too soon, thinking they were fully grown, only to find the hearts rather small. How can you tell when they've stopped growing?

If you're uncertain about your lettuce's readiness for the salad, test for firmness by gently pressing the head with the back of your hand. Do not pinch or squeeze the lettuce, as the hearts are easily bruised.

Choice of deterrents

What's the best way to stop birds and slugs enjoying my lettuces?

Most garden experts decided some time ago that chemical repellents had little effect on birds. Their conclusion gave rise to a number of mechanical deterrents, including such variations on the old scarecrow theme as inflatable dummies. Recorded and amplified whines and bangs are available, and kestrel-like shapes suspended from captive helium-filled balloons, though none of these are really practicable in the small garden. For this there is a variation on the kestrel motif, a dummy hawk that sways about on the top of a tall, flexible pole. Or you might try humming lines, which – stretched tightly between supports – vibrate in the wind, emitting an ultrasonic sound that birds find unpleasant. Suspend the lines above the plants, supported by canes arranged in a zigzag formation across the rows.

Alternatively, string black cotton over the rows, or cover the lettuces with cloches, frames or wire mesh.

Slug control is rather less of a hit or miss affair. There are a number of products on the market, all of which are fairly successful though they work in different ways.

Water at the base

Should lettuces be watered from directly overhead or is it better to keep the leaves dry? How much water do they need in hot, dry weather?

Plants get most benefit from water that is applied directly to where it can be put to maximum use: the root zone. There is little point in spreading water all over the site where much of it cannot be taken up by the crop. This is particularly important in warm, dry spells, when you should give 2-3 gallons per square yard each week, directing the water around the base of the plants.

Otherwise, wait until two weeks before the crop is ready to harvest and then apply 3-4 gallons per square yard. This watering will probably have to be an overhead one, because much of the soil surface will be covered by the leaves of the lettuces.

Dressing for colour

How do you get really dark green lettuces? Mine always look so pale and washed out compared with the ones on the seed packets.

The colour of lettuce can vary a great deal – from light to medium or dark green. Many of the butterhead types, such as 'Hilde II', 'Reskia' and 'Suzan', are naturally light green. However, if the varieties you are growing are not meant to be pale, they may lack colour because of a lack of nitrogen in the soil. A deep soil with a good supply of nutrients is essential for a good-quality crop.

Two or three weeks before sowing or planting, apply general fertiliser at 3-4oz per square yard. If this is done correctly, it is not generally necessary to give any further treatment. However, a high-nitrogen liquid feed would certainly help summer-maturing crops on light, poor soils. Use a proprietary liquid feed and apply it around the base of the plants. Water the ground first so that the feed spreads rapidly through the soil.

LILIES

Fading flowers

After only a few years of blooming, my lilies are deteriorating. What can I do to revive them?

Not a lot. It's almost impossible to revive fading lilies, and in almost every case it's a waste of time. The best thing to do is to dig them out and start again with new plants.

Lilies need a sheltered spot and a crumbly, well-drained soil. Too much damp, and too rich manure or compost around the bulbs will lead to poor flowering and general loss of vigour. So will virus diseases.

Choose the right types of lily as well. Start with the Madonna lily, *Lilium candidum*, and the tiger lily, *L. tigrinum*. Mid-Century hybrids, too, are reliable and will tolerate a heavier soil than most other lilies.

Once you have had success with these easy-to-grow varieties, experiment with the more temperamental types.

Planting time

When is the right time to plant lilies? Some experts say autumn. Others say spring.

Plant in November – that's the right time for lilies. You can delay planting until the end of March, provided that you keep the bulbs in dry peat or sawdust to prevent them drying out and shrivelling. Nevertheless, there's less risk of them rotting or shrivelling if you leave them to spend the winter in the ground. The Madonna lily, *Lilium candidum*, is an exception. Ideally, this should be planted a little before the end of August, to give it time to produce its energy-generating rosette of foliage before winter.

Choosing bulbs

Lily bulbs are expensive. What should I look for to make sure I am getting a good buy?

Good, tight scaling on the bulb is the first thing to look for. Don't buy if:

- The scales are loose or soft.
- The bulb skin is damaged.
- There are signs of mould, generally seen in the form of sunken, brown spots.
- The bulb feels dry and brittle.

Be wary of bulbs that are offered in cardboard boxes; look at them carefully. Lily bulbs should be stored in peat, sawdust or wood shavings and should be kept in one of these until sold.

Be careful too about bulbs that are prepacked in polythene bags. These can be perfectly good buys, but in warm shops condensation may form inside the bags and cause premature sprouting.

Lily bulbs are sometimes waxed before being put on sale, to prevent them from drying out. There is nothing wrong with bulbs treated in this way as long as they have been kept in cool, dry conditions.

Big flowers are not necessarily produced by the biggest bulbs. Lilies are among the most diverse of flower species. Some of the tallest North American varieties spring from the tiniest bulbs and some short Asiatic blooms sprout from bulbs like tennis balls. So check species before you buy, and don't be dazzled by the size of bulb alone.

Dividing Madonnas

I have some overcrowded clumps of Madonna lilies in my garden. Can I lift and divide them?

You can, but you need to take more care than with other lilies which remain dormant through the winter months.

Madonnas are the only lilies that produce a rosette of foliage in autumn, which they keep throughout the winter. Because of this habit, the best time to divide the clumps is in August or September, when the leaves have died back but before the basal foliage forms. Lift the clumps gently, preferably when the ground is moist, and ease the bulbs and roots apart. It is important to keep the roots damp as you divide up the clump. Drying out will check future growth. Replant at once.

Cut blooms

I am planning to grow some lilies for flower decoration at my local church. Which are the most suitable types and how are they best grown?

Choose the Easter lily, *Lilium longiflorum*, with its lovely white trumpet and golden anthers on a tall, firm stem. It is only half-hardy in Britain, being a native of Japan, so it is essentially a greenhouse plant, but it does take well to growing in pots.

The natural species can be raised easily and quickly from seed, reaching flowering size in 18 months. If you grow from bulbs – as you have to do for named varieties such as 'White Queen', which won't grow true from seed – you will get blooms for a cut display the summer after planting.

Plant the bulbs in autumn in groups of three in 10in pots filled with a soil-based compost mixed 3-to-1 with sedge peat. Keep the pots in a cool dark place for the first ten weeks or so to develop a healthy root system, then bring them into the light. The plants can be brought on with a little mild heat, but no more than 16°C (about 60°F). Too much heat and too little light will produce straggly growth and poor flowers. The blooms, topping 3ft stalks, will open roughly six weeks after the buds become visible, so you will be able to forecast with some precision when the flowers will be ready to present to the church.

The bulbs can be used a number of times before losing vigour, but at any sign of virus, discard them and start again with new ones. This lily is prone to virus, and poor bulbs produce poor blooms.

Shady spot

I have a shady spot in my garden, overhung by trees. Can I grow lilies there?

Yes – indeed, they'll do well there as long as it's not too dry. You can try any of the modern Mid-Century hybrids.

Lilies are heavy feeders and will not like being too close to the trunk of the tree, where competition from the tree's roots will be fierce. Plant them towards the edge of the shade canopy. Dig in some well-rotted compost or manure in autumn, and in spring mulch the area with a 1in thick layer of the same material or of something similar such as peat or chopped and composted bark.

Self-supporting

My garden is in North Devon, and even in summer it can be buffeted by some fairly exuberant breezes. Are there any lilies I can grow there which don't require staking?

No lilies enjoy being blown about, but quite a number can endure even strong breezes without staking. Try the Mid-Century hybrids, such as 'Destiny', which has lemon-yellow flowers, or 'Enchantment', which has orange-red blooms. These hybrids, mostly crosses between hybrids of *Lilium* x *hollandicum* and *L. tigrinum*, are fairly tough and will hold up on their own without stakes. So will the short-stemmed *L. formosanum* 'Pricei' and the handsome, purple, turk's-cap lily, *L. mar-*

ENCHANTING *The Mid-Century hybrid 'Enchantment' normally needs no staking.*

tagon. The ice-white Madonna lily, *L. candidum*, and the bright orange tiger lily, *L. tigrinum*, will also stand without support.

If your garden is very exposed and windy, try to create some shelter with shrubs or fences before planting lilies.

Greenhouse lilies

Can I grow lilies successfully in the greenhouse?

Yes, they will love it if you give them plenty of light and ventilation and shield them from direct sun. They will reward you with long-lasting blooms unblemished by wind or rain, and their fragrance, too, will be best appreciated in this enclosed environment. Plant the bulbs in a peat-based compost, and in separate pots for each variety. Don't choose tall varieties, for it is difficult to stake tall lilies growing in pots.

As soon as flower buds show, begin weekly feeds, using a standard liquid house plant fertiliser. Stop feeding as soon as the blooms fade, or the bulbs will become soft and difficult to keep over winter.

Some indoor lilies drop a lot of pollen, which can stain the petals. Enthusiasts often clip off the pollen-bearing anthers as soon as they appear to keep the flowers fresh and clean-looking.

Planting in grass

Are there any lilies which will grow happily in grass?

Only the turk's-cap lily, *Lilium martagon*, will really take to naturalising in grass. It grows no more than 2-3ft tall, needs no staking and produces handsome purple flowers in late June and early July. The best grasses to plant lilies in are the fescues, which are not gross feeders, so will not rob the bulbs of vital nutrients, and which do not grow so high that they will hide the flowers. Even so, give the bulbs a spring feed of bone meal at the rate of 2oz to the square yard, just to make sure they don't go short of nutrients.

L. tigrinum, *L. henryi*, and *L. davidii* will also grow in grass, but not so happily as the turk's-cap lily.

Longer season

My lilies give a glorious show for about four weeks, then fade away to nothing. In other gardens I have seen lilies in bloom all summer. Can you recommend some varieties that I can enjoy for rather longer?

Most lilies flower in July and August, but with planning you can get a continuous show from June to September.

Start with the Madonna lily, *Lilium candidum*, which throws out its handsome white spikes in June. The bright orange *L. bulbiferum* opens up at about the same time, although it's not at its best until July. To extend the season, plant *L. speciosum*, which has white, red and pink varieties. Try the varieties 'Melpomene' and 'Rubrum', both of which in a good year will last into early October. The orange tiger lily, *L. tigrinum*, and its vivid yellow variety 'Flaviflorum' will often do the same.

Planting in lime

I have a very limy soil. Are there any lilies which will tolerate this?

You could try the Madonna lily, *Lilium candidum*, or any of the Bellingham hybrids – American varieties which come in mixed colours. They will grow in a limy soil and do not mind sun or shade. Give them a good base of well-rotted compost when you plant, and keep them watered regularly.

Two other lilies will survive limy soil with care. They are the purple-flowered *L. martagon*, and *L. amabile*, a similar flower which has orange-red blossoms spotted black.

Growing from seed

Can I grow lilies from seed?

Yes, but it is a long, slow business and not as reliable as dividing clumps or propagating from bulb scales (see *Plants from scales*, page 228). You have to be of a patient disposition to grow lilies from seed; some varieties take up to seven years to flower.

Growers argue about whether it is better to sow seed in spring or autumn. Some varieties do not germinate until after a hard frost, others will germinate with or without frost. The safest bet is to sow in autumn if it's seed you have gathered yourself – when you know the seed is fresh – and to sow in spring if you're using bought, packaged seed.

Mix up 3 parts of soil-based compost with 1 part of peat and add a little sharp sand or grit to keep it open and free-draining. Sow thinly, just cover the seed with the mixture and place the tray or pot in a cold frame. Some lilies germinate quickly. Others, such as *Lilium auratum* and *L. rubellum*, will not show for at least a year, until the seed has formed a tiny bulb under the soil.

After sprouting, lilies of all species tend to become congested. So lift and tease them apart as soon as they are big enough to handle. Put them separately into 2½-3in pots and leave them for a year. They can then be moved into larger pots or planted out, depending on vigour and variety.

Rockery plants

Are any lilies suitable for a rock garden?

Very few – and don't bother with any of the spectacular varieties. They are just too big. Stick to one of two varieties: *Lilium pumilum*,

Plants from scales

I'm told that it's possible to propagate lilies from pieces of the bulb. How is this done?

It is called scaling, and the time to do it is in early autumn.

Lift the bulbs after the plants have finished flowering, some time in September, and pick out a particularly plump, healthy one. Strip off any dry or damaged outer scales around the bulb, then carefully separate those that are left. From an average-sized bulb, you should be able to take 12-24 firm scales, easing each one away and making sure that it includes a tiny piece of the hard base plate of the bulb.

Prepare seed trays with a mixture of a soil-based compost such as John Innes No 3, mixed 3-to-1 with sedge peat. Insert the scales, base down, to about half their depth and set the trays in a propagator, ideally one fitted with a soil-warming cable that you've set to 10-13°C (50-55°F). Small bulblets will form at the base of the scales; these will produce shoots and leaves by the middle of the following summer.

The young bulbs can then be potted up individually and left in a cold frame. In three to five years, depending on variety, they will grow into mature plants and reach flowering stage. You can then plant them out in their flowering positions at some time between autumn and spring, ideally in October.

1 *Strip off dry outer scales and separate the rest, making sure that each contains a piece of the bulb's hard base.*

2 *Half bury the scales in a mixture of peat and compost, and keep them at a temperature of about 10-13°C (50-55°F).*

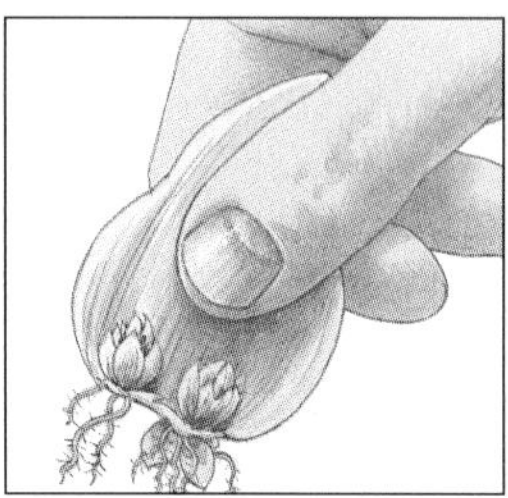

3 *Tiny new bulbs will form on the scales. Pot the bulbs up separately when leaves appear from them the following year.*

also known as *L. tenuifolium*; and *L. formosanum* 'Pricei'. *L. pumilum* is a bright red martagon type that grows only 15in high. It likes a cool, moist root run and an open position. It looks good among short, shrubby plants that will shade the roots and, in late summer, conceal its fading foliage.

L. formosanum 'Pricei' reaches to only 12in, and has white trumpet blooms flushed with purple. It flowers from seed in only nine months, so it's often treated as an annual. The variety is much hardier than its parent species, *L. formosanum*. Don't mix them up. The species will do well only in the shelter of a cold greenhouse.

Twisted leaves

My lilies, which I planted two years ago, flowered well until this year, when they grew to only about 6in and the leaves became twisted and mottled. What is the matter?

They have a virus disease. There are several, all of which cause stunted growth and twisted foliage. The viruses are passed on by sucking insects such as aphids, so pest control is the best preventative. For your lilies which already have the virus, though, there is no cure. Burn them or put them in the dustbin. Don't compost them.

Spray lilies regularly with a systemic insecticide such as dimethoate as soon as they sprout – in early spring – and keep spraying, as often as recommended in the manufacturer's instructions until late summer. This will control the aphids – a good idea whether the lilies are infected or not – and help prevent viral infection.

Sometimes, bulbs bought from a shop or garden centre are already infected. There is no way of telling until the growth twists and distorts. Any lilies that do show signs of virus should be burnt or thrown away at once. Otherwise, aphids will transmit the disease to neighbouring plants and could devastate the entire lily bed in a single summer.

Alarming as all this may sound, lilies are relatively trouble-free. But just in case, here is a checklist of other ills that sometimes come their way.

- **LILY BEETLE** Watch for holes in leaves, buds, stems, flowers and seed capsules. It can be eliminated by spraying with malathion or resmethrin, and repeating the dose every two or three weeks for the remainder of the season.
- **LILY BOTRYTIS** A disease that causes wilting and produces red-brown spots on leaves. Spray fortnightly with benomyl from spring onwards and destroy plant debris in autumn.
- **SLUGS AND SNAILS** Holes and chewed-out pits in bulbs and shoots, and slimy trails near the plants are the symptoms of a slug or snail raid. Slug pellets are the cure.
- **TULIP GREY BULB ROT** One of the most serious diseases of bulbous plants; the symptoms are rotting or rotted bulbs which are covered with a whitish mould that spreads to the surrounding soil. Destroy infected bulbs and do not grow lilies in the same spot for at least five years.

Leaf bulbs

Mini-bulbs have grown on the stems of some of my lilies. Can I grow full-sized bulbs from them?

Yes, although it will take time. You find these bulblets forming in the leaf axils – the spots where the leaf stalks join the stem – on *Lilium bulbiferum* and *L. tigrinum*. They are black or deep maroon, and do look like tiny lily bulbs. They're called bulbils.

Leave them on the plant until the leaves turn yellow in about September. Then pick them off. Once gathered, the bulbils can be planted at once, but you risk losing the young plants in a harsh winter. It's better to put the bulbils with a little damp peat in a polythene bag, and store them in a refrigerator until the spring.

Plant them in moist peat-based compost in seed trays in March, setting them with their noses just beneath the surface. Stand the trays in a cold frame. As soon as leaves form, feed the plants every three weeks – a standard liquid house plant fertiliser is fine. Keep feeding until the end of July; feeding any later will make the bulbs soft and vulnerable to disease. Pot up the young plants individually in 2½-3in pots in autumn and leave them in a cold frame for a couple of years. You will get the first flowers three or four years after planting.

LOGANBERRIES

A gentler loganberry

Is there a thornless form of loganberry in the same way that there's an 'Oregon Thornless' blackberry?

You must be thinking of the loganberry that goes under the somewhat bureaucratic name of LY654. It's not only thornless but it crops heavily, too.

With most cane fruits, the thornless varieties yield lower crops than those with thorns. But the LY654 crops just as heavily as the thorn-bearing LY59, which in its day came first in a trial and was declared the only loganberry worth growing in our climate.

Trying something different

I like to experiment with new fruit bushes and new tastes. Have there been any interesting developments in recent years?

You might consider the tayberry. Like the loganberry, it's a cross between a raspberry and a blackberry and tastes like a loganberry. It was bred in Scotland at what was then the Scottish Horticultural Research Institute and was released in the late 1970s. Its main advantages over the loganberry are that it's hardier and bears almost twice the weight of fruit of a comparable loganberry plant.

Specifically, it is a cross between the American blackberry 'Aurora' and an unnamed seedling raspberry.

The tummelberry is the hybrid offspring of the tayberry with another blackberry/raspberry cross. It gets its name because the River Tummel is a tributary of the River Tay. It yields about 8lb of fruit per plant – a little less than the tayberry – but is slightly more hardy and the fruit ripens about a week later, starting in late July. The berries are slightly shorter than tayberries and taste a little sharper.

Then there's the sunberry, a cross between the raspberry 'Malling Jewel' and *Rubus ursinus*, a related cane fruit. It was raised in Kent at the East Malling Research Station, and produces dark purple fruit. It tastes like a loganberry or tayberry and comes between them for hardiness, but is more vigorous than either. The sunberry was released to the general public in 1985, and is available from some of the larger garden centres and from nurseries specialising in soft fruit.

ALL ABOUT CARING FOR CANE FRUITS

Loganberries, tayberries, sunberries – in fact all hybrid cane fruits – are cultivated in the same way and all need the support of a permanent post and wire system, in much the same way as raspberries and blackberries.

One thing to remember is that they're very shallow-rooted and benefit from a moisture-retaining mulch of garden compost or manure in the spring, especially in the drier East and South of the country. Aim to cover an area 2ft wide down the row and make the mulch anything up to 4in thick. It doesn't matter if the mulch touches the stems.

Treat them to a dressing of Growmore each spring – 2-4oz per square yard – to ensure good crops and an ample supply of new canes for the following year.

Try to give them a sheltered and sunny position and, if your district is known to have cold winters, protect the canes before the worst of the winter weather. Wrap them securely in straw or sacking. This is a rather tedious job, but it can make the difference between life and death in a bad winter. If you bundle the canes together before wrapping, they will be even better protected.

If you have had loganberries for ten years or more, think seriously about replacing them with the hardier tayberries.

MARJORAM

Fresh or dried?

I'm not sure when to pick marjoram. Do the leaves have to be dried before use?

There's no need to dry the leaves at all. Indeed most cooks prefer to use the herb fresh, and to keep plants growing in pots on a windowsill through the winter in order to have a fresh supply all year round (see *How to keep marjoram going through winter*, this page).

You can pick stems and leaves from outdoor plants from July to September. With indoor plants you can, of course, pick at any time of the year. Indoors or outdoors, choose the largest leaves – they have the most flavour – and aim to harvest them just before the flower heads open. The best time of day to gather the herb is around mid-morning on a dry day, when the sun is not too hot and the oil content of the leaves is at its peak.

If you want to store the leaves for later use, there are two ways to preserve them: drying and freezing. To dry marjoram, cut off 9in long stems about 2in from the ground, and tie them into bundles. Hang them upside down in a dark, warm spot such as an airing cupboard. Leave them for a week or so until the leaves feel crisp and papery. Rub them between your hands to crumble the leaves. Discard the stems and store the leaves in screw-top jars.

To freeze marjoram, strip the leaves from the stems, wash and finely chop the leaves and sprinkle a teaspoonful into each compartment of an ice-cube tray. Top the tray up with water and put it in the freezer. Once the water has frozen, you can pack the cubes in polythene bags in the freezer. To use the herb, simply drop a cube into the saucepan while you're cooking. There's no need to thaw it. Some cooks blanch herbs before freezing by putting them in boiling water for a minute or two to kill off any bacteria. But this is unnecessary and, moreover, tends to weaken the flavour.

How to keep marjoram going through winter

Can I grow marjoram outdoors or does it have to be grown in pots inside?

In Mediterranean countries, where marjoram comes from, the winters are mild and the herb is naturally perennial – that is, it grows outside year after year without any problem. In Britain, however, where the weather is that much harsher, it can survive only mild winters outside. Pot marjoram is the hardier of the two common types of marjoram (the other type is sweet or knotted marjoram). But even pot marjoram is likely to survive the British winter outdoors only if you happen to live in the South or West.

To improve the survival chances of any plant you decide to leave outdoors, cut it back by two-thirds before it dies down in winter and cover it with a 6in layer of peat, leaf mould or straw.

The only sure way to keep your marjoram going from year to year, though, is to bring it indoors or into the greenhouse over winter. This means either taking cuttings or potting up whole plants from your garden. Both methods have the bonus of providing you with a supply of fresh leaves all through winter.

If you prefer cuttings, take them during August. Cut 2-3in long pieces from non-flowering sideshoots, strip off the leaves from the bottom inch of each cutting and set half a dozen cuttings around the edge of a 6in pot in a half-and-half mixture of peat and sand. Put a polythene bag over the pot to keep in moisture (see picture, page 21). When you see new growth, it'll mean the cuttings have rooted and can be transferred individually to 3in pots of potting compost. Put the pots in a greenhouse or on a bright but not sunny windowsill.

Alternatively, to pot up a whole plant, simply dig it up in autumn, divide it into pieces about 2in across and put each piece into a 3in pot indoors.

If all this seems like too much bother, grow marjoram from seed every year or buy young plants in pots from a garden centre. Sow seeds in pots or pans of seed compost in February or March. Lightly cover them with compost and place the pots or pans in a greenhouse or in a light but shaded spot in the house. Harden off the young plants before transplanting them outdoors in May. Set the plants 12-18in apart each way. You can also sow seeds outdoors in late April. Sow them in drills 9-12in apart. Thin out the seedlings and plant them 9in apart as soon as they are large enough to handle – usually when they are a couple of inches tall.

Telling marjoram apart

What are the differences between sweet marjoram and pot marjoram?

The main difference is that sweet marjoram (*Origanum majorana*) – also known as knotted marjoram – is said to be better for cooking. Its more pungent aroma also makes it suitable for a potpourri.

Pot marjoram (*O. onites*) is slightly hardier than the sweet, but not so much hardier that it needs any less careful treatment.

Wild marjoram (*O. vulgare*) is better known as the culinary herb oregano. As its name suggests, it grows wild in Britain. It has a more biting taste than the other types of marjoram, which makes it ideal for dishes like spaghetti bolognese. All three need to be grown in exactly the same way.

MARROWS (See also COURGETTES, page 103)

Help with pollination

For several years my marrows, grown from seed, have flowered successfully but failed to set. What am I doing wrong?

Marrows are normally pollinated by insects. However, you may have to pollinate them by hand if it is rainy or cold when the flowers are fully open. If the problem persists well into the season, despite good weather, it could be that your site is too exposed to wind. This tends to discourage pollinating insects, such as bees, from lingering.

The solution is to shelter the bed with some kind of fence, hedge or windbreak, and to sow your seeds a little later in spring to take advantage of milder weather. You can also help the pollination process by doing it yourself. Pick off a male flower (one without the bulge of an embryonic marrow behind it), peel off the petals and push the stamen firmly into the female flowers. Each male can pollinate two or three female flowers.

Protection from frost

When is the best time to set out marrows and can they be grown under cloches?

The ideal time to plant out marrows without protection is when there is no further risk of frost. In warmer parts of Britain this can be from late May onwards. In Northern areas, however, it is safer left until early June. The plants can certainly be grown under cloches, and this can bring the cropping period forward by a few weeks. Provided they are picked regularly, marrows can be harvested from July until October – or even from June with cloches.

You'll get the earliest crop from sowing in early April. Sow a single seed into a 3in pot, using a peat-based potting compost. Push the seed ¾in down into the compost. Maintain a temperature of 18-21°C (about 65-70°F) to encourage quick and even germination. Grow the plants on a bright windowsill or in a greenhouse – plenty of light makes for sturdy growth. About five weeks after sowing, harden the plants off gradually over a period of about two weeks, then plant them outdoors in late May or early June. Keep them covered with cloches until all risk of frost has passed.

Make a second sowing indoors in the second half of April for transplanting outside without protection later in June. Alternatively, if the weather is very warm, you could sow seeds directly into the ground in the first half of May.

A crippling disease

Last year mildew crippled my marrows. Is there a safe spray around which isn't harmful to bees?

Powdery mildew attacks the leaves and stems of marrows, turning them white and eventually causing them to wither prematurely. It can, as you say, be a crippling disease, but it can be controlled. Spray with benomyl or thiophanate-methyl, at the intervals recommended on the packet, at the first sign of infection.

As for protecting bees, that's not a question of what you spray so much as when you spray it. The best time to spray is around early to mid-evening, when few insects are on the wing and bees tend not to be active. Thoroughly wet the stems and buds, and the underside as well as the upper surface of the leaves. By the time the bees return the next day, the chemical will have been absorbed by the plant and the bees will be able to work unharmed.

Successful storage

The marrows I was storing for winter turned to pulp. How could this have been prevented?

By growing traditional varieties such as 'Long Green Bush' to start with. Their skins become leathery but the flesh stays firm and fresh and tends to sweeten with age. Some of the newer F1 hybrids, by contrast, tend to be rather thin-skinned, and do not store as well. This is especially true of varieties which are usually grown for courgettes.

High temperatures or frost are other risks. Both will quickly turn stored fruits to pulp, especially if they're not ripe. The best test for ripeness is that the skin should be quite hard. When rapped with the knuckles, the marrow should sound hollow.

Store marrows individually in nets in a cool, airy, frost-free place such as a garage. They should keep until February. Check them regularly and use immediately any which show signs of deterioration.

Fruit or vegetable?

Some folk say that marrows are vegetables, others that they're fruits. Who's right?

They all are. Marrows are vegetables both in the ordinary shopping sense of a plant that you cook and eat as part of a main course, not a dessert, and in the schoolroom sense of animal, vegetable and mineral.

But they're also fruits, because botanists use the word to mean the parts of a plant that contain its seeds. By that definition, an apple is a fruit, as you would expect; but so is a tomato, corn on the cob and a runner bean, which you might not. And sticks of rhubarb, which you'll find in the fruit section of your supermarket, are actually plain vegetables.

MEALY BUGS

White bugs in the greenhouse

Several of my greenhouse plants are badly infested by colonies of tiny, whitish bugs that drape strings of sticky white fluff about the leaves. I've tried spraying with soapy water, but without too much effect. What are these creatures, and how do I get rid of them?

They're mealy bugs – tropical or subtropical insects that have found ideal environments in heated greenhouses in this country, where they are able to thrive and multiply throughout the year.

They're a real pest, for both young and adults feed upon the sap of plants and excrete sticky honeydew.

Look out for them in the crowns of plants, around leaf axils and in other hideaway situations. As for getting rid of them, spray thoroughly with diazinon or malathion and repeat the dose, if necessary, at fortnightly intervals.

In the case of small plants, or house plants, that become infected, paint the mealy bug colonies with a solution of either one of the same insecticides. Use a small, watercolour paintbrush. This will give control, but stay vigilant in case there are further assaults.

An interesting non-chemical alternative is to use a biological control method: introduce the Australian ladybird *Cryptolaemus* into your greenhouse. The ladybirds eat the mealy bugs, and also lay their eggs inside them. You can buy the ladybirds from a number of specialised nurseries.

Attractive as this idea may sound, there are a couple of problems. It takes an enormous number of mealy bugs to satisfy the ladybirds' appetite, and if the ladybirds can't get enough, they eat each other. Moreover, you'll need to buy more ladybirds for each attack, since once the predators have eaten all the bugs, they will eventually starve to death. For further information, contact Natural Pest Control, Watermead, Yapton Road, Bognor Regis PO22 0BQ.

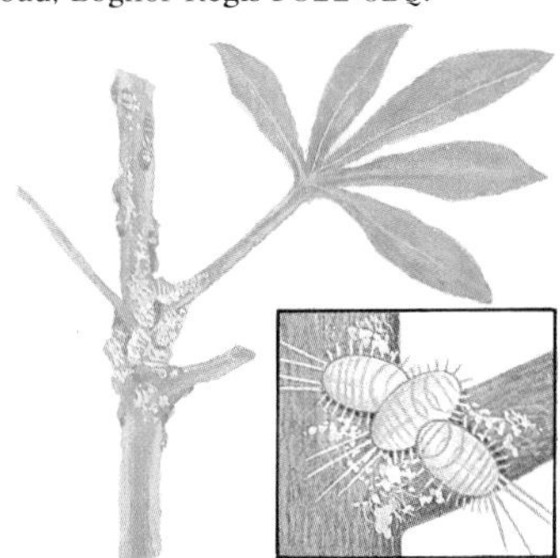

IMMIGRANT PIRATES *Mealy bugs, imported by accident from warmer climes, have found a home from home in Britain's heated greenhouses and on indoor windowsills.*

MINT

Spearmint for sauce

Which is the best mint for making mint sauce?

Spearmint, the common 2ft tall garden variety known to botanists as *Mentha spicata*, is the one you want. Its strong flavour does wonders for new potatoes as well as combining happily with vinegar in mint sauce.

There are several other varieties of mint worth growing, too – each with its own strengths. Try some of these, for instance:

Apple mint (*M. rotundifolia*) Height 2-3ft; woolly-leaved; best for drinks.

Peppermint (*M. piperata*) Height 2ft; very dark leaves; use for tea and summer drinks.

Ginger mint (*M. gentilis*) Height 12in; beautifully variegated golden and green leaves; adds a hint of ginger to salads.

Pennyroyal (*M. pulegium*) Height 1in; small-leaved, creeping, attractive at the front of a herb bed, but of no value in the kitchen; cut it back hard each year in early April to prevent it straggling.

Eau-de-cologne mint (*M. citrata*) Height 12-18in; brush against a plant and savour the perfume; hold a bunch of leaves under the tap for a scented bath.

All the varieties will grow in almost any soil, although a rich, moist loam is ideal. If the soil is poor, add a dressing of well-rotted compost or manure in early spring.

Mint also tolerates shade more than most

other herbs, so you can usefully place the taller varieties at the back of a bed, where other herbs won't thrive. Set the plants about 12in apart.

Deadly pimples

My mint plants are looking straggly and have developed orange pimples on the leaves and stems. What is causing this?

Mint rust. And it is a killer. The rust fungus spreads throughout the plant; it is not confined to the little pimples. The only answer is to uproot the plants, burn them and start again with new stock on a fresh site. To prevent attacks in future, the best method is to keep your plants young by taking cuttings every two or three years and growing the new plants in a fresh site. For some reason, it seems to be mainly old plants that are vulnerable to the disease.

Stopping the invasion

I'm forever plucking out shoots of mint from all over my herb bed. Is there a variety which will grow where it's put?

Not really. Most types, if they are not checked, will spread quickly and take over the herb garden. To prevent this invasion, grow each plant in an old bucket or a 12in plastic pot which has had most of its bottom cut out, and sink the pot almost to its rim in the ground.

Each autumn, lift out the pot or bucket and trim off any roots and shoots that are escaping from it.

The plants die down each winter and reappear at the end of March, producing leaves which are ready for picking by June.

Mint plants soon exhaust the soil. Every three years make a fresh home for them by renewing the soil in the bucket or pot. Stock the pot with plants created by dividing the old plants in March, or by taking 3-4in long cuttings of basal shoots in April-May.

MOLES

Dealing with unwanted visitors

My carefully nurtured lawn is marred by heaps of soil, the handiwork of moles. Is there any way I can get rid of them, preferably without hurting them?

People have mixed feelings about these furry little animals. The fact remains that they can and do cause considerable damage in a garden, not only by their unsightly molehills but by tunnelling under shrubs, causing soil collapse and the death of roots.

They can be discouraged from spoiling your lawn by depriving them of their primary food – earthworms – with a proprietary wormkiller. Elsewhere play upon their main weakness: a sensitivity to noise and smell. Rags soaked in creosote and pushed down a run will discourage them, as will bottles buried upright up to their necks in the earth – the thrumming caused by any breeze across the open bottlenecks is unpleasant to the moles' ears.

Probably the most effective deterrent is to treat the runs with a harmless chemical based on aluminium ammonium sulphate, which is also used to drive away cats. The ground must be soaked and, once the moles have gone elsewhere, a barrier treatment of the material must be put down along the boundary to prevent them coming back.

An old country trick is to put rose or bramble shoots vertically down a run. This acts in the same way as a barbed-wire fence does in deterring human trespassers. Some people believe in planting caper spurge, *Euphorbia lathyrus*, in the borders. Moles are said to find the roots unpleasant and usually move on, though firm evidence for this is lacking.

Deterrents do not always work, though, and you may feel that you have to take more drastic steps. There are a number of options you can consider, none of them very pleasant. Mole traps, for instance, are still legal but hard to come by. Proprietary smokes vary in effectiveness; to work well they need to be placed near the central nest where moles spend most of their time. Farmers have also been known to lead a hose from a car exhaust pipe down one of the tunnels. Letting the engine run for ten minutes or so ensures that lethal carbon monoxide penetrates the whole network.

Fertile mounds

Can the soil from molehills be used for anything in the garden? It seems so nice and crumbly.

Molehill soil can be used outdoors, but not for indoor pot plants. To use it indoors, you'd need to boil it with water, a little at a time, in a saucepan to get rid of weed seeds, diseases and pests.

Since this is a long and messy process, it's much easier just to buy commercially sterilised soil or compost.

For outdoor planting, molehills are fine ready-made mounds of crumbly soil. It can be used for planting trees and shrubs, or for flowers in beds, tubs or window boxes. When planting seeds, make a deeper and wider drill than usual, and half fill it with the molehill soil. Sow the seeds, then cover them with more of it.

MULBERRIES

Making a home for silkworms

I have a mulberry tree in my garden. Does this mean I can cultivate silkworms?

There are three types of mulberry: *Morus nigra* (the black mulberry); *M. alba* (white mulberry); and *M. rubra* (red mulberry). The best silk comes from silkworms raised on the white mulberry. The fruit from this, however, is of poor quality.

Your tree is most likely to be a black mulberry, because that is the most commonly grown species in Britain. This yields the biggest and best fruit, and is just about acceptable to silkworms.

Making silk, though, is a time-consuming and difficult process. You need to buy the silkworms (about 15 would be a good number to start with, taking into account the cost and the amount of food available) from a silk farm, because silkworms no longer exist in the wild.

Once you've bought the silkworms, your problems have only just begun. You will not be able to breed from the insects – they need specially controlled temperatures. You also need to keep them indoors – Britain is just too cold for them outside – and to feed them two or three times daily on chopped mulberry leaves.

After 30-35 days, a healthy silkworm caterpillar will spin itself a cocoon which may contain 2-3 miles of silk. To collect this silk, you need to boil the cocoon in water (incidentally killing the insect inside), then unwind the thread and card it. Some animal lovers may find the boiling repugnant.

The output from 15 silkworms would in any case be very little – about enough to make a handkerchief.

400 years old – and still fruiting

I understand that mulberries live for ages. Does this mean that they take a long time to start producing fruit?

It's true that they can be very long-lived trees. At Syon Park in Middlesex, for instance, there is a mulberry tree dating from 1548. So they can certainly live for at least

400 years. Despite this longevity, they don't take especially long to start bearing fruit. Ten years is probably the upper limit, with six or seven years perfectly normal.

The trees are sometimes grown trained against a wall. Alternatively they can be grown on a lawn, where their often gnarled shape makes them very attractive.

Can I eat them?

Are mulberries edible or just decorative?

They are certainly edible. Though they're never likely to be as popular as strawberries and raspberries, they are very pleasant with stewed apple and other desserts.

Like blackberries, they contain largish pips. If you want to remove these try the traditional method: boil the mulberries until they are a pulp, then strain them through a muslin cloth into a pan.

One easy way to hold the cloth while you're pouring is to tie it to the legs of an upturned stool or chair.

MULCHING

Merits of mulching

I have often wondered if the layer of pulverised bark put by many local authorities around parkland shrubs is for decorative purposes only, or are there other reasons for doing this?

The practice of mulching – that is, covering the ground above the roots of shrubs and other plants with a layer of compost, peat or other material, which can be pine bark but which could also be black plastic – is done for several purposes. Beauty is not always one of them.

Firstly, the mulch acts as a blanket and helps to prevent the moisture in the soil evaporating during hot weather. It keeps the soil and surface roots at an even temperature during weather changes.

Secondly, mulching with properly composted material improves the fertility of the soil. The bulky layer of material slowly builds up the humus content of the upper soil layer as it decays and is taken down into the soil by worms. Some mulches, however – notably pulverised bark – deprive the soil of nitrogen if they're not composted before use.

Thirdly, any mulch, if applied in a suitably thick and unbroken layer on the ground, goes a long way towards smothering weed seedlings before they have a chance to emerge.

The best for the ground

Suggestions, please, on which materials are best to mulch with.

Any material that you use as a mulch must fulfil three basic requirements: it should have a loose texture so that air can reach the plants' roots through it; it mustn't blow away in a wind; and it mustn't clog together when wet. Despite these restrictions, the list of suitable substances is still a long one. The cost and availability of the materials will quickly narrow your choice, though.

There are two mulches that are absolutely free. The first is a layer of loose soil, an inch or two deep, created simply by stirring up the surface with a hoe. When this tilth dries out, it forms an effective barrier to water evaporation from the firmer ground below and weeds are destroyed in the process of creating it. This mulch does not, however, add any nutrients to the soil.

The fall of leaves in autumn provides the second natural mulch, if gathered up and allowed to rot down into a leaf mould. This can then be spread around the base of shrubs and ferns because the leaf mould gives some protection from frost and, in its slow decay, returns nutrients to the soil. Don't leave low-growing rock garden plants smothered in fallen leaves, though. That will merely encourage fungal diseases and slugs.

These suggestions apart, the main materials for mulching are farmyard manure, garden compost, peat, straw and pulverised bark.

Farmyard manure, bark, compost and straw must be well rotted before being put on the ground. The process of rotting down uses large quantities of nitrogen. So if you spread these substances unrotted, they take the nitrogen they need from the soil, denying it to nearby plants. If you have to use the mulching material before it is completely rotted, sprinkle onto it a high-nitrogen fertiliser such as sulphate of ammonia at the rate of 2-3oz to the square yard to restore the missing nutrient. Don't worry about weed seeds in the compost or manure (there are likely to be some in it no matter how well you've rotted it down). You will smother more weeds on the ground than you will ever introduce with the mulch.

Bark and peat can prove to be expensive mulches when used in large quantities. You could compromise by mixing them with another cheaper material that may be readily obtainable near your home.

Any of the following materials, for instance, will be useful if you can get hold of them: spent mushroom compost, spent hops, brewery waste, seaweed, wool shoddy, sawdust and wood shavings. Sawdust and wood shavings need to be composted in the open for at least a year before being used.

Black plastic sheeting also makes a type of mulch since it does keep in moisture and keep down weeds.

Where to mulch

Do I need to mulch all of my garden or are there certain parts that would benefit the most?

If possible, mulch any bare soil, except in the rock garden or around annual seedlings until they are well established. But cost – if you have to buy the mulching material – and difficulty of access to the ground around the plants may prevent you from doing this.

The sections that will benefit most from a regular yearly mulch are the garden's long-term residents: the shrubs, roses, fruit trees and bushes, especially the surface-rooting raspberries, and strawberries. In all these instances the plants remain in the same place year after year and there is usually room to work around them.

The herbaceous border and vegetable garden would also appreciate a mulch, after you do your planting out. Take particular care laying mulch around young stems (see *How close for comfort?* on page 234).

The best for looks

Which is the best-looking material to use for a mulch in the flower garden?

Peat and bark are probably the most attractive mulches for a flower garden. There are several other attractive options which will still keep the soil cool and moist, and keep weeds under control. For instance, where herbaceous plants and shrubs are grown, try a 1-2in layer of grit, gravel, shingle, granite chippings or ornamental blue flints. Even crushed bricks can look good. When it is necessary to dig the ground, the chippings can be incorporated into the soil. But this type of mulch is not suitable for smaller plants and vegetable gardens.

The ground-cover option

Can I grow ground-cover plants as a mulch or will they take too much out of the soil?

These plants do not really mulch; they only prevent weeds from growing and the soil from losing too much moisture. They do, however, provide a living and extremely decorative cover to the ground, particularly in shrub borders. Obviously, though, this sort of feature isn't always suitable. You'd never, for instance, use it in a vegetable patch.

Don't be too concerned that the ground cover will grow at the expense of the main shrubs. In the early years, when all the ground-cover plants are growing hard and filling up the available space between the shrubs, they are well away from their larger neighbours and not competing for food. By the time the ground-cover plants do form a

PLASTIC MULCH
Black plastic warms the ground and suppresses weeds on crops such as strawberries. Set out plants through slits cut in the sheet.

complete carpet, the shrubs will have deep and extensive root systems and will be well able to look after themselves. If anything, it's the ground-cover plants that will suffer with their shallower roots.

Mulching with mowings

Like many other gardeners with a large lawn, I have a nagging problem of what to do with the constant supply of fresh lawn clippings. Could I use them as a mulch and solve my dilemma once and for all?

Sorry, but no. You'd do better to compost them first on an ordinary garden compost heap. Raw grass mowings have several snags. On an exposed site they tend to blow all over the place in dry weather. And in wet weather in any garden, they clump together and hinder the passage of air to the roots of the growing plants. Moreover, there are seldom enough clippings, however big your lawn, to put down an effective mulch over an entire border or shrubbery. So the job looks permanently incomplete.

Mowings can also be guaranteed to contain weed and grass seeds which, if the mulch is less than 2in thick, will give little weed-smothering effect while promoting the growth of grass. A layer more than 2in thick, on the other hand, may bind together and prevent rain getting through.

Be particularly careful about grass from a lawn you've sprayed with a weedkiller. Until at least the third mowing after the treatment, don't even compost the mowings; throw them away or burn them.

The right thickness

How thick should I make my mulch?

On a herbaceous border, around roses, shrubs and other established plants, an evenly forked 2-3in deep layer is best. Smaller plants and young plants require a thinner layer, about 1in deep. The straw mulch between raspberry canes, currants and gooseberries is most effective when in a layer 3-4in deep.

The ideal situation would be to cover as much ground as possible with mulch. But if you haven't got enough to go round, spread the appropriate depth around each individual plant. Leave the rest of the garden uncovered rather than applying a too-thin layer all over it.

At the other extreme, don't be too generous with the mulch. One that is too thick becomes just another rooting zone for weeds and will cut down on the amount of air and water able to get through to the soil and the roots beneath.

When to spread

When is the best time of year to mulch my garden?

Spring. If you live in the South, then about the middle of April; a week or two later if you live in the North. At this time of year, the weeds haven't become established and the ground is moist. Don't mulch any earlier than this, because it is also important for the ground to be warmed up by the sun before mulching. Once applied, a mulch acts as an insulating blanket.

If spring is impossible, mulching is still worth doing at other times of the year. The only thing is that it will be harder work: you'll have to clear the ground of weeds and water the soil before you can lay the mulch.

Rain and the action of earthworms will very gradually integrate the mulch with the top soil layer. Keep a check on the mulch during the year and if necessary renew it regularly during the growing season to keep a permanent covering of the right depth.

Feed first

I may want to fertilise my flower border later in the year, after mulching, but I'm worried that the feed won't get to the roots. Do I have to fork the mulch out of the way first?

No. Just as water will seep through any mulch – except unbroken black plastic or a very thick layer of raw grass clippings – any fertiliser will wash through, too. One suggestion, though. Try next year to put on your fertiliser – particularly a granular fertiliser such as Growmore – before applying the mulch. That way the nutrients have a shorter distance to travel and will get to the plants' roots more quickly.

How close for comfort?

I am getting conflicting advice from my neighbours about the effects of letting a mulch touch plant stems. Should the mulch be in direct contact with them?

On the whole, no. Leave a 1-2in gap. Most young flowers and vegetable plants are liable to suffer if an organic mulch such as compost or manure is in direct contact with them. It may infect them with any disease the mulch contains. Incompletely rotted compost could also burn the stems.

Any plant that's grown as a grafted variety on a rootstock – most roses and fruit trees, for instance – runs an extra risk if any mulch is piled up against its stem. The covering can induce the grafted variety to develop roots of its own from above the union with the rootstock. These roots can change the nature of the plant. On a fruit tree, for instance, the new roots will overpower the dwarfing effect of the rootstock, and encourage the tree to grow larger.

MUSHROOMS

Other fungi

I love the taste of mushrooms. Are there other edible fungi and can I grow them at home?

Yes, and no. There are other edible fungi growing in the wild, and some are as tasty as the cultivated mushroom, but growing them at home is really out of the question.

Many fungi need a specific wood, usually decaying, off which to feed. They will grow only where a delicate balance of nature exists: the right organic matter; the right amount of shade and moisture; the right light; and the right temperature. You could not hope to re-create the exact conditions in the garden.

You can, of course, go out in the wild looking for edible fungi, but don't take any chances – they could be fatal. Never eat any fungus unless you have positively identified it as an edible species. Don't be convinced by those old wives' tales, such as: 'If fungus turns a silver spoon black during cooking, it is deadly; if the cap peels you can eat it.' The chances are it isn't . . . and you can't.

Commoner edible fungi you may find in the wild include: grisettes (4½in high); parasol mushrooms (5-6in); horn of plenty, also called trumpet of the dead (3in); chantcrelles (2½in); and blewit (2½in).

Outdoor planting

I fancy growing mushrooms in my lawn. But though I've twice bought kits and sprinkled the spore as instructed under the turf, nothing has ever come up. What has gone wrong?

Cultivating mushrooms outdoors is a gamble – yours just hasn't come off. It's hard to be sure why.

The soil may be too dry, the spot you chose too warm, the earth under your lawn not rich enough, or it could simply be the weather. A growing season of dry days followed by fairly heavy dews seems to be the best, and no amount of planning can guarantee that. All you can do is eliminate as much of the element of chance as possible.

Plant on a damp day around the end of July. Choose a lightly shaded part of the lawn with a base soil that you have enriched a month earlier by spreading well-rotted manure on the grass.

Skim off 1in of turf and lay it to one side. Scoop out the top 1in of soil and lay the blocks of mushroom spawn, each about 2in across, into the space.

Set the blocks about 12in apart. Replace the soil and turf, treading it down firmly.

The spawn will spread under the lawn during July and August. About a month after planting, apply a dressing of superphosphate to stimulate growth. You will get the best results after a summer that is warm but not too dry.

Once cropping starts in September, you will not be able to cut that part of the lawn, or treat it against weeds, so there are disadvantages. You should have more success and less bother growing them under cover in controlled conditions.

How to harvest

Should mushrooms be pulled or cut, or doesn't it matter how they are picked?

They should be snapped off at the base, or twisted free of the soil.

Snap them off when they are clustered together on one thick stem; twist them out when they stand alone. Make sure the mushrooms are dry before you start.

Disturb the compost or soil as little as possible when you harvest, and cut off any broken stalks left behind with a sharp knife. Fill in any holes in the compost to encourage further cropping.

ALL ABOUT GROWING MUSHROOMS FROM KITS

FRESH button mushrooms can be grown at home indoors from simple kits. Picked regularly, they can go on providing a crop for six to eight weeks.

● **WHAT YOU GET** Each pack has a growing container – either a box made of cardboard or polystyrene, a plastic tub, or a heavy-gauge polythene bag.

It also has the mushroom spawn, a coarse, straw-like compost and a bag of 'casing' – a mixture of peat and chalk or peat and lime. The compost and casing can be spread in the garden as a valuable soil conditioner after you've grown your harvest on it.

● **WHAT YOU DO** Follow carefully the instructions on the kit you buy. Cultivation is in three stages:

First, mix the mushroom spawn with the strawy compost and put it in the growing container in a spot where the air temperature is a fairly constant 18°C (about 65°F). This will encourage the growth of the mycelium, a web of white, thread-like filaments.

The second stage of cultivation happens about two weeks later, when the mycelium threads appear on the surface of the compost. That's when you add the casing mixture, without which the mycelium won't go on to produce the fruiting bodies we call mushrooms. Spread the mixture on top of the compost.

The third stage – when the mycelium appears on the surface of the casing mixture – consists of watering the container lightly and reducing the temperature around it to about 16°C (about 60°F).

About three weeks after you add the casing mixture, the first mushrooms begin to appear, initially as pinhead-sized growths.

Check moisture levels each day and follow carefully the watering instructions with your kit. Some need more water than others. You'll have to keep the growing container out of the sun to prevent it drying out, but there's no need to keep it in total darkness.

● **WHAT YOU'LL HARVEST — AND WHEN** The first mushrooms are normally ready to be picked about three to four days after the first pinhead growths appear. A new flush – as each wave of growth is called – can be picked about a week later.

The first picking will probably be the largest. Each subsequent flush of mushrooms will be smaller than the one before. After six to eight weeks, by which time the compost will be exhausted, you may have picked six flushes with a total weight of up to 4lb.

Some kits, however, may yield rather less, and in anything but the best conditions may produce as little as 1½lb of mushrooms. At kit prices, which in 1987 were around £5-8, this is considerably more expensive than buying commercially grown mushrooms in the shops – but, on the other hand, it's a lot more fun.

ONIONS

Seed or sets?

I don't understand why some gardeners grow onions from seed, while others use sets. Which is better?

It is impossible to say which is the better method. Each has its advantages and disadvantages, and in the end it is up to you to make the choice.

Sets are immature onion bulbs specially grown for planting and consequently more expensive than seed. On the credit side they can be planted in early spring, when the soil is still too cold for sowing. There is even one variety of set, Unwin's 'First Early', which is designed to be planted in autumn. Sets are also much easier to handle than tiny seeds, and they will not have to be thinned or transplanted. The food reserves within the sets mean that they take a shorter length of time to mature than seeds, which need to be germinated before they can start taking in nutrients. Sets also seem to be less likely to suffer from onion fly.

The biggest drawback of sets, apart from their cost, is that they are more likely to flower prematurely, or 'bolt', than onions grown from seed. There is no reliable way to eliminate this risk; small sets and modern varieties seem to be just as vulnerable as large sets and older varieties.

If you decide to grow onions from seed, you will have more varieties to choose from and, of course, you will also have the option of using the thinned seedlings as spring or salad onions.

Stunted bulbs

My main onion crops never seem to grow large and round. They are healthy enough but small, and the bulbs look stunted. Am I preparing the soil properly?

If your onions are merely stunted – and not diseased – don't worry unduly. Yes, it is possible that the condition of the soil is not good enough to produce large, round, firm globes. But bear in mind that onion-growers who exhibit their prize bulbs at shows usually cultivate their crops under totally contrived conditions – in special soil, for instance, and in a spot which is completely protected from the weather.

Another point is that onion bulbs grow naturally in different shapes, sizes and colours. Some have a flattened shape, others are globular. Skin colour varies from almost pure white to bright red. Flavour, too, ranges from very strong to very mild. So you might get better results by growing a different variety next year.

In kitchen gardens it is traditional and beneficial to plant onions in the same place every year, unless signs of disease such as white rot make a move imperative. Either way, choose an open, sunny spot which doesn't get waterlogged.

Dig this area thoroughly in autumn, turning in plenty of well-rotted garden compost or manure as you go. If your soil is very acid, add a few handfuls of lime to it. A week or two before you sow your seeds or plant your sets, sprinkle on a general fertiliser such as Growmore at the rate of about 4oz per square yard. Choose a fine day for sowing or planting and rake the surface level. Then tread over the area with your heels to make the bed firm and rake it over again to produce a fine, crumbly surface.

If you use this soil preparation procedure and your seeds or sets are healthy, you should have more-than-adequate bulbs at the end of the season.

Soil quarantine

I've heard that onions should not be grown on the same piece of ground more than once every ten years. Is this true and if so, why?

The advice is not strictly valid, as onions can be grown with some success on the same piece of ground for many years. It is only when the crop starts getting attacked by a soil-borne pest or disease that the ground must be kept free of onions and related crops such as leeks for a quarantine period, to let the predator die out. Of course, gardeners whose plot is too small for any kind of crop rotation must either take a chance and grow onions repeatedly on the same piece of ground or abandon the crop for a while if it becomes diseased.

The length of the quarantine period depends on the problem. For rust disease, it's at least four years. If downy mildew is the problem, grow the onions on a different site each year, avoiding badly drained areas altogether. For shanking, or stem and bulb eelworm, the quarantine period is at least five years. For smut and white rot, it's at least eight years.

For details about how to recognise all these diseases, see *Tears in the shed*, opposite.

Exhibition standard

For years I have marvelled at the really big exhibition onions seen at local and county shows. How can I achieve the same sort of standard?

Generally, the target to aim for is a large solid onion of good shape, with a relatively slender neck and clear skin. To achieve this, the soil must be cultivated deeply, with heavy dressings of manure. The seed should be sown under glass in January to give the plants as long a growing season as possible. As soon as the seedlings are large enough to handle, transfer them to trays. Set them 2in apart each way. As the weather improves, leave the trays outdoors for longer and longer periods each day until, by the middle of April, the seedlings are sturdy enough to be planted out.

Choose a position in full sun, but protected by a wall or hedge from cold winds. At the planting stage (and subsequently throughout the growing season) watch out for pests

Rope trick

How do I make a rope of onions?

Onions will store relatively well in shallow trays, net bags, or even old nylon tights. However, making a rope is the best way to store them, because it allows air to circulate without restriction right around the bulbs. This prevents the bulbs from becoming affected by fungal rot diseases which thrive in damp, stagnant air.

To make a rope, first remove the flaky outer skin and the dead roots from the onions. Knot the necks of two medium-sized bulbs with string. Keeping the dead leaves pointing upwards, continue tying more bulbs – two or three at a time – to the gathered foliage with the string, until the rope of onions is the length you want.

The completed rope can be stored in any shed or outhouse as long as the onions are kept dry. Cold alone will not damage them.

As bulbs are needed in the kitchen, cut them off at the neck, so that they can be removed without damaging the rope. Take the onions from the top of the rope first and work downwards.

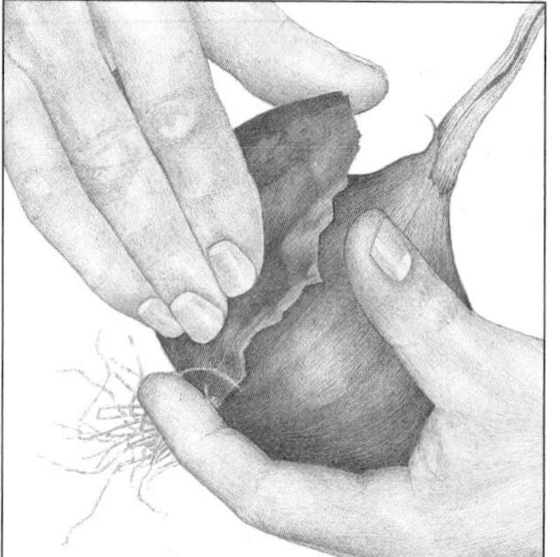

1 *Trim off dead roots and flaking outer skins, but leave the leaves intact.*

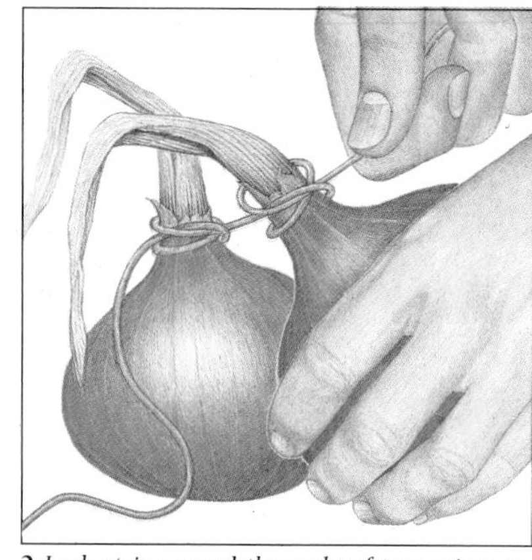

2 *Lash string round the necks of two onions to form the base of the rope.*

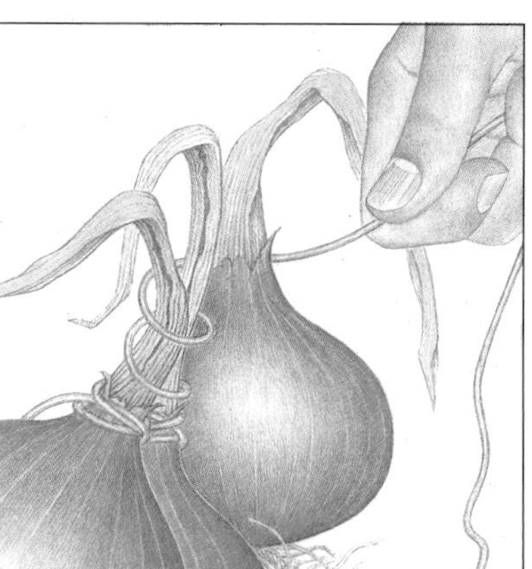

3 *Wind the string tightly round the leaves, binding in more bulbs as you go.*

4 *Tie a knot round the topmost bulbs and hang the completed rope in any dry place.*

and diseases, and take action as necessary (see *Tears in the shed*, this page).

When planting, make planting holes 6in apart with 9in between rows. The holes should be deep enough to let the roots fall in vertically, with the white portion of the bulb buried and only the green parts above the surface; plant the seedlings firmly. After the bulbs have made some growth, scratch out the soil round them with a finger to allow them room to expand.

Feed the onions with a high-nitrogen fertiliser once every two weeks from planting out until the end of July to promote growth. After this, switch to a high-potash feed to harden the bulb tissues and aid ripening.

Running to seed

Some years my onions run to seed prematurely. Why does this happen and how can I prevent it?

When onions produce their flower heads prematurely – a phenomenon known as 'bolting' – it can be due to a number of different factors. It may be because the seed was sown too early, or perhaps the onions were planted during an excessively cold spring. Perhaps, also, the soil into which the roots penetrated was too loose; onions prefer a firm soil.

Onion sets are specially treated to discourage bolting, although the process is only partially effective. The little bulbs lose some moisture in the process and it turns their outer skin pale brown. For this reason, they need planting in warm, moist soil. Some gardeners start them into growth in individual pots to avoid cold, rough soil.

If your onions do start to bolt – and you can tell because part of the leading shoot begins to swell into a flower bud – cut off the flower stalks and lift the bulbs at once. Do not let them stay in the ground until all the normal plants are beginning to ripen; bulbs that have bolted will not get any bigger. Use them in the kitchen as soon as possible because they won't keep.

Bending the leaves

What's the best way to ripen maincrop onions before storing them? Some people bend the tops over; others lift the bulbs and lay them in the sun to ripen.

A successful harvest depends on good ripening. So onions should always be lifted and dried in the sun before storing. The practice of bending the leaves over before the bulbs are lifted from the garden – once done to hasten ripening by exposing the bulbs to more sunlight – is not recommended by many expert gardeners these days. Bending the leaves, they say, damages the onion, and reduces the bulb's storage life.

When the time is right, onion leaves will die back on their own, turning yellow and toppling over. At this stage, easing up each bulb slightly with a hand fork speeds up the ripening process. Leave them like this for about a fortnight, and then, on a dry day, lift the bulbs carefully with a fork. Onions which are not needed for immediate use in the kitchen must be dried. The best way to do this is to spread them out on trays or sacking and leave them outdoors to catch the heat of the sun. Bring them indoors if the weather turns wet.

Drying in this way should be done as fast and as thoroughly as possible – about two weeks should be sufficient depending on the size of the bulbs and the air temperature. Once drying is complete, inspect the bulbs and take out any soft, spotted, scratched, bruised or thick-necked ones. These will not store, and should be set aside for immediate kitchen use.

At all stages make sure you handle the bulbs with great care: even a tiny cut or bruise can become a foothold for rot in store.

Bred for pickling

I want to grow onions for pickling. Can any type be grown – and harvested before the bulbs are too large – or are there special varieties for this purpose?

Any kind of onion can be pickled. But if you pickle a variety that is not recommended for the purpose, you take a chance that the end product will not be of top quality. It may be soft and squashy, or brown and discoloured. Over the years a number of onion varieties have been specially bred for pickling, and it is always advisable to go for these.

The ideal pickling or cocktail onion has small, silver-skinned bulbs (often known as 'button' onions). Three good varieties for this purpose are 'Paris Silverskin', 'Quicksilver' and 'The Queen'. Some gardeners find shallots the best types of onion for pickling. They are certainly tasty, if milder than the special pickling varieties.

Sow pickling onions between March and late June. The seedlings need not be thinned. Harvest the bulbs when they are about the size of marbles.

Growing shallots

We often eat shop-bought shallots and find them quite appealing. Is there any special technique needed to grow them?

Shallots are easy to cultivate, requiring more or less the same conditions as onions grown from sets. However, the end product is rather different. While you harvest one large onion from one set, from one small shallot bulb you will harvest a bunch of between six and twelve small bulbs.

Planting should be done on a fine day in February or March, in ground prepared as for normal onions. Plant the sets about 9in apart in rows about 15in apart. Leave each small bulb so that its tip is just showing above the surface of the ground.

In summer, the onset of ripening is signalled by the leaves slowly turning yellow. When the leaves are completely yellow, lift the bulb clumps and dry them in the same way as onions. Separate the bulbs and tie them into bunches for autumn and winter storage, but put aside a sufficient number for planting the following February.

Among the best varieties of shallots are: 'Giant Yellow' (good-sized, mild-flavoured bulbs that keep well); 'Hâtive de Niort' (an outstanding exhibition variety); and 'Sante' (a heavy-cropping variety whose large, round bulbs have a reddish-brown skin). For more advice, see *Shallots*, page 309.

Hardy spring onions

I love spring onions in my summer salads. But are they hardy enough to be sown in autumn for winter salads?

Generally, the first spring onions for summer salads should be sown in March and you can go on sowing until August for later and later crops. One of the best varieties for this purpose is 'White Lisbon'. When pulled green it has a lovely mild flavour.

For still later sowing, to yield salad onions in March or April, choose the related variety 'White Lisbon/Winter Hardy', which, as its name implies, can withstand heavy winter frost. The seed should be sown directly outdoors in autumn, in drills about ½in deep and with 12in between rows. This variety is not suitable for spring sowing.

Tears in the shed

This year I had a marvellous crop of onions. I harvested them at their prime and stored them according to the book, in boxes of crumpled wire-netting in a dry, airy shed. Yet I see that in several of the boxes there are onions with grey mould around the stem bases, and even a few bulbs that are going soft and rotten. What did I do wrong?

Probably, nothing. The trouble is almost certainly neck rot, a very common bacterial disease of onions in store. There's not much you can do about it, although if you remove and burn all bulbs showing signs of the disease, you may save the remainder. In future, don't store onions whose necks are fleshy and green.

For such seemingly robust vegetables, onions are subject to a surprising number of maladies. Here are the more usual.

- **STEM AND BULB EELWORM** A soil-borne pest that causes leaves to swell and distort, kills young plants and softens the bulbs of older ones. Burn infested plants, and do not grow onions or other susceptible crops such as peas, beans or strawberries on the same site for at least three years. It may help, too, to plant onion seeds rather than sets.

• **ONION FLY** Yellowing leaves, plants dying or failing to develop, and maggots in stems are the symptoms. Infested plants must be destroyed. Dig the bed over in winter to expose the insects' dormant pupae to the cold and to birds. Dust the soil with bromophos or diazinon before planting. Dust established seedlings with HCH in June or July.

• **CUTWORM** The name given to the caterpillars of several species of moth. They chew plants at ground level, often severing the stems. Destroy severed seedlings, but use the unaffected bulbs of mature plants immediately. Apply bromophos before sowing or planting, and again on young plants.

• **WIREWORM** Symptoms not unlike those of cutworm – leaves gnawed at ground level. Give the same treatment as for cutworm.

• **RUST** Brings out orange spots and blotches on leaves. Destroy affected plants, and do not grow onions or leeks on the same site for at least four years.

• **DOWNY MILDEW** Grey mould on leaves leading to die-back and shrivelling and bulbs turning soft. Spray with mancozeb at fortnightly intervals. Do not store infected bulbs or plant onions on the same site again for at least five years.

• **WHITE ROT** Yellow, wilting leaves are accompanied by fluffy white mould with black spots on bulb bases. The bulbs themselves become soft and slimy. There's no reliable cure, though you could try calomel or treating the soil with Armillatox. Burn diseased plants and do not grow onions there again for at least eight years.

• **SMUT** Named for its black blotches on bulbs. It also distorts and thickens the leaves of young plants. Lift and burn infected onions. Since the initial infection is always on the first leaf, seedlings raised in a disease-free seedbed can safely be planted in ground that has contained smut-infected plants. But do not sow onion or leek seeds in the plot for at least eight years.

• **SHANKING** Leaves turn yellow, slime appears between bulb scales. Lift and burn diseased plants. Do not grow onions on the same ground for at least five years.

ORCHIDS

Increasing your stock

What is the best way to propagate orchids?

In the wild, certain types of orchids – the epiphytes – lodge on tree branches, obtain their moisture from the air, and store it in fleshy, rounded organs called pseudobulbs, which grow from the bases of the plants. Orchids with this ability include cymbidiums and calanthes. Several other types, particularly cattleyas and dendrobiums, have long, stem-like pseudobulbs, which sprout leaves from their joints.

Use the pseudobulbs to raise new plants. Detach those growing on their own, or cut stem-like pseudobulbs into sections about 4in long, and plant them in small pots containing a peat-based orchid compost. Warmth and high humidity are essential to encourage rooting; ideally use a heated propagator or cover the pots with polythene and stand them on a light but shaded windowsill during the summer.

On the right scent

I'm thinking of taking up orchid growing in a modest sort of way. But though I love the exotic appearance of the flowers, I'm a little disappointed by their lack of fragrance. Are there, in fact, any scented orchids?

Yes, many orchids are very heavily scented, especially the sumptuous flowers of the cattleyas and their relatives.

Cattleyas are native to Central and South America, and have beautifully frilled and fringed lips. Altogether, there are about 30 species, which grow on trees and rocks – they're known as epiphytes and lithophytes. In this country they do very well in moderately heated greenhouses.

Many odontoglossums are also sweetly scented. They are strong, tough plants, comparatively untroubled by disease. They are usually modestly priced and will grow in 5in pots. A single flower spike will carry as many as 15 or 20 blooms; some hybrids carry several hundred. The flowers retain their full perfection for up to three months.

Some cymbidiums, too, are scented; try the large, white *Cymbidium eburneum* or the equally grand *C. tracyanum*, which is yellow with reddish lines.

Water ration

The gardening books say that orchids need very little water, but they don't explain how much is 'little' for an orchid. Can you advise?

An excellent rule is 'when in doubt about watering, don't'. In the depths of winter, you should water no more than every two or three weeks, and in summer when the weather is very hot, every two or three days will do. Thoroughly soak the plants and allow the water to drain away, then don't water again until the compost is nearly dry.

Use rainwater whenever possible and store it in a tank or bucket. If you have orchids hung on pieces of bark, these can be taken down and dipped in the water for a few minutes before being hung up again; make sure that they don't drip on any plants below. Spray your plants with rainwater on warm summer days.

Water early in the morning, so that the compost has time to dry out before the cool of the evening.

Pause in winter

I didn't like to say anything, but I noticed that some of my mother's precious orchids were shedding their leaves. The time was late autumn, but I've never heard that orchids are deciduous. Are they?

Some are. The genus lycastes, for example, sheds its leaves in winter, an indication that the plants are beginning their resting period. Let them rest, now that their year's growth is completed, by restricting watering to no more than once in two or three weeks, though the soil should never be allowed to dry out completely. Give the plants fresh air when there is no frost about.

The shape of things to come

The pseudobulbs at the base of my cymbidium orchid are growing full and strong. Do these indicate the numbers of flowers I'm likely to get?

They could be flowers in the making – or they could be leaves. During the late summer months, the pseudobulbs on cymbidiums, as on many other orchids, begin to produce new growths. If these growths are round, bullet-shaped, and soft at the end to the touch, they will become flower spikes. If they're flat and elongated, they will grow into young leaves.

Piqued paphiopedilum

My paphiopedilum orchid has not flowered this year. Have I done something to upset it?

Paphiopedilums, or slipper orchids, normally flower once a year beginning, in the Northern Hemisphere, about December. The flowers should last for up to ten weeks in perfect condition.

If you had a very large plant which you recently divided or repotted, the resultant shock might prevent it flowering for some time – and that can be a problem when these orchids should be repotted every other year in as small a container as possible.

Avoid either over-watering or under-watering; the compost should be kept just moist. Check that the plant is well ventilated, too, but clear of draughts, and that the correct temperatures are maintained.

Some paphiopedilums like a cool house, while the mottled-leaved varieties need a minimum winter temperature of 13°C (55°F).

The deceivers

Even as a child, wandering in the woods, I was struck by the extraordinary appearance of wild orchids – quite unlike that of any other flower. Why are they so different?

Orchids are highly adapted to attracting the bees, wasps, flies, moths, beetles and even birds which are essential for their pollination. The flowers' colours, scents, markings and shapes are all designed to attract, and even to deceive. The orchid may, for example, look and, due to the hairs on its petals, feel like a female bee. The male bee, when it attempts to mate, is covered with pollen which is then carried to the next flower.

Other orchids smell of rotting carrion to attract flies, or are heavily scented or brightly coloured to resemble butterflies. Some British wild orchids look like moths, spiders, and even frogs. These remarkable plants are protected by law, but they are sometimes available from specialist growers.

Repotting pays

My odontoglossum orchid has flowered bravely for two out of the three years we've been together. But this year the roots seem to be bursting the container. Should I repot it and if so, when?

Your odontoglossum should be repotted every other year, if possible when the new growth can just be seen at the base of the leading bulb.

Usually the right time is during the spring or autumn months, depending on your plant's growing cycle. Use a pot one size larger than the existing one, and a proprietary orchid compost.

Orchids for everyone

I have always longed to grow some orchids, but have only a small, unheated greenhouse. Would I be wasting my time to try?

Cymbidiums will grow in an unheated greenhouse provided the winter is not too severe, but the best orchids to try would be the hardy or half-hardy European and Far Eastern varieties. Try *Bletilla striata* or the cultivated varieties of pleione. These orchids will also grow outdoors if they're sheltered with cloches during severe weather.

Orchids defined

I've seen dozens and dozens of flowers all called 'orchids', yet bearing little or no resemblance to one another. So what exactly is an orchid?

Orchids belong to one of the largest of all families of flowering plants, and are found in every part of the world except Antarctica. They grow in snow, and in tropical jungles, at sea level and high in mountain ranges. Two Australian species, *Rhizanthella gardneri* and *Cryptanthemis slateri*, spend their entire lives buried in the ground, where they flower, reproduce and die in darkness.

There are, in fact, some 20,000 orchid species in the world, and about 60,000 hybrids, a number which increases almost daily. These orchids vary in size from a fraction of an inch to 8ft or so in height; some have luxuriant foliage while others have no leaves at all.

What distinguishes the orchid from all other plants is the flower. Orchid flowers have three petals; two laterals of equal size; and a lip, or labellum, which is usually quite different. The lip may be brilliantly coloured with beautiful markings, or have a furry surface, raised lines or frilled edges; sometimes it is exaggeratedly large and shaped like a slipper, or even a bucket. This design is intended to attract insects, which slide or fall into the sticky depths of the flower, from which they cannot escape without becoming covered in pollen.

The lip is the top part of the floral segment when the orchid is in bud, but, in order to catch these pollinating insects, it needs to be at the bottom of the flower when it opens. In order to achieve this, the stalk twists round 180 degrees, which means that most orchid flowers are, in fact, upside down.

The three sepals, which on other plants are the green leaf-like structures enclosing the bud, are, in the orchid, often as brightly coloured as the petals themselves. Again,

WHAT CAN GO WRONG WITH ORCHIDS

Symptoms	Cause	Action
Flower buds drop off or shrivel	1 Too early fertilisation 2 Gas or paint fumes 3 Under-watering 4 Draught 5 Too much sun 6 Temperature too low	1 Exclude bees and other pollinating insects from the greenhouse. 2 Air the greenhouse before planting orchids; check that heaters are working. 3 Increase humidity in hot weather by spraying greenhouse interior two or three times a day. 4 Check that ventilators are not blowing directly onto plants. 5 Increase shading. 6 Increase heat.
Leaves scorch or turn yellow	1 Sudden excessive heat from direct sun or greenhouse heater 2 Over-watering	1 Increase shading; check greenhouse temperature. 2 Water earlier in the day and make sure that no water is left on the orchids at night.
Spoiled flowers	1 Aphids 2 Slugs or snails	1 Spray with derris, pirimicarb or malathion. Repeat two weeks later if necessary. 2 Put down slug pellets or some beer in a tin on the floor; the creatures are attracted to it and drown.
Leaves, pseudobulbs and stems shrivel; whitish scales on leaves	Mealy bugs	Spray with derris, dimethoate or malathion; if colonies are small, paint one of these insecticides onto the scales with a small brush. If necessary, continue the treatment at fortnightly intervals.
Yellowish speckling or cloudy white mottling on leaves	Red spider mites	Spray with derris, dimethoate or malathion. Even when rid of the infestation, continue to spray once a month as a precaution.
Leaves show light or dark spots	1 Wet compost, stagnant air or temperature too low 2 Plant is growing old	1 Check growing conditions. 2 Remove marked leaves.
Spotted leaves, stunted growth	Virus disease	Burn infected plants.
Black-tipped leaves	Temperature too high or too low; draughts	Check growing conditions; cut out black portions with a sharp knife.

unlike other flowers which have separate male and female organs, the orchid has the stamens, or male organs, and the style, or female organ, fused together so that the ovary lies below the floral part.

The ovary resembles part of the stalk until fertilisation takes place, when it swells up and develops into an obvious seed pod.

Orchids for outdoors

I don't think I can spare the space to grow orchids in my greenhouse. Are there any that can be grown in the garden?

There are many hardy orchids, including 53 species and ten subspecies and varieties which are native to Britain. Some, such as the man orchid, *Aceras anthropophorum*, and the autumn ladies' tresses, *Spiranthes spiralis*, make their homes on open grassland. For others, such as the bird's-nest orchid, *Neottia nidus-avis*, the natural habitat is woodland, so they are difficult to keep alive in the open garden. But they will do well in a wooded

ALL ABOUT GROWING ORCHIDS

With the exception of a few hardy and half-hardy types, most orchids may be divided into three groups: cool house; intermediate house; and hot house. Hot house orchids are too difficult and expensive for the average gardener to grow, and are therefore omitted here.

Cool house orchids

Probably the best plants for the cool house are among the genera brassia, coelogyne, dendrobium, laelia, maxillaria, odontoglossum, oncidium, paphiopedilum and cymbidium. These give marvellous results for very little effort and, most important, are tolerant of mistakes.

Winter temperature in the cool house should never fall below 9-10°C (48-50°F), although the plants will survive at a few degrees lower if the growing compost is kept fairly dry and the atmosphere is not too damp. In summer, the maximum temperature needs to be no more than 24°C (75°F).

Intermediate house orchids

You needn't use the whole greenhouse. Instead, divide off a small section where the winter temperature can be kept to a night-time minimum of 13°C (55°F) and a daytime minimum of 16°C (about 60°F). In summer, the minimum night temperature should be 16°C (about 60°F), and the daytime temperature should be between 21 and 27°C (about 70-80°F). In an intermediate greenhouse it is possible to grow a wider selection of paphiopedilums, including the marble-leaved varieties, special hybrids from the odontoglossum group, 'pansy orchids' (miltonias) and above all, the richly scented cattleyas.

Caring for orchids

Wherever you grow your plants, there are some common features to be borne in mind.

All orchids thrive on humidity which must be balanced with the temperature, so that as heat increases the atmospheric humidity rises as well. For good growth the humidity should be on average between 75 and 80 per cent. To achieve this, the soil, path and staging can be damped down early in the morning and also in the middle of the day if the weather is hot. Do not spray the water on the plants themselves.

Place the plants on humidity trays on top of inverted saucers to protect them from the wet gravel on floor or ground. Give an overhead spraying of rainwater, but do it early enough for the plants to dry off before the nightfall temperature drops.

Ventilation is essential, but draughts are death to orchids. Slow electric greenhouse fans keep the air moving while preserving humidity, yet do not cause draughts. Box ventilators let into the walls below the staging and with fine mesh gauze to keep insects out are probably the ideal. Some form of shading during the summer months is necessary, because direct sunlight can burn the foliage, but plants should still have maximum indirect light. Spray the glass with a coat of greenhouse shading paint, or, if you're feeling expensive, fix roller blinds.

Correct watering is the most important factor in determining success or failure in growing orchids. Nearly all cultivated orchids like the compost to dry out almost completely between waterings. It is important to ensure swift drainage to prevent the roots from rotting; on the other hand the compost must not become so dry that plant growth is slowed and the pseudobulbs begin to shrivel. Should this happen, a good soaking will plump them up again. The deciduous varieties shed their foliage when their resting time arrives; as the leaves turn yellow, watering should be reduced. From the time when the leaves fall until fresh growth appears, it should be reduced to a minimum – say, once a fortnight or so.

Repotting should always be carried out in the spring months, when the plant is at its most active.

Orchids grow best in special orchid compost which usually contains no soil and is based on a mixture of sphagnum moss, peat and osmunda fibre with a little charcoal added. The raw ingredients are often difficult to buy separately, so the easiest answer is to buy a proprietary orchid compost.

Feeding is not essential, but it is beneficial when given to plants growing well during the summer months. Most pot plant feeds are suitable and may be added to the water or applied as a foliar feed. A high-nitrogen feed in spring will stimulate growth, and a high-potash one, such as a tomato fertiliser, given later on, will encourage flowering.

Propagating orchids

Growing orchids from seed was once regarded as a nigh-impossible task. An orchid pod contains up to 4 million seeds as fine as dust. In natural conditions, these may be carried on the wind for hundreds or even thousands of miles until a few of them settle by chance near a root fungus called mycorrhiza. The seeds can germinate without the fungus, but they need it to go on growing after that.

In the 1920s, it was discovered that orchid seeds could be made to germinate artificially by sowing them in Knudson's Formula 'C', a sterile medium containing trace elements. Since then, growers have been able to breed new hybrid plants in far greater quantities than ever before. These new plants greatly surpass the original species in colour, shape and size, as well as being far easier to grow and in a wider variety of conditions.

Another form of propagation is to remove the meristem, or growing tip, from a plant and place it in a growing medium. The meristem tissue grows like a seedling and produces plants which are genetically identical to the parent.

It is also possible to propagate orchids by division. A small plantlet appears on the pseudobulb or stem which, if left, will usually send roots into the air. These small plants can be cut off with a sharp knife and planted in pots containing loose compost that give the roots plenty of air. Give a very small amount of water in the form of a fine spray until the roots have settled.

Orchids such as cymbidiums, cattleyas and odontoglossums have pseudobulbs. These storage organs are formed from swollen stem tissue and resemble egg-shaped bulbs. Each season, new growth starts from a dormant 'eye' at the base which becomes another pseudobulb growing beside the first. In autumn, when the season's growth has finished, the rootstock can be cut but left in the pot until the following spring; the bulb immediately behind the cut will begin to grow and can be planted separately.

Cuttings may be taken from some varieties of orchid. For example, a side branch from a vanda can be cut off and potted up when the aerial roots growing from it have reached about 3in long.

Tips for beginners

- Join an orchid society where, for a small annual subscription, you can share the knowledge gained by experienced growers.
- Begin by growing hybrids which have been specially bred for the greenhouse.
- When your first orchids bloom, remove the flowers after two or three weeks so that they don't sap the strength of the plants. The cut flowers will live for several weeks in water.
- Orchids which like cool conditions may not flower if there is not a marked drop in temperature at night. Leave a little ventilation in your greenhouse, but avoid draughts.
- To prevent damage by pests and diseases, make sure that all weeds and dead and decaying matter are removed from the greenhouse and from the immediate vicinity.
- Make sure your greenhouse is well insulated. If necessary, line the greenhouse with polythene sheeting stretched tightly about 2in away from the inside of the glass.
- To maintain humidity in the greenhouse, put a layer of plain soil over the floor. It is easier to keep this damp than gravel.
- Open-slatted greenhouse staging is best. It will allow air to circulate freely and prevent plants from becoming waterlogged.

patch or in an unheated greenhouse, where the hardy Mediterranean orchid species will also thrive.

It is illegal to collect British orchids from the wild, but some are sold, perfectly legally, by specialist dealers.

Among the plants available are the lady's slipper orchids (cypripedium), as well as coeloglossum, epipactis, gymnadenia, himantoglossum, ophrys, orchis and spiranthes. Some of these bear lovely old common names: frog orchid, bee, spider and butterfly orchids, for instance, the scented, musk and spotted orchids, and the helleborine.

Bletilla striata, a species from the Far East, which has rose-pink flowers, will also grow well outdoors, but should be protected from hard frosts with cloches.

The cultivated varieties of pleione, a genus from the Himalayas, China and South-east Asia, are also well worth growing. They have a shallow root run, so plant the pseudobulbs to no more than half their depth in a compost that has plenty of coarse sand for good drainage. Try some of the named varieties of *Pleione formosana*, such as 'Clare' or 'Oriental Splendour'.

ORGANIC GARDENING

The pros and cons of going organic

What are the real advantages – and disadvantages – of organic gardening for the ordinary home gardener?

Basically, organic gardening is gardening without using any kind of factory-made chemical fertilisers, pesticides, weedkillers or fungicides. Instead organic gardeners use only garden compost and organic fertilisers and sprays – those made from animal or vegetable matter.

Organic gardeners believe, in common with many chemical-using gardeners, that to produce healthy plants you need a healthy, crumbly and nutritious soil. Where the two groups differ is in the methods they advocate to achieve this end.

For organic gardeners, it is centrally important that the soil should be rich in humus – decaying vegetable and animal matter – and thickly populated with living organisms such as worms and bacteria to break the humus down into plant nutrients. Using chemicals, organic gardeners believe, interferes with this complex process. In the end, they say, the chemical interference destroys most of the organisms in your soil – and your plants suffer as a result.

Organic fertilisers and compost, on the other hand, add organic matter to provide humus as well as nutrients for the plants. Plenty of organic matter in the soil also means that a plant's roots can penetrate it more easily – and the plant will be healthier and stronger as a result.

The principal advantage of organic gardening is that you can be sure that fruit and vegetables grown in this way are free from the effects of all the chemicals which are generally used in growing fruit and vegetables commercially.

Many organic gardeners claim that these chemicals are at best unnecessary – and at worst actually harmful to our health. Many anti-chemical gardeners also believe that the taste of organically grown fruit and vegetables is better.

Organic gardening's principal disadvantage is that without chemical sprays the plants are bound to suffer more from pests and diseases – some apples will tend to be maggoty, for example, and lettuces may have more slugs. Organic fertilisers also tend to be more expensive than inorganic ones and, because they're less concentrated than inorganic feeds, can take longer to apply.

Organic fertilisers

Which fertilisers are organic? Are they used in the same way as inorganic ones?

Essentially, organic fertilisers are those made only from animal and plant matter. Hoof and horn, for example, the principal organic nitrogen fertiliser, is made as its name suggests from the ground-up hooves and horns of cows. Organic gardeners also sometimes use fertilisers such as rock phosphate, which, though not made from animals or plants, are nevertheless 'natural' rather than manufactured.

Organic fertilisers are applied in the same way as inorganic ones, but they are seldom so concentrated and generally about twice as much has to be applied. It is also important to remember that although organic fertilisers will continue to be effective for longer than inorganic ones, they are slower to act in the first place.

Organic fertilisers have the advantage of being less likely to damage plants if too much is applied.

Popular organic fertilisers, with the percentages of nitrogen, phosphorus and potassium (potash) they contain, are: hoof and horn (14:2:0); dried blood (12:0:0); soot (3-6:0:0); bone meal (4:20:0); rock phosphate (0:30:0); and wood ash (0:0:5-10).

The most popular general organic fertiliser – roughly equivalent to the inorganic fertiliser Growmore (7:7:7) – is probably fish meal (6-10:6-12:1). But it is usually better to use one of the ready-made mixtures of dried blood and fish and bone meal. They give plants a more balanced diet.

Ashes for plants

I know wood ash is good for plants. What about coal ash?

As you say, wood ash from indoor fires or a bonfire is an excellent and quick-acting organic source of potash; it contains about 5-10 per cent potassium (potash). But keep it dry before use. If it is left to get wet, the potash will soon be washed out. Apply a spadeful of wood ash to each square yard.

The ashes of coal, coke and other fossil fuels, however, aren't nearly so good for plants. They have no fertiliser value and are of some benefit as a soil conditioner only if they contain small cinders and clinker to lighten the soil. Coal and coke ash are best for this – and they're most useful on clay soils. Sandy soils don't need lightening. Other fossil fuels tend simply to burn to a fine, dust-like ash which can do more harm than good by filling up the pores in the soil and making it sticky.

This ash is not even worth adding to a compost heap. It's best put in the dustbin.

Dodging the digging

I'm told that there is a method of organic gardening that involves no digging. How does it work?

It uses what are known as raised beds and was originally developed to cultivate exceptionally heavy land which was difficult to dig. The essence of the method is that after a crop you simply clear away as much of the crop debris as possible – without bothering to turn the soil. Then you put down a layer of organic matter on top. This covers whatever debris is left and gives you a clean surface to sow or plant in.

The raised-bed method is especially suitable for cultivating vegetables that like soft ground – primarily root vegetables such as carrots and parsnips. The vegetables that do not grow well in raised beds are those, such as brussels sprouts and winter cabbage, that like hard ground.

To make raised beds, divide the area you wish to cultivate into strips about 4ft wide with 1½-2ft paths between each strip. Then single-dig or double-dig each strip (see *Digging*, page 121). The digging is just to establish good drainage and to make sure that while the bed is still quite low the plants have plenty of well-broken soil in which to put down roots. It should be the last time you have to do any digging.

Cover each strip with at least 3in – preferably more – of garden compost or composted manure. If you are using fertiliser, apply it at this stage and rake it in. Place boards round the edge of the raised bed to keep the soil in. Plant or sow in short rows across the width of the beds.

After the crop, lightly rake the surface of the bed to remove the worst of the debris, putting the debris on the compost heap. Cover the bed with another 3in or more of compost and repeat the process.

People sometimes express the fear that raised beds will get out of hand, rising several feet above the surface of the ground. This will not happen. Even well-rotted compost will continue to rot down and shrink long after it has been put on the bed. The raised-bed method need not be an exclusively organic method. You can use it, if you wish, with chemical fertilisers and sprays.

Anti-pest bugs

I understand that you can buy bugs that will feed on pests such as whitefly and keep them under control. Is this true? If so, how well do they work?

There are two such bugs commonly used – one attacks whiteflies and the other red spider mites. But you can use them effectively only in greenhouses – in the garden the bugs will disperse themselves far too widely. Moreover, the bugs work only if introduced within a day or two of the pests appearing. If the infestation becomes too advanced, you will have to resort to more drastic measures such as spraying. If introduced in time, the anti-pest bugs will keep whitefly and red spider mite down to harmless levels – but they will never completely eliminate the pests.

The anti-whitefly bug is *Encarsia formosa*, a tiny chalcid wasp, less than one-fortieth of an inch long. It lays its eggs in whitefly scales – whiteflies at an immature stage. When the encarsia larvae hatch out of the eggs, they eat away the inside of the scale, thus killing it. Encarsia attacks only whitefly, ignoring all other insects whether beneficial or harmful.

The other bug is called *Phytoseiulus persimilis*. It is a predator which feeds on red spider mites – and looks strangely like them, though slightly larger. Each one can eat as many as five adult mites or twenty young ones in a day. The predators breed much faster than the mites, too, so that the mites are soon outnumbered.

Encarsia and phytoseiulus are usually sold by mail order. Ask at your local garden centre or contact the Royal Horticultural Society by writing to the Secretary, PO Box 313, 80 Vincent Square, London SW1P 2PE; telephone 01-834 4333. The bugs have to be introduced to the greenhouse afresh each year. Various other predators and parasites are available to commercial growers – but these are the only two that are widely available to amateurs.

This method of using other bugs to keep pests under control is known as biological control and can also be used by non-organic gardeners. A drawback for non-organic gardeners is that biological control prevents them from using most insecticides – because both bugs are very susceptible to most sprays. This could lead to a build-up of other pests. The most likely is greenfly, but that pest can be dealt with quite easily by spraying with pirimicarb. Pirimicarb, which is not an organic spray, does not affect either encarsia or phytoseiulus.

Other pests, though, are more difficult to deal with. You might simply have to use the appropriate insecticide – and forget about the anti-pest bugs.

Outdoors, although encarsia and phytoseiulus aren't effective, there are a number of other creatures you should always encourage – because they at least help to keep pests under control, if incompletely.

The principal ones – all illustrated below – are ladybirds, hoverflies and lacewings (which attack greenfly), ichneumon flies (which attack caterpillars) and devil's coach-horses, violet ground beetles and centipedes (all of which attack several common pests). Try to avoid spraying when there are plenty of these creatures in your garden.

Anti-pest plants

Is it true that some plants help to keep pests away?

It is certainly true that just as some plants tend to be particularly attractive and susceptible to certain pests, so others tend to be particularly repellent to them. Tomatoes and fuchsias, for example, generally attract whitefly, while nasturtiums usually repel them.

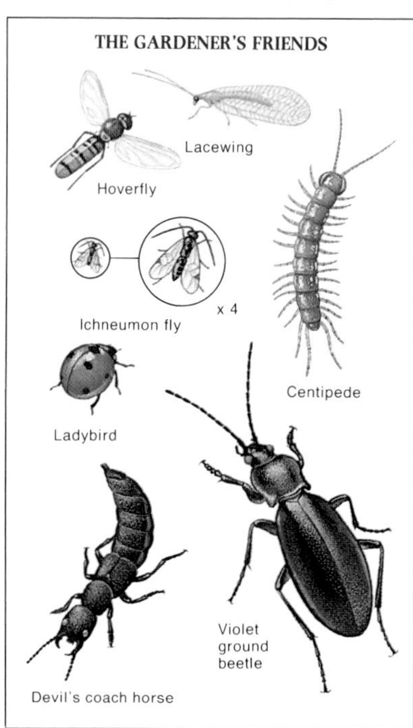

However, planting repellent plants is a far from certain method of pest control. It will never cure an outbreak of a particular pest – at most it will help (with other methods of pest control) to prevent one. Even then it won't always work – not every tomato or fuchsia is attacked by whitefly and equally not every nasturtium repels them.

The two most effective repellent plants are garlic and tagetes (French and African marigolds). Planted among rose bushes, garlic can help to discourage greenfly. Tagetes can help to deter whitefly when planted in a greenhouse. Nasturtiums can help to deter whitefly and greenfly in a greenhouse, but they have the unfortunate habit of attracting their relative, the blackfly.

Other traditional measures which are claimed, but not proven, to keep diseases at bay include burying bits of rhubarb in the ground among brassica plants. This is said to discourage club root. Hanging moth-repellent rings or mothballs in peach trees is said to help to prevent leaf curl.

Weed control

How can I keep down weeds in a chemical-free garden?

The best thing is to try to discourage weeds from springing up in the first place. There are a number of ways to do this. One is to make sure when sowing not to break the soil up to a finer tilth than necessary. Weed seeds are generally tiny, and so need a fine, crumbly surface layer or 'tilth' to germinate. When sowing larger seeds, such as pea or bean seeds, the surface can be left fairly lumpy – and this may help to discourage the germination of weed seeds.

Another method is to put down in spring a 3-4in thick layer of manure or garden compost as a mulch around well-established plants – not seedlings. This will smother weeds and have the additional benefits of helping the soil to retain moisture and of supplying the ground with organic matter.

For a shrub or herbaceous border, you could also plant ground-cover plants: ivy, for example, or one of the spreading dead nettles such as yellow archangel, *Lamium galeobdolon*. Ground-cover plants will both keep down weeds and look decorative. But they will take some years to be large and dense enough to be effective, so you will have to use other methods of weed control until then.

Consider, for instance, planting the marigold species *Tagetes minuta*. According to some organic gardening researchers, it is a natural weedkiller, capable of destroying even such tenacious weeds as bindweed, ground elder and couch grass.

If, in spite of all your preventive measures, weeds do spring up, you will simply have to return to some of the rules and methods that were normal 30 or 40 years ago before most modern weedkillers were available. The most important of the rules is: get rid of the weeds while they're young. The older they are, the more difficult they are to kill; and it is important to destroy them before they set seed and start a new generation.

Probably the best tool for weeding is the hoe – provided it's used carefully and shallowly to avoid damaging the roots of your garden plants. It's effective, doesn't use chemicals and, once you've bought the hoe, it's free. A hoe is not so valuable, though, if the soil is very wet. A hoe tends, in these circumstances, simply to pull weeds out of the ground so that they will root again elsewhere, rather than cut lethally through the stems. The only non-chemical alternatives to weeding with a hoe are weeding by hand or, more drastically, weeding with a flame gun. These garden flamethrowers can be bought in garden or DIY centres, or can in many parts of Britain be rented from tool hire shops.

Be careful when disposing of weeds. Make sure your compost heap is hot enough to kill any seeds – otherwise the weeds will simply be reintroduced when you spread the compost on the beds. Lay out any perennial weeds such as docks, ground elder or bindweed in the sun to dry and die before putting them on the compost heap. Alternatively, put them in the dustbin or burn them.

Organic seeding and potting

Are any of the proprietary seed and potting composts organic? If not, what can I use instead?

Very few are completely organic. The entire John Innes range of soil-based composts, for example, contains added chemical materials. John Innes seed compost contains superphosphate – an inorganic fertiliser – and the potting mixes have superphosphate and another inorganic fertiliser, sulphate of potash. Most other proprietary brands of seed and potting composts include inorganic materials such as urea-formaldehyde.

One of the few completely organic seed and potting mixtures is Stimgro, introduced into Britain in 1986. It is based on a composted mixture of cow manure and peat with nothing chemical added.

If you can't find an organic compost, it is possible to make your own – though professionally made ones are usually better. Mix three parts of moss peat with one part of horticultural sand. For every cubic foot of compost add ¾oz of ground chalk. If you wish, you can add organic fertilisers to provide nutrients, but it's usually simpler to feed the seedlings or cuttings with manure water once they have begun to develop roots.

You can make manure water by hanging a muslin bag full of manure in a bucket of water until the water turns the colour of dark ale. Most manures, fresh or partially decomposed, are suitable.

Diminished returns?

Does organic gardening mean reduced yields?

Yes. Without modern chemical insecticides and fungicides your crops are bound to suffer more from pests and diseases – particularly when you have just started gardening organically. Organic methods of pest and disease control, although effective, are never as completely effective as the modern chemical methods. So your crops will never be quite as large and the individual fruits or vegetables will never be quite as unblemished.

If you use the raised-bed system, you may also find that your crop yields are smaller for the first few years, until the topsoil on the bed is about 12-18in deep. This will be because the underlying soil is too hard for the plants' roots to penetrate it properly, although you can minimise this risk by digging the ground very thoroughly before the beds are laid down.

Having said all that, though, you may feel that reduced yields are a small price to pay for food you know to be entirely uncontaminated by any man-made chemical. Moreover, provided you cultivate the soil well, work plenty of organic matter into it and use effective organic fertilisers and methods of pest and disease control, there is no reason why after a few years your crops shouldn't be perfectly acceptable and the yield very nearly as high as when gardening with chemicals.

How to keep pests and diseases away

If I can't use chemical sprays, how do I stand a chance of keeping my plants free from pests and diseases?

As with all gardening, whether organic or not, prevention is better than cure. The most important thing is to provide the best possible growing conditions – so that plants are healthy and more resistant to disorders. If possible, choose varieties that are either immune or resistant to common pests and diseases. More and more such varieties are now being bred. They include, for example, among raspberries the varieties 'Malling Delight', 'Malling Leo' and 'Malling Orion', which are largely resistant to aphids carrying raspberry virus diseases, and among potatoes the varieties 'Maris Piper', 'Cara' and 'Pentland Javelin', which are more resistant to eelworms.

Avoid conditions that favour the development of pests and diseases by paying attention to hygiene. Don't leave diseased or pest-infested leaves lying about on the ground or on the plant – rose leaves plastered in black spot, for example. In winter, be especially careful not to leave fallen brassica leaves lying around – they make a perfect home for slugs and snails. In most cases, infected plant remains can go on to the compost heap, but if they're infected with soil-borne diseases, such as club root or white rot, burn them. The compost may not generate enough heat to kill the disease organisms.

Watch out, too, for plants and weeds infected with common pests or diseases that could be passed on to your flowers or vegetables. Club root, for example, as well as attacking brassicas, attacks other plants in the *Cruciferae* family, such as wallflowers and weeds like hairy bittercress and shepherd's purse, any of which can serve as a reservoir for the disease. The disease could then easily be brought into your garden by one of these plants or weeds – so be quick to remove any infected specimen.

Careful crop rotation (see page 105) will also be of some help.

In a greenhouse, be careful not to overcrowd plants. Overcrowding encourages fungus diseases. Make sure there is plenty of ventilation in winter as well as summer. Cold, damp and, especially, stagnant air encourages diseases such as grey mould. In summer, prevent your plants from drying out and wilting in the heat by spraying water over the plants and onto the floor of the greenhouse several times a day. This discourages red spider mites.

If, in spite of these precautions, your plants are attacked by pests, there are some proprietary organic sprays you can use. These organic sprays include: rotenone, made from the ground roots of some species of derris, a tropical climber, and used against caterpillars, aphids and other insects; and pyrethrum, made from the flower heads of a species of chrysanthemum and used to control several insect pests, including aphids.

Homemade sprays, which many organic gardeners swear by, include: soapy water as a spray against aphids; and, again to get rid of aphids, some elder, rhubarb or wormwood leaves boiled in water. One traditional recipe is: chop up 1lb of elder or rhubarb leaves or 8oz of wormwood leaves and simmer for half an hour in two pints of water. Strain, then add a further four pints of water. Allow the mixture to cool, then spray it on aphid-infested plants as often as necessary.

As a last resort against aphids, some organic gardeners recommend nicotine – but use it only as a last resort because it is highly poisonous. Boil 2oz of cigarette ends with their filters in a pint of water for about 30 minutes. Strain and dilute with 4 pints of cold soapy water. Spray the infested leaves thoroughly.

Whether, or how well, these homemade sprays work is a subject gardening experts still argue about. The pro-organic lobby insists that they do. Others argue that what works is the jet of liquid – its force simply knocks the aphids off the plants – and that a spray of water would work just as well. The scientific case remains unproven, so the best answer is probably to experiment to see what works in your garden.

PAMPAS GRASS

Slow to grow

Can I raise pampas grass from seed?

Yes, you can cultivate the ordinary pampas grass species, *Cortaderia selloana*, in this way. But you won't be able to grow any of its cultivated varieties such as 'Silver Spire' from seed. If you do want to grow them, you'll have to buy the plants, or divide and replant existing clumps.

Sow the seeds thinly in a seed tray. The fine-bladed, delicate seedlings look like any other grass at first. As soon as they are large enough to handle, prick them out and plant them two or three to a pot in 3in pots. When they are growing well, divide them up again one to a pot. Stand these out in a frame until the following spring, by which time they should be ready to plant out.

The only drawback to growing pampas grass in this way is that it'll be several years before the young plants produce plumes. Some gardeners put a figure of seven years on this period, but there is no scientific evidence for the belief. How long it actually takes for plumes to appear depends on where you've set the plants and how well you look after them.

Pampas portions

Can you tell me how to split up my pampas grass? I'd like to give some to my neighbour and replant smaller clumps elsewhere in my garden.

Don't do anything until early spring. The time to divide your pampas is when you see the new season's growth coming out from the previous year's sheaths. This is usually in late February in the South, early March in colder areas.

Lift the grass carefully, keeping as much earth on its roots as you can manage. With a big clump, you'll have to dig a trench at least 12in deep all round the clump, then work two garden forks beneath the roots and rock them loose. Split the clump into four or five portions; you might do it with a spade, but you may well need an axe.

Pampas grass dislikes being disturbed, though, so don't expect all the portions to succeed. To improve their chances, cut the foliage on each portion back to 3-4in from the base and start them off in boxes of potting compost in a cold frame. Later in the year ease the plants out of the box and look at the edge of the compost. When you can see roots showing, it's time to put the plants out in their permanent positions.

Spring clean

How can I keep my pampas grass looking good?

All you really need to do is trim it down with shears in early spring, and methodically remove the dead centres from the grassy tussock. The new shoots can then grow freely. Pampas leaves have very sharp, cutting edges so always wear protective gloves for this job. If you make this a yearly task, it shouldn't become too daunting.

Alternatively, you can get rid of the dead foliage by setting fire to it in the spring. This may seem an extreme way of tidying, but the pampas grass will survive perfectly well so long as you are careful. It would take quite a blaze to kill its dense crown. Make sure that no new season's shoots are emerging or these will get singed and the first few leaves will have charred tips. Put some newspaper at strategic places underneath the grassy clump. If possible, burn it on a breezy day to get the job done quickly. The ash left at the end will help to fertilise the plant.

Retrieved in time

I have a very old clump of pampas grass which I'm afraid I haven't looked after for years. Would it be a good idea to feed it?

As it happens, pampas is one plant that needs very little attention. If your plant is so neglected, though, that it has become spread out – the young portions seeking fresh nutrient-rich soil and the centre a tangled mass of old, dying foliage – then it's a wasted effort to feed it, and you would do better to replace the plant completely.

Perhaps your situation isn't as bad as this. To prevent it getting that way, put fertiliser in the centre of the clump each spring after you have removed the old, dead growth. Bone meal or hoof and horn – a couple of generous handfuls for a plant that has been established for four or five years – will provide all the food necessary to keep it in a neat, tight condition.

If your pampas is growing on free-draining sandy soil, it might be a good idea to mulch it with garden compost, peat or pine bark. This isn't advisable on heavier, clay soil, however, because the damp conditions that any mulch encourages may cause parts of the grass to rot at ground level.

Once you've nursed your pampas grass back to health, all it needs is to be watered in dry spells and kept free from weeds.

PARSLEY

French and curly

What is the difference between French parsley and ordinary parsley?

French parsley (also called Continental or flat-leaf parsley) is a plain, uncurled variation of ordinary parsley. It probably bears a close resemblance to the original species first brought to England from Sardinia in the Middle Ages. It is a rather coarse plant with dark green leaves and a stronger flavour than the more familiar curled parsley.

Most gardeners nowadays grow curled parsley, whose crimped, serrated leaves are popular as a garnish. The crested varieties developed by plant breeders are now known as moss-curled, a term that aptly describes their appearance. The sad thing about parsley is that its popularity as a garnish means that far more of it is left on the side of the plate than is eaten. Yet parsley added to soups and stews does wonders in bringing out flavours, and parsley sauce is practically inseparable from salt beef and white fish.

Coarse parsley

My parsley does well for one year, but after that it becomes coarse and starts flowering. How can I stop it?

Parsley is a biennial plant – that is, it grows from seed one year, lives through the winter and then flowers, sets seed and dies in the following summer. In its first year, the plant produces the lovely soft foliage that is ideal for cooking. Winter weather will make the leaves stringy and unpalatable, unless protected by a cloche. In spring, the plant produces fresh growth which soon develops flowering stems. Once these appear, there will be less and less usable foliage, and what there is takes on a strong, almost rank taste.

So flowering is just part of the plant's natural growth cycle, and there is nothing you can do to stop it. To be sure of a succession of fresh parsley, you must sow fresh seed each spring. Alternatively, if you leave your parsley in the ground, it will seed itself each year, allowing you to treat it effectively as a perennial. It'll be killed off only in a very severe winter.

Old gardeners' tales

Everyone tells me I should pour boiling water over parsley seed before sowing it. Can this be right – and if so, what good does it do?

This is just one of a host of old wives' tales about sowing parsley. Ignore it, as you would the one that says a husband should never allow his wife to plant it if he wants to remain master in his own house. Pouring boiling water over the seed is far more likely to kill it off than encourage it to germinate. Another old myth advises that boiling water should be poured along the seed drills before sowing. Even though this may not actually do any harm, it will not do a lot of good either, merely semi-sterilise the ground.

Like most members of the *Umbelliferae* family, parsley seed deteriorates quickly and has a low germination rate. The best way to get it to germinate is to buy fresh seed every year and sow it, in optimum conditions, at the right time of year.

Even on light soils, it is advisable not to sow before April. Make allowances for poor germination by sowing the seed generously in ½in deep drills, thinning the young seedlings out as they develop.

You can also raise parsley indoors in seed trays. If you do, put the trays in a warm spot until the seedlings emerge. Many gardeners find that in a temperature of about 21°C (70°F) parsley can be persuaded to germinate in as little as two weeks, compared with the two months it can take outdoors. Transfer the seedlings to pots when they're 1-1½in tall – when, as traditional gardening advice has it, they're large enough to handle. Take great care when you transplant seedlings because they resent disturbance and have a tendency to run to seed when moved.

PARSNIPS

Easy storage

My garden shed is now full of potatoes, carrots and onions that I've lifted this autumn. What am I to do about my parsnips – the leaves have withered and I'm sure they are ready for lifting?

You needn't worry. One of the many good things about these vegetables – apart from their delicious flavour – is that you can leave them in the ground until you need them. They are normally ready from October onwards, which is when the foliage starts to die, but the crop is very hardy and the roots can be left throughout winter, even if the ground freezes. However, it is a good idea to cover the bed with a layer of straw as the foliage dies down. This will stop frost turning the ground rock-hard, making it almost impossible to dig out the roots. Another useful tip is to dig a trench alongside the row with a fork so that you can get at the roots more easily and lift them intact.

If you have any roots left in the ground in March, lift them and heel them into a smaller patch of spare ground, or store them in dry sand. This will stop them sprouting and also make space for your spring crops.

The right soil

My soil is quite heavy and full of clay and gets very waterlogged in autumn and winter. Can I grow parsnips on it?

No, not right away. Though parsnips will grow on most garden soils, they do best on one that is stone-free, light, loamy and deeply cultivated. Like all winter crops, they need a well-drained soil that will not get waterlogged – apart from anything else, it increases the risk of canker. But don't despair. Work at your clay following the instructions under *Getting a start on clay soil*, page 73, and you should have no trouble. You will probably have to add lime as well; clay is often, though not always, acidic. You should aim for a nearly neutral soil of pH 6.5-7.0, which suits parsnips best.

Once you've got your soil right, do not over-manure or use nitrogen-rich fertilisers. Parsnips need little nitrogen – and freshly manured ground can cause the roots to fork. Your best course is to grow them on ground that was well-manured for a previous crop.

A few weeks before sowing, apply a balanced general fertiliser to the bed, at 1½-2oz per square yard, and work it into the top few inches with a fork.

Prize-winning parsnips

Every year I enter some of my garden produce in our annual village fête competition. I've been successful with some of my vegetables but I just can't match the other gardeners' prize-winning parsnips for such long, straight roots. What's the secret of their success?

The answer is soil preparation and a lot of care – it's quite fussy, but if you're an enthusiastic exhibitor, here is one technique.

Take a 30in diameter drum – an old galvanised metal or plastic dustbin will do. Clean it thoroughly and knock out the bottom. Place the drum in position on the bed and fill it with 4 parts by volume of washed, coarse, sharp sand mixed with 1 part of peat or spent growing-bag compost. Firm and water the mixture. If you want very long, thin-shouldered roots, fill the drum with sand alone; for broad shoulders, add more peat to the mixture. If the soil below the drum is heavy, mix in plenty of coarse sand so that the long roots can be withdrawn intact when it comes to harvesting.

Now use a crowbar or stout stake to make four equally spaced cone-shaped holes in the mixture and into the garden soil below. Using a 2 gallon bucket as a measure, make up a growing medium of 1 part of finely sieved garden soil, 1 part of washed coarse sand and 1 part of sieved sphagnum moss peat. To this add 1oz of sulphate of potash, 1oz of fine-grade calcified seaweed and a good dose of bromophos. Mix the lot thoroughly and fill the holes with it, compacting the mixture with a stick.

Dust the seeds with a proprietary seed dressing, then sow three or four to each position in February or March. To help germination, cover each site with a 2lb jam jar set upside down. Thin to the strongest seedling when the first true leaves appear, then replace the jars until the plants are about 3in tall. Start liquid feeding at that stage, and repeat every fortnight. Parsnips do not need too much water, so keep watering to a minimum – that will also encourage the roots to lengthen in search of moisture. However, don't let them dry out completely.

At harvesting time, you can let the soil dry so that it is easy to pull the roots out. Alternatively, take away a few handfuls of the growing medium from around the shoulders of the roots and flood the positions. Allow the water to drain and pull the parsnips wet. The best varieties to grow for exhibition include 'Tender and True', 'Impact', 'Hollow Crown Improved' and 'Cobham Improved Marrow'.

Diseased roots

I was told that parsnips are one of the easiest vegetables to grow, but this autumn my first crop has developed brownish-orange patches of rot on the shoulders of the roots, and the leaves have brown spots. What is it?

Yes, parsnips are easy, but that doesn't mean that there isn't a villain lurking in the wings waiting to pounce. In your case, it's parsnip canker, a widespread and fairly common fungal disease, especially in wet weather. The fungus produces dark brown, black or purplish-black wounds, often with orange flecking, on the lower part of the root.

There is no effective chemical control for canker, but the chance of the disease getting a hold can be minimised by good husbandry. Make sure you have a deep, rich, fairly light soil – with added lime if it is acid. Don't plant parsnips in the same ground two years running – try a four-year rotation. And keep down carrot flies, which can damage the roots and provide sites for the fungus to infect, by treating the seed drills with bromophos powder at sowing time, and watering the crop in August with a spray-strength solution of diazinon.

If the trouble persists after all these efforts, try growing a variety that shows good resistance to canker. Among the best are 'Avonresister' and 'Model' (both highly resistant), and 'Cobham Improved Marrow', 'Gladiator', 'Offenham' and 'White Gem' (all moderately resistant).

PATHS AND PAVING

A gravel drive

I love the sound of gravel being crunched under a car's wheels, but is it a sensible choice for a drive? Doesn't it get messy?

Gravel is cheaper to buy and to lay than stone or brick-block paving. And many people prefer its texture and look, even when cost is no object. In general, there is no need for it to look messy: a light raking from time to time will usually keep it trim. But you should be aware of one or two problems. Young children – toddlers especially – love playing with gravel and have a habit of spreading it about the garden. Also, you have to take special care with any gravel adjoining a lawn, because stray pebbles can damage your mower's blades.

The main problems, though, are the hollows which are sometimes gouged out when a car turns or reverses. These can look untidy, even revealing your undersurface or hardcore. The best remedy is not to keep raking the same gravel back into place. Instead, keep a bag of gravel in the garage or shed, and if a hollow appears tip in some fresh pebbles, using a rake to blend the new gravel with the old.

You can get gravel in different colours: white, brown or black – even grey-blue, maroon or yellow. You can also buy it in different sizes, pebbles ranging from ¼in to 1in in diameter. The smallest, known as pea gravel, is probably the most popular and looks best in a formal setting. But you must rake it regularly to keep it looking neat. The larger ½in gravel is more practical for general purposes. Garden furniture and shoe heels are less likely to sink in, and the pebbles, being bigger and heavier, are less easily displaced.

To make a gravel drive, excavate its whole area to a depth of about 10in. Spray the bottom with a path weedkiller (see *Choosing the right weedkiller*, page 368). Lay 6in of hardcore, sloping it across the width of the drive at about 1 in 80 to help rainwater drain away. Roll the hardcore. Shore up the sides with an edging strip of plastic or wood, positioning it so that its top edge is level with the adjoining earth. That way you can mow the grass to the edge without obstruction. Spread a 1in layer of sharp sand to fill any gaps in the hardcore and to make a smooth base for the gravel. Roll the sand down firmly. Lay ½in of gravel and roll it flat to bed it firmly in the sand. Spread another ½in of gravel on top and roll again. There should now be a gap of 2in between the finished level of the gravel and the borders. This will ensure that no gravel gets thrown up onto the lawn or caught in your mower. Rake the gravel whenever it gets bumpy, and spray it once a year with weedkiller.

A hard drive

I want to lay a hard drive, and cannot make up my mind between concrete and asphalt. What are the pros and cons of each?

In part, you must choose according to the sheer look of the two types of drive. Concrete is grey or straw-coloured, rather stark in appearance and prone to staining from algae and moss. Asphalt comes in tones of grey, black and red.

Asphalt does not so readily suffer from algae or moss, but it is prone to staining from oil drips. These oil stains won't come out of asphalt (though they can be got out of concrete by using an appropriate cleaner).

The two surfaces have some things in common. In both cases, you have to prepare the site, level it and put down a 6in thick hardcore foundation. But while any home gardener can, with a little expertise, lay the concrete on top, traditional hot asphalt is a trickier material.

It has to be mixed, heated, spread and rolled in precisely the right way, using specialised equipment – and that's a job best handled by a professional firm.

Alternatively, you could use cold asphalt, which can be bought in bags from DIY stores, or you could use other materials such as paving slabs or bricks.

Weeds in the cracks

Weeds are constantly sprouting up between the stone slabs on my patio. No sooner have I got one batch up than a new crop starts to appear. Is there a way of getting rid of them permanently?

No. Your only options are weeding by hand or using chemicals. Chemical treatment is more efficient, in the sense that its effect will last longer. However, it does not last for ever.

The most powerful chemical weedkiller suitable for patios, paths and drives is sodium chlorate, which stays active in the ground for up to a year. In its raw form, the substance is highly flammable, and the type sold in shops usually contains an ingredient to suppress the fire risk. The weedkiller comes in powdered form and you mix it with water before applying it with a watering can through a special attachment known as a dribble bar. You have to take care, though, because sodium chlorate will kill almost any living plant. It also tends to creep sideways through the soil, so it can't be used close to a lawn or flowerbed.

A number of less toxic weedkillers are also available for paths and patios. They usually contain paraquat, diquat, aminotriazole, sodium salts or simazine, and they work well enough for shorter periods of time.

Slippery stones

My paving slabs tend to get green and slippery, especially in wet weather. Walking on them can be positively dangerous – is there a solution?

There are three types of 'mossy' growth which can cause this problem. The first is algae, a green or black slime made up of countless microscopic plants. It thrives in damp conditions and you find it especially under the drip-line of trees, where rain falls from their canopy of leaves. It is often at its worst in spring after a long, wet winter.

The second type is lichen, which occurs in leaf-like plates of mossy growth. It is brown, or nearly black, when moist. But when dry, the surface fades to grey and curls up to reveal a white underside.

The third type is true moss, which grows in green cushions on paths as well as on walls, roofs and in lawns. Moss thrives chiefly in damp, shady places.

Getting rid of any of these growths is not a particularly difficult job. Tar oil, for example, can be applied to the affected area. Alternatively, try scrubbing it with a solution of household bleach or Jeyes Fluid. You won't get rid of it forever this way, but you should be able to clear it for several months. In the long term, the only way to diminish the problem is to expose the area to more sun. You can do this by cutting back any bushes or foliage that shade the area.

A utility path

I want to make a path from my back door to a vegetable plot at the far end of my garden. It doesn't have to look particularly ornamental, just as long as it is hardwearing and not too expensive.

Obviously, a grass path will quickly get worn away, while loose chippings and gravel are awkward with, for example, a heavy wheelbarrow. You really need a solid path, and that gives you four options: concrete, paving slabs, brick blocks and asphalt.

Among these, brick blocks and paving slabs will offer you a wide range of colours, shapes and textures. However, they tend to be rather expensive. If you really don't care about the look, you might consider asphalt. You can buy cold asphalt from DIY stores.

Alternatively, you could have a concrete path. You can buy concrete ready-mixed or, more economically, mix it yourself (see *All about mixing your own concrete*, opposite). A width of 3ft will give you ample room for a wheelbarrow, and the concrete should be at least 2in thick.

Mark out the path and dig an 8in deep trench. Save the topsoil for use elsewhere in the garden. Lay 6in of hardcore, broken bricks, clinker or any other builder's rubble on the bottom. Ram down your foundation, and make a frame with 2in by 1in timber, to hold the concrete mixture. Use a spirit level to ensure a slight tilt for drainage, and hammer in pegs on the outside to keep the timbers in place. For a shortish path you can probably mix the concrete in an old wheelbarrow, but for convenience you may prefer to rent a mixer. Pour the concrete for the path in 4yd sections and leave a strip of hardboard between each section to act as a contraction joint. If, instead of concrete, you use tarmac, asphalt, ash, bricks or paving slabs, adjust the depth of the trench to suit the varying thicknesses. Slabs and bricks will need a 1in layer of sand or mortar as a bed on top of the hardcore.

Scalped verges

I've laid a path through my lawn, slightly lower than the grass level as the gardening books advise. The trouble is that as I mow over the path's edge, my mower's wheels tend to drop so that the grass gets butchered.

You were right to set your path into the lawn at a lower level. Otherwise you would constantly be damaging your machine's blades as you mowed up to the edge. But the difference in level need not be as great as yours seems to be. If your path is only ½-1in lower than the lawn, your mower shouldn't scalp the grass when you mow over the edge.

If your pathway is much deeper, though, lay a plank of wood on the path when you mow, so as to raise the path to the same level as the earth. Alternatively, consider resurfacing your path to raise it permanently to within 1in of the lawn.

Grass paths

I'd like to plant a grassy path between shrub borders, but I'm worried that it would start to look untidy if used as a true thoroughfare. How can I prevent the grass from getting worn away?

Grass paths can look beautiful, especially in older properties where concrete, for example, would be quite out of place. And grass is versatile, too. A broad, straight grassy walk between shrub borders creates a rather formal atmosphere, while nothing is more delightfully informal than a narrow grass path meandering between mixed herbaceous plantings. You can also achieve a satisfying contrast in texture by mowing a winding path of neatly cut grass through an area where long shaggy grasses and wild flowers are allowed to thrive.

You are right, though, in assuming that a grass path is not entirely trouble-free. Obviously, it will be unsuitable where children's bikes are used a lot, or where muddy boots and heavily laden wheelbarrows are likely to pass incessantly. Nevertheless, as long as the path is intended only for occasional foot traffic, there is no need for it to get worn.

When laying out your path, make sure that it is at least the width of your lawnmower. Ideally, it will be at least double or treble the width, so that the grass will be easy to cut thoroughly, and it will take a wheelbarrow when necessary. Moss and mud are the two main hazards, and to guard against them you must ensure that the soil receives adequate drainage and air. Spike the grass path every spring and autumn, making holes 4-6in deep and roughly the same distance apart. This will help moisture and air to reach the roots. You should also feed the grass with a high-nitrogen fertiliser in spring and summer, and a high-potash fertiliser in autumn. Grass needs nitrogen in spring to promote leaf growth, potassium in autumn to toughen the stems.

Lastly, don't be tempted to cut the grass very short, or it will be worn away all the more easily. Never cut it lower than ¾in in high summer, or below 1¼in when there is risk of drought, or below 1¼in in spring and autumn when growth is slow.

ALL ABOUT MIXING YOUR OWN CONCRETE

CONCRETE does not have the beauty of, for example, mellow brickwork or natural stone. But for certain utility jobs in the garden it is invaluable. You can use it to make fence-post settings and floor slabs, foundations for a shed or a driveway for a car. You can buy ready-made products for small jobs, but when you are covering a large area, it always works out cheaper to buy the individual components and mix them up at home.

Concrete has four basic ingredients: cement; clean river sand or sharp sand; aggregate (pebbles, stones and shingle); and water.

For any jobs requiring layers of concrete 3in or more thick, use a standard, general-purpose mix. The proportions are 1 part of cement, 2 of sand and 3 of aggregate. To find out what volume you need, measure out the area and multiply it by the depth (a car driveway will need to be at least 4in thick). Having obtained your cubic measurement, add another 10 per cent for wastage. It is infuriating to have to stop halfway through a job in order to buy more supplies.

For a driveway or any other large job, buy ready-mixed concrete, which can be delivered to your door, or hire a small mixer from a local tool hire shop. Mixing large quantities of concrete by hand is very heavy work, but with small quantities, it's not too difficult.

- Mix the ingredients dry on a smooth surface. Measure out your sand first, then the aggregate then the cement.
- Make a crater in the heap, and add a small quantity of water. It is not easy to specify the exact amount. The vital thing is to add only as much water as you need to bind the dry ingredients together. You need a stiff paste – nothing sloppier than that.
- Turn the mix into the water, and keep turning and adding small quantities of water until the whole heap has an even consistency and colour.
- To judge if the concrete is ready, draw your spade along the mixture making a row of ridges. If the ridges stay in position, the mix is about right. If they crumble at the edges, add a little more water. If they collapse like soft mud, add more dry ingredients.

Firm foundations

I'm laying a path of paving slabs, and the books tell me it will need a good foundation. But they seem to differ on what makes a good foundation. Should I use sand? Sand and cement? Hardcore?

There certainly are a number of ways in which slabs can be laid, and they all have their different merits. Obviously, the ground supporting your path must be firm and even, or the paving slabs will rock. So it is usually a good idea to begin by laying down a 6in thick layer of hardcore – that is, clean brick rubble or broken concrete. Hardcore is especially necessary on clay and peaty soils, which are notoriously unstable. Consolidate the hardcore by ramming it down with a tamper, or use a garden roller.

You'll find it hard to lay slabs directly onto the uneven surface of the hardcore. For better results you need a layer of finer material on top, and for this purpose lay down 1in of coarse builder's sand. Rake the sand level, roll it, and lay your paving slabs directly on top.

Start laying the paving from an inside corner (if the path starts from a building). Having put the first slab in position, tap it down with the wooden handle of a club hammer or wooden mallet, until it lies flat in its bed. As you add the next slabs, keep them all level with one another.

Many gardeners lay their slabs on loose sand in this way. The danger, though, is that rain will wash sand away so that slabs wobble and corners start sticking up at angles. Smaller slabs, especially, become quickly dislodged, as do slabs supporting heavy traffic.

One solution is to 'spot-bed' the slabs, by applying a lump of sand-and-cement mixture to each corner of the slab's underside, and to the middle of the underside. This helps the stone to grip its bed more firmly. And its advantage is that when settlement does occur you can still lift slabs to make adjustments as necessary.

However, for the strongest foundation, you need to lay the slabs on a bed of sand and cement, or of concrete. This is really essential for slabs smaller than 9in square, and for any slabs used to carry the weight of a car – on a driveway, say. The cement mixture should be stiff, not wet or sloppy. And, before the mixture sets, brush any blobs from the surface of the slabs, or they will leave lasting stains.

Brick patterning

I love patterned brick paths, especially the ones in herringbone. Are there any special problems in making them?

A wide variety of bricks and blocks is available, in different colours and shapes. The visual effects can be very pleasing indeed, but they cost time and money.

Bricks are the most expensive form of paving, and you cannot safely use the ordinary household variety. Soft, porous house bricks tend to soak up rainwater and crack at the first sign of frost. The best bricks are hard, dense and resistant to rain and frost alike; but they don't come cheaply.

It is probably best for a beginner not to attempt too elaborate a design, because some blocks will almost certainly need cutting. In the popular herringbone pattern, for example, you have to cut bricks diagonally to make the edges of a path – although you can hire special cutting tools to make the job easier. In addition, it is best not to try to cover a large area. Bricks look perfect for a short, cottage path, but their scale is wrong for a broad sweep.

To lay a brick path, excavate first to a depth of 7in *plus* the thickness of the bricks. Lay a 6in hardcore base. On top lay a 1in bed of sand-and-cement mix. You can buy this in ready-made form or, more cheaply, you can mix it up yourself; 1 part of cement to 4 parts of sand will be about right. Lay the bricks on the mixture (for pattern ideas, see the pictures on page 102).

Leave a gap of about $\frac{3}{8}$in between the bricks. Fill the gaps with the same mixture of sand and cement. But this time, use it almost dry to avoid the risk of staining the bricks. Tamp the mixture down between the bricks with a stick and finish the joints by running a length of bent rod along them. This should leave the grouting looking tidy and just below the level of the bricks' surface. Then wipe each brick with a clean, damp cloth. Finally, consolidate the surface, preferably with a plate vibrator (the machines can be hired by the day).

Paths for children

Our two small children are always running about the garden and falling over on our hard concrete paving. They'd ruin a grass path, but can you suggest anything else which might leave fewer cuts and bruises than stone or concrete?

Parents have long been looking for a miracle pavement which is hard-wearing – without being hard. Many playgrounds now use thick rubber matting for this purpose, but it's likely to be expensive for a large area. Sand is not much help, either. It gets waterlogged in the rain, becomes quickly discoloured and gets trodden into the house.

One solution is to use shredded or pulverised bark. This material, often used as a soil conditioner, is springy enough to prevent those nasty knocks. And, laid to a depth of 4-6in, it will give you a well-drained surface which won't become slippery in the wet.

Cobbles

We are laying out a new garden, but aiming for an old-fashioned effect. Cobbled paving looks quaint – is it practical, too?

Frankly, cobbles can be a nuisance in a garden. Wheelbarrows, prams, pushchairs and wheelchairs may all need to travel along the path at some time or another, and you may well find the bumpy surface irritating. Cobbles are uncomfortable, too, underfoot, and particularly awkward for elderly walkers. So if you do want to have them, use them only in nooks and crannies. They make interesting infilling material – around a tree, for example – where it may be difficult to cut larger paving materials. Or use them in the triangles left at the edge of a diamond-shaped pattern of flat slabs. But where you're going to be walking, use ordinary paving slabs or the small types known as setts or pavers.

You can lay cobbles just like paving slabs, in a bed of wet sand and cement over a hardcore base. Alternatively, push them into a bed of dry sand and cement – mixed in the ratio of 4 parts of sand to 1 of cement – and water them with a sprinkler from above. It takes much longer for the mixture to dry by this method, so you have longer to make adjustments and to ensure that each pebble is clean before the cement hardens.

Natural stone

What is the best sort of natural stone to use for a patio?

Four main types of rock occur naturally in Britain: sandstone, limestone, granite and slate. You may live in an area where one or other is prevalent, in which case it makes sense to go for that. Your local stone will probably harmonise best with its surroundings – and you should be able to obtain it more cheaply from a local quarry than from a garden centre or stone merchant.

Savings in price can be dramatic: stone bought from a quarry can be as much as ten times cheaper per ton than it would be if bought elsewhere. Besides, you can often pick out precisely the pieces you want, arranging for delivery at a modest price. Quarries are listed in telephone directories' *Yellow Pages*, and you may find it well worth your while to travel some distance to find one rather than rely on local shops. The different stones, though, do have different qualities which you should take into consideration. Sandstone is formed, as its name implies, from millions of particles of sand. It makes a hard and durable rock, and the fine sandstones, such as Yorkstone, are particularly suited to paving. Colours include shades of yellow, cream, blue-grey and pink.

Limestone (like chalk) is formed from the calcium-based shells of marine creatures. It occurs in shades ranging between pale grey and bright yellow, has a natural grain and weathers beautifully (as the golden villages of the limestone Cotswolds bear witness). Nevertheless, being a soft rock it does soak up water, is prone to frost damage and wears down quickly in heavy use.

Granite is an ancient volcanic rock. Composed of masses of tiny crystals, it is famed for its hardness, and is ideal for paths and patios. It comes in a range of pinks and greys, and is often sold as small blocks known as setts. Slow to weather and resistant to water, it might seem the perfect stone for a garden. It is, however, very expensive.

Finally, there is slate. This is a metamorphic rock formed when geological forces subjected beds of sediment to such pressure that they metamorphosed, or changed in structure. Slate is resistant to water, weathers well and can be found in a variety of colours including shades of blue, brown, green, black and grey.

Downcast about uplift

I laid my own front garden path with heavy tiles set directly into the soil. It looked very smart in the summer, but with the onset of winter the tiles have lifted, some have cracked, and the gate which swung freely before now gets jammed on them. What's gone wrong?

It sounds like a classic problem of drainage. When the ground beneath a path is poorly drained, it tends to soak up a lot of rainwater. In winter, the water freezes and expands, so that the path is physically lifted. This is almost certainly what caused the gate to jam. And the process of freezing and thawing, expanding and contracting, can exert such pressure that even good-quality tiles may crack. The problem is particularly acute with clay and other heavy soils; it is less common on lighter, more sandy ground.

Unless you are happy to live with cracked slabs and a shaved-off or repositioned garden gate, you will really have to start again. This time, lay down a good foundation of hardcore or gravel. Ideally, bed the tiles on top of the foundation in a mixture of 4 parts of sand to 1 of cement, and fill in the joints with the same mixture so that no water penetrates the path from above.

The path itself should be set at a slight gradient sloping away from the house to ensure that it sheds surface water quickly.

PEACHES AND NECTARINES

Indoors or out?

Can peaches be grown outdoors in this country?

They can, and as far north as the Midlands – but you must train the tree against a south or west-facing wall or fence that gets plenty of sunshine and offers protection from the chilling effects of the wind. Such a wall keeps the tree at a relatively even temperature by absorbing heat during the day and releasing it at night – rather in the manner of a night storage heater.

This warmth and shelter is particularly important at the beginning of the season to protect the new growth and blossom from frost damage; peaches sometimes start into growth and blossom as early as February, though more often in March.

At the other end of the season, the tree needs all the sun, warmth and shelter it can get if the peaches are to ripen properly and develop their flavour.

You *can* get some marvellous peaches in this way, but all in all it's probably better to grow peaches in a greenhouse. It lengthens the growing season, giving the fruit a longer time to ripen. A greenhouse will also enable you to grow some of the more delicate – and delicately flavoured – varieties.

Off the wall

I want to grow peaches in my greenhouse, but don't have a wall that's suitable to train a tree against. What should I do?

Grow it in a pot as a dwarf pyramid – a pyramid-shaped tree with branches coming from a single central stem. The best tree to buy is one that's two or three years old, and has already been started off as a dwarf pyramid. It is better to buy a tree growing in a container – rather than a bare-rooted one – because the root system will be restricted, rather than widely spreading, and so will be disturbed less when the tree is transferred to your greenhouse pot from the container.

Plant between November and March, in about an 11 in pot with drainage holes at the bottom. Cover the holes with crocks before putting in the compost. A compost that contains loam is better than a peat-based one; it weighs more, giving the tree greater stability, and protects the roots from possible waterlogging. John Innes No 3 is a good choice. Plant the tree firmly, and give it a good watering.

One of the advantages of a potted peach tree is that you can move it inside or out as the weather dictates. On the whole, it is best to keep it in when frost threatens, when the tree is in blossom and when the fruit is ripening; otherwise, keep it outdoors for most of the rest of the year. Just the same, if it's at all possible, it's better to train a peach tree against a wall – even in a greenhouse. A wall-trained tree requires less work and attention and produces more fruit than a potted pyramid.

Grower's calendar

Can you give me some idea of the year-round routine when growing a peach tree in the greenhouse?

In autumn and winter, there's very little to do at all, apart from sprinkling a handful of bone meal around the roots, together with a weak solution of tomato fertiliser. You're not growing it under glass to force it into early fruiting, but because you stand a better chance of getting a good crop at the normal time than if the tree were growing in the open. So far as the peach tree is concerned, you can let the greenhouse temperature drop as low as you like in winter; the tree's natural annual cycle requires a cold spell. Even when there are signs of growth in February, the temperature should not be allowed to rise above about 18°C (65°F).

But from March onwards, the tree will need more attention. While it is in blossom, keep the air in the greenhouse moving – to avoid fungus diseases – and don't let the night temperature sink below 7°C (45°F). You should also fine-spray the flowers with water on sunny days to encourage pollen release; pollinate the flowers by hand.

In April and in the following months, keep the air in the greenhouse moist by spraying the floors and staging with water. This keeps the temperature down and discourages red spider mites. As the weather gets hotter, it becomes increasingly important to keep the peach tree cool by shading the outside of the glass with blinds or shading paint, and by increasing humidity with regular sprays of water – at least once a day, and more in really hot weather. Open all greenhouse vents, the door too, and make sure that the roots of the tree get plenty of moisture.

Give a feed of liquid fertiliser once a month from June to August.

Picking a peach

Could you give me a checklist, please, of the best varieties of peaches and nectarines to grow, indoors and out?

The rule of thumb for outdoor trees of both peaches and nectarines is that if you live in the North – though no farther so than the Midlands – plant a variety that ripens by mid-August. If your home is in the balmier South, you can choose one that ripens in September. The nectarine, incidentally, is a 'sport' – that is, a natural mutant – of the peach. Both are members of the species *Prunus persica*. Nectarines are smooth-skinned, in contrast with furry-skinned peaches, and have a richer, slightly sharper flavour. Occasionally, a peach tree will produce, alongside its more usual fruit, a single nectarine from a mutant bud.

Nectarines and peaches are grown in exactly the same way. Nectarines are gener-

PICK OF THE PEACHES AND NECTARINES

Name	Picking time	Remarks
'Duke of York' (peach)	Mid-July	Cream skin with red flush. Large, tender fruits with melting greenish flesh. Hardy
'Hale's Early' (peach)	Late July to early Aug	Yellow skin with red flush. Delicately flavoured, pale yellow flesh. Hardy
'Peregrine' (peach)	Early Aug	Crimson skin. Richly flavoured, creamy flesh. Hardy; one of the best all-rounders
'Rochester' (peach)	Early Aug	Gold skin with red flush. Large, finely flavoured fruit with yellowish flesh. Hardy; one of the best outdoor varieties
'Bellegarde' (peach)	Early to mid-Sept	Gold skin with crimson flush. Richly flavoured, creamy flesh. Borderline case for growing outdoors in the South; otherwise under glass
'Sea Eagle' (peach)	Late Sept	Yellow skin with crimson mottling. Large fruit, with well-flavoured, pale yellow flesh. Best grown under glass
'Early Rivers' (nectarine)	Mid-July	Pale yellow skin with red flush. Richly flavoured fruit, tender and juicy; yellow flesh. Reasonably hardy
'Lord Napier' (nectarine)	Early Aug	Yellow skin, with russet flush. Large, richly flavoured fruit; pale green flesh. One of the best nectarines for growing outdoors

ally just as hardy as peaches – despite a commonly held belief to the contrary. The fruit of both is ripe – and ready for picking and eating – when the flesh around the stalk yields to a gentle pressure of the fingers. For advice on which varieties to grow, see the chart on page 249.

Basic training

All the authorities are unanimous in saying that peach trees should be grown against a wall. But what's the best way of doing this?

Fan training is far and away the best – the idea being that you end up with a tree whose main branches are spread against the wall in a fan shape, or like the splayed-out fingers of a hand.

You can begin either with a maiden (one-year-old) tree, or one that is two or three years old and has already been started as a fan. Buying an older tree will cut out the business of early training, and will give you fruit a little earlier. Either way, before you plant the tree, you should stretch a series of 14 or 16-gauge galvanised wires along the wall, leaving a 6-9in space between wires. Plant bare-rooted trees in autumn, and container-grown trees at any time.

If your choice is a maiden tree, in the May after planting cut back the main stem to about 2ft above the ground, making your cut just above a growth bud. In the following summer, select two sideshoots, one on either side of the main stem, about 9in above the ground. Leave these two shoots, but pinch off all the others.

Tie two 5ft canes into the supporting wires to support the two selected sideshoots. Place one cane on either side of the main stem, each pointing upwards and outwards at roughly 45 degree angles from the main stem at the points where the shoots join. Tie the two shoots to the canes, so that they will train along them. When the shoots are 18in long, cut out the main stem above the point where the shoots join it, and pinch off any new sideshoots.

Late in the following winter, cut the two side branches back to 18in long, then leave the tree until the summer, letting new shoots grow from the two branches.

When most of these new shoots are 4in long, select three or four on each of the branches; choose shoots that are evenly spaced out, and growing from the top or bottom of the branches, rather than those that are growing either towards the wall or away from it. Leave the selected shoots, but pinch out all other new ones.

Tie the shoots that are left to further canes attached to the supporting wires, at angles of about 20-30 degrees from the two main branches. Late in the following summer, trim all the branches back to 2-2½ft.

In the years that follow, repeat the process of tying in new shoots and removing surplus ones in summer, then trimming the tied-in shoots late in winter, until the wall space is covered. An average, fan-trained tree will reach to about 8ft in height by 20ft wide in ten years.

From the fourth spring you should be able to allow short fruiting shoots to form from the permanent branch system. Choose shoots growing either from the top or bottom of the main branches at about 6in intervals and pinch out all the others. Towards the end of the summer, tie the fruiting shoots onto the supporting wires. If any are more than 18in long, nip out the tips.

The shoots will not bear fruit until the next summer; unlike apple and pear trees, peach trees produce fruit on the previous year's growth. If a good number of fruits are set, thin them out by cutting off the surplus fruits when they're about the size of hazelnuts so that there is at least 9in between each fruit. Once the fruiting shoots have borne their fruit, they can either be kept and tied in to become main ribs of the fan, or cut back to the little cluster of buds at the base.

If you begin with a two or three-year-old partly trained tree, then the whole process is advanced by a year or so.

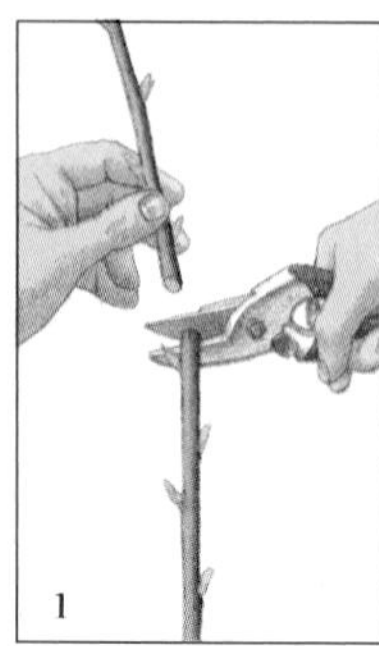

STARTING THE FAN *On a one-year-old tree, cut the main stem back to 2ft from the ground in the May after you plant it (**1**). Allow two sideshoots to develop, and train them along angled canes. Trim off the main stem above the sideshoots (**2**).*

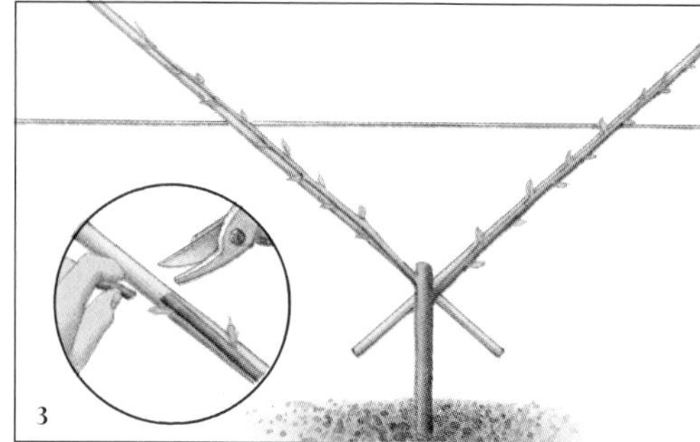

WINTER TRIM *Late in winter, prune the two branches to about 18in each, to encourage the formation of more branches. Make each pruning cut just above a bud (inset picture).*

FILLING THE FAN *Pinch out any shoots that grow towards or out from the wall. Aim to leave only three or four evenly spaced shoots on each branch. Train the selected shoots up more canes tied to wires on the wall.*

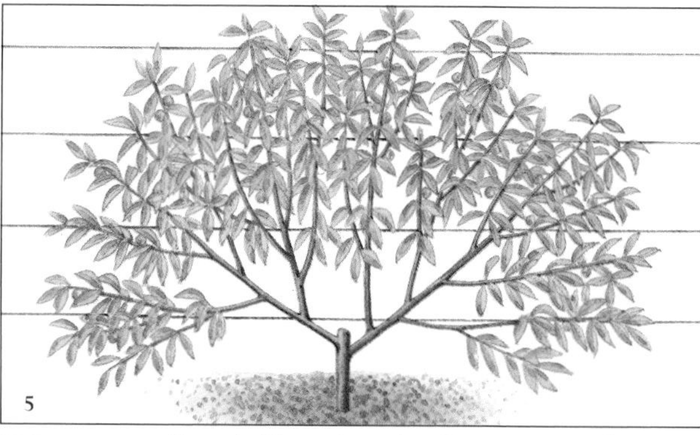

READY TO FRUIT *Keep pinching out surplus shoots, tying in the rest in summer and pruning them back in late winter until the wall is covered. A fan tree may take ten years to spread 20ft, four years to start fruiting.*

Red, blistered leaves

My five-year-old peach tree has been doing splendidly until late June this year, when many of the leaves turned red and blistered. What can I do?

Your tree has peach leaf curl, a fungal disease that attacks peaches, nectarines and almond trees, too. Almost every peach or nectarine tree grown outdoors suffers from it. It will not kill your tree – at the very worst, it will do no more than wipe out the leaves and crop of a single year. It is relatively easy to control, although you are unlikely ever to get rid of it completely.

There are three lines of attack you can try. You can spray the tree with a copper-based fungicide at leaf-fall and again in February, just after growth has started. Or you can apply three sprays of a systemic fungicide such as benomyl at fortnightly intervals from the time the first symptoms appear in early summer. When you've got the disease under control, you can try a little preventive medicine. The spores of the fungus that cause peach leaf curl are spread largely by rain, and if the foliage is given some shelter the disease spreads less rapidly. So if your tree is wall-trained, give it a little roof, or a sheet of polythene, stiffened with battens, that sticks out a couple of feet from the wall.

Peaches can suffer from several other diseases and pests. These are the common ones, along with details of how to spot them and what to do about them:

- **MILDEW** Young shoots develop white tips. To control the disease, spray with a systemic fungicide such as benomyl.
- **DIE-BACK** Shoots die back from the tips. There is no chemical treatment for this disease, which can be caused by bacteria or fungi. Instead, prune dead shoots back to clean wood and burn all the clippings.
- **LIME DEFICIENCY** Fruits have split stones. Treat by sprinkling garden lime around the tree. Sprinkle ½lb per square yard over the whole area beneath the branches.
- **GREENFLY, BLACKFLY** Small winged and crawling insects visible; leaves may become sticky and curled; shoots may bend at the tips. Treat by spraying with a systemic insecticide such as dimethoate.
- **RED SPIDER MITES** Older leaves gradually turn a bronzed yellow colour, dry out and die. Spray the tree with malathion, derris or dimethoate.

Grown from the stone

What are the chances of growing a peach tree from a stone?

The peach is one of the very few fruit trees that will produce good crops when grown from seed. This is true even of a seed taken from a peach bought at the greengrocer's, and when you do eventually get a crop from it, the fruits will normally be carbon copies of the parent. So choose a handsome peach to start with.

Open the hard shell and remove the seed. It's best to do this with a small hacksaw; if you try to smash the shell open you risk crushing the seed as well. Alternatively, you can leave the seed in the shell, but it will certainly take months and will probably take years for the shell to break down sufficiently for the seed to germinate.

When to sow is also a matter of choice. You can sow the seed in spring so that it has the whole growing season to germinate and grow. Or you can sow the seed in autumn and leave it outside – a thorough frosting may encourage germination, particularly if you've left the shell on. You can sow it in a pot of seed compost in the greenhouse, on a windowsill, or in garden soil in the open. All ways are successful. Seedling trees take longer to start fruiting than budded or grafted ones, so it may be five or six years before you see your first fruit.

HAND POLLINATION *Spread pollen between the flowers with a soft brush. Trim off surplus fruits to leave 9in between them.*

A partner for pollinating

Do peach trees have to be pollinated by other varieties like apples? Will I have to plant a second peach to ensure that the first one crops?

Fortunately for gardeners, peaches and nectarines are largely self-fertile and there's no need to plant another tree. But there is a pollination problem. Peaches flower very early in the year – late March to early April – when there are few pollinating insects about. This means that even outdoor peaches may sometimes have to be pollinated by hand. For indoor peaches, it is always essential.

Do this pollinating by gathering pollen from one flower on the tip of a camel-hair paintbrush, and pass it gently across the centre of another flower to transfer the pollen to its stigma. Repeat the process each day, ideally at noon, throughout the flowering season, until most of the blossoms are pollinated and no new flowers are opening.

It can be a wearisome task, especially on a large tree – but it is necessary.

PEARS

Small trees for a small garden

Our garden is really quite small, but we should like to grow a pear tree. Is there a specially small one you could recommend?

Pears generally grow more vigorously than apples, and there are none that could really be described as dwarf. The smallest, when fully grown, would probably reach a height of 10-12ft. Most pears from nurseries have been grafted onto quince rootstock; 'Malling Quince C' has a moderately dwarfing effect, and any pear you choose should be growing on this rootstock.

'Williams' Bon Chrétien' or 'Packham's Triumph' grown on 'Malling Quince C' may suit your case. A snag, of course, is that most pears are self-sterile, which means that you or a neighbour would have to grow another variety nearby in order to pollinate the first one (see also *Pollinating partners*, page 252). This may compound, rather than offer a solution to, your space problem. One way around it would be to grow 'Conference'; this tree is at least partly self-fertile, though it will produce better crops in company with another variety.

Alternatively, why not grow a family tree – that is, a tree which grows more than one variety of fruit? It is a matter of grafting another variety onto, say, your 'Conference'; 'Onward' would be a good one to choose. It's a fascinating and fairly simple business – to find out how to do it, see *Grafting*, page 160. In that way, you would get two trees in one, each happily pollinating the other.

Two other tips that may help to keep your tree small. Go easy with the high-nitrogen fertilisers, which promote growth. Use bone meal instead. And keep your pruning as light as you can. Its eventual effect is to encourage shoots at the expense of fruit.

Uncertain fruiting

Why does my pear tree fruit very well some years, then have two or three years when the crop is fairly light? Should I prune it?

Perhaps, if your tree is getting crowded. Pears can stand hard cutting back, so never hesitate to remove overcrowded branches.

The same applies to fruiting spurs, which pear trees produce in abundance. Too many will sap the energy of your tree, so thin them out in July. This may well improve fruiting performance (see also *Pruning*, page 269).

Another possible cause of your problem could be late frosts, or colder-than-usual spring winds that may have scorched some of the blossom. If your tree is a large one, and in an exposed position, there's not much you can do to protect it. There's a chance, too, that adverse weather conditions might have reduced the number of pollinating insects about at blossom time. Again, unless you can shelter the tree to some degree so as to encourage insects to linger near it, all you can do is hope for more mild springs.

Pollinating partners

I know that it's often necessary to plant more than one variety of apple tree to ensure a good crop. Is it just as important with pears?

If anything, it's more important. With pears as well as apples, one variety needs to be pollinated by another to produce a good crop. Apple trees are fairly common, and there may well be a suitable tree of a different variety in a neighbouring garden – in which case you don't have to grow a second tree to pollinate yours. There are not nearly so many pear trees about, though, so the chances are you'll have to plant another variety yourself. Most varieties of pear will cross-pollinate, provided that their flowering times overlap by at least a few days. But the flowering periods of some overlap for longer, and are therefore especially suitable for pollinating each other. Combinations that have stood the test of time include:

- 'Williams' Bon Chrétien' with 'Conference', 'Doyenné du Comice' or 'Joséphine de Malines'.
- 'Beth' with 'Doyenné du Comice', or 'Williams' Bon Chrétien'.
- 'Onward' with 'Conference' or 'Williams' Bon Chrétien'.
- 'Beurré Superfin' with 'Doyenné du Comice'.
- 'Conference' with 'Doyenné du Comice', 'Packham's Triumph' or 'Williams' Bon Chrétien'.
- 'Doyenné du Comice' with 'Williams' Bon Chrétien', 'Beth', 'Conference' or 'Beurré Superfin'.
- 'Joséphine de Malines' with 'Conference'.

STORING PEARS

Most varieties of pear are ready to pick at around the same time – in September or October. Once they are picked, though, the time they take to ripen varies considerably. Some, like 'Williams' Bon Chrétien', ripen within a few weeks; others, such as 'Glou Morceau', may not ripen until January. Long-ripening pears, especially, need careful storage.

- Store all pears in a place that has a cool, even temperature: as cool as you can make it, though above freezing point. The air should be free to circulate and the atmosphere should not be too dry. A cellar, larder or garage might do, but don't be tempted to use an attic where the temperature fluctuates widely.
- Lay the pears, unwrapped, in a single layer on a shelf or tray.
- Leave the pears in the cool place until the period in which they become ready for eating (see the chart opposite for the dates). About 10-14 days before you want to eat them, bring them inside, into a temperature of around 18°C (65°F), to finish ripening. When ready, they will give slightly to gentle finger pressure.
- Even though the pears are being stored in a cool place, keep an eye on them. Some may start to ripen before being brought inside – in which case use them immediately before they spoil.

Pruning pears

Do pear trees need pruning?

Prune them in the same way as apple trees (see *Apples*, page 13), but less heavily in the early years. Established trees of some varieties, such as 'Williams' Bon Chrétien', tend to produce large-branched fruiting spurs which should be thinned out during late winter, or in July, leaving three or four plump fruit buds.

A wall-trained pear

I've a long, south-facing wall that cries out for an espaliered fruit tree, and I'd like to try a pear. Which variety should I choose and how should I train it to the wall?

Choose a really top-quality pear – one that does best in a warm, sunny spot. Two suitable varieties, both with excellent flavour, are 'Glou Morceau' and 'Joséphine de Malines'. Another exceptionally good pear you could try is 'Doyenné du Comice'.

What you aim for in planning an espalier is an eventual pattern of a central vertical stem with pairs of branches reaching out horizontally along the wall, from opposite sides of the main stem, at roughly 12in intervals. Before planting the tree, run a series of wires along the wall, anchoring them with vine eyes and wire strainers. There should be a 12in gap – about four courses of brick – between the wires; the bottom wire should be 18in from the ground. The height to which you let the espalier grow will depend on the wall, but 8ft high by 15ft wide is a good average size.

Plant the tree in winter. You can save yourself a lot of effort if you buy a three or four-year-old tree that has already been started as an espalier; you will also be able to get fruit from it within a couple of years. But if you want to train the tree yourself, get a two-year-old one which has two opposing sideshoots and a vertical, central stem. After planting, tie the two horizontal shoots to the bottom wire; they will become the espalier's lowest pair of branches. Then cut the central stem, or 'leader', 2in above the next wire up.

TOP TIERS *An espaliered pear looks good and grows well, trained on wires against a sunny wall. This tree is a 'Conference'.*

During the growing season, the leader will continue to grow upwards and the two side branches outwards, and a number of new-shoots will grow from the leader. In the summer, choose the two shoots closest to the second wire up, and tie them to the wire; these will become the next pair of side branches. Leave the other shoots alone for the present.

In the winter, cut the leader 2in above the third wire and cut back all sideshoots that are not tied onto the wires to 4-5in long. Continue building up the espalier in this way until it has reached the size you want. From then on, cut back any new shoots to ½in long each summer.

How to beat the birds

In late summer each year my pears are badly pecked by birds. This lets wasps into the fruit, and last season I lost perhaps two-thirds of my crop. What can I do to stop this?

If your tree is small, and you can reach most of the fruits with a ladder, try putting small cardboard collars, about 2in across, around the stem of each pear. Birds nearly always start pecking at the stalk end, and the collars will usually put them off – so long as you get the collars on at the first sign of pecking. But it must be admitted that it's a finicky and time-consuming job.

An alternative and much simpler method, if the tree is small, is to throw a net over it; but do check to see that no birds are trapped inside. With a larger tree you may have to consider using one of the chemical deterrents based on aluminium ammonium sulphate. These will do something towards keeping the birds at bay, but will not help the fruit in the upper parts of the tree – the parts that the spray cannot reach.

So switch your sights to the wasps instead. The best way to get rid of them is to find and destroy their nest (see *Wasps*, page 359). Failing that, jam jars half filled with beer or watery jam and hung among the branches can be very effective. The wasps are drawn by the sweet liquid and drown in it.

Ready for the picking

Exactly when is a pear ready to be picked? If I leave them until they're ripe, either they fall off or the wasps get them.

Never leave pears to ripen on the tree. If you do, they lose too much moisture and end up fluffy and dry; or, as you say, they become a target for wasps. On the other hand, if you pick them too soon, they will never ripen properly. The perfect time to pick a pear is when it has reached its full size, but before it has started to ripen. At this point, it should part readily from the tree when lifted and twisted. If it has to be dragged off, and takes a bunch of leaves with it, it's clearly not ready. If it falls into your hand, you've probably left it too long.

Here are the times when you would normally expect to pick the principal varieties of pear: 'Williams' Bon Chrétien', 'Beth' and 'Onward' in September; 'Beurré Superfin' in September or October; 'Louise Bonne of Jersey' and 'Doyenné du Comice' in October; and 'Conference' and 'Joséphine de Malines' in October or November.

Which trees to grow

To round off my orchard, I've just got room for a couple of pear trees. Which varieties should I grow?

There are a number of excellent pear varieties, and which you choose is largely a matter of which flavours you prefer. The chart on the right shows the characteristics of some of the most reliable varieties. They are listed in the order in which they ripen.

When choosing which pears to grow, bear in mind that the two trees must be varieties that will pollinate each other (see *Pollinating partners*, opposite). It is also a good idea to grow one that ripens early – say a 'Beth' – and one that ripens later, such as 'Doyenné du Comice'. In that way you will have a supply of pears lasting for months rather than just a few weeks.

Some pears are of a low, spreading habit; others are taller and more upright. It is easier to care for spreading trees, and easier to pick fruit from them. On the other hand, upright trees take up less room. For details of which variety has which habit, see the chart.

Hard pears

I have a large pear tree in the garden. It crops well but its fruits never ripen, no matter how long I store them. What can I do to make them ripen?

Nothing. If, as you say, it is a large tree with fruit that won't ripen, then you've almost certainly got the best known of all cooking pears, 'Catillac'. These pears are not meant to soften. In fact, their ability to stay firm even when stored until April is their main virtue; it prevents them from falling to pieces when cooked.

To be sure that your tree is a 'Catillac', examine the blossom next time it's out. The flowers should be noticeably larger than those of other pear trees.

Banana-like pears

Many of my 'Conference' pears are shaped more like bananas than pears. What's wrong?

These oddly shaped fruits are the result of 'parthenocarpy', or virgin birth – that is, they have developed from flowers that were never fertilised. The seeds have failed to develop in the fruitlet, and the surrounding flesh has not been stimulated into growth. 'Conference' is the only common pear variety that produces these freak parthenocarpic fruits. Other varieties, if unfertilised, produce nothing at all.

The only way to try to stop this happening is to improve pollinating conditions. Make sure there's a pear tree of another variety nearby, and if possible, provide a windbreak during the flowering period to encourage pollinating insects to linger on the tree. So long as your tree produces only a few parthenocarpic fruits, it's not worth bothering about. The fruits are perfectly edible. You may be interested to know that bananas, seedless grapes and oranges, and most cucumbers, are all parthenocarpic.

Brown plague

Recently, some of the pears on my trees have developed pale brown patches surrounding rings of whitish spots, and in one or two the disease spread so far that the fruits simply shrivelled up to nothing. What's the cause?

It's a disease called brown rot that can also occur in pears in store. There's not much chance of your saving this year's crop, but it won't do the tree any lasting damage. To prevent the disease spreading further, destroy all rotten or withered fruit on the tree, on the ground or in store. When you're next pruning the tree, make sure to cut out

PICK OF THE PEARS

Name	Ready for eating	Remarks
'Beurré d'Amanlis'	Early Sept	Yellow skin. Vigorous, spreading growth. Hardy
'Williams' Bon Chrétien'	Sept	Greenish-yellow skin. Crops regularly. Hardy
'Beth'	Mid to late Sept	Yellow-green skin with red flush. Rich, sweet and juicy
'Merton Pride'	Mid to late Sept	Green skin. Crops regularly. Upright growth
'Onward'	Late Sept to early Oct	Yellow-green skin with orange flush. Crops well even when young
'Gorham'	Late Sept to Oct	Yellow skin. Upright growth
'Beurré Superfin'	Oct	Yellow skin. Moderately upright growth. Susceptible to scab disease
'Conference'	Oct	Green and russet skin. Prolific crops. Sweet, juicy fruit
'Louise Bonne of Jersey'	Late Oct	Yellow-green skin with red flush. Hardy and vigorous
'Doyenné du Comice'	Late Oct to Nov	Pale yellow and russet skin. Outstanding fruit, but not a heavy cropper.
'Packham's Triumph'	Nov	Pale yellow skin. Upright, compact growth
'Winter Nelis'	Nov to Dec	Yellow-green skin. Spreading growth. Small, tasty fruit
'Glou Morceau'	Dec to Jan	Yellow skin. Upright growth. Best trained against a wall
'Joséphine de Malines'	Jan to early Feb	Yellow skin, sometimes with a red flush. Spreading growth. Small fruit
'Catillac'	Dec to Apr	Green skin. Standard cooking pear. Large, hard fruit. Resistant to scab disease

all dead wood. Spray with benomyl in late August or early September; this will reduce the chances of the fruits rotting after they have been picked and stored.

Brown rot is the worst of the common problems that are likely to beset your pear trees. The others are:

- **PEAR SCAB** Causes black spots on leaves and fruit. Spray with a systemic fungicide such as benomyl every ten days.
- **APHIDS** Watch out for puckered leaves and twisted shoot tips. Get rid of the creatures by spraying with a systemic insecticide such as dimethoate.
- **PEAR LEAF BLISTER MITE** Minute pests that raise yellowish-green blisters on leaves. Spray with thiophanate-methyl at the end of March.
- **PEAR MIDGE** Tiny grubs appear in fruitlets. To discourage them, spray with fenitrothion before and after the flowers open. But don't spray while the flowers are open; otherwise you'll kill pollinating bees, and without them no fruit will set.
- **PEAR SUCKER** Leaves become sticky in summer. Spray with dimethoate.
- **CATERPILLARS** The signs are holes in leaves and fruitlets. Spray with permethrin.
- **FIRE BLIGHT** A serious disease, which must by law be reported to the nearest office of the Ministry of Agriculture. For details, see *Fire blight*, page 136.

Feeding pears

There's some disagreement in my neighbourhood about the how and when of feeding pear trees. Can you settle it?

It is certainly important to get the feeding pattern right. Any pear tree, wrongly or poorly fed and watered, is quite capable of dropping its whole crop prematurely. The best regime is this. Pear trees need no feeding during the first year after planting. Thereafter, in January or February, give each tree 1oz of sulphate of potash to the square yard. Each March give 1oz of sulphate of ammonia per square yard, plus a further ½oz if the tree is in grass. Every third year, also in January or February, sprinkle 2oz of superphosphate to the square yard.

In each case, when applying the fertilisers, keep them clear of the trunk and scatter them over an area slightly larger than that covered by the branches. An additional light mulch of well-rotted manure or compost applied around the trunk in spring will help to promote sturdy growth.

Finally, keep the trees well watered. Pears are sensitive to drought, and in dry periods between May and July, you should give them 4 gallons of water per square yard per week.

PEAS

Newspaper sponge

My neighbour plants his peas in a trench lined with old newspapers. What good does this do?

The newspapers lining your neighbour's trench help the soil to retain moisture. Peas are deep-rooting and need deep, rich, fertile soil that is free-draining yet also holds moisture if they are to produce a good crop.

Although your neighbour's newspaper does help to hold the moisture in his soil, it doesn't improve the soil's fertility or do much for its structure, so he should really add some form of organic matter as well.

Instead of newspapers, it is usually better to dig a 2in layer of well-rotted farmyard manure or garden compost into the soil in the autumn or early winter. This helps to retain moisture *and* improves the structure of the soil and its fertility.

Too much too soon

My peas last year were very disappointing. The plants produced a lot of leaf but not many pods. I kept them well watered, but do you think they needed more feeding?

No – quite the opposite. Far from needing extra feeding, the problem with your peas was probably that they made too much growth because you gave them too much water or too much high-nitrogen fertiliser *at the wrong time*.

Peas do need a lot of water. But if they are watered heavily at the beginning, or fed with large amounts of high-nitrogen fertiliser, they will produce lots of leaf and stem and not many flowers – and hence not many pods. Once you've sown the seed, keep the soil moist until the seedlings have become established. After that, give no more water until the plants start to flower. Water them only if they show signs of wilting in a drought. Once flowering starts, water the plants twice weekly around the base at a rate of 1-2 gallons per square yard.

Grow to suit yourself

Is it worth growing your own peas these days, now that frozen peas are not very expensive?

You won't save much money by growing your own peas. The yield is quite small for the area taken up, especially if soil conditions are poor or the weather is hot and dry. If you are looking to save money, it would probably be better to choose a crop with a better return, such as runner beans or tomatoes. But the flavour of freshly picked peas is much better than any fresh peas sold by greengrocers, and most people would say better than frozen peas, too. This is because the sugar in peas starts to turn to starch as soon as the peas are picked. The longer they have to wait before being eaten, the less good the flavour.

There are three ways of growing peas. You can make one small sowing that will provide you with just enough to eat over the two or three weeks that the peas are ready. Alternatively, you can sow batches of peas every two or three weeks to provide fresh peas from the end of May until autumn.

Sowing in batches, you could expect a yield of about 30lb on a 10ft row. The cost will be for 1½ pints of seeds (or its equivalent in seed packets), six barrowloads of manure and about ½lb of Growmore.

Alternatively, you may prefer to sow your peas in one large batch and then freeze the surplus. You can then clear the ground and use it for something else. However, you won't be able to eat many of the peas fresh, and your frozen peas will not necessarily taste better than commercially frozen peas.

Sow the seeds 2-3in apart in 2-3in deep, flat-bottomed drills, 6-8in wide. The distance between the drills should be roughly the same as the eventual height of the variety you are growing: this can be as little as 12in for some of the dwarf varieties or as much as 5ft. The plants can be grown without supporting sticks, but yields will be better if the pods are kept off the ground.

Make sure all your sowings are protected from birds, especially in the early stages (for ideas on how to do that, see *Birds*, page 28).

Late sowing

What is the latest time to sow peas outside? Will they grow during the winter if they're cloched over?

The latest you can sow peas for picking the same year is June-July. Sow the seeds at intervals of two or three weeks and they will be ready for picking in early September, continuing through until the end of October. In areas where there is a risk of early frost, it will be necessary to finish the crop under cloches or field frames.

Peas will also grow through the winter under cloches. You won't get a crop for picking during the winter months, but if you plant in October-November or February-March, the peas will be ready for picking in April-May. There are likely to be some losses, though. Crops sown very late or very early usually escape the ravages of birds and pea moths, which affect maincrop peas. On the other hand, in wet summers slugs can be a problem, attacking seedlings above and below ground and sometimes feeding on the lowest pods. A firm seedbed will help to limit slug activity as well as encouraging quick germination. Another danger with late crops is drought. It is particularly important to sow in deeply cultivated fertile soils which are free-draining, yet retain moisture. Powdery mildew is also likely to be a problem with late peas.

Choose early varieties for both late and early sowing. Round varieties (those that remain smooth when dried) such as 'Feltham First' are quick-maturing and hardier than the wrinkled (marrowfat) varieties. But marrowfat types, such as 'Little Marvel' and 'Kelvedon Wonder' (which has a high resistance to mildew), have better flavour. Other marrowfat varieties worth trying are 'Hurst Beagle' and 'Progress No. 9'.

Polythene protection

I sowed my peas evenly, but the germination was gappy. Why is this?

Probably because you sowed them too early in the year without protection. Peas will actually germinate in temperatures as low as 5°C (41°F), but they take a long time about it, especially if the soil is wet as well as cold. When germination is slow, you get high losses – and so gaps – because of damage by mice, and because fungal and bacterial diseases attack the seeds.

Little, if anything, is gained by sowing too early. In warm parts of the country don't sow until late February – not until March in colder parts. For the best results, to speed up germination and protect from frost, cover the rows with cloches or field frames.

As an alternative, the whole area can be covered with a floating cloche – a transparent, perforated film, specially designed for the purpose (see *Floating cloches: the pros and cons*, page 82). Once you've sown the seed, mark out where the edges of the film will be and dig a 4in deep trench. Lay the film directly over the bed, placing the edges in the trench. Turn the soil back into the trench and firm it with your feet to hold down the film. Don't stretch the film tight. As the seedlings emerge, their foliage lifts the film to form a loose tunnel – a floating cloche. Remove the cover before the plants get too large, three to four weeks after sowing.

Peas in pots

I would like to grow early peas in pots in my heated greenhouse. How do I set about it?

By growing under glass you can have a crop of fresh peas ready for late spring. For the earliest crop, sow the seeds between October and early December. The most suitable pots are 8-10in in diameter. Peas can also be grown in borders, growing bags or deep boxes.

Put about 2in of gravel in the bottom of the pot for drainage, and half fill the pot with John Innes No 1 potting compost. Sow about eight seeds to a pot, then cover them with ½in of compost. When the seedlings are 1-2in high, thin them to leave the five strongest. Once the plants are established, give them as much light and ventilation as possible, and keep them free from frost. Do not keep them much warmer than this, otherwise they become susceptible to damage and disease.

As the plants grow, top-dress them with compost until the pots are filled to within 1in of the top. Then stake the plants, tying each growth separately. Add longer brushwood sticks later in the spring if necessary.

Give plenty of ventilation when the plants are in flower. Immediately the pods have set, feed the plants about once a fortnight with a balanced liquid fertiliser such as a house plant fertiliser.

Suitable dwarf peas are 'Little Marvel' and 'Progress No. 9', both wrinkled marrowfat varieties, and the round varieties 'Meteor' and 'Feltham First'. Medium and tall varieties can also be used, and they are more productive than dwarf peas. They rarely reach full height when grown in a pot, and you may need to pinch out the growing points after a fair number of flowers have opened. The side growth may also need removing. This treatment will sometimes be necessary with strong-growing dwarf varieties, but not with compact dwarf varieties.

Edible pods

Mangetout peas are usually very expensive in the shops. What makes them different from ordinary peas? Are they much more difficult to grow? Are there any other kinds of peas with edible pods?

Mangetout means literally 'eat all'. The pods remain soft and tender even when ripe, unlike ordinary peas which are lined with a thin, tough membrane which dries as the pea ripens – finally splitting to eject the peas.

Mangetout peas can be treated like french beans, topped and tailed then cooked whole, or they can be eaten raw because they are very sweet.

Mangetouts are hardier than most people realise. In warmer parts of the country they can be sown in the autumn, outdoors, or in an unheated greenhouse or in polythene tunnels, for an early crop. For a main crop, sow them outdoors from March to June and grow them just like ordinary peas. Pick them when the pods are about 3in long and still flat, before the seeds can be seen.

Three good mangetout varieties are 'Sugar Dwarf Sweet Green', which grows to about 3ft high, the 20in high 'Norli', and 'Oregon Sugar Pod', which grows to about 3½ft.

There is another type of pea with edible pods – the asparagus pea. Ornamental bushy plants, about 18in high, have delicate clover-like foliage and red flowers like sweet peas. They produce four-winged pods which are eaten raw when young. When older, they can be cooked and eaten in salads. They usually become inedibly tough when longer than 1½in.

Grow asparagus peas in a sunny position in light, well-drained soil. Before planting, apply general fertiliser at 1-2oz per square yard. In early May, after the frosts are over, sow 4-6in apart directly into the ground in 1in deep drills, 12in apart. Keep them weed-free, especially in the early stages, and don't water much until the flowers have developed, then water them regularly. The plants usually need to be tied to pea sticks.

Sugar snap peas fall halfway between ordinary garden peas and mangetout. When they are young, they can be cooked just like mangetouts. When they are older and the peas have developed in the pods, they can be stringed and cooked like french beans or the peas can be shelled. Grow them like mangetouts. For advice on varieties, see *Pick of the peas*, page 256.

Stems for compost

Is it safe to add pea stems to a compost heap?

Yes – virtually anything from the vegetable garden will break down in a compost heap, including pea stems (haulms). The only things that should be avoided are diseased material because the heat inside the heap may not be great enough to kill the bugs. Therefore, don't compost pea haulms affected with downy and powdery mildew, foot rot or sclerotinia disease. Burn such material to reduce the risk of spreading the disease or carrying it over to the next season.

Mix the pea haulms well with other ingredients before putting them on the heap. This is one of the keys to successful composting. Mixing up the ingredients in any compost heap helps to provide a balanced diet for the micro-organisms that turn vegetable waste into rich compost.

Self-supporting

How successful are peas that are said to need no supporting? Do they really stand up by themselves?

Self-supporting peas are varieties in which the leaves are converted to tendrils. They are leafless or semi-leafless and look a little like barbed wire. Such variations occur naturally in ordinary peas every now and then and they have been developed by plant breeders trying to improve vining peas which are grown commercially for canning and drying.

Vining peas are wrinkle-seeded (marrowfat) peas with a high sugar content. They are at their best for picking for only about 24 hours before they start to deteriorate. They often start to collapse and the foliage begins to rot before that point is reached. The self-supporting peas do not collapse because they support each other with intertwining tendrils. The first varieties developed had a relatively low yield per plant because they were intended for high-density use in fields. Varieties developed more recently, however, have a much better yield.

Varieties worth trying which stand up well, all semi-leafless, are 'Bikini' (very good for freezing) and 'Eaton', which are earlies, and the maincrop varieties 'Markana' (unattractive to birds) and 'Poppet'.

Drying time

Should peas for drying be left on the plant or picked while they are still fresh?

Leave them as long as possible on the plants – until the foliage begins to turn yellow and the pods start to wrinkle. Then pull up the plants and tie the stalks together in loose bundles.

Hang them in a dry shed or well-ventilated building so that the air can get through them. When the pods are crackly and snap open easily, shell the peas and store them in jars. Peas for drying have never been widely grown in gardens. Even when they were most popular, during the Middle Ages, they were considered a field crop rather than suitable for the kitchen garden. There has been a revival of interest, though, in dried peas as a protein source. Peas suitable for drying include 'Dun Pea', 'Maro' (resistant to downy mildew), and 'Progneta'.

Summer pests

My pea pods are infested with little pale yellow grubs. What are they, and what can I do to get rid of them?

The grubs are the caterpillars of the pea moth. This is a widespread pest of members of the pea family. During June and July, the moths lay their eggs on the leaves of pea plants in flower. When the caterpillars hatch, they eat into the young pods and feed on the peas. After about a month the caterpillars leave the pods and, as the weather cools, they make themselves cocoons in the soil. They hatch into moths in the spring.

Since egg-laying is mostly during June and July, the best way to avoid the pest is by sowing very early, so that the peas are picked by the end of June.

Chemicals can be used to protect plants that are in flower during June and July, particularly on sites that were infested the previous season. Spray as soon as the plants come into flower, and then again 14 days later. Use a foliar spray: fenitrothion (wait at least a fortnight after spraying before harvesting); or permethrin (leave a three-week gap between spraying and harvesting).

Several other species of caterpillar, apart from the pea moth, attack leaves and peas, usually during July and August. Treatment is the same as for pea moth.

Pea moth is not the only pest to affect peas. Two of the most important are birds and, in the country, field mice. They eat the seeds before they have a chance to germinate. See *Birds*, page 28, for methods of keeping off birds. Set traps for mice.

These are the other common pests and diseases that afflict peas:

- **PEA APHID** The growing points are damaged, the leaves and pods become yellow and malformed and the yield is reduced. Aphids can also carry leaf roll and pea mosaic virus. Apply a foliar spray such as dimethoate, pirimicarb, malathion or fenitrothion. See also *Aphids*, page 12.
- **PEA AND BEAN WEEVILS** These insects cause U-shaped notches in the leaf edges of young plants, and the growth may be damaged. Older and quick-growing plants can usually tolerate damage, which is rarely severe enough to need treatment. A good seedbed will encourage quick germination and growth and reduces the amount of shelter available for the weevils.
- **PEA CYST NEMATODES** They cause poor stem and root growth and yellow patches in the crop. The problem is often aggravated by fungal root rot. Don't replant the site with peas for at least four years.
- **PEA MIDGES** The leading shoots and flower buds are deformed or dead, there is poor shoot growth, flowers drop off and pods grow small and misshapen. Don't sow any more peas that year. Check for adult midges on the crop in early June and spray, if necessary, with dimethoate or fenitrothion.
- **PEA THRIPS** They cause silvery mottled areas on the leaves and pods; they also cause stunted plants, blind flowers and distorted pods. Check for signs of damage in June and July, especially in dry spells. Spray affected plants with dimethoate. Don't grow peas on that site again for at least four years.
- **DOWNY MILDEW** This fungus causes fluffy grey-brown growth on the undersides of the leaves, pale yellow-green leaves on young plants, and stunted growth. The plants die, and there are no seeds in the pods. Burn affected plants, and spray the remainder with a fungicide such as triforine.
- **FOOT ROT** The disease causes blackening of the stem base and roots, and leaf spotting. Burn the affected plants and keep the site

PICK OF THE PEAS

Type of pea	Name	Height	Remarks
GARDEN PEAS			
First earlies (sow Jan–Mar or Oct–Nov for picking May–June)	'Feltham First'	18in	Round-seeded. Hardy and very reliable.
	'Meteor'	18in	Round-seeded. Curved and pointed pods. Heavy cropper. Very hardy and quick-growing.
Second earlies (sow Mar–Apr for picking June–July)	'Hurst Green Shaft'	2½ft	Wrinkled. Pointed pods usually borne in pairs. Heavy cropper with good flavour. Resistant to downy mildew and fusarium wilt.
	'Early Onward'	2ft	Wrinkled. Large, well-filled, blunt pods. Vigorous grower but short-jointed. Heavy cropper.
Maincrop (sow Apr–May for picking July–Aug)	'Antares'	2-2½ft	Wrinkled. Pods usually borne in pairs. Heavy cropper. Very reliable. Compact.
	'Alderman'	5ft	Wrinkled. Robust plants with large, pointed pods. Excellent cropper over a long season.
MANGETOUT (SUGAR PEAS) (Sow Apr–May for picking Aug–Sept)	'Sugar Dwarf Sweet Green'	3ft	Pointed pods. Very sweet and tender. Exceptionally heavy cropper.
	'Norli'	20in	Bush type. Early, membrane-free pods. Heavy cropper.
PETIT POIS (Sow Apr–May for picking Aug–Sept)	'Cobri'	2ft	Must be picked when very young.
	'Waverex'	18in	Delicious eaten raw. Also suitable for freezing.
SUGAR SNAP (Sow Apr–May for picking Aug–Sept)	'Sugar Rae'	2ft	Maincrop with long, bright green pods. Remains in good condition for several days after picking.
	'Sugar Snap'	4-6ft	Thick pods. Very sweet.

free of peas for at least four years. See also *Foot rot*, page 144.

• **STEM NEMATODES** Affected stems are stunted, with blackened bases and generally poor growth. Keep weeds, such as bindweed, knotgrass, mayweed and chickweed, that harbour stem nematodes, under control. Don't plant peas again on that site for at least four years.

• **FUSARIUM FOOT ROT** The lower leaves start to wilt and the plants die in well-defined patches. The roots and stems turn black or brown. Burn affected plants. The risk of infection can be reduced with a long crop rotation – leave a four-year gap before replanting on the same site. Avoid compacted soils and waterlogged sites.

• **FUSARIUM WILT** There is a greyish bloom to the leaves before the plants turn yellow from the bottom upwards. The leaves are rolled and brittle and there is a pale orange-brown discoloration within the base of the stem and the taproot. Burn affected plants. See also *Fusarium wilt*, page 149.

• **LEAF AND POD SPOT** The disease causes premature ageing of plants, disfigured pods, and slightly sunken pale brown spots on leaves and pods. Burn affected plants after severe attacks. The disease is carried in seeds or waste matter, so never save the seeds from affected plants. Don't replant the site with peas for at least four years.

• **POWDERY MILDEW** Leaves and pods are covered with a white powdery growth. It is worst in dry weather when there are heavy dews. Powdery mildew particularly affects late varieties and crops. Burn the diseased plants to prevent spread. See also *Powdery mildew*, page 268.

• **ROOT ROT** Causes the seedlings to collapse just after they emerge. The roots are decayed and the taproot blackened. Do not replant the site with peas for at least four years. To avoid root rot, make sure the soil is well drained and keep it in good condition by digging in plenty of organic matter. Use a fungicidal seed dressing to prevent future attacks.

• **PEA MOSAIC VIRUS** Causes mottled leaves with pale green or yellowish-green depressed areas between the veins. The disease is spread by aphids. See also *Aphids*, page 12.

• **SCLEROTINIA DISEASE** Stems rot and collapse. Black resting spores are present on or in the stems. Burn the affected plants. Don't replant the site with peas for four years.

Incidentally, an attack by any of these pests or diseases does not necessarily mean that you have to throw out your pods as well as your plants. Provided the peas themselves have no obvious damage, they'll be safe to eat even if the plants that bore them are a write-off.

PEPPERS

Top crop

How many peppers can you get from one plant?

Yields can vary a great deal, depending on the variety and how well it's grown. A single sweet pepper plant can produce as many as 30 fruits. Normally, though, you can expect only six to ten fruits per plant. Moreover, it's not usually worth going simply for the maximum number of fruits, because they can become misshapen and damaged by pressing against each other. It's better to thin the overcrowded ones as they grow, and harvest fewer but better-quality ones.

Pick the fruits regularly as they ripen in August and September. But never take all the fruit off a plant at once, because this can stimulate growth of shoots and leaves at the expense of further fruit. You can pick the fruit green (some varieties remain this colour even when mature) or leave them to mature to red or yellow. Those that do change colour normally take about three weeks to do so if they're growing in a greenhouse. Among the varieties which consistently carry the heaviest crops are 'Bell Boy' (green at maturity), 'Gypsy' (red) and 'Gold Star' (yellow). If you want to grow peppers outdoors – something that's worth doing only in milder parts of the South and West of Britain – go for 'Canape'.

Hot and mild

Is it possible to make ordinary pepper or a hot pepper spice from dried capsicums?

No. The ordinary ground pepper you sprinkle on your food is made from the dried fruit of an entirely unrelated plant, *Piper nigrum*, a woody vine native to Indonesia. When the fruits are ground whole, the result is black pepper. If the shells are removed first, the result is white pepper.

As for the hot pepper spices, the answer again is no. Capsicums, or sweet peppers, have a relatively mild flavour, whether you eat them raw in a salad or cooked. It would be unorthodox to dry and crush them, and it wouldn't turn them into pungent peppers anyway. All sweet peppers are the fruit of a naturally occurring subspecies known as *Capsicum annuum grossum*. The hot peppers – from which we get the mouth-searing, eye-watering spices of chilli powder, cayenne pepper and paprika – are all forms of another subspecies, *Capsicum annuum acuminatum*.

Both subspecies do best in the shelter of a greenhouse, and both are grown in the same way. If you want to try your hand at growing the hot types, one of the best varieties is 'Cayenne Chilli'.

A pinch of pepper

Do sweet peppers need pruning?

No. All they need is a single pinch. When the plants are about 6in tall, nip off the central growing point with your fingers. This encourages the plant to produce bushy sideshoots. It also improves cropping. The plants don't normally need sophisticated supports either. Simply fix a 2½ft cane in the soil beside each plant and tie the stem to it.

Where to grow them

Where's the best place for peppers: the greenhouse or the garden? Are they difficult to grow?

It depends on where you live. In the South, peppers can be grown in the garden, like sweet corn and outdoor tomatoes – although they need a hot summer to produce large crops. In the North, they'll always do better under cover. They will happily grow alongside tomatoes in a greenhouse, because both thrive in the same sort of temperature and humidity.

The crop is not difficult to grow. You can start by raising your own from seed or by buying young plants in pots. Peppers are ready for planting out as soon as the first flowers show.

Grow the crop either directly in the border soil or in 8-10in pots, or put four plants in a growing bag. Keep the soil moist for the first week or two after transplanting, to encourage the roots to become established.

Spray the plants with water every day or so in dry, hot conditions in order to help the flowers set and to discourage red spider mites. When the fruits are about the size of a walnut, start giving the plants a weekly feed with a standard tomato fertiliser.

You can start picking when the fruits are about the size of a tennis ball. Cut the peppers off with a knife or secateurs. Pick them about once a week in order to encourage further fruits to grow.

Provided you don't strip the plant completely of fruit, the more you gather, the greater the yield – six to ten fruits per plant ordinarily, but potentially up to 30. Store surplus fruits in the refrigerator or freezer.

Pepper problems

What caused my red peppers to develop soft patches and rot?

Basically, sweet peppers suffer similar problems to tomatoes, but they are especially prone to aphid attack and botrytis. There is also the odd problem specific to peppers, such as sun scald, which seems to be the trouble in your case. In bright sunlight, soft, light-coloured areas develop on the exposed surface of the fruits. These areas eventually become slightly sunken and dry out to assume a bleached, papery appearance; they may also be attacked by botrytis, the grey mould fungus (for details of how to combat the fungus, see *Grey mould*, page 176).

The problem is not uncommon in bright, sunny weather but it seldom causes serious losses. There's nothing you can do to rescue affected fruits; discard them. Protect the rest by shading the greenhouse, or shade the plants themselves if they are outside.

One other problem you might encounter is red spider mite – a microscopic insect whose telltale signs are pale mottling and bronzing of the leaves. You can sometimes also see faint webs on the leaves. Spray with rotenone (derris) as soon as you notice the symptoms. Since the mites are particularly active in hot, dry weather, spraying the plants with water regularly should keep them away thereafter.

PETAL BLIGHT

Disease or damp?

Some of my chrysanthemums are looking very sorry for themselves – tattered, and with watery brown spots on the petals that spread until the petals rot, crumple up and drop off. Is this a disease or simply a by-product of an awful summer?

Both. Petal blight is a disease, and quite a serious one, though it's at its most virulent in prolonged wet seasons and in greenhouses where there's too much humidity. The disease can be troublesome on dahlias, cornflowers, anemones and globe artichokes as well as on chrysanthemums.

Affected flowers can't be treated. They must be destroyed. Greenhouse plants can be protected by lowering the humidity – open doors and vents, and cut down on watering. Outdoors and indoors the disease can also be prevented by spraying or dusting with mancozeb just before the flower buds open. Repeat the dose at fortnightly intervals throughout the flowering season.

BEDRAGGLED BLOOMS *Petal blight is a disease that destroys the flowers of chrysanthemums and several other species. Its effects are exacerbated by wet weather and high humidity.*

PINKS AND BORDER CARNATIONS

(For greenhouse types, see CARNATIONS, page 43)

Taking cuttings

Can you tell me how to take cuttings from my pinks and how long will it be before the plants flower?

The propagation of pinks from cuttings is simplicity itself, yet in part is unique. For the 'cuttings' of pinks are of two types: one called a cutting in the conventional way; and the other a piping. A cutting is made by pulling off a shoot, cutting it cleanly just below a node or joint, and removing the lowest leaves.

A piping, in contrast, is not cut from the plant at all; it is pulled out from the top of a young shoot. Sections of the shoots pull apart very easily, rather like lengths of drainpipe.

Take cuttings and pipings in late June or early July from healthy young shoots. Dip the bases of the cuttings in a hormone rooting powder, and place them in trays in a half-and-half mixture of sand and sterilised loam. Either cover the trays with propagator covers or place them in a closed cold frame for a month or two for roots to form. Keep a daily eye on the cuttings during this period to make sure that they're not drying out or being attacked by any pests or diseases (for details of common problems, see *Carnation collapse*, this page).

It is often suggested that the young plants should be planted out in their flowering positions in the autumn. In fact you will get better plants if they are first potted on into 3in pots of soil-based potting compost, kept in the cold frame, and finally planted out in the spring.

The first flower or two should appear that season, though your pinks will not reach full flowering potential for two or three years. Eventually the plants may become straggly. When this happens, dig them up completely in the autumn, pull them apart, and immediately replant the healthiest pieces. Alternatively, replace your stock every few years from cuttings or pipings.

Easy-care carnations

I want to grow carnations this year but I don't want the bother of staking them. Can you recommend any short cuts, or any varieties that don't need staking?

The name carnation to many people conjures up visions of the large-flowered forms seen in florists and used for wedding buttonholes. These are all forms of the perpetual-flowering carnation, most of which are grown in commercial greenhouses.

They can be grown satisfactorily in garden greenhouses, too, but they require time, patience and expertise – with careful stopping, disbudding and staking.

Much simpler and at least as rewarding are the outdoor relatives of the perpetuals, the various types of pinks and border carnations. Bought as young plants, they will flower in the first year, and the pinks require no staking at all.

The main groups of pinks are the old-fashioned laced and border varieties and their modern relatives, the Allwoodii pinks and the Alpine or rock-garden pinks. These can all be left to their own devices, apart from a trimming back of straggly growth after flowering. None usually requires any disbudding or staking.

If a few taller blooms tend to flop, place small split-cane flower sticks round each clump, and lightly tie the flowers up with soft twine. After three or four years, dig up and divide the clumps in autumn, and replant the best shoots.

In a good soil, the minimum of fertiliser treatment should be given. Simply top-dress early in spring with a light sprinkling of bone meal, a scattering of fresh soil, or both.

Border carnations can be grown in much the same way as pinks, but they certainly do need staking. Remove the small side buds to produce fewer but better blooms. Border carnations tend to deteriorate fairly rapidly. Replace them with fresh stock every four or five years.

Among other types you might consider are annual carnations, which are raised from seed. Sown in seed compost in January or February at a temperature of about 16°C (60°F) and planted out in May, they make superb bedding plants, flowering from July to the first frosts of autumn.

Two other easy-to-grow groups are: the familiar biennial and also annual sweet williams; and the so-called Japanese pinks, which are forms of *Dianthus heddewigii*. Japanese pinks are generally raised from seed, too, and treated as half-hardy annuals (for advice, see *Half-hardy*, page 11).

Carnation collapse

Three clumps of my formerly sprightly carnations are looking decidedly the worse for wear. Many of the leaves have wilted almost to the point of collapse, and the entire plants look generally feeble. What can the matter be?

It sounds like soil-borne wilt disease; you could confirm it by cutting open a stem or two to see if there are dark streaks visible in the tissues. The only guaranteed way to get rid of wilt is to abandon your plants, buy new ones and grow them in another bed. But it's also worth trying to restore your existing plants to health and vigour by replacing the soil in the carnation bed or by shifting the plants to another part of the garden. If they're growing in the greenhouse border, dig them out, wash off the old soil and replant them in pots of fresh compost. Actually, you've been unlucky, for pinks and carnations are fairly trouble-free as a rule. There are, however, a few possible problems, apart from soil-borne wilt.

- **LEAF MINER LARVAE** The signs are whitish streaks and blotches on the leaves. Spray at once with a systemic insecticide such as dimethoate.
- **VIRUS** Infection shows in distorted leaves and stems, and in small, feeble flowers. Dig up and burn diseased plants and obtain new stock. Keep aphids under control; they spread virus diseases.
- **BUD ROT** Flower buds turn soft and brown and fail to open, especially during rainy spells. Destroy infected buds and spray the plants with a systemic fungicide such as benomyl. If you've had this trouble before, or if your neighbours suffer from it, spray the plants each year anyway, whether or not you see signs of rot.
- **TORTRIX MOTH CATERPILLARS** Flowers, buds and shoots are draped in a cobweb-like covering. Remove the caterpillars by hand or spray with permethrin.
- **APHIDS** Shoots and buds are infested with small insects. Spray with dimethoate, malathion, permethrin or fenitrothion.
- **RUST** Small, yellow-brown pustules appear on leaves. Spray plants or drench the soil with fungicide containing thiram. If the trouble persists, destroy affected plants and replace them with new stock.
- **THRIPS** Masses of small, light flecks appear on flower petals. Spray with permethrin, malathion or rotenone (derris).

Forgotten beauty

Years ago we used to grow laced pinks. How do they differ from border carnations and are they still obtainable?

The laced pink has become an almost forgotten plant in the English garden, and only a handful of nurseries still supply it. In garden centres you will probably find modern Allwoodii pinks, which are actually hybrids between the pink and the perpetual-flowering carnation. You may also find pinks labelled 'old-fashioned', but these are almost certain to be (like the varieties 'Mrs Sinkins', 'Inchmery', and 'Sam Barlow') garden or border pinks – attractive enough, but not the same as the genuine laced pink.

The true laced pink is a hardier, older plant – sometimes called Tudor pink, although it probably has little of the original Tudor strain in it – that became most popular in the unlikely surroundings of the Lancashire and Paisley cotton mills in the late 18th and early 19th centuries.

The laced pink has a single main flush of bloom in June with a smattering of flowers later in the summer. The name 'laced' comes from the petals, which are marked with white against dark crimson, red-brown, mauve or pink in a lace-like pattern. The blooms have a heady clove-like perfume that seems to epitomise the English cottage garden. They require no staking, no disbudding, and only an occasional tidying up. Varieties you are likely to find these days – though only in a large garden centre – are:

'London Lovely' – white with mauve lacing and darker eye.
'London Glow' – deep crimson with white edging.
'London Poppet' – white with a hint of pink, dark red edge, dark red eye.
'Laced Joy' – deep pink with crimson edging and crimson eye.
'Laced Prudence' – white with crimson edging.
'Laced Romeo' – white with red-brown edging.
'Dad's Favourite' – white with red-brown edging and darker eye.

OLD LACE *Laced pinks, a traditional garden favourite, look frilly and delicate. But they're also tough plants that need little attention. This variety is 'Dad's Favourite'.*

PLUMS

What's the difference?

Can you tell me what the differences are between plums, gages and damsons?

Primarily colour. Gages are green or yellow. Most plums are purple. Both can be eaten fresh or cooked. Damsons are smaller than either plums or gages and are generally cooked to make fruit cheeses and jams.

Cross-pollination

Do plums need pollination partners in the same way that apples do?

All fruit trees crop better when pollinated by another variety of the same fruit. Some will not crop at all unless cross-pollinated. Self-fertile trees, on the other hand, will carry reasonable crops on their own pollen – though nothing compared to the crops they bear when cross-pollinated.

The self-fertile plum varieties include 'Victoria', 'Denniston's Superb', 'Czar', 'Merryweather Damson', 'Early Transparent Gage', 'Oullin's Gage' and 'Marjorie's Seedling'. 'Cambridge Gage' is partially self-fertile; it produces only a small crop on its own pollen. 'Coe's Golden Drop' and the 'Old Greengage' must be cross-pollinated to produce any fruit. 'Denniston's Superb' and 'Coe's Golden Drop' are good pollinating partners. 'Czar', 'Victoria' and 'Merryweather Damson' also go well together, as do 'Old Greengage' and 'Marjorie's Seedling'.

Getting the best from a new plum tree

I've just bought a plum tree – my first. What kind of care will I have to give it to get the best out of it in the years ahead?

Not a great deal. As with other fruit trees, give it a winter feed of fertiliser in February or March, so that there is time for the nutrients to be washed down to the roots before growth starts in the spring. Growmore, with its 7 per cent each of nitrogen, phosphate and potash will do fine. Late winter is also generally the best time to prune the tree. Once the main framework of branches has been formed after four or five years, this annual pruning should simply be a matter of removing any dead, diseased or damaged shoots or branches.

You may also have to do a little extra pruning in the summer when dead and diseased branches are easier to spot.

Don't pick the fruit until it is ripe, or nearly so. It loses quality if picked too early. Dessert plums in particular are best left to ripen on the tree. Eat them as soon as they're ripe – no variety will store for any length of time.

One of the biggest hazards to plums is spring frost damage; to find out how to protect your tree, see *Poor fruiting*, page 260.

Probably the worst pest to affect plums is aphids, which attack from midsummer onwards. Spray with a systemic insecticide such as dimethoate when the pest is first seen. Another problem can be red plum maggots, which are the tiny red caterpillars of the plum fruit moth. To control them, give the tree a thorough spray with tar oil winter wash around Christmas or spray with permethrin during late June.

How to keep finches away

My plum tree produces very little blossom in spring and even less fruit each summer. How can I make it more productive?

Sounds very much like the work of bullfinches. The lack of fruit is the result of lack of blossom, and the reason for this, almost certainly, is that bullfinches, or perhaps tits, have been stripping the buds in early spring. This is a very common problem, especially in rural areas where there are woods within a few hundred yards.

During the greater part of the year you will probably see nothing, although in the early winter you may well see one or more likely a pair of bullfinches flitting about in the trees. Then, once the weather turns hard and the birds' natural food runs out – or there is snow on the ground – they will leave the woods and come in large numbers to neighbouring gardens to feed. You can tell that they have been eating your buds by the bud scales lying beneath the trees. In the following spring, too, trees that have been attacked by them will have quite long shoots (often a foot or more) completely without leaves or blossom.

A bird repellent containing aluminium ammonium sulphate can be helpful in keeping off the bullfinches – provided you apply it early in winter before they attack. Alternatively, cover the tree with a net. Glittery and noisy birdscarers will work for a few days, but the effect soon wears off as the birds get used to them.

Poor fruiting

I get plenty of blossom on my two six-year-old 'Victoria' plum trees but very little fruit. What's the trouble?

The problem could be either that the blossom isn't being adequately pollinated, or that it's being damaged by spring frost. As the 'Victoria' is a self-fertile variety, which normally carries a good crop even without pollination, it's more likely in this case to be frost.

Plums, like peaches, blossom early in the year, usually by April, and so are particularly vulnerable to spring frosts. Small trees can be protected quite easily by throwing something light like old bed sheets, or polythene, over them on nights that threaten to be frosty. Larger trees have to take their chance – but your six-year-old trees should still be small enough for the method to be practicable.

As for the other possible cause of the problem, it could be that conditions for effective pollination and fertilisation don't exist in your garden when the trees are in blossom. This is usually because the site is too exposed to the wind. Anything you can do to provide more shelter will help – even if it means putting up temporary windbreaks on the windy side of the garden.

It is also possible that your trees need to be pollinated by another variety of plum – although this is less likely with 'Victoria' trees, because they normally produce reasonable crops even when not cross-pollinated. But if there are no other plums of a different variety in the neighbourhood, it may be worth planting one to be sure (see also *Cross-pollination*, page 259).

Training a fan

I've seen plum trees trained into all sorts of shapes and patterns. Is this just for show, or are there practical advantages?

The traditional way of growing fruit trees, including plums, is as 'standards', 'half-standards' or 'bush' trees. These are large trees, whose trunks alone are 6ft, 4ft and 2ft tall respectively. Now, however, plums, like apples and pears, are increasingly grown as dwarf pyramids or trained as fans. These are more suited to today's smaller gardens.

Fan-trained trees are the more practical. Their growth is more open, so the branches are easier to get at and manage. Fans carry heavier crops for their size than traditional trees, and the quality of their fruit is often a good deal better. They also take up a fraction of the space of traditional trees.

Fans are trained either against a wall or onto canes and wires in the open garden. Before planting the tree, stretch a series of wires horizontally at 6in intervals across the wall or between stout posts.

Buy a one-year-old tree and plant it in winter. In the following February, cut it back to 2ft high, then in the summer select two sideshoots opposite each other 9-12in from the ground. Remove all other sideshoots. When the two remaining sideshoots are 18in long, tie them into the wires at a 45 degree angle to the central stem. Remove the central stem above the sideshoots so that the tree now forms a Y-shape. Remove any other sideshoots as they appear.

SPACE SAVER *A fan-trained tree takes up much less room than a free-standing one. This is a 'Victoria' plum, growing on a 'Pixy' rootstock.*

In the second February, cut back the two side branches so that they are once more 18in long. In the summer, select three new shoots on each of the two branches. Two of the shoots on each branch should be growing from the top of the branch and the other from the bottom. Keep these shoots but remove all the others.

In the third February, cut back all eight branches to 2ft long. In the summer select new shoots growing from the top and bottom of these eight branches. Together with the eight original branches, these new shoots will form the main ribs of the fan. The number of new shoots you retain after this depends on the room available for the fan. These new shoots will not need pruning in the following February.

In subsequent summers, stop all new shoots when they have made six or seven leaves, by nipping out the bud at the tip. These shoots will produce a few fruits the following summer but the main crop will come the summer after that. Once the fruit has been picked, cut back the shoots that have fruited by half. If there are gaps in the tree's framework of branches, fill them by allowing suitable new shoots to grow.

Damson without blossom

We have a ten-year-old damson tree that was grown from a pip. There hasn't been a sign of a flower yet. How much longer will we have to wait?

You should be seeing something any year now. If you bought a tree grafted onto a rootstock from a nursery, you would have to wait five to seven years before it flowered. If you had one growing on its own roots, it would be seven to ten years before it flowered. But one grown from a pip may not flower for as much as 12 years.

If you're impatient, you may be able to turn the plant's energies from growth to flowering and fruiting. Apply sulphate of potash fertiliser in the spring, and sow grass beneath the tree. The grass deprives the tree of nitrogen and, in a sense, forces a crisis upon it. All plants are genetically structured to react to threats of overcrowding, lack of food and so on by reproducing themselves before possible extinction. So if you worry your tree a little, it may flower sooner. Ring-barking – which is the practice of cutting off a ½in wide strip of bark extending half to two-thirds of the way round the trunk – is often used to encourage fruiting, and it works for the same reason.

The sulphate of potash helps by giving the tree an extra shot of potassium – the main nutrient involved in flowering and fruiting. Incidentally, a tree grown from a pip is almost certainly a product of cross-pollination, so there's no way of telling in advance whether the fruit you finally get will be worth the wait.

Pale, silvery leaves

For the last two springs, one large branch on my plum tree has failed to flower with anything like the same intensity as the remainder of the tree. The contrast is extraordinary, and continues to be so, since the leaves on that branch are pale and silvery. What's wrong?

This sounds like silver leaf – a fungus disease whose spores attack plum trees during the winter. The spores enter the tree through wounds – pruning cuts, for example. If the disease gets well established, it will kill the tree. Another symptom is brown staining on the diseased branches of the tree.

If the disease has so far affected only one branch, you should be able to save the tree by cutting off the diseased bough. Make sure to cut right back to sound wood; no brown-stained, diseased wood should be left on the tree. Paint the wound afterwards with a pruning sealant and destroy the branch. However, a tree with more than about one-third of its branches diseased is probably not worth saving – cut it down and burn it. There's no chemical cure for silver leaf.

To prevent silver leaf from getting established in the first place, prune the tree as much as possible during the summer when the spores are at their least active. It's also easier to spot already infected branches at this time.

Plums for gardens of every size

I adore plums, but the trees are largish and my garden is small. Can you suggest any varieties that won't take the place over?

If you have a small garden, it's best to buy a plum growing on the semi-dwarfing rootstock 'Pixy'. You can be almost sure that the height of a tree grown on 'Pixy' rootstock will be below 10ft – no more than two-thirds of the size of a mature tree grown on its own roots. Plums can also be trained into shapes suitable for a smaller garden (see *Training a fan*, opposite).

The great all-rounder is the 'Victoria' – easily the most widely grown variety of plum. It is reliable, easy to grow and produces good crops of reasonably flavoured fruit. There are a number of varieties that may excel the 'Victoria' in flavour, though few can rival it for general performance. Still, if you're a plum fancier, it would be a pity to limit yourself to a single tree. Moreover, all varieties will produce a better crop if they are cross-pollinated. A number of sound garden varieties are listed on the chart below in the order in which they come into season.

Shrivelled, brown plums

My plum trees fruit prolifically, but dotted among the healthy fruits this year were quite a number that were brown and shrivelled. Is this serious?

Very serious indeed. Pick the shrivelled plums off and destroy them. Don't even leave them on the ground underneath the trees. These shrivelled fruits are carrying brown rot fungus, one of the worst diseases to attack any fruit trees.

If the diseased plums are left on or even just near the trees, they will release a new generation of brown rot spores to carry on the disease for another year.

Brown rot attacks fruit through the slightest wound in its skin at any time during the summer after the fruit is half grown. Once one fruit is infected, the disease will spread rapidly until, by picking time, many more will be diseased and useless.

The disease can also attack blossom, turning it brown and wilted.

You won't be able to eradicate an established outbreak of brown rot, but you should be able to stop it spreading.

The first step is to pick off any shrivelled fruits as soon as you see them. Then spray the trees with benomyl or thiophanate-methyl when the fruits are about the size of a cherry, and follow with two more sprays at fortnightly intervals.

PICK OF THE PLUMS

Name	Ready for picking	Colour	Remarks
'Czar'	Late July	Purple	Cooking variety. Good flavour
'Victoria'	Aug	Bright red	Cooking and dessert variety. Reasonable flavour
'Opal'	Early Aug	Dark purple	Cooking and dessert variety
'Oullin's Gage'	Early Aug	Golden	Dessert variety. Sweet, mild flavour
'Denniston's Superb'	Mid-Aug	Green-yellow	Dessert variety. Good flavour
'Early Transparent Gage'	Mid-Aug	Green	Dessert variety. Good flavour
'Cambridge Gage'	Late Aug	Green	Dessert variety. Good flavour
'Merryweather Damson'	Late Aug, Sept	Black	Good for dessert and bottling. Good flavour
'Old Greengage'	Late Aug, early Sept	Green and russet	Dessert variety. Excellent flavour, but difficult to get good crops
'Marjorie's Seedling'	Late Sept	Purple	Cooking variety
'Coe's Golden Drop'	Late Sept, early Oct	Yellow with red spots	Dessert variety. Rich, sweet flavour

PONDS AND POOLS

Cotton-wool killer

My goldfish are covered with a cotton-wool-like growth. What is it, and how can I cure it?

After the winter, when their energy reserves are low, goldfish are often attacked by fungus, especially if they have scales missing or an open wound. Fungus can occur at any time, though, mostly as a secondary infection after fish have been treated for white spot or anchor worm, two pests which damage tissue. Fungus appears as a greyish film or cotton-wool-like growth, in severe cases spreading to the mouth and gills and ultimately causing death. If seen early it is relatively easy to clear up, although infected small fish or fry are best destroyed.

Fungal cures are sold by pet shops; most are based on methylene blue or malachite green, in which the fish are dipped for a few moments. If the maker's instructions are followed, your fish should soon be healthy again. Some people prefer to use a salt bath, which is cheap but long-winded and does not guarantee success. It depends on the use of rock or sea salt – never table salt – dissolved at 1 tablespoon to a gallon of water. The fish are immersed in this solution for a couple of days, the strength being increased gradually to a maximum of 3 tablespoons to a gallon until the fungus falls away.

Fish food containing an anti-fungal ingredient such as saprolegnil will discourage the disease, although it has little effect on severe infection. Some of the diseases embraced by

HOW TO BUILD A POOL

THE easiest method of constructing a pool is probably to use a liner. Choose an open, sunny site in your garden, within easy reach of the hose or other water supply, and think about the shape of the pool. Rectangles, circles or kidney shapes are fine, but avoid crosses, narrow waists or dumbbells – they restrict the circulation of water in the pool. Mark out the shape on the ground with pegs and string or, if the shape is curved, with the garden hose pegged down into the shape you want.

Outline the shape with a half-moon turf-cutter, and remove the turf. Now start digging. The centre of the pool must be about 3ft deep, but leave a ledge round the edge no more than 9in deep to accommodate your shallow-water plants.

Smooth all surfaces, being careful to remove sharp stones. Line the pit with an inch of sand and smooth everything again. If you can't make sand stay in place on steep parts of the sides, use instead thick wads of wet newspaper plastered into position like *papier-mâché*.

There are a number of materials available for lining your pool. Polythene is cheap, but won't last very long. Nylon-reinforced PVC, more expensive, will last about ten years. The most expensive choice, butyl rubber, will probably outlive you. To discover the amount of material you will need, measure the maximum length and width of the pool and add 2ft plus twice the maximum depth to each of these measurements. Thus, if your pool is 12ft long by 6ft wide and 3ft deep, you would need a liner measuring 20ft by 14ft. The extra 2ft should leave you with a comfortable overlap for when you come to finish off the edges.

Spread the liner over the bottom of the pool and up the sides, leaving at least 12in of overlap round the edge of the pool. Weigh the overlap down with bricks, and gradually fill the pool with water. The weight of the water will press and stretch the liner until it fits snugly into the shape of the pool.

When the pool is full, cut around the liner, leaving about 6in of overlap. Press and pleat the liner into any corners it hasn't reached, and fill any gaps with sand. Surround the pool with ornamental stone slabs, so that they completely cover the lining overlap, and protrude an inch or so over the edge of the pool. Tread everything well down, brush off the edges, and your pool is ready for planting. Always keep the pool full of water, both for the sake of the plants and because direct sun will rot the liner.

Instead of using a liner, many people prefer to use a preformed fibreglass pool shape. The advantages are that these pools are long-lasting, and come with ledges and curves built in. But they are more expensive, and packing up the ground beneath to marry precisely with their bumps and hollows can be quite a chore. As for lining the excavation for the pool with cement, that's hard, heavy and messy work.

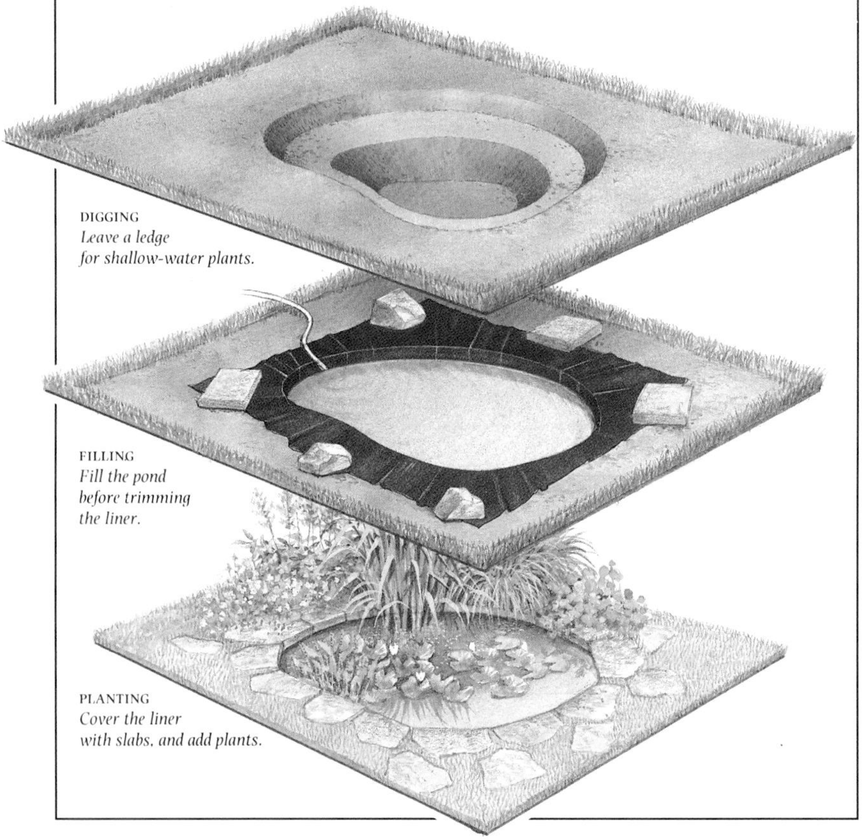

DIGGING
Leave a ledge for shallow-water plants.

FILLING
Fill the pond before trimming the liner.

PLANTING
Cover the liner with slabs, and add plants.

the term 'cotton-wool fungus' also attack goldfish eggs and uneaten fish food, so keep up pool hygiene.

Thinning a crowd

My water lilies are very crowded and showing few flowers. Should I divide them?

Too few flowers and too much leafy growth, often rising above the surface, are usually signs of overcrowding. With most water lilies this occurs after three or four years, although some smaller hybrids may last six or seven years without attention.

Late spring or early summer is the ideal time to divide the plants. Lift them from the water, wash off all compost, and remove any adult foliage. Most water lilies consist of a main rootstock with several side branches. Retain these vigorous side growths and discard the older central portion, even when a growing point is evident. Each side growth is potentially a new plant, so replant only one into each basket.

Remove and destroy

What has caused the roots of my water lily to go soft and smelly?

It sounds like root rot. Yellow cultivated varieties with mottled foliage seem to be the most susceptible, but the disease can strike without discrimination.

Remove and destroy damaged plants immediately, because they are a source of infection. If you can take out the fish, do so. Then protect any uninfected plants by impregnating the water with copper sulphate. Place some crystals in a muslin bag, tie the bag to a stick, and drag it through the water until the crystals dissolve. After 24 hours, drain the pool, rinse it and fill it with fresh water before putting the fish back; copper compounds are poisonous to fish.

How to wash out flies

The water lilies on my pond are infested most years with clouds of small black flies, but I don't want to spray the flies in case I harm my goldfish. What should I do?

The flies are undoubtedly water-lily aphids. Once the plants have become infested, the only thing you can do is to spray the leaves forcefully with a jet of clear water to wash the flies into the pool, where, with luck, the fish will eat them.

Because the aphids migrate to plum and cherry trees for the winter, it is easier to break their life-cycle there rather than in the pool. Eggs laid in the fissures of bark can be destroyed by spraying with a tar oil winter wash. This is the spray which is widely used for apple and pear trees in winter, and it can be safely applied during the dormant period.

If you do the spraying thoroughly, you should have far fewer aphids to worry about next year.

A jumping friend

Will frogs cause problems with the fish in my pond?

Not likely. These friendly amphibians generally live quite happily with the fish, snails and other creatures in a garden pond. Very occasionally a lone male frog will attach itself to a fish during the breeding season, clasping it around the gills and causing severe damage. But the minimal risk in having frogs is far outweighed by the pleasure they give and the good work they do by feeding on garden pests.

Finding a compost

Is there a special compost for aquatic plants?

The best compost is clean soil from a garden free of artificial fertiliser. Generally, the heavier the soil the better. Irrespective of its source, it must be put through a coarse sieve to remove twigs, weeds or leaves that might decompose and foul the water.

Never use soil from low-lying land or a stream-side. Although it might seem suitable, it will probably contain the seeds of pernicious aquatic weeds, which are very difficult to eradicate once established. Coarse bone meal or hoof and horn are the only suitable fertilisers to incorporate in your compost, because they dissolve fairly slowly and do not taint the water. A generous handful for every planting basket, thoroughly mixed into the compost, should do.

Feeding a water lily

How do I feed a water lily without polluting the water?

Special water-lily fertilisers are now made in perforated sachets that merely need pushing into the soil of the plant container. You can also make your own 'pills' by mixing a handful of coarse bone meal with enough wet clay to bind it. Both release nutrients for the plant while causing no pollution.

Fishing for snails

Something is eating chunks out of the leaves of my water lilies. Could it be a fish?

Extremely unlikely, although some fish do occasionally nibble at the foliage of submerged plants to provide green matter for their diet. The most likely culprit is a mollusc known as the great pond snail, *Lymnaea stagnalis*. This is frequently sold as a snail for the garden pool. While it will generally eat algae and organic debris, including fish eggs, it can also damage young water-lily pads by chewing them.

WATER-LILY EATER *The great pond snail lays its eggs in sausage-shaped masses on the undersides of submerged leaves.*

ALGAE EATER *The white ramshorn, which grows to less than ⅓in long, is a valuable scavenger, eating algae and plant debris.*

When such snails are established in a pool there is only one method of control. Float fresh lettuce leaves on the surface in early evening. Remove them next morning – with considerable numbers of snails feeding underneath. Great pond snails can be recognised by their spiralled, pointed shells, which are up to 2in high. Their egg deposits, often found on submerged plant foliage, are distinctive cylinders of jelly, quite unlike the flat sticky pads of the useful ramshorn snail. Removal of the eggs is an effective means of controlling the population.

Repairing a crack

Can a concrete pool be repaired?

Yes – but remember that the repair will always be a point of potential weakness. Drain the pool and chip out a V-shaped trench along the crack with a cold chisel. Roughen the surface to provide a key for the new concrete. Make a dry mixture of 1 part by volume of quick-setting cement, 2 parts of sand, and 3 parts of gravel, then add water until it's a stiff grey paste.

Soak the old concrete with water. Then fill the crack with your mixture, smoothing it with a trowel. After drying, paint a neutralising agent over the raw surface to eliminate any problem with lime in the water. Finally, paint on a plastic pond sealant, extending some way across the old concrete.

Green-water problem

The water in my pond is very green despite having a fountain working all day. What more can I do?

It is a common misconception that if you have a fountain a pool will automatically become clear. While a working fountain with a filter on the pump will help, the only reliable way to keep the water clear permanently is to plant submerged oxygenating plants such as the Canadian pondweed, *Elodea canadensis*. The plants absorb mineral salts from the water, competing with and eventually starving out the primitive green algae which also feed on the salts.

While you're waiting for the oxygenating plants to become established, you may be able to remove some of the algae by hand. The easiest way is to use a fork round which you have wrapped some chicken wire. Sweep the fork back and forth across the pond, and twist it to scoop up as much of the slimy algae as you can. Do this once a week until the water stays clear without help.

To create a balance from the outset, put in submerged plants at one bunch to every square foot of surface area of open water. Apart from a short period in spring, when the temperature rises and the plants have not started into growth, the pool should remain clear.

Oxygenating plants

I have tried to establish submerged oxygenating plants in my pool by dropping the bunches into the deepest part – without success. I thought they just fed on mineral salts in the water and could be left to their own devices?

Submerged plants do absorb mineral salts, but with few exceptions they must be allowed to root into a growing medium: otherwise they float around and are pulled about by the fish.

Some plants such as the common hair grass, *Eleocharis acicularis*, are clump-forming and must be planted in soil. Others such as curled pondweed, *Lagarosiphon major*, and spiked milfoil, *Myriophyllum spicatum*, are sold in bunches as unrooted cuttings fastened with strips of lead. These will root quickly if planted in clean garden soil in a planting basket. But make sure that the lead weights – which need to be left on the cuttings to hold them underwater while they root – are buried in the compost. In time, the stems will rot where they touch the lead, so you need to encourage roots to form from the section above the lead. Otherwise, when the stems rot through, the tops of the plants will come floating to the surface. Prevent fish from disturbing the compost by covering it with a layer of pea shingle.

Smelly water

My pond gets very murky and evil-smelling in hot weather. How can I keep the water clean and fresh?

The smell usually means something is decomposing. This deoxygenates the water and can kill fish and snails as well as causing unpleasant smells. The commonest cause is an accumulation of dead leaves, not only of water plants but from surrounding trees. So it is vital in autumn to cover the pool. A strawberry net spread across it for two or three weeks will catch most leaves.

In a small pool, a dead fish or mussel could be the problem. Or it could simply be uneaten fish food decomposing on the bottom. Either way, you must act swiftly or the trouble will multiply. Clean out the pool at once.

Scavenger patrol

I have been told to put a scavenger fish in my pool or it will always be murky. What kind of fish should I buy?

Scavenger fish will have little effect upon your murky waters – which are caused either by fish stirring the bottom or an imbalance of plant life. The role of scavengers is to clear up uneaten fish food which might otherwise pollute the water as it decomposed. They are also useful predators of harmful aquatic insects. Catfish are often offered by garden centres for this role, but are totally unsuitable, being ferociously carnivorous. A better choice for a scavenger would be tench, carp or gudgeon.

POND PATROL *Scavenging tench, which mostly eat insects and plant debris, can survive in water with a low oxygen content.*

POTATOES

Doubtful economy

Can I double up on my seed potato stock by cutting them in half before planting?

This is an old chestnut that comes up every year in the gardening magazines, and the consensus of advice is: don't do it, for a whole heap of reasons.

Halving the seed potato, generally speaking, halves the number of sprouts, so in order to obtain the same yield from a given area, you have to plant cut seed closer together than uncut. Then, too, the cut surfaces of both halves bleed, reducing the moisture that encourages sprouting, while the open wounds invite slugs, rot and disease. Some diseases, such as leaf-roll, are actually spread by the gardener's knife, if the blade has not been sterilised beforehand.

If, nevertheless, you want to divide your seed potatoes – and if you accept that this will give you smaller, although more, potatoes – cut them through lengthways. Choose a spot between the eyes, leaving an equal number of eyes on each side, and slice down to within ½in of the base; then withdraw the knife. That way, you will minimise moisture loss from the cut, and the surfaces will be better protected, by each other, from airborne infection.

Leave the cut tubers for about a week, which gives the cut halves time to stop bleeding and callus over. Just before planting, gently pull the two halves apart, so that when in the ground each will bleed only from a tiny wound ½in across.

Roll out the barrel

I don't think I've got room for a row of potatoes in my back garden. Would it be possible to grow a patch of potatoes instead?

Perfectly possible; but a much better space-saving idea for the small garden would be to grow them in a barrel. It's not a new idea, but it's been improved upon recently. There are now PVC barrels available that can be taken apart at the end of the season for easy storage. There are bonus reasons, too, for raising the plants in this way. Potatoes grown in barrels are nearly always free of surface blemishes and scab and, of course, they're fairly inaccessible to slugs. Neither is it a difficult process.

You'll get the best results if you follow this growing routine.

Use a barrel 4ft or so high set in a sheltered, sunny spot and, if there are no holes in the bottom, drill a few for drainage. To improve drainage still further and give the barrel stability, put in a 2-3in layer of stones or rubble. Cover the rubble with a 4-5in layer of well-rotted compost or farm manure, and add a 4oz sprinkling of Growmore. Top up with a 1in layer of John Innes No 3 potting compost.

In late March, lay four 3oz seed potatoes of a first early variety on the compost. Place them an equal distance apart and about 6in inward from the sides of the barrel. Cover the tubers with a further 3in of John Innes No 3. On chill evenings, if there's any danger of frost, cover the top of the barrel with newspaper or lightweight polythene.

The plants will grow quickly during April and May. As the stems lengthen, add further layers of compost enriched with Growmore to each 6in of stem height. Each morning, give about a gallon of water to each plant. Irregular or insufficient watering may cause the tubers to grow cracked or lumpy.

When the foliage begins to show above the rim of the barrel, insert a few canes around the edge. Tie them tc the plants to give additional support. The appearance of flower buds signals that young tubers are forming. They will be ready for harvesting in early June. Gently brush away the compost layers to reach the tubers; each plant will yield about 4-5lb of potatoes.

Not all potato varieties are suitable for growing in barrels; maincrop varieties, for example, give a very disappointing performance. It is better to stick to first early varieties such as 'Arran Comet', 'Arran Pilot', 'Duke of York', 'Epicure', 'Foremost', 'Maris Bard' and 'Ulster Sceptre'.

Definitions

Just to settle the question I'm too shy to ask in garden centres – exactly what is the difference between first early, second early and maincrop potatoes?

The three classifications – with the further subdivisions of early and late maincrop – were originally devised for the benefit of farmers, to indicate the times when particular varieties should be lifted to give the best commercial return. They do not necessarily signify the period when a particular variety reaches maturity, nor do they preclude the growing of the variety outside the period of its group. But loose as they are, the classifications do help the gardener who is trying to plan his year. Roughly, the divisions work like this:

FIRST EARLY Plant in late March (early March in the South-West, early April in the North). Harvest in June or July.

SECOND EARLY Plant between early and mid-April. Harvest July-August.

MAINCROP Plant in the second half of April. Lift a few potatoes in August if they're required for immediate use, but the bulk of the crop – for storing and winter use – should not be harvested until early October.

For suggestions on which varieties to grow in each group, see *Which variety*, this page.

In general, the first and second earlies are varieties which grow best in the long daylight conditions of early and midsummer. The earlier the variety, too, the faster the growth rate – and the earlier the foliage dies down, the lower the yield.

Both groups are usually grown for immediate consumption, because they are thin-skinned and do not store well. They include the 'new' potatoes, which are earlies that have been lifted before the skins have hardened. A potato whose skin does not come off when rubbed with the hand has no right to be called new.

Also within the early groups is a number of varieties which produce fine-tasting potatoes for winter storing if they're allowed to grow on, though the crops may not be as heavy as those yielded by maincrop varieties, whose longer growing period stretches into early autumn. For this treatment, try the first early variety 'Maris Bard', or the second early varieties 'Wilja' and 'Estima'.

On the whole, if you're short of space, it's probably best to grow early varieties. These are more expensive to buy in the shops than the maincrops, but you get fresh new potatoes straight from the garden – the best of all reasons for growing your own.

Sprouting peel

I was astonished to see that some of the potato peelings on my compost heap have sprouted, and that the sprouts have even put on leaves. If I left them to grow on, would they turn into real potato plants?

Yes they would, but fairly feeble ones since they do not have the food reservoir of the whole tuber to back them up. Nevertheless, it is from the peel of the tuber that the potato plant grows, or at least from the parts of the peel that have 'eyes' – embryonic sprouts – embedded in the surface.

The warmth, moisture and nutrients which are contained in your compost heap will stir the sprouts into action, though it is likely that the resultant stems and leaves will shortly wither away and die.

If you would like to amuse the children, or yourself, by trying this means of propagation under more controlled conditions, cut slices of peel, each containing an eye, from a shop-bought potato. Pot up each cutting, eye upwards, in a 3in pot of compost, and place them on the kitchen windowsill. Green shoots – similar to the ones sprouting from your compost heap – quickly appear, and when they have grown to a height of 6-9in, put the plants outside during the day to harden off.

When all danger of frost is past, plant the young potatoes out, water them well for a week or two, then treat them in the same way as more conventionally raised potatoes. Eventually you will get a crop. Not much of one, but you will have proved a point. Potatoes will grow from peel.

Lime level

Each year, I lime my allotment to sweeten the soil, but the chap who has the next plot tells me that this is a bad idea if I'm growing potatoes. Is he right?

Though potatoes will grow in most soils, they prefer an acid one and, in fact, the best crops are grown at a pH level of 5.0-6.0. Regular liming will gradually raise the pH of your soil, and if it reaches a level of 6.5 or above, then the ground is really too alkaline to produce good potato crops. High alkalinity also encourages potato scab disease.

On the whole it is best to avoid liming the ground you're going to plant potatoes in and, to keep the incidence of disease down, practise crop rotation instead. It wouldn't be a bad idea to test the pH level of your soil in any event. To find out how to do this, see *All about pH*, page 6.

Greenhouse potatoes

I should like to steal a march on the neighbours – and the greengrocer – by growing some really early new potatoes. What do you think about growing them in the greenhouse?

Not much, unless you're already heating the greenhouse for something else. To maintain a heat of 10°C (50°F) for three months or so just for potatoes would make them pretty expensive. But, assuming you are heating the greenhouse for other things as well, then they're not a bad idea. If you plant in January, you should be able to get some new potatoes around mid-April – that is, at least six weeks before the first ones from the garden, though not of course before those imported from warmer climes.

For greenhouse growing, choose early sprouting varieties which produce many small potatoes rather than a few large ones, for the smaller ones will mature faster. They should also be varieties whose foliage is compact, to save space. There are quite a number to choose from: 'Arran Comet', a high yielder with a waxy texture; 'Civa', yellow-fleshed and delicious; 'Duke of York', also yellow but mealy; 'Epicure', a magnificently flavoured heavy cropper; 'Maris Bard', with white flesh and skin; and 'Ulster Sceptre', another high yielder.

Get the seed potatoes a few weeks before planting, and leave them lying loose in an old egg box or in a tray at about their growing temperature – 10°C (50°F) – and in full light. The object is to induce them to sprout, which they will in a couple of weeks or so. When the new shoots are about ½in long, the tubers are ready for planting. This planting can be done in a barrel, growing bags or pots. Bags, however, tend to spread a bit, and in a greenhouse 8in pots are probably the best method. Half fill each pot with a rich potting compost, firm it gently, and lay a tuber on top, one to each pot. Cover the tubers with a further 2in of compost. Maintain the recommended temperature, keep the compost moist but not waterlogged, and allow the growing plants to enjoy whatever daylight there is at this time of year. When the shoots appear, and as they grow, top-dress with more compost, a little at a time, until it is within an inch of the rim.

Wait until the plants are in full flower, then gently scrape back the compost. If the potatoes are somewhere near the size of table-tennis balls, they are ready for harvesting; if not, replace the compost and give them a little longer.

The moment to pick

There's a lot of advice in all my gardening books about harvesting and storing potatoes, except for one thing. Nobody says how you tell when potatoes are ready for lifting.

A lot of it is rule of thumb and experience. But – as a rough guide – with first and second earlies, wait until the plants are in full flower, then gently scrape away the soil. If the tubers are about the size of hen's eggs, then they're ready for harvesting as new potatoes. If you want them larger, leave them until the foliage dies down.

Leave maincrop potatoes until the foliage has browned and withered, then cut off the stalk and leaves. Allow the tubers to remain in the ground for a couple of weeks, then turn them up to the surface and leave them to dry for a few hours. Pack them in trays or sacks and store them in a dark, dry, frost-free place. They'll last there right through the winter.

Which variety to grow

When I see seed potatoes piled up and labelled in the garden centre, I'm afraid I'm usually baffled. Can you give me some idea of the varieties I ought to be growing?

Unfortunately, the answer cannot be straightforward, since some potatoes will do better in one district than in another. The best thing is to seek local advice – from a garden centre or a knowledgeable friend – before making your final choice of variety. However, here are some old favourites that you shouldn't go far wrong with.

FIRST EARLY (for early summer harvesting)
'Arran Pilot' – floury texture.
'Home Guard' – round tubers; good on heavy soil.
'Pentland Javelin' – white flesh, good flavour.
'Foremost' – heavy cropper, firm texture.

'Ulster Chieftain' – often the earliest of all; floury texture.
SECOND EARLY (for harvesting in mid-summer)
'Ben Lomond' – floury and flaky.
'Craig's Royal' – smooth and waxy.
'Kerr's Pink' – good on heavy soil.
MAINCROP (for autumn harvesting)
'Desirée' – heavy cropper, fine flavour.
'Golden Wonder' – among the best of all for roasting or chips.
'King Edward' – heavy, dependable cropper, good cooker.
'Pentland Crown' – heavy cropper, good all-round cooker, scab-resistant.
'Pentland Dell' – good cropper, blight and disease-resistant.

Bigger for baking

Of all the many ways to cook potatoes, my family likes baked best. How can I guarantee that I get a good crop of the right shape and size for this cooking method?

Weather, soil type and a good composting in the autumn before planting can all have an effect on potato sizes. But the most important single factor is the variety you plant. The old-fashioned second early 'Great Scot' produces a heavy crop of round, white-fleshed tubers that many people vow are the best of all for baking.

Then there's the maincrop variety 'Maris Piper', another good cropper that produces largish tubers and is an excellent all-round cooker. For appetites that enjoy a challenge, try 'Pentland Squire', an early maincrop plant that bears large crops of truly enormous potatoes that keep well and cook beautifully.

Avoiding frost

The first of my early potatoes are often nipped by frost. What precautions can I take to avoid this?

If it happens quite often, it may be that you are planting your potatoes in a 'frost pocket' – or, perhaps, in part of the garden where the shadows linger over-long in the morning. Always plant potatoes in a sunny spot if possible and, if there is any danger of frost remaining when the first shoots appear above ground, rake a little soil over them for protection.

Christmas bonus

I have a fancy for serving fresh, home-grown new potatoes with the Christmas turkey. Can this be done?

There is no guarantee, and perhaps you'd better have some stored maincrop potatoes standing by just in case. But yes, it can be done. When lifting your first early crop of new potatoes in late June, plant some of the tubers in a warm part of the garden and grow them on in the normal way until early October. Then cover the plants with cloches, and with luck you should have some new potatoes on Christmas Day.

Just for fun, you could even plant a few of this Christmas generation of new potatoes in January, in pots in the greenhouse, to get another batch of extra-earlies (see *Greenhouse potatoes*, page 265), although to keep planting on in this manner tends to encourage disease.

Family trouble

There's an old gardening saying that tomatoes and potatoes should never be grown together. Is this really valid, and if so, why?

It is valid, and the reason is that the two plants are closely related, both being members of the botanical family *Solanaceae*. This means that both are liable to attack by many of the same pests and diseases, and one might easily infect the other if the plants were grown close together.

Tomato blight, for example, is caused by the same fungus that gives rise to potato blight. So infected potatoes, growing near indoor or outdoor tomatoes, are very likely to pass the disease on to them.

Potato cyst eelworms, a notorious pest, will thrive just as happily on tomatoes. If they get into either crop, you would not be able to grow potatoes or tomatoes in the infected site for at least seven years.

Potatoes for free

Instead of buying seed potatoes, why don't I simply keep a part of this year's crop and plant it next year?

No reason at all, if you mean exactly what you say. The humble spud is, after all, immortal. Each crop is a 'clone', a genetically identical replica of its parent. So if you start with a 'King Edward' seed potato, you will get a crop of 'King Edward' tubers, any one of which can be used next year to grow another crop of 'King Edward' – and so on, indefinitely.

Well, that's the principle. In practice, growing from one crop to another, year after year, leads to a build-up of diseases, including potato blight, the scourge that caused the terrible Irish famine in the 1840s. The only way to circumvent this build-up problem is to plant seed potatoes which have been grown in disease-free areas, many of which are in Scotland whose climate is too chill for the insects that often spread the diseases. That, incidentally, is why so many potatoes have Scottish names – 'Arran Pilot', 'Arran Banner', 'Pentland Crown', and so on.

Perhaps the best idea is to compromise and buy new, disease-free seed potatoes every second or third year. Since the disease build-up takes several years to become serious, you'd be pretty safe planting small tubers from this year's crop as next year's seed potatoes. You should get away with it a second time, too. But thereafter, unless you restock with new seed potatoes, your yields will drop dramatically.

Another way to raise potatoes is to grow them from real seed – not seed potatoes. If you allow your potato plants to grow on, they produce tomato-like fruits on the stalks. These contain seeds which you can dry and plant in the following spring.

In two years the seeds will grow into plants that will produce tubers. But this is worth doing only for curiosity value. Don't expect anything wonderful, since the seed will be a genetic mongrel – a mixture of two genes derived from your own and neighbouring crops, and there's no way of telling what sort of tubers you'll get.

For a fuller explanation of how and why this genetic mingling happens – even with seed from a crop of a single variety – see *Why F1 seeds are OK*, page 308.

Black spots

My potatoes looked perfect until my wife cooked them. Then they turned black. What's wrong?

It might be because you've been storing them in too warm conditions, but more likely it's due to potash deficiency. Always store potatoes in a cool, dark place, and next year give your plants an occasional feed of liquid tomato fertiliser to counteract whatever is causing the potash deficiency.

This is one of quite a number of diseases that can beset the potato grower. Here are some other common complaints.

- **POTATO BLIGHT** Can destroy all foliage in August in a wet season; tubers rot in store. Early symptoms are brown patches on the leaves with white mould on the underside. Destroy affected plants and do not store infected tubers. Pregnant women should not eat the tubers, but they are safe for other people. Spraying with mancozeb in July, and again at fortnightly intervals in wet weather, slows the spread of the disease.
- **SOFT TUBERS** Tubers that look all right on the outside feel soft to the touch. Usually caused by the plant taking up water from the tubers in a dry spell. Prevent it doing so by generous watering – about 4 gallons per square yard – in dry weather.
- **VIRUS DISEASES** There are a number of these. The usual symptoms are mottled leaves or leaves that roll inwards and turn brittle. Plant only tubers certified to be disease-free, and spray with dimethoate to control the aphids that spread the diseases. Provided the tubers are in good condition, it is safe to eat the crop from infected plants.
- **MAGNESIUM DEFICIENCY** Leaves turn yellow, then brown and brittle. Leaf growth

is stunted, too, although the tubers remain edible. Prevent by regular feeding during the growing season with liquid fertiliser containing magnesium.

- **SCAB** Scabby patches on the skins of tubers. These are merely disfiguring and do not affect the eating quality of the potatoes. Rotate crops in future and do not lime the potato bed before planting. Alkaline soil encourages scab.
- **GANGRENE** Dark brown hollows appear in the skins of stored tubers, whose flesh then rots. Destroy affected tubers, and store only sound ones in future. Store in cool but frost-free conditions.

Slow to sprout

In the past few years my seed potatoes have taken a long time to sprout. How can I hurry them up?

Potato tubers are usually dormant for 5-20 weeks after harvesting, and during this period they will not sprout – unless subjected to chemical treatment or to high temperatures. Early varieties generally have a shorter dormant period than maincrops, though even within this group there are differences in sprouting times between one variety and another.

The length of the dormancy period also depends on the conditions under which the seed tubers were produced. The earlier the parent plant was planted and harvested, the earlier the offspring tubers will sprout.

Speeding sprouting is really a matter of temperature control. Once the period of natural dormancy has ended, sprouting will start at temperatures above 4°C (about 40°F), though some maincrop varieties will not start below 9°C (48°F). The higher the temperature, the faster the rate of sprout growth. A certain amount of light, though not direct sunlight, is also required to ensure greening of the sprouts and sturdy growth.

Hollow in the middle

Why is it that perfectly normal-looking tubers sometimes have hollow centres? I've looked for pests, but can't see any.

There are no pests, or diseases for that matter, involved in this anomaly, which is known as hollow heart. The disorder starts with the death of a small area of the pith cells. This vacant area enlarges as the tuber grows, resulting in the hollow centre. The symptoms occur more frequently in large tubers and often occur along with other tuber deformities.

The problem is usually associated with rapid foliage growth, encouraged by high temperatures and high moisture levels at the time the tubers begin to grow. High levels of nitrogen, which also encourage stem growth, increase the likelihood of hollow heart, too. Potato varieties differ markedly in their susceptibility to hollow heart. 'Pentland Squire', for instance, is particularly prone.

CHIPS FOR EVERYONE

Long before Columbus, the natives of the High Andes grew potatoes, which they called *batadas*. The Spanish conquistadores tasted them, liked them, and took them – along with gold, slaves and anything else they could lay their hands on – and by 1570 potatoes were more or less established as an edible vegetable in Spain. The English approached the tubers more cautiously, despite Sir Francis Drake's earnest advertisement in the late 16th century that 'potatoes be the most delicate rootes that may be eaten and doe farre exceed our passeneps (parsnips) or carets'. The few people who did grow them were probably more intrigued by the plant's reputed aphrodisiac qualities than by its flavour.

How the innocent potato gained this sensual reputation is a mystery, but it was passed on to its relative, the tomato, when that plant began to be widely grown in Britain a century later. That was why the Jacobeans and the French called the tomato 'love-apple'. Potatoes are variously said to have been brought to Ireland by Sir Walter Raleigh or by a storm-driven survivor of the Spanish Armada. Whatever route it came by, the Irish seized eagerly upon the vegetable, finding in it a food source that would flourish in poor soil and a soggy climate. Sustained by the potato, the population multiplied over the next three centuries, until the 1840s when the failure of several crops in succession brought Ireland to starvation and destitution. The cause was potato blight, a disease that devastated the crops of other European nations as well. But none was as dependent on the potato as Ireland, where famine killed around a million people, and drove many more into exile.

Potatoes made their principal entry into England via Ireland, and were being grown by Lancashire smallholders in the late 17th century. They, and Liverpool seamen, evolved lobscouse, the meat and potato stew whose name, shortened to 'Scouse', has since become the label of every Liverpudlian. The tubers took root up and down the Western counties of Britain, but as late as the mid-18th century no one would grow potatoes in Hampshire without being paid a subsidy. In the end, it was the potato's sheer versatility that won the day, but it was left to a Frenchman to point this quality out. He was Antoine-Auguste Parmentier, an 18th-century economist and cookery writer, who began a notable public-relations exercise by winding potato flowers in Queen Marie Antoinette's hair. He pursued it by giving a dinner of dishes, and even coffee, made entirely from potatoes.

Reassured, the British took to potatoes in earnest, and now consume about 15,250 tons a day – that is, 10oz a day for every man, woman and child. There are some 300 varieties available, in all shapes and colours, and there may soon be a 301st. Plant breeders in the USA were, in the mid-1980s, trying to develop a hybrid plant which would produce tomatoes on its stems and potatoes on its roots.

Slug control

Even though I put down slug pellets, my potato crop, when I dug it up, was still riddled with slug holes. How can I deal with this menace?

Slug pellets are the correct treatment for ordinary slugs. But if your problem is keeled slugs, a species which lives underground and attacks maincrop tubers in August, you may have to lay down black polythene sheeting around the plants as well. For details, see *How to guard potatoes*, page 322.

Two other pests commonly afflict potato crops: potato cyst eelworm; and wireworm.

- **POTATO CYST EELWORM** Weak, stunted plants lose their lower leaves. Upper leaves wilt during the day. Only tiny tubers are produced. Destroy infected plants. Rotate crops in future and do not grow tomatoes or potatoes on the same site again for at least seven years.
- **WIREWORM** Shiny, orange or yellow caterpillars riddle tubers with tunnels. The pests are most common in new beds, particularly beds that have been recently under grass. Rake bromophos into the soil before planting, and harvest tubers as soon as they are ready (see also *Wireworms*, page 377).

Return on investment

Is there any rule of thumb for figuring out how many seed potatoes I need to plant to get, say, a sackful of potatoes? And how much space will I need to devote to the crop?

If by a sackful you mean the average potato sack, which contains 25kg – half a hundredweight, or 56lb – then here's a rough guide. About 6½-7lb of seed planted in rows totalling 45ft in length will yield some 52lb of early potatoes. For maincrop, sow 4lb of seed potatoes in one or more rows totalling 25ft in length to get a harvest of around 50lb.

Yields vary greatly according to variety, your cultivation methods and the weather, but those are reasonable estimates.

Cold store

My potatoes were fine when I lifted them, but now about a quarter of them have turned black and rotten in store. Have they some sort of disease?

Probably not. It sounds much more like frost damage resulting from your potatoes being stored in too cold a place. If potatoes are kept in temperatures that fall to below −2°C (28°F), the water contained in the cells of each tuber freezes and expands, rupturing the cell walls and destroying the tissue of the potato. When the thaw comes, the tuber collapses into a soggy mass that quickly begins to rot. There's not much you can do about the damaged potatoes, but you can save the others if you move them into a cool, dry and *frost-free* place.

The magic potato

It's said that potatoes are a marvellous crop for ridding soil of weeds. Is this true and if so, how does it work?

Quite simply. It's the work you do in cultivating the ground, planting and earthing up that clears the ground of weeds. The potato has nothing to do with it. In fact, if you were to plant the seed potatoes in weed-infested ground and did nothing about removing the weeds, it is certain that the crop would suffer in the competition for water and nutrients.

Certain weeds, too, are alternative hosts for a number of pests and diseases that attack potatoes, among them potato cyst eelworm and the peach and potato aphid. Sadly, there's only one magic formula for getting rid of weeds – and that's hard work.

POWDERY MILDEW

Ghostly roses

I know that roses are liable to catch anything that's going, and I'm not inexperienced at dealing with their complaints. But a couple of my plants recently have been exhibiting a symptom that's new – a sort of whitewash coating on the leaves and stems. Is it serious, and what do I do?

If this is your first encounter with powdery mildew, then you're lucky, for it's by no means uncommon. It affects not only roses, but apples, michaelmas daisies, begonias, gooseberries, strawberries, grapes and a host of other plants as well. It's a disease that gets around.

The best thing to do is to cut out and burn badly affected shoots in the autumn to prevent the spores surviving the winter on the shoots, and to spray with benomyl or thiophanate-methyl at three-weekly intervals from April to September. This should give adequate control. If you dislike using chemical sprays around the garden, you could grow some of the many rose varieties that are resistant to mildew. Most garden centres carry a selection.

DUSTY DISEASE *Roses, grapes and a large number of other plants are subject to attack by powdery mildew. But vigilance and prompt treatment will usually save them.*

PRIVET

Filling the gaps

Can I take cuttings from my privet hedge to produce new plants to fill gaps?

Yes, and fairly easily, too. Leave part of the hedge unclipped for a summer to provide a stock of hardwood shoots. Cut more shoots than you think you'll need in the autumn. Trim the bottom of each shoot straight across just below a node (the spot where a leaf stalk joins the stem), and the top of the shoot diagonally just above a node, so that the cutting is 12in long. Remove the leaves on the bottom two-thirds of the cutting.

In the warmer parts of Britain, the cuttings can be rooted in ordinary garden soil in a sheltered bed (insert about half their length into the soil).

Elsewhere root them in a cold frame in a half-and-half mixture of peat and sand. Move the rooted cuttings into a nursery bed in the spring and plant them out the same autumn, or, better still, one year later.

Of the common privet species, *Ligustrum ovalifolium* roots well in the open garden. But *L. japonicum* and *L. lucidum* are more tender and are best rooted in a cold frame.

How to cut the trimming

My summer seems to be spent largely in keeping the privet within bounds. Are there any ways to avoid this chore?

The need for regular trimming is one of the biggest drawbacks to privet. It can't 'make do with only one cut each year. Two are the absolute minimum, in July and October. Even then, the hedge is likely to appear unkempt for much of the summer.

The only short cut is a limited one: to spray on a growth-retarding chemical. These chemicals are plant hormones, or similar substances, that temporarily slow down the lengthening of the shoots. This means less growth and hence less clipping. The most widely available product contains a substance called dikegulac sodium, but it works better on some hedges than on others (it is not limited to privet), and it works better at some times of the year than others. To get the best results, therefore, it's important to follow the maker's instructions precisely. You won't find that these sprays will end your trimming chore. But because you need clip a treated hedge only once a year instead of twice, they may help to give you a little more spare time in summer.

BOTTOM-HEAVY *Slope the sides of a privet hedge to lessen the area in shade around its base.*

By the way, when you do clip your privet, cut it so that it's narrower at the top than the bottom – not like an inverted pyramid. That way the hedge will cast less shade on the ground either side of it (allowing more plants to grow), and in winter it will shed any burden of snow more readily.

Question of safety

I've been thinking of planting a privet hedge but I understand that it is poisonous and I'm worried about my young children. Should I choose some other type of hedge?

Yes, but not because of any safety risks. Privet berries are poisonous, but no more so than the seeds and berries of other plants grown widely in gardens, such as yew, laburnum and euphorbias. In any case, provided privet is not allowed to flower and set fruit, which it normally isn't as a hedging plant, there won't be any berries to tempt a toddler.

Moreover, of course, it's always worth discouraging children from eating any garden plant without an adult's permission. Poisonous or not, it may be contaminated by soil-borne organisms, or it might recently have been sprayed with some chemical that could upset a child's delicate digestive system.

No, the reasons for avoiding privet are altogether simpler: it needs a great deal of clipping; it impoverishes the soil nearby; and, to many gardeners' eyes, it is unpardonably dull. Consider instead a rose hedge, or a honeysuckle, or an ornamental plum such as *Prunus* x *cistena*, which has red-purple leaves and white flowers in spring (see also *Hedges*, page 186).

Bad neighbours

My privet hedge is an invaluable screen to my garden but I can't persuade anything to grow close to it. What am I doing wrong?

Nothing, apart from having chosen privet as your garden boundary. Mind you, you're not alone. Despite the present popularity of the faster-growing Leyland cypress as a hedging plant, privet has been popular for so long that it must outnumber all other types of garden hedge in Britain.

Privet – or to give it its proper name, *Ligustrum ovalifolium*, Japanese privet – has two great advantages as a hedge. The plants grow densely and close together, and they're evergreen so they form a year-round screen.

But there's a price to pay. Privet roots suck moisture and nutrients from the soil over a wide area either side of the hedge, and leave the ground too impoverished for most other types of plant. It is this simple fact that accounts for the reluctance of plants to grow near privet; there is no evidence for the widespread belief that the roots somehow poison the soil to keep other plants away. But though most plants don't like privet for a neighbour, some will tolerate it. On the shady side of the hedge you could try *Euphorbia cyparissias* (the cypress spurge) or *E. robbiae*, *Geranium macrorrhizum*, *Helleborus foetidus*, *Iris foetidissima*, lunaria (honesty), *Pachysandra terminalis*, teucrium, valerian and *Viola labradorica*.

On the sunny side, where it will be even drier, you might succeed with erodium, euphorbias again, *Iris unguicularis*, nepeta, salvia or stachys.

Whatever you plant near privet, you will need to feed it regularly, water the area thoroughly and apply a mulch. In addition, each spring drench the area thoroughly with a hose and follow this with a top-dressing of Growmore at about 2oz per square yard (a good handful). Then apply a thick mulch while the soil is wet, to keep the moisture in.

The only slight snag with this procedure is that it can sometimes be self-defeating. For although it certainly improves the growing conditions near the hedge, it will also stimulate the growth of the hedge itself. And that will make the privet yet more efficient at raiding the surrounding soil for food and water.

You may, in the end, have to resign yourself to having a yard-wide corridor either side of the privet with nothing on it except grass (because its shallow roots will grab the rain and dew before the privet) or, perhaps, a cosmetic layer of bark chippings.

Hedging options

What are the best varieties of privet for hedging and as a free-standing shrub?

The privet seen most commonly for hedging is *Ligustrum ovalifolium*, a Japanese species. If you ask for privet at a garden centre, this is the plant you will almost certainly be sold, but it's not the best. A more attractive species is another Japanese plant, *L. japonicum*, which has larger, very shiny leaves, somewhat like those of a camellia, a more compact habit than its relative and slightly slower growth. It makes a good hedge, though it needs even more trimming than *L. ovalifolium*. And grown as a shrub it produces cascades of white flowers in late summer.

L. lucidum has more elongated leaves and forms an attractive small tree, again with cascading white flowers. But one of the best privets for growing as a shrub has to be the golden privet: *L. ovalifolium* 'Aureum'.

Finally, a privet to stay away from for either purpose (hedging or shrub): *L. vulgare*. It is only partly evergreen and of fairly open habit. It has very dull foliage and produces miserable flowers and black fruits.

PRUNING

Root pruning

Why do people sometimes prune the roots of trees and shrubs?

There are two types of root pruning, and the first is easy enough to understand. Sometimes, when you buy a bare-root plant, the roots may be long and straggly. If you can allot the plant only a limited amount of space, some cutting back will be necessary. With a bare-root rose bush, for example, you can safely trim straggling roots back to about 9in in length to make planting easier. The operation will give you a chance to remove any dead, diseased or damaged roots. It will also shock the plant into throwing out some new roots and shoots.

The second form of root pruning is applied to established trees and shrubs. When a plant such as a plum tree is producing a lot of vigorous green vegetation without much flower or fruit, the reason may be an overdeveloped root system. Cutting back the roots will cause the excessive green topgrowth to slacken off, and should improve the yield of blossom and fruit. Do the job in winter when the plant is dormant. Dig out a trench round the tree or shrub 2-5ft from the stem, and cut through the thickest roots as you come to them. Fill in the trench immediately afterwards to prevent the exposed roots from drying out. If the tree is large, do the job in two stages: dig a trench halfway round the trunk the first winter; and do the other half a year later.

TRENCH CUT *To prune the roots of a mature tree or shrub, open up a deep trench about the width of a spade and 2-5ft from the trunk. Tackle the job in winter.*

ROOTS TO LEAVE *As you dig, try not to damage thin feeding roots you come across. Cutting them will do little to help jolt the plant into producing more flowers or fruit.*

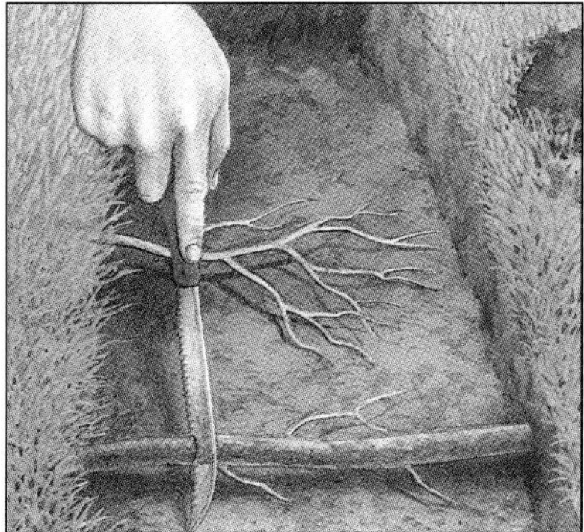

ROOTS TO SEVER *Chop or saw through the thick roots as you find them, then fill the trench again. On large plants, prune half the roots one year, half the next.*

Flowering shrubs

When should I prune my flowering shrubs – and is it really necessary anyway?

Pruning is rarely necessary for a plant's survival. In fact, evergreen shrubs – unless they are part of a hedge or you wish to restrict their size – should generally be left unpruned except for occasionally removing any dead or damaged stems. This is best done in spring, when growth is most vigorous (see *All about pruning shrubs*, page 272). On deciduous shrubs, however, pruning needs doing as an annual routine, not for the plants' health but to get the best yield of flowers.

Most of these woody plants produce their flower buds only on young or one-year-old wood. So it makes sense to cut out the old wood which has already blossomed. This allows the plant to devote its energy to producing new young wood stocked with flower buds. Leave the old wood in place and the shrub will waste strength supporting flowerless shoots. As for the best time to prune, it will depend on whether the plant blooms on the fresh young wood growing during the current year or whether it blooms on wood produced the year before.

To take two different examples, the popular buddleia, known as the butterfly bush, *Buddleia davidii*, blooms on wood of the current year. You can cut it almost down to the ground in early spring: the fresh young shoots will then grow up and flower copiously in late summer.

However, the equally popular flowering currant, *Ribes sanguineum*, blooms on stems grown the previous year. It would be disas-

Taking off a large branch

One of my apple trees has a large, sickly looking branch. It should really be cut off, but it is so thick – well over 6in – that I am worried about the shock to the tree. Won't it suffer by the sudden loss of so much wood and foliage?

An established tree will never be harmed by the sudden loss of an individual limb. If a branch has to come off for whatever reason (it may simply be growing at an awkward angle), don't be afraid of removing it. The important thing, though, is to cut it right back to the point where it joins the trunk. This will mean that all the tree's energy will be diverted to branches elsewhere. With a branch of this thickness you will obviously need a saw, and you may find that an ordinary carpenter's saw will tend to get jammed in the fibre of the wood. Use instead a proper gardener's pruning saw: it will save your strength – and your temper.

The best approach is to cut off the branch in manageable stages, until you have a stub 12-18in long. Don't leave the stub: it will look ugly, it may get in the way, and it will rarely serve as a foundation from which a whole new branch can spring.

To tackle a thick stub, begin by making a cut underneath and sawing up through about one-third of the branch's thickness close to the trunk. Then finish the job by cutting down from above. If you try to cut entirely from above, you run some risk of tearing a strip of bark and wood from the tree's side as the heavy stub falls away. If you're worried about it crushing plants below as it drops, tie a rope firmly round it, loop the rope over a higher branch and get a helper to hold the other end well away from the tree. Your helper can then control the branch's descent precisely. After the branch has been removed, trim the edges of the wound down to a smooth surface, using a knife. This will encourage a neater callus to form, with better and quicker healing. Finally, paint on a sealant.

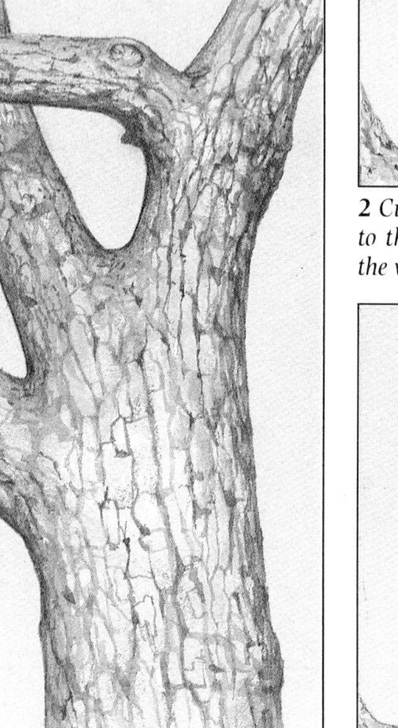

1 *To remove a large branch from a tree, saw off manageable sections of it until you're left with a stub 12-18in long.*

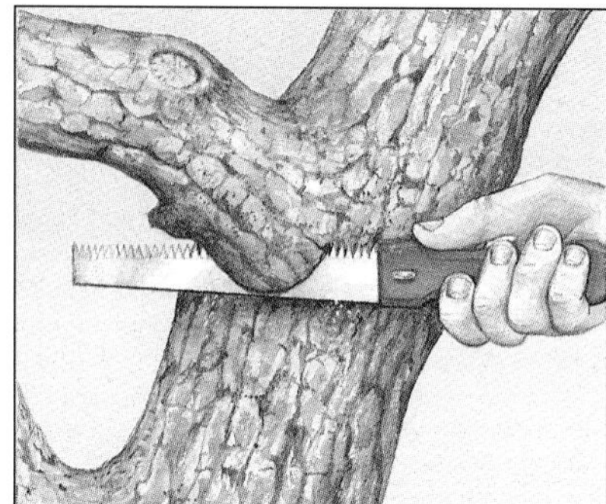

2 *Cut upwards into the stub as close as you can to the trunk of the tree. Cut about one-third of the way through the branch.*

3 *Tie the stub to a higher branch so that it cannot fall on plants beneath, then cut through the rest of the stub from above.*

4 *Trim off with a sharp knife any ragged edges around the wound, and any torn wood where the saw cuts met.*

5 *Paint the bare wood with a pruning sealant, or with any household paint, to protect the tree from frost and disease.*

trous to cut the entire plant hard back in early spring, since you would lose the whole stock of flower buds. This shrub and others of its type are best pruned as soon as possible after the flowers have faded.

The principles of pruning

Every time I read an article on pruning, or hear an expert talk about it, I seem to get different advice. How can I tell who is right?

They may all be, because exactly where and how much to prune has to depend on the health of the individual plant and what you want it to look like in the coming year. Once you know *when* to prune your roses or shrubs – and for details on that, see *Roses*, page 286, and *All about pruning shrubs*, page 272 – the routine job of doing it each year presents no particular problems. The following principles are sound, straightforward, and common to all plants and all experts.

First, remove unhealthy growth wherever you find it, along with any obviously straggly and misshapen shoots. Dead and diseased wood should be cut away and burned before problems spread, and the stragglers should be removed, too, because they are wasting the plant's energy. They won't produce decent fruits or flowers, and it is better to invest the plant's resources in the healthier stems.

Next, open up the heart of the plant. When a rose or shrub becomes overcrowded it is often the middle which suffers most. Prune so that air and sunshine can reach all the stems, ripening wood and swelling buds. Watch out in particular for any branches that are crossing one another. Cut one or the other out, or they will become damaged by chafing.

Be sure to cut cleanly. And lastly, when pruning to length (rather than removing a whole stem), end with an outward-facing bud where possible. The bud is the growing point from which a fresh young shoot or flower will spring. If you cut too far from it, the purposeless piece of stem beyond will become disease-prone and wither. Equally, if you cut *too* close, you run some risk of damaging the bud itself. Aim to cut about $\frac{1}{4}$in beyond it.

Thereafter, pruning is as much a matter of taste as a haircut. Decide on the shape and size you want, and cut to achieve that.

Cutting back a big cherry tree

An ornamental cherry tree in our garden has grown more than 30ft high, and is blocking out the sun. Is it possible to cut it back without spoiling its looks forever?

The job can be done – but it will be heavy work, and the tree's looks are bound to suffer for a while. Cutting a tree of this size inevitably involves working high up with a ladder, and perhaps a chain saw, too. It is really a job for two people, in which safety is the prime consideration. Unless you know how to handle a chain saw and have a good head for heights, you would do better to contact a professional tree surgeon.

As for the tree itself, seriously reducing the size of its canopy – by as much as half, say – will come as a severe shock to its system. The shock could in fact kill it if the cutback is done all at one go. So for the health of the tree it will be best to spread the pruning over a two-year period at least.

Do one side of the tree in the first year; the other side the next. Do both halves in late summer – July or August. You may well have an odd-looking tree for that first year but it will benefit in the long run. Cutting in two distinct stages like this allows you to balance the cuts evenly. If you lop off branches in a more patchy fashion, you may lose the overall shape.

How hard to cut

Sometimes, one of my shrubs will throw out particularly vigorous shoots which upset the general shape of the plant. Should I prune them back extra hard?

No – do the reverse. Prune them only lightly.

It may seem slightly illogical, but the basic principle operating here is to prune hard when you want to encourage vigorous growth. Prune lightly, or not at all, to slow down the growth rate. 'Vigour' in gardening terminology has a specific meaning: the yearly rate at which woody growth expands. And pruning stimulates vigour, even in the weaker shoots.

That is why the rose catalogues, for example, advise you to prune the most vigorous varieties, such as 'Peace', only lightly. Otherwise you will get a forest of stems without necessarily gaining more flowers, because the shoots will all be competing for the same air, sunlight and nutrients in the soil.

Pruning rambler and climbing roses

I have bought both rambling and climbing roses for my new garden. Will I be able to prune them all in the same way?

No. To a casual observer, ramblers and climbers may seem much the same: after all, they are both forms of rose which can be trained to scale heights, scrambling up walls, pergolas and so on. Nevertheless, there are some differences in their looks – and even more marked distinctions in their flowering habits.

Ramblers – such as 'American Pillar' and 'Albertine' – have long stems which carry huge trusses of small flowers. When in bloom they tend to form more colourful masses than climbers. But all the flowers come in one flush, and it may last no longer than two weeks. Ramblers also require more maintenance. The flowers are borne on one-year-old stems, so these stems should be removed completely after flowering (usually in late summer). With many ramblers you should cut back these stems to ground level.

Climbers – such as 'Piccadilly' and the Bourbon climber 'Zéphirine Drouhin' – have stiffer stems, with smaller trusses of flowers than ramblers. But the individual flowers are larger, and the plants have two or more flushes of bloom during the season. The flowers are carried on sideshoots, on a framework of mature wood. You should not remove any of the framework of mature wood as long as it is producing healthy flowers. Instead, deadhead all faded flower trusses and in late autumn or early winter merely cut back the sideshoots which have borne flowers, removing perhaps a quarter of the stem length. For additional information about pruning roses, see *Roses*, page 286.

Cutting climbers

We've got several climbers on the walls of our house and on the garden fences. How often should they be pruned?

Leave most climbers unpruned until they get too large, then prune flowering types after flowering. Prune non-flowering climbers in spring or summer. Most climbing plants do not need the careful precision of rose pruning. They need only to be trimmed back to the size you want.

Self-clinging climbers, such as ivy or climbing hydrangeas, can be trimmed on the wall.

Climbers that use supports, such as honeysuckle and clematis, can be pruned more thoroughly if they're first detached from the supports to make cutting and clearing of the prunings easier.

If the main stems look extremely old and bare, cut them out completely and replace them with some of the younger stems – either shoots growing from ground level or from low down on the old stems. Climbers that can be pruned by this method include actinidia, campsis, *Clematis armandii*, *C. macropetala*, *C. montana*, *Hydrangea petiolaris*, aristolochia, eccremocarpus, *Lonicera periclymenum*, parthenocissus, *Jasminum officinale*, *Passiflora caerulea*, *Polygonum baldschuanicum*, schizophragma, *Solanum crispum* and vitis (grape vines).

Tools for the job

There are a lot of overgrown shrubs in our new garden. Which pruning tools do you think we should buy out of the large array offered at the garden centre?

Your first investment should be a good pair of gardening gloves. On any big pruning job you will be carrying a lot of coarse or prickly foliage to the bonfire, and you will need to protect your hands. Also, be sure to get a good wood sealant – any household paint will do. In severing the thicker branches – particularly if you cut them flush with the trunk – you leave wounds through which frost and disease can enter and do damage unless a sealant is applied.

As for the pruning tools themselves, the main all-purpose implement is a pair of secateurs. There are two types, single and double-bladed, which have slightly different merits. The single-bladed type has one hard metal blade which cuts through to a soft metal anvil. It's a very adaptable tool, though the anvil tends to wear out in time.

Double-bladed secateurs have blades which bypass one another like those of scissors (though only one blade has a cutting edge). The double-bladed types tend to last longer than the single ones, but they do have one drawback: you can't really snip with the tips of the blades – a cut must be made at the middle.

Loppers, or long-handled secateurs, are useful for cutting out old, hard wood which is too thick and tough for ordinary secateurs. The longer handles give you extra leverage and reach, but you need to use both hands. Loppers will easily slice through wood up to

ALL ABOUT PRUNING SHRUBS

There are six main methods of pruning, matching six main categories of shrubs: those which flower before midsummer on last year's wood; those which flower after midsummer on the same year's stems; winter-flowering shrubs; evergreens; those with colourful stems; and small-leaved shrubs.

Whichever method is used, bear in mind these general points:

- Make sure your tools are sharp.
- Do not leave jagged edges or crushed tissues. Trim them off with a knife.
- Always cut out dead or diseased wood, crossing and chafing branches and weak, spindly shoots.
- Always remove to ground level, to a good, outward-facing bud or to sound wood, depending on the plant.
- Paint all wounds more than an inch across with a wood-sealing compound, or any household paint, to prevent disease spores getting into the plant's tissues.

For details on how to prune roses, see *Roses*, page 286.

For details on how to prune fruiting plants, look under the name of the fruit – *Grapes*, for instance, on page 162.

SHRUBS WHICH FLOWER ON OLD WOOD
WHEN TO PRUNE As soon as flowering is over.
HOW TO PRUNE Cut back flowering shoots to just above a strong bud and remove old and spindly shoots to ground level. This will encourage fewer but larger flowers and keep the shrub's growth within bounds.
WHICH TO PRUNE *Buddleia alternifolia*, chaenomeles, cytisus, deutzia, forsythia, *Jasminum nudiflorum*, *Kerria japonica*, philadelphus, prunus, ribes, *Senecio greyi*, *Spiraea* x *arguta*, tamarix (spring-flowering), *Weigela florida*.

SHRUBS WHICH FLOWER ON NEW WOOD
WHEN TO PRUNE In early spring, when the severe weather is over and new growth is beginning.
HOW TO PRUNE Cut back hard. Remove all the previous year's shoots that have flowered, back to two or three buds or shoots from their base. Do not cut back into the older wood (unless you want to get rid of a branch altogether), as new shoots may not grow from the stump.

After pruning, mulch with a 2in layer of rotted manure or garden compost. Sprinkle on 2oz (2 heaped tablespoons) of a general fertiliser such as Growmore to each square yard.

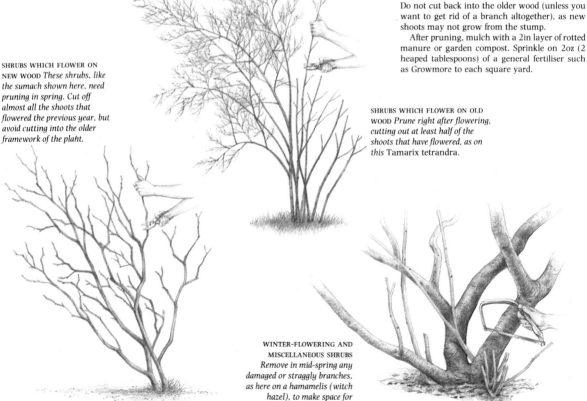

SHRUBS WHICH FLOWER ON NEW WOOD *These shrubs, like the sumach shown here, need pruning in spring. Cut off almost all the shoots that flowered the previous year, but avoid cutting into the older framework of the plant.*

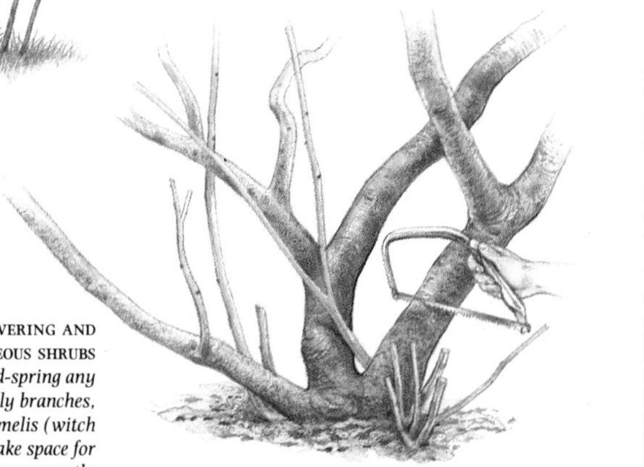

SHRUBS WHICH FLOWER ON OLD WOOD *Prune right after flowering, cutting out at least half of the shoots that have flowered, as on this* Tamarix tetrandra.

WINTER-FLOWERING AND MISCELLANEOUS SHRUBS *Remove in mid-spring any damaged or straggly branches, as here on a hamamelis (witch hazel), to make space for strong young growth.*

about $\frac{3}{4}$in thick. Pruning saws are needed to cut thicker wood. An ordinary carpenter's saw is not really suitable for green, living wood because its cutting teeth get clogged up with moist sawdust and the blade jams in the damp fibres.

Pruning saws are specially designed with wide-set and splayed teeth to keep the saw unclogged and cut wider than the thickness of the blade.

Other items tend to have specialised uses. A pruning knife, for example, is really for the skilled and experienced gardener. It does cut the most slender stems very cleanly, and can be used to trim any rough-edged pruning wounds. However, it is only too easy to nick your finger with the blade, and secateurs do most jobs just as well.

At the other end of the scale is the powered chain saw. This is an expensive item of equipment, normally hired by the day or the weekend. Don't use one unless you know exactly how to handle it – they can kill. Get the hire shop to give you clear instructions and a demonstration, too. You'll need a chain saw only when you have a lot of large branches – more than 4in thick – to cut. In such cases, ropes, ladders and a helper, too, will often be needed. For pruning on this scale, it may make more sense to call in a professional.

WHICH TO PRUNE *Buddleia davidii*, *Caryopteris* x *clandonenis*, ceanothus (deciduous types), *Colutea arborescens*, *Fuchsia magellanica*, *Hydrangea paniculata*, leycesteria, passiflora, sumach, sambucus, tamarix (summer-flowering).

WINTER-FLOWERING AND MISCELLANEOUS SHRUBS

WHEN TO PRUNE Deadhead regularly, tidy in April and prune in summer.

HOW TO PRUNE In mid-spring (April), remove any branches that are diseased, damaged or overcrowded. Cut out, too, any branches which have no flower or growth buds visible. In summer, cut back all branches that have flowered to two or three buds from where they join another branch. Do this unless you want to let the flowers develop into fruits – as, for example, on cotoneasters. In this case, do not prune in summer. Instead, leave the fruiting branches and trim them in mid-spring when you carry out your tidy-up.

WHICH TO PRUNE Abelia, abutilon, amelanchier, berberis, chimonanthus, clethra, corylopsis, cotoneaster, daphne, *Enkianthus campanulatus*, escallonia, euonymus, genista, hamamelis, *Hydrangea macrophylla*, *Jasminum officinale*, *Kolkwitzia amabilis*, *Potentilla fruticosa*, *Stranvaesia davidiana*, symphoricarpos, syringa, tree peony and deciduous viburnum.

EVERGREEN SHRUBS

WHEN TO PRUNE Remove dead wood in spring and deadhead, but do not prune until the shrub has become overgrown or is bare at the base. This condition usually takes quite a few years to develop. When pruning is necessary, do it in spring or, in the case of flowering shrubs, after flowering.

HOW TO PRUNE An overgrown or leggy evergreen plant will be given new vigour by having its main branches sawn off to within a few inches of the ground. Paint the wounds and mulch round the roots with compost or rotted manure, plus 2 tablespoons of general fertiliser such as Growmore to the square yard.

WHICH TO PRUNE Arbutus, aucuba, azara, *Buxus sempervirens*, callistemon, camellia, carpenteria, evergreen ceanothus, *Choisya ternata*, elaeagnus, escallonia, x *Fatshedera lizei*, *Garrya elliptica*, *Griselinia littoralis*, evergreen hebe, *Itea ilicifolia*, ilex, *Laurus nobilis*, mahonia, olearia, *Pernettya mucronata*, *Phlomis fruticosa*, photinia, pieris, *Prunus laurocerasus*, pyracantha, rhododendron, *Ruscus aculeatus*, santolina, taxus (yew) and ulex (gorse).

SHRUBS WITH COLOURFUL STEMS

WHEN TO PRUNE In early spring before the buds break. This will ensure a rich display of ornamental stems in the following autumn and winter.

HOW TO PRUNE Reduce stems to within 2in of their bases, from which fresh shoots will appear.

WHICH TO PRUNE Cornus, particularly *C. alba* 'Sibirica', rubus and salix (if you prefer, you can prune every second February, or cut half the stems each year).

SMALL-LEAVED SHRUBS

WHEN TO PRUNE After flowering.

HOW TO PRUNE Trim off dead spikes with shears or secateurs, but do not go into old wood as this can lead to die-back.

Winter-flowering heaths and heathers should be trimmed in early spring, while species that flower in summer or autumn need trimming in late winter.

It's a good idea to go over the tall-growing varieties lightly with shears in the late autumn, or before new growth starts, to prevent the plant becoming leggy.

WHICH TO PRUNE Calluna, daboecia, helianthemum, helichrysum, erica, lavender, *Lonicera nitida*, *Salvia officinalis*, *Spartium junceum*, vinca.

EVERGREEN SHRUBS *Pyracanthas, like other evergreen shrubs, need drastic pruning only if they are leggy or overgrown. Otherwise, just trim off dead wood in spring.*

SHRUBS WITH COLOURFUL STEMS *To encourage the growth of vividly coloured young stems, prune hard in early spring before the buds break. On large plants, like this willow, you may need to use loppers.*

SMALL-LEAVED SHRUBS *Prune lavender and other shrubs with small leaves after flowering. The easiest and quickest way to do the job is with garden shears rather than secateurs.*

QUINCES

Growing demand

Are quinces difficult to grow?

They are among the simplest of fruit trees to grow. They can be grown trained against a wall – which doesn't even need to be a sunny one – or in the middle of the garden. The trees tend to get out of hand, if you don't prune back crowded branches in the winter. In a really good soil they can reach 18ft high, although the average is nearer 10ft. None of the quince varieties needs to be pollinated by another variety.

Quinces grow best in soil without too much lime or chalk. Like plums, they suffer from deficiencies of trace elements in strongly alkaline soils.

Fruiting versus flowering

Can I make quince jelly from the fruit of an ornamental quince?

Yes. The trouble is, it's not worth doing. The best quince jelly comes from the fruiting quince, *Cydonia oblonga*. The most widely grown variety is probably 'Vranja', which has large, pear-shaped fruit. Other good varieties are 'Champion' and 'Meech's Prolific'. The last one grows more slowly than the others, but carries fruit earlier – often after three years instead of five or even seven.

The ornamental quince, also called the japonica, belongs to a completely different but closely related genus, chaenomeles. It is grown purely for the sake of its flowers. Although its fruits are perfectly edible, they have little flavour, and are seldom more than a couple of inches across. They bear roughly the same relationship to proper quinces that crab apples bear to good cooking apples.

The best thing to do with the fruits of the japonica is to use them for their fragrance, not their flavour. Pick them when they're just turning from pale to dark yellow, usually in the autumn. Keep a bowlful in your sitting room. They have an attractive, sweet smell that soon spreads through the room. They'll last between two and four weeks.

From one stock, many fruits

I've heard of family apple trees and pear trees where several varieties are grown on the same tree. Can I do the same thing with my quince?

Easily; but far more useful would be to graft one or more pear varieties onto your tree – to give you a mixed pear and quince tree. After all, every pear tree you buy now has been grafted onto a quince rootstock.

Choose reliable pear varieties, such as 'Conference', to graft onto your quince. For details of how to do it, see *Grafting*, page 160.

HOW TO MAKE QUINCE JELLY

WITH its pleasantly lemony flavour, quince jelly is excellent on buttered toast, or with pork, game or apple pie. This recipe makes 4–5lb of jelly.

4lb quinces
Sugar
Juice of 2 lemons

Wash the quinces, roughly chop them and place them in a heavy-based pan with just enough water to cover the fruit. Bring to the boil, cover the pan, and leave to simmer for 1-1½ hours until the fruit is very soft.

Scald a square of muslin and tie the corners to the legs of an upturned stool. Place a bowl beneath the muslin, and ladle the fruit and liquid into the bag formed by the muslin. Leave to strain for about four hours. Do not squeeze the bag or the jelly will be cloudy.

Heat the oven to 110°C (225°F) or gas mark ¼. Measure the strained juice and weigh out 1lb of sugar for each pint of liquid. Place the sugar in an ovenproof dish in the middle of the oven to warm through for 15 minutes.

Warm the juice on top of the stove in the heavy-based pan and add the lemon juice. Stir in the warm sugar. Bring the jelly to the boil and cook rapidly for 10-15 minutes until the mixture reaches setting point.

To test for setting point, put a spoonful of the jelly onto a chilled saucer. Leave the saucer in the refrigerator for a minute, then take it out and tip it gently. If the surface of the jelly wrinkles as it runs, the jelly has reached setting point. If it doesn't, continue boiling it and try again five minutes later. Skim the jelly if necessary, put it in pre-warmed pots, leave to cool and seal.

RABBITS

Discouraging rabbits

How can I keep rabbits out of my garden?

Shoot or gas them, or build a rabbit-proof fence. The first two demand skills which, if you had them, would make the question unnecessary in the first place. So this leaves the fence – expensive but essential to ward off these pests, each one of which will eat a pound or more of your fresh greens per day.

The fence must be at least 4ft high and of 1in or 2in mesh wire-netting. Buy a roll 5ft wide, because the bottom 6in or so of wire will have to be buried in the ground and angled outwards. This will stop the rabbits as they try to burrow under the fence. They may have another try farther along, but they will eventually give up and your vegetables will be safe.

Some measure of control can be achieved by chemical deterrents based on aluminium ammonium sulphate. They usually come in powder form. You will have to lay a barrier of this at least 3ft wide all the way around the section of the garden you want to protect. Repeat the treatment every two weeks, and again after rain. Not every rabbit will be put off, but it will make a significant reduction in the numbers feeding at your expense.

Among old country deterrents is a creosote-soaked string stretched right around the plot at a height of about 4in. Rabbits dislike the smell of creosote, and often sheer off. Another one is to find the rabbit holes and push crumpled newspaper down them. It is said the rabbits are frightened by the noise the paper makes as they trample it on their way into their burrows, and will then retire to a more congenial neighbourhood.

Compost boost

Can the straw and droppings from our pet rabbits be used on the compost heap?

Yes, it can. The nitrogen-rich droppings will help to activate the heap, warm it up, and help it to decompose more quickly. The straw will also add bulk to the heap. The same is true of the droppings of other vegetarian family pets, such as guinea pigs, hamsters, mice and chickens. So add these to your heap as well, if you have them.

The droppings of carnivorous pets, such as cats and dogs, are less valuable to a compost heap, but adding them won't do the heap or your garden any harm. Put them in the centre of the pile – where they will decompose most quickly – and cover them with vegetable waste to keep flies off and minimise any unpleasant smell.

Easy weeders

I have a weedy patch in my garden that is very difficult to control. Would my children's rabbits get rid of the weeds if I penned them into the patch?

They certainly would. Move the pen along as the rabbits strip each section. You will get effortless weed control and the ground will be manured as well. The change of diet should appeal to the rabbits, too.

RADISHES

Spindly plants

A lot of my radishes never come to anything because the plants remain spindly instead of thickening up. Where am I going wrong?

You're overcrowding them. Radishes won't thrive if the seedlings – at any stage whatever – become overcrowded or drawn.

Try to sow the seeds where you want the finished plants. Space them at ½-1in intervals in shallow drills, ½in deep, and leave 4in between the rows. The idea is to avoid thinning out altogether, if possible.

Unless the soil is already moist, water the bottom of the drills and allow them to drain before sowing. This encourages quick germination and early seedling growth.

If the weather stays dry once the seedlings are up, water them once a week, using about 2 gallons per yard of row. This should maintain a balanced rate of growth. Overwatering can lead to excessive leaf growth.

Winter crop

Are the radishes that grow during the winter anything like the salad varieties? Are they fussy about their soil?

Winter radishes are much larger than their summer counterparts, and they come in a variety of hues, with red, brown, pink or even black skins. Both round and long types are available, and they can be eaten either raw in salads, or cooked, like turnips. Some of the long varieties grow to over 2ft in the right soil conditions. Like the summer varieties, they do best in sandy, fertile, well-drained soils. They can be grown in heavy clay soils, but not in soggy ones.

Unlike summer varieties, winter radishes take several months to reach maturity – and they need space to grow. Sow them in July or early August, in shallow drills. Don't be too lavish with the seeds; try to space them 2-3in apart in the drill. Thin the seedlings to leave individual plants 8in apart. You'll also need to leave more space between the rows – 12-15in is about right.

Try any of these varieties for a winter crop: 'Black Spanish Long'; 'Black Spanish Round'; 'China Rose'; 'Mino Early'. All should be ready for harvesting from October onwards.

How to stop bolting

Why do radishes sometimes run to seed in the summer?

Probably because you're growing the wrong variety for the time of year. It's important to distinguish between the four main groups of radish: quick-maturing forcing types, such as 'French Breakfast' (which can also be grown in summer); early, non-forcing types, such as 'Cherry Belle', 'Sparkler' and 'Scarlet Globe'; maincrop and summer types, such as 'Saxa', 'Prinz Rotin' and 'Pink Beauty'; and winter types, such as 'Black Spanish Long'.

Growing any of these at the wrong time invariably leads to problems, such as plants running to seed, going to leaf prematurely, making too much leafy growth at the expense of the root, or developing coarse, woody roots. The secret of success with radishes is to choose the right type – and then grow the crop fast, watering generously throughout. Sow forcing types from January, early non-forcing types from March, maincrop types from April, and winter types in July or early August.

A head start for earlies

How early in the year is it safe to sow radishes, and would any variety be all right?

Radishes can be sown outside from February through to September. But for the very earliest crops, sow the seed of a forcing variety in cloches or frames in January. Not only will you get an earlier harvest, you'll get better yields and quality.

The best roots are grown in full sun. Prepare the ground by digging the soil over to the depth of a spade's blade, and incorporating plenty of peat – as much as a bucketful for every three buckets of soil if you can spare it. Peat is better than compost or manure for radishes, because they may otherwise develop forked roots.

Apply ground limestone, where necessary, to raise the soil pH to 6.5-7.0, and rake in a base fertiliser, at 3oz per square yard, a few weeks before sowing.

Any old variety won't do. For early sowing, choose only quick-maturing varieties suitable for forcing, such as: 'French Breakfast' (crisp, crunchy, mild and sweet; red with white bottom); 'Ribella' (round, bright red roots; fresh and crisp); 'Sparkler' (round red with white tip; very quick-growing); and 'Saxerre' (round, scarlet roots).

RASPBERRIES

How to keep raspberries upright

Do all raspberries have to be tied into a post-and-wire support system?

Summer-fruiting varieties need a permanent support system; autumn-fruiting ones don't.

Before planting summer raspberries, sink a 2in by 2in, 8ft tall post 2ft into the ground at each end of a row. Stretch two 13 gauge galvanised wires between the posts, one wire 2ft above the ground and the other 4½ft. The posts should be braced with struts for extra strength, and if the row is longer than about 12yds you should give further support by spacing smaller posts about every 3yds between the outer ones.

Tie the canes into the wires with string or soft twine. For tidiness, many gardeners think it a good idea to put in a second bottom wire running parallel to the first one – but on the other side of the post. The raspberry canes are then trained up between the two lower wires and tied to the top wire.

Autumn raspberries do not grow as tall as summer ones, and need to be supported only during the later part of the year – after they have reached about 3ft high – to prevent them being blown about and damaged. To do this, drive a 6ft post 2ft into the ground at each end of the row.

Run two lengths of stout twine between the posts, one on either side of the row of canes, and 2-3ft high so that they hold the canes securely. Leave the twine in place until the canes are pruned in March.

Which varieties?

Which are the best varieties of raspberry for my small garden and what sort of weight can I expect from each plant?

However small your garden, the size of raspberry canes remains the same; but there are new dwarf varieties, so your choice really depends on whether you want summer-fruiting raspberries (which ripen in July or August) or autumn-fruiting ones (which ripen between August and November) – or both. The raspberries you see in garden centres are usually summer-fruiting ones.

The principal summer raspberries that crop reliably and have a good flavour are 'Malling Promise', 'Malling Admiral' and 'Leo'. 'Malling Promise' starts to ripen early in the summer. 'Malling Admiral' fruits in mid to late summer, and 'Leo' comes in late, fruiting nearly until the end of August. Other summer varieties include 'Glen Clova' (with excellent flavour), 'Malling Jewel' (reliable and with good flavour), 'Malling Delight' (also with good flavour), 'Malling Orion', 'Glen Prosen' and 'Malling Enterprise'.

The principal autumn-fruiting raspberries are 'Zeva' and 'Autumn Bliss'. 'Zeva' was for many years regarded as the best, but it has recently been superseded by 'Autumn Bliss' which carries, on average, twice the crop. 'Autumn Bliss' and all the Malling varieties were developed in Kent at the East Malling Research Station.

The sort of crop you can expect depends on a number of variables, such as soil and weather. However, a healthy, well-established row of summer raspberries will yield about 4lb of fruit per yard of row. Autumn raspberries bear smaller crops produced over a longer period.

Where to grow raspberries

Do raspberries need to be grown in a sunny position – or will they tolerate shade?

Almost all dessert fruits do best in a sunny position – and raspberries are no exception. They'll tolerate a little shade, but it won't improve the crop at all.

Sunshine is needed both for the fruit to ripen and to increase the sugar content. Sunshine also helps to ripen the plants' shoots so that ample, strong fruit buds are formed for the following year.

Late summer-fruiting raspberries, such as 'Leo', and all autumn-fruiting ones, especially, need to be grown in sunny positions. That late in the year, they need all the sun that's going. Plants grown in dense shade usually have thin, drawn-out shoots and poor crops.

Pruning

When should raspberries be pruned?

It depends whether they are summer or autumn raspberries. Summer raspberries fruit on canes that grew up in the previous year; thus, in any year you will have two kinds of canes, those that are carrying fruit and others that are simply growing – the ones that will fruit next summer. Immediately after fruiting, prune summer raspberries by cutting the canes that bore fruit right back to the ground. This lets air and light in to next summer's canes.

After pruning, tie the new canes to the top and bottom wires, spacing them about 4in apart along the top wire. Tie in only the strongest and best of the new canes, and cut out any rejects. In the following spring, shorten any canes growing higher than 9in above the top wire.

The canes of autumn-fruiting raspberries grow and fruit in the same year, so they require a different pruning system. Do not cut the canes after fruiting; leave them instead to give the rootstocks some protection during the winter. Then, in March, cut them down to the ground.

You can, in fact, leave the canes to fruit another year, which they will do very early in the summer – but this is not generally a good idea. It will lead to reduced crops in the autumn and you run the risk of carrying diseases over to the new canes.

Traditionally, summer varieties are shortened to 9in immediately after they are planted in November. This stops them forming too many berries in the first year and so helps them to get established and develop strong young canes. Autumn varieties should be left alone after planting until March; then cut them down to the ground in the same way as mature plants.

TIPS FOR GROWING TOP BERRIES

- Buy raspberry canes only from a reputable nursery and make sure they are certified as virus-free.
- Choose a site that is sunny and sheltered from the wind. Preferably, the soil should be slightly acidic (pH 5.0-6.5). Raspberries dislike chalky soil.
- A few months before planting, clear the site and dig trenches about 12in deep and 30in wide. Fork in as much manure or compost as possible to provide humus, then fill in the trenches.
- Don't stint on feeding your canes. In early March, apply 4oz of Growmore per square yard, then mulch with well-rotted compost, manure or pulverised bark.
- Control pests and diseases. Aphids, which spread raspberry viruses, are the most dangerous pest. As soon as you see any, spray the canes with fenitrothion, dimethoate or pirimicarb.
- Keep weeds out of the rows by regular shallow hoeing. Remove all suckers.

Deteriorating plants

My raspberries fruited beautifully for the first few years I had them, but then began to deteriorate, and die back in bits and pieces. At the same time, the crops got lighter and some of the leaves became mottled, wrinkly and brittle. Can you help, please?

Only up to a point. Your plants have obviously been attacked by one of the raspberry virus diseases, probably raspberry mosaic virus. There is no cure: all you can do is to dig up and burn the infected row, and replant in the autumn. If possible, don't replant in the same place – because if you haven't succeeded in getting rid of all the old roots, infected suckers may come up with the new plants and spread the virus to them.

To reduce the risk, plant one of the varieties that is less susceptible to virus. A disadvantage of 'Glen Clova', otherwise an excellent plant, is that it is particularly prone.

'Malling Jewel' is an unusual variety because it can become infected by virus and yet be none the worse for it, continuing to produce perfectly satisfactory crops. It can, however, spread the disease to other plants, and so shouldn't be grown with susceptible varieties. Like other soft fruits, raspberries seem to have rather more than their fair share of enemies. Here are some of the other most common ones.

- **GREY MOULD** Makes fruits turn grey and mouldy. Destroy affected fruits (see also *Grey mould*, page 176).
- **SPUR BLIGHT** Affects buds on fruiting canes so that they fail to develop. No reliable cure available; burn infected canes.
- **CANE SPOT** The symptoms are purple patches on canes, leaves and flower stalks. Spray with benomyl, but not at fruiting time.
- **GREENFLY** This universal pest causes raspberry shoot tips to become puckered and stunted. Keep it off by spraying with dimethoate or pirimicarb.
- **RASPBERRY BEETLE** Look for small, white grubs burrowed into ripe fruit. Keep them away in future by spraying with rotenone (derris) at flowering time.

Raspberries for freezing

Which raspberry varieties are best for freezing?

Most raspberries will freeze very well. The best, which stay firm and sweet after thawing, include 'Glen Prosen', 'Glen Clova', 'Malling Orion', 'Malling Admiral', 'Malling Jewel', 'Malling Joy', 'Malling Enterprise' and 'Leo'. 'Malling Enterprise' is considered the best raspberry for freezing, but has little else to recommend it; it crops lightly and its flavour when fresh is unexceptional. Avoid freezing 'Malling Delight', whose fruits fall to pieces and go mushy when thawed.

Non-stop raspberries

My family and I adore raspberries, but the fruiting season is so short. Is there any way of extending it?

By planting the right combination of varieties, you should be able to have fresh raspberries from the end of June right through to early November. Start the season with 'Malling Promise', the earliest of the summer varieties, which fruits for a month or so from about the third or fourth week of June. Continue with 'Malling Admiral'. It starts fruiting a few days after 'Malling Promise' and carries on until about the second week of August. Alternatively, plant a few 'Leo', the latest of the summer varieties, which doesn't start fruiting until the third or fourth week of August. 'Malling Joy', which fruits from mid-July to mid-August, would be another possibility.

Finally 'Autumn Bliss' will carry you through to the autumn mists. It starts fruiting in early August before 'Leo' and sometimes even 'Malling Joy' have finished, and goes on until early November when the cold brings its activities to a close.

If you're still not tired of them, you could freeze your summer surplus fruits and have raspberries all year round.

REDCURRANTS

Good fruiters

Which are the best red and white currant varieties to grow in a garden where every inch matters?

You need heavy croppers which will have a good lifespan and not take up too much room. Choose from this list.

'Red Lake' is a mid-season variety that should be ready for picking in the third week of July. It makes a vigorous bush and crops well. It is the most widely grown commercial redcurrant.

'Stanza' is a new Dutch redcurrant variety which bears prolific crops at an early age. In trials in Kent it produced almost three times as much fruit in the first two years as other varieties. One disadvantage – it flowers in May, about ten days before 'Red Lake', so there is a danger of frost damage in some areas.

'Redstart' is an even newer redcurrant and not available everywhere. It does not crop as heavily as 'Stanza' in its early years, but it has much larger berries. It flowers between 'Red Lake' and 'Stanza', and is ready for picking in mid-August.

'White Versailles' is the standard white currant and the one most commonly grown. There isn't a better one.

When to prune

What are the differences between red, white and blackcurrants – or should I treat them all the same?

The only real difference is the colour. They all need the same feeding, watering and care – until it comes to pruning.

Red and white currants both fruit best on spurs formed on older, established branches. So they need to be pruned in the same way. In late June, trim all new shoots to about 4-5in. Then in early winter, cut the new shoots again, this time back to about 2in.

Blackcurrants fruit on wood that grew the previous year. So prune them after fruiting each year to encourage rapid growth of the new shoots which will carry the next year's crop. Each autumn, cut out completely about one branch in three. All the branches you cut out should be of old, dark wood that has already fruited. Leave as many of the light brown new shoots as you can.

Training currants

Can I train a redcurrant against a wall, and if so, how do I do it?

Yes, you can train white or redcurrants against a wall or a fence. Train them into a U-shape. Start with a young bush and in the first season keep only two main shoots that are growing in opposite directions. Train them sideways and upwards against the wall or against canes and wires spaced about 12in apart.

In early winter, trim back all new sideshoots to about 2in to encourage spur growth – the growth on which the fruit will appear. Prune new growth on each of your two main branches by one-third, or by a half if growth is slow, in the early years. Once the bush has reached the size and shape you want, treat new growth on these branches as new sideshoots and cut it back each year to 2in.

This type of training is no good for blackcurrants. Because they fruit on young wood, they need to be grown into a full bush with new growth – not spurs – encouraged (see *Blackcurrants*, page 29).

RHODODENDRONS

Tips on transplanting

If pruning back a rhododendron can be risky, is moving it any safer?

One of the best things about rhododendrons is that they are fairly easy to move. Even quite large bushes can be transplanted successfully.

You *can* move at almost any time of year, apart from the depths of winter when the ground is frozen or waterlogged. Even if you are doing the job in late spring or summer you will need to take care after the move to keep the plant well watered and shielded against strong sunlight during the next growing season.

From the plant's point of view, the ideal planting time is early autumn when the roots can establish themselves before the winter sets in.

To lift the plant from its present site, first dig a circular trench in the soil around it. If the plant is no bigger than 3-4ft across, dig up a ball of soil with it about 2-3ft wide and 12in deep. If the plant is larger, the ball should be larger, too. For example, with a plant that has a 10ft spread, you should aim for a rootball 4-5ft across. Try to damage as few roots as possible. Don't hack wildly; gently prise the plant out of the soil by getting your spade under the rootball, and when you do have to cut roots, cut them cleanly.

Before lifting the plant, make sure the new hole is dug to the right size and mix plenty of humus into the bottom soil: peat, manure, well-rotted compost or one of the compost mixes specially formulated for planting trees and shrubs. No bone meal though; rhododendrons dislike the alkaline calcium that bone meal contains. Use superphosphate instead.

Never set rhododendrons too deeply in the soil. Take particular care that the old soil mark on the stem is at the same level in its new location.

Fill in the soil around the rootball and, as you do so, loosen the soil at the sides of the hole with your spade. Tread the plant well in, but keep your boots off the rootball itself. Lastly, give the ground a good watering. This is all-important: the roots must have moist soil if the plant is to become properly established.

Removing dead flower heads

Why do gardening books tell you to take the dead flower heads off rhododendrons? After all, the plants don't get deadheaded in the wild, and they bloom there.

There are certain flowering plants – and the rhododendron is one – for which deadheading is always strongly recommended. Yes, the plants do bloom in the wild. But they do not bloom so copiously as in a well-maintained garden. Basically, deadheading prevents the plant from wasting its energy producing seeds. Remove the seedheads (which often look unsightly anyway) and all that energy is lavished instead on the next season's crop of flower buds. It's not a very arduous chore.

Most flower heads can be snapped off by hand once the knack is learned. Just take the whole flower head in your hand and break it off between finger and thumb. With the largest varieties, though, it is probably better to use two hands because some force is needed. Don't use secateurs; you may damage the shoots.

Some large-leaved rhododendrons grow into enormous bushes in time, when the sheer number of trusses, and their inaccessibility, make a thorough deadheading impracticable. Still, the simple rule for rhododendrons is to deadhead as many trusses you can – you won't be disappointed with the results.

Pruning an overgrown bush

My rhododendron is much too big for my garden; it blots out half our sunlight. Would the plant be damaged if I pruned a lot of it back?

It rarely makes sense to try to reduce the overall size of a rhododendron. The plants lose their natural shape and as often as not start looking distinctly maimed: however carefully you've done it, it still looks naked. Obviously, it is a good idea to remove old or straggly wood, and you can promote growth in a young plant by lightly pruning its stems in spring. But a grand assault does not rejuvenate rhododendrons in the way that it often does with, say, roses. In fact, an established bush, pruned back to half its size in a single operation, would take years to recover and would look pretty awful until it did.

Still, if the plant *is* too big and you don't want to remove it entirely, you might as well give pruning a try. Do it in early spring, or immediately after flowering. Cut back to the trunk, or to a healthy young stem, because dead stumps encourage disease. Above all, cut back only a little at a time so as to leave as much foliage as possible. Live with each alteration for a while; too fierce pruning will leave you with nothing more than a pathetic skeleton of a bush.

Rhododendrons for chalky soils

My small local gardening centre doesn't stock rhododendrons; they say the soil in our area is too chalky. Does that mean I can never grow a rhododendron without moving house?

It is true that rhododendrons do not thrive in chalky soil. In fact, like camellias and heathers, their dislike of it is proverbial. And there isn't much point in trying to change your soil's character: for example, by digging in lots of chalk-free topsoil from elsewhere, or by enriching it with acid peat.

This rarely works because the slightest trace of your local chalk or lime seeping in will quickly turn the plant's leaves pale and yellow. In a short time the rhododendron will wither and die.

There is only one practicable way to grow rhododendrons in your area, and that is to grow them in tubs. There are several small varieties which can be grown in tubs – or in large pots or urns. Dome-shaped bushes are particularly suited to container-growing, and the best of these are probably the hybrids which are listed as *Rhododendron yakushimanum*. Their neat shape and large trusses of flowers give them a pampered, almost artificial look which admirably suits, for example, a patio area.

Tender varieties

I've been told that some rhododendrons can be killed by frost or cold winds and should be grown only in a greenhouse. Which are they, and how can I tell before I buy?

Among the thousands of rhododendrons commercially available in Britain, only a handful are 'tender' – meaning that they're easily damaged by the cold. It's not easy to recognise them just by their appearance, but since most nurseries label their stock, you're not likely to buy a tender form by mistake.

Tender rhododendrons are suited only to the fortunate few with really large conservatories or greenhouses. In such a position, it would be possible to grow, for instance, *Rhododendron* 'Fragrantissimum' which produces highly fragrant, rose-pink blooms with a white flush in early spring; it can reach a height and spread of 10ft or so. A number of other rhododendrons can be grown in this way, but they are specialists' plants and not easy to obtain.

MULTIPLYING RHODODENDRONS

The best ways to propagate rhododendrons are by layering or by cuttings.

Layering

- This is often regarded as the better method; and it is certainly the simpler. Start in winter by pruning some of the lowest branches to encourage vigorous young shoots to grow. Spread a circle of peat around the plant and fork it in.
- Next summer, dig out a 4-6in trench in the circle and mix in a little sharp sand to aid rooting. Choose a few of the lowest, strongest shoots, cut halfway through each at a leaf joint and peg them down into the trench so that the cut section is buried.
- Firm the shoots in and water them well. Leave them for a year or more, so that they take root. Then sever each new plant from its parent, but leave it where it is. Move the young plants to their permanent site the following spring.
- Another way of doing the same thing is to sink pots of half-and-half peat and sharp sand into the ground and then peg the shoots into the pots rather than the open ground. Plants rooted in this way probably suffer less disturbance when they are eventually lifted.
- Rhododendrons whose stems are too stiff or too high to be bent down to ground level can be propagated by air layering (see *All about layering*, page 110).

Cuttings

In July, cut 4in lengths from the tips of some of the plant's young new shoots. Remove the lower leaves. Cut any remaining large leaves in half (this reduces their surface area, so reducing moisture loss). Trim off the stem bottom just below a leaf joint.

- Push the cuttings into a tray of rooting compost made up of equal parts by volume of peat and sharp sand. Be careful not to compress the mixture when you are pushing the cuttings in.
- Place the tray in a propagator or enclose it in a plastic bag to create a mini-greenhouse. Ideally, you need an electric propagator, so that you can maintain a bottom temperature of 21°C (70°F).
- After some time – it may take six weeks or six months, according to variety – the cuttings will throw out some new leaves, a sure sign that they have rooted. At this stage, pot the new plants singly in 3in pots of peaty compost. Give the plants some protection from winter frosts and summer sun, and plant them out in the following autumn.

Rhododendrons and azaleas: telling them apart

Garden books sometimes link rhododendrons and azaleas as though they were one and the same. At other times they distinguish between them. How do the plants differ – if at all?

The genus rhododendron is made up of about 1000 natural species and many more thousands of hybrids and varieties. Its members range from creeping rock plants barely 2in high to trees towering up to 80ft.

Azaleas are a largish group within the great rhododendron community. At one time, they were classified as a separate genus, then botanists decided that their similarities were greater than their differences and reclassified them altogether as rhododendrons. There *are* botanical differences between the plants, but they would not at once leap to the eye of the layman.

Deciduous azaleas, for example, are the only deciduous rhododendrons to have scaly leaves, while evergreen azaleas are not true evergreens, in that the leaves that form on the lower parts of the shoots in spring each year are shed in winter.

Despite the botanists, a great many gardeners continue to differentiate between the two groups. For them a 'rhododendron' is usually a big spring-flowering shrub with long, glossy evergreen leaves. Azaleas are generally smaller and are sometimes deciduous.

But these rules do not hold firm in all cases. There are giant azaleas and dwarf rhododendrons, for example, and the confusion is compounded because some varieties are still sold under their old names as well as the new. The popular deciduous plant often sold as *Azalea pontica*, for instance, also goes under the correct botanical name of *Rhododendron luteum*.

Nibbled leaves

Something has taken large chunks out of the leaf edges of my rhododendron. If an insect is causing the problem, I've never seen it.

Rhododendrons are relatively free from pests. The symptoms, though, do suggest an attack by weevils. This pest is a type of beetle which eats only the edges of leaves. It feeds by night, hiding during the day – which is why you have never seen it.

The chemical antidote is to dust or spray the affected leaves, and the surrounding soil, with an insecticide containing HCH. But there is another method, much used by keen entomologists, which is just as effective, particularly on small infestations. Go out after dark with a torch, and place a tray immediately beneath the nibbled branches. Give the plant a sharp tap. Many – perhaps all – of the weevils will drop onto the tray, and they can then be disposed of.

For the small garden

I have a tiny town garden with 3ft wide borders. Are any rhododendrons small enough to fit?

During the past 40 years or so, a good many plant breeders have been concentrating on the production of miniature rhododendrons. The smallest modern rhododendron hybrids grow to only 2-3ft in height, needing borders of roughly the same width.

Into this category fall the hardy rhododendrons 'Jenny' and 'Elizabeth', both strong cardinal reds and very reliable – though 'Elizabeth' may grow to 6ft in perfect conditions. 'Bow Bells', another miniature, is deep cerise in bud, opening to soft pink within, while 'Blue Tit' has flowers of a lavender-blue which intensifies with age.

'Chikor' rarely grows over 2ft in height, and bears clusters of yellow flowers. For a violet-blue, choose 'Intrifast' and, for a rose-pink, go for 'Treasure'. 'Treasure' is a ground-hugging hybrid which forms a kind of flattened mound. It was bred from *Rhododendron forrestii repens* – a good choice in itself, with bright scarlet flowers set against pale green foliage.

Many of these rhododendrons have small flowers to match their small size. And delightful as they are, they may not look much like typical rhododendrons to the layman. The very hardy *R. yakushimanum*, though, is different. Despite a height and spread of only 2-3ft, it has full-sized foliage and flowers.

The bush is very neat and compact, with leaves rolled distinctly downwards, and the flowers are carried in upstanding clusters. The buds are rose-pink, but as the blooms open they pale to white. Over the years, this valuable plant has been developed by specialist plant breeders to increase its range of colours. 'Percy Wiseman' is rather taller, and has beautiful blooms of cream and peach-pink. 'Apple Blossom' (also known as *R. yakushimanum* 'Hoo') is a subtle pink with a white throat to each flower.

RHODODENDRONS FOR YEAR-ROUND COLOUR

The great flowering month for many rhododendrons is May. But you can also enjoy the plants all year round by selecting your varieties with care. The ten varieties listed here will, between them, provide a display of colourful flowers or foliage right through the calendar.

Name	Flower colour	Jan	Feb	Mar	Apr	May	June	July	Aug	Sept	Oct	Nov	Dec
Rhododendron mucronulatum	Rose-purple	•	•	•									
'Christmas Cheer'	Pink in bud, fading to white		•	•	•								
'Cilpinense'	White, flushed pink			•	•								
'Blue Diamond'	Lavender-blue				•	•							
'Cynthia'	Rose-crimson with blackish-crimson markings					•	•						
'Sarled'	Creamy-white					•	•						
'Polar Bear'	Pure white, with a light green flush within the blooms						•	•					
'Azor'	Soft salmon-pink							•	•				
R. luteum (also sold as *Azalea pontica*)	Yellow spring flowers; crimson, purple and orange leaves in autumn					•				•	• (foliage)	•	
R. nobleanum album	Pink in bud, opening to white	•	•	•	•								•

RHUBARB

Choosing the variety

Which are the best and easiest varieties of rhubarb to grow?

Until the late 1970s, the choice of rhubarb varieties was very limited. It was confined to a handful of established varieties developed before the Second World War. In the 1970s, though, commercial growers began to take a new interest in the crop and several new varieties were developed at the Stockbridge House Experimental Horticultural Station, near Selby in Yorkshire. The names given to them are prefixed either with Stockbridge or Cawood, a small town nearby. Stockbridge varieties can be grown outdoors or forced in gentle heat in the late autumn. Cawood ones are designed only for growing outdoors.

Of the new varieties, the best all-rounder is probably 'Stockbridge Arrow', which has largely replaced the traditional 'Victoria' on commercial holdings, and is held by many gardeners to outclass even the popular traditional 'Hawke's Champagne'. For growing outdoors only, 'Cawood Castle' is probably better; it's a heavy cropper and produces long, fleshy sticks. The most attractive variety, with bright red sticks even after cooking, is 'Cawood Delight' – but it's not a very heavy cropper. If you want a variety purely for forcing so that you can pick it as early in the year as possible, the best is still the traditional variety, 'Timperley Early' – but, like 'Cawood Delight', it's not a heavy cropper. All these varieties are easy to grow in most soil types and climates.

When to pick rhubarb

Can you pick rhubarb all the year round or is there a 'close season'?

Essentially rhubarb is a spring and early summer crop. If you force it in a frost-free greenhouse, you should be able to start picking in early February. The earliest outdoor rhubarb is usually ready for picking in March, or if the winter has been mild, the very end of February. You can then go on picking until mid-June – at which point the plants should be left to recover for the next season. Three or four plants provide enough sticks for the average family.

If you want to force rhubarb in the greenhouse, one of the best places to put the plants is under the staging. This space is usually fairly empty in winter. Plant the crowns in December straight into the ground about 9in apart or in wooden fruit boxes of seed or potting compost that has already been used once. You should be able to begin picking four or five weeks after planting.

To produce pink and tender sticks, you must keep the plants in the dark. This is best done by draping black polythene over the staging to form a kind of cave. Failing that, put upturned buckets or large cardboard boxes over the plants. Don't let the temperature in the greenhouse rise above 10°C (50°F) in January, or above 13°C (55°F) in February and March. If the greenhouse gets too hot, the sticks will be thin and tasteless. Once the plants stop producing good sticks, throw them out. Outdoor plants will be producing by then, and the forced plants will be worn out.

Outdoor plants can also be gently forced so that you can pick them a week or two before the main, unforced crop is ready. Dig them up in autumn and replant them in December (see *Frosted sticks*, below). Soon after Christmas, cover them with a layer of straw or with upturned buckets or dustbins. Heap manure or straw round the buckets to generate extra warmth.

If you want supplies of rhubarb over a still longer season, you'll have to freeze part of the crop. Chop the sticks into 1-2in lengths, place them on a tray and freeze them loose. Store the frozen pieces in plastic bags. They freeze excellently.

RHUBARB TIPS

RHUBARB does not like waterlogged land – but it will grow well in almost any other type of soil. Before planting, dig the ground deeply and incorporate plenty of garden compost or well-rotted manure.

- Never pick rhubarb during the first growing season after planting. In the second season, pick over each plant only two or three times. Thereafter pick normally.
- A rhubarb plant can go on producing good crops for 20 years. But for best results, it's best to replace plants about every ten years.
- The only common disease with rhubarb is crown rot, a fungal infection that rots buds at the tips of the shoots and causes blackened holes in the rootstock. Leaves become spindly and discoloured, and die early. There's no cure for crown rot. Dig up any affected plant and burn it. Grow new plants on a different site.

Frosted sticks

An old neighbour used to say that rhubarb had to be dug up every autumn so that it was thoroughly frosted before being replanted. Is this true?

It's partly true – but do it only with plants you are going to force in the warmth. If you try it with ordinary outdoor rhubarb, you'll simply damage and possibly destroy the plant's ability to produce a crop next year.

What you should do is dig up only a few strong plants that you want to force early in the following year; dig them up in about November after their leaves have died off. Lay them on top of the soil to expose their roots to the frost. Leave them there until December, then replant them under cover (see *When to pick rhubarb*, page 279).

The plants need to be exposed to the cold in this way to make them enter winter dormancy – and they need to go through the dormant phase before they will respond to warmth by putting up fresh sticks. So if you want them to sprout prematurely, you have to make them dormant prematurely – and lifted, exposed plants will receive the necessary dose of cold well before those still in the ground. The best varieties for forcing are those which require the least amount of cold to make them dormant: 'Timperley Early' and the Stockbridge varieties.

De-flowering

Every year from June onwards, my rhubarb sends up flower stalks. Do I have to remove them?

On the whole it's better to cut the flower stalks down as close to the crown (rootstock) as possible. The stalks tend to weaken the plant at the time of year when it should be building up its strength after the picking season. But it isn't absolutely essential and many people leave them. The flowers can look strangely attractive.

ROCK GARDENS (See also ALPINES, page 8)

The best soil

What is the best kind of soil for a rock garden?

In the ideal rock garden, each planting pocket is isolated from its neighbours, so that each plant gets precisely the right soil for its needs. But perfection is difficult to achieve, and you will do very well with a good general-purpose mixture of 3 parts, by volume, of clean garden soil, 1 part of sedge peat and 2 parts of grit. You can then adjust the mixture here and there to suit the needs of individual species. For example, high alpine plants require as much as half the mix, by volume, to consist of grit. These are plants which root naturally in shale containing scarcely any organic matter. If you buy them from a nursery or garden centre, they may well come in little pots of gritty compost which contain all the nutrients they need. They hate a damp soil, and in some cases a free-draining pocket of almost pure grit may be just right.

You also have to consider the nature of your own garden soil and the grit you are adding to it. Some rock plants hate lime, and will not grow if your garden soil contains it. Others are lime-lovers, and for these you may need to prepare a special mixture containing limestone grit.

In short, the general-purpose mixture suggested here is only for guidance – in particular cases you may still need to match soils to individual plants. To check the special needs of any particular plant, look it up in *Plants at a glance*, pages 378-441.

Constructing a rockery

I am thinking of making a rock garden at the end of my back lawn. The site faces south, and gets plenty of sun, though it's shaded by the house when the sun is low. Would it be difficult, and how do I set about it?

Rock gardens are not difficult to make – but making them can be very hard work. They are not just mounds of earth with rocks sticking out. Rather the opposite, in fact – a framework of rocks filled in with a conglomeration of rubble, stones and compost. And a plot 12ft square, for example, could call for two or three tons of rock.

Your choice of position looks good – the site should always be where it can benefit from full sunlight for at least a good part of the day. Good drainage is important, so first prepare the site as described in *The importance of drainage*, page 285. Next, select rocks for the base, arranging them so as to form a low plateau, in the shape you require. The outer rocks should act as a retaining wall, defining the shape.

Take account of any strata lines in the rocks, so that they all 'flow' in the same direction – usually horizontally. A stone placed 'on edge', with vertical lines, spoils the effect. Furthermore, once a rock has been set in position in the base, it will be all but impossible to remove later.

Once the base has been laid, fill the gaps and crevices between the rocks with a mixture of two-thirds stones or shale, and the rest gritty soil to ensure good drainage – this is very important. Old bricks and broken roof tiles also make excellent filling when camouflaged with a good depth of stony soil. When the base is filled in, start placing the remaining rocks in position (again ensuring the strata lines run in the same direction), until you achieve the sort of height and shape you have in mind.

Finally, excavate the pockets and crevices which will house your alpine plants and fill them with suitable soil or compost (see *The best soil*, this page). If you are new to rock gardening it might be wise to defer planting the more tricky kinds, concentrating first on those which provide plenty of colour and thrive in well-drained, gritty soil (see *Rockeries for everywhere*, page 284).

Penstemons for the cold

I planted penstemons in my rockery last year, and they all died over winter. Can any species be relied on to survive cold weather?

Penstemons are a group of attractive herbaceous and shrubby plants which bear flowers rather like those of snapdragons. The

HILL OF PLENTY Mimulus cupreus *'Whitecroft Scarlet' blazes beyond green pillows of saxifrage and a mauve fringe of* Armeria maritima *and thyme.*

tall border species are particularly prone to damage by frost and cold winds, and they are usually raised from cuttings each year to get round this problem.

There are, however, several so-called alpine species which are suitable for rock gardens. Most of them originate from North America – and are reasonably hardy.

One of the best for a rock garden is the narrow-leaved *Penstemon pinifolius*, a little gem with bright green foliage and slender, orange-red flowers. *P. scouleri* has larger foliage and more substantial flowers of bright lilac. This is a neat, shrubby plant that will flourish in a well-drained, sunny position. There is a white form called 'Alba' and a purplish-pink hybrid known as 'Six Hills'.

Plant these rockery species in a loose, gritty soil; they will die if their roots are in waterlogged ground that becomes frozen in winter. The plants are also liable to searing by winter winds, and, though this is a less crucial problem, their survival can never be guaranteed. As a precaution, many gardeners take a few cuttings in late summer and keep them in a cold frame over winter, providing a vigorous young reserve to replace any dead or damaged plants.

Success with lithospermum

I've grown Lithospermum diffusum *'Heavenly Blue' for years as a ground cover in my rock garden where its flowers indeed glow a paradisiacal blue all summer long. Its fast, mat-forming character would be an equal boon in other parts of the garden, but I've had no luck with cuttings. Any tips?*

Lithospermum diffusum, now renamed *Lithodora diffusa*, is a very popular rockery plant and comes in two varieties: 'Heavenly Blue' and 'Grace Ward', which has slightly bigger flowers. Both bloom from June to October, and theoretically you should be able to increase them by cuttings at any time during the growing season. But lithospermum can be oddly mulish, and it seems that for most gardeners there are only three weeks – in late July and early August – when cuttings can be taken with any great chance of success. So here's what you do.

In the last week of July or the first week in August, take a few non-flowering shoots at leaf joints, each no more than 2in long. Remove the lower leaves, and dip the base of the cuttings in a hormone rooting powder. Place the cuttings in a tray of compost made up of equal volumes of peat and perlite (or peat and sharp sand).

Keep the compost moist with soft water. But don't spray from overhead; the leaves are covered with fine hairs which trap a lot of moisture that could cause the cuttings to rot before they can take root.

Rooting should take place in about three weeks. Once this has happened, pot the cuttings individually in a lime-free potting compost. Even within the recommended three-week period in late July and early August, there seems to be an optimum time for taking cuttings – and it cannot be gauged in advance, or just by looking at the plants. So, for the maximum chance of success, take three batches of cuttings – one each week over the three-week period.

Snowflakes for spring

For novelty's sake, I've tried growing spring snowflakes in my rock garden. But they've come up stunted and there are very few flowers – what's gone wrong?

The spring snowflake, *Leucojum vernum*, is a bulbous plant which looks much like a snowdrop – though it's a couple of inches taller than the snowdrop's 6in. The other difference is that a snowdrop has three long and three short white petals; the snowflake's six petals are all the same size.

Spring snowflakes *look* very much at home in a rock garden. The trouble is that they are moisture-lovers – and a rock garden, with its free-draining soils, is not really their natural habitat. To get the best out of your bulbs, you must plant them in pockets of compost which should be kept permanently moist. They should then flower reliably in February or early March.

Bother-free rock gardening

I am laying out a rock garden during a few days' holiday, but once it's done I won't have too much time to spend on it. I'd like it to be well covered, colourful and, above all, trouble-free. What plants do you suggest? The site, by the way, is in full sun.

Three names occur immediately, all beginning with A: aubrieta, arabis and alyssum. These are robust, spreading plants which form hummocks, carpets and tumbling cascades of colour in the rock garden every spring. Aubrieta mostly comes in shades of blue. 'Bengal Strain', for example, has very dark blue, semi-double flowers; 'Dr Mules' is deep violet; while 'Bridesmaid', to ring the changes, is pale pink.

Arabis caucasica (also known as *A. albida*) is white, and an exuberant, almost invasive grower. But the pink variety 'Rosabella', the double-flowered white 'Flore Pleno', and 'Variegata' with its variegated foliage, are more controllable.

Alyssum is yellow. Both the bright yellow species *Alyssum saxatile* and the paler lemon variety 'Citrinum' are reliable.

Between them, these three plants will cover your rocks in no time. Some of the mossy saxifrages are almost as rampant, especially *Saxifraga caespitosa*, whose sparkling pink flowers rise from carpets of bright green foliage in April. Varieties include the red 'Holden Seedling' and 'Winston Churchill'. All are excellent value.

You might also consider the perennial candytuft, *Iberis sempervirens*. This shrubby evergreen with handsome shiny foliage produces wide heads of white flowers in May and June. There is a good dwarf form too, 'Pygmaea', which is useful where space is limited; and a pink perennial candytuft, *I. gibraltarica*, which flowers in April and May.

Finally, give a thought to a mat-forming plant known as snow-in-summer (*Cerastium tomentosum*). This is a beautiful, spreading species with silvery-grey leaves and starry white flowers in summer. Gardening books tend to be snooty about cerastium because it spreads extraordinarily fast and will quickly smother any delicate little alpine. It is often referred to as 'weed-like' or 'invasive'; but for sheer rampant coverage of a large patch of bare rock you could scarcely do better.

Rockery primulas

Are all primulas suitable for a rock garden?

The primulas are an enormous group of plants which range from the common primrose and cowslip to species from the Himalayas. Some are best suited to growing indoors, others to the dampness of a bog garden, still others to the herbaceous border. It is not always easy to assign a particular plant to its place, but in seeking out primulas for a rock garden it makes sense to go for the so-called alpine varieties.

In general, they are small, and do best in rocky clefts approximating to those in their native mountain screes. Alpine primulas have a reputation for being difficult to grow. But if you stick to the old favourites offered by most garden centres, you shouldn't have much trouble. In particular, all the varieties of *Primula* x *pubescens* are reliable and will give a wonderful show in April or May. They include the brick-red 'Rufus', the violet-blue 'Mrs J.H. Wilson' and the milky-white 'Harlow Car'. Try, too, the varieties of *P. marginata* which also bloom in April and May in shades of mauve and blue.

All that these primulas need is a sunny position, adequate drainage and a soil-based compost with plenty of grit added. They also benefit from a top-dressing of grit or fine gravel. Every three or four years in early spring, the plants should be lifted, divided and replanted to spread them around and retain their vigour. Plant the divisions at once in their permanent sites.

Weeds among the rocks

Some of the weeds in my rockery have burrowed beneath the stones and seem to have shot roots down to the bowels of the earth. Do I have to dismantle the whole affair to get them out?

Deeply rooted and persistent weeds are very difficult to control in a rock garden – even with modern weedkillers. The main problem is how to kill them without damaging the plants you've been cherishing. A systemic weedkiller based on glyphosate is probably the best weapon. It is absorbed into the sap stream. From the leaves it travels around the plant, killing foliage, stems and roots without affecting the surrounding soil. But how to apply it?

Obviously, you can't simply spray from above since you might easily smite your rockery plants at the same time. You must instead apply it to each weed with a small paintbrush. Or use a weed-stick – a hollow walking stick, loaded with a chemical, which, when pressed into a weed, squirts it without spraying the others round about.

Either of these methods will wipe out the deep-rooted weeds without your having to take the rocks apart. Once the weeds are dead, remove their remains by hand.

Cliffhangers

I have a most unusual garden in that it ends in a 15ft high old quarry face, and I've long been intrigued with the notion of creating a cliff garden there. Which plants should I choose?

A good choice would be some of the hybrids derived from *Lewisia cotyledon howellii*, which put out 2in wide pink flowers from April to June. The lewisia's favourite habitat is a vertical cleft between rocks where it can grow sideways. If it's planted conventionally upright, its leaf bowl tends to collect water which rots the crown. Plant lewisias on their sides and the rain drains safely away.

Other contenders would be houseleeks – sempervivums – some saxifrages of the type known as encrusted, and ramondas. Push the young plants into crevices with as much compost as the space will take. If the plants look like falling out, hold them in place with staples or bent wire – the wire can be removed as soon as the plants take hold. The seeds of some other species can be sown directly into crevices so long as they are watered properly. These include all of the aubrietas, arabis, *Erinus alpinus* and the soapwort *Saponaria ocymoides*, which produces a cascade of pink flowers from May to July.

But before planting anything, do consider how sunlight strikes the rock. For plants to thrive, a cliff garden really must face west or south. Few plants will populate a rock face with an easterly or northerly aspect.

A multiplying investment

I think dwarf bulbs are the best investment for spring colour in a rock garden. But can you suggest some that will look after themselves, don't need lifting, and will just quietly multiply year by year?

There are many easy-going dwarf daffodils suitable for a rock garden, some of which are described in *For a rock garden*, page 112. As well as these, you might consider angel's tears, *Narcissus triandrus albus*. This has delightful bell-like blossoms of icy white, but you must make sure that it has a particularly well-drained pocket in the rock garden. It won't tolerate damp conditions.

Grape hyacinths are always popular. The species *Muscari armeniacum* multiplies so freely that it can become a nuisance, but there are a number of better-behaved varieties, including the lovely, free-flowering 'Blue Spike'. Another valuable blue-flowering plant is *Scilla tubergeniana*, an early bulb, whose pale blossoms brighten up the dull days of February.

For a similar pale blue slightly later in spring, go for *Puschkinia libanotica*, the striped squill; its delicate little petals are striped with a darker blue, and the plant soon fills any vacant pocket in the rock garden.

Crocuses are well suited to this environment. The numerous varieties derived from *Crocus chrysanthus* provide in early spring a cavalcade of colours – among them yellows, blues, whites, purples and bronzes. Another lovely bulb is *C. susianus*. It provides bright golden flowers in early spring. Other crocus species, including *C. speciosus* and *C. zonatus* (also known as *C. kotschyanus*), flower in autumn.

Dwarf tulips tend to be rather temperamental, and are not usually recommended among the bulbs which can be left to their own devices in the rock garden. Nevertheless, the yellow and white *Tulipa urumiensis* can be relied on. Make sure that it is planted in gritty, free-draining compost at the outset, and it will colonise any sunny corner you give it.

All dwarf bulbs appreciate a generous application of bone meal during the growing season. Apart from this, the only attention you need give them is to divide and replant them every four or five years. When clumps become overcrowded, the bulbs become starved of nutrients and produce fewer and smaller flowers.

Slug control

Slugs wreaked havoc in my rock garden last summer. How can I prevent the same thing happening again?

There are several precautions you can take. The key with slugs is hygiene. They are night-time feeders that hide during the day under rotting leaves and in other cool, moist places. If you keep your rock garden tidy, then the problem is greatly reduced. Removing weeds also aids slug control. Slugs do not travel long distances in order to feed, and if you deprive them of daytime shelter you'll see a lot fewer of them.

It also helps to surround any vulnerable plants with a generous layer of grit or rock chippings. Slugs dislike crossing sandy or gritty soil. However, the traditional antidote of laying a ring of soot or coarse ash around each plant makes no particular sense. The circles look ugly, quickly become pasty in wet weather – and do no good to the rock plants themselves.

Another time-honoured and more successful remedy is to put half grapefruit skins upside down on the soil near vulnerable plants. Turn them over each morning and you should find slugs and snails aplenty. They can then be removed and destroyed – or let loose on waste ground where they present no threat to garden plants. For details of chemical control methods, see *Slugs and snails*, page 322.

Multiplying saxifrages

A mossy saxifrage in my rock garden is beginning to encroach upon the plants around it. If I trim it back, can I grow new plants from the cuttings?

Yes. Mossy saxifrages and similar plants which produce rosettes of foliage are quite easily increased from cuttings. The most vigorous young growth is found at the edge of a clump so your trimmings will make ideal material. Even the tiniest young rosettes from the edge will root better than rosettes from the centre. At the middle of a clump, rosettes often have crisp, dead leaves at the base, and a harsh wiry stem that is not inclined to put down new roots at all.

Remove individual rosettes after flowering; June and July are the best months for most saxifrages. Place them, each with a tiny portion of stem, in a pan of silver sand. Put the pan in a cold frame, or on a cool window ledge in the house – the cuttings need light but no heat. Once they have rooted, set them individually in gritty, well-drained potting compost.

Growing the cuttings in silver sand produces a lively root system very quickly. With some species, though, you may find that the roots afterwards fail to adapt properly to the potting compost. If you find that the plants tend to deteriorate in their pots, treat the next batch of cuttings in a different way. Mix 1 part by volume of peat with 3 parts of silver sand before filling the pan.

Rejuvenating aubrietas

I planted my rock garden three years ago, and my young aubrietas and arabis spread out in good, compact hummocks. But recently, they have lost that smooth, rounded look, and the clumps have bare, stringy stems at the centre. Should I replace them?

Aubrieta and similar plants should last a good five or six years before you need consider replacing them. Probably it's not the plants that are exhausted – it's the soil. Like some saxifrages, these plants spread outwards, seeking nutrients and exhausting them as they go. After a while, the centre of the plant naturally dies out, while the edges flourish as they colonise fresh soil. The remedy is to feed the centre of the plant before it starts to deteriorate, though you must feed very carefully or the new growth will be distorted. Quick-acting fertilisers and liquid feeds are out. Instead, use bone meal or hoof and horn, which are long-lasting and slow-acting. Feed each sizable clump, immediately after flowering, by scattering onto it a generous handful of the fertiliser. Precise quantities are hard to specify. You should aim to apply enough for it to be visible as speckles, but not as an uninterrupted white layer. Let the rain water it in, but if no rain falls within a couple of days, use a sprinkler or watering can.

Apart from this feeding, you will help the plant to maintain a compact outline if you remove the seedheads after flowering. Basically, this prevents the plant from wasting its resources on manufacturing unwanted seeds and keeps the clump clear of inferior, straggly seedlings. Run a pair of shears over the seedheads, and trim off any stray or unsightly rosettes. If the job is completed by midsummer, the plant will produce fresh, tight growth.

Instant weathering

The freshly quarried stones in my rock garden look rather stark. Is there any quick way of getting them to look weathered and mature?

Try using a blend of milk and cow dung. When the two ingredients are mixed to the consistency of runny porridge and painted onto exposed rocky surfaces, colonies of green algae soon appear. The method also works on walls, and milk makes a far better partner in the mixture than water.

Winter casualties

Every winter I lose a number of rock garden plants. The symptoms are always the same – tops become detached from the roots, and the roots look as if they are decaying. Is this frost damage?

It is much more likely to be winter wetness. Far more rock garden plants are lost each winter to the damp than to frost. Waterlogging causes rotting in the base of the stem, roots and leaves; plants with furry leaves are particularly vulnerable because their foliage tends to retain moisture rather than let it run off.

The right soil and adequate drainage are essential if your rock garden plants are to survive (see also *Soil structure*, page 324, and *Drainage*, page 123). If you have inherited a rock garden consisting of no more than a mound of earth with rocks sticking out, you may have to think of major structural alterations (see *Constructing a rockery*, page 280). Once the soil and drainage are right, you can provide further protection for specially vulnerable plants by building open-sided shelters for them. An open-ended cloche, for example, or a sheet of glass raised on bricks and weighted at the corners to stop strong winds lifting and smashing it, will keep off direct rain while allowing moisture to reach the plant from the ends.

Do make sure, though, that cold air can circulate freely inside the shelter. Many of these plants come from mountainous regions and tolerate low temperatures. A closed shelter will cause abnormally soft growth which is vulnerable to disease.

Phlox for free

How do you take cuttings of alpine phlox?

Alpine phlox are scrambling plants with soft leaves and masses of brightly coloured flowers. They usually bloom during May and June, and all are easily rooted from stem cuttings taken immediately after flowering.

In choosing cuttings, avoid shoots that have flowered, because these are often harsh or wiry. The best cutting materials are strong, non-flowering, sideshoots (those branching off from the main stem), which have been produced during the current season. Take cuttings no more than 2in long, severing them just below a leaf joint. Strip off the lower leaves.

Push the cuttings ¼in deep – just enough for them to stand independently – into pans of a half-and-half mixture of peat and perlite (or peat and sharp sand). Water the cuttings and stand the pans in a cold frame, or in a box with a sheet of glass over the top.

Keep the box sealed, but at least twice daily wipe any condensation from the glass because droplets of moisture falling on the cuttings can cause rotting. Most of the cuttings will root within a couple of weeks and can then be potted individually into 3in pots. If a particular phlox variety fails to root properly, try taking cuttings with a 'heel' – that is, with a strip of wood from the main stem. Instead of cutting the shoot off at a leaf joint, tear it away to obtain the heel.

When potting the plants individually, use John Innes No 1 potting compost, and mix in about one-third by volume of sharp sand to help drainage. Grow the plants on in a garden frame for the winter. The result should be good-sized plants suitable for planting out in the rock garden in early spring.

Shrubs for the rockery

My rock garden is covered with tumbling and scrambling plants. It looks restless, and I'd like to add a shrub or two to give it more backbone. Which are the most suitable – and least likely to outgrow their position?

The obvious choices are found among the dwarf conifers. But you have to be careful with them, since many are slow-growing rather than true miniatures. Some of the specimens which look cosy at the garden centre will grow to formidable size after 20 years or so. For trees that are permanently suited to your rockery, see *Dwarf conifers*, page 127. They're well worth growing. Being evergreens, they will enliven your rock garden throughout the winter months and look even more splendid when draped with snow. There are several dwarf berberis which are evergreen, too, including *Berberis* x *stenophylla* 'Gracilis Nana'. This is a tiny form of the popular *B.* x *stenophylla*, much treasured for the abundance of golden flowers it produces in April.

Another evergreen choice is the slow-growing, tiny-leaved holly, *Ilex crenata*, of which

ROCKERIES FOR EVERYWHERE

Because so many rock plants are natives of the open scree, many gardeners believe that a rock garden can be built only on a sunny, well-drained site. But it is also possible to make one work in far less promising spots. Check this list for plants that will thrive in your rockery.

Name	Height	Flowers
Plants for a damp sunny position		
Arenaria balearica	1in	White (Mar–July)
Linnaea borealis	2in	Pink (May)
Phlox subulata and varieties	3in	Pink, red, white (Apr–May)
Saxifraga 'mossy' species and varieties	3-9in	Pink, red, white (Apr)
Plants for a damp shady position		
Dodecatheon meadia	9-12in	Rose, purple (May–June)
Hepatica nobilis	3in	Blue (Feb–Apr)
Primula auricula and varieties	6in	Yellow, blue, purple, green, white (Mar)
Primula juliae and hybrids	6in	Wine, purple, pink (Feb)
Shortia galacifolia	6in	Pink (Apr)
Soldanella alpina	3in	Purple (Mar–Apr)
Uvularia grandiflora	9in	Yellow (May)
Vancouveria hexandra	9in	White (May)
Plants for a well-drained sunny position		
Achillea tomentosa	6in	Yellow (July–Sept)
Alyssum saxatile	9-12in	Yellow (Apr)
Anacyclus depressus	3in	Pink-flushed white (June–Aug)
Arabis caucasica	9in	White (Mar)
Armeria caespitosa	9in	Pink (Apr)
Aster alpinus	6-9in	Purple-blue (June–July)
Aubrieta deltoidea and varieties	3-5in	Mauve, blue, pink (Mar)
Campanula species and varieties	3-12in	Blue, white (May–Sept)
Dianthus alpinus	4in	Pink (June)
Dianthus deltoides and varieties	4-6in	Pink, red, white (June)
Erinus alpinus	4in	Pink (Apr)
Gentiana acaulis	3in	Blue (May–June)
Helianthemum nummularium and varieties	6-9in	Yellow, orange, pink, red, white (June)
Helichrysum bellidioides	3in	Fawn (July)
Hypericum polyphyllum	6in	Yellow (July–Aug)
Iberis sempervirens	9in	White (May–June)
Lewisia cotyledon	9in	Pink, red (May–June)
Lithospermum 'Heavenly Blue'	6-9in	Blue (July)
Penstemon pinifolius	6in	Orange (July)
Saxifraga 'encrusted' species and varieties	6-12in	White, pink (May–July)
Sisyrinchium brachypus	6in	Yellow (June)
Thymus serpyllum and varieties	2in	Pink, red, white (June–July)

there are numerous varieties. These include the gold-leaved 'Golden Gem', the variegated 'Aureovariegata' and the black-fruited 'Convexa'. None of them has prickly leaves – they look, in fact, rather more like box than holly. Though they are slow-growing, they must be clipped regularly to contain their height and spread.

Among the deciduous shrubs you will find miniature versions of many popular varieties. Three excellent choices are: *Forsythia viridissima* 'Bronxensis'; the rose-pink *Spiraea japonica* 'Alpina'; and the scented Korean lilac, *Syringa velutina*.

Making the most of shade

With our new house we've inherited an ancient rock garden, which is shaded for much of the day. We don't want to take it apart and move it, but what about the shade? Don't most rock garden plants need full sunshine?

You're right; not many of the classic rock garden plants will tolerate shade. Their ancestral home is bare scree and stony hillside, under open skies. However, there are shade-loving rock plants as well; for some ideas, see the chart opposite.

The smaller ferns would also make excellent material for your setting. Consider, for example, the soft green dwarf lady fern, *Athyrium filix-femina* 'Minutissima', or the hardy maidenhair ferns *Adiantum pedatum* and *A. venustum*, or the fancy varieties of the native British evergreen fern *Polypodium vulgare*, such as 'Ramo-cristatum'.

Among the shrubby plants, dwarf gaultherias and vacciniums will do well, and the creeping white-flowered, dwarf dogwood *Cornus canadensis* is perfect. There are, too, quite a number of dwarf bulbs that are perfectly happy in shaded positions, especially the smaller squills, such as *Scilla sibirica*. The *type* of shade will also contribute to your choice. If it is created by deciduous trees, the rock garden will be open to the sky in early spring, so that many crocuses, eranthises, snowdrops and reticulate irises can all be expected to prosper.

The type of soil, too, will affect your selection; if you create moist, peaty pockets, you can plant the lovely white wake robin, *Trillium grandiflorum*, and the blue Virginian cowslip, *Mertensia virginica*.

Too much juniper

The prostrate juniper I planted in my rockery a few years ago, and was so proud of, is now taking over. Should I try to prune it back?

Some varieties of prostrate juniper do cause problems in rock gardens. If you catch them just in time you can sometimes limit the problem by cutting back each year into the past season's growth. However, more severe pruning rarely works. Cutting back the old wood distorts the plants' natural shape, and fresh growth will not break evenly from the severed stumps. The sensible thing to do with your already overgrown shrub is to dig it up, find a more relaxed place for it, and replant with a less invasive variety – *Juniperus horizontalis* is one of the best behaved.

Pinks a-plenty

I want to increase my alpine pinks. Should I sow seeds? Or take cuttings?

It depends which kind of pinks you want. Most species can be raised from seed, as can the mixed hybrids. However, named varieties, such as 'Little Jock' and 'La Bourbille', are best propagated from cuttings.

Sowing is best done in summer, though it can be done in spring. Fill pans with seed compost mixed with about a quarter by volume of grit. Spread on it a top layer of fine compost only. The seeds should start to germinate within a couple of weeks. Prick out the seedlings into trays when they show their first true leaves. Transfer them into individual pots when they are about 2in tall, using potting compost mixed with coarse grit for drainage. The seedlings will need the protection of a cold greenhouse or a cold frame over winter before you plant them out the following spring.

Cuttings are best taken in summer. Choose strong shoots, sever them close to the main stem, and strip off the lower leaves, leaving three or four pairs of leaves at the top. Sever the cuttings again just below the topmost joints that have been stripped of their leaves, and push them no deeper than the base of the first leaf into pans that have been loosely filled with John Innes No 1 potting compost and topped up with a 1in deep half-and-half mixture of peat and coarse sand. Water the pots and put them in a cold frame, a cool greenhouse, or under cover in a cool spot with plenty of light. They should root in 18-30 days, after which they may be hardened off for a couple of weeks before planting out in their permanent sites.

The importance of drainage

My garden soil is a heavy clay. All the books tell me that rock plants do best on a light, loose soil. Does that mean that I can't have a rock garden?

Not at all. A rock garden is, in effect, an artificial creation independent of the rest of the garden, with special soil added to suit the needs of the plants you want to grow (see *Constructing a rockery* and *The best soil*, page 280). So the type of soil you happen to have already doesn't really matter. Nevertheless, good drainage is vital for any rock garden – rock plants have evolved to suit stony mountainsides where water does not linger – so clay is the most problematic soil because, with its dense texture, it holds water much longer than other soils.

What you will have to ensure is that the soil beneath your proposed rock garden drains freely. With most soils you can do this by breaking up the ground with a fork and adding plenty of coarse rubble, covered by a layer of smaller rubble. Old bricks and roofing tiles, broken up, make excellent free-draining filling. But in the case of a clay soil like yours, you will have to dig out the site to a depth of about 12in. Slope the bottom of the hole away from the centre of the proposed site and fill it with coarse hardcore before starting to build your rockery on top.

Types of stone

Does it matter what kind of stone I use in my rock garden? Is the choice crucial when selecting the plants I'd like to grow?

People often worry that certain types of stone may alter the soil's acidity or alkalinity in their rockeries. For example, it is a common belief that limestone can damage lime-hating plants. In reality, such worries are largely groundless: even the softer limestones dissolve far too slowly to alter significantly the alkaline content of the soil in rock garden pockets. Nevertheless, it is safer to grow lime-loving plants in limestone rock gardens.

So far as looks are concerned, the type of stone *does* matter, since plants always harmonise best with the rocks of their natural habitat. Sandstone enhances such acid-loving plants as heathers. Limestone sets off pinks and other lime-loving plants. Sometimes, a perfectly vigorous and healthy plant can look oddly wrong in a particular rock garden. The answer may be that it is naturally unsuited to the colour or texture of its stone backdrop.

Choose the colour scheme that pleases you best. As a guide, many gardeners feel that blue, white and yellow plants and flowers harmonise especially well with craggy white or greyish limestone, while warm reds and oranges blend in with the ruddier tones of sandstone. With hypertufa, which is a greyish granite colour (see *Homemade rock*, below), the method of planting in small pockets restricts you to tight, cushion-type plants, and wide splashes of colour are not possible. Whatever your taste, take the time to study rock plants against rocks rather than in isolation before making your selection.

Homemade rock

Someone was telling me the other day about the wonders of tufa – a rock on which you can actually grow plants. Sounds ideal for a rockery: can I get some?

Not easily – but it's not difficult to make a lookalike substitute. Tufa is a soft and porous magnesian limestone which can be easily shaped and drilled to take plants. It absorbs and retains water so readily that plants can take root in the rock itself, though a little compost is needed in the prepared holes. However, it is quite expensive and difficult to obtain.

Much better – and cheaper – is to make some hypertufa, an imitation rock which can be moulded to a desired shape, drilled like real tufa and is receptive to a wide variety of plants. Simply mix 2 parts of sand, 2 parts of peat and 1 part of cement, adding water until the mixture is like a stiff porridge. You can make it into any shape you like to suit your garden. One of the easiest ways is to dig an irregular hole in the garden and apply a 2in thick layer of the mixture to the bottom and sides to make a basin shape. When it has set, lift it out, turn it upside down and wash off the soil to leave a rough-faced, artificial rock. Alternatively, mould the mixture, 2in thick, over a wooden fruit box. Then chip it to give a roughcast or irregular appearance. Being hollow, these 'rocks' are lighter and easier to handle than real ones. Hypertufa can also be used to cover a glazed sink or trough. Score the glazing with a chisel, apply a coat of epoxy glue to provide grip, then plaster the mixture over it. Again, it can be modelled and chipped into a natural appearance, and with a little weathering it will look like a genuine rock-hewn container.

To root a rock plant in either tufa or hypertufa, drill a small hole about 1in deep, at a slight downward angle, and insert a seedling. Pour in sharp sand mixed with a little compost to cover the roots, then water well. Plants with fibrous roots are best, for these will eventually grow into the rock itself.

ROOT APHIDS AND ROOT MEALY BUGS

Troublesome on pot plants

Many of my plants are turning yellow and wilting, and I'm told this is due to root aphids. What's the best treatment?

Root aphids are just one member of the all-too-numerous aphid family of pests. As the name implies, root aphids live underground, where they create havoc by feeding on roots. This prevents nutrients from reaching the plants, whose growth becomes weak and stunted. The leaves also begin to show the symptoms you describe. Pot plants in greenhouses or in the home, such as cacti, hippeastrums, vines, camellias and primulas, are frequent targets of root aphids. But the pests also go for lettuces and outdoor flower plants. The danger period is late summer and autumn outdoors, and any time of year under glass. The only treatment is to soak the infested root systems with a spray-strength solution of malathion or diazinon, and to keep doing it weekly until the plants perk up again.

Root mealy bugs cause the same symptoms, although they are different insects, and can be dealt with in the same way.

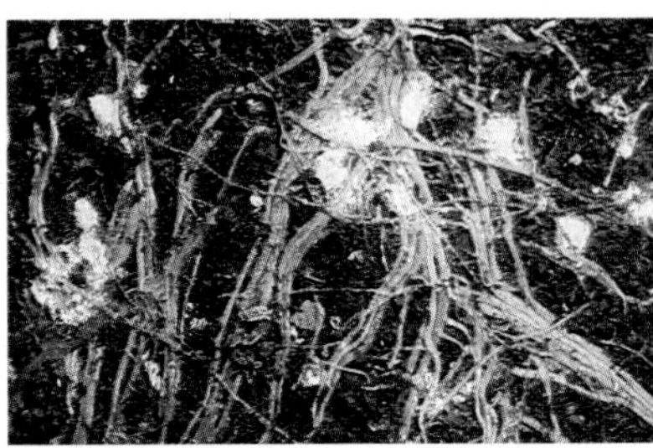

ROOT SAPPERS *Colonies of wax-covered root aphids – each usually less than $\frac{1}{8}$in long – can be a serious threat to plants indoors and out.*

ROSES

Site and soil

Will roses grow in any kind of soil and situation, or do they have certain preferences?

Roses will grow in most soils. But they grow best in rich soils which contain plenty of organic matter. They favour a slightly acid to neutral soil (pH 6.5-7) and are not happy on the more strongly acid, peaty soils in which rhododendrons flourish. Roses also favour slightly heavy soils – those with a fairly high proportion of clay – because such soils provide good anchorage, plant foods and moisture. They do not do so well on sandy or chalky soils.

As for light, most roses enjoy full sun or light shade. A few varieties, however, such as 'New Dawn' and 'Mermaid', will do quite well against shady north-facing walls.

Few gardeners are blessed with the perfect soil, but some are luckier than others and can content themselves with minor soil modifications.

Bare-rooted or potted

What is the best way of buying roses, with bare roots or in pots?

So far as plant quality is concerned, there's not much in it. A healthy rose properly planted should get off to a good start whether it's a container-grown or a bare-rooted specimen. The time of year, though, should have significant bearing on your choice. Late autumn – October and November – is the ideal time for planting bare-root roses, and nurseries and garden centres are stocked to capacity with young dormant plants whose roots are devoid of soil. Bare-root roses are cheaper than pot-grown, because you're not buying the pot and soil; there is also the advantage of being able to see if they have a well-developed root system and a strong union or neck. The union is the part between roots and the stem where the plant was budded.

Bare-root plants should be set out as soon as possible after buying; they can be shallowly planted for a short period – this is called heeling in – but it is much better to plant them straightaway, so that the roses can settle and begin to make new roots before winter.

Buying roses in spring and summer is a different matter; by then the best bare-root roses have usually been sold, and the remainder will have suffered in quality since they were lifted the previous autumn. It is unwise to buy bare-root roses after the end of March or early April. You cannot expect a bare-root rose to make new roots as well as producing leaves and flowers if it is planted at this time of the year. Pot-grown roses can, however, be safely bought at any time of the year. Provided that the plant is moved from container to ground with its rootball intact, it should continue to grow without a check.

Make sure, though, that any plant you buy in a container has actually been grown in it. It is not unknown for bare-root roses which have been lifted in autumn but which remain unsold by Christmas to be transferred to pots in late winter and then sold as higher-priced container-grown specimens.

It is quite easy to check if a rose is actively growing in the pot or merely contained in it. Simply grip a piece of stem and move it about. If the whole plant responds by moving loosely in the soil, it is a fake. If the whole pot moves, the rose is firmly rooted and a true pot-grown specimen.

Rose terminology

None of my books explains the collective names used to describe roses. What is the difference between a Modern shrub, a Hybrid tea and a Cluster-flowered rose?

In a changing world, the classification of many plant groups, including roses, is also undergoing change, supposedly to make it easier for the gardener or buyer to differentiate between the various types. At present, rose classification is expressed in new as well as in old names, but until the new system is fully accepted and integrated into gardening language, there is bound to be some confusion.

There are eight main groups of roses whose divisions are chiefly determined by growth and flowering habits. The list begins with the rose ancestors from which most of the modern hybrids have been bred.

• **WILD ROSES** is the group which was formerly called Species roses; it covers all the true species that occur naturally in the wild, as well as hybrids between them, whether natural or induced by gardeners. For many years eclipsed by more showy groups, Wild roses are now regaining popularity and are valued for their handsome foliage, for their frequent tolerance of pests and diseases, and for their usually single flowers, frequently scented, followed in many cases by brilliantly coloured hips.

Wild or Species roses range from such giants as the 40ft high *Rosa filipes*, which is one of the ancestors of the modern 'Kiftsgate' climbers, to the dog rose (*R. canina*), widely used as rootstock for modern bush roses, and the 12in *R. chinensis* 'Minima', the parent of the Miniature roses. Strong favourites among the Wild roses are *R. moyesii* and its improved hybrid form *R. moyesii* 'Geranium', and 'Canary Bird', an improved clear yellow hybrid form of *R. xanthina*.

• **OLD GARDEN ROSES** is the new name for the group previously known as the Old-fashioned roses. These shrub roses were developed before modern types and include: the Moss and Gallica hybrids; the China and Centifolia (cabbage) roses, both with deep red blooms and attractive flask-shaped hips; and the Damasks and the Rugosas. All were introduced in the early 1800s.

Most are tall shrubs with large, many-petalled flowers, heavily scented. They usually have a shorter flowering season than Modern shrub roses and some are vulnerable to attack by mildew and black spot.

• **MODERN SHRUB ROSES** are chiefly hybrids between the first two groups. Their diversity of shape and growth and informality of habit make them unsuitable for growing in a rose bed. They are best planted in a shrub border or as single specimens where they will have room to develop and can be viewed in isolation.

They form a large group which includes such lovely roses as 'Fountain', which stands to 6ft with crimson, fragrant flowers and dark green foliage, and 'Fred Loads', more than 7ft tall and with large clusters of orange, scented flowers. A fairly recent introduction (1982) is 'Mountbatten', very vigorous and upright, easily reaching 5ft, with glossy, light green foliage and trusses of double, bright yellow, scented flowers.

• **LARGE-FLOWERED ROSES** These are the popular bush roses formerly known as Hybrid tea roses. They bear large flowers, one or occasionally a few to a stem, flowering from early summer until autumn, and excellent as cut flowers. With their formal, restricted growth habit they are ideal for planting in rose beds. The group includes many well-tried favourites, including 'Grandpa Dickson', and new introductions are constantly adding to the wide range of colour, scent and growth habit.

• **CLUSTER-FLOWERED ROSES** is the new and cumbersome name for the group that used to be known as Floribundas. They vie for popularity with the Large-flowered roses, the main difference being in the arrangement of the flowers which, on the Cluster-flowered, grow in trusses on the tips of branching stems. They bloom throughout the summer, but need more attention by way of deadheading than Large-flowered types; old flower heads spoil the appearance of the plant and slow down the formation of new flowering stems. Popular examples include the $3\frac{1}{2}$-5ft tall 'Queen Elizabeth'.

• **MINIATURE ROSES** have undergone no name change. They are a group of roses that rarely grow more than 10-12in high. They are delicately branched, with tiny flowers of Large or Cluster-flowered type, and are suitable for raised beds, rockeries, pots and troughs. They can also be planted as an edging to a bed of bush roses or as low outer groups of three or more. Among the many Miniatures available are the red, sweetly scented 'Starina' and the bicoloured, perfumed 'Baby Masquerade'.

• **CLIMBING ROSES** have also retained their group name. They include roses of a climbing habit but which need the support of a wall, fence or trellis, with the framework stems tied in. Climbing roses flower on shoots made in the current year; those derived from the Wild and Old garden roses have one flush of bloom only, in early summer, while modern

Pruning for health and vigour

There seems to be any number of theories about rose pruning. Are there any standard rules?

Certain basic principles do indeed apply to the pruning of roses – and of other woody shrubs as well. Pruning encourages the formation of new and strong flowering stems, it maintains the health of a plant by removing dead and diseased wood, and it improves the plant's shape.

These general rules apply to *all* groups of roses, so before you tackle a bush or climber, take note of these simple steps:

1 Remove all dead and diseased wood right back to the base.

2 Cut out weak and spindly shoots; they will never be strong enough to support a head of flowers.

3 On all bush and shrub roses, aim for an open centre. Remove completely all tangled and crossing branches (on climbing types, train the branches apart instead).

4 Prune to achieve a balanced shape.

When you prune, always cut back to a dormant bud. Later this will grow into a new shoot; and if you always prune to an outward-facing bud you will be able to give the plant the open-centred shape that suits it best. Make all cuts just above the bud and slanting down, away from it.

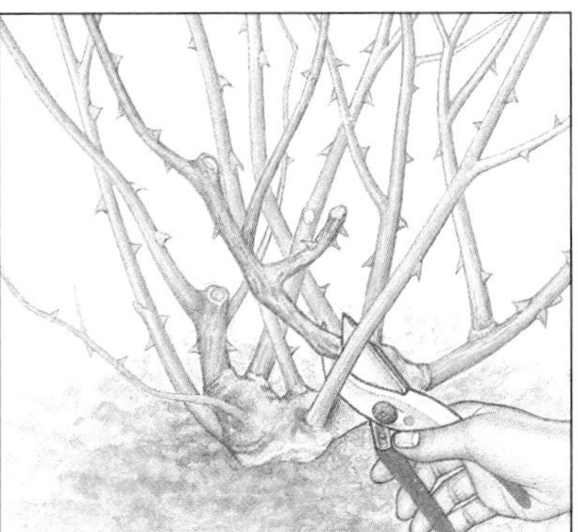

DEAD WOOD *To prune a bush rose – or any other woody shrub – start by removing completely all dead or diseased branches.*

WEAK WOOD *Cut off, too, any spindly stems, particularly if they lie at a low angle. They'll be too weak to support good blooms.*

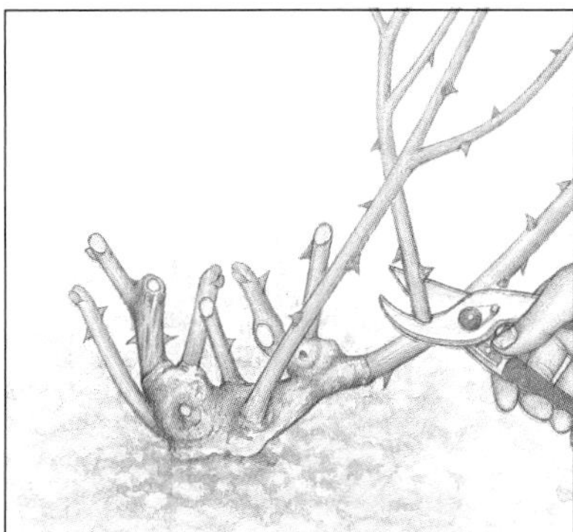

CROSSING WOOD *Remove at its base one of any pair of crossing stems. Cut back the stems that are left to outward-facing buds.*

varieties flower throughout summer and autumn. A Climber should be trained with a permanent framework of main stems from whose lateral shoots the flowering wood is produced.

Some Climbers, derived from Large or Cluster-flowered roses, bear the same name as the bush roses, but it is prefixed by the word 'climbing' as in 'Climbing Piccadilly' (scarlet-yellow), 'Climbing Fragrant Cloud' (coral-red) and 'Climbing Blessings' (pink). The majority of Climbers have their own specific names, including such popular roses as 'Compassion' (large, pink to apricot, double flowers), 'Golden Showers' (bright yellow) and 'Swan Lake', which is one of the best white climbers, with almost pure white double flowers.

• **RAMBLER ROSES** are often confused with the Climbers, but they differ in one important aspect: Ramblers flower on long stems produced in the previous year. They have no permanent framework of branches because every year after flowering the old flowered stems should be cut out from the base and the young canes, that will flower next year, tied in. The flowers are more numerous but smaller than on the Climbers, and often appear in small clusters on arching sprays all along the canes. The flowers all appear more or less at the same time in early summer, although a few blooms may recur later on. Rambler roses create images of old cottage gardens with their sprays of small double flowers and delicate leaves, though many of the older varieties are vulnerable to mildew and need regular spraying. One of the most spectacular and long-established Ramblers (introduced in 1921) is the vigorous 'Albertine' with pink, double, fragrant blooms. 'Dorothy Perkins' is even older (1901), but with its arching sprays of small double, pink blooms, has never lost its popularity despite being very prone to mildew.

The kindest cuts

Which kind of secateurs are better for pruning?

It doesn't matter which type you use. Both of the types available – anvil and scissors – do a perfectly good job, on roses and other plants. What does matter is where you cut (see *Pruning for health and vigour*, page 287) and that you keep the tool sharp so that it slices rather than crushes the stem.

Chalk and roses

My soil is pretty chalky. Should I try to grow roses in it, or give up the idea and try something else?

For chalky and other thin soils that do not provide good anchorage, choose short-growing roses that will not suffer too much from wind rocking. Compact bush roses of the Cluster-flowered type include 'City of Belfast', which has large trusses of bright scarlet flowers, and 'Tip Top', almost a Miniature, with large salmon-pink, scented flowers.

Among the Large-flowered bush roses, the following are of equally neat and compact habit: 'Colour Wonder', which has freely produced orange-pink bicoloured flowers; and 'Ophelia', whose fragrant, pale pink blooms shade to yellow. Or you might choose some Miniatures like 'Colibri', which has

New roses from cuttings

Is it possible to raise roses from cuttings? If so, will they do as well as, say, roses bought from nurseries?

It's certainly possible, but whether they will do as well as bought plants is another matter. With the exception of the Wild or Species roses and some of the Old garden roses and their hybrids, roses in general – and especially the Large and Cluster-flowered types – do not do well from cuttings. They generally lack the vigour of those that are grafted onto a suitable rootstock. However, this can be an advantage with Miniature roses which sometimes grow too large if grafted onto vigorous stock plants.

On the other hand, roses grown on their own roots never produce suckers, thus disposing of the chore of constantly removing the vigorous shoots that grow from grafted rootstock. Also, since little labour and no cost is involved in propagating a few roses from cuttings, why not give the method a try? If you do, multiply your chances of success by taking at least a dozen cuttings for each plant you want. Each one should be about 12in long and cut in late August or September, from a healthy sideshoot that grew that year. Make a sloping cut above the top bud of each cutting and a square one just below the bottom bud. Remove all foliage and the remaining buds, except for two or three near the top bud; push off all prickles with the thumb, taking care not to damage the skin of the cuttings.

Prepare a V-shaped trench, about 9in deep, in good, crumbly soil. Put a 1in deep layer of sharp sand in the bottom and set the cuttings in the trench, with the base of the cuttings resting on the sand. Gently fill in the trench and tread the soil firm.

By the following spring, at least some of the cuttings should begin to produce a few shoots and leaves, and by the end of the summer, with luck, a few may have rooted. In November, lift the rooted cuttings, complete with rootball, from the trench and transfer them to their permanent growing positions, planting them to the depth of the previous soil marks.

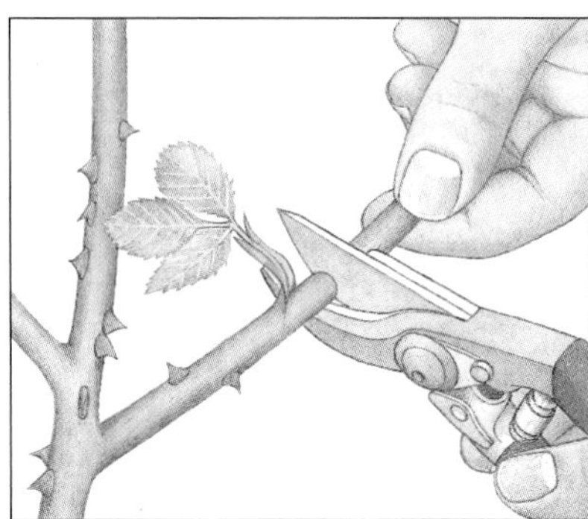

TAKING *In late summer or early autumn, cut off healthy sideshoots which grew that year.*

TRIMMING *Cut the top end just above a bud, the bottom just below one, to leave a 12in long stem.*

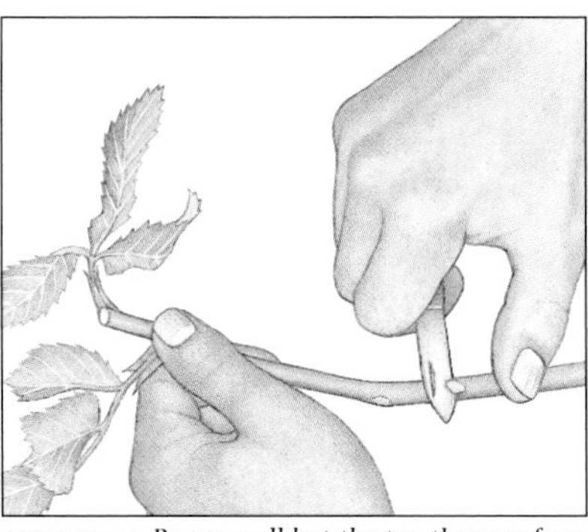

DISBUDDING *Remove all but the top three or four buds, and all the leaves and thorns.*

PLANTING *Set the cuttings on sand, with about 4in above ground. Leave them for a year.*

small orange-yellow flowers. Ground-cover roses might suit you. They are particularly good on shallow soils and help to hold down top-dressings of manure and garden compost: 'Nozomi' quickly forms a dense prostrate cover, studded with small, single, pink flowers; 'Snow Carpet' is similar but with double, pure white blooms.

A danger signal with roses on chalk is leaves that turn yellow in summer. This often indicates iron deficiency which should be corrected with an application of sequestered iron. Regular watering is also important during summer.

Many gardeners on chalky soil create beds raised above the ground, not just for roses but for lime-haters like heathers. These beds are especially suitable for sloping ground where a low wall of, say, peat blocks or railway sleepers can be built across the slope and the space behind filled with non-chalky soil and compost to form a terrace. This works well, provided you top up the bed regularly with additional soil and compost or manure.

Roses from seed

Can I grow roses from hips? What are the chances of success, and how long does the process take?

It is certainly possible to raise roses from hips filled with fertile seeds although the progeny is uncertain unless two selected parents have been hand-pollinated, and even then the seedlings may turn out to be mutants or throwbacks to long-lost ancestors. Wild (Species) roses and other roses grown on their own roots are most likely to yield strong seedlings, but remember that the bees that pollinated a flower had probably visited other roses and may well have transferred pollen from a different type. The seeds inside the hip can be of a different variety from the mother plant, and might even realise the dream of every amateur rose breeder: a new hybrid rose.

Check a few ripe hips in late autumn to see if they contain tiny hard seeds covered in fine hairs. Collect a few healthy-looking hips and leave the rest for the birds.

Break the selected hips open so as to expose the seeds; it is not necessary to separate the seeds from the fleshy seed case. The hard outer covering of the seeds must be softened before germination can begin, and exposure to cold, known as stratification, does this most effectively. You can simulate stratification by placing the broken hips in a small tray covered with polythene or clingfilm and setting it in the refrigerator for about two months. Alternatively, cover the bottom of a seed tray with sharp sand, scatter the seed on top and cover with more sand to a depth of about 2in. Place the tray outside in the garden or in an unheated cold frame where it will be exposed to winter weather. Make sure to cover the tray with fine wire mesh to deter birds, mice and cats.

In January, after a period of frost, remove the seeds from the sand, or the refrigerator, and separate them from the fleshy seed cases. Sow the seeds thinly in a tray of free-draining seed compost and cover them with about ½in of sharp sand. Replace the wire protection and stand the tray outdoors in a slightly shaded spot or a cold frame. Some of the seeds will probably germinate in the first year, but others may take several years. When a good proportion of the seedlings have developed two or three true leaves, prepare a nursery bed for the young plants. Carefully separate the seedlings in spring and plant them in rows 10in apart each way.

Keep the bed free of weeds, and water it thoroughly during dry spells. After two or three years the seedlings should have grown into sturdy young plants producing their first flowers. Only then can you select the ones you want to keep and grow on. Destroy any plants that appear weak or are covered in mildew or black spot.

Finally, carefully lift the roses of your choice and plant them in their permanent positions. There is a remote chance that you might have produced a new rose. If it looks promising, contact the Royal National Rose Society in St Albans for advice about trialling and registering it as a new variety.

Roses for beginners

I am a newcomer to gardening and would like some suggestions for trouble-free rose varieties that even a beginner can grow with some chance of success.

It is quite easy, even for a novice gardener, to grow a superb display of roses that will flower from May or June until the arrival of cold weather. In mild winters and sheltered spots it is even possible to pick a few blooms for the table on Christmas Day.

The following are all well-tried varieties of sturdy bush roses, growing about 3ft high and flowering more or less continuously. The Large-flowered bush roses (Hybrid tea) mainly bear one spectacular bloom on each stem and are ideal as cut flowers. They come in a range of colours and include: 'Grandpa Dickson', large yellow flowers on upright stems; 'Alec's Red', classic-shaped red flowers, very fragrant; 'Blessings', pure pink flowers, sometimes singly, sometimes in clusters; and 'Whisky Mac', amber-yellow blooms with dark foliage.

Cluster-flowered bush roses (Floribunda) have trusses of flowers on each stem. Try: 'Anne Harkness', large clusters of apricot flowers on tall stems; 'Arthur Bell', golden-yellow, fragrant flowers, glossy leaves; 'Evelyn Fison', bright red flowers; and 'Iceberg', a large, vigorous and spreading bush with masses of pure white flowers. All these widely available varieties are easy to grow and will flower well even in the first year after planting. Watch out for signs of greenfly and thrips which damage leaves and flowers and stunt growth. The common rose diseases, mildew, black spot and rust, also attack and disfigure the foliage; in severe cases the leaves fall off. However, all these complaints are fairly easy to control, and the appropriate remedies, some in combinations of fungicides and insecticides, can be bought at garden shops and garden centres. Ideally, you should anticipate problems by spraying according to the manufacturers' instructions before the various plagues arrive, but this is expensive. If you apply the appropriate spray when the first symptoms appear, this will do nearly as well.

Don't leave dead flowers on the bushes – snip them off as soon as they have faded. Deadheading, as this process is called, encourages a continuous flower display. Follow the advice in *Pruning for health and vigour* on page 287, and *Pruning: spring versus autumn* on page 293, and you should get a display to be proud of.

Trouble-free roses

I lead a very busy life, and simply don't have the time for the pruning, mulching, spraying, deadheading and all the other cosseting that the books say roses demand. Are there no roses, whatever the type, that will look after themselves and still be attractive?

All roses, like other plants, will do better with a little loving kindness and attention. Left entirely to themselves they will deteriorate as they run out of nutrients and become cluttered with dead and spindly shoots that invite disease and pests. Left unchecked, the spores of black spot and rust will overwinter in the soil, preparing to launch renewed attacks on the already weakened plants in the spring. With everything against them, the roses simply cease flowering altogether.

This sad fate would certainly overtake neglected modern roses. But some of the Wild (Species) and Old garden roses are made of sterner stuff and require less attention; they need the minimum of pruning, and as long as they remain strong they are remarkably free of pests and diseases. Their greatest drawback, which led to their being eclipsed by modern bush roses, is their short flowering season, usually only a few glorious weeks in early summer, though some put out a repeat show later on. In addition, many grow as shrubs, 5ft high or more, and need more space to spread than the stiffly formal Large-flowered roses. Even so, many of the Old garden roses have survived the competition; they may have to be sought out from specialist nurseries and are more expensive than the run-of-the-mill modern roses, but they are well worth the seeking.

Nevertheless *all* roses are hungry plants, and while the Old roses need the least attention, they do need a top-dressing, at least once a year in spring, of well-rotted manure or garden compost.

You could do worse than try the easy Rugosa hybrids, distinguished by attractively crinkled, light green foliage on prickly stems. Most bear small clusters of richly fragrant flowers in high summer, but not infrequently you may have intermittent, or even continuous, flowering throughout the season.

Some Rugosas produce decorative hips, and if you prefer these to a second flowering, there is no need to deadhead. The following plants are still available, more than 70 years after their introduction: 'Roseraie de l'Hay', a compact 5ft high shrub that produces fragrant, crimson double flowers throughout summer; and 'Schneezwerg' ('Snow Dwarf'), which has a similar growth habit, with white, semi-double flowers.

The polyantha roses are small, easily cared for shrubs, that show delightful clusters of flowers through most of the season. Their descendants are the modern Cluster-flowered bush roses, but 'Cécile Brunner', one of the oldest hybrids, which first appeared in 1881, still rivals them in popularity. It grows no more than 2ft high and wide, and has slender, hairy stems and downy leaves that provide a background for the soft pink flowers; it is also available as a 10ft climber, though in this form it blooms less profusely.

Hedges and barriers

We want to plant a rose hedge round our front garden. Obviously, we should like to grow a really attractive variety, but just as important is that the hedge should grow densely enough to keep dogs out. Any suggestions?

Many roses are excellent for hedging, the choice ranging from the thicket-forming Rugosa and Hybrid musk roses to the more open but still impenetrable Cluster-flowered (Floribunda) and Modern shrub roses.

The best hedging roses are the vigorous types which grow upright rather than spread sideways. Plant the hedge during the dormant season, setting the roses a little closer than their natural spread.

Allow plenty of room for the hedge to grow outwards. Do not plant right against the boundary, especially if this adjoins the pavement where the thorns might snag the clothes of passers-by.

For a small hedge up to 3ft high, plant Cluster-flowered varieties such as 'Korp' (orange-scarlet, small double flowers, very thorny), or 'Arthur Bell' (golden-yellow, fragrant). Or grow Large-flowered (Hybrid tea) types like 'Alec's Red' (large red, fragrant), or 'Whisky Mac' (amber-yellow, fragrant).

For a taller hedge up to 5ft high, choose between the Cluster-flowered 'Masquerade' (large flower trusses, yellow buds opening pink, turning red), 'Southampton' (double, apricot-orange, fragrant), the Large-flowered 'Alexander' (vermilion-scarlet) and the sweet-scented Hybrid musk 'Penelope' (pink-apricot, fading to cream).

Some of the Modern shrub roses are excellent for hedges 6ft or more high, including 'Fountain' (deep red, scented) and 'Heidelberg' (bright red). The Cluster-flowered 'Queen Elizabeth' (pure pink) would suit, too.

For a hedge of dense growth and up to 7ft tall, nothing can beat a mixture of Rugosa roses. Try 'Alba' (white), 'Rubra' (near purple), or 'Scabrosa' (rose-pink).

The ultimate height of the hedge will depend on soil condition and care after planting. Keep the hedge clear of weeds, mulch and feed it annually, and water it regularly in dry weather. Trim the hedge lightly to shape in spring.

For more recommended varieties, see *Pick of the hedging roses*, page 191.

Elegant hips

Our garden is particularly good in autumn, and we are thinking of adding to the effect by planting a bed of roses whose berries will give us a blaze of colour late in the year. Which varieties would be best for this?

The berries, or hips, produced by modern hybrids are usually green and not very interesting. For a spectacular autumn show of bright, shiny berries in many shapes and sizes, and in colours that range through orange, crimson and scarlet to black, you really need the Old garden (Old-fashioned) and Wild (Species) roses.

The trouble is that these lofty and vigorous plants are not really suitable for a rose bed that would fit into the average modern garden. To appreciate the full effect, of flowers or hips, they should be seen massed, with low shrubs or perennials in front and a hedge at the back.

However, let's assume you do have enough room, and begin by planning the size and position of the bed. It should be at least 8ft wide and as long as you can manage. Dark foliage, such as that of holly, laurel or Leyland cypress, would make the perfect backdrop for showing up the flowers as well as the hips. If a hedge is inconvenient in this site, create the background with dark green ivy grown up a fence or trellis. Either hedge or ivy will need to be trimmed a couple of times a year, so allow room to move along the back of the rose border. A sunny position is the best, although roses will grow quite well anywhere as long as they receive some sun for part of the day to encourage flowers and hips. Allow plenty of room between plants to allow each to develop a natural shape, without running into each other in a tangled mess.

A spacing of 4ft between the larger varieties and 3ft between smaller is about right, though more space may be needed for very vigorous roses such as *Rosa macrophylla*. Prepare the border by thorough digging and by mixing in plenty of well-rotted manure or garden compost. Remove all perennial weeds like couch, bindweed and ground elder; if they are persistent, spray with a weedkiller based on glyphosate and give it time to work before the final preparation and planting.

Mark out the position for each plant with a cane, and rearrange the canes until the positions look right from every angle. Dig a large hole for each plant and fork in manure or compost with a handful of bone meal: plant each rose firmly, treading the soil down around the plants. Use the previous soil mark as a guide to depth of planting. If there is no obvious mark, set the rose so that the graft union is just below the firmed soil surface. Some of the shrubby Wild roses may have been grown from cuttings, and if there is no clear soil mark or graft union, plant so that the shoots are just above soil level.

The following roses are outstanding for their hips, although some of the largest might be better grown as specimen shrubs rather than in a rose bed.

R. farreri persetosa (which grows to 6ft) – pink, single flowers in profusion in May and June; small ovoid, bright red hips.

R. hugonis (7ft) – creamy-yellow, scented flowers; fern-like foliage and black hips.

R. macrantha (5ft) – single blush-pink and scented flowers on trailing branches; round red hips.

R. macrophylla (to 10ft) – deep pink flowers in clusters; it produces bright orange-red, bottle-shaped hips.

R. moyesii 'Geranium' (8-10ft) – single scarlet flowers; large red, bottle-shaped hips.

R. pendulina (4ft) – single deep pink flowers; pear-shaped red hips.

R. pomifera (4-6ft) – pink flowers; very large mahogany-red and bristly hips.

R. spinosissima (syn *R. pimpinellifolia*) *lutea* (4ft) – canary-yellow flowers; round black-purple hips.

Some of the finest berrying roses are found among the Rugosas, outstanding for their large single flowers with conspicuous golden stamens and for their clusters of large, round and shiny red hips: *R. rugosa* 'Alba' (6ft), pure white, fragrant; 'Frau Dagmar Hastrup' or 'Frau Dagmar Hartopp' (3ft), delicate pink; and 'Rubra' (7ft), mauve-pink.

Updating Old roses

I love the look and scent of Old-fashioned roses, but am put off by their short flowering season. Are there similar roses among the modern hybrids, but with a longer flower display?

The classification of roses is changing and roses are being regrouped. The Old-fashioned roses were formerly listed in their separate groups, such as Moss, Bourbon and Damask. For ease of selection, all these hybrids are now collectively known as Old garden roses, though within this classification they keep their former names. Don't dismiss the Old roses for having only one main flowering period. It isn't always so, but in any case, even those which flower once only in a season are so exquisite in form and scent that they more than compensate for their short life. And, of course, you get the marvellous garden jewellery of their hips in autumn. True, many are vigorous and tall-growing and some get mildew, but many are resistant to black spot and rust which is more than can be said for modern roses. The old roses are not so quick to start flowering from young plants, and often take several years to produce enough mature wood on which to bear their huge displays of flowers. Like other roses, they need looking after with mulching, feeding and watering; but pruning should be less drastic and consist of removing dead and weak shoots only.

Damask roses are among the most fragrant of the Old shrub roses, with heady-scented blooms in June and July. 'Ispahan', compact and up to 6ft tall, flowers only once in a season, but the display of richly fragrant, bright pink, double blooms, borne in large clusters, continues for at least six weeks. 'Quatre Saisons', one of the oldest roses, produces its fully double, scented, pink blooms in early summer, with a repeat performance later on; and 'Comte de Chambord', with pink-lilac, quartered, fragrant blooms, flowers more or less continuously.

The Centifolia (cabbage) and Moss roses have double flowers, often nodding downwards on arching branches and covered with a mass of moss-like, often soft, bristles. They flower only once. 'Rosa de Meaux' is a short Centifolia type, growing to about 3ft and with small pink flowers, sweetly scented. 'Henri Martin', a Moss rose, grows to about 5ft and bears clusters of semi-double, light crimson flowers, fading to pink. 'Mousseline', also a Moss rose and sometimes listed as 'Alfred de Dalmas', flowers in early summer and again later on. The blooms are in clusters and are double, soft pink and fragrant. They are produced on compact plants, 4-5ft high.

The China roses are an interesting group first introduced in the middle of the last century and valued for their long flowering season, attractive foliage and compact growth. They produce flowers throughout the summer and have some very attractive forms.

'Mutabilis', 7ft or more tall, produces large single flowers that start reddish-copper, then change to crimson as the flowers fade, giving a multicoloured effect. Flowering is continuous throughout the summer.

Many Modern shrub roses, which are usually repeat or continuous-flowering, have retained the massed blooms, colour and fragrance of the old roses. Carefully selected and positioned for height and colour, they make outstanding border or specimen shrubs. 'Ballerina', 4ft high and wide, sometimes listed as a Hybrid musk rose, produces huge clusters of scented, pale pink flowers with a white eye; they're recurrent throughout the season. 'Marjorie Fair' is a close relative of 'Ballerina' and is very similar except that the flowers are bright red with a white eye.

'Erfurt', a compact shrub, 4-5ft high, has fragrant, semi-double, clear pink blooms with conspicuous golden anthers. The flowers are borne in clusters from June to September.

'Alec's Red', a 3ft Large-flowered (Hybrid tea) bush rose with typical foliage, bears double 'old-fashioned' crimson flowers that are richly fragrant.

'Baroness Rothschild', 4ft high, is a hybrid perpetual rose, but has foliage similar to 'Alec's Red' and large cupped flowers, rose-pink with a silvery sheen on the reverse of the petals. It, too, is highly scented and repeat-flowering.

Miniature roses

I have tried several times to grow Miniature roses in a trough, but they never do well. Am I wasting my time?

All roses, including Miniatures, grow best when they have a well-anchored root system. There is no reason why they should not thrive in a trough provided that it is at least 8-10in deep and filled with medium to heavy loam mixed with well-rotted garden compost. Good drainage is very important, so make sure that the trough has several drainage holes and space below the bottom of the trough to allow excess water to drain away; set the trough on a bed of pebbles.

In spring and summer, Miniature roses will suffer if allowed to dry out – they are seriously affected by drying winds, in or out of troughs – and this can result in flower buds and leaves dropping off.

You should pay particular attention to roses grown in such restricted spaces as troughs and window boxes. Apply a liquid fertiliser every four weeks, otherwise growth will cease and leaves become discoloured. Choose a fertiliser specially formulated for roses or shrubs, and avoid any fertiliser that is high in nitrogen.

Every spring remove the top layer of soil in the trough, and fork in some rose fertiliser before topping up with fresh compost or soil. Every three or four years, the soil should be thrown out and replaced by fresh loam or loam-based compost. Carefully prise out the roses, prune the tops and trim the roots. Clean the trough thoroughly and check it for cracks. Make up a fresh growing medium of loam, garden compost and rose fertiliser, mixing it thoroughly before replanting the roses in the trough.

Never overdo fertilising, and follow the manufacturer's instructions; overfeeding causes the roses to grow soft and leafy, producing no flowering wood, and the plants become vulnerable to such diseases as mildew and black spot. In addition, high concentrations of fertiliser in a restricted space can be toxic to the plants; the leaves discolour and drop off.

A few worms will find their way into the trough and are beneficial; they can be an aid to drainage. Watch out for ants; they tend to build nests and disturb the soil round the roots, causing them to dry out, especially in small troughs. If you spot any ants, apply an ant powder to the soil surface and lightly work it into the top inch.

Exhibition roses

For several years now I've been entering roses for the local show, but getting absolutely nowhere. I don't know if I'm growing the wrong varieties, or the right ones wrongly. Please help.

Growing roses for local competitions is good fun and adds a new dimension to the enjoyment of these lovely plants. First decide which classes you want to enter, then choose your varieties.

Depending on show rules, roses can be entered in a number of classes, such as Modern garden, Old garden, and Miniature roses; within each class are certain subdivisions. Modern garden roses, for instance, are often divided into such classifications as single blooms, Large-flowered roses, and Cluster-flowered, or Floribunda.

Until you gain some experience of growing and showing exhibition roses, it is probably best to concentrate on the easiest group, Modern garden roses. Having decided on the class and on the rose varieties, stake out a fair-sized patch of your garden which will be dedicated only to the growing of roses. Roses for competition need extra attention, with space for easy access for disbudding and other jobs. Space the roses farther apart than for ordinary planting, allowing at least 3ft between plants to prevent them from brushing one another. Choose three plants of each variety rather than a single bush to obtain a better choice of blooms.

Some easy-to-grow, Large-flowered bush roses that should stand a chance of winning a place include: 'Grandpa Dickson', with its upright habit and large yellow flowers; 'Fragrant Cloud', which has shapely red and fragrant blooms; and 'Big Chief', that puts forth large crimson flowers and handsome foliage.

Suitable exhibition varieties among the Cluster-flowered bush roses include: 'Anne Harkness', a tall, upright bush producing large clusters of apricot flowers, and dark green foliage; and 'Evelyn Fison', with its vigorous glossy green leaves and trusses of vivid red blooms.

Much mystique surrounds the cultivation of exhibition plants, with many a tale of closely kept secret techniques reckoned to be sure to produce winners. Special fertilisers and other sprays are all part of exhibition lore, and no doubt you will develop a few magic formulas of your own. That apart, it is essential that growth should be healthy and continuous, with a good supply of plant nutrients in the form of manure or compost, and with regular applications of rose fertiliser. Do not exceed the recommended doses; overfeeding results in lots of leaves and shoots, but few flowers, and soft growth is likely to be attacked by pests and diseases. Inspect the plants daily and act at the first sign of greenfly or mildew. Develop a spraying programme based on the manufacturer's recommendations and stick to it. Some sprays can leave blemishes on foliage and flowers, and it's a good idea to check with the manufacturer that their product is suitable for exhibition blooms.

During dry weather, water thoroughly over the entire root area, but keep water off the developing blooms. Water droplets may stain the flowers. As the young blooms develop, it may be necessary to disbud some varieties in order to encourage a few flowers of the right size. Take out unwanted buds early, or they will leave a scar.

Standard roses

I know what they look like, but how are bush and standard roses given their different forms?

Most modern roses are the products of a union between two different but compatible partners: one for the roots and the other for the topgrowth. Intense breeding has resulted in varieties with uniformity of flowers, foliage and habit, but such crosses often have weak roots and are grafted onto a rootstock of a different variety of proven vigour, frequently *Rosa canina* or *R. rugosa*. Grafting, or budding as it is also known, is the propagation method used by commercial rose growers; the only difference between a bush and a standard rose is the point at which the chosen variety is grafted onto the rootstock.

In grafting, a single bud of the chosen variety is inserted in summer under the bark of the stem of the stock plant; the union, or neck, is secured with rubber bands or clips to hold the joint together and to prevent water and disease spores from entering. Bud and stock marry quite quickly, and after a few weeks the bud will have swollen so much that the rubber must be loosened if it has not already rotted and fallen off. In the following spring, the stem of the stock plant is cut back to just above the union with the budded variety, which will begin to produce the shoots that form the maiden bush for sale in the autumn.

On bush roses, a single bud is grafted low down onto the stem of the rootstock. On standard roses the technique is slightly different. For a start, the rootstock plant, of exceptional vigour, must be grown on in the nursery as a single-stemmed, straight plant until it reaches a height of 6-7ft. All buds on the stem are rubbed out, so that at the time of grafting the rootstock plant consists of a tall bare stem with a head of foliage; the chosen variety is grafted in at about 3-4ft from ground level. Three buds are inserted under the bark round the bare stem, and each tied in place. Early the following spring, the rootstock plant is cut down to the top bud, and shoots develop from all three buds to form a well-shaped maiden standard.

Most standard roses are grafted with Large-flowered or Cluster-flowered varieties, so you can buy a 'Peace' or 'Iceberg' rose either as a bush or as a standard. Weeping standards are less common – and more expensive; they are grafted, at a height of about 5ft, with a Rambler rose variety such as the creamy-white 'Albéric Barbier' or the rose-pink 'Dorothy Perkins'.

Roses in the sun

I'm thinking of retiring to the Mediterranean. Which of my favourite roses can I continue to grow there?

Some of the oldest and most famous rose breeders and growers have nurseries in the Mediterranean area, so you will have no problem buying roses there.

But when it comes to growing, you may have to adapt your ideas a little. The hot, baking summers of the Mediterranean, with temperatures soaring to 30°C (86°F), are hard on roses. The air is dry and hot, the soil dries out quickly and often there is a watering ban just when moisture is most needed. But if you can keep the soil damp with sprinklers in the cool of evening, and make sure the plants have adequate nutrients, you will still have a summer display of roses. Otherwise, if you are forced to stop watering, they will leap to life when the autumn rain arrives, and you will have your display long after the English roses have finished.

Much of the Mediterranean soil is poor and stony, and it pays to use plenty of manure when preparing the soil and planting. Apply a deep mulch afterwards to prevent moisture loss, keep down weeds and release nutrients. Supplement feeding in summer with liquid rose fertilisers, supplied through a hose end diluter when watering.

Most countries have strict laws governing the importing of plants, and it's really best to buy fresh stock when you get to your new home.

Many of the more popular British varieties are listed in Continental catalogues under their English names, such as 'Ena Harkness', 'Grandpa Dickson', 'Orange Sensation' and 'Dorothy Perkins'. Others have merely undergone a translation of the name: in France, for example, 'Iceberg' is known by the French equivalent of 'Fée des Neiges'. That most famous of all roses, 'Peace', was bred in France by Francis Meilland in 1939; in his homeland it bears the name of 'Mme A. Meilland'.

Pruning a new rose

What's the best way to prune a newly planted rose?

A container-grown or bare-root rose needs hard pruning in the first spring after planting, both to allow it to divert some vigour into root growth, and to encourage strong shoots from the base to establish the main framework.

First remove any damaged, dead and weak shoots right back to the junction with the main stems or the rootstock. Then prune Large-flowered (Hybrid tea) types back to about 4in above ground, always to an outward-facing bud. Cut back new Cluster-flowered (Floribunda) roses to 5-6in, and Miniatures to 2-3in.

Newly planted Old-fashioned shrub roses should not be pruned, apart from the obvious removal of dead, damaged or badly placed shoots; they flower on stems made in the previous year. Neither should Climbers, Ramblers and Species roses be pruned in the first year after planting, apart from removing any weak or damaged shoots and about 3in from the tips of the stems.

Summer pruning and deadheading

There are few garden tasks more boring than the summer-long chore of deadheading roses. Is it really necessary?

It is a sad fact of gardening life that if you want continuity of bloom, you must both deadhead your roses and prune them in summer. By cutting off each dead bloom you encourage the next bud in the bunch to open and at the same time stimulate growth in buds lower down the stem. When all the flower buds in a cluster have opened, there will be no more growth at the end of that stem. However, more flowers open on the short stems produced from the buds below the old flower head.

Regular deadheading encourages rapid growth from such buds, and on some rose varieties the young shoots will have bursting flower buds by the time the last bit of deadheading is finished. By then there will be a piece of woody stem left that supported the first flush of the cluster above, and some rose bushes may develop an uneven growth pattern, with blooms appearing at different heights. This is when summer pruning is carried out. When the last flowers in a cluster are fading, cut the whole stem back to just above a swelling bud from which a new shoot will grow and carry the next flush of bloom. Do not cut back too hard, generally no more than 12in, though this varies with different varieties. Correctly timed, deadheading and summer pruning will ensure a continuity of flowers on Large-flowered (Hybrid tea) and Cluster-flowered (Floribunda) roses. Some perpetual-flowering Climbing roses also benefit by this treatment.

If roses are not deadheaded they often produce seedheads or rose hips. On modern hybrids this is no advantage as the hips are rarely attractive; but on older hybrids and Wild (Species) roses, hips can be a spectacular addition to the autumn display. They can persist for most of the winter and are an important source of food for birds.

When deadheading, by the way, it's a good idea to collect the less damaged petals and place them in a bowl to add colour and fragrance to the house. Potpourri would last longer and give off a stronger scent, but it is complicated to make and a bowl of rose petals by themselves will serve nearly as well.

Rose-hip syrup

I have a collection of Old and Species roses that produce the most glorious display of differently coloured hips in autumn. Are these the kind of hips you can make rose-hip syrup from? Or does it have to be the wild variety?

Either would do equally well, as would a mixture of the two. If you don't get enough hips to make the syrup from your garden roses, you can supplement them with dog rose hips from the hedgerows. It is important that both kinds should be full and ripe when picked; unripe hips are lacking in juice. Leave them on the plants until they are burnt by the first frosts and feel soft to the touch.

Nicholas Culpeper, the 17th-century herbalist, pronounced rose-hip syrup 'a conserve of a pleasant taste . . . it binds the belly, stays defluxions from the head upon the stomach and dries up the moisture and aids digestion'. In other words, it is rich in Vitamin C. Here's how you make it.

2lb ripe rose hips
6 pints water
1lb sugar

Wash the hips, remove the stalks and calyces, and put the hips through the coarse blade of a mincer. Add them to a pan containing 4 pints of boiling water, bring back to the boil, and remove the pan from the heat.

Allow to stand for 15 minutes, then strain through a jelly bag. Extract as much juice as possible. Return the pulp to the pan with a further 2 pints of boiling water. Bring back to the boil and remove from the heat. Leave for 10 minutes, then strain through a clean jelly bag.

Mix the two juice extracts, and boil in a clean pan until reduced to about 2 pints.

Add the sugar, stirring constantly until it has been dissolved. Bring the mixture to the boil and keep it at boiling point for 5 minutes. Pour into clean, warm bottles and seal at once with sterilised stoppers or corks. Use small bottles, if possible, for the syrup does not keep long once opened.

Removing suckers

How should I get rid of rose suckers? My neighbour says they should be pulled off, rather than cut. Why is that?

They should certainly be removed. Modern roses in general are not grown on their own rootstocks, but on those of more vigorous plants such as the dog rose (*Rosa canina*). Sometimes the rootstock puts forth shoots of its own – which are called, rather unfairly, 'suckers' – and since these shoots are more vigorous, they would eventually swamp the grafted rose on top.

There are two schools of thought concerning the method of removal. One maintains that they must be pulled out of the rootstock so that they cannot grow again. But the force required to do this may disturb the root and leave a wound through which disease could enter. The other way is to cut the sucker off at ground level – though this is in effect pruning it, encouraging it to flourish even more strongly next year.

So compromise; pull as much of the sucker out of the ground as you can without disturbing the roots of the plant, and then cut it off. You may have to repeat the exercise next

Pruning: spring versus autumn

Should roses be pruned in the autumn or in the spring?

This will vary with the type of rose you're dealing with. But most commonly the right answer is: both. Large-flowered (Hybrid tea) and Cluster-flowered (Floribunda) bushes, particularly in windy gardens, benefit from being tidied up and shortened back in November so that they are not rocked and blown about by the wind during the winter. This involves removing old flower heads and shortening all strong shoots by about one-third. Don't prune all the way in autumn, though. Frost will probably burn the top few inches, which can be removed as part of the main pruning in spring. In March, prune the bushes more thoroughly by cutting out all weak shoots and any that have been damaged or killed during the winter. Cut all strong shoots back to within 6-9in of the ground, but cut weaker shoots back harder, to about 4in, to encourage them to produce a stronger shoot. In general, the weaker the variety, the harder the pruning. The old gardeners' saying 'Let your worst enemy prune your roses' is a useful reminder that most people are too gentle with their plants. Climbing roses should be pruned at the same times. Their autumn trim involves removing dead flower heads and tying in long shoots so that they are not blown about. In March, remove weak shoots altogether and cut others back to form spurs 2-4in long. These will produce more flowering shoots in the following summer. Any new, long shoots that have not flowered should be tied in to form part of the permanent framework.

Ramblers have a short and glorious flowering period in midsummer and then finish (Climbers, by contrast, bloom all summer). They bloom best on long shoots that grew the previous year. After flowering, these shoots should be cut back to the ground to make room for new ones. Prune weeping roses in the same way as Ramblers, standard roses in the same way as bushes.

Whenever you prune roses, make sure that all cuts are close to a bud, otherwise the part of the shoot above the bud will die back later. This is especially important in the autumn because cut ends are far more liable to fungal attack during the winter. It is a wise precaution to treat all saw cuts with a sealant – any household paint will do.

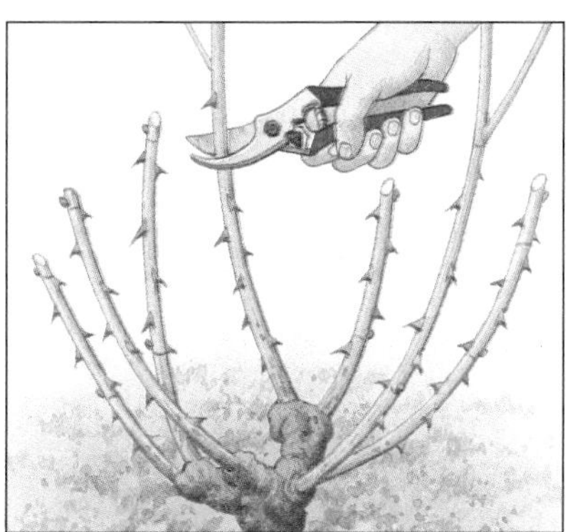

LIGHT PRUNING *If your bush rose is of average growth, prune it lightly each year to produce a good display.*

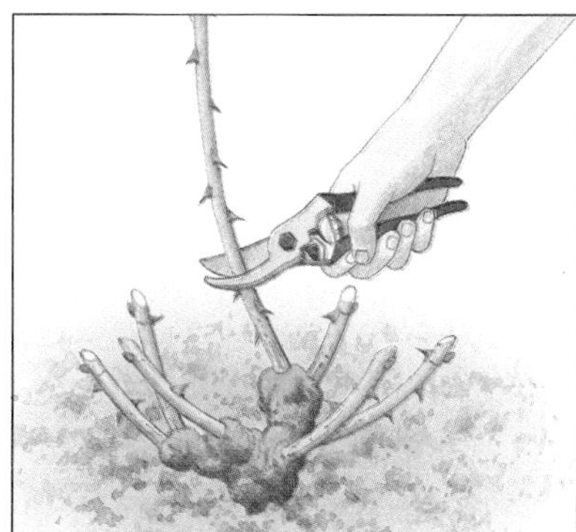

HARD PRUNING *If you want to grow large, well-formed roses, though few in number, prune your bush back hard annually.*

year, but by then the sucker's growth will have been substantially weakened.

The way to tell a sucker, incidentally, is that it usually, but not always, carries its foliage in groups of seven small leaflets – the badge of the wild rose – as opposed to the five larger leaflets of cultivated roses. Any suspect shoot should be traced back; if it comes from the rootstock, it's a sucker.

Rejuvenating a pillar rose

My 'American Pillar' rose has grown so large that it is pulling down the trellis. If I prune it hard back, will it shoot again from the base?

'American Pillar' is an extremely vigorous rambling rose; like other Ramblers it should be pruned annually after flowering to allow the new shoots to mature ready for next year's display. 'American Pillar' should respond to hard summer pruning by producing a mass of young shoots, but such a profusion of new shoots may not ripen enough to withstand a hard winter. It would be better to prune back to the base in spring and allow the new stems to mature during the summer, ready for flowering the following year. It will mean sacrificing that year's flowering display, but will give you better results in the long run.

While waiting for the new shoots to grow, build a support out of something sturdy like larch poles. Tie in the lower stems horizontally; this encourages profuse flowering in the following year and makes for easier pruning after flowering.

Recurring greenflies

I keep spraying my roses against greenfly, but they always come back. Is there a lasting cure?

Not really; greenflies, a type of aphid, have a particular fondness for roses, favouring especially the tips of new shoots and developing flower buds. Frequent spraying with insecticide helps but cannot be guaranteed to deter the greenfly for good, and if just a few escape they will multiply so fast that within a few weeks you'll be back to square one. It is essential that the plants are sprayed thoroughly, covering upper and lower leaf surfaces, as well as stems and flower buds. When you spray the roses, check nearby plants; many greenflies are winged and migrate from one host to another.

Begin the spraying programme in spring, as soon as the first greenfly appears. Systemic insecticides such as dimethoate, which are absorbed by the plant tissues, are excellent, but as the plants grow, repeat applications become necessary – as often as every two weeks in a bad year. Never mix more insecticide than you can use up in one treatment; watered down, it loses its effectiveness within a couple of days (see also *Aphids*, page 12 and *Chemicals*, page 53).

Inevitable diseases

Are black spot and mildew on roses inevitable?

Very nearly. All varieties are prone to these two fungus diseases to a greater or lesser extent, but avoiding those which are particularly susceptible will help. For example, 'Frensham' gets mildew badly and 'Fragrant Cloud' is a favourite target of black spot.

Regular and frequent spraying with a systemic fungicide such as triforine is the most successful control and, for mildew, this should start as soon as the leaves are open in the spring. It should be carried out every 10-14 days until late summer.

Because the spores of black spot need a relatively high temperature – about 21°C (70°F) – to germinate, the disease rarely appears before June, so spraying need not normally start until then. However, the sensible course is to start in the spring and use a specific rose fungicide which will control both diseases at once.

There are many specific sprays available, and some even have an insecticide included to cope at the same time with a third almost inescapable nuisance – greenfly.

Don't overlook underplanting

What are the pros and cons of underplanting roses?

There are several pros and only one important con. The principal aims of growing other plants below and around roses are to make use of the empty ground and to show the roses off to best advantage. The normal system is to use fairly low-growing annual bedding plants, such as pansies in the spring and begonias in the summer.

The only significant disadvantage is that the extra cultivation involved in planting and removing these plants can disturb the roses. But that problem can be overcome simply enough by placing the bedding plants around the edges of the rose bed rather than crowding them up to the stems of your roses. Try, for instance, silvery lamb's tongue (*Stachys lanata*), steel-blue rue (*Ruta graveolens*) or the silver-grey hummocks of old-fashioned pinks. One common worry – that the bedding plants will rob the roses of nutrients – you can safely ignore. Rose roots collect most of their nutrients from far deeper levels in the soil than any bedding plant will reach.

Old gardeners' tales

Is it true that bonfire smoke, marigold and garlic plants will keep greenfly off roses?

These methods of controlling greenfly and other pests are all part of gardening folklore, though they should not be entirely dismissed. Bonfire smoke may well contain all sorts of ingredients harmful to greenfly, but dense smoke can be unpleasant to humans, too, and in many areas local by-laws prohibit the lighting of bonfires altogether.

Marigolds are said to be helpful in controlling perennial weeds like couch and ground elder. It is quite likely that the unpleasant scent of marigolds is off-putting to greenfly, and that the roots contain useful chemicals that discourage weeds and soil-borne pests, but research has not so far produced conclusive proof.

Garlic and pyrethrum are also said to be useful in pest control. An extract of the pyrethrum plant – a kind of chrysanthemum – grown in Uganda is still used in the manufacture of a fast-acting, non-persistent insecticide also called pyrethrum. Adherents of natural pest control insist that a single garlic clove planted beside each rose bush will slay all greenflies; many gardeners believe that the roots of the roses absorb a substance from the garlic that is so repellent to the pests that not even the eggs will hatch.

Pest control using natural extracts and harmless predators is the subject of much research, and natural products will probably become more generally available in the future.

Black spot tips

The black spot season is with us again. Is there any way of ridding my roses permanently of this disfiguring and persistent disease?

Almost certainly not. Just in case there are any rose growers who do not know black spot when they see it, it generally manifests itself as dark brown or black spots on the leaves. Sometimes the spots merge together to form larger blotches, but they are always irregular in outline, often with a yellowish halo which eventually extends to turn the whole leaf yellow. Diseased leaves fall prematurely, and severe attacks encourage dormant buds to produce weak shoots in autumn, so reducing the vigour of the bush in the following spring.

The disease spreads quickly during warm, damp weather. It's often carried by rain splashes, or on hands or tools. Fortnightly spraying with triforine or propicanizole helps to control it, as does spraying the bushes in November with Armillatox. Garden hygiene is also important. Burn fallen leaves and old prunings immediately. Then, too, you might grow some of those varieties with a strong resistance to the disease, among them the popular 'Alec's Red', 'Blessings', 'Peace' and 'Uncle Walter'. All these things help, but in general, black spot is almost as much a part of roses as their scent.

Probably only greenflies are a greater trouble on roses, but there are a number of other menaces that are by no means uncommon. They include:

- CAPSID BUGS These sucking insects

tatter and distort the leaves and buds. Get rid of them by spraying with an insecticide such as malathion or diazinon.

- **LEAF HOPPERS** The signs are a pale mottling on the leaves, whose edges may curl to reveal insect skins on the undersides. Spray with malathion, and pick off and destroy leaves with curled edges.
- **THRIPS** Flowers are damaged by minute black insects which can be seen on light-coloured varieties. Spray with rotenone (derris), malathion or dimethoate.
- **MILDEW** Appears as a white powder on leaves and young shoots, most frequently where the ground is dry. Spray with triforine or benomyl. Glossy-leaved varieties are thought to be the most resistant.
- **RUST** In spring and summer, this twists and distorts leaves and shoots, which are also covered by an orange powder. Spray both sides of the foliage with mancozeb or thiram. Remove and destroy affected parts and, if the disease persists, destroy the plant.
- **MINERAL DEFICIENCY** Yellowed leaves drop prematurely, the flowers are few and short-lived, and new growth is thin and weak. These symptoms may result from drought or from iron deficiency, so water the plants well during dry periods, mulch annually and feed regularly. If your soil is limy, apply sequestered iron.
- **CATERPILLARS AND ROSE CHAFERS** Holes or tattered petals visible as flowers open. Spray with HCH or malathion.
- **FROST DAMAGE** The symptoms, also caused by cold winds, are black or purple-tipped shoots and leaves. Cut back to healthy wood when all danger of frost is past. If the symptoms persist from year to year, do your spring pruning later. Do not feed the plants in late summer; this encourages the soft growth that is most liable to damage.

Downhill roses

A lot of my roses seem to be deteriorating at the same time – poor growth, fewer flowers. Am I not feeding them properly, or is it simply time they were replaced?

Roses are very long-lived plants, and with careful pruning and regular feeding they should thrive for many years. It is not unusual to hear of roses still flowering well after 20 years. If you don't prune properly and regularly, roses lose vigour and gradually decline; the signs are dead wood, weak shoots and few flowers.

Before you dig up your roses, give them one more chance: prune them hard in spring and take out all dead wood and weak shoots. Afterwards, burn all the prunings to prevent the spread of disease. Lightly prick over the soil, remove all weeds, and scatter a rose fertiliser around the bases. Spread a layer of well-rotted manure or compost, at least 2in deep, over the whole rose bed. If the weather is dry during the vital growth period of May and June, put a sprinkler on the rose bed for 20 minutes once a week to ensure that the fertiliser reaches the roots. This also helps to keep the mulch damp.

Another possibility is that your plants are suffering from rose sickness, which occurs when roses planted in a bed that has long supported roses suddenly fail to thrive. However, without extensive and expensive soil analysis at a laboratory, it would be difficult to be sure. The disease is thought to be a physiological disorder: a combination of mineral imbalance, viral disease, microscopic pests and an accumulation of other problems. It affects only roses.

Rose sickness can be overcome by sterilising all the soil in that particular bed, but as this is a lengthy and laborious process, not easily undertaken by an amateur gardener, the most sensible solution is to move the roses to a fresh site. However, if that is not feasible, dig up and burn the old roses when they have finished flowering and give the bed a thorough overhaul in autumn by trenching or double digging. It is very important to mix plenty of well-rotted manure or garden compost into the bottom of each trench and to turn each spadeful of soil upside down into the trench to bury seeding annual weeds.

Leave the newly dug bed over winter to settle down and to allow frost to break down the soil clods. In spring, re-plant the bed with new roses, adding manure or compost mixed with a dressing of bone meal to each planting hole.

Roses that fight back

I see that some roses are advertised as being disease-resistant. Can they really fight off all rose diseases, and are they worth the extra money asked for them?

What the advertiser might more accurately say is that certain varieties are resistant to one or both of those rose scourges – black spot and mildew. Thanks to research and scientific breeding, most of the fungus diseases have been almost eliminated in many of the most popular roses. 'Peace', for example, is generally free from mildew, though it may suffer from rust, while the climbing 'Zéphirine Drouhin' is rarely seen with black spot, but almost invariably has mildew.

For such blessings, it is well worth paying a little extra. However, disease-resistant roses cannot be expected to remain immune for ever if grown in close proximity to others which habitually suffer from fungus diseases. While disease-resistant types should require no fungicides, this is only true as long as the health of the plant is maintained with annual mulching and feeding, regular deadheading and watering. And, sadly, the rose that is resistant to greenfly is yet to be bred.

It is generally thought that bright, glossy foliage offers the best resistance to rose diseases. But breeders, eager to develop hybrids with disease-free leaves, exquisite flowers and superb colour, often have to sacrifice some other feature, such as scent. If you want a rose garden that has the lot – beautiful blooms, delicious scent and healthy foliage, opt for the roses of your choice and treat them regularly with a combined fungicide and insecticide.

Rain spoilage

My rose bed was a mass of lovely flowers until a heavy shower spoilt them. Are all roses susceptible to rain damage?

The large showy blooms, and especially the double types, are particularly vulnerable to damage by rain, and white roses appear to suffer most of all. Single roses and small or Cluster-flowered types tend to be less vulnerable.

To minimise the problem, don't plant roses close to trees or eaves where they can be damaged by drips after rainfall. Any damaged blooms should be snipped off as soon as possible so that the plant can develop new flowers. If you leave wet petals tangled in a cluster of buds they may damage the young emerging flowers.

Hours and flowers

My neighbour tells me that roses need six full hours of bright sunlight a day to produce their best flowers. Is this true?

No. And given the weather of some British summers, it's just as well. Roses are what botanists call 'day-neutral' plants – meaning that they don't need any particular period of light or dark to start them flowering. Chrysanthemums, by contrast, are short-day plants – they begin producing flower buds only when they have at least 12 hours of continuous darkness each day (see *All-year chrysanthemums*, page 68).

If roses are given a reasonable diet of nutrients, any reasonable amount of light and adequate warmth, they'll flower at any time of year – with or without sunshine. The crucial factor is temperature, not light. That's why roses will sometimes begin to flower in a very mild winter, when they're not getting anything like six hours of sunshine a day.

All modern rose varieties – including the Old-fashioned varieties – can, in fact, have too much sunlight, or, to be more precise, too much warmth. A bush set against a south or west-facing wall, for instance, will produce an earlier but poorer crop of flowers than an identical bush in a cooler spot in the open garden, or a bush which is in light shade for part of the day.

The extra warmth from the wall merely accelerates the flowers' development and decline, giving you earlier flowers but shortening the time each bloom stays open.

PICK OF THE ROSES

All the plants mentioned on these two pages are readily available, well-tried and reasonably disease-resistant. The heights given are necessarily approximate, being based on those achieved by well-pruned plants growing in average soil in the Southern half of the country. In the balmy West they may grow higher, while in chilly, exposed parts of the North and East they will probably stand shorter. Some climbing roses – 'Blessings', for example – carry the same name as the bush variety from which they developed. They are distinguished here by the letters in brackets after the name.

Colour	1-2ft	2-2½ft	2½-3½ft
White	Easter Morning (M) Pour Toi (M) Snow Carpet (M)	Bianco* (CF) Margaret Merril* (CF) Memoriam (LF) Pascali (LF) Silver Wedding (LF) Virgo* (LF) Yorkshire Sunblaze (CF)	Grace Abounding (CF) Iceberg (CF) Ice White (CF) Polar Star (LF) Princess of Monaco (LF) Pristine* (LF)
Pink	Angela Rippon (M) Dearest* (CF) Pink Sunblaze* (M) Royal Salute (M) Tip Top (CF)	Ballet (LF) Cécile Brunner (O) Golden Slippers (CF) Mullard Jubilee* (LF) Ophelia (LF) Petit Four (CF) Silver Jubilee (LF) Susan Hampshire* (LF) The Fairy (S) Wendy Cussons* (LF) Yesterday* (CF)	Admiral Rodney* (LF) Blessings* (LF) Chicago Peace (LF) City of Leeds (CF) English Miss* (CF) Mala Rubinstein* (LF) Mischief (LF) Pink Parfait (CF) Scented Air* (CF) Sweet Promise (LF)
Red	Fire Princess* (M) Little Buckaroo (M) Starina* (M) Topsi (CF) Trumpeter (CF) Wee Man (M)	Anna Ford* (CF) Beautiful Britain (CF) Big Chief (LF) Cheshire Life (LF) City of Belfast (CF) Deep Secret* (LF) Duke of Windsor* (LF) Fragrant Cloud* (LF) Marlena (CF) National Trust (LF) Red Planet (LF) Sarabande (CF) Summer Holiday (LF)	Alec's Red* (LF) Alexander (LF) Chorus (CF) Ernest H. Morse* (LF) Evelyn Fison (CF) John Waterer (LF) Korp (LF) Lilli Marlene (CF) Papa Meilland* (LF) Precious Platinum* (LF)
Yellow	Baby Bio (CF) Gold Pin (M) Josephine Wheatcroft (M) Kim (CF) Yellow Sunblaze* (M)	Grandpa Dickson (LF) King's Ransom* (LF) Korresia* (CF) Peer Gynt (LF) Simba (LF) Sunblest (LF) Yellow Cushion* (CF) Yellow Pages (LF)	Allgold (CF) Arthur Bell* (CF) City of Gloucester (LF) Fragrant Gold* (LF) Fred Gibson (LF) Gold Crown (LF) Peace (LF) Summer Sunshine (LF) Sunsilk (CF)
Apricot/ tangerine	Colibri* (M) Darling Flame* (M) Peek-a-Boo (M)	Alpine Sunset* (LF) Glenfiddich (CF) Judy Garland (CF) Just Joey (LF) Tenerife* (LF) Whisky Mac* (LF) Zambra (CF)	Anne Harkness (CF) Apricot Silk (LF) Diorama* (LF) Doris Tysterman (LF) Fragrant Delight* (CF) Lady Sylvia* (LF) Perle d'Or* (O) Woburn Abbey* (CF)
Bicoloured	Baby Masquerade (M) Little Flirt* (M) Magic Carousel (M) Stars 'n' stripes* (M)	Candy Stripes* (LF) Colorama (LF) Colour Wonder (LF) Harry Wheatcroft (LF) Redgold (CF) Sue Lawley (CF)	Chivalry (LF) Double Delight* (LF) Escapade* (CF) Eye Paint (CF) Kronenbourg (LF) Masquerade (CF) Matangi (CF) My Choice* (LF) Rose Gaujard (LF) Southampton (CF)

'Blessings'
Large-flowered rose

'Iceberg'
Cluster-flowered rose

'Angela Rippon'
Miniature rose

'Ballerina'
Modern shrub rose

PICK OF THE ROSES

C = Climber; CF = Cluster-flowered (Floribunda); LF = Large-flowered (Hybrid tea);
M = Miniature; O = Old roses; R = Rambler; S = Modern shrub;
W = Wild (Species); * = Scented
(For an example of each of these eight rose categories, see the pictures below and opposite)

$3\frac{1}{2}$-5ft	5-7ft	7ft +	Colour
Elizabeth Harkness* (LF) Frau Karl Druschki (O) Mme Hardy* (O)	Blanc Double de Coubert* (O) Prosperity* (O)	Félicité et Perpétue (R) Iceberg (C) Mme Alfred Carrière* (C) Nevada (S) *R. filipes* 'Kiftsgate'* (W) Sander's White* (R) White Cockade (C)	**White**
Ballerina* (S) Frau Dagmar Hastrup (*or* Hartopp)* (S) Lavender Lassie* (S) Old Blush (O) Pink Grootendorst (S) Queen Elizabeth (CF)	Fantin-Latour* (O) Königin von Dänemark* (O)	Albertine (R) Aloha* (C) Bantry Bay (C) Blessings* (C) Dorothy Perkins (R) François Juranville* (R) Pink Perpétue (C) Sarah van Fleet* (S) Zéphirine Drouhin (C)	**Pink**
Charles de Mills (O) Dorothy Wheatcroft (CF) Fountain* (S)	Heidelberg (S) Roseraie de l'Hay* (S) *R. moyesii* 'Geranium' (W)	Altissimo (C) Crimson Shower (R) Danse du Feu (C) Ena Harkness* (C) Excelsa (R) Paul's Scarlet (C) *R. moyesii* (W) Sympathie* (C)	**Red**
Chinatown* (CF) Golden Wings* (S) Mountbatten* (CF)	Frühlingsgold (S) *R. xanthina* 'Canary Bird' (S)	Casino (C) Dreaming Spires* (C) Emily Gray* (R) Goldfinch* (R) Leverkusen (C) *R. hugonis* (W) Royal Gold (C) Wedding Day* (R)	**Yellow**
Buff Beauty* (O)	Fred Loads* (S)	Compassion* (C) Meg* (C) Schoolgirl* (C)	**Apricot/ tangerine**
Adolf Horstmann (LF) Erfurt* (O) Molly McGredy (CF) Rosa Mundi (O)	Frühlingsmorgen* (S) Joseph's Coat (S) Variegata di Bologna* (O)	American Pillar (R) Dortmund (C) Handel (C) Piccadilly (C)	**Bicoloured**

Rosa hugonis
Wild rose

'Zéphirine Drouhin'
Climber

'Albertine'
Rambler

Charles de Mills'
Old rose

RUNNER BEANS

Setting problem

What is the secret for getting runner beans to set well? Mine produce magnificent flowers, but not many turn into beans.

At least you're halfway to producing good crops: a frequent complaint by many gardeners is that they can't get their beans to flower. Reluctance to flower is usually the result of over-generous feeding and watering.

The root of your setting problem may be that your beans are growing in a chilly or windy part of the garden, that bees and other pollinating insects shun. Next year, try another part of the garden, or make a windbreak of plastic netting or plant a sheltering row of Jerusalem artichokes upwind of where you plan to put your beans.

The traditional method of getting beans to set is to spray or syringe the plants with water when they are in full flower. Yet according to the Institute of Horticultural Research at Wellesbourne, who have been conducting experiments over several years, there is little evidence that this has any effect on pollination and it sometimes actually seems to discourage setting. You would probably get a better result by watering the soil thoroughly in dry weather. This will help the flowers to last longer, so increasing the chances of pollination.

If your entire garden is too draughty to encourage bees, then you might do better to abandon the traditional red-flowered runner beans and try some of the self-pollinating white or pink-flowered varieties instead. 'Sunset' (pale pink), or the white-flowered 'Mergoles' or 'White Achievement' may suit your case – and they have the added advantage of being early croppers.

Wigwams or rows?

What's the advantage of growing beans wigwam fashion, rather than in straight rows? Do they crop better that way?

The main advantage is that the wigwam saves space in a small garden. Four to ten poles, each supporting one plant, spaced 6-12in apart at the base and tied together near the top is a convenient way to grow runner beans if you're short of room or if you only want a small crop.

A minor bonus is that you'll get a larger number of straight beans – the ones that have grown hanging down inside the wigwam without becoming entangled with stems or foliage. Of course, their skins will be pale, due to their being shielded from the light by the surrounding leaves; but they will taste none the worse for that. Nevertheless, if you have the room, there's no doubt that the most productive way to grow runner beans is in twin rows. Space the rows 2ft apart – the supports should stand at least 6ft tall – and allow 6in between each plant. This method should yield around 6lb of beans per foot of double row.

Beans reborn

The other day, when clearing out my old bean plants, I wondered if they might grow again if I left them in the ground until next year. Do you think they would?

In a balmier climate they certainly would. Their roots are really fleshy tubers – similar to dahlias but not so plump – and are quite capable of storing sufficient food during the summer to see them through the dormant months to the spring. Unfortunately, the tubers won't survive our winters outdoors, so if you want to keep them, you'll have to dig them up in autumn and store them in a frost-free shed or greenhouse in pots or deep boxes of peat or compost. Lightly water the compost occasionally to prevent the tubers from shrivelling.

When the new shoots appear in spring, let the tubers get plenty of light. In May, harden them off over a period of two or three weeks by moving them outdoors during warm days and bringing them in at night. Gradually increase the length of time you leave them outside, and set them out in the garden in late May or early June when the risk of frost is virtually over.

Runner beans kept over the winter in this way will normally flower and crop two or three weeks earlier than plants raised from seed. But they won't be so vigorous and the yield will be much lower.

ALL ABOUT RUNNER BEANS

- Runner beans do best in slightly alkaline soil that drains freely but won't dry out in summer. A sunny, reasonably sheltered position encourages pod setting.
- Prepare the soil in autumn or winter by digging an 18in deep trench and covering the bottom with a 6in layer of moisture-retentive compost, rotted manure, or garden and kitchen waste (see *Deep feed*, page 300).
- To ensure a harvest from late July onwards, sow the seeds under glass in late April and set out the plants four weeks later or when the last frosts are over. Raise the plants in individual peat pots or flower pots to minimise root disturbance when transplanting.
- Alternatively, sow outdoors between early May and early June, depending on when the chance of frost is gone from your district, for a harvest between August-October. Rake Growmore into the soil 10-14 days before sowing, at the rate of 1-2oz per sq yd.
- Space the plants 6in apart, providing 6-8ft high canes, bean poles or plastic nets as supports. Allow 2ft between double rows with 3ft pathways between each pair of rows.
- Loosely tie the stems in to their supports to encourage earlier climbing; when doing so, always twist the stems anticlockwise.

Black bean riddle

Each autumn I keep some of my bean crop to plant as seeds in the following spring. But this year, I see that some of the beans I kept are completely black, instead of the normal pinky-brown. Are they diseased?

No. What's happened is that bees or other insects have transferred pollen from different varieties in nearby gardens to your plants, cross-pollinating the flowers. You now have a new variety.

But don't get too excited, because it is not uncommon for black seeds to develop, and the plants aren't likely to crop any better. However, it could be interesting to see how they fare – grow them alongside your normal variety and compare the results.

Indoors or out

Is it better to start runner beans off in seed trays indoors, or to sow them directly into the bed outdoors?

It's safer to sow the seeds in individual flowerpots or peat pots in the greenhouse, cold frame, or perhaps on a sunny windowsill indoors.

Outdoor sowings can fail if the weather and soil remain wet and cold for the first two to three weeks after the seeds have been sown. If the soil temperature is below 10°C (50°F), runner bean seeds will have to struggle for several weeks to germinate, and it's likely that many will rot. For this reason, it's best to delay outdoor sowings until early May in the South and West, and until late May or early June in colder areas. Cloches placed over the sowing area at least two weeks beforehand will help the soil to warm up more quickly and the plants can remain covered until they outgrow the cloches.

Indoor sowings can begin in late April. Allow four weeks between sowing and setting out the plants in the garden – transplanting should be done when the risk of frost is virtually over, normally late May or early June, when the plants are at least 3-4in high.

Seed trays are often used to raise runner beans, but the trays' lack of depth causes grave disturbance to the roots when the plants are divided. Sowing the seeds in individual 3in or 3½in diameter flowerpots reduces the transplanting shock. Better still, use tall peat pots which can be set out intact, leaving the roots to grow through the sides of the pots into the surrounding soil with no disturbance at all.

How to dry beans

I always find some dried runner bean seeds at the end of the season. Are they edible?

Yes – but only if they're cooked. Like red kidney beans, they can cause stomach upsets if they're eaten raw. You cook them like *haricots secs* (dried french beans). For details of how to prepare them safely, see *Cook for safety*, page 144.

To dry runner beans for winter use, shell them when the pods are brittle, and let the beans dry out in a sunny place indoors for a few days. Then store them in jars. Any you don't eat before the spring can be used to grow next year's crop.

Net versus poles

A neighbour tells me that beans grown on plastic netting will do far better than on the canes and poles I use. Is this true?

The beans couldn't care less and will do equally well on either. The netting has a certain appeal in that it involves rather less work than the old-fashioned method, and is maybe a little cheaper.

A disadvantage is that however tightly you've strained the wires, as the plants grow, they cause the nets to sag, reducing the overall height of the plants and sometimes allowing some of the lower beans to rest on the soil. So make sure your main posts are rigid (see the picture on the right) and, if your net runs are especially long, put in further supports for every 6ft of length.

Removing the tangled stems from the netting in the autumn can be a chore, but it's lessened if you cut them out with secateurs while they are still pliable. Don't wait until they are dry and hard.

Is small beautiful?

Dwarf runner beans seem a lot less trouble. But will they give me as good a crop as the tall climbing types?

For yield, the dwarf varieties can't begin to compare with the climbers. You'd be lucky to get 10-15lb from a 10ft row of dwarf beans – where a standard variety might give twice this weight. Also, the pods borne on dwarf plants are much shorter and often less straight than those grown on tall varieties, and they are more likely to be splashed by mud and nibbled by slugs.

The advantage of dwarf varieties is that they don't require canes, poles or netting, though it's sometimes necessary to provide 2ft sticks to stop the plants flopping over. One way to get the best of both worlds is to plant the tall varieties 'Scarlet Emperor', 'Sunset' or 'Kelvedon Marvel'. They can be grown as dwarf plants by pinching out the tip of the main stems when they are 12-15in high and thereafter pinching out the sideshoots every week. Space the plants 2ft apart to allow for their bushy habit and provide twiggy sticks to hold them upright.

Short and curling

Whatever runner bean variety I grow, the pods are stunted and try to turn into corkscrews. How can I get them to grow long and straight?

It's all a matter of good gardening. Most runner bean varieties are capable of producing straight pods 12-15in long, and 'Enorma', 'Streamline' and 'Prizewinner' will exceed 18in if the plants are given good conditions.

A sheltered, sunny position and deeply dug soil enriched with peat, well-rotted stable manure or garden compost will encourage sturdy pod growth.

From the time the pods start to form, give plenty of water. If the soil dries out it will check development. During dry weather it may be necessary to apply 1-2 gallons of water per square yard every three or four days to keep the soil moist.

Thin the pods by taking two or three from each cluster when they are between 1in and 2in long. Those that remain will get a bigger share of the available nutrients, and could grow up to 6in longer than they would if you didn't thin. Pods that get tangled in netting or their own stems won't grow as long and straight as those hanging without restriction. So keep an eye on the plants and release any small pods in danger of entanglement before the damage is caused.

Cool, clear water

Can you give me a watering programme for runner beans, please? Mine always seem thirsty.

The rules are simple. Hold back on the watering of young plants until they flower, since over-watering them encourages the growth of leaves and stems at the expense of flower buds – though, of course, you should never allow the soil to dry out to the point where the plants actually wilt.

Beans need water most when they are flowering and producing pods. Nevertheless, even at this stage, you would be unwise to keep the soil permanently saturated. Roots made lazy by the abundance of moisture fail to stretch out in search of nutrients. This can lead to poor crops and even to root rot, especially if the soil is on the heavy side and doesn't drain freely.

So what you do, according to the Institute of Horticultural Research at Wellesbourne, near Stratford-upon-Avon, is this: throughout the flowering and pod-growing periods, give your runner beans 1-2 gallons of water per square yard twice a week.

For good beans, you will have to follow this watering routine even in wet summers, since the dense foliage of the plants deflects rain from the root area.

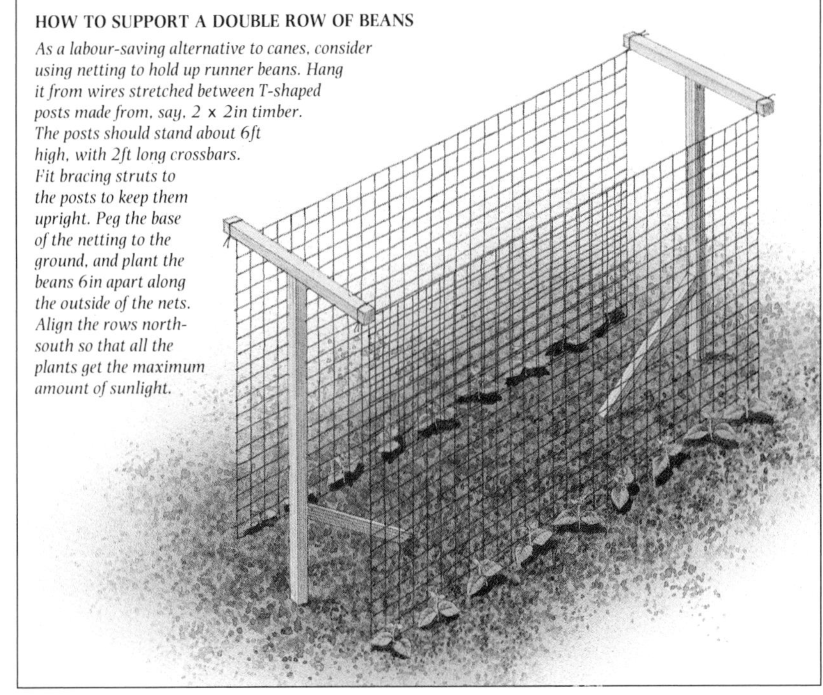

HOW TO SUPPORT A DOUBLE ROW OF BEANS

As a labour-saving alternative to canes, consider using netting to hold up runner beans. Hang it from wires stretched between T-shaped posts made from, say, 2 x 2in timber. The posts should stand about 6ft high, with 2ft long crossbars. Fit bracing struts to the posts to keep them upright. Peg the base of the netting to the ground, and plant the beans 6in apart along the outside of the nets. Align the rows north-south so that all the plants get the maximum amount of sunlight.

Deep feed

Will beans get a better boost from deep-dug manure, or, as I've been told, from a quick surface feed of, say, Growmore?

They need a bit of both, really, though the deep-dug manure is the more important. The loosened soil will help the roots to grow downwards to find the rich organic matter and the extra moisture the plants need.

To make sure that the roots have this rich organic base, dig a trench in late winter, and make it about 18in deep and 2ft wide. In fact, there's no need to use compost or manure. Simply leave the trench open and throw in vegetable peelings, egg shells, fallen leaves, newspapers, old telephone directories, anything that breaks down into moisture-retentive compost; this does not include the coated paper of colour magazines.

When you have accumulated a loose layer 6in or so deep along the length of the trench, top up with soil to ground level, and you're almost ready to plant. About ten days or a couple of weeks before doing so, lightly rake in Growmore fertiliser at 1-2oz to the square yard to help the beans get off to a good start.

Living space

How far apart should runner beans be planted? The advice on the seed packs seems to differ.

The actual spacing within the rows should be governed by the number of rows you're planning and the room between them. For example, a 6in spacing between plants is fine if you grow one row on its own, or two rows 2ft apart. A path at least 3ft wide should separate each pair of rows. On the other hand, a 9in spacing is better for the plants if they are going to be grown in twin rows only 18in apart with 3-4ft paths.

Experiments conducted by the Institute of Horticultural Research have shown that the more even the plant arrangement, the higher the yield is likely to be. For example, the researchers found that 2ft twin rows separated by 3ft wide paths gave a 12 per cent higher yield than a 12in twin row and a 4ft path. This finding held good whether the plants in each row were 6in, 12in, 18in, 24in or 30in apart. Their experiments also showed that planting two runner beans at each cane, instead of one, could lower the yield by up to 20 per cent.

Thrifty beans

I'm on a small economy drive and would like to save some of my runner beans to plant as seed next year. How do I go about it?

In late August choose one or two clusters of long, straight healthy pods and allow them to develop their seeds. At first, the pods will turn dark green, shiny and bulging from the swelling seeds within. After about four to six weeks, when the seeds have finished growing, the pods will become brittle and straw-coloured. At this stage, cut the pods from their stalks and leave them to dry out in a sunny place indoors for several weeks.

When the pods are quite dry, remove all the seeds, but keep only those which are large and undamaged – watch out for and discard any that have small round holes because they may contain seed beetle grubs. If you store your seeds in an airtight container – a biscuit tin, for example – in a dry, cool room, they should remain viable for at least two years. The worst possible way to store seeds is to put them in a paper envelope and leave them on a shelf in a greenhouse or shed. The damp atmosphere encourages fungus moulds to grow on the skins and eventually kill the seeds.

A good strain of home-saved seeds selected each autumn can crop just as well as named varieties purchased each year.

Pests and diseases: how to keep them away

My runner bean seedlings are like gorgonzola cheeses. Holes are everywhere – in the seed leaves and in the stems. What can I do about it?

It sounds as if your beans are being raided by the tiny, $\frac{1}{8}$in long, white maggots of the bean seed fly. Throw out damaged seedlings and sow a new batch. Prevent damage to them by sprinkling into the seed drills an insecticide based on diazinon, phoxim or bromophos. Try, too, to keep the new plants growing quickly. That way, they will pass more rapidly through the vulnerable seedling stage. If it's any consolation, the bean seed fly does at least do its damage early enough for you to consider starting again. Some other common bean troubles are more difficult to handle.

- **BLACK BEAN APHID** Thick colonies of blackfly infest the shoots and undersides of leaves during the summer, reducing the vigour of the plants. Wash them off with a forceful jet of water from a hosepipe, and remove very badly infested leaves. Alternatively, spray with pirimicarb.
- **SEED BEETLE** Look out for small round holes in the bean seeds. Don't sow any which are affected; germination will be slow and the seedlings weak.
- **ANTHRACNOSE** Pods and stems develop brown spots and patches, which frequently turn pink in wet weather. Leaves discolour before withering. Dwarf beans are the varieties worst affected by the disease, especially in cool, wet summers. Remove and burn affected plants. Spray the remainder at ten-day intervals with benomyl, thiophanate-methyl or carbendazim.
- **FOOT AND ROOT ROTS** These fungus diseases, which blacken and rot the roots and lower stems, build up in the soil if beans are grown in the same spot for several years. The leaves turn yellow and the plants collapse. Remove diseased plants and do not grow beans in the same place for at least five years. Alternatively, try treating the soil in autumn with Armillatox.
- **HALO BLIGHT** Leaves on seedlings and young plants bear small brown spots which later become ringed by a characteristic yellow halo. Affected plants become stunted and the pods may develop greasy spots. To check the disease's spread, remove and burn infected plants; spray the rest with a copper compound before the first pods develop. Avoid, in future, soaking seeds before sowing in order to hasten their germination. Because the disease is carried on the seeds, this technique can allow one infected bean to contaminate a whole batch.
- **NO FLOWERS** Excessive water and fertiliser tends to encourage lush growth at the expense of flowers. If your beans develop few flowers, stop watering and feeding at once. Next year, limit your feeding to one dose of a low-nitrogen fertiliser just before sowing or planting. Until the plants flower, water the soil only when the top 3in or so of ground dries out. Once flowers form, water freely to help to swell the crop.
- **POOR SETTING** Occasionally bean pods may fail to develop because sparrows damage the flowers. Consider using nets or a chemical deterrent to keep the birds away. See also *Setting problem*, page 298.

Chop or not?

I have a tidy mind, and when my runner bean plants straggle over the path, I'm inclined to cut them back. Does this do any harm?

The stems are quite tough and are not likely to rot where they've been cut, but you can't expect a record crop if you remove a lot of flowering growth. Most gardeners use supports which rise about 6-8ft above the ground, even though it's not unusual for the plants to grow another 2ft or so taller. Pinching out the tip of the main stems when they reach the top of their supports checks their upward progress, and encourages the growth of sideshoots. These sideshoots benefit from the nutrients that would otherwise have gone towards main stem growth, and are thus encouraged to produce earlier flowers and crops.

If you don't want your beans to stand too tall, the length of the stems can be increased by training their lower parts to grow horizontally instead of vertically. Wait until the plants are about 2ft high. Then, carefully unravelling 15-18in of the stem and keeping it just above the ground, twist it anticlockwise around a horizontal string, then up another string 12-18in farther along the row. By layering each plant in this way, you can let each main stem grow a foot or two longer before it outgrows its supports.

RUST

Chrysanthemum killer

I've heard that there's a killer disease of chrysanthemums called white rust. What are its symptoms, and how do I protect my plants against it?

White rust – *Puccinia horiana* – is indeed a killer, though not one you should lose too much sleep over. British import and quarantine controls have made encounters with it fairly rare.

Just in case you do meet it, the first symptom is yellowish blotches on the top surfaces of the leaves. These develop brown centres, while the undersides develop dirty pink pustules that turn white.

There is no cure, and you must destroy infected plants. But before doing so, you are obliged by law to report the presence of the disease to the Ministry of Agriculture, Fisheries and Food. The ministry's office will be listed in your local phone book under 'Agriculture'.

Patchy pelargoniums

The leaves of my geraniums – pelargoniums, to be precise – have suddenly developed brown, powdery rings on their undersides. Is this the dreaded rust, and if so what do I do about it?

Yes, it is rust but it's not so dreaded as all that – at least not the variety that hits pelargoniums. There is no need to destroy the plants unless the disease persists into next year, though infected leaves must be removed and burnt.

If the pelargoniums are under glass, reduce the humidity by ventilating the greenhouse. Indoors or outdoors, give the plants a fortnightly spray of thiram.

RUST ON THE RAMPAGE *Bright orange patches forming on the underside of rose leaves are a symptom of rose rust, one of a group of fungal diseases that attack a wide variety of plants. Treat by spraying with a fungicide.*

ALL ABOUT GETTING RID OF RUST

RUST is the all-embracing name given to a large number of fungal diseases, some of which have lengthy and complex life cycles. The name is also applied to the symptoms of the diseases – generally brown, orange or yellow powdery masses of spores which develop on affected leaves and stems, and occasionally on flowers and seed pods as well. Rust is not usually a killer, but it affects a great many plants, and treatment often differs. These are the main groups affected and how to treat them.

- PLANTS UNDER GLASS Chrysanthemums and carnations are the most vulnerable. Rusts are encouraged by high humidity, so increase ventilation. Remove infected leaves and destroy severely diseased plants. Spray the rest with thiram.
- ROSES The danger signal is bright orange pustules on branches, leaves and hips. Spray regularly with thiram or a copper compound. Destroy badly infected plants.
- SWEET WILLIAM *(Dianthus barbatus)* Very susceptible, particularly in rich soil. The signs are pale green spots on the topsides, brown spore masses on the undersides of leaves; flowering is poor. There is no treatment. Don't grow sweet williams in manured plots.
- HOLLYHOCKS Nearly all hollyhocks acquire the telltale orange pustules on leaves, stems and seed pods; but, unsightliness apart, rust has little effect on the plants. Best to sow new hollyhocks each year. Spray the seedlings with thiram.
- ANTIRRHINUMS Destroy infected plants at the first sign. Ask for, and grow, resistant varieties.
- HYPERICUMS (including Rose of Sharon) Treat in the same way as roses.
- PLUMS Upper sides of leaves develop tiny yellow spots, while the undersides turn brown. The leaves drop off early, which may weaken young trees. Spray with a copper compound or thiram when the fruits are half grown, and again after harvest. Plums are infected by the same species of rust that attacks anemones, wild or cultivated. Do not grow the two plants near each other.
- CONIFERS Rust on needles is not important, but swellings and the twiggy growths on branches known as 'witches' brooms', which are often caused by rust, should be cut out 6in below the infected area. Do not grow junipers near sorbus species such as whitebeam and mountain ash – some rusts need both groups as host plants, and cannot survive if either one is missing.
- OTHER TREES AND SHRUBS Rust will be troublesome only if the plants are poorly fed or thirsty. Mulching and watering will usually put matters right.
- MINT Very susceptible to a species of rust that in spring causes swollen, distorted stems bearing red spores. Destroy the plants and, to prevent future attacks, burn off the withered top growth of the mint clump each winter. Alternatively, establish a healthy new mint bed by washing cuttings in cold water, then immersing them for ten minutes in water heated to about 46°C (115°F) before planting out – though in time they may still become infected. Savory is also prone to this type of rust.
- OTHER VEGETABLES AND HERBS Rust is most likely to appear on plants suffering from potassium deficiency. Feed with a high-potash fertiliser to minimise the risk.

SAGE

Windowsill herb

Can I grow sage on the kitchen windowsill?

A great idea, for there are few plants with a wider range of culinary uses. Sage and onion stuffing apart, the herb admirably complements such rich meats as pork and duck. Whole leaves may be laid on joints during roasting, while chopped fresh leaves are often added to kebabs, pickles, salads and cheese. Sage tea was drunk all over Europe long before the other kind came from China, and in the Middle Ages was considered the remedy for practically everything from falling hair to cholera.

The leaves were also put among clothes to discourage moths and mice.

Sage should be perfectly happy in a 6in pot on the kitchen windowsill, though it tends to be short-lived as an indoor plant. Once it starts to get woody and untidy in appearance, propagate new plants from cuttings and start again. Plant your sage in John Innes No 2; it does not require anything stronger and does not enjoy rich composts.

Sage advice

A friend wants to take cuttings from my sage, but neither of us is sure if the plant can be propagated in this way. If it is possible, when is the best time to do it?

You can take sage cuttings from non-flowering shoots at any time from mid to late summer. Cuttings taken directly from fresh young shoots will often root quite successfully, but it is better to use a heeled cutting. To obtain a heeled cutting, tear off (don't cut) a small shoot of last season's growth in such a way as to leave a sliver, or 'heel', of the woody stem attached.

Sage cuttings will root easily in a pan containing a mixture of either peat and sharp sand, or peat and perlite, in equal volumes. Before planting, dip the bottoms of the cuttings in a hormone rooting powder. This will speed up the rooting process and give some protection against fungal diseases. Water regularly, keeping the compost moist but not sodden, but don't get water on the hairy foliage of the young plants. In still, humid indoor conditions, this encourages the appearance of leaf spots and causes the leaves to fall off prematurely.

Once your cuttings have rooted, pot them up individually in 3in pots, using John Innes No 2. Always take many more sage cuttings than you need. Even in ideal conditions only a small percentage of them will root.

SAND

Bone dry

My garden is more or less pure Surrey sandstone, and to make matters worse it is on a slope, so it is forever drying out. What can I do to keep it moist?

Dig in all the bulky organic matter – well-rotted manure or compost – that you can find, and grow ground-cover plants to limit moisture loss by evaporation. Both will help to make your soil act less like a sieve and more like a sponge. If the slope is severe enough you may have to consider terracing it, holding back the soil and the moisture with stones.

On a gentle slope, your best solution may simply be to keep your plants – vegetables or flowers – mulched throughout the warm spells. Firm the soil between the rows and the plants early in the season, and mulch it with about 3-4in of peat or pulverised bark, or a mixture of both. On shrubs and roses, you can mulch with well-rotted garden compost or farmyard manure.

In the early spring, dig in bulky organic material such as chopped straw and farmyard manure. These are the general rules to follow on sand:

DON'T dig your soil until early spring. Autumn digging followed by frosts tends to break sandy soils up even more.

DON'T plant moisture-loving species such as mimulus, cornus or rhododendron hybrids.

DO tread down your soil after digging to slow evaporation and hold the water in.

DO grow ground-cover plants such as hypericum, heathers and ivy. Their roots will help to stabilise the soil – and stable soil is better able to trap moisture in its pores.

Endless watering

My soil is so sandy that I have to keep watering it almost endlessly in summer. Is there a time-saving way to do it?

A hose and sprinkler is as good a method as any. The cheap rotary sprays, which spin round under pressure from the water supply, are perfectly satisfactory. Oscillating sprinklers, which water in a square or rectangular pattern, are more expensive but do a better job more quickly.

Some gardeners puncture holes in an old hosepipe and run it round the vegetable patch and the flowerbeds and just turn on the tap for a comprehensive soaking. Simple, but effective. Or you can buy special perforated hoses to do the same job.

The most elaborate system is to lay underground pipes through the garden with pop-up valves which automatically spring upwards and start spraying as soon as you turn the tap on.

Long term, the only way to save watering time – and, possibly, money if water meters should become widespread in Britain – is to build your soil's ability to hold moisture. That means adding plenty of soil-conditioning, bulky organic matter such as manure and compost – the more the better.

Sand-lovers

I have heard it said that sandy soil is good for growing cauliflowers, so I am thinking of putting some in my sandy patch. Is this true, and if so, why?

It is partly true. Cauliflowers that mature in summer and autumn need to be grown quickly, and they will do this in a sandy soil because their roots can reach speedily through the loose and airy ground structure.

But sandy soil alone is not enough. Cauliflowers also need access to the moisture and richness contained in well-rotted manure or compost. Cauliflowers that are allowed to take a long time to grow, and which mature slowly, often finish up with curds no bigger than a tennis ball. And that happens more commonly on heavy clay soils.

Other vegetables that like the free-draining and loose structure of sand are carrots and all the other root crops, and peas and beans. But you'll still have to water and feed them – they need their nutrients, too.

Summer puddles

The soil in my area is very sandy, yet I still get puddles of water lying around, even after summer rain, in a way you would expect only on clay. What is happening?

Soil compaction. It is most likely on the lawn, which gets trodden on much more than the flowerbeds or vegetable patch.

Soil particles and organic debris are probably blocking the channels and air pores through which the water would normally drain. The solution is simple: spike the lawn in autumn or spring with an ordinary garden fork. Press the tines in about 4in, wiggle the handle to ease the soil apart, lift and do the same again at intervals of about 4in all over the compacted area.

If the puddles are lying on cultivated areas, the problem is probably more deep-seated. The puddles are likely to be the result of a 'pan', a compacted layer of soil about 12in underground. The pan is not letting water through, and so the moisture is building up and flooding the growing zone. The solution then is hard work: double dig the whole area next spring. For details of how to do this, see *How to double dig a bed*, page 121.

Hungry plants

I have fed my garden soil plenty of fertiliser and watered the plants regularly, yet they still appear half starved. What do I do now?

Work in some chopped-up farmyard manure or well-rotted garden compost. You have the classic sandy soil growth problem: not enough organic matter in the soil. The structure is too open – too much like a sieve, and not enough like a sponge. As a result, water, nutrients and all that expensive fertiliser you are throwing on is simply being washed through into the subsoil, where it's beyond the reach of the roots. Feed in the organic matter *every* time you dig your ground. That way you can cut down on fertiliser and your plants will lose that hungry look.

How to lighten soil

Clay soils are described as heavy, sandy soils as light. So, can I lighten my heavy soil by adding sand? And does it matter which sort of sand I use?

Yes, you can lighten any soil by adding sand, though you'd need tens of tons of it to do an entire garden. And yes, it does matter which sort you use. Choose horticultural grit, which is a coarse sand with particles up to 4mm (about $^1/_6$in) across. Make a half-and-half mixture of sand and peat and scatter it on between autumn and spring at the rate of about a bucketful to the square yard. As worms mix it with the ground beneath, it will liven up the clay and give your plants a much better soil structure to grow in.

Don't use a finer grade of sand, and don't use sea sand. It is too fine and its salt will do your plants no good. Peat, manure and lime can all be used as well to improve a heavy soil, but their effects, though valuable, are temporary. Sand's effects are permanent.

The reverse of this argument, by the way, is not true: it is never sensible to spread clay on a sandy soil in order to make it heavier. The best answer to that problem is to dig in bulky organic matter such as peat, manure and compost.

The right sand

Is there a difference between lawn sand and other sands?

There certainly is, and it's important not to mix them up. Lawn sand is a mixture of sulphate of ammonia, sulphate of iron and fine sand. It's spread on the lawn at the rate of about 4oz to the square yard to keep down moss and give the lawn a boost (sulphate of ammonia is a high-nitrogen fertiliser). The sand is nothing more than a medium to carry the two chemicals and make them easier to spread.

Lawn sand is of no use elsewhere in the garden. It won't do a lot to counteract any clay in your soil – lime would be more useful for that – and its fertiliser content could overload your ornamental plants and vegetables with nitrogen, giving you too much leaf and too few flowers.

Root mixture

Cuttings, I am told, root best in a half-and-half mixture of peat and coarse sand. Does that mean any kind of sand?

No, it doesn't. The job of the sand in the peat mix is to keep the mixture free-draining and let in the air so vital to early root formation. Fine sand is no good. Its tiny particles would do nothing to help water to drain out or to let air in. You need sand with coarser particles, 3-4mm ($^{1}/_{8}$-$^{1}/_{6}$in) across.

You needn't stick to sand. Horticultural grades of perlite and vermiculite, which you can buy in most garden centres or shops, do an even better job and the grading is better controlled. Perlite is a type of volcanic ash. Vermiculite is mica that has been expanded by great heat.

Don't be tempted to use builders' sand or sea sand. Both are too fine for the job you want done (they will tend to keep water and air out of the mixture), and sea sand contains harmful sodium salts.

True grit

There is a material called horticultural grit for sale at our garden centre. What is it used for?

It gives added drainage to seed and potting composts. Horticultural grit is usually quartzite which has been crushed and then screened, so that the particles are 3-4mm ($^{1}/_{8}$-$^{1}/_{6}$in) across. Mix it in the compost and you can even decorate the surface with it after potting – it gives a neat and finished look to house plants.

In winter, you can also scatter it on icy paths and drives to make them less slippery.

Vanishing goodness

I'm told that, in wet spells, valuable plant foods are leached out of the soil by the rain – and that this is particularly serious on sandy soil. How do I stop it?

On borders you do it by digging in enough bulky organic matter, such as well-rotted manure or compost, to soak up and hold in the moisture and nutrients. On lawns you do it by spiking the ground with a garden fork, then scattering fine peat over it and brushing it into the holes.

Mind you, these treatments won't stop it permanently or completely. Sandy soil will always need more fertiliser than clay soil because, however much you improve its structure, nutrients will always be 'leached out' – washed away – by rain.

Sand-seekers

Can you tell me some flowers which will thrive on extremely sandy soil?

Choose your favourites from this list – you will see there are quite a lot of sand-lovers. One word of warning: sandy soil is often acid. Where plants will thrive only on acid sand, and not on alkaline sand, this is noted after the plant.

Shrubs and climbers Bamboo, aucuba, azalea (for acid sand only), berberis, broom, buddleia, calluna (acid only), ceanothus, chaenomeles, choisya, cistus, colutea, coronilla, cortaderia, cotinus, cotoneaster, daphne, deutzia, elaeagnus, erica (acid only), escallonia, euonymus, fuchsia, garrya, genista, hebe, helianthemum, hippophae, hydrangea, hypericum, juniper, lavender, ligustrum, lonicera, magnolia, mahonia, philadelphus, phlomis, piptanthus, potentilla, pyracantha, romneya, rosemary, sage, santolina, senecio, spiraea, tamarix, viburnum, wisteria and yucca.

Hardy perennials Achillea, anchusa, anthemis, armeria, aster, aubrieta, bergenia, campanula, chrysanthemum, dianthus, echinops, euphorbia, geranium, gypsophila, hemerocallis, kniphofia, limonium, lupin, mallow, nepeta, oenothera, onopordum, poppy, phlox, salvia, saxifraga, sedum, sempervivum, solidago, thyme and verbascum.

SAVORY

Summer collapse

Why does my summer savory so often keel over at the base and then die?

Summer savory is particularly susceptible to wet soil conditions. In clay soils, it often 'damps off' – rots and collapses at ground level – especially in wet summers. Seeds are usually sown straight into the ground where the plants are wanted, and the seedlings are then thinned out. But if you have recurring trouble with damping off, it is a good idea to sow a few seeds in pots, and then remove all but the strongest seedlings.

Grow the seedlings on in 3in whalehide pots, in a mixture of 3 parts John Innes No 1 to 1 part sharp sand, or grit. This will give them a free-draining compost that should overcome any damping-off problems. Then, in late April or May, tear off the base of the whalehide pot, and plant the savory, pot and all, directly into the garden. Make sure that both the rim of the pot and the level of the compost inside are slightly higher than the surrounding soil. This will stop the plant becoming too damp.

Savouring the difference

What is the difference between winter and summer savory?

Summer savory is a bushy, annual plant, no more than 12in high. It has slender stems, sparsely covered with tiny green leaves, and small, delicate pink or lilac flowers. Sow the seeds in open ground from April onwards, thinning the seedlings to 6-9in apart when large enough to handle.

Winter savory is a perennial, shrubby plant which can also be sown in its permanent site, usually in August. Scatter the seed on the surface of the soil, and do not cover it up. This is one of the few types of seed that need light to germinate. You can also propagate established plants by lifting and dividing them in March. Winter savory has purplish-pink flowers from July to October and, apart from its culinary value, is a useful addition to the flower border. Both summer and winter savory like an open position in free-draining soil.

Both savories have a spicy, peppery flavour and are widely used in soups, egg dishes, salads and in bean dishes. They are widely thought to aid digestion, and are often used to complement such dishes as roast pork and cucumber salad. Summer savory has probably the better flavour. It was introduced to this country by the Romans, who chopped the leaves and mixed them with vinegar to make a sauce.

SCAB

Gladioli plague

I went to replant my gladioli the other day, but some plague had been there before me. Several corms were completely rotted, and a good half of the others were pitted with craters that looked as if they had been varnished over. The point is: should I plant the less damaged corms in the hope that they will flower?

No. Your gladioli have scab, which, though it has the same common name as the scab on apples and pears, is a bacterial not a fungal disease.

Burn all the rotted corms, along with any others that show the slightest sign of damage. Soak the remaining healthy corms for a quarter of an hour or so in a benomyl solution, and plant them somewhere else in the garden – well away from their previous site, where the bacteria will have spent the winter in the soil.

Next year, when digging up your corms for winter storage, clean them off, give them another benomyl soak, and store them in an airy, cool but frost-free place.

The traditional, and quite correct, advice is that you should plant your gladioli in a different place each year. But for those who don't have that much room in their gardens – and nowadays that's most of us – following these rules will give you the best chance of keeping the disease at bay.

Pitted potatoes

Anyone, I was told, could grow potatoes, but my first crop is sending me straight back to the greengrocer. All the skins are scarred and covered with rough-edged scabs that in places almost join together. I'm very disappointed.

You can at least comfort yourself with the knowledge that the damage is only skin deep. Beneath its evil appearance each potato is perfectly edible and will taste just as good as ever. Your crop is suffering from common scab, a fairly mild fungal disease that is most prevalent in lighter soils in dry weather.

Ignore it, and chip or mash the potatoes. But burn the peelings rather than throw them on the compost heap. Next year, dig plenty of compost into the soil before planting; but do not add lime because it encourages the disease. In addition, plant scab-resistant varieties such as 'Arran Pilot' 'Pentland Crown' or 'Maris Peer'.

Common scab has a much deadlier relative known as powdery scab. The symptoms of this fungal disease are round scabs which burst open to release a powdery mass of spores. Affected tubers become deformed and develop an unpleasant, earthy flavour.

There is no cure for powdery scab, which can strike at any time during the growing season, nor any way of preventing it. All you can do is destroy diseased tubers and plants, and not plant potatoes in the same site for several years – maybe as much as ten years, though the severity of infection dwindles with each year that potatoes are not present in the ground. Fortunately, powdery scab is a much rarer disease than the common variety your potatoes have.

Brown crusting on apples

My apples, growing plump and rosy until recently, suddenly developed unsightly patches of brown crust on their skins. Most of the fruits seem to be affected to some degree, from which I assume that the tree itself is diseased. Is this the case, and what do I do about it?

The tree is diseased, but only in a surface sort of way. What it has is scab, a very common fungal disease in apples, crab apples, pears and sometimes in pyracanthas. There would have been earlier symptoms, but you might have missed them.

The fungus's spores lie dormant through the winter in fallen leaves and debris, and are carried onto the trees by wind and rain splash. In spring, they attack young shoots, which develop small blisters; later these burst, showing as small, circular scabs.

The spores multiply and move on to attack the growing foliage, where they form olive-brown patches and may cause premature leaf fall. Finally, as the fruits grow, the spores settle on the skins, with the results you describe. Although disfiguring, the scabs make no difference to the flavour, so as far as your own apples are concerned, you needn't let them bother you. In any case you cannot cure the condition, though you might be able to do something towards preventing its recurrence next year. These are the steps to take:

- Burn the leaves fallen from infected trees in autumn.
- Cut out and destroy scabbed twigs in winter.
- Spray the tree at fortnightly intervals between bud opening and petal fall with benomyl or carbendazim.

BANE OF FRUIT FARMERS *The fungal scab disease that attacks apples and pears is not so much a danger as a disfiguring nuisance, because it scars the fruit. Successive heavy infestations can, however, weaken young trees, and the disease can make commercial crops unsaleable.*

SCALE INSECTS

Sticky, sooty, encrusted leaves

My small bay tree, from which I take bay leaves for cooking, is looking distinctly unwholesome. The leaves are sticky and sooty, and small waxy, brownish-yellow scales have developed on the undersides of the leaves and on the stems. Obviously the plant is sick; can I cure it?

It's probably not feeling too well, but it suffers not from disease but an infestation of scale insects. The scales you see are waxy, honeydew secretions beneath which colonies of females spend almost their entire lives laying their eggs and hatching them out. The young, known as crawlers, emerge on outdoor plants in summer, and on indoor ones at any time of year, to move on and spread the infestation.

The sooty appearance of your leaves is probably caused by a mould which grows on the insects' secretions.

The answer is to catch the crawlers when they're hatching. In late May, spray outdoor plants with malathion, taking particular care to spray the undersides of the leaves, where the insects settle.

Alternatively, you can spray a deciduous tree or shrub in winter with a tar oil wash. That won't help your bay tree, though, because it's evergreen.

If your bay tree, or any other infested plant, is being grown in a greenhouse or indoors, you could also wash off the scales with a soft cloth dipped in soapy water.

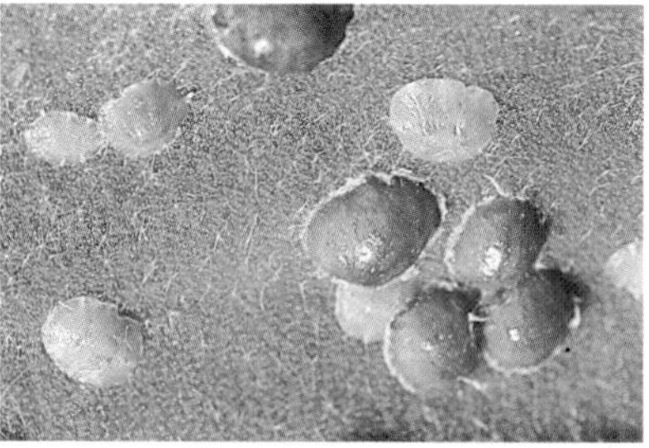

SCALE ARMOUR *Sap-sucking scale insects protect themselves, their eggs and their young beneath a waxy brown, yellow or white secretion which they glue to the undersides of leaves.*

SCORCH

Young leaves wither in spring

As spring advanced, I was startled to see that some of the young leaves on my ornamental maple looked exactly as though someone had waved a blowtorch across them. They were browned and shrivelled at the edges, and sometimes the whole leaf had turned brittle, brown and papery. Is it a disease? And what can I do about it?

It's not a disease. It's a condition called scorch, caused most often by extremes of temperature. In maples and beeches, scorch is the effect of unseasonably cold winds upon tender young leaves. It can give the trees a distinctly autumnal appearance. Similar symptoms appear on greenhouse and house plants in summer, though there the cause is lack of water and too much sun. Move the house plants away from the window, shade the greenhouse panes and keep the soil moist.

Damage from chemical sprays can also produce scorch effects in outdoor plants, but there's little that can be done about them – or, indeed, about your maple.

All you can do, if you can reach them, is to pick off the damaged leaves. This will at least help to reduce the risk of disease or fungus gaining a foothold on the tree. And next time you plant ornamental maples, do it in a more protected part of the garden.

AUTUMN IN SPRING *Maple and beech foliage may be browned like autumn leaves by cold winds in spring. Similar symptoms can be caused in greenhouse plants by too much sun.*

SEEDS

Wallflowers from seed

Can I grow wallflowers from seed – and, if I can, should I start them indoors or out?

Wallflowers do best if they're sown and grown outdoors. Sow the seed any time between late May and early July, making ½in deep drills with the edge of a hoe in a nursery bed. Be sure the soil is moist – if not, water it thoroughly before sowing.

Water the seedbed whenever the soil looks dry – which can be at least twice a week if the weather is dry. Wallflower seedlings generally emerge a week or so after sowing. As soon as they are up, dust them with an insecticide to prevent attacks by flea beetles. Plant them out in their flowering site in October and they will flower in the following spring and early summer.

Where to sow hardy annuals

Can I sow hardy annual flower seeds straight into open ground outside?

Provided the soil is right, yes. Go by the soil conditions rather than by any precise calendar date suggested on the seed packet. The soil needs to be moist but not sodden, crumbly but not dust-dry.

If the soil has been well weathered over the winter, resist the temptation to knock it down into a fine tilth until just before sowing. If you prepare the seedbed days in advance, there's always the risk that a heavy shower will compact the surface and make sowing more difficult. But it is important to make sure the soil is firmed immediately before sowing. Loose, puffy soil is just as unsuited for seeds as hard, compacted ground. For the best seedbed, shuffle your feet across the soil without stamping it down, and finish off by gently raking the surface. If you are going to use a fertiliser – and this depends on what you're growing; nasturtiums, for instance, flower better in unfertilised soil – scatter it on at the raking stage.

Damping off

How can I stop emerging seedlings damping off?

Pay extra attention to garden hygiene. Damping off – a fungus disease – causes devastation among many seedlings, especially asters and antirrhinums. Seedlings come up and then collapse at the base and die. Unsterilised compost and damp growing conditions aggravate the disease. Use a proprietary seed compost in a light, well-ventilated working area, and you will go a long way towards eradicating damping off.

Don't sow seeds thickly, either. Thinly sown seeds are less susceptible. Another useful precaution is to water seed trays with Cheshunt compound. If you spot established seedlings succumbing to the disease, try watering with benomyl.

THREE WAYS TO SOW SMALL SEEDS EVENLY

PURPOSE-BUILT seed spreaders can be expensive. Here are three cheap ways to achieve the same results.

1 To distribute small seeds such as grass over a large area, mark out the ground into yard-wide strips with pegs and string. Sprinkle half the seeds along the strips, the other half across the strips. Use the same technique for spreading fertiliser.

2 To sow small seeds in a seedbed, mix them with four times their own volume of silver sand, then sprinkle the mixture along each row. Rows are better than block sowing because they are easier to mark. The sand-and-seed mixture will show up clearly against the dark soil.

3 A variation on the last method, for sowing rows in a seedbed, is to mix small seeds with ordinary wallpaper paste – though be careful to choose a paste that does not contain fungicide. Spoon the mixture into an old plastic bag, snip off one corner and squeeze the mixture out through the hole just as if you were icing a cake.

No need to nick

Every year I spend hours chipping my sweet pea seeds to speed up germination. Is there an easier way to do this, other than nicking each individual seed with a penknife?

Yes, there is. Nicking the seeds is laborious and may well be a waste of time. Not because it doesn't work – it does – but because there are easier ways of achieving the same result. The aim, as with any seed, is to get the sweet pea to germinate quickly to reduce the risk of rotting. The problem is that sweet peas, like some other seeds, have very hard coats – and it takes water a long time, unaided, to seep through the coats to trigger the seeds into growth.

Chipping the seeds with a knife is one method of helping to open a doorway for water. But there are easier ways, such as rubbing them between sheets of sandpaper or shaking them in a jar. For details, see *Getting started*, page 334.

Compost for seeds

Does it matter what compost I use for my indoor seeds – whether it's a John Innes soil-based type or one of the peat-based brands?

Yes, it does matter. John Innes seed compost is a safe bet for most plants raised indoors, but some germinate and develop faster in a peat-based mixture. Peat-based composts are ideal for larger seeds such as salvia and french marigold. And, mixed with about a quarter as much sharp sand, they can be quite satisfactory for alpine varieties.

But be wary of soilless composts that are all peat, with added nutrients. It isn't, for instance, normally a good idea to sow fine-seeded flowers like lobelia and petunia in these composts. This is because the composts are very fibrous, which often leads to air pockets developing near the surface – and tiny seeds can die in such pockets.

If you're uncertain which to use, stick to John Innes seed composts. Your seedlings may take a little longer to develop, but the final plants will be just as good.

Ordeal by fire

You can now buy the seeds of species that come from dry tropical zones where, I'm told, it takes a bush fire to break their dormancy – plants like the lovely South African protea. I've tried raising such seeds in the past, but had little success. Is there a practical way of providing their baptism by fire?

Put them in a metal kitchen sieve, over a lighted candle – a few seconds is long enough. The rounded, hard-coated seeds will jump about at first, like Mexican jumping beans. When they stop, they're ready for sowing.

Very hairy seeds like those of the protea need all the hairs burnt off before they will germinate. You can do this either as before, in a sieve over a candle, or by running a cigarette lighter over them. Then sow them in a frost-free greenhouse.

When it's worth soaking

I've heard that seeds of members of the pea and bean family should be soaked in water before sowing. Is this true – and if it is, what good does it do?

The only advantage in soaking the seeds of legumes such as peas and beans is to speed up germination. And it doesn't work with every member of the family. Dwarf french beans, for instance, have a tendency to 'drown' – they become waterlogged and die. But soaking garden peas, runner beans and broad beans for about 24 hours before sowing gives you a head start of three or four days over conventionally sown, dry seeds.

How deep to sow

Gardeners are always arguing about how deep to sow seeds. How precise do I have to be about this?

As a general rule, cover most seeds with about their own depth of soil or compost. The exceptions are fine seeds and the odd few, such as begonias and celery, that require light to germinate. Mix fine seeds with a little dry silver sand, trickle them over the compost, and don't cover them at all.

The exact depth of the soil is not critical, but it's wise to keep within the range suggested. A typical $\frac{1}{4}$in seed, for instance, will germinate tolerably well if it's covered by anything between about $^{1}/_{10}$in and 1in of soil; it's unlikely to grow at all if it's right on the surface or 6in down.

Seeds that come in from the cold

Some seed packet instructions tell you to freeze the contents, to get the seeds to germinate. Do I put the packet in the refrigerator or the deep freeze?

The deep freeze. Gardeners don't like it, but it's the only way, with some seeds, to break the dormancy and get them to germinate. And it's no good just putting the unopened packet in the freezer: you must first sow the seeds in a tray of seed compost, water them and then put the whole thing in the freezer. If it all seems too drastic a course of action, consider the rationale behind it.

Seeds that need this kind of treatment come from plants that live in mountainous regions or shady places. Take, for instance, a classic example – the lovely, white-flowered Christmas rose, *Helleborus niger*, which flowers in winter and early spring. It flourishes in rich organic soil and dappled shade. In the wild, when it is in flower, there is no leaf canopy on the trees nearby and the plant thrives. But the seeds develop and ripen in early summer, at about the time the surrounding trees have come into full leaf. In some seasons, the resulting shade and virtual exclusion of rain mean that the soil is dry and that any seeds falling onto it fail to germinate.

These seeds become effectively dormant, and then warmth and moisture alone are not enough to break their dormancy. Germination remains inhibited until the spring heralds more favourable conditions. Meanwhile autumn arrives, the leaf canopy overhead disappears and rain falls to moisten the soil. But it is still cold and hostile to germinating seedlings. Winter brings more damp and cold, especially frost. But frost acts on the resting seeds like a signal, telegraphing the near arrival of spring, with all its advantages of light, warmth and moisture. Frost, in fact, breaks the chemical inhibitor in the seeds and allows them to germinate as soon as suitable conditions come along. Placing the seeds in a deep freeze creates a similar effect.

Three weeks of freezing, followed by up to six weeks in the warm, will usually promote germination. If nothing happens after six weeks, put the seeds back in the deep freeze for a further three weeks before bringing them out into the warm again. Some seeds have a double dormancy pattern and need two fake 'winters' in order to germinate.

When to water a seedbed

Local experts say I should water a seedbed before sowing, not after. I can't see what difference it can make – can you?

Yes, although it's not a major difference. The reasoning behind the experts' view is that you shouldn't do anything to make it more difficult for the seeds to grow.

If you water a seed drill or a seed tray before sowing, you can make sure that water gets to the soil or the compost with which the seeds will actually be in contact. You can then sow the seeds and rake loose soil or scatter loose compost over them to keep the moisture in. The seeds themselves will be thoroughly moist, and the loose layer above will give the fragile seedlings an easy passage to the surface.

If you water after you've sown and covered the seeds – particularly if you drop the water on from several feet up – you run two risks. First, you may not put on enough water to reach the seeds. Second, the falling drops could compact the soil surface and turn it into a barrier, which could slow down or stop the seedlings' growth.

More important, though, than whether you water before or after sowing is that all seeds need moisture to germinate. If you sow them in dry soil or compost, they'll just remain dormant until it becomes moist. And the longer they lie inactive, the more likely they are to be attacked by pests or diseases. Also, brisk germination is essential if you want an even crop or flower display.

But a word of warning: once you start watering a seedbed in dry weather, make sure that you keep it up. Seeds are encouraged to germinate by moist conditions. The resulting seedlings will soon perish if you forget to water them

Warm start

I've been told to start my seeds off in the airing cupboard. They do germinate, but they are always yellow and sickly. Why?

You're leaving them in too long. An airing cupboard is a useful place to germinate seeds which need a high temperature to get started – but it's no good for growing the resulting seedlings.

Once seeds germinate, the seedlings need full daylight to thrive and produce good, short-jointed green plants. So as soon as you spot those bulges in the compost of your seed trays that signal the presence of emerging seedlings, take them out into the light. Even one day in warmth and total darkness will lead to pale, spindly seedlings which will take a long time to recover.

Coping with tiny seeds

How can I get even germination of small seeds like primulas?

Use a good seed compost and sow the seeds indoors. Very few of the species with fine, dust-like seeds will do as well if you sow them outdoors in open ground. Once you've prepared your compost in seed pans or trays, mix the seed with a little dry silver sand – just add it to the seed packet and shake it about. Seed and sand should then be fairly evenly mixed and you can trickle the mixture gently onto the compost.

This not only helps to distribute the seed evenly, but you can see, from the sand, which areas are covered. Don't cover fine seeds like these with compost; leave them on the surface. And always water from below, by standing the pans or trays in water. If you water from above, the seeds will just tend to float to the edge of the tray.

Pellets: the pros and costs

Pelleted seeds always seem to be much more expensive than the ordinary kinds. Are they worth the extra money?

The idea behind pelleted seeds is that they are easier to handle, by virtue of their size. Obviously the cost of encapsulating seeds in the clay-like pelleting material means that individual seeds are more expensive. However, there is less waste because the seeds can be placed – and spaced – more accurately from the outset. With ordinary seeds, there is generally a lot of waste with crowded seedlings. On top of that, there is all the time it takes to prick them out or thin them. So on balance, plant for plant, pelleted seeds are no more costly than unpelleted ones.

One tip, though. If you're using pellets, give the compost slightly more water than you would normally use before sowing. The moisture ensures that the coating breaks down quickly – and lets the seeds get off to a good start.

ALL ABOUT VEGETABLE SEEDS

Name	Average life of seeds (*years*)	Average days to germination (*open ground*)	Average time to mature from sowing (*weeks*)
Beans, Broad	2	21	20–26
Beans, French	2	14	9+
Beans, Runner	2	14	13+
Beetroots	3	13	9–13
Broccoli	3	8	39–50
Brussels sprouts	3	8	26–31
Cabbages, Early	3	8	17+
Cabbages, Late	3	8	21+
Carrots	3	16	11–14
Cauliflowers	3	8	13–17
Celeriac	2	8 (indoors)	26–30
Celery	2	8 (indoors)	26–30
Chicory	3	9	17–21
Cucumbers	3	9	10–13
Kale	3	8	29+
Kohl rabi	3	7	11–14
Leeks	2	14	29–34
Lettuces	3	7	9–13
Marrows	3	7	9–13
Onions	2	14	21–30
Parsnips	2	17	21–30
Peas	3	10	11–17
Radishes	3	6	3–6
Salsify	2	12	19–24
Summer spinach	2	11	7–13
New Zealand spinach	2	11	10–12
Swedes	3	8	21+
Sweetcorn	3	9	17+
Tomatoes	5	7 (indoors)	14+
Turnips	3	8	7–12

Saving seeds

I have several half-full packets of vegetable seeds left over from last year. Can the seeds be used this season?

Stored in the dry, most vegetable seeds remain good for two or three years, even though the packet has been opened. For details of particular crops, see the chart on the left. The best place to keep the seeds is in a fridge or in an airtight jar in a cool, dry place such as a shed or garage.

Germination rates gradually decline, however, so if you have any doubts, make a test sowing of, say, 20 seeds in a seed tray indoors. The result will show whether it is worth sowing the rest in the garden. You can apply the same principles to saving the seeds of flowers.

Watch the soil, not the calendar

How can I tell when the ground is just right for sowing?

With difficulty. In the end, it's something you learn largely by trial and error. It varies on different soils and you will need two or three seasons' experience before you're sure of the best time for sowing in your own garden. There are two main factors to watch: crumbliness and moisture.

First, the soil needs to be loose and crumbly and have what gardeners refer to as a good 'tilth' – meaning that its surface layer should be about the consistency of breadcrumbs.

Second, it should not be dust-dry, because seeds need moisture to germinate. On the other hand, it must not be so wet that they are likely to rot before they have a chance to germinate.

Get these two elements right and your seeds will romp away. Get them wrong and your seeds will suffer – even if you sow on exactly the date given on the seed packet or in a gardening book.

Fruits from pips

Can I grow fruit trees and bushes from pips?

You can, but don't bother – except for fun. The reason is that, being hybrids, most fruit varieties will simply not come true from seed. The offspring will vary enormously, both from each other and from the parent varieties. And it won't be just the character of the fruit that differs from the parent. Other features will vary widely, too – and unpredictably. These might include the time of flowering, the ripening of the fruit and even the vigour of the plant. Propagating fruit 'vegetatively' – by cuttings, division or grafting – is the only way to get new plants which are identical to the parent stock (see *Cuttings*, page 107, and *Grafting*, page 160).

If you do, nevertheless, want to grow some pips, treat them as you would any other seeds. Sow them in a pot or tray of seed compost, cover them with a sheet of glass and a sheet of paper (to keep moisture in and light out) and put the container in a warm place such as a windowsill or airing cupboard. As soon as the first seedlings emerge, take off the paper and glass and grow the plants on in the light. Move temperate-latitude plants such as apples and pears outdoors in spring. Grow hot-climate plants such as avocados and oranges in a greenhouse or as house plants.

Why F1 seeds are OK

Are F1 vegetable and flower seeds worth the extra money they cost?

Without a doubt. Most fruits and vegetables grown around the world by modern farmers and gardeners are hybrids – varieties created, often artificially, from interbreeding two or more separate strains. Over generations of selective breeding and cross-fertilising, hybrid plants can be tailored to have almost any set of characteristics. They may have consistently larger fruit, for instance, faster growth or greater resistance to pests and diseases.

Plants which have been bred selectively for generations so that they always grow true to type from seed, however, tend to lose their vigour. They grow feebly because of inbreeding. But if two true-breeding varieties are crossed, the first resulting generation – known as Filial 1, or F1 for short – has the dominant qualities of its parents, plus vastly increased vigour. As a result, F1 seeds can produce more abundant crops than either of their parent varieties.

The generation descended from the F1 has almost as much vigour as the F1, but less uniformity, because about one plant in four will display what are called recessive characteristics, derived from the original varieties but submerged in the F1 generation (see the chart on the left). These second-generation plants – known as F2 hybrids – are also widely grown because no laboriously controlled cross-pollination is needed, and so the seeds are cheaper to produce.

Later generations than the F2 can be grown as well, but they are usually sold only as mixtures because the genetic structure is by then so scrambled that few of the resulting plants grow true to type.

The genetic principles used by modern plant breeders to create all hybrids, including F1 and F2 strains, were discovered by an Austrian monk named Gregor Mendel (1822-84). He published his results, largely based on experiments with garden peas, in 1866, but his discoveries were ignored until other researchers confirmed them in 1900, 16 years after his death. Mendel found that all genetic characteristics, in animals as well as plants, are carried in pairs. He also found that where two opposed characteristics – such as tallness and shortness – are carried by the same plant, one of the factors will consistently dominate. It is this consistency which explains why plants grown from F1 seeds are so uniform.

HOW F1 AND F2 PLANTS DIFFER

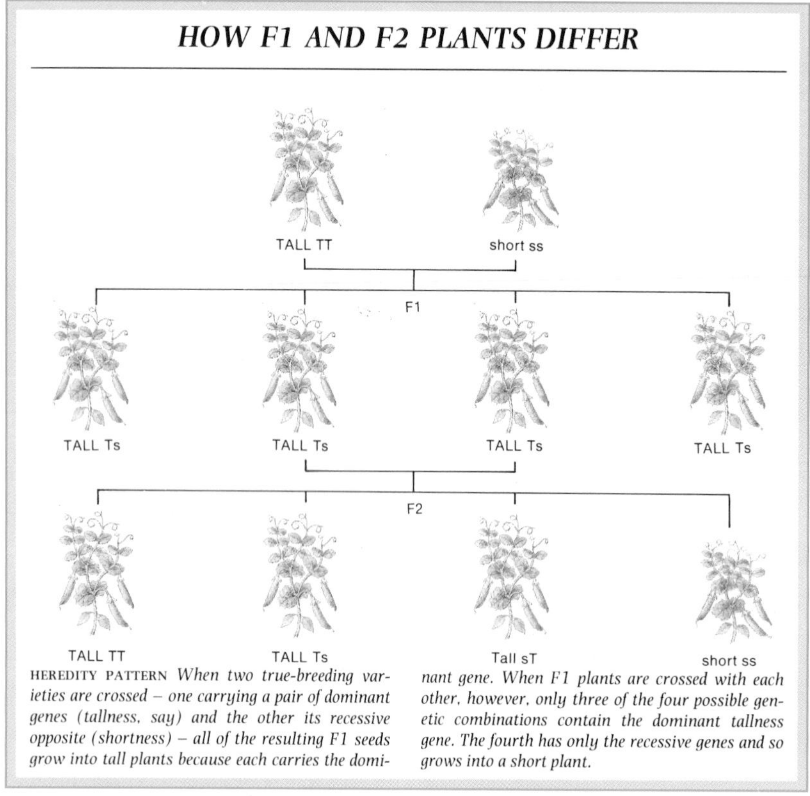

HEREDITY PATTERN *When two true-breeding varieties are crossed – one carrying a pair of dominant genes (tallness, say) and the other its recessive opposite (shortness) – all of the resulting F1 seeds grow into tall plants because each carries the dominant gene. When F1 plants are crossed with each other, however, only three of the four possible genetic combinations contain the dominant tallness gene. The fourth has only the recessive genes and so grows into a short plant.*

SHADE

In the shade

A large tree growing in my neighbour's garden hangs majestic but light-obscuring limbs over several square yards of my territory. Since I don't want to amputate the branches, can you suggest a few shrubs that might grow in their shade instead?

Your problem, or that of your shrubs, in such a situation is two-fold: lack of light; and lack of nutrients, since most of the food and water are taken by the tree. Establishing shrubs in its shade will be an uphill fight, a matter of regular mulching, watering and foliar feeding. But it's worth a try. Some of the following evergreens might do well, but plant them as close as possible to the edge of the tree's leaf canopy.

Aucuba japonica (3-5ft high) Several good variegated varieties available including *A. j.* 'Maculata'.

Daphne pontica (3-5ft) Bright green leaves. Yellow flowers April-May.

Euonymus fortunei 'Emerald 'n Gold' (2-3ft) Green, gold and pink foliage.

Mahonia aquifolium (3-5ft) Yellow flowers in winter. Reddish leaves.

Prunus laurocerasus (6ft) Vigorous, spreading growth. White flowers in April.

Skimmia japonica 'Fragrans' (3-5ft) Aromatic, white flowers in spring.

Viburnum davidii (2-3ft) Compact mound. Blue fruits if shrubs of both sexes are grown.

Alternatively, one deciduous shrub worth trying is a North American one: *Rubus odoratus*. It grows 6-7ft high and has velvety, large bright green leaves. It bears purple-red flowers between June and September.

Under the spreading cypress tree

We have a very awkward north-facing corner in the garden, overshadowed by a large cypress fir, with a wall on two sides and a lawn in front. Is there anything that can be persuaded to grow and add some colour under this permanently funereal tree?

There are many plants which are tolerant even of deep shade – even though some of them adapt by an increased size of leaf, often at the expense of the flower. The soil under a large cypress will tend to be very dry and should be thoroughly dug over two or three weeks before planting and mulched with a 3-4in thick layer of peat, well-rotted manure or compost. The digging will help to open up soil which has probably become sour and compacted under the drip of the tree, and the mulch will help it to retain moisture better. Check the soil, too, with a testing kit to see how acid it is. Add lime, if necessary, to raise the pH level to at least 5.5. Most of the best plants for this spot will not do well if the soil is more acid than this – if, in other words, the pH level is below 5.5. For details on how to check and adjust your soil's pH level, see *Acid soils*, page 6. Finally, at planting time, hoe into the ground a general fertiliser such as Growmore at a rate of 2oz per square yard. Once you've prepared the ground, try these herbaceous perennials: convallaria (lily of the valley); *Iris foetidissima* 'Citrina'; *Polygonatum multiflorum* (Solomon's seal); digitalis (foxglove); *Euphorbia wulfenii*; and *Helleborus orientalis* (Lenten rose).

For ground cover, add evergreen periwinkle (*Vinca minor*), which has bright blue flowers from March until July, and sometimes intermittently until October.

A watery solution

Would a pond be a sensible option for a shady part of the garden?

This depends on what kind of a pond you want and whether the shade is caused by shrubs, trees or a neighbouring building. Plants with floating foliage, such as water lilies, are intolerant of shade, but if your pond is informal with, perhaps, an overspill, you can have a bog garden which allows for a wider variety of interesting plants.

If the shade comes from trees rather than buildings, your pond will be easier to maintain if the trees are evergreen, not deciduous. Fallen leaves must always be removed from any pond because, if left, apart from being unsightly, they'll foul the water. Thin out the branches of shrubs a little to allow some sunshine through and so increase the varieties of pond plants you can grow.

Try some of these plants in your bog garden: astilbe; *Acorus calamus*; *Alisma plantago-aquatica*; *Aponogeton distachyus*; *Butomus umbellatus*; *Calla palustris*; *Caltha palustris*; *Iris cristata*; *I. delavayi*; *Leucojum aestivum*; ligularia; *Lysimachia nummularia*; *Lysichiton americanus*; *Mentha aquatica*; *Myosotis palustris*; *Primula bulleyana*; *P. denticulata*; *P. florindae*; *P. sieboldii*.

For more details on how to build and plant up a pond, see *Ponds and pools*, page 261, and *Water gardens*, page 360.

Colour for yew

Is there anything which will grow under a yew hedge where the soil is very dry and there is not too much light?

Surprisingly, daffodils will grow tolerably well there, so long as the hedge is kept clipped. So will the brilliant yellow St John's wort (hypericum), and snowdrops.

PLANTS THAT SHINE IN THE SHADE

These plants will do equally well in acid or alkaline soil unless otherwise marked. For further suggestions for plants that will grow well in shade, see *Colour*, page 84.
P = perennial, A = annual or biennial, C = climber, S = shrub.

Plants for damp shade
Alchemilla mollis (P)
Amelanchier lamarckii (S) Acid soil only.
Anemone blanda (P)
Aquilegia 'Blue Bedder' (A)
Aruncus sylvester (P)
Arundinaria nitida (S)
A. viridistriata (S)
Azalea (S)
Bergenia 'Silberlicht' (P)
B. 'Bressingham Salmon' (P)
Caltha palustris (P)
Camellia x *williamsii* 'Donation' (S)
C. japonica 'Contessa Lavinia Maggi' (S) Both acid soil only.
Campanula latifolia (P)
Chaenomeles speciosa (S)
Clematis montana (C)
Convallaria (P)
Desfontainea spinosa (S) Grow in mild or sheltered areas only.
Digitalis ambigua (P)
Euphorbia wulfenii (P)
Filipendula ulmaria (P)
Fritillaria meleagris (P)
Garrya elliptica (C)
Geranium maculatum (P)
Helleborus niger (P)
Hydrangea petiolaris (C)
Iris foetidissima (P)
Ligularia clivorum (P) Light shade only.
Lunaria annua (A)
Meconopsis betonicifolia (P)
M. cambrica (P) Both best in acid soil.
Nicotiana affinis (A) Light shade only.
Paeonia mlokosewitschii (P) Best in semi-shade.
Polygonum baldschuanicum (C)
Rheum palmatum 'Rubrum' (P)
Rhododendron (S) Acid soil only.
Viola labradorica (A)
Zantedeschia aethiopica (P) Hardy only if grown in 6-12in of water.

Plants for dry shade
Aconitum 'Arendsii' (P)
A. orientale (P)
Brunnera macrophylla (P)
Cyclamen hederifolium (P)
C. coum (P)
Digitalis lutea (P) Best in semi-shade.
Euphorbia cyparissias (P)
Geranium endressii 'Claridge Druce' (P)
Hedera colchica 'Dentata Variegata' (C)
Lonicera japonica (C)
Macleaya cordata (P)
Omphalodes cappadocica (P)
O. alba (P)

SHALLOTS

Flowering shallots

Why do some shallots flower and not others? Should the flowering stems be cut off?

The larger the bulb, the more likely it is to flower – though it can depend upon temperature, too. Storing the bulbs at less than about 7°C (45°F) in winter, or planting them out when the weather and soil are still quite cold, can trigger the process. So it's wise to keep bulbs in a cool room indoors, at a temperature around 10°C (50°F), until you plant them out in late winter or early spring.

Don't let the bulbs get too warm, though. If you delay planting out until late April, when weather and soil are normally warmer, fewer bulbs will flower – but you'll get a poorer crop.

As for the flowers, cut the stems off as soon as you spot them and as low down as possible, because they sap the vigour of the developing bulb. Once shallots have produced flower stems, they shrivel more quickly in storage.

How to store the crop

What's the best way to store shallots?

Lift them when their leaves have turned yellow and withered – usually in July or August. Separate the clusters and remove any soil or loose leaves. If the weather's fine, leave them outside for a week or two to dry out. If it's wet, keep them under cover.

Once the bulbs are dry, spread them up to three bulbs deep, in shallow containers – seed trays or wooden tomato boxes are ideal. Alternatively, hang them in nylon stockings from the roof of a frost-free shed or garage. Keep them cool, or they'll start growing again. Keep them dry, too; damp air will turn them mouldy. In ideal conditions, they should stay firm for up to eight months.

Saving shallots for next year

Is it worthwhile using home-grown shallots to start off my crop next year?

Certainly – as long as the plants have stayed healthy and vigorous all season, and the harvest was good. The shallots sold by garden centres and nurseries are usually certified free from a virus disease known as shallot yellows. Leaves of infected bulbs develop short, yellow streaks at the base, which sometimes spread to cover the whole area of the base. The leaves often become stunted, and the bulbs don't grow. The virus is carried by greenfly which have fed on infected onion, leek or shallot plants.

Choose your seed bulbs from healthy shallots weighing around ⅓oz – about the size of a large marble – when you lift them. Store them in a cool, dry, frost-free place until February or March, and then replant them. Plant them in the same way as newly bought bulbs – for cultivation details, see *Growing shallots*, page 237.

If birds are a problem, start the bulbs under cover in trays of moist peat. Plant them out when their shoots emerge; by then the birds should leave them alone.

Bulbs that won't grow

Each year I grow shallots, only to find in the autumn that all the bulbs are still the same size as the ones I planted. What am I doing wrong?

Nothing at all. You're doing well, in fact, to grow them to the same size – the bulbs you've bought from the garden shops are already fully grown, and they've been raised in optimum commercial conditions.

Unlike onion sets – really just baby onions – which reach their mature size only in the second year, shallots mature in just one season. But they rarely become any fatter. Instead they produce more bulbs of the same size. Plant shallots between February and early April and you should find their numbers have multiplied 10 to 12 times by the time you lift them in the summer.

SHOTHOLE

Holes in leaves, but no insects

My beetroot and spinach have both begun to develop an amazing number of holes in their leaves, but, search as I might, I cannot find the creatures responsible. Have you any idea what they could be – and what spray I should use to get rid of them?

Most likely in this case, insects are not responsible. What your plants have is a disease, or rather a condition, called shothole. The condition gets its name because the leaves look as though they've been peppered with shotgun pellets. As well as in beetroot and spinach, it also occurs in horseradish and in plums, peaches and cherries, too. The cause of shothole is somewhat uncertain. Sometimes it seems to be due to bacteria, at other times to fungus. In its most severe form, on cherries, weeping wounds develop all over the tree and in time the tree can die. In this case the cause is a strength-sapping disease known as bacterial canker.

The disease is very hard to eradicate but it can be controlled in fruit trees by spraying them three times at three-week intervals with a copper compound, starting in August after harvesting. A spray when the petals fall is also advisable, although this can cause damage in certain varieties of tree.

On vegetables, try spraying with a fungicide such as mancozeb.

PEPPERED LOOK *One possible cause of shothole on cherries is soggy ground. Discourage the disease by improving the drainage nearby.*

SHRUBS

Blind philadelphus

We have two apparently healthy mock orange shrubs. Everyone says they're easy to grow but in the last four years neither has produced so much as a single flower – plenty of shoots and leaves, though. What should we do?

Mock orange – philadelphus – is a very undemanding shrub which does well on most soils, even on chalk. It likes a sunny position but doesn't mind light shade either. Therefore, the most likely reason for lack of flowers is simply that the shrubs are too young. Just leave them alone for a year or two and they'll probably come around.

You don't say which philadelphus you have, but most likely it's the popular *Philadelphus* 'Belle Etoile'. This can grow to 10ft, and so may easily take four years and more to settle down into a flowering rhythm. By the way, go easy with the pruning. Philadelphus flowers next year on this year's young shoots, so be careful not to cut them out. In late July, or thereabouts, take out the shoots which have flowered, and with them any thin or weak shoots. If the bushes are getting too crowded you can also remove from the centres any shoots which show no flower buds, or have lost their terminal bud. This will improve air circulation.

Brightening a wall

Could you suggest three or four low-growing shrubs to brighten up the retaining wall of a small garden?

You don't say which way the wall is facing but presumably you want to create a screen, or at least put some expression on the blank face of the wall. There are many shrubs that would do; but only you can decide which flowering period would best suit your garden, and what shrub heights you require. Here is a short selection of deciduous (D) and evergreen (E) shrubs that you could choose from, according to the siting of the wall.

NORTH OR EAST-FACING

Spring-flowering: *Camellia japonica* (E, height 5ft); *Euonymus fortunei* (E, 2-3ft); *Chaenomeles japonica* (D, 3-5ft); *Daphne odora* (E, 1-3ft).

Summer or autumn-flowering: *Choisya ternata* (E, 5-10ft); *Grevillea rosmarinifolia* (E, 6ft); *Pyracantha coccinea* (E, 10-15ft).

Winter-flowering: *Garrya elliptica* (E, 6-10ft); *Mahonia aquifolia* (E, 5-8ft); *Viburnum foetens* (D, 4-8ft).

WEST-FACING

Spring-flowering: *Fothergilla major* (D, height 5-10ft); *Prunus cistena* (D, 3-6ft).

Summer or autumn-flowering: *Kolkwitzia amabilis* (D, 6-10ft); *Potentilla fruticosa* 'Katherine Dykes' (D, 2-4ft).

Winter-flowering: *Viburnum fragrans* (D, 8-12ft); *Daphne odora* (E, 1-3ft).

SOUTH-FACING
Spring-flowering: *Berberis thunbergii* 'Atropurpurea Nana' (D, height 3-6ft); *Corylopsis spicata* (D, 3-4ft).
Summer or autumn-flowering: *Prunus tenella* 'Fire Hill' (D, 5-8ft); *Cistus corbariensis* (E, 2-5ft).
Winter-flowering: *Viburnum tinus* (E, 3-10ft); *Erica carnea* (E, 1-3ft).

Quince questions

Three years ago I planted a Japanese quince against a south-facing wall, but so far it has shown no signs of flowering. Is it unhappy in this situation, and should I move it?

Don't touch it. It's in exactly the right spot. All you have to do is give it an annual mulch – spread a 1-2in thick layer of peat or compost around the stem in spring – and the flowers will turn up in a year or two.

Berries not for children

I have a new, raw wall that would be much improved by a shrub planted against it. But with small, inquisitive children around the place I'm a bit worried about poisonous berries. What do you suggest?

Pyracantha or cotoneaster would be safe enough. But many shrubs and trees are not. Thorn apple, daphne, yew, laburnum, honeysuckle, the Chilean potato tree and snowberry are all bad news. So, too, while on the subject, are many other plants such as ivy, rhubarb leaves, green potatoes, mistletoe, foxglove, and lily of the valley. Fortunately, most of these will induce vomiting rather than permanent harm. All the same, if a child shows any symptoms of poisoning – vomiting, diarrhoea or stomach pains – telephone your doctor at once, or take the child to the nearest hospital. Take leaves or fruit from the suspected plant with you, to speed the correct treatment.

Always impress upon children that they can't assume that just because they see birds or animals eating a plant, that means it's safe for humans. As often as not, it isn't.

Boosting old hydrangeas

I'm afraid that my 20-year-old hydrangea bush is now past its best. I'd be sad to lose it, but if its time is up, I could use the space. Or should I give it another chance?

Most certainly. Look after *Hydrangea macrophylla* properly, and it might easily outlive you. It sounds as if your plant has been left to its own devices for too long, but it's not by any means beyond redemption.

Start the revival treatment in March or April. Cut out the very old wood and shorten the younger shoots as far as an active bud to encourage new growth. A year or two of this treatment will give it a new lease of life. You may not get any flowers for two or three years, but in the end you will get a display more glorious than ever. Fertiliser will not be of any particular help. But if your hydrangea is really on the downward path, or you'd like some insurance, carry the line on with a few of its offspring (see *Hydrangea blue, hydrangea pink*, page 316).

Staking out

Is it always necessary to stake shrubs?

Generally, it's quite unnecessary. A shrub, almost by definition, has many stems arising at or below ground level. These support one another, and provided the shrub is firmly planted, no further support is needed.

Certain shrubs, however, such as some varieties of the Japanese maple, *Acer palmatum*, have only single stems, and like young trees, are top-heavy. In these cases, staking is a good insurance policy.

Feeding times

I've had all kinds of advice – especially from gardening catalogues – but I wonder if you could suggest a really sound feeding programme for shrubs?

This is an aspect of shrub cultivation that is surprisingly often overlooked. Like all plants, shrubs do better if regularly fed, and there is an excellent three-step programme you could adopt.

Begin at the planting stage by incorporating bone meal or superphosphate in the compost or in the loose soil at the bottom of the planting hole. This will provide sound, long-lasting nourishment for the young shrub's roots.

Next, during the years of active growth, give the plant an annual spring feed of general fertiliser, such as Growmore. One ounce to the square yard sprinkled around the base will suffice. In addition, a 1-2in layer of peat, bark or compost spread around the base will protect the shallower roots from drought.

Finally, when the shrub is mature, it may well be surrounded by lawn, or underplanted, possibly, with perennials. The grass or other plants will then take the lion's share of any fertiliser you scatter on the surface, leaving the shrub's deeper roots with very poor returns indeed.

So it's best to feed a mature shrub with a general fertiliser early, say in March, before the competition gets moving, and there is time for the rain to wash the food down to the shrub's roots.

If this is inconvenient, or you've missed early spring, there are a number of foliar feeds specially designed for shrubs on the market. These feed the plant via the leaves, and are best sprayed on when the foliage is newly opened and at its most receptive.

Multicoloured lilac

I've just noticed the most extraordinary thing. Some of the branches of next-door's lilac bear white flowers, while others carry the usual lilac-coloured ones. Is it a new species?

Sadly, no. Quite a number of trees and shrubs occasionally display such eccentricities. Probably what happened in this case was that long ago your neighbour or his predecessor bought a white lilac, which is a cultivated variety. Frequently such cultivated varieties are grafted onto a rootstock of the common lilac (*Syringa vulgaris*) – which has lilac flowers – to give added vigour. The old roots are vigorous indeed, and sometimes throw up 'suckers', or shoots, on their own behalf. If these are not detected at an early stage, the owner often assumes that they are a part of the main plant, and allows them to grow to flowering size.

So this is probably what happened. The plant you describe started off as a white variety clamped to *S. vulgaris* rootstock. Suckers developed, and are now putting forth the pale purple flowers of the rootstock alongside the white blooms of the grafted scion.

All of which just goes to show how important it is to take out any shoots on a grafted plant which arise from below ground level. Tear them off, or cut them right back to the root from which they sprang. If you leave any kind of a stump on a sucker, it will react like any other pruned stem by producing bushy sideshoots, which merely multiplies the problem.

Good buys

The young shrubs for sale in the local garden centre are ranked in battalions. Do you have any tips for selecting the best?

Most shrubs nowadays are sold in containers, which means they can be planted at almost any time of year. Medium-sized specimens are the best ones to buy. Large plants often take a long time to get established and small ones, as often as not, are recently rooted cuttings, which will take ages to present a reasonable display in the garden.

Look, too, for a well-shaped shrub with even, bushy growth all round the base. A lopsided or spindly shrub can take years of careful pruning to get back into shape.

When you find a plant of the right size and shape, lift it by its stem. If the plant and soil come easily together out of the container, then move on, for the plant is not well established. Also avoid plants whose roots have grown through the base of the container or spread over the surface of the soil; these have been cramped for too long. However, a few small roots breaking through the side of plastic-sheet containers are a good sign – the plant is well established. Above all, make sure that the plant you buy has rich dark green foliage with leaves down to the bases of the stems. Plants with leaves that are shrivelled, distorted or scorched around the edges must be shunned, and so must those with bare, leafless stems – except, of course, in winter.

It doesn't matter if there are a few weeds or even green algae on the surface of the soil, but if it is covered with a dense growth of weeds, then discard the plant.

Bare-root plants are usually cheaper than container-grown, and can be a very good buy. But avoid any with shrivelled or discoloured stems, with buds beginning to grow, or with small, white, fresh roots growing into the packing. Abnormal stems could indicate a diseased or carelessly grown plant; and fresh growth on a bare-root shrub means that it will be slow to get established in your garden.

Highly scented

My wife has a special fondness for honeysuckle, and I'd like to buy a few for our anniversary. Which are the most sweetly scented, and are there any problems in growing them?

Both types of honeysuckle – bush and climbing – contain fragrant species and varieties. Among the climbers, try *Lonicera periclymenum* (yellow flowers June-Sept), or *L. caprifolium* (pinkish-white flowers June-Oct). Among the bush types, consider *L. fragrantissima* (height 6-9ft, creamy flowers Dec-Mar), or *L. rupicola* (height 4-6ft, lilac flowers May-June).

Both types are very undemanding, requiring only a moderately rich well-drained soil. The climbers do best in light shade, and the bush types in full sun. Plant bare-root versions of both types between September and March. Container-grown plants can, however, be planted at any time of year.

The climbers need only an occasional pruning to keep them in shape, but the shrubby types should be lightly trimmed after flowering, to cut out the wood that has flowered. If you find the berries decorative, delay pruning until winter or early spring.

Of shrubs and the sea

In beginning a seaside garden, I'm quite aware that as with paintwork and cars, many plants are not too keen on salt breezes. But I've got to start somewhere, so would you recommend some shrubs for my situation, please?

It would be an ill site that treated every shrub unkindly, and, though living by the sea incorporates problems of spray damage and high winds, severe frosts are much less likely by the coast and earlier crops can be grown.

Some shrubs cannot abide salt; others thrive on it and are happy, too, in the relatively frost-free conditions. If you choose shrubs from among this last group, you will have the basis of a very attractive and even unusual garden.

One maritime shrub which can stand and enjoy anything the sea can throw at it is the evergreen *Escallonia macrantha*. This has glossy leaves and red flowers, and can be grown as a windbreak hedge or as a specimen plant. It will flourish even in the teeth of a spray-laden gale. Other evergreen shrubs that do well by the seaside include:

Arbutus unedo (strawberry tree) – height 15ft. Produces white/pink flowers, Oct-Dec.
Choisya ternata – 6ft. Fragrant white flowers, Apr-May.
Elaeagnus pungens 'Maculata' – 10ft. Striking gold-centred leaves.
Griselinia littoralis – up to 25ft. Glossy green leaves. Excellent for hedging.
Any species of *Hebe* – for instance *H. salicifolia*, which bears long spikes of lilac flowers, June-Aug.
Pittosporum tenuifolium – 15ft. Pale, wavy-edged leaves.

Special pleaching

On visits to stately gardens, I have been much impressed by the ingenuity and grace of their pleached walks. Might it be possible to imitate them on a smaller scale, or is it very difficult?

Not at all difficult, though posterity is more likely to enjoy the fruits of your labour than you are. At its simplest, pleaching is a method of training trees or shrubs into covered avenues or tunnels. The system is also used to convert single trees into strangely shaped novelties.

The fashion seems to have begun in the 17th century, when there was a passion for lime walks. Avenues of lime trees were planted about 10ft apart, and with 10ft between trees in a row. The trees were allowed to grow until they had firm woody stems, and were then all topped at the same height to encourage the growth of many side branches. Some of these were fastened to canes, or to a wire frame which would direct further growth along the side walls and upwards to form an arch. All other branches were cut back to the trunk.

The branches forming walls and roof were intertwined and, in the fullness of time, grafted themselves to one another. As they lengthened, the branches became further entwined into the framework; so did the sideshoots that made the sides and roof more solid. Gradually, a growing, flowering tunnel was formed and kept in shape by judicious pruning. A splendid 180ft long example may be seen at Bodnant Garden in North Wales, though there the tunnel is composed of laburnums. In May and June, when the long golden clusters of flowers hang down from the almost solid roof, the effect is quite breathtaking.

The young shoots of most trees and shrubs are so elastic that they can be quite easily twisted round each other or around wire frames of almost any shape. You could also try intertwining different plants that are already established in your garden. Traditionally, lime, hazel, laburnum and yew were used for the tunnels and arbours, but any shrub or small tree with whippy young branches can be pleached.

Mostly for the birds

I don't share the feelings of exasperation that some gardeners seem to have about birds. Can you suggest a few shrubs that are pleasing to the eye and whose fruit will attract more birds to my garden?

It's a lovely idea, but do remember that birds don't distinguish between the plants grown for their benefit and the ones you were hoping to keep for yourself. So far as they are concerned everything in the garden is fair game, and if you encourage them you may find it a waste of time to grow fruit bushes, strawberries or cherries – unless you build a fruit cage as well.

To answer your question, here are a few shrubs that are attractive to humans and birds alike. Within the list, 'E' signifies evergreen, and 'D' deciduous.

Aucuba japonica 'Variegata' (E, height 6-10ft) Variegated foliage, red berries.
Berberis thunbergii (D, 6ft) Bright red berries.
Callicarpa japonica (D, 3ft) Violet berries in autumn.
C. bodinieri (D, 6ft) Lilac flowers in July, followed by violet berries.
Cotoneaster horizontalis (D, 6ft) Good wall or ground cover. Red berries.
Pyracantha coccinea 'Lalandei' (E, 12ft) Masses of red berries.
Symphoricarpos racemosus (D, 8ft) White berries. Birds take them only in severe winters.
Viburnum opulus (D, 15ft) Clear red berries.

While you're waiting for the shrubs to develop, you can encourage birds, especially tits, in your garden by hanging net bags of peanuts, half a coconut, or the bone from a weekend roast (they like the fat), from the branch of a tree. In winter, scatter grain, seeds and bits of fruit on the lawn, rather than an unrelieved diet of bread. Bread is particularly bad for birds in the nesting season, when the adults will take it back to their young in the nest and can choke them with it. In frost and in drought give water, but in summer leave birds generally to their own devices. They're used to it.

Standing up for camellias

I love camellias, but they have a reputation for being very difficult to grow. Is this so, or do you think I might try one or two?

Pay no attention to the reputation. At heart, camellias are easy-going. Just take a little care with their planting and positioning. A chalky or alkaline site is not for them, and before planting, you should incorporate at least a couple of buckets of peat or lime-free compost in the soil at the base of the hole. September to October or March to April are the best planting times. An ideal situation could be where the camellias would avoid the early morning sun, get a little shade, and be protected from cold winter winds. Even so, they will do quite well in a north-facing border, provided they do not get too dry.

Camellias like a moist climate, and in hot, dry spells will benefit from overhead spraying. No pruning is required other than the removal of dead wood and faded flowers. You might like to try one of the following varieties; they all flower early in spring, and are relatively trouble-free.

Camellia x *williamsii* 'Donation' (6-10ft high) Pink, semi-double flowers.

C. japonica 'Adolphe Audusson' (6-10ft) Scarlet, semi-double flowers.

C. j. 'White Snow' (6-12ft) White, single flowers with gold stamens.

Maple leaves forever

In all my life, I've never seen anything to rival the colours of the New England woods in autumn. Most brilliant of all were the maples. Would it be possible to grow one or two in a small British garden?

Most maples (acers) are large trees, but there are some small ones, and even shrub maples which will give not only autumn colour but a splendid display through the summer as well. The best of these shrub maples is *Acer palmatum* 'Dissectum atropurpureum', a 2-5ft high mound of soft, feathery, purple leaves. Another eye-catcher is the golden *A. japonicum* 'Aureum', which grows to about 3ft. Both shrubs are deciduous.

The only difficulty in growing them is that the delicate leaves require some protection from high winds, and, if possible, need a little shade to avoid sun scorch in summer.

If your garden is large enough to take small trees, *A. cappadocicum* 'Aureum' is very decorative. Its red leaves turn to gold as the season progresses. The young leaves of *A. pseudoplatanus* 'Brilliantissimum' are a showy shrimp-pink. Both trees grow very slowly, taking about 20 years to reach 25ft.

Over-enthusiastic pruning

All the books say you should prune forsythia after the flowers fade in late spring. I did this to my large shrub two springs ago, cutting it back almost to the ground. It has not bloomed since. Have I damaged it irreparably?

The point about pruning is to encourage new shoots and foliage to grow – though it's usually at the expense of flowers. In pruning forsythia, you should remove crowded shoots and some of the oldest wood each spring. By cutting the whole shrub down to the ground you have got rid of all the flowering wood as well, and you may have to wait three or four years before flowers reappear.

When you have to prune old or over-large flowering shrubs, you should always spread the operation over as much as four or five years. In this way, you will encourage growth without losing the display.

New brooms

Despite the sentiment expressed in the old song, 'The bonnie, yellow broom', I've always considered it a rather unbeautiful shrub, and short-lived at that. Or have I simply been growing the wrong varieties?

Diamonds may be forever, but assuredly broom is not. Within a relatively few years, the old wood becomes brittle; the long, wand-like branches are then too heavy for the strength of the fork so they split or snap off, and the shrub dies.

Nevertheless, there are some magnificent brooms, and since the plants will grow in almost any soil, there is a place for broom in every garden. The toughest is *Cytisus scoparius* 'Burkwoodii', which bears crimson, red and yellow flowers in May and June, while its relative *C. s.* 'Andreanus' is yellow and crimson. In season, the flowers completely cover the long, whippy stems. But to ensure their reappearance next season, you must each year cut the stems hard back after flowering. Be careful not to cut into old wood; wounds there rarely heal and will probably prove fatal to the plant. But once the plants become hard-wooded and leggy, it's best to discard them and restock.

Just to show what brooms can do, you might also like to try *C. battandieri*, a 15ft tall wall shrub. It has silvery-green leaves and yellow flower spikes that smell of pineapples. In contrast, the purple-flowering *C. purpureus* is a delightful plant that rarely grows to even 1ft.

Backs to the wall

A few years ago, I planted a pyracantha close by a wall of the house. Having reached adolescence, it now waves wild branches and is obviously in need of control and support. But how are these best provided?

There are several methods. Most garden centres stock special nails with soft metal strips attached to the heads. You bang the nails into the wall, and loosely bend the strips about the stems to direct growth. Or you could stretch plastic-covered wires across the wall with galvanised nails and tie the branches into the wires.

Another way, which is excellent for all kinds of climbers, is to fix two or three 6in deep blocks to the bottom of the wall and hinge the bottom of a trellis to them. Fix similar blocks to the top of the wall, and hook the top end of the trellis to them. The branches and shoots of the plant can then be woven or tied into the trellis.

The beauty of this system is, that when you come to repaint the wall, trellis, plant and all can be gently lowered to the ground with a minimum of damage and labour. The 6in clearance provided by the blocks keeps the shoots away from the wall. It also gives you enough room to tie in the growing branches without losing fingernails.

Golden thought

I thought of giving my aunt and uncle a golden shrub to commemorate their golden wedding. Any suggestions?

Two outstanding golden shrubs come at once to mind. Either would fit your bill, since all they ask is a sunny or slightly shaded spot

THE SHRUB PLANTER'S GUIDE

Follow these ten straightforward rules to give any shrub you plant a flying start.

1 Always make the planting hole about 6in deeper and 12in broader than the roots of the shrub.

2 Cover the bottom of the hole with a 3-4in thick layer of peat mixed with a little of the surrounding soil or compost.

3 Stir in a heaped handful of bone meal, unless you're planting a lime-hater, such as rhododendron. In that case, use superphosphate.

4 If a stake seems necessary, drive it into the base of the hole before you insert the plant. Put the stake on the windward side of the plant to reduce the risk of chafing.

5 Insert the shrub gently, and gradually fill the hole with a half-and-half mixture of soil and peat to which a further handful of bone meal (or superphosphate) has been added.

6 Shake the shrub up and down from time to time as you fill the hole, and firm down the soil with your fists or feet to ensure there are no air pockets among the roots.

7 Bury the plant up to the soil mark on the stem. Create a saucer-like depression around the stem to direct rainwater to the young roots. This is particularly valuable in sandy soils, which do not retain water well.

8 For the first three years, while the roots are getting established, put a 3in layer of compost around the base of the plant each spring. Add a sprinkling of general fertiliser such as Growmore.

9 Water generously in dry spells for the first year particularly, giving each plant up to 4 gallons of water at a time. You may need to water as often as once a week in a summer drought, but a better guide is to use a trowel to look at nearby soil 3-4in below the surface. If it's dry, the plant needs watering.

10 If the plant is in a windy spot, set a plastic mesh or sacking screen around it to protect it from drying winds during the first couple of years.

in almost any reasonable soil. Neither needs regular pruning. So one or the other of these would interpret your idea exactly:
Philadelphus coronarius 'Aureus' (3-6ft high) – its gold-yellow spring foliage turns green-yellow in summer.
Ribes sanguineum 'Brocklebank' (2-5ft) – gold leaves; pink flowers Apr-May.

The same idea can be used for a silver wedding. Two shrubs with silver-grey foliage are *Santolina chamaecyparissus* (1½-2ft high) with feathery leaves and yellow flowers in July, and *Senecio* 'Sunshine' (3-4ft) which is evergreen and produces yellow flowers in June.

Alternatively, try an elaeagnus: the evergreen *E. pungens* 'Maculata', for its glossy, gold-splashed leaves; or the deciduous *E. commutata*, for its silvery berries.

Disappointing sumach

On an autumn visit to New England a few years ago, I was totally captivated by the clear, singing colours of the sumachs. On my return I bought one, but so far, though the leaves change colour in autumn, they are rather dull and hardly mirror the sumachs of Vermont. Is it my fault, or the weather's?

Sumachs have been renamed recently, and in the resulting confusion, you may have been sold the wrong plant. The brilliantly coloured sumachs of New England are *Rhus typhina* and *R. glabra*, respectively the stag horn sumach and the smooth sumach. These make shrubs 10-15ft high and bear long pointed leaves which go bright red in sunny autumn weather.

Another shrub which used to be called rhus is the smoke bush, now classified as *Cotinus coggygria*. This 3-8ft high bush has oval, purple leaves that turn orange-red in autumn, and are seen at their best in the variety called 'Flame'. From July to October, this and all other cotinus varieties bear long panicles of flowers that slowly fade from purple to smoky-grey. But the shrubs do not grow wild in the USA.

In any case, it would be hoping for too much to expect the sumachs in Britain to colour up as vividly each year as they do in the States. We do not have the long, dry, clear autumns of New England which encourage the colours.

Nevertheless, the plants can be exciting here, too, if the weather is right; in wet autumns they just look homesick.

HOW TO MULTIPLY YOUR SHRUBS

There are several ways to increase your shrub stock. The methods most widely used are hardwood cuttings, softwood cuttings, tip cuttings and layering. Of these, hardwood cuttings are the most likely to succeed, especially with deciduous shrubs. But with certain species, the other methods may produce better plants more quickly. The sections below explain how to carry out each technique, and which plants it works best with. Whatever method you choose, bear in mind these general points:

- Collect more cuttings than you think you'll need. The chances are that some will fail.
- To give your cuttings the best possible chance, insert them in a half-and-half mixture (by volume) of peat and coarse sand.
- Cuttings with leaves need a humid atmosphere, so keep them in a propagator, or in a pot covered with a transparent plastic bag.
- All cuttings require plenty of light – but not direct sunlight, which will scorch them.

If you are uncertain which method to use, or you don't have time to watch over the propagator, try hardwood cuttings first.

HARDWOOD CUTTINGS

After the leaves have fallen and the plant has stopped growing, choose woody, hard stems of the current season's growth and cut them with secateurs near the base.

Trim each stem to about 10-12in in length. Remove the tip by a sloping cut, and trim the bottom of the cutting with a horizontal cut below a node – the spot where a bud or leaf is attached to the stem. Make the top cut just above a leaf node, the bottom cut just below a leaf node. Most cellular activity takes place at these nodes, and the trimming encourages the lowest node to throw out roots, the uppermost one to throw out shoots – increasing the chance of success. All leaves on the lower two-thirds of the cutting should be removed. Large-leaved varieties such as cherry laurel tend to lose moisture rapidly; this can be reduced by slicing each leaf in half with a razor blade or sharp scissors. Do not remove all the leaves, though; they help to manufacture food for the cutting while it is rooting.

Plant the hardwood cuttings in a well-dug site protected from north and east winds and in semi-shade. Make a slit in the soil by inserting a spade to full depth and then pulling forward a few inches. Lay a 1-2in layer of coarse sand in the bottom. Dip the bases of the cuttings in hormone rooting powder and plant them 3-4in apart with two-thirds underground. Leave 2ft between the rows. Push soil into the trench, water the cuttings well and tread them in firmly.

Severe frosts may loosen the cuttings; push them down with thumb or finger and in early spring firm the soil again. The easier-rooting cuttings – such as ivy, privet and salix (willow) – will be ready for lifting and setting in their permanent site after a year. Slower-rooting species need a further year.

Be guided by the new growth that appears on the cuttings: ample, healthy new growth is a sure sign that a cutting has rooted well.

Plants suitable for hardwood cuttings
Buddleia davidii, cornus, ivy, privet, lonicera, paeonia, chaenomeles, salix, sambucus, symphoricarpos and tamarix.

SOFTWOOD CUTTINGS

These cuttings are taken between early summer and autumn from the current year's growth which has become moderately firm but is still growing. Softwood cuttings are green at the tip and the base. Semi-ripe cuttings are green at the tip and slightly woody at the base (see *The*

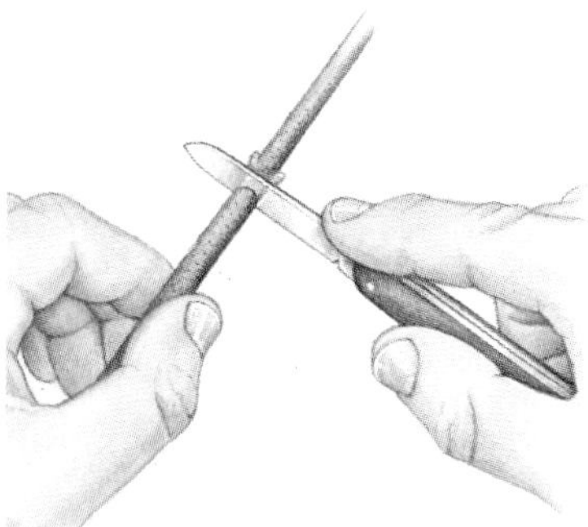

HARDWOOD CUTTINGS *Trim the base of the cutting just below a leaf node, the tip just above a node. Cut the base off square, the tip on a slant, to make it easy to see which end is which.*

SOFTWOOD CUTTINGS *One way of taking a softwood or semi-ripe cutting is to tear it off with a 'heel' – a small piece of the parent stem. The heel helps to stop sap draining out.*

TIP CUTTINGS *Young shoots taken as tip cuttings in early summer will root in weeks rather than months. But, while they're rooting, they need extra care: high humidity and warmth.*

Winter glow

I like the idea of winter colour in the garden, so last spring I bought a dogwood (Cornus alba 'Westonbirt') *for the sake of its bright red stems. What should I do to ensure that its brilliant colour is shown to best advantage?*

It's the young stems of dogwood that have the colour. So you should establish a regular pruning routine to stimulate the production of new branches each year. This is very simple: all that is required is that the young shoots are cut back either to the main stem or to ground level in March or April.

Given such treatment, the shrub will never reach its full height, of course, but you will have the strong winter colour you want. The ultimate size of your shrub can be determined by the severity of the pruning. Incidentally, there are quite a few other shrubs with coloured bark in winter. One or two of them might provide an interesting contrast to your dogwood. For example, try:

Cornus alba 'Elegantissima' (plum-coloured bark).
C. stolonifera 'Flaviramea' (green-yellow bark).
Leycesteria formosa (sea-green bark).
Rubus cockburnianus (purple bark with a white bloom).
Salix daphnoides (purple-black bark with a white bloom).
S. alba 'Chermesina' (orange-scarlet bark).
S. a. 'Vitellina' (yellow bark).

All of these shrubs are deciduous, so there are no leaves to block your view of the winter display.

Stripes, bars and blobs

Why are some shrubs variegated? It makes them more decorative but surely it can't be natural?

Plants become variegated – that is, produce white or gold patches upon their normally green leaves – for a variety of reasons. The most common, probably, is virus infection. *Aucuba japonica*, the spotted laurel, for instance, owes its attractive spots to a virus disease.

But although this is the most widespread cause of variegation, it very rarely produces the decorative stripes or patterns so sought after at garden centres. These are more likely to arise where some of the cells in the growing tip of the plant lose, for genetic reasons,

language of cuttings, page 108). Cut off sideshoots about 6-8in long, remove the leaves from the lower half and trim them horizontally just below the lowest leaf node.

Alternatively, pull off the sideshoots whole with a heel – a sliver of the main stem – attached to prevent sap draining away.

Whether the base has a heel or not, cut off the soft tip above a leaf node to leave a cutting 2-4in long. Dip the base in rooting powder and insert the cutting in a tray or pot so that the lowest remaining leaves are just above the soil surface. Set the cuttings 1-2in apart – five or six will fit comfortably around the edge of a 6in pot.

Water them well and put them in a cold frame, or cover the pot with a transparent bag.

Softwood cuttings take three to nine months to root.

Plants suitable for softwood cuttings

Andromeda, arbutus, aucuba, buddleia, buxus, callistemon, camellia (also suitable for leaf-bud cuttings, see page 109), chaenomeles, choisya, colutea, cornus, corylopsis, cotinus, cytisus, deutzia, elaeagnus, enkianthus, euonymus, garrya, gaultheria, heaths and heathers, ivy, hibiscus, hypericum, ilex, jasminum, kerria, kolkwitzia, lilac, lavandula, lonicera, olearia, osmanthus, pernettya, philadelphus, phlomis, photinia, pieris, pittosporum, potentilla, prunus (ornamental species), pyracantha, rhus, roses, rubus, senecio, skimmia, spiraea, ulex, viburnum and weigela.

TIP CUTTINGS

Try this method if you wish to take cuttings in early summer, though it is a fussy operation which demands constant care and attention.

Select shoots with four or five pairs of leaves and sever each shoot beneath the pair of leaves nearest the main stem. A 5in pot filled with cuttings compost or a half-and-half mixture of peat and coarse sand will take about ten cuttings. Dipping the cuttings in rooting powder will help, but is not necessary.

Plant them in holes made with a dibber, firm in and water well. Cover the pot with a transparent bag and keep it in a warm spot in a greenhouse or cold frame, but out of direct sunlight.

Never let the compost dry out. The plants should root in three to six weeks, but they will need to be grown on in the pot for at least a year before being planted out. Because the cuttings usually grow very slowly, it is rarely necessary to repot them.

Plants suitable for tip cuttings

Erica, calluna, conifers, callicarpa, fuchsia, hypericum and mahonia.

LAYERING

Layering is an ingenious way of propagating shrubs without a cold frame or greenhouse. Basically, a flexible branch is bent into the ground and encouraged to grow roots of its own before it is severed from the parent plant. One of the easiest methods is what horticulturists call simple layering (for details of other layering techniques, see page 110). This is how it works.

Choose only first-year branches which have not yet flowered. Between April and August, or in autumn, prepare the ground by filling a small hole with peat, coarse sand and soil, and bend a branch towards it, about 12in from the tip.

Strip off the leaves where the branch touches the ground. Notch the underside or twist it to injure the tissue. Dig a hole 6in deep in the prepared ground beneath the notched section and partly fill it with an equal-parts mixture of peat, soil and coarse sand.

Peg the notched part into the hole and cover it with the mixture. Stake the tip.

Make sure the spot never dries out, and within 12-15 months the layered branch should have rooted. You can check progress by gently scraping the soil away to have a look, and patting it back in place if the roots are still undeveloped.

Once the roots have formed a rootball about the size of the top growth of the tip above them, sever the new plant and its root from the parent branch and set it in its permanent home.

Plants suitable for layering

Camellia, chimonanthus, cassiope, cornus, corylopsis, cotinus, fothergilla, heaths and heathers, kalmia, lonicera, osmanthus, paeonia, philadelphus, pieris, rhus and viburnum.

LAYERING *Layered shoots root more reliably than ordinary cuttings because they continue to get some nourishment from the parent plant during the year or so they take to root. They can be severed and moved when a sizable rootball has grown.*

their ability to produce chlorophyll. Chlorophyll is the green pigment in plants that absorbs energy from sunlight.

The pattern shown by leaves or stems suffering from such a loss will depend on the location and number of the deviant cells. If these cells occur at the outer parts of the leaves, then the foliage will have white or yellow edges, or even stripes.

On the other hand, if the deviant cells are in the thicker part of the leaves, then the leaves will have white or golden centres. This is what happens in 'Goldheart' ivy, for instance, and in the widely grown oleaster, *Elaeagnus pungens* 'Maculata'.

These variegations can sometimes be hereditary, and so be transmitted through the seeds. But they are usually not hereditary; the variegated form then has to be 'cloned' – that is, propagated by cuttings.

Variegation actually harms plants, and few plants so affected would survive in the wild. This is because the loss of the ability to form chlorophyll reduces the efficiency of the food manufacturing process in the leaves, for which both light and chlorophyll are necessary.

To compensate for this reduction, it is wisest to grow variegated plants in full sun. It's also sensible to grow variegated plants away from any frost pockets in your garden. In the severe frost of 1982, much less damage was done to green plants than to their variegated relatives.

The general rule is, grow them in exactly the same way as their normal relatives, but coddle them a little more. If a totally green shoot appears on a variegated bush, prune it back to the main stem; if left, it would outgrow and eventually swamp the variegated part of the plant.

Hydrangea blue and hydrangea pink

I would like to take cuttings of my hydrangea, which is a lovely deep blue, but have been told that the resulting plants will be pink. Is this true and how should I take the cuttings?

Blue hydrangeas will produce blue-flowered cuttings if the new plants are grown under the same conditions as the parent. Usually, however, plants raised from hydrangea cuttings are taken to another site and since it's the soil content which determines the colour of the flowers, they may well change to pink.

The reason for the colour change is not fully understood, but it's usually said that the blue colour comes from acid soils and the pink from limy, alkaline soils – the reverse, curiously, of the colours you may remember from school chemistry experiments with litmus paper.

Hydrangeas are very easily propagated from cuttings of semi-ripe wood. At the end of July, cut off 10in long sections of young sideshoots which have not flowered, yet have a good collection of leaves. Remove all the leaves except the top pair, and dip the base of each cutting in rooting powder.

Insert the cutting into a pot or box of sandy, well-drained soil, preferably in a cold frame, leaving only the tip of the cutting and the two leaves above the surface.

If you do not have a cold frame, use a deep pot. Stick four short canes in around the side of the pot and open a clear polythene bag over the framework. Secure the bag to the pot with an elastic band or string. Stand the whole thing in a bright place, but out of direct sunlight. Inspect your cuttings regularly, make sure that they don't get too wet, and remove any leaves that turn yellow. You will know the cuttings have rooted when the tip or sideshoots start to grow, usually in the following spring. They can then be moved to their permanent home.

Perpetual youth

How is it that beech hedges keep their leaves all winter, while beech trees drop theirs in autumn? Are they different species?

Beech trees and hedges are the same species and the difference is due simply to the way they are treated. The juvenile, or first-formed leaves of most plants often have different shapes and even a different physical makeup from the mature adult leaves. The regular trimming a beech hedge gets stops it forming adult foliage. But juvenile beech leaves do not readily produce the particular cells which, by their death, cause the adult leaves to fall in autumn. So the juvenile foliage remains on the beech until spring, and a beech hedge is, in effect, a row of permanently juvenile trees.

This effect can sometimes be seen on young beech trees in winter, when the top adult leaves have fallen and the lower, juvenile leaves are still present.

Juvenile leaves are found in many other species as well. They are particularly obvious in ivy, where juvenile leaves are lobed and adult leaves are oval. The cider gum, *Eucalyptus gunnii*, shows the same phenomenon, and is often cut back to maintain its attractive oval juvenile leaves.

Imitation of spring

I am told that if you cut small branches of flowering currant in February and put them in water in the house they will come into flower. Are there any other shrubs you can treat in this way?

Flowering currant (ribes) will certainly flower if treated in this way. But, interestingly, the flowers will often be white even if the flowers remaining outdoors are dark red. The reason for this is that the biochemical mechanisms which produce the red pigment do not operate at the higher temperatures indoors. The same treatment will work for any of the early spring-flowering shrubs which form their flower buds in late summer or early autumn, such as *Daphne mezereum* and *Viburnum tinus*. Normally, they open in spring after a cold spell followed by higher temperatures, and you are mimicking these conditions in the house.

You can do the same thing with forsythia, winter jasmine, witch hazel and other winter-flowering shrubs. Even shoots of lily of the valley can be brought early into flower by this method.

Hoe? No

I keep down weeds among my shrubs by hoeing but am occasionally brought up short as I stub the hoe on a root. Am I doing serious damage, and should I find some other means of keeping the weeds down?

Many shrubs, among them rhododendrons, azaleas, pieris, camellias, and all heathers and roses, have their roots near the surface, and can be damaged by deep hoeing.

There are two kinds of damage possible. One is the damage to, or even the killing of, surface roots caused by the soil surface drying out after being broken up by the hoe. The other occurs when you are hoeing around grafted plants such as roses, lilacs or flowering cherries, where a wound on the rootstock will encourage the production of inferior suckers from the roots. Your roses might become briars and your lilacs become swamped by ancestral privet.

If you must hoe among shrubs, try to disturb no more than the surface inch or so of soil. This is just as destructive to weeds as deep hoeing, and much less destructive to the shrubs you're trying to protect. Probably the best solution is to mulch your shrubs heavily with layers as much as 2-3in thick of peat, bark or compost so that the weeds are smothered, or at least so that they form only shallow roots.

If you don't mind using chemicals and have no underplanting, any weedkiller containing dichlobenil will, if applied in April, keep the bed free of most weeds until autumn. If you do use chemical weedkillers, be sure to apply them before the leaves of the shrubs open. If that is impossible, take special care that none of the spray or dust touches the leaves of your valuable plants.

Green for survival

How long do evergreen shrubs keep their leaves and what's the point of a plant being evergreen anyway?

There are two kinds of evergreens. The most common kind is the large-leaved group that includes rhododendron, viburnum, euonymus and skimmia. The other, and obviously different, group is the one whose members have very small needle-like leaves, such as heather, brooms and all conifers. Leaves vary in the length of time they live. Large, glossy, evergreen leaves are usually shed all the year round, though mainly in spring. Conifer needles may last for many years until the parent twig develops into a small branch and becomes encased in bark.

It's of no great advantage for a plant in a temperate climate to be evergreen, but since leaves manufacture food, it enables these plants to continue making food and a little growth during the winter months when deciduous plants are totally dormant. It is thought that evergreen leaves developed as a water-conservation device in areas with long, cold winters where the soil and the water in it were frozen for months. Evergreen plants could continue to gain nourishment through their leaves in situations where deciduous trees that had shed their leaves would die. It is probably for this reason that the forests of high latitudes are coniferous.

The space between

Gardening books always tell you how much space to leave between two identical plants. But nobody seems to explain how much space I should leave between dissimilar neighbours – in a shrub border, say. Is there a straightforward way of working it out?

Yes, there is. Many formulas have been advanced to solve this difficulty, but the simplest is 'the rule of three'. Under the rule, you add the final *heights* of any two neighbouring shrubs, and divide the total by three. The answer is the planting distance.

Thus, if shrub A grows 6ft tall and shrub B grows 4ft tall, then the total is 10ft. Divide by three and you get 3ft 4in. Call it 3½ft and you have about the right spacing to leave between those two shrubs.

Burying treasure

When establishing my shrubbery, is there any reason why I shouldn't make food reservoirs for my plants by burying garden rubbish deep below their roots?

Buried garden rubbish will add to the future humus content of the soil. But there are snags. If, say, you don't bury the weeds sufficiently deeply – 3ft or more – they may start to grow again, and then you will be faced with the problem of weeds mixed with the roots of your shrubs. Deep-rooted weeds, such as couch grass, ground elder, bracken or mare's tail in such a situation would be practically ineradicable.

But then, if you bury the weeds very deeply, they will take a long time to break down to humus. And when they do, cavities may well be left in the soil which can induce the shrubs to sink and break their tender roots. It might also cause a temporary nitrogen shortage, because decomposition requires nitrogen, so depriving the shrubs. It is not until the process of decomposition is complete that the chemical becomes fully available again for the plants. It is probably wiser to start a compost heap, provided you omit the weeds and the mowings from lawns that have been treated with weedkiller.

A gift yucca

My mother-in-law has just given me a yucca that's far too big for the sitting room. Can I plant it in the garden?

You can and should, especially if you live in the South. What you probably have is *Yucca recurvifolia*, which puts out 6ft panicles of creamy flowers between August and October. It is hardy and long-lived, and does particularly well in poor sandy soil in seaside gardens, though any well-drained garden soil will suit it. Plant it out in April in a sunny site. The long, strap-like leaves are very handsome, but it is unlikely to flower until the woody trunk reaches 3ft high.

Coddling a buddleia

I'm thinking of growing a buddleia. Does the plant need special protection from hard frosts?

You haven't said which kind of buddleia you're thinking of. If it's *Buddleia davidii*, the lovely butterfly bush, or *B. alternifolia*, with its sweetly scented lavender-blue flowers, then neither of these needs much protection. Both reach up and out to 15ft or so and are fairly hardy. When they're young, you could protect them in winter with a layer of peat or straw spread over the crowns; otherwise leave them to their own devices. It might be worth mentioning that *B. alternifolia* flowers on old wood, so should be pruned back to within two or three buds of the parent stem immediately after flowering. *B. davidii*, on the other hand, flowers on new wood, so you should cut all last year's stems back to two or three buds from their base in March.

A number of other buddleias, however, are only half-hardy in Britain. They include the pink-flowered *B. colvillei* and the orange-yellow *B. globosa*, both of which grow to around 10ft. These need to be grown against a west-facing or south-facing wall where they will have the maximum amount of warmth before the sun sets. If your district is really cold, you'd probably do better to choose the hardier species.

Bark round the bushes

All the books tell me to mulch my shrubs, but my small compost heap does not provide enough for the job. What else could I use?

Bark or sawdust would be excellent for the job. For a long time there was a reluctance among gardeners to use powdered or shredded tree material, since it was feared that it might carry honey fungus disease. The processes now used in commercial bark and timber production, however, have eliminated this possibility, making them perfectly safe. When mulching with these materials, you should also sprinkle on a high-nitrogen fertiliser to help the decomposition of the mulch into humus. A couple of handfuls to the square yard would do.

In time, the mulch will break down to add valuable humus and some nutrients to the soil. The breakdown rate depends on the mulching material. Compost takes about six months, peat a year or more. Sawdust and bark may take two to five years, depending on the size of the fragments. Sprinkle on more high-nitrogen fertiliser every year until the sawdust and the bark have broken down completely.

The glory of calico

On a recent walk through a stately garden, I was captivated by the gorgeous pink display put forth by a considerately labelled calico bush. What are my chances of growing it?

Pretty good, provided you have or can provide fairly acid soil. The calico bush, *Kalmia latifolia*, which is an evergreen, can reach 10ft high. It is an acid-loving plant which needs to be grown in a light soil that is free of lime. If you don't already have an acid soil, put plenty of peat in the planting hole and in the planting mixture.

In many ways the bush is like a rhododendron, and if you can grow the one, you can grow the other. Kalmia will thrive in partial shade and should be mulched with at least a 2in thick layer of peat each spring.

No regular pruning is required, but for the first five years or so trim off the faded flower clusters in July to stop the seeds forming. If the bush becomes straggly, cut out old or dead wood in April.

Pretty bush, pretty simple

My 'new' old cottage has an abelia bush growing by a wall, about 5ft tall with little pink and white trumpet-shaped blossoms. It is so pretty I would like another. Can I propagate from it, and when is the kindest time to prune?

Propagation is pretty simple for most species of abelia. Pruning is even simpler: it isn't necessary, though overgrown shoots may be thinned out after flowering. This would be in October for your plant which, from its description, is *Abelia grandiflora*.

To propagate, take some 3-4in cuttings from the current season's wood in July. Plant three or four in a half-and-half mixture of peat and sand in a 3in pot. Place the pot in a cold frame, on a warm windowsill or in a greenhouse. The cuttings should be ready for planting out in the following spring.

PICK OF THE SHRUBS

Choosing the right shrub for a particular spot in the garden can be a bewildering business. Most shrubs will *tolerate* most sorts of conditions, but they won't necessarily *thrive* in all conditions. Some prefer clay to sand or vice versa. Some do well only on an acid soil. Some are at their best in full sun, and refuse to flower in shade. This chart is designed to help you through the maze to the shrub that's just right for your needs. You can use it in two ways: to check on the ideal soil and light conditions for a particular shrub that you're thinking of planting; or to find a shrub that meets a particular set of conditions – a medium-sized plant, say, that flowers in winter and will thrive in a shady spot on alkaline soil. The 'Peak display' season marked for each plant is the one in which it looks its best. Shrubs that are at their peak in more than one season – for instance, those which bloom in summer (June–August) and produce berries or colourful foliage in autumn (September–November) – are marked in both. Figures for the spread of a plant are given only for shrubs which are usually grown to fill an area rather than for their height.

	Soil		Texture			Light						Peak di			
Name	Acid	Alkaline	Sand	Clay	Loam	Sun	Semi-shade	Shade	Height at maturity	Flowers and foliage	Fruit and berries	Spring	Summer	Autumn	Winte
Abelia floribunda	●			●		●			Up to 5ft	Rose-white, scented		●	●		
Abelia triflora	●			●		●			Up to 15ft	White, scented			●		
Acer japonicum 'Aureum'	●		●					●	Up to 20ft	Golden foliage, turning crimson				●	
Acer palmatum 'Atropurpureum'	●				●	●			Up to 15ft	Bronze-red foliage				●	
Andromeda polifolia	●			●			●		6-12in/ spread 12in	Pink-white		●	●		
Aralia elata	●			●	●		●	●	8ft	White			●	●	
Acuba japonica 'Crotonifolia'		●	●	●			●	●	6-12ft	Variegated foliage					●
Berberis darwinii	●	●	●	●	●	●	●	●	8-10ft	Evergreen, orange		●			
Berberis x *stenophylla*		●	●					●	8-10ft	Yellow		●			
Berberis thunbergii 'Atropurpurea Nana'		●			●	●			1-1½ft/ spread 6ft	Red-purple foliage		●			
Buddleia alternifolia		●	●			●			12-20ft	Lavender-blue			●		
Buddleia davidii 'Royal Red'		●			●	●			9ft	Red, purple			●	●	
Callistemon salignus (hardy only in sheltered sites)	●				●	●			5-8ft	Yellow			●		
Camellia japonica 'Adolphe Audusson'	●		●				●		6-12ft	Blood red					●
Camellia japonica 'Contessa Lavinia Maggi'	●				●		●		6-12ft	Pink		●			
Caryopteris x *clandonensis*	●			●			●		2-4ft/ spread 2-4ft	Blue			●	●	
Cassiope lycopodioides	●				●			●	2-3in/spread 1-1½ft	White		●			
Cercis siliquastrum		●			●	●			15-20ft	Rose-purple		●			
Chaenomeles speciosa 'Cardinalis'		●	●	●				●	6ft	Deep red		●			●
Chaenomeles speciosa 'Nivalis'		●	●	●				●	6ft	White		●			●
Chimonanthus praecox		●		●		●			10ft	Yellow, scented					●
Choisya ternata	●			●		●			5-6ft	White, scented; evergreen		●			
Clethra alnifolia	●			●				●	6ft	White			●	●	
Colutea arborescens	●			●		●			8ft	Yellow	Copper seedpods		●	●	
Cornus alba 'Elegantissima'		●		●			●		8-10ft	Variegated; red stems in winter					●
Cornus alba 'Sibirica'	●				●		●		8-10ft	Bright red stems					●
Cornus canadensis	●				●			●	4-6in/ spread 2ft	White			●		
Cornus kousa chinensis	●		●				●		10ft	Yellow; red autumn foliage				●	
Cornus mas		●	●			●			8-12ft	Golden-yellow		●			●
Corylopsis willmottiae	●	●		●	●		●		10ft	Yellow, scented		●			
Cotoneaster horizontalis	●				●	●			2ft/spread 6-7ft	Pink	Red berries		●	●	

Name	Soil: Acid	Soil: Alkaline	Texture: Sand	Texture: Clay	Texture: Loam	Light: Sun	Light: Semi-shade	Light: Shade	Height at maturity	Flowers and foliage	Fruit and berries	Peak display: Spring	Peak display: Summer	Peak display: Autumn	Peak display: Winter
Cytisus x *beanii*	●	●	●	●	●	●			1½-2ft/ spread 3ft	Yellow		●			
Cytisus x *kewensis*	●	●	●	●	●	●			1-2ft/ spread 4ft	Pale yellow		●			
Cytisus nigricans	●	●	●	●	●			●	3-4ft	Yellow			●	●	
Cytisus x *praecox*	●	●	●	●	●	●			5-6ft	Pale yellow		●			
Daboecia cantabrica	●				●	●			3ft	Purple-red			●	●	●
Daphne x *burkwoodii* 'Somerset'	●	●			●		●		3-4ft	Pink, scented		●	●		
Daphne mezereum		●	●			●			5ft	Purple-pink		●			●
Daphne odora 'Aureomarginata'		●			●			●	5-6ft	Pale purple		●			●
Elaeagnus pungens 'Maculata'	●			●				●	8-12ft	Green and gold foliage					●
Enkianthus campanulatus	●		●					●	8ft	White; red autumn foliage		●		●	
Erica carnea varieties	●	●	●		●	●	●		1ft/ spread 2ft	Various		●			●
Erica x *darleyensis*	●		●				●		2ft/ spread 3ft	White, pink or purple		●			●
Escallonia 'Apple Blossom'	●		●			●			5ft	Evergreen; pink			●	●	
Escallonia macrantha	●		●			●			6-10ft	Evergreen; red			●	●	
Eucalyptus gunnii	●		●				●		45ft	Silvery-grey young foliage			●		
Euonymus alatus 'Compactus'	●				●			●	6-8ft	Green; red autumn foliage			●	●	
Euonymus japonicus 'Ovatus Aureus'		●			●	●			10-15ft	Yellow-pink foliage				●	
Fatsia japonica		●		●				●	8-15ft	White				●	
Forsythia x *intermedia* 'Lynwood'		●		●				●	8ft	Yellow		●			
Forsythia x *intermedia* 'Spectabilis'	●	●	●	●			●		8ft	Yellow		●			
Forsythia ovata	●	●		●	●	●			4-5ft	Gold					●
Fothergilla monticola	●				●	●			6-8ft	White		●			
Fremontodendron californica (hardy only in sheltered sites)		●	●			●			8-12ft	Golden-yellow			●	●	
Garrya elliptica 'James Roof'	●		●					●	8-15ft	Grey-green catkins					●
Gaultheria procumbens	●		●		●		●	●	3-6in/ spread 3ft	Evergreen; pink or white	Red berries		●	●	
Gaultheria shallon	●		●	●			●	●	4-6ft	Pink	Purple berries	●	●		
Genista aetnensis	●		●			●			15-20ft	Yellow			●		
Genista lydia	●		●			●			2-3ft/ spread 6ft	Yellow		●	●		
Griselinia littoralis	●				●	●			10-25ft	Evergreen, shiny foliage					●
Halesia carolina	●				●	●			15-20ft	White		●			
Hamamelis mollis 'Pallida'	●			●		●			6-8ft	Yellow, scented					●
Hebe brachysiphon		●	●			●			6ft	White; evergreen			●		
Hedera helix 'Hibernica'		●	●					●	50-100ft	Evergreen					●
Hoheria sexstylosa		●			●		●		10-15ft	Evergreen; white			●		
Hydrangea macropyhlla 'Nikko Blue'	●	●	●	●	●			●	4-6ft	Blue (especially on acid soils)			●	●	

continued overleaf

continued from page 319

Name	Soil: Acid	Soil: Alkaline	Texture: Sand	Texture: Clay	Texture: Loam	Light: Sun	Light: Semi-shade	Light: Shade	Height at maturity	Flowers and foliage	Fruit and berries	Peak d: Spring	Peak d: Summer	Peak d: Autumn	Peak d: Wint
Ilex cornuta		•		•			•		5-8ft	White or green	Red berries				•
Indigofera gerardiana (hardy only in sheltered sites)	•				•	•			5-6ft	Red-purple			•	•	
Jasminum nudiflorum		•	•				•		10ft	Yellow		•			•
Kalmia latifolia	•		•					•	6-10ft	Pink			•		
Kerria japonica	•				•		•		4-6ft	Orange-yellow		•			
Leptospermum scoparium	•		•			•			6-10ft	Red			•		
Ligustrum ovalifolium 'Aureum'		•			•			•	12-15ft	Gold foliage; white flowers			•		
Lonicera fragrantissima		•			•		•		6ft	White, scented		•			•
Lonicera x *purpusii*		•			•	•			6ft	Cream		•			•
Lupinus arboreus	•		•			•			2-4ft/spread 2-4ft	Yellow			•		
Magnolia stellata	•			•	•	•	•		8-10ft	White, scented		•			
Mahonia aquifolium	•	•	•	•	•		•	•	3-5ft	Yellow	Blue-black berries	•			
Mahonia bealii	•	•	•	•	•			•	6-8ft	Yellow					•
Mahonia x 'Charity'	•	•	•	•	•	•			8-10ft	Yellow					•
Mahonia japonica	•	•	•	•	•		•	•	8-10ft	Yellow, scented		•			•
Myrtus communis	•				•		•		8-10ft	White, scented			•		
Osmanthus decorus	•			•				•	6-10ft	White, scented		•			
Osmanthus delavayi 'Latifolius'	•				•			•	6-8ft	Evergreen; white, scented		•			
Paeonia lobata	•				•		•		2ft/ spread 2ft	Deep red			•		
Paeonia lutea		•	•		•	•	•		4-6ft	Yellow, scented			•		
Paeonia lutea 'L'Esperance'		•	•		•	•	•		4-6ft	Yellow			•		
Parrotia persica	•				•			•	10-18ft	Crimson, amber and gold autumn leaves				•	
Pereskia aculeata		•		•				•	Up to 30ft	White, pale yellow or pink					•
Philadelphus x 'Avalanche'	•	•	•	•	•	•	•		3-5ft	White			•		
Philadelphus 'Beauclerk'	•	•	•	•	•	•	•		6-8ft	White			•		
Philadelphus coronarius 'Aureus'	•	•	•	•	•	•	•		6-9ft	White; golden foliage			•		
Photinia x *fraseri* 'Red Robin'	•			•				•	7-10ft	Young foliage red		•			
Picea glauca 'Albertiana Conica'	•		•				•		4ft	Grass-green					•
Pieris 'Forest Flame'	•				•			•	6-12ft	White; young foliage orange-red		•			
Pieris formosa 'Forrestii'	•		•				•		6-12ft	Young foliage bright red		•			
Potentilla fruticosa 'Katherine Dykes'		•	•				•		4ft	Yellow			•	•	
Potentilla fruticosa 'Tangerine'		•			•		•		2ft/ spread 5ft	Orange			•	•	
Prunus lusitanica		•	•					•	15-20ft	White, scented			•		
Prunus 'Shimidsu Sakura'		•			•	•			10-15ft	Pink-tinged buds, opening to white		•			
Prunus subhirtella 'Autumnalis'		•			•	•			20-30ft	White		•			•
Prunus triloba		•		•		•			10-15ft	Pink, double		•			

Name	Soil: Acid	Soil: Alkaline	Texture: Sand	Texture: Clay	Texture: Loam	Light: Sun	Light: Semi-shade	Light: Shade	Height at maturity	Flowers and foliage	Fruit and berries	Peak display: Spring	Peak display: Summer	Peak display: Autumn	Peak display: Winter
Pyracantha crenulata rogersiana	●			●				●	8-10ft	White	Orange berries		●		
Rhododendron 'Elizabeth'	●		●					●	2-3ft/spread 3-6ft	Scarlet		●			
Ribes sanguineum 'King Edward VII'	●			●		●			6-9ft	Crimson		●			
Ruscus aculeatus		●		●				●	2-3ft/spread 2-3ft	Evergreen	Red berries				●
Salix alba 'Chermesina'		●		●			●		15-25ft	Orange-red twigs		●			●
Sambucus racemosa 'Plumosa Aurea'		●		●			●		8-10ft	Golden foliage	Scarlet berries	●	●		
Sarcococca humilis	●	●	●	●				●	2ft/ spread 2ft	Evergreen; white, scented					●
Senecio x 'Sunshine'	●			●			●		2-3ft/ spread 4ft	Yellow flowers; grey foliage			●	●	
Skimmia japonica 'Rubella'	●		●	●			●		3-5ft	Pink	Bright red berries		●	●	
Skimmia reevesiana	●			●		●			1½-3ft/ spread 3-4ft	Cream	Crimson berries		●		
Spiraea x *arguta*		●		●			●		6-8ft	White		●			
Stephanandra incisa prostrata		●			●			●	1½-3ft/ spread 4ft	Green			●		
Symphoricarpos albus		●			●			●	5-7ft	Pink	White berries			●	●
Symphoricarpos orbiculatus		●		●				●	5-6ft	Pink	Pink-purple berries			●	●
Symphoricarpos 'White Hedger'		●			●			●	5-7ft	Pink	White berries				●
Syringa x *josiflexa* 'Bellicent'		●	●	●	●	●	●	●	12-15ft	Rose-pink		●	●		
Syringa microphylla		●	●	●	●	●	●	●	4-5ft	Lilac, scented			●	●	
Syringa microphylla 'Superba'		●	●	●	●	●	●	●	6-8ft	Rose-pink, scented		●	●	●	
Syringa palibiniana		●	●	●	●	●	●	●	5ft	Lavender-purple		●			
Syringa vulgaris 'Congo'		●	●	●	●	●	●	●	8-12ft	Pink, scented		●			
Syringa vulgaris 'Primrose'		●	●	●	●	●	●	●	8-12ft	Pale yellow, slightly scented		●			
Tamarix tetrandra	●		●			●			10-15ft	Pink		●			
Vaccinium corymbosum	●				●			●	4-6ft	Pink-tinted white	Blue berries		●	●	
Vaccinium vitis-idaea	●				●			●	6in/spread 1½ft	White or pale pink	Red berries		●	●	●
Viburnum x *burkwoodii*		●		●		●			8ft	Evergreen; white, scented		●			
Viburnum davidii	●	●		●			●		2-3ft/spread 4-5ft	Evergreen; white flowers	Turquoise-blue berries		●		●
Viburnum farreri		●			●		●		9-12ft	White, scented					●
Virburnum opulus 'Compactum'		●		●	●		●	●	6ft	White	Red berries		●	●	
Virburnum plicatum tomentosum 'Lanarth'		●		●			●		8-10ft	White		●			
Viburnum plicatum tomentosum 'Mariesii'		●		●		●			8-10ft	White			●		
Virburnum tinus		●	●			●			7-10ft	Evergreen; pink-white		●			●
Weigela 'Abel Carriere'		●		●		●			5-6ft	Rose-pink			●		
Weigela florida		●	●				●		6ft	Rose-pink			●		
Weigela florida 'Foliis Purpureis'		●			●	●			5ft	Pink; purple foliage			●		
Weigela florida 'Variegata'		●		●			●		3ft/spread 3-4ft	Pale pink; variegated			●		

SILVER LEAF

Plum tree at risk

My neighbour says he's worried by the silvery sheen that has appeared recently on a few of the leaves of my 'Victoria' plum. He thinks it might affect his trees. Is he right?

He may be. What your tree probably has is a fungal disease called silver leaf. Plums are particularly prone to it. But so, too, to a lesser degree, are pears, cherries, lilacs and other trees and shrubs.

However, you can't be sure that your tree has it until you cut off a branch – at least 1in thick – on which the silver leaves appear. Moisten either of the cut ends, and if a brown or purple stain appears within a few minutes, then your tree has the disease. The disease is not actually infectious at this stage; that happens after about a year when it has killed a branch and a flat, layered, purplish-to-fawn fungus forms on the dead wood. The fungus throws out spores, some of which will land on minute wounds in other susceptible trees. That's why your neighbour is worried.

Damp weather is the time of greatest danger. The only cure is to cut back infected branches – those with silvery leaves – to at least 6in below the point where the stain shows. Then cover the wound with fungicidal paint. After that, feeding and general care may restore the tree to health. It is not necessary to destroy the tree unless the disease becomes really widespread in it.

SILVER WARNING *Leaves showing a silvery sheen may mark the presence of a deadly fungal disease. But prompt action can save it.*

SLUGS AND SNAILS

Chemical concern

What's the safest chemical method for getting rid of slugs and snails?

Modern chemical methods of controlling the pests – most commonly slug pellets or liquid slug and snail killers – are largely based on one of two substances: metaldehyde and methiocarb. Both are also poisonous to fish and other animals, although scientific research suggests that hedgehogs, which eat large numbers of slugs, are rarely harmed by metaldehyde in their prey.

One way to cut the risks is to use a liquid product rather than the conspicuous pellets or paste. Another is to make the chemicals inaccessible to larger animals – by spreading them under a propped-up tile, say.

The risk of pellets

Is there any way I can get rid of slugs and snails without poisoning every other animal in sight, including my own pets?

Yes, but remember the old saw that there's no reward without risk. The more you try to get rid of the pests completely, the greater the risk to other animals; and the more safety-conscious you are, the more survivors there will be among the pests. The trouble really is that almost any substance poisonous to slugs and snails is poisonous to other creatures, too. Non-chemical methods, on the other hand, tend either to be less reliable or to involve a lot more work.

Still, there are some non-chemical approaches worth trying. First, try cleaning up the places, such as thick foliage and plant debris, where the pests hide during the day – they are active mostly by night.

Alternatively, if you can't get rid of the hiding places, get rid of the pests. Pick them off by hand as they emerge in the evening, and drop them into a bucket of water.

A third strategy is to forget the pests and concentrate simply on keeping them away from your plants. Sprinkle a barrier of fine ashes, soot or spiny twigs such as gorse – all of them are uncomfortable for slugs and snails to cross. Or fill saucers with beer and bury them up to their rims close to the plants. Prop an old slate or tile over them to keep the rain out. Slugs and snails drawn by the smell start drinking the beer, become unconscious, and drown in it.

Another method is to place empty grapefruit halves upside down near the threatened plants. Slugs will be attracted to the pungent fruit and will gather beneath the halves. Dispose of the catch each morning.

How to guard potatoes

I've no problem with slugs on most of my garden plants, but my potatoes are devastated by them. What's the answer?

Your problem is almost certainly the type called the keeled slug. It's particularly difficult to fight because it spends most of its life underground, effectively beyond the reach of slug pellets.

You could of course work large numbers of pellets into the soil around your crop. That would keep the slugs away, but many gardeners understandably fight shy of using such large doses of chemicals.

Dusting the seed potatoes at planting time with soot will help to protect them, but it won't keep the slugs off the new crop. Avoiding susceptible varieties – particularly 'Maris Piper', 'King Edward', 'Desirée' and 'Pentland Crown' – will help, too, if you know that your soil has a large population of the slugs. Another tip is to dig your soil in autumn and leave it rough for the winter; that will help to expose large numbers of the pests to the killing cold. It's also worth lifting maincrop varieties promptly each year because the worst of the slug damage normally happens late in the season.

Since your problem is so severe, though, your best bet is to grow only early varieties, and to grow them under sheets of black polythene laid on the ground over the whole bed at planting time.

Sprinkle slug pellets on the soil before you lay the plastic, and lift the sheets from time to time to renew the bait.

The beauty of this system is that the new potatoes form on top of the soil under the plastic. So the slugs have to surface to feed – and there the pellets are, waiting for them. The plastic doesn't look exactly beautiful in the garden, even when it's partly concealed by the plants (cut a cross in the sheet to let each plant through as it surfaces). But it has two useful bonuses: it keeps pets and other animals away from the pellets; and it saves all that work of earthing up.

LITTLE PERFORATIONS *Tattered holes in leaves, and slime tracks, are the tell-tale signs of a raid by slugs and snails.*

SNOWDROPS

Giant snowdrops

A garden down the road contains a patch of grass that in late winter is carpeted with snowdrops which are taller and have much larger flowers than the usual ones. Are these easy to grow, and where do I find them?

The doubles and the giants are just as vigorous as the sturdy single-flowered *Galanthus nivalis*, the familiar and much-loved snowdrop. You can find them in most garden centres.

Make sure you get the right type, though, because some of the less common varieties will struggle in the open, or in grass, and would do better in a sheltered spot in the rock garden. For the wide-open spaces, try the large hybrid *G. n.* 'S. Arnott', which is both tough and vigorous.

Spring move

The sages tell us that we must divide and plant snowdrops as soon as they finish flowering. But surely as bulbous plants they should be planted in the autumn?

Not in this case. With snowdrops you get the best results by planting them while they are still green. That is, immediately after flowering and before the leaves begin to fade. Look in the garden centres and nurseries in February or March and you will see that this is the time when snowdrops are most commonly offered for sale, though you can also buy dry bulbs in autumn.

If you want to multiply your own stock, follow the nurserymen's example, and dig up and divide the clumps as soon as flowering is over. Do it carefully so that each bulb is separated with its roots and leaves intact. Replant the bulbs immediately so that they do not dry out.

Seed time

Small yellow fruits, which I assume to be seed pods, are hanging from the stems of my snowdrops. If I sow them, will they produce more snowdrops?

Yes, but it's a slow process – three years or more from seed to flower. The secret of success is to sow as soon as the seeds are ripe. You'll know when this is, because the fruits will exude a jelly-like substance; this contains the ripe seeds.

Don't try to separate the seeds from the jelly. Spread it onto a tray of John Innes seed compost. Sprinkle a light covering of compost over the jelly and put the tray in a cool place.

By autumn, you should have a number of onion-like plants, though germination is often erratic. Bulbs capable of flowering will be produced by the end of the third year, and some will bring forth flowers in the following spring.

If there's no sign of growth by about October, put the tray in the freezer for a week or ten days, then take it outdoors and leave it in a warm and sunny position. With luck, the brief freeze will trick the seeds into thinking that winter has come and gone, and should trigger germination.

Good in grass

Why do most people grow snowdrops in the lawn rather than in flowerbeds? Don't they get in the way when you begin mowing?

They're usually grown in grass because that's where many gardeners think they look best. But there's no reason in principle why you shouldn't grow them in a flowerbed if you prefer.

As to whether they get in the way, like naturalised daffodils can do, the answer is on the whole, no. Snowdrops flower before the grass starts growing, so by the time you get the lawn mower out, the flowers have long gone and the foliage is beginning to fade as well. By the time you get to the second or third cut of spring, the foliage should be pretty well dead – so you can safely mow straight over it.

Mind you, it's important to mow round the plants for as long as the leaves stay green. As with most bulb plants, it is the leaves that help to feed the bulb and make for a good show next season.

To plant dry, shop-bought snowdrops in turf in autumn, simply cut a large X or H in the lawn across the spot you want, undercut the turf between the cuts and roll it back. Fork over the soil beneath and sprinkle into it a handful or two of bone meal. You can plant the bulbs at precise spacings if you want, but there's no need to. You can achieve a more natural look by scattering the bulbs at random over the prepared area, and planting them where they fall. Cover each bulb with 1-2in of soil, then replace the turf. The common snowdrop, *Galanthus*

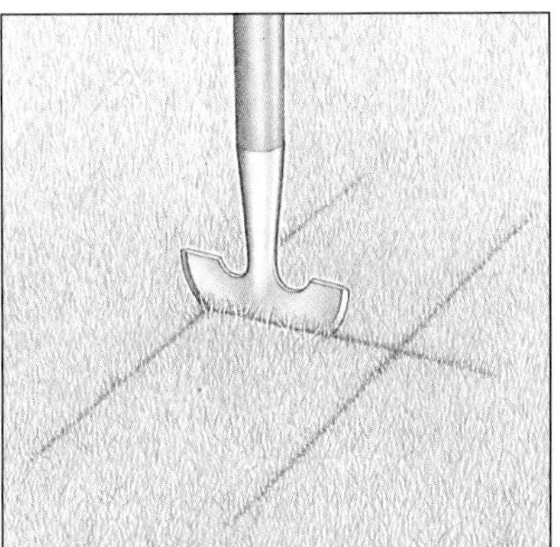

1 *To plant snowdrops in grass, cut an H or X shape about $1\frac{1}{2}$in deep in the turf with an edging tool or a spade.*

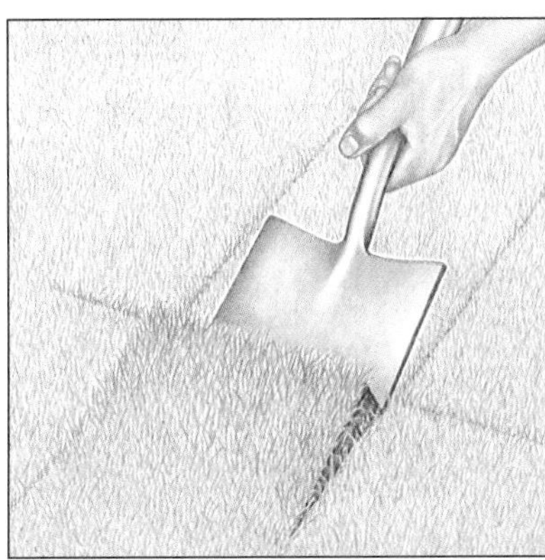

2 *Undercut the edges of the turf between the cuts, and roll the grass back to expose the soil beneath.*

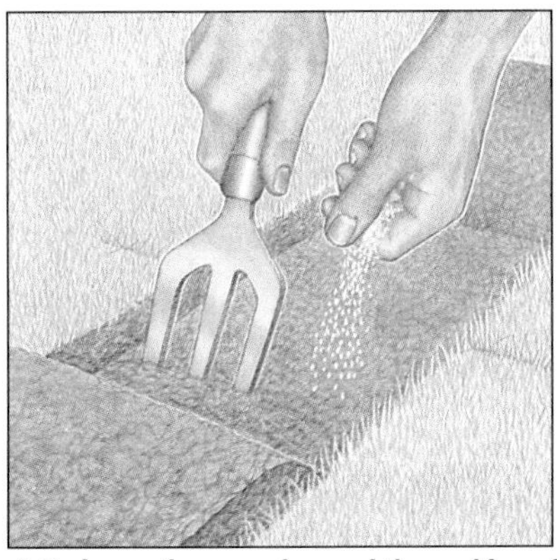

3 *Fork over the exposed ground thoroughly and mix into it a couple of handfuls of bone meal to stimulate the bulbs' root growth.*

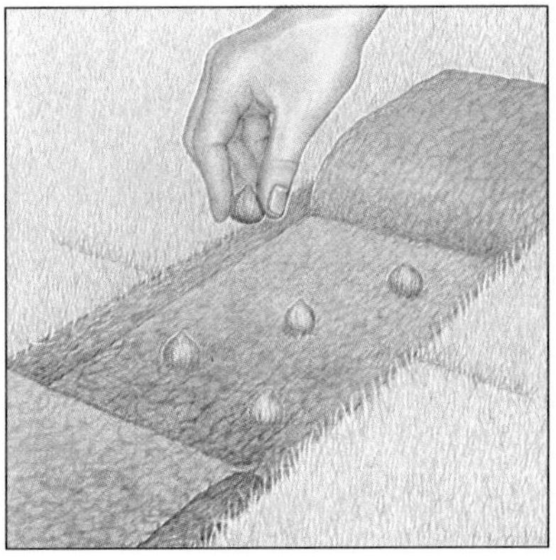

4 *Scatter the bulbs or place them in the positions you want. Bury them 1-2in deep, then unroll the lifted turf over the area.*

nivalis, is one of the best to grow in grass. It settles in more quickly than some of the more showy varieties, and, once established, comes up reliably year after year.

If you're transplanting your own or bought bulbs into a lawn in spring – and they still have leaves on – don't bury the leaves. Use a bulb planter to take out 2-3in deep cores of turf and soil, and leave the foliage jutting out when you replace the plug over the bulb.

PICK OF THE SNOWDROPS

Name	Height/Spacing	Flowers
Galanthus elwesii	4-10in/4-8in	Large white, single (Feb-Mar)
G. nivalis (common snowdrop)	4-8in/3-6in	White, single (Jan-Feb)
G. n. 'Atkinsii'	6-8in/3in	Large white, single (early Jan)
G. n. 'Flore-plena'	4-6in/3in	White, double (Jan-Feb)
G. n. 'S. Arnott'	9-12in/3in	Large white, single (Jan-Mar)

SOIL STRUCTURE

What makes soil?

What do experts mean when they talk about soil texture and soil structure?

Soil texture is a description of the size and type of mineral particles that make up the soil. Soil structure is the way in which the particles are held together. Soil is a mixture of broken-down rock particles and crystals held together by water and organic matter. There are two extreme types:

Sand – the ground-down particles of sandstone rock; they are relatively large, from about 0.02mm (0.0008in) up to about 2mm (0.08in) in diameter.

Clay – a mixture of fine particles at least one-tenth the size of the smallest sand grains; they're less than 0.002mm (0.00008in) across, and made of aluminium silicate and soda, potash and lime crystals.

Soils with a high proportion of sand are said to be light. Those with a high proportion of clay are known as heavy. Between these extremes lie mixtures of the two. The soil in your garden will probably be somewhere towards the middle of the range.

Many soils also contain chalk or limestone. These soils can be light or heavy (see *Chalk versus limestone*, page 53).

The structure of the soil is determined by the material that holds these particles together. This is a mixture of organic matter in various stages of decomposition, micro-organisms, bacteria and water.

Changing soil patterns

In a country as small as Britain, I would have expected the soil to be much the same everywhere, yet there are obviously many different types. How did this happen, and is there an 'ordinary' soil?

The nature of surface soil depends chiefly on the nature of the underlying rock. Several different types of rock stretch across Britain: sedimentary sandstone, chalk, limestone, clay and shales, for example, as well as the volcanic rocks granite and basalt.

Millions of years of weathering of these rocks have produced the basic soils of each region. In addition, some rocks and soils were bulldozed across the country, then dumped erratically, by the great glaciers of the Ice Age, which about 10,000 years ago ended their southward march roughly along the line of the River Thames. Local accidents of geology and biology – a crumbled outcrop of chalk, the crushed remains of a rotted primeval forest, the deposited silt of a riverbed which changed course – add to the complex jumble, changing the soil between one village and the next. Even from garden to garden, a soil can change – where an orchard once grew, where a builder stored clay bricks, or where an underlying rock course holds water.

So, the answer to the other part of your question is that there is no such thing as an ordinary soil. All soil is different.

Kindly frost

Why is frost good for the soil?

Water expands when it freezes, forcing soil particles apart. As the ground thaws, the water shrinks to its normal volume and air rushes in. This is part of the natural phenomenon of weathering.

It is particularly important in heavy clay, when you dig your soil roughly in autumn and leave it for the winter. Frost turns the water in the ground to ice, repeatedly stretching the clay apart and cracking it open, so that as the weather warms the soil falls broken into a good tilth. Even the toughest clay will have its structure considerably improved by the action of frost.

This is not so important with a sandy soil. It is often as well not to dig this type of soil until spring, or you may open up the soil too much, so that its nutrients leach out and you have to correct the excessive drainage with large doses of organic material.

The garden's ideal mix

What is loam?

This is the ideal soil, the one all gardeners aim for. It drains freely, yet holds water and nutrients. It is soft and crumbly and easy to dig. Plants thrive in it. Hardly anyone is lucky enough to have it. Scientists have a formula for it. They take as their basic guide the following measurements:

Clay is a soil with particles less than 0.002mm (0.00008in) in diameter. *Silt* is 0.002-0.02mm. *Fine sand* is 0.02-0.2mm. *Coarse sand* is 0.2-2mm. *Gravel* is 2mm (0.08in) upwards.

On this basis, a medium loam, the best of all soils, is ideally a mixture of: 8.8 per cent of coarse sand; 45.1 per cent of fine sand; 19 per cent of silt; 16.1 per cent of clay; and 11 per cent of moisture and organic matter. Even if you have got it, you won't be able to define it like that.

Any loam, heavy or light, is fine for the garden and you will know it by its balance of fine and medium particles, by its slight stickiness, by the way it breaks up easily as you dig, and by the way it holds its moisture and does not bake hard in the sun.

To get it, you need to add plenty of manure or well-rotted compost to your soil – and, on clay, lime as well.

Why lime likes to be alone

Gardening books always say that lime should go on separately from fertilisers. But the books I've seen never say why. Can you help?

The reason for the advice is chemical. Many fertilisers contain nitrogen (which is vital for leafy growth) in the form of compounds based on ammonia – a chemical made of nitrogen and hydrogen. Lime unlocks these compounds, releasing the ammonia. Since ammonia is a gas, it then blows away in the wind, taking the nitrogen with it.

Mixed with one common high-nitrogen fertiliser, sulphate of ammonia, lime has an even more drastic effect. First it drives off the ammonia, so that the fertiliser becomes valueless. Then it mixes with the sulphur left behind (the sulphate part of the fertiliser). Since lime makes soil more alkaline and sulphur makes it more acidic, the two chemicals cancel each other out, destroying the purpose of adding the lime.

Lime should not go on with manure, either. It deprives manure of nitrogen, and thus slows down the rate at which it decomposes into valuable humus (see also *Using lime wisely*, page 73).

Identifying soil

How do I discover what kind of soil I have?

Look at it. Feel it. Dig it. And note which plants do well in it.

● **LOOK** Dark soils are usually rich in organic matter. Pale grey soils suggest chalk with little organic material.

Yellow and red soils are normally sandstone soils that drain well, need feeding and may be acidic. Yellow or orange sticky soils are usually clay. There may be plenty of nutrients in them, but there won't be much air. Brown soils are generally clayey loam – pretty good soils if they are kept open and drained. Dark, flaky soil is often peaty, and that usually means it's acidic.

● **FEEL** Pick up the soil and smear it between your finger and thumb. If it feels smooth but lumpy, it's clay. If it is gritty, it's coarse or medium sand. If it is silky and slippery, it's silty clay. If it sticks to your boots, it's clay; if it doesn't, it's sandy. If it blows about in the wind, it's fine sand. If you crush it in your hand and it falls apart as you open it, it's too sandy. If it clings loosely together, you have loam, the ideal garden soil.

● **DIG** If the soil sticks to your spade and turns over in shiny lumps, it is clay. If you can turn it over immediately after rain and it still falls apart, it is sandy.

● **PLANTS** Look around – and not just in your garden – at the natural plants that grow. In heavy clays with a lot of water in the soil, you will find rushes, sedges, moss and algae. In rich fertile soil there will be stinging nettles, sow-thistle and groundsel. In lime or chalk – and that means an alkaline soil – clover and wild clematis, or old man's beard, will flourish. On acid land, you will find heathers and sorrel doing well.

There is one other test you can carry out. Dig a small pit in the garden, 2-3ft deep, cutting the sides cleanly and vertical. Look at the soil layers. The top layer, anything up to 12in deep, should be crumbly, dark and full of organic matter. The next layer will usually be lighter in colour because it has less organic matter in it. If it is coarse and gritty, it is sandy. If it is hard, compacted and shiny when wet, it is clay. Beneath it you should find the parent material from which the upper soil is derived.

While the pit is dug out, you can test the drainage of your soil. Fill the pit with water. If it is all gone in 24 hours, drainage is good. If there is still some there after 48 hours, drainage is poor.

Basic material

Does soil type determine soil texture?

The type is the basic material your soil starts out with. A soil that has been naturally created over thousands or millions of years by the breaking down and steady weathering of sandstone rock won't change its type or its texture. It will always be a sandy soil. Over more and more years – but not in your lifetime – it will merely become a finer sandy soil. Clay is a mixture of soft, sedimentary rocks and crystals that tends to lie in level layers in the bottoms of valleys and on plains. It is much less likely to be affected by weathering. It will always remain clay, with the texture of clay.

The structure of the soil – how the particles are held together – is what man can change. Nature does the job itself, to some extent. Micro-organisms, falling and then rotting vegetation, and rainfall all change the structure of soil. Man changes it further by adding manure, compost, sand and peat. Structure can be called the living part of soil – the texture never changes.

Corridors of life

Good soil structure, the gardening experts keep telling us, is important for garden soil. Why?

Good structure creates in the soil the corridors of life which enable the plants to grow. The structure is created by moisture and organic material in the soil: the rotted compost, vegetable matter and micro-organisms which hold together – and keep apart – the particles that make up the mineral part of your garden's soil.

This organic matter opens cracks and fissures – the corridors – in the soil, by holding clumps of clay particles apart and keeping grains of sand together. Along these corridors run air, water, dissolved minerals and nutrients that feed and succour plants. It is in these corridors that the roots form.

Without the organic material, rainwater and plant food would drain straight through sandy soil. Without the organic material, air would be locked out of clay and there would be nowhere for the roots to develop.

The experts are right. Keep your soil structure good. It's not difficult if you regularly dig in well-rotted compost and manure.

Why feeding won't help

I have given my soil good applications of fertiliser, but it is still rock hard in summer and sopping wet in winter. What am I doing wrong?

Your soil structure is all wrong, and no amount of fertiliser will change that.

Fertiliser provides the soil with plant food but does nothing for the structure of the soil. Your soil obviously has a high proportion of clay. Start by digging it well in the autumn (see *Digging*, page 121). As you turn it, work in plenty of bulky organic matter such as well-rotted manure or compost.

At least three months later, sprinkle on lime – about 2oz per square yard. It will make the clay particles clump together to form larger, more workable grains.

Do all this once a year and you will control and, in time, correct both problems: there will be no more compacting in summer, and no more soggy patches in winter. You won't even need to apply quite so much fertiliser because of the nutrients in the organic material you have added.

SPINACH

Runaway leaves

Have you any tips on how to prevent spinach from bolting in the summer?

You can't actually stop summer spinach varieties from 'bolting' – running to seed and flowering. Spinach is an annual plant and so its natural pattern is to complete its lifecycle within one growing season – and that can mean just eight weeks from sowing.

What you can do is *delay* the moment when the plant begins to form flowers, and at the same time ensure that you get more, and better, leaves for picking. To do this, you need fertile, moisture-retentive soil, strong plants – and plenty of water. If the soil's sandy and free-draining, dig in generous quantities of peat, well-rotted compost or manure, preferably in the autumn. This will help it to retain more water in the summer. Increase the fertility by raking in about $3\frac{1}{2}$oz of Growmore per square yard a few days before sowing.

Try to grow spinach in a slightly shaded position, perhaps between rows of peas or broad and runner beans. Strong, direct sunshine for more than a couple of hours a day encourages earlier flowering.

Sow, between March and May, in drills 12-15in apart, and very thinly, because crowded plants become spindly and tend to run to seed more quickly. As soon as the seedlings are large enough to grasp, thin them out to 3in apart. When the remaining plants meet in the rows, thin them again to 6in – the thinnings will be large enough to eat by this time. Some gardeners prefer to thin the plants to a final spacing of as much as 12in to get larger, but fewer leaves. It is essential, either way, to keep the soil moist throughout the life of the crop. Any shortage of water, especially in hot weather, increases significantly the likelihood of early flowering.

Spinach likes a lot of water, and, in dry weather, you need to give it up to 4 gallons per square yard a week, in two or three applications, to ensure steady growth.

Yellow leaves

Does spinach prefer acid or alkaline soil? I used lime last year and the leaves turned yellow.

Many books tell you to apply lime before sowing spinach, but it's often unnecessary. Spinach will put up with slightly acid, neutral and even slightly alkaline conditions – in other words, a pH anywhere between about 6.5 and 7.5. Most soils are acid: that is, they have a pH below the neutral point of 7.0. But very acid conditions are more harmful to spinach than strongly alkaline soils – hence the traditional advice.

If a soil test shows your soil to be very acid, apply sufficient lime, in the autumn or winter before you intend sowing, to bring the pH level to at least 6.5 (see *How much garden lime to use*, page 8).

Too much lime, on the other hand, will prevent iron and other trace elements in the soil from being taken up by the plants. This leads to a condition known as lime-induced chlorosis, where the leaves turn yellow between the veins. That seems to be what happened to your plants. If it happens again, water around the plants with a sequestered iron compound, to help the leaves to recover. The lime you put on will gradually wash out of the soil, so you may not have the same problem next year. If necessary, dig in peat before sowing again, because peat is acidic.

Winter spinach

Is winter spinach sufficiently hardy for the Midlands?

Not without protection. It's not tough enough on its own to cope with frost and ice. But a covering of cloches, from late October to March, should see it safely through the winter. Even in milder areas, some form of protection is advisable.

Sow the seeds of winter spinach in a sunny position in late August. You should be able to start picking the outer leaves about 12 weeks later. To keep up a steady supply of new leaves, pick over each plant lightly. Picking more than a quarter of the leaves at any one time will seriously weaken the plants.

For winter use, choose varieties which resist early flowering and bolting, such as 'Broad Leaved Prickly' or 'Sigmaleaf'.

Beetroot masquerading as spinach

Are spinach and spinach beet the same?

No. Spinach beet, which is also called perpetual spinach, is a type of beetroot with dark green leaves that taste rather like spinach when cooked. It's a biennial plant – meaning that it completes its natural lifecycle in two years – and it's far less likely to run to seed on dry soils than ordinary annual spinach. To grow it, sow between March and July in ½-1in deep drills drawn 15in apart. Thin the seedlings to about 8-12in apart and cover the plants with cloches in the autumn to keep up a steady supply of leaves for autumn and winter use.

STEM AND BULB EELWORMS

When leaves are twisted

My patch of naturalised daffodils has been a disappointment this year. Flowers are far fewer, and many of the leaves are pale, twisted and dotted with spots. Is there a spray or feed I can give to restore the plants to health?

What you describe are the classic symptoms of a stem and bulb eelworm attack. To confirm the gloomy diagnosis, dig up one or two daffodils and cut the bulbs horizontally in half. If they are soft, and have dark rings in the middle, then your plants are infested for certain.

Not that you will see the creatures, for they are microscopic; nevertheless, they do a remarkable amount of damage. They attack not only daffodils and narcissi, but onions, phlox and tulips as well, leaving bulb and plant tissues soft and rotten. There *is* a cure, but it won't be much comfort to you. When the bulbs are dormant, and provided they're not too badly infected, you can immerse them for three hours in water kept at a steady temperature of 44°C (112°F).

The trouble is, of course, maintaining the temperature. You might succeed with the technique if you watched pot and thermometer very carefully throughout the three essential hours, but it hardly seems worth while. Better to burn all the infected plants and a few of their neighbours as well. As for the remainder, leave them until next season and see how they get on.

If you buy more daffodils, or other plants susceptible to attack, plant them elsewhere in the garden. The old plot will remain infected for at least three years, and there is no effective chemical treatment.

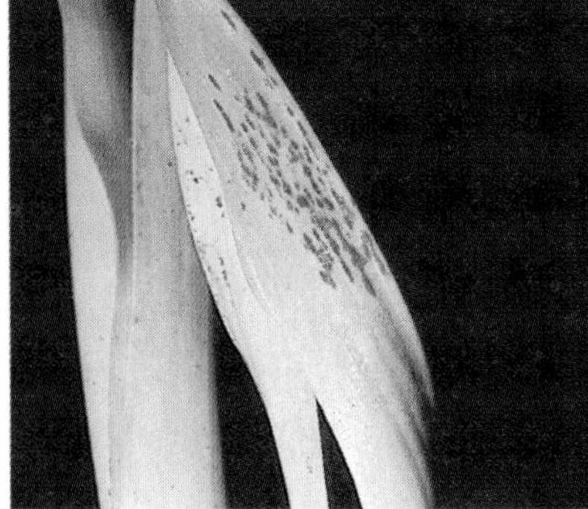

MICROSCOPIC MENACE *Yellowing, distorted or spotty leaves and rotting bulbs in daffodils and other bulbous plants are signs of infestation by the tiny stem and bulb eelworm. There is no practicable cure for affected plants.*

STEM ROT

Brown patches, yellow leaves

Just as they were coming to full growth, about a third of my tomato plants were struck by a blight of some kind that turned the lower leaves yellow. Another, and I suppose related, symptom is that sunken brown patches surrounded by small, blackish spots have appeared at the base of the stems. What's causing the problem, and is it curable?

The disease, or more correctly the symptom, is called stem rot. It can be caused by any one of several fungi which attack carnations, lobelias and godetias as well as tomatoes, indoors and out, giving rise in each case to very much the same symptoms as you describe. If the rot is well advanced, as it appears to be on your tomatoes, there's little you can do but destroy the plants. Burn them or put them in the dustbin – not on a compost heap. But with plants that are not too badly affected, you could try cutting out the diseased area and painting over the wound with a benomyl solution.

Spray the lower stems of surrounding plants with benomyl as well. Before planting tomatoes in the greenhouse next year, thoroughly sterilise the interior.

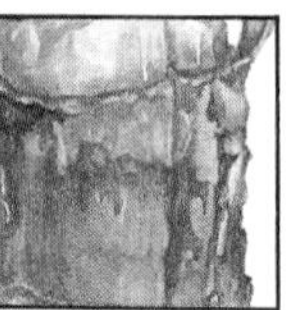

KILLER CANKER *Unchecked, stem rot is fatal to greenhouse tomatoes and several other plants.*

STRAWBERRIES

Strawberries for ever

Gardening magazines occasionally mention perpetual strawberries, and I've even seen them advertised in garden centres. But what are they, exactly?

Perpetual strawberries are what many people call autumn strawberries, and others, more old-fashioned folk, 'remontant' strawberries, from the French 'to climb again' – a reference to the plants' ability to flower and fruit repeatedly all summer and autumn long.

Modern varieties of perpetual strawberries will indeed do this if left to their own devices, but it's a better idea to stop early fruiting by disbudding the plants until the end of May. This is particularly the case if you're growing summer varieties as well. If you let the perpetual strawberries behave as they want to, they'll begin flowering and fruiting at the same time as the summer plants, consuming energy that would be best directed into producing a large crop in autumn when the summer varieties have finished. They will continue producing until October or November, when the colder weather and reduced light puts a stop to them. Prolong late cropping by putting cloches or polythene tunnels over the plants until they've produced their last strawberry for the year.

There is an excellent range of autumn – or perpetual – varieties available. Here are some of the best:

'Aromel' Medium to large fruits of good flavour. Crops well and produces runners freely. Best grown for only one year.

'Gento' Carries the largest fruits of any perpetual. Tends to have a summer and an autumn flush rather than a continuous crop. Runners carry fruit when still young. Good flavour.

'Marastar' A new French variety that is the first perpetual to be resistant to mildew and to some extent to grey mould. The fruits are medium sized and of good flavour. Heavy cropper.

'Ostara' Especially useful for heavy early autumn crops. Good flavour, but susceptible to mildew.

Autumn melancholy

I'm very disappointed with my autumn strawberries. They start fruiting at the same time as the maincrop varieties and, by the autumn, seem to have run out of steam. What's wrong with them?

Nothing, probably. The problem lies in the fact that the term 'autumn strawberry' is really a misnomer. There's no such thing. The plants that are sold as 'autumn fruiting' are really 'perpetual fruiting', in that they can flower and fruit all summer and autumn long. The varieties that are generally sold for autumn fruiting include: 'Aromel', 'Gento', 'Marastar', 'Ostara', 'Hampshire Maid' – and the almost forgotten 'Red Rich', 'Sans Rivale' and 'St Claude'.

Left to their own devices, all these varieties will start flowering in the spring, at the same time as the summer-fruiting kinds, and will therefore fruit at the same time, too. But unlike the summer varieties, which produce only a single flush of flowers, the perpetuals will carry on flowering and fruiting until the frosts put a final stop to their activities in October or November, by which time the fruits will be pretty feeble. So, if you want them to produce only a single, top-quality crop in autumn, all you have to do is stop the spring flowers developing. Do this by pinching off all the flowers that are produced before June. Not a bad memory-jogger is the Chelsea Flower Show – carry out the final disbudding during the weekend after the last day of the show. All the flowers that are produced from then on can be allowed to develop into fruits.

Substitutes for straw

Living as I do in a London suburb, I find it impossible to get straw to put round my strawberries. Is there an alternative or, come to that, need I bother at all?

You most certainly need to do something, or the strawberries will probably become riddled with grey mould. That's the disease that turns all the berries into little grey balls of fungus. All this is caused by rain, which spatters the strawberries with mud and provides the damp environment that the mould loves. What you could do is to cover the plants with cloches, or with a polythene tunnel. This certainly keeps the rain off, but unless you give plenty of ventilation the plants will get too hot and produce lank, soft growth.

Covering the ground beneath the plants with barley straw is the traditional way of protecting the berries, but there are several modern alternatives that will do a perfectly efficient job, and save you the bother of tracking down straw. The best of these are the so-called strawberry mats. They are made of bituminised paper, about 10in across, and have a hole in the centre and a slit from this to the edge, so that they can be slipped round the base of the plant to shield the fruits from contact with the soil. An alternative is black polythene sheeting. This kills the weeds under it by depriving them of light and, at the same time, it keeps the berries off the ground. Puddles of water may gather on the polythene, so cut small slits where they form to let them drain away and, at the same time, water the plants. If you wish to go to a little extra expense, there is some excellent ready-slitted black polythene on the market.

Early berries for the bride

My daughter is getting married next June and I should like to provide my own strawberries for the wedding breakfast. Is it possible to obtain a crop that early, and how do I ensure that they will be ready for the great day?

This means advancing the crop by about a month, which is perfectly possible and there's more than one way of doing it. The most important single factor common to all of them is the choice of variety. Obviously, it's got to be an early one, and the most reliable early one is 'Cambridge Vigour'. Since it also has one of the best flavours, this is certainly the one to go for. If you can't find it, grow the much more easily found 'Cambridge Favourite'. It fruits about a week later, and though the flavour isn't as good, the crops are usually heavier.

Buy new plants in August or September and pot them into 5in or 6in pots. Allow a plant for each guest at the wedding; this may sound a lot, but it's safer to have too much fruit than not enough. Leave the plants outdoors until late February, then bring them indoors, into a greenhouse that is heated just enough to keep it frost-free. After that, simply make sure that the plants don't run short of water. Provide heat only if there's a risk of frost during or after flowering. Good ventilation is vital, to ensure that the temperature never rises above about 16°C (60°F). If it gets too hot, all you'll get is a lot of leaf and very little fruit.

During flowering, encourage bees and other pollinating insects into the greenhouse by leaving the ventilators and door open whenever there's no chance of frost. As added insurance, you can use the traditional method of a rabbit's tail or camel-hair brush to pollinate the flowers by hand (see *What can go wrong*, page 329). Insufficient pollination is a far greater risk than too little heat. No feeding will be necessary until the first fruitlets are forming; then, feed with a liquid tomato fertiliser once a week.

Given luck and reasonable weather, you should be picking strawberries at the end of May, and getting ready for the main crop 10-14 days later. If the timing looks as though it isn't going to be quite right, either increase the ventilation to hold the crop back or introduce heat at night to speed it up. But do bear in mind that it's much easier to delay cropping than it is to advance it. Your plants will be exhausted after their forced fruiting, so throw them away; they won't be fit for planting outside. Another way to get early strawberries is to buy the plants, already in pots, before the end of February. From then on, follow the same method, except that you may have to start by potting the plants into larger pots; they're hardly likely to be in the 5 or 6in sizes when you buy them.

These two methods are the only really reliable ways of ensuring that you will have strawberries in June, but as a challenge you might be able to do something with plants already growing in the open. These would have to be early-variety 'maiden' plants, which have never fruited before, planted during the previous August or September.

At the end of February, cover them with 18in high and wide glass or Perspex cloches. After that, treat them in much the same way as if they were growing in the greenhouse. Polythene tunnels are another possibility, though they only provide enough protection to advance the crop by about a fortnight. Glass and Perspex cloches, or a cold greenhouse, will bring them forward by a month. Don't use plants older than maidens; they're too large to be any good for forcing.

Keeping the birds off the berries

Is there any way of protecting strawberries from blackbirds and thrushes, which won't tangle and entrap the birds?

There is no reason why birds, strawberries and other soft fruit should not co-exist in the same garden. The best devices for keeping them apart are nets, and the best of these is undoubtedly the fruit cage – a permanent structure with a metal frame and wire-netting sides. The top should be nylon or plastic netting, which can be removed when protection isn't required. Netting spread over the plants also works quite well and is considerably less expensive. Support it on canes with jam jars or tins over the tops; alternatively, make hoop supports from the stiff wire coathangers that breed profusely in your wardrobe. Don't let the netting rest on the plants; the birds will reach through to the detriment of both fruit and birds. Unless the netting is stretched tight, the birds may easily become trapped in it.

Some people stretch lengths of black cotton among the plants, the idea being that when the birds bump into something they can't see, they get frightened and clear off. This can be very effective when stretched along rows of seeds and seedlings but, with plants as large and tempting as strawberries, it's fairly useless. It's also likely, if slack, to ensnare birds rather than frightening them off – especially if you use strong nylon thread. They can carry lengths of it away on their feet, becoming more and more entangled. Hanging strips of glittering and noisy silver paper over the bed usually works well to begin with but, unfortunately, the birds soon get used to them. A fairly new product in the garden centres is the 'humming line', a plastic line that is stretched above the plants to be protected. When the wind catches it, it sets up a low reverberation that frightens the birds. On calm days, of course, it remains silent. But if you haven't got a fruit cage, maybe the best thing to try is a combination of the humming line and a net stretched tight over canes.

Strawberries at Maytime

Each spring my greenhouse is half empty, and I wonder if it would be a good idea to use the space to force a few early strawberries?

An excellent idea – and one that is well within the capabilities of any gardener with even a basic knowledge of greenhouse gardening. Not least of the joys, if you are a strawberry addict, is that it will enable you to bring forward the season of these delicious fruits by at least a month.

For the method of cultivation, see the answer to the question *Early berries for the bride*, on page 327, but in your case you might be able to broaden the scope by experimenting with a wider range of varieties.

'Cambridge Vigour' and 'Cambridge Favourite' are certainly the best for forcing, but you might also try the heavily fruiting 'Maxim'. Don't be put off by the large size of the berries; the flavour is surprisingly good. You can also add some colour to the greenhouse by using different containers. Terracotta strawberry barrels are very attractive, but they do tend to be expensive. Tower pots are a good proposition; they can be built on top of one another as tall as you like, making quite a feature and, at the same time, saving an immense amount of bench space. There are several different ones available, ranging from self-watering models to much cheaper plastic types. Less aesthetic, but very practical, is to use old growing bags – each will take 8-10 plants.

After fruiting, the plants really won't be fit for planting outside and should be thrown away; they will have been completely worn out by their efforts.

Getting the timing right

What is the best time of year to plant strawberries? I've only a small garden and want to get the best crop I can.

Maincrop summer varieties fruit in July, and should be planted as soon as new plants can be raised from the current year's runners. This is usually from late July onwards, but in any case, for the best results, planting should be completed by mid-September. If it isn't, the crop in the first year suffers. The average crop weight from a July runner raised in a pot and planted out during August or September should be about 8oz. From a freshly dug runner planted in October or November, the weight would be around 4oz and, if planting were delayed until the spring, the yield could be as little as 2oz.

Perpetuals – the so-called autumn-fruiting varieties – are different in that, because they fruit much later, they can also be planted later: up to the end of March, in fact.

Chop or not?

My neighbour cuts all the leaves off his strawberry plants after they've fruited. They don't seem any the worse for this drastic treatment, but are they any better for it? And why is he doing it?

This used to be a favourite practice of commercial growers, but it's largely fallen out of favour now. The reason for doing it is that the plants may have picked up pests or diseases during the time, just before picking, when the number of sprayings had to be cut back. The simplest way of getting rid of the pests was to take off the leaves and destroy them. Often, and for the same reason, the straw bedding round the plants was burnt at the same time. The appearance in recent years of safer and more effective sprays has enabled commercial growers to continue spraying almost until picking, making it unnecessary to remove the leaves.

Though such sprays are available to amateur gardeners, amateurs tend to use them far less often than professional growers. There is, therefore, some point in you scalping your strawberry plants after fruiting, since your plants may have picked up more pests than the heavily treated crop on a fruit farm. In addition, scalping encourages the plants to grow new leaves to strengthen them before winter. And it certainly doesn't do them any harm.

Multiplying your stock

Is it a good idea to propagate my own strawberries? And how do I do it?

It is certainly quite easy to do, and many gardeners do it when the time has come to scrap one strawberry bed and plant another. This usually happens every three years, for the life of a strawberry bed, either summer or perpetual fruiting, is no longer than this.

Provided that your old plants are free from pests and diseases, it is a simple matter to propagate new ones from the plantlets that form on the 'runners' – creeping stems – which strawberry plants send out in the summer. All you have to do is to peg the plantlet to the ground until it takes root about a month later, when it can be severed from the parent plant. Or better still, plunge a few 3 or 4in pots of used seed or potting compost in the soil around the parent plants, and get the plantlets started in those.

Either way, once the roots have formed, the plantlets will be ready for their permanent positions after they have been severed from the parent. Summer varieties should be planted out as soon as they are ready – that is, in mid to late summer – but perpetual varieties can safely be left in their pots until the following spring.

That's *how* you propagate strawberries. As to whether it's a good idea, it's probably generally better to buy new plants. They don't cost very much, they'll be certified virus-free, and they'll usually crop more heavily than plants raised at home.

Does deblossoming help?

I was told the other day that strawberries should always be deblossomed in their first year. Is this so, and if it is, why?

Gardening folklore usually has a modicum of truth in it, but this is an exception to that rule. Preventing the plants from fruiting until they've been established for nearly two years is never worth doing, especially when you consider that the life of a strawberry bed is only three years at most; by deblossoming in the first year, you're taking away a third of the bed's cropping life.

The legend may have arisen out of the fact that perpetual-fruiting varieties should be prevented from flowering until the end of May, to ensure good autumn crops.

The berry that never was

I seem to remember, years ago, reading about climbing strawberries. What happened to them?

You did indeed see them advertised but there isn't, and never has been, such a thing as a climbing strawberry. The ones that were described as 'climbing' were generally the French variety 'Sans Rivale', or something very similar. These varieties produced flowers and fruits on young runners almost from the moment the runners formed. The 'climbing' was induced by gardeners who tied these flowering runners to nets or trellises placed behind the plants. Had the runners been left to themselves, they would have behaved in exactly the same way as the runners of any other variety: trailed across the ground and then rooted into the soil.

Getting the most out of strawberries

How long can I depend on getting good crops from my strawberry plants? And is there any difference in length of cropping life between the summer and perpetual varieties?

The short answer is three years and, no, it's the same for summer and perpetual varieties.

As a rule, strawberries carry their largest fruits in their first, or maiden, year, but the crop weight tends to be light. The second year is usually best, when the plants produce fruits that are only slightly smaller, but the total crop is heavier. In the third year, the fruit size is smaller still but the total crop weight reaches its maximum. After that, the fruit size remains fairly constant, but the crop weight drops, due to the increased incidence of virus disease.

It's really a waste of time planting anything other than a 'maiden' plant – that is, one that has never flowered or fruited, and was produced at the end of a runner from its parent plant during the previous summer. This applies to plants both for indoor and outdoor use. Older plants will take longer to establish, will carry only light crops in their first summer, and thereafter will probably have no more than one good season.

Though second-year plants look large and healthy, it is a false economy to plant them. It's much better to buy or raise new plants every three years, except in the case of early or forced greenhouse varieties which should be replaced every year.

Freezing strawberries

Strawberries are notoriously poor freezers. Are there in fact any varieties that I might successfully freeze for winter use?

Not many. The trouble is that, when strawberries freeze, the water in their cells expands into ice, rupturing the cell walls like burst pipes. Then, when the fruits are defrosted, they collapse into more or less of a mush. But though the shape is gone, the flavour remains relatively unaffected, and the mush can be converted into delicious purées, ice creams and other dishes.

Canada has produced a new race of strawberry varieties that have been specially bred for freezing but, as so often happens, when a new characteristic is bred into plants, some older virtue is lost. Research showed that firmer-fruited varieties were best at keeping their shape after thawing, so firmness was intensified in the new strain. Unfortunately, it resulted in a strawberry that was unacceptably hard and of a not too sparkling flavour when fresh, though it froze and thawed quite well. So far, only one of these Canadian varieties, 'Totem', is widely available to amateurs. It holds its shape after thawing better than any other strawberry, and has a good but not outstanding flavour.

One tip for frozen strawberries of the more old-fashioned kinds is to use them in a fruit salad. Place the strawberries, still frozen, at the bottom of the bowl and put the other unfrozen fruit on top. The strawberries will thaw out, but since they haven't been handled in a thawed state, they will retain something of their original shape.

TWELVE RULES FOR SUCCESS WITH STRAWBERRIES

1 Choose a variety that will suit your conditions best, in a greenhouse or outdoors.
2 Buy the plants from a reliable source that certifies them to be virus-free.
3 Order the plants early in the year so that they arrive early in the planting season.
4 Plant summer varieties from late July until mid-September. Plant perpetual (autumn-fruiting) varieties in spring.
5 Prepare the ground about a month before planting, adding plenty of well-rotted compost or manure.
6 Protect the developing fruits from mud splashes by strewing straw about the plants or surrounding them with strawberry collars, before the fruit touches the ground.
7 Carry out thorough pest, disease and weed control.
8 When propagating from your own plants, do so only from the healthiest parents.
9 Use only one-year-old plants for early crops under glass.
10 Apply a liquid feed – such as tomato fertiliser – to greenhouse plants at weekly intervals from fruit formation to harvest.
11 Disbud perpetual varieties until the end of May to ensure a good autumn crop.
12 Use cloches or polythene tunnels to protect the fruits of autumn varieties from early October onwards.

What can go wrong

I have just grown strawberries under glass for the first time and many of the fruits turned out lopsided and misshapen. What went wrong? Have I got a poor batch of plants?

No – poor pollination is the problem. Insects haven't been able to get at the plants as they would outdoors to do the job. The answer for next year is to pollinate by hand – it's quite simple and not too time-consuming. Just take a soft camel-hair paintbrush (you can buy one from an art materials shop) and gently stroke each flower in turn to transfer pollen from one plant's flowers to another.

That problem is simply cured – but it could have been worse. Slugs are another cause of fruit damage. So, outdoors, are birds. Make a point, therefore, of netting your outdoor plants against birds and sprinkling pellets to knock out slugs. And while we're on the topic of pests and diseases, there are several other things that could go wrong with your plants. Here are the main ones:

- **APHIDS** Can curl the leaves and distort the blossoms and flower stems. Treat by spraying with pirimicarb or dimethoate.
- **RED SPIDER MITES** Stunt the plants and cause leaves to turn bronze, wither and fall. Spray with pirimiphos-methyl or malathion.
- **GREY MOULD** Fruit rots and becomes covered in grey, velvety mould. Prevent by spraying with benomyl, repeating two or three times every two weeks from when the first flowers open. Remove any diseased fruits to prevent spread by contact.

• **MILDEW** Dead patches appear on the upper sides of leaves, accompanied by whitish fungus on the undersides and on flower trusses. Spray with benomyl three times at two-week intervals from the first sign of the symptoms. Prevent the disease from reappearing next year by burning old leaves after harvesting; spray again with benomyl in late summer or early autumn.

• **RED CORE DISEASE** Infects the roots, turning them brown or black with a red core. Affected plants are stunted with small, wilted leaves. Fruiting is poor or non-existent. There is no cure, so burn all affected plants.

• **YELLOW EDGE VIRUS** Leaves are small and cupped, with yellow edges. There is no cure; burn all affected plants. As a preventative, spray against aphids, which spread the disease.

• **CRINKLE VIRUS** Produces red or purple patches on the leaves, which become puckered and may also have yellow edges. Burn all affected plants. As a preventative, spray against aphids, which spread the disease.

Starting from seeds

My garden centre has strawberry seeds for sale. I'm quite intrigued, but what are the resulting plants like?

Strawberry seeds are a bit of a gimmick, but quite fun for all that. Like most other kinds of fruit raised from seed, the offspring are of course going to be variable. Not startlingly so in this case, since most seeds come from the old alpine type of strawberry, and not from the large-fruited modern hybrids. Good alpine strains, such as 'Alexandria' and 'Baron Solemacher', can be raised and they do fruit freely. However, there is also one modern, large-fruited variety available – called 'Sweetheart' – that does come true from seed. Even so, some plants will have bigger fruits than others, and the ripening period will vary more than between plants propagated from runners.

Strawberry seeds are often sold on the notion that you can go from seed to fruit in one year. It's not impossible, but it does mean sowing the seeds in heat in January or early February. Otherwise, sow the seeds in autumn or spring in a cool greenhouse or a cold frame. Pot the seedlings on and plant them in their final positions as soon as they outgrow a 3in pot. They will fruit from July to October of the following year.

SWEDES AND TURNIPS

Why swedes and turnips are best grown apart

Should swedes and turnips be grouped together with other root vegetables when planning crop rotation?

Swedes and turnips are an exception to the general rule that root vegetables should move around the vegetable patch as a group. The reason is that they belong, botanically, to the brassica family, along with greens such as cabbages, brussels sprouts and cauliflowers.

All of these plants are very susceptible to the serious fungus disease known as club root. One of the best ways to control club root is to make sure that brassicas are not grown on the same patch year after year.

If you grow swedes and turnips with other root vegetables, you will, on an orthodox crop rotation plan, be growing brassicas on the same spot two years out of three – leading to a build-up of the disease in the soil. It's better instead to group swedes and turnips with the other brassicas, since they all thrive on the same treatment (see *Crop rotation*, page 105).

How to grow tender swedes

My swedes seemed to grow normally but were far too tough to eat. What caused this?

Probably some form of check while they were growing. You must give swedes – and other vegetables grown for their roots, such as carrots, turnips and beetroot – ideal conditions if they're to grow steadily without any setbacks. If the plants stop growing at any stage, their roots turn quite woody and may become inedible.

The answer lies in the soil. It should be light, well-drained and fertile, and should contain a fair amount of rotted compost dug in several months before sowing. The roots are likely to fork if they come into contact with fresh manure, so it's wise to grow swedes (and other root vegetables) on a site that was manured the previous season for another crop.

Keep the soil moist during dry weather, particularly in July and August when the roots should be swelling quickly. If the soil dries out, growth will stop and the skins of the roots will harden – with the result that they'll split when rain or watering starts the plants growing again. The Institute of Horticultural Research (formerly known as the National Vegetable Research Station) at Wellesbourne, Warwickshire, recommends giving swedes about 2 gallons of water per square yard each week.

The swede is commonly regarded as being at its best in midwinter, and certainly it is hardy enough to survive in the ground until required for the kitchen. But to taste really tender swedes, try digging up a few in October, before they reach maximum size.

Swedes for beginners

Which varieties of swede do you recommend for someone who has never grown them before?

For yields, 'Marian' is outstanding and, most important, has good resistance to club root and mildew – qualities often lacking in other varieties. It has globe-shaped roots with attractive, purple-skinned flesh. It can be harvested from October onwards as the roots are needed in the kitchen.

'Best of All' is also popular because it is extremely hardy and keeps well if lifted and stored for the winter. Like 'Marian', it is ready for harvesting from October and it has yellow-fleshed roots with purple skin, but the foliage is more compact.

For a quick-maturing variety, try another swede with purple-topped roots: 'Western Perfection'. This can be lifted from September, a month before other varieties would normally be ready.

Tops for harvesting

It seems a shame to waste turnip leaves after we've eaten the roots. Are they safe to eat?

Yes, they are, and tasty, too. But it's no good taking leaves from plants dug up in the autumn or early winter – they'll be too

EARLY TURNIPS UNDER CLOCHES

You can grow deliciously tender turnip roots, 1½-2in across, in as little as six weeks from a February sowing under cloches.

Choose a sunny part of the garden and dig the soil in the autumn. Apply lime to deter club-root disease, particularly if the soil pH is below 5.5. The ideal range for turnips is 5.5-7.0.

About three weeks before you plan to sow, cover the soil with cloches to help to warm and dry it. Seven days before sowing, rake the soil into breadcrumb-sized particles, scatter about 2½oz of Growmore per square yard, and dust the soil with bromophos to control soil-borne pests.

Sow the seed thinly about ½in deep in drills 9-12in apart. It's essential to use varieties that mature early, such as 'Milan White Forcing' and 'Purple Top Milan'. Slow-growing varieties are more likely to run to seed and spoil the roots. When the first rough turnip leaves appear, thin the seedlings to 4in apart and dust their leaves with HCH to ward off flea beetles. Keep the soil moist and free from weeds, and ventilate the cloches in sunny weather.

Start pulling the roots in May when they're about 2in across. The crop should be cleared within three weeks.

tough to eat. And it's not a good idea, either, to harvest younger leaves in the summer, because you'll just slow down the development of the growing roots.

If you want to harvest the tops, sow a maincrop variety such as 'Green-top White' in August or September, and grow it to provide the tops as spring greens in March and April.

Sow the seeds thinly in drills 3in apart, and leave all the plants to grow on. There's no need to thin them, as you would need to do if you were growing them for their roots. When the leaves are about 4-6in high in the spring, cut them off close to the main stem. You should be able to harvest them several times before the plants become too weak to sprout again.

When the plants do run out of leaves, there's a bonus. You can dig up the roots and eat them, too. Because of the close spacing, and because your harvesting will have diverted more of the plants' energy to the leaves, the roots will be pretty small. But they'll be no less tasty than full-sized ones.

You can also eat swede shoots like turnip tops. Lift the roots in the winter, trim their tops and plant the roots closely together in wooden boxes filled with damp peat. Keep them in a cool, fairly dark room – a shed or garage – and the partly blanched shoots will be quite tender when cooked.

Keeping out rot

Is there a special way to keep turnip roots? I carefully surrounded mine with peat in boxes and kept them dry, but they turned soft and slimy inside, well before the winter was up.

Your turnips were suffering from soft rot – a disease to which turnips and swedes are both very susceptible. It gets into growing plants, as well as stored roots, through wounds made by careless hoeing or by birds, slugs or other pests.

The roots are worst affected when they're stored, because the disease spreads quickly from the neck or crown, even when the outer skin remains intact. Chemicals don't help to prevent or control soft rot, but skilful growing can reduce the likelihood of attack. Follow these rules to improve your chances of a rot-free harvest in the future.

- Always rotate the crops, so that turnips and swedes aren't grown on the same ground again for at least four years. The disease lives in the soil and rotation will help to starve it out.
- Although turnips and swedes like a rich soil, don't put on large amounts of farmyard manure just before you sow – it can lead to soft growth more prone to infection.
- If you notice the disease on any roots you harvest, lift the rest of the crop at once. Consign severely affected roots and all the topgrowth on even slightly affected plants to a dustbin or a bonfire – don't be tempted to compost them.
- Use at once any roots which are only slightly affected. Don't store them, and don't compost the peelings.
- Check swedes and turnips in store about once a week. Remove any infected roots to minimise the spread of disease.

SWEET CORN

Two is enough

How many cobs should you get from one sweet corn plant? Because my plants were quite large, I expected a bumper crop and was disappointed to discover they only had two each.

Two is the usual number. Occasionally you'll only get one. You'd be lucky indeed to grow a plant that produced three cobs. The height and spread of sweet corn plants have no bearing on the number of cobs.

Sideshoots, also known as tillers, sometimes grow from the base of the main stem during the summer months, and these can make the plants quite bushy. But don't be deceived by them – sideshoots rarely flower and so cannot usually bear fruit.

It's best just to leave them alone because they help to strengthen the plant. If you cut them off, they'll only start growing again and thus divert more energy from the main stem. And you risk damaging the plant's roots if you pull them up.

Cobs for the North

Is it worthwhile attempting to grow sweet corn in the North?

Yes. If you choose hybrid varieties bred to mature early in colder areas, you can grow sweet corn just as successfully as gardeners in the South, where the summers are warmer and longer.

Modern hybrids generally produce cobs slightly smaller than older varieties – but it's worth sacrificing size for more reliable ripening. You still need a sheltered, sunny spot, whatever variety you grow, and it's wise to delay planting out the young plants until late May or early June, when the risk of frost is minimal. Even a slight frost can kill or severely damage the young plants.

Set the young plants 15-18in apart each way. Alternatively, sow the seeds in their growing position at the beginning of May, but cover the site with cloches two or three weeks beforehand to warm the soil.

For reliability, 'Earliking' is unsurpassed, and its 6-8in long cobs usually ripen towards the end of August, even in indifferent summers. 'Earlibelle' grows more strongly, and its cobs are up to 2in longer, although they may not ripen until early September. Also good for the Midlands and North are 'First of All', with firm, 6in long cobs, and 'North Star', a variety noted for the sweetness of its large cobs. Both ripen from late August onwards.

When to pick

I was pleased with the size of my sweet corn cobs last year, but they were so tough and chewy we couldn't eat them. Why did this happen?

Either you left harvesting them too late, or you left too long a period between picking and cooking them.

To sample sweet corn at its best, you must pick the cobs within two or three days of their reaching the peak of perfection. And, once picked, it's vital to cook them within 24 hours. The natural sugar in them starts converting to starch minutes after they're picked. Cobs with a high starch content look quite normal on the dinner table, but, as you've discovered, they're dreadful to eat: tough and doughy.

Harvest the cobs when the 'silks' – the tassels of the female flowers at the tips of the cobs – have completely withered and turned brown or black. This is usually in August or September, about a month after the silks start to wither.

Unfortunately, not all the cobs ripen simultaneously, so you'll have to test each one individually, every two or three days. To do this, gently part the leaves surrounding the cob and pierce one of the fatter grains with your fingernail. If a pale, watery liquid oozes out, the cob is not yet ready to harvest. But if the liquid is thin and creamy-white, pick the cob immediately. Grasp it with one hand and twist it downwards, pulling it away from the stem. Cobs whose grains slowly exude a thick, white liquid when pierced are past their best. They're still edible, but they will be tough when cooked.

Early corn in pots

Does sweet corn transplant successfully? I am wondering about raising plants in pots to bring them on early.

Yes, but bear in mind that if the roots become too disturbed during the transplanting process, the plants will take a long time getting established – and then growth and cropping can suffer.

For best results, sow individual seeds in peat pots. Then you can set out the young plants intact, and the roots will grow through the walls of the pots into the surrounding soil. Alternatively, raise the plants in 3in clay or plastic pots and transplant them to their prepared site in May or June.

Sow the seeds in a propagator or greenhouse, starting in mid-April in the South and West, and from early May in the Midlands and North. Keep the temperature at about 13-18°C (55-65°F), and the seedlings should appear in seven to ten days.

Warm start for seeds

I can never get all my sweet corn seeds to grow, which is very annoying because they are quite expensive. What's the best way to ensure good germination?

Make a start in April or May by lining the bottom of a small plastic container – a sandwich box will do – with three or four layers of absorbent kitchen paper. Run clean tap water into it to dampen the paper, then drain off the excess water. Lay the seeds about ¼in apart on the paper.

Stretch cling film over the container, or cover it with aluminium foil, to keep the humidity in, and put it in an airing cupboard, a propagator or any other place where you can maintain a steady temperature of about 21°C (70°F). Leave the container there until the seeds 'chit' – that is, they start to sprout. This could be in as little as 48 hours – though some seeds take a day or two longer.

As the seeds sprout, gently transfer them from the container and sow them individually, 1in deep, in small peat pots of seed compost. Keep the pots at a steady temperature of between 13°C and 18°C (about 55-65°F) until late May or early June. Harden them off for seven to ten days, to accustom them to the lower temperatures outdoors, then plant them out in the garden.

Sowing outdoors

Will sweet corn succeed outside, or do the plants have to be raised in a greenhouse and then moved to their growing position?

Provided you take simple precautions, garden sowings will flourish. Choose a sunny, reasonably sheltered spot and, two or three weeks before you plan to sow – in May or early June – cover the prepared soil with cloches to warm it. Using the corner of a rake or draw hoe, mark out the positions for the plants (normally 15-18in square), and then sow three seeds in each position, 1in deep and close together. Replace the cloches. When the seedlings emerge, remove the two weakest plants, leaving the strongest one to grow on. Keep the cloches in place until the plants grow too big to fit under them.

Blocks, not rows

I've got enough room for a row of sweet corn. How far apart should the plants be?

Whatever you do, don't grow sweet corn in single rows – it's highly unlikely you'll get a good crop. The plants are pollinated by the wind, which blows pollen from the male flowers at the tips of the stems onto the female flowers at the tips of the cobs. Grow the plants in a rectangular block and the wind will pollinate them far more effectively than if they were set out in single or double rows. Plan your block of sweet corn to grow end on to the prevailing wind. This will allow pollen to drift more evenly through the plants. Space short varieties 15in apart each way, tall varieties 18in square.

SWEET PEAS

Some good, some bad

I grow sweet peas along the edge of my vegetable plot and more against the house wall. I prepare the soil in exactly the same way for both sites, but the plants by the house never do very well. They look sickly, and struggle up to no more than 3ft, while those in the vegetable bed thrive and soar. Why the difference?

Simply a matter of siting. Sweet peas like the wide open spaces – the open part of the garden, where they can get plenty of air and full sunshine. The shade of trees and tall buildings does not appeal to them at all, though if you can find them a place with some shelter from the prevailing winds so much the better. Wind can do much damage to the delicate flowers.

Obviously, the sweet peas at the edge of your vegetable garden are enjoying ideal conditions: good soil with plenty of humus, and an open position in full sun. Your other plants, however, next to the house, are probably getting too much shade. The soil is probably not as fertile as that of the vegetable plot, and the nearby house foundations may well be cramping the roots.

Because they are rapid, vigorous growers, with many stems in continuous flower, sweet peas are immensely hungry and thirsty. Ideally, at some time in the autumn before planting, the soil should be dug over to a depth of at least 2½ft – sweet peas are deep rooters, so yours might easily be hitting the house foundations. It used to be the custom to dig trenches for sweet peas, but nowadays most garden experts reckon that it is better to dig the whole area. A narrow trench can easily become a drain in heavy rains, and though sweet peas thrive in a cool soil, they hate being waterlogged.

When the digging is done, incorporate hefty quantities of organic matter – well-rotted manure or compost. A few handfuls of bone meal thrown over the lot will give an extra fillip and your sweet peas will be off to the best possible start. Follow a programme of regular feeding, and never let the roots dry out.

Saving seeds

Sweet pea seeds are expensive. If I save the ones from this year's plants and sow them, will I get the same results as from shop-bought seeds?

If you let a few flowers set seed, and plant the seeds, next year's results will be just as good as this. However, if you follow the same course year after year, the plants often tend to become less and less sturdy and produce fewer flowers whose colours steadily fade. But until the deterioration occurs, there's no reason why you shouldn't keep using saved seed from year to year, particularly if you're growing mixed plants for general display.

Here's how you go about it. Take seeds only from the strongest plants and wait until the pods are dry and brown before picking them off. Lay the pods on sheets of newspaper and leave them to dry for several weeks in a warm, sunny but well-ventilated place. When the pods are dry, break them open and extract the seeds; some of the pods will have split open during drying and have already released their seeds. Store the seeds in airtight, labelled jars and keep them cool. Some gardeners even favour the idea of storing them in a refrigerator. When the time comes, plant them in exactly the same way as you would packeted seeds.

Tackling tendrils

According to my old gardening manual, the tendrils on sweet peas should be 'cut off with a pair of garden scissors'. But a friend who grows excellent sweet peas is quite shocked at the idea of snipping tendrils. Who is right?

It depends what you want from your sweet peas. Gardeners who aim to take prizes at the local show usually recommend that all sideshoots should be pinched out, tendrils snipped off and flowers removed at the instant of fading. The idea is that sideshoots, tendrils and flowers running to seed take energy which ought to be directed towards producing bigger and better blooms, and it is true that no flower responds better to such painstaking care than the sweet pea.

Tendrils support the weak stalks of the plant by attaching themselves to canes, netting, twiggy branches or whatever else is available. If you remove them, you will have to replace their support with liberal quantities of gardener's twine or wire rings. But if all you want out of your sweet peas is a pretty garden display and some flowers for cutting, leave the tendrils to do their job. They do it very efficiently and will save you much of the labour of tying in.

Everlasting sweet peas

What's the advantage of 'everlasting' sweet peas? Are they treated in the same way as the annual types?

The best-known 'everlasting' – that is, perennial – sweet pea is *Lathyrus latifolius*. Once established, it dies down at the end of each year, and reappears again each spring. It can easily climb up to 10ft, and if you are planting more than one, set them about 18in apart.

The flowers are generally rose-purple – though white, red and violet forms also exist – and appear continually between late spring and early autumn. While they are obviously of the same family, the everlasting pea flowers lack the frills of the highly colourful annual hybrid types; nor do they have their scent.

Another everlasting pea is the Persian variety, *L. rotundifolius*. This is smaller, growing to about 6ft. It carries clusters of rose-pink blooms from June to August and is easily distinguished from *L. latifolius* by its round, paired, dark green leaflets.

Annual and everlasting sweet peas are grown in quite different ways. The annuals are sown, and then planted outdoors in spring for summer flowering. Everlasting pea seedlings, however, are generally planted outdoors between October and March, and are often allowed to ramble among tall shrubs. That's the way to see them at their best, making a splendid contribution to the garden that the annuals could not emulate. Cut the current year's growth down to ground level in November and they will be raring to go again in spring.

Giving support

What's the foolproof method of supporting sweet peas?

It's by no means unusual to see a row of superb plants ruined because their supports were not strong enough to withstand midsummer gales. If you are to get the best from your tall sweet peas, you must provide them with good support – something the tendrils can really cling to as they climb.

Whatever kind of support you use, set it up before the sweet peas are planted. If you want to display your flowers at local shows, or you would like your garden to be filled with sweet peas of exhibition standard, one of the best methods of support – and very simple to erect – is a 6ft high length of strong, plastic netting, or wire mesh.

Stretch it along the prepared site and secure it to a stout wooden post at each end. The posts should be about 8ft long, of which 2ft has been driven into the ground. Now thread two lengths of strong wire through the mesh, 12in and 6ft above the ground, and staple the ends to the posts. This will help to hold the net steady. For extra sturdiness, push a few tall bamboo canes into the soil at intervals between the posts, and tie them to the wires and netting.

On the other hand, if all you want is a reasonable display of summer blooms, you may not wish to go to such lengths. For ideas on simpler alternatives, see *Space-saving tips for sweet peas*, page 334.

PICK OF THE SWEET PEAS

Name	Colour	Scent
'Royal Wedding'	White	Heavy
'White Leamington'		Medium
'Hunter's Moon'	Cream	Heavy
'Cream Southbourne'		Heavy
'Champagne Bubbles'	Pink on cream	Heavy
'Pink Bouquet'		Heavy
'Terry Wogan'		Light
'Alan Titchmarsh'		Medium
'Cyril Fletcher'	Pink on white	Heavy
'Southbourne'		Light
'Catherine'		Light
'Dynasty'	Rose and carmine	Faint
'Gypsy Rose'		Light
'Diana'	Orange and salmon	Faint
'Brian Clough'		Faint
'Sheila Macqueen'		Light
'Nancy College'		Medium
'Red Arrow'	Red	Faint
'Blaze'		Light
'Blue Danube'	Blue	Medium
'Evensong'		Heavy
'Noel Sutton'		Medium
'Blue Mantle'		Medium
'The Doctor'	Mauve	Heavy
'Midnight'	Purple and maroon	Faint
'Black Prince'		Light
'Milestone'		Medium
'Royalist'		Light
'Southampton'	Lavender	Light
'Royal Baby'		Heavy

Conflicting advice

According to the gardening books and magazines, some gardeners sow sweet peas under glass in autumn and plant them out a few weeks later. Others sow in autumn under glass but plant them out in spring. Then there's a school that sows in spring under glass and plants out later, while a breakaway group sows directly outside – in either autumn or spring. So what should I do?

It's true. Even the experts can't agree on the ideal time to sow sweet peas. In an attempt to settle the argument a few years ago, the Consumers Association conducted some sowing tests. From the tests, whose results were published in March 1983, it appeared that gardeners in the South wishing to grow flowers for exhibition would do best if they sowed directly into the ground in autumn – provided the ground was thoroughly prepared beforehand.

The seeds germinated readily, and the seedlings were sturdy enough to survive a fairly cold winter. All grew on to produce vigorous plants with long stems and a wealth of fine flowers. Wet, early summers often have a disastrous effect upon sweet peas – the buds drop off – but there was no sign of this with the autumn-sown plants.

But at the same time, it was agreed that for non-exhibiting gardeners, sowing under glass in spring produced perfectly acceptable results.

If you live in the North, however, autumn sowing, either indoors or out, is inadvisable; you'd do better to wait until spring when the weather and soil conditions are more favourable. The question then is whether to sow in pots under glass, or directly into the garden. Tests in Northern gardens showed that seeds sown directly outside gave the worst results of all. Germination was poor. Those that did grow produced weak plants which did not begin to flower until mid-July and lost many buds in early summer. To sum up: if you live in the North, sow sweet peas under glass in spring, and then plant out. In the South, sow into an outdoor bed in autumn for best results.

Knee-high peas

If I could, I'd fill the house with vases of cut sweet peas. The trouble is that in my small garden a sweet pea support frame would look ridiculous. What about the non-climbing varieties?

The choice is limited, but there are some semi-dwarf or dwarf varieties that might fill the bill. Semi-dwarf types are bushy, and require only minimal support – pea sticks maybe, or a wire-mesh fence if you have one. They would look well in a herbaceous border and are quite spectacular in large pots, tubs or even growing bags.

Mostly these varieties come in mixed strains, rather than in single colours. Among the best are the 'Jet Set' and 'Knee-Hi' strains, which carry half a dozen or so nicely placed blooms on each 3ft high stem.

Then there is 'Snoopea Mixed', which has thin acacia-like leaves and no tendrils. Though no more than 2ft in overall height, 'Snoopea' carries a wealth of full-sized blooms on 8-9in long stems.

The foot-high dwarf varieties can be grown in pots or window boxes and can even be used as edging in flower borders. 'Bijou' spreads to about 15in and has large, frilly flowers, usually four or five to a stem. 'Burpee's Patio Mixed' comes into flower before other dwarfs, and is highly fragrant.

Fairly new on the scene, 'Little Sweetheart' is a tiny gem that has a height and spread of only 9in. Nevertheless, it flowers prolifically in shades of red, pink, rose, white, purple, lilac and blue.

Underplanting

My sweet peas climb to the expected 6-7ft in height, but the bottom 3ft or so is a not too attractive tangle of leaves and stems. This is particularly so towards the end of the season. What can I grow to improve the balance of flowers and greenery?

Almost any tall summer bedding plant could be used to conceal the lower 2-3ft of sweet peas. What it is, is a matter of personal taste. But do remember that sweet peas need plenty of sunlight throughout their growth, even when they are only a few inches high. So take care that they are not overshadowed by plants growing nearby.

If your sweet peas are of mixed colours, the best bet might be to offset them with front plants of a single colour. Try pot marigolds (*Calendula officinalis*), which have yellow or orange blooms and vary between 12in and 2ft in height. Then there are the carnations, which are usually grown and treated as annuals or biennials. Of these, a good choice might be the variety 'Scarlet Luminette', which has slightly scented double blooms borne on 2ft stems.

A plant that would catch everyone's eye is the spider flower (*Cleome spinosa*), with its spiky, pink-purple flower heads standing 2-3½ft high. Almost as self-assertive are the deep blue flowers of *Centaurea cyanus* 'Blue Diadem' – a form of annual cornflower reaching nearly to the same height.

Finally, if you are growing sweet peas in single colour groups, why not make a contrast by underplanting with an edging of dwarf, or semi-dwarf, mixed sweet peas? This piling of colour on colour will provide an impressive banking effect.

Outdoor sowing

I don't have a greenhouse; how do I go about sowing sweet peas directly outdoors?

Outdoor sowing is worth doing at all only in the South. In the North, it's much better to sow under cover (see *Conflicting advice*, page 333). The cover doesn't have to be a greenhouse. It could be a cold frame, a cloche or even an indoor windowsill. The best time for outdoor sowing is in the autumn – October or early November – but there's still a good chance of success up to early April.

Either way, sow the seeds in prepared ground about 1in deep and 8-12in apart. As with indoor sowing, it pays to treat the seeds before sowing, to soften or crack their hard coats and thus speed germination (see *Getting started*, this page).

Space-saving tips for sweet peas

Can you suggest a good way of growing sweet peas in a limited space?

Make a sweet pea wigwam with pea sticks or bamboo canes. Sow two seeds by the foot of each cane, and thin to the better one.

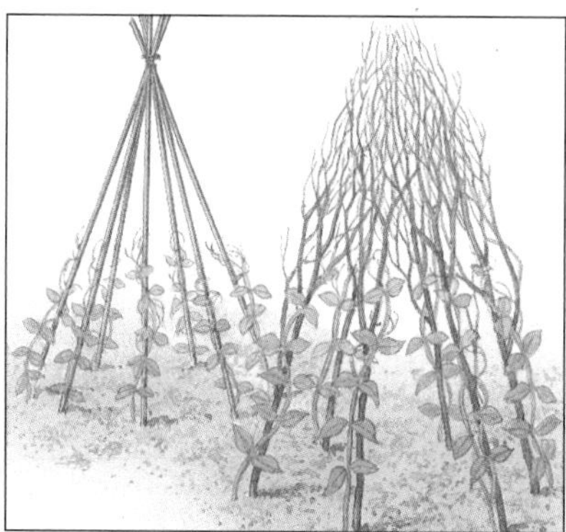

HIGH PEAS *Thrust the lower ends of canes firmly into the soil, and tie the tops together. Pea sticks don't need tying.*

Alternatively, if you've sown the seeds earlier in a greenhouse, set out one plant by each cane. Tie the peas up the sticks as they grow and you'll have a colourful garden feature that will last through late spring and summer. Another attractive notion is to let the plants ramble over a tall shrub or to train them over a wire arch or up a trellis.

Getting started

Growing sweet peas is one thing, making them germinate quite another. I suppose there's a knack that has somehow escaped me. What can it be?

If you're sowing indoors for planting out later, there are indeed a couple of tricks that will help to boost the germination success rate. In all of them, timing is crucial. Late February or early March is the period in which the success or failure of this year's sweet peas will be determined.

One idea is to put your sweet pea seeds between two layers of moist blotting paper 24 hours before you intend to sow. After that time you will see that some seeds have swelled while others have not. Those which have not swelled are the ones with the harder coats; they need tougher treatment to ensure germination. You can, for instance, nick each seed once with the tip of a sharp knife, or gently file it, on the side opposite the scar which denotes where the roots and shoots will emerge. This will allow water to enter more quickly when the seed is sown.

You could nick or file the seeds before they are soaked, but at that stage you won't know how many actually need the rather fiddly treatment. The soaking should save some work.

Another method – and one that's a good deal easier than nicking the seeds individually – is to tip the seeds out of the packet and sandwich them between two sheets of medium-grade sandpaper. Briskly slide the sheets up and down about ten times so that the abrasive sand cracks the seed coats.

A similar effect is achieved by putting up to 50 dry seeds in a jam jar and shaking it vigorously for 30-60 seconds. As the seeds bounce against each other and hit the glass, their seed coats become crazed and the hairline cracks will allow water to pass through more easily, speeding germination when the seeds are sown.

Peat-based composts suit sweet peas best. Fill 3in pots or special sweet pea tubes with the compost. Soak the compost, then sow the seeds in pairs, sinking them no more than ½in deep into the compost and covering them. Put the containers into a propagating frame, or a plastic bag, to prevent them drying out, and maintain them in a temperature of about 15°C (about 60°F).

After five or six days, the seedlings will begin to break through the surface of the compost. Remove and discard the weaker seedling of each pair, and move the containers to a cold frame or to an unheated part of the greenhouse in order to start the hardening-off process. Full sun, however, is essential if the seedlings are not to become drawn and leggy.

One final tip: since sweet peas have deep roots, it makes sense to start them off in deep containers. In place of special sweet pea tubes for this purpose, consider using the cardboard tubes from old toilet rolls or kitchen rolls. When the time comes to plant the seedlings out, they can go into the ground tubes and all. That way the roots won't be disturbed, and the tubes will rot into the soil during the summer.

Colours you can't have

Though sweet peas come in many shades, I've never seen a yellow variety, or a black one. Do they in fact exist, and if not, why not?

Just one of those things, like the elusive blue rose. Among hybrid sweet peas there is indeed no true yellow or black. Black is a rare colour among flowers, as is black foliage. Nevertheless there are a few deep maroon sweet peas that are almost black. There is, for instance, the relatively new variety 'Midnight', which one catalogue describes as 'easily the finest dark maroon, almost jet-black'. It has large, frilly flowers of perfect shape on long, stout stems. Then there is 'Black Prince', just about the nearest to black yet seen in sweet peas; it's a rich and velvety black-maroon.

There is a naturally yellow species, *Lathyrus luteus*. This is a small perennial, native to the Mediterranean, which has been used, together with others, in the breeding of new varieties. But in 1987 there was no garden form which reproduced its colour. The closest approximations are 'Hunter's Moon', which is a rich deep cream, almost lemon-yellow, and 'Cream Southbourne'. This has huge creamy blooms borne on strong stems.

Sweet pea problems

The sweet pea seeds I sow outdoors have mostly vanished. They seem to have been dug up. Could birds be responsible?

Birds are more likely to nibble the flowers and buds of sweet peas (you can keep them off by covering the plants with a net). Your problem is more probably mice. The solution is to lay traps or poison. Alternatively, if children or pets use the garden, shake the seeds in a jar or bag with sand which has been dampened with paraffin. Then sow as usual. The lingering smell will repel mice without any risk to pets or children.

Other common problems are:

- **APHIDS** The tiny insects, which are usually white, leave sticky patches on stems and leaves. Spray with dimethoate, malathion, permethrin or fenitrothion.
- **SLUGS** Seedlings chewed in winter and spring. Guard plants with slug pellets.
- **THRIPS** Leaves and petals become silvery and finely mottled. Spray with rotenone (derris), malathion or dimethoate.
- **MILDEW** Grey furry patches on the undersides of leaves are the marks of downy mildew. A white powdery coating on leaves and stems signals the presence of powdery mildew. Treat both by spraying with thiophanate-methyl or benomyl.
- **FOOT OR ROOT ROT** Leaves yellow and wither. Stem bases decay, and plants eventually collapse. Dig up infected plants and burn them or throw them away. Cut down on watering, because waterlogging encourages the disease. To stop further attacks, treat the soil with Armillatox in autumn.
- **VIRUS** Plants become stunted, shoots die back, and leaves and flowers may become discoloured or distorted. There is no treatment. Destroy infected plants, then wash tools thoroughly. Spray against aphids as well, because they spread virus diseases.

SWIFT MOTH CATERPILLARS

Raiders among the roots

When digging over my herbaceous border, I noticed that every few turns of the fork brought up inch-long and fairly unpleasant-looking caterpillars – slow-moving creatures with dirty-white bodies and brown heads. Appearance apart, is there anything against them from the gardening point of view?

Yes. These are swift moth caterpillars, which feed on the roots of a wide range of plants – most vegetables, strawberries, peonies, daffodils, irises, dahlias and delphiniums among them. The creatures are particularly fond of old herbaceous borders. When disturbed, they have a characteristic habit of wriggling hurriedly backwards.

Watch out for groups of plants that quickly wilt, then die. The caterpillars also feed upon the roots of nettles and docks, and it is upon these plants that the female swift moth often lays its eggs.

Good weed control and frequent turning over of the soil is the best prevention, but if infestation is serious, work HCH dust or bromophos into the ground around the plants.

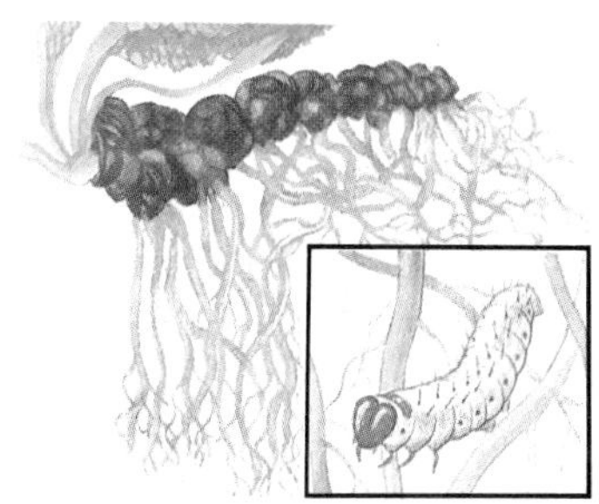

DWELLERS IN DARKNESS *Swift moth caterpillars live underground, feeding on roots.*

TARRAGON

How to beat the frost

I find it difficult to keep tarragon through the winter. Occasionally it survives, but most seasons it never re-appears. What am I doing wrong?

The most common cause of winter fatalities is waterlogging, although French tarragon does appear to be less hardy than the Russian variety and can be killed by a sharp frost. Planting in an open, well-drained position should help its chances of survival, as will the protection of a cloche from late autumn on. As a precaution, take several 2in or 3in cuttings in late summer and keep them in a cold frame for the winter.

These cuttings can take over if your plant does not survive, and they will give you plenty of fresh leaves for the kitchen.

France v Russia

Everyone tells me that French tarragon is better than Russian tarragon – but also that it is more difficult to grow. What is the difference?

According to most botanists, French and Russian tarragon are both forms of the same species, *Artemisia dracunculus*. The French variety has a more aromatic tang. But it does also seem to be less hardy and, since it does not set seed in this country, it has to be propagated by cuttings in spring or summer, or by dividing plants in spring.

French tarragon grows to 3ft high, and has dark green, shiny and fragrant leaves, that are used in béarnaise sauce and in many chicken dishes. The Russian version is slightly taller and has leaves of a paler green. It can be grown from seed, but many gardeners feel that there is little point in growing it at all, since its flavour is not appealing enough for it to be used as a substitute for French tarragon.

THRIPS

Silvery scars on leaves or pods

My peas were doing very well until the weather turned warm. Soon, pods and leaves were covered by a silvery mottling and became malformed and stunted. Is the problem too much sun, or am I getting the watering wrong?

None of these things. If you look closely, you will see that the silvery mottling is actually minute bites. They are made by tiny insects, called thrips, which are particularly troublesome on peas in warm weather. Similar symptoms can appear at this and other times on privet, gladioli, irises, onions and leeks, and on many greenhouse plants including tomatoes. The main hazard is not in the scarring itself, but in the way it exposes the plant to other problems, especially virus diseases.

At the first sign of silvering on peas or any other plants, spray or dust with HCH, malathion, derris or nicotine. Spray a second time ten days later if a lot of the bites still show silver. Don't pick peas until at least two weeks after the last spray. Check the label on the bottle for detailed advice about safety precautions.

SILVER LEAF *Tiny silvery scars – here caused by onion thrips on a leek – can make plants vulnerable to viruses.*

THYME

Fragrant footsteps

I've been told that some varieties of thyme can be grown in the cracks between paving stones where they will give off their scent when trodden on. Sounds a good idea; but how do I get them to grow in the cracks to begin with?

The creeping thymes grown in paving cracks bear little resemblance to the culinary kind. They are mostly derived from the low, sprawling shepherd's thyme, *Thymus serpyllum*, which you can buy, grown in 3in pots, from most alpine nurseries. Obviously, these are too large to push into paving cracks, but you can break them up and plant small, rooted pieces individually in a compost composed of equal parts of sharp sand and peat, or peat and perlite.

Now prepare the paving area where you want the thyme to grow. Gently lift each paving slab and replace the debris in the cracks with John Innes potting compost No 1. This will give the plants a good start. When the young plants are ready, insert them between the slabs with an aquarium planter – a two-pronged stick used for putting aquarium plants in tropical fish tanks. Water the plants regularly for several weeks after planting, until you are sure they have taken. For the first few months, avoid walking on them. When they are well established, a moderate amount of crushing underfoot will do them little harm.

Trying time

I've tried again and again to get thyme cuttings to root, but with little success. When is the right time to take them?

You can make the attempt at any time during the growing season, though success is never guaranteed. Use individual shoots, stocky, short-jointed, and no more than $1\frac{1}{2}$in long. While you can root large pieces of thyme, they make unruly and unsatisfactory plants. Smaller cuttings may take longer to get established, but in the end they make more vigorous and better-looking plants.

Take thyme cuttings from non-flowering new growth which is not too soft. If the stems are very green and succulent they often rot before they root. On the other hand, cuttings from older, woody stalks often do not root, and lose all their leaves.

If you have no luck with cuttings from this in-between, 'semi-ripe' stage, try taking them with a 'heel'. To do this, choose suitable short shoots and tear them off their parent branches, pulling off with them a small portion of the old wood. This piece of older wood, known as a 'heel', helps troublesome cuttings to root (see *The language of cuttings*, page 108).

Insert the cuttings in pots containing equal parts of peat and sharp sand, or peat and perlite, and place the pots in a well-ventilated frame or on a bright but shaded windowsill. Once rooted – and you'll be able to tell because the shoots will start to make new growth – cuttings can be potted up individually and then plunged in a peat or sand bed in a cold frame over winter. Plant them out the following spring.

Be generous with the amount of space you allow for thyme in your herb bed, for it is a very useful plant. It is a principal ingredient in *bouquets garnis*, and on its own is widely used to flavour sausages, stews, stuffings and even to enliven creamed potatoes. It is also said to be invigorating: Roman legionaries, according to legend, bathed in thyme-scented water as a bracer before battle.

TOMATOES

Skin split

My tomatoes have been doing so well, but the other day I noticed that some of the skins were starting to split. Is there a remedy?

Splitting is usually caused by unsettled weather coupled with lack of watering. In cold or dry seasons the fruits develop slowly and the skins become hard.

When a warm or wet spell follows, development accelerates, but the tomatoes are unable to expand without splitting their skins. The only treatment is to water regularly and never let the compost dry out.

Curly leaves

My greenhouse tomatoes are soaring, but though the leaves look green and healthy, they seem reluctant to open, and remain curled up. Is it some sort of blight?

No. Actually it's one of several problems that very often plague the small greenhouse owner and pass the large commercial houses by. The curled-up leaves are due almost entirely to the big contrast between day and night temperatures. The plants make a surplus of food during the warmth of the day, but cannot absorb it at night because the low temperature slows down their biological activity. The result is a stop-start growth pattern which produces the curly leaves you see. This is not such a problem with outdoor tomatoes, where the day and night temperature range is not so great.

Summer temperature control is very difficult in a small greenhouse where night temperatures may plunge to below 10°C (50°F), then during a sunny day may easily climb to 35°C (95°F). This is too great a contrast for tomatoes to be happy in – or any other plant, for that matter.

To alleviate the problem, you need to flatten the temperature peaks. To cool the plants by day, cover the glass with a plastic shade-cloth, or paint with shading paint. Then, if you have any heating in your greenhouse and can control it, set your thermostat to 10°C (50°F) to cushion the night-time fall.

Another way to cool the greenhouse is to sprinkle water on the path inside, but be careful not to overdo it. Excessive humidity can encourage fungal diseases. On hot, sunny days remember to open all the ventilators and leave the door open as well.

Tomato droop

I think one of the tomato plants in my greenhouse border is about to die. The leaves are hanging and limp, though the other plants look healthy. What is wrong?

Wilt is the problem, either the type known as fusarium or the one called verticillium. These fungal diseases affect a plant in similar ways, by attacking the water-conducting tissues in the stem; eventually they will kill it. To prevent the wilt spreading, you must carefully dig out the plant and burn it.

Because both diseases are soil-borne, remove all the surrounding soil as well, and replace it with sterilised compost – if you have spotted the wilt early enough, you may be able to stop the fungus spreading to adjacent healthy plants.

Drench these plants with a solution of a systemic fungicide such as benomyl, and repeat a fortnight later. It won't guarantee their immunity, but the only other alternative is to destroy the lot – which means no tomatoes that year if you are well into the season.

To avoid future problems, always use clean, sterilised soil or new peat-based compost.

Truss stop

My outdoor tomatoes are doing well, and are just forming their fifth truss, with the fruits on it about pea size. Is this the time to stop them?

Yes. Stop them now by pinching out their growing tips. Five trusses is the limit for outdoor cordon tomatoes in the South of the country – many good gardeners choose to stop their outdoor tomatoes after four, and three is more common in the North. The fifth doesn't usually get to the stage your plants are at until late August or early September, when there will be little time for them to become fully formed and to ripen.

To encourage your fifth-truss fruits to swell, and to make sure that the fruits lower down ripen fully, a useful trick is to remove the ties and supports about now, lay the plants down on straw (without breaking the stems) and cover them with cloches. That way, you effectively create a mini-greenhouse around the plants, which can keep the fruits developing and reddening for as much as a month longer than they would without the shelter.

Insect raiders

Some of my greenhouse tomato plants have suddenly had their leaves eaten away almost to a skeleton overnight. What is the pest and how can I get rid of it?

You've got a bad attack of tomato moth caterpillar, a greenhouse pest in the main, and you're lucky not to have your fruit and stems damaged as well. Look among the leaves and you will probably find them covered in dozens of small green caterpillars – they turn brown as they grow, which they will do rapidly unless checked.

Obviously, the best preventative is to spot the pest before trouble starts – check the undersides of the leaves regularly for clusters of small eggs. Crush these before they hatch. But once you've got the grubs, spray with fenitrothion and destroy damaged fruit.

The tomato moth caterpillar is not the only insect that can have a go at your tomatoes. Sticky, yellow leaves are probably caused by aphids – they will attack both under glass and outdoors. Spray with malathion and fumigate (in the greenhouse) with HCH cones, but use derris or pyrethrum close to fruiting time. Another sticky-leaf problem, where the leaves of greenhouse tomatoes are covered in patches of honeydew, on which grow patches of black mould, could be caused by whitefly. The leaves also become pale and curled, but you can be sure of the cause by gently moving the plants – clouds of whitefly will rise into the air.

Combat the problem with a permethrin spray at three-day intervals over three weeks. That's seven sprays in all and should destroy the pest at all stages of its development. An alternative is to fumigate the greenhouse, three times at seven-day intervals, with a permethrin smoke.

Other insects which could take a fancy to your plants include the following:

- **RED SPIDER MITES** The leaves of greenhouse plants curl and become spotted and bronzed. Groups of minute red spiders are found under the leaves. Fumigate with HCH smoke cones or spray with pirimiphos-methyl. A dry atmosphere encourages the pest so spray the plants with water regularly.
- **EELWORMS** Prevalent indoors. Plants wilt in the sun and yellow and dead patches develop on the lower leaves. Destroy the plants and change or sterilise the soil.
- **SPRINGTAILS** Young greenhouse plants develop holes and scrape marks on the leaves. Apply HCH dust carefully to the soil around the plants.
- **THRIPS** Found outdoors and in the greenhouse. Commonly known as thunderflies, thrips pierce plant tissues and suck the sap, with the result that leaves become finely mottled with a silvery appearance. Treat by spraying the plants with malathion, repeating the dose 14 days later. Use derris close to harvest time.

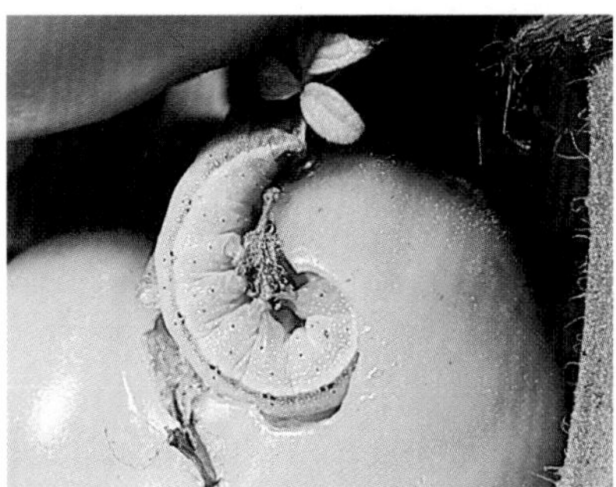

TOMATO MOTH *The moth's small green and brown caterpillars can devastate a crop.*

Feeding times

I'm a newcomer to tomato growing. Mine are about 15in high with fruits just visible on the first truss. The books say I should start feeding about now. Is this right, and what's the best thing to give them?

If the plants are growing in well-prepared greenhouse border soil, they will be happy without additional feeding until the tomatoes on the first truss are the size of small marbles. At this stage start feeding with one of the proprietary tomato liquid feeds, applied every seven to ten days in accordance with the instructions on the label.

But if you are rearing your plants in growing bags or pots, then the picture is rather different. In this case, it is better to start feeding as soon as the flowers on the first truss have 'set' – meaning that they have been fertilised and are visibly starting to shrivel. Feed every four or five days, again using a proprietary tomato fertiliser.

Stick close to the manufacturer's instructions wherever your tomatoes are growing. Overfeeding a plant is just as harmful as starving it, so if you do accidentally overfeed, thoroughly water the growing bag or the soil around the plant to dilute or wash out the surplus fertiliser.

Perfect tomato plants

I have no heated greenhouse, and therefore buy tomato plants rather than grow them from seed. However, I've bought quite a few duds down the years. What should I look for in a good tomato plant?

Always go for plants which are being grown in individual pots. Avoid plants which are growing in groups in a seed tray; when you separate them at planting time, you're bound to damage some of the roots and thus cause a considerable setback in growth. The ideal pot-grown plant is sturdy, with no more than 1-1½in between leaf joints, dark green and shows no hint of flowering. It should be about 8in high, 6in across and have a stem about as thick at its base as your little finger. The rootball on such a plant will have enveloped the compost in the pot so that transplanting can be carried out with the minimum of disturbance.

Check, though, that the plant is not trailing long streamers of roots from the pot's drainage holes. If it is, this means that the plant has become pot-bound – a condition which, like damaged roots, will tend to check the plant's growth.

No growth

My first greenhouse tomato trusses have set on time and according to the rules. But having reached about the size of matchheads, the fruits refuse to grow any further. What's wrong?

It's a malady known as dry set. What has happened is that, during the fertilisation period, the pollen has dried out. When this occurs, only minute fruits are formed. It's usually the result of a dry atmosphere and high temperature. It can also be caused by infertile pollen, but low humidity is the usual cause. There's nothing you can do to rescue the affected fruits. But you can prevent the same thing happening on later trusses by levelling off the midday temperature. Open the ventilators full out in sunny weather, and damp down the floor in the heat of the day. A gentle spray of water on the plants and flowers will also help, but don't overdo it; fungal diseases love damp, too.

Cutting back

'Pinch out the sideshoots of greenhouse tomatoes', says the book, but they look pretty delicate to me. Is there a knack?

All tomatoes grown as single-stemmed plants, known as cordons, produce sideshoots in the leaf axils – that is, between the leaf stalks and the main stem. These must be removed to keep the plant growing upwards and to prevent it from growing into a less-productive bush shape. The sideshoots should be removed as soon as they can be seen. Do it gently, using your thumb and finger or a pair of nail scissors. You must be careful not to damage the fruit trusses as you work. Remember that these trusses grow out of the main stem between the leaf stalks. If you miss a sideshoot for a time and it grows large, cut it out as soon as you spot it, and dust the wound with sulphur to keep out disease.

TWENTY TIPS FOR TOP TOMATOES

OUTDOORS

1 Choose a sunny site and, if possible, one screened from north and east winds. Beside a wall facing south-west would be ideal.
2 Prepare the site thoroughly. Dig in plenty of well-rotted compost or farmyard manure.
3 Let the site settle for a couple of weeks. Then just before planting, fork in a general fertiliser – Growmore, for instance – at the rate of 2oz to the square yard.
4 Plant out the tomato plants in late May or early June.
5 Set cordon types – such as 'Moneymaker' or 'Alicante' – 1½-2ft apart. Put a 5ft cane by each plant and tie the stem to it.
6 Set bush types – such as 'Red Alert', 'Pixie' or 'Sigmabush' – 2½-3ft apart and tie the main stem of each plant to a 2ft cane. Once the plants are established, cover the soil beneath each plant with straw or bracken to protect the fruits from mud splashes.
7 Remove all sideshoots from cordons as they appear, and tie in the main stem firmly to the supporting cane. Stop the leading shoot after the fourth or, at most, the fifth fruit truss (the third in the North of the country). Do not remove any sideshoots from bush tomatoes; when the fruits appear, thin out some of the stems to encourage ripening.
8 Give both types a weekly liquid feed after the first fruit has grown to pea size, and water as necessary. Do not let the soil dry out.
9 After mid-July, spray plants with a fungicide, such as a copper compound, to combat potato blight. If aphids appear, spray with pyrethrum or derris.
10 Regularly check the ties of cordon types, and re-tie as necessary. In late summer, make sure that plants are secure; the developing fruit trusses will make them top-heavy.

INDOORS

1 Plant cordon types – such as 'Moneymaker' and 'Alicante' – into the greenhouse border. If the borders are 'tomato sick' (see *Changing ground*, this page, for details), plant them in growing bags, rings or pots.
2 Plant tomatoes in well-heated greenhouses in mid-March to early April; in moderately heated houses, mid-late April; in cold houses, early May to end May.
3 Water very carefully from the start; never let the soil or compost become sodden.
4 Set a short, stout cane – about 2ft high – beside each plant and join it to the roof with a double string. Tie the plants to the canes.
5 Gently pinch off all sideshoots from the plants as they appear.
6 As the plants grow, twist the string around the stems.
7 Start liquid feeding with a proprietary fertiliser when the fruits on the first truss have grown to the size of peas. Plants in growing bags, rings or pots should be fed every four or five days, those in borders every seven days.
8 On hot sunny days, lightly spray greenhouse paths with water at midday to create a little humidity.
9 Ventilate the house well. High temperatures and excessive humidity promote disease problems.
10 Stop the leading shoots by late August or after six trusses, whichever is first. Remove any brown, withered lower leaves.

Changing ground

I've grown tomatoes in my greenhouse border for a few years now. I always feed the soil well with liquid fertiliser, but last year the crop was pretty miserable and I had a good many plant failures, too. What's the matter?

Probably your ground is 'tomato sick'. What has happened is that the soil has developed a poor structure as a result of constant liquid feeding. Over the years, there has been a build-up of salts, plant acids and toxic products from both the plants and the fertilisers, all of which have made the soil sour.

In addition, pests and diseases that attack tomatoes specifically may also be there, transmitted from an earlier crop and now spreading through the border.

Tomatoes grow best in soils that have not known tomatoes before, and you can return to that happy state in one of three ways. You could remove the soil completely to a depth of at least 2ft and replace it with fresh soil from the garden. Or you could sterilise the present soil with Jeyes Fluid (for the method, see *Ring culture*, opposite).

If all this seems a bit elaborate, then the simplest solution is to lay out a few growing bags along the border and grow the tomatoes in them. This method shuts out all soil-borne diseases completely – and at the end of the season you can mulch the garden with the compost in the bags.

Tomatoes in May?

I have a fancy to grow a few really early tomatoes. How should I set about it? I have a well-heated greenhouse, by the way.

With a really well-heated greenhouse, you should be able to pick tomatoes as early as mid-May.

Sow the seeds in late December or early January in a temperature of at least 16°C (60°F). Pot up the seedlings individually in 3in pots in mid-January. Move them on to 4in or 5in pots three to four weeks later, and about five to six weeks after that – towards the end of March – plant them out into the border soil or a growing bag. Once they're there, grow them on as normal. It's worth remembering the importance of light at all these stages – for successful development, seeds, seedlings and young plants must receive the maximum possible.

All this potting and repotting may seem clumsy, but it does result in better plants. Plants which are moved into over-large pots tend to suffer because the unused compost around their roots becomes stagnant. Each time you repot, handle the young plants only by the leaves as far as possible, so as not to bruise the tender stems. As for heating, it's vital not to let the night-time temperature drop below 14°C (58°F) at any stage, or to let the daytime temperature climb to more than 24°C (75°F). If the greenhouse gets too warm and there is not enough light, the plants will become leggy; if too cold, they'll be stunted and bushy.

Alternatively, if all this seems rather daunting, you could buy young plants from a nursery between mid-March and May.

Magnesium check

I've been giving my tomatoes regular feeds with liquid fertiliser, but I notice that some of the lower leaves are yellowing between the veins, and I think the yellow is advancing. What's the trouble? I'm sure it can't be in the way I've been watering.

Magnesium deficiency is the culprit. Magnesium is included in some tomato fertilisers, but not all.

Check the label on yours, and if magnesium isn't listed, change to a fertiliser that does have it. At the same time spray your plants with a solution of Epsom salts.

Mix the spray at a rate of 3oz to 1 gallon of water, adding a few drops of washing-up liquid. Repeat the dose every seven to ten days until the leaves are all green, and at the same time cut the tomato fertiliser by half. When the plants are once again green and healthy, resume normal feeding.

Ring culture

A friend has been extolling the advantages of growing tomatoes by ring culture. Sounds interesting. How do I go about it?

'Ring culture' is another method of growing tomatoes which can be used when greenhouse border soil has become 'tomato sick'. It is interesting, or at least novel, to most people, and a lot less work than totally replacing the border soil, or sterilising it.

You begin by taking off the top 6in of border soil and replacing it with a layer of coarse, weathered ashes, gravel, shingle, or coarse sand. For extra protection against infection, spread a plastic sheet over the undersoil before adding the new layer, but stab the sheet here and there with a garden fork to aid drainage.

Now comes the 'ring' part. There are bottomless 9in bituminised paper pots on the market, but it's easy to make your own by stapling roofing felt into cylinders about 9in high and 9in across. Or knock the bottom out of a big plastic flower pot or bucket. Sink the rings about 2in deep into the aggregate to give stability, and about 18in apart. Fill the rings with potting compost to within 2in of the tops. Leave the rings for a few days to allow the compost to warm up, then plant one tomato plant in each ring, firming them well in and watering them – this will be the first and last time you water the pot. The plants will rapidly root down through the pot into the aggregate layer, which acts as a reservoir and provides a cool base. From now on, you water the aggregate around the bases of the rings, but pour liquid feed into the compost in the pot.

At the end of the growing season, or in spring well before planting next year's tomatoes, use the old compost as a garden mulch, clean the rings and water the aggregate with a chemical steriliser such as Jeyes Fluid – follow the manufacturer's instructions about the strength of the dose. After watering on the chemical, cover the soil with plastic for four to five days, then remove the plastic and ventilate the greenhouse well. It is essential that this sterilisation is carried out annually.

Green to red

Is there any truth in the old legend that red tomatoes will ripen green ones stored alongside them?

Most gardening folklore contains a nugget of sound sense, and this maxim is no exception. Red or ripe tomatoes give off a gas called ethylene which will hasten the ripening of green ones. Wrap the green tomatoes separately in tissue paper and store them together in a drawer – putting one or two red ones with them. Check them daily and remove them as they ripen – otherwise you'll have a rotting mess and a drawer to clean.

Alternatively, if you've eaten all the red tomatoes, put a ripe banana in with the green tomatoes. Ripe bananas give off ethylene in the same way as red tomatoes.

Fiction or fact?

My sister and I bought tomato plants at the same place, at the same time and planted them in exactly the same way. Yet, a couple of months later, her plants are twice the size of mine. Is it possible that some people actually possess 'green fingers'?

There's little doubt of it. We all know people who are able to sow seeds, take cuttings and grow plants with much better results than the general run. It's all a matter of doing things at the right time. Gardening is both a science and an art, and it's how you apply your knowledge of gardening techniques that counts in the end.

If plants are grown under laboratory conditions – that is, sown, planted out and potted on in exactly the same way at the same temperatures and at the same time – there is little difference between them. Your sister cannot have followed the same course as you; if she had, your tomato plants would be the same. Probably she has a feel for plants and is able to sense their requirements, so that she waters and feeds them in exactly the way they need. What you'll have to do is watch her and learn from her.

Bigger tomatoes

Last season, my tomato plants produced too many flowers too late in the year – and a disappointing crop. What should I do next year to make sure I get large, firm tomatoes?

Stop the plants before they outgrow their strength. Outdoors, this simply means cutting off the growing point once four, or at the most five, trusses have set. This is the limit for plants in the South; in the North, where it is cooler and development is slower, three trusses is more common. In the case of greenhouse plants, you can allow six trusses to form before stopping the plant.

STOPPING POINT *Cut off the growing tip on outdoor plants after three to five trusses have set.*

Where to start

Can I grow tomatoes from seed outdoors or must I start them off in a greenhouse?

No – don't sow them outdoors; it never works. By late May or early June, when other gardeners are planting out their outdoor plants, yours will still be small seedlings. You're unlikely to get a good crop of fruit because they will simply never catch up.

The seeds should always be started off in a greenhouse or even in the house, to give them a flying start. If you want only a few plants it is better to buy them, ready to plant out, in late spring or early summer.

Leaf stripping

Every year I get conflicting advice from my gardening friends about whether or not to remove the leaves from my tomato plants to help ripen the fruit after the trusses have set. What should I do?

It is a common fallacy that leaf removal will help the fruit to ripen more quickly by exposing the tomatoes to the sun. In fact, the speed of ripening depends on the prevailing temperature and not on direct sunlight.

Indeed, direct sun on the fruits can be positively harmful – especially in a greenhouse – by overheating them and turning them a blotchy, orange-yellow – sometimes with a hard, green ring at the stalk end, known as greenback.

Remember, also, that the leaves are the factory where the sun's energy is used to convert chemicals into food for the plant – the process known as photosynthesis. It's a kind of industrial sabotage to remove the leaves – you're cutting back the plants' chances of strong growth.

Nevertheless, you should break off the first few lower leaves at the base of the plant as they wither and brown – this will help air to circulate and lower the risk of disease that might develop in the rotting vegetation.

In your greenhouse, too, it's a good idea to remove the lowest leaves – they will in any case probably be overshadowed by more vigorous growth from above. These early leaves may be withering and therefore becoming more susceptible to rotting and disease. Removing them will also make it easier to get at the container for watering.

You may also find that the foliage on greenhouse plants becomes very thick. In these circumstances, to reduce the risk of fungal disease developing in the still, trapped air, remove a couple of leaves here and there from each plant, to open them out a bit and let air circulate freely.

Fruit – black and blotched

The stem end on some of my greenhouse tomatoes has turned black and some of the fruit has fallen. Have I got a bad batch of plants or is it something I am doing wrong?

The condition is called blossom end rot and I'm afraid it's your fault. You are either watering irregularly or else you are not following the instructions carefully when making up your liquid fertiliser feed. All you can do is remove the rotted fruits and water and feed with more care in future. Watering and feeding regularly are also important if you don't want other fruit disorders to set in. For example, fruit with yellow or orange blotches which fails to ripen can result from nutrient deprivation, although it is also caused by direct sunlight overheating the fruit (see *Leaf stripping*, page 339). You can't do anything about the fruit that is already blotched, but you can ensure that other trusses don't go the same way by shading and ventilating the greenhouse, and by feeding the plants regularly.

Greenback – fruit on which the stalk end does not ripen and remains hard and green – also results from overheating by direct sunlight, although it can sometimes be caused by potash deficiency. To remedy, shade and ventilate the greenhouse, and feed with a high-potash fertiliser.

Bronzing of the fruit is a different kettle of fish. This is a virus disorder and the only sensible course of action is to lift and burn the affected plants. The fruit is not worth saving – it's not very palatable.

A rotten attack

My greenhouse tomatoes have developed a grey, velvety mould near the stalk end on some of the fruits, on the scars where I've removed sideshoots and on a few damaged leaves. Some of the stems have started to rot as well. Can I rescue the plants?

The heavy ash-grey mould is a sure indicator of botrytis – a fungal disease that gets into the plant through the stumps of carelessly trimmed leaves and shoots. It may occur outdoors as well. Yes – you can do something about it. First remove the diseased fruits before they infect their neighbours. Then cut back diseased leaves and sideshoot stumps to the stem with a sharp knife. Do the same with any rotted sections of the stem. Spray the wounds with benomyl, then fumigate the greenhouse with tecnazene.

Keep the atmosphere as dry as possible, giving plenty of ventilation day and night. Remove two or three lower leaves to allow free air circulation. There are several other diseases that could hit your plants. These are the common ones.

- **LEAF MOULD** It usually starts among the lower leaves with yellow patches developing on the tops and a purple-brown, felt-like mould on the undersides. Ventilate the greenhouse and remove the affected leaves; spray with mancozeb.
- **TOMATO MOSAIC VIRUS** One of the main virus afflictions, resulting in yellow-mottled and curled leaves – they sometimes become almost fernlike. Brown vertical streaks appear on the stems and the plant's growth is usually checked. Destroy the affected plants, roots and all.
- **POTATO BLIGHT** Usually affects only outdoor crops. Brown areas appear on the leaves and dark streaks on the stems. The leaves die – in wet weather the fungus thrives, and appears as a mass of white threads on the underside of the leaves. Fruit may also be attacked.

Destroy the affected plants. As a preventative, spray healthy plants with a copper compound every two weeks from July until the end of the growing season.

- **DIDYMELLA STEM ROT** Brown scars and slimy black dots appear on the stems just above ground level. Burn infected plants and spray the lower stems of the remainder with a copper-based fungicide. Burn these plants at the end of the season and thoroughly disinfect the greenhouse.
- **OEDEMA** Bumps and blotches appear on the stem and occasionally on the leaves, caused by excess moisture in the soil or the atmosphere. To counteract, increase the greenhouse ventilation and reduce the humidity. Using a petroleum oil to control red spider mite can also cause oedema on tomatoes – in which case discontinue spraying at once.
- **PHYTOPHTHORA STEM ROT** The first sign is brown or black fungus followed by a white, fluffy growth on the main stem. It's usually encouraged by the careless application of fertiliser. There is no cure; burn all affected plants and sterilise or renew the soil for the next season.

TOOLS

(For powered tools, see CULTIVATORS, page 107, and LAWN MOWERS, page 218)

Choosing tools

I'm just starting on my first garden. How do I judge what tools I really need, and which are just expensive luxuries?

Start with the basics. Buy a strong spade, a digging fork, a rake, a Dutch hoe (see *What hoe?* opposite), a trowel, a hand fork, a pair of shears, some secateurs and a garden line (which can be a couple of wooden pegs and a long piece of string). With these – and a lawn mower – you can do most things in the garden. Over the years, you will accumulate other tools as well. There are some good labour-saving tools around that are worth saving up for.

But think before you buy, and don't buy for novelty's sake. Such tools very often gather rust at the back of the shed once the owner discovers that old-fashioned basic tools do the job just as well.

Be wary, for example, of expensive, motorised cultivators. With some of them, you can lose as much time in maintenance as you gain on the ground. Also, though these machines can dig, they won't give you a better tilth than you can get with a good spade, a good fork, a rake, and some steady exercise.

No rust

What are the advantages of buying stainless-steel tools?

They don't go rusty, so they last longer. And so they should, because they cost a good deal more – often twice as much – as ordinary steel tools.

Don't imagine that stainless-steel tools don't need cleaning after use. They do. All tools should be cleaned, and especially so at the end of the season, when they are put away for winter. The simplest way to guard them against deterioration during the damp of winter is to wipe them over with an oily rag before you put them away.

There is one disadvantage with stainless-steel tools. They lose their sharp edges more quickly than ordinary steel. This does not matter too much with forks and spades, hoes and trowels. But it does with shears and secateurs. So stick to the hard steel versions when buying these – and clean and oil them after use.

What hoe?

I'm bewildered by all the different types of hoes on sale at the garden centre. Do they all do different jobs, or are they simply meant to suit different preferences?

They do different jobs. There are three main types: the Dutch; the draw; and the onion.

The Dutch hoe is generally used with a push-pull action, with the gardener stepping backwards as he works so that no footmarks are left. It's ideal for weeding between rows, especially among shallow-rooting crops and flowers.

It not only cuts down weeds, but gently breaks up the surface, reversing the tendency of many soils to form a waterproof crust of compacted earth after heavy rain.

The Dutch hoe is also versatile because you can turn it over and use it like a draw hoe for chopping at tougher weeds or for earthing up vegetables.

The draw hoe is used by chopping down into the soil and pulling it towards you. You can avoid leaving footmarks by walking backwards or by standing in one gap between vegetable rows and hoeing in the next. This type of hoe can go down quite deep and can chop through larger weeds than a Dutch hoe. It's also the best tool for earthing up potato ridges and for taking out planting drills.

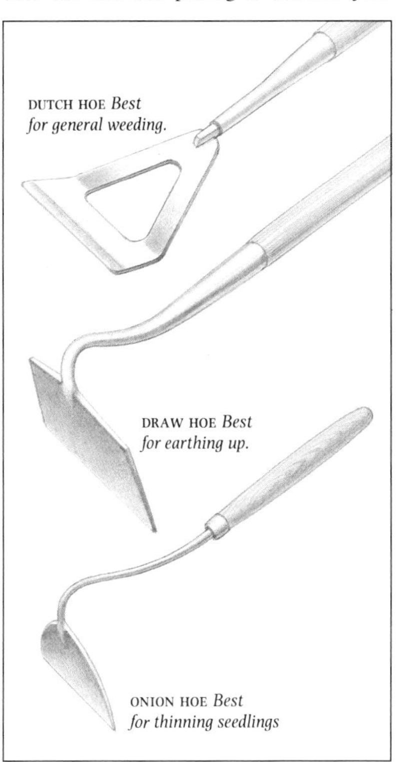

DUTCH HOE *Best for general weeding.*

DRAW HOE *Best for earthing up.*

ONION HOE *Best for thinning seedlings*

On hard, stony ground where constant collisions with rocks can jar hands and arms painfully, consider buying a type of Dutch hoe in which the blade is connected to the handle by a single arm, not a double one. The single arm acts as a stiff spring, which has the effect of cushioning the blow when you hit a rock in the soil.

The onion hoe has a narrow blade and a short handle, which is generally only about 12in long. It's used for thinning out seedlings and for getting in between plants that are close together.

Hoes are basically cutting tools so you need to sharpen them regularly. When buying a Dutch or draw hoe, get one that won't make you stoop. As a rough guide, with the hoe held vertically, the top should be about level with your eyes.

Keep close

How close and how deep is it safe to hoe?

As close as you can to your garden plants, but no deeper than about $\frac{1}{2}$in.

At this depth you will cut off the weeds at their roots and disturb the soil sufficiently to prevent a crust from forming. Any deeper, and you risk damaging the roots of the plants you want to keep. The tool for this job is the Dutch hoe.

Always keep the blade of your hoe sharp. It is meant to cut through the weeds, not push them through the soil.

A choice of power

Are electrically driven garden machines as good as petrol ones?

Yes, they are just as good. They can also be quieter, cleaner and cheaper to run – and they start more easily.

This is certainly true of hedge cutters, trimmers, weeders and light cultivators. The main disadvantage is the long and unwieldy cable, probably with one or more extensions if you are working at some distance from the power point.

When joining up the extensions before use, always plug into the power point last, and disconnect from the power socket first after use. Make sure the lead has a clear unimpeded run from socket to tool.

If you use a reeled extension cable, always pull out the full length of the reel even if you don't need it all. In use, any electric cable gets warm, and if you leave cable wound on the reel, the trapped heat can build up to the point where the insulation melts, causing a short circuit.

Fit a circuit breaker – one type is called a residual current circuit breaker (RCCB) – with all electrical equipment for use in the garden. The circuit breaker is designed to cut off the power instantly if there is a short circuit or if you get an electric shock. Keep the lead clear of the tool by draping it over

SAFETY TIPS FOR GARDEN TOOLS

EVERY year around 420,000 people in Britain get hurt in accidents outdoors at home – about one in seven of the 3 million people who, each year, are injured badly enough at home to need some form of medical treatment.

Many of the 420,000 victims are gardeners, and many of the accidents need not happen. Follow these simple rules to make your garden a safer place.

- Keep sharp-edged tools sheathed and out of the reach of children when not in use, preferably under lock and key.
- Never leave a fork or rake lying on the ground prongs upwards. If you tread on the prongs, the handle can fly up and strike you in the face.
- Keep power tools switched off and unplugged when they are not in use, so that they cannot be started accidentally.
- For the same reason, switch off and unplug power tools before cleaning, adjusting or lubricating them.
- With petrol-driven tools, remove the lead from the spark plug before working on them, to prevent any chance of the motor starting up by accident. Otherwise, a motor mower, for example, may spring into life when the blades are turned by hand.
- Do not use electric tools outdoors in the rain – the wet may cause a short circuit and give you a severe shock.
- Never use tape to join loose power cable, indoors or out – the joint may pull apart and it's not waterproof. Use purpose-made waterproof connectors instead.
- Push a mower away from you – never pull it – and mow across slopes, not up them. That way there is less risk of the mower running over your foot.
- When using mowers and trimmers, always wear stout shoes and trousers. Wear goggles when using trimmers – they can throw up small stones and dust.
- Hold electric mower trigger switches on by hand – never tie them down.
- Look out for a symbol showing two squares, one inside the other, when buying electrically powered tools. It means that the tool is doubly insulated.
- Make sure all cable attached to electrical tools used outside is orange. The colour stands out well against the greens and browns of the garden and you are therefore less likely to trip over it or cut through it.
- Never use an extension lead thinner than the lead attached to the tool, otherwise the extension lead may well overheat.

your shoulder while working, and never use electrically powered tools in the rain.

Don't touch blades immediately after switching off; electric tools continue to run for several seconds. For information about petrol or electrically driven lawn mowers, see *Lawn mowers*, page 218.

The fork dilemma

Should I use a spade or a fork for digging?

A clean, sharp, well-balanced spade is the perfect digging tool. It cuts through the soil, holds it while you turn it, and drops it where you want it.

But there are times when you will need to use a fork. For example, very wet or compacted clay soil will stick to a spade, making digging impossible.

The ideal thing to do would be to leave the soil to dry out. But, to save time, you can use a fork. It will still be an arduous task, but the prongs of the fork will slide through clay where a spade would clog.

Otherwise, a fork is used mainly to break up the surface soil – after the spade has done the spadework.

The right handle

Tools come with a variety of handles. Why the difference? What are the advantages and disadvantages?

Spades and forks have closed Y-shaped, D-shaped or T-shaped heads to their handles.

The older-style D-shaped wooden handles were inclined to be weak at the junction of the D and the stem and have now, in wooden-handled tools at least, largely given way to the closed Y-shape, which has a bolt or strengthening rod at the point where the Y divides. Well maintained, these tools will last a lifetime.

The T-shaped handle has no split, but a cross-piece fixed at the top. Many gardeners find it awkward to use, because it can catch in your clothes as you dig. It seems to be a regional design, being much more popular in the North than in the South. The edging iron, or half-moon, has a standard T-handle as do some shovels. The reason seems to be to allow a better push with the hand.

As to which is best, go simply for the handle that feels most comfortable.

Beyond that personal choice, pain-free gardening – particularly digging – is more a matter of how you work rather than what you work with. For advice on how to ease the task, see *Digging*, page 121.

The big push

Should a wheelbarrow be pushed or pulled?

Never mind what builders do; in a garden a barrow should be pushed. You have more control over it and you can see where the wheels are going.

Pull it behind you, and it can tip over before you can correct it, apart from leaving a lasting impression of your passing on the edging plants.

Buy a galvanised iron barrow, with a pneumatic tyre. It is light and long-lasting, and a pneumatic tyre makes less of a crease in the lawn than a solid one. A galvanised iron barrow can also be used as an impromptu and movable barbecue, with the coals in the barrow and an old oven shelf laid across the top. Put bricks under the back legs if necessary to make the rim level.

You can also buy barrows which have a large ball instead of a wheel; they make for easy progress over soft ground.

If you have lots of leaves to move in autumn, get a barrow which has a removable extension top. It will enable you to transport larger cargoes with less spillage.

Whatever barrow you buy, keep the axle well greased. There is nothing more infuriating than a squeaky barrow. Incidentally, always leave an empty wheelbarrow facing the way you *next* want to go. That way, you won't risk putting your back out turning the barrow after it's loaded.

On the edge

Edging shears and edging irons – the half-moon ones – seem to be intended to do the same job. Which should I buy?

The shears are essential; buy an edging iron only if you can't borrow one.

They *don't* actually do the same job. The shears cut the grass along the edges of the lawn. The half-moon cuts the soil. So, you need the shears all summer long – each time you mow, really. The edging iron you may need no more than once a year.

When using an edging iron, stretch a garden line tightly along the direction of the cut, or lay a board along the edge of the lawn to use as a guide.

With both tools, cut at a slight angle away from the lawn. This will give a firmer edge to the turf and prevent it crumbling so readily into the border.

Saving seedlings

Whenever I hoe around seedlings, I invariably chop off a number of them by accident. What can I do to avoid this?

One way is to lay angle irons or boards down each side of the row and hoe between them, or put upturned flower pots over the seedlings for the duration of the operation. Otherwise, hoe only as near to the plants as is safe, then do the rest by hand. Don't rush the job.

Better still, follow the maxim: hoe before you sow. If you've done a thorough job of clearing the ground of weeds and breaking up the surface before sowing, you shouldn't need to hoe again until the seedlings have grown into sturdy – and more easily avoidable – plants.

TORTRIX MOTH CATERPILLARS

Rolled-up leaves

On my chrysanthemums, I notice that the edges of a number of leaves have been pulled together by silken threads to form funnels. In some cases, several leaves have been joined together in this way. What's doing it?

It's the industrious caterpillars of tortrix moths, which pull leaves about themselves with silken webs. Thus protected from insect predators, they can set about eating the leaves at leisure – and not only the leaves of chrysanthemums, but of carnations, heleniums, phlox and other herbaceous plants, too. The caterpillars are also common on trees and shrubs – especially species of ivy, laurel, privet and euonymus – and on all kinds of greenhouse and house plants. They live on and in their leafy hiding places for six to eight weeks and then pupate; the adult moths appear about a month later.

There are several species, all broadly similar. Outdoor plants are most likely to be attacked in early summer. Indoors, plants are at risk all year round.

Tortrix caterpillars are a serious pest and must be got rid of. It's not easy. The rolled-up leaves are quite a good defence against spraying as well as predators, and the only sure method is to pick off the leaves – caterpillars and all – by hand. Alternatively, you could try thorough and forceful spraying with HCH, derris or pyrethrum.

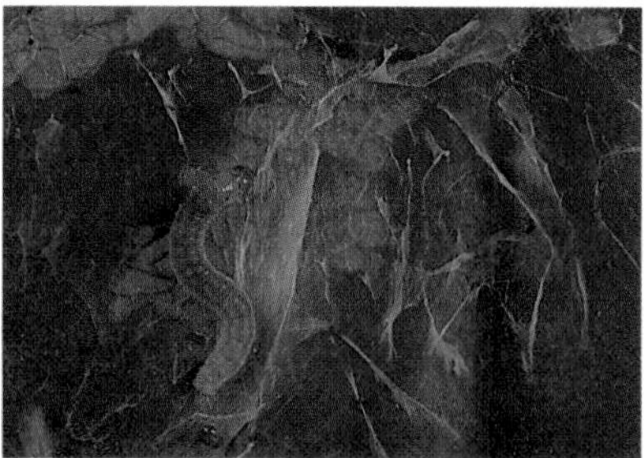

GNAWED AND LODGING *Tortrix caterpillars – which are usually yellow or green, and which grow to about $\frac{3}{4}$in long – chew holes in the leaves they draw about themselves with silk to make their homes.*

TOWN GARDENS

Town vegetables

I should like to grow vegetables, and other plants I can eat, but all I have is a patio-sized patch and most of it is covered with concrete. Any ideas?

Try these:
1 Trail runner beans up a trellis against a wall, both for the beans and the exotic, scarlet flowers.
2 Sow climbing nasturtium and let it wander among your shrubs; chop the leaves and flowers and use them raw to pep up a salad.
3 Train 'Merton Thornless', a luscious, big blackberry, along your rear fence.
4 Plant tomatoes, aubergines, cucumbers, peppers, courgettes and lettuce in growing bags or, for a better display, in 10in tubs.
5 Set half a dozen Swiss chard plants in tubs. They'll keep the family supplied with fresh spinach from June until September.
6 Grow the sugar pea, or mangetout, in a container. The plants look particularly good against an edging of a decorative herb such as golden marjoram. 'Oregon Sugar Pod' is a good late summer cropper.
7 Fill a tub or a tower pot with strawberry plants. Wild Alpine varieties such as 'Red Alpine' give summer colour and autumn fruit. 'Royal Sovereign' is a good mid-season choice.
8 Use another tub or a barrel to grow an early crop of potatoes. After they're harvested, you can use the compost again for a later crop of, say, leeks or onions grown from sets.
9 Finally, pot out some herbs. Rosemary, sage, parsley, thyme, mint and chives are all attractive plants. Add a splash of blue with hyssop.

SMALL IS BEAUTIFUL *Colour overflows a tiny terrace: yellow begonias; red and white busy lizzies; the grey-green foliage of senecio; and, on the walls, wisteria and purple clematis.*

Winter colour

My little town garden looks grey and dull in winter. What can I plant to liven it up?

You will find a wide choice of colourful winter shrubs at most garden centres – and in your sheltered garden, protected from the worst of the weather by surrounding houses and walls, most will flourish.

Try making a feature of the autumn cherry, *Prunus subhirtella* 'Autumnalis', which can grow to 15ft. Masses of pale pink blossoms clothe its fragile bare branches in winter. Or choose *Chimonanthus praecox*, which grows to about 10ft high and wide. Its tawny yellow flowers, with their deep purple base, will fill your garden from December to February with sweet, exotic perfume.

Shrubs you can plant include: *Viburnum* x *bodnantense*, whose bright pink flowers, appearing from November to February, will stand the coldest spells; and *Mahonia lomariifolia*. The prickly leaves of the hardy mahonias give magnificent autumn colour; this one also has bright yellow spires of flowers in February.

Another candidate is *Daphne odora*, a glossy evergreen with trumpet-shaped pink flowers. The variety 'Aureomarginata' has variegated leaves.

Climbers are ideal for brightening up a garden where land is at a premium. Among the best for colour on almost any soil are *Jasminum nudiflorum*, which will cover a north wall with starry yellow flowers from November to February, and *Lonicera fragrantissima*, the winter honeysuckle, which has creamy flowers with a heady scent.

The rich pink *Cyclamen hiemale* will give colourful ground cover around the shrubs in December; *C. coum* will do the same in January. Snowdrops, snowflakes and the Algerian iris (*Iris unguicularis*) will liven up February. And, on a dry or acid soil, don't forget the heathers (for suggested varieties, see *Pick of the heathers*, page 180).

For more ideas on what to grow see *Colour*, page 84, and *Shrubs*, page 310.

Hidden corners

My garden is long, straight and narrow. How can I give it some mystery, with interesting nooks and crannies?

You need walls, hedges, some masking shrubs and a meandering path.

Start at the house with a paved, sitting-out area and, perhaps, a small herb garden (see *Herbs*, page 194). Cut this off from the rest of the garden with a low wall or hedge.

Lay your path to wander in and out of some tall shrubs or evergreens, and hide parts of the garden behind trellises supporting climbers or roses.

Build a water garden with a pond, perhaps partly hidden behind a rockery and some not too tall evergreen shrubs or conifers. For details on how to lay out a pond, see *Ponds and pools*, page 261. For suggestions on conifers for a small garden, see *Dwarf conifers*, page 127.

Your path could eventually lead to a small informal garden with old-fashioned Bourbon roses, or even to another, sunny paved area with a bench and a surrounding of spring bulbs.

Around each bed or twist in your path set some feature plant that cannot be seen from the house. You can thereby create corners that bloom at different times of the year to give continuous interest.

Decorative food

My garden is just 30ft by 15ft and full of flowers. There is one apple tree, but no room for a vegetable patch. What can I plant that will give fresh food without spoiling the overall look?

Choose your favourite vegetables, but plant them in clumps in the flowerbeds instead of in rows, and make a feature of their looks. Globe artichokes, for instance, will reach 4ft at the back of a bed, giving magnificently shaped silver foliage, and those delicious flower buds fruit in their second or third year if properly fed. Sweet corn can be grown as an ornamental grass in a mixed border. In front, you could choose among green curly kale, ruby chard, and the ornamental but still tasty cabbages, which come in shades of green, silver, pink and mauve. Even the foliage of the humble carrot can add a bright and feathery touch to an ornamental bed. Rosemary and chives give blue and purple flowers, and mix well with the soft yellow of variegated mint. These and other herbs make attractive edging plants for a flowerbed.

Try tomatoes in tubs, too. The variety 'Tigerella' has dramatically striped yellow and orange fruits, and they taste good as well. Golden zucchini could be planted beneath them.

You could also trail a vine through a trellis or pergola. The black grape 'Chambourcin' and the green one 'Seyve Villard White' will both do well in tubs. In a sunny, sheltered garden, they will eventually yield up to 8lb of grapes a year and the leaves are a lovely colour in autumn. For details on how to care for vines, see *Grapes*, page 162.

Bright backyard

My backyard is small and square with depressing brick walls. What can I do to brighten it up?

There are two ways. First, you can paint the walls. Second, you can hide the walls with flowering shrubs and climbers.

Paint – especially white paint – will immediately make the area brighter. Put in a small pool with a fountain, too, to add more sparkle. You could even back the pool with a mirror set in an arched trellis, to give extra depth and perspective. Make sure you use a heavy-duty mirror with a silver back protected by several coats of red oxide bitumastic paint. Cover the edges with tape to prevent water getting in.

A spotlight set to bounce light off the water can make the whole arrangement outstandingly attractive in the evening. Set the pond off with a white *Iris laevigata* and a few brightly coloured Koi carp.

Shrubs and climbers can be staggered to give new perspectives to the garden. Make some raised beds from old bricks or treated wooden logs to give height to parts of the garden. Then build your display around a few simple but outstanding plants.

Try, for instance, a spring-flowering *Camellia japonica*, whose shiny green leaves are offset by white, pink or red flowers. Or a *Pieris* 'Forest Flame', with its young red growth and later creamy flowers giving months of interest. Or, perhaps, a hydrangea, whose extravagant flower heads make a show lasting well into autumn.

Line the walls with trellises – again painted white – and train climbers up them (for suggestions, see *Climbers*, page 76). Fill shady corners with the cheerful and resilient busy lizzies, or with *Vinca minor* 'Alba', a periwinkle, which will form an evergreen mat with starry white flowers. Liven sunny spots with pots of geraniums or tuberous begonias.

Garden mural

My daughter is something of an artist and has offered to paint a mural on one of the walls in our backyard. Is this practical, or would the damp ruin it?

With proper preparation, it can be done and it could add a fascinating dimension to your home.

If the wall is brick, it will need to be rendered first with a smooth skin of cement. If it is already cement, then check that it is

ALL ABOUT WINDOW BOXES

STRONG support is the first requirement for a window box. Few house window ledges are wide enough to hold a box. Take a close look at your windows before building one.

● If your windows open outwards, mount the box on brackets below the window and hold it in place with a strap of strong wire firmly attached to the wall. You can then open the windows and plant and water the box from above.

Sash windows, or those which open inwards, make planting and watering much easier – but boxes still need to be firmly fixed against the walls, and this also applies to boxes placed on top of a wall or at the side of a balcony. A winter storm could otherwise topple your box into the street.

● Good window boxes can be made of wood, and the harder the wood the longer the box will survive. Teak, oak, iroko or cedar will all last longer than a softwood such as pine. Whichever wood you use, treat it with preservative to prevent rotting, and treat the outside with clear varnish to show off the grain.

Plastic boxes are cheaper and lighter than wood, but choose heavy-duty ones. Sunlight tends to make plastic brittle and, in time, thin plastic may crack or break.

Glass-fibre boxes are tough and long-lasting. If you find them not so attractive as wood, fill them with plants which trail to hide the box.

● Fit your window box the full length of the ledge and make it as deep as possible, at least 8in. In a shallow box, roots become crowded and the compost dries out quickly.

● You can either fill the box directly with compost or use a removable liner. Alternatively, you can grow all the plants in pots, and stand the pots in the window box. If you choose a liner, make sure it is strong enough to lift out with the contents intact when the plants need to be removed or replaced. This will save you detaching the box from its supports and bringing it in at the end of each season. Just lift out the liner and replace it with new soil and new plants. If you are bringing on your own plants, you can even have them ready in a second liner and simply switch liners.

● Because even large window boxes dry out rapidly, it's vital to keep a regular eye on the watering. In high summer on a south-facing wall, you may need to check each box every day. Aim to keep the soil moist, but don't let it become waterlogged.

● Plan the planting of each box – scale is as important in a window box as in a garden. Consider including evergreens for winter interest and as a background for colourful summer annuals. Consider, too, running climbers up the wall from the sides of the box.

HOW TO PLANT UP A HANGING BASKET

HANGING baskets will cheer up a dark corner or brighten a porch or passageway, and they are simple to make.

Line a wire basket with sphagnum moss and fill it with peat-based compost. Then fill it with your favourite summer annuals and bedding plants – arranged, ideally, so that they form a mound of colour, with the tallest plants in the centre and short or trailing species around the edge. You can even push plants in through the moss liner into the sides of the basket to form almost a complete globe of colour.

Petunias, fibrous-rooted begonias, busy lizzies and marigolds do particularly well in hanging baskets. So do nasturtiums, dropping their trumpet flowers into mid-air, trailing lobelia and wandering pelargoniums.

Regular watering is vital. Suspended in air and warmed on all sides by the sun, baskets can dry out in a matter of hours. Put a few lumps of charcoal in the moss base to help to hold in moisture – and top up each basket with water at least once a day. Fix each basket to a wall with a firmly sited hook and a strong chain. And adjust the height so that you can reach it easily to give it its daily soaking.

even and that there are no cracks which need filling in.

When the cement or filler is completely dry, coat it with a masonry stabiliser or neutraliser to prevent alkali in the wall from damaging the painting. Your daughter, being an artist, will know that the rapid-drying acrylic paints, which give a permanent waterproof finish, are the ones to use for an outdoor mural like this.

She will also, of course, have her own ideas about what she wants to paint, but a landscape or architectural view would give the garden most perspective, and could make it seem much larger than it really is.

An acrylic varnish will seal the work when it is finished. Plant beds or containers in front of the mural to add to the three-dimensional *trompe l'oeil* effect.

Softening angles

My garden is small and triangular, ending in a sharp point. What can I do to bring harmony and balance to this shape?

Turn it into an asset. Make the head of the triangle a focal point that may even make the garden seem larger.

Start by separating the end of the triangle from the house with an arched trellis or a pergola. A pergola can be bought in kit form. Once in place, cover it with scented climbers, a fragrant honeysuckle or a free-flowering old rose. Use the trellis or pergola to frame a feature at the point of the triangle. Depending on the size of your garden, this feature could be a garden swing, a seat, a rockery, a fountain, a statue, or a single tree.

This tree could be an *Acer pseudoplatanus* 'Brilliantissimum', which can grow in time to a height of 35ft. Its rich coral-pink spring leaves fade to pale green in summer, then turn brilliant red in autumn.

Or consider planting *Stuartia malacodendron*, which can grow to 15-20ft and is covered in August with white, cup-shaped flowers with purple anthers. It, too, has brilliant red autumn foliage, and the piebald bark gives it interest even in winter.

Plant the rest of the garden in broad borders and let the flowers overflow their beds, giving a meandering effect that will soften the garden's shape.

Soothing colours

I have read of a white or grey garden. Would it be practical in a small town backyard?

Yes, but it does need to be backed by a cool green, or the effect may become funereal.

Frame the beds with clipped box hedges or pot out some evergreens to give background and height to your garden.

Choose white-flowering evergreens, such as *Camellia* 'Narumi-gata', or the glossy-leaved *Fatsia japonica*, which blooms in October.

Beds can be filled with a mixture, including: *Anaphalis cinnamonea*, which has papery-white flowers; *Artemisia absinthium* 'Lambrook Silver', a bushy, silky form of wormwood; and *Stachys lanata*, the lamb's tongue, with its fleecy leaves and woolly white spires.

Herbs can add a silvery touch. Plant the grey-leaved curry plant (*Helichrysum angustifolium*), sage (*Salvia officinalis*), and the silvery-leaved *Thymus drucei*, the original wild thyme. If the garden is big enough, find room for a white lilac, white-flowering buddleia, or the ground-spreading rose 'Partridge', which is only a few inches high and has a spread of as much as 10ft. For more ideas on plants to fit a particular colour scheme, see *Colour*, page 84.

Paint the wall

My garden is a 5ft by 20ft space alongside the kitchen. What can I do to brighten this gloomy little area?

Paint the walls white or cream, and line them with trellis and hanging baskets filled with herbs and flowers.

Red peppers, with their exotic fruit, can ramble along the trellis. Let an ivy such as *Hedera helix* 'Goldheart', with its splash of gold on each leaf, clamber on its own on the walls. It won't mind sharing a pot with a clematis such as 'Marie Boisselot'. Fill some pots with lavender, petunias and begonias. Stick to a fairly simple colour scheme for your plants – yellow and cream, say, or green and cream, or lavender and white.

You can even make a miniature water garden by filling an old tank or a big ceramic bowl with water and miniature lilies. Pump water from the tank to a bronze mask or lion's head on the wall, and let the water spout from the mask back into the tank. Add a few fish for interest.

A scent of flowers

I have always wanted a scented garden, but I have only a little space. Would this be possible?

Yes, a scented garden will adapt well to a small area. Try any of the plants in the chart on this page, all of which are fragrant and will thrive in the shelter of an urban garden without swamping it.

FLOWERS FOR A SCENTED GARDEN

Name	Flowers and peak fragrance
Butterfly bush (*Buddleia davidii*)	Lilac-purple (July–Oct)
Common primrose (*Primula vulgaris*)	Yellow, red or blue (Mar–Apr)
Daphne mezereum	Pink-purple (Feb–Apr)
Hyacinth (*Hyacinthus orientalis*)	Pink, blue or white (Apr–May)
Lily of the valley (*Convallaria majalis*)	White bells (Apr–May)
Madonna lily (*Lilium candidum*)	Pink-white, gold centre (June–July)
Mock orange (*Philadelphus* 'Beauclerk')	White (June–July)
Snowdrop (*Galanthus nivalis*)	White-green (Jan–Feb)
Sweet pea (*Lathyrus odoratus*)	Pink, purple and white (June–Sept)
Sweet william (*Dianthus barbatus*)	Pink, red and white (June–July)
Viburnum carlesii	Waxy white (Apr–May)
Wallflower (*Cheiranthus cheiri*)	Yellow, orange, red or purple (Apr–June)
White jasmine (*Jasminum officinale*)	Pure white (June–Sept)
Winter sweet (*Chimonanthus praecox*)	Lemon-yellow, carmine centre (Dec–Feb)

Balcony blooms

There is no garden with the flat I live in, but it does have a balcony. What can I plant there and what are the pitfalls?

You can make a good show with pots, but first you must check the structure of your balcony. Make sure that the floor is strong enough to support the weight of tubs full of earth. Look for the points where the balcony is reinforced, probably at the sides, and place your largest pots there close to the wall – not out near the edge.

Watering is another problem. Containers dry out quickly in the warmth of a sheltered balcony. Small pots will need watering daily. You can set up, quite inexpensively, a timed watering system linked to your plumbing, so that you won't have to worry if you are away for any length of time. But make sure that water does not drip down onto your neighbours beneath.

Check, too, that high winds can't blow small pots over the edge, with potentially lethal consequences for passers-by. If you're in any doubt, use pots that can't slip between the railings, or move them well away from the edge, or group them in larger, more stable containers such as a window box lined with about 2in of sand.

As for what to plant, that depends largely on your taste. Petunias, however, are tough enough to survive neglect and still give a lively show. Ivy-leaved geraniums, too, will throw cascades of pink, red or white flowers even in drought conditions until the first frosts of autumn. Train a flowering rose such as 'Pink Perpétue' up a trellis and let a clematis, say 'Nelly Moser', twine among it. A pot of runner beans will give you bright scarlet flowers and fresh vegetables.

Basil and variegated thyme make a fine show in pots. Plant, too, the delicious little cherry tomato 'Gardener's Delight' in a tub or growing bag, with an edging of alyssum. And don't forget hanging baskets. Support them on sturdy brackets attached to the walls – don't hang them over the edge of the balcony – and let busy lizzies and trailing lobelia trail out of them.

Labour-saving tips

I work long hours and have little time to spend on my small town garden. How can I design it for maximum leisure and minimum attention?

Try one or more of these ideas. The more you use, the less time you will need to devote to gardening.

1 Forget grass. Pave the garden, using an attractive combination of surfaces such as brick, cobbles and gravel. Or consider York stone, paving slabs or even large terracotta tiles.

2 Forget vegetables and fussy annuals. Go for medium-sized shrubs that need little pruning or maintenance. Many will grow happily unattended in large spaces left between the paving material. Try sweet-smelling Mexican orange blossom (*Choisya ternata*), which doesn't mind some shade; *Arundinaria palmata*, the hardy bamboo; and *Viburnum davidii*, an evergreen with white, scented blooms and turquoise autumn berries.

3 Use self-watering pots. A wick fed into the compost from a reservoir keeps the soil moist while you relax. Camellias, azaleas and tree peonies will flourish with no attention in these conditions.

4 Build a small, raised pond. Once it is filled and planted, all you need to do is sit by it (see *Ponds and pools*, page 261).

5 Set a statue, a bench or an urn in a framework of trellis to give a feature that need only be looked at.

Pots and crocks

Why do gardening books always advise me to put crocks in the bottom of my pots? Is it really necessary?

Tradition is largely the answer to your first question. The belief is that a layer of broken crocks in the bottom of the pot aids drainage, and to some extent mirrors the structure of the earth, with topsoil lying above rocky inert subsoil.

In fact, however, if you put two identical plants in identical pots, with crocks in the bottom of one and no crocks in the other, both plants will normally grow just as well as each other. So crocks aren't necessary – with one small proviso.

Clay pots usually have a single hole in the bottom; the larger the pot, the larger the hole. And that means that, when you water, you run the risk of washing some of the compost out of the pot. So there is some point in putting one or two crocks in the bottom of a clay pot, just to keep the compost in.

Plastic pots, on the other hand, usually have several small holes in the bottom. So there is little risk of losing the compost, and little need for crocks.

TREES

A fine dividing line

My local garden centre describes some of its stock as large shrubs, and others as small trees. What's the difference?

It's often difficult to pinpoint the exact difference. The Oxford English Dictionary defines a tree as a 'perennial plant with a single, woody, self-supporting stem or trunk, usually unbranched for some distance above the ground', and a shrub as a 'woody plant smaller than a tree and usually divided into separate stems from near the ground'.

A tree stem may occasionally divide lower down, but still above ground level, while most shrubs divide from below or just above ground level.

Size is another tricky point. Experts have laid down that a large shrub can be 15ft or more and a small tree 15-30ft in height.

You can, of course, settle this tricky question for yourself by the way you prune your large shrub or small tree. Take the amelanchier, for example; if trained up on a single stem it becomes a small tree, or it looks equally well as a multi-stemmed large shrub.

In short, many plants can be grown either as small trees or as large shrubs – depending simply on how hard you prune them.

A question of colour

Last winter I planted an ornamental cherry tree which, according to the label, had pink flowers. This spring it produced pink flowers – and white ones as well. Is this unusual?

Unfortunately it isn't. Most ornamental cherries are propagated by budding onto *Prunus avium*, the wild cherry, or onto the cherry rootstock called 'Colt', both of which have white flowers.

So your pink blossoms come from the variety – the one you wanted – and the white ones from the original rootstock.

Your pink-and-white mixture is most likely to occur when the ornamental variety is top-worked – that is to say, when budding has been carried out about 5ft from the ground onto the stem of the rootstock. A shoot from the rootstock may then have been mistakenly left to grow away.

If you notice this in time, say within a year or two of purchase, the offending branch can be cut out with little damage to the tree. But be warned – the white-flowered rootstock is generally more vigorous than the ornamental variety and will eventually take over if nothing is done to control it.

Cutting it out after several years will harm the appearance of the tree. So it's probably wiser to leave the pink and white flowers to grow together – and enjoy them both.

Magic on the bough

The mystical properties of mistletoe have always fascinated me, and I've decided to grow some on my apple trees. How do I set about this, and will it harm the trees?

Mistletoe (*Viscum album*), though a parasite, does not harm its hosts. It grows wild in Britain as far north as Yorkshire, mainly on apple trees, limes and poplars. Britain imports several tons from Normandy every Christmas to satisfy the demand for festive decorations. The Druids called it the 'Golden Bough' and used it in their rites.

They believed that the berries contained the seminal fluid of the sacred oak, and that mistletoe held the life of the host tree when the tree seemed to die in winter.

It was long believed that a sprig of mistletoe fastened over the door would protect the house from storms, which accounts for the country name of thunder plant. Mistletoe has also long been associated with Christmas when a kiss beneath a bunch will bring happiness and good luck in the coming year.

Mistletoe is quite easy to grow, provided you start it on the right kind of host tree – preferably apple or lime. It is propagated by seed, and is done by bursting the white translucent berries into a cut on a fairly young branch during January or February.

This will release a sticky substance, which hardens and attaches the single seed securely. In nature, the seeds are usually transported by birds, most of all by mistle thrushes. Mistletoe plants are either male or female, so a lone plant won't bear fruit. Not all seeds are viable, and you may have to try several times before one takes.

In spring, the seed germinates and puts out suckers that run deep into the bark and draw nourishment from the tree. The mistletoe also feeds itself from its green leaves, through photosynthesis.

A clump of mistletoe will take a few years to establish itself. The plants do not normally fruit until they are several years old.

Mistletoe does not need pruning, and is generally free from pests and diseases.

A tree for all seasons

I've got room for a small tree in my garden, but I want something that will be attractive all year round. Any suggestions?

Choose a tree that has more to offer than just its flowers. One that has pretty foliage, bright autumn colour, and attractive bark and fruit, or at least a couple of these attributes, will add up to a plant for practically all seasons.

The chart on this page lists an amelanchier, two crab apples, four cherries, a Kashmir rowan and a stuartia, any of which will give lasting pleasure in a small garden.

The stuartia, which has a grey flaking white bark, prefers an acid soil. All the rest will thrive in any reasonable soil.

The last bough

This spring, it became apparent that my venerable 20ft apple tree was dead at last. How can I take it down with safety and tidiness?

The safest and tidiest thing you can do is to inform your local council that you intend to take the tree down. In many areas you are not allowed to take out trees without the proper authority, and the council may wish to satisfy itself as to the tree's state before allowing you to take a saw to it. In most boroughs, it is the Planning Department which takes the greatest interest while others allocate such matters to the Parks Department or even to a Tree Preservation Officer.

The legal aspect settled, the tidiest way of bringing a tree down is to call in a tree surgeon, but if you are determined to go it alone you will need a ladder, gloves, a hand axe or lopper, a sharp saw and a piece of strong rope at least twice as long as the tree is tall. A 20ft apple tree is no forest giant, but cutting it up can be hard work with dull tools. You could of course hire a chain saw, which would do the job in no time, but these machines can be horrifyingly dangerous in unskilled hands.

Begin with the lowest branch and lop the branches off in manageable lengths. Chop the twigs off with a saw or axe and pile them for burning. A bonfire is permissible even in a smokeless zone, provided it is not a nuisance to other people, but don't let it smoulder too long, or light it when the neighbours are hanging the washing out.

You can deal with the trunk in two ways. Cut it down in sections to a 3ft stump which can be winched out by a tree surgeon, or cut it down almost to ground level in one go, leave the stump for a year to dry out, then break it up with an axe or wedges.

A few tips about cutting techniques. Always undercut each branch first. Saw some way into the underside, close to the main stem, then start a new cut into the topside a little farther out. As you proceed with this cut, the one underneath will close up, opening the topside cut and making it easier for your saw to go through. Without the undercut, the branch might break and swing to one side, knocking you off the ladder, or rip a strip from the trunk below, leaving an ugly scar. With the undercut, the branch will break cleanly and drop straight to the ground. If the bough is heavy, lash it to a stout branch higher up before starting to cut. When the bough is cut through, lower it gently to the ground.

Use a similar technique to deal with the trunk. Tie one end of your long rope to the trunk near the top. Chop or saw a 45 degree wedge out of one side of the trunk, the side you wish the tree to fall. The wedge should extend about one-third of the way through the trunk. Now make a straight cut through from the other side, a little above the wedge. When the trunk begins to waver, get right out of the way in case the base kicks backwards as it topples. Then get family or friends to haul on the rope, pulling the trunk towards the wedge cut. Make sure that your helpers are well beyond the area where the tree will fall.

If you've followed these tips, the tree should drop exactly where you want it.

The beauty of bark

Every winter I admire the bare, pale silver trunks of some birches near my home. Are there any other trees with attractive bark which I can grow in my small garden?

There are a large number of trees that are grown principally, if not entirely, for the beauty of their bark. This is particularly the case with certain deciduous species which,

TREES FOR ALL SEASONS

	Flowers		Fruit			Size after	
Name	Colour	Month	Colour	Month	Autumn colour	20 years	Shape
Amelanchier lamarckii	White	May			Orange-red	20ft	Broad
Malus 'Golden Hornet'	White	May	Yellow	Oct-Dec	Russet-brown	20ft	Pyramidal
Malus 'John Downie'	White	May	Red	Sept-Dec	Russet-brown	20ft	Conical
Prunus x *hillieri* 'Spire'	Pink	Apr-May			Orange-red	25ft	Conical
Prunus 'Kursar'	Deep pink	Mar-Apr			Golden-yellow	20ft	Broad
Prunus 'Okame'	Deep pink	Mar			Golden-yellow	15ft	Broad
Prunus sargentii 'Rancho'	Pink	Apr			Russet-red	20ft	Conical
Sorbus cashmiriana	Pink flush	May	White	Oct-Jan	Russet-red	20ft	Pyramidal
Stuartia pseudocamellia	White	July			Orange-red	20ft	Conical

AUTUMN BRILLIANCE *Japanese maples, like this one, have outstanding autumn colours.*

TREES FOR AUTUMN COLOUR

Exactly when deciduous trees put on their full autumn colour depends very much on local conditions and on day-by-day changes in temperature and sunlight. In the following list, the autumn leaf colour is given and the expected height of the tree after 20 years. The height figure is based on average growing conditions in Britain. Trees marked (A) prefer acid soil.

Name	Leaf colour	Height after 20 years
Acer capillipes	Orange/red	20ft
Acer griseum	Orange/russet	18ft
Acer japonicum 'Vitifolium'	Scarlet	15ft
Acer pensylvanicum (A)	Butter yellow	30ft
Amelanchier lamarckii	Scarlet	20ft
Betula albo-sinensis var *septentrionalis*	Yellow	25ft
Cercidiphyllum japonicum (A)	Yellow-red	20ft
Fagus sylvatica 'Dawyck Gold'	Rich copper-brown	25ft
Malus tschonoskii	Crimson/purple	22ft
Nyssa sinensis (A)	Crimson	15ft
Nyssa sylvatica (A)	Orange-crimson	18ft
Oxydendrum arboreum (A)	Purple	15ft
Parrotia persica	Crimson/gold	15ft
Picrasma quassioides (A)	Yellow/orange	16ft
Prunus 'Okame'	Yellow/orange	14ft
Prunus sargentii	Orange/crimson	18ft
Sorbus commixta	Copper-red	20ft
Sorbus 'Embley'	Orange/crimson	22ft
Stuartia pseudocamellia (A)	Orange/red	16ft
Taxodium ascendens 'Nutans'	Copper-brown	14ft

having shed their leaves, bring brilliance and variety to the garden in winter.

The colours and textures range from white to pink and amber, and from silky smooth to rugged and flaking.

Some of the most attractive are grouped below according to colour. Unless otherwise indicated, all are deciduous and do well in ordinary soil. Some show their bark colours to the best advantage if pollarded. To find out how to do this, see *An old art with new uses*, page 351.

- **White**: *Betula papyrifera*, *B. utilis* 'Sauwala White', *B. u.* 'Grayswood Ghost'.
- **Grey-white**: *Betula pendula*, *Stuartia pseudocamellia* (peeling bark, prefers acid soil).
- **Pink-white**: *Betula ermanii*, *B. jacquemontii*, B. 'Jermyns'.
- **Snake bark, white-green**: *Acer capillipes*, *A. davidii* 'George Forrest', *A. hersii*, *A. pensylvanicum* (prefers acid soil).
- **Snake bark, shrimp pink**: *Acer pensylvanicum* 'Erythrocladum' (prefers acid soil).
- **Coral pink**: *Acer palmatum* 'Senkaki'.
- **Mahogany**: *Acer griseum* (peeling bark), *Prunus serrula*.
- **Cinnamon-brown**: *Acer triflorum* (peeling bark), *Arbutus menziesii* (evergreen, prefers acid soil).
- **Cinnamon-brown, pink**: *Betula nigra*.
- **Orange-brown, pink**: *Betula albo-sinensis septentrionalis*.
- **Amber-brown**: *Prunus maackii*.
- **Purple, black**: *Salix acutifolia* 'Blue Streak' (pollard for best effect).
- **Orange, scarlet**: *Salix alba* 'Chermesina' (pollard for best effect).
- **Golden-yellow**: *Salix alba* 'Vitellina' (pollard for best effect).
- **Violet**: *Salix daphnoides* (pollard for best effect; see the chart on page 351).
- **Orange**: *Sorbus aucuparia* 'Beissneri'.

A wood of your own

I have a fancy to establish my own small bit of woodland. I want the trees to complement one another, yet the effect should be entirely natural and native to the countryside. Which trees should I plant?

Much of the charm of our landscape depends on the patterns made by trees, whether in leaf or with bare twigs etched like black lace against the winter sky.

A silver birch (*Betula pendula*) covered in hoar frost is one of the great beauties of winter, the pale bark being particularly attractive between October and March. The tree will reach a height of about 20ft in ten years and 35ft in 20 years. Silver birches may live for 80 years and when fully grown may stand 60-80ft tall.

You should also plant a few trees that bear berries, so as to attract birds to your woodland (for ideas, see the chart opposite).

Sorbus aucuparia, the rowan or mountain ash, has large clusters of creamy-white flowers in late spring and leaves that turn yellow and then red in the autumn. The bright red berries attract a host of birds, especially thrushes and blackbirds.

Sorbus aria, the whitebeam, has less spectacular berries but most attractive oval leaves which are white on the underside and shiny greyish-green on top.

The glossy leaves of the evergreen holly (*Ilex aquifolium*) would add a cheerful note to your scheme; another advantage is the plant's adaptability. For the best effect, it is necessary to buy two holly trees, for a female will produce its red berries only if a male tree is nearby. The berry display is at its best between October and February.

A hazel, *Corylus avellana*, will bring its crop of nuts to your garden in autumn and a cascade of yellow catkins in February and March. A mature hazel will reach up to 20ft with a spread of 15ft or more.

It can be grown as a single stem tree, but is most impressive as a multi-stemmed shrub. This is achieved by coppicing – the regular cutting back of shoots to the base.

Trouble with lichen

My trees are covered with moss and lichen. Are they harmful, and if so, how do I get rid of them?

It's a safe bet that you live fairly deep in the country, somewhere on the damp, western edge of Britain. Mosses grow in wet conditions and, like lichens, can thrive only in clean air.

Mosses are primitive plants which absorb water through their entire surface and grow in the winter when the weather is cool and wet. Spore capsules are produced in the spring, and the plant gradually withers as summer advances.

Lichens are 'epiphytes' – meaning that they draw their nutrients from the surrounding air rather than from the soil.

Lichens and mosses are not harmful to trees and in most instances are not worth removing; in fact, many of them are extremely attractive. The Japanese have created beautiful gardens whose principal theme is mosses.

So: do you really want to get rid of these interesting plants? You might wish to do so, perhaps, if your trees have colourful bark now hidden by lichen. Provided the trees are deciduous, you can easily remove the growth with a tar-oil wash in winter, when the trees have lost their leaves. This treatment is generally recommended as a means of getting rid of the overwintering eggs of insect pests, but it is just as effective against mosses and lichens.

If you are not keen on using chemicals – tar oil will scorch vegetation as effectively as a fire – then a little hard work with a bucket of water and a scrubbing brush will solve your lichen problem.

Keeping aphids at bay

The aphids in my lime trees have covered the car and the back windows of the house with a horrible, sticky layer of honeydew. Is there any way I can get rid of the pests once and for all?

There is no way to get rid of them once and for all, but it's no bad thing to cut down the aphid population if you can. In Britain, there are more than 500 species of aphid, many of which are specific to one plant species or genus, while others attack closely related groups of plants.

They feed on young plant growth and produce an abundance of sticky honeydew which encourages sooty mould to form. But perhaps their worst aspect is that they transfer viruses from one plant to another; for this reason alone, you should certainly take all the countermeasures you can. Tar-oil washes will kill overwintering aphid eggs, but should be used only on deciduous trees when they are completely dormant during December and January.

Tar oil is an effective if messy method, but it should be undertaken only if adequate precautions are taken. Do not spray on windy days, and cover nearby evergreen plants and grass; tar oil will burn any foliage it touches. It has a similar effect on human skin, so wear protective clothing.

A number of other chemicals can be used in the growing season, from May to October. Pirimicarb is excellent, in that it slays only aphids and does not harm beneficial insects. Then there are the systemic insecticides, mostly based on dimethoate. When using these, read the manufacturer's instructions carefully and follow them to the letter.

Mainly for the birds

I'm a keen birdwatcher and would like to plant a tree that would bring birds to my garden during autumn and winter. Any ideas?

Planting a berrying tree – a rowan, say – will beautify your garden, provide birds with roosting cover and food, and give you the pleasure of watching them as well.

Berries are taken by only a few species, most commonly by thrushes and blackbirds; however, a severe winter will bring more unusual visitors such as the strikingly crested waxwings that have been driven south from their breeding grounds in northern Europe.

Another ploy is to plant seed-bearing flowers such as sunflowers and michaelmas daisies and leave their dead stems standing for a while after the growing season is over. The packed seedheads will prove a tasty attraction.

A few creature comforts such as a bird table or bath might also be provided, along with plenty of titbits if the winter is severe. As for which berry trees to grow, strong avian favourites include cotoneaster, holly, rowan, hawthorn and cherry. A selection from the list at the foot of this page would give you a contrast in berry sizes and colours. The hollies (species of ilex) are evergreen, the rest deciduous.

Waiting for magnolia

Ten years ago, my mother planted a magnolia against a south-facing wall of the house. It is now 15ft high and 8ft across but, though it seems healthy enough, it has never flowered. Is it ever likely to?

This species is most probably *Magnolia grandiflora*, an evergreen with large leathery leaves introduced from the southern states of America in the early 18th century.

Normally, it is propagated by cuttings or grafting, in which case flowering can be expected within a few years of planting. Trees raised from seed tend to take a good deal longer.

If your mother's tree was raised from seed, another year or two's wait may well reward your patience with fragrant, creamy-white flowers as much as a foot across. These appear in summer and last well into autumn.

My willow won't weep

My ten-year-old weeping willow drooped most elegantly until a year or so ago when the branches suddenly began to grow upwards. How can I make it weep again?

This is just part of the willow's growth pattern, a pattern that may easily continue until it reaches 70ft or more. The tree generally grows on a single stem of up to 8ft, which then divides into a number of upright branches. The branches form the basic support for a random framework of sideshoots which tumble over to droop to the ground. It is

TREES WITH ATTRACTIVE BERRIES

Name	Colour
Crataegus x *grignonensis*	Red
Crataegus x *lavallei*	Orange/red
Ilex x *altaclerensis* 'Camelliifolia'	Red
Ilex aquifolium 'Amber'	Amber/yellow
Ilex aquifolium 'Bacciflava'	Yellow
Malus 'Golden Hornet'	Yellow
Malus 'John Downie'	Yellow/red
Malus 'Red Sentinel'	Red
Sorbus aucuparia 'Xanthocarpa'	Amber/yellow
Sorbus cashmiriana	White
Sorbus sargentiana	Scarlet

this combination of ascending branches and trailing shoots that characterises the willow.

So, if you have sufficient space, leave the tree to continue its upward spurt; it will settle down to produce weeping shoots again before long. If, however, you feel that the tree is getting too tall, you could trim back the upward-growing branches. This will encourage the willow to increase its spread and resume its weeping habit.

A sweetly scented garden

My sight isn't what it was, and I wonder if you could recommend a few trees that could be grown chiefly for their fragrance?

It's a matter of personal preference really, for each of us has a different sense of smell. But under any circumstances, fragrance is a major element to consider when planning a garden.

Careful choice of plants will ensure that the garden is full of scent for almost the entire year, though even sweetly scented plants may vary considerably in their output according to weather conditions and even the time of the day or night. Some plants are best in the early morning, while others are fragrant after a shower. In some cases, the scent is sharpened after a cold spell in autumn, while other plants are more fragrant after dark.

On the whole, shrubs are more notable for their scent than trees. But there are some trees that are famed for fragrance of flowers, foliage or both. The chart at the top of this page lists some of the best.

TREES FOR FRAGRANCE

FLOWER SCENT Name	Peak time	Flower colour
Ligustrum lucidum	Aug-Sept	White
Magnolia kobus	Apr-May	White
Magnolia salicifolia	Apr-May	White
Malus coronaria 'Charlottae'	May-June	Pink
Malus hupehensis	May	White
Prunus 'Amanogawa'	Apr-May	Pink
Prunus mume 'Beni-shidon'	Mar-Apr	Pink
FOLIAGE SCENT **Name**	**Peak time**	**Leaf colour**
Laurus nobilis	All year round	Green
Laurus nobilis 'Aurea'	All year round	Golden-yellow and green
Populus x *candicans* 'Aurora' (needs pollarding for best results)	May-June	Green-cream (flushed with pink)
Thuja occidentalis 'Fastigiata'	All year round	Green

Spare that cherry tree

The people who are buying my house have agreed that I can take my 10ft flowering cherry with me. The only problem is, how to move it without damage?

With care, there's no reason why the tree – and you – should not survive the move. At some stages you will certainly need an extra pair of hands: those of your accommodating buyer, perhaps. The roots of a 10ft cherry could safely be cut back to 1½-2ft long, which means a rootball about 4ft across. So start the operation by marking out a 4ft circle around the tree.

Do this by tying a 2ft length of string to the base of the trunk. Tie a sharp peg to the end of the string and use it to scratch a circle around the tree. If it's in the lawn, use an edging tool to cut the turf within the circle into sections: remove the sections and put them to one side for later replacement.

Dig a trench 15in deep outside the circle and gradually undercut so that a ball of soil 12in deep is left surrounding the roots. Trim any damaged or dead roots with secateurs.

Slide a sack or a polythene sheet under the rootball, bring up the ends and tie them around the trunk. This will help to keep the rootball in one piece and prevent the roots from drying out.

In your new garden, clear the site selected for the cherry and mark on it a circle 18in larger than the rootball – that is, about 5ft 6in across. This time, stick a peg in the ground where the trunk of the cherry will be, and use a 2ft 9in length of string to measure out the circle.

Dig a pit 15-18in deep. Place the topsoil to one side, breaking it up as you go, and add to the mound peat, leaf mould or well-rotted compost. Fork over the subsoil, and add well-rotted manure or more compost.

Loosen the sides of the pit by jabbing them with a fork, particularly if the subsoil is clay; this will help the roots to grow out into the surrounding soil.

Remove the sack or plastic and plant the cherry at the same depth as before. Check this by getting someone to steady the tree in the pit while you lay a cane across the hole: the cane should be level with the old soil mark above the roots; add or remove soil accordingly. Many people plant their deciduous trees too deeply and then wonder why they are not growing strongly.

As you refill the pit with soil, tread each layer well in. When the roots have been covered, scatter two handfuls of sterilised bone meal over them and add a bucket of peat for good measure.

Fill in the rest of the hole, treading as you go, until the old soil mark on the trunk is just visible. Level the ground with a fork and mulch with 2in of forest bark or peat to keep the newly planted tree moist and prevent weed growth. Water roots and foliage well during the first season. Light watering will cause surface roots to grow upwards in search of moisture. A 10ft tree will require double staking until it is firmly established in its new home: hammer the stakes in deeply on opposite sides of the rootball, and tie them to the trunk with rubber slings pulling in opposite directions.

Before the tree starts to grow again in the following spring, check the soil. Frost may have caused lifting, in which case you will need to firm down the soil again by treading it all over.

Acacias for everyone

A friend has a most attractive acacia tree – its creamy flowers look spectacular when they burst into colour each June. I would like to grow one, but my soil is much drier and stonier than hers. Is it possible?

Yes, you can grow one – but hers is not a true acacia. Your friend has a false acacia – *Robinia pseudoacacia*, or locust tree. This is the tree that was planted along so many suburban Acacia Avenues in the 1930s, mostly because it would grow almost anywhere. It thrives in poor soil and even poorer atmospheric conditions.

True acacias, which include gum trees, African thorns and Australian wattles, do not grow in Britain. False acacias came from North America in the 17th century, and in the 19th their timber was used for tool handles, in preference to ash.

The tree's handsome appearance has ensured its continuing popularity, and you can find them at most garden centres. Plant it at any time between October and March, preferably in well-drained soil and in a reasonably sunny, sheltered spot. It needs little moisture and does not have to be pruned. But bear in mind that it may grow to 30ft in 8-10 years and spread to 15ft.

A touch of the country

I live in a city, and in a terrace house with a small garden. All the same, I should like to plant a tree: one that is tall enough to be a feature yet not so wide that it will shut out the light. Any suggestions?

Your specifications are fairly exacting. Most trees, even small ones, develop a spreading crown which will shut out light during at least part of the year. This makes it difficult to grow other plants underneath them, or even nearby.

The shading effect will be welcome on a hot summer's day when you want to sit outside, and then there's the privacy that a luxuriant tree gives.

To enhance the effect, you might train ivy up the garden walls and plant one or two well-placed shrubs. The combination will give your garden character and make it seem bigger than it really is.

So what you need is a tree that is tallish and slim, is tolerant of city atmosphere, has attractive foliage or flowers, and will not put out spreading root systems which could undermine the house or penetrate the drains.

Any of these trees – *Juniperus virginiana* 'Skyrocket', *Malus* 'Van Eseltine', *Prunus kurilensis* 'Ruby' or *Pyrus communis* 'Beech Hill' – would fit the bill.

Red spots on limes

Many of the leaves of the lime trees outside my house are disfigured by small red spots. Are the trees in danger?

These are the tiny, conical galls of the nail gall mite (*Eriophyes tiliae*) which cause little or no damage to healthy trees, even when the mites settle on them in vast numbers. There are many forms of eriophyid mites, most of which are less than 1/100in long. They live in colonies, and a single leaf may support thousands of individuals. The creatures feed on the plant tissue, and the action stimulates the production of the galls.

The appearance of the red spots in May and June worries many gardeners, but it is not necessary to do much about it. The galls will protect the mites from the effect of chemical sprays, though a dose of benomyl in the spring when they are moving to new feeding sites will bring their numbers down.

Some people with an eye for colour even like the contrast of the bright red spots against the fresh green of the young leaves.

An old art with new uses

I was reading the other day how country craftsmen used to 'pollard' and 'coppice' trees to harvest wood for charcoal, sheep folds, furniture and many other purposes. Does anyone still do this?

Coppicing and pollarding are ancient methods of obtaining a continuous supply of timber from the same trees.

In coppicing, trees are cut down to near ground level, leaving a stump called the coppice stool. The straight shoots which spring up from the stool are harvested every few years, according to the timber size that is required and the use that is going to be made of it.

Traditionally, coppiced wood was used for building and fencing, for hurdles, broom-making, charcoal and for bark used in tanning. Some 90,000 acres in Britain are still devoted to coppicing; for pulpwood, wood-turning, fencing and firewood. The principal trees harvested in this way are alder, poplar, eucalyptus, southern beech, ash, lime, oak and sweet chestnut: many thousands of sweet chestnut saplings are required each year for fencing. Lesser amounts of hazel are used for hurdle making, garden fencing and thatching spars, while osiers are cut for basket weaving.

Pollarding differs only in that the stump or stool is left 6ft or more high so that the young shoots will be out of reach of browsing animals. It is quite often used as a technique for ornamental effect, especially on trees whose young growth is attractive either in its stems or leaves.

This effect probably requires a century or two to achieve, but even in a smaller garden and with more limited time, pollarded and coppiced trees can be very attractive.

The necessary cutting with secateurs or loppers is best done in February, March or early April, depending on the state of the season and the species. Willow stems can be cut back completely to the stool every year to give a constant supply of colourful young shoots. Poplars similarly treated will provide a display of bright new foliage.

The trees listed in the chart on this page take readily to coppicing or pollarding. The bright stems of two or three planted together would make a wonderful splash of colour in the spring or winter garden.

Basic buying

Please settle the old argument as to whether, when buying a deciduous tree, it is better to buy one that is container-grown, or one with bare roots?

The answer is not straightforward, since your choice depends on a number of factors.

Pot-grown plants (including those sold in polythene bags) are actively growing when bought and can be planted at any time as long as the ground is not frozen, flooded, or baked hard and dry. A container-grown tree is also easy to deal with, and it need not be

TREES FOR POLLARDING AND COPPICING

Name	Main interest	Colour of main interest	Time of year for main interest	Pruning instructions (prune all species Feb-Apr)
Corylus avellana 'Aurea'	Leaf	Yellow	Apr-June	Six-year-old stems to 9in
Corylus avellana 'Contorta'	Twisted stems and catkins	Yellow	Nov-June	Six-year-old stems to 9in
Corylus maxima 'Purpurea'	Leaf	Purple	Apr-Oct	Four-year-old stems to 9in
Eucalyptus gunnii	Leaf	Silvery-blue	All year round	Two-year-old shoots to 18in
Populus x *candicans* 'Aurora'	Leaf	Creamy-yellow and green	June-Oct	Two-year-old shoots to 2ft
Populus 'Serotina Aurea'	Leaf	Golden-yellow	May-July	One-year-old shoots to 2ft
Salix alba 'Chermesina'	Stem	Orange and scarlet	Oct-Mar	One-year-old shoots to 9in or on a stem to the desired height
Salix alba 'Vitellina'	Stem	Golden-yellow	Oct-Mar	One-year-old shoots to 9in or on a stem to the desired height
Salix daphnoides	Stem	Purple and violet	Oct-Mar	Two-year-old shoots to 9in or on a stem to the desired height
Salix sachalinensis 'Sekka'	Flattened stems	Polished brown	Oct-Mar	Two-year-old shoots to 9in or on a stem to the desired height

planted straight away, although you must ensure that the compost is kept moist. A common fault is that the tree may have become pot-bound, with the root system wrapping itself round the base of the pot. Such a tree, after planting, may fail to develop spreading roots and become unstable. If you find you've bought a pot-bound tree, slash through the tangled roots three or four times with a sharp knife to encourage new roots to grow from the cuts.

Bare-root trees have well-developed root systems, and are lifted from the nursery beds during the dormant period from November to March. Trees taken from open ground do best if planted before Christmas; they establish themselves more quickly and will be more tolerant if growing conditions are tricky during the following summer.

Plants with thick, fleshy roots like magnolias do better if lifted in February or March. But whenever a bare-rooted tree was lifted, plant it as soon as you can after buying. If bad weather holds you up, prevent the roots from drying out by covering them with sacking or heavy-duty polythene, or by heeling the tree into a temporary trench. This should be a spade-deep, V-shaped trench with one vertical side. Lay the tree against the sloping side of the trench, cover the roots completely and firm in.

In the end, it matters little whether the plants are container-grown or bare-rooted, so long as they are properly looked after. The choice is yours. Buy the type which fits better into your gardening timetable.

Witches' brooms

The old birch tree at the bottom of the garden has several large twiggy lumps growing from the upper branches. At first I thought they were birds' nests, but they're too solid. What are they, and will they harm the tree?

This deformity is known as a witches' broom – an over-generous growth of shoots caused by a fungus called *Taphrina turgida*.

It is frequently seen on birches and also occurs on cherries, plums, hornbeams, ornamental prunus and several types of conifer. Some of the foliage may show blisters.

Witches' brooms do not really harm a tree, though in extreme cases they can become enormous and take over much of the crown. Most of the leaves would then be in the shade, to the detriment of growing stems and roots.

Crop losses are likely on fruit trees as the brooms do not bear fruit. Neither do the bumps improve the looks of the ornamental trees. In both these cases it would be better to get rid of them. In winter, cut off the affected branches at a point 6in below the brooms. Burn the branches and paint the wounds to seal them.

You can obtain new dwarf trees from witches' brooms on conifers. In late summer or early autumn, take a shoot from a broom one year old, dip it in rooting powder and plant it in a cold frame in a 50:50 mixture of peat and sharp sand. Late in the following spring, transfer the cutting to a pot and keep it there for one or two years before planting it out in a rockery or tub.

Alternatively, graft the cutting onto the stump of another tree of the same species (see *Grafting*, page 160).

The kindest cut

Gardening books tell me to paint a sealant onto every large pruning cut, but I've heard that rubbing the wound with soil works just as well. Still further advice recommends leaving the cut uncovered in order to let it breathe. Which is right?

Even among foresters there is considerable debate. For many years it was the invariable advice that wounds in trees should be painted in order to keep out bacteria and fungi. Recent research, however, is casting doubts on this practice.

It suggests that trees have long evolved their own defences against disease. If you look closely at the point where a small branch joins a larger one, or at the junction of a large branch with the trunk, you will see a slight ridge on the upper side of the branch.

This is known to botanists as the 'branch bark ridge', while a similar bulge on the underside of the branch is the 'branch collar'. Provided that an angled cut is made outside these points, no damage will be done to the tree's internal chemical protective layer, and you need not bother to paint.

But if you cut flush with the stem, the tree's heartwood will be open to attack; in this case, painting will be necessary. Any household paint will do – it doesn't have to be a specialised sealant.

And what about rubbing soil on the wound? All this does is camouflage the cut – it is of no benefit to the tree at all.

Sure sign of heart rot

A fawn, shelf-like fungus has appeared on an old tree stump in the garden. First of all, what is it? And is it harmful to pets or plants?

It's called bracket fungus from its shelf-like shape, and it's generally harmless. These wood-rotting fungi, which may grow to a foot or more across, appear from July until the end of the growing season in about October. They are sure signs that the heart or inner wood of the host tree is rotten.

The spores enter dead trees and start to break down the wood, or enter a living tree – usually an old one – through a wound and feed on the sap. This weakens the tree, which eventually dies; the fungus then consumes the dead wood. So to find bracket fungus on a dead stump is quite normal. Trees nearby will come to no harm provided they are healthy. All the same, you would be well advised to remove the stump; as well as bracket fungus, dead wood attracts honey fungus, a killer of many plants.

One situation in which bracket fungus might be dangerous is if it appears on a large tree near a house, since it can rot the tree from within and cause it to keel over without warning. If you find it on a living tree, remove the diseased branches; if it appears on the main stem, cut out both fungus and rotting wood and coat all wounds with fungicide paint.

Instant orchards

My children and their friends have become intrigued at the notion of growing their own orchard from pips. I've told them they're being rather optimistic, but what in fact are their chances?

Since apples, pears and plums grow naturally in this country, their chances are really quite good. The only trouble is that the seedlings are unlikely to reach fruiting age for many years, by which time the children may have lost interest. The more exotic plants – oranges, dates, lemons and so on – are unlikely to grow outdoors in our climate, though you could raise some interesting and attractive house plants.

Many fruit and nut seeds germinate better if they have been chilled, so put them in a moist peat and sand mixture in the refrigerator for two or three weeks. After that, sow the seeds singly in pots or trays in the house at about 13°C (55°F) and, when they germinate, pot them on.

Peanuts are also fun to grow. They need a rather higher temperature, but will flower and fruit in a greenhouse at 21°C (70°F) in the same year that they were sown. Crack the shells before planting them about an inch deep in moist seed compost.

A forest from scratch

My children collect conkers each year, and we always wonder whether we can grow from them. Can you give us some advice?

Think twice before you plant conkers in your garden, unless you have a spare acre or two. You – or the occupiers of your house in 20 years or so – will find that a horse chestnut in the backyard can be somewhat overwhelming.

Growing from seed can be fun, and satisfying to a child's sense of curiosity. There are plenty of native plants in the hedgerow which can be propagated by seed and are a better size for the garden.

There are a few rules to be observed when sowing tree seeds. After collecting, do not leave the seed lying about – it will soon dry out. Oily seeds, like conkers and acorns, are best planted straight away, and often other seeds gathered from the ground have already begun to shoot. These too should be planted at once, but if you're delayed for some reason, put the seed in a sealed polythene bag and put it in the refrigerator (not the freezer) until you are ready to deal with it.

Sowing can be carried out from October to April. Fill a pot or seed tray with seed compost, either soil or peat-based, and sow on the firmed level surface. A fine, dust-like seed, such as birch, will not need covering, but bury larger seeds – such as conkers – under ½-1in of compost.

Spread a fine layer of washed grit on top of the compost to prevent the soil caking or moss forming in the year or more that tree seeds take to germinate. This is not necessary in the case of the very fine seed. Make sure the compost is kept moist.

Place the pot or seed tray in a sheltered area or cold frame out of direct sunlight, and check regularly to see if germination has taken place. When germination occurs, most tree seedlings will produce two seed leaves – more in the case of conifers – followed by the first true leaves. Lift out the seedlings, taking care not to damage the roots, and grow each of them on singly in its own pot, in potting compost.

Nature lesson

We have just moved to a new housing estate encroaching upon old parkland. A large number of the original trees remain, for which we are very grateful, though they do create planting problems. How can we best make use of the semi-desert that exists in the trees' shade?

If the trees were growing in their natural woodland setting, there would be no problem. Though the great roots draw nutrients and moisture from the soil in enormous quantities, year by year the trees replace the goodness with fallen leaves, making a rich, organic layer in which smaller woodland – and therefore shade-loving – plants will grow. Though the architects were thoughtful enough to leave the original trees when building your estate, it would seem that they must have felt it necessary to clear away the valuable leaf litter beneath them. The best thing you can do is to re-create at least a small part of a tree woodland environment.

Do this by mulching your dry, shaded areas with well-rotted garden compost or manure, spent hops, leaf mould gained from the trees, and with pulverised bark or peat. Keep the layer going by repeating the treatment every spring. The resulting mulch will prevent the ground from losing too much moisture, keep down weeds and feed shade-loving plants.

A wide range of plants can be grown in shade – shrubs, herbaceous plants and bulbs, along with mosses and ferns. For some ideas on what to grow, see *Plants that shine in the shade*, page 309, and *Pick of the ground-cover plants*, page 177.

Stumped for an answer

The previous owner of my house did not think it necessary to remove tree stumps. How can I get rid of them?

A moderately sized stump can be winched from the ground as long as there is at least 3ft of stump left above ground to attach the cable to, and a secure anchorage point close at hand.

The actual process of winching is best left to a contractor. So, too, is operating a stump grinder. The machine is costly to hire but solves the problem quickly. It will chew up a stump of any size into small chips which can be disposed of easily.

Don't use chemicals on stumps unless they are still alive and you wish to stop them sprouting. To do this, make a few deep axe cuts in the top of the stump and soak it with a brushwood killer mixed with a light oil such as paraffin.

Best of all – why not leave the stumps and instead make use of them as settings for climbing or scrambling plants such as clematis, ivy and honeysuckle – or, if it is a large, hollow stump, as a raised bed for a mass of summer bedding plants?

Putting a name to it

I can see why rare plants which have no common names should need to be identified by Latin ones. But what's wrong with calling a chestnut a chestnut?

It depends which chestnut you're talking about. In the genus Aesculus there are 13 species, which include the familiar horse chestnut, the Indian horse chestnut and a round-topped shrub that the Americans call red buckeye. The genus also contains a large number of varieties of these species, and the problem, as with other genera, is how, when describing the species, to distinguish one plant from another.

Since there are at least 250,000 species of flowering plants alone, not to mention 6000 or so ferns and countless mosses, liverworts and fungi, it would be impossible to allocate to each of them a common name that would be acceptable in every language. Hence botanical names, which by international agreement signify the same plants in every tongue. Common or local names given to plants are far more ancient than the botanical ones, but they do of course change from country to country and even from district to district. So, for gardeners, the naming of a plant begins with its genus – roughly its surname – the group of closely related plants to which it belongs. This is followed by the species name, which identifies the particular plant within the group. Thus the red buckeye is known botanically as *Aesculus pavia* (the genus name followed by the species name).

Naturally occurring and cultivated varieties are also identified in this system, as are hybrids, in which one species has been crossed with another. In the case of the common horse chestnut, *A. hippocastanum*, this is how the three categories would be identified: *A. h. laciniata* (a naturally occurring variety identified by a three-part name all in italics); *A. h.* 'Baumannii' (a cultivated variety or cultivar, identified by the varietal name in inverted commas and in ordinary type); and *A.* x *carnea* (a hybrid, denoted by the multiplication sign).

This Latin-based system of classification, not only of plants but of all living things, was evolved by the Swedish biologist Karl von Linné (1707-78). By some odd quirk, he himself is now better known by the Latinised version of his name, Carolus Linnaeus.

Boosting the growth of a tree

In many parts of the countryside, I have seen new avenues being created out of young trees being grown within plastic tubes. Is this a more efficient way of planting trees than growing them in the open?

The growing of deciduous trees in translucent tubes began in 1979. Briefly, they create mini-hothouse conditions, protect the young plants and make them grow faster for the first years of their life.

The tubes carry out these functions very well. The Forestry Commission found that they generated temperatures of up to 48°C (118°F) with 100 per cent humidity levels without damaging the plants. The most responsive trees were oak, sweet chestnut, hawthorn and the small-leaved lime, whose rates of growth were usually double during their first two or three years. The Forestry Commission has also been carrying out tests with conifers, and the results generally have been good. For some reason or other, how-

TREE SHELTERS *Tubular plastic tree shelters act like mini-greenhouses – sheltering seedlings from wind and speeding their growth.*

ever, beeches are an exception, and do not respond well to this treatment. Some 1,500,000 plastic tree shelters were used during the 1984/5 planting season. They are designed to last five years, the amount of time it takes for the tree to grow above the 45in high shelter which has given it support and protection while the stem thickened.

If you try this form of planting yourself, leave the tube in place until it disintegrates, otherwise the stem may snap. Within five years, your tree should be sturdy and well.

The root of the problem

I should like to plant a tree in my smallish garden, but I'm a bit worried about the effect it might have on the drains or the foundations of the house. Are my worries justified?

Most of us used to think that trees and houses co-existed quite happily. The Great Drought of 1976 put an end to that illusion. At that time, millions of pounds were paid out in insurance claims for subsidence damage caused by the shrinking or swelling of soil beneath houses. Certain soils, particularly clays and peats, are liable to shrink in very dry conditions, and then to expand again just as rapidly at the first touch of moisture – with disastrous results to the house standing on top. In a drought, tree roots hasten the rate of drying out.

Willows and poplars are most frequently blamed for damaging foundations. They are greedy for moisture, and their roots will drive through almost anything to find it. But if they can be planted near a sufficient and constant water supply, they will generally behave themselves. However, they should not be planted near new or small houses – nor should other large trees, such as oak, ash, lime, plane, beech and sycamore.

To be on the safe side, find out the ultimate height of the tree you want and plant it at least one and a half times this distance away from the building.

Tale of a tub

My town garden is almost entirely paved. Can you suggest any trees that I might grow in large tubs?

Quite a wide range can be grown in this way, though do remember that tubs restrict growth, and because of this, the trees will be shorter-lived than if they had been planted in a garden. They will, in fact, become pot-bound, and repotting a sizable tree is a fairly difficult operation.

Plant your trees in John Innes No 3 compost, rather than in a peat-based compost. This will give them firmer support and retain water and nutrients better. Top-dress the compost every March or April by scraping off the top 2 or 3in and replacing it with fresh compost; this will help to maintain the correct nutrient levels.

Water the trees regularly, especially in warm weather, and ask a neighbour to take care of this when you are away on holiday. A vigorous plant will also need a feed of liquid fertiliser every two weeks during the summer.

Drainage is important: make sure there are pebbles and drainage holes in the base of the tub and see that it is raised off the ground so that excess water can drain away.

You can expect a slow-growing tree in a large tub, say a halved wooden beer barrel, to last for ten years or more. The tub will restrict root development and slow the rate of growth still further, so keeping the tree in proportion with its surroundings.

A tub complete with tree and soil is extremely heavy, but is still mobile if handled with care. In severe winters when roots and foliage may become frosted – evergreens are very vulnerable to this – move the tub to a sheltered spot, or hang netting or hessian on a framework around the tree to protect it.

If a tree gets too big, or you feel like a change, pass it on to a friend who can plant it out in his garden. The chart on this page contains a list of trees suitable for tubs: four evergreens – two cypresses, a juniper and a sweet bay (laurus); and five deciduous trees – three crab apples (malus species), a Japanese cherry and a Japanese apricot.

TREES FOR TUBS

Name	Principal interest	Peak display
Chamaecyparis lawsoniana 'Columnaris'	Grey-green foliage	All year
Cupressus sempervirens 'Green Spire'	Green foliage	All year
Juniperus chinensis 'Kaizuka'	Green foliage	All year
Laurus nobilis 'Aurea'	Yellow foliage	All year
Malus 'Cowichan'	Red flowers (red fruits)	May-June (Sept-Dec)
Malus 'Crittenden'	Pink flowers (scarlet fruits)	May-June (Oct-Mar)
Malus 'Elise Rathke'	White flowers (yellow fruits)	May-June (Oct-Dec)
Prunus 'Kiku-shidare Sakura'	Deep pink flowers	May
Prunus mume 'Beni-shidon'	Deep pink flowers	Feb-Apr

Acid rain: the bitter argument

Deep passions are being roused by the damage that acid rain is doing to trees on the Continent. Is it likely to harm British woodlands – or the trees in my garden, come to that?

At present it seems unlikely that acid rain will damage British woodlands, though we can never be sure. But in other European countries, the problem is an urgent one, and the solution a good deal more difficult to find than had once been supposed.

Research into the phenomenon in Sweden in 1983 indicated that acid rain by itself had little effect on trees, and that damage began to occur only in areas where the pH level of the soil was below 3.

Gardeners measure soil alkalinity or acidity on a pH scale of 1 to 14, the mid-point of 7 being neutral. Values above 7 are alkaline and below 7, acid; garden soils are rarely above 8 or below 4.5 (see also *Acid soils*, page 6). For comparison, 'pure' rainwater in Britain has a pH of 5.6, which in some districts may drop as low as 4.6; but even this is still well outside the level at which damage may occur. Even when trees are planted on soils with a low pH there appears to be little evidence of damage caused by acid rain alone.

So what happened in the stricken conifer forests of Central Europe and Scandinavia? A final explanation has yet to be found. It seems that a number of factors interacted in a way that we do not fully grasp. Soil problems, low temperatures, drought and ozone levels in the atmosphere all appear to have contributed: a complexity of conditions that does not occur in this country.

Quite what part industrial pollution in Britain has played in this problem is not certain. Scientists do not, for instance, yet understand why the effects should have become apparent only in the past few years when British homes and factories belched out far more pollution a century ago.

In search of the ideal tree

My local garden centre spoils me for choice, since whenever I look for a tree, there is a row of a dozen or so seemingly identical ones available. How do I tell the good from the mediocre?

Choose a tree with the same care that you would choose a piece of furniture for your house. It is going to be a dominant feature in the garden for a long time.

A strong, well-balanced plant with a good, fibrous root system will stand a better chance than a scrawny one with poor roots. So have a look at the roots if that is possible, and never buy a tree whose roots have been left in the open to dry out.

Even with container-grown trees, there are a few points to watch. A thick root growing downwards from the base of the container, or exposed roots on the surface, are indications that the plant has been in the container too long and will not grow away successfully.

Next, look at the stems and branches. Trees are generally sold as 'standards' with a 5ft to 6ft clear stem before the branches start, or as 'feathered' trees which have a central stem with sideshoots all the way up.

In either case look for a sturdy, evenly distributed branch system with a central leading shoot; avoid trees whose branches are heavier or denser on one side than on the other. If some of the leaves are shrivelled, discoloured or shot with holes, the tree is diseased or under insect attack, so leave it well alone. Check for frost damage to foliage, and to roots; evergreens sold in pots are particularly prone to this. The danger signals are leaves that turn brown or drop off after a spell of hard frost.

Some nurseries give a plant guarantee. Some will even replace a tree if it dies within six months of purchase, provided you have kept the receipt and it is apparent that the tree has not been neglected.

Saplings need support

I have bought a sturdy 6ft tree from the garden centre. Do I need to stake it?

Yes. It will not have much of a root spread, whether a pot-grown or bare-rooted plant. Either way, it will be at risk of being blown over or knocked about by the wind, so inhibiting the roots from taking hold.

For your 6ft tree you will need a stake 2in thick and tall enough to drive 2ft into the ground, yet leaving sufficient stake to support the stem up to the point where the branches start. Drive the stake into the bottom of the hole before you settle the tree in beside it, otherwise you could damage the root system. Or you might fix two stakes, one on either side of the tree and fitted with slings pulling in opposite directions. This is ideal for a large tree that has been planted in a windy position.

Tie the tree firmly in to the stake, or stakes, but avoid strangling it. Use plastic or webbing straps which have plastic or rubberised buffers that fit between tree and stake to prevent chafing. These have enough give to prevent strangling the tree, and are easily adjusted as the tree grows.

Another way is to wrap hessian several times round the stake and then around both stake and stem, to provide a protective layer between the two. Secure the hessian with strong, rotproof string. Never use plastic string or wire as these will bite into the trunk as its girth increases. Check the ties at least twice a year, and always after strong winds. Slacken them off a bit if they are constricting the thickening trunk.

After about two years, the tree should be strong enough to stand alone.

Sizing up a planting hole

Are there any rules about how big and deep the hole should be when planting a young tree?

As a general rule, the larger the tree, the larger the hole you will need. An 8ft tree, for instance, will require a hole 3-4ft wide and 2ft deep. Make sure you have at least a foot wide clearance around the roots. If you squash them into too small a hole, the tree will have difficulty in growing.

When a conifer takes off

My prostrate conifer has suddenly grown upwards. What can I do about it?

The short answer is: if you don't want your conifer to grow tall, prune it down to size. But the more interesting question might be: what causes the change to happen? Dwarf or slow-growing conifers are fascinating plants. On the one hand they seem extremely docile and easy to train, while on the other they have a tendency to surprise you by reverting to ancestral habits.

Many of them are closely related, and it is not difficult to grow a new prostrate variety. All you have to do is to select a ground-hugging shoot on a normally upright growing plant and take a cutting. Alternatively, graft the cutting onto a rootstock of the same species (see *Grafting*, page 160).

Once the cutting is growing independently the new plant will remain prostrate, though it may in time go back to its original habit and grow upwards. This is most likely to be seen in species such as firs (Abies) and spruces (Picea). The general principle is that a cutting from an upright shoot will produce an upright plant, while a ground-hugging shoot will give a prostrate plant.

Sad cypress

My cluster of Lawson cypress has died after only three years – why?

It is unusual for these fairly tough trees to die so young. Weather is not usually the cause; they can recover even from severe drought, unless they are growing on a dry sandy soil. Scorched foliage due to wind chill is only a temporary setback, but waterlogged ground can cause death. Incorrect transplanting may also prove fatal, but the most common cause of death is phytophthora root disease, a fungus which attacks a wide range of ornamental plants. Lawson cypress is particularly susceptible.

The disease is most common on heavy, wet soils; the inner foliage turns brown and the browning quickly spreads to the rest. A Lawson cypress that looks healthy in June may be totally brown by October. Root systems close to the stem will by then be dead as well. If the tree is left, mushrooms of honey fungus may appear, a sign of secondary invasion rather than the cause of death. If your trees show any of these symptoms, dig them out and burn them.

TUBERS

Dividing begonias

The tubers of my begonias are becoming large and rather woody. Can I divide them?

It is possible to divide begonia tubers and get them to flower again, but it's a bit hit and miss. You would almost certainly do better with stem cuttings, and multiply your stock more swiftly at the same time.

In the spring, plant the tubers in a good peaty compost in trays, and give them gentle heat – 18-21°C (about 65-70°F) – to encourage them to sprout. When the stocky, short-jointed basal shoots are about 2in high, cut them off. You can leave a heel of the parent tuber attached to the cutting if you prefer, but it's not essential (for advice on techniques, see *Cuttings*, page 107, and *How to multiply your shrubs*, page 314). Dip the bases in hormone rooting powder, and set the cuttings in a half-and-half mixture of sharp sand and peat, or peat and perlite. Keep them in a warm, moist atmosphere, and they will root quite readily.

Allow the cuttings to grow throughout the summer, and by late autumn, each will have produced a new tuber.

Thus from a single old tuber, you may have produced as many as five new plants – a much better deal than the two you would have gained from division. Your new plants will give you several years of splendid flowers before it is necessary to begin the next round of cuttings.

Storing dahlias

What's the best way to store dahlia tubers?

Keep them dry and keep them frost-free. Probably the safest method is to pack them in peat in wooden boxes – old tomato trays if you can get them. But the real secret of keeping dahlias successfully through the

WHAT CAN GO WRONG WITH FLOWERING TUBERS		
Symptom	**Cause**	**Action**
Tubers soft and slimy	Bacterial soft rot	Burn the tubers.
Decay and blue-green mould on tubers	Blue mould rot	Dip the tubers in benomyl solution for 15-30 minutes before planting. Dust with sulphur before storing.
Damaged tubers with tiny, hairy white mites	Bulb mite	Destroy the tubers. Mites attack only damaged tubers. Gentle handling of tubers when planting and lifting is the best preventative.
Damaged tubers; slime trails	Slugs or snails	Sprinkle slug pellets around the plants.
Small round holes in tubers; thin yellow larvae	Wireworm	Work HCH dust into the soil before planting.
Plants yellow or die. A web of violet-purple strands visible at the base of tubers	Violet root rot	Burn affected plants and tubers. Do not plant tubers in the bed again.

winter is in the lifting. Here's how to do it.
DON'T lift until the plants have been hit by a really hard frost. Chop off the foliage when flowering is over, but leave at least 9in of stem above ground to await the freeze. A gentle frost won't do. It must be hard enough to seal the main stem of the plant. Any green and decaying tissue remaining could harbour infection that would rot the tubers in their winter store.
LIFT the tubers carefully by easing a fork underneath. Cut off any damaged tissue with a sharp knife and seal the wounds with a dusting of sulphur.
DON'T wash soil off the tubers, shake it off. Any dampness will encourage mould to spread during the storing period. When the tubers are dry, trim stems and roots and core out the stems' centres with a screwdriver. For details of how to do this, see *To lift or not to lift*, page 115.

Now pack the tubers in peat in wooden boxes – tomato trays are ideal. Make sure the peat is not quite bone dry, but certainly not damp enough to start any growth. It is important to ensure that air continues to circulate about the tubers – the main reason for using tomato trays. Their corner supports, standing higher than the sides, allow the air to pass between the trays even when they are stacked.

Right way up

I have some begonia tubers, but have forgotten which way up they should be planted. Would you remind me, please?

Coarse and concave upwards; round and smooth down. The new flower and leaf shoots will sprout from the hollow bowl of the concave side.

Plant the tuber so that this concave side shows above the surface – don't bury it.

Begonias do best if planted in 3in deep boxes of moist peat in March or April at a temperature of 18°C (about 65°F). As the leafy shoots grow, move the tubers on into 4in pots of potting compost, and then into 6-8in pots. From the time when the flower buds first become visible until the end of flowering, give your begonias a fortnightly feed of liquid fertiliser.

If you still have any misgivings about which way is up, plant the tubers on edge in the peat until the shoots sprout and reach up to the light. That will resolve what lingering doubts you have.

Greenhouse lilies

I have been given some white arum lily tubers. Wonderful. But how do I grow them? Can I plant them outdoors?

In this country, they'll do best in a cold greenhouse. There, you can most nearly reproduce the warm, damp conditions of their South African habitat.

Plant the tubers of this lovely lily, *Zantedeschia aethiopica*, straight into the greenhouse border or in 6in pots in a predominantly peaty compost, in September.

Keep the growing plants frost-free and in March or April flower buds will begin to appear among the luxuriant foliage. From then on, feed the plants fortnightly with a tomato fertiliser. Spray against greenfly, too.

When flowering has ended, put the plants outdoors and keep them well watered until July, after which the watering should be gradually cut back until the leaves turn yellow. Then stop watering altogether to let the plants dry off.

In late September, lift and repot the tubers in new compost and bring them back into the greenhouse. They may well have produced offsets, which can be potted separately and treated in the same way as the parent tubers.

A dwarf version of the arum lily, called 'Crowborough', is hardy enough to risk leaving outside over winter.

TULIPS

Plants for windy sites

Our garden is very exposed, and our tall tulips take a beating from strong winds in April and May every year. Are there any varieties that would be more suitable for the position?

Yes – many bulb merchants offer collections of early and mid-season tulips of short and sturdy growth, which are ideal for windy spots. They average 9-15in in height, while many of the dwarf tulips are shorter still. As a bonus, the miniatures and dwarfs are also suitable for rockeries, or for planting in the front of beds and borders.

The dwarfs are mainly derived from *Tulipa kaufmanniana*, *T. greigii* and *T. fosteriana*, though there are also one or two true species which give a fine spring display and are well worth planting – even if they do look rather different from modern hybrids. All are very hardy and do best in open, sunny spots, in fertile, free-draining soil.

T. kaufmanniana and its hybrids – also known as water-lily tulips because of the shape of the flowers – will give you the earliest show, coming into flower in March and continuing well into April. They rarely grow to more than 10in and are among the few tulips that will naturalise successfully in grass. The parent itself is quite modest, appearing in various shades of white, cream or pink. The hybrids have stronger colours. The yellow and orange-striped 'Stresa' is one of the most popular. 'Brilliant' is scarlet with a yellow base, 'The First' is a cool icy white, and 'Cesar Franck' is carmine edged with yellow. The hybrids from the cross between *T. kaufmanniana* and *T. greigii* provide an added touch of interest: the leaves are mottled and streaked with purple-brown.

T. greigii itself is an attractive plant, about 9-12in high, with scarlet cup-shaped flowers and broad blue-grey leaves veined and marbled with mauve. Among its many beautiful hybrids, which in most cases flower in early April – a little later than the kaufmanniana hybrids – are the vivid orange-red 'Bokhara' and the red and white 'Plaisir'.

Slightly taller, but still of sturdy character, are the hybrids of *T. fosteriana*, which flower in about mid-April. Few of them surpass the fiery red, large-flowered 'Madame Lefeber' (also known as 'Red Emperor'), a much improved form of the species. For a cooler look, try 'Purissima' (milky white) or 'Albas' (blush pink).

Dwarf tulip species suitable for exposed sites include the 6in *T. tarda*, a resilient, multiflowered plant with starry gold and white blooms in March. Equally short is *T. clusiana chrysantha* (better known as *T. chrysantha*), whose red and creamy-yellow flowers appear in April. Although much taller (12-18in), the multiflowered *T. praestans* is fairly wind-tolerant; it has brilliant red blooms, seen at their most intense in the variety 'Fusilier'.

Potted black

During a recent gathering of gardening friends, a heated discussion developed about a black tulip. Does such a plant exist?

Since 'tulipmania' first seized Europe in the mid-17th century, horticulturists and plant breeders have tried to raise a black tulip. The closest they came, until quite recently, was the deep purple-black Darwin hybrid, 'La Tulipe Noire'. This masqueraded as a black tulip and was often sold as such – to the great disappointment of most buyers.

At last, however, recent experiments in Holland have produced the first true black-flowered tulip. The work of a Dutch nurseryman named Gert Hageman, it is the result of a union between 'Wienerwald' and 'Queen of the Night'. In 1986 a single bulb was exhibited, but thanks to modern propagation techniques it is expected to be increased fairly quickly and to become available – at a price – to amateur gardeners during the 1990s. The new bulb will probably get its final name about the time it goes on sale – in the meantime it goes under its breeder's code of 08.35.79.

How deep to plant

Everybody seems to have different ideas about how deep to plant tulip bulbs. What's the straight answer?

Plant the bulbs so that their tops are covered by about 5-8in of soil. On a clay soil, go for the shallow end of that range; set the tops 5-6in below the surface. On sandy soil, set the tops of the bulbs 7-8in deep.

If you're in doubt about the category your soil falls into, cover the bulbs with 5in of soil. If you're planting small offsets from a mature bulb, put them in holes deep enough so that the offsets are covered by 2-4in of soil, while they grow to flowering size. Some gardeners believe, wrongly, that tulips can be planted successfully at almost any depth because offsets will form naturally at a depth that suits them. In fact, however, this process of natural migration happens too slowly to be of much use to tulips. It's safer to stick to the recommended range of depths.

HOW TULIPS ARE CLASSIFIED

Modern tulips are hybrids, and breeders are constantly adding new varieties. Because of their vast numbers, the hybrids are classified in various 'divisions', characterised by flower type and flowering period. Each division contains numerous named varieties, often in a wide range of colours. This chart lists the commonly used divisions, and identifies the characteristics of each.

Division	Use	Height	Flowering period
Single Early	Forcing and bedding	9-20in	Mid-Apr to early May
Double Early	Forcing and bedding	10-15in	Mid-Apr
Triumph	Bedding	18-20in	Late Apr
Darwin Hybrids	Bedding	24-28in	Late Apr-May
Rembrandt	Bedding	24-26in	May
Lily-flowered	Bedding and mixed border	20-24in	Late Apr-May
Cottage	Bedding	24-28in	Mid to late May
Parrot	Cut flowers and mixed border	20-24in	May
Double Late	Cut flowers and mixed border	18-24in	Mid to late May
T. kaufmanniana hybrids	Border, rock gardens and for naturalising	8-10in	Mid-Mar to early Apr
T. fosteriana hybrids	Border and rock gardens	10-15in	Mid-Apr
T. greigii hybrids	Border and rock gardens	9-16in	Early to mid-Apr
Single Late	Bedding	24-28in	May
Fringed	Mixed border	20-24in	Early May
Viridiflora	Mixed border	9-24in	Early May
Species	Border and rock gardens	4-26in	March to late May

A BURNT-OUT CASE *There's no cure for the devastating virus disease of tulip fire.*

Tulip fire

The leaves of my tulips look sickly. They have reddish streaks and blotches that look as though they are scorched, and the stems are deformed. What is wrong, and can I cure it?

The symptoms you describe are typical of the first steps of the devastating virus disease known as tulip fire. You may already have also noticed the later symptoms – the leaves will be covered in grey mould and be starting to rot at soil level.

There's no cure for this disease. Dig up and burn all infected plants, and any neighbouring tulips, immediately. Do not use the same site for tulips again.

Blindness – permanent or temporary?

The tulip bulbs I planted in the autumn, at the correct depth of 4in, produced no flowers in the spring. Will they flower next season, or is the lack of blooms permanent?

Plenty of foliage but no flowers – known as blindness – is most commonly found among tulip and daffodil bulbs.

The immediate cause of the blindness may be a very severe winter which has damaged or killed the embryo flower buds, resulting in leaves but no flowers.

If that's the cause, the problem is likely to be temporary. Provided that you let the foliage develop and die away naturally to help the bulbs to recover their strength, flowering should return to normal next year.

However, the blame may lie in the quality and size of the bulbs you have bought. There are very few real bargains when it comes to buying bulbs. You get only what you pay for. Tulip and daffodil bulbs are graded for size, so select the largest you can afford. If you order by mail from reputable nurseries, they will always state the bulb size in their catalogues. 'Top size' and 'first size' are other descriptions used for 4-5in circumference tulip bulbs guaranteed to flower in their first season.

Small offsets from mature tulip bulbs usually yield only foliage for the first couple of years. However, if you plant them 2-4in deep and 3in apart in rows 9in apart in a nursery bed of good loam, water them regularly, and feed them with a general liquid fertiliser every three weeks from the time the leaves emerge until early June, they will reach flowering size in a year or two.

If you suddenly get blindness among long-established clumps of tulips, the usual reason is starvation or overcrowding. To cure it, lift the bulbs, dig the ground and work in a general fertiliser such as Growmore, and replant the largest bulbs – about 6-8in apart for large varieties, and 4-6in apart for the small species.

Treat the smaller, undernourished bulbs in the same way as young offsets. They'll take a year or two to get back into top form, but will in time recover.

After the show is over

My tulips are marvellous while they're in flower, but once the display is over the bare stems and drooping leaves look very unsightly. Is it all right to cut them back to the ground?

No – about the worst thing you can do to your tulips is to remove the foliage before it has died back naturally. The bulbs will grow weak and you will have no flowers the following season.

While the stems and leaves are green, they act as the plant's power station, generating energy which is stored in the bulb. The energy will later be used to produce next year's flower and foliage.

So the most you should do is snip off the faded blooms with about 2in of stem. This will stop the plants wasting energy on trying to set seed, and also keep the ground clear of rotting fallen petals.

It is equally important to keep the foliage strong and healthy, since tulips, like other bulbs, use a lot of energy in flowering and need plenty of nourishment to build up strength for the following year. So feed your tulips with a general liquid fertiliser every two or three weeks from the moment the leaves show through the soil until they start to turn yellow.

If you don't want a mass of unattractive foliage after flowering, or if the plants are getting in the way of summer bedding, lift them and heel them in on some open, sunny, spare ground. Leave the foliage undisturbed, except for watering and feeding, until it fades naturally. At this stage you can carefully lift the bulbs, dry them off, remove the dead stems and leaves, and store the bulbs in a cool, dry place until you are ready to replant them in autumn.

If, however, you can put up with the foliage, leave the bulbs where they are. By not moving them after flowering, you avoid the risk of damaging the roots and thereby lessening the bulb's ability to soak up energy for the following year.

VERTICILLIUM WILT

Wilting tomatoes

The most extraordinary thing is happening to my tomatoes. Each day the leaves and sideshoots droop, but every night they spring up again. Are they not getting enough water, or is the day too hot for them? Or what?

It sounds as though they're suffering from verticillium wilt, a soil-borne fungal disease which attacks not only tomatoes but also michaelmas daisies, carnations in greenhouses and some shrubs, such as maples and sumachs. The wilting is caused by blockage of the stem tissues that conduct water to the leaves and by the build-up of toxic substances. The blockage is not complete, so a little water can get through. During the warmth of the day, more water evaporates through the leaves than the plant can replace through the stem – so the plant wilts. At night, though, cooler temperatures mean less evaporation. As a result, the water supply catches up with the needs of the shoots and leaves – and the plant appears to perk up again.

In shrubs, the disease causes branches to die back, but rarely kills the whole plant; simply cut off the affected branches and paint the resulting wound with fungicidal paint. But in the case of flowering plants and your tomatoes, there is no cure.

Your tomatoes will die anyway, and the best thing to do is to dig them up now and burn them, and put the soil in which they grew in the dustbin. Spray nearby healthy plants with a benomyl solution to stop the disease spreading, and repeat the dose two weeks later. If the plants are growing in a greenhouse, sterilise it at the end of the season and use growing bags in future.

Infected carnations and michaelmas daisies must be treated in the same way.

UP-AND-DOWN TOMATOES *Tomatoes and other plants which wilt during the day, but appear to recover after sunset, are probably victims of verticillium wilt, a soil-borne disease which only shrubs are likely to survive.*

VINE WEEVILS

Ragged rhododendrons

My two rhododendrons have recently acquired a ragged appearance due to the large holes that some creature is making in their leaves. It can't be small, judging by the size of the holes, though despite a long search I can find nothing. What's doing it and, more important, how do I stop it?

The vine weevil is to blame, a blackish-brown beetle that comes out at night and chews holes in the edges of the leaves of rhododendrons, polyanthus, clematis, vines, strawberries, raspberries and many other plants. Indoors, its white larvae, which can be up to ⅓in long, attack the roots of such pot plants as cyclamens and begonias.

During the day, the weevils disappear into the soil or burrow into fallen leaves, which is why they're not so easy to find. You can take advantage of this habit by leaving pieces of folded sacking or rolls of corrugated paper on the ground beneath your shrubs. The weevils will burrow into them, and you can get rid of insects and hideouts together.

For lasting defence, clear away plant debris and apply a persistent insecticide to the foliage, soil and potting composts – a spray or dusting of HCH, for example.

LATE DINER *The vine weevil eats the edges of rhododendron leaves by night, and those of many other plants, too. Its larvae attack the roots of several species, especially indoors.*

VIRUSES

Dahlia disaster

I kept my dahlia tubers through the winter without loss. But now they are growing, at least a third of the plants seem stunted, and quite a number of leaves have yellow or brownish rings on them. Am I over-feeding or under-feeding the plants, or what?

It has nothing to do with feeding. Almost certainly, your dahlias have a virus disease and, sadly, there is no cure. Dig the infected ones up and burn them. This may prevent the disease spreading not only to the remaining dahlias, but to your chrysanthemums, clematis and many other border plants, too.

Then spray the survivors with a systemic insecticide such as dimethoate to get rid of the aphids that are probably spreading the disease. One of the problems with virus diseases is recognition, since the same disease can cause different symptoms on different plants, and it is quite possible for a plant to suffer from more than one virus at the same time. However, colour changes in leaves, stems and flowers, abnormal growths, distortion, stunting and wilting are all signs of likely infection. Whatever the virus or viruses responsible, there is only one course to take: as with the affected dahlias, dig out the plants and burn them.

The viruses enter the plant tissues through wounds, which may be caused through careless handling or during propagation or planting, but the most likely villains are the tiny creatures that feed on plants – aphids, eelworms, whiteflies, thrips and the like.

The best defences are thorough spraying, good garden hygiene, and restocking with plants certified to be virus-free.

TWISTED GROWTH *Tattered, underdeveloped flowers indicate virus infection. So, too, do blotched leaves, stunted or distorted plant growth and wilting, as here on a tomato plant.*

WASPS

How to avoid being stung

I have a fear of being stung by wasps when picking fruit. Can I prevent this, or at least reduce the risk?

Prevention, not unusually, is the best cure. Try to find the wasps' nest, and, having done so, provided the nest is on your own property, telephone your local council's health department. The Pest Control Officer will usually destroy the nest free of charge. If you're in a hurry, call in a pest control firm who will do the job faster, but for a fee.

Wasps are rarely the first invaders of fruit. They are not often seen early in the year because they concentrate on killing insects and aphids, which they feed to their young. In return they feed on the sweet saliva produced by the larvae. Later in the year, when the queen wasp has stopped laying eggs, the wasps look for sweetness elsewhere. They generally turn to fruit only after it has already been damaged by birds, disease or insects. The wasps are attracted by the sweet smell of the juice.

To keep wasps away from the fruit, the trick is to keep the initial attackers away – by spraying against pests (see under particular pests or plants) and protecting the fruit from birds (see *Birds*, page 28). Plums and pears are particularly vulnerable; their softness makes them more liable to damage than apples, and they are much juicier.

If your problem is no greater than a few wasps on an afternoon patrol, try the old and very effective remedy of hanging a jar filled with watery jam or beer in each tree. These attract the wasps, which plunge in and drown when they cannot escape from the jar. Otherwise, wear gloves when picking fruit and have a tube of antihistamine cream to hand. This is usually all the treatment that a wasp sting requires, but if you have lasting pain or continuing swelling, consult a doctor.

Good in parts

What is the point of wasps? I've just had a picnic ruined by them and they've chewed my plums. Do they have any beneficial part to play in the scheme of things, or are they a nuisance through and through?

For most of their lives, wasps are entirely benign, and the gardener especially has good cause to be grateful to them. What happens is this. The queen mates in autumn, then hibernates until spring. Mated queens are the only wasps to survive the winter. On awakening, she seeks out a suitable nest – an old mouse hole, perhaps – and a source of dry wood, often an old fence. She chews shavings from this into a pulp which she uses to build cells in the nest. In each cell she lays an egg which hatches out a grub.

The grubs, known as larvae, are fed by the queen with chewed-up insects until they pupate, and they emerge a week or so later as worker wasps – infertile females. These female workers enlarge the nest and tend the next generation of larvae while the queen continues to lay eggs. By August, the colony will have grown to about 2000 individuals; and their effect on the garden will have been completely beneficial. The workers will have destroyed vast numbers of insect pests to feed the grubs, which in turn will have fed the workers with a sweet, sticky saliva.

Then, towards the end of August, the queen builds larger cells which hatch out male wasps and new queens. After this, she stops laying altogether, and the colony begins to deteriorate. With no grubs to feed them, the workers go off in search of other sources of sugar, at just about the time when your plums and pears are at their most succulent, when you're starting to make jam and when you're holding the last picnics of summer. You and the wasps are suffering from a clash of imperatives, which is a pity because up until now you have had interests in common.

But even as you reach for the antihistamine cream to soothe your stings, you can console yourself with the thought that the wasps' days are numbered. As the days shorten and become chillier, the workers and the males die. All that remain are the newly mated queens who go into hibernation and begin the cycle all over again.

How to destroy a nest

There's a wasps' nest burrowed deep into a bank at the bottom of my garden, and its inhabitants have been plaguing me for a long time. How do I destroy it?

With caution; wait until dusk, when the last stragglers have returned to base, before doing anything. Any wasps coming home and finding you at work on their nest are liable to attack and sting you.

Most wasp-killers on the market are powders based on carbaryl dust. Shake the powder into the entrance of the nest, according to the manufacturer's instructions, place a stone over the hole, and retire to a respectful distance. Do not be tempted to study the results of your handiwork until at least 24 hours have passed. This type of nest, a burrow in a clear and obvious place, is the only kind you should tackle. If the nest is hanging from a branch, tucked into a corner of a shed or attic, or situated in a hollow tree, you would do much better to call in the Pest Control Officer from the local council's health department, who will normally remove it for nothing, or a commercial pest control firm, who will charge.

The deceivers

There are a number of small wasps in my garden that fly in a most peculiar manner, stopping dead in mid-air for several seconds. Do these wasps sting?

They are almost certainly not wasps, but hoverflies of the genus Syrphus, and they don't sting. They certainly look like wasps, though. In fact, this is a case of animal mimicry, a not uncommon phenomenon in which one animal evolves over thousands of generations to resemble another. This particular example is one of Batesian mimicry – so called after the 19th-century British naturalist Henry Bates – in which a harmless or edible creature protects itself by coming to resemble a poisonous or dangerous one.

Thus the harmless and edible hoverfly has evolved to resemble a wasp, which birds have learned to avoid. Actually, the resemblance is fairly superficial, since, unlike a wasp, the hoverfly has only one pair of wings and no wasp waist; but the disguise is good enough to keep the birds away. Another kind of hoverfly, *Volucella bombylans*, has adapted to look like a bumblebee – not to deceive birds, but to deceive the true bumblebee in whose nest it lays its eggs. Presumably the bumblebee allows it to do this, believing it to be one of its own kind. *Volucella bombylans* lives in woodland.

The hoverflies in your garden, incidentally, should not be harmed. They, or rather their young larvae, consume vast quantities of greenfly – sap-sucking insects which damage many garden plants.

WASP *Most wasps, including the common wasp,* Vespula vulgaris, *have four wings and a distinctively small wasp waist.*

HOVERFLY *The hoverfly has a thick waist, a striped thorax and two wings fewer than a wasp. It doesn't have a sting, either.*

WATER GARDENS

How to control reedmace

I planted wild reedmace along the side of our stream. It is now spreading like wildfire and smothering all the neighbouring plants. How can I get it under control?

Reedmace is an aquatic plant widely known, incorrectly, as bulrush. It has tall grey-green leaves and bold flower spikes whose chocolate-brown poker heads are much loved by flower arrangers. There are two wild species in Britain: *Typha latifolia* and *T. angustifolia*. Both are handsome but have such a vigorous root system that they are a menace in all but the largest water gardens.

If you are planting reedmace, it is wise to go for one of the smaller species such as *T. stenophylla*, which is much more delicate both in habit and appearance. However, if a wild reedmace is already established, there is one way of controlling its spreading. Cut any new shoots below the water level. They are hollow and, filled with water, will rot away. You must keep cutting regularly, though, or clumps will soon extend their frontiers again.

Winter interest

My bog garden looks flat and dead in winter. What can I do to give it a bit of interest at that time of year?

Shrubs can give you both height and colour – and there are several that don't mind getting their feet wet. The obvious choices are the brightly stemmed varieties of cornus, or dogwood. They will grow to well over 8ft if left to themselves. But to obtain the most vivid stems, you should cut them to the ground each spring, just as the buds begin to break. The best are *Cornus alba* 'Sibirica', which has coral-coloured stems, the bright red-stemmed *C. a.* 'Westonbirt', and *C. stolonifera* 'Flaviramea', whose winter bark is a bright greeny-yellow.

Finally, you might consider the swamp cypress *Taxodium distichum*. This is a remarkable conifer – partly because it is deciduous, and partly because it relishes wet ground and will even grow standing in water. The foliage turns a bright orange-brown in autumn, and though these trees eventually attain heights of more than 30ft, they take many years to do so.

Stabilising a bank

A fast-moving stream flows through the bottom of our garden which is fine apart from the erosion of the banks when the stream swells after rain. Are there any plants that might help to hold the soil together?

Many plants are capable of stabilising the banks – the problem is getting them established. The best solution is usually to cover the banks with strong wire netting, using sturdy pegs to hold it down. Plants can then be pushed through the mesh, and once their roots intermingle they will help to withstand further erosion.

To make a dense, impenetrable carpet, put in the common brooklime, *Veronica beccabunga*; water mint, *Mentha aquatica*; or creeping jenny, *Lysimachia nummularia*. Spread soil over the netting at planting time. Once the bank has been stabilised, you can cut holes here and there in the netting to put in larger plants purely for ornament.

It is generally better to use plants with ready-developed root systems, rather than trying to plant unrooted cuttings. But there is one exception. If you have a longish stretch of bank, it is a good idea to establish willows at regular intervals to strengthen it. These will root very happily from cuttings pushed through the wire and into the soil. Good varieties include *Salix alba* 'Chermesina' and *S. daphnoides*. Both can be cut back hard in February to encourage the growth of brightly coloured young stems.

Changing water levels

The stream in our garden has very changeable water levels. Under normal circumstances the water is little more than 6in deep, but it rises by over 3ft after heavy rains. Grass grows on the banks happily enough, but I've had difficulty establishing other plants.

Widely fluctuating water levels present special problems. When the water line is liable to shift at any minute, you can never be sure where young plants can safely be placed. The use of netting along the sides of the stream will prevent gradual soil erosion (see *Stabilising a bank*, this page); but it cannot protect plants against drowning or being washed away in sudden flood.

There are however a few species which if sown on a moist patch of soil by the water's edge, quickly form flowering plants, and don't mind being covered by water for a while.

Best for this purpose probably are the mimulus family. Go for the brightly coloured hybrids derived from *Mimulus luteus* and *M. cupreus*. They need no prepared seedbed. Just sow the seeds where they are to flower, during late April or May. Though the plants rarely grow more than 18in high, they are memorable for their pouched blossoms of yellow, orange or red often spotted and splashed with brown. Despite their tropical appearance, many of these hybrids can be relied on to survive the winter.

Water plantains can be sown in the same way and will quickly colonise large areas. *Alisma plantago-aquatica* is the most popular.

Another group of plants you might try are the arrowheads. One of the best species is the white-flowered *Sagittaria japonica*. It comes in two forms: single and double.

An excellent choice too for this situation is the flowering rush, *Butomus umbellatus*. It is not; in fact, a true rush, though it resembles one. Growing from a hard rootstock, it is a narrow-leaved perennial with bold, rose-pink flower clusters. Tiny bulbils cluster along the stem, and planting is simply a matter of pushing rootstock or bulbils into the wet soil in their flowering position.

Damage by ducks

Wild ducks from a local park sometimes visit our garden. We like to see them, but they have damaged some of our water plants. Are there any kinds we could plant which would be safe?

Ducks eat a wide range of aquatic plants – and they do damage, too, by trampling on them. Young and newly established plants are most at risk, and if you want to grow any of the showier water plants you would be wisest to shoo the ducks away. However, if you like to see your feathered visitors, the rushes, sedges and grasses are usually safe, and many are decorative as well.

One of the finest waterside grasses is *Glyceria aquatica* 'Variegata', a handsome plant which grows up to 3ft tall. The foliage is cream and green, with a rich pink tinge when the first growth appears in spring. The plant also flowers, but the plumes are rather sparse and not particularly interesting. *Typha stenophylla*, one of the reedmaces, is another sturdy, almost duck-proof plant.

Ducks can do a lot of damage to water lilies. But pond lilies of the genus nuphar, which often grow wild, are very resistant. Their little yellow flowers are not as attractive as those of true water lilies – the nymphaeas – but their floating pads are just as pleasing as those of the grander species.

All water gardens need submerged oxygenating plants (for suggestions, see *Oxygenating plants*, page 263). Most of them will be safe from ducks. But wild ducks, mallards, are basically dabblers, or surface feeders, so you should avoid the water crowfoot, *Ranunculus aquatilis*, and the water violet, *Hottonia palustris* – both of which produce floating, as well as submerged, leaves.

A poolside bog garden

I want to make a bog garden next to my pool. How can I keep it permanently moist?

It really depends on whether you have built your pool already, or whether you are starting pool and bog together from scratch.

A bog garden is a marshy area devoted to such moisture-lovers as hostas, astilbes, water irises and bog primulas. Its soil must be kept permanently damp, and starting from scratch will certainly give you fewer problems. All you have to do is make sure that your pool liner is large enough to stretch under the bog garden, too (see *Ponds and pools*, page 261). The bog garden itself should be an area dug out about a foot deep. Build a retaining wall of loose bricks or stones to separate it from the main pool. Next, put down a layer of gravel and fill the bog garden with a good peaty soil. This can be made up of the excavated soil mixed with an equal volume of coarse peat. The soil surface in the bog garden should be at least 2in above the water level in the pool. Water from the pool should now moisten the soil through the barrier; it will get soaked up and retained by the peat, but any excess will drain away.

If you have built the pool already, don't tamper with it to try to get a flow going. You will have to make the bog garden as an entirely separate unit: dug out, lined and filled with peat and soil mix as before. The lining will prevent water from draining away immediately. But you will have to water it regularly by hose or watering can if it is not to dry out through evaporation.

Dividing bog plants

Some of my bog plants have become very crowded this summer. The clumps need to be lifted and divided. Should I do it straight away? And if so, how?

Leave them for the time being. The best time to divide bog plants is in early spring when new growth is just beginning to appear.

Some bog plants have fibrous roots. Divisions can often be pulled apart by hand, or prised apart with a hand fork. Others, including astilbes, have to be dissected with a sharp knife. With these, even though the divisions end up looking like diced chunks, each will grow happily enough, provided that it has at least one strong shoot and a piece of root. Some plants, such as hostas, produce a lot of shoots and can be split up into surprisingly small units if a lot of new plants are required. Size doesn't matter; the important thing is that each piece has a shoot and some root.

The best material is usually around the edges of clumps, where growth is young and vigorous. The heart of the clump is often composed of the oldest growth, which is best discarded if space is limited.

WATERSIDE COLOUR

The shallow waters around the edge of a pool are the places for what botanists call marginal aquatic plants. The soil there should be at least 9in deep and be permanently covered by about 3in of water. With a little planning, you can have waterside colour from March right through to September. Try basing your display on some of these easy-to-grow plants.

Name	Height	Flower colour and season
Alisma plantago-aquatica	3-3½ft	Pinkish-white (June-Sept)
Butomus umbellatus	1½-2½ft	Rose-pink (July-Sept)
Calla palustris	8-10in	White (Apr-May)
Caltha palustris	12-18in	Yellow (Mar-May)
Caltha palustris 'Plena'	12in	Double, yellow (Mar-May)
Caltha polypetala	3ft	Yellow (Mar-May)
Iris laevigata	2-3ft	Blue (June)
Iris laevigata 'Alba'	2-3ft	White (June)
Iris laevigata 'Rose Queen'	2-3ft	Pink (June)
Iris laevigata 'Variegata'	2-3ft	Blue (June); variegated leaves
Menyanthes trifoliata	8-12in	White or pink (Apr-June)
Mimulus ringens	18in	Blue (June)
Myosotis scorpioides	8-10in	Blue (May-July)
Pontederia cordata	2-3ft	Blue (Aug-Sept)
Ranunculus lingua 'Grandiflora'	2-3ft	Yellow (May-June)
Sagittaria japonica	1½-2ft	White (July-Sept)

WEEDS

Elder in a border

What is the best way of getting rid of ground elder in a well-established herbaceous border?

If the weed is not widespread, it can be killed by painting the leaves with a chemical called glyphosate. This is available as a gel, complete with applicator brush. The effect will start to show in a week to ten days. The chemical is not effective through roots, so any falling on the soil will be harmless, but be careful not to touch the topgrowth of cultivated plants.

If the infestation is extensive, and particularly if the ground elder has grown up among the crowns of plants, it would be quicker and cheaper to dig up the whole area, removing the weed as you go, and at the same time taking the opportunity of dividing the herbaceous plants for replanting or discarding. Before replanting, though, wait for three or four weeks to allow any stray roots of ground elder you've left behind to sprout. When the shoots appear, paint the young foliage with the same chemical.

Christmas trees?

On starting the basic digging in a neglected border of our new home, I found shoots like miniature Christmas trees with long roots. How should I deal with them?

This is a weed commonly called horsetail. Botanically it's a species of equisetum, several of which invade gardens. Horsetail is a very primitive, ancient plant, and the shoots can grow up to 2ft tall, so that a clump can look like a small forest.

The deep roots, really underground stems, are wide-ranging, and breaking off a shoot above ground merely stimulates dormant buds on the roots into growth. That's why gardeners so often find that the more they cut the weed back, the worse the problem gets. Horsetail is a spore-bearing plant, like a fern, not a flowering plant. But it spreads chiefly by extending the underground stems, not by distributing spores.

Control is difficult. With small patches, quick removal of the shoots while still tiny will prevent the weed spreading and in time will destroy it. Alternatively, try spraying with glyphosate, repeating if necessary since it is not easy to get a good cover on the needle-like leaves. Try, also, mixing 1 pint of paraffin with every 3 pints of glyphosate spray; the paraffin helps to break down the waxy coating on the leaves and lets more of the chemical in.

When digging, as in your case, remove and destroy all the roots you can find. If you can then leave the ground fallow for a season, any missed roots will sprout and you can spray them or dig them out.

How to tell weedkillers apart

I'm confused by all the weedkillers on the market. What are the real differences, and do I need them all?

There are three main types of weedkiller: contact weedkillers, which are applied to the leaves; 'translocated' or systemic types, which are mainly applied to the leaves but also sometimes work by being absorbed through the roots; and residual types, which are applied to the soil.

There are also total weedkillers, which may be absorbed through the leaves, roots or the soil, but which kill all plants – weeds or cultivated.

Contact weedkillers, such as paraquat, kill only the leaves they actually touch.

Translocated or systemic weedkillers such as glyphosate, 2,4-D and mecoprop are absorbed either through the leaves or roots, then circulated in the plant via the sap so that the entire plant dies.

These weedkillers are also called 'selective' weedkillers because they affect only broad-leaved plants, or narrow-leaved plants such as grasses – not both.

Residual weedkillers are applied to the soil and must be absorbed into the roots. They remain effective for up to a year. Into this category come sodium chlorate, dichlobenil, simazine, and atrazine.

Many proprietary weedkillers contain the same chemical under different brand names, and you are unlikely to need more than two or three. Paraquat and glyphosate are probably the most generally useful to the gardener. Sodium chlorate kills almost all plants but tends to creep sideways in the soil – making it risky to use near cultivated plants. Simazine lasts longer in clean soil and stays put.

Airborne invaders

An enormous number of seedlings are coming up all over my garden in the spring. They have two small leaves 1in long and then two larger ones, heart-shaped with toothed edges and one end pointed. The young leaves are reddish-green. What are they?

The seedlings are likely to be those of the sycamore (*Acer pseudoplatanus*), a fast-growing tree which produces winged seeds in late spring.

The seeds can be carried long distances by the wind. Their germination rate is almost 100 per cent and their growth is such that one seedling can be 12in high by autumn, with a correspondingly deep taproot, and a well-established, 2-3ft high sapling by the second autumn.

It's therefore important to get rid of the seedlings while they are still small and loosely rooted. Look for them lurking at the base of shrubs and roses – along with seedlings of ash, hawthorn and oak. If you find you have great numbers of seedlings growing on your flowerbeds, paraquat spray will kill them, but keep it away from the topgrowth of cultivated plants.

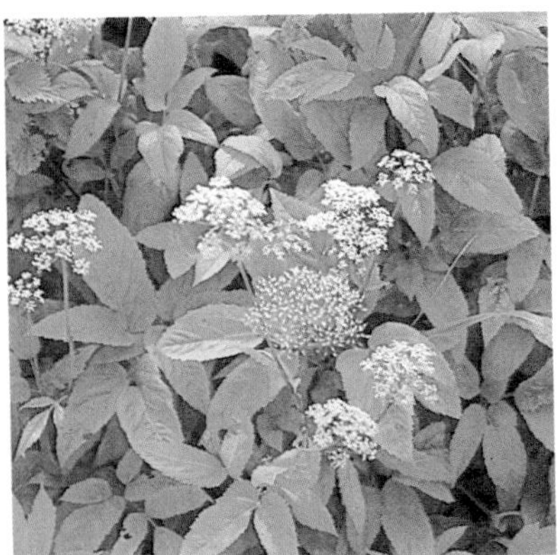

GROUND ELDER *Treat with glyphosate gel.*

HORSETAIL *Control is difficult. Try digging.*

FIELD WOODRUSH *Healthy grass will control it.*

Coarse and hairy

After a wet winter I find a kind of coarse grass growing in my lawn. The fine grasses become thin, and this tufty growth appears to be spreading. What can I do?

Your coarse and unwelcome visitor is probably field woodrush, *Luzula campestris*, which likes soils that are wet and acid and short of nutrients. It has stiff leaves about $\frac{1}{8}$in wide, 1-2in long and with a fringe of long hairs. If allowed to grow, the plant develops clusters of brownish flowers.

Grass in good condition will compete successfully with it, so regular feeding, aeration and top-dressing will help to keep it down, especially as it cannot survive regular mowing. Mecoprop, found in many proprietary lawn weedkillers, will have some effect. But if the infestation is small, it is often quicker to remove it by hand, and to reseed bare patches at once.

How to get rid of chickweed

I am thinking of sowing a few vegetables in my thriving bed of chickweed. What will stand the competition?

If you have no vegetables growing there at the moment, the chickweed can easily be killed by spraying with a solution of paraquat. If the spraying is done in bright sunlight, the weeds will start to die at once, and as soon as they are all dead the bed can be sown or planted, because the weedkiller is inactivated on reaching the soil and has no effect on roots.

Paraquat is useful for controlling both annual and perennial weeds. Groundsel, shepherd's purse, petty spurge, plantain, white clover and hairy bittercress will all yield to it, particularly if they're sprayed while they're still young.

Try to spray any or all of these weeds before they flower. Once a weed flowers it will seed itself rapidly – and that means you'll have to spray all over again.

Tangled in bindweed

Can you tell me how to get rid of bindweed growing among blackcurrants and gooseberries?

Bindweed, *Calystegia sepium*, is a perennial, climbing, native plant with attractive, trumpet-shaped white flowers. It also has deeply penetrating, white, brittle roots, which when broken off readily grow into new plants.

That's the bad news. The good news is that it responds well to glyphosate. Among blackcurrants and gooseberries, the best method is to paint individual leaves of bindweed with glyphosate gel as soon as the weed starts to grow vigorously in spring. Be careful not to contaminate the topgrowth of the fruit bushes. Don't try digging out the bindweed; you will never get rid of the roots, and you will damage the bushes. If the infestation is particularly severe, you may need to repeat the treatment a month later.

Killing couch

Is there a way of getting rid of couch grass once and for all? I've tried everything including sieving every inch of soil, but it always comes back.

Couch grass (*Elymus repens*), also called twitch grass, scutch, or wicks, is a native British grass which spreads rapidly by its white, creeping underground stems. Even 1in pieces broken off will root again.

Its sharp-pointed roots can penetrate right into the centre of a plant and can in time become so mixed up with it that you may have to tear the whole lot apart to get all the roots and stems out.

There are three weapons available that might help you to gain the upper hand. Toughest is glyphosate, a chemical which acts through the leaves and is taken right down to the roots. By way of a bonus, it kills a lot of other weeds as well, and, for a drawback, a good many cultivated plants, too. So be careful when using it round the borders. Glyphosate-based weedkillers may be bought as liquid concentrates for spraying, as gel for brushing on weeds among plants, and as a weed-wiper that can be brushed onto weeds growing in borders. When using glyphosate in the vegetable garden, allow two or three weeks between spraying and cultivating, planting or sowing, to give the couch time to die.

Dalapon will kill couch and other annual and perennial grasses, too. This also acts through the leaves, and it has an advantage in that you can use it among fruit and some vegetables, provided you are careful to follow the instructions on the label. Watch out for wind-drift when spraying among established plants; dalapon can damage their foliage. You will be able to begin cultivating vegetable beds or new lawns ten days after spraying, but at least 12 weeks must elapse before you can sow or plant.

Another option you could consider is to use alloxydim sodium, a grass weedkiller that may be sprayed among other plants with impunity, since the chemical will have no effect upon them. It attacks only couch grass, and then only at the young leaf stage of growth. Therefore, it's the ideal weapon in situations where the couch has become entangled among shrubs and perennials.

So, on an empty allotment, new border or lawn site occupied by many different weeds including couch, use glyphosate to kill them all, and begin sowing or planting soon afterwards. Among fruit bushes, or on ground where couch or other grasses are a problem, use dalapon.

In the border, or where the couch is strangling plants and cannot be treated separately, use alloxydim sodium.

Of course, none of these or other weedkillers are sold under their chemical names, though those names will appear somewhere on the label. For the brand names of products containing these chemicals, see *Choosing the right weedkiller*, page 368.

In future, if you want to keep couch out of a particular area – beside a couch-infested lawn, say – set up a physical barrier such as a lawn edging or a concrete drainage gully. Provided the barrier extends at least 6in underground, the shallow roots of the couch should be unable to get beneath it.

BINDWEED *Digging won't help; use glyphosate.*

COUCH GRASS *Try dalapon or alloxydim sodium.*

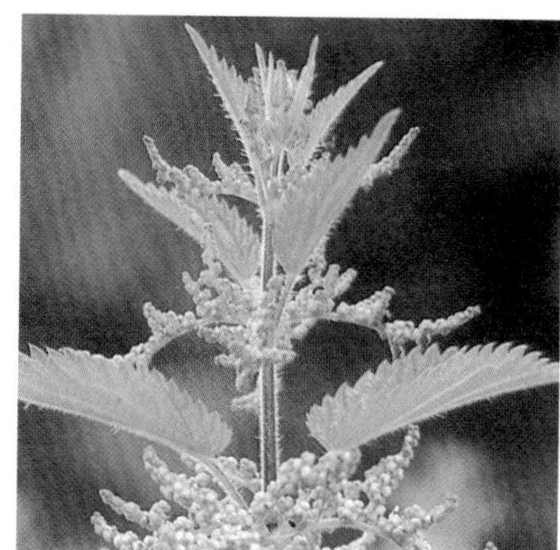

NETTLES *Pull up annuals before they flower.*

Grasping the nettles

Our strawberry patch has been invaded by nettles. Any suggestions?

If they are the annual nettles, pull them up – wearing gloves, of course – in mid-spring while they're still young and before they flower. Perennial nettles have spreading tenacious yellow roots, and are better painted with glyphosate gel, also while they're young. Try to catch them when they're about 8-10in tall. Once the nettles are dead, spread a 1-2in thick mulch of compost, straw or peat round the strawberries to smother any more seedlings.

Clearing a mess

I recently took over an allotment which had been disused for years. It's infested with dock, nettles, coarse grass and brambles. What's the best way to clear it up?

The quickest way is a blanket spray with glyphosate. Pick a windless day so that the spray does not drift onto your neighbour's cultivated patch. To be effective, the spray has to fall on the leaves and stems. So, if the weed cover is very dense, a second spray may be necessary after the top layer has withered.

The cheapest way would be to cut the topgrowth down by hand, then dig the ground, clearing out weeds and roots as you go. You can destroy them by digging them in – provided you bury them at least 10in down – but the taprooted weeds such as dock and dandelion are better removed and burnt or composted. A mechanical cultivator will do the job more quickly, but it's less cheap and it has the drawback that many of the cut weeds will re-root. Brambles will have to be dug out anyway.

As to which of these methods is better, that's up to you. But remember one cautionary thought whichever method you pick: a plot that's been neglected as long as yours will be alive with weed seeds, many of which will germinate as a result of your initial onslaught. Be prepared, therefore, for a tough couple of years until you get them under control.

Clearing the pond

The surface of our pond is covered in a tiny light green leaf and there are masses of bits of green, hairlike material in the water. How can these be removed without harming the pond plants?

The leaf covering your pond is likely to be duckweed (*Lemna minor*), while the hairlike substance is an alga – probably blanket weed, silk weed or flannel weed. Chemicals would kill them, but would also damage the cultivated pond plants and fish.

The best method of control for duckweed is either a child's shrimping net or careful raking, repeated regularly – as often as once a week, if necessary – during the summer. Blanket weed is best removed by hand, because it is often tangled up with other plants. Both weeds make good compost-heap material.

To keep algae at bay in future years, add more oxygenating plants such as the Canadian pondweed, *Elodea canadensis*; it will help to starve out algae by competing with them for food and light.

A clear, clean drive

As spring advances, so do the weeds, making my drive ever more forlorn. Is there a way of getting rid of them without harming some long-established shrubs and perennials along the edges of the drive?

The ideal time to begin treatment is in March or April, before the weeds get started. The construction of your drive will determine whether you should use a liquid or a granular weedkiller. On a hard surface – stone, say, or tarmac where the weeds come up through the cracks – it's best to use a liquid spray that will penetrate all the crannies. On gravel and other loose surfaces, granules are better, for they will more readily work down into and among the small stones. Most weedkillers are available in both liquid and granular forms, but their chemical constituents work in different ways. Some, like simazine and dichlobenil, act on weeds only at the germination stage. Others, such as aminotriazole and atrazine, attack weeds at both the germinating and growing periods of their lives. Go for a brand of proprietary weedkiller that contains both kinds of ingredients.

Whatever you do, don't use sodium chlorate in your situation. It will certainly clear the drive, but it may then be washed off into the soil, where it may creep sideways and devastate the front garden.

The right time

I put a combined weed-and-feed dressing on my lawn in June, but the only effect was to turn the grass brown. What was wrong?

Probably the timing. You need the soil to be moist and the grass and weeds growing well in warm temperatures – conditions most likely in middle to late spring. In a hot, dry summer spell, growth is slow or non-existent, and weedkillers will hardly be absorbed. The result: an excessive concentration of chemical on or under the surface of the grass, leading to the scorched look.

Next time, spread the dressing in spring or, if you must do it in summer, during a spell of rainy weather. Alternatively, water the lawn thoroughly first.

Plant and let die

Is it true that there are plants that will kill weeds?

Yes. Some plants, such as marigolds, do seem to secrete substances from their roots that act as weedkillers on some persistent weeds such as couch grass and bindweed. Moreover, a blanket of any ground-cover plant can kill most weed seedlings by denying them light, moisture and nutrients.

Four kinds of marigold are widely claimed to be able to kill weeds by secreting chemicals: the French marigold and the African

DUCKWEED *Skim from ponds with a net or rake.*

OXALIS *Dig it out with its rootball intact.*

YELLOW DOCK *Good for the skin, say herbalists.*

marigold, both annual plants and both species of tagetes; a related plant, *Tagetes minuta*; and the English or pot marigold, which is a species of calendula.

Most of the ideas about the power of these and other plants to kill weeds come from people who claim that it works for them. As yet, there is no formal scientific confirmation of this power but, given the increasing interest in chemical-free gardening, it can only be a matter of time before researchers – amateur and professional – explore a view that so many gardeners already accept.

Harrassed by yarrow

Can you help with a weed in my lawn? The roots are tough, and the dark green leaves are feathery. They lie flat to form a matted patch, effectively preventing the grass from growing.

You have given an exact description of yarrow, *Achillea millefolium*. When not growing in a lawn it has a basal rosette of leaves, from the centre of which grows a flowering stem 12-18in tall, topped by a cluster of tiny white flowers. If there are only a few patches, deal with them by slashing through the roots in a crisscross fashion with a sharp knife and clear the debris.

Larger areas should be sprayed with the hormone weedkiller 2,4-D or mecoprop. Repeat the treatment if the weed reappears. The best time for action is early May. Daisies can be dealt with in the same way.

Weeding among vegetables

What can I do to give my vegetables a better start when weed seedlings among them grow so much faster?

Try digging the ground over thoroughly some weeks before you plan to sow vegetables. Leave it fallow and, when the weeds germinate, hoe them off, repeating the process every few days until the vegetables need to be sown. If you can leave the plot fallow for a whole summer, hoeing it regularly should eliminate practically all the weeds, except those that blow in, without the need to use chemicals at all.

Growing early potatoes will also help, because the regular cultivation they need in the early stages will ensure destruction of nearby weeds (for details on how to care for potatoes, see *Potatoes*, page 264). Or consider using a mulch of black plastic, cutting slits in it to plant your vegetables through, while denying light and air to the weeds.

If the weed seedlings form a clearly defined cover between the rows, you could use a chemical method: paraquat. Use a dribble bar to apply the chemical. If you use a spray gun, some is bound to get onto the vegetables as well, and it will kill them.

How to stamp out colt's-foot

I have a grassy bank overrun by a weed which has large, rounded leaves, toothed at the edges and white underneath, with yellow flowers in late February. How can I clear it out and plant some shrubs?

This is likely to be colt's-foot, *Tussilago farfara*. It's extremely difficult to control because of its creeping stems. A blanket spray with glyphosate when the weed is in full leaf will deal with most of it, and a further treatment with a gel should wipe it out – this is essential before you plant shrubs.

The great escaper

In one of my flowerbeds is a weed with a pretty clover-like leaf and sometimes pinkish-purple flowers. As fast as I dig it up it reappears, and I despair of ever getting rid of it. Can it be kept under control?

The plant is likely to be a garden 'escape' weed, *Oxalis corymbosa*. It was introduced to Britain from South America and the Far East as an ornamental plant. These days it is often found in the gardens of old town houses where the soil has been cultivated for many years and there is shelter and warmth.

It has a fat translucent taproot 1-1½in long, with clusters of tiny brown-skinned bulbils. The bulbils – immature bulbs – are easily knocked off by hand weeding and will quickly root if not removed. In fact, hand weeding has to be so careful that you should dig up the weed complete with its lump of soil and put it all in the dustbin. Otherwise spray with glyphosate while there is plenty of leaf present, and be prepared to treat dormant bulbils as they come to life – maybe for the next year or two.

How to put helxine out of business

A thick mat of a plant with tiny, green round leaves and brittle stems keeps forming on my rockery and is invading the lawn at its foot. How can I get rid of it?

Mind-your-own-business (*Helxine soleirolii*) seems to be the name of your trouble. This apparently fragile weed spreads by rooting at the leaf joints, and when the brittle stems break off, the roots are often left behind to sprout again. You can kill it with paraquat or glyphosate. If you pull it out by hand, don't compost it; it can start growing in the heap. Throw it away or burn it.

Unprecious pearl

The spaces between slabs on my patio are infested with a sort of moss. It's dark green with thin thread-like stems, 1-2in long and lying flat on the ground. What should I do?

This sounds like a weed called pearlwort, *Sagina procumbens*. It is also frequently found on lawns. Superficially it is like moss, with its thready stems forming a matted patch. But close examination will show that it has small round green balls attached to the stems, from which come minute white flowers. These flowers quickly produce seed, and since the plant can flower all year round and germinate even in a mild winter, it can go on spreading right round the calendar. Pearlwort also roots along its stems, so it quickly colonises even areas unsuitable for other weeds. Paraquat and diquat spray will

COLT'S-FOOT *Spray and paint with glyphosate.*

MIND-YOUR-OWN-BUSINESS *Treat with paraquat.*

PEARLWORT *Spray with paraquat and diquat.*

deal with it. The spray is best applied from a dribble bar attached to a watering can. Or use a knife to lever up the roots from between the cracks.

Making a weed-free lawn

My lawn is green – but mostly on account of the weeds in it. Would you advise killing the weeds and re-seeding, or digging it all up and starting again?

To kill the weeds without killing the grass, you'll have to use a hormone weedkiller such as 2,4-D or mecoprop. These affect the germination of grass seed, though, so you would have to wait at least four weeks to sow new grass if you used 2,4-D and until the following spring if you used mecoprop. It might be better to kill both grass and weeds with a paraquat and diquat mixture. You can then dig over the ground and re-seed in a matter of days.

If time is not so important, dig up the entire lawn, taking the grass and weeds off as turves and stacking them upside down in a heap to rot into loam. You can sow the new lawn at once and, in a year or so, you'll have a sizable quantity of weed-free compost which you can spread on the borders or brush into the lawn.

Both these options will give you the chance to start your lawn again from scratch. But if they sound like an awful lot of work – and they are – there is a third alternative. Simply leave the lawn as it is and mow it – closely, regularly and at least once a week. In time, the weeds will be weakened by the constant cutting and the grass will be able to fight back. It may take several years to get the weeds down to the point where you can attack them individually, and you will never get a top-quality lawn, but you will have a perfectly serviceable family play area.

Paving the way

We would like to clear an area where we propose to build a patio and ensure weeds do not grow through after the paving is laid. Can you recommend a weedkiller?

Clear the area with a mix of paraquat and diquat for annual and small weeds, or with glyphosate or dichlobenil for perennial weeds. If the weeds are the kind with tenacious and creeping roots, such as ground elder, you may need to repeat the application. Paraquat and diquat, and glyphosate, should be sprayed onto the leaves and stems; dichlobenil is absorbed through the roots and so must be dissolved in the soil moisture.

Sodium chlorate is a much riskier chemical to use. It can 'creep' horizontally through the soil into any adjacent flowerbed and lawn – killing everything it touches. Remember that all the roots, as well as the topgrowth, have to be destroyed, or there will be trouble after the paving is down.

When the weeds are dead, water the area with a solution of simazine, which will kill any weed seeds trying to germinate, and this will be effective for at least 12 months. Simazine has the advantage that it stays exactly where it is put. It does not leach through the soil or 'creep' sideways.

Weeds can be useful

I remember as a child how dock leaves were used for rubbing on nettle stings. Do other weeds have any positive uses like that?

Yes, they do. Nettles themselves make first-class compost. Fresh nettles added to rainwater and left for a few weeks make a good fertiliser for plants; and young nettle leaves can be cooked and eaten like spinach.

A cover of annual weeds actually helps – like any other mulch – to keep the soil moist in hot weather and, if the weeds are dug in before they flower, provides a valuable 'green manure'. As for the old belief in docks as an antidote to nettles, there does seem to be some medical basis for it. Both *Rumex obtusifolius* (broad-leaved dock) and *R. crispus* (yellow dock) are used by modern herbalists to treat some skin complaints.

Guarding your fruit

We grow all our own soft fruits, but the battle against weeds such as thistles, docks and creeping buttercups is never-ending. What do the professionals do?

On commercial plantations of bush and cane fruits and strawberries, the ground is cleared completely of weeds before planting, with a blanket spray of a total weedkiller such as glyphosate or dichlobenil, and kept clear after planting with simazine.

In your case, where the weeds are already present, the best method would be to kill the weeds with glyphosate, painting on the gel form of the chemical to avoid damage to your fruit. Once the weeds are dead, either keep the ground clear with a heavy covering of peat or well-rotted garden compost, or use simazine at the strength recommended by the manufacturer.

Weeds for wildlife

What kinds of wild plants would it make sense for me to encourage for the sake of butterflies, bees and other insects, and provide shelter for hedgehogs, frogs and perhaps birds? How can I create a mini-conservation area?

What we call weeds – and 'weed', after all, simply means any plant you don't want in a particular spot – are often native or wild plants. And often they are very attractive to Britain's native creatures such as bees, butterflies and other insects. Scabious, for instance, lady's-smock, foxglove, primrose and honeysuckle are all big crowd-pullers in the insect world. Native grasses left to flower and seed will attract a second collection of insects and, if the mixture is allowed to grow naturally, it will in time provide shelter for hedgehogs and other small mammals such as mice, voles and shrews.

If you have a pond you may have frogs, tadpoles and newts. Birds will be attracted by suitable nesting sites – for instance, in well-established honeysuckle or hawthorn – anywhere, in fact, where there are lots of twiggy shoots well covered by foliage. Food-providing plants such as elder, the guelder rose, the spindle, blackberries and the wayfaring tree attract birds as well. Numerous other plants will attract butterflies and moths (see *Butterflies*, page 38).

To create such a conservation area you can obtain special seed mixtures from specialist seedsmen. Prepare the soil in the same way as for any seedbed and, once germination has begun, try to ensure that the stronger species do not swamp the others. Try to provide shelter round the edges and take advantage of already established bushes and trees.

For more suggestions about ways of turning all or part of your garden into a haven for native British plants and animals, see *Wild gardens*, page 370.

Weeding without chemicals

Weedkillers are expensive these days – especially if they don't work properly. Is there a cheaper alternative?

In general, the cheaper alternatives are more time-consuming. Mulching is a useful way of keeping weeds at bay and, if there are weeds present already, you can choke out the small ones at least by covering with a thick blanket of a mulch such as rotted garden compost, peat or spent mushroom compost. The mulch must cover the weeds completely; even the smallest part exposed to light will enable them to live and spread. Black plastic sheeting is also effective as a mulch. Lay it around existing plants or spread it over the whole of an unplanted area and set your plants in the ground through slits you cut in it. Bury its edges to keep out all light.

Grassing and then regularly mowing an area infested with weeds will eventually eradicate them, since they cannot withstand the constant removal of topgrowth. Digging them in at least 6in deep will also kill them. But weeds whose roots extend widely, such as bindweed, couch grass and ground elder, may cause more trouble if they're buried. Deal with them instead by digging them out individually or by treating them with a systemic chemical such as glyphosate.

Hoeing seedlings out is a job best done on a sunny day; in damp weather some might re-root themselves.

Finally, to keep weeds at bay – at least in a flowerbed or shrub border – never leave bare soil where a weed is removed. Put or sow a cultivated plant immediately in the space to help to deny any passing wind-blown weed seed the chance of a new home.

Safety control

What effects do weedkillers have on the soil? I'm worried about my vegetables absorbing potentially harmful chemicals?

All weedkillers break down in the soil over varying periods, depending on the chemicals they contain. During those periods, they can be a danger. But the packet will specify any minimum time you should leave between spraying and harvesting. As time goes by, all weedkillers gradually disperse and disintegrate. Unlike some toxic metals, such as mercury, they don't accumulate in your vegetables or in you.

Besides, all weedkillers on the market have to pass stringent government safety tests before they can legally be sold. Provided you use a weedkiller precisely as directed, it won't harm your plants, your pets or you.

Eliminating suckers

In my lawn some shoots appear to be sprouting from tree roots close to the surface. Even if they are mown off small, new ones take their place. How can I stop this happening?

The shoots are suckers from tree roots close to or at the surface, or from trees which are particularly vigorous. Poplar, cherry, plum and willow are prone to this. The safest way to stop the suckers is to twist or tear them off at their point of origin, though they may reappear at other spots. Spraying with paraquat or 2,4-D will kill the suckers, but it might also damage the parent.

What's in a name?

I never know the names of weeds, but does it matter? Surely I can use any weedkiller on any weed and get results?

You will get results of a kind, but in many cases the results won't amount to adequate control. Of course it isn't essential to know the name of every weed that appears. Provided you know how a particular weedkiller works, and the type of weed it deals with, you can cope even with unknown weeds.

Weeds can be divided into two groups – those which spread mainly by seed, and those which reproduce vegetatively. The seed-spreaders are mostly annuals: plants which germinate, flower and die in one growing season (such as chickweed, speedwell and groundsel). A few are perennials – dock and dandelion, for instance.

Weeds which spread vegetatively tend to be much more persistent. They have long creeping roots or underground stems – colt's-foot and bindweed, for example – or above-ground stems which root at leaf joints – such as creeping buttercup, cinquefoil and clover. Or they may have corms or bulbs like lesser celandine and oxalis.

So any plant which is small and easily pulled up is likely to be an annual or a young perennial, and it can be killed with paraquat. Anything which is difficult to pull up, and which proves to have masses of root, swollen roots or bulbs is perennial and needs treating with a systemic weedkiller such as glyphosate, dichlobenil or mecoprop. Plants with grass-like leaves need a specialist chemical: diquat for annual grasses; and dalapon for couch grass and similar perennial species.

Carry on fighting

I clean up my weeds every autumn, but by the end of March there is a thriving cover, especially in the vegetable garden. Are there any short cuts in dealing with them?

Weeds are mostly native plants, so they have a built-in resistance to hard winters. Many also produce seed which is shed in late summer and autumn and germinates between then and the following spring. When weeding in autumn, try to remove every single specimen, however tiny and newly germinated. It is the ones you miss that will develop insidiously for the rest of the autumn and in mild spells in winter to produce a mat of new growth in spring.

The best ways to limit the problem are to hoe every few weeks during winter, to put down a residual weedkiller such as simazine, or to use a mulch such as black plastic sheeting, peat or a thick layer of bracken.

Vulnerable daffodils

I'd like to use a selective weedkiller early on in spring on my lawn, but will it harm the naturalised daffodils growing there?

Yes. A selective weedkiller such as 2,4-D or mecoprop, designed for use on lawns, should in theory not affect bulbs because they are, in botanical terms, narrow-leaved plants. In practice, however, it will because the leaves are broad enough to absorb a significant amount of the chemical. Moreover, because these weedkillers can remain in the soil for considerable lengths of time, they can affect the bulbs directly, causing distorted flowers, no flowers or even death.

For these reasons, never use this type of weedkiller anywhere near your bulbs – and don't use it at all unless the leaves are up and you can see precisely where the bulbs are. Far better to avoid spraying with any selective weedkiller and to go instead for a spot weeder, which you can paint directly onto the weed leaves. The job will take longer, but your daffodils will be safe.

Spot weeding

How can I spray small patches of weed in the lawn without harming the nearby rosebeds?

The best way is to 'spot' treat them. This ensures that the weedkiller is applied directly to each patch, and that there is no risk of spray drift. Spot treatment can be with an aerosol form of 2,4-D and mecoprop, in which the nozzle of the aerosol is aimed at a few inches' range directly at the centre of the weed patch.

Otherwise one of the weedkiller 'canes' can be used, by which a solution is either squirted into the heart of the patch or wiped onto it with a chemical-soaked wick. A third, more laborious, method is to paint the gel form of glyphosate onto the patch by hand.

How to weed a hedge

The bases of my two hedges – one of privet, the other a mixture of beech and hornbeam – have been invaded by ivy and brambles. What is the best way of cleaning them out?

Weeds at the base of a hedge are often the perennial kind, such as ground elder, couch grass and perennial nettles. Ivy is a frequent interloper, saplings flourish, and brambles sprout from seed dropped by perching birds.

Control of these weeds is important, because the competition can weaken the growth of the hedge.

Forking out the weeds is one method, but it can disturb the hedge roots. So chemicals are often the best option. Before spraying, clear out all debris, such as dead twigs, large stones, rotted stumps, weak growth from the hedge, and fallen birds' nests.

Then paint glyphosate onto the young leaves of the weeds. That way, you should be able to kill even the toughest of the weeds without harming the hedge plants.

Old weeds on a new lawn

When I grew my lawn from seed, I had a lot of difficulty in eradicating weeds and getting the grass to establish. How can I prevent this on a new lawn I am planning?

Weeds germinating with the lawn grasses are inevitable. But if the area is left fallow during the summer before you sow, the weed seedlings can be hoed off as they germinate. Then, when the lawn is down, any surviving weeds will be young and less able to withstand the frequent cutting. If you can't wait, the weed seedlings can be killed as they germinate with a mixture of 2,4-D and mecoprop used at half the normal strength.

CHOOSING THE RIGHT WEEDKILLER

Where the weeds are	What the weeds are	Chemical	Trade names	Notes
Uncultivated areas, waste ground	All types of weeds	Aminotriazole, simazine	Super Weedex (Fison's)	Use only where planning not to plant for a year
		Aminotriazole, 2,4-D, diuron, simazine	Hytrol (Agrichem)	
		Aminotriazole, MCPA	Fison's New Improved Problem Weeds Killer	
		Simazine, diuron	Total Weedkiller Granules (May & Baker)	
		Sodium chlorate	Boots Sodium Chlorate Weedkiller, ICI Sodium Chlorate, Murphy Sodium Chlorate (Fison's)	Use type containing fire depressant. Do not use over tree roots. Persists for up to eight months
		Sodium chlorate, atrazine	Atlacide Extra Dusting Powder (Chipman)	As sodium chlorate but persists at least 12 months
	Grass weeds, including couch grass	Dalapon	Couch and Grass Killer (Synchemicals), Herbon Dalapon (Atlas Interlates)	Persists about three months
		Alloxydim sodium	Weed Out (May & Baker)	Persists two or three months
	Woody weeds, ivy, sucker growths from old tree stumps	Ammonium sulphamate	Amcide (Albright and Wilson)	Persists two or three months
		2,4-D, mecoprop, dicamba	New Formula SBK (Synchemicals)	Persists about three months
Paths	Germinating weeds, moss	Simazine	Weedex (Fison's)	Apply in early spring. Effective for several months
	All types of weeds	Paraquat/diquat, simazine, aminotriazole	Pathclear (ICI)	Apply in early spring. Effective for several months
		Aminotriazole, MCPA, simazine	Fison's Path Weedkiller	
		Aminotriazole, atrazine	Murphy Path Weedkiller (Fison's)	
		Aminotriazole, MCPA	Fison's Path Spot Weedkiller	
Fruit	Established annuals	Diquat/paraquat	Weedol (ICI)	
	Germinating weeds, established annuals and perennials	Dichlobenil	Casoron G4 (Synchemicals)	Apply in early spring. At rates safe to use, some weeds are only checked
		Glyphosate	Murphy Tumbleweed, Murphy Tumbleweed Gel, Murphy Tumbleweed Ready to Use (Fison's)	Do not use among soft fruit. Keep solution or gel off topgrowth of fruit trees. Prevent drift
	Grass weeds, including couch grass	Dalapon	Couch and Grass Killer (Synchemicals) Herbon Dalapon (Atlas Interlates)	Use in winter only
		Alloxydim sodium	Weed Out (May & Baker)	Use in winter only. Persists two or three months
New or understocked garden pools	Green algae			No safe chemical control. Establish a natural balance of water plants, fish and molluscs (see *Ponds and pools*, page 261, and *Water gardens*, page 360)

CHOOSING THE RIGHT WEEDKILLER

Where the weeds are	What the weeds are	Chemical	Trade names	Notes
Tree and shrub borders	Established annual weeds and small perennials	Diquat/paraquat	Weedol (ICI)	Will not control large or well-rooted perennials
	Established perennials, established and seedling annuals	Dichlobenil	Casoron G4 (Synchemicals)	Apply early spring. Persists several months. Risk of damage with some trees and shrubs
		Glyphosate	Murphy Tumbleweed, Murphy Tumbleweed Gel, Murphy Tumbleweed Ready to Use (Fison's)	Keep solution or gel off topgrowth of trees and shrubs; prevent drift
Roses	Established perennials, established and seedling annuals	Dichlobenil	Casoron G4 (Synchemicals)	
		Glyphosate	Murphy Tumbleweed, Murphy Tumbleweed Gel, Murphy Tumbleweed Ready to Use (Fison's)	Keep solution or gel off topgrowth of roses; prevent drift
Bulbs in borders	Established annual weeds and small perennials	Diquat/paraquat	Weedol (ICI)	Use only after bulb foliage has been removed and the point of emergence covered with soil
Bulbs in turf: see Lawns	See Lawns	See Lawns	See Lawns	Minimal risk of damage if weedkiller is applied when bulbs are fully dormant
Lawns	All types of weeds	2,4-D, dicamba	Bio Lawn Weedkiller (pbi) Fison's Lawn Spot Weeder Green Up Weedfree Spot Weedkiller for Lawns (Synchemicals)	Apply in spring as grass becomes vigorous
		2,4-D, dichlorprop, mecoprop	Boots Lawn Weedkiller	
		2,4-D, mecoprop	Supertox Lawn Weed Spray (May & Baker)	
		MCPA, dicamba	Fison's Turf Weeds Killer	
		Mecoprop, 2,4-D	Verdone 2, Verdone 2 Spot Weedkiller (ICI)	
	Moss	Dichlorophen	Bio Moss Killer (pbi) Murphy Super Moss Killer and Lawn Fungicide (Fison's) Mosstox-Plus (May & Baker) Moss Gun (ICI)	Controls moss for one growing season, but cultural attention is also needed to remove the causes of moss growth (see *Lawns*, page 209)
		Chloroxuron, ferric sulphate, urea	Tumblemoss (Fison's)	As dichlorophen, but also feeds grass
	Various weeds and mosses	Ferrous sulphate heptahydrate (lawn sands)	Green Up Mossfree (Synchemicals)	Lawn sands only check weed growth; less effective than dichlorophen for moss

WHITE ROT

Eight years' quarantine

The end of my spring onions was signalled by yellow, collapsing leaves and confirmed, after I pulled up a few plants, by a fluffy white mould on the bulbs. A neighbour tells me that mouldy nose is the cause, a disease that's not only incurable, but highly infectious. Is he right?

Very much so. Mouldy nose, or as it's more usually called, white rot, is a fungal disease. It's bad at any time in the growing season, but in warm weather, among overcrowded spring onions or onion seedlings, it's a disaster. It attacks onions, leeks, shallots and garlic with near-equal enthusiasm, and there's not much you can do about it other than hauling the plants out of the ground and burning them. Nor should you plant any kind of onion in the same ground for the next eight years; the tiny black spores of the fungus will survive in the soil through at least seven winters.

Your best answer is to move your onion beds each year, and before you plant, scatter calomel in the drills. Alternatively, try drenching the soil with Armillatox.

The onion variety 'Bedfordshire Champion' is said to be fairly resistant to white rot. But you can't win; despite this advantage, the variety is very susceptible to another fungus, downy mildew.

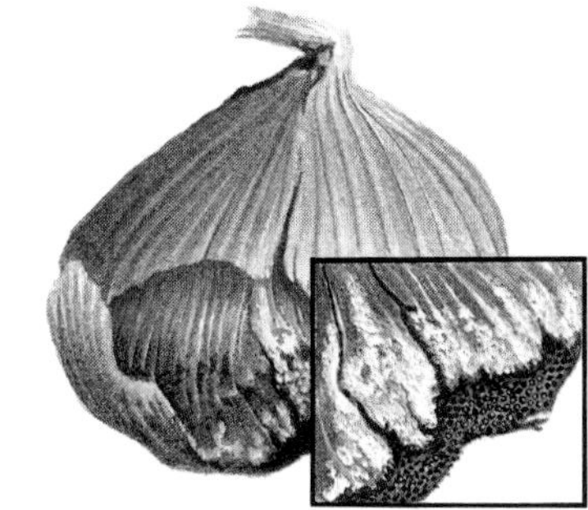

WHITE DEATH *A fluffy white fungus and rot spreading over the base and roots of onions are a sure sign of white rot, a killer disease.*

WILD GARDENS

New plot

I've just bought an old house with a neglected garden and I'd like to grow wild flowers in it. Where do I start?

With the soil. Cut down the grass and weeds in the autumn and clear them from the site. Skim off the top 2in or so of soil with the remaining plants in it and pile the clumps upside down. It's worth removing some of the surface soil in this way because garden soil, however neglected, tends to be much too rich and too fertile for most wild flowers.

Dig over the ground, removing weed roots. In three to four weeks – or in early spring if you start work late in autumn – a new crop of annual weeds and shoots from perennial weeds will appear. Wipe them out with a once-over application of a non-selective weedkiller such as glyphosate or, if you prefer, weed by hand.

Prepare the ground as if for a lawn, treading it flat and raking it. If the soil contains a lot of clay, sprinkle garden lime on at the rate of 2oz per square yard. Sow with a mix of grass and wild flower seeds. You can buy suitable seed mixtures from some garden centres or from specialist wild flower nurseries. For suggestions about suitable meadow plants for different soil types, see the charts on pages 371-3.

Add annual cornfield flower seed (for suggested varieties, see *Flowers of the cornfields*, page 375). This will help to settle your new meadow and give a spectacular first-season show when little else is in flower. Cut cornfield flowers before they set all their seed, to prevent them competing too strongly in future years with the other grassland species you've sown.

Now, back to the heap you made with the topsoil. It can be used as a raised bed to grow wild plants that need a richer soil, or for conventional garden plants. It can also be turned into a compost heap, giving valuable dressing for any fruit or vegetables you may decide to grow.

Poor – but good

I have been told that wild flowers do not need rich soil or fertilisers. Is this true?

Yes. Most wild flowers do better on relatively poor soils. The main exceptions are cornfield weeds which prefer a richer earth. Clustered bellflower (*Campanula glomerata*), for instance, is a tiny plant with huge flowers on the thin soil of chalky grasslands. But where fertilisers from neighbouring farmland drift into its environment it shrinks into a shadow of its former glory – with rank, coarse foliage and tiny, pale flowers. Herb-robert (*Geranium robertianum*) and ivy-leaved toadflax (*Cymbalaria muralis*) are at their best on a dry sunny wall, where they take on deep red or purple hues.

In rich soil, the coarse grasses drive out the finer grasses and the broad-leaved meadow plants, and dandelions and nettles crowd out less familiar species. That's why it's always worth skimming the top 2in or so of soil off any area you want to turn over to wild flowers. The flowers will thrive, you'll be spared the expense of fertiliser, and you'll have more fertile loam to use on your cultivated species.

Shallow soil

My garden has shallow soil over chalk and will grow very little. Would I have more success planting it with wild flowers?

Almost certainly. Soil over chalk – and the various types of limestone – is generally shallow, well-drained and therefore fairly dry, and with high levels of calcium compounds. It is unsuitable for most garden plants, but many native species have adapted to it, including species not found on other soils in Britain.

Plant your own meadow with species whose natural home is downland or limestone (see *Meadow plants for chalky soils*, opposite). Where you need a path, try hoary plantain (*Plantago media*), wild thyme (*Thymus drucei*) and selfheal (*Prunella vulgaris*), all of which tolerate close cutting and trampling. There is probably native chalk grassland nearby, so other species may find their way into the garden – possibly even wild orchid species, such as the early purple orchid (*Orchis mascula*), pyramidal orchid (*Anacamptis pyramidalis*) or the spectacular bee orchid (*Ophrys apifera*).

Woodland or hedgerow trees and shrubs which tolerate chalky soils include the field maple (*Acer campestre*), box (*Buxus sempervirens*) and spindle (*Euonymus europaeus*). Choose, too, climbers such as traveller's-joy (*Clematis vitalba*) and herbaceous plants like the wood anemone (*Anemone nemorosa*) and red campion (*Silene dioica*). You can also buy seed of the relatively rare oxlip (*Primula elatior*) to grow in light shade.

Informal lawn

Maintaining my large lawn has become an increasing problem. Is there a low-maintenance solution?

Try turning part or all of it into an informal lawn or wild flower meadow. To start with, just stop mowing. You may be surprised to find what is in your garden.

As well as the white flowers of daisy (*Bellis perennis*) and white clover (*Trifolium repens*), you may find the purple flowers of selfheal (*Prunella vulgaris*) and the blue of one or more speedwells (species of veronica). The lawn probably also contains less desirable dandelions (*Taraxacum officinale*) and great plantain (*Plantago major*). Change the look of the lawn with versatile grassland species such as the ox-eye daisy (*Leucanthemum vulgare*) or yarrow (*Achillea millefolium*). Remove a patch of turf in early autumn, and scatter on the exposed soil seed mixed with sharp sand. Rake and tread it in lightly.

For greater success with expensive seed, sow into prepared beds, or in seed trays using a soil-based compost. Move young plants into the lawn the following autumn, using a bulb planter. If your garden soil is fairly moist, add bought corms of meadow saffron (*Colchicum autumnale*) and fritillary (*Fritillaria meleagris*), both of them rare native species.

More ambitiously, remove a section of the turf and sow meadow plants suitable for your type of soil (see the charts on pages 371-3). In a few years, a relatively sterile lawn which needs cutting every weekend can be transformed into a flower-rich meadow needing only a few cuts each year.

Making a hedgerow

I am tired of clipping an uninteresting hedge to keep it in shape. Is there another way of dealing with it, other than grubbing it out?

Turn it into a hedgerow, and create a whole new wildlife world in your garden. Let some of the plants already there grow out to see what you have got. Replace the ones you don't like with native species, such as hawthorn, hazel, holly and buckthorns.

Add interest by planting among them climbers and trailers such as traveller's-joy (*Clematis vitalba*), black bryony (*Tamus communis*), woody nightshade (*Solanum dulcamara*), brambles and dog roses (*Rosa canina*). Near the hedge, but clear of its root complex, plant some woodland herbaceous species, such as red campion, hedge garlic (*Alliaria petiolata*) or snowdrops. For more ideas, see *Flowers of the woodlands*, page 376.

One cautionary note: hedgerows take up a lot of space, so you will still need to cut out some branches from time to time to prevent it getting out of hand. Avoid doing this pruning at nesting time in spring, so that you don't disturb the animals and birds who will soon move in to make their homes.

Collecting seed

I want to get wild flowers for my garden. Can I take seeds or plants from the countryside?

Never dig up plants in the countryside for your garden – they are protected by law (see *Law*, page 205). It is a criminal offence even to take seeds or cuttings from 62 particularly rare species (see *Wild plants protected by law*, page 374). It is, however, not an offence to take seeds from other wild plants – provided, of course, that you have the permission of whoever owns the land they're growing on. If you do want to collect seeds or cuttings in the wild, the simplest place to find them is on road verges, embankments and waste ground. Make a point, though, of not collecting seeds when there are only one or two of the plants at a particular site.

If you think rare plants are threatened – by building development, say – ask the landowner for permission to remove a plant or seeds. Whenever you do collect seeds in the wild, sow them in soil-based compost outdoors at once.

Many wild flowers will establish themselves naturally in a garden without your having to forage for them. Seeds may be wind-blown, or carried by birds, animals, pets or even in your clothes. These botanical hitchhikers could include enchanter's nightshade (*Circaea lutetiana*), goosegrass (*Galium aparine*) and herb bennet (*Geum urbanum*). Squirrels may drop hazel or walnut seeds. Birds carry the seed pips of blackberries, sea buckthorn, ivy, firethorn and cotoneaster.

You can also get pot-grown wild flowers from some nurseries, or seeds from some garden centres. Or you may be able to collect seeds for nothing from a neighbour's weeds.

Not for the lazy

Must I be a gardening expert to grow wild flowers? And do they need very different treatment from cultivated plants?

It's not difficult to grow wild flowers – but it's not a soft option for a lazy gardener, either. All gardening is about making the plants you want succeed where you want them; and wild flowers need care like any other plants.

There are differences, though, in the kind of care they need. Mostly they need poorer soil than cultivated species, so don't fill the ground with compost and nutrients. Many will grow in close association with other wild plants, as in a hay meadow. These will need little maintenance apart from an annual mowing in July.

Where you will need some expertise is in your choice of plant, and where you place each species. For suggestions about which plants will do best on your soil, see the charts on pages 371-3. Germination, too, is more complex in wild flowers than in cultivated varieties. Most wild flowers, for instance, germinate only when triggered by the right conditions or series of events. This natural dormancy has been largely bred out of most cultivated garden plants.

Some seeds need time to mature internally before they will germinate. These include quaking grass, harebell and greater knap-

MEADOW PLANTS FOR CHALKY SOILS

Name	Height	Flowers
GRASSES		
Quaking grass (*Briza media*)	8in-1½ft	Inconspicuous (June-July)
Red fescue (*Festuca rubra*)	4in-2½ft	Reddish spikelets (May-July)
Yellow oat-grass (*Trisetum flavescens*)	8in-1½ft	Yellow spikelets (May-June)
BROAD-LEAVED PLANTS		
Clustered bellflower (*Campanula glomerata*)	2-8in	Purplish-blue (May-Sept)
Common milkwort (*Polygala vulgaris*)	4in-1ft	Blue, pink or white (May-Sept)
Cowslip (*Primula veris*)	4in-1ft	Deep yellow or orange-spotted (Apr-May)
Greater knapweed (*Centaurea scabiosa*)	1-3ft	Reddish-purple (July-Sept)
Horseshoe vetch (*Hippocrepis comosa*)	4in-1½ft	Yellow (May-July)
Lady's bedstraw (*Galium verum*)	6in-3½ft	Bright yellow (July-Aug)
Maiden pink (*Dianthus deltoides*)	6in-1½ft	Rose-coloured, often with pale spots (June-Sept)
Mouse-ear hawkweed (*Hieracium pilosella*)	2in-1ft	Pale yellow (May-Aug)
Small scabious (*Scabiosa columbaria*)	6in-2½ft	Bluish-lilac (July-Aug)
Yellow-wort (*Blackstonia perfoliata*)	6in-1½ft	Bright yellow (June-Oct)

weed. Many of the pea family, including the vetches and the common bird's-foot trefoil, have a tough seed coat that will not absorb water until it has rotted. You can speed up the process by chipping seeds individually with a knife, or shaking a handful of them vigorously in a jar, or by rubbing them between two sheets of sandpaper.

The fleshy parts of berries need to be stripped off before sowing the seeds, in order to reproduce at least in part the seeds' natural pattern of germinating after passing through an animal's gut.

The seeds of cowslip, great burnet and members of the carrot family germinate best if they spend months at around freezing temperatures. Others need freezing nights, but days at around 15°C (60°F) – close to spring weather. These include lady's bedstraw, oxeye daisy and common toadflax.

Others depend on the presence of another species before germination. Parasitic broomrapes, eyebrights and yellow rattles need host plants such as centaureas or members of the pea family. Orchids depend on a fungus in the soil. As a general rule, sow wild flower seeds outside in autumn – and don't be disappointed if some take more than a year to germinate.

Beware these plants

Are there any plants I should avoid growing in a wild garden?

Take care with the vigorous self-seeders and the plants which spread underground, throwing out new stems from their roots. Unseen, they may choke out other species that are more attractive but less aggressive.

These invaders include hedge bindweed (*Calystegia sepium*), couch grass (*Elymus repens*), ground elder (*Aegopodium podagraria*), pale toadflax (*Linaria repens*), creeping thistle (*Cirsium arvense*), blackthorn (*Prunus spinosa*) and rosebay willowherb (*Epilobium angustifolium*). Vigorous grasses such as cock's-foot (*Dactylis glomerata*), perennial rye (*Lolium perenne*) and tor-grass (*Brachypodium pinnatum*) will also squeeze out other plants if you let them multiply.

Watch out, too, for aerial raiders – plants whose seeds are spread by the wind, such as dandelions and some daisies. Other plants, although wild, should never be grown. Ragwort (*Senecio jacobaea*), for instance, is poisonous to livestock and is banned by the Ministry of Agriculture.

Spindle (*Euonymus europaeus*) is the winter host plant for the black bean aphid, and barberry (*Berberis vulgaris*) is the winter home of a fungus that attacks cereal crops. Don't plant either near farmland.

Town and country

I have a small town garden, most of which is paved. Is there any way I can grow wild flowers?

Yes. Grow them in concrete or clay containers – the larger the better to even out fluctuations in the water supply. Store rainwater from gutters for use in the pots – tap water can be lethal to some species.

Cornfield wild flowers will grow in most garden soils (for suggested species, see *Flowers of the cornfields*, page 375). Alternatively, put a very sandy soil in some of your pots and you could grow sand-dune flowers such as the dwarf burnet rose (*Rosa pimpinellifolia*) or the purple milk-vetch (*Astragalus danicus*). In other pots, use lime-rich soil to simulate chalk grassland and grow downland meadow plants. A rich, peaty mix will support the common cottongrass (*Eriophorum angustifolium*), bog asphodel (*Narthecium ossifragum*), or even insect-eating plants such as sundews and butterworts. You could also try to create a tiny pond, with floating frogbit (*Hydrocharis morsus-ranae*); but drain it each year, because it may freeze solid in winter, and that could crack the container.

Off the ground, you could fill hanging baskets or window boxes with wild ground-ivy (*Glechoma hederacea*), ivy-leaved toadflax (*Cymbalaria muralis*) and wild ivies.

Mountain favourites

I like the plants which grow in the mountain regions of Scotland and Wales. Will they grow in my lowland garden?

Yes, if you get the conditions right. That will mean a very free-draining soil, best achieved with a raised bed, a rockery or a gravel garden. Brick, concrete or stone rubble, buried under a sandy soil, will readily support plants which normally grow on cliffs and scree, such as purple saxifrage (*Saxifraga oppositifolia*), Dovedale moss (*Saxifraga hypnoides*) and the mountain pansy (*Viola lutea*). The ideal bed is built on a 12-15in thick base of rubble. On that spread a 3-4in layer made up of 6 parts (by volume) of garden soil mixed with 1 part of peat and 1 part of horticultural grit or coarse sand.

In a garden with chalky soil, you may need to make a peat bed – using lime-free soil, peat and grit in the same proportions – or to grow the plants in containers. It's the soil, not the altitude, which matters.

Other plants from lower altitudes which can be grown in the same way include Cheddar pink (*Dianthus gratianopolitanus*) and the common rock-rose (*Helianthemum chamaecistus*). Use only commercial seed for Cheddar pink – it is illegal to take this rare native from the countryside. All these wild moun-

MEADOW PLANTS FOR SILTY OR SANDY SOILS

Name	Height	Flowers
GRASSES		
Fine bent (*Agrostis tenuis*)	8in-1½ft	Inconspicuous (June-Aug)
Meadow brome (*Bromus commutatus*)	1-3ft	Inconspicuous (June)
Smooth meadow-grass (*Poa pratensis*)	6in-3ft	Inconspicuous (May-July)
BROAD-LEAVED PLANTS		
Agrimony (*Agrimonia eupatoria*)	1-2ft	Yellow (June-Aug)
Cuckoo flower (*Cardamine pratensis*)	6in-2ft	Lilac-coloured (Apr-June)
Great burnet (*Sanguisorba officinalis*)	1-3ft	Dark crimson (June-Sept)
Large bird's-foot-trefoil (*Lotus uliginosus*)	6in-2ft	Yellow and red (June-Aug)
Meadow buttercup (*Ranunculus acris*)	6in-3½ft	Golden-yellow (May-July)
Meadowsweet (*Filipendula ulmaria*)	2-4ft	Creamy-white (June-Sept)
Meadow vetchling (*Lathyrus pratensis*)	1-4ft	Yellow (May-Aug)
Ragged-robin (*Lychnis flos-cuculi*)	1-2½ft	Bright pink (May-June)
Sorrel (*Rumex acetosa*)	8in-3½ft	Inconspicuous (May-June); crimson foliage
White campion (*Silene alba*)	1-3½ft	White (May-Sept)

tain plants need much the same sort of care as cultivated alpine plants. So if you've already tried growing rock garden plants, you should have no trouble.

Garden cornfield

Can I create in my garden the effect of the lush cornfields I remember from childhood?

Yes; many seed firms keep lists of cornfield species. The plants can be added to a formal bed, or put in a bed of their own, or sown in any bare and open spot. Dig out any perennial weeds first, then plant the cornfield seeds in autumn for best results.

You can choose from numerous old favourites which have been purged from farmland by weedkillers and deep ploughing. For ideas, see *Flowers of the cornfields*, page 375.

Wild orchard

Can I make my orchard double up as a wild garden?

Yes, it can make a perfect site for a meadow garden. In a new orchard with young trees, plant cornfield species. In an older orchard, where coarse grasses have established themselves, strip off some of the turf and sow a finer mix of wild grasses. Tougher species, such as ox-eye daisy, can be sown direct into the orchard and other wild species introduced to start with as pot plants. Bury the pots up to their rims, so that the plants can become established without having to fight – initially at least – for root space.

In a mature orchard with dense shade, introduce woodland species (see *Flowers of the woodlands*, page 376). Cut back the wild meadow in early autumn, leaving the orchard clear for harvesting.

Water meadows

My lawn has poor drainage and is repeatedly flooded. Can I grow wild flowers on it – and so save myself the expense of installing drainage?

If the problem is compacted soil, you can cure it by digging soakaway pits at low points, filling them with rubble and covering them over (see *Drainage*, page 123). Then you can go for meadow flowers.

If the soil is just heavy clay, add lime to improve its texture.

If you simply have a naturally high water table, then the problem is indeed incurable – and you can grow wild flowers on it. Go for the lovely wild plants that thrive in boggy soil and water meadows. Plant common meadow-rue (*Thalictrum flavum*), marsh-marigold (*Caltha palustris*), red rattle (*Pedicularis palustris*), ragged-robin (*Lychnis flos-cuculi*) and summer snowflake (*Leucojum aestivum*). You could also grow the fritillary (*Fritillaria meleagris*), a rare native with handsome chequered blooms. You can buy the bulbs from specialist firms.

Spotting seedlings

I've sown a packet of mixed wild flower seeds. How can I tell which seedlings are weeds and which ones I should keep?

Only by experience. Familiarise yourself with the common weeds of your area in their early stages of growth, and get hold of an illustrated book of British wild flowers (most libraries should have such books) to see what the leaves or stems of your flowers should look like. You should then be able to recognise at least the more distinctive species.

Leave any unknown seedling alone but keep an eye on it. In time you'll discover that you've added a new wild bloom to your collection – or that you've got an ugly plant you'd do better to get rid of next year. Either way, you'll learn something.

Attracting wildlife

What can I do to encourage wildlife to my garden?

Plant wild flowers – they provide the food which will lure the birds and animals.

Finches and sparrows will tease the ripe seeds from the handsome cotton thistle (*Onopordon acanthium*), from the spiky flower heads of the teasel (*Dipsacus sylvestris*) and from the long heads of the great plantain (*Plantago major*). Blackbirds and thrushes and their winter migrant cousins, fieldfares, love berried shrubs and climbers. Squirrels and mice will hunt out nut trees such as the common hazel.

Provide nesting boxes and safe havens for birds, bats, amphibians and reptiles. Think about slugs, snails and insects, too. You won't get hedgehogs and kestrels if you regularly poison their food supply with slug pellets and sprays. For details of how to attract butterflies, see *Butterflies*, page 38.

Garden trees

Are there any native trees that will not outgrow a modest-sized garden?

Choose from these native species, none of which should get out of hand in an average quarter-acre garden: aspen (*Populus tremula*); bird cherry (*Prunus padus*); common alder (*Alnus glutinosa*); crab apple (*Malus sylvestris*); guelder rose (*Viburnum opulus*); and the wayfaring tree (*Viburnum lantana*). The birches, such as *Betula pendula*, are also small

MEADOW PLANTS FOR CLAY SOILS

Name	Height	Flowers
GRASSES		
Meadow barley (*Hordeum secalinum*)	1-2ft	Inconspicuous (June-July)
Meadow foxtail (*Alopecurus pratensis*)	1-3ft	Inconspicuous (Apr-June)
Sweet vernal grass (*Anthoxanthum odoratum*)	8in-1½ft	Inconspicuous (Apr-June)
BROAD-LEAVED PLANTS		
Betony (*Stachys officinalis*)	6in-2ft	Reddish-purple (July-Sept)
Bird's-foot-trefoil (*Lotus corniculatus*)	4in-1½ft	Yellow streaked with red (June-Sept)
Cat's-ear (*Hypochoeris radicata*)	3-10in	Bright yellow (June-Sept)
Dropwort (*Filipendula vulgaris*)	6in-3ft	Creamy-white (June-July)
Field scabious (*Knautia arvensis*)	10in-3½ft	Bluish-lilac (May-June)
Goat's-beard (*Tragopogon pratensis*)	1-2½ft	Yellow (June-July)
Hardheads (*Centaurea nigra*)	6in-2ft	Reddish-purple (June-Sept)
Meadow crane's-bill (*Geranium pratense*)	1-2½ft	Violet-blue (June-Sept)
Musk mallow (*Malva moschata*)	1-2½ft	Rose-pink (July-Aug)
Ox-eye daisy (*Leucanthemum vulgare*)	8in-2½ft	White with yellow centres (June-Aug)

and cast only light shade. You could also try coppicing – cutting trees back almost to ground level and allowing them to regrow from the stumps. Even large trees such as oak and beech can be treated this way. In addition the English oak supports up to 300 species of insect, so it will draw a whole wildlife system to your garden.

One word of caution, though: don't plant any big trees near a house or wall, especially in heavy clay soil. The roots can damage the foundations. As a rule of thumb, plant any tree at least as far from the house as one and a half times its *eventual* height.

Keep them apart

Can I turn my traditional garden into a wild garden without losing my favourite plants?

Most cultivated garden plants look somewhat garish in a wild garden. So it is usually best to keep them apart.

Prepare a special area, perhaps away from the house, where your wild flowers can grow and be seen in something like their natural habitat. Lay a wild meadow, for instance, that changes gradually into a woodland edge in the shade of your shrubs or a hedge. Alternatively, if you want a cottage-garden look, some wild flowers will fit in well: corn marigold, for instance, foxglove, mulleins, pinks and soapwort. Plant also Jacob's ladder (*Polemonium caeruleum*) and lily-of-the-valley (*Convallaria majalis*), both of which are also widely grown as garden plants.

Flowering wall

I am building a new stone wall in my garden. How can I make it look natural?

Leave pockets in the wall that can be filled with compost in which plants can be rooted. Larger holes at the foot of the wall can provide living space for animals. And to encourage moss, mix a forkful of manure with milk in a bucket, then paste it thinly onto the wall with an old brush.

You can fill the crevices you create with rusty-back fern (*Ceterach officinarum*), maidenhair spleenwort (*Asplenium trichomanes*) and wall-rue (*Asplenium ruta-muraria*). Larger ferns, such as common polypody (*Polypodium vulgare*) and the hart's-tongue fern (*Phyllitis scolopendrium*), will also do well.

Among the wild flowers you can naturalise into your wall are biting stonecrop (*Sedum acre*), English stonecrop (*Sedum anglicum*), navelwort (*Umbilicus rupestris*) and herb-robert (*Geranium robertianum*). Choose a self-clinging climber such as ivy (*Hedera helix*) to ramble among them.

Worried neighbour

My neighbour is worried that my wild flower garden is going to over-run into his garden. What can I do to prevent this happening?

Avoid growing as much as possible species with seeds that are dispersed by the wind, such as dandelion, groundsel and willow herb. And block the spread of plants with creeping roots by setting them behind ponds, paths, walls and drives. If you have nettles or brambles near a boundary fence, sink overlapping strips of galvanised iron vertically beneath the fence to stop the root systems spreading across the boundary.

Finally, remind your neighbour that since your land is full of wild flowers there is no room for the common garden weeds which are such a nuisance in his own garden.

Hiding the shed

The corner of my garden, which I am turning into a wild garden, contains the garden shed and an unsightly fence. What plants can I use to hide them?

Pick any native climbers. The native honeysuckle (*Lonicera periclymenum*), hops (*Humulus lupulus*) and the narrow-leaved everlasting pea (*Lathyrus sylvestris*) will all do the job. You could even choose the large bindweed (*Calystegia silvatica*) or hedge bindweed (*Calystegia sepium*), with their large, white and occasionally pink funnel-shaped flowers. But make sure they are not going to spread to valuable ground.

Ivy will give year-round cover. Blackberries will give an autumn crop. Box can also be trained, with careful pruning, to make an attractive disguise.

Shady garden

My garden is overshadowed by trees. Which are the best wild flowers for these conditions?

You've got the ideal conditions for many of Britain's oldest wild flowers. Ferns and sedges will love it. So will wood melick (*Melica uniflora*), asarabacca (*Asarum europaeum*), which has lustrous, cyclamen-like leaves, and arums such as *Arum maculatum*.

Where hungry tree roots have sucked all the moisture from the soil, add leaf mould to the ground and plant common dog violet (*Viola riviniana*) and sweet violet (*Viola odorata*).

A pond can cause a problem beneath trees because it fills with autumn leaves. But you could bury a pool liner (see *Ponds and pools*,

WILD PLANTS PROTECTED BY LAW

These are the 62 species specially protected because of their rarity by the Wildlife and Countryside Act 1981. Removal from the wild of any part of these plants – including the seeds – is an offence. The maximum penalty is a fine of £1000 for each plant collected.

Adder's-tongue spearwort (*Ranunculus ophioglossifolius*)
Alpine catchfly (*Lychnis alpina*)
Alpine gentian (*Gentiana nivalis*)
Alpine sow-thistle (*Cicerbita alpina*)
Alpine woodsia (*Woodsia alpina*)
Bedstraw broomrape (*Orobanche caryophyllacea*)
Blue heath (*Phyllodoce caerulea*)
Brown galingale (*Cyperus fuscus*)
Cheddar pink (*Dianthus gratianopolitanus*)
Childing pink (*Petrorhagia nanteuilli*)
Diapensia (*Diapensia lapponica*)
Dickie's bladder-fern (*Cystopteris dickieana*)
Downy woundwort (*Stachys germanica*)
Drooping saxifrage (*Saxifraga cernua*)
Early spider-orchid (*Ophrys sphegodes*)
Fen orchid (*Liparis loeselii*)
Fen violet (*Viola persicifolia*)
Field cow-wheat (*Melampyrum arvense*)
Field eryngo (*Eryngium campestre*)
Field wormwood (*Artemisia campestris*)
Ghost orchid (*Epipogium aphyllum*)
Greater yellow-rattle (*Rhinanthus serotinus*)
Jersey cudweed (*Gnaphalium luteoalbum*)
Killarney fern (*Trichomanes speciosum*)
Lady's slipper (*Cypripedium calceolus*)
Late spider-orchid (*Ophrys fuciflora*)
Least lettuce (*Lactuca saligna*)
Limestone woundwort (*Stachys alpina*)
Lizard orchid (*Himantoglossum hircinum*)
Military orchid (*Orchis militaris*)
Monkey orchid (*Orchis simia*)
Norwegian sandwort (*Arenaria norvegica*)
Oblong woodsia (*Woodsia ilvensis*)
Oxtongue broomrape (*Orobanche loricata*)
Perennial knawel (*Scleranthus perennis*)
Plymouth pear (*Pyrus cordata*)
Purple spurge (*Euphorbia peplis*)
Red helleborine (*Cephalanthera rubra*)
Ribbon-leaved water-plantain (*Alisma gramineum*)
Rock cinquefoil (*Potentilla rupestris*)
Rock sea-lavender (*Limonium paradoxum*)
Rock sea-lavender (*Limonium recurvum*)
Rough marsh-mallow (*Althaea hirsuta*)
Round-headed leek (*Allium sphaerocephalon*)
Sea knotgrass (*Polygonum maritimum*)
Sickle-leaved hare's-ear (*Bupleurum falcatum*)
Small alison (*Alyssum alyssoides*)
Small hare's-ear (*Bupleurum baldense*)
Snowdon lily (*Lloydia serotina*)
Spiked speedwell (*Veronica spicata*)
Spring gentian (*Gentiana verna*)
Starfruit (*Damasonium alisma*)
Starved wood-sedge (*Carex depauperata*)
Teesdale sandwort (*Minuartia stricta*)
Thistle broomrape (*Orobanche reticulata*)
Triangular club-rush (*Scirpus triquetrus*)
Tufted saxifrage (*Saxifraga cespitosa*)
Water germander (*Teucrium scordium*)
Whorled Solomon's-seal (*Polygonatum verticillatum*)
Wild cotoneaster (*Cotoneaster integerrimus*)
Wild gladiolus (*Gladiolus illyricus*)
Wood calamint (*Calamintha sylvatica*)

page 261) and give yourself a marsh garden with marsh-marigold (*Caltha palustris*), pendulous sedge (*Carex pendula*), royal fern (*Osmunda regalis*) and marsh fern (*Thelypteris palustris*).

At the edge of the woodland, statuesque mulleins and cotton thistle (*Onopordon acanthium*), with their pastel flowers, look marvellous against a dark backdrop of shady foliage.

Economy gardening

I have only a limited budget for gardening. Should I try growing wild flowers?

Apart from seeds and the labour of preparation, wild flower gardening is not expensive.

You don't need fertilisers, weedkillers, pesticides, a greenhouse or a garden frame. You don't need a cylinder mower or expensive bags of potting composts.

You do, on the other hand, need a rotary mower that can be raised to give a 3in cut – wild flowers won't stand close mowing. Alternatively, you need a scythe – if you can work out how to use it. And you need the flowers. Buy pot plants if you want your garden established quickly, and spend some of your limited budget on a few native shrubs or small trees. Ponds can be expensive, too, but even a small one can add a rich set of habitats to any wild garden.

Wild herbs

Can I get double value from my wild garden by growing plants for eating and herbal use?

Yes. This is probably how British gardening began – with the planting near a house of wild plants which were used daily in the kitchen or for medicinal purposes.

Some edible plants grow well in a meadow garden. These include thyme, sorrel and dandelion, which can be used in salads or as a vegetable. The lower leaves of sea kale (*Crambe maritima*) and its stalks are edible.

Nettles (*Urtica dioica*) lose their stinging properties after being cooked for a few minutes. Tansy (*Tanacetum vulgare*) and feverfew (*Tanacetum parthenium*) will grow by a hedge or on a grassy bank. Blue-flowered chicory (*Cichorium intybus*) can be used as a vegetable, and its thick roots can be ground up for use as a coffee substitute. Watercress (*Nasturtium officinale*) planted in a garden pond will give you a peppery addition to salads. One easy way to tell which plants have traditionally been used in herbal medicines is to look at their Latin name. If it contains the word *officinale* or *officinalis* – as watercress does, and dandelion (*Taraxacum officinale*) – the plant was almost certainly being used by apothecaries as far back as the Middle Ages. The name comes from *officina* – the word for the medical storeroom in a medieval monastery.

CORNCOCKLE *The flowers of* Agrostemma githago *used to be common in cornfields.*

FIELD POPPY *Deep ploughing and weedkillers have made this flower rare on farmland today.*

Homely logs

If I leave old logs in my garden as a refuge for wildlife, will fungi form that can kill off my trees and shrubs?

Fungi breaks down dead wood; it rarely attacks a healthy plant. But watch out for one particular fungus that can be a problem. The honey fungus (*Armillaria mellea*) has black, bootlace-like fungal 'tentacles' which spread under the bark of dead wood, but can also push their way many feet through the ground to attack live trees and shrubs. Where you see it, burn the infected wood; there is no effective treatment. In autumn the fungus produces edible toadstools 2-4in high, each with a honey-coloured cap roughened by darker scales and with a yellow-flecked ring near the top of the stalk.

Life in the pond

How can I encourage the greatest range of wildlife to adopt my garden pond?

Start planning for wildlife with the design. A pond needs to be at least 2ft deep at one point, so that there is always a body of water that will not freeze. It will then provide a winter haven for hibernating amphibians and the resting stages of aquatic plants. Build gradually shallowing edges, so that there is space for birds to bathe and drink and for amphibians to get in and out of the water.

Dig some mud from the bed of an established lake or canal and lay it in the bottom of the pond to introduce a whole range of microscopic life. Native water snails will help to keep down the algae during summer. Tadpoles are vegetarian in early life. Put fine-

FLOWERS OF THE CORNFIELDS

Name	Height	Flowers
Corncockle (*Agrostemma githago*)	1-3½ft	Reddish-purple (June-Aug)
Cornflower (*Centaurea cyanus*)	8in-3ft	Bright blue, pink or white (June-Aug)
Corn marigold (*Chrysanthemum segetum*)	1-3½ft	Golden (July-Sept)
Field poppy (*Papaver rhoeas*)	8in-2ft	Scarlet (June-Aug)
Pheasant's eye (*Adonis annua*)	4in-1½ft	Scarlet and black (July)
Scentless mayweed (*Matricaria maritima*)	6in-2ft	White with yellow centres (July-Sept)
Shepherd's needle (*Scandix pecten-veneris*)	6in-1½ft	White (Apr-July)
Venus's looking-glass (*Legousia hybrida*)	2in-1ft	Reddish-purple or lilac (May-Aug)
Wild pansy (*Viola tricolor*)	6in-1½ft	Bluish-violet, yellow or white (Apr-Sept)
Woad (*Isatis tinctoria*)	1½-4ft	Yellow (July-Aug)

leaved plants such as spiked water-milfoil (*Myriophyllum spicatum*) into the water for them to feed on. Newts wrap their eggs in the leaves of plants such as water starwort (*Callitriche stagnalis*).

Duckweeds and other floating water plants grow quickly, suppressing microscopic algae and giving shade for water dwellers. Goldfish love to hide beneath the plate-sized leaves of the water lily (*Nymphaea alba*).

The nymphs of dragonflies and damselflies go through their metamorphosis to beautiful adults among waterside plants such as bogbean (*Menyanthes trifoliata*), flowering-rush (*Butomus umbellatus*), hemp-agrimony (*Agrimonia eupatoria*) and yellow flag iris (*Iris pseudacorus*). So plant some of these species, too, to attract the insects.

WHAT IS A WILD GARDEN?

DON'T imagine a wild garden to be a wilderness. A wild garden needs as much care as any other type of garden if it is not to become overwhelmed by plants which have adapted to richer, cultivated land nearby. Wild does *not* equal neglected.

There are no fixed rules about what makes a wild garden. Instead of growing the highly developed, nursery-bred specimen plants that fill most of our gardens, the wild gardener plants the natural, wild flowers of the countryside in mixed communities where they live together as they would in the fields and hedgerows.

These flowers have subtler colours and more delicate flowers. And, free of herbicides and insecticides, they attract into the garden the native wildlife of the country. The efforts of the wild gardener can thus make a real contribution to conservation.

Even in a small garden, it is perfectly possible to reproduce the delights of an English meadow, the busy life of a rural hedgerow, the soft and quiet colour of a woodland edge, or the rich, squelchy beauty of a bog-marsh.

Soil preparation is the key to successful wild flower gardening. Most natural plants live – and thrive – in a much less rich soil than the pampered garden favourites. Get the soil right, which largely means *not* adding fertiliser or compost, and you get your wild garden right.

Having said all that, wild gardening is something of a misnomer, because most of Britain's present population of wild flowers are not actually native to Britain.

Many were brought in by people – either deliberately as crops or ornamentals, or accidentally as strays in crop seed, or entangled in imported wool, or in the fur or feathers of migrating animals.

The successful plants found their own niche in the landscape and have developed into the strains we now call British wild flowers.

Most of these plants are now readily available as seeds from seed merchants and even in plant form from some specialist nurseries, such as that of John Chambers at 15 Westleigh Road, Barton Seagrave, Kettering, Northants NN15 5AJ; telephone Wellingborough (0933) 681632.

Wild arrangements

I love flower arranging with fresh and dried flowers. Are there any wild flowers I can plant that would be suitable?

Dozens. For fresh spring flowers, grow bluebells, cowslips, lily-of-the-valley or even the exotic-looking fritillary. There are also many attractive summer-flowering meadow plants, including long-stemmed ox-eye daisies (*Leucanthemum vulgare*) and field scabious (*Knautia arvensis*). Yarrow and yellow rattles can be dried for winter arrangements.

In summer, cut stems of cornflowers and corn marigolds. In autumn, collect seedheads of corncockle, poppies and dry annual grasses such as native hare's-tail (*Lagurus ovatus*) and greater quaking grass (*Briza maxima*).

Many hedgerow and meadow species of the carrot family have attractive seedheads – sweet cicely (*Myrrhis odorata*), for example, and wild angelica (*Angelica sylvestris*). Other useful dried flowers include meadow grasses, teasel (*Dipsacus sylvestris*) and sprays of 'old man's beard' which are the seeds of *Clematis vitalba*. The seedheads of reedmace (*Typha latifolia*) look good, too – they dry best if they're picked young.

There are also the colourful, though poisonous, autumn berries of black bryony (*Tamus communis*) and woody nightshade (*Solanum dulcamara*), the hips of the dog rose, and the autumn leaf sprays of field maple and guelder rose. Foliage plants include ferns such as the hard shield-fern (*Polystichum aculeatum*), and wild ivy.

Colour: how to get a long display

I would love wild flowers in my garden, but I don't think they will be as colourful or last as long as cultivated species. Are there varieties that will give a year-long display?

No, but wild flowers can give you colour from spring to late autumn. Individually, few of the blooms will match up to cultivated garden favourites, but seen together they can still be impressive.

Little can better the brilliance of a cornfield full of poppies, or the delicate effect of a late summer meadow with pastel clouds of pink, lavender and blue. Spot the subtlety in form and colour of the grasses and sedges. Wild flowers just need to be looked at differently from the more familiar and more flamboyant blooms of cultivated plants.

To get a long display, use the charts of meadow and woodland plants on pages 371-6. Choose plants that have a variety of flowering times. Go, for instance, for bulbs to get spring colour before the leaves unfurl on the deciduous trees.

Mow part of the summer meadow in spring to give you an area for autumn colour, planting there flowers such as cyclamen (*Cyclamen hederifolium*) and meadow saffron (*Colchicum autumnale*) or plants carrying a late display of berries.

Wild flowers bring you a bonus as well – you never know what will appear from year to year. Slow-germinating seeds in the mixture you sow will spring up unexpectedly. So will wind-borne seeds that have blown in over your fence. Within a few years,

FLOWERS OF THE WOODLANDS

Name	Height	Flowers
Bluebell (*Endymion nonscriptus*)	8in-1½ft	Blue (Apr-June)
Foxglove (*Digitalis purpurea*)	1½-4½ft	Pinkish-purple (June-Sept)
Lily-of-the-valley (*Convallaria majalis*)	6-8in	White (May-June)
Primrose (*Primula vulgaris*)	3-6in	Pale yellow (Mar-May)
Red campion (*Silene dioica*)	1-3ft	Rose-coloured (May-June)
Solomon's seal (*Polygonatum multiflorum*)	1-3ft	White and green (May-June)
Stinking iris (*Iris foetidissima*)	1in-3ft	Purple and yellow (May-July)
Wild daffodil (*Narcissus pseudonarcissus*)	8in-1ft	Yellow (Feb-Apr)
Wood anemone (*Anemone nemorosa*)	2in-1ft	White or pink (Mar-May)
Wood sorrel (*Oxalis acetosella*)	2-6in	White and lilac (Apr-May)

you may have more than a hundred species growing in a meadow area that was once just a patch of lawn. The diversity of species will surprise you – and you will be making a direct contribution to the conservation of Britain's native plants.

Spreading plants

Are there ways of encouraging wild flowers to spread?

Wild flowers should propagate by themselves, but you can help the process by collecting seed and sowing it into pots outdoors or into seedbeds prepared in your meadow area. Sow all such seed as soon as you collect it.

Other methods are much the same as for garden plants. Clumps of herbaceous plants such as wild marjoram and ox-eye daisy can be divided early in spring. Cowslips can also be split. Rhizomatous plants such as galingale, Solomon's-seal and irises can be lifted and pieces of rhizome taken for new plants. Clumps of bulbs of bluebells and ramsons can be lifted and divided after they die down in summer.

Cuttings can be taken from native pinks. Mountain plants – such as mountain avens and moss campion – can be propagated in the same way by using a gritty compost. English stonecrop can be grown from its fleshy leaves, which root at the base.

Mowing the meadow

What must I do when the flowering meadow part of my garden begins to look untidy after the flowers are finished?

Mow it, leaving 3-4in of uncut stems. And don't collect the clippings. This is a vital stage of the wild flower meadow. Leave the cut grasses and flower stems where they fall so that the seeds can ripen and fall off into the ground to give next year's crop.

Rake off the resultant hay about three weeks after cutting and before it rots – enriched soil is not good for most wild flowers. The hay can be used as animal feed – for rabbits, say – or put on a compost heap. Leave part of the meadow uncut, perhaps a bank, because some butterflies spend the winter as a chrysalis on dead stalks.

The timing of the mowing depends on the weather and the plants you have sown. The usual time is July. But spring meadows, with cowslip, fritillary and the cuckoo flower (*Cardamine pratensis*), should be mown after the end of July. Use the area thereafter as a rough lawn, and cut it twice more, once in mid-August and again in early September.

Summer meadows, with burnet, greater knapweed and ox-eye daisy, need cutting towards the end of September. Give them another tidy-up in November.

WIREWORMS

Watch out for wilting

The crops in my new vegetable bed have been a disappointment. The potatoes have holes drilled through, and the stems of my lettuces and tomatoes have been gnawed through underground. I occasionally see a few slow-moving yellowish worms among the roots of my plants. Are these the culprits?

They are indeed. As so often with garden insects, fast means friendly – and slow means trouble. That is, the slow movers are generally vegetarians, chewing away at your plants, while the speedier creatures, such as centipedes, are carnivores that make your life easier by preying on the vegetarian pests. Your problem is wireworms. They're most often a problem in plots that have been dug out of grassland in the past year or so. Wireworms also attack the stems of most flowering plants and seem to have a particular fondness for carnations and chrysanthemums. Apart from seeing the creatures when digging, wilting is the only sign of possible infestation in both flowers and vegetables.

An old-fashioned but effective way of controlling wireworms, and a few other pests like millipedes, too, is to punch holes in the bottoms of tin cans, fit the rims with wire handles, fill the tins with vegetable peelings and sink them in the ground. Every few days, haul them out and destroy the contents. Otherwise, scatter bromophos, HCH or diazinon around plants likely to be affected.

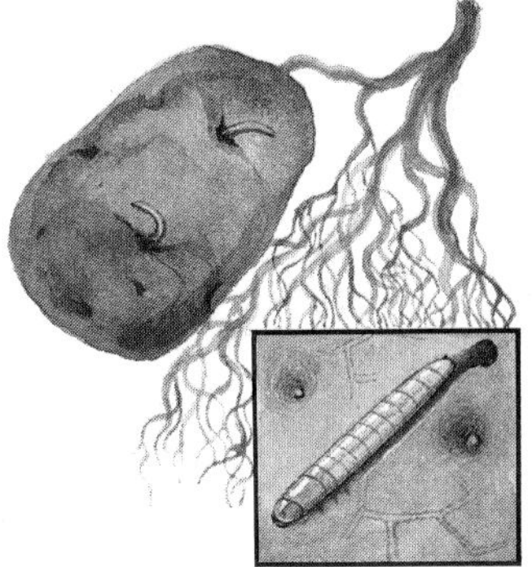

WIRY INVADERS *Named for their tough, shiny skins, wireworms, which can be 1in long, are not true worms but the larvae of click beetles.*

WORMS

Out, casts

My once immaculate lawn is now punctuated by worm casts that are unsightly and unpleasantly slippery if trodden on; the problem is particularly pronounced after rain. How do I get rid of the worms, or at least persuade them to go elsewhere?

Your worms are only declaring their role in the scheme of things. They obtain nourishment by passing soil and the vegetable matter contained in it through their bodies: a life-long task. It is estimated that a worm eats its own weight in soil every day and that the worms in a single acre will, in the course of a year, move 18 tons of soil from the depths to the surface.

The worms' action aerates the ground, helps to create humus and plays a vital part in fertilising and rejuvenating the soil. For the most part, this activity takes place underground, but a few species occasionally bring their most recent meals of soil to the surface and deposit them there in the coiled pyramids known as casts. They seem particularly inclined to do this in showery weather, though why is not certain.

Perhaps the best thing to do is to let the casts dry before brushing the nutritious soil over the lawn as a top-dressing. There is an objection to this in that the worms might have brought weed seeds to the surface with them. But, unless the problem is very acute, you can afford to live with it.

If, on the other hand, the worms are seriously disfiguring your lawn, it is possible to get rid of them. The trouble is that you cannot attack the cast-making species without hurting the other worms as well, and to annihilate them all would do your soil no good. You could drive the creatures out of the ground temporarily with irritants such as permanganate of potash, dissolved in water and sprinkled on the grass at the rate of 1oz per gallon per square yard, or 1oz of derris dust to the square yard, sprinkled on dry and watered in. This will bring the worms to the surface, where they can be collected and dropped into the compost heap. A more permanent method is to use a worm-killer based on chlordane or carbaryl.

Finally, if you don't like the chemical approach, you could try a traditional remedy which is said to work well: hold a morris dance on your lawn, or any other kind of energetic dance for that matter. The worms are said to interpret the thumping feet as the vibration of a heavy shower. So they pop to the surface – where they can be brushed up.

PLANTS AT A GLANCE

A READY-REFERENCE GUIDE TO POPULAR SPECIES AND HOW TO GROW THEM

Abelia
Abelia x *grandiflora*

Abutilon
Abutilon vitifolium

Acacia
Robinia pseudoacacia 'Frisia'

Acaena
Acaena microphylla

PLANTS in this guide are listed under the names by which most gardeners know them. Thus, for example, hollyhock appears under its common name, not under its botanical name, althaea. Similarly, the common or false acacia is listed under acacia rather than under its less familiar botanical name, robinia. But euonymus appears under its botanical name, not under its less familiar common name of spindle tree. And the vigorous ground-covering species of the genus achillea are listed at the front of the alphabet rather than at the back under their common name, yarrow.

Each entry begins with examples of popular species or varieties within the genus, and gives brief details of how to care for and propagate the plants. The entry ends with a list of pests and diseases to which the plant is vulnerable. The list of potential problems is often formidably long, but your plant is very unlikely to suffer from more than one or two of them - and may never suffer from any.

Detailed descriptions of pests and diseases, and of how to cure them appear in the main question-and-answer section of the book. Those which attack a wide range of plants – aphids, for example – have their own entries, and appear here in SMALL CAPITAL letters. Less widespread problems are dealt with under the plants they commonly affect: apple canker, for instance, is covered under apples. Many of the plants described here are also dealt with in the main part of the book. Widely grown plants, such as apples, potatoes and roses, appear under their own names. Less common ones may appear under the group to which they belong such as *Bedding plants, Rock gardens, Shrubs* or *Trees*. To find more detail on any particular plant, consult the index.

Abelia

Bushy, semi-evergreen or deciduous shrub.
Examples *A. floribunda* Height up to 10ft, spread 4ft. Magenta-rose flowers produced May-July. *A.* x *grandiflora* Height 5-6ft, spread 4ft. Pink-white flowers July-Oct.
Plant Sept-Oct or Mar-Apr in ordinary soil in sheltered, sunny position.
Propagate by taking 3-4in long cuttings of the current season's wood in July. The cuttings should be ready for planting out in the following spring.
Care May require winter protection in colder parts of the country – a covering of sacking, or a layer of bracken or peat over the base. Thin overgrown shoots after flowering to encourage new growth. That apart, no regular pruning is needed.
Pests and diseases Generally trouble-free.

Abutilon

Tender shrub.
Examples *A. megapotamicum* Height and spread 6-8ft. Yellow and red flowers May-Oct. *A. vitifolium* Height 8ft, spread 5ft. Mauve flowers May-Oct.
Plant *A. megapotamicum* in May, *A. vitifolium* May or Sept, in ordinary, well-drained soil, preferably against a warm, sunny wall.
Propagate by cuttings of young sideshoots May-Aug.
Care Give roots winter protection with straw or bracken; remove frosted or dead shoots Mar-Apr.
Pests and diseases SCALE INSECTS, MEALY BUGS.

Acacia (Robinia pseudoacacia)

Decorative, fast-growing tree.
Example *R. p.* 'Frisia' Height 30ft plus, spread up to 15ft. Leaves golden-yellow Apr-May, turning green-yellow in July. Cream, fragrant flowers July. The tree produces numerous thorny suckers.
Plant Oct-Mar in ordinary soil, and in reasonably sheltered, sunny position. The tree is tolerant of low rainfall and atmospheric pollution.
Propagate by planting suckers in a nursery bed Oct-Feb. When well-rooted, one or two years later, plant out in permanent positions Oct-Mar.
Pests and diseases SCALE INSECTS.

Acaena

Hardy perennial, widely used for ground cover.
Examples *A. buchananii* Height 1-2in, spacing 2ft. Tight, dense foliage with russet burrs from July onwards. Grey-green leaves. *A. microphylla* Height 1-2in, spacing $1\frac{1}{2}$-2ft. Dense bronze-green leaves with crimson burrs and seed heads from July onwards.
Plant Sept-Mar in well-drained soil in full sun or partial shade.
Propagate by division Sept-Mar.
Pests and diseases Generally trouble-free.

GARDEN TIP
Acacia

To encourage a new robinia to settle quickly into your garden, make a point of buying a container-grown specimen, not a bare-root one. Although robinias do not mind poor soil, and shrug off polluted air, they are likely to suffer a setback to their growth if their roots are disturbed during the transplanting operation. Using a container-grown tree minimises this risk.

Acanthus
Acanthus mollis

Achillea
Achillea filipendulina

Actinidia
Actinidia kolomikta

Aechmea
Aechmea fasciata

Aethionema
Aethionema pulchellum

African lily
Agapanthus orientalis

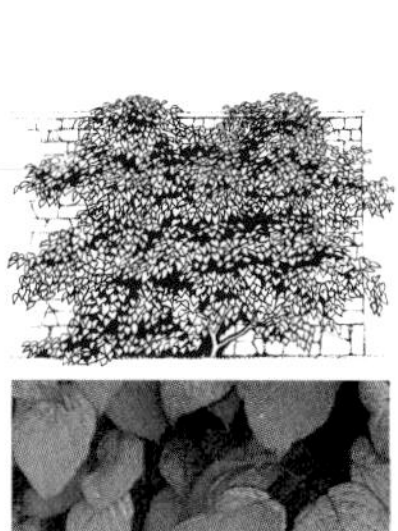
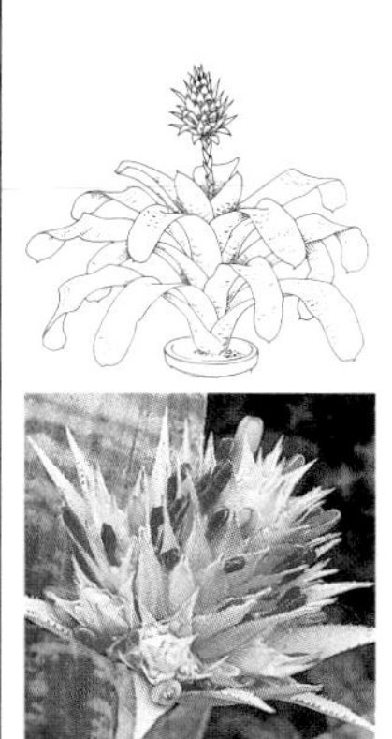

Acanthus

Hardy border perennial.
Examples *A. longifolius* Height 2-3ft, spacing 2ft. Lilac flower spikes, 12in long, produced in June-July. *A. mollis* Height 3ft, spacing 3ft. Purple and white flower spikes, 18in long, July-Aug.
Plant in sunny position and in deep, well-drained soil.
Propagate by root cuttings in winter and by seed in spring. Overcrowded plants may be divided and replanted Oct-Mar.
Care Cut stems back almost to ground level after flowering.
Pests and diseases Generally trouble-free.

Achillea

Good ground cover; can be invasive.
Examples *A. millefolium* 'Cerise Queen' (yarrow) Height 2½ft, spacing 15in. Tiny white to cerise flowers June-Sept. *A. filipendulina* Height and spread 3ft. Clusters of lemon flowers July-Sept. 'Gold Plate', height 4-5ft, spread 2ft, has deep yellow flowers. *A. tomentosa* Ground-cover plant. Height 6-9in, spacing 12in. Densely packed bright yellow flower heads July-Sept.
Plant Oct-Mar in well-drained soil in sunny position.
Propagate by root division in Mar. Plant root portions immediately.
Pests and diseases Generally trouble-free.

Actinidia

Climber.
Examples *A. chinensis* (Chinese gooseberry) Height 30ft. Creamy flowers June-Aug, followed by edible egg-shaped fruits. *A. kolomikta* Height 6-12ft. Dark green, heart-shaped leaves with pink or white tips. Round white flowers in June.
Plant Nov-Mar, preferably in rich loam, but not in soils that are chalky, poorly drained or lacking humus. Plant against a wall or old tree. Male and female flowers of *A. chinensis* grow on separate plants, so plant specimens of both sexes to ensure pollination.
Propagate by cuttings July-Aug, in a greenhouse with bottom heat and mist propagation. Alternatively, sow seed in spring in a cold frame.
Care Pinch out growing points of young plants to encourage spreading growth.
Pests and diseases CATS.

Aechmea

Greenhouse or house plant.
Example *A. fasciata* Height 2ft. Tubular pink flowers in Aug.
Plant in late spring indoors or in a greenhouse in pots containing lime-free compost. For the first summer, keep the rosette filled with water, or at least moist.
Propagate by severing stolons (lateral stems) or sideshoots when they are one-third the size of the parent and plant them in the same compost mixture.
Care Water young plants freely during the growing period, and feed with half-strength liquid fertiliser. When fully grown, keep rosettes and soil just moist.
Pests and diseases Generally trouble-free.

Aethionema

Dwarf rock garden shrub.
Examples *A. grandiflorum* Height 6in, spread 18in. Pink flowers May-July. *A. pulchellum* Height 6-9in, spread 12in. Dark pink flowers May-July.
Sow in Mar in cold frame or greenhouse. Pot on May-June and plant out in well-drained soil and in sunny position Oct-Mar.
Care Remove stems after flowers fade.
Pests and diseases Generally trouble-free.

African lily (Agapanthus)

Clump-forming hardy perennial.
Examples *A. orientalis* Height 2½ft, spacing 18in. Vivid blue flower heads July-Sept. White and double blue forms available. *A.* 'Headbourne Hybrid' Height 2-2½ft, spacing 15-18in. Violet-blue to pale blue flowers July-Sept.
Plant Apr, in fertile, well-drained soil and in sunny but sheltered position. Set the crowns of the plants about 2in below ground level. Once planted, do not disturb.
Propagate by division Apr-May.
Care Water well during growing season and cut back stems to ground level after flowering. In cold sites protect plants Oct-Apr with 6-9in layer of bracken, or a 2-3in layer of ashes or sand.
Pests and diseases Generally trouble-free.

GARDEN TIP
Achillea

The brightly coloured flowers of some achilleas can be used for winter decoration indoors long after their garden display is over. The best candidates for this treatment are varieties of *Achillea filipendulina*. Their flat flower heads can be air-dried or treated with silica gel to preserve them almost indefinitely. For details on how to do this, see *Four ways to preserve your flowers*, page 142. Tall varieties of achillea, a hardy perennial which is also known as yarrow, will return with renewed vigour in spring if you cut them down to ground level in November.

African violet
Saintpaulia ionantha

Agave
Agave americana 'Variegata'

Ageratum
Ageratum houstonianum

Ajuga
Ajuga reptans 'Atropurpurea'

Allium
Allium moly

Almond, ornamental
Prunus dulcis

African violet (Saintpaulia ionantha)

House or greenhouse plant. Height 4in, spread 6-9in. Flowers can appear at any time of year, but most abundantly June-Oct.
Plant in peat compost indoors or in a greenhouse. Keep the compost only just moist and keep water off the leaves. Place plants in bright light but not direct sunlight.
Propagate June-Sept by leaf cuttings. Take cuttings with 2in stalks and insert stalks into half-and-half mixture of peat and sand. Enclose potted cuttings in propagator or plastic bag for 7-10 weeks until they root.
Care Repot established plants that are growing too big for their pots every other year in Apr; feed with half-strength liquid manure every 14 days May-Sept.
Pests and diseases Tarsonemid mites. Yellow rings on leaves are caused by water splashes.

Agave

Greenhouse or house plant.
Example *A. americana* Height 4ft. Grey-green, spiny dark leaves.
Plant indoors or in a greenhouse; in summer place the pots in a sunny position outdoors.
Propagate by removing offsets from the edge of the rosettes, drying them for several days, and planting them in John Innes No 2.
Care Water freely in growing season; repot in bigger pots, if necessary, in Apr; keep at 5°C (about 40°F) in winter.
Pests and diseases MEALY BUGS, ROOT MEALY BUGS.

Ageratum

Half-hardy annual bedding plant.
Example *A. houstonianum* Height and spacing 12in. Numerous hybrid varieties available with blue, mauve, pink or white flowers.
Sow seeds under glass Mar-Apr, and plant out May-June in sheltered, sunny position.
Care Deadhead regularly to prolong flowering period.
Pests and diseases FOOT ROT, root rot.

Ajuga

Perennial ground cover.
Examples *A. genevensis* Height 12in, spacing 6in. Blue, pink or white flowers June-July. Can be invasive. *A. pyramidalis* Height 9in, spacing 6in. Spikes of blue flowers with purple bracts in May. *A. reptans* Height 12in, spacing 18in. Blue flowers June-July. *A. r.* 'Atropurpurea' has purple leaves.
Plant in ordinary soil at any time except when soil is frozen or waterlogged. *A. genevensis* requires a sunny site, *A. pyramidalis* and *A. reptans* both do best in a moist, partly shaded situation.
Propagate by division at any time.
Pests and diseases Generally trouble-free.

Allium

Bulbous perennial.
Examples *A. moly* Height 12in, spacing 4in. Bright yellow starry flowers June-July. *A. ostrowskianum* Height 12in, spacing 3in. Star-shaped, rose-coloured flowers in June.
Plant bulbs Sept-Oct. Cover them to about four times their own depth – about 4in of soil above a 1in bulb, say – in well-drained soil and on a sunny site.
Propagate by dividing bulbs in autumn or spring if they become crowded. Replant immediately in moist soil.
Care Deadhead flowers, leaving the stems to feed the bulbs. Remove dead leaves and stems in autumn.
Pests and diseases SLUGS, WHITE ROT.

Almond, ornamental (Prunus)

Highly decorative tree or shrub.
Example *P. dulcis* Height 12ft, spread 15ft. Clear pink flowers Mar-Apr before leaves.
Plant in site sheltered from cold winds, in early autumn or spring and in any good, well-drained soil, preferably with a touch of lime.
Care In country districts, protect young trees from hares in winter by surrounding the trunks with chicken wire. Avoid digging or hoeing deeply near the trunk. Ornamental almonds, like other prunus varieties, are shallow-rooting plants.
Pests and diseases BIRDS, APHIDS, CATERPILLARS, honey fungus, leaf spot, POWDERY MILDEW.

GARDEN TIP
African violet

Many African violets are now sold with labels declaring that the plant is protected under the Plant Varieties and Seeds Act 1964. The Act allows plant breeders effectively to patent a variety they've bred.
But the protection does not mean that it is illegal for you to take cuttings from the plant – for your own use or to give away to friends. The Act merely makes it illegal, on pain of a fine of up to £400, for you to *sell* the cuttings without the breeder's permission.

Aloe
Aloe variegata

Alyssum
Alyssum maritimum

Amaryllis
Amaryllis belladonna

Amelanchier
Amelanchier lamarckii

Anemone
spring-flowering
Anemone coronaria 'De Caen'

Anemone
summer and autumn-flowering
Anemone x *hybrida*

Aloe

Greenhouse perennial.
Example *A. variegata* (partridge-breasted aloe) Height 12in. Dark green, white-banded leaves; orange flowers in early summer.
Propagate in summer by removing offsets (sideshoots), allowing them to dry for a few days and repotting them. Or sow seeds indoors or in a greenhouse in Mar. Repot established plants, if necessary, in Apr.
Pests and diseases MEALY BUGS, ROOT MEALY BUGS.

Alyssum

Dwarf plant for growing in rock garden or border.
Examples *A. maritimum* (also called *Lobularia maritima*) Border annual. Height 6in, spacing 12in. White, lilac or purple flowers June-Sept. *A. saxatile* (gold dust) Perennial. Height 12in, spacing 18in. Golden-yellow flowers produced Apr-June.
Sow perennial seeds in compost in a cold frame in Mar. Plant out in any ordinary garden soil in full sun from Sept. Sow annuals in flowering site Mar-Apr.
Care Cut perennials back hard after flowering. Deadhead annuals regularly by trimming.
Pests and diseases SLUGS, FLEA BEETLES, downy mildew.

Amaryllis

Tender bulbous perennial.
Example *A. belladonna* Height $2\frac{1}{2}$ft, spacing 12in. Pink trumpet-like flowers Sept-Oct.
Plant bulbs June-July, 6-8in deep in well-drained soil. Best site is against a south-facing wall.
Propagate by lifting mature plants when leaves turn yellow in summer; divide bulbs and replant immediately.
Pests and diseases Narcissus fly maggots, bulb scale mites.

Amelanchier (June berry)

Tree or shrub with year-round interest.
Example *A. lamarckii* Height and spread 10ft. White starry flowers in Apr followed by edible black berries in June. Brilliant autumn foliage. *A. lamarckii* is sometimes sold under the name *A. canadensis*.
Plant Nov-Mar in any good, moisture-retentive soil, in sun or partial shade.
Propagate by separating rooted suckers from the parent plant Oct-Mar.
Pests and diseases FIRE BLIGHT.

Anemone, spring-flowering

Border perennial.
Examples *A. blanda* Height 6in, spacing 4in. Blue flowers Feb-Apr. Pale blue, mauve, pink and white forms also available. *A. coronaria* 'De Caen'. Height 12in, spacing 4in. White, blue or red flowers Mar-Apr (or later with successive planting).
Plant Sept-Oct, 2in deep in sun or partial shade; *A. coronaria* does best in a position which is in full sun.
Propagate by division, or by separating offsets from parent plants after topgrowth has died down in late summer.
Pests and diseases FLEA BEETLES, CATERPILLARS, CUTWORMS, SLUGS.

Anemone, summer and autumn-flowering

Border perennial.
Example *A.* x *hybrida* Height 2-4ft, spacing 18in. White or pink flowers Aug-Oct.
Plant Oct-Mar in well-drained but moisture-retentive soil and in a spot which is in partial shade.
Propagate by dividing and replanting during mild weather Oct-Mar.
Care Avoid disturbance for several years after planting. Cut stems down to ground level after flowering. But if your garden is on an exposed site, or in colder parts of Britain, you can leave the dead stems on until spring to give the plant some extra protection against frost.
Pests and diseases See *Anemone, spring-flowering*.

GARDEN TIP
Anemone, summer and autumn-flowering

Don't expect varieties of *Anemone* x *hybrida* to burst into full bloom the first year you plant them. They can take a year or two to get established after a move. Once they do settle in, however, they flower very freely. Among the best varieties is 'Honorine Jobert', whose 2-3in wide white flowers wave atop 4ft stems; this variety is the one often sold as *Anemone japonica*. Two other attractive varieties are 'Queen Charlotte', whose pink and semi-double flowers reach to a height of about $2\frac{1}{2}$ft, and the 2ft tall, pink-flowered 'September Charm'.

Angelica	Antirrhinum	Aponogeton	Apple	Apricot	Aquilegia
Angelica archangelica	*Antirrhinum majus*	*Aponogeton distachyus*	'Cox's Orange Pippin'	'Moorpark'	*Aquilegia vulgaris*

Angelica

Biennial herb.
Height 10ft, spacing 3ft. Yellow-green flowers July-Aug. Candied leaf stalks used in confectionery and cake decoration.
Plant Mar, in moist, humus-rich soil and in sun or partial shade.
Harvest leaf stalks for candying May-June and side growths in Aug.
Propagate from fallen seeds. They germinate freely, producing dozens of seedlings.
Care If seedlings are not required, remove flower heads as soon as they appear, to increase the foliage and prolong the plant's life.
Pests and diseases Generally trouble-free.

Antirrhinum (Snapdragon)

Annual or short-lived perennial border plant.
There are two main groups: the Nanum group, which grows to 18in and flowers from July to the first frosts; and the Nanum Compactum group, which grows to 6in. Both groups of varieties are derived from *Antirrhinum majus*.
Sow under glass Feb-Mar and plant out in early summer, in well-drained soil enriched with manure and in sun or light shade. Alternatively, plant out bought bedding plants when the last frosts have passed. Set Nanum varieties 10-12in apart, Nanum Compactum varieties 9in apart.
Care Stake tall varieties. To induce side branching, pinch out growing points of all antirrhinums when the plants are 3-4in tall.
Pests and diseases APHIDS, BUMBLE BEES, FOOT AND ROOT ROT, GREY MOULD, RUST.

Aponogeton

Perennial water plant.
Example *A. distachyus* (water hawthorn, Cape pondweed) Water depth 2ft, surface spacing 18in. Floating leaves appear in spring, followed by white hawthorn-scented flower clusters.
Plant Apr-June in loam enriched with bone meal at the bottom of the pond. The tubers should be covered by at least 18in of water to ensure protection from ice.
Propagate by division in spring.
Pests and diseases Generally trouble-free.

Apple (Malus sylvestris or M. domestica)

Fruit tree.
Apples are divided into cooking (C) and dessert (D) varieties.
Examples 'Bramley's Seedling' (C) large green fruits, usually tinged with red; susceptible to late frost; flowers mid-season. 'Cox's Orange Pippin' (D) russet-skinned fruit; susceptible to disease and frost; flowers mid-season.
Plant bare-root specimens Nov, container-grown plants at any time. Soil should be deep, moisture-retaining and enriched with compost. The site should be sunny but sheltered from cold winds.
Pruning See *How to prune apple trees*, page 15.
Pollination See *Pollination partners*, page 17.
Care Water the trees in prolonged dry weather May-July and give annual dressing of high-nitrogen and high-potash fertiliser Jan-Feb.
Pest and diseases BIRDS, codling moths, apple sawfly, APHIDS, capsid bugs, CATERPILLARS, apple canker, apple mildew, apple scab, honey fungus.

Apricot (Prunus armeniaca)

Fruit tree.
Example 'Moorpark' Height 12ft, spread 10ft. White flowers Feb-Mar; fruits Aug.
Plant Oct-Nov in ordinary, fertile soil. Even in warmer parts of the country, apricots do best if fan-trained against a south-facing wall.
Pruning Strengthen the framework of young trees by shortening leading shoots in Mar.
Care Pollinate the flowers by hand with a camel-hair paintbrush. Cover the pollinated blossoms with fine muslin bags for protection against spring frosts; the bags can be left on until the fruits appear.
Give the trees a winter feed of bone meal and a high-potash fertiliser.
Pests and diseases Glasshouse red spider mites, SCALE INSECTS, SILVER LEAF.

Aquilegia (Columbine)

Border perennial.
Example *A. vulgaris* (granny's bonnet) Height 2ft, spacing 12in. Grey-green foliage. Blue, pink, yellow, red, white or purple flowers are produced in May-June.
Plant Sept-Mar in well-drained leafy soil and in sun or partial shade.
Propagate by division Oct-Mar.
Care Cut stems to ground level after flowering.
Pests and diseases APHIDS, leaf spot.

Asparagus
Asparagus officinalis

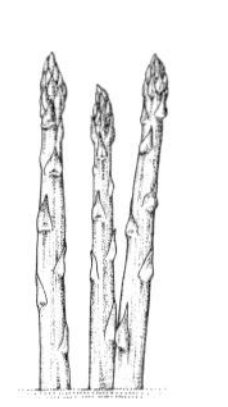

Aspidistra
Aspidistra elatior

Astilbe
Astilbe x arendsii

Aubrieta
Aubrieta deltoidea

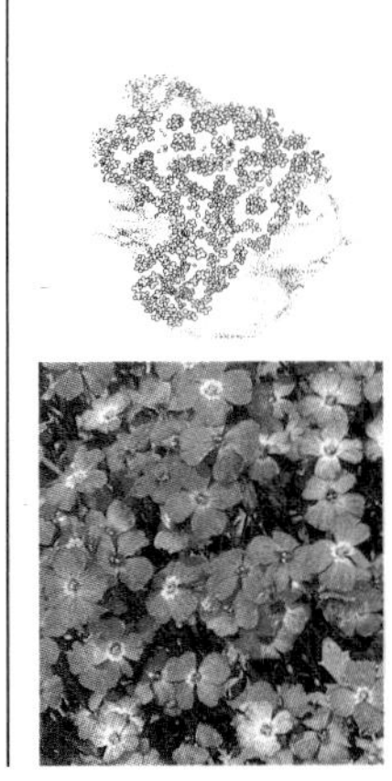

Autumn crocus
Colchicum speciosum

Azalea
Rhododendron

Asparagus (Asparagus officinalis)

Perennial vegetable.
Examples 'Connover's Colossal' and 'Kidner's Pedigree' – both best grown from plants. 'Brocks Imperial' and 'Martha Washington' – best grown from seed.
Plant one-year-old crowns 2ft apart on a ridge in a prepared trench in early Apr. Dig trenches 12in wide and 8in deep. Mix sand with the excavated soil, and using the mixture make a 3in high ridge at the bottom of the trench. Spread the roots of each crown down the sides of the ridge and cover the crowns with 2-3in of soil. Continue to keep them covered as growth develops. Alternatively, sow seeds in Apr, ½in deep in a bed prepared with well-rotted manure or compost. When the seedlings are 6in tall, thin them to 12in apart. Seed-raised plants may take four years to reach harvesting size.
Harvest In the first year of cropping (the second year after planting one-year-old crowns), take only two or three shoots from each plant in mid-May. When the bed is established, you can safely extend the harvesting period from late April or early May to the first half of June. Cut stems about 4in below the surface of the piled-up soil.
Pests and diseases Asparagus beetle, frost damage, violet root rot.

Aspidistra

House plant with year-round foliage.
Example *A. elatior* Height 12in, spread 2ft. Dark green leaves up to 20in long; inconspicuous purple flowers Aug.
Plant in Mar in 6in pots of compost.
Propagate by division Mar-Apr.
Care Aspidistras thrive in most living-room temperatures and conditions. Water freely in summer and wash leaves occasionally. Keep compost just moist in winter. Repot in progressively larger pots every two or three years, and in summer give occasional weak feeds of standard liquid house-plant fertiliser.
Pests and diseases Glasshouse red spider mites, SCALE INSECTS.

Astilbe

Hardy border perennial.
Example *A.* x *arendsii* Height 3ft, spacing 2ft. Feathery pink, white and red flowers June-Aug.
Plant in groups Oct-Mar, in moist, fertile soil, in sun or partial shade.
Propagate by division Mar-Apr.
Care Mulch in late spring and water freely in dry weather. Cut stems to ground level in autumn.
Pests and diseases Generally trouble-free.

Aubrieta

Evergreen border or rock garden perennial.
Example *A. deltoidea* Height 4in, spread 2ft. Flowers, in various shades of purple, Mar-June.
Plant Sept-Mar in rockeries, on dry-stone walls or between paving, in well-drained, limy soil and in full sun.
Propagate Sept, by division.
Care Trim after flowering to encourage neat growth.
Pests and diseases White blister, downy mildew.

Autumn crocus (Colchicum)

Bulbous perennial.
Examples *C. autumnale* Height 6in, spread 9in. Rose-lilac flowers Sept-Nov. *C. speciosum* Height 10in, spread 12in. Rose-purple, white, or purple-veined flowers Oct-Nov.
Plant July or early Aug, in any well-drained soil. Plant *C. autumnale* 4in deep, *C. speciosum* 6in deep.
Propagate by separating and replanting corms June-July.
Pests and diseases SLUGS.

Azalea (Rhododendron)

Flowering shrub.
Once regarded as a separate genus, azaleas are now grouped botanically with rhododendrons. The popular evergreen hybrids have an average height and spread of 5ft, and flower in May.
Plant Sept-Apr in well-drained but moisture-retentive sandy loam. Rhododendrons cannot tolerate chalk, or a soil in which their roots dry out. Give plenty of peat, and plant in sites sheltered from the wind and from early morning sun.
Propagate by layering July-Aug. Sever rooted shoots from the parent plant two years later.
Care Give an annual mulch and a spring feed of general fertiliser. Deadhead the plants with finger and thumb, not secateurs.
Pests and diseases CATERPILLARS, azalea gall, chlorosis, honey fungus, rhododendron bud blast.

GARDEN TIP
Aspidistra

If you're beginning to despair of making anything grow well indoors, consider the aspidistra. It'll tolerate extremes of temperature, shrug off gas fumes and thrive on a diet of neglect and bad light – which is largely why it was so popular as a house plant in the dim, gas-lit rooms of Victorian homes. One of the most attractive members of the family is a variegated variety, *Aspidistra elatior* 'Variegata'. Its leaves are striped with cream.

Balm	Bamboo	Basil	Bay	Beech	Beetroot
Melissa officinalis 'Aurea'	*Arundinaria japonica*	*Ocimum basilicum*	*Laurus nobilis*	*Fagus sylvatica*	*Beta vulgaris conditiva* 'Detroit'

Balm (Melissa officinalis)

Perennial herb with lemon-scented leaves.
Example *M. o.* 'Aurea' (golden balm) Height up to 4ft. Lemon-scented leaves. Small white flowers June-July.
Sow seeds outdoors late Apr to early May. Use well-drained soil, preferably in full sun.
Propagate by dividing and replanting roots Oct or Mar.
Care In autumn cut all growths hard back to near ground level. Cover roots with straw or bracken in cold areas in winter.
Pests and diseases Generally trouble-free.

Bamboo (Arundinaria)

Clump-forming ornamental grass.
Examples *A. japonica* (Japanese bamboo) Height 15ft, spread 6-8ft. Glossy, dark green, sharp-pointed leaves. Forms thickets; not suitable for small gardens. *A. nitida* Height 9-10ft, spread 4ft. Fast-growing with purple stems. It has never been known to flower in cultivation. *A. variegata* Height up to 4ft, spread 6ft. Dense thicket-forming species with zigzagged canes and white-striped leaves.
Plant Apr-May in good moist soil in sunny site.
Propagate by dividing and replanting clumps in Apr.
Care Give shelter from cold winds.
Pests and diseases Generally trouble-free.

Basil (Ocimum basilicum)

Culinary herb; half-hardy annual. Height 2-3ft. Aromatic leaves used in cooking. Small white flowers Aug.
Sow ½in deep in May, in drills 15in apart. Thin out seedlings gradually to 12in apart.
Care Water in dry weather but let soil dry out between waterings. Pinch off the white flowers as soon as they appear – usually in Aug – to encourage the growth of more leaves. Harvest fresh leaves July-Sept. Leaves can also be dried or frozen to preserve them for winter use.
Pests and diseases Generally trouble-free.

Bay (Laurus)

Evergreen shrub.
Example *L. nobilis* (sweet bay) Height and spread – if unrestricted – 18ft. Glossy, aromatic leaves used whole in cooking. *L. n.* 'Aurea' has gold leaves. Both male and female plants have inconspicuous yellow-green flowers in April, but only female plants bear purple-black ½in long berries.
Plant Mar-Apr in ordinary soil in a sunny, sheltered position. Or grow standard or half-standard shrubs in 18in tubs containing potting compost, and move tubs to sheltered places in cold weather.
Propagate by heel cuttings Aug-Sept.
Care Prune and shape tub-grown bays in summer.
Pests and diseases SCALE INSECTS.

Beech (Fagus)

Tree and hedging plant.
Example *F. sylvatica* Height and spread 40ft. *F. s.* 'Cuprea' has copper leaves, *F. s.* 'Purpurea' purple-red ones. Autumn foliage is retained through winter, particularly if the plants are trimmed in late summer.
Plant Oct-Mar in well-drained soil and in sunny position. Beeches do not thrive on damp clay soils. For hedging, the best results are from 12in plants spaced 18in apart.
Care Remove the top quarter of all shoots after planting, to encourage beech hedges to become more bushy. Remove tips again in the following year and thereafter trim to shape July-Aug.
Pests and diseases SCALE INSECTS, weevil, apple canker, bracket fungi, CORAL SPOT, honey fungus, SCORCH.

Beetroot (Beta vulgaris conditiva)

Annual vegetable.
There are two main types – globe and long-rooted. Globe beetroots are less prone to bolting and can be sown earlier than the long-rooted type. 'Avonearly' and 'Boltardy' are good early globes; for autumn and early winter, try 'Detroit'. Long beets – used as maincrop for winter storing – include 'Cheltenham Green Top' and 'Cylindra'.
Sow thinly in ¾in deep drills, allowing 12in between rows. Thin the seedlings to 4-5in apart for globes, 8in for long-rooted varieties. Make successive sowings from late Mar or early Apr to July. Soil should be well-dug and manured, with a top-dressing of general fertiliser added just before planting.
Harvest early globes as required from June. Maincrops can be left in the ground for winter use, or lifted in Nov and stored in boxes of peat or sand. Twist off the leafy tops for storage, but take care not to damage the roots, which bleed easily.
Pests and diseases Mangold fly, SWIFT MOTH CATERPILLARS, SCAB, violet root rot.

Begonia
Begonia semperflorens 'Organdy Mixed'

Berberis
Berberis x *stenophylla*

Bergenia
Bergenia crassifolia

Birch
Betula pendula

Bluebell
Endymion nonscriptus

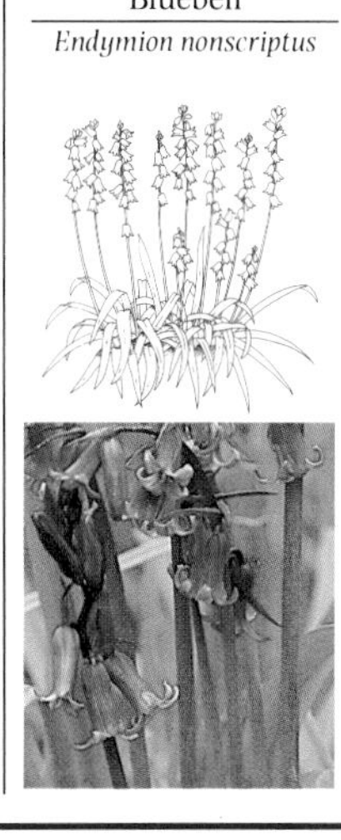

Borage
Borago officinalis

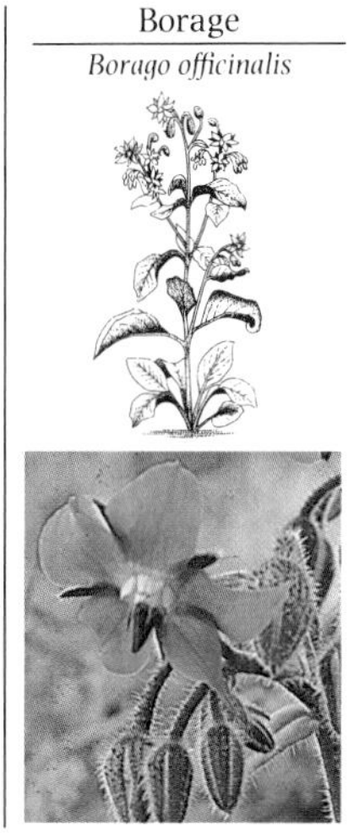

Begonia

Tender border perennial.
Examples *B.* x *tuberhybrida* Height 1-2ft, spacing 12-15in. Large, rose-like flowers in a range of colours, June-Sept. *B. semperflorens* Height and spread 6-9in. Glossy bright green or dark purple leaves. Red, pink or white flowers, June-Sept.
Plant tubers hollow side uppermost in any good, well-drained soil, and in sun or light shade. Harden the plants off in a cold frame in May before planting out in early June.
Sow *B. semperflorens* Feb-Mar under glass at a temperature of 16°C (about 60°F). Prick seedlings into boxes and harden off in a cold frame before planting out in late May.
Propagate by dividing and repotting tubers and taking cuttings in Apr.
Care Lift tubers in mid-Oct when the foliage has died down, and store them indoors through winter in boxes of almost dry peat.
Pests and diseases Weevils, tarsonemid mites, POWDERY MILDEW, damping-off, tomato spotted viruses.

Berberis (Barberry)

Decorative shrub.
Examples *B. buxifolia* Height and spread up to 6ft. Dark green evergreen foliage. Yellow flowers Mar-Apr followed by blue-black berries. *B.* x *stenophylla* Height and spread 10-12ft. Evergreen. Gold flower plumes in Apr followed by purple berries. *B. thunbergii* 'Aurea' Height and spread 4ft. Deciduous. Golden foliage. Yellow flowers June-July, then scarlet berries.
Plant evergreen types Sept-Apr, deciduous Oct-Mar in ordinary soil; evergreens in sun or shade, deciduous in sun. For hedges, plant 15in high plants 2ft apart; cut back all shoots by a quarter.
Propagate by semi-hardwood cuttings July-Sept.
Care Keep young plants well-watered. *B. buxifolia* requires a site with some shelter from winter winds. Clip hedges annually – evergreens after flowering, deciduous in late summer.
Pests and diseases Honey fungus.

Bergenia

Hardy perennial border plant.
Examples *B. cordifolia* Height and spacing 12in. Clusters of dark lilac, bell-shaped flowers Jan-Apr. *B. crassifolia* Height and spacing 12in. Pale pink, bell-like flowers Jan-Apr.
Plant Oct-Mar in sun or part shade. Leave undisturbed until over-crowding makes division necessary.
Propagate by division Sept-Oct or Mar.
Pests and diseases Leaf spot.

Birch (Betula)

Graceful, deciduous tree.
Example *B. pendula* (silver birch) Height 30ft plus, spread 12ft. Weeping tree whose bark is silver slashed with black.
Plant in loamy soil and in sun or shade Oct-Mar, though the trees will do reasonably well in most situations.
Pests and diseases CATERPILLARS, sawflies, bracket fungi, RUST.

Bluebell

Native perennial.
Examples *Campanula rotundifolia* (Scots bluebell; harebell in England) Height 6-12in, spread 18in. Bell-like flowers, slate to blue-purple, June-Aug. *C. r.* 'Alba' is pure white. *Endymion nonscriptus* (also known as *Scilla nonscripta, S. nutans* and *Hyacinthus nonscriptus*. This is the common English bluebell; it's also known in Scotland as the wild hyacinth) Height 12in, spacing 4in. Purple-blue flowers, Apr-June.
Plant endymion bulbs 4-6in deep in moist soil, well enriched with organic matter. Best in partial shade.
Propagate by lifting and dividing clumps after flowering or when dormant.
Pests and diseases RUST.

Borage (Borago officinalis)

Annual herb.
Height 3ft, spacing 12in. Deep blue flowers June-Sept. Its flowers and leaves are mostly used to flavour summer drinks.
Sow Apr, in almost any soil, preferably in well-drained ground and in a sunny position. Thin seedlings to 12in apart.
Harvest flowers and young leaves only when required.
Propagate by self-sown seedlings; the plant can be invasive.
Pest and diseases Generally trouble-free.

GARDEN TIP
Birch

Don't plant birches near flower borders or fences. The trees all have widespreading shallow roots that can get in the way of cultivating your bed or could damage a fence. For the same reason, make a point of watering your trees during long periods of dry weather. Wild birches often grow on acidic, sandy soils. But the trees will also thrive on any reasonable soil, and in sun or dappled shade.

Box	Broad bean	Broccoli	Broom	Broom	Brunnera
Buxus sempervirens	*Vicia faba*	*Brassica oleracea botrytis*	*Cytisus scoparius*	*Genista pilosa* 'Prostrata'	*Brunnera macrophylla*

Box (Buxus)

Dense-leaved hedging shrub.
Example *B. sempervirens* Height 6-10ft, spread 6ft.
Plant Sept-Oct or Mar-Apr in ordinary soil and in sun or light shade. For hedges, space 12in tall plants 12in apart. Remove one-third of each leading shoot immediately after planting or in the following Apr to promote bushy growth.
Propagate by taking 3-4in long cuttings in Aug-Sept. Insert the cuttings in pots of peat and sand in a cold frame. Grow on for two years before planting out.
Prune to required shape Aug-Sept.
Pests and diseases Box suckers, leaf spot, RUST.

Broad bean (Vicia faba)

Annual vegetable.
There are three types: Longpod varieties such as 'Exhibition'; Windsor varieties such as 'Unrivalled'; and late-sowing Longpod varieties such as 'Aquadulce Claudia' and 'The Sutton' (dwarf). All but dwarf varieties grow 3ft or more high.
Sow in open ground Nov-Dec for early crop, or under cloches in Jan-Feb. Or transplant seedlings in Mar. Medium-heavy soils best but any fertile, well-drained soil suits. Dress acid soil with lime. Prepare the bed before planting by digging 2 spits deep, working well-rotted manure into bottom spit at 1 bucket per sq yd. Sow seeds 6in apart in 3in deep drills, with rows 2ft apart, or 15in for dwarfs.
Harvest Pick pods as soon as seeds are $\frac{3}{4}$in across. After harvesting cut tops down, but leave roots in soil to release their nitrogen.
Pests and diseases SLUGS, bean fly maggots, APHIDS, anthracnose of dwarf bean, black root rot, rhizoctonia.

Broccoli (Brassica oleracea botrytis)

Annual vegetable.
There are three types: purple-sprouting such as 'Christmas Purple' (ready for harvesting Jan-Feb); white-sprouting such as 'Early White' (ready for harvesting Mar-Apr); and calabrese (green-sprouting) such as 'Express Corona' which is ready for harvesting from early autumn to first frosts.
Sow in well-manured soil, Mar-May, in $\frac{1}{2}$in deep drills 12in apart. In spring, give a top-dressing of lime, and of general fertiliser two weeks before planting. Thin seedlings to about 12in apart.
Harvest when the spears are 4-6in long, but before the flower buds have opened. Cut the central spears first, to encourage the side ones to develop. Cropping should continue for about six weeks.
Care Water well in dry spells. Protect from birds.
Pests and diseases See *Cabbage*, opposite page.

Broom (Cytisus)

Shrub.
Examples *C. battandieri* Height 15ft, spread 8ft. Fragrant yellow flowers May-June. *C. scoparius* Height and spread 8ft. Flowers in various colours May-June.
Plant in peaty soil in autumn or spring. *C. battandieri* does best in rich loam against a south-facing wall.
Propagate by heel cuttings Aug-Sept.
Care Cut back flowered stems to new shoots in summer.
Pests and diseases Gall mites.

Broom (Genista)

Shrub.
Examples *G. aetnensis* (Mount Etna broom) Height and spread 15ft. Light green leaves. Gold-yellow flowers July-Aug. *G. hispanica* (Spanish gorse) Height 2-4ft, spread 4-6ft. Dark green leaves. Golden flowers June-July. Hardy only in the South. *G. pilosa* Height 18in, spread 2-3ft. Also creeping form, height 3in, spread 3-4ft. Mid-green leaves, yellow flowers May-July.
Plant in full sun. Genistas do best in poor, sandy soil.
Propagate by heel cuttings in Aug.
Care Pinch out growing tips on young plants after flowering. No regular pruning needed.
Pests and diseases Generally trouble-free.

Brunnera

Hardy perennial.
Example *B. macrophylla* Height and spacing 18in. Pale blue flowers Apr-June. The variety *B. m.* 'Variegata' has cream-edged leaves.
Plant Oct-Mar in any ordinary garden soil, ideally in light shade. Brunneras do well under trees.
Propagate by dividing and replanting roots in Oct-Mar. Or take root cuttings Oct-Nov and insert in half-and-half mixture of peat and sand in a cold frame. Plant out rooted cuttings May-June.
Care Remove stems after flowering, and prune out any stems of *B. m.* 'Variegata' that revert to the green foliage of the species.
Pests and diseases Generally trouble-free.

Brussels sprouts (Brassica oleracea gemmifera)

Annual vegetable.
Examples On light soils and in windy positions, try small-growing varieties such as 'Peer Gynt' or 'Achilles', both ready in Oct. On medium to heavy soils, good varieties include 'Early Half Tall', ready in Sept, 'Fasolt' (Nov-Feb), 'Perfect Line' (Dec-Jan), and 'Citadel' (Dec-Mar).
Sow sprouts in a sheltered seedbed in Sept for transplanting the following year. Sow seeds thinly in $\frac{1}{2}$in drills 6in apart. Transplant to permanent bed in batches mid-May to mid-June to ensure succession of crops. Permanent bed should be deeply dug and well enriched with manure or compost. Just before transplanting, add 3oz of Growmore per sq yd. Sprouts should not be grown in ground that grew brassicas the previous year.
Pick sprouts from the bottom of the stem upwards as they ripen. A second crop often develops from the stem upwards if they are harvested in this way.
Pests and diseases APHIDS, cabbage whitefly, CATERPILLARS, CABBAGE ROOT FLY, downy mildew, CLUB ROOT, frost damage, leaf spot.

Buddleia

Decorative shrub.
Examples *B. alternifolia* Height 12-20ft, spread 15-20ft. Lavender-blue scented flowers in rounded clusters June. *B. davidii* (butterfly bush) Height 9ft, spread 7-12ft. Scented arching flower spikes July-Oct. The flowers are extremely popular with butterflies.
Plant Oct-Nov or Mar-Apr in full sun in any ordinary soil.
Propagate by 9-12in long hardwood cuttings Oct-Mar, or by 4-5in long semi-ripe heel cuttings July-Aug.
Care Feed only on very poor soil to avoid encouraging excessive foliage. Prune *B. davidii* in spring, cutting back to the lowest buds of the previous year's growth. Remove flowered shoots of *B. alternifolia* after flowering.
Pests and diseases Generally trouble-free.

Busy lizzie (Impatiens)

Half-hardy annual.
Examples *I. balsamina* Height and spacing 6-15in. Flowers June-autumn. *I. walleriana* (also known as *I. holstii*) Height 2ft, spacing 6-15in. Scarlet flowers Apr-Oct.
Sow Mar under glass at a temperature of 16°C (about 60°F). Prick seedlings into pots and harden off before planting out in late May, in sun or partial shade.
Pests and diseases APHIDS, SLUGS.

Cabbage (Brassica oleracea capitata)

Annual vegetable.
Examples Spring cabbages 'Durham Early', 'Harbinger'; summer cabbage 'Primo'; autumn and winter cabbages 'January King', 'Large Blood Red'.
Sow summer cabbages in early spring; autumn and winter cabbages in late spring; and spring cabbages in late summer and autumn – the types are named after their harvesting season. Start them in trays under glass or in a seedbed and transplant to permanent sites when large enough to handle. Transplant summer cabbages Apr-May; autumn and winter varieties June-July; spring cabbages Sept-Oct. Cabbages do well in any ordinary soil which has been 'sweetened' with 4oz of carbonate of lime added per sq yd in spring.
Harvest Grown in succession, cabbages can be harvested throughout the year.
Pest and diseases APHIDS, CABBAGE ROOT FLY, FLEA BEETLES, CATERPILLARS, CLUB ROOT, damping-off, frost damage.

Calandrinia

Grown as annual border plant.
Example *C. umbellata* Height 6in, spacing 9-12in. Clusters of crimson flowers July-Sept.
Sow Apr in rockery or border, in open, sunny site and in light, sandy soil. Thin out to required spacing.
Pests and diseases Generally trouble-free.

Calceolaria

Rock garden and bedding plant.
Examples *C. biflora* (alpine species) Height 6-12in, spacing 12-18in. Yellow flowers July-Aug. *C. integrifolia* 'Sunshine' (bedding species) Height 12in, spacing 9in. Yellow flowers June-Oct.
Plant out *C. i.* 'Sunshine' in Apr in any reasonable garden soil. Does best in full sun. Because raising from seed is difficult, bedding displays are best created from bought plants.
Sow alpine species July or Mar on surface of seed compost in a cold frame or greenhouse. Grow on in frost-free frame and plant out in Apr of following year.
Propagate alpine species by dividing and replanting in Apr, *C. integrifolia* by cuttings Aug-Sept.
Care Remove faded flower stems from alpine species after flowering and protect plants in winter with glass.
Pests and diseases APHIDS, SLUGS.

Callicarpa	Callistephus	Camellia	Campanula	Canary creeper	Candytuft
Callicarpa rubella	*Callistephus chinensis*	*Camellia japonica*	*Campanula carpatica*	*Tropaeolum peregrinum*	*Iberis sempervirens*
	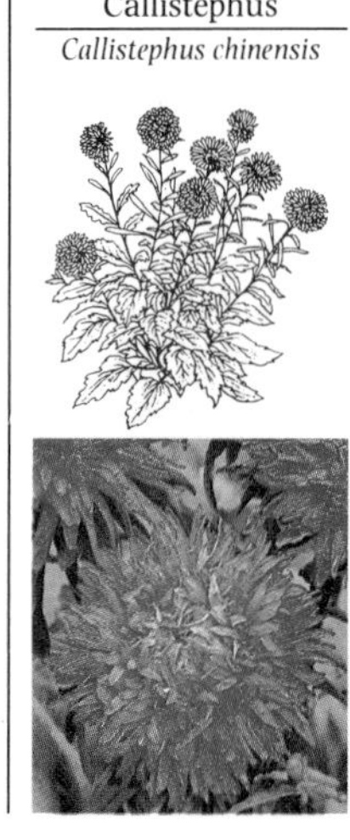				

Callicarpa

Deciduous tree or shrub.
Examples *C. bodinieri giraldii* Height and spread 6ft. Lilac flowers produced in July, followed by purple berries. *C. rubella* Height 7-10ft, spread 5-6ft. Pink flowers produced in July followed by red-purple berries.
Plant Oct-Mar in any good soil and in sunny, sheltered position; best against a south-facing wall.
Propagate by heel cuttings July-Aug.
Care In cold gardens, cover lower parts of young plants in winter with straw or bracken. Cut previous year's growth back to young wood in Feb.
Pest and diseases Generally trouble-free.

Callistephus (China aster)

Half-hardy annual.
Example *C. chinensis* Numerous varieties available including: dwarf strains (height 8-9in) such as 'Pinocchio Mixed'; and the Lilliput strain (height 15in). Taller varieties include: 'Powder Puff Mixed' (height 2ft). All varieties produce flowers in shades of pink, red, purple and white from July to first frosts.
Sow seeds under glass in Mar. Harden off seedlings and plant out in May. Plants thrive in any well-drained garden soil in an open, sunny position.
Care Large varieties may require staking. Deadhead to improve flowering of sideshoots.
Pests and diseases APHIDS, CATERPILLARS, callistephus wilt, tomato spotted wilt virus.

Camellia

Decorative shrub.
Examples *C. japonica* Height 12ft, spread 8ft. Varieties include 'Adolphe Audusson' (semi-double, scarlet flowers), 'Arejishi' (salmon-pink), 'Nobilissima' (peony-flowered, white). Flowers produced Mar-Apr. *C. reticulata* 'Captain Rawes' Height 15ft, spread 12ft. Red flowers Feb-Apr. *C.* x *williamsii* 'Donation' Height 8ft, spread 6ft. Silver-pink flowers Nov-Apr. One of the hardiest and best of camellias.
Plant Sept-Oct or Mar-Apr in lime-free soil in sun or light shade. *C. reticulata* does best fan-trained against a warm west-facing wall, or in a cool greenhouse in colder areas.
Propagate by taking 3-4in long cuttings July-Sept, or by layering *C. reticulata* in Sept.
Care Prevent frost damage to flower buds by covering with polythene. Mulch with 2in layer of leaf mould or peat in spring. Protect from morning sun by not planting against east-facing walls.
Pests and diseases BIRDS, MEALY BUGS, bud drop, frost damage, honey fungus.

Campanula

Perennial rock garden and border plant.
Examples *C. carpatica* Height 12in, spacing 15in. Blue, white and purple flowers July-Aug. *C. persicifolia* Height 1-3ft, spacing 12-15in. White, blue or purple-blue flowers June-Aug.
Plant in well-drained soil and in sun. Does well in rockery, dry wall or between paving.
Propagate by division Mar-Apr.
Pests and diseases SLUGS AND SNAILS, FROGHOPPERS, tomato spotted wilt virus.

Canary creeper (Tropaeolum peregrinum)

Vigorous climbing annual.
Height 12ft, spacing 15in. Vigorous climber with yellow flowers produced July-Oct.
Sow two or three seeds in the flowering site in Apr, later removing all but the strongest seedling. Does best in reasonably well-fertilised soil and in a sunny position against a wall or dead tree.
Pests and diseases APHIDS, tomato spotted wilt virus.

Candytuft (Iberis sempervirens)

Rockery evergreen.
Height 9in, spread 2ft; dense heads of white flowers which are produced in May-June. Varieties include 'Little Gem' (height 4in, spread 9in), 'Snowflake' (height 6-9in, mat-forming), and 'Plena', which has double flowers.
Plant Sept-Mar in a sunny position. Plants do well even in poor soil.
Propagate by 2in long softwood cuttings June-Aug.
Pests and diseases FLEA BEETLES.

GARDEN TIP
Carrot

To avoid sowing tiny carrot seeds thickly, mix them with a little peat or sand, then sow the mixture. From an early variety, you can expect to harvest about 8lb of carrots from a 10ft row. From a maincrop, you could get 10lb. To grow perfect show-bench carrots, go for the variety 'St Valery'. Use a broom handle to make a deep cone-shaped hole, and fill it with potting compost or growing bag mixture. Sow three seeds in the top and thin to the strongest seedling. Feed the plant every 7-10 days and keep the ground moist.

Canterbury bell
Campanula medium

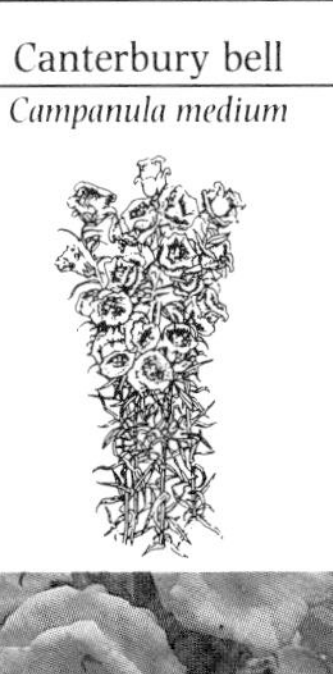

Caraway
Carum carvi

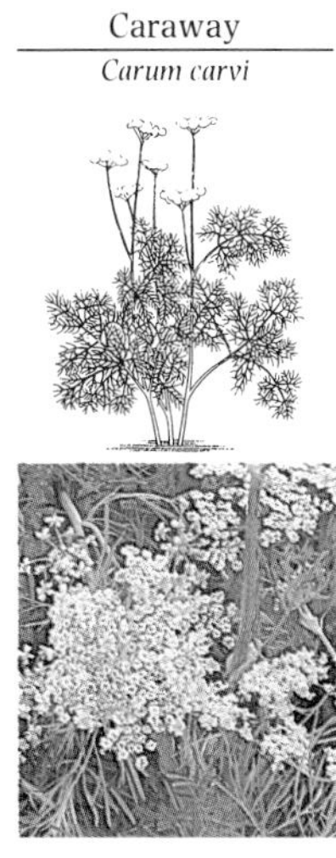

Carnation, border
Dianthus caryophyllus 'Bookham Sprite'

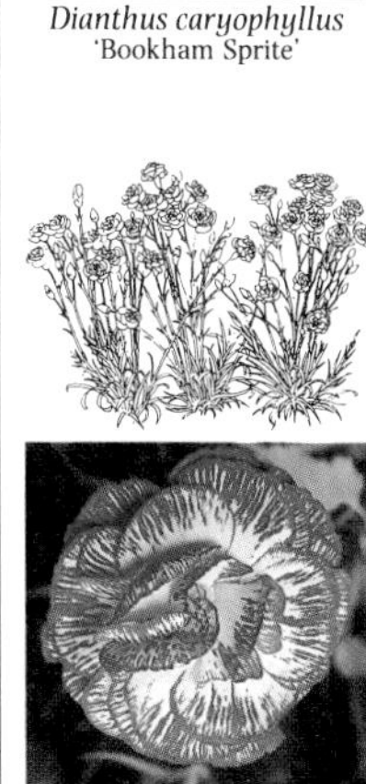

Carrot
'Chantenay Red Cored'

Caryopteris
Caryopteris x *clandonensis*

Cauliflower
'Polaris'

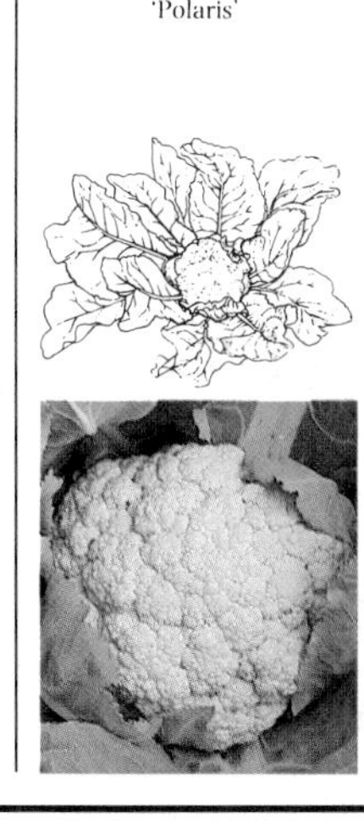

Canterbury bell (Campanula)

Back-of-the-border biennial.
Example *C. medium* Height 3ft, spacing 12in. Flowers May-June. Varieties include 'Bells of Holland' (pink, blue and white flowers).
Sow Apr-June for flowering the following year. Plant out in well-drained soil in sunny position.
Care Deadhead regularly. Stake tall plants in exposed sites.
Pests and diseases SLUGS, SNAILS, FROGHOPPERS, leaf spot, tomato spotted wilt virus.

Caraway (Carum carvi)

Biennial herb.
Height 3ft, spacing 12in. Ferny leaves. Minute white flowers June-July are followed by seed heads, which are dried and used in cooking.
Sow Sept or Mar in any fertile, well-drained soil, preferably in full sun. Do not feed or top-dress.
Harvest when the seeds are ripe. Cut the stalks at ground level and tie into bundles; hang these in a shed until the seeds are dry, when they can be rubbed off. Place a sheet of paper under the bundles to catch the seeds, which should be stored in airtight jars.
Pests and diseases Generally trouble-free.

Carnation (Dianthus)

Perennial border plant.
Example *D. caryophyllus* Height 1-2ft, spacing 12in. Pink, red, yellow, purple and white flowers July-Sept. Numerous varieties available, some of which are scented.
Sow Mar-Apr in seed compost indoors or in a greenhouse. Harden off in a cold frame and plant out in May in any well-drained garden soil which is not acid. Plants do best in full sun.
Propagate by layering young plants in July-Aug.
Care Stake tall plants. Disbud flower stems in June.
Pests and diseases APHIDS, carnation fly, BIRDS, THRIPS, CATERPILLARS, carnation ring spot, carnation stem rot.

Carrot (Daucus carota)

Annual vegetable.
There are three types: short-rooted types such as 'Amsterdam Forcing'; intermediate-rooted, early-maincrop ones such as 'Autumn King' or 'Chantenay Red Cored'; and long-rooted, later-maincrop types such as 'St Valery'.
Sow in deep soil, in sun or partial shade, and in ½in deep drills 9-12in apart. Do not add manure to soil; it can cause forking. Thin crowded seedlings to final 3in intervals. For succession, sow short-rooted carrots Feb-Mar, and intermediate and long-rooted types at two-weekly intervals from Apr to mid-July.
Harvest as required from June. Carrots for winter storing can be dug up in mid-Oct and stored in outdoor clamps, or in deep boxes of sand in a dry shed.
Pests and diseases CARROT FLY, APHIDS, splitting, violet root rot.

Caryopteris

Decorative shrub.
Example *C.* x *clandonensis* Height and spread to 4ft. Aromatic, grey-green leaves; bright blue flowers produced in Aug-Sept. Varieties include 'Ferndown' (deep blue or mauve flowers) and 'Kew Blue' (blue).
Plant Sept-Oct or Mar-Apr in ordinary garden soil, in a sunny position.
Propagate by cuttings Aug-Sept.
Care In cold areas, grow plants against a wall or fence. Cut previous year's growth back hard in Mar.
Pests and diseases Generally trouble-free.

Cauliflower (Brassica oleracea botrytis)

Annual vegetable.
There are four types: early-maturing (ready for harvesting May-June) such as 'Polaris'; mid-season (ready June-Aug) such as 'Rocket'; late-maturing (ready Sept-Dec) such as 'Conquest'; and Australian late-maturing (ready Sept-Dec) such as 'Kangaroo'.
Sow early and mid-season cauliflowers in seed compost Sept or Jan and germinate at around 16°C (about 60°F). Plant out young plants early Apr onwards, allowing 1½-2ft each way per plant. Sow later groups in outdoor beds Mar-May. Plant all cauliflowers in a sunny position and in rich loam or in lighter soils that have been well-manured. Non-limy soils should be given a dressing of about 4oz per sq yd of garden lime in spring.
Harvest in the morning when the dew is still on the plants. Break leaves over curds if necessary to shade them or to delay maturity.
Pests and diseases BIRDS, CABBAGE ROOT FLY, downy mildew, CLUB ROOT, wire stem, frost damage, leaf spot.

Ceanothus
Ceanothus x 'Gloire de Versailles'

Cedar
Cedrus atlantica

Celeriac
Apium graveolens rapaceum

Celery
'Green-snap'

Centaurea
Centaurea montana

Chamaecyparis
Chamaecyparis lawsoniana

Ceanothus

Flowering shrub.
Examples *C.* x 'Autumnal Blue' Height and spread 8-10ft. Evergreen. Blue flowers July-autumn. *C. azureus* Height and spread 4-6ft. Deciduous. Needs a sunny wall. Long, fluffy plumes of deep blue flowers July-Sept. *C.* x 'Gloire de Versailles' Height and spread 6-8ft. Deciduous. Powder-blue, fragrant flowers June-Oct.
Plant Sept or Apr-May in light and ideally non-alkaline garden soil. Can be grown in an open, sunny position, but does best trained against a south or west-facing wall or fence.
Propagate by heel cuttings in July-Aug.
Care Shorten previous year's growths of 'Autumnal Blue' in Apr. Cut deciduous varieties back hard in Apr.
Pests and diseases SCALE INSECTS, frost damage, honey fungus.

Cedar (Cedrus)

Slow-growing tree.
Examples *C. atlantica* 'Glauca' (blue Atlas cedar) Height 50ft, spread 15ft. *C. deodara* (deodar) Height 40ft, spread 10-15ft. *C. libani* (cedar of Lebanon) Height 40ft, spread 25ft.
Plant cedars in any ordinary, well-drained soil; they thrive especially in coastal gardens. Plant Nov or Apr, choosing plants about 18in high. Incorporate leaf mould, peat and bone meal when planting.
Care Feed young plants with general fertiliser in Apr.
Pests and diseases Honey fungus.

Celeriac (Apium graveolens rapaceum)

Annual vegetable.
Examples 'Claudia' (non-branching roots); 'Globus' (large rooted); 'Marble ball' (disease-resistant, good storer).
Sow Apr in a sheltered, sunny seedbed. Thin out as necessary, and plant out in permanent site in June, allowing 12in each way per plant. Remove any side growths that appear Sept-Oct when the roots begin to swell.
Harvest Nov-Dec. Draw soil round roots in Nov to keep tops blanched if leaves are also being harvested. Store roots in boxes of sand or soil in cool, dry shed.
Pests and diseases CARROT FLY, cucumber mosaic virus, cherry leaf spot.

Celery (Apium graveolens)

Annual vegetable.
There are four types: white varieties such as 'Prizetaker White', 'Solid White'; pink varieties such as 'Superb Pink', 'Unrivalled Pink'; red varieties such as 'Giant Red', 'Hopkin's Fenlander'; and self-blanching varieties such as 'Golden Self-blanching' and 'Green-snap'.
Plant shop-bought young celery plants (white, pink or red varieties) 9in apart May-June in a 12in deep by 18in wide trench which has been heavily manured in spring. Plant self-blanching varieties 9in apart May-June in a well-manured flat bed. When trenched plants are 12-15in high, tie stems loosely together with raffia, and fill in soil to halfway up the stems. Three weeks later, use further soil to make firm slopes up to the base of the leaves. Or tie loose sleeves of black plastic round the stalks, and extend the sleeves as the plants grow. Protect late varieties against frost with straw or bracken.
Harvest trench-grown plants about eight weeks after the first earthing-up. Self-blanching varieties are ready about mid-Aug.
Pests and diseases CARROT FLY, celery fly, SLUGS, cucumber mosaic virus, celery leaf spot, damping-off.

Centaurea

Border plant.
Examples *C. cyanus* (cornflower) Height 9in-3ft, spacing 9-15in. Annual. Pink, red, blue or white flowers June-Sept. *C. dealbata* Height 2ft, spacing 18in. Perennial. Pink flowers June-July and again in autumn. *C. montana* Height 2ft, spread 18in. Perennial. White, pink, purple flowers May-July.
Plant Oct-Mar in fertile, well-drained soil and in sun or partial shade.
Propagate by division Oct-Mar every two or three years.
Care Support tall plants with twigs. Cut all stems to the ground in autumn.
Pests and diseases POWDERY MILDEW.

Chamaecyparis (False cypress)

Dense-leaved conifer.
Examples *C. lawsoniana* (Lawson cypress). Many sizes and varieties available, with foliage ranging from dark green to pale grey, gold and blue-green. *C. l.* 'Elegantissima' has pale yellow shoots and silvery-grey foliage. *C. obtusa* (Hinoki cypress) Height 25ft, spread 6ft. Slow-growing; dense, rich green foliage.
Plant Oct in light, sandy soils or Apr in heavy clay soils, in open sun or light shade.
Pests and diseases Honey fungus.

Chamomile
Anthemis nobilis

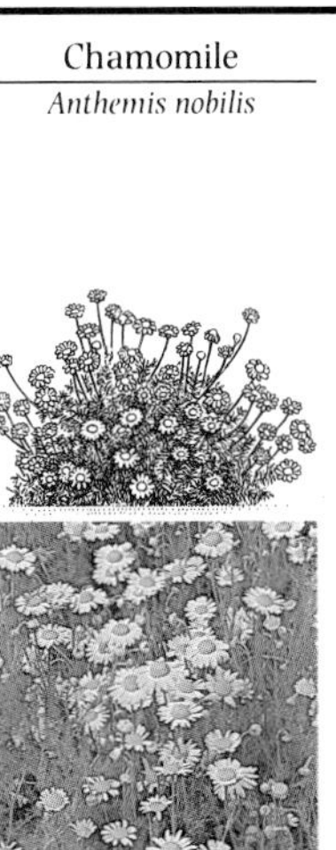

Cherry, fruiting
Prunus avium

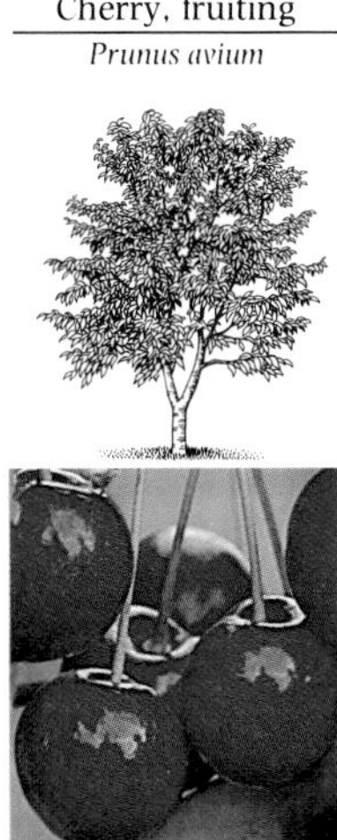

Cherry, ornamental
Prunus x 'Pink Perfection'

Chervil
Anthriscus cerefolium

Chicory
Cichorium intybus

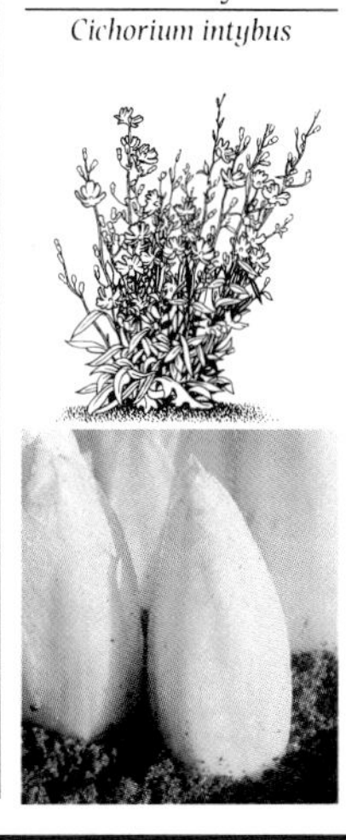

Chionodoxa
Chionodoxa luciliae

Chamomile (Anthemis)

Spreading ground-covering perennial.
Examples *A. nobilis* (also called *Chamaemelum nobile*; common chamomile) Used for making small, fragrant lawns. Height 9in, spacing 15in. Daisy-like flowers June-Aug. The non-flowering variety 'Treneague' requires least mowing. *A. sancti-johannis* Height 18in, spread 15in. Bright orange flowers June-Aug.
Plant *A. sancti-johannis* Sept-Mar in a sunny position in well-drained soil. For a chamomile lawn, set *A. nobilis* plants about 6in apart each way Mar-Apr.
Propagate by division Sept-Mar.
Care Mow chamomile lawns once or twice a year to remove long stems. Support *A. sancti-johannis* with twigs in exposed positions.
Pests and diseases Generally trouble-free.

Cherry, fruiting (Prunus)

Deciduous fruit tree.
Examples *P. avium* (sweet cherry) Height 40ft, spread 30ft. Flowers Apr-May; fruits, yellow to black, July-Aug. Numerous varieties available. 'Stella' (height 10ft) is best for smaller gardens and is self-fertile. *P. cerasus* (acid cherry) Height 20ft, spread 15ft. 'Morello' flowers Apr-May, fruits July-Aug, after six to ten years' growth.
Plant fan-trained trees at four years old, bush trees at two years. Plant both types Nov-Feb. Sweet cherries require deep, fertile loam; acid cherries are less demanding. Both do best in an open site, but neither thrives in frost pockets or at more than 500ft above sea level.
Care Shorten the leaders of all young trees by half in winter. Prune acid cherries by half throughout their lives.
Pests and diseases BIRDS, APHIDS, bacterial canker, honey fungus, silver leaf.

Cherry, ornamental (Prunus)

Deciduous flowering tree.
Examples *P.* 'Kiku-shidare Sakura' (Cheal's weeping cherry) Height 10ft, spread 6ft. Double, deep pink flowers Mar-Apr. *P.* x 'Pink Perfection' Height and spread 20-25ft. Double rose-pink flowers produced in Apr. *P. subhirtella* Height and spread 20-30ft. Pale pink flowers produced Mar-Apr.
Plant early autumn or spring, in ordinary, well-drained soil.
Pests and diseases BIRDS, APHIDS, CATERPILLARS, honey fungus, leaf spot, POWDERY MILDEW.

Chervil (Anthriscus cerefolium)

Grown as annual herb.
Height 18in, spread 12in. White flowers are produced in June-Aug in the plant's second year of life – it dies after flowering. Aromatic leaves used in cooking.
Sow in any type of soil Mar-Aug, in sun or partial shade. Thin seedlings to 6in, then 12in each way.
Propagate by allowing one or two plants to self-seed.
Care If seeds are not required, pinch out flower heads. In severe winters, protect plants with cloches.
Pests and diseases Generally trouble-free.

Chicory (Cichorium intybus)

Annual vegetable.
Usually grown for its leaves, used in winter salads, but occasionally for its tall bright blue or pink flowers that appear July-Oct. Reliable salad varieties include 'Witloof' and 'Crystal Head'.
Sow Apr-May in $\frac{1}{2}$in deep drills in ground which has been well dug in early spring and (except on limy soils) top-dressed with 6oz of garden lime per sq yd. Thin seedlings to about 9in apart. In Nov, when the leaves are dying down, lift the roots, cut off the foliage and store in a frost-free but cool place.
Force a few roots at a time for chicons (the white, crisp and slightly bitter leaf hearts) by planting them upright 2-3in apart in pots of sand or light soil. Cover them with boxes or pots to exclude all light, and place in a temperature of about 10°C (50°F). Cut the chicons when they are 5-6in long.
Pests and diseases SWIFT MOTH CATERPILLARS, SLUGS.

Chionodoxa

Bulbous perennial.
Example *C. luciliae* Height 6in, spread 4in. Light blue, white-centred flowers Feb-Mar. There is a white form, *C. l.* 'Alba', and pink forms, *C. l.* 'Rosea' and 'Pink Giant'.
Plant bulbs in autumn, 2-3in deep in ordinary, well-drained soil and in a spot which is in full sun.
Propagate by dividing crowded bulbs when the foliage has died down.
Pests and diseases SLUGS, smut.

Chives	Choisya	Christmas rose	Chrysanthemum annual	Chrysanthemum perennial	Cineraria
Allium schoenoprasum	*Choisya ternata*	*Helleborus niger*	*Chrysanthemum carinatum*	*Chrysanthemum maximum*	*Senecio maritimus*

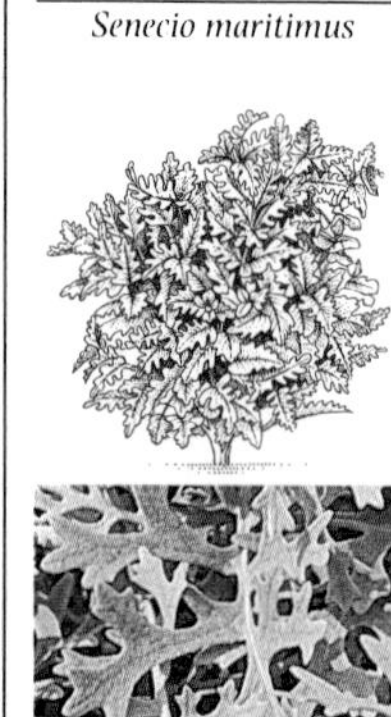

Chives (Allium schoenoprasum)

Perennial herb.
Height 10in, spread 12in. Globular, rose-pink flower heads June-July. Onion-flavoured leaves used in cooking.
Plant Sept-Oct in any well-drained garden soil, or in pots or window boxes. Or sow seeds in Mar in ½in deep drills, thin to 6in apart and transplant to permanent position in May.
Propagate every four years in Sept-Oct by dividing clumps with a knife. Replant bunches of shoots 12in apart in freshly manured ground.
Harvest by cutting leaves close to the ground when they have reached their full height. Use fresh, dried or frozen.
Pests and diseases RUST.

Choisya (Mexican orange)

Decorative shrub.
Example *C. ternata* Height and spread 6ft plus. Aromatic, glossy green trifoliate leaves; scented white flowers are produced in Apr-May and intermittently until winter.
Plant Apr-May in well-drained soil and in sheltered position in full sun or partial shade. In cold areas, best grown against a south-facing wall.
Propagate by cuttings in Mar.
Care Remove frost-damaged shoots in Mar.
Pests and diseases Frost damage, honey fungus.

Christmas rose, Lenten rose (Helleborus)

Perennial shrub.
Example *H. niger* (Christmas rose) Height and spread 18in. White flowers with golden centres Dec-Mar. *H. n.* 'Potter's Wheel' has particularly large flowers.
Plant Oct in deep, moist soil and partial shade.
Propagate by division in Mar. Once planted, hellebores should not be disturbed.
Pests and diseases Leaf spot.

Chrysanthemum, annual

Border plant.
Example *C. carinatum* Height 2ft, spread 12in. Single flowers, June-Sept, have purple discs surrounded by petals banded in different colours. Varieties include: 'Monarch Court Jester', large single flowers in a wide range of colours; 'Double Mixed', double flowers; and 'Northern Star', white, golden-centred, single.
Sow Mar-Apr. For early summer flowers, sow in autumn in cold greenhouse and pot seedlings on into 5in pots.
Pests and diseases Chrysanthemum leaf miner, chrysanthemum stool miner, CAPSID BUGS, CATERPILLARS, SLUGS, SNAILS, chrysanthemum virus, leaf spot, PETAL BLIGHT, POWDERY MILDEW, root rot, RUST.

Chrysanthemum, perennial

Border plant.
Examples *C. rubellum* Height 2½ft, spread 18in. Single pink, fragrant flowers Aug-Oct. *C. maximum* (shasta daisy) Height 2½-3ft, spread 12-18in. Single white flowers, with golden-yellow centres, June-Aug.
Plant Sept-Apr in sunny position and in well-drained, preferably limy soil.
Propagate by division in Mar-Apr every third year, or take 2-3in long cuttings of basal shoots in Mar-Apr.
Care Tall varieties of *C. rubellum* often require pea-stick support. Cut stems of all perennials to ground level in Dec.
Pests and diseases See *Chrysanthemum, annual.*

Cineraria (Senecio maritimus or S. bicolor)

Annual border plant.
Height 2ft, spacing 12in. Woolly, silvery-white leaves and stems; yellow flowers July-Sept.
Plant May, or when frost danger is past, in any soil and in sunny position. Or sow seeds in potting compost Feb-Mar in a temperature of about 16°C (about 60°F). Prick out into pots and harden off in a cold frame before planting out in May.
Pests and diseases APHIDS, THRIPS, chrysanthemum leaf miner, POWDERY MILDEW, tomato spotted wilt virus.

GARDEN TIP
Chives

Because chives die down each winter, consider bringing part of a clump indoors in autumn and growing it on in a pot on the kitchen windowsill. Harvest the leaves regularly to encourage steady growth. Alternatively, chop fresh leaves in summer or autumn and spread them in the sections of an ice tray. Top up the tray with water, then freeze the whole lot. Whenever you want the taste of fresh chives in winter, simply toss one or more chive cubes into your saucepan.

Clarkia
Clarkia elegans

Clematis
Clematis 'Nelly Moser'

Cleome
Cleome spinosa

Comfrey
S. x *uplandicum*

Convolvulus
Convolvulus tricolor

Coreopsis
Coreopsis tinctoria

Clarkia

Hardy annual bedding plant.
Example *C. elegans* Height 2ft, spacing 12in. Double flowers July-Sept. 'Mixed' variety has white, lavender, purple, scarlet and pink flowers; single-colour varieties also available.
Sow in flowering position in Mar, in medium, slightly acid loam and in sunny positions; thin out seedlings to 12in. Avoid heavy feeding.
Pests and diseases GREY MOULD, FOOT ROT, root rot.

Clematis

Climbing shrub.
Examples *C. tangutica* Height 15-20ft. Yellow lantern-like flowers late summer to autumn, followed by silky seed heads. Early flowering hybrids bloom May-June. Height about 10ft. Varieties include 'Barbara Jackman' (red-purple), 'Lasurstern' (blue) and 'Nelly Moser' (pink and crimson). Late-flowering hybrids bloom June-Sept. Height to 15ft. Varieties include 'Duchess of Albany' (pink).
Plant in deep, enriched soil Oct-Mar. Best against a west-facing wall with ground cover to shade roots. Place pea sticks by young plants to help them grow up to trellis or other support.
Propagate by taking semi-ripe cuttings in July, or by layering in Mar (sever from parent plant one year later).
Care Water in dry spells. Mulch in spring. Prune late-flowering hybrids back to 12in from ground level in spring.
Pests and diseases SLUGS, APHIDS, EARWIGS, clematis wilt, POWDERY MILDEW.

Cleome (Spider flower)

Annual bedding plant.
Example *C. spinosa* Height 3-4ft, spread 18in. Pinky-white flowers, July to first frosts. Varieties include 'Helen Campbell' (white) and 'Pink Queen'.
Sow under glass in Mar at about 18°C (about 65°F). Prick out seedlings into pots and harden off before planting out in May. Flowering site should be in fertile soil enriched with humus and in full sun.
Pests and diseases APHIDS.

Comfrey (Symphytum)

Perennial border plant.
Examples *S. caucasicum* Height 2ft, spread 18in. Bell-like flowers, pink then blue, Apr-June. *S. grandiflorum* Height 8in, spread 15in. Ground-cover species with white, tubular flowers Apr-May. *S.* x *uplandicum* Height and spread 3ft plus. Long, purple, tubular flowers June-Aug.
Plant Oct-Nov or Mar-Apr in ordinary garden soil, in sun or shade.
Propagate by dividing roots Oct or Mar.
Care *S. caucasicum* may require staking. Cut back flower stems of all species after flowering.
Pests and diseases Generally trouble-free.

Convolvulus

Border annual or perennial.
Examples *C. tricolor* (annual species) Height 12-15in, spread 6-9in. Rich blue flowers with yellow or white throats July-Sept. Varieties include *C. t.* 'Blue Flash' (blue with yellow centres, and in mixed colours). *C. althaeoides* (perennial species) Height 3in, spread 3ft plus. Prostrate or climbing plant with pink to purple flowers July-Sept. Can be invasive, but dies back in Sept.
Sow annual species in Apr in flowering site. Plant perennial species Apr-May. All species require well-drained soil in sunny position.
Propagate perennial species by taking $1\frac{1}{2}$-3in long heel cuttings June-Aug. Pot rooted cuttings into 3in pots, grow them on in a frost-free greenhouse or cold frame and plant them out the following May.
Care Remove seed heads of annual species regularly to encourage flowering.
Pests and diseases Generally trouble-free.

Coreopsis

Back-of-the-border annual, sometimes listed as Calliopsis.
Examples *C. drummondii* Height 2ft, spacing 12in. Bright yellow flowers with deep purple centres July-Sept. Crimson and scarlet strains also available. *C. tinctoria* Height 1-2ft, spacing 9-12in. Bright yellow flowers with purple and brown centres July-Sept.
Sow in flowering site – ideally a sunny position in fertile, well-drained soil – Mar-June.
Care Cut back early-flowering stems to encourage second blooming. Stake tall plants.
Pests and diseases FROGHOPPERS, SLUGS.

Corydalis	Cotinus	Cotoneaster	Crab apple	Crocosmia	Crocus
Corydalis lutea	*Cotinus coggygria*	*Cotoneaster horizontalis*	'John Downie'	*Crocosmia masonorum*	*Crocus vernus*

Corydalis

Medium-sized perennial.
Example *C. lutea* Height 8in, spread 12in. Yellow flowers Apr-Nov.
Sow Mar-Apr in ordinary soil, in sun or shade. Plants thrive on old stone walls, where they self-seed profusely.
Care Keep in check by uprooting any surplus self-sown plants.
Pests and diseases Generally trouble-free.

Cotinus (Smoke tree)

Shrub grown for its decorative foliage.
Examples *C. coggygria* Height and spread 8ft plus. Light green leaves that may colour brilliantly in autumn. Small purple flowers July. *C. c.* 'Royal Purple' has dark plum-purple foliage which reddens in autumn.
Plant Oct-Mar in any ordinary soil and in a sunny position. Do not feed often. In rich manured soil, the plants will not develop their most brilliant autumn colours.
Propagate by 4-5in long heel cuttings Aug-Sept or by layering shoots in Sept and severing from the parent plant one year later.
Pests and diseases POWDERY MILDEW, VERTICILLIUM WILT.

Cotoneaster

Shrub grown for flowers, fruit and foliage.
Example *C. horizontalis* Height 2ft, spread 7ft. Deciduous. Bank or wall-hugging plant with pink flowers in June, followed by red berries and bright autumn foliage.
Plant Oct-Mar in any ordinary soil, in sun or light shade.
Propagate from heel cuttings July-Aug, or by layering autumn or spring.
Care Remove straggly shoots from deciduous plants in Feb and from evergreens in Apr. Trim hedges in Aug.
Pests and diseases APHIDS, BIRDS, FIRE BLIGHT, honey fungus, silver leaf.

Crab apple (Malus)

Smallish, decorative tree.
Examples *M. coronaria* 'Charlottae' Height 12ft, spread 6ft. Fragrant pink flowers May-June; brilliant autumn foliage. *M.* 'John Downie' Height 12ft, spread 6ft. White flowers in May; glossy red and yellow fruits.
Plant in any good soil, in sun or light shade.
Propagate only by grafting, in Mar or July-Aug.
Care Mulch young trees. Remove dead and straggly shoots in Feb; but established trees need no regular pruning.
Pests and diseases APHIDS, CATERPILLARS, fruit tree red spider mites, codling moth, apple scab, honey fungus.

Crocosmia

Summer-flowering bulb.
Examples *C.* x *crocosmiiflora* (montbretia) Height 2ft, spread 6in. Trumpet-shaped flowers July-Sept. Colours range from yellow and orange to deep red. Several varieties available. *C. masonorum* Height 2½ft, spacing 6-9in. Leaves appear pleated. Orange flowers July-Aug.
Plant in well-drained soil in a warm site or one that is protected by nearby herbaceous perennials.
Propagate by dividing overgrown clumps after flowering or in spring.
Care Leave foliage as protection until Mar, and cover crowns with bracken, leaves or peat in winter.
Pests and diseases Generally trouble-free.

Crocus

Border perennial.
Examples *C. chrysanthus* and hybrids (winter-flowering species) Height and spread 3in. White, gold, mauve or blue flowers, some striped, Feb. *C. vernus* (spring-flowering species) Height 5in, spacing 4in. Many varieties available with white, lavender, blue, silvery or purple flowers, some striped, in Mar. *C. speciosus* (autumn-flowering species) Height 5in, spacing 4in. Lilac, rose, white and lavender-flowered varieties available, all blooming in Oct. *C. sativus* (saffron crocus) Height and spacing 4in. Purple flowers Oct.
Plant autumn-flowering types Aug-Sept, other types Sept-Nov. Set corms 2-3in deep, or 6in deep on sandy soils.
Propagate by division when leaves turn brown or while dormant.
Pests and diseases LEATHERJACKETS, mice, BIRDS, APHIDS, gladiolus dry rot, gladiolus scab, blue mould.

Cucumber greenhouse	Cucumber ridge or outdoor	Cup and saucer plant	x Cupressocyparis	Cupressus
'Vercor'	'Burpee'	*Cobaea scandens*	x *Cupressocyparis leylandii*	*Cupressus macrocarpa*
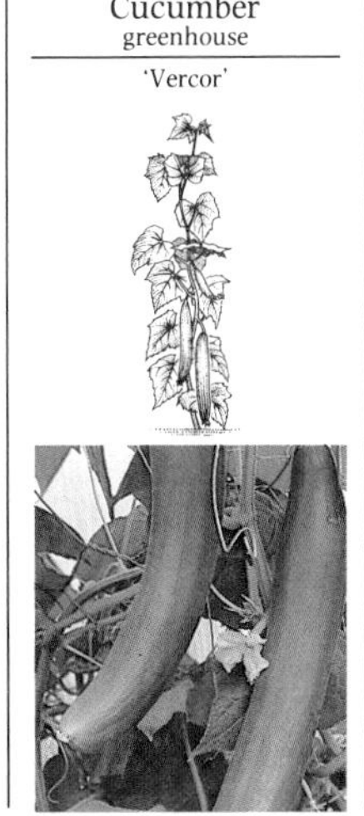	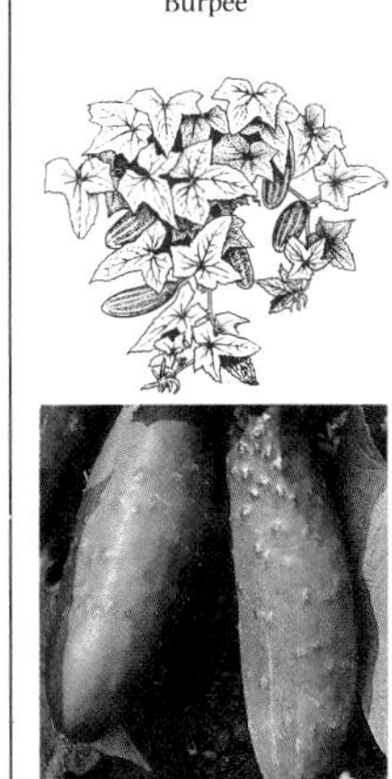			

Cucumber, greenhouse (Cucumis sativus)

Salad vegetable.
Greenhouse varieties: 'Butcher's Disease Resisting', 'Conqueror', 'Sigmadew', 'Vercor'. Climbing height 8ft plus.
Sow greenhouse cucumbers late Feb-Mar. Push seeds edgeways into 3in compost-filled peat pots, one seed to each pot. Place the pots in a propagator, above the greenhouse heater, or in the airing cupboard at a temperature of at least 21°C (70°F).
Plant the seedlings and their peat pots into soil rich in compost and manure or into growing bags when two true leaves have developed. Stake each plant to aid its climb to support wires strung across the bed about 12in from the glass. Pinch out the tips of leading shoots when the plants have reached the greenhouse roof. Tie resulting sideshoots to the wires. If no cucumbers appear on the sideshoots by the time they have grown to a length of 2ft, pinch out the shoots' tips. Pinch out fruiting shoots two leaves beyond a female flower. Remove all male flowers (those with no miniature cucumber behind them) to prevent pollination – fertilised fruit can taste bitter.
Shade plants from strong sunlight, and water well. Keep the greenhouse ventilated and maintain humidity by spraying the floor twice a day. When the fruit begins to swell, give the plants a fortnightly feed of liquid fertiliser.
Harvest June-Sept before the fruit reaches maximum size – roughly, when the sides are parallel.
Pests and diseases Red spider mites, woodlice, anthracnose of cucumber, gummosis of cucumber, cucumber mosaic virus, GREY MOULD, POWDERY MILDEW, root rot, VERTICILLIUM WILT.

Cucumber, ridge or outdoor (Cucumis sativus)

Salad and pickling vegetable.
Outdoor varieties: 'Bedfordshire Prize', 'Burpee', 'Long Green Ridge', 'Nadir', 'Apple-Shaped' (round, yellow), 'Venlo Pickling' (gherkin).
Sow Groups of three or four seeds 1in deep and 3in apart in late May in the centre of planting stations set 2ft apart. Prepare planting stations by filling spade-deep holes with a mixture of well-rotted compost or manure and soil. As the seedlings grow, remove the weaker ones and leave the strongest to grow on alone. Pinch out the growing tip of each remaining plant when it has put out six or seven leaves; this will encourage the fruit-bearing sideshoots. Do not remove male flowers – fertilisation is essential on outdoor cucumbers. Transfer pollen with a camel-hair paintbrush from developed male flowers (thin stalks) to the females (bulging stalks which will become cucumbers).
Alternatively, pick a male flower and shake it over the female blooms. If a shoot produces no fruit by the time the seventh leaf appears, pinch out the tip.
Water the plants frequently, give regular feeds of liquid fertiliser and protect with slug pellets. As the fruits ripen, place boards beneath them to keep them off the ground.
Harvest July-Sept, taking the fruits before they reach full maturity.
Pests and diseases See *Cucumber, greenhouse.*

Cup and saucer plant (Cobaea scandens)

Climbing shrub.
Height 20ft plus, spread 2ft. Vigorous climber, purple and green flowers produced in May-Oct. *C. s.* 'Alba' has green-white flowers.
Sow seeds edgeways Mar-Apr under glass in 3in pots of potting compost. Plant out, when frost danger is past, against pergola or trellis in ordinary soil and sunny, sheltered position.
Care Water freely in dry spells.
Pests and diseases APHIDS.

x Cupressocyparis leylandii (Leyland cypress)

Dense-leaved conifer.
Height 50ft, spread 15ft. Fast-growing; used as specimen tree, for windbreaks and for hedging. Several varieties available, including 'Castlewellan' (feathery foliage and rich yellow-green new growth), 'Leighton Green' (rich green leaves; good for hedging) and 'Robinson's Gold' (bright yellow).
Plant Apr-May in any deep soil and in sun or partial shade. Plants $1\frac{1}{2}$-2ft high are the easiest to establish, but trees up to 8ft can be used if well staked. For hedges, allow $1\frac{1}{2}$-2ft between young plants.
Propagate by cuttings Sept-Oct.
Care Trim hedges in Sept.
Pests and diseases Generally trouble-free.

Cupressus (True cypress)

Decorative conifer.
Example *C. macrocarpa* (Monterey cypress) Height 50ft, spread 15ft. Red-brown bark, dark green foliage and gold flowers. *C. m.* 'Donard Gold' is a fast-growing, golden-leaved variety.
Plant Sept-Oct or Apr in ordinary well-drained soil and in position sheltered from cold winds. Plants $1\frac{1}{2}$-2ft high are easiest to establish.
Propagate Sept-Oct by 3-4in long cuttings of sideshoots.
Pests and diseases APHIDS, mites, GREY MOULD, honey fungus.

Currant	Cyclamen	Cyperus	Daboecia	Daffodil	Dahlia
Blackcurrant	*Cyclamen hederifolium*	*Cyperus alternifolius*	*Daboecia cantabrica*	Narcissus	Small cactus

Currant (Ribes)

Fruit bush.
Height and spread about 5ft, spacing between bushes 5-6ft. Red and white currants can also be grown as cordons with 15in between plants, 6ft between rows. Varieties include: Blackcurrants – 'Laxton's Giant' (early) and 'Wellington XXX' (mid-season). Redcurrants – 'Laxton's No1' (early) and 'Red Lake' (mid to late season). White currants – 'White Versailles' (early).
Plant in moisture-retentive but well-drained soil, in sun or partial shade, preferably in autumn.
Propagate by hardwood cuttings in autumn. Use 8-10in long cuttings for blackcurrants, 12-14in cuttings for red and white currants.
Care Firm bushes after frost. Mulch in spring with rotted compost or manure. Protect ripening fruits from birds with netting.
Pests and diseases BIRDS, blackcurrant gall mite, APHIDS, American gooseberry mildew, GREY MOULD, honey fungus.

Cyclamen

Tuberous perennial.
Examples *C. europaeum* (also called *C. purpurascens*) Height and spacing 4in. Fragrant, carmine flowers July-Sept. *C. neapolitanum* (also known as *C. hederifolium)* Height and spacing 4in. Mauve, pale pink or white flowers Aug-Nov.
Plant in well-drained soil containing plenty of leaf mould or peat, in shade and shelter from cold winds. Woodland conditions are ideal.
Care Mulch with 1in layer of leaf mould annually.
Pests and diseases APHIDS, mice, VINE WEEVILS, tarsonemid mites, black root rot, cucumber mosaic virus, GREY MOULD.

Cyperus

Perennial water plant.
Examples *C. alternifolius* (umbrella grass) Water depth 6in, height 2ft, spread 18in. Dense thicket of leaves and stems. Feathery green flower heads June-Sept. *C. vegetus* Water depth 6in, height 2ft, spread 12in. Green plumes Aug-Sept.
Plant Apr-June in 5-8in perforated pots of rich soil in pond shallows and in sun or partial shade.
Propagate by detaching and replanting young growths Apr-May.
Care Remove old flower heads before seeds ripen. Remove old foliage in spring, not autumn, so as to provide winter shelter for birds.
Pests and diseases Generally trouble-free.

Daboecia

Long-flowering heath.
Example *D. cantabrica* (St Dabeoc's heath) Height and spread to 3ft. Dark green leaves with silvery undersides. Purple-pink flowers May to early winter. Named varieties available with white, pink, purple, crimson or streaked flowers.
Plant Mar-May or Oct-Nov in any lime-free soil. Lighten clay soils with sharp sand or peat and enrich all soils with bone meal.
Propagate by 1-2in long cuttings taken in July-Oct.
Pests and diseases Generally trouble-free.

Daffodil (Narcissus)

Bulbous perennial.
Daffodil varieties (also known as trumpet narcissi) are distinguished from other narcissi by their central trumpets, which are as long as, or longer than, the surrounding petals. Height 12-18in. Flowers Mar-Apr. Varieties include: 'Dutch Master' and 'King Alfred' (yellow); 'Beersheba' and 'Mount Hood' (white).
Plant bulbs Aug-Oct in any well-drained soil, in sun or light shade. Set bulbs 3-12in apart in holes which are at least three times the depth of the bulb. Do not remove the leaves until they are completely brown.
Propagate by lifting clumps of bulbs in July-Aug. Divide each clump and plant out offsets immediately.
Pests and diseases STEM AND BULB EELWORM, tarsonemid mites, narcissus fly maggots, SLUGS, arabis mosaic virus, narcissus fire, GREY MOULD.

Dahlia

Tuberous perennial.
Numerous varieties available in two main groups: border and bedding. For recommended varieties, see pages 119-20.
Plant border dahlias mid-Apr to late May in well-drained soil enriched with compost and bone meal and in an open, sunny position. Sow bedding dahlias under glass Feb-Mar and harden off in a cold frame from mid-Apr before planting out when danger of frost is over. Bedding dahlias thrive in medium to heavy soil and an open, sunny position.
Propagate border dahlias by dividing tubers in Mar.
Care Stake border dahlias and lift tubers in autumn for winter storage in a frost-free place.
Pests and diseases APHIDS, CATERPILLARS, CAPSID BUGS, EARWIGS, cucumber mosaic and tomato spotted wilts, damping-off, GREY MOULD, PETAL BLIGHT.

Daisy
Bellis perennis 'Monstrosa'

Daphne
Daphne cneorum

Day lily
Hemerocallis fulva 'Kwanso'

Delphinium
D. elatum hybrid

Deutzia
Deutzia scabra 'Plena'

Dicentra
Dicentra spectabilis

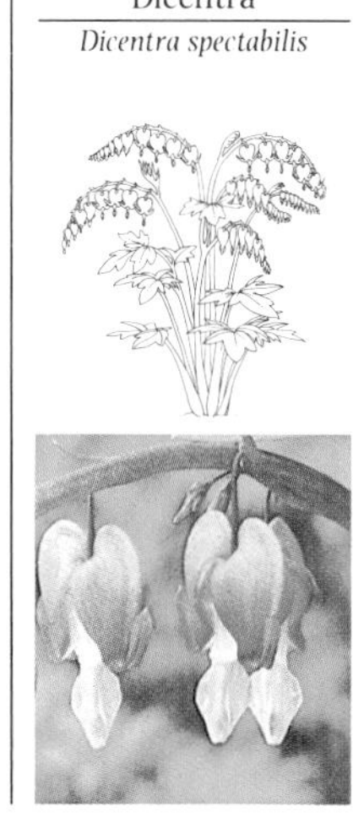

Daisy (Bellis)

Hardy border perennial, often grown as a biennial.
Example *B. perennis* (common daisy) Height 3-6in, spacing 6-9in. Varieties include 'The Pearl' (white), 'Rob Roy' (red), 'Dresden China' (pink), 'Pomponette' (white to crimson) and 'Monstrosa' (large flowers in white, pink or red). All the varieties flower Mar-July.
Plant out seedlings Oct-Nov in any fertile garden soil, in sun or partial shade. Sow seeds May-June.
Propagate by division in Mar.
Care Deadhead regularly to prevent the growth of self-sown seedlings.
Pests and diseases Generally trouble-free.

Daphne

Low spreading shrub.
Examples *D. cneorum* Height 6in, spread 2ft. Evergreen. Rose-pink, fragrant flowers May-June. *D. mezereum* Height 5ft, spread 4ft. Deciduous. Fragrant pink, purple or white flowers Feb-Apr, followed by red berries.
Plant Sept or Mar-Apr in ordinary soil sheltered from cold winds.
Propagate by heel cuttings July-Aug. Evergreens can also be propagated by layering in spring.
Pests and diseases APHIDS, cucumber mosaic virus, leaf spot.

Day lily (Hemerocallis)

Back-of-the-border perennial.
Examples Hemerocallis hybrids Height 3ft, spacing 2ft. Dozens of varieties available, including 'Pink Damask' (pure pink), 'Stafford' (red with yellow centres) and 'Golden Chimes' (yellow). The flowers, which are produced from June to Aug, can be up to 7in across.
Plant Oct-Apr in good soil, in sun or partial shade.
Propagate by division Oct-Apr.
Care Cut stems to near ground level after flowering.
Pests and diseases Generally trouble-free.

Delphinium

Tall annual or perennial plant. Perennial varieties, which flower June-July and in autumn (height 3-8ft, spacing 1½-2½ft), are derived from *Delphinium elatum*. They include: 'Vespers' (blue-mauve), 'Mighty Atom' (Lilac), 'Pink Sensation' (pink) and 'Galahad' (white). Annual varieties, often called larkspurs, flower June-Aug (height 1-4ft, spacing 18in). They are derived from two species, *D. consolida* and *D. ajacis*, and include: 'Giant Imperial' (mixed colours, height 4ft), and 'Dwarf Rocket' (mixed, height 12in).
Plant perennial and annual varieties in well-drained but moisture-retentive soil, in sunny spot sheltered from wind. Annual varieties will tolerate light shade.
Propagate perennial varieties by dividing and replanting clumps Mar-Apr. Propagate annual varieties by sowing in flowering site in Sept or Mar-Apr; thin to required spacing.
Care Support tall plants with pea sticks or canes. Mulch in early spring. Water freely in dry spells. Remove faded flower spikes to encourage a second blooming. Cut stems of perennial varieties back to ground level in autumn.
Pests and diseases SLUGS, SNAILS, crown rot, root rot, cucumber mosaic virus, POWDERY MILDEW, STEM ROT, GREY MOULD.

Deutzia

Decorative shrub.
Example *D. scabra* Height to 10ft, spread to 6ft. White cup-shaped flowers June-July. *D. s.* 'Plena' has double white flowers with a rosy glow; *D. s.* 'Rose of Rochester' has double white flowers tinted pink.
Plant Oct-Feb in any well-drained soil, in full sun or dappled shade. Shelter from north winds.
Propagate by 10-12in long hardwood cuttings in Oct.
Care Remove old flowering stems in July to encourage new growth.
Pests and diseases Generally trouble-free.

Dicentra

Adaptable perennial.
Example *D. spectabilis* (bleeding heart) Height 1½-2½ft, spacing 1½-2ft. Deep pink and white flowers produced in Mar-May.
Plant Oct-Mar in any well-drained, compost-enriched soil. Good in sunny border or as ground cover under trees.
Propagate by carefully dividing the brittle roots Oct-Mar. Once plants are established, leave them undisturbed as long as possible.
Pests and diseases Generally trouble-free.

GARDEN TIP
Daisy

As well as making fine edging plants, daisies can also be grown easily in a window box. Or grow them in 3½-4in pots and keep them in a frost-free greenhouse to provide flowers in winter.
Incidentally, the flower gets its common name from its habit of opening and closing with the sun. The word is a corruption of 'day's eye'.

Dill
Peucedanum graveolens

Dimorphotheca
Dimorphotheca aurantiaca

Dogwood
Cornus kousa chinensis

Echinops
Echinops bannaticus

Echium
Echium lycopsis

Elaeagnus
Elaeagnus pungens

Dill (Peucedanum graveolens)

Annual herb.
Height 3ft, spacing 12in. Yellow flower heads June-Aug. The aniseed-flavoured leaves and seeds are used in cooking.
Sow in any well-drained fertile soil in a sunny position, making successive monthly sowings Mar-July to ensure constant summer supply.
Harvest leaves as required. They can be dried or frozen. Collect seeds when the seed heads are turning brown in Aug. Spread them on paper until the seeds are dry enough to shake loose easily. Store in airtight jars.
Propagate by allowing the plant to self-seed, which it does readily.
Pests and diseases Generally trouble-free.

Dimorphotheca (Cape marigold)

Border plant. Both perennial and annual species are available.
Examples *D. annua* Annual. Height 12-18in, spacing 6-12in. Cream-white, gold-centred flowers, purple on the underside, June-Aug. *D. aurantiaca* (star of the veldt). Perennial. Height 18in, spacing 12in. Bright orange flowers with brown, blue-edged centres June-Sept. *D. ecklonis* Perennial. Height 2ft, spacing 12in. Purple-pink flowers with deep blue centres July-Aug.
Sow in the flowering site in May and thin out as required.
Propagate *D. aurantiaca* by 3in long semi-ripe cuttings taken in July-Aug. Root cuttings in pots of peat and sand in cold frame. Plant out in the following May.
Pests and diseases GREY MOULD.

Dogwood (Cornus)

Shrub; grown for summer flowers, autumn leaf and winter bark.
Examples *C. alba* Height and spread 10ft. Inconspicuous yellow-white flowers May-June, followed by white berries. Foliage turns red or orange in autumn and current season's stems are bright red in winter. *C. florida* (flowering dogwood) Height 15ft, spread 20ft. Green flowers surrounded by white petal-like bracts (modified leaves) in May. Blooms are followed by strawberry-like fruits. Brilliant autumn foliage. *C. f.* 'Rubra' has pink bracts. *C. kousa* Height and spread 8-10ft. Purple-green flowers surrounded by white bracts in June. Strawberry-like fruits in Sept. *C. k. chinensis* has larger bracts and the foliage turns crimson in autumn.
Plant Mar-Apr in moist soil, in sun or partial shade.
Propagate by heel cuttings July-Aug. Alternatively propagate *C. alba* by replanting rooted suckers in Nov.
Care Cut *C. alba* back to within a few inches of the ground in Apr.
Pests and diseases Generally trouble-free.

Echinops (globe thistle)

Tall perennial border plant.
Example *E. bannaticus* Height 3-4ft, spacing 2ft. Globular heads of grey-blue flowers July-Aug.
Plant Oct-Mar in ordinary, well-drained soil and in a sunny position.
Propagate by root division Oct-Mar.
Harvest flowers to dry for winter decoration.
Care. Cut stems to ground level in Oct. Dry flowers for winter decoration. Wear gloves when handling the plant – it can cause a rash.
Pests and diseases Generally trouble-free.

Echium (Annual borage)

Colourful bedding plant.
Example *E. lycopsis* (or *E. plantagineum*) Height 3ft, spacing 18in. Blue tubular flowers on spikes, June-Aug. Hybrids such as the 12in high 'Blue Bedder' and 'Dwarf Hybrids' are available in a variety of colours.
Sow Mar or Sept in the flowering site – preferably sandy, dry soil and in open sun. Thin out seedlings to required spacing in Apr.
Pests and diseases Generally trouble-free.

Elaeagnus

Shrub. Evergreen and deciduous species available.
Examples *E. multiflora* Height 10ft, spread 12ft. Deciduous shrub with yellow-white flowers Apr-May. Edible orange-red fruits ripen in July. *E. pungens* Height and spread to 12ft. Evergreen shrub producing silvery flowers Oct-Nov, sometimes followed by orange fruits. Widely used for hedging.
Plant deciduous species Oct-Dec, evergreens in Apr or Sept, in ordinary or poor soils including chalk. For hedging, space young plants 15-18in apart.
Propagate evergreen species by 3-4in long cuttings Aug-Sept. Propagate deciduous species by sowing seed in seed compost July-Sept.
Care Remove pure green-leaved shoots from variegated forms of *E. pungens* whenever they appear. Trim established hedges in June and Sept.
Pests and diseases Leaf spot.

Elder
Sambucus racemosa 'Plumosa-aurea'

Endive
'Exquisite Curled'

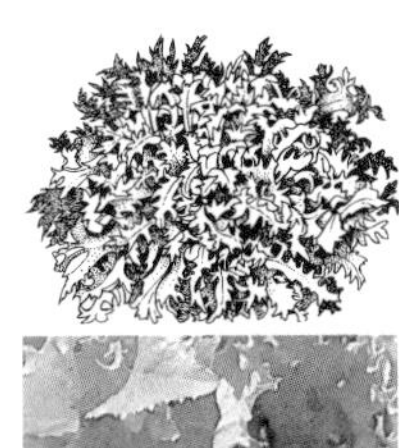
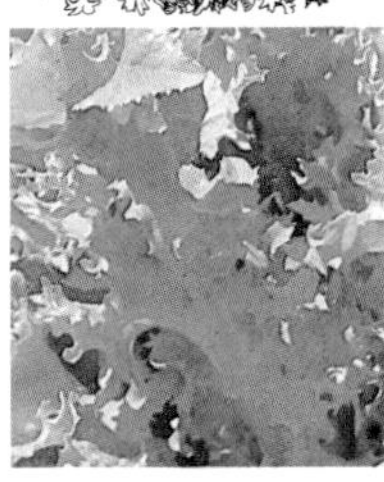

Epimedium
Epimedium grandiflorum 'Violet Queen'

Eremurus
Eremurus elwesii

Eryngium
Eryngium alpinum 'Improved'

Escallonia
Escallonia x *iveyi*

Elder (Sambucus)

Shrub. Can be invasive.
Example *S. racemosa* Height and spread 10ft. Yellow-white flowers Apr-May followed by scarlet berries June-July. The flowers and fruits of all species are widely used in country wine-making.
Plant in any fertile soil Oct-Mar.
Propagate by 10-12in long hardwood cuttings Oct-Nov.
Pests and diseases APHIDS, arabis mosaic virus.

Endive (Cichorium endivia)

Late autumn and winter salad plant. Curly-leaved varieties include 'Moss Curled' for early sowing and 'Exquisite Curled' for late summer harvesting. Plain-leaved varieties include 'Batavian Broad Leaved' for autumn and winter use.
Sow seeds thinly in ½in deep drills 15in apart. Thin seedlings to 12in apart. Make first sowing in Apr, and thereafter at monthly intervals until mid-Aug for continuous supply. Endives do best in a sunny spot on light, well-drained soils.
Harvest the plants three or four months after sowing. Blanch them first by covering them with inverted pots whose drainage holes have been blocked to exclude all light. The endives will be ready for harvesting after about a week of blanching in summer, or up to three weeks in autumn or winter.
Pests and diseases Generally trouble-free.

Epimedium

Perennial border plant.
Example *E. grandiflorum* Height and spacing to 12in. Carmine, violet or yellow-spurred flowers in June. *E. g.* 'Rose Queen' has crimson flowers. Foliage and flowers of all species are widely used by flower arrangers.
Plant Sept-Mar in moist sandy loam and in partial shade.
Propagate by root division Sept-Mar.
Care Give a top-dressing of peat or compost in spring and remove old leaves before flower spikes form in Mar.
Pests and diseases Generally trouble-free.

Eremurus

Perennial; not for small gardens.
Example *E. elwesii* Height 6in-10ft, spacing to 3ft. Fragrant, pink flowers on long spikes in May. *E. e.* 'Albus' has pure white flowers.
Plant Sept-Oct in well-drained loam, positioning the crowns so that they are covered by 6in of soil. Choose a sunny position, though preferably without morning sun.
Propagate by division Sept-Oct.
Care Mulch annually with rotted manure or compost Sept-Oct. Cut down stems after flowering.
Pests and diseases Generally trouble-free.

Eryngium

Back-of-the-border perennial.
Examples *E. alpinum* Height 2ft, spacing 15in. Steel-blue flowers surrounded by spiky bracts July-Aug. *E. maritimum* (sea holly) Height and spacing 18in. Silver-blue leaves; metallic-blue flowers July-Sept.
Plant Oct-Apr in ordinary soil and in sunny position.
Propagate by root cuttings in Feb, or by sowing seeds in compost in a cold frame in Mar-Apr. Propagate *E. alpinum* by division in Mar.
Care Cut stems to ground level after flowering finishes. Harvest the flowers for drying for winter decoration before they fade.
Pests and diseases Generally trouble-free.

Escallonia

Shrub: tender in most parts of Britain.
Examples *E.* x *iveyi* Height 10ft, spread 8ft. White flowers July-Aug. Should be grown as a wall shrub except in warmer Western districts. *E. macrantha* Height 6-10ft, spread 6ft. Crimson flowers June-Sept. Hardy only in the South and West. Widely used for hedging in coastal gardens. Escallonia varieties – such as *E.* 'Donard Seedling', *E.* 'Donard Star', *E.* 'Glory of Donard' and *E.* 'Slieve Donard' – are hardier than the species. Height of these named varieties 5-8ft, spread 5-6ft.
Plant Oct or Mar-Apr in any ordinary soil and in sunny position. For hedging, use 12in plants spaced 18in apart.
Propagate by taking 3-4in long heel cuttings of non-flowering shoots Aug-Sept.
Care For hedging, remove top quarter of all shoots immediately after planting to promote bushy growth. Trim established hedges lightly.
Pests and diseases SILVER LEAF.

Eschscholzia	Eucalyptus	Euonymus	x Fatshedera	Fennel, common	Fennel, Florence
Eschscholzia californica	*Eucalyptus gunnii*	*Euonymus alatus*	x *Fatshedera lizei*	*Foeniculum vulgare*	*Foeniculum vulgare dulce*

Eschscholzia

Annual bedding plant.
Example *E. californica* (Californian poppy) Height 12-15in, spacing 6in. Orange-yellow flowers June-Oct. Varieties in many other colours also available.
Sow Sept or Mar in flowering site and thin out young plants as necessary.
Care Gather cut flowers before the buds open.
Pests and diseases Generally trouble-free.

Eucalyptus (Gum tree)

Fast-growing, decorative tree.
Examples *E. gunnii* Height in ten years 50ft, spread 15ft. Juvenile foliage round, blue-green to silver. Later leaves become lance-shaped and darker. Maintain juvenile foliage by pruning off the previous year's growth in early spring before new growth starts. White flowers July-Aug. *E. niphophila* (snow gum) Height and spread in ten years, up to 20ft. Grey or green glossy leaves. White flowers in June, but the tree's chief attraction is its snakeskin bark.
Plant June-July in well-drained soil which is neither sandy nor chalky. Plants about 12in tall are easiest to establish.
Care Stake young plants firmly for the first five years, and in cold areas tie sacking or straw around the stem during the first winter to protect the tree from winds. Prune in early spring and summer to maintain shape. To form a rounded bush, keep cutting back the 'leading shoot' – the shoot at the tip of the plant. Left unpruned, this topmost shoot will suppress the growth of sideshoots.
Pests and diseases Damping-off, botrytis, SILVER LEAF.

Euonymus (Spindle tree)

Shrub; deciduous and evergreen species available.
Examples *E. alatus* Height and spread 8ft. Deciduous. Crimson or scarlet leaves and purple berries in autumn. *E. japonicus* 'Aureopictus' Height 10-15ft, spread 5ft. Evergreen. Gold-variegated leaves. Good for hedging.
Plant evergreens Sept-Oct or Apr-May, deciduous Oct-Mar, in ordinary soil and in sun or partial shade. For hedging use 12in high plants, spaced 18in apart. Evergreens do best in a sheltered position; variegated forms do best against walls.
Propagate by 3-4in long heeled cuttings Aug-Sept.
Care Prune hedges of *E. japonicus* in Apr and Aug-Sept. Tidy up deciduous species by thinning out shoots in Feb.
Pests and diseases APHIDS, SCALE INSECTS, CATERPILLARS, honey fungus, leaf spot, POWDERY MILDEW.

x Fatshedera

Hardy shrub.
Example x *F. lizei* Height 4-8ft, spread 4ft. Evergreen used for ground cover. Shiny, dark green lobed leaves. Pale green flowers Oct-Nov, but these will open outdoors only in the warmest autumns.
Plant Sept-Oct or Mar-Apr in any ordinary garden soil and in sun or shade.
Propagate by 4-5in long cuttings of tips or sideshoots July-Aug.
Care For ground-cover plants, peg upright shoots to the ground when 18in long. For tall shrubs, pinch out young shoot tips regularly and support the plants with stakes.
Pests and diseases Generally trouble-free.

Fennel, common (Foeniculum vulgare)

Perennial herb.
Height 5-8ft, spacing 1-2ft. Aromatic herb with fine, blue-green ferny leaves. Tiny yellow flowers July-Aug. Young leaf stalks can be cooked in the same way as celery; the seeds, which taste of aniseed, and the leaves are used as flavouring.
Plant in well-drained soil and in a sunny position.
Harvest fresh leaves as needed. For winter use, freeze leaves or lift clumps in Oct and grow in pots indoors.
Propagate by sowing in shallow drills 15in apart Mar-May – and thinning seedlings to 12in – or by dividing established plants in spring.
Pests and diseases Generally trouble-free.

Fennel, Florence (Foeniculum vulgare dulce)

Annual herb and vegetable.
Height 2ft, spacing 9-12in. Similar to common fennel, but with a bulbous base that can be used as a sweet, aniseed-flavoured vegetable. Leaves are used as flavouring.
Sow Apr in shallow drills 20in apart in fertile, well-drained soil and in a sunny position. Thin seedlings to 9-12in. As the stems swell, earth up or cover them with paper collars to blanch them.
Harvest by cutting the swollen leaf bases July-Sept when they are about the size of a tennis ball. Use leaves for the kitchen in the same way as those of common fennel.
Pests and diseases Generally trouble-free.

Fig	Forget-me-not	Forsythia	Fothergilla	Foxglove	Freesia outdoor
Ficus carica	*Myosotis sylvatica*	*Forsythia x intermedia*	*Fothergilla major*	*Digitalis purpurea*	*Freesia x kewensis*

Fig (Ficus carica)

Fruit tree; tender in most parts of Britain.
Height (for a wall-trained tree) 10ft, spread 15ft; for a bush type, 15ft by 10ft. Both types will produce ripe fruit in the warmer South and West. 'Brown Turkey', bearing brownish fruits, does best under glass or fan-trained against a wall. 'White Marseilles', the best outdoor bush, has pale green fruits.
Plant Nov-Mar in 12in pots sunk in the ground with the rims protruding above the soil. Fill the pots with soil mixed with a couple of handfuls of bone meal. Support fan-trained trees with horizontal wires 12in apart and up to 10ft high.
Harvest Aug-Oct when the ripe fruits hang downwards. On outdoor trees remove all obvious fruits in autumn. Leave tiny fruits to develop the following year.
Propagate by layering in summer; sever the rooted shoots from the parent plant 12 months later.
Care Check root growth every other year in winter by lifting the pot. Prune away any roots which have grown through the pot's drainage holes. Mulch mature trees Apr-May. Prune out crowded shoots in Mar. Stop fruit-bearing growths at four to six leaves in June.
Pests and diseases WASPS, CORAL SPOT, GREY MOULD.

Forget-me-not (Myosotis)

Annual and perennial plant, usually grown as biennial bedding plant.
Examples *M. alpestris* Height 3-8in, spacing 6in. Fragrant, azure flowers with yellow eyes Apr-June. Varieties include 'Ultramarine' (deep blue), the compact 'Blue Ball', and 'Carmine King' and 'Rose Pink' (both pink). *M. sylvatica* Height 12in, spacing 6in. Fragrant, blue flowers May-June.
Sow in cold frames or seedbeds Apr-May and plant out in Sept into a moist but well-drained, partly shaded site.
Pests and diseases GREY MOULD, POWDERY MILDEW.

Forsythia

Spring-flowering shrub.
Examples *F.* x *intermedia* Height and spread 8ft plus. Clusters of golden-yellow flowers Mar-Apr. *F.* x *i.* 'Spectabilis' is suitable for hedging. *F. suspensa* Height and spread 10ft. Bright yellow pendulous flowers Mar-Apr.
Plant in ordinary soil, in sun or partial shade. For hedging, space young (1½-2ft tall) plants 18in apart. After planting, cut back the top third of all shoots to promote bushy growth.
Propagate by 10-12in long cuttings of the current season's growth in Oct. The drooping tips of *F. suspensa* often root when they touch the ground. Sever rooted tips in Oct and replant in flowering positions.
Care Shorten shoots after flowering; trim hedges in Apr after flowering.
Pests and diseases BIRDS, honey fungus.

Fothergilla

Decorative shrub.
Examples *F. gardenii* Height 2-3ft, spread 3-4ft. Mid-green leaves turn crimson in autumn. Scented catkin-like cream flowers Apr-May. *F. major* Height and spread 8ft. Scented cream flower spikes in May.
Plant Oct-Nov or Mar in light, moist, lime-free soil enriched with compost, and in sun or light shade.
Propagate by layering in Sept; sever rooted shoots from the parent plant two years later.
Pests and diseases Generally trouble-free.

Foxglove (Digitalis)

Perennial or biennial border plant.
Example *D. purpurea* Height 3-5ft, spacing 1½-2ft. Flowers June-July. Varieties include *D. p.* 'Excelsior' (white, cream, pink or purple flowers) and *D. p.* 'Foxy' (white, cream, pink or red).
Sow outdoors May-June by scattering on surface. Add a thin layer of damp peat. Transplant to flowering sites in Sept. Foxgloves do well in any soil that does not dry out and is in partial shade.
Care Cut off central spike after flowering to encourage flowering sideshoots. Cut perennial species back to ground level in Oct.
Pests and diseases Crown rot, root rot.

Freesia, outdoor

Bulbous plant; usually grown as annual.
Example *F.* x *kewensis* (or *F.* x *hybrida*) Height 12in, spacing 4in. Scented funnel-shaped flowers Aug-Oct. Red, yellow, white, lilac and blue varieties available.
Plant only corms specially developed for outdoor use in Apr, 2in deep in light sandy soil and in full sun. Propagation is not possible with outdoor freesias. Discard corms after flowering and buy new ones.
Care Water well in dry spells.
Pests and diseases APHIDS, CATERPILLARS.

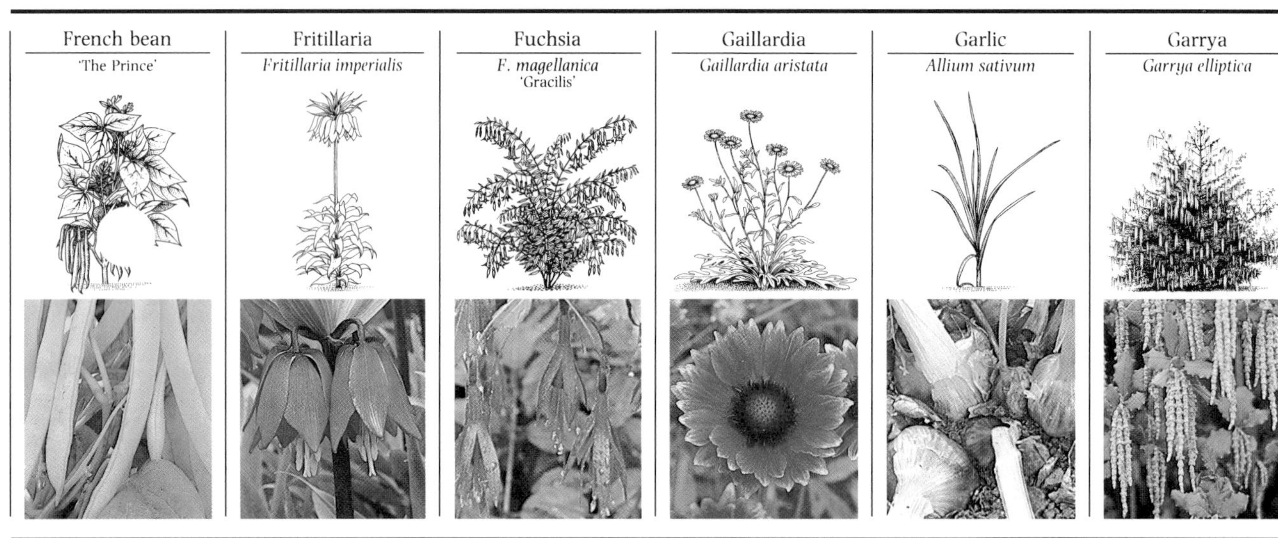

French bean (Phaseolus vulgaris)

Annual vegetable.
Flat-podded dwarfs: 'Masterpiece', 'The Prince' 'Canadian Wonder'. Pencil-pods: 'Cordon', 'Tendergreen' (dwarf). Haricot: 'Comtesse de Chambord'. Flageolet: 'Chevrier Vert'. Only the seeds of haricot and flageolet types are eaten. On other types, the pod is eaten as well.
Sow seeds 2-3in apart in 2in deep drills drawn 18in apart. Thin to 6in apart when first pair of true leaves shows. For early June crop sow seeds under cloches mid-Mar. Keep under cover until end of May. For main crop sow outdoors third week in Apr in South, early May in North; then sow once monthly until mid-July. Light, well-drained soil is best. Add lime to acid soil. Prepare soil before sowing by digging it deeply in autumn. Work in 1 bucket of well-rotted manure per sq yd. Dwarf non-climbers are self-supporting but may need sticks in exposed beds. All climbers need tall pea sticks.
Care Water freely in dry weather, mulching with grass cuttings or moist peat. In Oct put cloches over the last sowings for Nov crops. After harvesting cut tops down, but leave roots in soil to release their nitrogen.
Pests and diseases See *Broad bean*, page 386.

Fritillaria (Fritillary)

Bulbous border plant.
Examples *F. imperialis* (crown imperial) Height 2-3ft, spacing 9-15in. Tulip-shaped hanging flowers in Apr. *F. meleagris* (snake's head) Height 18in, spacing 6in. Bell-shaped flowers Apr-May.
Plant Sept-Nov, 4-6in deep (8in for *F. imperialis*), in fertile, well-drained soil in sun or partial shade. *F. meleagris* will also grow in turf.
Propagate by offsets, which can be separated from the parent plant after the foliage has died down in summer.
Care Fritillarias do best when left undisturbed for at least four years. Cut stems down to ground level after they die back in summer.
Pests and diseases Generally trouble-free.

Fuchsia

Almost hardy flowering shrub.
Example *F. magellanica* Height 4-6ft, spread 2-4ft. Crimson and purple flowers July-Oct. Numerous varieties, hardy in the South, are available. Numerous hybrid varieties, most derived in part from *F. magellanica*, are available, including 'Abbe Farges' (lilac flowers), 'Alice Hoffman' (rose and white), 'Empress of Prussia' (scarlet), 'Gracilis' (slender, crimson and purple). All flower July-Oct.
Plant May-June in rich, deep soil.
Propagate by cuttings in Aug or by root division in late spring or autumn.
Care Water in dry spells, mulch in late spring. Protect roots in winter with bracken, straw, peat or leaf mould. Cut frost-damaged branches to near ground level Mar-Apr.
Pests and diseases Generally trouble-free.

Gaillardia (Blanket flower)

Spectacular bedding and border plant.
Example *G. aristata* Height $2\frac{1}{2}$ft, spacing 18in. Large daisy-like flowers July-Oct. Hybrid varieties include 'Burgundy' (deep red), 'Dazzler' (orange with maroon centre), 'Goblin' (yellow and red, dwarf type), 'Mandarin' (flame orange and red) and 'Wirral Flame' (red with gold-tipped petals).
Sow Apr in flowering site. The plants do best in light soil and sun, but will tolerate any reasonable garden soil and light shade.
Care Provide pea sticks for tall or heavy-headed plants. Deadhead to prolong flowering period.
Pests and diseases Downy mildew.

Garlic (Allium sativum)

Bulbous perennial herb.
Height 1-3ft, spacing 9-12in. Small, white, red-tinged flowers in June. The bulb, made up of bulblets or cloves, is widely used in cooking.
Plant bulbs or cloves in spring 3in deep in a light, well-manured soil and in a sunny position. Pinch out flower heads to prevent diversion of nutrients from the forming bulbs. Make a second planting in Oct if required.
Harvest when the foliage turns yellow in Aug. Lift the bulbs and allow them to dry in the sun. Tie them into bundles and store them in a cool, dry, frost-free place. Alternatively, plait them into strings (for details on how to do this, see *Rope trick*, page 236).
Propagate by retaining the best bulbs to provide cloves for next year's planting.
Pests and diseases WHITE ROT.

Garrya

Evergreen shrub.
Example *G. elliptica* Height 8-15ft, spread 6-12ft. Grey catkins Feb-Mar.
Plant Apr in well-drained soil and preferably in full sun against a south or west-facing wall. In severe winters, protect plants from frost with bracken, or shelter with a polythene screen, during their first winter.
Propagate by 3-4in long heel cuttings of sideshoots Aug-Sept or by layering in Sept. Sever the rooted shoots from the parents about two years later.
Pests and diseases Generally trouble-free.

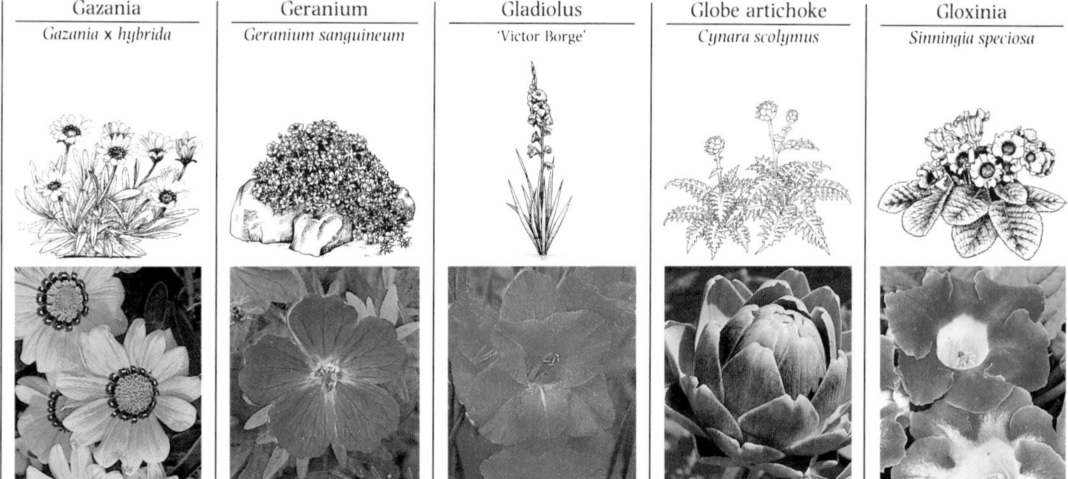

Gazania

Perennial, but grown as annual. **Example** *G.* x *hybrida* Height 9-15in, spacing 12in. Daisy-like flowers in a wide range of colours June-Oct. Single-colour varieties such as 'Ministar Yellow' and 'Red Hybrid' are available, but multicoloured seed mixtures are more popular.
Sow under glass Jan-Feb at a temperature of 16°C (61°F). Prick out the seedlings into 3in pots and harden off before planting out in June. Any soil will do, but full sun is essential.
Propagate by cuttings July-Aug.
Pests and diseases GREY MOULD.

Geranium (Crane's-bill)

Perennial border plant.
(For the popular bedding and pot plants commonly called geraniums, see *Pelargonium*, page 420.)
Examples *G. pratense* Height 1½-2ft. Flowers July-Sept. Varieties include 'Album' (white), 'Flore-pleno' (double blue) and the dwarf hybrid 'Johnson's Blue' (light blue flowers May-Aug). *G. sanguineum* (bloody crane's-bill) Height 6-9in, spread 18in. Ground-cover plant. Crimson-magenta flowers June-Sept.
Plant Sept-Mar in well-drained, compost-enriched soil, in sun or light shade.
Propagate by division Sept-Mar.
Care Support tall plants with pea sticks. Cut stems to ground level in autumn.
Pests and diseases SLUGS, RUST.

Gladiolus

Summer-flowering bulb.
Hundreds of varieties in dozens of colours available in four main categories:
Large-flowered hybrids Height 3-5ft, spacing 4-6in. Single and multi-coloured forms available.
Butterfly hybrids Height 2-4ft, spacing 4-6in. Numerous colours, many with contrasting throat markings.
Primulinus hybrids Height 1½-3ft, spacing 4-6in. Hooded flowers in wide colour range.
Miniature hybrids Height 1½-3ft, spacing 6in. Slightly smaller blooms than primulinus types.
Plant corms in two-weekly succession Mar-Apr (for continuous display), in well-drained soil and open sunny site. In heavy soil, plant at least 4in deep; in light soil, at least 6in deep.
Propagate by dividing off cormlets during winter storage for planting in Apr.
Care Lift corms when the foliage begins to turn yellow-brown, before the first frost. Cut off the main stem an inch or two from the corm, clean and dry the corm and store for the winter in a cool but frost-free place. Alternatively, leave corms in the ground and protect them from frost with straw or bracken.
Pests and diseases THRIPS, APHIDS, SWIFT MOTH CATERPILLARS, CORE ROT, cucumber mosaic virus, gladiolus dry rot, gladiolus scab, gladiolus yellows, HARD ROT, leaf spot, storage rot.

Globe artichoke (Cynara scolymus)

Perennial vegetable.
Perennial grown as a vegetable and for decoration. Height 5ft, spacing 3ft. Thistle-like flowers produced in summer.
Plant Apr in fertile, well-cultivated and well-manured soil and in sheltered, sunny position.
Harvest the edible flower heads, while still in the bud stage, from June onwards. Cut heads at top of stems first to encourage heads on sideshoots to develop. The young leaf shoots, called chards, blanched like celery, are also edible. After harvesting the heads, cut the plant back to promote growth. When the shoots are about 2ft high, tie them together and blanch for five or six weeks by covering them with black polythene.
Propagate by rooted suckers, detached and potted Apr or Nov.
Care In Nov, cut the stems back to 18in, draw soil up the stems, and cover the area with a 6in layer of straw or bracken. Remove the layer after frost danger is past.
Pests and diseases PETAL BLIGHT.

Gloxinia (Sinningia speciosa)

Tuberous house or greenhouse plant. Height 9in, spread 12in. Violet or purple flowers May-Aug, or all year round with planned sowing.
Numerous varieties, often known as florists' gloxinias, are available. They include 'Emperor Frederick' (scarlet flowers with white edges), 'Emperor William' (purple and white) and 'Mont Blanc' (pure white).
Sow Feb-Mar in seed compost and germinate at 21°C (70°F). When the second leaves develop, pot the seedlings individually into 2½in pots of potting compost and when established lower the temperature to 18°C (about 65°F). Pot on as necessary.
Propagate by leaf cuttings June-July.
Care Grow plants in a shaded greenhouse in humid atmosphere and with a minimum temperature of 18°C (about 65°F). Keep plants moist throughout the flowering period.
Pests and diseases FOOT AND ROOT ROT, physiological disorder (yellow rings on foliage, caused by incorrect watering), tomato spotted wilt virus.

Golden rod	Gooseberry	Grape	Grape hyacinth	Gypsophila	Hamamelis
Solidago x *hybrida* 'Peter Pan'	'Careless'	*Vitis vinifera* 'Black Hamburgh'	*Muscari armeniacum*	*Gypsophila elegans*	*Hamamelis mollis*
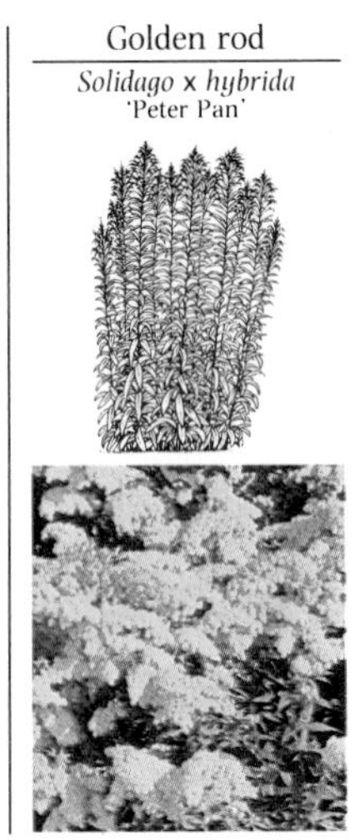					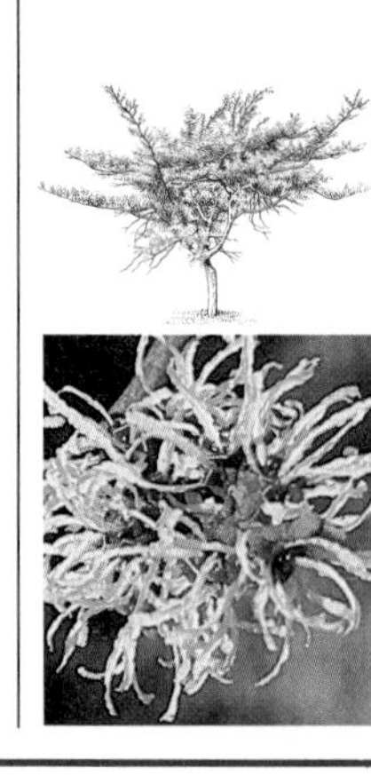

Golden rod (Solidago)

Perennial border and rock garden plant.
Examples *S. brachystachys* Height 6in, spread 12in. Plumes of tiny golden flowers Aug-Sept. Rock garden or border edge.
Hybrid garden border varieties, chiefly derived from *S.* x *hybrida*, include: 'Golden Gates' (height 3ft, spacing 2ft; golden flowers in Sept), 'Golden Wings' (height 6ft, spacing 3ft; deep yellow flowers Aug-Sept).
Plant Oct-Mar in ordinary soil and in sun or partial shade.
Care Stake tall plants to half their height. Cut down all flower stems Oct-Nov.
Pests and diseases TORTRIX MOTH CATERPILLARS, POWDERY MILDEW.

Gooseberry (Grossularia uva-crispa)

Fruit bush.
Height 4-5ft, spacing 4-6ft. Varieties include: 'Careless' (mid-season cooking type, yellow-green berries); 'Keepsake' (early dessert or cooking type, large green berries); 'Leveller' (mid-season dessert or cooking type, large yellow-green berries); 'Whitesmith' (mid-season, large white berries, dessert or cooking).
Plant two or three-year-old bushes Nov-Mar in well-drained but moisture-retentive soil, in full sun or partial shade. Avoid sites liable to frost or strong summer winds.
Harvest berries May-Aug.
Propagate by cuttings in Oct. Plant out one year later, Nov-Mar.
Care Apply a mulch of compost in spring. Give annual winter feed of 1oz sulphate of potash per sq yd and a Mar feed of 1oz sulphate of ammonia per sq yd. Remove suckers from bushes grown on a 'leg' (single stem). Avoid spring frost damage by covering bushes in Apr with fine muslin. Prune in spring to space branches for easier harvesting.
Pests and diseases BIRDS, gooseberry sawfly, American gooseberry mildew, cluster cup rust, GREY MOULD, honey fungus.

Grape (Vitis vinifera)

Fruit tree.
Height and spread of wall-trained varieties, 15ft. (Cordons) 2ft by 4ft. Outdoor varieties include: 'Riesling Sylvaner' (light yellow grapes of the Alsatian type, ripening in Oct); 'Siegerrebe' (large golden grapes of muscat flavour, ripening in Oct); 'Black Hamburgh' (sweet, blue-black grapes, ripening mid-season; best planted against a sunny wall).
Plant wall-trained vines in any free-draining, well-manured soil against a south-facing wall, Oct-Feb. Set plants 5ft apart and train them up wires secured to the wall 12in apart. On open ground, plant vines Oct-Feb in fertile, well-drained soil and in sun – preferably on a southern slope. Set the plants $4\frac{1}{2}$ft apart with 3ft between rows. Firmly stake each plant and join the stakes with wires running along the rows.
Propagate in Feb by eye cuttings – that is, cuttings with a single eye or bud.
Care Mulch established vines annually in Mar. Prune cordon-grown plants just before leaf fall, cutting all sideshoots back to two or three buds. For detailed pruning advice, see *Grapes*, page 162.
Pests and diseases MEALY BUGS, SCALE INSECTS, honey fungus, magnesium deficiency, oedema, POWDERY MILDEW, scald, shanking, splitting.

Grape hyacinth (Muscari)

Proliferating spring bulb.
Example *M. armeniacum* Height 8-10in, spacing 3-4in. Deep blue flowers with white rims Apr-May. Varieties include 'Cantab' (light blue) and 'Heavenly Blue' (bright blue).
Plant bulbs Aug-Nov so that the tops are about 3in deep. They will thrive in any well-drained soil, ideally in full sun. Shade encourages more leaves but fewer flowers.
Propagate by dividing crowded clumps after the leaves turn yellow. Otherwise, leave them to spread by themselves.
Pests and diseases Smut.

Gypsophila (Baby's breath)

Border plant: annual and perennial species available.
Examples *G. elegans* Height 18in, spacing 12in. Tiny, starry flowers June-Sept. Varieties include 'Covent Garden' (white) and 'Rosea' (bright pink). *G. repens* Height 6in, spread 2ft. Mat-forming rock garden species. Minute white or pink flowers July-Aug.
Sow seeds of *G. elegans* in flowering site Sept or Mar and thin seedlings as necessary. Plants thrive in any well-drained, preferably chalky, soil in a sunny position.
Propagate *G. repens* by 2in long cuttings of sideshoots or basal shoots Apr-May.
Pests and diseases Generally trouble-free.

Hamamelis (Witch hazel)

Decorative perennial.
Example *H. mollis* (Chinese witch hazel) Height and spread 10ft. Bright yellow, fragrant flowers Dec-Feb, followed by the hazel-like leaves, which turn yellow in autumn.
Plant in neutral or acid moisture-retentive soil and in sun or light shade. Incorporate plenty of peat or manure in heavy soils.
Propagate by layering in Sept. Sever rooted shoots two years later.
Care Prune straggly branches on established plants after flowering.
Pests and diseases Generally trouble-free.

Heath	Heather	Hebe	Helenium	Holly	Hollyhock
Erica carnea 'December Red'	*Calluna vulgaris*	*Hebe* x 'Midsummer Beauty'	*Helenium autumnale*	*Ilex aquifolium* 'Argenteo-marginata'	*Althaea rosea*

Heath (Erica)

Shrubby ground cover.
Examples *E. ciliaris* (Dorset heath) Height 18in, spread 2ft plus. Bell-shaped flowers, July to winter, range from white to pink to purple. Many varieties available. *E. carnea* Height to 12in or prostrate, spread 2ft. Ground-cover plant with white or pink flowers Nov-May. Many varieties available. *E. cinerea* (bell heather) Height and spread 9-12in. White, pink, red, maroon or mahogany flowers June-Oct. Many varieties available.
Plant Mar-May or Oct-Nov in peaty, acid soil, and in full sun. *E. carnea* will also tolerate chalky soil.
Propagate by cuttings July-Oct.
Pests and diseases SCALE INSECTS, leaf spot.

Heather (Calluna, ling)

Perennial dwarf shrub.
Example *C. vulgaris* Height and spread $2\frac{1}{2}$ft. Leaves range in colour from green to grey to orange and red. White, pink or purple flowers July-Nov or later.
Plant Mar-May or Oct-Nov in any lime-free soil. Add 2in top-dressing of peat and 4oz per sq yd of bone meal.
Propagate by cuttings July-Oct.
Care Water in spring and dry spells. Add an annual dressing of peat.
Pests and diseases Heather die-back, honey fungus.

Hebe

Long-flowering shrub.
Example *H. salicifolia* Height and spread 5-10ft. White, lilac, purple flowers June-Aug.
Plant Sept-Oct or Apr-May in any fertile soil and in full sun. Best grown in sheltered gardens or in frost-free maritime districts.
Propagate by 2-4in long cuttings of non-flowering shoots in July-Aug.
Care Deadhead all species when flowering is over.
Pests and diseases Downy mildew, honey fungus, leaf spot.

Helenium (Sneezewort)

Good border perennial.
Example *H. autumnale* Many varieties available including 'Moerheim Beauty' (height 3ft, spacing 2ft, bronze-red flowers July-Sept); 'Butterpat' (height 3ft, spacing 2ft, golden-yellow flowers Aug-Sept); 'Golden Youth' (height $2\frac{1}{2}$ft, spacing 2ft, pure yellow flowers June-July).
Plant Oct-Apr in any ordinary soil.
Propagate by dividing clumps in autumn or spring.
Care Stake plants with canes or pea sticks in exposed gardens. Deadhead flowers to encourage second flush of blooms. Cut down dead stems in Nov.
Pests and diseases SLUGS, TORTRIX MOTH CATERPILLARS.

Holly (Ilex)

Evergreen tree or hedging.
Example *I. aquifolium* Height 18-25ft, spread 8-12ft. Many varieties available, including: 'Argenteo-marginata' (silver-edged leaves; females produce large crops of red berries if a male plant is nearby); and 'Pendula' (a weeping form which grows 8-12ft high).
Plant Sept-Oct or Apr-May in ordinary soil and in sun or light shade. Good in maritime or city sites. For hedges, plant 18in high saplings 2ft apart.
Propagate by heeled 2-3in long cuttings of current year's growth Aug-Nov.
Care Trim hedges annually in Apr, and prune specimen trees to shape in July-Aug.
Pests and diseases BIRDS, hares, holly leaf miners, honey fungus, leaf spot.

Hollyhock (Althaea)

Annual, biennial and perennial species available.
Examples *A. ficifolia* Height 6ft, spread 2ft. Yellow flowers June-Sept. *A. rosea* Height 4-6ft as an annual, 9ft as a biennial; spread up to 2ft. Pink, dark pink, red or white flowers July-Sept.
Plant To grow as biennials or perennials, sow seeds outdoors, 9in apart in shallow drills, June-July. Transplant to 2ft apart Sept-Oct. To grow as annuals, sow in flowering position in Apr – in rich soil in sheltered, sunny position, or raise earlier under glass.
Care Water freely in dry weather. Stake tall plants and those in exposed positions. For perennials, apply annual mulch of manure or compost Cut stalks down to 6in after flowering.
Pests and diseases CATERPILLARS, CAPSID BUGS, RUST.

GARDEN TIP
Grape hyacinth

If you find you keep damaging dormant grape hyacinth bulbs while hoeing, try experimenting with the depth at which you plant. The traditional advice is to cover the bulbs with about 3in of soil, but it's worth trying a few at slightly deeper levels – 4-6in, say – to get them out of range of your hoe.
You may also find that the extra depth improves their performance on your soil. Plant researchers have found that, on some soils, some bulbs – particularly large-trumpet daffodils and some species of tulip – actually do better if they're planted twice as deep as normal.

Honesty
Lunaria annua

Honeysuckle, climbing
Lonicera periclymenum

Honeysuckle, shrub
Lonicera nitida 'Baggesen's Gold'

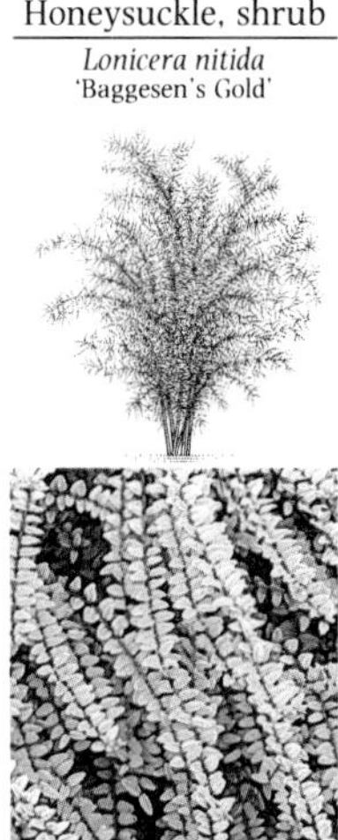

Hornbeam
Carpinus betulus

Horse chestnut
Aesculus x *carnea*

Horseradish
Armoracia rusticana

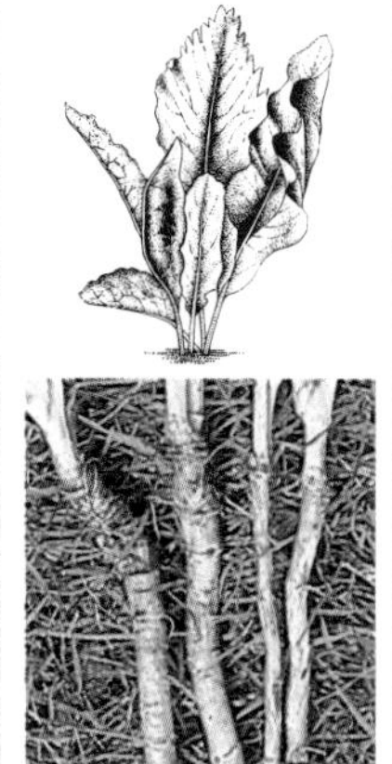

Honesty (Lunaria)

Herbaceous biennial.
Example *L. annua* Height 2ft, spacing 12in. Purple or white flowers Apr-June, followed by silvery, disc-shaped seed pods, which are widely used in flower arrangements.
Sow outdoors in nursery bed May-June. Plant out in Sept into ordinary soil, preferably in partial shade.
Care Cut seed pods in Aug, before autumn gales begin.
Pests and diseases CLUB ROOT, white blister.

Honeysuckle, climbing (Lonicera)

Climbing shrub.
Examples *L. japonica* (Japanese honeysuckle) Height 30ft. Evergreen. White to pale yellow fragrant flowers June-Oct. *L. periclymenum* (woodbine, honeysuckle) Height 20ft. Deciduous. Yellow-red flowers July-Aug followed by red berries.
Plant *L. japonica* Apr-May. *L. periclymenum* Sept-Mar in ordinary soil enriched with humus, in sun or partial shade.
Propagate by taking semi-hardwood cuttings July-Aug; by serpentine layering Aug-Sept (see *All about layering*, page 110).
Care Occasionally thin out old wood after flowering, or in early spring.
Pests and diseases APHIDS, leaf spot, POWDERY MILDEW.

Honeysuckle, shrub (Lonicera)

Sweetly fragrant shrub; evergreen and deciduous.
Examples *L. fragrantissima* Height and spread 6ft. Deciduous. Strongly scented, creamy flowers Dec-Mar. *L. nitida* Height and spread 6ft. Dense, evergreen shrub used for hedging. Tiny, insignificant yellow flowers Apr-May, followed by translucent violet berries.
Plant Sept-Mar in well-drained soil and in sun or partial shade. For hedging, set young plants 9-12in apart.
Propagate by hardwood cuttings Sept-Oct, or by layering Aug-Nov. Sever rooted shoots from parent plant a year later.
Care Give a light mulching in spring. Thin out old wood occasionally after flowering. Reduce young hedging plants by half on planting, trim young shoots during the summer following, and cut the plants back by half each year until the desired height is reached. Thereafter, trim in May and Sept to maintain shape.
Pests and diseases APHIDS, leaf spot, POWDERY MILDEW, SILVER LEAF.

Hornbeam (Carpinus)

Deciduous tree; often used for hedging.
Example *C. betulus* Height 25ft, spread 15ft. Catkins Apr-May, followed by nuts. Tree used for hedging. Varieties include 'Fastigiata' (densely conical), 'Incisa' (small, deeply toothed leaves) and 'Purpurea' (leaves purple when young).
Plant Nov-Mar in ordinary soil and in sun or partial shade. For hedging, space plants 20in apart.
Propagate by seed sown outdoors Sept-Oct in nursery beds. Plant out three or four years later.
Care Clip hedges annually in July.
Pests and diseases Honey fungus.

Horse chestnut (Aesculus)

Deciduous tree; not for small gardens.
Examples *A.* x *carnea* (red horse chestnut) Height 50ft, spread 30ft. Rose-pink flowers May-June. *A. hippocastanum* (common horse chestnut) Height 30ft, spread 10-15ft. White flowers in May. *A. pavia* (red buckeye) Height 20ft, spread 15ft. Bright red flowers in June.
Plant both types Oct-Mar in any fertile soil and in a sunny or partially shaded position.
Propagate species by seed sown outdoors in a nursery bed Sept-Oct. Grow seedlings on for two or three years before transplanting to permanent positions. Propagate varieties and hybrids, such as *A.* x *carnea*, by grafting one-year-old shoots in Mar onto rootstocks of *A. hippocastanum*.
Pests and diseases SCALE INSECTS and leaf spot.

Horseradish (Armoracia rusticana)

Perennial root herb; can be invasive. Height 2ft, spread 18in.
Plant Feb almost anywhere, but it does best in manured ground. Plant 9-12in roots upright 12in apart with the tops about 2in below the surface. Leave 18in between rows. Once established, it is difficult to eradicate and it is best to replant it annually.
Harvest Dig up roots as required during the summer. For winter use, lift in early winter (before topgrowth dies back and the roots become hard to find) and store in boxes of soil or sand. Use thicker roots for the kitchen, and thinner roots for replanting in Feb.
Pests and diseases Arabis mosaic virus, leaf spot, white blister.

Hosta	Hyacinth	Hydrangea	Hypericum	Iris	Ivy
Hosta sieboldiana	*Hyacinthus orientalis* 'Jan Bos'	*Hydrangea macrophylla* (Hortensia type)	*H.* x 'Hidcote'	*I.* 'Carnaby' (Tall Bearded Hybrid)	*Hedera helix* 'Goldheart'
		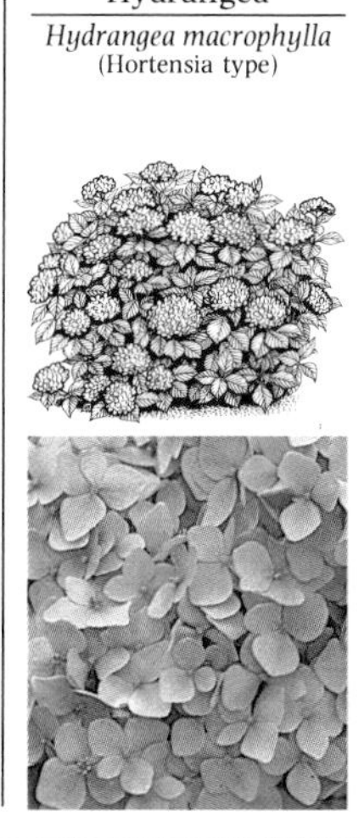			

Hosta

Summer border plant.
Examples *H. albo-marginata* Height and spread 18in. White-edged leaves. Lilac, violet-striped flowers July-Aug. *H. sieboldiana* Height and spread 2ft. Large blue-green leaves. White-purple flowers Aug. *H. undulata* Height and spread 2ft. Has wavy, oblong leaves with white centres. Lilac-coloured funnel-shaped flowers produced in Aug.
Plant Oct-Mar in moisture-retentive soil which has been enriched with peat or compost. A spot in partial shade is best.
Propagate by dividing and replanting crowns in Mar.
Pests and diseases SLUGS.

Hyacinth (Hyacinthus orientalis)

Spring bulbs for borders and pots. Height and spread 6-9in.
Popular varieties 'Carnegie', 'L'Innocence', 'Mme Kruger' (white); 'Amsterdam', 'Jan Bos', 'Lady Derby' (pink or red).
Plant out pot-grown Christmas bulbs in Mar-Apr, 6in deep. If left undisturbed they will flower in the garden for many years to come. Plant out other bulbs 5-6in deep in autumn.
Propagate by slitting the base of the bulb to encourage the growth of bulblets. It is best not to use bulbs prepared for Christmas for propagation.
Pests and diseases STEM AND BULB EELWORMS, narcissus fly maggots, grey bulb rot, soft rot, storage rot, VIRUSES.

Hydrangea

Deciduous flowering shrubs and climbers.
Examples *H. macrophylla* Height and spread 6ft plus. Shrub. Pink or blue florets July-Sept. *H. petiolaris* (Japanese climbing hydrangea). Superb cover for a north-facing wall. Height up to 60ft. Creamy flowers June.
Plant both types Oct-Nov or Mar-Apr in loam enriched with well-rotted manure or peat, and in a sheltered position.
Propagate by cuttings of vigorous sideshoots June-July.
Care The flowers of blue forms of *H. macrophylla* tend to lose colour on alkaline soils. Restore acidity with annual feeds of peat and sequestrene. Pink forms fade on acid soil; treat with ground limestone.
Pests and diseases Very occasionally chlorosis and honey fungus.

Hypericum

Ground-cover and shrub species available.
Examples *H. calycinum* (rose of Sharon) Height 18in, spread indefinite. Forms a dense, ground-covering carpet. Bright gold flowers June-Sept. *H.* x 'Hidcote' Height 6ft, spread 5ft. Semi-evergreen shrub. Golden flowers July-Sept.
Plant Oct-Apr in fertile, well-drained soil and in a sunny position.
Propagate *H. calycinum* by division Oct-Apr, *H.* 'Hidcote' by heeled cuttings July-Sept.
Care Cut *H. calycinum* back almost to ground level every few years in Mar to keep it compact. Shorten *H.* 'Hidcote' to within a few buds of old wood in Mar.
Pests and diseases RUST.

Iris

Wide range of bulbous and rhizomatous perennials.
There are three main groups: bulbous types such as *Iris danfordiae*, which grow to 4-6in and flower in Feb; bearded types such as the Tall Bearded Hybrids, which grow to 2-3ft and flower in May-July; and beardless types such as *I. sibirica*, which grow to 3ft and flower in May-June.
Plant in sunny, well-drained position. Set non-bulbous (rhizomatous) types half into the ground; set small bulbous types 2-3in deep, large ones 4in deep. Plant bearded types in July, beardless types in late autumn or Apr, bulbous types in Sept.
Propagate all types by dividing and replanting – bearded types after flowering, beardless types in autumn or Apr, bulbous types after the foliage has died back or in early autumn.
Pests and diseases Bearded and beardless types may be affected by arabis mosaic virus, leaf spot, rhizome rot and RUST. Bulbous types may be affected by blue mould, grey bulb rot, iris mosaic virus, iris scorch and leaf spot.

Ivy (Hedera helix)

Attractive and sometimes invasive climber, some types of which can grow to a height of 100ft. Also grown for ground cover.
Plant Sept-Mar in almost any soil or site. Peg shoots to the ground at first.
Propagate July-Aug by cuttings from tips of shoots.
Care Prune back unruly shoots Feb-Mar and summer.
Pests and diseases SCALE INSECTS, bryobia mites and leaf spot.

Japanese cedar	Japanese maple	Japonica	Jasmine	Jerusalem artichoke	Jonquil
Cryptomeria japonica 'Elegans'	*Acer palmatum*	*Chaenomeles speciosa*	*Jasminum nudiflorum*	*Helianthus tuberosus*	*Narcissus jonquilla*
					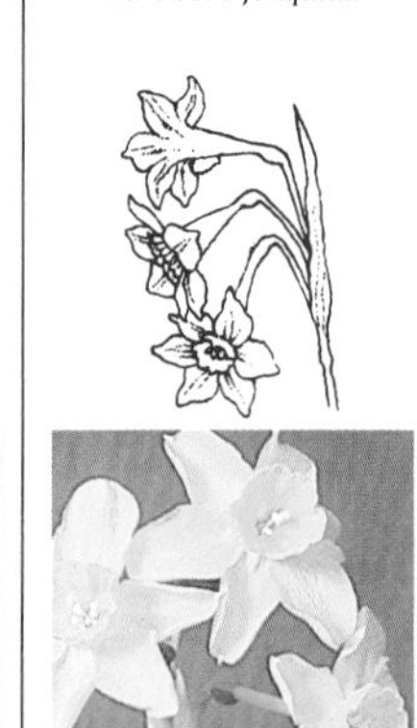

Japanese cedar (Cryptomeria japonica)

Tree; the varieties listed here are suitable for small gardens.
Example *C. j.* 'Elegans' Height 15ft, spread 10ft. Ground-sweeping branches whose leaves are blue-green in summer and bronze or purple in winter. 'Nana' and 'Compacta', height and spread 3ft, are dwarf forms of 'Elegans'.
Plant in any ordinary soil; but trees do best in deep, slightly acid and dampish soil and in sunny sheltered position. Plant Oct-Nov on sandy soil, Apr on heavy clay soils.
Propagate by 2-4in long cuttings taken in Sept.
Pests and diseases Generally trouble-free.

Japanese maple (Acer palmatum)

Tree; grown for highly decorative foliage.
Height 15ft, spread 8ft.
Examples *A. p.* 'Atropurpureum' Bronze-red foliage. *A. p.* 'Senkaki' Coral-red bark and yellow autumn foliage. *A. p.* 'Osakazuki' Orange, crimson and scarlet autumn foliage.
Plant Oct-Mar in well-drained but moist, neutral-acid soil and in sun or partial shade. *A. p.* 'Senkaki', grown for autumn foliage, should be planted in a spot sheltered from autumn winds.
Propagate by grafting in Mar.
Pests and diseases Red spider mites, APHIDS, honey fungus, SCORCH, tar spot, VERTICILLIUM WILT.

Japonica (Chaenomeles speciosa)

Grown for flowers and fruits.
Height and spread 6ft plus. Flowers Jan-Apr; green-yellow fruits, used in preserves, produced in autumn.
Varieties include: 'Apple Blossom' (pinky-white flowers), 'Aurora' (rose), 'Umbilicata' (deep rose-pink flowers) and 'Cardinalis' (crimson).
Plant Oct-Mar in any soil, and in a sunny position. The shrubs do best trained against a wall.
Propagate by 4in long heel cuttings of sideshoots July-Aug. Or layer long shoots in Sept; separate from parent plant two years later.
Care Prune wall-trained plants in May after flowering, cutting back previous season's growth to two or three buds.
Pests and diseases BIRDS, FIRE BLIGHT.

Jasmine (Jasminum)

Sweetly fragrant shrub.
Examples *J. nudiflorum* (winter jasmine) Height and spread 10ft. Yellow flowers Nov-Feb. *J. officinale* Height and spread 20ft. Fragrant white flowers June-Sept.
Plant Oct-Apr in any ordinary soil, preferably against a south, south-west or east-facing wall.
Propagate *J. nudiflorum* by hardwood cuttings in Nov. *J. officinale* by heel cuttings July-Aug.
Care Prune out dead or weak growth after flowering. Cut back flowered shoots on *J. nudiflorum* at the same time to within 3in of the base.
Pests and diseases APHIDS, MEALY BUGS, GREY MOULD.

Jerusalem artichoke (Helianthus tuberosus)

Perennial root vegetable.
Grown for its edible tubers, used as a winter vegetable or in soups; the tall foliage makes a useful summer screen. Height 12ft. The best cooking variety is 'Fuseau' (height 5-6ft). Plants can be grown from egg-sized tubers bought from greengrocers or supermarkets.
Plant tubers Feb-Mar, 15in apart in 5in deep drills set 3ft apart. The plants thrive almost anywhere, in ordinary soil and in sun or partial shade.
Harvest as required, from Oct through the winter.
Propagate by growing on unharvested tubers.
Pests and diseases SLUGS, SWIFT MOTH CATERPILLARS, sclerotinia disease.

Jonquil (Narcissus)

Sweetly scented, spring-flowering bulb.
Height 7-14in; flowers Apr. Jonquils have several fragrant flowers on each stem and a central cup which is shorter than the surrounding petals (the reverse of daffodils).
Numerous single and double hybrid varieties are available in several shades of yellow, including 'Sweetness' (yellow) and 'Golden Sceptre' (deep yellow).
Plant bulbs Aug-Sept in any well-drained soil, in sun or light shade. Set bulbs 3-12in apart in holes which are at least three times the depth of the bulb. Do not remove the leaves until they are completely yellow.
Propagate by lifting clumps in July-Sept. Divide each clump and plant out offsets immediately. It is also possible to propagate by seed. But seeds take three to five years to reach flowering size, and are unlikely to resemble the parent plant exactly.
Pests and diseases STEM AND BULB EELWORMS, tarsonemid mites, narcissus fly maggots, SLUGS, arabis mosaic virus, narcissus fire, GREY MOULD.

Juniper	Kale	Kalmia	Kerria	Kniphofia	Kohlrabi
Juniperus virginiana 'Skyrocket'	*Brassica oleracea acephala* 'Frosty'	*Kalmia latifolia*	*Kerria japonica* 'Pleniflora'	*Kniphofia galpinii*	'Early Green'

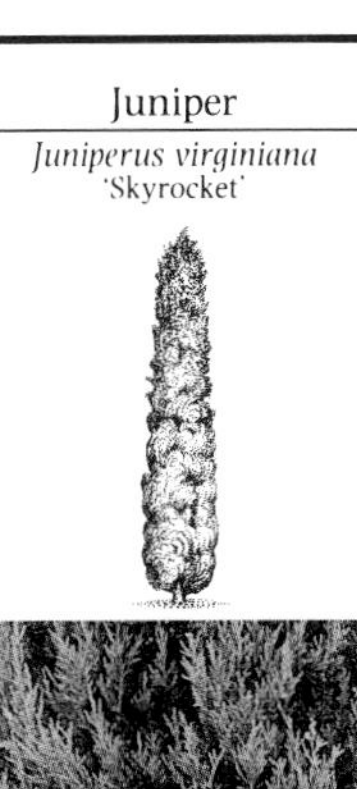
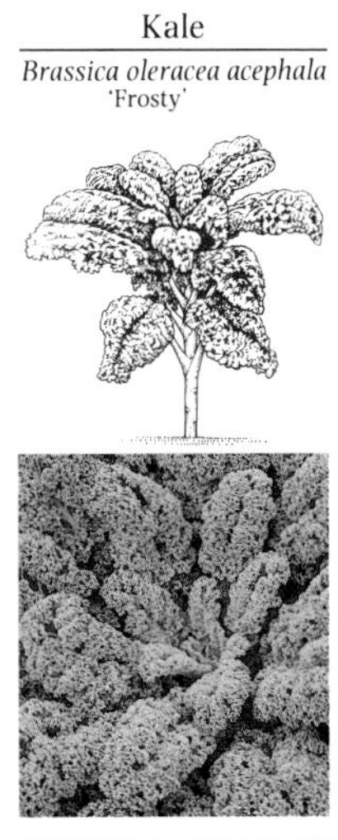

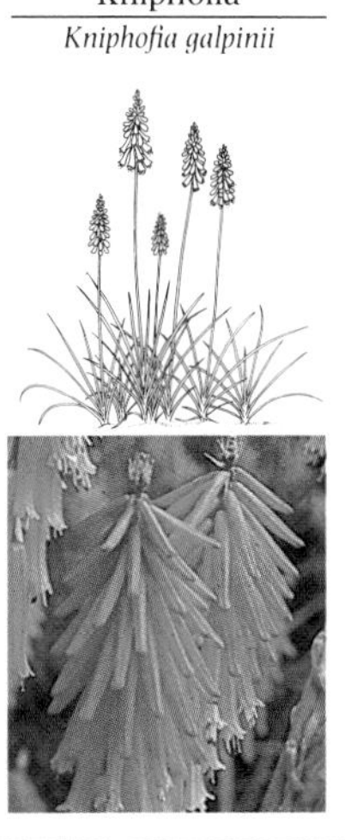
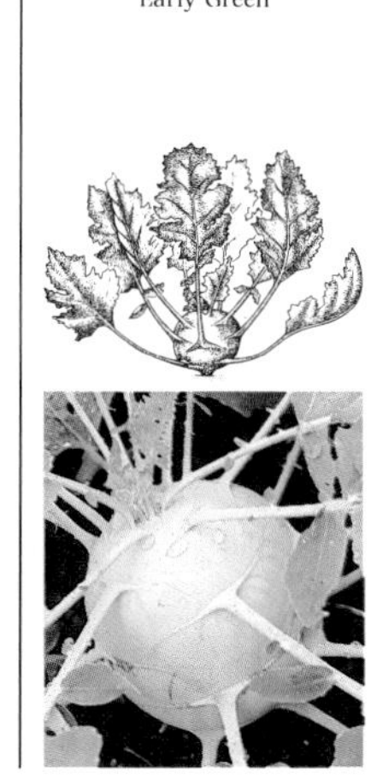

Juniper (Juniperus)

Fragrant, evergreen conifer.
Examples *J. virginiana* 'Skyrocket' Height 20ft, spread 2ft. Slow-growing. Forms a slim, blue-grey spire. *J. horizontalis* Height 12in, spread 6ft. Widespreading, blue-green ground cover.
Plant Apr in almost any garden soil and in sun or light shade.
Propagate by cuttings in Sept.
Pests and diseases SCALE INSECTS and caterpillars of the juniper webber moth.

Kale (Brassica oleracea acephala)

Annual winter vegetable.
Varieties include: 'Frosty' (curly-leaved; height 12in) and 'Cottager's' (crimped-edged, purple-tinged leaves; height 2ft). Rape kale varieties – which are similar in appearance to the curly-leaved types – include 'Favourite' and 'Ragged Jack'.
Sow in a seedbed in mid-May and thin seedlings as they grow.
Transplant to final quarters in July, allowing 2ft each way per plant. They do best in well-drained, well-manured loam.
Harvest Christmas onwards, taking the centre of each plant first. Continue harvesting until Apr.
Pests and diseases CATERPILLARS, FLEA BEETLES, damping-off, wire stem, violet root rot.

Kalmia (Calico bush)

Flowering shrub; do not grow it where animals browse.
Example *K. latifolia* (calico bush, mountain laurel) Height 10ft, spread 8ft. Evergreen. Crinoline-shaped pink flowers in June. Leaves are poisonous to cattle.
Plant Sept-Oct or Apr-May in moist, peaty, lime-free soil and in partial shade.
Propagate by cuttings in Aug.
Care Trim off faded flower clusters.
Pests and diseases Generally trouble-free.

Kerria (Jew's mallow)

Spring-flowering shrub.
Example *K. japonica* Height and spread 4-6ft. Deciduous. Orange-yellow, rose-like flowers Apr-May. Varieties include: 'Pleniflora' (bachelor's buttons), which has double flowers and grows to 8-12ft; and 'Variegata', which grows to 3ft and has single yellow blooms.
Plant Oct-Mar in ordinary soil in sun or partial shade. Thrives against walls in cold areas.
Propagate by 4-5in long cuttings of sideshoots Aug-Sept.
Care Mulch late Apr. Cut back flowered stems to new growth after flowering.
Pests and diseases Generally trouble-free.

Kniphofia (Red hot poker)

Vivid border perennial; good for naturalising.
Examples *K. galpinii* Height and spacing 2ft. Brilliant orange flowers Sept-Oct. *K. uvaria* Height 3-5ft, spacing 2-4ft. Flowers July-Oct. Hybrid varieties include 'Alcazar' (orange), 'Gold Else' (yellow), 'Royal Standard' (red and yellow) and 'Maid of Orleans' (cream).
Plant in sun and in ordinary but well-drained soil, Oct or Apr.
Propagate by division in spring, but only from well-established plants.
Care Mulch in late spring. Protect young plants from cold winters with a 6in layer of straw or bracken. Disturb even established plants as little as possible. Even tall varieties need no staking. But all varieties flower for longer if faded flower spikes are cut off near their base. Tie the remaining leaves together in Nov-Dec to protect the crowns from excess moisture and frost.
Pests and diseases THRIPS.

Kohlrabi (Brassica oleracea caulorapa)

Annual vegetable.
Vegetable grown for its swollen stem, which resembles a leafy turnip. The flavour, too, is turnip-like. A large form is grown as cattle food. Small, quick-growing forms are more suitable for the kitchen. Varieties include: 'Early Green' and 'Green Vienna' (early-maturing; sow in spring or summer); 'Purple Vienna' (late-sowing variety); and 'Rowel' (sweet-fleshed F1 hybrid).
Sow in shallow drills 15in apart in any fertile, well-drained soil. Thin seedlings to 6in apart when third leaves appear. Make successive sowings from Mar to late Aug to ensure continuous supply.
Harvest when the stems are the size of tennis balls. Seeds planted in Mar produce a June crop.
Pests and diseases CLUB ROOT.

Kolkwitzia
Kolkwitzia amabilis

Laburnum
Laburnum x *watereri* 'Vossii'

Lady's mantle
Alchemilla mollis

Lamium
Lamium maculatum 'Beacon Silver'

Lavender
Lavandula spica

Leek
'Musselburgh'

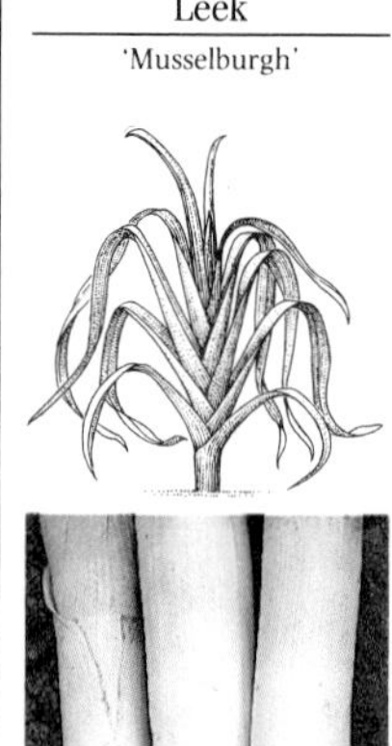

Kolkwitzia

Deciduous shrub.
Example *K. amabilis* (beauty bush) Height 6-12ft, spread 4-10ft. Deciduous. Peeling brown bark. Pale pink and yellow foxglove-like flowers May-June. *K. a.* 'Pink Cloud' has richer, clear pink flowers.
Plant Oct-Nov or Mar in well-drained soil and in full sun.
Propagate by 4-6in long heel cuttings of sideshoots July-Aug.
Care After flowering, cut out the older flowering stems.
Pests and diseases Generally trouble-free.

Laburnum

Good town tree; but poisonous in all its parts.
Example *L.* x *watereri* 'Vossii' Height 15ft, spread 12ft. Bright yellow flowers late May. All parts of the tree are poisonous, most especially the seeds and pods which should be collected and destroyed if children or pets use the garden.
Plant Oct-Mar in well-drained soil and in sun or partial shade.
Propagate by grafting in Mar.
Care Stake young trees.
Pests and diseases LEAFCUTTER BEES, leaf miners, SILVER LEAF.

Lady's mantle (Alchemilla)

Border perennial which forms dense clumps.
Example *A. mollis* Excellent for cut flowers. Height 18in, spacing 15in. Starry, yellow-green flowers June-Aug.
Plant Oct-Mar in a sunny or partially shaded position, in any moist but well-drained soil.
Propagate by dividing and replanting clumps Oct-Mar. The plants also produce self-sown seedlings.
Care Cut stems back to about an inch above the ground in late autumn.
Pests and diseases Generally trouble-free.

Lamium (Dead nettle)

Border perennial; can be invasive.
Examples *L. maculatum* Height and spacing 12in. Silver-striped leaves. Pink-purple flowers in May. *L. m.* 'Album' has white flowers, 'Aureum' golden leaves, 'Beacon Silver' silvery leaves, pink flowers, and 'Roseum' shell-pink flowers. *L. orvala* (giant dead nettle) Height 2ft, spacing 12in. Pink-purple flowers May-June. Not invasive, unlike most other dead nettles.
Plant Oct-Mar in almost any soil or degree of shade. Excellent plant for ground cover. Only *L. maculatum* 'Aureum' requires rich soil.
Propagate by root division Oct-Mar.
Care Trim the plants after flowering to maintain dense leafy ground cover.
Pests and diseases Generally trouble-free.

Lavender (Lavandula)

Low, sturdy, fragrant shrub.
Example *L. spica* (old English lavender) Height and spread 3-4ft. Pale blue flowers July-Sept. *L. s.* 'Hidcote', height and spread 2ft, is more compact and has deep purple flowers.
Plant Sept-Mar in ordinary soil in sunny position. For hedges, set young plants 9-12in apart.
Propagate by 3-4in long cuttings of non-flowering shoots in Aug.
Harvest whole flower stalks for drying before the flowers are fully open. Hang the flowers in bunches to dry in a cool, airy place and, as the colour fades, strip them from the stalks.
Care Trim flower stalks in late summer. Cut straggly plants hard back in Mar-Apr and trim hedges to shape, also in Mar-Apr.
Pests and diseases FROGHOPPERS, GREY MOULD, honey fungus, leaf spot, SCAB.

Leek (Allium porrum)

Annual vegetable.
Numerous varieties available, including: 'Early Market', 'Prize-taker' and 'The Lyon' (all ready for harvesting Sept-Nov); 'Musselburgh' and 'Argenta' (both ready Nov-Jan); 'Yates Empire', 'Royal Favourite' and 'Winter Crop' (all ready for harvesting Feb-Apr).
Sow Mar in $\frac{1}{2}$in deep drills set 6in apart in a seedbed. When the plants are about 8in tall, in June-July, transplant to growing positions in deeply dug, richly manured soil. Add lime, 4oz to the sq yd, to acid soil. Make 6in deep holes, drop the seedlings in and fill the hole with water to settle them in. Space early and mid-season plants 6in apart, late varieties 9in. Rows should be 15in apart.
Care Blanch to increase length of white stems by drawing up soil, tying paper collars round stems or by setting a bottomless black plastic bag round each plant.
Pests and diseases Onion fly maggots, WHITE ROT.

GARDEN TIP
Laburnum

Although laburnum is poisonous, particularly to small children, it's unlikely to cause them much more than a stomachache. According to the National Poisons Information Service, nobody has ever died of eating the plant.

Lettuce
'Suzan'

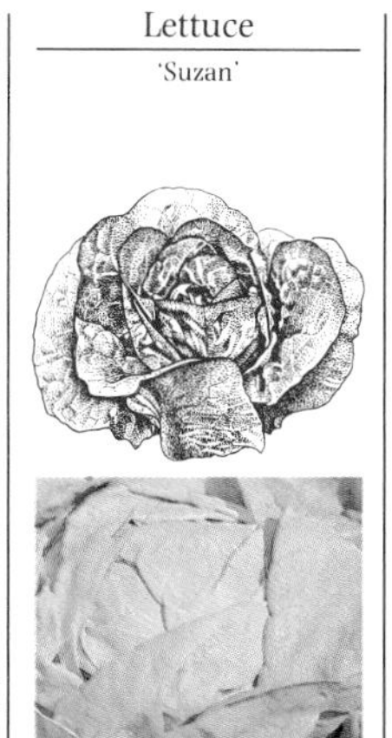

Ligularia
Ligularia dentata

Lilac
Syringa vulgaris

Lily
Lilium martagon
'Album'

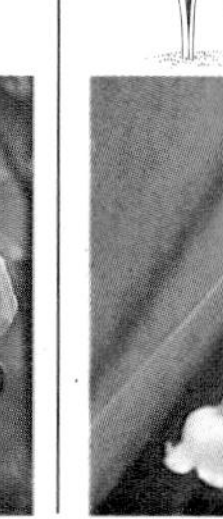

Lily of the valley
Convallaria majalis

Lettuce (Lactuca sativa)

Annual salad vegetable.
There are two main groups, cos and cabbage lettuces. Cos are taller and roughly oblong; cabbage are round and divided into further groups – the smooth-leaved butterheads and the crimped-leaf crispheads.
Summer-maturing varieties include the butterhead types 'Cobham Green', 'Continuity' and 'Suzan' and the crispheads 'Webb's Wonderful' and 'Windermere'. Cos types are 'Buttercrunch', 'Lobjoit's Green Cos', 'Vaux's Self-folding Green' and 'Little Gem'.
For growing in the open through winter to mature in spring, sow hardy butterheads such as 'All the Year Round', 'Arctic King' and 'Imperial Winter' under cloches in cold areas and always in a sheltered site. The butterhead varieties 'Kloek', 'Kwiek' and 'May Queen' are better grown in a greenhouse.
Sow lettuce seeds thinly in shallow drills in the growing site – any fertile, well-drained soil. Summer lettuces require soil that has already been well-manured, but for winter crops, drainage is more important; lighten heavy soils with peat or compost. Grow greenhouse plants at a minimum temperature of 10°C (50°F).
Harvest Aug-sown plants Nov-Dec, plants sown Jan-Feb in Apr-May. Oct-sown plants will be ready for cutting in Jan, Feb and Mar. Always cut lettuces early in the day, using a sharp knife just below the bottom leaves. Harvest plants showing signs of bolting first.
Pests and diseases APHIDS, SLUGS AND SNAILS, CATERPILLARS, damping-off, GREY MOULD, VIRUSES, sclerotinia disease.

Ligularia (sometimes sold as Senecio)

Back-of-the-border perennial.
Example *L. dentata* Height 3-5ft, spacing 3ft. Heart-shaped leaves; orange-yellow flowers July-Aug. *L. d.* 'Desdemona' has orange-red flowers and purple-flushed leaves. *L. d.* 'Othello' is more deeply coloured.
Plant Oct-Apr in ordinary, preferably moist, soil and in partial shade.
Propagate by division Apr-May.
Care Cut plants to ground level in Nov.
Pests and diseases APHIDS, THRIPS, chrysanthemum leaf miner maggots, POWDERY MILDEW, tomato spotted wilt virus.

Lilac (Syringa)

Sweetly scented shrub; good for cut flowers.
Examples *S.* x *josiflexa* 'Bellicent' Height 15ft, spread 12ft. Rose-pink fragrant flower spikes May-June. *S. vulgaris* Height 12ft, spread 10ft. Flowers May-June. Varieties include: 'Blue Hyacinth' (blue flowers); 'Congo' (rich lilac-red); 'Marechal Foch' (carmine); and 'Massena' (deep purple).
Plant Oct-Nov in any fertile soil, in sun or partial shade. Good in town gardens.
Propagate by 3-4in long heel cuttings of semi-ripe shoots in summer. Or graft buds from varieties of *S. vulgaris* onto rootstock of common privet in July.
Care Deadhead. Thin out crossing and weak branches Oct onwards. Rejuvenate overgrown bushes by cutting them back to 2-3ft high in winter. Remove suckers July onwards.
Pests and diseases CATERPILLARS, SCALE INSECTS, die-back, frost damage, lilac blight, SILVER LEAF.

Lily (Lilium)

Bulbous border plants.
An enormous group of plants ranging in height from a foot or so to a majestic 8ft plus. They are sometimes categorised by flower forms into three groups: bowl-flowered, trumpet-flowered and Turk's-cap-flowered.
Bowl-flowered types include *L.* 'Imperial Crimson' (height 5-7ft, spacing 12-15in, deep crimson and white flowers in Aug, fragrant). Trumpet-flowered types include *L. candidum* 'Madonna Lily' (height 3-4ft, spacing 9in, white, June-July, fragrant). Turk's-cap-flowered types, which have swept-back petals, include *L. martagon* (Turk's-cap lily, height 3-5ft, spacing 9in, rose-purple with dark spots, July; *L. m.* 'Album' has white flowers); and *L. tigrinum* (tiger lily, height 4-6ft, spacing 9in, orange blooms spotted with dark purple, Aug-Sept).
Plant unbruised, unwithered bulbs preferably in Oct, though late summer to early spring will do. Plant stem-rooting lilies with the tops of the bulbs at least 6in below the soil surface. But plant other types such as *L. candidum* with their tops only about 2in below the soil surface. Put a sprinkling of sand at the bottom of the hole and spread the roots. Pick a sunny site, but ideally one with ground shading from other plants, and with shelter from the wind.
Propagate by division of mature clumps in Oct.
Care Deadhead before seeds form. Cut dead stems to ground level.
Pests and diseases LEATHERJACKETS, lily beetle, mice, millipedes, BASAL ROT, lily disease, mosaic virus.

Lily of the valley (Convallaria)

Spring-flowering border perennial.
Example *C. majalis* Height 6-8in, spread 2ft plus. White, bell-like, scented flowers Apr-May. Varieties include 'Fortin's Giant' (white, large-flowered) and 'Rosea' (pink).
Plant crowns singly, pointed ends uppermost, in partial shade and in ordinary soil enriched with leaf mould or compost, Sept-Oct.
Propagate by division Oct-Mar.
Care Top-dress annually with compost or peat in summer when the leaves die down.
Pests and diseases SWIFT MOTH CATERPILLARS, GREY MOULD.

Limnanthes
Limnanthes douglasii

Lithospermum
Lithospermum diffusum

Lobelia
Lobelia erinus 'Cambridge Blue'

Loganberry
Rubus x *loganobaccus*

Love-in-a-mist
Nigella damascena 'Miss Jekyll'

Love-lies-bleeding
Amaranthus caudatus

Limnanthes

Border and rock garden annual.
Example *L. douglasii* (poached egg flower) Height 6in, spacing 4-6in. Scented, funnel-shaped flowers, white with yellow centres, July-Aug.
Sow seeds shallowly in flowering site Sept or Mar. Thin as necessary. Plants do best in rockeries and along the edges of paths and paving.
Propagation The plants are prolific self-seeders and may reproduce for years.
Care Sept-sown plants require cloche protection in cold areas.
Pests and diseases Generally trouble-free.

Lithospermum

Mat-forming perennial.
Examples *L. diffusum* Height 4in, spread 2ft. Mat-forming rockery ground cover with deep blue flowers June-Oct. Varieties include 'Grace Ward' (intense blue) and 'Heavenly Blue'. *L. oleifolium* Height 6in, spread 12in. Sky-blue flowers May-Aug.
Plant Apr in full sun and in sandy soil with peat or leaf mould added. Plant *L. diffusum* only in lime-free soil.
Propagate by $1\frac{1}{2}$-$2\frac{1}{2}$in long heeled cuttings in July-Aug.
Pests and diseases Generally trouble-free.

Lobelia

Popular as an edging for annual beds.
Example *L. erinus* Height 6in, spacing 4in. Pale blue or white flowers from May to first frosts. Many varieties available in white, red and different shades of blue. Also trailing varieties, such as 'Blue Cascade', 'Red Cascade' and 'Sapphire'.
Plant May in rich, moist soil in shelter and partial shade. Or sow in Feb, under glass, at a temperature of 16°C (about 60°F), and harden off before planting out in May.
Pests and diseases Rhizoctonia, STEM ROT.

Loganberry (Rubus x loganobaccus)

Large fruit bush; needs space. Height 6ft, spread 8ft. A cross of probably accidental origin between cultivated blackberry and raspberry. Sweet, claret-coloured fruits produced July-Aug on shoots of previous season's growth.
Plant Oct-Mar in sunny but sheltered, or part-shaded, site, in ordinary soil enriched with compost or manure. Train the plants to strong wires set 2, 4 and 5ft above ground level. Cut canes back to 12in high after planting. Later string the new growths to the wires. No fruits can be expected the first year.
Propagate by pegging branch tips to the ground July-Aug. Sever from the parent plant and plant out in Mar.
Care Give winter dressing of potash-rich fertiliser and a further dressing of nitrogen-rich fertiliser in Mar.
Pests and diseases Raspberry beetle, cane spot, crown gall, GREY MOULD, rubus stunt, RUST, spur blight.

Love-in-a-mist (Nigella)

Space-filling annual bedding plant. Height 9-18in, spacing 9-12in. Flowers July-Sept.
Example *N. damascena* Several varieties available, including: 'Miss Jekyll' (blue flowers, height 18in); 'Persian Jewels' (mixed, 18in); and 'Dwarf Moody Blue' (blue, 6in).
Sow in Sept or Mar-Apr in flowering position. Thin to required spacing. The plants thrive in sun or light shade in any well-drained soil.
Care Deadhead regularly.
Pests and diseases Generally trouble-free.

Love-lies-bleeding (Amaranthus)

Back-of-the-border annual bedding plant.
Example *A. caudatus* Height 3-4ft, spacing 18in. Drooping crimson flowers July-Oct. *A. c.* 'Viridis' has pale green flowers.
Sow Apr, ideally in a sunny site and in deep soil which has been enriched with manure. Thin seedlings as necessary.
Pests and diseases APHIDS.

GARDEN TIP
Lobelia

Trailing varieties of lobelia can be used to turn a wire hanging basket into a globe of colour. To do this, plant up the top of the basket in the ordinary way. Then make holes with your fingers in the moss lining around the sides and even underneath the basket. Push a small clump of young lobelia plants through the wire into each hole, making sure that the roots are in contact with the compost in the centre of the basket. As the plants grow, the flowers will spread to form a living bowl.

Lupin (Lupinus)

Ideal for giving stature to the perennial border.
Example *L. polyphyllus* hybrid (Russell strain) Height 3-4ft, spacing 18in. Flowers May-July. Varieties include: 'Blue Jacket' (blue and white); 'Lady Fayre' (pink); 'Lilac Time' (lilac).
Plant Oct-Mar in well-drained soil enriched with peat and a general fertiliser, in sun or light shade.
Propagate by basal cuttings Mar-Apr.
Care Mulch with peat or garden compost and top-dress with general fertiliser in spring. Cut dead stems to ground in autumn.
Pests and diseases Black root rot, cucumber mosaic virus, honey fungus, POWDERY MILDEW.

Lupin, tree (Lupinus arboreus)

Colourful flowering tree; thrives in seaside gardens.
Height and spread 2-4ft. Fragrant pale yellow flowers June-July. Varieties include: 'Snow Queen' (white); 'Golden Spire' (deep yellow); and 'Mauve Queen' (light purple).
Plant Oct-Mar in well-drained but poor soil, in a sheltered spot and in full sun. Plants thrive in coastal areas.
Propagate by cuttings planted in a cold frame in summer, or sow seeds in spring.
Care Shorten stems Mar-Apr. Deadhead faded flowers. Cut all flowering stems to ground level in Nov. Take cuttings regularly since plants live for only a few years.
Pests and diseases Black root rot, cucumber mosaic virus, honey fungus, POWDERY MILDEW.

Lychnis (Campion)

Border perennial; grown for flowers and foliage.
Examples *L. coronaria* (rose campion) Height 2ft, spacing 12in. Silver-grey leaves; magenta or white flowers, July-Sept. *L. flos-jovis* (flower of Jove) Height 2ft, spacing 12in. Silver foliage; purple or red flowers produced in June-Aug.
Plant Oct-Mar in ordinary, well-drained soil in sun or light shade.
Propagate by basal cuttings Apr-May or sow seeds Mar-Apr.
Care Deadhead to prevent self-seeding. Mulch in Mar. Remove dead stems in autumn or spring.
Pests and diseases APHIDS, FROGHOPPERS, VIRUSES.

Magnolia

Deciduous or evergreen tree.
Examples *M. grandiflora* Height 15ft, spread 10ft. Evergreen. Large white flowers July-Sept. *M.* x *soulangiana* Height 10-15ft, spread 10-18ft. Deciduous. White and purple flowers Apr-May. The variety 'Rubra' has purple-red flowers.
Plant preferably in neutral to acid soil, though *M. grandiflora* and *M. soulangiana* will both tolerate lime. Spring-flowering species do best against a south or west-facing wall.
Propagate by layering in early spring.
Care Mulch with compost or manure in spring. Remove outward-pointing shoots from *M. grandiflora* in Apr.
Pests and diseases Frost damage, GREY MOULD, honey fungus, leaf spot.

Mahonia

Hardy evergreen shrub.
Examples *M. aquifolium* (Oregon grape) Height 5ft, spread 6ft. Dark glossy leaves; yellow flowers Mar-Apr. *M. japonica* Height 10ft, spread 12ft. Dark glossy leaves; lemon-yellow flowers with lily-of-the-valley scent Jan-Mar.
Plant Sept-Oct or Apr-May in any good soil and in sun or light shade.
Propagate by 3-4in long tip cuttings in July, or sow seed when it is ripe – usually in Aug.
Care Feed with high-potash fertiliser in spring and summer. Mulch in Apr. If *M. aquifolium* is being grown as ground cover, prune back to 6in in Apr to encourage bushy growth.
Pests and diseases Leaf spot, POWDERY MILDEW, RUST.

Maidenhair fern (Adiantum)

Perennial fern.
Examples *A. pedatum* Height 18in, spacing 2ft. Pale green, drooping fronds that die back at the first frosts. *A. venustum* Height 6-10in, spacing 9-12in. Pale green fronds turn gold-brown at first hard frosts, but remain intact during winter.
Plant Apr, in partial shade and in a soil enriched with peat and bone meal. Plant rhizomes of *A. venustum* no more than 2in deep, *A. pedatum* no more than 1in.
Propagate by division Mar-Apr. Cut the rhizomes into pieces, each with a growing point, and pot in a mixture of equal parts of peat, soil and sand. Keep the pots moist and in shade.
Care Apply a top-dressing of bone meal each spring.
Pests and diseases Woodlice, ROOT MEALY BUGS, leaf-blotch eelworms.

Mallow (Lavatera)

Annual shrub.
Example *L. arborea* (tree mallow) Height 4-6ft, spacing 18in. Rose-purple flowers July-Aug. *L. a.* 'Variegata' has red flowers and white marbled leaves. Though naturalised in many coastal districts, the plant is not fully hardy in cold areas.
Sow Sept or Apr in flowering site, a sunny but sheltered spot. Avoid rich soil; it encourages excessive leafy growth. The seeds should be only just covered. Thin seedlings in May.
Propagate by self-sown seedlings.
Pests and diseases Leaf spot, RUST.

Malva (Mallow)

Perennial border plant.
Examples *M. alcea* Height 4ft, spread 2ft. Mauve flowers July-Oct. *M. moschata* (musk mallow) Height 2ft, spacing 18in. Mid-green leaves that give off a musky smell when crushed. Rose-pink flowers May-Sept.
Plant Oct-Mar in sun or light shade and in ordinary, even poor, soil.
Propagate by sowing seed in a greenhouse or cold frame Mar-Apr, or by taking 3in long cuttings of basal shoots in Apr.
Care Support tall plants. Cut down stems in autumn.
Pests and diseases RUST.

Marigold (Calendula)

Annual bedding plant.
Example *C. officinalis* (pot marigold) Height 1-2ft, spacing 12in. Varieties include 'Geisha Girl' (2ft high, bright orange), 'Lemon Queen' (18in, yellow) and 'Fiesta Gitana' (12in, mixed pastel colours). All flower June-Oct.
Sow seeds in flowering site Mar-Apr, or Sept for flowering in late spring.
Pests and diseases CATERPILLARS, cucumber mosaic virus, POWDERY MILDEW, RUST.

Marigold (Tagetes)

Annual bedding plant.
Example *T. patula* (French marigold) Height and spacing 6-12in. Dark crimson or yellow single flowers from June to first frosts. Many varieties, mostly smaller than the species, single and double. Brilliant colour range includes gold, orange, mahogany and combined colours.
Sow under glass Mar-Apr at a temperature of 18°C (about 65°F). Pot on, and harden off before planting out in May in a sunny spot.
Pests and diseases GREY MOULD.

Marjoram (Origanum)

Perennial herb.
Example *O. majorana* (sweet marjoram) Height 2ft, spacing 12in. Grey leaves. Mauve, pink or white flowers June-Sept. The flowers and leaves, both sweetly aromatic, are used in cooking and in *potpourris.*
Plant in spring, in ordinary, well-drained soil and in a sunny position.
Harvest fresh as required. For drying or freezing, cut sprigs just before the flowers open.
Propagate by basal cuttings Apr-May, or sow seed Mar-Apr.
Care Cut the plant back by two-thirds before winter, and trim in the growing season to prevent spreading.
Pests and diseases Generally trouble-free.

Marrow (Cucurbita pepo)

Annual vegetable.
Varieties include: 'Long Green Trailing' (very large, dark green fruits with pale stripes); 'Long White Trailing' (heavy cropper, good for storing); 'Green Bush' (medium-sized dark green fruits that can be cut young for courgettes, good flavour); 'Custard Marrow' (squash variety, white or yellow fruits); and 'Atlantic Giant' (very large pumpkin variety).
Plant in May, in prepared soil. Two weeks earlier, take out a spadeful of earth where each plant is to be grown. Work a bucket of manure into the bottom of the hole and return the soil, leaving a slight crest on top to aid drainage. Plant two seeds 1in deep in each crest. After germination, remove the weaker of the two seedlings. Allow about 2ft spacing each way between bush marrows, about 3ft between trailing varieties.
Harvest July-Oct when the fruits are 9-12in long and when the skins yield to pressure. A few late marrows, however, may be left on the stalk until Oct. These can be stored for a few weeks by hanging them in nets in a dry, frost-free place.
Care In dull weather fertilise female flowers (those with a tiny marrow behind the bloom) by hand by dabbing them gently with a male flower. Water around the plants, not over them.
Pests and diseases APHIDS, cucumber mosaic virus, GREY MOULD, POWDERY MILDEW.

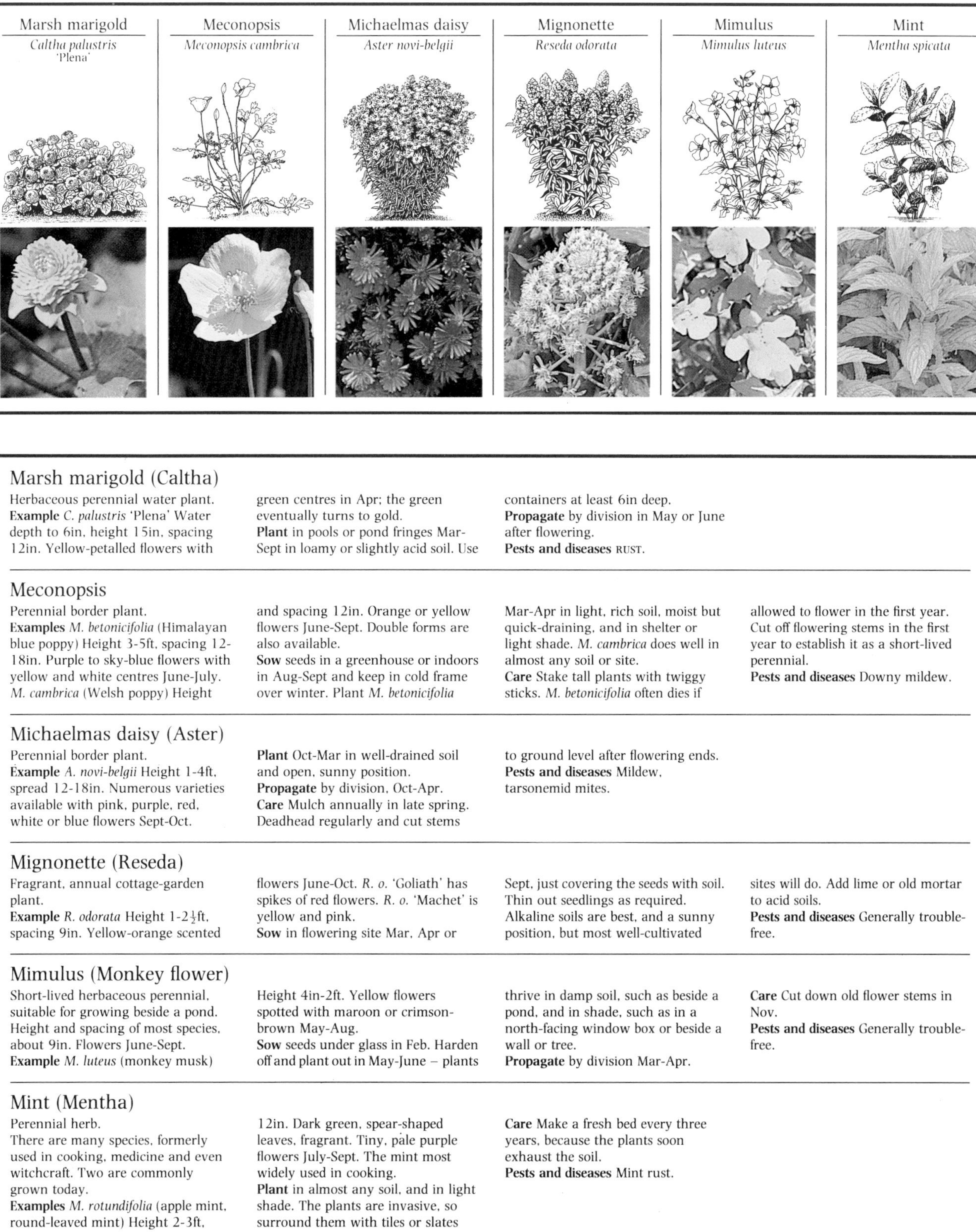

Marsh marigold (Caltha)

Herbaceous perennial water plant. **Example** *C. palustris* 'Plena' Water depth to 6in, height 15in, spacing 12in. Yellow-petalled flowers with green centres in Apr; the green eventually turns to gold.
Plant in pools or pond fringes Mar-Sept in loamy or slightly acid soil. Use containers at least 6in deep.
Propagate by division in May or June after flowering.
Pests and diseases RUST.

Meconopsis

Perennial border plant.
Examples *M. betonicifolia* (Himalayan blue poppy) Height 3-5ft, spacing 12-18in. Purple to sky-blue flowers with yellow and white centres June-July. *M. cambrica* (Welsh poppy) Height and spacing 12in. Orange or yellow flowers June-Sept. Double forms are also available.
Sow in a greenhouse or indoors in Aug-Sept and keep in cold frame over winter. Plant *M. betonicifolia* Mar-Apr in light, rich soil, moist but quick-draining, and in shelter or light shade. *M. cambrica* does well in almost any soil or site.
Care Stake tall plants with twiggy sticks. *M. betonicifolia* often dies if allowed to flower in the first year. Cut off flowering stems in the first year to establish it as a short-lived perennial.
Pests and diseases Downy mildew.

Michaelmas daisy (Aster)

Perennial border plant.
Example *A. novi-belgii* Height 1-4ft, spread 12-18in. Numerous varieties available with pink, purple, red, white or blue flowers Sept-Oct.
Plant Oct-Mar in well-drained soil and open, sunny position.
Propagate by division, Oct-Apr.
Care Mulch annually in late spring. Deadhead regularly and cut stems to ground level after flowering ends.
Pests and diseases Mildew, tarsonemid mites.

Mignonette (Reseda)

Fragrant, annual cottage-garden plant.
Example *R. odorata* Height 1-2½ft, spacing 9in. Yellow-orange scented flowers June-Oct. *R. o.* 'Goliath' has spikes of red flowers. *R. o.* 'Machet' is yellow and pink.
Sow in flowering site Mar, Apr or Sept, just covering the seeds with soil. Thin out seedlings as required. Alkaline soils are best, and a sunny position, but most well-cultivated sites will do. Add lime or old mortar to acid soils.
Pests and diseases Generally trouble-free.

Mimulus (Monkey flower)

Short-lived herbaceous perennial, suitable for growing beside a pond. Height and spacing of most species, about 9in. Flowers June-Sept.
Example *M. luteus* (monkey musk) Height 4in-2ft. Yellow flowers spotted with maroon or crimson-brown May-Aug.
Sow seeds under glass in Feb. Harden off and plant out in May-June – plants thrive in damp soil, such as beside a pond, and in shade, such as in a north-facing window box or beside a wall or tree.
Propagate by division Mar-Apr.
Care Cut down old flower stems in Nov.
Pests and diseases Generally trouble-free.

Mint (Mentha)

Perennial herb.
There are many species, formerly used in cooking, medicine and even witchcraft. Two are commonly grown today.
Examples *M. rotundifolia* (apple mint, round-leaved mint) Height 2-3ft, spacing 12in. Pale green leaves; purple flowers July-Sept. Excellent for mint sauce. *M. spicata* (common mint, spearmint) Height 2ft, spacing 12in. Dark green, spear-shaped leaves, fragrant. Tiny, pale purple flowers July-Sept. The mint most widely used in cooking.
Plant in almost any soil, and in light shade. The plants are invasive, so surround them with tiles or slates buried on edge, or plant them in a bottomless bucket sunk in the ground.
Propagate by division in Mar.
Care Make a fresh bed every three years, because the plants soon exhaust the soil.
Pests and diseases Mint rust.

Monkey puzzle tree	Monkshood	Morning glory	Mulberry	Narcissus	Nasturtium
Araucaria araucana	*Aconitum napellus*	*Ipomoea tricolor* 'Heavenly Blue'	*Morus nigra*	N. 'Jack Snipe' (Cyclamineus type)	*Tropaeolum majus* 'Whirlybird'
	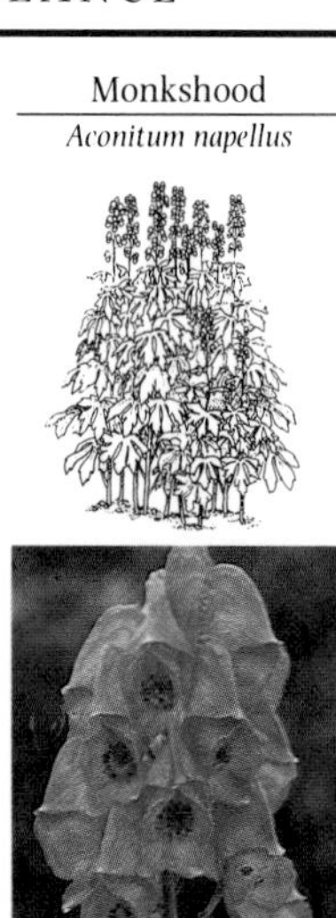	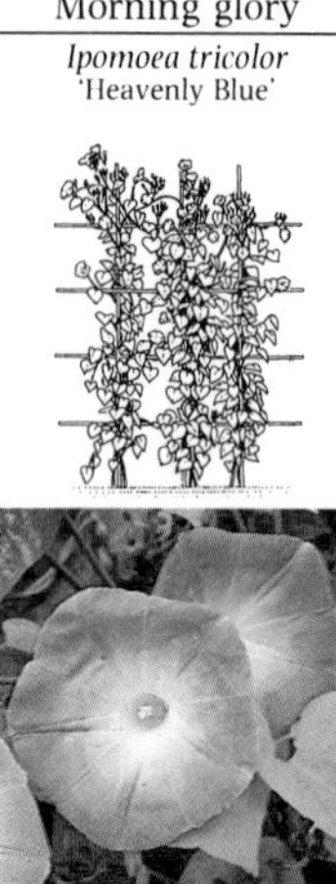			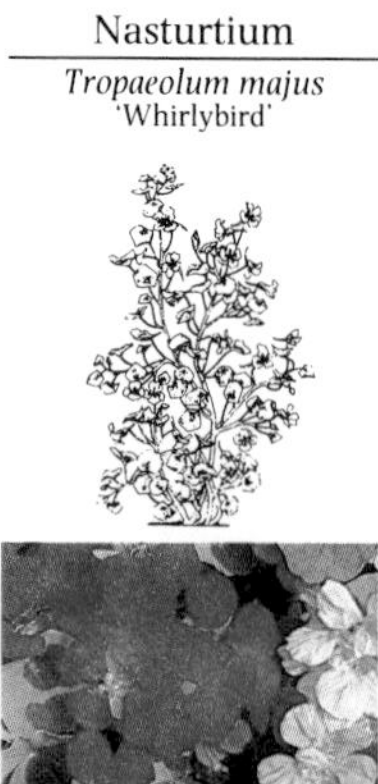

Monkey puzzle tree (Araucaria araucana)

Tall conifer suitable only for a large garden.
Height up to 70ft. Generally, the tree takes six to ten years to achieve 4ft, then grows 12in a year thereafter. Sweeping branches with dark green, spiny, overlapping leaves. Male trees produce catkins, females globular cones.
Plant Oct-Nov in most soils and conditions. Ideally, use only plants less than 12in high.
Pests and diseases Honey fungus.

Monkshood (Aconitum)

Perennial herbaceous border plant. All parts of all species are poisonous.
Examples *A. napellus* Height $3\frac{1}{2}$ft, spacing 15in. Deep blue flowers with high hoods July-Aug. *A. wilsonii* Height 6ft, spacing 18in. Amethyst-blue flowers with tall hoods, Aug-Sept.
Plant Aug-Mar in deep, moist soil in partial shade.
Propagate by division Oct-Mar.
Care Mulch annually in spring after the second year. Cut down flowering stems in Oct.
Pests and diseases Generally trouble-free.

Morning glory (Ipomoea)

Annual or perennial climber.
Example *I. tricolor* (also known as *I. violacea* and *I. rubro-caerulea*) Perennial usually grown as annual. Height 8ft, spread 12in. Flowers, produced July-Sept, are bright purple-blue to blue when they open in the morning, but fade as the day goes on. *I. t.*'Heavenly Blue' has sky-blue, white-throated flowers, which are produced in July-Sept.
Plant in May, in light, rich soil and in sunny position. A sunny wall or fence is ideal; otherwise provide pea sticks for support.
Care Deadhead to prolong flowering period.
Pests and diseases APHIDS, THRIPS.

Mulberry (Morus)

Deciduous fruit-bearing tree.
Example *M. nigra* (black mulberry) Height 15-20ft, spread 10-15ft. Slow-growing. Small, green-yellow catkins May-June, followed by dark red, loganberry-like fruits, ripening Aug-Sept.
Plant Nov in deep, rich loam and in a sheltered site. In the North plant it against a warm, south-facing wall.
Propagate in autumn or early spring by 12in long cuttings planted in the growing site with only two or three buds above ground.
Pests and diseases Canker, die-back.

Narcissus

Bulbous perennial.
Numerous varieties available (see also DAFFODIL and JONQUIL), including: 'Ice Follies' (large-cupped type) Height 1-2ft, white petals, lemon-yellow cup; 'Barrett Browning' (small-cupped type) Height 12-18in, orange-cupped white flowers. Tazetta types (best grown in pots) and triandrus types usually have several flowers on each stem. Varieties include: 'Thalia' (triandrus type) Height 6-18in, white flowers; and 'Soleil d'Or' (tazetta type) Height 18in, yellow flowers. Cyclamineus types have long, trumpet-shaped cups and petals that sweep up and back. Varieties include 'Jack Snipe' Height 8-15in, cream-white petals, rich yellow cup. Dwarf types such as *N. bulbocodium* and 'February Gold' (both with yellow flowers) grow to 8in or less.
Plant bulbs Aug-Sept in any well-drained soil, in sun or light shade. Set bulbs 3-12in apart, in holes which are at least three times the depth of the bulb. All narcissi flower in Feb-May. Do not cut down foliage until leaves are completely brown.
Propagate by lifting clumps of bulbs in July-Sept. Divide each clump and plant offsets from the edge of the clump immediately.
Pests and diseases STEM AND BULB EELWORMS, tarsonemid mites, narcissus fly maggots, SLUGS, arabis mosaic virus, narcissus fire, GREY MOULD.

Nasturtium (Tropaeolum)

Bedding plant and climber.
Example *T. majus* Height 6in-6ft, spacing 6-18in. Brilliant red, yellow or orange flowers are produced June-Oct. Annual. Varieties include: 'Tall Mixed' and 'Climbing Mixed' (both 6ft high); trailers such as 'Scarlet Gleam' and 'Golden Gleam' (12in, double flowers); and dwarfs (6-9in) such as 'Red Roulette', 'Empress of India' (dark red), 'Whirlybird' (mixed colours) and 'Tom Thumb' (mixed colours).
Sow seeds about $\frac{3}{4}$in deep in compost under glass in Feb or in Apr in the flowering site – ideally a sunny spot. Set out plants raised under glass in May.
Pests and diseases APHIDS, THRIPS, red spider mites, spotted wilt virus.

Nemesia
Nemesia strumosa 'Fiesta'

Nemophila
Nemophila maculata

Nerine
Nerine bowdenii

Nicotiana
Nicotiana affinis 'Lime Green'

Oak
Quercus coccinea 'Splendens'

Olearia
Olearia x *haastii*

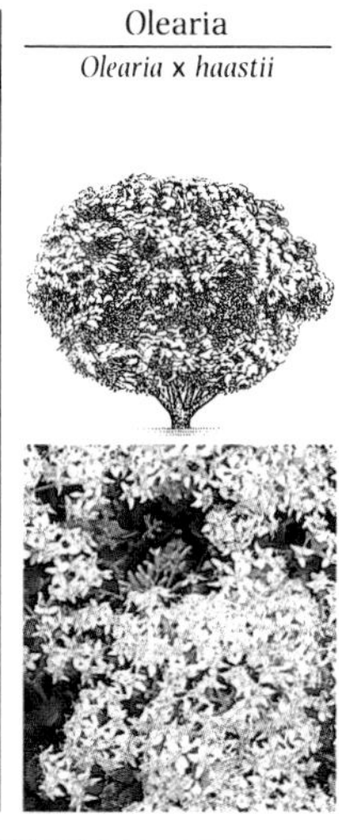

Nemesia

Bedding plant.
Example *N. strumosa* Height 9-18in, spacing 6in. Varieties include: 'Blue Gem' (blue); 'Fiesta' (orange); 'Fire King' (crimson); and 'Sparklers' (mixed colours). All flowers produced June-Sept.
Sow indoors or in a warm greenhouse in Mar, and plant out in May. Alternatively in mild areas sow outdoors in Apr, in any reasonable garden soil in sun or light shade. The plants prefer lime-free soil.
Care Pinch out growing tips of seedlings to encourage branching. Water well in dry weather. Deadhead regularly.
Pests and diseases FOOT ROT, root rot.

Nemophila

Annual bedding plant.
Examples *N. menziesii* syn. *N. insignis* (baby blue eyes) Height 9in, spacing 6in. White-centred sky-blue flowers June-Aug *N. maculata* Height and spacing 6in. Purple-spotted white flowers June-Aug.
Sow in flowering position in Sept or Apr. Thin seedlings in Apr. The plants do best in moist soils, especially sandy loams, in sun or light shade. But blooms do not last as cut flowers.
Pests and diseases APHIDS.

Nerine

Bulbous perennial.
Example *N. bowdenii* Height 2ft, spacing 6in. Pink flowers Sept-Oct.
Plant bulbs Aug or Apr, 4in deep, in well-drained soil in full sun – preferably near a south-facing wall. Protect bulb sites in winter with a mulch of straw, bracken or peat.
Propagate by lifting and dividing clumps of bulbs every four or five years in spring.
Pests and diseases MEALY BUGS, VIRUSES.

Nicotiana (Tobacco plant)

Fragrant annual border plant.
Example *N. affinis* syn. *N. alata* Height 9in-3ft, spacing 9-12in. Flowers June-Oct. Garden varieties and hybrids derived from the species include: 'Lime Green' (yellowish-green blooms, height 2½ft); 'Red Devil' (red, 18in); and 'Tinkerbell' (mixed colours, 9in).
Sow indoors or under glass Feb-Apr. Plant out, when frost danger is past, in any well-drained soil in sun or light shade – ideally near a window so that the flowers' intense evening fragrance wafts indoors.
Care Stake tall varieties in exposed spots.
Pests and diseases APHIDS.

Oak (Quercus)

Large tree.
Examples *Q. coccinea* (scarlet oak) Height 25-30ft, spread 10-15ft. Hardy and fast-growing. Mid-green leaves turn scarlet in autumn. *Q. c.* 'Splendens' has particularly bright autumn colouring. *Q. ilex* (evergreen oak, holm oak) Height 15-20ft, spread 10-15ft. Evergreen, with rugged bark; not suited to very cold districts of the East or North.
Plant *Q. ilex* Sept-Oct or Apr-May, *Q. coccinea* Oct-Mar in ordinary well-drained soil in sun or part shade. To establish hedges of *Q. ilex*, set young plants 2ft apart. Pinch out growing points to promote bushy growth.
Propagate by acorns in autumn. Start the seedlings in pots of seed compost in a cold frame.
Care Help to establish young trees by giving an annual mulch for the first two or three years. Trim hedges in Apr.
Pests and diseases CATERPILLARS, oak phylloxera, bracket fungi, canker, die-back, frost damage, honey fungus.

Olearia (Daisy bush)

Evergreen shrub, suitable for seaside gardens.
Example *O.* x *haastii* Height and spread 8ft. White, daisy-like flowers July-Aug.
Plant in any reasonable soil and in full sun. Intolerant of severe frost, but thrives in industrial and coastal areas, even those open to winds.
Propagate by taking 4in long semi-ripe cuttings of sideshoots in Aug.
Care Remove any dead shoots in Apr.
Pests and diseases Generally trouble-free.

GARDEN TIP
Nasturtium

Like Californian poppies (*Eschscholzia californica*), nasturtiums are ideal in a labour-saving garden. The plants give of their best on poor soil, and they need no feeding at all. Indeed, feeding simply encourages more foliage to grow at the expense of the flowers.
Consider, for instance, planting a climbing variety in a sunny spot close beside a shrub, in soil which has been impoverished by the shrub's roots. The plants will rapidly clamber over and through the shrub – thereby saving you even the trouble of staking them.

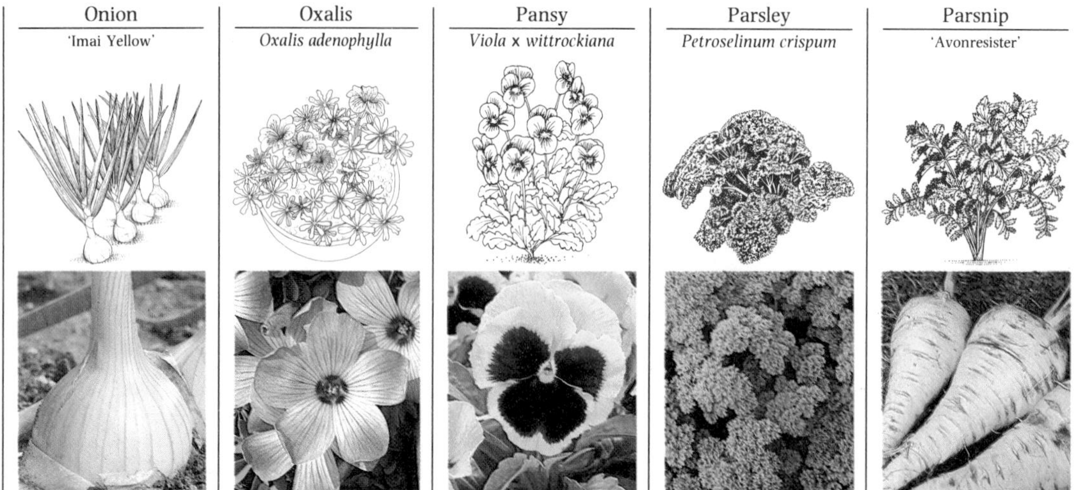

Onion (Allium cepa)

Bulbous vegetable.
Varieties include: 'Ailsa Craig' (big bulbs, but poor keeper); 'Autumn Queen' (flattish, good for autumn sowing); 'Bedfordshire Champion' (large, good keeper but mildew-prone); 'Hygro' (big, good storer); 'North Holland Blood Red' (red-skinned); 'Reliance' (large, good for Aug sowing); 'White Spanish' (large, flat, good keeper); 'White Lisbon' (quick-growing salad onion, silvery-skinned); and 'Paris Silver Skin' (good for pickling if harvested when the bulb is marble-sized). Japanese varieties, which can be harvested from late June onwards, include 'Express Yellow', 'Imai Yellow' and 'Senshyu'.
Sow traditional varieties in Mar or early Apr in rows 12in apart. Thin seedlings to 2in apart, then 4in, using the thinnings for salads. Water freely until bulbs start to ripen, then stop. Sow salad onions in July in the North, Aug in the South for harvesting Mar-May. Sow pickling onions Mar-Apr on light, poor soil for a July harvest. Sow Japanese varieties in late July and thin to 6in apart. Alternatively, plant sets (immature bulbs) of Japanese varieties in late Sept or Oct.
Harvest salad onions as required. Others are ready when the leaves turn yellow. When the foliage dries, lift the bulbs and leave them to ripen in the sun for about a month. Store, plaited into ropes or in boxes, in a cool, airy place.
Care Prepare the ground by digging in plenty of manure in autumn and adding peat or coarse sand to improve drainage. Sprinkle garden lime onto all but limy soils. Two weeks before sowing, rake the ground to a fine tilth and sprinkle a general fertiliser.
Pests and diseases Onion fly, STEM AND BULB EELWORMS, downy mildew, VIRUSES, WHITE ROT.

Oxalis

Rock garden plant.
Examples *O. adenophylla* Height 3in, spread 6in. Crinkled grey foliage; cup-shaped, satin-pink flowers May-July. *O. chrysantha* Height 2-3in, spread 12in. Mat-forming species with funnel-shaped golden flowers June and Sept. *O. enneaphylla* Height 3in, spread 6in. White flowers June-July. *O. e.* 'Rosea' has pale pink flowers.
Plant in any well-drained soil, preferably with some peat added, and in sun or light shade. Excellent for rock gardens. *O. chrysantha* should be planted where its roots can find shelter beneath a rock. It is not as hardy as the others.
Propagate by division after flowering has finished.
Pests and diseases Generally trouble-free.

Pansy (Viola x wittrockiana)

Perennial bedding plant usually grown as an annual.
Height 6-9in, spacing 9-12in. Many varieties in many colours. The two main groups are winter-flowering types, which bloom from late autumn to early spring in mild and protected sites, and summer-flowering types, which bloom May-Sept.
Sow July-Aug in a cold frame and transplant to flowering site Mar-Apr. Or sow outdoors in a nursery bed and transplant Sept-Oct.
Pests and diseases Cucumber mosaic virus, leaf spot, pansy sickness, RUST.

Parsley (Petroselinum crispum)

Perennial herb.
Height 1-2ft, spacing 9in. The densely curled leaves are used in cooking and in *bouquets garnis*. Flowers are produced in the second summer, but most of these should be nipped out to prevent too much self-seeding.
Sow ½in deep in well-drained, fertile soil and in sun or partial shade. Make a first sowing in Apr and a second in Aug. Germination can be slow – up to two months.
Harvest Pick regularly for a continuous supply of fresh leaves. To dry, dip the sprigs in boiling water then place in a warm oven until crisp. Crush and store in airtight containers when cool. Leaves can also be gathered and frozen from June onwards.
Pests and diseases CARROT FLIES, celery fly, leaf spot.

Parsnip (Pastinaca sativa)

Hardy biennial vegetable grown as an annual for its sweet-tasting pale yellow roots.
Varieties include: 'Avonresister' (small, good flavour, canker-resistant); 'Dobie's Exhibition' (long, white-skinned, good flavour); 'Improved Hollow Crown' (heavy cropper); and 'Lisbonnais' (fine-textured).
Sow Feb-Mar in deep, rich soil, preferably ground that was manured in the previous year. Make the drills 1in deep and 18in apart; thin the seedlings to 9-12in apart.
Harvest after the first frost, and when the leaves die down in autumn. Lift as required, or lift all roots in Dec and store in a clamp. Roots left in the ground until spring will start to make new growth.
Pests and diseases Celery fly, parsnip canker.

Passion flower (Passiflora)

Perennial climber.
Examples *P. caerulea* (common passion flower) Climber, height 20-30ft. Blue-purple and white flowers June-Sept. The arrangement of petals and stamens in the flower is said to symbolise the Crucifixion. Edible yellow fruits are produced in warm summers. *P. c.* 'Constance Elliott' has pure white flowers and is hardier than the species. *P. umbellicata* Height 20ft. Purple-brown flowers July-Sept.
Plant in a greenhouse border or in 10-12in pots or tubs. Or, in the South and West, plant in a sheltered, sunny spot outdoors in any ordinary soil.
Propagate by taking 3-4in long sections of stem in July-Aug.
Care For the first two or three winters, protect the roots of outdoor plants with straw or bracken. Tie young growths to supporting strings or wires until the tendrils have taken hold. Mulch, and thin out overgrown plants at ground level, in Mar.
Pests and diseases Cucumber mosaic virus.

Pea (Pisum sativum)

Annual vegetable.
Early varieties (ready May-June) include: 'Feltham First', 'Histon Mini', 'Meteor' and 'Kelvedon Wonder' (all 18in high); 'Hurst Green Shaft' and 'Onward' ($2\frac{1}{2}$ft); and 'Eaton' and 'Poppet' (both can be grown without sticks).
Maincrop varieties (ready July-Aug) include: 'Dwarf Greensleeves' ($3\frac{1}{2}$ft); and 'Lord Chancellor' (4ft).
Late varieties (ready Sept onwards) include: 'Kelvedon Wonder', 'Pioneer' and 'Progress No. 9' (all $1\frac{1}{2}$-2ft high).
Sow in drills 6in wide and 3in deep. Set rows between 2ft (for 18in high varieties) and $3\frac{1}{2}$ft apart (for 4ft plants). Sow early varieties in Nov or Feb-Mar, later ones Apr-May.
Harvest as soon as the peas are ready. When cropping is finished, put the foliage on the compost heap, but leave the roots in the ground to provide nitrogen.
Care As soon as the seedlings are through, hoe to kill weeds. Provide twiggy pea sticks, leaning inwards on either side of the row. Mulch in summer to aid moisture retention.
Pests and diseases APHIDS, CATERPILLARS, THRIPS, damping-off, FUSARIUM WILT, GREY MOULD, manganese deficiency, POWDERY MILDEW, root rot.

Peach (Prunus persica)

Fruit tree.
Average height and spacing for fan-trained trees, bushes and half-standard trees, 20ft.
Varieties include: 'Duke of York' (large yellow and crimson fruits mid-July); 'Hale's Early' (medium-sized yellow-red fruits late July); 'Peregrine' (large, crimson, juicy fruits early Aug), and 'Rochester' (large yellow-fleshed fruits mid-Aug).
Plant Oct-Nov in medium, well-drained soil, in shelter and sun. When planting against a wall, set trees about 9in out. Each tree requires a wall space 6-8ft high, with horizontal wires set 12in apart.
Harvest when the fruit feels slightly soft about the stalk. Best eaten immediately, but can be stored in a cool place for up to a week.
Propagate by stones – those from peaches bought from a greengrocer can be used, but they will not be as successful as varieties bred for the British climate. Plant Sept-Oct in pots of seed compost, setting the seedlings out one year later; or plant them straight into the growing site.
Care Protect flowers from frost with hessian, which can also be left as protection against birds. Mulch in spring. Thin fruits to an eventual 9in apart, starting when they first appear. Cut out or tie back any shoots that are shading the fruits. When fan-training young trees, cut back to buds pointing in the required direction in Feb.
Pests and diseases APHIDS, BIRDS, WASPS, bacterial canker, honey fungus, peach leaf curl, peach mildew, SILVER LEAF.

Pear (Pyrus communis)

Fruit tree.
Average height and spacing: bush type 10-12ft; standard 12-15ft; espalier 8ft high, 10-15ft wide; dwarf pyramid 8-10ft high, 3-6ft wide.
Varieties include: 'Conference' (juicy, dark green and russet fruits ready Oct-Nov. Best pollinated by 'Williams' Bon Chrétien' or 'Joséphine de Malines'); 'Dr Jules Guyot' (heavy cropper; pale yellow-russet fruits ready in Sept. Best pollinated by 'Conference' or 'Fertility'); and 'Fertility' (heavy cropper, crisp dull yellow fruits ready Oct. Best pollinated by 'Dr Jules Guyot' or 'Winter Nelis').
Plant Nov-Mar in deep, well-drained soil. Avoid sites subject to spring frosts or to salt-laden winds.
Harvest pears when the fruit parts easily from the tree. Ripen the fruits in a cool place. When the flesh around the stalk begins to soften, bring the fruits into a temperature of 16°C (about 60°F) for a few days before eating.
Propagate by grafting only.
Care Water young trees freely to get them established. After the first year, give an annual mulch and feed of general fertiliser Jan-Feb. Thin fruits to one or two a spur in June. Prune established trees in the same way as apple trees; young trees need little pruning. For pruning details, see *How to prune apple trees*, page 15.
Pests and diseases APHIDS, BIRDS, pear leaf blister mites, apple canker, BROWN ROT, FIRE BLIGHT, frost damage, honey fungus, pear scab.

Pelargonium	Penstemon, alpine	Penstemon, border	Peppers	Periwinkle
Pelargonium x *hortorum* 'Brocade'	*Penstemon rupicola*	*Penstemon* x *gloxinioides*	*C. annuum grossum*	*Vinca major*
			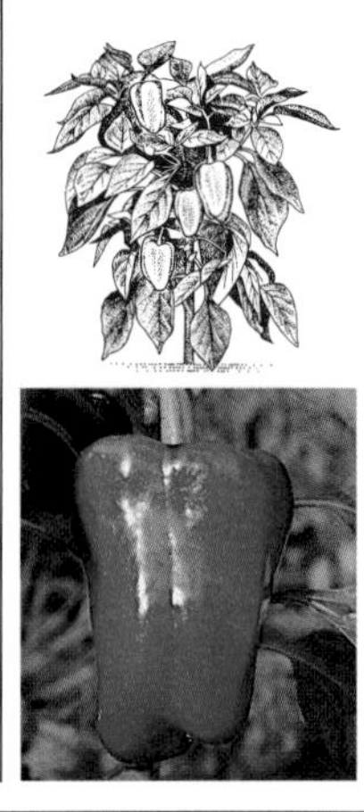	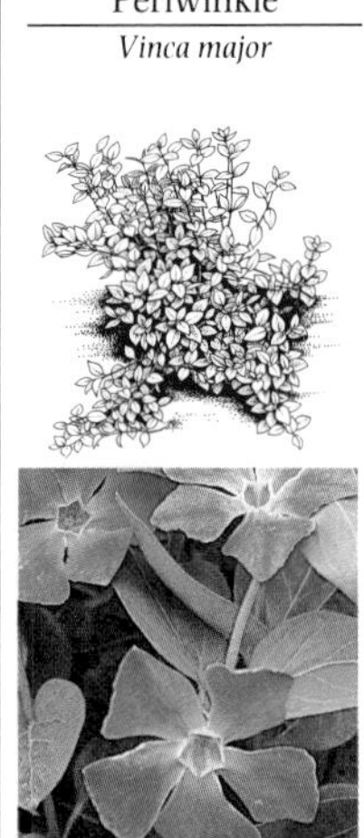

Pelargonium (Geranium)

Bedding, greenhouse or pot plant.
Examples *P. peltatum* (ivy-leaved geranium) Trailing stems 3ft plus long. Carmine flowers May-Oct. White, pink, crimson, mauve varieties available. *P. tomentosum* (peppermint geranium) Height 1-2ft. Hummock-forming, low-climbing species, with small white flowers June-Sept. The pale green, hairy leaves emit a strong peppermint scent when bruised. *P.* x *domesticum* (regal pelargonium) Height 15-24in. Pink to purple flowers May-Oct. Varieties include: 'Aztec' (bright red veined with purple); 'Carisbrooke' (rose frilled with maroon); 'Joan Morf' (ruffled white petals shading to pink); and 'South American Bronze' (bronze edged with white). *P.* x *hortorum* (zonal pelargonium) Height 6in to 6ft. Flowers May-Oct. Dozens of varieties available in a colour range that includes white, pink, vermilion, orange, scarlet and rose. Varieties include 'King of Denmark' (rose-pink); 'Modesty' (white); 'Brocade' (pink).Varieties grown specifically for their foliage include: 'Maréchal MacMahon' (maroon leaves zoned in pale green); 'Distinction' (green leaves edged with a fine dark line); and 'Verona' (pale bronze leaves). Dwarf and standard varieties are also available.
Plant pelargoniums into bedding schemes from late May onwards; *P. tomentosum* looks best in hanging baskets. All species should be taken indoors for winter before the first frosts.
Propagate by 3in cuttings in July for standards, in Sept for large bush types. Or, to make smaller plants, take cuttings in Mar.
Care Before moving plants into pots for the winter, cut all growths back by one-third.
Pests and diseases Black root rot, GREY MOULD, LEAFY GALL, RUST.

Penstemon, alpine

Rock garden plant.
Examples *P. menziesii* Height 9in, spread 15in. Violet-purple flowers in June. *P. rupicola* Height 4in, spread 12in. Carmine flowers in May. *P. scouleri* Height 12in, spread 18in. Dark rose flowers June-July.
Plant Oct-Mar in rock garden, paving or peat bed and in sunny position.
Propagate by $1\frac{1}{2}$-$2\frac{1}{2}$in cuttings of non-flowering sideshoots July-Aug.
Care No winter protection is needed for alpine species; all are hardy.
Pests and diseases Generally trouble-free.

Penstemon, border

Front-of-border plant.
Examples *P. barbatus* Height 3ft, spacing 18in. White, pink or carmine flowers June-Aug. *P.* x *gloxinioides* Height 12in, spacing 18in. Red flowers July-Aug.
Plant Mar-Apr in well-drained, well-manured soil, and in sun and shelter.
Propagate by 3in cuttings of non-flowering sideshoots Aug-Sept.
Care Mulch lightly in spring. Cut plants to just above ground level in Oct and protect crowns from frost during the winter with straw, bracken or cloches.
Pests and diseases Generally trouble-free.

Peppers (Capsicum)

Vegetable fruit.
Examples *C. annuum acuminatum* Height $1\frac{1}{2}$-3ft, spacing 18in. Produces chilli, cayenne and paprika fruits. Culinary varieties include 'Californian Wonder', 'Cayenne Chilli' and 'World Beater'. *C. a. grossum* Height and spread 12-18in. The large fruits are green, but ripen to red or yellow. Good culinary varieties are 'Bull-nosed Red' and 'Bull-nosed Yellow'.
Sow seeds in seed compost in Mar, and raise indoors or in a warm greenhouse. Harden off and plant out in late May or June in well-drained soil, enriched with rotted compost or manure, and in a sheltered site against a sunny south-facing wall. Alternatively, grow in a greenhouse border.
Harvest Aug-Sept.
Care Syringe leaves daily during flowering season. Give dilute liquid feed at ten-day intervals during fruiting period. Stake tall varieties. Shade greenhouse plants lightly in hot weather.
Pests and diseases Glasshouse red spider mites (under glass), CAPSID BUGS.

Periwinkle (Vinca)

Mat-forming ground-cover plant.
Examples *V. major* (greater periwinkle) Height 12in, spread 4ft. Purple-blue flowers May-July with an occasional second flush Sept-Oct. *V. minor* (lesser periwinkle) Height 4in, spread 4ft. Blue flowers Mar-July, occasionally to Oct. Varieties include 'Alba' (white), 'Albo-plena' (double white), 'Atro-purpurea' (purple) and 'Burgundy' (wine-red).
Plant in ordinary but well-drained soil Sept-Mar, in partial shade.
Propagate by division Sept-Apr.
Pests and diseases Cucumber mosaic virus, RUST.

Pernettya	Petunia	Philadelphus	Phlomis	Phlox, alpine	Phlox, annual
Pernettya mucronata	*Petunia* x *hybrida* Nana Compacta	*Philadelphus coronarius* 'Aureus'	*Phlomis fruticosa*	*Phlox subulata* 'G.F. Wilson'	*Phlox drummondii*

Pernettya

Evergreen shrub.
Example *P. mucronata* Height and spacing 3-5ft. Glossy, dark green leaves. Small white, bell-shaped flowers May-June. Clusters of fruits appear in autumn and last through winter. Varieties include 'Alba' (white fruits), 'Atrococcinea' (red-purple) and 'Rosea' (pink). Pernettyas are usually unisexual so male and female plants must be grown together to produce fruits, but 'Bell's Seedling' is hermaphrodite and will produce berries by itself.
Plant Sept-May in lime-free soil, preferably peaty loam, in sun or light shade. Set plants in groups to ensure pollination.
Propagate by 2in long cuttings Sept-Oct.
Care Cut back leggy plants hard in late winter, to encourage new bushy growth. Otherwise, no regular pruning is needed.
Pests and diseases Generally trouble-free.

Petunia (Petunia x hybrida)

Half-hardy annual suitable for tubs and window boxes.
Many varieties available in four main groups:
Multiflora varieties are bushy, with a height and spread of 6-12in.
Grandiflora varieties are bigger, but with fewer flowers, sometimes double and/or frilled; they are susceptible to rain damage.
Nana Compacta varieties grow to only 6in.
Pendula varieties have long, trailing stems suitable for a hanging basket.
All groups produce flowers from June to the first severe frosts in a range of colours including yellow, cream, white, pink, red, mauve and blue.
Sow Jan-Mar in a temperature of at least 15°C (59°F). Plant out in a sunny site in any ordinary soil when frost danger is past.
Care Deadhead regularly to promote more flowers.
Pests and diseases APHIDS, cucumber mosaic virus, tomato spotted wilt virus, FOOT ROT, root rot.

Philadelphus (Mock orange, Syringa)

Fragrant shrub.
Example *P. coronarius* Height 6-9ft, spread 6-8ft. White, cup-shaped flowers, scented like orange blossom, June-July. *P. c.* 'Aureus' has golden leaves, especially when grown in shade. Hybrid varieties (height and spread 6-8ft or less) include: 'Belle Etoile' (white flowers with purple blotch); 'Virginal' (double white); and 'Avalanche' (height 3-5ft, single white).
Plant Oct-Mar in ordinary, well-drained soil, in sun or partial shade.
Propagate by 12in long hardwood cuttings Oct-Nov.
Care Thin old wood after flowering, retaining young shoots; these produce the following year's flowers.
Pests and diseases Leaf spot.

Phlomis

Herbaceous border perennials and evergreen shrubs.
Examples *P. fruticosa* (Jerusalem sage) Height 4ft, spread 2ft. Evergreen shrub with grey woolly leaves. Yellow flowers June-July. *P. russeliana* Height 2½-4ft, spacing 18in. Herbaceous perennial with large, wrinkled leaves. Yellow flowers June-July. *P. samia* Height 3ft, spacing 2ft. Green-grey leaves. Creamy flowers, sometimes marked with green and pink, May-June.
Plant Oct-Apr in a sunny position. *P. fruticosa* requires light, well-drained loam, but any ordinary soil will do for *P. samia* and *P. russeliana*.
Propagate *P. fruticosa* by cuttings Aug-Sept; *P. samia* by root division Oct or Mar.
Care Cut *P. samia* down to ground level in Oct.
Pests and diseases Generally trouble-free.

Phlox, alpine

Perennial rock garden plant.
Examples *P. adsurgens* Height and spread 12in. Salmon-pink flowers June-July. *P. douglasii* Height 3in, spread 18in. Dense mat of leaves. Pale lavender flowers May-June. *P. subulata* (moss phlox) Height 3in, spread 18in. Dense, leafy mat. Pink or purple flowers Apr-May. Varieties include 'G.F. Wilson' (milky blue), 'Apple Blossom' (pink) and 'Temiscaming' (magenta).
Plant in May in well-drained soil with peat or leaf mould added. Best sites are a dry-stone wall or rockery, ideally in a spot in full sun.
Propagate by basal cuttings in July.
Pests and diseases SLUGS, eelworms, leaf spot, LEAFY GALL, POWDERY MILDEW.

Phlox, annual

Annual border plant.
Example *P. drummondii* Height 6-15in, spacing 9in. Flowers June-Sept. Varieties include 'Large-flowered Mixed', 'Beauty Mixed' and 'Twinkle' (star-shaped flowers), all with mixed colours.
Sow under glass in Mar and germinate at 15°C (59°F). Harden off and plant out in May in an open, sunny site. Or sow directly in flowering position in Apr.
Care Deadhead to prolong flowering.
Pests and diseases SLUGS, leaf spot, powdery mildew.

Phlox, perennial	Phygelius	Physalis	Pieris	Pine	Pink, annual
Phlox maculata 'Alba'	*Phygelius capensis*	*Physalis alkekengi*	*Pieris formosa* 'Forrestii'	*Pinus sylvestris* 'Beuvronensis'	*Dianthus chinensis* 'Pink Charm'
		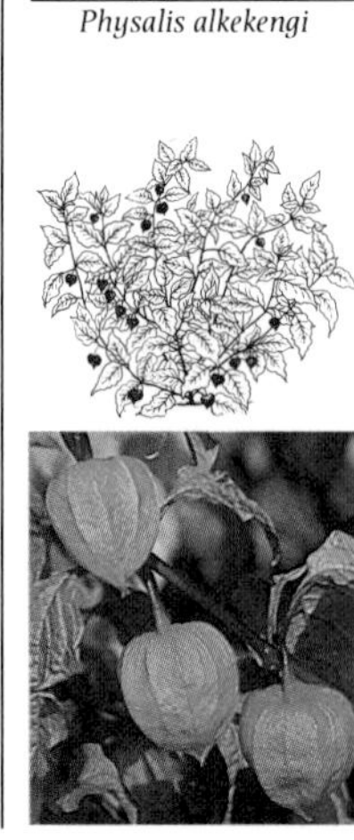			

Phlox (perennial species)

Perennial back-of-border plant.
Examples *P. maculata* Height 2-3ft, spacing 18in. Purple flowers July-Sept. *P. m.* 'Alpha' has pink flowers. *P. m.* 'Alba', white. *P. paniculata* Height 2-4ft, spacing 18in. Varieties include 'Brigadier' (scarlet), 'Dodo Hanbury Forbes' (pink), 'Graf Zeppelin' (red and white) and 'Harlequin' (purple with variegated foliage). All flower July-Oct.
Plant Oct-Mar in fertile soil, in sun or partial shade.
Propagate by division of mature clumps Oct-Mar, or by ½in long root cuttings Feb-Mar.
Care Mulch well in spring. Stake tall plants or those in exposed sites. Cut flower stems back to 2-3in above ground level in autumn.
Pests and diseases Eelworms, SLUGS, leaf spot, LEAFY GALL, POWDERY MILDEW.

Phygelius

Herbaceous border plant.
Examples *P. aequalis* Height and spacing 2ft. Evergreen. Orange flowers July-Oct. *P. a* 'Yellow Trumpets' has yellow flowers. *P. capensis* Height 3ft, spacing 2ft. But can grow to 6ft high against a wall. Rust-red flowers July-Oct. *P. c.* 'Coccineus' has scarlet flowers.
Plant Apr in light soil and in a sheltered, sunny position. Secure *P. capensis* to a trellis if grown against a wall.
Propagate by root division Mar-Apr.
Care Remove dead wood and cut back to shape or to ground level in Apr each year.
Pests and diseases Generally trouble-free.

Physalis

Border plant often grown for use as dried winter decoration.
Example *P. alkekengi franchetii* (Chinese lantern) Height and spacing 2ft. White flowers July-Aug, followed Sept-Oct by bright red papery 'lanterns', each containing an edible orange berry. *P. a. f.* 'Gigantea' grows to 3ft, 'Nana' is a dwarf variety.
Plant Mar-Apr in any ordinary soil in sun or partial shade.
Propagate by dividing clumps Mar-Apr.
Care The plant is invasive; to control numbers, cut underground runners with a spade in autumn. Cut fruiting stems when the lanterns begin to show colour and hang them upside down in a cool spot away from sunlight to dry. Remove the withered leaves when dry, and use the stems and lanterns in dried flower arrangements.
Pests and diseases Generally trouble-free.

Pieris

Evergreen shrub, suitable only for lime-free soil.
Examples *P. floribunda* Height and spread 4-6ft. White flowers Apr-May. *P. formosa* Height 12ft, spread 15ft. Copper-red young leaves. *P. f.* 'Forrestii' and *P. f.* 'Wakehurst' have bright red young leaves. All have white flowers Apr-May. *P. japonica* Height and spread 6-10ft. Leaves are copper when young, green later. White flowers Mar-Apr.
Plant in moist, lime-free soil in partial shade in Oct, Mar or Apr.
Propagate by 3-4in semi-ripe cuttings in Aug, or by layering branches in early summer.
Care Top-dress with peat in Apr.
Pests and diseases Generally trouble-free.

Pine (Pinus)

Coniferous tree.
Examples *P. mugo* 'Gnome' Height after ten years, 2ft. A prostrate variety of the mountain pine and suitable for a large rock garden. *P. nigra* Height after ten years 25ft; eventual height 60ft, spread 20ft. Hardy, lime-tolerant, straight-trunked tree; good as windbreak. *P. strobus* (Weymouth pine) Height after ten years 15-20ft; eventually 50ft with 15ft spread. Blue-green foliage. *P. n.* 'Nana', a dwarf form, grows to 6ft high. *P. sylvestris* 'Beuvronensis' Height 3ft, spread 4ft. Slow-growing dwarf version of the Scots pine. Low rounded bush, best grown at the summit of a rockery with the lower twigs cut away to show the rough, red trunk.
Plant Nov-Mar in full sun; most do best in well-drained acid soils and are indifferent to exposure.
Propagate varieties by grafting only.
Pests and diseases ADELGIDS, sawfly larvae, GREY MOULD, RUST.

Pink, annual (Dianthus)

Border plant.
Example *D. chinensis* and hybrids (Indian pink) Height and spacing to 12in. Varieties include 'Baby Doll' (crimson, rose and white flowers), 'Pink Charm' (pink), 'Queen of Hearts' (scarlet) and 'Merry-go-round' (white with scarlet centre). All flower from June to first frosts.
Sow Jan-Mar in compost under glass, and in temperature of about 13°C (55°F). Harden off and plant out in May in sunny position. Plants prefer limy or neutral soil.
Care Pinch out growing tip of young plants to encourage bushy growth.
Pests and diseases APHIDS, carnation fly, BIRDS, CATERPILLARS, THRIPS, FUSARIUM WILT, leaf rot, POWDERY MILDEW, VERTICILLIUM WILT.

Pink, perennial	Pittosporum	Plum, edible	Plum, ornamental	Polyanthus
Dianthus alpinus	*Pittosporum tenuifolium* 'Silver Queen'	'Early Laxton'	*Prunus* x *blireana*	*P.* x *tommasinii*
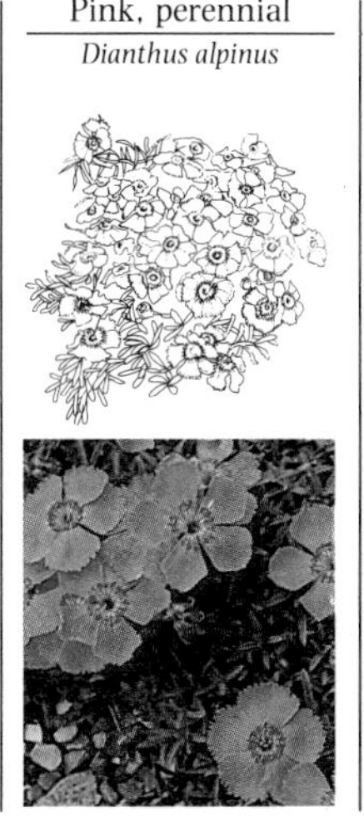	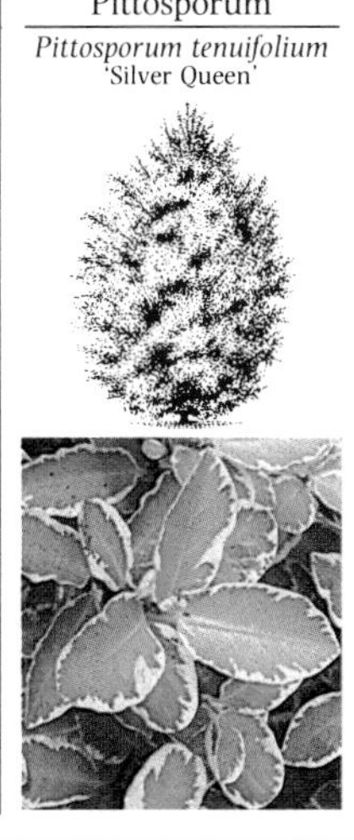			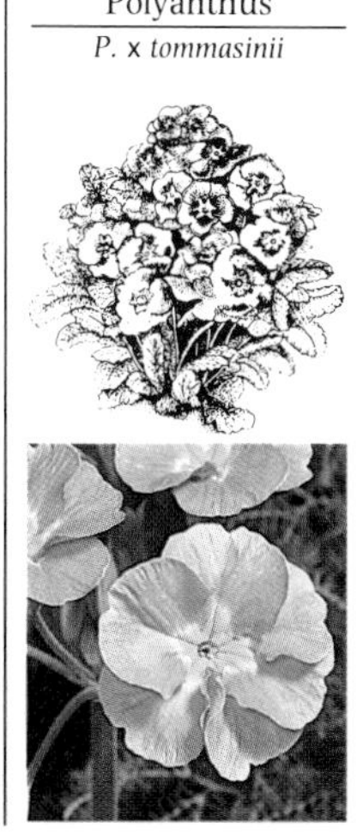

Pink, perennial (Dianthus)

Perennial border or rock garden plant.
Examples *D.* x *allwoodii* Height 10-15in, spacing 9-12in. Flowers June-July and Sept-Oct. Numerous varieties available. *D. alpinus* Height 4in, spacing 6in. Purple to pink flowers May-Aug. *D. deltoides* Height 9in, spacing 12in, white, pink, red flowers June-Sept. *D. haematocalyx* Height 6-12in, spacing 4-6in. Pink-purple flowers with yellow reverse from July to first frosts.
Plant Mar to Sept-Oct in well-drained limy soil and in sun or light shade. Plants thrive in a rockery, on a dry-stone wall or between paving.
Propagate by 3-4in long cuttings of sideshoots June-Aug, or by layering sideshoots June-Aug (sever the shoots from the parent plant after six weeks).
Pests and diseases see *Pink, annual*, opposite page.

Pittosporum

Half-hardy evergreen shrub.
Examples *P. crassifolium* Height 15ft, spread 6ft. Maroon flowers Apr-May followed by white seed capsules. The shrub is used for hedging in Cornwall and the Scilly Isles; elsewhere it requires the protection of a warm wall. *P. tenuifolium* Height 15ft, spread 5-7ft. Vanilla-scented, brown-purple flowers in May, followed by round fruits Aug-Sept. Also used for hedging in mild districts and grown for its light green, glossy, wavy-edged foliage by flower arrangers. *P. t.* 'Silver Queen' has silver-green foliage.
Plant pot-grown plants Apr-May in fertile soil in a sheltered position. Young plants used for hedging should be set 18in apart; clip off growing tips at least twice in the first season.
Propagate by taking 3-4in long heel cuttings from sideshoots in July. Place them in a frame with a bottom temperature of about 18°C (65°F), and when rooted grow on in a cold frame for two years before planting them out in their permanent positions.
Care Shear hedges to shape Apr and July. Protect specimen shrubs with polythene sheeting during severe winter spells.
Pests and diseases Generally trouble-free.

Plum (Prunus domestica)

Fruit tree.
Of the three main types – gages, plums and damsons – gages have the sweetest flavour, but require a warm, dry site and do best when grown against a wall. Plums are early-flowering and therefore cannot stand late frosts. Damsons, generally used in preserves, come from trees that are much hardier and flower later than the other two.
Average heights and spreads of all three types are: bushes 15 x 12ft; half-standards 20 x 15ft; standards 25 x 20ft; fans 8 x 5ft. Even self-fertile varieties do best when grown in the company of pollinator varieties. Many varieties available including: 'Kirke's' (purple dessert plum, ready mid-Sept. Best grown on a wall and with 'Czar', 'Golden Transparent' or 'Laxton's Gage' as pollinator, flowers mid-season); 'Laxton's Gage' (golden-yellow dessert gage, ready mid-Aug. Self-fertile, but best grown with 'Early Laxton', flowers mid-season); 'Farleigh Damson' (small, black cooking damson, ready mid-Sept. Best grown with 'Cambridge Gage', 'Czar' or 'Golden Transparent').
Plant in deep, well-drained heavy loam in autumn, in bare ground where the tree does not have to compete with grass for moisture.
Propagate by grafting only.
Care Mulch every one or two years with manure and give a top-dressing of general fertiliser in spring. Prune young trees in early spring, established trees in summer.
Pests and diseases APHIDS, BIRDS, plum sawfly, bacterial canker, BROWN ROT, honey fungus, SHOTHOLE, SILVER LEAF.

Plum, ornamental (Prunus)

Deciduous tree.
Examples *P.* x *blireana* Height 10ft, spread 5ft. Purple foliage. Rose-pink blooms in Apr. *P. cerasifera* 'Nigra' (cherry plum) Height 12ft, spread 8ft. Black-purple leaves. Pink flowers Mar-Apr. Fine specimen tree, also used for hedging. In maturity, bears cherry-sized plums.
Plant early autumn or spring in any soil, ideally in full sun. Plant *P. cerasifera* hedges in Oct, using 1½-2ft high plants, spaced 2ft apart.
Propagate by 3-4in heel cuttings of current season's shoots taken in July. Insert cuttings in half-and-half mixture of peat and sand in a propagating case with a bottom temperature of 16-18°C (about 60-65°F).
Pests and diseases BIRDS, APHIDS, CATERPILLARS, honey fungus, leaf spot, POWDERY MILDEW.

Polyanthus (Primula x tommasinii or P. variabilis or P. polyantha)

Bedding plant.
Height 6-12in, spacing 12in. Many different varieties available including those categorised as the Pacific strain (numerous colours) and Goldlace strain (yellow-edged petals). Flowering period of all varieties grown outdoors is Mar-May.
Plant Oct-Mar in fertile, well dug and manured ground, in sun or light shade.
Propagate by division after flowering.
Pests and diseases BIRDS, CATERPILLARS, FOOT ROT, GREY MOULD, leaf spot.

Polygonatum	Polygonum	Polypodium	Poppy, annual	Poppy, perennial	Potato
Polygonatum multiflorum	*Polygonum baldschuanicum*	*Polypodium vulgare* 'Cornubiense'	*Papaver rhoeas*	*Papaver orientale* 'Perry's White'	'Pentland Javelin'
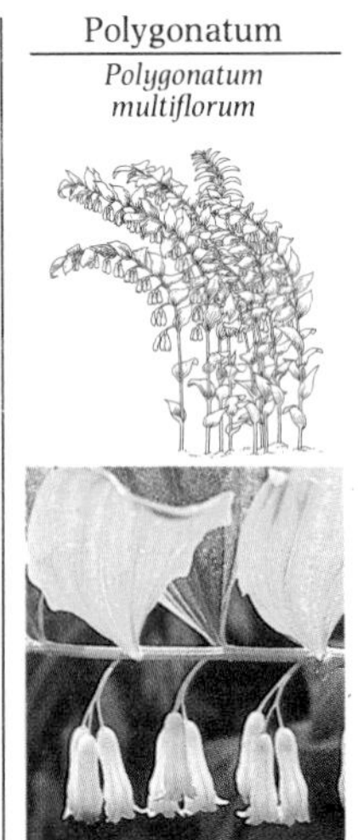					

Polygonatum

Herbaceous perennial suitable for a shady border or for cut flowers.
Examples *P. odoratum thunbergii* Height 18in, spacing 12in. Green-tipped white flowers Apr-May. *P. o. t.* 'Variegatum' has green-edged leaves. *P.* x *hybridum* (also known as *P. multiflorum;* Solomon's seal) Height 2-4ft, spacing 12-18in. White flowers June.
Plant Sept-Mar, ideally in moist peaty soil and in partial shade, though Solomon's seal will do reasonably well anywhere.
Propagate by dividing and replanting roots in Oct or Mar.
Care Cut down all plants in Nov.
Pests and diseases Sawflies.

Polygonum (Knotweed)

Herbaceous border plant or climber.
Examples *P. bistorta* 'Superbum' (snakeweed) Height 3ft, spacing 2ft. Mat-forming plant with pink flowers May-June and often a second flush in late summer. *P. baldschuanicum* (Russian vine, mile-a-minute). One of the most vigorous of climbers, it may easily grow 15ft a year to reach an eventual height of 60ft or more. Excellent for screening and often grown over old trees and outhouses. Pink or white flowers July-Sept.
Plant *P. bistorta* Oct-Mar in rich moist soil in sun or part shade, *P. baldschuanicum* Mar-Apr in almost any situation. Pinch out the Russian vine's growing points to encourage branching, and give initial support on twiggy sticks.
Propagate *P. bistorta* by division Oct or Mar; *P. baldschuanicum* by hardwood cuttings Oct-Nov.
Pests and diseases APHIDS.

Polypodium

Perennial fern.
Example *P. vulgare* Height 15in, spread indefinite. Mid-green fern with elegantly drooping fronds. *P. v.* 'Pulcherrimum' and *P. v.* 'Cornubiense' have finely dissected fronds.
Plant Apr-May in sun or partial shade when the new fronds begin to appear. Stony ground with added humus is best. Set the rhizomes just beneath the surface, anchoring them with bent wire or stones.
Propagate by dividing the rhizomes Apr-May.
Pests and diseases RUST.

Poppy, annual (Papaver)

Border plant.
Examples *P. alpinum* (alpine poppy) Height and spread 4-10in. Rockery plant producing white, yellow or orange flowers May-Aug. *P. nudicaule* (Iceland poppy) Height 1½-2½ft, spacing 12-18in. Fragrant white or yellow flowers in summer. Numerous varieties in other pastel hues available. *P. rhoeas* (field poppy) Height 2ft, spacing 12in. Flowers red with black centre, June-Aug. Many varieties available, including 'Shirley Single Mixed' and 'Shirley Double Mixed' in shades of rose, white, salmon and crimson. *P. somniferum* (opium poppy) Height 2½ft, spacing 12in. Large white, pink or purple flowers June-Aug. Several garden varieties available, including 'Peony-flowered Mixture' (double flowers, mixed colours).
Sow in flowering site Mar, Apr or Sept, just covering the seeds with soil. Thin seedlings as necessary.
Pests and diseases Downy mildew.

Poppy, perennial (Papaver)

Border plant.
Example *P. orientale* (oriental poppy) Height 3ft, spacing 2ft. Quick-spreading border plant producing bowl-shaped scarlet flowers with black blotches May-June. Many varieties available, including 'Perry's White' (white), 'Mrs Perry' (pink), 'Marcus Perry' (scarlet), 'Salmon Glow' (double orange) and 'Goliath' (red).
Plant Oct, Mar or Apr in ordinary soil and in a sunny position.
Propagate by root division Mar-Apr. Root cuttings can also be planted in a cold frame in winter.
Care Stake plants as they grow. Deadhead to promote a second flowering.
Pests and diseases Downy mildew.

Potato (Solanum tuberosum)

Root vegetable.
Early varieties include 'Arran Pilot', 'Home Guard', 'Pentland Javelin' and 'Sutton's Foremost'. Second-early varieties include 'Ben Lomond' and 'Craig's Royal'. Maincrop favourites are 'King Edward', 'Red King', 'Pentland Crown' and 'Majestic'.
Plant sprouted tubers (seed potatoes) 4-5in deep. Almost any kind of soil will do, provided that it has been well dug and manured in autumn. Early and second-early varieties can be planted in the South and West in Mar, in the North mid-Apr. Set the tubers 12in apart in rows 2ft apart. Plant maincrop varieties in late Apr, 15in apart with 2½ft between rows.
Harvest early potatoes only as required. Lift the main crop in Oct and store them for winter in paper bags in a cool, dry place.
Care When the shoots are about 6in tall, draw up the soil to form 6in high sloping ridges on each side of the rows. Draw up a further 1in of soil a month later and again three weeks after that.
Pests and diseases APHIDS, SLUGS, common scab, potato blackleg, potato blight, powdery scab.

Potentilla
Potentilla nitida

Potentilla
Potentilla fruticosa

Primula, alpine
Primula auricula

Primula, border
Primula denticulata

Privet
Ligustrum ovalifolium 'Aureomarginatum'

Pulmonaria
Pulmonaria rubra

Potentilla (Rock cinquefoil)

Mat-forming rock garden plant.
Example *P. nitida* Height 2-3in, spread 12in. Mat-forming. Pale pink flowers with near-crimson centres in July-Aug. Silvery, silky leaves. *P. n.* 'Rubra' has deep rose flowers. Good rockery plant.
Plant Oct-Mar in ordinary but well-drained soil and in a spot which is in full sun.
Pests and diseases Generally trouble-free.

Potentilla (Shrubby cinquefoil)

Deciduous shrub.
Example *P. fruticosa* Height and spread 5ft. Yellow, starry flowers May-Aug. Varieties include 'Abbotswood' (height 2½ft, white), 'Elizabeth' (3ft, yellow) and 'Red Ace' (2ft, vermilion).
Plant Oct-Mar in light, well-drained soil and in full sun.
Propagate by heeled cuttings of sideshoots Sept-Oct.
Care After flowering, remove tips of dead flowering shoots.
Pests and diseases Generally trouble-free.

Primula, alpine

Rock garden plant.
Examples *P. auricula* Height and spacing 6in. Flowers Mar-Apr. Many colour variations available. *P. juliae* Height 3in, spread 12in. Mat-forming; flowers Mar-May. Many colours available. *P. minima* Height 2in, spread 5in. Large pink flowers produced in Apr-May.
Plant Sept-Mar in well-drained gritty soil containing plenty of humus.
Propagate by dividing clumps after flowering finishes.
Pests and diseases APHIDS, CATERPILLARS, crown rot, FOOT ROT, GREY MOULD, leaf spot, RUST.

Primula, border

Herbaceous border plant.
Examples *P. denticulata* (drumstick primrose) Height 12in, spacing 9in. Globular flowering heads in a wide range of colours Mar-May. Varieties include 'Alba' (white) and 'Ruby' (rose-purple). *P. japonica* (Japanese primrose) Height 2½ft, spacing 12in. Magenta flowers May-July. Varieties include 'Postford White' and 'Rosea' (deep pink). *P. vulgaris* (native primrose) Height 6in, spacing 9in. Yellow flowers, Mar-Apr. White, pink and red sub-species available.
Plant in moist, fertile soil Oct-Mar in sun or light shade.
Propagate by dividing clumps after flowering finishes.
Pests and diseases BIRDS, APHIDS, CATERPILLARS, VIRUSES, GREY MOULD, leaf spot, RUST.

Privet (Ligustrum)

Evergreen and deciduous shrubs widely grown as hedging plants.
Example *L. ovalifolium* Height 10-15ft. Evergreen except in the hardest winters. Creamy, scented flowers in July. *L. o.* 'Aureo-marginatum' (golden privet) has glossy green leaves with yellow borders. The leaves of *L. o.* 'Variegatum' are edged pale yellow or cream.
Plant Oct-Apr in any ordinary soil, in sun or shade. For hedging, choose plants 1-3ft high, spacing them 18in apart. Cut back all shoots by half in Apr, and in the following years, in Sept, cut all new growths back by half until the required height is reached.
Propagate by 12in hardwood cuttings in Oct. Insert cuttings in ordinary soil in a sheltered spot; plant out rooting cuttings about one year later in Oct-Apr.
Care Clip established hedges at least twice a year, in May and Sept.
Pests and diseases Leaf miners, THRIPS, honey fungus, leaf spot.

Pulmonaria (Lungwort)

Front-of-border or ground-cover plant.
Examples *P. angustifolia* Height and spacing 12in. Sky-blue, funnel-shaped flowers in Apr. *P. a.* 'Azurea', *P. a.* 'Mawson's Variety' and *P. a.* 'Munstead Blue' have darker blue flowers. *P. officinalis* (Jerusalem cowslip, lungwort) Height and spacing 12in. White-spotted leaves. Blue-purple, funnel-shaped flowers Apr-May. *P. rubra* Height and spacing 12in. Red flowers Mar-May. *P. r.* 'Bowles' Red' has salmon-pink flowers and makes good ground cover.
Plant Oct-Mar in ordinary soil and in shade. Mulch with peat.
Propagate by dividing and replanting roots Oct-Mar.
Pests and diseases Sawfly larvae.

GARDEN TIP
Poppy

To extend the life of cut poppies – annual or perennial – in flower displays, follow two rules.
First, pick only the stems whose buds are just beginning to show colour. Flowers which are already open when they're picked will quickly fade.
Second, immediately after cutting, seal the stems to keep the sap in. Do this either by searing the stem base in a flame for 20 seconds, or by dipping the base in boiling water for one minute.

Pyracantha
Pyracantha coccinea 'Lalandei'

Pyrethrum
Pyrethrum roseum

Quince
'Portugal'

Radish
'Crimson French Breakfast'

Ranunculus
Ranunculus acris 'Flore-pleno'

Raspberry
'Glen Clova'

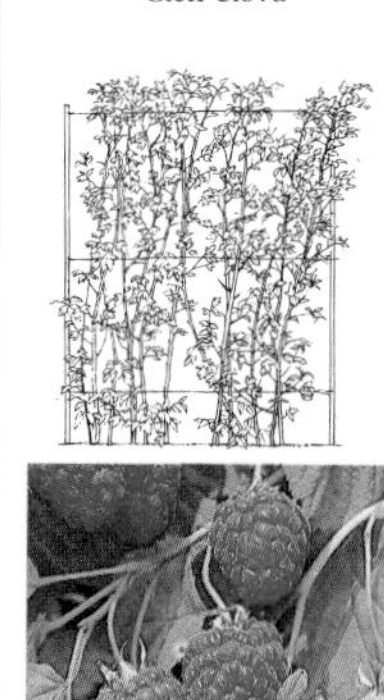

Pyracantha

Spiny evergreen shrub.
Examples *P. angustifolia* Height 10ft, spread 8ft. Creamy flowers June-July followed by bright orange berries. *P. atalantioides* Height and spread 10-15ft. White flowers in June, followed by crimson berries. *P. a.* 'Aurea' has bright yellow berries. *P. coccinea* Height and spread 10-15ft. Mid-green leaves. White flowers in June followed by bright red berries. *P. c.* 'Lalandei' has orange-red berries.
Plant pot-grown plants Oct-Mar in any fertile, well-drained soil, in sun or partial shade. Tie wall-trained plants into trellis or wires. Set hedging plants 15-24in apart.
Propagate by semi-ripe heel cuttings taken in July-Sept.
Care Clip wall plants and established hedges May-July.
Pests and diseases Woolly aphids, SCALE INSECTS, FIRE BLIGHT, pyracantha scab.

Pyrethrum (Feverfew)

Herbaceous perennial, suitable for a sunny border.
Example *P. roseum* (also known as *Chrysanthemum coccineum*) Height 3ft, spacing 18in. Many varieties available including 'E.M. Robinson' (pale pink, single flowers), 'Bressingham Red' (crimson, single) and 'Lord Rosebery' (red, double). All flower May-June.
Plant Oct-Mar in light, well-drained soil and in full sun.
Propagate by dividing clumps Mar or July after three or four years of growth.
Care Stake with pea sticks; water freely. Remove flower stems when blooms fade to prolong flowering.
Pests and diseases Generally trouble-free.

Quince (Cydonia oblonga)

Deciduous fruit tree.
Height 15ft, spread 10ft. Self-fertile tree with crooked branches and dark green foliage that turns yellow in autumn. White-pink flowers in May, followed in autumn by pear-shaped fruits which are used mainly in preserves. Varieties include 'Portugal' and 'Vranja'.
Plant late Oct-Nov preferably in moist, loamy soil and in sun or against a sheltered wall or fence. Fruits on outdoor trees rarely ripen in colder districts in the North.
Harvest early Oct, and store fruits in a cool, frost-free store. Do not store close to other fruits which may become tainted by the quince's scent.
Propagate Oct-Nov by 12in long heeled hardwood cuttings. Insert in nursery bed and grow on for two or three years before planting out. Long branches can be layered Sept-Oct; sever from parent tree one year later.
Care Thin out crowded branches in winter. Prune wall-trained trees to shape in winter.
Pests and diseases BIRDS, codling moth, apple sawfly, APHIDS, CATERPILLARS, CAPSID BUGS, apple mildew, BROWN ROT.

Radish (Raphanus sativus)

Peppery-flavoured root vegetable, generally eaten raw in salads. Varieties include 'Crimson French Breakfast', and 'Sparkler'.
Sow Mar onwards at three-weekly intervals in fertile, well-drained soil. Sow seeds 1in apart in ½in deep drills set 4-6in apart.
Harvest when the roots are about the size of a 5p coin. Radishes are at their best when young.
Pests and diseases FLEA BEETLES.

Ranunculus (Buttercup, bachelor's buttons)

Border or rock garden plant.
Examples *R. aconitifolius* 'Flore-pleno' Height 2ft, spacing 12-18in. Double white flowers May-June. *R. acris* 'Flore-pleno' Height 2½ft, spacing 12-16in. Yellow, double flowers June-Aug. *R. ficaria* 'Aurantiacus' (lesser celandine). Dwarf rockery plant with orange-yellow flowers Mar-Apr.
Plant Sept-Apr in ordinary, moisture-retentive soil in partial shade.
Propagate by dividing and replanting in autumn or spring.
Pests and diseases Generally trouble-free.

Raspberry (Rubus idaeus)

Fruit bush.
Height 6-8ft, usually trained on supporting wires. There are two groups: summer-fruiting (July-Aug) and autumn-fruiting (mid-Sept on). For summer varieties, try 'Glen Clova' and 'Malling Jewel'. For autumn-fruiting varieties, consider 'Zeva', 'Autumn Bliss' or 'September'.
Plant young canes about 2ft apart in Nov in rich, well-drained but moisture-retentive soil, in sun or partial shade. Plants will not thrive in dry or alkaline soils without the addition of peat, compost or manure.
Propagate by transplanting young sucker shoots Nov-Mar.
Care Control annual weeds by shallow hoeing. Water well when the fruits are ripening and apply a mulch in Apr to conserve moisture. Give a feed of Growmore or a high-potash fertiliser – such as tomato fertiliser – in Mar. In Feb, prune off the top of summer-fruiting varieties, and cut autumn-fruiting varieties back to ground level.
Pests and diseases Raspberry beetle, maggots, APHIDS, cane blight, cane spot, crown gall, GREY MOULD, honey fungus, raspberry virus disease, spur blight.

Rhododendron

Evergreen or deciduous shrub. Among hundreds of varieties the most useful for general garden planting are the hardy, evergreen hybrids (see also *Azalea*, page 383). Average height and spread is 6ft, but it can be more in moist, sheltered sites. Most popular varieties flower in May-June. Varieties include: 'Britannia', 'Cynthia', 'David' and 'Doncaster' in various shades of red; 'Lavender Girl' (pale lavender); 'Moonshine Supreme' (rich yellow); 'Mrs W.C. Slocock' (creamy-apricot); 'Purple Splendour' (purple with black markings); and 'Unique' (peach).
Plant Sept-Apr in well-drained but moisture-retentive acid loam. The shrubs do not tolerate lime, nor can they flourish where their roots dry out, so provide plenty of moss peat when planting. Plants do best in sites sheltered from cold winds.
Propagate by layering July-Aug. Sever rooted shoots from parent plant two years later.
Care Mulch and give a feed of general fertiliser in spring. Deadhead plants with finger and thumb, not secateurs.
Pests and diseases Rhododendron leafhopper, rhododendron bugs, CATERPILLARS, azalea gall, chlorosis, honey fungus, rhododendron bud blast, SILVER LEAF.

Rhubarb (Rheum rhaponticum)

Perennial fruit, grown for its red stems, which are used as a cooking fruit from Feb to June. The leaves contain oxalic acid and are poisonous. Varieties include 'Timperley Early' (thin-stemmed, early-maturing), 'Hawke's Champagne' (deep red, good cropper) and 'The Sutton' (large-stemmed, main crop).
Plant crowns in Mar in ground that has been deeply dug and well-nourished with manure or compost and with wood ash and bone meal a few weeks earlier. Allow 3ft between plants, and set the crowns sufficiently deeply for the top buds to be covered by 2in of soil.
Harvest Feb-June by pulling three or four fully grown stems at a time from any one crown. Do not take any stems at all in the first season.
Propagate by dividing the crowns after about five years.
Pests and diseases STEM AND BULB EELWORMS, SWIFT MOTH CATERPILLARS, crown rot, frost damage, honey fungus, leaf spot.

Ribes (Flowering currant)

Border shrub.
Examples *R. sanguineum* Height 6-9ft, spread 5-7ft. Varieties include 'Pulborough Scarlet' and 'King Edward', both with deep crimson flowers May-June, followed by blue-black berries Sept-Oct. *R. speciosum* Height 6-10ft, spread 4-5ft. Brilliant red, almost fuchsia-like flowers Apr-June. Outside the mildest areas, it requires the shelter of a warm wall.
Plant Oct-Mar in any ordinary soil, in sun or light shade.
Propagate by hardwood cuttings Oct-Nov.
Care Top-dress with compost or manure in Apr. Cut out old wood in May. Prune back flowered shoots after flowering ends.
Pests and diseases APHIDS, leaf spot.

Rock jasmine (Androsace)

Rock garden perennial.
Examples *A. lanuginosa* Mat-forming alpine. Height 2½in, spread 18in. Pinkish, primrose-like flowers June-Oct. *A. sarmentosa* Height 4in, spread 2ft. Rose-pink flowers Apr-June.
Plant Mar-Apr in sunny position in sharply drained soil with limestone grit or coarse sand added.
Propagate *A. lanuginosa* by taking 2in long basal cuttings in June. Insert cuttings in sand in a cold frame and plant out in Apr. For *A. sarmentosa*, detach single rosettes in June, insert in sand in a cold frame and plant out in Apr.
Pests and diseases APHIDS, ROOT MEALY BUGS, BIRDS.

Rodgersia

Herbaceous perennial, often grown for foliage as well as flowers.
Examples *R. pinnata* Height 3-4ft, spacing 2½-3ft. Flowers in white or shades of red in July. *R. tabularis* Height and spacing 3ft. Creamy flowers in July.
Plant rhizomes Mar-Apr in moist, well-mulched soil in partial shade and sheltered from strong winds. Set the plants so that the crowns are covered by 1in of soil.
Propagate by division Mar-Apr.
Care Remove faded flower stems.
Pests and diseases Generally trouble-free.

Romneya (Tree poppy)

Herbaceous perennial.
Examples *R. coulteri* Height and spacing 4-6ft. Large white flowers with golden stamens July-Sept. Not suitable outdoors in colder regions of Britain. *R. trichocalyx* Height and spacing 3ft. Smaller, but otherwise similar to *R. coulteri*. Also not suited to colder regions.
Plant Apr-May in moderately well-drained soil, enriched with compost, in a sheltered, sunny position.
Propagate Apr-May by replanting rooted suckers.
Care Avoid disturbing established plants. Romneyas can be invasive, and may be troublesome in a herbaceous border.
Pests and diseases Generally trouble-free.

Rose	Rosemary	Rudbeckia	Runner bean	Ruta graveolens	Sage
'Fragrant Cloud'	*Rosmarinus officinalis*	*Rudbeckia fulgida* 'Deamii'	*Phaseolus coccineus*	'Jackman's Blue'	*Salvia officinalis*
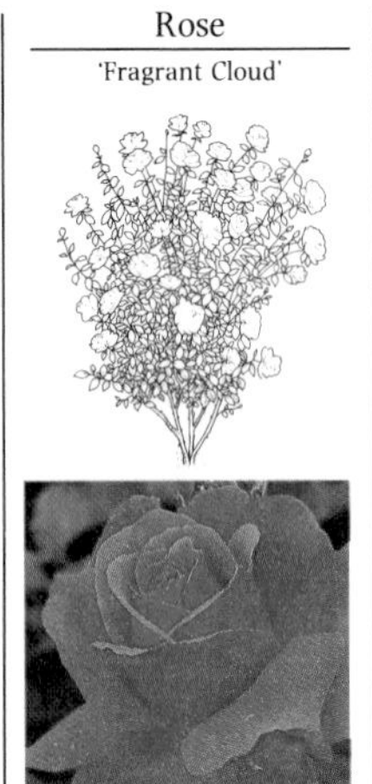			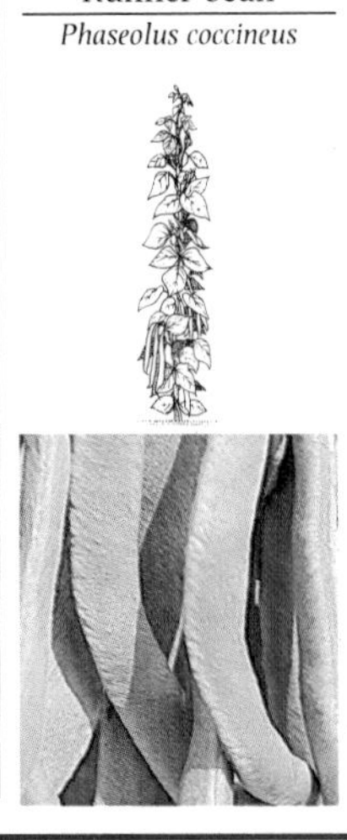		

Rose (Rosa)

Deciduous shrub or climber.
Hundreds of varieties available in many hues and forms. The main divisions are Species roses, Old-fashioned roses, Hybrid teas (Large-flowered Bush), Floribundas (Cluster-flowered Bush), Modern shrub roses, Climbers, Ramblers and Miniature roses. Within these divisions there are numerous sub-divisions, hybrids and varieties, whose numbers increase each year (for advice on which varieties to grow, see *Pick of the roses*, page 296).
Plant Oct-Apr in ground containing liberal amounts of well-rotted manure or compost and preferably in full sun.
Propagate most types by 9-12in long heel cuttings Aug-Sept.
Prune all types regularly for best results. Make all cuts immediately above a bud. Remove dead or diseased wood, and damaged or crossing shoots whenever they are seen. Otherwise prune in autumn or spring. Always prune to an outward-pointing bud (for further details, see *Roses*, pages 286-97).
Pests and diseases APHIDS, CATERPILLARS, LEAFHOPPERS, chafer beetles, black spot, frost damage, GREY MOULD, POWDERY MILDEW, RUST.

Rosemary (Rosmarinus officinalis)

Evergreen herb.
Height and spread 6ft. Mauve flowers Mar or Apr to Sept.
Examples *R. o.* 'Albiflorus' has white flowers, *R. o.* 'Pyramidalis' is of pyramidal habit, *R. o.* 'Jessop's Upright' is erect and has pale mauve flowers. The grey-green leaves of the species and varieties are strongly and sweetly aromatic and are used fresh or dried for flavouring.
Plant Mar in ordinary, well-drained soil and in a sunny position.
Propagate by cuttings of mature shoots in Sept or Mar.
Care Prune off dead growths in Mar each year and cut back overgrown bushes by half in Apr.
Pests and diseases Generally trouble-free.

Rudbeckia (Coneflower)

Bedding and border plant. Common name comes from the cone-shaped centre of the daisy-like flowers.
Examples *R. fulgida* Height and spacing 2ft. Perennial species. Yellow-orange flowers with brown cone-shaped centres July-Sept. *R. f.* 'Deamii' has yellow flowers. *R. f.* 'Goldsturm' has yellow flowers with dark brown centres July-Oct. *R. hirta* (black-eyed susan) Height 1-3ft, spacing 12-18in. Annual species. Golden-yellow flowers with brown-purple central cones Aug-Oct.
Sow annual species under glass Mar-Apr, or in mild areas sow outdoors in mid-Apr. Perennial species are better propagated by root division Oct-Mar. All species thrive in any reasonable garden soil, in sun or light shade.
Care Support with canes. Mulch in spring. Water in dry spells. Cut dead stems to ground level in autumn.
Pests and diseases SLUGS AND SNAILS.

Runner bean (Phaseolus coccineus)

Annual vegetable.
Varieties include 'Hammond's Dwarf Scarlet' (non-climbing bushy type); 'Best of All' and 'Streamline' (both climbers).
Sow seeds outdoors under cloches in mid-Apr, 2in deep, 9in apart, in rows 2ft apart for bush varieties, or in double rows 12-15in apart for climbers. Allow one pole per seed for climbers. Most soils are suitable, but dig clay soils deeply in winter, manuring well. For light or sandy soil, dig trenches 1½-2ft wide and about 2ft deep, adding layers of manure or compost at the bottom.
For early crops, sow seeds singly in peat pots in a greenhouse or indoors in early Apr. Plant out in second half of May, or in early June in colder areas.
Harvest July-Sept.
Care Pinch out growing tips at pole height. Pick pods before beans swell to encourage continuity of production of pods.
Pests and diseases See *Broad bean*, page 386.

Ruta graveolens (Rue)

Evergreen shrub.
Height 2-3ft, spacing 18in. Low shrub with aromatic leaves once widely used as flavouring. Clusters of sulphur-yellow flowers June-July and later. *R. g.* 'Jackman's Blue', height 2ft, spacing 15in, has bright blue-grey foliage.
Plant Sept-Mar in ordinary, well-drained soil and in sunny position.
Propagate by cuttings of sideshoots in Aug. Insert them in pots of a half-and-half mixture of peat and sand. Plant out in the following Mar.
Pests and diseases Generally trouble-free.

Sage (Salvia officinalis)

Evergreen herb.
Height 2ft, spacing 15in. Small violet-blue flowers June-July. The plant is grown for its green-grey aromatic leaves, used as flavouring. Forms with purple or variegated leaves are also grown as ornamentals and ground cover.
Plant Mar-Apr in well-drained light soil and in a sunny position.
Propagate by heel cuttings in Sept.
Care Pinch off flowers to encourage leaf growth. Trim plants regularly to prevent them becoming leggy.
Harvest leaves as required for the kitchen. They do not dry well.
Pests and diseases CAPSID BUGS, GREY MOULD, POWDERY MILDEW.

Salsify	Salvia, annual	Salvia, perennial	Saponaria	Saxifrage	Scabious
'Mammoth'	*Salvia splendens* 'Blaze of Fire'	*Salvia haematodes*	*Saponaria ocymoides*	*Saxifraga moschata*	*Scabiosa caucasica*

Salsify (Tragopogon porrifolius)

Root vegetable, grown for its yellow, tapering, edible roots whose flavour has been likened to both asparagus and oysters.
Sow Apr in ground that has been well dug and manured in the previous year – recently manured ground may induce the roots to fork. Sow the seeds 1in deep in drills 15in apart. When the seedlings appear, thin them to an eventual distance of 9in. Keep the bed well watered.
Harvest roots from mid-Oct, lifting them as required. Leave some roots until spring when they will produce the green shoots known as chards. Cut these when 5-6in long and serve raw like chicory in salads.
Pests and diseases White blister.

Salvia, annual

Bedding plant.
Examples *S. splendens* Height and spacing 9-15in. Spikes of clear scarlet flowers produced from July to first frosts. Purple, white, pink and mixed varieties also available. *S. horminum* Height 18in, spacing 9in. Pale pink or purple flowers and bracts (which can be dried for winter decoration) are produced June-Sept. Blue, carmine, white, red and mixed varieties also available.
Sow Jan-Mar in seed compost under glass. Harden off in a cold frame before planting out in May.
Care Pinch out tops when 2-3in high to encourage bushy growth.
Pests and diseases Generally trouble-free.

Salvia, perennial

Bedding or border plant.
Examples *S. haematodes* Height 3ft, spacing 2ft. Purple spikes of flowers July-Sept. *S.* x *superba* Height 2ft plus, spacing 1½-2ft. Rich, blue-purple spikes produced July-Sept.
Plant Oct-Mar in well-mulched, well-drained soil and in a sunny site.
Propagate *S.* x *superba* by root division every three years Oct-Mar. *S. haematodes* is short-lived and is best increased by seeds sown in a cold frame Mar-Apr.
Care Mulch in spring. Support tall plants in exposed sites. Deadhead regularly and cut all stems back to ground level in autumn.
Pests and diseases Generally trouble-free.

Saponaria

Rock garden or border plant.
Example *S. ocymoides* Height 3in, spacing 12in. Prostrate perennial. Rose-pink flowers July-Sept. Pale to mid-green leaves. *S. o.* 'Compacta' is a slower-growing variety with darker leaves.
Plant in any fertile soil Oct-Mar.
Propagate by division of underground runners Oct-Mar.
Care Cut back strong plants after flowering to encourage a second display. Stake tall plants.
Pests and diseases Generally trouble-free.

Saxifrage (Saxifraga)

Rock garden plant.
A wide range of low-growing plants usually divided into three groups: encrusted, mossy and cushion.
Examples *S. cochlearis* Height and spacing 9in. Encrusted type. White flowers on red stems May-June. *S. paniculata* Height and spacing 12in. Encrusted type. White flowers May-June. *S. p.* 'Rosea' is pink. *S. moschata* Height 3in, spread 18in. Mossy type. Starry flowers Apr-May. *S. m.* 'Pixie' has red flowers; *S. m.* 'Peter Pan' is pink; *S. m.* 'Cloth of Gold' has white flowers above gold leaves. *S. burseriana* Height 2in, spread 12in. Cushion type. Pure white flowers, Feb-Mar. *S. b.* 'Sulphurea' is yellow with grey leaves. *S.* x 'Cranbourne' Height 1in, spread 12in. Cushion type. Grey-green leaves with clear pink flowers, Mar-Apr.
Plant Mar-Apr in well-drained, gritty soil in shade. Encrusted saxifrages prefer full sun and a dry-stone wall or rockery situation.
Propagate by dividing well-established clumps in Mar.
Care Cut stems to ground level in Nov.
Pests and diseases APHIDS, RUST.

Scabious (Scabiosa)

Bedding or border plant.
Example *S. caucasica* Height 2-3ft, spacing 18in. Lavender flowers June-Oct. *S. c.* 'Clive Greaves' is mid-blue, *S. c.* 'Bressingham White' and *S. c.* 'Miss Willmott' are white, and *S. c.* 'Imperial Purple' is deep violet.
Plant Oct-Apr in well-drained, limy soil in full sun.
Propagate by division Mar-Apr.
Care Mulch in spring. Cut down stems in autumn.
Pests and diseases SLUGS AND SNAILS, root rot, POWDERY MILDEW.

Schizanthus
Schizanthus x *wisetonensis*

Scilla
Scilla sibirica

Scorzonera
'Russian Giant'

Sedum
Sedum spectabile

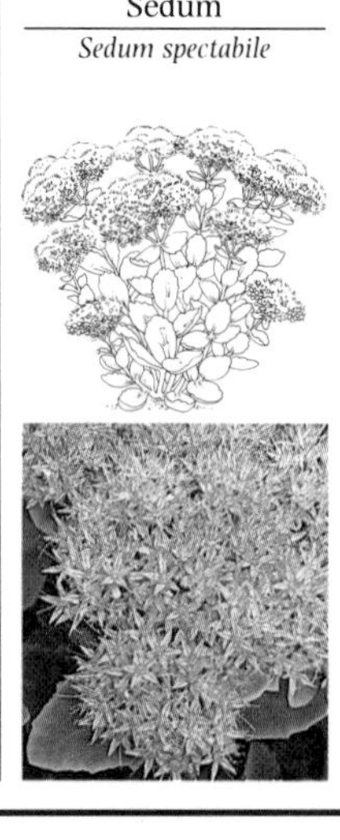

Sempervivum
Sempervivum arachnoideum

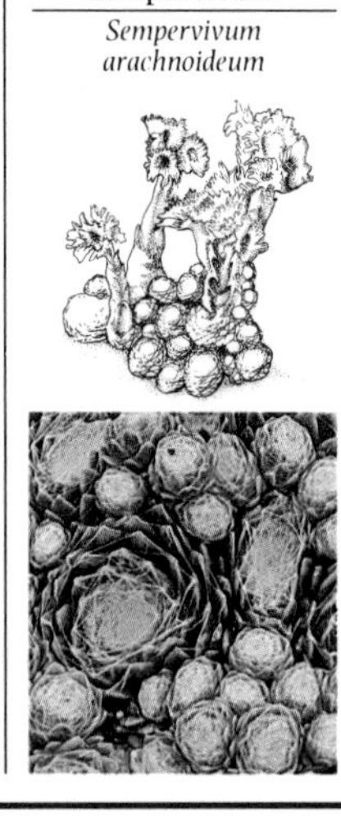

Shallot
'Hâtive de Niort'

Schizanthus (Poor man's orchid, butterfly flower)

Greenhouse or annual border plant.
Example *S.* x *wisetonensis* Height 18in, spacing 12in. Annual hybrid with orchid-like range and combination of colours including rose, pink and crimson.
Sow Apr directly into the flowering site. Plants do best in light, well-manured soil in a sunny but sheltered site.
Care Twiggy supports may be needed for taller plants.
Pests and diseases APHIDS, crown and foot rot, tomato spotted wilt virus.

Scilla

Bulbous perennial.
Examples *S. bifolia* Height 8in, spacing 3in. Starry blue – occasionally pink or white – flowers in Mar. *S. sibirica* Height 6in, spacing 4in. Brilliant blue flowers in Mar. *S. s.* 'Alba' is white. *S. s.* 'Spring Beauty', deep blue. *S. s. taurica* is pale blue.
Plant the bulbs haphazardly in any ordinary, well-drained soil and in a sunny or partially shaded spot.
Propagate by lifting established plants when the leaves die down and replanting the offsets.
Pests and diseases APHIDS, STEM AND BULB EELWORMS, RUST, smut.

Scorzonera (Scorzonera hispanica)

Root vegetable.
Scorzonera has a delicate, asparagus-like flavour similar to that of salsify. 'Russian Giant' is a favourite variety.
Sow Apr-May in ½in deep drills in rows 15in apart. Any fertile, well-drained ground will do, in sun or shade; plants do best in a plot manured for a previous crop. Thin the seedlings to about 10in.
Harvest in Oct, lifting the roots as required. Any left in the ground will grow on and can be harvested in the following autumn.
Pests and diseases White blister.

Sedum

Rock garden plant.
Examples *S. acre* (biting stonecrop) Height 2in, spread 12in plus. Mat-forming species, best on dry walls. Flat yellow flower heads June-July. *S. a.* 'Aureum' has bright yellow shoot tips Mar-June. *S. spathulifolium* Height 2-4in, spread 9in plus. Mat-forming evergreen with yellow flower heads May-June. *S. spectabile* (ice plant) Height and spacing 12-18in. Border perennial with large pink flowers Sept-Oct. *S. s.* 'Carmen' is carmine, *S. s.* 'Meteor' deep red.
Plant Oct-Apr in ordinary, well-drained soil in full sun.
Propagate by division Oct-Mar.
Care Break previous season's dead stems off in spring.
Pests and diseases APHIDS, SLUGS, crown rot, root rot.

Sempervivum

Rosette-forming evergreen succulent, widely grown on dry-stone walls and in rock gardens.
Examples *S. arachnoideum* (cobweb houseleek) Height 1in, spread 12in plus. Alpine with rosettes of leaves linked with cobweb-like threads. Bright rose flowers June-July. *S. tectorum* (common houseleek) Height 2-3in, spread 12in. Rose-purple flowers in July. *S. t.* 'Commander Hay' has purple-red leaf rosettes with green tips; *S. t.* 'Othello' has deep red rosettes. *S. t.* 'Silverine' is silver-grey.
Plant Sept-Apr in ordinary, well-drained soil in sunny spot.
Propagate by lifting and replanting offsets Sept-Oct or Mar-Apr.
Pests and diseases BIRDS, RUST.

Shallot (Allium ascalonicum)

Onion-like bulb vegetable often used for pickling.
Varieties include 'Dutch Yellow', 'Dutch Red', 'Giant Yellow', 'Giant Red' and 'Hâtive de Niort'.
Plant bulbs in Feb-Mar in well-drained soil previously manured. Set them 9in apart in rows 15in apart with the tips of the bulbs level with the surface.
Harvest in mid-July when the foliage turns yellow. Lift the clumps and leave them to dry and ripen in the sun for a few days. Turn them daily. Separate the bulbs when they are completely dry. Store in boxes in a dry, cool but frost-free place. Save a few good bulbs for next year's planting.
Care At the end of June, aid ripening by pulling the soil away from the base of the clumps of bulbs.
Pests and diseases Onion fly, STEM AND BULB EELWORMS, downy mildew, virus disease, WHITE ROT.

Silene
Silene acaulis

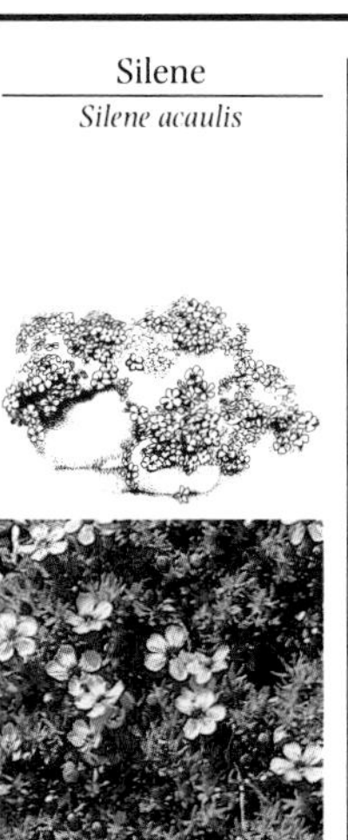

Silver fir
Abies koreana

Sisyrinchium
Sisyrinchium angustifolium

Skimmia
Skimmia japonica

Snowdrop
Galanthus nivalis

Snowflake
Leucojum vernum

Silene (Campion)

Rock garden or bedding plant.
Examples *S. coeli-rosa* (rose of heaven) Height 18in, spacing 6in. Annual species. Rose-purple flowers with white centres June-Aug. *S. c.* 'Candida' is pure white. *S. c.* 'Oculata Nana Compacta' is a dwarf strain. *S. acaulis* (moss campion) Height 2in, spread 18in. Mat-forming perennial. Bright pink flowers May-June. *S. maritima* (sea campion) Height 6in, spread 12in. White flowers July-Sept. *S. m.* 'Flore-pleno' is double. *S. pendula* Height 6-9in, spacing 6in. Annual with pale pink flowers May-Sept depending on when the seeds were sown. *S. p.* 'Compacta Mixed' is double salmon-pink or crimson; *S. p.* 'Triumph Mixed' is pink, salmon or orange.
Sow annuals Sept or Mar-Apr in the flowering site and thin seedlings to the required distance. All silenes thrive in ordinary, well-drained soil in sun or partial shade.
Plant perennials Sept-Mar.
Propagate perennials by 1-2in long cuttings in July-Aug. Propagate *S. maritima* from cuttings of basal shoots in Apr.
Pests and diseases Generally trouble-free.

Silver fir (Abies)

Evergreen conifer.
Examples *A. homolepis* (Nikko fir) Height 25ft, spread 10-15ft. Columnar shape. Bark pink and grey, purple cones, leaves pale green and silvery. *A. koreana* (Korean fir) Height 15ft, spread 10ft. Slow-growing and produces flowers and cones when only 3-5ft high. Leaves dark green and silver. Crimson, pink or green flowers in May, followed by blue-green cones.
Plant young trees in autumn or late spring, in slightly acid soil and in sun or light shade. Not recommended for areas with polluted air.
Propagate by seeds sown in Mar. Move seedlings to permanent positions two or three years later.
Care Prune to maintain a single leading shoot. Apply a mulch of peat or compost annually in early May.
Pests and diseases ADELGIDS, die-back, RUST.

Sisyrinchium

Rock garden plant.
Examples *S. angustifolium* (blue-eyed grass) Height and spacing 9in. Violet flowers May-Oct. *S. douglasii* (spring bell) Height 10in, spacing 6in. Purple, bell-like flowers in Mar.
Plant Sept-Mar in well-drained, well-mulched soil in full sun.
Propagate by division Sept or Mar.
Care Cut off dead growth in autumn.
Pests and diseases Generally trouble-free.

Skimmia

Evergreen shrub.
Example *S. japonica* Height 3-5ft, spread 5-6ft. Evergreen. Creamy flowers Mar-Apr followed by bright red berries Aug-Sept. The male form *S. j.* 'Fragrans' has strongly scented white flowers.
Plant Sept-Oct in any ordinary, well-drained soil, in sun or partial shade. Plants are tolerant of atmospheric pollution. Plant male and female forms to get the best display of flowers and berries.
Propagate by heel cuttings of sideshoots July-Aug or by seed removed from the berries and sown when the berries are ripe.
Pests and diseases Frost damage.

Snowdrop (Galanthus)

Bulbous perennial.
Examples *G. elwesii* Height 4-10in, spacing 4-8in. Large white flowers with deep green inner petals Feb-Mar. *G. nivalis* (common snowdrop) Height 4-8in spacing 3-6in. Grows tallest in rich soil and partial shade. White flowers with green markings Jan-Feb. *G. n. reginae-olgae* flowers in Oct. *G. n.* 'Flore-plena' is double.
Plant Sept-Oct in ordinary soil and in partial shade; bulbs do best in heavy loam in grass under trees.
Propagate by dividing bulb clusters after flowering.
Pests and diseases STEM AND BULB EELWORMS, narcissus fly maggots, GREY MOULD.

Snowflake (Leucojum)

Bulbous perennial.
Examples *L. aestivum* (summer snowflake) Height 2ft, spacing 8in. Green-tipped white flowers Apr-May. *L. autumnale* (autumn snowflake) Height 10in, spacing 4in. White flowers with a pink flush July-Sept. *L. vernum* (spring snowflake) Height 8in, spacing 4in. White, green-tipped flowers are produced Feb-Mar. They are easily confused with snowdrops. *L. v.* 'Carpathicum' has yellow-tipped petals.
Plant bulbs of *L. aestivum* and *L. vernum* at least 4in deep in moist soil and in light shade, in early autumn. Plant *L. autumnale* in summer or after flowering in autumn, at least 2in deep and in well-drained soil in full sun.
Propagate by division only when the plants are becoming crowded.
Pests and diseases Generally trouble-free.

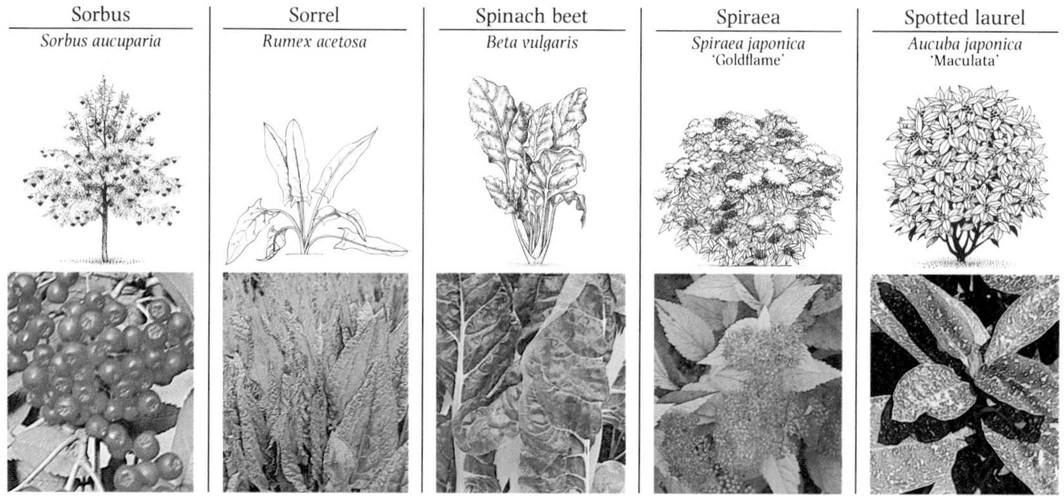

Sorbus

Tree, widely grown as a decorative feature in small gardens.
Examples *S. aria* (whitebeam) Height 20ft, spread 15ft. Russet and gold leaves in autumn. Cream flowers May-June followed by scarlet berries in Sept. *S. a.* 'Majestica' has larger leaves and fruits. *S. a.* 'Lutescens' has creamy young foliage, turning silvery later. *S. aucuparia* (rowan, mountain ash) Height 25ft, spread 12ft. Green-grey leaves turn orange and yellow in Oct. White flowers May-June are followed by orange berries in Aug. *S. a.* 'Asplenifolia' has fern-like leaves. *S. a.* 'Beissneri' has amber or orange bark. *S. a.* 'Edulis' has larger, edible fruits.
Plant Oct-Mar, in sun or partial shade, and in any ordinary soil. *S. aucuparia* will not thrive in shallow alkaline ground.
Propagate by removing the seeds from the berries in Oct and sowing them in potting compost in a cold frame. Plant the seedlings in nursery beds a year later and in their final positions three years after that.
Pests and diseases Apple canker, FIRE BLIGHT, honey fungus.

Sorrel (Rumex)

Perennial herb.
Examples *R. acetosa* (common sorrel) Height 12-18in, spacing 9in. Mid-green, arrowhead-shaped leaves, sharper in flavour than French sorrel. *R. scutatus* (French sorrel) Height 12-18in, spacing 6in. Tiny green-red flowers in early summer. The grey-green leaves are used in salads or are cooked and served like spinach.
Sow Apr in any fertile, well-drained soil, in sun or light shade. Draw the drills 18in apart and thin seedlings to 3in, then to 6in.
Harvest young leaves only; older ones tend to be more acid. Best used fresh, but can be dried or frozen.
Care Pinch out flowering stems to encourage new leaf growth.
Propagate by dividing established plants in Mar, Apr or Sept.
Pests and diseases Generally trouble-free.

Spinach

Annual vegetable.
A general word used to describe several plants, all grown for their edible leaves. They include: annual spinach (*Spinacia oleracea*), whose dark green leaves can be harvested all year round; New Zealand spinach (*Tetragonia expansa*), which is smaller-leaved but less hardy than the annual species; and spinach beet, also known as perpetual spinach or sea kale beet (*Beta vulgaris*). *B. v.* 'Ruby Chard' has red stalks and is often grown as a decorative border plant. The most versatile annual variety is 'Sigmaleaf', which can be grown for harvesting in summer and winter.
Sow annual spinach in moist, well-manured soil in partial shade. Make the first sowings early Mar in the South, late Mar in the North, in drills 1in deep and 15in apart. Thin plants to 6in, then to 12in. Make successive sowings at three-week intervals until July. Sow winter crops in Aug and Sept for harvesting Oct-Apr. Pick leaves when ready, taking two or three only from each plant to maintain the supply.
Sow New Zealand spinach in May, in light, well-drained soil in a sunny position. Allow 3ft between rows and 2ft between plants. Water well. After five or six weeks pick leaves as required, taking a few from each plant.
Sow spinach beet in Apr in the same way as annual spinach. Make a second sowing in early Aug for autumn and winter crops.
Pests and diseases New Zealand spinach can be attacked by millipedes; otherwise it is trouble-free. The others may be affected by mangold flies, cucumber mosaic virus, damping-off, downy mildew, leaf spot and manganese deficiency.

Spiraea

Flowering shrub.
Examples *S. japonica* Height and spread 3-5ft. Rose-pink flowers in late summer. *S. j.* 'Bullata', 12in high, has crimson flowers. *S. j.* 'Goldflame' has gold-flushed leaves. *S.* x *arguta* (bridal wreath, foam of May) Height and spread 6-8ft. White flowers Apr-May.
Plant Oct-Mar in fertile soil and in sun. For hedging, plant shrubs 15-24in apart. Cut back previous season's growth to within 6in of the ground.
Propagate by dividing roots Oct-Mar.
Care Trim established hedges after flowering.
Pests and diseases Sawfly.

Spotted laurel (Aucuba japonica)

Shrub with year-round interest. Height 12ft, spread 7ft. Olive-green, starry flowers Mar-Apr; scarlet berries autumn-spring. *A. j.* 'Crotonoides' has gold-barred leaves. *A. j.* 'Fructo-alba' has yellow-white berries. *A. j.* 'Maculata' is the common variegated form and has yellow-spotted leaves.
Plant in ordinary soil Sept-Oct or Mar-Apr, in sun or partial shade. To ensure cross-pollination, plant one male to three females.
Propagate by 4-6in long heel cuttings of sideshoots Aug-Sept.
Pruning None needed.
Pests and diseases Generally trouble-free.

Spurge *Euphorbia griffithii*	Star of Bethlehem *Ornithogalum nutans*	Stephanandra *Stephanandra incisa* 'Crispa'	Stock annual *Matthiola incana*	Stock night-scented *Matthiola bicornis*	Stock Virginian *Malcolmia maritima*
					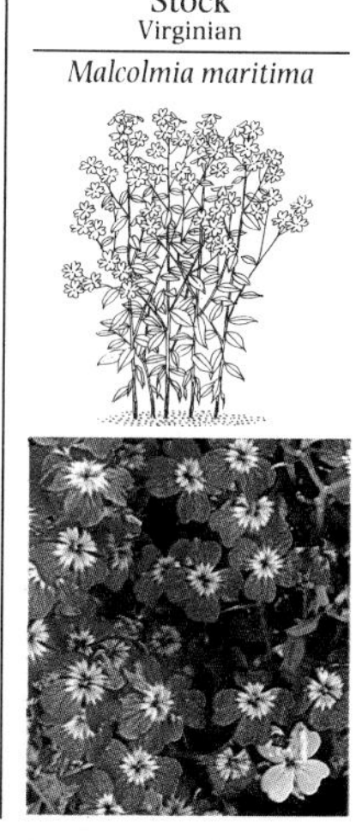

Spurge (Euphorbia)

Perennial for the herbaceous border.
Examples *E. griffithii* 'Fireglow' Height 2-2½ft, spacing 2ft. Brilliant orange bracts May-June. *E. polychroma* Height 18in, spacing 2ft. Bushy evergreen with bright yellow heads of bracts Apr-May.
Plant Sept-Apr in ordinary soil and in sun. The plants make good ground cover.
Care Cut faded flower stems to ground level to promote bushy growth. Wear gloves when pruning; euphorbia sap can irritate sensitive skins.
Pests and diseases Black root rot, die-back.

Star of Bethlehem (Ornithogalum)

Quick-spreading bulbous perennial.
Examples *O. balansae* Height and spacing 4in. White flowers with green stripes Mar-Apr. Good for rockeries. *O. nutans* Height 15in, spacing 6in. White and green bell-shaped flowers Apr-May. *O. umbellatum* Height 12in, spacing 8in. Green-striped white flowers Apr-May.
Plant Oct in borders, short grass or rockeries. Set in ordinary soil and in sun or shade, except *O. balansae*, which requires full sun.
Propagate by lifting and separating bulbs when the leaves die down in summer (*O. umbellatum* can be invasive).
Pests and diseases Heterosporium fungus.

Stephanandra

Flowering shrub; bright autumn colour.
Example *S. incisa* Height 7ft, spread 6ft. Bright yellow autumn foliage. Star-like greeny-white flowers in June. *S. i. prostrata* (height 2ft, spread 4ft) makes good ground cover; the flowers are flushed with pink.
Plant Oct-Mar in any ordinary soil in sun or partial shade.
Propagate by detaching rooted suckers Oct-Mar.
Care Thin out old wood Feb-Mar.
Pests and diseases Generally trouble-free.

Stock, annual (Matthiola)

Excellent filler for annual beds.
Examples *M. incana* (annual varieties) Height 1-2½ft, spacing 9-12in. Scented single and double flowers June-July. Numerous varieties available – mostly sold as Ten Week stocks or East Lothian stocks – in a range of sizes and in shades of pink, yellow, red, lavender and white. *M. incana* (biennial varieties) Height 18in, spacing 9in. Numerous varieties available – usually sold as Brompton Stocks – producing single or double flowers in shades of pink, purple, yellow or white in Mar-May.
Sow annual varieties under glass Feb-Mar. Harden off in cold frame and plant out Apr-May in well-drained soil, preferably slightly alkaline and in sun or partial shade. Alternatively, sow in flowering site in Apr.
Sow biennial varieties June-July in a cold frame or greenhouse and plant out the following spring in the same sort of soil and position as the annual varieties. East Lothian stocks can be grown either as annual or as biennial flowers.
Care Stake tall plants. Deadhead to encourage longer flowering.
Pests and diseases CATERPILLARS, APHIDS, CLUB ROOT, damping-off, downy mildew, GREY MOULD, STEM ROT.

Stock, night-scented (Matthiola bicornis)

Fragrant annual.
Height 15in, spread 9in. Spikes of lilac flowers that perfume the entire garden on July-Aug evenings when the flowers open. The flowers are closed during the day.
Sow Apr in flowering position, ideally in fertile, slightly alkaline soil in sun or light shade. Since the plant has a somewhat untidy daytime appearance, it is often grown among the more colourful Virginian stock, *Malcolmia maritima*.
Pests and diseases See *Stock, annual*, this page.

Stock, Virginian (Malcolmia maritima)

Annual, widely grown as bedding and edging plant.
Many varieties available, including 'Dwarf Mixed' (height 6in) and separate colours such as 'Red' (10in). Height of most varieties 8in, no spacing normally necessary. Showy, scented flowers in shades of red, yellow, rose or white are produced about four to six weeks after sowing and continue for six to eight weeks.
Sow thinly in flowering site, only just covering the seeds. Make successive sowings Mar-July to maintain flowering continuity. Sow again in Sept for Apr blooming. Almost any soil or site will serve, but plants do best in full sun.
Propagation The plants self-seed prolifically if left undisturbed.
Pests and diseases Generally trouble-free.

Stranvaesia	Strawberry	Strawberry tree	Sumach	Summer savory	Sunflower
Stranvaesia davidiana salicifolia	*Fragaria* x *ananassa*	*Arbutus unedo*	*Rhus typhina*	*Satureja hortensis*	*Helianthus annuus*
	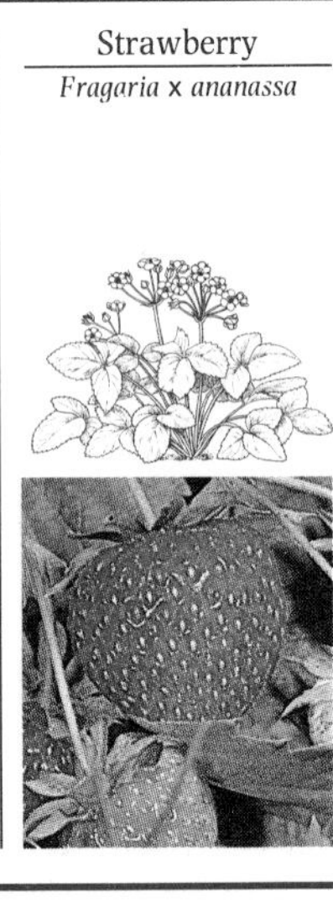			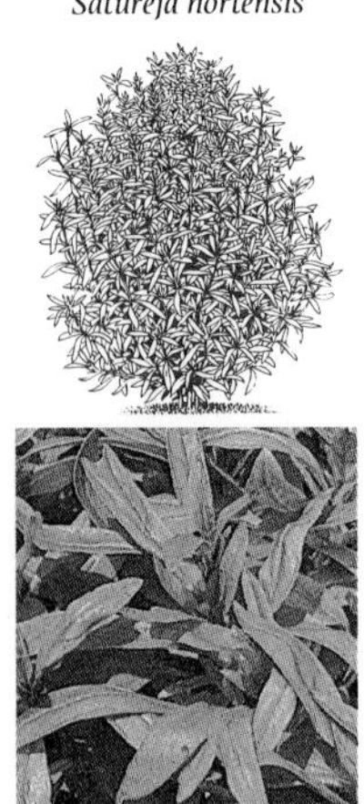	

Stranvaesia

Large shrub for year-round interest. **Example** *S. davidiana salicifolia* Height and spread 12-18ft. Some of the dark green leaves turn crimson in Sept. White, hawthorn-like flowers in June. Crimson berries ripen Aug-Sept, lasting into winter. *S. d. s.* 'Fructuluteo' has yellow berries.
Plant in any reasonable soil, in sun or partial shade.
Propagate by layering in spring; sever rooted branches one or two years later.
Pests and diseases FIRE BLIGHT.

Strawberry (Fragaria x ananassa)

Perennial fruiting plant.
Two main types: single-croppers that produce once in summer; and ever-bearing or perpetual strawberries that crop June-Oct. These are less hardy than the single-crop types. Many varieties of both are available.
Plant 18in apart in rows 18in apart, in a sunny spot with the crowns level with the surface. Firm the plants in. Before planting, dig the ground deeply and work in some well-rotted manure or compost. Fork in a general fertiliser at 3oz per sq yd in spring.
Propagate by pegging runners to the ground from June onwards. Sever from the parent plants when they have rooted.
Care Water regularly in dry spells and when the fruit is ripening. Before the fruit touches the ground, scatter slug pellets around the plants and fit strawberry mats – which fit around the plant at ground level – to prevent the fruit touching the soil. You can make your own mats by cutting discs of tarpaper or plastic, and slitting them so that they fit round the stem. Or give similar protection with clean straw. Protect from birds with nylon netting stretched over canes.
Harvest strawberries by snapping the stalks; do not touch the easily bruised fruits.
Pests and diseases BIRDS, SLUGS, strawberry beetle, APHIDS, eelworm, GREY MOULD, leaf spot, strawberry mildew, red core, strawberry virus diseases, yellow edge.

Strawberry tree (Arbutus)

Ornamental shrub and tree.
Examples *A. andrachne* Tender when young. Height 15ft, spread 8ft. Cinnamon-red bark, leathery leaves. White flowers Mar-Apr followed by strawberry-like and edible though insipid fruits. *A. unedo* Ornamental tree; hardy in mild, sheltered situations. Height 15-20ft, spread 10ft. White or pink flowers Oct-Dec, often at the same time as the edible orange-red fruits.
Plant Oct or Mar-May in lime-free soil in sunny position, sheltered from cold winds. *A. unedo* is lime-tolerant.
Propagate by 3-4in long semi-ripe heel cuttings in July.
Care Protect young trees and shrubs in winter with straw.
Pests and diseases Leaf spot.

Sumach (Rhus)

Shrub; brilliant autumn colour.
Examples *R. glabra* (smooth sumach) Height 9ft, spread 6ft. Pale red flowers in July. The leaves flare to brilliant red in early autumn. *R. typhina* (stag's horn sumach) Height and spread 15ft, small, pinkish flowers June-July, followed by clusters of yellow fruits. Foliage takes on shades of red, yellow and purple in autumn.
Plant Oct-Apr in ordinary soil and in a sunny position.
Propagate by replanting suckers from Oct onwards.
Care If autumn foliage only is desired, cut stems to ground level Feb-Apr.
Pests and diseases Die-back, VERTICILLIUM WILT.

Summer savory (Satureja hortensis)

Annual herb.
Height 12in, spacing 9in. Spikes of tiny lilac flowers, June-Sept. The spicy, strongly aromatic leaves are used in cooking, and as an ingredient of *potpourris*.
Sow Apr in shallow drills 12in apart, in any fertile, well-drained soil. Thin seedlings to 9in apart. For a winter supply, sow a few seeds in pots and stand them in the kitchen.
Harvest fresh as needed. Leaves and shoots can also be dried or deep-frozen in Aug.
Pests and diseases Generally trouble-free.

Sunflower (Helianthus)

Back-of-the-border annual and perennial.
Examples *H. annuus* (annual) Height 10ft, spacing 18in. The flowers, borne in July-Sept, can be 12in plus across. *H. a.* 'Flore Pleno' is double, *H. a.* 'Autumn Beauty' (3ft high) sulphur-yellow, and *H. a.* 'Russian Giant' yellow. *H. decapetalus* (perennial) Height 4-6ft, spacing 1½-2ft. Varieties include: 'Loddon Gold' (5ft high, double, golden); 'Soleil d'Or' (5ft, semi-double, yellow).
Sow annuals and perennials Mar-Apr in well-drained soil and a sunny position, or plant perennials Oct-Nov or Apr. Cut perennials almost to ground level after flowering.
Propagate perennials by division Oct-Apr.
Care Stake large plants; deadhead to prevent self-seeding.
Pests and diseases GREY MOULD, sclerotinia disease.

Swede
'Chignecto'

Sweet chestnut
Castanea sativa

Sweet corn
'Kelvedon Glory'

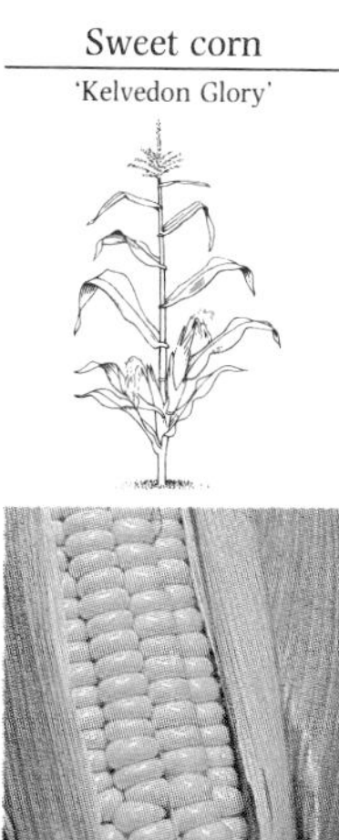

Sweet pea
Lathyrus odoratus

Sweet william
Dianthus barbatus
'Summer Beauty'

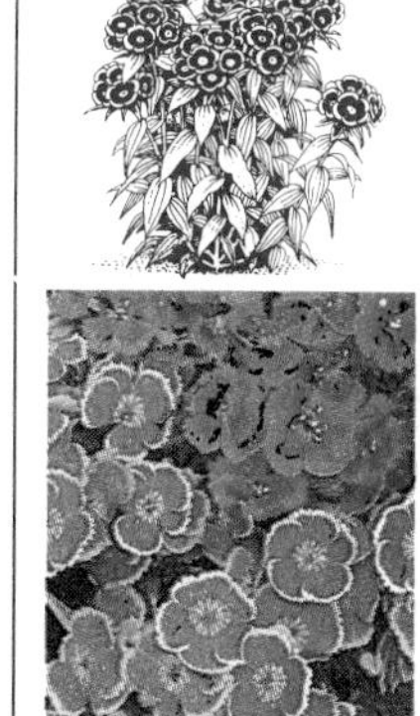

Sycamore
Acer pseudoplatanus
'Brilliantissimum'

Swede (Rutabaga, Brassica napus napobrassica)

Mild-flavoured, yellow-fleshed annual root vegetable grown for use in winter.
Varieties include: 'Chignecto' (disease-resistant, stores well); 'Marian' (high yield, good flavour, disease-resistant); 'Purple Top' (reliable, widely available, good storer); 'Mancunian Brown Top' (slow-growing, but excellent storer); and 'Western Perfection' (quick-growing, ready in Sept).
Sow mid-May in the South, mid-June in the North. Make drills 1in deep, 18in apart. Thin seedlings to 12in apart. Grow in any good, fertile soil except acid.
Harvest as required autumn-spring. Store a few in a cool, frost-free place for use when the ground is frozen.
Pests and diseases FLEA BEETLES, boron deficiency, CLUB ROOT, damping-off, downy mildew, soft rot, splitting, violet root rot.

Sweet chestnut (Castanea sativa)

Tree; not for small gardens. Height 30ft, spread 20ft in 20-25 years, eventually much larger. Pale green-yellow flowers in July, followed by spiny burrs containing edible nuts.
Plant Oct-Mar in any good soil and in an open, sunny position.
Propagate by ripe seeds sown outdoors in Oct. Transplant three or four years later to permanent positions.
Pests and diseases Generally trouble-free.

Sweet corn (Corn-on-the-cob, Zea mays)

Annual vegetable.
Height 4-5ft, spacing 18in.
Recommended varieties include: 'Early Xtra Sweet' (large, high sugar content, but do not grow near other varieties as cross-pollination spoils the flavour); 'Earliking' (large cobs, good in Northern areas); 'North Star' (best in Northern districts and in cool, wet summers); and 'Kelvedon Glory' (mid-season, heavy cropper, good flavour).
Sow in groups of three in fertile, manure-rich soil in a sunny position in late May. Remove the two weaker seedlings, leaving one to grow on its own.
Harvest in Aug-Sept, about a month after the silky tassels begin to turn brown. Test for ripeness by gently pressing the seeds. They are ripe if a milky juice squirts out. Cook the cobs immediately after picking; they have the best flavour then. They may be frozen if first wrapped in plastic film.
Pests and diseases BIRDS.

Sweet pea (Lathyrus odoratus)

Sweetly fragrant annual.
Numerous varieties available in three main groups: Spencer varieties, hedge varieties and dwarf varieties.
Spencer varieties, such as 'Gaiety' and 'White Ensign'. Height 6-10ft. Four or five flowers are carried on each stem, June-Sept. Dozens of varieties in a huge colour range available.
Hedge varieties, such as 'Knee-hi' and 'Jet Set'. Height 3ft, needing little support. Many varieties available. Flowers June-Sept.
Dwarf varieties, including 'Bijou', 'Snoopea' and 'Little Sweethearts'. Height 12in; no support required. Wide colour range. Flowers June-Sept.
Sow Sept, Oct or Mar in well-drained, well-manured soil. Soak the seeds in water for at least 12 hours before planting. Thin out the seedlings to 6in apart in Apr. Provide support – bushy sticks or wire netting – for taller varieties.
Care Deadhead to promote further flowering.
Pests and diseases SLUGS, THRIPS, bud-drop, downy mildew, FOOT ROT, FUSARIUM WILT, GREY MOULD, LEAFY GALL, POWDERY MILDEW.

Sweet william (Dianthus barbatus)

Short-lived perennial, usually grown as a biennial.
Height 6in-2ft, spacing 8-10in. Single or double flowers in various colours June-July. Varieties include 'Auricula-eyed Mixed' (18in high), 'Indian Carpet' (10in), 'Summer Beauty' and 'Wee Willie' (6in), all in mixed colours.
Sow in open ground in a sunny spot May-July and transplant seedlings to flowering positions in Oct.
Alternatively, for flowers the same year, plant under glass in Mar at room temperature, harden off and plant out in May. 'Wee Willie' must be grown as an annual.
Care Remove flower stems immediately after flowering to encourage plants to bloom for a second year.
Pests and diseases APHIDS, carnation fly, carnation ring spot, RUST.

Sycamore (Acer pseudoplatanus)

Tree; not suitable for small gardens.
Example *A. p.* 'Brilliantissimum'. Good windbreak tree, height 20ft, spread 15ft. Slow-growing; spring foliage is coral-pink, changing to pale green in summer. *A. p.* 'Worlei' Height 35ft, spread 15ft. Bears yellow foliage from spring to July.
Plant Oct-Mar in well-drained but moist soil and in sun or partial shade. Thrives in coastal gardens.
Propagate Seedlings from wind-borne seeds sprout prolifically.
Pests and diseases APHIDS, gall mites, honey fungus, SCORCH, tar spot, VERTICILLIUM WILT.

Tamarisk	Tarragon	Tellima	Thalictrum	Thorn	Thrift
Tamarix tetrandra	*Artemisia dracunculus*	*Tellima grandiflora*	*Thalictrum aquilegifolium*	*Crataegus laevigata*	*Armeria maritima*
		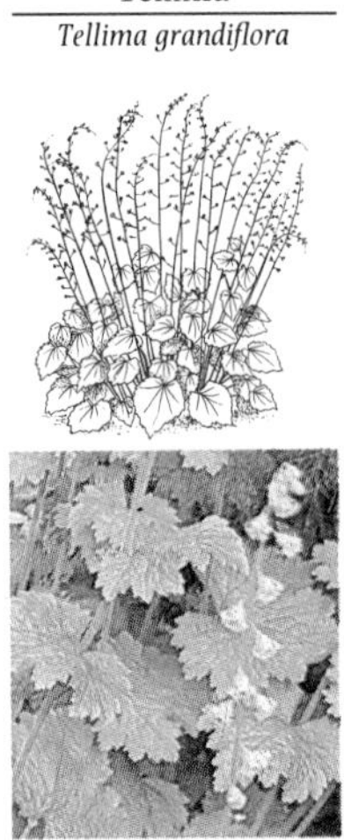			

Tamarisk (Tamarix)

Tough, long-lived shrub.
Examples *T. pentandra (T. hispida)* Height and spread 15ft. Tiny pink flowers in Aug. *T. p.* 'Rubra' has deep rose flowers. The shrub is exceptionally hardy and makes a good windbreak in maritime areas. *T. tetrandra* Height and spread 10-15ft. Bright pink flowers in May.
Plant in any ordinary, lime-free soil Oct-Mar. For a windbreak, set young plants of *T. pentandra* 2ft apart, and trim them back to a height of 12in after planting.
Propagate by taking 9-12in long hardwood cuttings in Oct. Insert in sandy soil outdoors. Plant out in permanent positions one year later.
Care Prune *T. pentandra* Oct-Feb, and *T. tetrandra* after flowering. In both cases remove at least half the previous season's growth.
Pests and diseases Generally trouble-free.

Tarragon (Artemisia dracunculus)

Perennial herb.
Height 2ft, spacing 12in. Tiny greenish flowers appear in Aug in clusters above the grey-green, strongly aromatic leaves that are used fresh or dried as an ingredient in *fines herbes, bouquets garnis*, sauces and vinegars.
Plant Oct-Mar in sandy, sharply drained soil and in a sunny though sheltered position.
Harvest the leaves mid-June to end of Sept. Sprigs may be dried or deep-frozen.
Propagate by severing and replanting rhizomes in Mar-Apr or by taking cuttings in summer.
Pests and diseases Generally trouble-free.

Tellima

Ground-covering perennial for the herbaceous border.
Example *T. grandiflora* Height 1½-2ft, spacing 18in. Bell-shaped green-yellow flowers Apr-June, but tellimas are mostly grown for the ground-cover qualities of their bright green foliage.
Plant Sept-Mar in ordinary soil and partial shade.
Propagate by division Sept-Mar.
Pests and diseases Generally trouble-free.

Thalictrum

Back-of-the-border perennial.
Examples *T. aquilegifolium* Height 2-3ft, spacing 12-18in. Fluffy mauve or purple flowers May-July. *T. a.* 'Album' has white flowers, *T. a.* 'Purpureum' light purple and *T. a.* 'Thunder-cloud' dark purple. *T. dipterocarpum* Height 4-5ft, spacing 18in. Sprays of mauve and yellow flowers June-Aug. *T. d.* 'Album' is white; *T. d.* 'Hewitt's Double' has double mauve flowers.
Plant Mar-Sept in ordinary soil, in sun or light shade, though plants do best in rich, moist soil.
Propagate by division Mar-Apr.
Care Stake tall plants. Cut plants back to ground level in Nov. Top-dress with a 1-2in thick layer of well-rotted manure, peat or compost in Mar.
Pests and diseases Generally trouble-free.

Thorn (Crataegus)

Tree; makes a near-impenetrable hedge.
Examples *C. crus-galli* (cockspur thorn) Height 15ft, spread 20ft. Viciously thorned branches carry glossy green leaves that turn scarlet in autumn. White flowers in June followed by red haws that may last to New Year. *C. laevigata* (*C. oxyacantha*, Midland hawthorn, may) Height 30ft, spread 20ft, though often shortened for hedging. White, pink or red, single or double heavily scented flowers in May; followed by crimson haws in autumn.
Plant in winter in almost any soil and in an open position. The trees withstand exposure and extremes of wet and dry weather.
Propagate *C. crus-galli* by seed sown in autumn after removing the flesh of the ripe berry. Seed takes 16-18 months to germinate. Propagate *C. laevigata* by grafting in spring.
Prune hedges July-Aug.
Pests and diseases CATERPILLARS, FIRE BLIGHT, honey fungus, POWDERY MILDEW, RUST.

Thrift (Armeria)

Hummock-forming perennial.
Examples *A. caespitosa (A. juniperina)* Height 3in, spacing 9in. Grey-green leaves and stemless pink flowers in May. *A. maritima* Height and spread 12in. Forms a leafy hummock and bears pink flowers May-July. White and red forms also available.
Plant Sept-Apr in ordinary soil and in full sun.
Propagate by dividing clumps Mar-Apr. Or take 2in long cuttings of basal shoots July-Aug, and insert them in a half-and-half mixture of peat and sand in a cold frame.
Care Remove faded flower heads to improve appearance.
Pests and diseases RUST.

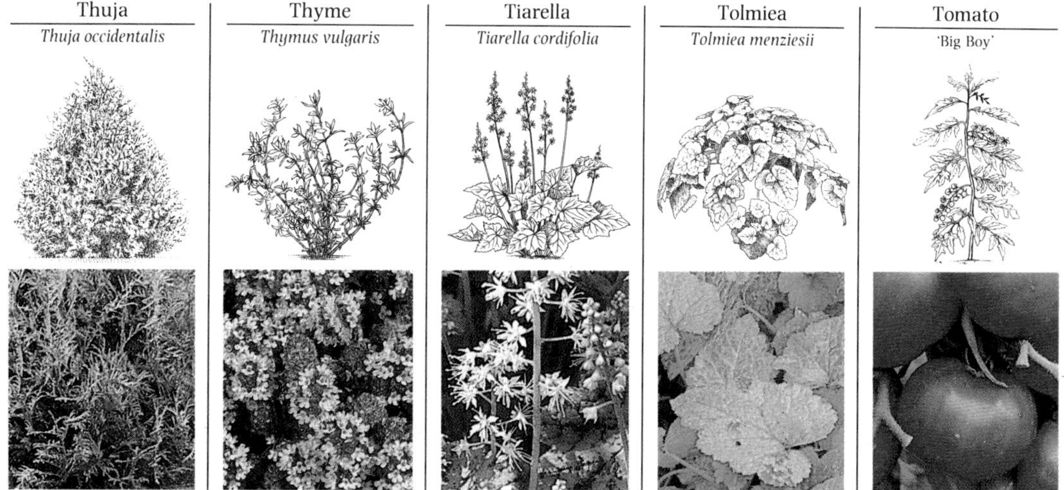

Thuja

Conifer; excellent for small and medium-sized gardens.
Example *T. occidentalis* (white cedar) Height 25ft, spread 15ft. Greeny-yellow foliage. Varieties available include some of the best conifers for small gardens, such as: *T. o.* 'Globosa' (height and spread 2-3ft, compact, with dense grey-green foliage in flat sprays); *T. o.* 'Umbraculifera' (height and spread 6ft, blue-green foliage); and *T. o.* 'Hetz Midget' (height and spread 12in, dark green ball shape good for small rockeries, very slow-growing).
Plant Nov-Mar, preferably in moist soil and in sun and shelter, though any reasonable soil and site will do.
Propagate by taking 2-4in long tip cuttings Sept-Oct.
Care Apply a general fertiliser in spring.
Pests and diseases Generally trouble-free.

Thyme (Thymus)

Perennial herb, widely used for flavouring and decoration.
Examples *T. praecox arcticus* (*T. serpyllum*, wild thyme) Height 2in, spread 2ft. Dense, mat-forming plant with red, pink or white flowers in summer. *T. p. a.* 'Albus' has white flowers, *T. p. a.* 'Pink Chintz' is pink and *T. p. a.* 'Coccineus' is crimson. *T. vulgaris* (common thyme) Height 4-8in, spacing 9-12in. Mauve flowers in June. Excellent as an edging plant in rockeries; also grown for its aromatic leaves, used in cooking, scents, liqueurs and antiseptics. *T.* x *citriodorus* (lemon-scented thyme) Height and spacing 12in. Lemon-scented, decorative version of common thyme, used in cooking and *potpourris*. Silver and gold-leaved varieties available.
Plant Oct-Mar in any well-drained soil and in a sunny position.
Propagate by dividing plants in Mar, or Aug-Sept, and replanting immediately.
Care Crop flower heads to maintain bushy growth.
Pests and diseases Generally trouble-free.

Tiarella

Adaptable perennial ground cover.
Examples *T. cordifolia* (foam flower) Height and spacing 12in. Carpeting ground cover with creamy flowers May-June. *T. wherryi* Height and spacing 12in. Maroon-flecked leaves. Creamy flowers June-Sept and later.
Plant Oct or Mar-Apr in moist soil and in shade. Good beneath trees, and for winter interest since the plants retain their leaves all year round.
Propagate by division Oct or Apr.
Pests and diseases Generally trouble-free.

Tolmiea

Perennial for indoor pots or outdoor ground cover.
Example *T. menziesii* (piggy-back plant) Height 6in, spread 15in. Indoor plant or ground cover that produces young plants on the leaves. Spires of greenish, red-flushed flowers in June.
Plant Oct-Mar in well-drained, humus-rich soil, ideally in partial shade.
Propagate by pegging leaves to the soil where they will root readily.
Pests and diseases Generally trouble-free.

Tomato (Lycopersicon lycopersicum or L. esculentum)

Annual fruiting plant.
Greenhouse favourites include 'Moneymaker', 'Ailsa Craig' and 'Alicante'. Good for indoors, too, are the Beefsteak varieties – $\frac{3}{4}$lb to 1lb giants such as 'Big Boy' and 'Dombito'.
The first three are also excellent outdoor cordon varieties, as are the heavy-cropping 'Outdoor Girl' and 'Sweet 100', with its bite-sized fruits. Bush varieties include the sweetly flavoured 'Red Alert', heavy-cropping 'Sleaford Abundance' and the disease-resistant 'Alfresco'. For a delicious novelty, try the cherry-sized 'Tiny Tim'.
Sow indoor tomatoes Feb-Mar, outdoor varieties Mar-Apr, 1in apart in boxes of seed compost, and germinate them at a temperature of 16°C (about 60°F). When the seedling leaves are fully expanded, pot the plants into potting compost. Harden off before planting into the greenhouse border Apr-May, or outdoors May-June. The site should be warm and sheltered and the ground well manured. Stake taller varieties, tying the plants in as they grow. Water freely.
When the first flower trusses have set, feed once a week with a proprietary tomato fertiliser. For more detailed growing instructions, see *Tomatoes*, page 336.
Harvest fruits as they ripen. Those that are still green when the cold weather begins can be wrapped in paper and placed in a drawer to ripen. Store them near a red tomato or a ripe banana – both give off ethylene gas, which speeds ripening.
Pests and diseases CATERPILLARS, potato cyst eelworm, APHIDS, blossom end rot, damping-off, FOOT and ROOT ROT, greenback, GREY MOULD, leaf mould, magnesium deficiency, potato blight fungus, stem canker, tomato virus diseases.

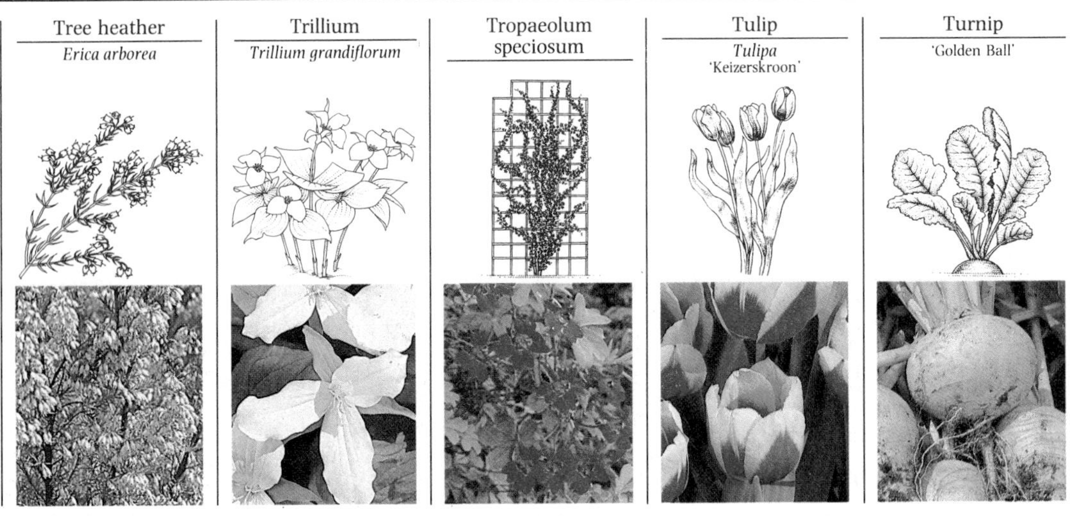

Tree heather (Erica)

Tough flowering shrub.
Example *E. arborea* Height 8-12ft, spread 6-8ft. White flowers Mar-June. Intolerant of exposed sites and limy soil.
Plant Mar-May or Oct and Nov, preferably in acid soil with peat and bone meal added.
Propagate by taking 1-2in long cuttings July-Oct or by layering in Mar, severing from parent plants after a year.
Care Top-dress with peat in spring.
Pests and diseases SCALE INSECTS, leaf insects.

Trillium

Shade-loving perennial.
Examples *T. grandiflorum* (wake robin) Height 12-18in, spacing 12in. White flowers, later flushed rose-pink, Apr-June. Double white and pink varieties available. *T. undulatum* (painted wood lily) Height 12in, spacing 9in. White flowers with purple centres Apr-June. The leaves and petals of all trilliums are arranged in threes.
Plant Aug-Sept in moist but well-drained soil in partial shade, setting the rhizomes in groups and sufficiently deep so that they are covered by 3-4in of soil.
Propagate by dividing the rhizomes autumn-Mar.
Pests and diseases SLUGS.

Tropaeolum speciosum (Flame creeper)

See also *Nasturtium*, page 416.
Tender climber.
Height 10-15ft, spread 2-3ft.
Twining perennial with large scarlet flowers July-Sept.
Plant rhizomes horizontally Nov or Mar in acid or neutral soil, with peat, compost and sand added. Flame creepers do best in full sun, but lower growths and roots require shade. A good planting site would be the shady side of a bush, hedge or wall, allowing the upper growth to climb over the top. Does best in Northern and Western areas and in cool, moist parts of the South.
Propagate by dividing rootstocks in Mar.
Care Top-dress with compost or manure each spring before growth begins. Support young growths with twiggy sticks. In cold areas, protect roots with straw or bracken in winter.
Pests and diseases APHIDS, THRIPS, VIRUSES.

Tulip (Tulipa)

Elegant, bulbous perennial.
Hundreds of different varieties available in many forms and colours: all flower Mar-May. Types of tulip include:
Single early Height 9-20in, spacing 4in. Flat-opening flowers, Apr-May.
Double early Height 10-15in, spacing 6in. Peony-like, often frilled flowers, Apr.
Triumph Height 18-20in, spacing 6in. Sturdy, angular flowers, late Apr.
Darwin Height 24-28in, spacing 8in. Large, round flowers, Apr-May.
Lily-flowered Height 20-24in, spacing 6in. Long flowers bending outwards at the petal tips, Apr-May.
Cottage Height 24-28in, spacing 6in. Tall, round flowers, May.
Parrot Height 20-24in, spacing 8in. Big, fringed flowers, often with twisted petals, May.
Kaufmanniana hybrids Height 8-10in, spacing 5in. Ideal for rockeries. Star-shaped flowers, Mar-Apr.
Plant Nov-Dec at least 6in deep in well-drained, preferably alkaline soil and in a sheltered position.
Propagate by lifting the tulips and removing the offsets when the leaves begin to wither.
Pests and diseases APHIDS, mice, SLUGS, STEM AND BULB EELWORMS, VIRUSES, blue mould, grey bulb rot, tulip fire.

Turnip (Brassica rapa)

Annual root vegetable, which can be grown almost all year round.
Early (fast-growing) varieties include 'Purple Top Milan' and 'Golden Perfection'. Summer varieties include the globular 'Sixweeks' and 'Snowball'. A good winter variety is the easy-to-store, yellow-fleshed 'Golden Ball'.
Sow mid-Mar for early crops, Apr-May for summer crops, July-Aug for winter types, allowing 9in between summer turnips and 12in between winter varieties. Sow in fertile soil with deep-dug compost. Give a top-dressing of phosphorus-rich fertiliser (such as superphosphate) and bone meal just before sowing.
Harvest summer turnips when young and as required. Harvest winter turnips in the same way, or lift them in Nov and store them in a dry, frost-free place.
Care Water well in dry spells.
Pests and diseases FLEA BEETLES, CLUB ROOT, damping-off, downy mildew, soft rot, splitting, violet root rot.

Ursinia	Vaccinium	Verbascum, alpine	Verbascum, border	Verbena	Veronica, alpine
Ursinia anethoides	*Vaccinium corymbosum*	*Verbascum* x 'Letitia'	*Verbascum* x *hybridum*	*Verbena* x *hybrida* 'Delight'	*Veronica prostrata*

Ursinia

Tender perennial border plant.
Example *U. anethoides* Height 18in, spacing 12in. Orange-yellow daisy-like flowers with purple central discs June-Sept. The flowers close in the evening and in dull conditions. Several varieties available in a range of orange shades.
Sow under glass in Mar at a temperature of 16°C (about 60°F). Harden off in a cold frame before planting out in May into a sunny site and preferably sandy soil, though any reasonable soil will do.
Care Provide twiggy support to protect tall plants from wind.
Pests and diseases Generally trouble-free.

Vaccinium

Flowering shrub with edible fruits.
Examples *V. corymbosum* (blueberry) Height 4-6ft, spread 6-8ft. Deciduous. White, pink-flushed flowers May-June, followed by blue-black edible berries that ripen Aug-Sept. The foliage turns brilliant red in Oct.
V. vitis-idaea (cowberry, mountain cranberry) Height 6in, spread 18in. Evergreen. White or pale pink flowers May-June, followed by dark red edible berries that often last into winter. Grown mainly as an ornamental and as ground cover. Can be invasive.
Plant Oct-Mar in peaty, lime-free soil, in sun or partial shade.
Propagate by division Oct-Mar.
Pests and diseases Generally trouble-free.

Verbascum, alpine

Low-growing rock garden perennial.
Examples *V. dumulosum* Height and spread 6-12in. Shrubby plant with clear yellow flower spikes produced in June-July. *V.* x 'Letitia' Height 9in, spread 12in. Velvety leaves; yellow flowers June-Aug.
Plant alpine species, often called rock mulleins, in Oct or Mar-Apr in ordinary soil and in full sun. Plants do best in dry walls or rockeries.
Propagate May-July by 2in long heel cuttings set in a cold frame during winter.
Care Shelter plants from rain in winter with a sheet of glass.
Pests and diseases Generally trouble-free.

Verbascum, border

Perennial for the rear of the herbaceous border.
Example *V.* x *hybridum* Height 3-6ft, spacing 2ft. Varieties include: 'Gainsborough' (4ft high, yellow flowers); 'Pink Domino' (3-4ft, rose).
Plant border species, often called mulleins, in Oct or Mar-Apr in ordinary soil and in sun.
Propagate Feb-Mar by 3in long root cuttings set in a cold frame.
Care Stake tall plants. Deadhead to encourage further flowering. Cut plants to ground level in Nov.
Pests and diseases Generally trouble-free.

Verbena

Long-flowering border annual.
Example *V.* x *hybrida* Height 6-18in, spacing 12in. Clusters of flowers June to first frost in red, blue, lilac, white and pink. Single-colour and mixed varieties available.
Sow under glass Jan-Mar at a temperature of 18-21°C (about 65-70°F). Harden off in a cold frame before planting out in May, in any fertile soil in sunny, open position.
Care Deadhead to encourage longer flowering.
Pests and diseases APHIDS, tarsonemid mites.

Veronica, alpine

Rock garden perennial.
Examples *V. filiformis* Height 1in, spread 3ft plus. Pale blue flowers Apr-July. Can be troublesome, though, particularly if it spreads to lawns. *V. prostrata* Height 4in, spread 18in. Rich blue flowers May-July. Varieties, which are widely available, include *V. p.* 'Alba' (white) and *V. p.* 'Mrs Holt' (pink).
Plant Sept-Mar in ordinary soil in a sunny position. Plants do best in a rockery.
Propagate by division Mar-Apr.
Pests and diseases POWDERY MILDEW.

GARDEN TIP
Verbena

Lemon verbena is related to the colourful border annual, but is not a member of the genus verbena, despite its common name. Known to botanists as *Lippia citriodora*, it was introduced to Britain from Chile in the 18th century, and is now widely grown as a herb in sheltered spots outdoors or in cool greenhouses.
The leaves of lemon verbena can be used to make a lemon-flavoured herb tea which is said to soothe congestion in the nose and lungs. To brew the tea, steep a teaspoonful of the leaves, fresh or dried, in a cup of boiling water for 3-5 minutes.

Veronica, border	Viburnum	Virginia creeper	Wallflower	Water lily
Veronica spicata	*Viburnum* x *burkwoodii* 'Anne Russell'	*Parthenocissus tricuspidata* 'Veitchii'	*Cheiranthus cheiri*	*Nymphaea* 'Escarboucle'

Veronica, border

Perennial for the front of the herbaceous border.
Example *V. spicata* Height 6-18in, spacing 6-12in. Flowering spikes in shades of blue June-Aug. Varieties include 'Alba' (white), 'Barcarolle' (pink) and 'Pavane' (2ft high, deep rose flowers).
Plant Oct-Apr in ordinary, well-drained soil, in sun or partial shade.
Propagate by division Mar-Apr.
Care Support tall varieties in exposed positions. Cut plants to ground level in Nov and divide every three years.
Pests and diseases POWDERY MILDEW.

Viburnum

A collection of shrub species for year-round interest.
Examples *V.* x *bodnantense* 'Dawn' Height and spread 9-12ft. Deciduous. Rose-flushed white flowers borne on bare wood Dec-Feb. One of the most dependable of winter-flowering shrubs. *V.* x *burkwoodii* Height 6-8ft, spread 12ft. Semi-evergreen. Waxy, scented white flowers, Mar-May. *V. plicatum tomentosum* Height 10ft, spread 15ft. Deciduous. White flowers in May; wine-red autumn foliage.
Plant *V.* x *burkwoodii* Sept-Oct or Mar-May, the others Oct-Mar in good, moist soil and in sun.
Propagate by layering long shoots in Sept. Sever them from the parent plant about one year later.
Care Thin out old wood on evergreen species in early May, on deciduous types after flowering finishes.
Pests and diseases APHIDS, whiteflies, frost damage, honey fungus, leaf spot.

Virginia creeper (Parthenocissus)

Perennial climber.
Examples *P. henryana* Height 25-30ft. Attractive silver-veined leaves that turn brilliant red in autumn. Requires a warm sheltered wall except in the mildest areas. *P. inserta* (common Virginia creeper) Height or spread up to 40ft. Best trained to horizontal supports, from which it trails in a graceful hanging curtain. The leaves turn bright red in autumn. *P. quinquefolia* (true or common Virginia creeper) Height up to 70ft. Hardy, self-clinging; impressive on tall tree tops, and on walls and fences too – though there it must be kept under control. *P. tricuspidata* 'Veitchii' Height up to 50ft. Self-supporting. Grows rapidly once established.
Plant by digging a pocket 2ft square and 18in deep against a wall or tree. Fill it with a mixture of loam and compost and plant out a pot-grown Virginia creeper in mild weather Nov-Mar. Pinch out the growing points of vertically growing species. Support plant with twiggy sticks until it becomes self-clinging.
Propagate by taking 10-12in long hardwood cuttings in Oct-Nov. Insert them to half their length in a sheltered outdoor border.
Care Remove overcrowded growth in summer.
Pests and diseases APHIDS, SCALE INSECTS, weevils, honey fungus.

Wallflower (Cheiranthus)

Highly popular border biennial that can be perennial in mild areas.
Examples *C. cheiri* Height 8-24in, spacing 10-12in. Numerous varieties available, including dwarf and giant strains, and in various hues of red, yellow, mahogany, pink, orange or purple. All flower Apr onwards. *C.* x *allionii* (Siberian wallflower) Height 15-18in, spread 12-15in. Similar to *C. cheiri*, but flowers May-June.
Sow seeds in May and plant out 12in apart in nursery bed in July. Transfer the young plants to their flowering positions in early Oct.
Care Pinch out growing points of plants when 4in tall to encourage bushy growth.
Pests and diseases CABBAGE ROOT FLY, CLUB ROOT, downy mildew, LEAFY GALL.

Water lily (Nymphaea)

Tuberous perennial for water gardens.
Numerous varieties available from specialist nurseries in shades of white, yellow, pink and red, and with a surface spread of between 12in (miniature types) and 4½ft (large types). Established plants normally begin flowering May-July, depending on water temperature, and continue until late Sept.
Plant tubers or rhizomes Apr-June in the muddy base of a pool or in perforated containers. Set miniature types in 4-6in of water, medium types in 12-18in, large types in water up to 2½ft deep. Thin overcrowded plants Apr-May.
Propagate by dividing rhizomes or tubers Apr-May.
Pests and diseases APHIDS, water lily beetles, CATERPILLARS, leaf spot, STEM ROT.

Weigela	Willow	Wisteria	Yew	Yucca	Zinnia
Weigela florida 'Bristol Ruby'	*Salix* x *chrysocoma*	*Wisteria sinensis*	*Taxus baccata*	*Yucca filamentosa*	*Zinnia elegans*

Weigela

Long-lived flowering shrub.
Example *W. florida* Height and spread 6ft. Light green leaves. Pale pink flowers May-June. *W. f.* 'Variegata' is more compact than the species. *W. f.* 'Bristol Ruby' has dark red flowers.
Plant Oct-Mar in any fertile soil in sun or partial shade.
Propagate by taking 10-12in long cuttings of current season's shoots in Oct. Insert the cuttings in a bed outdoors, and plant in permanent positions one year later.
Care Cut one or two old stems on mature plants back to ground level after flowering, to encourage new young growths.
Pests and diseases Generally trouble-free.

Willow (Salix)

Water-loving tree. Unsuitable for growing near buildings.
All willows are hardy, quick-growing, decorative and avid for moisture, making them a mixed blessing in a small plot.
Examples *S. caprea* 'Pendula' (Kilmarnock willow) Height and spread 10ft. Weeping habit; long, silky catkins in early spring. *S. matsudana* 'Tortuosa' Height 20ft, spread 15ft. Non-weeping; has curly, contorted twigs, leaves and branches. *S.* x *chrysocoma* (common or golden weeping willow) Height and spread 25ft. Spectacular hybrid suited to larger gardens near water.
Plant Oct-Feb in moist soil and in a sunny position. Large trees do best near a pool. Do not plant near foundations or drains.
Propagate by 9-15in long hardwood cuttings Oct-Mar.
Care Remove dead wood Nov-Feb.
Pests and diseases CATERPILLARS, APHIDS, SCALE INSECTS, anthracnose of willow, bracket fungi, honey fungus, RUST.

Wisteria

Prolifically flowering climbing shrub.
Examples *W. floribunda* 'Macrobotrys' Height up to 30ft on a wall or tree. Blue or purple flowers in plumes 1½-3ft long May-June. *W. sinensis* Height up to 100ft. Fragrant lilac flowers in racemes 8-12in long. The most popular wisteria. *W. s.* 'Alba' has white flowers.
Plant Oct-Mar in almost any soil, giving plenty of root space, beside a south or west-facing wall. Provide a permanent support and tie the growths in until the stems gain hold.
Propagate by cuttings in late summer, or layering in autumn or spring.
Care Cut back all growths to within two or three buds of the base of the previous year's growth in Feb. When controlling large plants, cut young growth back to within five or six buds of the base in July.
Pests and diseases BIRDS, APHIDS, THRIPS, bud-drop, chlorosis, honey fungus, leaf spot.

Yew (Taxus)

Slow-growing, evergreen tree, popular for hedging. It is poisonous to livestock.
Examples *T. baccata* (English yew) Height 40ft, spread 35ft. Dark green needle-like foliage; bright red fruits in summer. *T. b.* 'Fastigiata' (Irish yew) Height about 15ft, spread 2ft. A neat column of dark green, almost black needles. *T. b.* 'Fastigiata Aureomarginata' and *T. b.* 'Fastigiata Standishii' have golden foliage. All parts of all yews, except the red flesh of the fruits, are highly poisonous. Never plant trees near grazing land; they can kill livestock.
Plant in any soil, except swampy ground, in full sun or deep shade, Oct-Apr. The trees are hardy in almost any situation. For hedging, use 15in high plants set 15-18in apart.
Propagate named varieties by heel cuttings of sideshoots Sept-Oct. The species can be propagated by seeds taken from ripe berries and sown in a cold frame. Named varieties do not breed true from seed.
Pests and diseases SCALE INSECTS.

Yucca

Perennial flowering shrub.
Examples *Y. filamentosa* (Adam's needle) Height 2-2½ft, spread 3-4ft. Stiff, sword-like leaves; creamy bell-shaped flowers borne July-Aug in 3-6ft tall plumes (after two or three years). *Y. f.* 'Variegata' has yellow-edged leaves. *Y. recurvifolia* Height 3-6ft, spread 6-7ft. Creamy flowers produced in Aug-Oct.
Plant Apr or Oct in any ordinary, well-drained soil – including poor sandy soil – in full sun.
Propagate by taking rooted suckers in Mar-Apr.
Pests and diseases Leaf spot.

Zinnia

Half-hardy annual bedding plant.
Example *Z. elegans* Height 6-30in, spacing 12in. Numerous varieties in a wide range of colours available, including dwarf varieties. The smallest variety is 'Thumbelina' (6in high) and one of the largest is 'State Fair' (a dahlia-flowered type growing to 2½ft). All flower July-Sept.
Sow May into the flowering site, which needs to be rich, well-drained soil in a sunny but sheltered position.
Care Pinch out the growing tips of young plants to encourage branching. Deadhead to encourage the growth of more flowers.
Pests and diseases Cucumber mosaic virus, tomato spotted wilt virus, damping-off, GREY MOULD, seedling virus.

WHAT DOES IT MEAN?

A GUIDE TO THE LANGUAGE OF GARDENERS

Cross-references within the guide appear in SMALL CAPITALS.
Cross-references to other parts of the book are in italics and are followed by a page number – for example, *Soil structure*, page 324.

ACARICIDE Chemical spray against mites – especially red spider mites.

ACCLIMATISATION Getting plants used to conditions different from those in which they were grown (see HARDENING OFF).

ACID Soil with a pH level below 7.0 is said to be acid. Most plants will grow in acid soil – the level that suits the greatest number of plants is a pH of about 6.5. To make a soil less acid – often called 'sweetening' the soil – add limestone, which is most commonly available in the form of hydrated or garden lime (see PH).

AERATION Loosening soil by various mechanical means to allow air in – for example, a spiked roller may be used to aerate a lawn.

AERIAL ROOTS Roots growing from a plant stem which remain above ground. They sometimes absorb moisture from the air, and may also support a plant such as ivy, which clings by its aerial roots.

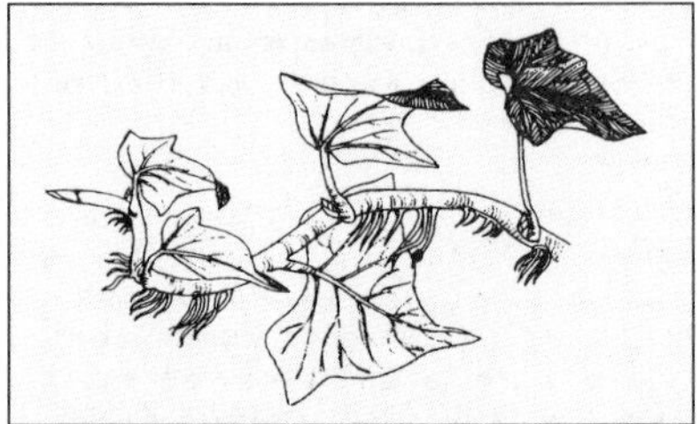

AERIAL ROOTS *They support or feed some plants.*

AIR FROST The freezing that takes place when the air temperature at a sheltered spot 4ft above the ground drops below 0°C (32°F). Air frosts are less common than ground frosts – but more damaging to plants if the low temperature persists (see also FROST and GROUND FROST).

ALGINATE Chemical soil conditioner made from seaweed, used to make heavy soil more crumbly.

ALKALINE Soil with a pH level above 7.0 is said to be alkaline. Most plants will grow in alkaline soil except those particularly suited to acid soil, such as rhododendrons and some heathers (see ACID).

ALPINE Term applied loosely to any small plant suitable for growing in rock gardens. More strictly, it applies to plants that grow naturally between tree and snow lines in alpine and other mountainous regions.

ALTERNATE Term applied to leaves that grow singly at different heights and on opposite sides of a stem.

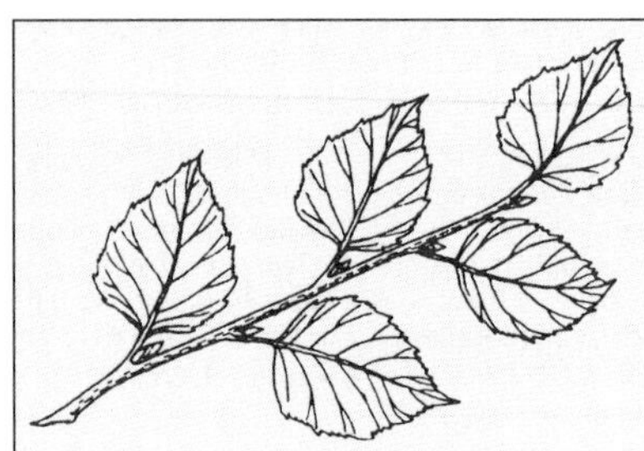

ALTERNATE *A common pattern of leaf growth.*

ANNUAL Plant that completes its life cycle from seed, through growth and flowering, to setting seed and dying within one growing season.

AQUATIC Plant that lives in water. It may, like a water lily, float on the surface and root on the bottom; it may float free, like a water hyacinth; or it may live completely submerged like the milfoil (*Myriophyllum* species), which also oxygenates the water.

ARBORETUM Collection of different species of trees and shrubs. Two well-known arboretums are at Ampfield, Hampshire, and Westonbirt, Gloucestershire.

AXIL Angle between a leaf, or leaf stalk, and a stem. An axillary bud is one that develops in the axil of the leaves.

BALL (or rootball) The compact ball of roots and soil of a well-developed open-ground or pot-grown plant. Any plant will transplant more readily if this ball is left unbroken. Shrubs may be bought as balled specimens, with their roots wrapped in sacking.

BARK-BOUND Trees stunted due to lack of moisture or nutrients may become bark-bound, because their bark hardens and so restricts growth. Such a tree may cure itself by splitting naturally along the trunk; otherwise, slit the bark vertically with a knife and seal the wound with grafting wax.

BATTER Method of trimming a hedge so that the sides slope inwards towards the top, making the top narrower than the base. It holds its shape better than one with vertical sides, particularly under a weight of snow.

BEDDING PLANTS Any plants raised in quantity for a temporary display. Planting, or bedding out, is commonly done twice a year, in late spring for a summer display and early autumn for a spring display.

BERRY Fruit in which the seeds are enclosed by a fleshy outer covering. Grapes and gooseberries are examples.

BIENNIAL Plant that needs two growing seasons to complete its life cycle. Leaves form during the first year, flowers and seeds the following season. Foxglove (*Digitalis*) is an example.

BISEXUAL Term applied to a plant which has both male and female organs in the same flower (see also PISTIL and STAMEN).

BLANCHING Keeping light from the stems of certain vegetables. This makes them more tender and tasty by preventing chlorophyll from being formed. Parts to be blanched can be earthed up, wrapped in thick paper or covered by a pot. Celery, leeks and chicory are commonly blanched.

BLEEDING Trees and plants are said to bleed when they lose sap through a cut. Bleeding is often most severe in spring, when the sap is rising.

BLIND A plant or stem without a flower bud or other terminal growth (see TERMINAL) is said to be blind. Usual causes are damage or disease.

BOLTING Prematurely running to flower or seed. Applies particularly to vegetables such as lettuce or beetroot, and is often caused by drought or poor soil.

BONE MEAL Organic fertiliser ideal for slow-growing crops, shrubs and herbaceous borders. But it causes an alkaline reaction in the soil (see ALKALINE) and is best avoided on acid-loving plants such as azaleas and rhododendrons.

BONSAI Japanese technique for growing decorative dwarf versions of trees such as pine, larch and maple in small containers. Roots are severely pruned and restricted; main stems are cut back repeatedly and trained into the required shapes by wires and strings.

BOTTOM HEAT Heating from a source placed deep in the soil below plants in a frame or greenhouse, to encourage cuttings to root more efficiently. Electrically heated cables are often used.

BRACT Modified leaf at the base of a flower stalk. Bracts are often brightly coloured – like the scarlet bracts of poinsettias – and sometimes mistaken for petals (poinsettia flowers are actually yellow and undistinguished).

BRASSICA Generic term for the cabbage family, which includes broccoli, brussels sprouts, kale, cauliflowers and turnips.

BREAK A sideshoot growing from an axillary bud (see AXIL). Pinching out the growing tips of a plant causes break buds to appear, promoting bushy growth. Rubbing off the natural break buds of plants such as chrysanthemums often results in better blooms at the tips of shoots.

BROADCAST Seeds strewn evenly over the ground, rather than sown in furrows, are said to be broadcast. Grass seeds, for example, are broadcast.

BUD Tightly condensed shoot from which leaves or flowers develop, and by which a plant grows rapidly in warm weather. A *crown bud* is a flower bud at the tip of a shoot and surrounded by other flower buds. A *dormant bud* is one that is inactive – especially on trees. A *fruit bud* (on a fruit tree) is one from which leaves, flowers and, finally, fruit develop. It is generally larger than a *growth bud*, from which only leaves or a shoot appear. An *axillary bud* is one which appears at an 'axil' – the joint between a leaf and a stem.

BULB A bud-like storage organ, usually underground. It is composed of fleshy scales, which are modified leaves or leaf bases. Unlike a CORM, a bulb always contains the young plant. Some bulbs, such as daffodils, are tightly encircled by scales which are themselves enclosed by thin, drier scales. Others, such as lilies, have quite open, separate scales.

BULBIL Small immature bulb, often formed at the base of mature bulbs or, as in some lilies, on stems above ground.

BULB FIBRE A mixture of peat, oystershell and charcoal in which bulbs are grown indoors for decoration. Bulbs raised in bulb fibre live on their own food stores and are exhausted after flowering.

BUSH Low shrub with no clearly defined main shoot, and with branches all forming near ground level. A *bush tree* – usually a fruit tree – is one with a trunk of 3ft or less before the lowest branches.

CAPSULE The dry, or nearly dry, seed case of certain plants which splits when ripe, scattering its contents. The seedheads of poppies and irises are capsules.

CATCH CROP Swiftly maturing crop grown in the interval between harvesting one main crop and sowing or planting the next. For example, lettuces and radishes can be grown after early potatoes are lifted and before spring cabbages are planted.

CATKIN Flower spike, often hanging but sometimes erect, of single-sex, stalkless flowers. Trees such as willow, birch and hazel bear catkins.

CERTIFIED STOCK Plants certified by the Ministry of Agriculture as free from certain diseases and pests, and true to their names. Applied, for example, to seed potatoes and strawberries.

CHALK See *Chalk*, page 52.

CLAMP Root crops such as potatoes, swedes and carrots can be stored in the open in clamps. To make a potato clamp, pile the potatoes into a pyramid and cover them with a 12in deep layer of straw, topped by a 9in thick layer of soil, for protection against frost. A chimney hole filled with straw on the top provides the necessary ventilation.

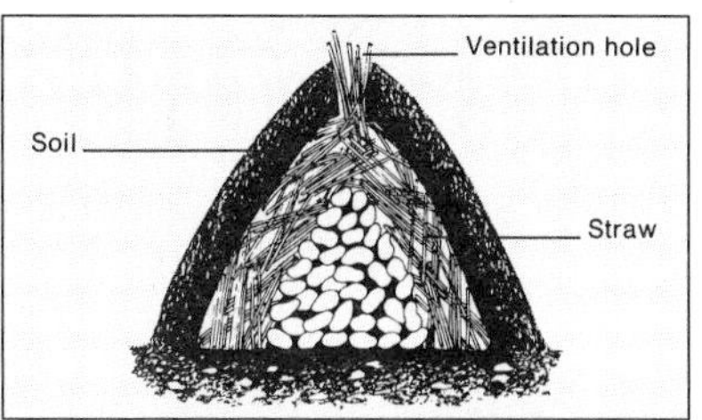

CLAMP *Potatoes protected against frosts.*

CLAY See *Soil structure*, page 324.

CLIMBER Climbers put out aerial roots, leaf stalks, tendrils or sticky suckers to attach themselves to supports such as walls, fences, trellises – even other plants – to reach for the sun.

CLOCHE Originally a cloche was a bell-shaped cover placed over a plant to aid propagation. The word is French for 'bell'. Modern cloches are made of clear plastic or sheets of glass, and are used mostly to protect early crops on open ground and to heat the soil before planting early crops.

CLONE One of a group of identical plants all raised from a single parent plant by vegetative propagation – by cuttings or division, for example, not from seeds. All 'Bramley's Seedling' apples are clones because they result from grafting material from the original specimen onto rootstocks.

COMPOSITE A member of the daisy family (*Compositae*). Their seemingly single flowers are made up of many smaller ones known as florets.

COMPOST This term has two meanings. It applies to a mixture of loam, sand, peat, leaf mould or other ingredients which is used for growing plants in pots. It applies also to a farmyard manure substitute made by carefully piling up grass cuttings and other plant remains, whose decaying process can be speeded by adding chemicals.

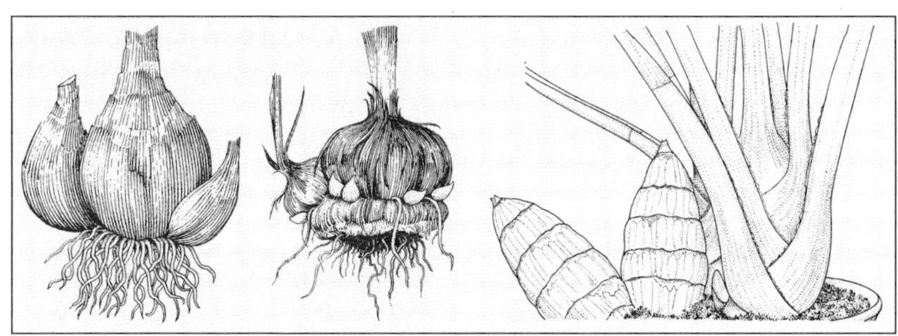

BULB *Three storage organs: a daffodil bulb and young bulbils (left); a gladiolus corm and young cormlets (centre); and pseudobulbs growing at the base of a cymbidium orchid (right).*

CONIFER Tree or shrub, mostly evergreen, which bears its seeds in cones. Pine, fir and cedar trees are conifers.

CORDON A term applied to a trained fruit tree whose growth is restricted by pruning to a single stem.

CORM The swollen, rounded, underground storage organ and stem of plants such as crocuses and gladioli. Sometimes it is enclosed in a papery skin, and looks rather like a bulb. At the top of a corm is the bud, and at the bottom are the old roots. The bud produces both shoots and new roots.

CROCKS Broken pieces of a clay flowerpot, often placed concave side down to cover the drainage hole of another pot or container.

CROP ROTATION A system by which different vegetable crops are grown on the same plot in consecutive years. This practice reduces the incidence of soil-dwelling pests, and ensures maximum use of the soil and any fertiliser and manure applied to it. One common three-year system rotates crops in three groups: onions, peas and beans; brassicas; and root vegetables.

CROWN The upper part of a rootstock from which shoots appear – as, for example, in rhubarb, peonies and lupins. Also applied to rhubarb roots lifted for forcing.

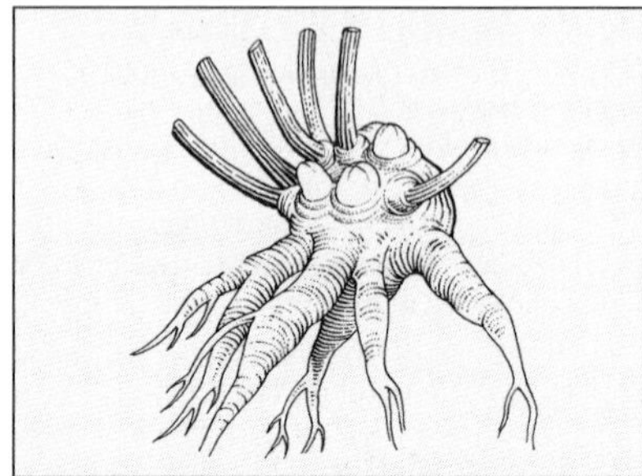

CROWN *The core of a herbaceous perennial.*

CULTIVAR Abbreviation of 'cultivated variety'. A plant variety that is and has been grown only in cultivation (see GENUS).

CUTTING Any part of leaf, bud, stem or root taken from a plant and used to propagate a replica of that plant. Unlike a plant grown from seed, a,plant grown from a cutting is genetically identical to the parent plant – what biologists call a 'clone'.

DAMPING DOWN Watering the floor and benches of a greenhouse or frame, usually in warm weather, both to increase the humidity and to lower the temperature.

DEADHEADING Removing dead or faded flowers from a plant, to tidy it up or to prevent it seeding and thus encourage new flowering. Violas, peonies, rhododendrons and roses are among plants which should be deadheaded regularly.

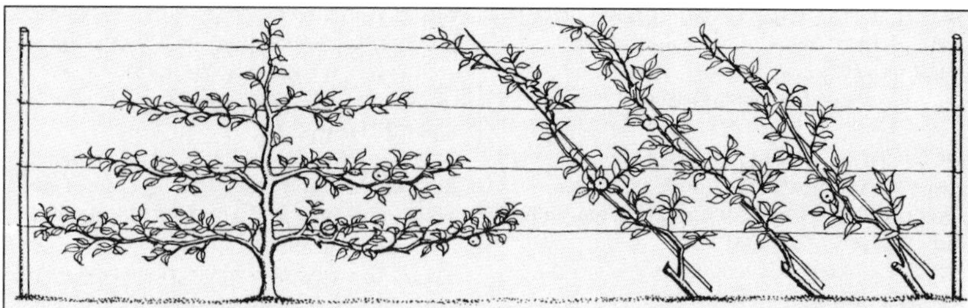

CORDON AND ESPALIER *Trained fruit trees. The cordons are on the right, the espalier on the left.*

DECIDUOUS Term applied to plants which shed their leaves in winter. Deciduous trees grown in the ground rather than pots should be planted or transplanted while leafless, from late October to early April.

DOT PLANT Tall plant used as a single specimen in a formal flowerbed, to contrast in height, colour and texture with smaller plants.

DOUBLE Term applied to a flower with more petals than usual. Double dahlias and double chrysanthemums are examples.

DRAWN Term for plants or seedlings which have grown long, thin and weak through overcrowding or lack of light.

DRILL Straight, narrow furrow in which seeds are often sown outdoors.

DWARF TREE See BONSAI.

EARTHING UP Piling up soil around plants to protect them against frost, sun or disease, or to blanch their stems. Potatoes are earthed up to stop the tubers turning green and bitter through exposure to light, and to protect them from frost and blight spores. Celery and leeks are earthed up to blanch their stems.

ESPALIER Fruit tree trained by pruning and tying to grow flat against a wall, fence or other support. The branches are usually trained in pairs, one each side of the trunk, and in tiers about 12-15in apart.

EVERGREEN Plant – usually a shrub or tree – which bears foliage all year.

EVERLASTING Term for flowers which retain their colours for a long time after being cut and dried – the helichrysum (strawflower), for example.

EXOTIC Any plant introduced to Britain from another country is called an exotic.

EYE Undeveloped growth bud, such as the eyes of potato or dahlia tubers. Alternatively the centre of a flower, especially if different in colour from the petals.

FAMILY See GENUS.

FASCIATION Abnormal plant growth in which several stems become flattened and fused together. Numerous genera are affected by fasciation including lilies, delphiniums and forsythias. It can be caused by a virus, by insect damage or through heredity. Often associated with rapid growth.

FASCIATION *The fused stems of a delphinium.*

FERTILISATION The fusion of a pollen grain nucleus (male) with an undeveloped seed, or ovule (female), to form a mature seed.

FLOWER A plant's reproductive structure, containing the female carpels, or ovaries, which eventually bear the seeds; and the anthers, which produce pollen, or male cells. These are usually surrounded by an inner ring of coloured petals and an outer protective ring of green sepals (though there are numerous variations of this pattern). Most plants bear flowers with both male and female organs, and are said to be 'monoecious'; others have single-sexed flowers on separate plants, and are 'dioecious'.

FORCING Making plants grow, flower or fruit before their natural time. Applies chiefly to plants grown for indoor decoration in winter, or for obtaining early crops of food plants such as lettuce or rhubarb. One method of forcing is to raise plants in a heated greenhouse; another, used for rhubarb, is to grow it in darkness.

FORM Term for a cultivated or naturally occurring variety of a species. *Clematis patens grandiflora*, for example, is a larger-flowered form of *C. patens*.

FORMALDEHYDE or **FORMALIN** Chemical solution of 40 per cent formaldehyde gas in water. It is used for sterilising greenhouse or potting soil, and for washing and sterilising greenhouse interiors. Dig over the soil and water with the prescribed amount of formalin; cover the soil with old sacks to retain the formalin vapour for at least 48 hours. Do not use the soil before the smell has gone. After seven days repeat the treatment. Clear all fumes before returning plants. Take care: formalin can irritate eyes, nose and mouth.

FRIABLE Crumbly soil, easily worked or raked, is said to be friable.

FROST In frosty weather, vulnerable plants can be protected from frost by covering them with an improvised awning or tent made out of, say, plastic or sacking. Alternatively bracken, peat, leaves or straw can be piled around their stems to protect the crowns and roots from frost; or seedlings can be covered with sheets of newspaper held in position with soil or stones (see also AIR FROST and GROUND FROST).

FRUIT Plant's seed-bearing organ – for example, a bean pod or a grape.

FUMIGATE To use poisonous fumes to kill pests and plant diseases in greenhouses and cold frames. Canisters or pellets can be lit to emit dense smoke, carrying insecticide, acaricide or fungicide agents to all parts of the enclosed area.

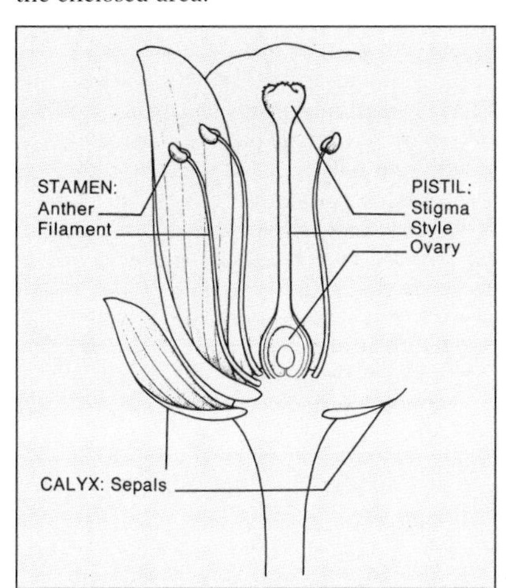

FLOWER *The reproductive heart of a plant.*

FUNGICIDE Any substance which will kill fungi. The old copper or sulphur-based chemicals have been largely replaced by more efficient organic compounds.

GALL Abnormal growth of plant tissue, usually caused by insects or bacteria, sometimes by fungi. Club root, a fungal gall, can severely damage cabbages, cauliflowers and other brassicas. Generally, however, galls do little harm.

GENUS Group of closely related plants. All the various SPECIES of horse chestnuts, for example, are grouped under the genus Aesculus. Related genera are grouped in turn into a family, in this case *Hippocastanaceae*. The common horse chestnut, like most plants, is identified by a genus and a species name, *Aesculus hippocastanum*. A natural VARIETY is identified by a third name in italics, such as *Aesculus hippocastanum laciniata*, and a CULTIVAR by quotation marks, as *Aesculus hippocastanum* 'Baumannii'. A cross or HYBRID between two species is identified by a multiplication sign: *Aesculus* x *carnea*, for example.

GERMINATION Sprouting. The first stage of development from a seed to a plant. It can be observed by placing a bean between damp blotting paper and the glass wall of a jam jar.

GLAUCOUS A term for the grey-blue colour of certain plants, or the bloom or patina on them. Examples are the foliage of the *Cedrus atlantica glauca* (Atlas cedar) and the white bloom on blue grapes.

GRAFTING Joining a stem or bud of one plant to the stem or stem base of another, to form a new plant. It is the usual method of propagating fruit trees and other plants from which cuttings are slow or reluctant to produce roots. Bud grafting is also a method of rapid propagation, as is the case with roses.

GREASE BAND A sticky, 4in wide flypaper-like band put around a fruit tree trunk, about 3ft off the ground, to trap winter moths and codling moths as they crawl along the trunk. Remove and burn the band in February.

GROUND COVER Carpet of low-growing plants, such as aubrieta and periwinkle, used to cover an area to suppress weeds.

GROUND FROST The freezing that takes place when the temperature at ground level drops below 0°C (32°F). Ground frosts happen more often than air frosts, but most plants will survive slight ground frosts in the early autumn or late spring when the period of low temperature is fairly short (see also AIR FROST and FROST)

HALF-HARDY Term for plants which cannot stand frost, and need greenhouse or cold-frame protection in winter. Also applied to shrubs and herbaceous perennials which can survive average winters outdoors, but must have a sheltered site or a mild-weather location.

HALF-STANDARD Any tree or shrub with a clear stem 2½-4ft high before its head of branches. A standard has a taller stem.

HARDENING OFF Gradually getting plants which have been raised under glass used to outdoor conditions. For example, they may be moved from greenhouse to cold frame, then gradually given more ventilation over a period of two or three weeks until tough enough to go outdoors.

HARDY Term for plants able to withstand normal winter frosts. However, a bad winter with severe frosts may still kill some.

HEAVY SOIL A soil with a high proportion of clay. A light soil is one with a high proportion of sand. You can get a rough idea as to whether your soil is heavy or light by stirring a tablespoon of it in a tall glass of water and leaving it to settle. The sand will settle first as a layer at the bottom, the clay will settle on top of it, and most of the humus content will remain floating. If the amount of clay sediment predominates, then your soil is heavy; if there is more sand, then it is light. The ideal would be loam, in which clay, sand and humus are in balance. Both heavy and light soils can be improved by digging in large quantities of peat, compost or manure. The organic matter breaks up heavy soils, helping to release the nutrients contained in the clay. In the case of light soils it acts as a sponge, retaining the nutrients that would otherwise be leached (washed) out.

HEEL The base of old wood or stem on a sideshoot that is pulled away from the main stem when making a heel cutting. Cuttings from some plants root more readily when a heel is attached.

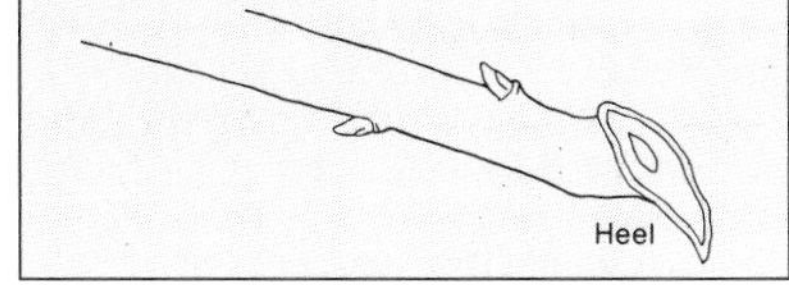

HEEL *One route to success with cuttings.*

HERBACEOUS A term for any plant which does not form a persistent woody stem. Such plants usually die down in winter, to grow again in spring from basal shoots. The term is chiefly applied to herbaceous perennials, although botanically it also applies to annuals and biennials.

HUMUS The dark brown residue of decayed vegetable matter. Often used also to describe partly decayed matter that is sweet-smelling, brown and crumbly, such as leaf mould or compost.

HYBRID Plant derived from crossing two varieties – often of the same species or genus – which has some of the genetic characteristics of each. A first-generation hybrid is known as an F1 (Filial one) hybrid (see page 308). Plants raised from the seeds of hybrids often do not breed true to type. In naming plants, a hybrid is indicated by a multiplication sign, thus: *Aesculus* x *carnea* (see GENUS).

HYDROPONICS Method of growing plants without soil, using dilute solutions of nutrients. The plants may be supported on fine wire mesh or capillary matting, with their roots suspended in the solution.

INORGANIC Term for any chemical compound which does not contain carbon. Inorganic fertilisers are mined or produced chemically, in contrast to organic ones, which are made from blood, bones and other once-living matter.

INSECTICIDE Substance used to kill garden insect pests. It may be available in liquid, powder, smoke or vapour forms.

INSECTIVOROUS Term applied to carnivorous plants which trap insects, absorbing them as food. Species of Drosera (sundew), for instance, trap them with long sticky glands on the leaf surface. The plants obtain nitrogen by digesting the trapped insects.

INTERCROP Fast-growing vegetable crop raised between rows of slower ones – for example, radishes sown between rows of peas, or lettuces between onions.

JOHN INNES COMPOST Soil-based compost made to formulas devised through research at the John Innes Horticultural Institute in Norwich. There is a seed compost used for raising seedlings, and sometimes to root cuttings, plus three potting composts. They are available from gardening shops or you can make your own, buying sterilised loam or using an electric steriliser:
Seed compost
Mix 2 parts sterilised medium loam, 1 part fibrous peat, 1 part coarse sand. To each bushel (2220cu in) of mixture add 1½oz superphosphate of lime and ¾oz ground chalk.
Potting composts
No 1 (for seedlings to move into from seed compost). Mix 7 parts medium loam, 3 parts peat, 2 parts sand. To each bushel of mixture add ¾oz ground chalk plus 4oz of a chemical mixture made up of 2 parts hoof and horn meal, 2 parts superphosphate of lime, 1 part sulphate of potash (all parts by weight).
No 2 (for potting on seedlings). Same mixture but double the quantity of fertilisers.
No 3 (for raising tomatoes, aubergines and other plants to maturity). Same as No 1, but treble the quantity of fertilisers.

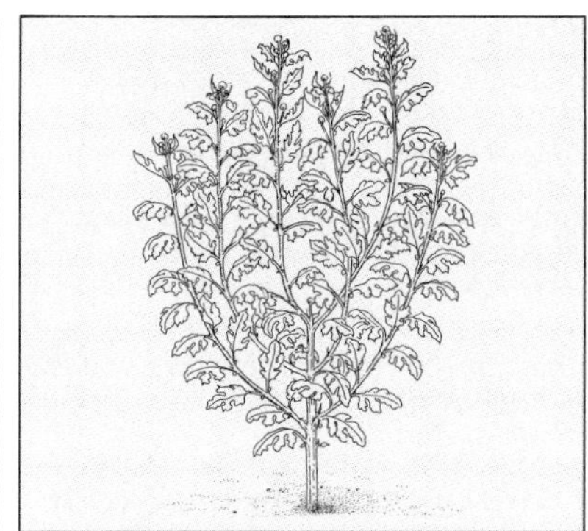

LATERAL *Sideshoots on a chrysanthemum.*

LATERAL Sideshoot or stem that grows from a bud on a larger stem.

LEACHING The removal of soluble materials, especially nutrients, from the soil by water draining through.

LEAF MOULD Compost made from dead, decaying leaves. To make it, stack autumn leaves – oak and beech are best – in 6in layers between layers of soil. A 2-3ft high heap decays to a fibrous mould resembling peat by the following autumn, and can be dug into the soil at 5lb per square yard.

LICHEN Primitive plant form often found growing on rocks and old trees. The grey-green encrustation, formed of algae and fungi, can be eradicated by spraying with a tar-oil wash.

LIGHT SOIL See HEAVY SOIL.

LIME Chemical (calcium) used to neutralise, or 'sweeten', acid soils. The usual forms are chalk, ground limestone, quicklime, and slaked lime.

LOAM Any reasonably fertile soil that is neither wet and sticky nor dry and sandy. It contains a blend of clay, humus, sand and silt, and is rich in minerals.

MANURES AND FERTILISERS Organic and inorganic substances added to soil to increase its fertility. Manures are usually of animal origin – often excrement mixed with straw – and are bulky. Bulky plant remains are known as compost. Fertilisers are more concentrated and may be organic – meaning of animal origin, such as dried blood or bone meal – or inorganic, meaning of mineral or manufactured origin such as ground chalk or ammonium sulphate. Inorganic fertilisers tend to be more expensive but faster-acting than organic ones. Green manuring is the practice of digging into the soil a leafy crop such as mustard.

MARGINAL Plant requiring constantly damp soil, as at the side of a pool.

MORAINE Rocky or gravelly debris left by a glacier. A moraine bed is used for growing high-altitude alpines.

MULCH Layer of rotted manure, leaf mould, compost, peat, straw, bark or sawdust spread on the soil around plants to conserve moisture, fertilise the roots and suppress weeds. Plastic mulches are also widely used to suppress weeds around such plants as potatoes and strawberries.

MUTANT Also known as a sport. Genetically aberrant plant or part of a plant. The mutation, which happens spontaneously, commonly takes the form of a variegated shoot or a flower of a different colour. Sports can be preserved and multiplied by cuttings.

NECTAR Sweet liquid, mostly occurring in flowers, that attracts pollinating insects.

NEUTRAL Soil that is neither acid nor alkaline, with a pH level of about 7.0.

NITROGEN Natural element occurring in soil and air, and used by plants primarily to make green foliage.

NODE Stem joint, sometimes swollen, from which leaves, buds and shoots grow.

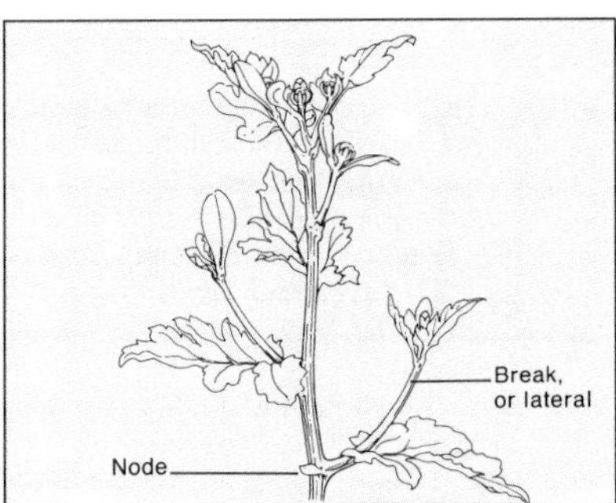

NODE *Growth points on a chrysanthemum plant.*

NYMPH Immature stage of certain insects, such as aphids. The nymphs resemble the adult, but lack adult wings.

OFFSET Young plants that develop naturally on a bulb or stem, and can easily be separated from the parent plant for propagation.

ORGANIC Term used for substances such as compost and manure, which are derived from the decay of once-living organisms.

OXYGENATOR Submerged aquatic plant that releases oxygen into water.

PAN Term with four distinct meanings in gardening: an underground layer of hard soil formed by frequent shallow mechanical cultivation to the same depth; a patch of surface soil which has been beaten hard by heavy rains or watering; a shallow pot used for growing seedlings or alpines; or a layer of ironstone that is found in some sandy soils and requires breaking up before the soil can be cultivated.

PARASITE Plant which lives on another and harms its host by taking part or all of its nourishment. Mistletoe, for instance, is a partial parasite on some trees.

PARTERRE Formal geometrical arrangement of flowerbeds. The style became popular in 16th-century gardens in France and Italy.

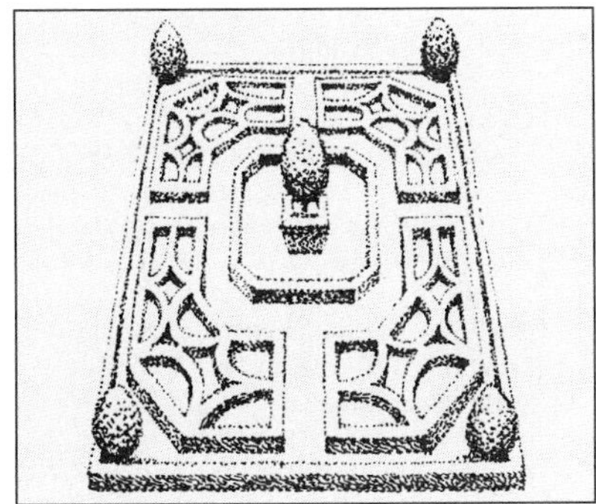

PARTERRE *From the French for 'on the ground'.*

PEAT Organic matter of low mineral content that, worked into soil, breaks down to form humus and improve the soil structure. Common or moss peat is largely derived from sphagnum moss from bogs; sedge peat, derived largely from the roots of sedges, forms in fens.

PERENNIAL Any plant which has a lifespan of more than two years. The term is commonly applied to herbaceous plants such as lupins and peonies, which put out new growth and flowers year after year.

PERGOLA Connected wooden arches forming a fence or canopy over which climbing or rambling plants are trained.

PERPETUAL Term applied to plants which bloom intermittently throughout the year.

pH Scale used to measure acidity. The letters stand for 'potential of Hydrogen'. A soil that is neither acid nor alkaline has a pH value of 7.0. Lower numbers mark increasing acidity; higher numbers mark increasing alkalinity. The full scale runs from 1 to 14, but most garden soils are within the range 4.5-8.0.

PINCHING OUT Also known as 'stopping'. The removal of the growing point of a stem to promote branching or to induce flower bud formation.

PISTIL Entire female reproductive organs of a flower. The organs consist of the ovary, stigma and, usually, the style.

PLUNGING Burying a pot plant and its container up to its rim in a bed of ashes, peat, sand or soil. The practice prevents plants drying out in summer and protects the vulnerable root systems of cuttings and seedlings from fluctuating temperatures.

POLLARDING Severe pruning of a tree back to its trunk and the stubs of its main branches. Willows and poplars are sometimes pollarded so that the resulting young shoots can be used for basket making.

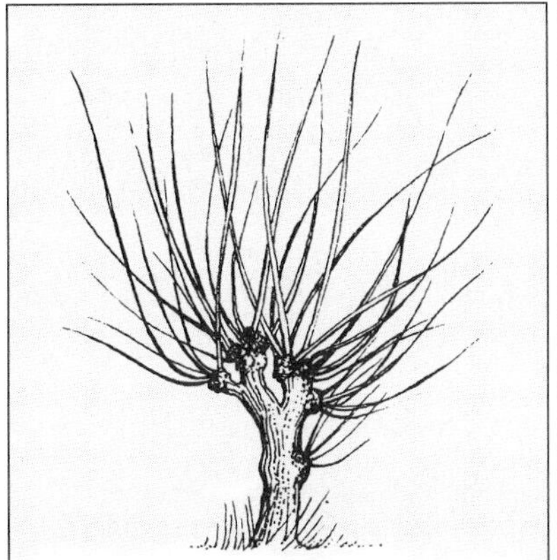

POLLARDING *Shoots on a pollarded willow.*

POLLEN Male cells of a plant. When transferred to the stigma of a plant of the same species – by gravity, wind or insects – the dust-like cells fertilise the seeds in the ovary.

POTTING Setting a plant in a pot. Potting up is used to describe the initial placing of plant and soil (or other potting mixture) in a container. Potting on is used to describe the transfer of a plant to a larger pot. Repotting is the process of transferring a plant to a pot of the same size – once its soil ball and roots have been reduced slightly to make room for fresh soil or potting mixture.

POTTING COMPOST Mixture of soil, peat, sand and nutrients used for pot plants. Soil-less composts contain peat and chemical nutrients.

PRICKING OUT (or off) Transplanting seedlings or cuttings from their initial site into larger containers or beds. Use a small, slim tool, such as a nail file, to pick out the seedlings, then drop them gently into a hole made with a slender dibber in their new environment. Firm in with dibber or fingers, and water to settle the soil.

PROPAGATION Increase of plants by any method. There are two categories: seminal propagation (sowing seeds); and vegetative propagation, which covers all the other techniques such as cuttings, grafting and layering. All vegetatively propagated plants are genetically identical to their parents – they are 'clones'. Plants raised from seed are entirely new plants that may differ from each other and from their parents – in the same way that children will differ from one another and from *their* parents (see also *Why F1 seeds are OK*, page 308).

PRUNING Cutting back plants, particularly those with woody stems such as roses, to restrict the size, to shape the plant, or to promote flower and fruit bud growth.

PSEUDOBULB A false bulb. The term is used of orchids to describe stem joints which swell with storage tissue, sometimes resembling bulbs.

PUPA Dormant transitional state between larva and adult of insects such as moths, butterflies and beetles.

REFLEXED Term used to describe petals or leaves which are sharply bent back on themselves.

RHIZOME Horizontally creeping underground stem which may also act as a storage organ.

RING-BARKING Removing part of a ring of bark from the trunk or a branch of an apple or pear tree, to restrict growth and encourage the development of fruit.

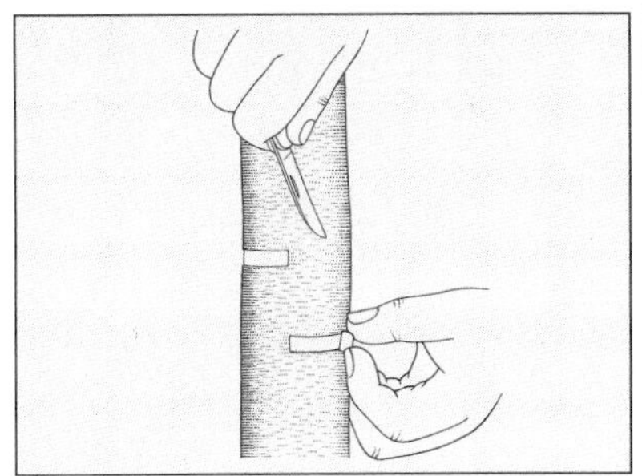

RING-BARKING *Cut in overlapping semicircles.*

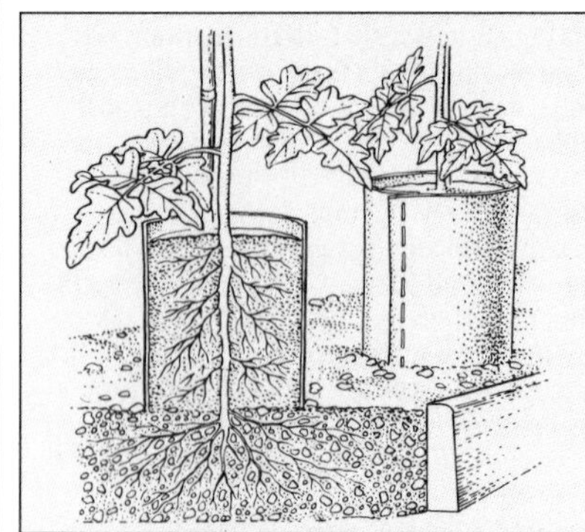

RING CULTURE *Two-tier roots on tomato plants.*

RING CULTURE Cultivation method used chiefly for greenhouse tomatoes and chrysanthemums. In essence, it creates plants with two tiers of roots: an upper tier of feeding roots, set in a bottomless pot (the 'ring'), through which the plant is given nutrients; and a lower tier, set in a free-draining aggregate such as boiler ash, through which the plant draws its water.

ROGUE A plant untypical of its species or variety.

ROOT RUN Area of soil occupied by a plant's roots.

ROOTSTOCK Plant upon which another (the SCION) is grafted. Flowering cherries, for example, are often grafted onto a rootstock of *Prunus avium*. The term is also applied to the crown and root system of herbaceous perennials and suckering shrubs.

RUNNER Stem which roots on contact with moist soil and forms a new plant. Strawberry and blackberry plants, for example, produce stems of this kind.

SCION Shoot or bud of one plant which is joined by grafting to the roots of another (the ROOTSTOCK).

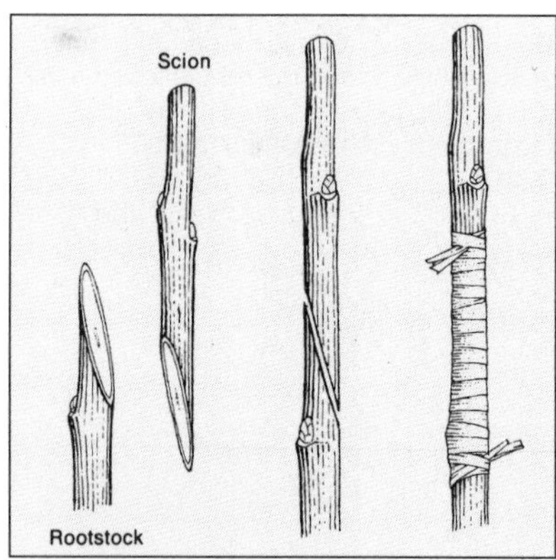

SCION *Splice grafting is one of several methods of joining two plants together.*

SCREE Heap or slope of rocky debris. A garden scree bed, used to grow some alpines and heathers, can be made by mixing coarse gravel or stone chippings with peat or soil.

SEED LEAF The first leaf, or the first pair of leaves, produced by a germinating seed.

SEEDLING Young plant with a single unbranched stem. The term is also applied to a slightly more mature plant which has been reared from seed.

SELF-COLOURED Term used to describe a flower of a single colour.

SELF-FERTILE Term used to describe a plant which will set seed when fertilised with its own pollen. A self-fertile tree, for example, is ideal for a small garden because it needs no pollinating partner.

SELF-STERILE Term used to describe a plant that requires a pollinating partner to produce seeds and fruit.

SET The term has two meanings. As a noun, it means a small onion, shallot bulb or potato tuber, which is planted out early in the season. As a verb, it describes blossom that has been fertilised, especially on a fruit tree.

SINGLE Flower with the normal number of petals.

SPECIES Unit of classification within a GENUS. Species have unique characteristics which consistently breed true to type from seed.

SPECIMEN PLANT Any plant grown where it can be seen from all angles. It is usually a tree or shrub.

SPHAGNUM (MOSS) Generic name for bog mosses that have unique water-retaining, aerating and cleansing properties. In a partially decomposed state, sphagnum moss is the main ingredient of moss peat.

SPIT The depth of a spade's blade – usually 10-12in.

SPORE Dust-like single-cell body by which ferns, fungi and mosses reproduce.

SPORT See MUTANT.

SPUR A word with two meanings: a short lateral branch of a tree (particularly on fruits such as apple and pear), which bears flowers; or a tubular outgrowth of a sepal or petal that produces nectar.

STAKING Using stakes or canes to support top-heavy plants or fragile saplings.

STAMEN Male reproductive organ of a FLOWER. It consists of the pollen-bearing anther and its supporting filament.

STIGMA Tip of the female reproductive organ. It secretes sticky fluid when it is ready for pollination.

STOOL Any plant which is used solely as a source of propagating material. A chrysanthemum stool, for instance, consists of the old roots and the basal shoots, which are taken as cuttings.

STOPPING See PINCHING OUT.

STRAIN Selection from an existing species or variety that is usually grown from seed.

SUBTROPICAL Term used to describe summer bedding plants native to the tropics, which require complete protection from frost – cannas, coleus and abutilons, for example.

SUCCULENT Any plant with thick fleshy leaves or stems, such as cacti and sempervivums.

SUCKER Shoot arising from below ground level. On grafted plants, suckers grow from the rootstock and must be cut or torn off at their point of origin on the roots if they are not to overwhelm the scion.

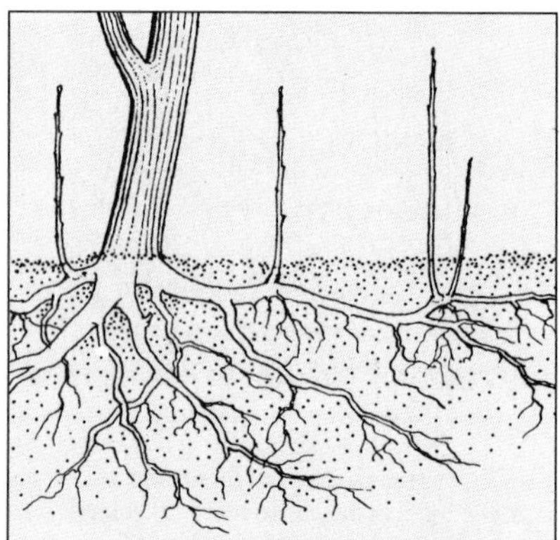

SUCKER *Shoots growing from underground tree roots can be a nuisance in lawns and beds.*

SYMBIOSIS A state in which two different organisms live together in mutual support – the algae and fungi that make up lichen, for instance.

SYSTEMIC INSECTICIDE Chemical compound that enters the sap of a plant when it is applied to the soil or sprayed onto the foliage. Sap-sucking insects are then destroyed, but other insects remain unhurt. The chemical will reach roots and leaf or flower buds which a non-systemic, or 'contact', spray could not penetrate.

TRUSS *A truss of flowers on a rhododendron (left) and of fruits on a tomato (right).*

TAPROOT Principal anchoring root of plants, especially trees.

TENDER Term used for any plant which is vulnerable to frost damage.

TERMINAL The shoot or bud growing at the tip of a stem or branch.

THINNING Removing some seedlings, flowers or fruit buds – in a vegetable crop, say, or on a fruit tree – to improve the growth and quality of the remainder.

TILTH Fine crumbly surface layer of soil. The ideal tilth for a seedbed is about the consistency of coarse breadcrumbs.

TOP-DRESSING Application of a layer, 1-2in thick, of soil, compost or peat to the surface around a plant. If the plant is in a tub or pot, the process involves removing a layer of the same depth to make room for the new one.

TOPIARY Art of clipping and training trees and shrubs into intricate shapes.

TRACE ELEMENT Chemical element, such as iron or zinc, that is essential for plant growth. Lack of these elements, which are normally present in small quantities in any fertile soil, can lead to deficiency diseases.

TRANSPIRATION The loss of water to the air from the leaves and stems of all plants.

TRUSS Cluster of flowers or fruits.

TUBER Thickened fleshy root or underground stem which serves as a food store and produces shoots. Potatoes are tubers; dahlias and begonias are tuberous plants.

TUFA Porous form of limestone that absorbs and retains moisture. It is sometimes used in rock or sink gardens, where small alpine plants can be grown on it. For details of how to make hypertufa, an artificial substitute, see *Homemade rock*, page 285.

TUNIC Fibrous outer skin of bulbs or corms such as crocus or gladioli.

UNISEXUAL Flower of a single sex.

VARIEGATED Decorative markings on leaves and sometimes petals.

VARIETY Variant of a species. It may arise naturally, as did *Rosa gallica officinalis*, the Red Rose of Lancaster, or as a result of selection by a plant breeder, as did *Rosa* 'Peace' (see CULTIVAR).

VEGETATIVE Propagation by any means other than by seed – for example, by cuttings, bulbs, tubers, division, layering and grafting (see *Cuttings*, page 107).

VERMICULITE Lightweight absorbent mica-type granules used for rooting cuttings and seedlings, and often used for storing dried-off dahlia tubers through winter.

WEEPING Term used to describe a tree or shrub of pendulous habit. The habit may be natural, as with a weeping willow, or induced, as in a weeping standard rose.

WILD GARDEN Informal style of planting which aims to simulate woodland or meadow. With careful initial preparation, wild gardens require minimal maintenance.

WINDBREAK Hedge, fence or wall which shelters plants by diminishing or blocking the wind.

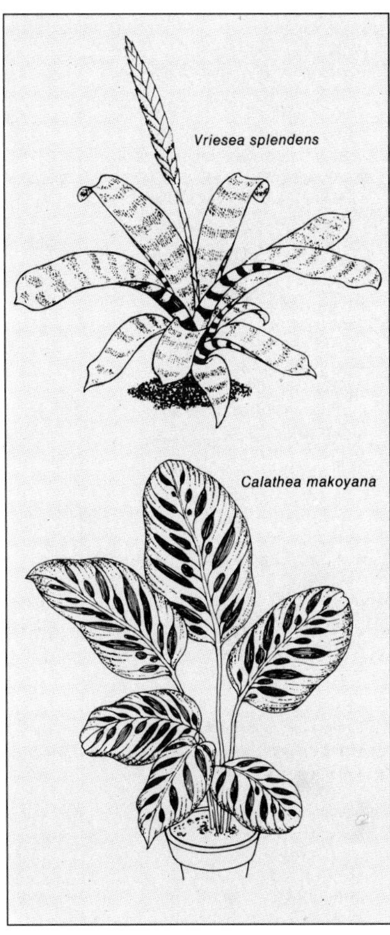

VARIEGATED *Two attractively marked plants.*

INDEX

Page numbers in **bold** type indicate a major treatment of a subject. Page numbers in *italic* indicate that the subject is illustrated.

B

C

D

E

F

M

N

Q

R

T

U

V

W

Y

Z

ACKNOWLEDGMENTS

Many organisations and individuals gave assistance during the preparation of this book, and the publishers would like to thank them all.

They include:
Alan Ball, Ceretech Ltd; Peter Bateman, Rentokil Ltd; I. Cannon, Armillatox Ltd; R.A. Chilton, Tarmac Roadstone Ltd; Kenneth Edwards, Ariel Industries PLC; Charles Fenwick, The Chelsea Gardener, London; Kathryn Hayward, Rockinghams Garden Centre, East Sheen; E. Heald, BTR Landscaper, Preston; ICI; The Institute of Horticultural Research (formerly the National Vegetable Research Station), Wellesbourne; Ministry of Agriculture, Fisheries and Food; Natural Pest Control, Bognor Regis; Rolawn Ltd; Royal Botanic Gardens, Kew; Royal Horticultural Society, Wisley; Royal National Rose Society, St Albans.

The publishers also acknowledge their indebtedness to the following books and journals, which were consulted for reference:

All-Colour Gardening Book, Arthur Hellyer (Hamlyn); *Alpine Garden Plants*, Will Ingwersen (Blandford Press); *The Book of the Rose*, Michael Gibson (Macdonald); *Botany: An Introduction to Plant Biology*, T. Elliot Weier, C. Ralph Stocking and Michael G. Barbour (John Wiley and Sons); *The Complete Book of Gardening*, edited by Michael Wright (Ebury Press and Michael Joseph); *The Complete Gardener*, W.E. Shewell-Cooper (Collins); *The Complete Handbook of Garden Plants*, Michael Wright (Michael Joseph and Rainbird); *Culpeper's Complete Herbal*, Nicholas Culpeper; *The Dictionary of Garden Plants*, Roy Hay and Patrick M. Synge (Ebury Press and Michael Joseph); *The Dictionary of Roses in Colour*, S. Millar Gault and Patrick M. Synge (Michael Joseph); *Directory of Garden Chemicals*, British Agrochemicals Association; *The Dried Flower Book*, Annette Mierhof (The Herbert Press); *The Englishwoman's Garden*, edited by Alvilde Lees-Milne and Rosemary Verey (Chatto and Windus); *The Expert* series, Dr D.G. Hessayon (PBI Publications); *A Field Guide in Colour to Beetles*, K.W. Harde (Octopus); *The Financial Times Book of Garden Design*, edited by Anthony Huxley (David and Charles); *The Gardener's Garden*, Jerry Harpur (Viking); *The Garden Planner*, consultant editor Ashley Stephenson (Book Club Associates); *Gardeners' Questions Answered*, Dr Stefan Buczacki (Collins); *Gardening Through the Year*, Arthur Hellyer (Hamlyn); *Geoffrey Smith's World of Flowers*, edited by Brian Davies (BBC); *The Hillier Colour Dictionary of Trees and Shrubs* (David and Charles); *An Illustrated History of Gardening*, Anthony Huxley (Paddington Press); *The Oxford Book of Invertebrates*, David Nichols and John Cooke (Oxford University Press); *Pests, Diseases and Disorders of Garden Plants*, Dr Stefan Buczacki and Keith Harris (Collins); *Plants for Connoisseurs*, Peter Coats (Condé Nast); *The Principles of Gardening*, Hugh Johnson (Mitchell Beazley); *The Royal Horticultural Society Dictionary of Gardening*, edited by Fred J. Chittenden (Oxford University Press); *Shrubs and Small Trees*, Geoffrey Smith (Hamlyn); *The Well-Furnished Garden*, Michael Balston (Mitchell Beazley); *The Wisley Book of Gardening*, edited by Robert Pearson (Collingridge); *Your Kitchen Garden*, George Seddon and Helena Radecka (Simon and Schuster).

The photographs listed below were provided by the following photographers and agencies.

The position of photographs on each page is indicated by the letters after the page number: *t* = top; *b* = bottom; *l* = left; *c* = centre; *r* = right.

The photographs in the *Dahlias* section are numbered.

The photographs in the *Plants at a glance* section read from left to right and have been lettered across the page: four pictures a-d; five pictures a-e; and six pictures a-f.

Front cover: *l* Harry Smith Collection, *tr* Pat Brindley, *br* Harry Smith Collection. **Back cover:** Kenneth Scowen. **1** Neil Holmes. **2** Sheila & Oliver Mathews. **4** Sheila & Oliver Mathews. **5** all pictures, Neil Holmes. **8** Ron & Christine Foord. **12** *t* Bruce Coleman/Kim Taylor, *b* A.G. Tree. **14** Photos Horticultural Picture Library. **23** Holt Studios Ltd. **29** Ron & Christine Foord. **34** *l* Harry Smith Collection, *c* National Vegetable Research Station, *r* A-Z Botanical Collection Ltd. **35** B & B Photographs. **43** A.G. Tree. **49** Harry Smith Collection. **69** Crown copyright. **70** *l* Harry Smith Collection, *cl* Harry Smith Collection, *cr* A-Z Botanical Collection Ltd, *r* A-Z Botanical Collection Ltd. **71** *l* Derek Gould, *cl* Derek Gould, *cr* Harry Smith Collection, *r* Eric Crichton. **84** B & B Photographs. **85** *t* Tania Midgley, *b* George Wright. **86** *t,b & tc* Tania Midgley, *bc* Sheila & Oliver Mathews. **86-87** Sheila & Oliver Mathews. **88** *l* Tania Midgley, *tr* Tania Midgley, *cr* Pat Brindley, *br* Bruce Coleman/Eric Crichton. **89** *t* Sheila & Oliver Mathews, *c* Bruce Coleman/Eric Crichton, *b* Tania Midgley. **90** *t* Sheila & Oliver Mathews, *cl* Eric Crichton, *cr* Harry Smith Collection, *bl* Ken Beckett, *br* Tania Midgley. **91** Tania Midgley. **92-93** Tania Midgley. **93** Michael Boys. **94** *l* Harry Smith Collection, *tr* Jerry Harpur, *br* Jerry Harpur. **95** Tania Midgley. **98** Neville Fox-Davies. **100** Neil Holmes. **118** 1 Harry Smith Collection, 2 Eric Crichton, 3 Biofotos, 4 A-Z Botanical Collection Ltd, 5 A-Z Botanical Collection Ltd, 6 C. Wooton Cupid, 7 Harry Smith Collection, 8 A-Z Botanical Collection Ltd, 9 Harry Smith Collection, 10 Harry Smith Collection. **129** B & B Photographs. **133** *l* Harry Smith Collection, *cl* Ken Beckett, *cr* B & B Photographs, *r* A.G. Tree. **136** Photos Horticultural Picture Library. **138** Camera Press. **145** B & B Photographs. **173** Pat Brindley. **176** B & B Photographs. **177** *l* Tania Midgley, *c* Eric Crichton, *r* Eric Crichton. **219** Harry Smith Collection. **222** A.G. Tree. **224** *t & b* B & B Photographs. **227** Eric Crichton. **252** Pat Brindley. **259** Pat Brindley. **260** Photos Horticultural Picture Library. **268** Robert J. Corbin. **281** Photos Horticultural Picture Library. **286** Ken Beckett. **296** *t* Bruce Coleman/Eric Crichton, *ct* Eric Crichton, *cb* Harry Smith Collection, *b* Eric Crichton. **297** *b* Ken Beckett, rest Eric Crichton. **301** A.G. Tree. **304** *t* Donald Smith, *b* Ron & Christine Foord. **310** Holt Studios Ltd. **322** *t* Donald Smith, *b* B & B Photographs. **326** B & B Photographs. **336** A.G. Tree. **337** A.G. Tree. **342** RHS. **343** Neil Holmes/Colin Wells-Brown. **348** Tania Midgley. **357** Holt Studios Ltd. **358** *t* Holt Studios Ltd, *b* A.G. Tree. **359** A.G. Tree. **360** both Richard Revels. **362** *l* Ken Beckett, *c* Eric Crichton, *r* Ron & Christine Foord. **363** *l* Sheila & Oliver Mathews, *c* A-Z Botanical Collection Ltd, *r* A-Z Botanical Collection Ltd. **364** *l* Biofotos, *c* A-Z Botanical Collection Ltd, *r* Holt Studios Ltd. **365** *l* Biofotos, *c* Ron & Christine Foord, *r* Biofotos. **375** *t* Biofotos, *b* Holt Studios Ltd. **378** a A-Z Botanical Collection Ltd, b Ken Beckett, c Pat Brindley, d Ken Beckett. **379** a Harry Smith Collection, b Pat Brindley, c Ken Beckett, d Harry Smith Collection, e Pat Brindley, f John Vigurs. **380** a Harry Smith Collection, b Harry Smith Collection, c Pat Brindley, d Ken Beckett, e Tania Midgley, f Harry Smith Collection. **381** a Harry Smith Collection, b A-Z Botanical Collection Ltd, c Harry Smith Collection, d Ken Beckett, e Tania Midgley, f Derek Gould. **382** a Harry Smith Collection, b Tania Midgley, c Tania Midgley, d Peter Stiles, e Robert J. Corbin, f Tania Midgley. **383** a Bruce Coleman/John Fennell, b Photos Horticultural Picture Library, d Pat Brindley, e Derek Gould, f Eric Crichton. **384** a Pat Brindley, b Harry Smith Collection, c Pat Brindley, d A-Z Botanical Collection Ltd, e Harry Smith Collection, f Harry Smith Collection. **385** a Ken Beckett, b Ken Beckett, c Neil Holmes, d Bruce Coleman/Roger Wilmhurst, e Ken Beckett, f Harry Smith Collection. **386** a Harry Smith Collection, b Harry Smith Collection, c Harry Smith Collection, d Ken Beckett, e Bruce Coleman/Mike Price, f Harry Smith Collection. **387** a Harry Smith Collection, b Ken Beckett, c Pat Brindley, d Harry Smith Collection, f Harry Smith Collection. **388** a Harry Smith Collection, b Harry Smith Collection, c Derek Gould, d Ken Beckett, e Pat Brindley, f Ken Beckett. **389** a Harry Smith Collection, b Pat Brindley, c A-Z Botanical Collection Ltd, d Harry Smith Collection, e A-Z Botanical Collection Ltd, f Pat Brindley. **390** a Kenneth Scowen, b Harry Smith Collection, c Harry Smith Collection, d Eric Crichton, e Tania Midgley, f Ken Beckett. **391** a Photos Horticultural Picture Library, b Harry Smith Collection, c Harry Smith Collection, d Harry Smith Collection, e Harry Smith Collection, f Eric Crichton. **392** a Tania Midgley, b Tania Midgley, c Harry Smith Collection, d Harry Smith Collection, e Harry Smith Collection, f Harry Smith Collection. **393** a Pat Brindley, b Tania Midgley, c Harry Smith Collection, d Harry Smith Collection, e A-Z Botanical Collection Ltd, f Harry Smith Collection. **394** a Pat Brindley, b Tania Midgley, c Harry Smith Collection, d Pat Brindley, e Pat Brindley, f Pat Brindley. **395** a Harry Smith Collection, b Pat Brindley, c Ken Beckett, d Ken Beckett, e Kenneth Scowen. **396** a Photos Horticultural Picture Library, b A-Z Botanical Collection Ltd, c A-Z Botanical Collection Ltd, d Harry Smith Collection, e Ken Beckett, f Tania Midgley. **397** a Neil Holmes, b Harry Smith Collection, c Tania Midgley, d Tania Midgley, e Harry Smith Collection, f Harry Smith Collection. **398** a Photos Horticultural Picture Library, b Pat Brindley, c Tania Midgley, d Harry Smith Collection, e Pat Brindley, f Pat Brindley. **399** a Pat Brindley, b Harry Smith Collection, c Derek Gould, d Ken Beckett, e Kenneth Scowen, f Bruce Coleman/Eric Crichton. **400** a Harry Smith Collection, b A-Z Botanical Collection Ltd, c Harry Smith Collection, d Harry Smith Collection, e Harry Smith Collection, f Harry Smith Collection. **401** a Harry Smith Collection, b Pat Brindley, c Pat Brindley, d Pat Brindley, e Tania Midgley, f Harry Smith Collection. **402** a Harry Smith Collection, b Harry Smith Collection, c Harry Smith Collection, d Harry Smith Collection, e Pat Brindley, f Ken Beckett. **403** a Harry Smith Collection, b Bruce Coleman/Hans Reinhard, c Eric Crichton, d A-Z Botanical Collection Ltd, e Pat Brindley. **404** a Pat Brindley, b Photos Horticultural Picture Library, c Tania Midgley, d Peter Stiles, e Pat Brindley, f Pat Brindley. **405** a Derek Gould, b A-Z Botanical Collection Ltd, c Sheila & Oliver Mathews, d Tania Midgley, e Robert J. Corbin, f Bruce Coleman/Eric Crichton. **406** a Harry Smith Collection, b Photos Horticultural Picture Library, c Harry Smith Collection, d Ken Beckett, e Harry Smith Collection, f Harry Smith Collection. **407** a Bruce Coleman/Eric Crichton, b Pat Brindley, c Pat Brindley, d Derek Gould, e Derek Gould, f Photos Horticultural Picture Library. **408** a Harry Smith Collection, b Tania Midgley, c Ken Beckett, d Photos Horticultural Picture Library, e Pat Brindley, f A-Z Botanical Collection Ltd. **409** a Photos Horticultural Picture Library, b Harry Smith Collection, c Tania Midgley, d Ken Beckett, e Harry Smith Collection, f Harry Smith Collection. **410** a Ken Beckett, b A-Z Botanical Collection Ltd, c Tania Midgley, d Pat Brindley, e Harry Smith Collection, f Harry Smith Collection. **411** a Harry Smith Collection, b Ken Beckett, c Harry Smith Collection, d Tania Midgley, e Peter Stiles. **412** a Harry Smith Collection, b Harry Smith Collection, c Kenneth Scowen, d Harry Smith Collection, e Photos Horticultural Picture Library, f A-Z Botanical Collection Ltd. **413** a Eric Crichton, b Bruce Coleman/A.J. Mobbs, c Harry Smith Collection, d A-Z Botanical Collection Ltd, e Derek Gould, f Ken Beckett. **414** a Tania Midgley, b A-Z Botanical Collection Ltd, c Harry Smith Collection, d Pat Brindley, e Ken Beckett, f Harry Smith Collection. **415** a A-Z Botanical Collection Ltd, b A-Z Botanical Collection Ltd, c Ken Beckett, d Pat Brindley, e Harry Smith Collection, f Harry Smith Collection. **416** a Pat Brindley, b Harry Smith Collection, c Harry Smith Collection, d Bruce Coleman Ltd/Bruce Coleman, e Ken Beckett, f Eric Crichton. **417** a Eric Crichton, b Eric Crichton, c Harry Smith Collection, d Harry Smith Collection, e Neil Holmes, f Eric Crichton. **418** a Pat Brindley, b Eric Crichton, c Eric Crichton, d Neil Holmes, e Harry Smith Collection. **419** a Tania Midgley, b Harry Smith Collection, c Tania Midgley, d Pat Brindley. **420** a Pat Brindley, b Ken Beckett, c Tania Midgley, d Harry Smith Collection, e Harry Smith Collection. **421** a Harry Smith Collection, b Eric Crichton, c Harry Smith Collection, d Ken Beckett, e Harry Smith Collection, f A-Z Botanical Collection Ltd. **422** a Harry Smith Collection, b Derek Gould, c Harry Smith Collection, d Harry Smith Collection, e Pat Brindley, f Pat Brindley. **423** a Eric Crichton, b Harry Smith Collection, d A-Z Botanical Collection Ltd, e A-Z Botanical Collection Ltd. **424** a Ken Beckett, b A-Z Botanical Collection Ltd, c Harry Smith Collection, d Harry Smith Collection, e Tania Midgley, f Harry Smith Collection. **425** a Ken Beckett, b Derek Gould, c A-Z Botanical Collection Ltd, d Harry Smith Collection, e Harry Smith Collection, f A-Z Botanical Collection Ltd. **426** a Neil Holmes, b Harry Smith Collection, c Harry Smith Collection, d Harry Smith Collection, e Photos Horticultural Picture Library, f Photos Horticultural Picture Library. **427** a Derek Gould, b Photos Horticultural Picture Library, c Derek Gould, d A-Z Botanical Collection Ltd, e Derek Gould, f Harry Smith Collection. **428** a Harry Smith Collection, b Derek Gould, c Eric Crichton, d Harry Smith Collection, e Eric Crichton, f Harry Smith Collection. **429** a Photos Horticultural Picture Library, b Tania Midgley, c Harry Smith Collection, d Ken Beckett, e Harry Smith Collection, f Harry Smith Collection. **430** a Harry Smith Collection, b Ken Beckett, c Harry Smith Collection, d Harry Smith Collection, e Pat Brindley, f Pat Brindley. **431** a Eric Crichton, b Eric Crichton, c Pat Brindley, d Eric Crichton, e A-Z Botanical Collection Ltd, f Harry Smith Collection. **432** a Harry Smith Collection, b Eric Crichton, c Harry Smith Collection, d Eric Crichton, e Harry Smith Collection. **433** a Harry Smith Collection, b Ken Beckett, c A-Z Botanical Collection Ltd, d Harry Smith Collection, e Pat Brindley, f Pat Brindley. **434** a Harry Smith Collection, b Bruce Coleman/N.G. Blake, c Pat Brindley, d A-Z Botanical Collection Ltd, e Pat Brindley, f Harry Smith Collection. **435** a Harry Smith Collection, b Eric Crichton, c Harry Smith Collection, d Eric Crichton, e Pat Brindley, f Derek Gould. **436** a A-Z Botanical Collection Ltd, b A-Z Botanical Collection Ltd, c Harry Smith Collection, d A-Z Botanical Collection Ltd, e Eric Crichton, f Pat Brindley. **437** a Pat Brindley, b Pat Brindley, c Harry Smith Collection, d Photos Horticultural Picture Library, e Harry Smith Collection. **438** a Harry Smith Collection, b Pat Brindley, c Ken Beckett, d Pat Brindley, e Pat Brindley. **439** a Harry Smith Collection, b Neil Holmes, c Pat Brindley, d Tania Midgley, e Pat Brindley, f Eric Crichton. **440** a A-Z Botanical Collection Ltd, b Tania Midgley, c Harry Smith Collection, d Neil Holmes, e Pat Brindley. **441** a A-Z Botanical Collection Ltd, b Photos Horticultural Picture Library, c Tania Midgley, d Harry Smith Collection, e Harry Smith Collection, f A-Z Botanical Collection Ltd.

TYPESETTING: SPRINT PRODUCTIONS LTD, LONDON
SEPARATIONS: MULLIS MORGAN LTD, LONDON
PAPER: C. TOWNSEND HOOK PAPER CO. LTD, SNODLAND
PRINTING & BINDING: GRAFICA EDITORIALE SPA, BOLOGNA

40.178.1